CRIMINAL INVESTIGATION
TWELFTH EDITION

CHRISTINE HESS ORTHMANN, M.S.
ORTHMANN WRITING AND RESEARCH, INC.

KÄREN MATISON HESS, PH.D.
NORMANDALE COMMUNITY COLLEGE

SGT. HENRY LIM CHO, M.A.
ROSEMOUNT POLICE DEPARTMENT (RETIRED)

SGT. JENNIFER MOLAN CHO, M.A.
DAKOTA COUNTY SHERIFF'S OFFICE (RETIRED)

 CENGAGE

Australia • Brazil • Canada • Mexico • Singapore • United Kingdom • United States

Criminal Investigation, **Twelfth Edition**
Christine Hess Orthmann,
Kären Matison Hess, Henry Lim Cho,
and Jennifer Molan Cho

SVP, Higher Education Product
Management: Erin Joyner

VP, Product Management, Learning
Experiences: Thais Alencar

Product Director: Jason Fremder

Product Manager: Michael W. Worls

Product Assistant: Martina Grant

Learning Designer: Natalie Goforth

Senior Content Manager: Betty L. Dickson

Digital Delivery Quality Partner:
Andy Baker

Director, Product Marketing: Neena Bali

Product Marketing Manager:
Ian A. Hamilton

IP Analyst: Deanna Ettinger

Production Service: Lumina Datamatics

Senior Media Designer: Erin Griffin

Cover Image Source:
iStockPhoto.com/ChakisAtelier

Interior image Source:
iStockPhoto.com/ChakisAtelier

For product information and technology assistance, contact us at
**Cengage Customer & Sales Support, 1-800-354-9706
or support.cengage.com.**
For permission to use material from this text or product,
submit all requests online at **www.cengage.com.**

Library of Congress Control Number: 2021946267

Student Edition:
ISBN: 978-0-357-51167-1

Loose-leaf Edition:
ISBN: 978-0-357-51170-1

Cengage
200 Pier 4 Boulevard
Boston, MA 02210
USA

Cengage Learning is a leading provider of customized learning
solutions with employees residing in nearly 40 different countries and
sales in more than 125 countries around the world. Find your local
representative at **www.cengage.com.**

To learn more about Cengage platforms and services, register or
access your online learning solution, or purchase materials for your
course, visit **www.cengage.com.**

Printed at CLDPC, USA, 01-22

Brief Contents

Section 5   Other Challenges to the Criminal Investigator   590

Appendixes   786

Contents

Chapter 3
Writing Effective Reports   74

Chapter 4
Searches   100

Chapter 5
Forensics and Physical Evidence 138

Chapter 6
Obtaining Information and Intelligence 198

Chapter 7
Identifying and Arresting Suspects   240

Section 3   Investigating Violent Crimes   286

Chapter 8
Death Investigations   290

Chapter 11
Crimes against Children   410

Chapter 16
Arson, Bombs, and Explosives   562

Chapter 19
Criminal Gangs and Other Dangerous Groups 686

Chapter 20
Terrorism, Extremism, and
Homeland Security   724

Chapter 21
Preparing for and Presenting Cases in Court   762

Appendixes   786

Preface

Welcome to *Criminal Investigation*, Twelfth Edition. Designed to be one of the most practical, hands-on, reliable textbooks you will ever read, *Criminal Investigation* presents the procedures, techniques, and applications of private and public investigation. The book seamlessly integrates coverage of modern investigative tools alongside discussion of established investigation procedures and techniques. The Twelfth Edition features updated, enhanced coverage of such important topics as terrorism and homeland security, cybercrime, forensics and physical evidence, federal law enforcement investigations, report writing, crimes against children, investigative photography and sketching, preparing and presenting cases in court, identity theft, and white-collar crime.

Forensics and crime scene investigation are increasingly popular components of criminal investigation courses today and are correspondingly emphasized in this text, which features complete coverage of digital fingerprinting, DNA evidence and databases, ballistics, body-fluid collection and examination, contamination of evidence, exhibiting evidence in court, and new technologies that are changing the way crime scenes are documented through photography, sketching, and so on.

Opportunities in investigations have altered since the terrorist attacks of September 11, 2001. New careers have opened up in federal law enforcement, and interest in working with federal agencies has grown among job seekers. This new edition increases its focus on federal investigations. It also delves more deeply into the fight against terrorism and the ways in which law enforcement—whether federal, state, or local—must be involved and must work collaboratively with other agencies to be effective.

Criminal Investigation can serve as an overview of the entire field or as a solid foundation for specialized coursework. Although the content of each chapter could easily be expanded into an entire book or course, this text provides the basic concepts of each area of investigation and will prove to be an invaluable reference long after students move on from the classroom.

ORGANIZATION OF THE TEXT

In Section 1, the student is introduced to the broad field of criminal investigation; to the elements of an effective, efficient investigation; and to the equipment, technology, and procedures that facilitate investigation (Chapter 1). Important court cases and decisions are cited and explained throughout the text.

Section 2 is designed to acquaint readers with various investigative responsibilities: documenting the scene by note taking, photographing, and sketching (Chapter 2); writing reports (Chapter 3); searching crime scenes and suspects (Chapter 4); identifying and collecting physical evidence for forensic examination (Chapter 5); obtaining information and intelligence (Chapter 6); and identifying and arresting suspects (Chapter 7).

Sections 3, 4, and 5 illustrate how these responsibilities are carried out in specific types of investigations. Section 3 discusses the basics in investigating violent crimes: death investigations (Chapter 8); assault, domestic violence, stalking, and elder abuse (Chapter 9); sex offenses (Chapter 10); crimes against children (Chapter 11); and robbery (Chapter 12). Section 4 discusses investigation of crimes against property: burglary (Chapter 13); larceny/theft, fraud, and white-collar crime (Chapter 14); motor vehicle theft (Chapter 15); and arson, bombs, and explosives (Chapter 16). Section 5 discusses other investigative challenges: computer crimes and their evolution into cybercrimes and the collection and analysis of digital evidence (Chapter 17); the dual threats of drug-related crime and organized crime (Chapter 18); the illegal activities of gangs and other dangerous groups, such as hate groups and cults (Chapter 19); terrorism, extremism, and homeland security (Chapter 20); and the culmination of investigations: preparing for and presenting cases in court (Chapter 21).

NEW TO THIS EDITION

The Twelfth Edition of *Criminal Investigation* has been completely updated with hundreds of new references.

We've also converted the Do You Know questions into more concrete learning objectives for each chapter. These statements will help instructors and students alike understand the outcomes they can expect from the chapter. Through the use of color, we capture the details of technical photographs and other instructional images, facilitating a more complete student understanding of the material. In addition to the inclusion in every chapter of a *Myth versus Fact* feature, which aims to dispel some of the common misperceptions surrounding the various topics discussed in the text, and a Technology Innovations feature to highlight some of the technological advances impacting the field of criminal investigation, the Twelfth Edition features the following chapter-by-chapter enhancements:

- **Chapter 1: Criminal Investigation: An Overview—** This chapter includes updated statistics throughout; a new discussion of the results of several studies involving recidivism, victimization numbers and rates, and forensic crime log backlogs; and a brief discussion of how the National Institute of Justice differentiates the different types of crime lab backlogs, as well as NIJ programs to reduce backlogs and increase efficiency.

- **Chapter 2: Documenting the Crime Scene: Note Taking, Photographing, and Sketching—**This chapter includes an updated Technology Innovation feature about 3-D crime scene mapping technology; new content from the FBI's Handbook of Forensic Services regarding aerial photography; and new content about technology used to produce electronic, computer-generated lineups. In addition, we converted a section of text discussing the different types of photographic equipment into a new table (Table 2.1).

- **Chapter 3: Writing Effective Reports—**This chapter was thoroughly reviewed to ensure the best-practices in report writing were presented.

- **Chapter 4: Searches—**The section on "Searches without a Warrant" was reorganized sightly to facilitate the flow of the discussion. The chapter includes two new terms (*attenuation doctrine, independent source doctrine*); many new cases—*Byrd v. U.S.*, 2018 (consent search), *U.S. v. Camou*, 2014 (warrantless search of cell phones), *U.S. v. Johnson*, 2019 (search incident to arrest: order is irrelevant), *U.S. v. Torres*, 2016 (inventory searches of vehicles), *U.S. v. Iwai*, 2019 (exigent circumstance searches), *Collins v. Virginia*, 2018 (warrantless searches of vehicles within the curtilage), *Arizona v. Evans*, 1995 (exclusionary rule exception involving clerical errors), *Bailey v. U.S.*, 2013 (detaining a person

who has left the immediate vicinity where a search warrant is being executed), *U.S. v. Whitaker*, 2016 (dog sniffs), *Murray v. U.S.*, 1988 (independent source doctrine), *Utah v. Strieff*, 2016 (attenuation doctrine), *Carpenter v. U.S.*, 2018 (warrantless search and seizure of cell phone records), *In re Search of a Residence in Oakland, California*, 2019 (challenge of technology and privacy rights), *U.S. v. Williams*, 2015 (using LRP to justify a *Terry* stop)—and an expanded discussion of the exclusionary rule, adding two new B-level headings: independent source doctrine and attenuation doctrine.

- **Chapter 5: Forensics and Physical Evidence—**This chapter includes a new photo of documentary evidence; several new Technology Innovations (portable forensic light source [Crime-lite XL to replace TracER], mobile fingerprint readers, DNA phenotyping); added three new terms (*digital evidence, primary transfer* [concerning DNA evidence], *secondary transfer* [concerning DNA evidence]); new content about voiceprints; an expanded section on collection of DNA evidence; a new section on individual skin-associated chemical signature evidence; additional coverage of the new forensic footwear database; an expanded discussion of the "Bite Mark" section to include teeth and lip prints, as well as consideration of the current legal challenges facing forensic bite mark analysis; a new discussion of the new drug analyzing technology called TruNarc; and a brief mention of protecting against infection from COVID-19. Additionally, Table 17.1 has been moved to this chapter (now Table 5.4) in the discussion of digital evidence that may be found when investigating various crimes.

- **Chapter 6: Obtaining Information and Intelligence—**The chapter includes several new terms (*implicit bias, microaggression*); an expanded "Knock and Talk" section to include the cases of *Florida v. Jardines* (2013), *State v. Huddy* (2017), *Kentucky v. King* (2011), *Michigan v. Frederick* (2019); new content from the HIG (High-Value Detainee Interrogation Group) regarding cross-cultural communication with victims, witnesses, and suspects; new content on implicit bias as a barrier to communication; new content regarding several interview and interrogation techniques (Reid, PEACE); a new Technology Innovation (VALT police interview recording software); a discussion of the case of *People v. Thomas* (2014), dealing with police use of coercive deception to gain a confession; updated information on false confessions; new content on voice stress analysis technology to detect deception; and a discussion of how NIEM is replacing GJXDM as platform to share information.

- **Chapter 7: Identifying and Arresting Suspects—** This chapter contains new information on show-up identification; an updated discussion of the FBI's National Center for the Analysis of Violent Crime (NCAVC); five new Technology Innovations (Integrated Biometrics Five-0 fingerprint biometric scanners, CrimeStat crime mapping software, TWS, ShotSpotter Flex, BolaWrap); new content on racial profiling and the use of gait analysis in developing and identifying suspects; a brief discussion of using single confirmatory photos in suspect identification; new content about photo arrays and DOJ procedures for conducting them; a discussion of the case of *United States v. Yang* (2020), which dealt with the constitutionality of using ALPR without a warrant to locate and identify suspects, and the use of social media in undercover investigations; a new mention that state laws vary regarding stop-and-identify; updated statistics and studies on police use of force; a new discussion of decision making models as options to replace use-of-force continuums; a discussion of the case of *Armstrong v. Village of Pinehurst* (2016), which set stricter guidelines in how police can deploy CEDs; and updated content regarding excited delirium.

- **Chapter 8: Death Investigations—**This chapter includes updated all UCR statistics; a new term (*cold case*); a new discussion of the differentiation between manner, cause, and mechanism of death; new content on excited delirium and sudden in-custody deaths; a new figure on Homicide Process Mapping and tasks to perform during the critical 48 hours after a homicide is reported to police; new content on forensic entomology and estimating time of death; a new case (*Mitchell v. Wisconsin*, 2019) that dealt with the legality of a warrantless blood draw from an unconscious individual suspected of drunk driving; updated the content on homicide clearances; and an updated section on cold cases.

- **Chapter 9: Assault, Domestic Violence, Stalking, and Elder Abuse—**This chapter, with crucial information for future law enforcement professionals who continue to be called on to respond to domestic and family violence calls, includes updated statistics throughout and new content on investigating domestic violence, as well as discussion of the evidence shown to increase criminal convictions rates; expanded content regarding investigating stalking; a new term (*cybersuicide*); and a restructured section

with updated content on investigating elder abuse. We also converted text discussing the types of intimate partner violence (IPV) into a table (Table 9.1).

- **Chapter 10: Sex Offenses—**This chapter includes updated statistics and two new terms (*sextortion, trauma bond*); discussion of a new case (*Karsjens v. Piper*, 2018) dealing with the civil commitment of sex offenders; and an updated date rape drug section, including the addition of GHB and Ecstasy. We heavily revised the section on human trafficking, updating statistics and adding new subsections on indicators of trafficking, recognizing traffickers, overlap with other crimes, gaining victim and witness cooperation, and questioning survivors of trafficking. Much of the "trafficking vs. smuggling" text was converted into a table.

- **Chapter 11: Crimes against Children—**This chapter includes updated statistics on child abuse and neglect; new content regarding how best to use anatomical dolls during forensic interviews of child abuse victims; mention of the amendment of CAPTA by the Victims of Child Abuse Reauthorization Act of 2018; and a list of different protocols for interviewing child victims of sexual assault. The discussion of the commercial sexual exploitation of children (CSEC) was reorganized, with a section added on sextortion and the live-streaming of child sexual abuse. We added content about the AMBER Alert Secondary Distribution (AASD) Program and a new Technology Innovation (Bark).

- **Chapter 12: Robbery—**This chapter includes updated crime statistics on robbery.

- **Chapter 13: Burglary—**This chapter includes updated statistics on burglary and a small addition on using rational choice theory to prevent burglary.

- **Chapter 14: Larceny/Theft, Fraud, and White-Collar Crime—**All crime statistics have been updated, and the chapter includes new content regarding wildlife theft and trafficking; new content on how to differentiate identity theft from identity fraud; new examples of recently investigated identity theft cases; and updates of the cases pertaining to environmental crimes. Two terms related to telephone scams (*jamming, sliding*) were deleted as they are no longer major problems with cell phones and free long distance, and one term was added (*identity fraud*).

- **Chapter 15: Motor Vehicle Theft—**This chapter includes updated statistics on the most common stolen vehicles and the most commonly cloned vehicles.

▪ **Chapter 16: Arson, Bombs, and Explosives**—The chapter contains updated statistics on arson and has been completely revised to reflect evolving fire science, including the most recent edition of *NFPA 921* (2021 Edition). It includes an expanded discussion regarding arsonist behavior; a restructured motivation section that better aligns with the current *NFPA 921* guidelines; a mention of the ATF's Fire Research Lan (FRL); new content regarding responding to a fire scene; and three new terms (*mass arson, serial arson, spree arson*).

▪ **Chapter 17: Computer Crime and Digital Evidence**—The chapter title was modified to include "Digital Evidence." In addition to updated statistics, new terminology (*dark web, deep web, ransomware, surface web*), and expanded content regarding IC3 and the types of complaints they handle, the chapter has a new section differentiating the layers of the web (surface, deep, and dark), new content regarding IPv6, a discussion of ransomware attacks, and content about the CLOUD Act. Two new tables are presented: 2019 Crime Types by Victim Count and Victim Loss (from the IC3 annual cybercrime report). Several new cases are discussed: *U.S. v. Microsoft*, 2018 (obtaining digital evidence from the cloud), *Van Buren v. U.S.*, 2020 (expansion of the CFAA), *U.S. v. Stanley*, 2014 (mooching another's IP address to commit cybercrime). The chapter also includes a mention of the USA FREEDOM Act and a new Technology Innovation feature about new tools to expedite digital evidence acquisition and analysis.

▪ **Chapter 18: A Dual Threat: Drug-Related Crime and Organized Crime**—This chapter includes updated crime statistics and a new term (*transnational organized crime*). The section titled "Classification of Controlled Drugs" was completely reorganized to group specific drugs into the same class (e.g., narcotics, stimulants). The chapter also contains a new section on fentanyl; new content on designer drugs (bath salts, synthetic opioids); a discussion of the use of Naloxone, a new paragraph about "drug-induced homicide" or "death by distribution" laws; updated content on transnational organized crime (TOC) and the IOC-2, and a new Technology Innovation feature about ACE-ID spectrographic drug identification. Table 18.2 was modified to include fentanyl, GHB, Rohypnol, Khat, methamphetamine, MDMA, and ketamine.

▪ **Chapter 19: Criminal Gangs and Other Dangerous Groups**—This chapter includes updated statistics regarding gangs and hate crimes; a new term (*security threat group*); a new section on "Gangs and Technology"; and new content on gang violence and gang-related homicides. It also differentiates hate crime from terrorism and extremism, and introduces a new Technology Innovation—the Gang Graffiti Automatic Recognition and Interpretation (GARI) App.

▪ **Chapter 20: Terrorism, Extremism, and Homeland Security**—Terrorism and homeland security are increasingly hot topics for law enforcement, and this chapter has been thoroughly updated, including the most recently available statistics and survey results regarding terrorism. "Extremism" now forms part of the chapter title to emphasize how radical ideology fits into the broader discussion of terrorism. Content pertaining to two Islamist terror groups (HAMAS, Al-Aqsa Martyrs Brigades) has been deleted due to their relative insignificance as direct threats to the homeland but there is a new paragraph on the Taliban. The discussion of domestic extremism and terrorism has been restructured and expanded, as that is currently the biggest threat to the United States, and it includes the reorganization of ideological categories (e.g., far-right, far-left, religious) to better align with those used by CSIS, START, and other entities that track, study, and respond to terrorism. Within the Domestic Terrorism section, the chapter includes expanded content regarding far-right extremism, including the Oath Keepers, Three Percenters, Proud Boys, and QAnon, and new content about Antifa in the section discussing far-left extremism. In addition to a new section on the USA FREEDOM Act, which replaced the USA PATRIOT Act in 2015, and new content pertaining to planning and preparing for a terrorist attack, several terms were deleted (*Islamic State of Iraq and the Levant [ISIL], technological terrorism*) and several terms were added (*boogaloo, extremism, targeted violence, terrorism*).

▪ **Chapter 21: Preparing for and Presenting Cases in Court**—This key chapter has been reviewed to be sure it helps prepare future investigators to defend their cases in a court of law, and a new term was added (*deposition*).

HOW TO USE THIS TEXT

Criminal Investigation is a carefully structured learning experience. The more actively you participate in it, the more you will learn. You will learn and remember more if you first familiarize yourself with the total scope of the subject. Read and think about the table of contents, which provides an outline of the many facets of criminal investigation.

Then follow these steps for *quadruple-strength learning* as you study each chapter.

1. Read the learning objectives (LOs) at the beginning of the chapter. These are designed to help you anticipate the key content of the chapter and to prompt a self-assessment of your current knowledge of the subject. Also, look at the key terms listed and watch for them when they are used.

2. Read the chapter while underlining, highlighting, or taking notes—whatever is your preferred study method. Pay special attention to information in the blue boxes or words that appear in boldface type. The former represent the chapter-opening LOs, and the latter comprise the key terms identified at the beginning of the chapter.

3. When you have finished reading the chapter, read the Summary—your third exposure to the chapter's key information. Then return to the beginning of the chapter and quiz yourself. Can you respond knowledgably to the learning objectives? Can you define the key terms?

4. Finally, in Sections 3, 4, and 5, complete the Application exercises at the end of each chapter. These exercises ask you to apply the chapter concepts in actual or hypothetical cases.

By following these steps, you will learn more information, understand it more fully, and remember it longer.

Note: The material selected to highlight using the quadruple-strength learning instructional design includes only the chapter's key concepts. Although this information is certainly important in that it provides a structural foundation for understanding the topic(s) discussed, you cannot simply glance over the highlighted boxes that correspond to each learning objective and summary and expect to master the chapter. You are also responsible for reading and understanding the material that surrounds these boxed features.

ANCILLARIES
For the Instructor

Online Instructor's Manual The manual includes learning objectives, key terms, a detailed chapter outlines, student activities, and media tools. The learning objectives

are correlated with the discussion topics, student activities, and media tools. The manual is available for download on the password-protected website and can also be obtained by emailing your local Cengage Learning representative.

Online Test Bank Each chapter of the test bank contains questions in multiple-choice, true/false, completion, and essay formats, with a full answer key. The test bank is coded to the learning objectives that appear in the main text, the section in the main text where the answers can be found, and Bloom's taxonomy. Finally, each question in the test bank has been carefully reviewed by experienced criminal justice instructors for quality, accuracy, and content coverage. The test bank is available for download on the password-protected website and can also be obtained by emailing your local Cengage Learning representative.

Cengage Learning Testing, Powered By Cognero This assessment software is a flexible online system that allows you to import, edit, and manipulate test bank content from the *Criminal Investigation* test bank or elsewhere, including your own favorite test questions; create multiple test versions in an instant; and deliver tests from your LMS, your classroom, or wherever you want.

Online Powerpoint Lectures Helping you make your lectures more engaging while effectively reaching your visually oriented students, these handy Microsoft PowerPoint® slides outline the chapters of the main text in a classroom-ready presentation. The PowerPoint slides are updated to reflect the content and organization of the new edition of the text and feature some additional examples and real-world cases for application and discussion. Available for download on the password-protected instructor companion website, the presentations can also be obtained by emailing your local Cengage Learning representative.

For the Student

Mindtap for Criminal Investigation With Mind-Tap™ Criminal Justice for *Criminal Investigation*, you have the tools you need to better manage your limited time, with the ability to complete assignments whenever and wherever you are ready to learn. Course material that is specially customized for you by your instructor in a proven, easy-to-use interface keeps you engaged and active in the course. MindTap helps you achieve better grades today by cultivating a true understanding of course concepts, and it includes a mobile app to keep you on track. With a wide array of course-specific tools and apps—from note taking to flashcards—you can feel confident that MindTap is a worthwhile and valuable investment in your education.

You will stay engaged with MindTap's video cases and career scenarios and remain motivated by information that shows where you stand at all times—both

individually and compared to the highest performers in class. MindTap eliminates the guesswork, focusing on what's most important with a learning path designed specifically by your instructor and for your Criminal Investigation course. Master the most important information with built-in study tools such as visual chapter summaries and integrated learning objectives that will help you stay organized and use your time efficiently.

Acknowledgments

We would first like to acknowledge Wayne W. Bennett, LLB (d. 2004), a graduate of the FBI National Police Academy and lead author on the first several editions of *Criminal Investigation*, a text originally based on his 45 years of experience in law enforcement and investigation. Bennett was the director of public safety for the Edina (Minnesota) Police Department as well as chief of police of Boulder City, Nevada. He taught various aspects of criminal investigation for more than 30 years and was coauthor of *Management and Supervision in Law Enforcement*, now in its seventh edition.

Second, we must acknowledge Kären Matison Hess, Ph.D. (d. 2010), the author who first developed this text with Bennett and carried it through eight very successful revisions, earning it the Text and Academic Authors Association's McGuffey Longevity Award in 2010. Dr. Hess was an instructor at Normandale Community College (Bloomington, Minnesota) who crafted a line of enduring, practical textbooks in the fields of law enforcement and criminal justice. In 2006, Dr. Hess was honored by the University of Minnesota College of Education and Human Development at the school's 100-year anniversary as one of 100 alumni who have made a significant contribution to education and human development. Without her tireless dedication to authorship and the education of criminal justice students, this text—and the many others she developed—would not have the 40-year track record of success that it does. Her passion and commitment will forever be an inspiration to us.

A number of professionals from academia and the field have reviewed the previous editions of *Criminal Investigation* and provided valuable suggestions, and we thank them all: Joel J. Allen, Western Illinois University; Thomas Allen, University of South Dakota; Captain Frank Anzelmi, Pennsylvania State Police; Greg Arnold, Manatee Community College; John Ballard, Rochester Institute of Technology; Robert Barthol, Chabot College; Kimberly Blackmon, Axia College of UOP, RETS College Online, and Central FL College Online; Alison McKenney Brown, Wichita State University; Jeffrey Bumgarner, Minnesota State University; Joseph Bunce, Montgomery College; William Castleberry, University of Tennessee at Martin; Walt Copley, Metropolitan State College of Denver; Edward Creekmore, Northland Community College; Elmer Criswell, Harrisburg Area Community College; Tom Cuda, Bunker Hill Community College; Stanley Cunningham, Western Illinois University; Andrew Dantschich, St. Petersburg Junior College; Chris DeLay, University of Louisiana at Lafayette; Everett Doolittle, Metropolitan State University; Thomas Drerup, Clark State Community College; Wayne Dunning, Wichita State University; Cass Gaska, Henry Ford Community College; Bruce Gordon, University of Cincinnati; Edmund Grosskopf, Indiana State University; Robert E. Grubb, Jr., Marshall University; Keith Haley, University of Cincinnati; George Henthorn, Central Missouri State University; Robert Hewitt, Edison Community College; John Hicks, Hocking Technical College; Ron Holt, Mercer University; Joanie Housewright, Texas Woman's University; Robert R. Ives, Rock Valley College; George Keefer, Southern Illinois University at Carbondale; Charles Thomas Kelly, Jr., Northwestern State University; Richard Kurek, Erie Community College North; James Lauria, Pittsburgh Technical Institute; Robert A. Lorinskas, Southern Illinois University at Carbondale; Todd Lough, Western Illinois University; David J. MacDonald, Eastfield College; Stan Malm, University of Maryland; Richard Mangan, Florida Atlantic University; Jane E. McClellan; Gayle Mericle, Western Illinois University; Michael Meyer, University of North Dakota; Jane Kravits Munley, Luzerne County Community College; Robert Neville, College of the Siskiyous; James F. Newman, Rio Hondo Community College; Thomas O'Connor, North Carolina Wesleyan College; William L. Pelkey, Eastern Kentucky University; Russ J. Pomrenke, Gwinnett Technical College; Ronald A. Pricom, New Mexico State University; Charles Quarles, University of Mississippi; Gregory E. Roth, Kirkwood Community College; Walter F. Ruger, Nassau Community College; James Scariot, Heald College; Shelley Shaffer, Keiser University; Jo Ann Short, Northern Virginia

Community College, Annandale; Joseph R. Terrill, Hartford Community College; Charles A. Tracy, Portland State University; Bob Walker, Trinity Valley Community College; Jason Waller, Tyler Junior College; and Richard Weber, Jamestown Community College.

We greatly appreciate the input of these reviewers. Sole responsibility for all content, however, is our own.

The authors also wish to thank the following individuals for adding valuable insight to the discussions concerning their respective areas of expertise: Jeffrey Liroff, Ray Fernandez, Timothy Kennedy, and Captain Tommy Bibb for their contributions on cargo theft investigations; John Lentini and retired Fire Chief Patrick Doheny for their critiques of arson investigations; Richard Scott and Detective Coreen Kulvich for their review of and input concerning computer crime and cybercrime investigations; Dan Christman, deputy director of the Snohomish County Medical Examiner's Office, for the use of some of his forensics photos in this text; and retired investigator Richard Gautsch for his careful review of the manuscript.

Additional special thanks go to Michael W. Worls and Betty L. Dickson, our product manager and content manager, respectively, at Cengage; and Katy Gabel, project manager at Lumina Datamatics.

Finally, thank you to our families and colleagues for their continuing support and encouragement throughout the development of *Criminal Investigation*, Twelfth Edition.

About the Authors

Christine Hess Orthmann, M.S., has been writing and researching in various aspects of criminal justice for more than 30 years. She is a coauthor of numerous Cengage books, including *Community Policing: Partnerships for Problem Solving* (8th edition), *Corrections for the Twenty-First Century, Constitutional Law and the Criminal Justice System* (7th edition), *Introduction to Law Enforcement and Criminal Justice* (11th edition), *Juvenile Justice* (6th edition), *Management and Supervision in Law Enforcement* (7th edition), and *Police Operations* (6th edition), as well as a major contributor to *Introduction to Private Security* (5th edition) and *Careers in Criminal Justice and Related Fields: From Internship to Promotion* (6th edition). She is a member of the National Criminal Justice Honor Society (Alpha Phi Sigma) and is a former reserve officer with the Rosemount (Minnesota) Police Department. Orthmann has a Master of Science Degree in criminal justice from the University of Cincinnati.

Kären Matison Hess, Ph.D., wrote extensively in the field of law enforcement and criminal justice. She was a member of the English department at Normandale Community College as well as the president of the Institute for Professional Development. Hess held a Ph.D. in instructional design from the University of Minnesota. Other texts Dr. Hess coauthored are *Criminal Procedure; Corrections in the Twenty-First Century: A Practical Approach; Introduction to Law Enforcement and Criminal Justice* (9th edition); *Introduction to Private Security* (5th edition); *Juvenile Justice* (5th edition); *Management and Supervision in Law Enforcement* (4th edition); *Community Policing: Partnerships for Problem Solving* (5th edition); *Police Operations* (4th edition); and *Careers in Criminal Justice: From Internship to Promotion* (6th edition).

Dr. Hess was a member of the Academy of Criminal Justice Sciences (ACJS), the American Association of University Women (AAUW), the American Society for Industrial Security (ASIS), the International Association of Chiefs of Police (IACP), the International Law Enforcement Educators and Trainers Association (ILEETA), the Justice Research and Statistics Association (JRSA), the National Council of Teachers of English (NCTE), the Police Executive Research Forum (PERF), and the Textbook and Academic Authors Association (TAA), of which she was a fellow and also a member of the TAA Foundation Board of Directors.

Sergeant Henry Lim Cho (retired) holds an M.A. in human services with an emphasis on Criminal Justice Leadership from Concordia University, St. Paul, Minnesota. He has worked in the field of criminal justice for more than 12 years, having held positions in private security, as a community service officer, police officer, and detective. He retired with the rank of sergeant from the Rosemount (Minnesota) Police Department. Sgt. Cho has experience as a use-of-force instructor and a crime scene investigator. His professional memberships include the Minnesota Police and Peace Officers Association, International Association of Identification—Minnesota Chapter, Minnesota Sex Crimes Investigator Association, High Technology Crime Investigation Association, and National White Collar Crime Center and Fraternal Order of Police. Sgt. Cho has published in the *Minnesota Police Journal*, appeared as a profile contributor in *Introduction to Law Enforcement and Criminal Justice* (9th edition), and is a contributor to *Police Operations* (5th edition) and *Introduction to Law Enforcement and Criminal Justice* (10th edition).

Sergeant Jennifer Molan Cho (retired) holds an M.A. in human services with an emphasis in Criminal Justice Leadership from Concordia University, St. Paul, Minnesota. She has spent more than 16 years in the criminal justice field, serving as a correctional deputy, deputy sheriff, school resource officer, gang investigator, and detective. She retired as a sergeant from the Dakota County (Minnesota) Sheriff's Office. She has extensive experience in gang and drug investigations, persons crimes, and white-collar crimes, and served as a union steward for several years. Sgt. Cho's professional memberships include the Minnesota Police and Peace Officers Association, Deputy Sheriff's Association, and International Gang Investigators Association. She coauthored and taught a juvenile diversion program for property offenders for the Dakota County Attorney's Office and appeared as a profile contributor to *Introduction to Law Enforcement and Criminal Justice* (11th edition). She has served as a subject matter expert on the CourXam Development Committee for *Introduction to Corrections* (2016), *Introduction to Law Enforcement* (2016), *Introduction to Criminal Justice Administration* (2016), and *Introduction to Criminal Procedure* (2016).

CRIMINAL INVESTIGATION

1 | Criminal Investigation: An Overview

Welcome to criminal investigation. What are you in for? Here's a glimpse . . .

New to law enforcement, rookie Police Detective Asha Mohammed responded to a homicide call and found herself standing over the body of a high school student. The 15-year-old girl had been brutally raped and murdered. Mohammed's world perspective that night would change forever. The 26-year-old detective had entered the police academy directly after completing her four-year college degree, and had graduated from the academy at the top of her class. She had finished her initial field training period on patrol and had just rotated into the investigative unit, the final step in probation that she needed to complete before being released on her own with her new partner.

Naive and inexperienced, Mohammed played a primary role in the pursuit, arrest, and conviction of the murder suspect. During the next five years with a metropolitan police department, Mohammed was involved in a variety of cases, including several undercover assignments. Her youthful appearance and cultural background allowed her access into a secretive Somali gang drug ring, and it didn't take her long to gain the trust of high-level dealers. During one investigation, Mohammed found herself in a hotel room with her informant, two dealers, and several gang members passing around a meth pipe. The leader of the gang asked Mohammed why she wasn't participating, and for the first time, she found herself in a position of fear, nearly overcome with the urge to flee.

Without any weapons or backup and nowhere to go, Mohammed had little choice but to try the drug, as the risk of

blowing her cover would have been deadly. Shortly afterwards she had to report the usage to her immediate supervisor and attend a mandatory detox and rehabilitation before being cleared to return to work. Through these experiences the young detective learned to rely on not only her communication skills, her intuition, street smarts, and attention to detail but also her survival instincts.

Over time, Mohammed came to understand that conducting tedious research for cases and sifting through filthy drug house trash cans were far more common elements of investigation than the excitement or intrigue shown on *NCIS* or *New York Undercover*. For an investigator, the ability to interview and write reports is vastly more important than how accurately they can shoot at the range or how skilled they are at tactical driving.

After several more years, Mohammed was eventually promoted to sergeant, supervising the general Investigations Unit. That same year, Mohammed led the investigation of a fellow police officer killed in the line of duty. This was her most difficult case, as the murder victim was not only an academy classmate of hers but also a close, personal friend. This made the case especially traumatic.

Several more years passed, and 15 years into her career, Sergeant Mohammed was promoted to captain. After getting her bars pinned on, Mohammed was assigned to command the entire investigative division, which included general investigations, homicide, gangs, drugs, sex crimes, property crimes, and white-collar crimes. In her second year as a captain, Mohammed led a highly publicized case that stunned everyone in the community. A young teenage boy was brutally beaten to death in an affluent neighborhood. There was overwhelming evidence against a neighbor who had a prior criminal history of violence, and no one in the community doubted his guilt, yet he remained un-charged, and the investigation stayed open. The community was outraged. Over the next three years, Mohammed and her team actively pursued and investigated the case, only to discover they had the wrong suspect.

This thumbnail sketch of one detective's career offers a glimpse into the world of the criminal investigator. Criminal investigation is a complex, sophisticated field, each aspect of which could constitute a book. This text includes the most basic aspects of criminal investigation. Section 1 presents an overview of criminal investigation and general guidelines to follow or adapt in specific circumstances, as well as basic considerations in the preliminary investigation, the most critical phase in the majority of investigations.

Investigators must be thoroughly familiar with crimes and their elements, modus operandi information, the major goals of investigation, the basic functions of investigating officers, and the investigators' relationships with other individuals and agencies.

Investigators do not operate in a vacuum but must relate to constitutional safeguards. They must also understand how case law determines the parameters within which they perform the investigative process. How these constitutional safeguards and case law specifically affect investigations is emphasized throughout the text.

Chapter 1
Criminal Investigation: An Overview

Learning Objectives

LO1 Summarize the primary goals of the criminal investigation.

LO2 Describe the basic functions performed by investigators.

LO3 Understand the intellectual, psychological, and physical characteristics possessed by an effective investigator.

LO4 Describe the key aspects of the initial investigation.

LO5 Explain how investigators decide whether or not to pursue a criminal investigation and what information they consider in this process.

LO6 Identify the various individuals and entities with whom successful investigators interrelate.

LO7 Describe some of the ways investigators can protect against civil lawsuits.

Introduction

On a cold January day in 2010, Livonia, Louisiana, police officer John Thibodeaux was patrolling the roads of Pointe Coupee Parish when he saw a car swerving between lanes. Officer Thibodeaux stopped the car and arrested the driver, 45-year-old Kevin Edison Smith, for drug possession. Under Louisiana law, police are authorized to take DNA samples during drug arrests, and Smith's DNA was entered into the national database. Little did Thibodeaux realize at the time that his stop would provide the missing piece to a murder mystery that had dodged Texas police for nearly 15 years.

On March 5, 1996, 13-year-old Krystal Jean Baker was last seen leaving a convenience store in Texas City, Texas. Krystal—who incidentally was the great-niece of Norma Jean Baker, aka Marilyn Monroe—was reportedly walking to a friend's house after a family spat at her grandmother's home. Her body was found later that day under a bridge in Chambers County. She had been sexually assaulted and strangled. DNA swabs were taken but led nowhere.

Several months after Smith's arrest in Louisiana, police in Texas City discovered the needle in the haystack they had been searching for—a DNA hit to match the sample gathered from the child victim. According to authorities, had Smith been pulled over in Texas for his offense, the case may never have been solved, because under Texas law, DNA can be taken only after an individual is convicted of certain sex offenses. In Louisiana, however, state law allowed DNA samples to be collected from suspects, not just convicted felons.

Some would say that the traffic stop and subsequent arrest were just plain luck. However, experience and alertness often play significant roles in investigation, and an observant police officer can initiate an important criminal investigation, sometimes without realizing it at first. Criminal investigation combines art and science

and requires extraordinary preparation and training. And in today's high-tech society, where information flows faster than ever and citizens expect results more quickly, investigators need to step up their technology and teamwork skills—they need an edge.

Because no two crimes are identical, even if committed by the same person, each investigation is unique. The great range of variables in individual crimes makes it impossible to establish fixed rules for conducting an investigation. Nevertheless, some general guidelines help to ensure a thorough, effective investigation. Investigators modify and adapt these guidelines to fit each case.

Investigators need not have superhuman reasoning ability. They must, however, proceed in an orderly, systematic way, gathering facts to analyze and evaluate. This chapter introduces decisions to be made and the actions to be taken. Subsequent chapters explain each step of the preliminary and follow-up investigations more fully.

A Brief History of Criminal Investigation

Contemporary criminal investigation owes its genesis to several notable individuals and events, the first significant one being the 1748 appointment of Henry Fielding as Magistrate of England's Bow Street. In 1750, as a response to widespread crime and disorder throughout his jurisdiction, Fielding formed the Bow Street Runners, which became the first paid detective unit.

Another noteworthy individual in the evolution of criminal investigation was Eugène François Vidocq, a former criminal turned crime fighter who is considered the father of modern criminology. In 1811, Vidocq organized a plainclothed civilian detective unit called

the Brigade de la Sûreté (Security Brigade), and in 1812, when the police realized the value of this unit, it was officially converted to the National Police Force, with Vidocq appointed head of the unit.

In 1833, Vidocq created Le Bureau des Renseignements (Office of Information), which combined private police and private investigation into what is considered the first private detective agency. Interestingly, most of the agents were ex-criminals. As head of the unit, Vidocq is often recognized as the first private detective in history. Vidocq is credited with introducing undercover work, ballistics, and criminology. He made the first plaster casts of shoe impressions and created indelible ink and unalterable bond paper. The exclusive Vidocq Society—a fraternal organization founded in 1990 whose members are both law enforcement professionals and nonprofessionals and meet monthly in a social setting to evaluate and discuss unsolved crimes, often homicides, officially brought to them by other law enforcement agencies—is named after him. Admission into this elite society is selective, with just over 150 individuals currently allowed to wear the distinctive red, white, and blue Vidocq rosette representing membership.

Also around this time, in 1842, England's Scotland Yard created an investigative branch.

Meanwhile, in the United States, the first municipal detective divisions were beginning to take shape. Allan Pinkerton, who immigrated from Scotland to the United States in 1842, played a significant historical role in modern police investigations. He was appointed the first detective in Chicago in 1849 and was a cofounder of the Northwestern police agency, which later became the Pinkerton National Detective Agency, whose symbol was a watchful eye and whose motto was "We never sleep." Pinkerton's agents were the forerunners for the U.S. Secret Service, and his agency was employed at the federal level for many famous cases, including protecting Abraham Lincoln in his presidency. Pinkerton developed several investigative techniques still used in law enforcement that include stings and undercover work, as well as the surveillance methods of shadowing and following targets or suspects. He was also known for working on a centralized database of criminal identification records that is now maintained by the Federal Bureau of Investigation (FBI).

Investigative units also began cropping up in other police agencies after Chicago's lead, with Detroit establishing a detective bureau in 1866, followed by New York in 1882 and Cincinnati in 1886.

The use of biometrics and identification systems in criminal investigation began in 1882, when French police officer Alphonse Bertillon, now considered the father of personal identification, unveiled a system known as anthropometry, in which offenders were identified by their unique physical measurements, as well as personality characteristics and individual markings, such as tattoos and scars. In 1884, Bertillon used his technique to identify 241 multiple offenders, demonstrating that the Bertillon system could successfully distinguish first-time offenders from recidivists. The system was quickly adopted by American and British police forces and remained a primary method of identifying suspects for more than three decades, when fingerprint analysis replaced it as more accurate means of identification.

Bertillon also standardized the criminal mug shot, advocated that crime scene pictures be taken before the scene was disturbed in any way, and developed "metric photography" to reconstruct the dimensions of a particular space and the placement of objects in it. Other forensic techniques credited to Bertillon include forensic document examination, ballistics, the use of molding compounds to preserve footprints, and the use of the dynamometer to determine the degree of force used in breaking and entering.

The field of criminalistics and forensics began taking shape in 1910, when Edmond Locard, a French criminologist, set forth his "exchange principle" stating that a criminal always removes something from a crime scene or leaves incriminating evidence behind. Under police leaders such as August Vollmer and J. Edgar Hoover, who is credited with molding the FBI into a credible national law enforcement entity, law enforcement and investigators in the United States began adopting Locard's exchange principle in 1932.

August "Gus" Vollmer, known as the father of modern policing, pioneered the movement to professionalize police by starting the first school in which officers could learn the laws of evidence. In 1905 he was elected town marshal of Berkeley, California, and in 1909 he became its first police chief. However, before officially becoming the chief, Vollmer was bringing innovation to criminal investigation. In 1907 he became the first American officer to implement the use of blood, fiber, and soil analysis in criminal investigations. In 1920 he was the first chief to have his department use the lie detector, an instrument developed by the University of California during a criminal investigation.

These early developments, as shown in Table 1.1, set the stage for a rapidly evolving field of criminal investigation in the United States. But what, exactly, *is* criminal investigation?

Definitions Pertinent to Criminal Investigation

An investigation is a patient, step-by-step inquiry or observation; a careful examination; a recording of evidence; or a legal inquiry. The word **investigate** is derived from the Latin word *vestigare*, meaning "to track" or "trace," a derivation easily related to police investigation. A **criminal investigation** is the process of discovering, collecting, preparing, identifying, and presenting evidence to determine what happened, whether a crime was committed, and who is responsible.

Criminal investigation is a reconstructive process that uses **deductive reasoning**, a logical process in which a conclusion follows from specific facts. Based on specific pieces of evidence, investigators establish proof that a suspect is guilty of an offense. For example, finding the suspect's watch at the scene of a burglary is one piece of evidence that supports the premise that the suspect was at the scene. An issue that might arise is whether the watch could have been planted there. Investigators need to anticipate what issues might arise and what evidence is needed to support the prosecutor's case. All issues in dispute must be supported by evidence. The more evidence an investigation yields, the stronger the proof of guilt. Equally important, however, is evidence establishing innocence.

Criminalistics refers to specialists trained in recording, identifying, and interpreting the minutiae (minute details) of physical evidence. A **criminalist** (aka crime scene technician, examiner, or investigator) searches for, collects, and preserves physical evidence in investigations of crime and suspected criminals. Criminalistics is a branch of **forensic science**, a broader field that encompasses the application of myriad scientific processes to the law, including legal inquiries conducted within the context of the criminal justice system (Fantino, 2007). The U.S. Department of Justice lists the following as the most common forensic science laboratory disciplines (2019):

- Molecular biology

- Chemistry

- Trace evidence examination (hairs and fibers, paints and polymers, glass, soil, etc.)

- Latent fingerprint examination

- Firearms and toolmarks examination

- Handwriting analysis

- Fire and explosives examination

- Toxicology

- Digital evidence

Other disciplines that may have a forensic applications include odontology, anthropology, serology, and photography. Practitioners involved in the disciplines of forensic pathology, forensic nursing, forensic psychology, forensic entomology, and forensic engineering are most often found in medical examiner or coroner offices, in universities, or in private practices (USDOJ, 2019).

The first determination in a criminal investigation is whether a crime has, in fact, been committed. Although everyone has a notion of what crime is, investigators must have a very precise understanding of what it means. Specific definitions of such terms as *crime, felony, misdemeanor, criminal statute,* and *ordinance* are found in case law.

A **crime** is an act or omission (of an act) that is forbidden by law and considered an offense against the state. In contrast to a tort, which is a private harm, a crime is a violation of a public right to which a government-sanctioned penalty is attached. The broader use of the term *crime* includes both felonies and misdemeanors, two general categories whose parameters are set based on the severity of an act and its recommended punishment. The more serious society considers a crime, the more severe the penalty. A **felony** is a serious crime, graver than a misdemeanor; it is generally punishable by death or imprisonment of more than one year in a penitentiary. A **misdemeanor** is a crime or offense that is less serious than a felony and is punishable by a fine or imprisonment of as long as one year in an institution other than a penitentiary. Misdemeanors are sometimes further subdivided into gross and petty misdemeanors, based on the value of the property involved and/or the severity of the offense.

A crime can be defined at the state or federal level through a **criminal statute**, a legislative act relating to prohibited conduct and attaching a penalty or punishment to that conduct. A crime can also be defined by an **ordinance**, an act of the legislative body of a municipality or county relating to all the rules governing the municipality or county, including misdemeanors. Statutes and ordinances list specific conditions, called the **elements of the crime**, that must occur for an act to be called a specific kind of crime. For example, a state statute might define burglary as occurring when (1) an accused enters a building (2) without the consent of the rightful owner (3) with the intent to commit a crime. An investigation must prove each element, even if the suspect has confessed. Sections 3 and 4 of this text discuss the elements of major crimes. Knowing these specific elements is essential to gathering evidence to prove a crime has been committed. Definitions of crimes and their penalties vary considerably depending on whether they occur at the municipal, county, state, or federal level. Consequently, investigators must be familiar with their area's criminal statutes and ordinances. For example, in some states, shoplifting is a felony regardless of the value of the property taken. In other states, however, the value of the shoplifted property determines whether the crime is a misdemeanor or a felony.

Because crimes and their penalties are established and defined by state and federal statutes and local ordinances, an act that is not declared a crime by statute or ordinance is not a chargeable offense, no matter how wrong it may seem. Designated crimes and their punishments change as society's attitudes change. In the past, for example, behavior associated with alcoholism was considered criminal, but

TABLE 1.1	**Major Advances in Criminal Investigation**
1750	First paid detective unit is formed in England—Fielding's Bow Street Runners.
1833	First private detective agency is formed in France by Vidocq.
1849	Pinkerton becomes the first American detective (in Chicago). Other municipalities across the country soon establish detective positions.
1868	DNA discovered.
1882	Alphonse Bertillon uses anthropometrics as a means of identification.
1893	First major book on investigation, *Criminal Investigation* by Austrian Hans Gross, is published.
1896	Edward Henry develops a fingerprinting system, which is adopted throughout England in 1900.
1908	Federal Bureau of Investigation (FBI) is established.
1909	Dr. Karl Landsteiner discovers the different human blood types and classifies them into A, B, AB, and O groups.
1910	Dr. Edmond Locard sets forth his "exchange principle."
1913	Professor Victor Balthazard publishes his classic article on firearms identification.
1920s	Calvin Goddard raises firearms identification to a science and perfects the bullet comparison microscope.
1923	August Vollmer establishes the first full forensic laboratory, in Los Angeles.
Early 1950s	James Watson and Francis Crick identify the structure of DNA.
1967	FBI creates the National Crime Information Center (NCIC), which has been called the lifeline of law enforcement. NCIC is a collective database that includes stolen items, identity of terrorists, and missing persons; runs 24 hours a day, 365 days a year; and is available to all American as well as international law enforcement.
1970s	FBI implements the Behavioral Science Unit, more commonly known as "criminal profiling." This criminal investigation technique seeks to understand the psychological characteristics of an individual as a way to predict future crimes as well as narrow down a profile of a likely suspect in a case.
1979	Herman Goldstein's Problem-Oriented Policing is published.
1985	Alec Jeffreys discovers the parts of the DNA structure that are unique in each person, making positive identification possible.
1986	First use of DNA typing in a criminal case, in England: DNA is used to clear a suspect in a murder. (A detective in the East Midlands read of the case and sought Jeffreys's help in solving the vicious murder and rape of two British schoolgirls. The police held a prime suspect in the case, a kitchen porter at an insane asylum who had confessed to one of the murders. They brought to Jeffreys semen samples from the murder scenes and a blood sample from the suspect. Jeffreys confirmed that the same person committed both crimes, but it was not the suspect the police held. On November 21, 1986, the kitchen porter became the first person in the world to have his innocence proven by DNA testing.)
1988	First use of DNA typing in a criminal case, in the United States, in which a criminal is identified by DNA (*Andrews v. State*, 1988). (Lifecodes Corporation [Stamford, Connecticut] performed the tests in the first case in the United States in which a criminal was identified by DNA. The trial of accused rapist Tommie Lee Andrews began in Orlando, Florida, on November 3, 1987. A scientist from Lifecodes and an MIT biologist testified that semen from the victim matched Andrews's DNA and that Andrews's print would be found in only 1 in 10 billion individuals. On November 6, 1987, the jury returned a guilty verdict, and Andrews was subsequently sentenced to 22 years in prison.)
1991	FBI forms CART (Computer Analysis and Response Teams) to investigate suspects' computers.
1994	CompStat (COMPuter STATistics) is developed in New York to reduce crime and manage personnel.
1997	Idea of "Touch DNA" is developed.
1998	FBI launches the Combined DNA Index System (CODIS), a database that stores DNA profiles submitted by law enforcement and private laboratories and is used to identify criminal suspects.
1999	FBI launches the Integrated Automated Fingerprint Identification System (IAFIS), a database that retains fingerprints taken from law enforcement and is used to identify suspects.
2011	FBI launches Next Generation Identification (NGI), a system upgrade to replace IAFIS that integrates a fingerprint database and incorporates other biometric identification methods, such as voice, facial recognition, iris recognition, fingerprint, and palm print.
2013	U.S. Supreme Court rules that DNA can be taken from persons under arrest. No conviction is required.
2017	Rapid DNA Act passes allowing DNA testing to be implemented when booking a suspect into jail.
2018	Clarifying Lawful Overseas Use of Data (CLOUD) Act established to speed access to electronic information held by U.S.-based global providers that is critical to our foreign partners' investigations of serious crime.

today many states regard alcoholism as an illness. However, driving while intoxicated is now considered a much more serious offense than it was previously. Additionally, our society has designated as crimes certain acts, such as computer fraud, that were unknown in earlier times.

Primary Goals of Criminal Investigations

The goal of criminal investigation would seem to be to solve cases. In reality, the goals of criminal investigation are not quite so simple. Investigators must first determine whether a crime has, in fact, been committed and then, if it has, systematically seek evidence to identify the individual or individuals who committed the crime, locate the individual or individuals, and obtain sufficient evidence to prove in court that each suspect is guilty beyond a reasonable doubt. If the investigation is of a property crime, an additional goal is to locate and recover the property that was taken. Procedures to accomplish these goals are the focus of the remainder of this text. However, it must always be remembered that determining the truth is more important than obtaining a conviction or closing a case.

LO1	Summarize the primary goals of the criminal investigation.

The primary goals of criminal investigation are to:

- Determine whether a crime has been committed.
- Legally obtain information and evidence to identify the responsible person.
- Arrest the suspect.
- Recover stolen property.
- Present the best possible case to the prosecutor.

As discussed, a criminal investigation is unwarranted if no crime has been committed. A legal arrest cannot be made for an act that is not defined by statute or ordinance as a crime. Thus, the first goal of an investigator is to assess whether the evidence corroborates a specific offense. Determining whether a crime has been committed involves knowing the elements of each major offense and the type of evidence that supports the offenses and ascertaining whether that evidence is present.

In addition to proving that a crime has been committed, investigators must determine when the crime occurred and who committed it. Determining when the event occurred is critical for checking alibis and reconstructing the **modus operandi (MO)**—the preferred method a criminal uses when committing his or her crimes. If the crime was committed by a repeat offender, recognizing an MO can help the investigator identify the responsible party or parties. For example, it was relatively easy to recognize the "work" of Jack the Ripper or the Washington, DC–area snipers. The peculiarities of each crime scene may be entered into an MO file and matched with characteristics of known perpetrators of previous crimes. However, investigators must always be vigilant for the potential for "copycat" offenders, and suspects should never be eliminated simply because their known MO does not fit the crime being investigated.

While committing crimes, people may make mistakes. They almost always leave some type of evidence. They may overlook tangible evidence such as a jacket, pen, purse, piece of paper, or card that connects them with a crime scene. Such evidence may be left for any number of reasons: carelessness, panic, underestimation of police capabilities, emotional or mental instability, or the influence of drugs or alcohol. More often, however, criminals leave trace evidence, less visible evidence such as fingerprints, small particles of glass or dirt, a faint footprint, body hairs, or clothing fibers. Investigators search for evidence using methods discussed fully in Chapter 4.

Sometimes, however, little or no evidence exists. Thus, not all crimes are solvable. For example, a theft committed by a transient who enters a house through an open door, takes food (larceny), eats it, and then leaves the area unseen is a crime not likely to be solved. A burglary committed by a person wearing gloves and whose footprints are washed away by a hard rain before police arrive will be more difficult to solve than if it had not rained. Often fingerprints are found but cannot be matched with any prints on file. Many cases have insufficient evidence, no witnesses, and no informants to provide leads. Solvability factors will be discussed later in this chapter.

Investigators learn to recognize when a case is unsolvable, but only after all **leads** (avenues bearing clues or potential sources of information relevant to solving the crime) have been exhausted. An FBI agent once remarked, "Any average person with training can pursue 'hot' leads. It is the investigator who can develop leads when the trail grows cold who is the superior investigator." A successful investigation is one in which

- A logical sequence is followed.
- All physical evidence is legally obtained and analyzed.
- All witnesses are effectively interviewed.

- All suspects are legally and effectively interrogated.

- All leads are thoroughly developed.

- All details of the case are accurately and completely recorded and reported.

Basic Investigative Functions: The Responsibility of All Police Personnel

Early police organizations were one-unit/one-purpose departments, with everyone performing generalized functions, including criminal investigations. However, over time, departments perceived a need for specialization because of

- The need to know about criminals and their MOs

- The amount of training necessary for learning and developing investigative techniques

- The frequency with which investigators had to leave their assigned shifts and areas during an investigation

- Patrol forces' heavy workloads

- A general administrative philosophy that supported specialization as a means of increasing efficiency and therefore solving more crimes

In larger police departments, specialization developed first in investigative functions and only later in other areas such as traffic, crime prevention, juveniles, and community relations. In most of these departments, the investigative division remains a separate unit under its own command and supervisory personnel. The officer in charge reports directly to the chief of police or a chief of operations. Department policy specifies the roles of and the relationships among the administrative, uniformed patrol, and investigative divisions. When these roles are clearly defined, the department can better achieve its common goals, with the investigative division fulfilling its assigned responsibilities in coordination with all other departments.

It is important to recognize that even in agencies where "investigations" are a separate division, they still exist within an integrated whole, with all levels of police administration and operations contributing to the success of criminal investigations. Administrative decisions affect the selection and assignment of personnel as well as the policies regulating their performance. According to the U.S. Bureau of Labor Statistics, detectives and criminal investigators comprised approximately 14% of all sworn law enforcement personnel in 2018 (n.d.).

Today, researchers are studying the extent to which specialization should remain, its effectiveness, the number of personnel who should be assigned to specialized investigative functions, and the selection and training required for such specialization. Several specific factors appear to support the training of *all* officers to perform investigative duties:

- Increasing competition for tax monies

- Possession of highly sophisticated equipment by some criminals

- More criminals using multiple MOs

- "Withdrawal syndrome" within the general public (i.e., the desire to remain uninvolved necessitates specialized training in interviewing techniques)

- Overwhelming workload of cases assigned to investigative personnel

- More intelligent, better-educated police recruits

- More police training available

The reality is that the majority of policing in the United States today occurs not in large, urban law enforcement organizations but in small agencies, serving relatively small jurisdictions, where departments do not have the "luxury" of a dedicated division of detectives. As such, the ultimate responsibility for criminal investigation lies with all police personnel, regardless of rank or title.

Uniformed patrol has traditionally been considered the backbone of the police department and has been responsible for the initial response to a crime. As first responders, patrol officers are required to perform at least preliminary investigations and are, in fact, in an ideal position to see an investigation through to its disposition. Experiments have shown that initial investigations by patrol officers can be as effective as those conducted by specialists. Involving frontline officers in the entire investigative process creates interest in crime prevention as well as investigation. In addition, giving patrol officers increased responsibility for investigating crimes frees detectives, in those agencies with such specialists, to concentrate on offenses that require more detailed investigations as well as on cases that require them to leave the community to conduct special interviews or to pursue leads. The result is a better investigation by the patrol officer of the more frequent, less severe crimes.

The trend toward having all officers assume a more active role in investigating crimes allows patrol officers more responsibility when responding to a call and enables them to conduct as much of the follow-up investigation as their shift and assigned areas of patrol permit. The importance of the patrol officer's investigative role cannot be overemphasized.

Regardless of whether departments have specialists or generalists, their goal is the same: solving crimes. Similarly, the investigative functions are the same, whether executed by a uniformed patrol officer or a detective in a suit and tie.

> **LO2** Describe the basic functions performed by investigators.
>
> Investigators perform the following functions:
>
> - Provide emergency assistance.
> - Secure the crime scene.
> - Photograph, videotape, and sketch.
> - Take notes and write reports.
> - Draft legal documents such as search warrants and subpoenas.
> - Search for, obtain, and process physical and digital evidence.
> - Obtain information from witnesses and suspects.
> - Conduct photographic and in-person lineups.
> - Identify suspects.
> - Conduct raids, surveillances, stakeouts, and undercover assignments.
> - Testify in court.

Most of these basic functions are discussed in detail in Section 2. What is important at this point is to realize the complexity of and interrelationships among the various functions performed by investigators and the skills they must develop.

Before looking at the characteristics of an effective investigator, it is prudent to briefly mention here the function of the crime scene investigator, or CSI, a specialist in the organized scientific collection and processing of evidence. CSIs not only develop, process, and package all physical evidence found at the crime scene and transport it to the lab for forensic evaluation, but they also attend and document autopsies, write reports, and testify in court about the evidence. And while CSIs are investigators, their role is limited to dealing with physical evidence and few, if any, of the other functions performed by a "generalist" criminal investigator. As such, further discussion about CSIs and the phenomenon known as the CSI effect is presented in Chapter 5.

Characteristics of an Effective Investigator

Although criminal investigation has become increasingly scientific over the past two centuries, investigators are frequently required to practice the "art" of investigation, that is, to rely on skill acquired by experience, study, and observation rather than on scientific principles. Investigators must develop the ability to see relationships between and among apparently unrelated facts and to question the apparently unquestionable. Effective criminal investigations require great attention to detail, an exceptionally suspicious nature at the appropriate time, considerable training in the classroom and the field, an unusual ability to obtain information from diverse types of personalities under adverse circumstances, and endless patience and perseverance. In short, a good investigator is knowledgeable, creative, patient, and persistent. Regardless of title, pay, or rank, investigative officers are more effective when they possess specific intellectual, psychological, and physical characteristics.

Intellectual Characteristics

Investigators must absorb training and apply it to their work. They must know the elements of the crime, understand and be able to apply investigative techniques, and be able to work with many different types of people. Exceptional intelligence is not a requisite trait of an effective investigator; objectivity, logic, and common sense are more important.

> **LO3** Understand the intellectual, psychological, and physical characteristics possessed by an effective investigator.
>
> Effective investigators obtain and retain information, apply technical knowledge, and remain open-minded, objective, and logical. They are well-organized and able to prioritize and manage cases effectively. They are also **culturally adroit**, that is, skilled in interacting across gender, ethnic, generational, social, and political group lines.

Investigators meet and talk with people from all walks of life—blue-collar workers and professionals, males and females, adults and juveniles—and must adjust their approach to each. In addition, each crime scene must be absorbed and recalled, sometimes months or years later. Thus, accurate, complete, and well-organized reports and records are essential.

Investigators also develop knowledge of and skill in investigative techniques such as interviewing and interrogating, photographing and sketching, searching, note taking, and numerous other areas discussed in Section 2. Such knowledge and skill are acquired through continuous training and experience, including academic classroom experiences, personal experiences, street learning, and learning from others in the field.

The abilities to obtain and retain information and to use investigative techniques effectively are worth little without the ability to reason through a case. The mental process involved in investigation is extremely complex. Logic is indispensable and often involves reverse thinking—that is, working the case backward. Why did an event happen? When? How? Who is culpable? Investigators must examine all possible cause-and-effect relations, find links, and draw conclusions—but only after they thoroughly explore all alternatives.

Decision making is continual and, to be effective, must be based on facts. When investigators review information and evidence, they concentrate on what is known (facts) rather than on what is only probable (inferences), and they eliminate personal opinions as much as possible. With sufficient facts, investigators can make valid inferences, from which they can logically draw definite conclusions.

A *fact* is an action, an event, a circumstance, or an actual thing done. In contrast, an *inference* is a process of reasoning by which a fact may be deduced (deductive reasoning). An *opinion* is a personal belief. For example, an investigator called to the scene of a shooting finds a dead man with a revolver in his hand (fact) and a suicide note on the table (fact). The officer might infer that the man committed suicide. The investigator might also hold the opinion that people who commit suicide are cowards. This opinion is irrelevant to the investigation. The inference, however, is critical. If the officer formulates a theory about the death based on suicide and sets out to prove the theory correct, much information and evidence may be overlooked or ignored. This is known as **inductive reasoning**, going from the generalization and establishing it by gathering specific facts. (Recall that criminal investigation is a reconstructive process that uses deductive reasoning.) Often both types of reasoning are required in an investigation.

Although investigators must draw inferences and form theories, they must also remain open-minded and willing to consider alternatives. Effective investigators guard against the tendency to become sold on a suspect or theory early in an investigation because such a mind-set creates an investigative myopia or shortsightedness, fostering the subconscious shaping of evidence or interpreting information to support their premature theory. Preconceived ideas hinder good investigation; objectivity is essential. Whenever an inference is drawn, its validity should be tested by examining the facts on which it is based.

The investigator seeks the truth, not simply proof of the suspect's guilt. Article 10 of the *Canons of Police Ethics* (International Association of Chiefs of Police [IACP]) states, "The law enforcement officer shall be concerned equally in the prosecution of the wrongdoer and the defense of the innocent. He shall ascertain what constitutes evidence and shall present such evidence impartially and without malice" (IACP, 1957).

Psychological Characteristics

Certain psychological characteristics are indispensable to effective investigation.

LO3 Understand the intellectual, psychological, and physical characteristics possessed by an effective investigator.

Effective investigators are emotionally well-balanced, detached, inquisitive, suspecting, discerning, self-disciplined, conscientious, and persevering.

Investigation is highly stressful and involves many decisions. Therefore, it requires emotional stability. Overly defensive or overly sensitive officers may fall victim to stress. Investigators must also absorb abuse and at the same time show kindness and empathy. Further, they must remain detached and uninvolved; otherwise, the problems of those with whom they are in contact will decrease their objectivity. Personal involvement with individuals associated with an investigation hinders the investigation and poses a direct threat to the investigator's emotional well-being.

Although remaining detached and objective, effective investigators are intimately involved with every aspect of the case. They do not accept things at face value; rather, they question what they hear and see. They use their knowledge of human nature to determine the truth of what is said. People often lie or tell half-truths, but this does not necessarily mean they are criminals. With experience, investigators develop a sense for who is telling the truth, who has important information, and who is acting suspiciously. The ability to distinguish the ordinary from the extraordinary and the normal from the suspicious is a hallmark of an effective investigator.

In addition, investigators must be self-disciplined and able to organize their time. Closely related to self-discipline is the willingness to persevere, to "stick with it" as long as is reasonable. Investigation often involves hours, days, or months of waiting and watching, of performing tedious, boring assignments that may or may not yield information or evidence helpful to the case. Thus, patience and perseverance are often the key to successful investigation. And although perseverance is desirable, it should not be confused with a stubborn refusal to admit a case is not likely to be solved. An investigator's ability to prioritize and manage cases, so as to devote more resources to those cases with a higher likelihood of being cleared, increases their effectiveness.

Investigators often experience cases in which facts, reason, and logic seem to lead nowhere. Yet, just when the case is about to be closed, an obscure newspaper item, an anonymous phone tip, an overheard remark at a social function, or even a series of events having no apparent connection with the case may provide leads for further investigation. Many cases are solved when investigators develop leads and pursue both relevant and seemingly irrelevant information. This is where the art of investigation supersedes the science of investigation.

Perseverance, coupled with inquisitiveness and intuition, is indispensable in difficult cases. Scores of experienced investigators attest to the value of **intuition**, a "sudden knowing" without conscious reasoning or apparent logic. Based on knowledge and experience, intuition is commonly referred to as *street sense*. It is the urge to proceed with no apparent valid reason, a "gut feeling" developed through experience.

Physical Characteristics

Age, height, and weight, unless they are extreme, are not important characteristics for investigators. However, some physical characteristics are important.

> **LO3** Understand the intellectual, psychological, and physical characteristics possessed by an effective investigator.
>
> Effective investigators are physically fit and have good vision and hearing. Undercover investigators must also "look the part."

Good health and a high energy level are beneficial because the hours spent performing investigative duties can be long and demanding. In addition to being physically fit, investigators are aided by keen vision and hearing. Investigators may have to listen to words during sobbing, moans, and hysteria; hear a very weak voice from a

seriously wounded or dying person; listen to more than one person talking at a time; or conduct an interview while a plane is flying overhead, machinery is operating, or heavy traffic is passing by.

Finally, investigators who are working undercover are often allowed a more "lenient" standard of physical appearance than are regular patrol officers, such as having piercings, tattoos, and copious facial hair, as a way of blending into the group they are investigating.

An Overview of the Investigative Process

A criminal investigation is usually initiated following either the personal observation of a crime by a police officer or the receipt of information from a citizen. Such information is received at police headquarters or central dispatch by phone, fax, email, text, radio, or direct report when a person steps up to make a complaint or report a crime. Crime information may also be called in or texted anonymously to a tip line. A police dispatcher relays the information to a patrol officer by radio, phone, or mobile computer in the officer's squad car, and the officer responds. Regardless of how the incident becomes known to police, this awareness of or reporting of a crime sets the investigative wheels in motion and is the first stage in a criminal investigation. The various stages of the investigative process, as well as the personnel involved, the official reports generated, and the victim's, complainant's, and suspect's roles are described in Table 1.2. It is important for the student to recognize that reports are involved in every stage of the investigative process and report writing consumes a substantial amount of an investigator's time.

The Initial Investigation and Police Contact

Most initial investigations, also referred to as preliminary investigations, begin the same way, and the same basic procedures are followed regardless of whether the first officer at the scene is a patrol officer, an investigator, or the chief of police.

The Initial Response

The first officer who responds, also known as the primary officer, is in charge until relieved by another officer. Department policy defines who is to respond as well as the duties of these individuals.

LO4   Describe the key aspects of the initial investigation.

The initial response is usually by a patrol officer assigned to the area where a crime has occurred.

The initial response is crucial to the success of an investigation. Although it is popularly believed that cases are won or lost in court, more cases actually are lost during the first hour of an investigation—the initial response period—than in court.

After notification, either through direct observation or departmental communications, the officer goes to the scene as rapidly and safely as circumstances permit. A crime-response survey conducted by the Law Enforcement Assistance Administration (LEAA) revealed that a response time of one minute or less is necessary to increase the probability of arrest at the scene. Most police departments, however, cannot assure their citizens of such a short response time, even for emergencies. To provide a one-minute response time, police agencies would need much smaller patrol areas, much larger staffs, computer-dispatched vehicles and personnel, and, thus, much larger budgets.

It is important to arrive at a crime scene rapidly because

- The suspect may still be at or near the scene.

- Injured persons may need emergency care.

- Witnesses may still be at the scene.

- A dying person may have a confession or other pertinent information to give.

- Weather conditions may change or destroy evidence.

- The integrity of the crime scene and evidence must be preserved.

The responding officers proceed to the scene as quickly as safety allows. Officers who injure themselves or someone else on the way to a call may create more serious problems than exist at the crime scene. They may, in fact, open themselves, their department, and even their city to civil and criminal liability. Many departments are developing necessary guidelines for rapid responses, replacing the assumption that all calls for service should be responded to as rapidly as possible.

The seriousness of a crime and whether it is in progress are important factors in driving speed and the

TABLE 1.2 A Brief Summary of the Investigative Process

Stage of Investigation	Police Role	Stage of Reports	Victim's/Complainant's Role	Suspect's Role
Initial Report	Dispatched to call for service	Recording of initial call/report	Reports the incident, requests police response	Sometimes interferes with the call
Initial Investigation/Police Contact	Arrive on scene and acquire information; may collect evidence	Incident reports and all applicable forms	Provides interviews and information about the incident and suspect; may provide evidence	Provides interviews and information about the incident; may provide evidence
Incident Review/Case Screening	Determine if further investigation is required after a review of the case	Police supervisor reviews the case for approval	Sometimes informed of case status	None
Follow-Up Investigations	Gather remaining information and evidence required for the case	Additional reports, additional interviews and evidence	Verifies and confirms information	Additional interviews and interrogations if cooperative and warranted
Case Preparation and Approval	Review the reports, coordinate the case with prosecution	Ready to submit for formal charging or court processing	None	None
Prosecution and Charging of Crime	Be available for court and testimony	Prosecution and court reports	Be available for court and testimony	In custody or present for court; if not present, have legal representation
Conclusion	Clear reports, release or purge evidence; close case with a disposition	File all complete reports into records	Retrieve any property used as evidence in the case	None

Source: Cho, H. L. Cho Research & Consulting, LLC. Copyright 2011.

rapidity of response. The use of emergency lights and siren may depend on the information furnished or may be dictated by department policy or state laws. A siren speeds arrival, but it also prompts the criminal to flee the scene. On the other hand, in a violent crime against a person, a siren alerting the offender may prevent further violence. Sometimes the victim, to avoid attracting attention, requests that no sirens and red lights be used. Some agencies and states, however, have policies or laws that require a responding officer to use both lights and siren together. Officers must know the specific laws governing their jurisdiction and whether they are allowed discretion in using lights and siren.

The route taken is also an important consideration. Officers should know which streets are under construction in their areas and avoid them. They must also choose between the fastest route and the route the suspect might use to leave the scene. When approaching a scene, officers should observe people leaving the scene and make mental notes of their descriptions. If two officers are in the patrol vehicle, one may write descriptions of people and vehicles observed leaving the scene. Many officers use in-squad video or digital recorders for such observations, permitting a single officer to record information while proceeding to the scene.

While driving to the scene, officers formulate a plan of action based on the type of crime and its location. An immediate response may be crucial because, even if no immediate arrest is made, the amount of information that can be obtained is directly related to the speed of response. Moreover, initial information is often the most important and accurate.

Many departments have found that sending several vehicles to a crime scene may not be the most effective approach. Instead, they implement a "bull's-eye," or target, approach, dispatching only a few vehicles directly to the crime scene (the bull's-eye). Other units are sent to observe traffic at major intersections radiating away from the crime scene in an attempt to intercept fleeing suspects. Success depends on broadcasting the suspects' descriptions rapidly and getting to the major intersections quickly. In many cases, such a response is more effective in catching the suspects than focusing all resources directly on the crime scene itself.

The Point of Arrival

When the first officers arrive, the scene may be either utter chaos or deserted. Regardless of the situation, the officers must take charge immediately and form a plan for proceeding based on the information they have at hand, which might not be much. The actions the first responders take at a crime scene can determine the value of the evidence for investigators and prosecutors.

People at a crime scene may be excited, apprehensive, or perplexed. They may be cooperative or uncooperative, confused or lucid. Therefore, officers must be flexible and understanding. Discretion and good judgment are essential because the greatest potential for solving the case lies with those present at the scene, even though many details of the crime may not be known at this stage. More decisions are made in less time at the point of arrival than at any other stage in the investigation, and this is when officers obtain most leads for subsequent action.

The initial response is a crucial stage in an investigation. The responding officer should obtain as much information from dispatch as possible before arriving on the scene.
© Henry Cho

Setting Priorities

Circumstances at the scene often dictate what is done first.

> **LO4** Describe the key aspects of the initial investigation.
>
> The priorities when arriving on scene are as follows:
> - Handle emergencies first to achieve scene safety.
> - Secure the scene to protect the integrity of the investigation.
> - Investigate.

The following guidelines can be adapted to fit specific circumstances.

Handling Emergency Situations

Sometimes emergencies dictate procedure. An emergency may include a dangerous suspect at or near the scene, a gravely injured person, or an environmental hazard such as downed power lines or chemical spills. Any of these emergencies can present a life-threatening situation for the officer and others, and their handling takes priority over other actions and situations. For example, if you arrive at a crime scene and the suspect begins to shoot at you, apprehending the suspect obviously becomes your first priority. In other instances, a person may be so seriously injured that without immediate aid, death is probable. Such an emergency takes precedence over all other procedures, unless officer safety or other public safety concerns preclude it. Then the scene must be secured before an officer administers aid.

Good judgment and the number of available officers dictate what should occur first if more than one emergency exists. Sometimes the decision is difficult. For example, if a victim is drowning, a suspect is running away, and only one officer is at the scene, the officer must make a split-second decision. Usually, saving life takes precedence. However, if the officer can do nothing to save the victim, the best alternative is to pursue the suspect. Apprehending the suspect may save other victims.

Responding to emergency situations causes the adrenaline to flow. At the same time, officers must plan their approach and remain extremely vigilant regarding the inherent danger associated with in-progress crimes. Officers should be preparing mentally for what they might encounter and continue to communicate with dispatch and other responding officers as new details arise.

One of the most important details to communicate is whether the suspect has fled the scene and could be, or is known for a fact to be, armed with a dangerous weapon.

Officers should also attempt to think like the suspect. They should decide which escape routes are probable and block them. Available information about the situation helps officers decide whether using lights and siren is advantageous to them or to the suspect. Officers should think about what they would do if they were the suspect and were cornered at the crime scene. If it is daytime, officers may be visible and the suspect not. If it is nighttime, officers may be able to take advantage of a darker area for their approach.

Flexibility is essential. The situation must be carefully assessed because each incident is different and requires different approaches and techniques. Officers should be cognizant that more than one suspect may be present.

Maintaining some physical distance can facilitate observation and give officers time to make decisions that will enhance their safety. In addition, reporting information as it becomes available helps backup know what they are coming into and offers other responding officers ideas on where they may need to go to secure a perimeter.

A Suspect at or near the Scene. If a call is made rapidly enough and officers can respond quickly, they may observe the crime in progress and arrest the suspect at the scene.

> **LO4** Describe the key aspects of the initial investigation.
>
> Any suspect at the scene should be detained, questioned, and then released or arrested, depending on circumstances.

Departmental policy determines whether the first officer at the scene thoroughly interrogates a suspect. Before any in-custody interrogation, an officer must read the *Miranda* warning to the suspect (a legality discussed in Chapter 6). Even if the policy is that officers do not interrogate suspects, officers often use discretion. For example, they may have to take a dying declaration or a suspect's spontaneous confession. If this occurs, a statement is taken immediately because the suspect may refuse, or be unable, to cooperate later. A more formal interrogation and written confession can be obtained later at the police department.

The suspect is removed from the scene as soon as possible to minimize the destruction of evidence and to facilitate questioning. The sooner suspects are removed, the less they can observe of the crime scene and possible evidence against them.

If the Suspect Has Recently Fled. If the suspect has just left the scene, immediate action is required. If the information is provided early enough, other units en route to the scene may make an arrest.

> **LO4** Describe the key aspects of the initial investigation.
>
> If a suspect has recently left the scene, officers obtain descriptions of the suspect, any vehicles, direction of travel, and any items taken, and then dispatch the information immediately.

As soon as practical, officers obtain more detailed information about the suspect's possible whereabouts, friends, descriptions of stolen items, and other relevant information regarding past criminal records and MOs. Such information can provide insight into where a suspect might go after committing a crime. For example, is the suspect a gambler or a heavy drinker? Could they be headed to a favorite bar? Do they have family living nearby? If a video from a responding squad car has captured the suspect vehicle's license plate, who is the registered owner, and where do they live?

If a Person Is Seriously Injured. Emergency first aid to victims, witnesses, and suspects is often a top priority of arriving officers. Officers should call for medical assistance and then do whatever possible until help arrives. They should observe and record the injured person's condition. When medical help arrives, officers should assist and instruct medical personnel during the care and removal of those injured to diminish the risk of contaminating the scene and losing evidence.

If a person is injured so severely that he or she must be removed from the scene, attending medical personnel should be instructed to listen to any statements or utterances the victim makes and to save all clothing for evidence. If the injured person is a suspect, a police officer almost always accompanies the suspect to the hospital. The humanitarian priority of administering first aid may have to become second priority if a dangerous suspect is still at or near the scene because others may be injured or killed.

If a Dead Body Is at the Scene. A body at the crime scene may immediately become the center of attention, and even a suspect may be overlooked. If the victim is obviously dead, the body should be left just as it was found but it and its surroundings protected. Identifying the body is not an immediate concern. Preserving the scene is more important because it may later yield clues about the dead

person's identity, the cause of death, and the individual responsible, as discussed in Chapter 8.

Environmental Hazards. Life-threatening emergency situations may also be present if a chemical spill has occurred, power lines have been downed, or any type of explosive device has detonated. Specific steps to take under these various scenarios is beyond the scope of this text, but common sense dictates that responders always be aware of the scene surroundings and potential hazards, stay upwind or outside the perimeter of possible contamination, and be ready to contact additional resources to help achieve scene safety. Utility companies may need to be summoned or hazmat teams deployed before a scene is truly safe to occupy. It is now common for first responders to undergo basic hazardous materials response training, and the Federal Emergency Management Agency (FEMA) offers numerous online courses for officers and agencies.

Protecting the Crime Scene

Securing the crime scene is a major responsibility of the first officers to arrive. Everything of a nonemergency nature is delayed until the scene is protected. The critical importance of securing the crime scene is better understood when one considers **Locard's principle of exchange**, a basic forensic theory that postulates that when objects come in contact with each other, there is always a transfer of material, however minute, between them. This evidence can easily be lost if the crime scene goes unprotected. At outdoor scenes, weather conditions such as heat, wind, rain, snow, or sleet can alter or destroy physical evidence. In addition, people may accidentally or intentionally disturb the scene. Additions to the scene can be as disconcerting to later investigation as the removal of evidence is.

Officers should explain to bystanders that protecting the crime scene is critical and that the public must be excluded. Bystanders should be treated courteously but firmly. A delicate part of public relations is dealing with the family of someone who has been killed. Officers should explain what they are doing and why and help family members understand that certain steps must be taken to discover what happened and who is responsible.

Crime scene protection can be as simple as locking a door to a room or building, or it can involve roping off a large area outdoors. Within a room, chairs or boxes can be used to cordon off an area. Many officers carry rope in their vehicle for this purpose and attach a sign that says "CRIME SCENE—DO NOT ENTER."

Officers setting up a crime scene perimeter should allow a wide enough area where they are confident most of the evidence will be, keeping in mind that a crime scene can always be made smaller; however, expanding it often proves more difficult. *Only* those officers directly involved in processing the crime scene should be allowed inside the crime scene perimeter. A buffer area should then be established around the crime scene area, where other officers and administrators, or other public officials, can be. Outside of that the buffer area is where the public and media may be allowed.

Sometimes other officers arriving at the scene can cause problems by ignoring posted warnings and barriers. *Ironically, police officers with no assigned responsibilities at a scene are often the worst offenders.* Arriving officers and everyone present at the scene should be told what has happened and what they need to do. Other officers can be asked to help preserve the scene, interview witnesses, or search for evidence. Officers not involved in processing the scene must be made aware that if they enter the actual crime scene they must complete a full report, a step that serves the dual purposes of maintaining the integrity of the scene and deterring unnecessary intruders.

A guard should be stationed to maintain security. If all officers are busy with emergency matters, a citizen may be asked to help protect the area temporarily. In such cases, the citizen's name, address, and phone number should be recorded. The citizen should be given specific instructions and minimal duties. The citizen's main duty is to protect the crime scene by barring entrance and to keep passersby moving along. He or she should not let any person into the area except police who identify themselves with a badge. The citizen should be relieved from guard duty as soon as possible and thanked for the assistance.

> **LO4** Describe the key aspects of the initial investigation.
>
> All necessary measures to secure the crime scene must be taken—including locking, roping, barricading, and guarding—until the preliminary investigation is completed.

Evidence should be protected from destruction or alteration from the elements by being covered until photographing and measuring can be done. Sometimes investigators must move evidence before they can examine it. For example, a vehicle covered with snow, dust, or other materials can be moved into a garage. In one case, a car used in a kidnapping was found four days later in a parking lot. Snow that had fallen since the kidnapping covered the car. To process the car's exterior for fingerprints, investigators took the car to a garage to let the snow melt and the surface dry. Evidence is discussed in depth in Chapter 5.

Conducting the Preliminary Investigation

After all emergency matters have been handled and the crime scene has been secured, the actual preliminary investigation can begin. This includes several steps whose order depends on the specific crime and the types of evidence and witnesses available.

> **LO4** Describe the key aspects of the initial investigation.
>
> Responsibilities during the preliminary investigation include
>
> - Questioning victims, witnesses, and suspects
> - Conducting a neighborhood canvass
> - Measuring, photographing, videotaping, and sketching the scene
> - Searching for evidence
> - Identifying, collecting, examining, and processing physical evidence
> - Recording all statements and observations in notes

Each of these procedures is explained in greater detail in Section 2. At this point, what is important is the total picture, the overview. In simple cases, one officer may perform all these procedures; in complex cases, responsibilities may be divided among several officers. Everything that occurs at a crime scene is recorded with photographs, videotapes, sketches, and complete, accurate notes. This record is the basis of future reports and is vital for future investigation and prosecution of the case.

Information may be volunteered by victims, witnesses, or suspects at or very near to the time of the criminal actions. Unplanned, spontaneous statements about what happened by people present at the scene are called *res gestae* ("things done") statements. **Res gestae statements** are unrehearsed statements made at the time of a crime concerning and closely related to actions involved in the crime. They are often considered more reliable and truthful than later, planned responses. *Res gestae* statements are generally an exception to the hearsay rule because they are usually very closely related to facts and are therefore admissible in court. *Res gestae* statements should be recorded in the field notes, and the person making the statements should sign or initial them so that there is no question of misunderstanding or of the person later denying having made the statement.

In addition to receiving and recording voluntary statements by victims and witnesses, investigators must go looking for information by conducting a neighborhood canvass as discussed in Chapter 6.

Determining Whether a Crime Has Been Committed and, If So, What Type.

As early as is feasible during the preliminary investigation, it is necessary to determine whether a crime has, in fact, been committed. Officers should observe the condition of the scene and talk to the complainant as soon as possible. After discussing the offense with the victim or complainant, the officers should determine whether a specific crime has been committed. If no crime has been committed—for example, the matter is a civil rather than a criminal situation—the victim should be told how to obtain assistance. If it is determined that a crime did occur, officers need to assess what type of crime or crimes were committed.

It is common for crime victims to misclassify what has occurred. For example, a citizen who comes home to find their back door kicked in and their new flat screen TV gone might report in their 9-1-1 call that they have been robbed. However, the responding officer determines that the crime was actually a burglary, not a robbery. As a general rule, burglary involves property being stolen from something tangible, such as a dwelling, whereas robbery involves property being stolen from a person by force or threat of force. The technical differences between some crimes are often unclear to laypersons, and thus the call an officer is responding to may actually turn out to involve a different crime entirely. In addition, state statutes differ in their definitions of the elements of certain crimes. For example, in some states, entering a motor vehicle with intent to steal is larceny; in other states, it is burglary.

Field Tests.

Investigators often want to know whether evidence discovered is what they think it is—for example, a bloodstain or an illegal substance. Field-test kits help in this determination. Field tests save investigators' time by identifying evidence that may have little chance of yielding positive results in the laboratory, and field tests are less expensive than full lab examinations. However, they are used on only a small number of specific items of evidence located at crime scenes. If a field test is affirmative, the evidence is submitted to a laboratory for a more detailed, expert examination whose results can then be presented in court.

Investigators can use field tests to develop and lift fingerprints; discover flammable substances through vapor and fluid examination; detect drugs, explosive substances on hands or clothing, imprints of firearms on hands, or bullet-hole residue; and conduct many other tests. Local, state, and federal police laboratories can furnish information on currently available field-test kits and may provide training in their use.

Establishing a Command Center.

In complex cases involving many officers, a command center may be set up where information about the crime is gathered and reviewed. This center receives summaries of communications, police reports, autopsy results, laboratory reports, results of interviews, updates on discovered evidence, and tips. Personnel at the center keep files of news releases and news articles and prepare an orderly, chronological progress report of the case for police command, staff, and field personnel. If the investigation becomes lengthy, the command center can be moved to police headquarters.

Dealing with the News Media.

A close, almost symbiotic relationship exists between the police and the news media. And while they depend upon each other, they are often seen as being at odds. Despite the need for cooperation, complaints from both sides are prevalent. Reporters complain that police withhold information and are uncooperative. The police complain that reporters interfere with cases and often sensationalize. It is important that the media and the police understand and respect each other's roles and responsibilities. Neither police nor media should regard the other as the enemy.

At any major crime scene or during any major criminal investigation, the media will be seeking all of the human-interest stories they can find. The media serve the public's right to know within legal and reasonable standards, a right protected by the First Amendment. The public is always hungry for news about crime. The police, on the other hand, are responsible for upholding the Sixth and Fourteenth Amendment guarantees of the right to a fair trial, the protection of a suspect's rights, and an individual's right to privacy. This often necessitates confidentiality. Further, making some information public could impair or even destroy many investigations. On the other hand, the police rely on the media to disseminate news about wanted suspects, to seek witnesses from the community, or to convey important information quickly to the public. Many cases are solved because of information from citizens.

In their quest for information, the media may target victims and witnesses. In some instances, victims are taken by surprise when the media shows up and safeguards have not yet been put in place to protect the victims' identities. And in some cases, victims or witnesses inadvertently reveal information that is being withheld from the media by law enforcement, as the police attempt to preserve the integrity of an investigation. A tool used by some police departments to protect both the privacy of victims and witnesses and the integrity of an investigation is a card telling these citizens how to deal with the media (Figure 1.1). The back of the card lists telephone numbers for the public information office and the victim services section.

Some departments use public information officers (PIOs) to interface with the media. Other departments assign the highest-ranking officer at the time of an incident or use written information releases. Still others allow virtually any officer involved in a case to address the media. Department policy commonly governs what information can be disseminated and who can release it. Officers must be aware of such policies and make sure to follow them. Officers who are not identified or trained as media liaisons should defer questions to a supervisor or speak with their supervisor prior to providing any information to the media. There might be facts or circumstances an officer is unaware of that may compromise the investigation or violate the data privacy act.

Media access to police information is neither comprehensive nor absolute. In general, the media have no right to enter any area to which the public does not have access, and all rules at cordoned-off crime scenes are as applicable to the media as they are to the general public.

Sometimes the media are directed to a certain area and advised of a time for a debriefing or an official press release. This protocol allows officers to process the crime scene without disruption, protects witnesses and victims from media pressure, and assures that all media are given current and accurate information. Such plans should be arranged as soon as possible during a preliminary investigation, as media often listen to scanners and can be quick to arrive on the scene.

Most members of the media understand the restrictions at a crime scene and cooperate. It is necessary to exercise firmness with those who do not follow instructions and even to exclude them if they jeopardize the investigation. Only facts—not opinions—should be given to reporters. The name of someone who has been killed should be given only after a careful identity check and notification of relatives. No information on the cause of death should be released; the medical examiner determines this. Likewise, no legal opinions about the specific crime or the suspect should be released. If officers do not know certain information, they can simply state that they do not know. The phrase "no comment" should be avoided because it implies you are hiding something. The benefit of a healthy relationship with the media is clear: "A good rapport with the media fosters a positive relationship with the general public. If you have a good partnership with the media, you generally have a good relationship with the public, because that's how the public gets information" (Garrett, 2007, p. 24).

Suggestions for dealing with the media include these: confirm the situation and verify information before giving any statement; position yourself with a provision for an easy exit; give a brief initial statement (5–10 seconds) with no questions answered and indicate police concern for the safety of those involved; establish your intent to return with additional information; and set the time for the return (Paris, 2007).

Additional advice for dealing with the media involves presenting a positive image, including marked patrol cars in the background and uniformed personnel actively engaged in the crime scene. Negative views to be avoided include body bags, yellow crime scene tape, hysterical victims and relatives, identifiable items such as addresses, evidence that needs to be kept confidential, and officers just standing around (Donlon-Cotton, 2007).

It is also imperative to recognize that in today's digital environment, data often flow instantaneously and in real time. If the media are unable to get information from the police, they may seek it from other sources, including witnesses who are willing to share statements and cell phone recordings, livestreaming social media feeds, or other social media posts. It is important that police keep a positive relationship with the media in the event that investigators need help accessing these sources.

Figure 1.1
Media advisory for crime victims and witnesses.
Source: Used by permission of the Fairfax County Police Department.

Providing an appropriate response to media questions can help an investigation, whereas poorly planned responses may actually hinder progress on a case.
Tom Carter/Alamy Stock Photo

A Final Consideration about Initiating Investigations

Although an investigations section may handle complex cases and those extending beyond the ability of patrol, patrol officers should handle a case from beginning to end whenever possible, including presenting it to the prosecutor, even if it means taking a case beyond the end of the shift (Stockton, 2006). Important benefits of this follow-through include

1. Patrol officers' effectiveness and expertise increase significantly.

2. Initial effort increases because officers know who is working on the follow-up.

3. Follow-up is timelier, resulting in more reliable witness interviews.

4. Job satisfaction increases.

When patrol officers know how to conduct an investigation, a department has investigators working around the clock.

Incident Review and Solvability Factors: A Critical Step in Managing Criminal Investigations

After the preliminary investigation has concluded, a review of the incident is conducted to determine whether the information gleaned thus far warrants further investigation. This screening process eliminates from the investigative workload those cases with a low potential for being solved or those that are determined to be unfounded. Police departments use case screening as a way to "maximize the effectiveness of their investigative and uniformed personnel, a critical need in the light of the fiscal constraints most municipalities face" (Cawley et al., 1977, p. 37). It is interesting to note that even four decades ago, law enforcement agencies were seeking ways to better utilize their limited resources in an effort to enhance productivity and effectiveness under tightening budgets, a situation that certainly continues to burden police managers today.

Many police departments screen investigations with a form that asks specific questions. If the answers to these questions are negative, the department either gives the case low priority for assignment or does not assign it at all. Factors that are considered when deciding whether to keep open or pursue an investigation further are called **solvability factors**, elements of information relating to a crime that are known to increase the likelihood of that crime being solved. For the purposes of this discussion, a case can be considered "solved" when a prosecutor is satisfied that sufficient evidence exists to charge a person with the crime (Coupe, Ariel, & Mueller-Johnson, 2019).

Among the most important solvability factors are the existence of one or more witnesses and whether a suspect can be named or at least described and located.

Other solvability factors include whether a vehicle can be identified; if stolen property is traceable through identification marks, unique characteristics, or serial numbers; if physical evidence is present; if there is a distinguishable MO; and whether crime analysis can help identify a suspect. The gravity of the offense and the possibility that the suspect may present a continued serious threat to others also factor into whether a case proceeds for investigation.

> **LO5** Explain how investigators decide whether or not to pursue a criminal investigation and what information they consider in this process.
>
> Case screening involves the systematic evaluation of solvability factors, such as the existence of witnesses and physical evidence, to determine which cases have the greatest likelihood of being solved and, thus, should be assigned for further investigation.

Even if a suspect is known or has confessed, an investigator must prove the elements of the crime and establish evidence connecting the suspect with the criminal act. Some cases require that suspects be developed, located, identified, and then arrested. Others begin with an arrest and proceed to identification. No set sequence exists, as the process is case dependent.

Whatever path the case investigation takes, an investigator must maintain accurate, thorough, up-to-date documentation of every step, from the initial report of or response to a crime, through the various stages of investigation, to the final disposition of the case. While many departments still use the manila file folder method of case management, technology is increasingly streamlining the process.

The Follow-Up Investigation

Preliminary investigations that satisfy all the investigative criteria do not necessarily yield enough information to prosecute a case. Despite a thorough preliminary investigation, many cases require a follow-up investigation. A need for a follow-up investigation does not necessarily reflect poorly on those who conducted the preliminary investigation. Often factors exist that are beyond the officers' control. For example, weather can destroy evidence before officers arrive at a scene, witnesses can be uncooperative, and evidence may be weak or nonexistent, even after a very thorough

Technology Innovations

Case Management Software

As with many aspects of law enforcement, computer software is enhancing the ability of investigators to track and prioritize tips and leads, develop an analytical time line, and manage the scheduling of tasks related to the investigation, such as follow-up interviews and evidence handling and analysis. Case Closed™, i-Sight®, EHS Insight, Trackops, and Perspective are only a few examples of software developers and providers of digital tools to help investigators manage their cases more effectively. While the specific capabilities of the different products vary, common features include programs that enable investigators to track cases, court status, evidence, and incoming tips; record incidents and manage leads; create and maintain a database of suspects, victims, witnesses, and informants involved in a particular case; identify crime trends; and generate reports. Many provide a mobile app that allows investigators to access software and databases from the field and create in situ audio and video files crucial to an investigation. In addition, some programs allow investigators from one agency or department to interface and collaborate with personnel from other organizations.

preliminary investigation. Other times, new information or evidence may come to light at a later time and require some follow-up.

The follow-up phase builds on what was learned during the preliminary investigation and can be conducted by the officers who responded to the original call or by detectives or investigators, depending on the seriousness and complexity of the crime and the size of the department. If investigators take over a case begun by patrol officers, coordination is essential.

Investigative leads that may need to be pursued include checking the victim's background; talking to informants; following up on leads provided by the public; determining who would benefit from the crime and who had sufficient knowledge to plan the crime; tracing weapons and stolen property; and searching MO, mug shot, and fingerprint files. Figure 1.2 provides an example of an investigative lead sheet that might be used in the follow-up. Specific follow-up procedures for the major offenses are discussed in Sections 3, 4, and 5.

Computer-Aided Investigation

Computers have significantly affected police operations. The role of computers in law enforcement and criminal investigation has evolved from being a useful aid (a nice thing to have) to being an essential tool (a *must* have). One of the biggest advances in using computer technology came in 1994 when William Bratton implemented the CompStat (Computerized Statistics, aka Compare Statistics) program in New York. From the beginning,

Investigative Lead Sheet

Case number _____ Lead number _____

Priority level: ☐ Low ☐ Medium ☐ High

Subject _____ Informant _____

Name _____

Address _____

Race _____ DOB _____ Sex _____

Height _____ Weight _____ Eyes _____ Hair _____

Identifying features _____

Employed _____ Occupation _____

Name _____

Address _____

Home telephone _____

Other telephone _____

How informant knows subject _____
_____

Telephone numbers Home _____ Work _____

Vehicle make _____ Year _____ Model _____ Color _____ Condition _____ Tag _____

Associates _____

ID confirmed ☐ Yes ☐ No How? _____

Details of lead _____
_____
_____

Lead received by _____ Date/Time _____

Lead # assigned _____

Lead status ☐ Good lead ☐ Questionable lead ☐ Suspicious informant ☐ Insufficient information

Lead assigned to _____ Date/Time _____

Findings _____
_____
_____

☐ Open lead ☐ Additional investigation required ☐ Subject has weak alibi
☐ Could not locate subject ☐ Other
☐ Closed lead ☐ Unfounded ☐ Subject has alibi ☐ Cleared by evidence ☐ Other

Other lead number references _____

Report completed ☐ Yes ☐ No Report# _____

Investigative supervisor _____ Date _____

Lead-room supervisor _____ Date _____

Figure 1.2
Investigative lead sheet.

Source: Steidel, S. E., ed. (2006, May). *Missing and abducted children: A law enforcement guide to case investigation and program management*, 3rd ed. Washington, DC: National Center for Missing and Exploited Children.

CompStat was hailed as an innovative managerial paradigm in policing, an information-driven strategy that stressed accountability at all levels of the police hierarchy. To achieve the goal of enhancing quality of life through reduced levels of crime, CompStat was built around four basic principles: (1) accurate and timely intelligence, (2) rapid deployment of resources, (3) effective tactics, and (4) relentless follow-up and assessment (Jang, Hoover, & Joo, 2010). CompStat 2.0 was released in 2016 with an upgrade that allows information to be shared almost instantly with other officers, the public, and the media (Figure 1.3).

Computers can help investigators efficiently access existing information such as fingerprint records and DNA tests, record new information and store it compactly for instant transmission anywhere, analyze the information for patterns (mapping), link crimes and criminals, manipulate digital representations to enhance the images, and re-create and visually track a series of events. Computers are also increasingly being used for electronic document management, allowing investigators to scan evidence captured from paper and attach audio and video clips to the case file. And, as already discussed, computers and software are helping investigators better manage their overall caseloads.

The ability to share data across jurisdictional lines is one of the most valuable benefits computers provide to investigators. In addition, the Internet has become an invaluable tool to criminal investigators, offering hundreds of thousands of websites and databases to aid informed investigators. One such resource is Thomson-Reuters's CLEAR® for law enforcement, established in 2008, which allows investigators to access numerous distinct public records databases in one central location, saving investigative time, enhancing the detection and analysis of crime patterns and trends, and helping connect the dots between incidents, individuals, and locations more efficiently and effectively. Through this website, investigators can find information about a subject's past addresses, vehicles, relatives, phone numbers, business affiliations, assets, and more. As an example of its many success stories, the application claims to have helped investigators locate information that led to finding a child who had been missing for eight years.

Crime Analysis, Mapping, and Geographical Information Systems

Using crime mapping, spreadsheet software, and advanced data analysis, crime analysis units have become integral partners in today's policing. Before the computer revolution, the traditional crime map consisted of a large representation of a jurisdiction glued onto a bulletin board with colored pins stuck into it. These maps suffered many limitations—they lost previous crime

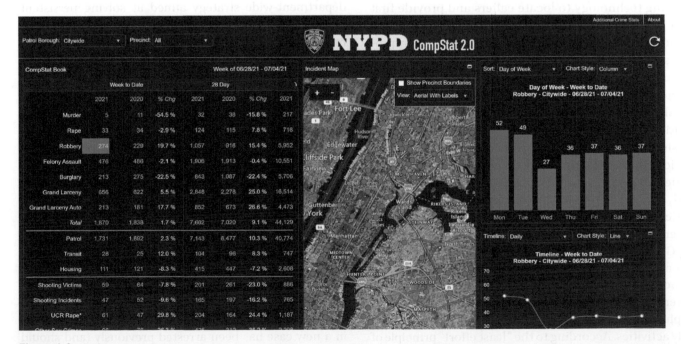

Figure 1.3

The New York City Police Department makes much of its crime data available to the public through CompStat 2.0, an online interactive experience that allows users to filter information by various parameters, including crime type, neighborhood, and day of the week.

New York City Police Department

patterns when they were updated, could not be manipulated or queried, and were difficult to read when several types of crimes represented by different colored pins were mixed together.

In addition to pushpin maps, investigators routinely used link charts to keep track of the people and places involved in a case, connecting index cards and photos with a maze of strings as relationships became established and details of an investigation emerged. The cumbersome pin maps and link charts have since given way to computerized crime maps and crime analysis programs. **Crime mapping** changes the focus from the criminal to the location of crimes—the **hot spots** where most crimes occur.

According to the National Institute of Justice (Hunt, 2019), "Mapping law enforcement report data can be an effective way to analyze where crime occurs. The resulting visual display can be combined with other geographic data (such as the locations of schools, parks, and industrial complexes) and used to analyze and investigate patterns of crime and help inform responses." This ability to visualize crime distribution provides intelligence and helps law enforcement direct resources to those areas in the community where they are most needed and, thus, will have the greatest impact.

Geographic Information Systems (GISs) and geographic profiling are other powerful tools for investigators: "Today the majority of law enforcement agencies use some degree of Geographic Information Systems/ mapping technology to locate callers and provide first responders with critical information before arriving on the scene. . . . In recent years GIS has evolved to provide significantly more information to improve safety and answer important questions during an emergency" (Wandrei, 2007, p. 61). GIS has moved beyond its traditional uses into the next trend in mapping technology— location intelligence: "Location intelligence solutions consist of a combination of software, data and expert services that help organizations leverage spatial capabilities without the need for a GIS expert" (Donahue, 2007, p. 32). Location intelligence includes automatic vehicle location (AVL) and global positioning systems (GPSs).

Geographic profiling is yet another advancement in mapping and is based on the theory that all people, including criminals, have a pattern to their lives. This pattern involves, among other things, a limited geographical area that encompasses the bulk of a person's daily activities. According to the "least effort" principle of human behavior, people travel only as far as necessary to accomplish their goals, so the most likely area for a crime is where an offender's desire for anonymity intersects with the offender's desire to stay within his or her comfort zone.

In addition to location, computer programs can help investigators uncover patterns in the timing of criminal events. Unfortunately, time analysis methods have lagged behind spatial analysis techniques and have proved more difficult to develop and implement thus far. The improvement of technology and the corresponding expansion of information now accessible to investigators have created a new set of challenges.

Data Mining

Although information is, indeed, the cornerstone of investigation, the plethora of information being generated can easily overwhelm an investigator. To be effective, investigators must know how to sift through the mountains of available information to find the data that pertain to their case, a process known as **data mining**. For example, data mining applied in a homicide case might allow investigators to more quickly develop a possible motive and thus expedite the identification of a suspect or help narrow the field of possible suspects.

A Brief Word about Problem-Oriented Policing

Problem-oriented policing (POP) can be defined as a department-wide strategy aimed at solving persistent community problems. Police identify, analyze, and respond to the underlying circumstances (problems) that create incidents and crime (Eck & Spelman, 1987). Data collected during criminal investigations can be extremely valuable to the problem-oriented policing that many departments are adopting. Investigators can analyze data to determine groups of problems rather than isolated incidents. Once specific underlying problems are identified, departments can seek alternative approaches to reduce or eliminate the incidence of particular crimes.

The subject of problem-oriented policing is beyond the scope of this text, but problem-solving strategies can be used in criminal investigations in many ways. One way is to expand collaborations by having investigators work more effectively with patrol officers and with other law enforcement agencies. Another way is to improve the quality of information in existing data systems, especially MO files. The likelihood that an offender in a new case has been arrested previously (and should be in the MO file) is greater than often thought. Although criminal investigations are, by nature, reactive, combining problem-oriented strategies with traditional investigative techniques can help investigators improve their ability to solve crimes and help them be proactive in preventing crime.

Investigative Liaisons within a Community Policing Paradigm

Investigators do not work in a vacuum but rely heavily on assistance from numerous other individuals and agencies, liaisons that work well within a **community policing** paradigm. Harkening back to 1829 in England, when Sir Robert Peel stated, "The police are the public and the public are the police," today's philosophy of community policing embraces the belief that "by working together, the police and the community can accomplish what neither can accomplish alone. The synergy that results from community policing can be powerful. It is like the power of a finely tuned athletic team, with each member contributing to the total effort" (Miller, Hess, & Orthmann, 2011, p. xix). The Community Oriented Policing Services (COPS) Office notes that community policing is not a program or collection of programs but, rather, an overarching "philosophy that promotes organizational strategies, which support the systematic use of partnerships and problem-solving techniques, to proactively address the immediate conditions that give rise to public safety issues, such as crime, social disorder and fear of crime" (*Community Policing Defined*, n.d., p. 3).

> **LO6** Identify the various individuals and entities with whom successful investigators interrelate.
>
> Using a community policing orientation, investigators form liaisons with uniformed patrol officers; dispatchers; the prosecutor's staff; the defense counsel; community corrections personnel; social services; physicians, the coroner, or medical examiner; laboratories; and citizens, including witnesses and victims.

Uniformed Patrol

Patrol officers are a vital part of the investigative process because they are usually the first to arrive at a crime scene and to have the opportunity to observe the scene before any disturbances occur. Uniformed officers are also the first to deal with victims and are in a unique position to develop trust with the persons involved. What patrol officers do or fail to do at the scene greatly influences the outcome of an investigation. In addition, the patrol officer, as the person daily in the field, is closest to potential crime and has probably developed contacts who can provide information.

A potential pitfall is lack of direct, personal communication between uniformed and investigative personnel, which can result in attitudinal differences and divisiveness. Communication problems can be substantially reduced by using a simple checklist describing the current investigative status of any cases jointly involving patrol and investigators.

Patrol officers want to know what happens to the cases they begin. Officers who have been informed of the status of "their" cases report a feeling of work satisfaction not previously realized, increased rapport with investigative personnel, and a greater desire to make good initial reports on future cases.

Dispatchers

In most cases, a police dispatcher is the initial contact between a citizen and a police agency. Most citizens call a police agency only a few times during their lives, and their permanent impression of the police may hinge on this contact and the citizens' perceptions of the police agency's subsequent actions.

In addition, the information obtained by the dispatcher is often critical to the officer, the victim, other citizens, and the success of the investigation. The accuracy of the information dispatched to the field officer or investigator may determine the success or failure of the case. The responding officer needs to know the exact nature and location of the incident. A direct radio, computer, or phone line should be cleared until the officer arrives at the scene. All pertinent descriptions and information should be dispatched directly to the responding officer.

As with working relationships with the media, the relationship between the police and dispatchers is not always positive: "There is no better example of a 'love-hate relationship' than the daily interaction between street cops and dispatchers. When things are going well, we love each other; when they're not, tempers flare, attitudes take a nosedive and we temporarily hate each other" (Brantner Smith, 2007). One reason for the discord is that dispatchers spend their shifts responding to crisis after crisis and rarely get to hear the outcome. Officers should be sensitive to this situation (Brantner Smith, 2007). Dispatchers constantly deal with rage, fear, and helplessness but must diffuse these elevated emotions while enhancing the caller's functionality and ability to answer questions or receive instructions (Bumpas, 2006, p. 20). Dispatchers are sometimes the lifeline for victims requiring assistance and the officers responding to a crime. Good working relationships with these individuals can go a long way in effectively responding to a crime scene.

Prosecutor's Staff

Another group of individuals with whom good working relationships are a necessity are prosecutors. Cooperation between investigators and the prosecutor's staff depends on the personalities involved, the time available, a recognition that it is in everyone's best interest to work together, and an acceptance of everyone's investigative roles and responsibilities. Given sufficient time and a willingness to work together, better investigations and prosecutions result. When investigators have concluded an investigation, they should seek the advice of the prosecutor's office. At this point, the case may be prosecuted, new leads may be developed, or the case may be dropped, with both the investigator and the prosecutor's office agreeing that it would be inefficient to pursue it further.

The prosecutor's staff can give legal advice on statements, confessions, evidence, the search, and necessary legal papers and may provide new perspectives on the facts in the case. The prosecutor's office can review investigative reports and evidence that relate to the elements of the offense, advise whether the proof is sufficient to proceed, and assist in further case preparation. The role of the prosecutor in investigations is discussed further in Chapter 21.

Defense Counsel

Our legal system is based on the adversary system: the accuser against the accused. Although both sides seek the same goal—determining truth and obtaining justice—the adversarial nature of the system requires that contacts between the defense counsel and investigators occur only on the advice of the prosecutor's office. Inquiries from the defense counsel should be referred to the prosecutor's office. If the court orders specific documents to be provided to the defense counsel, investigators must surrender the material, but they should seek the advice of the prosecution staff before releasing any documents or information. The role of the defense counsel is also discussed in greater depth in Chapter 21.

Community Corrections Personnel

Investigators may find it beneficial to have good working rapport with community corrections personnel because, often, people who are suspected of crimes have had prior run-ins with the law and may be on parole or probation for a previous crime. Actually, "The number of times a prisoner has been arrested in the past is a good predictor of whether that prisoner will continue to commit crimes after being released" (Langan & Levin, 2002, p. 10). A 9-year study that analyzed the offending patterns of nearly 68,000 randomly sampled prisoners released in 2005 across 30 states, and extrapolated those data to represent the more than 400,000 state inmates released that same year, found that

- Five out of six (83%) state prisoners were arrested at least once in the 9 years following their release.

- About 44% of prisoners (4 in 9) were arrested at least once during their first year after release, 68% had been arrested within 3 years of release, and 79% had been arrested within 6 years of release.

- During the first year following release, the percentage of prisoners released for a property offense who were arrested for any type of offense (including violent, property, drug, or public order offenses) was higher than the percentage of prisoners released for a drug or violent offense, a general pattern that persisted across the 9-year study period.

- At the end of the 9-year study period, 88% of property offenders had been arrested for a new crime, compared to 84% of drug offenders and 79% of violent offenders.

- The likelihood of former prisoners being arrested outside the state where they were released increased as years passed, with 8% of prisoners arrested for a new crime in another state during their first year of release, compared to 14% of prisoners who had been arrested in another state by the end of the ninth year following release.

- Younger prisoners (those age 24 or younger) were more likely to be arrested than older prisoners (those age 40 or older) during each year following release. For example, 28% of prisoners released at age 24 or younger were arrested during the 9-year study period, compared to 19% of those age 40 or older.

(Alper, Durose, & Markman, 2018)

From these data it becomes clear why probation and parole officers may be good sources of information for officers who suspect a repeat offender may be involved in their case.

Social Services

Social services, especially for investigators who specialize or work on family, domestic, and child-related crimes, can be valuable partners in helping elicit relevant information from suspects and victims. Investigators will often conduct child-victim interviews in tandem with trained social service personnel.

Physicians, Coroners, and Medical Examiners

If a victim at a crime scene is obviously injured and a doctor is called to the scene, saving lives takes precedence over all aspects of the investigation. However, the physician is there for emergency treatment, not to protect the crime scene, so investigators must take every possible precaution to protect the scene during the treatment of the victim.

Physicians and medical personnel should be directed to the victim by the route through the crime scene that is least destructive of evidence. They should be asked to listen carefully to anything the victim says and to hold all clothing as evidence for the police.

The coroner or medical examiner is called if the victim has died. Coroners and medical examiners have the authority to investigate deaths to determine whether they were natural, accidental, or the result of a criminal act. They can also provide information about the time of death and the type of weapon that might have caused it.

About 2,000 medical examiners and coroners' (ME/C) offices provided death investigation services across the United States in 2004 (Hickman, Hughes, Strom, & Ropero-Miller, 2007). These officers are responsible for the medicolegal investigation of deaths. They may conduct death scene investigations, perform autopsies, and determine the cause and manner of death when a person has died as a result of violence, under suspicious circumstances, without a physician in attendance, or for other reasons. In a typical year, ME/C offices handle about 4,400 unidentified human decedents, of which about 1,000 remain unidentified longer than one year. Nearly 1 million human death cases were referred to ME/C offices in 2004, of which about 500,000 were accepted (Hickman et al., 2007). Depending on the individual case, investigators and the ME/C may work as a team, with an investigator present at the autopsy. The ME/C may obtain samples of hair, clothing, fibers, blood, and body organs or fluids as needed for later laboratory examination.

Forensic Crime Laboratories

Many criminal investigations involve the processing of physical evidence through a forensic crime lab. All law enforcement agencies now have access to highly sophisticated criminalistic examinations through local, state, federal, and private laboratories.

The state crime laboratory is usually located either in the state's largest city or in the state capital and can be used by all police agencies of the state. The FBI Laboratory in Washington, DC, is also available to all federal, state, and local law enforcement agencies, with personnel available to provide forensic examinations, technical support, expert witness testimony, and training.

The National Institute of Justice (2008, p. 1) reports, "Television has given forensic science great public visibility, but provides viewers with the mistaken notion that crime laboratories provide results quickly. In truth, most crime laboratories have large case backlogs." Consider, for example, that in 2014, the nation's 409 publicly funded crime labs received an estimated 3.8 million requests for forensic service but completed 3.6 million requests, leaving an estimated 200,000 backlogged cases for that year (Durose & Burch, 2016). However, these labs went into 2014 carrying hundreds of thousands of backlogged cases from previous years, such that, despite having processed millions of requests during 2014, by the end of that year, U.S. crime labs still had an estimated backlog of 570,100 requests for forensic services.

Although no industrywide definition exists for how long a case must sit before it is considered "backlogged," with some labs allowing a 90-day time frame and others leaving it open-ended such that any sample that remains unanalyzed is considered backlogged, the National Institute of Justice (NIJ) defines a backlogged case as one that remains untested 30 days after it was submitted to the laboratory (Nelson, Chase, & DePalma, 2013). The NIJ (2010) differentiates between two types of backlogs:

- Casework Backlogs: forensic evidence collected from crime scenes, victims, and suspects in criminal cases and then submitted to a laboratory.

- Convicted Offender and Arrestee DNA Backlogs: DNA samples taken from convicted offenders and arrestees pursuant to federal and state laws.

The time-consuming nature of forensic evidence processing contributes heavily to casework backlogs, as such evidence must first be screened to determine whether any biological material is present and, if so, what kind of biological material it is. Only then can DNA testing begin. In addition, some samples can be degraded or fragmented or may contain DNA from multiple suspects and victims. By comparison, it is significantly easier and faster to analyze convicted offender and arrestee DNA samples because they are collected on identical media (usually a paper product), and the standardized collection methods in each state allow the laboratory to use automated analysis of many samples at once. Furthermore, unlike with forensic casework samples, the laboratory analyst does not need to "find" the DNA amidst the evidence (NIJ, 2010).

The NIJ has implemented several programs to reduce backlogs and improve efficiency. The DNA Capacity Enhancement and Backlog Reduction (CEBR) Program helps eligible states and local government:

- Process, record, screen, and analyze forensic DNA and/or DNA database samples

- Increase the capacity of public forensic DNA and DNA database laboratories to process more DNA samples, thereby helping to reduce the backlog of samples awaiting analysis

Often, a single case submission will include requests for forensic analyses of both DNA and non-DNA evidence. The DNA CEBR program does not, however, permit the use of funds for non-DNA disciplines. According to the NIJ (2019), the Forensic DNA Laboratory Efficiency Improvement and Capacity Enhancement program is intended to help address that gap by awarding funding to

- Enhance capacity and increase the efficiency of crime laboratories to process, record, screen, and analyze other forensic evidence in addition to DNA

- Decrease the turnaround time to process evidence

Citizens

Investigators are only as good as their sources of information. They seldom solve crimes without citizen assistance. In fact, citizens frequently provide the most important information in a case. Witnesses to a crime should be contacted immediately to minimize their time involved and inconvenience. Information about the general progress of the case should be relayed to those who have assisted. This will maintain their interest and increase their desire to cooperate at another time.

Citizens can help or hinder an investigation. Frequently, citizens who have been arrested in the past have information about crimes and the people who commit them. The manner and attitude with which such citizens are contacted will increase or decrease their cooperation with the police, as discussed in Chapter 6.

Witnesses

Witnesses are often the key to solving crimes. They can provide eyewitness accounts, or they can provide leads that would be otherwise unavailable. However, such testimony is often unreliable, with the results of one study estimating that as many as 75% of the defendants eventually exonerated through the use of DNA evidence were wrongly convicted in the first place because of erroneous eyewitness testimony (Sonenshein & Nilon, 2010).

Myth Eyewitness testimony is the most reliable form of evidence.

Fact Eyewitness testimony is notoriously faulty, as evidenced by three decades' worth of rigorous social science research. As of April 2020, 367 people had been freed from U.S. prisons based on DNA evidence presented by the Innocence Project, a nonprofit legal organization. Mistaken eyewitness identification—the single greatest cause of wrongful convictions in the United States—was found to have played a role in nearly three-fourths of the cases that were eventually overturned because of DNA testing.

Source: www.innocenceproject.org

Several states have passed legislation to create tougher standards for identifying suspects by witnesses, which is often considered one of the most problematic aspects of an investigation. Despite criticism and controversy regarding the value of eyewitness testimony, judges and juries accord significant weight to eyewitness evidence.

Key witnesses should be kept informed of the progress of the case and of their role in the prosecution, if any. If they are to be called to testify in court, their testimony should be reviewed with them, and they should be given assurances that their participation is important in achieving justice. Police officers must be aware of the problem of witness intimidation, which can also be directed at victims of crime.

Victims

Almost every crime has a victim. According to the National Crime Victimization Survey (NCVS), an estimated 3.3 million U.S. residents age 12 or older experienced roughly 6.3 million violent victimizations in 2018, and U.S. households experienced an estimated 13.5 million property victimizations that same year (Morgan & Oudekerk, 2019). Even so-called victimless crimes often have innocent victims who are not directly involved in a specific incident. The victim is often the reporting person (complainant) and often has the most valuable information. Yet, in many instances, the victim receives the least attention and assistance. Of the millions of people in the United States who are victimized every year, only a small percentage of these victims and family members obtain the services they need to manage the stress that develops when falling victim to crime (Oetinger, 2007). Jordan, Romashkan, and Werner (2007, p. 44) contend, "The law enforcement community has historically focused on the apprehension and prosecution of perpetrators, and although state laws define the rights and redress of victims of crime—such as the right to be treated with fairness, dignity and respect; to be informed and present throughout the entire criminal justice process; to be reasonably protected from the accused; and to be entitled to seek restitution—these individuals are very often neglected in the criminal justice system."

Police should keep victims informed of investigative progress unless releasing the information would jeopardize prosecuting the case or unless the information is confidential. The federal Victimization Bill provides matching-fund assistance to states for victims of some crimes. Numerous states also have victimization funds that can be used for funeral or other expenses according to predetermined criteria. Police agencies should maintain a list of federal, state, and local agencies; foundations; and support groups that provide assistance to victims. Police should tell victims how to contact community support groups. For example, most communities have support groups for victims of sexual offenses—if not locally, then at the county or state level.

In larger departments, psychological response teams are available. In smaller agencies, a chaplains' corps or clergy from the community may assist with death notifications and the immediate needs of victims.

Investigating officers should also give victims information on future crime prevention techniques and temporary safety precautions. They should help victims understand any court procedures that involve them.

Officers should tell victims whether local counseling services are available and whether there is a safe place they can stay if this is an immediate concern.

Major-Case Task Forces

Shrinking police budgets and the complications of modern-day crime have resulted in task forces becoming necessary for many crimes. "Task forces are critical when addressing multi-jurisdictional needs, investigating major cases impacting several agencies or when combating regional crime problems" (Boetig & Mattocks, 2007, p. 51). Federal, state, and local agencies are combining to form task forces to handle and investigate drugs, gangs, terrorism, violent offenders, Internet Crimes Against Children (ICAC), and human trafficking. Where appropriate, these task forces and their roles in investigation will be discussed in later chapters.

A *multidisciplinary* approach to case investigation uses specialists in various fields from within a particular jurisdiction. A *multijurisdictional* investigation, in contrast, uses personnel from different police agencies. Many metropolitan areas consist of 20 or more municipalities surrounding a core city. In a number of metropolitan areas, multijurisdictional major-case squads or metro crime teams have been formed, drawing the most talented investigative personnel from all jurisdictions. In addition, the services of federal, state, or county police agency personnel and probation and parole officers may be used.

Many agencies are developing special investigation units, focusing resources and training efforts on specific local crime problems. Other areas commonly investigated by special units include drug trafficking and gaming enforcement. In some major cases—for example, homicides involving multijurisdictional problems, serial killers, police officer killings, or multiple sex offenses—it is advisable to form a major-case task force from the jurisdictions that have vested interests in the case. All evidence from the joint case is normally sent to the same laboratory to maintain continuity and consistency. Murphy, Wexler, Davies, and Plotkin (2004, p. 13) observe, "Local law enforcement have long been scrutinized for how they handle large-scale, complex criminal investigations—often those involving serial, spree or mass murderers or violence against national leaders or celebrities. Many of these notorious crimes were investigated within a task force structure, involving multiple agencies, jurisdictions or levels of government. These crimes shared a number of characteristics that called for complicated, demanding investigations that challenged the agencies tasked with solving them in unprecedented ways."

In examining the lessons learned from the Washington, DC, sniper investigation, Murphy et al. (2004) were able to identify some critical aspects of a successful investigation, including thorough planning and preparation, advanced role definition and delineation of responsibilities, efficient information management, and a focus on effective communication. This investigation provides an excellent case study for further examination by students as it shows how complex an investigation can become in terms of the number of agencies and jurisdictions involved and the challenges of coordination and information sharing.

On the federal level, the Violent Criminal Apprehension Program (ViCAP) has been created within the FBI to study and coordinate investigation of crimes of interstate and national interest: "VICAP's mission is to facilitate cooperation, communication and coordination among law enforcement agencies and provide support in their efforts to investigate, identify, track, apprehend and prosecute violent serial offenders" (Murphy et al., 2004, p. 41).

Law Enforcement Resources

Investigators have several resources available at the federal level as well as at the global level.

Federal Law Enforcement Resources

Federal law enforcement agencies can provide numerous resources to aid local and state agencies involved in high-profile investigations. Federal agencies may have forensic experts that a local or state law enforcement agency does not employ in-house. For example, the Department of Homeland Security (DHS); Drug Enforcement Administration (DEA); the Bureau of Alcohol, Tobacco, Firearms, and Explosives (ATF); the FBI; and the U.S. Secret Service are available for such forensic expertise. Specialized response units, such as the FBI's Critical Incident Response Group (CIRG), the Rapid Deployment Logistics Unit (RDLU), and the Hostage Rescue Team (HRT), are also accessible by local and state law enforcement. The U.S. Marshal's Special Operations Group (SOG) is available for high-risk federal warrant investigations. In addition, the National Center for the Analysis of Violent Crime (NCAVC) Behavioral Analysis Unit (BAU) provides behavioral-based investigative and operational support: "BAU . . . provides assistance to law enforcement through 'criminal investigative analysis,' a process of reviewing

crimes from behavioral and investigative perspectives. BAU staff—commonly called profilers—assess the criminal act, interpret offender behavior and/or interact with the victim for the purposes of providing crime analysis, investigative suggestions, profiles of unknown offenders, threat analysis, critical incident analysis, interview strategies, major case management, search warrant assistance, prosecution and trial strategies and expert testimony" (Murphy et al., 2004, p. 41).

These and other federal resources available to investigators will be discussed throughout the remainder of the text.

INTERPOL

INTERPOL, whose correct full name is the International Criminal Police Organization (ICPO), was created in 1947 and has endured as the world's largest police organization while seemingly shrouded in a considerable level of mystique. INTERPOL consists of 194 member countries involved in providing investigators in agencies worldwide with up-to-date crime trend information. INTERPOL also helps member countries identify and locate criminals as well as providing assistance with the arrest of cross-border criminals.

Clearing a Case and the Remainder of the Investigative Process

An investigation typically ends one of several ways through a procedure referred to as clearing or closing the case. Following guidelines set forth by the FBI's Uniform Crime Reporting (UCR) Program (2018), an agency can close an investigation and clear an offense by arrest or by exceptional means:

> In the UCR Program, a law enforcement agency reports that an offense is cleared by arrest, or solved for crime reporting purposes, when three specific conditions have been met. The three conditions are that at least one person has been:
>
> - Arrested.
>
> - Charged with the commission of the offense.
>
> - Turned over to the court for prosecution (whether following arrest, court summons, or police notice).
>
>   . . . In certain situations, elements beyond law enforcement's control prevent the agency from arresting

and formally charging the offender. When this occurs, the agency can clear the offense *exceptionally*. Law enforcement agencies must meet the following four conditions in order to clear an offense by exceptional means. The agency must have:

- Identified the offender.

- Gathered enough evidence to support an arrest, make a charge, and turn over the offender to the court for prosecution.

- Identified the offender's exact location so that the suspect could be taken into custody immediately.

- Encountered a circumstance outside the control of law enforcement that prohibits the agency from arresting, charging, and prosecuting the offender.

Examples of exceptional clearances include, but are not limited to, the death of the offender (e.g., suicide or justifiably killed by police or citizen); the victim's refusal to cooperate with the prosecution after the offender has been identified; or the denial of extradition because the offender committed a crime in another jurisdiction and is being prosecuted for that offense. In the UCR Program, the recovery of property alone does not clear an offense.

Sometimes, despite even the most rigorous investigation, leads dry up and a case goes cold, at which time it can be classified as "open pending further information or leads." In such circumstances, the investigator will no longer actively pursue the investigation nor devote any more resources to it. Another possibility is that a case, after a more thorough investigation, is cleared because it is determined to be unfounded, such as when someone files a false report or, after more facts are revealed, it is established that no crime was actually committed. Finally, although an agency may administratively close a case, such a decision does not necessarily mean that the agency can clear the offense for UCR purposes.

As shown in Table 1.2, once an investigation has concluded with the clearance of the case, investigators still have several roles to fulfill. They must review their reports and coordinate with the prosecutor to prepare the case for court, and they must be available to testify if called on, sometimes several years following the conclusion of their investigation. These stages of the criminal investigation process will be discussed in the final chapter of this text.

A Word about Investigative Productivity

Productivity has been of interest in the police field for some time. Major opposition to a focus on productivity in police work may arise because of alleged "quota systems" in issuing traffic citations. Productivity involves considerably more than issuing citations, however. Nearly all jobs have some standard of productivity, even though the job may not involve a production line.

Criminal investigation personnel have traditionally been evaluated by the number and type of cases assigned to them, the number of cases they bring to a successful conclusion, the number of arrests they make, and the amount of property they recover. The evaluations should also assess how well the officers use investigative resources and how well they perform overall within the department and in the community. As discussed earlier, rigorous case screening can often increase investigative productivity.

An advantage of continuous evaluation of productivity is that updating case status is possible at any time. Such information is useful for investigating and for developing budgets, making additional case assignments, identifying MO similarities among cases, and responding to public inquiries.

Avoiding Civil Liability

Before concluding this overview of criminal investigation, it is worth briefly considering what can happen if investigators step outside their legal boundaries during an investigation or fail to act to uphold their full legal responsibility. Some might think the worst-case scenario is that the suspect walks free, but that would be only part of the bad news. The other part: the investigator finds that the shoe is on the other foot, as they have now become the defendant in a civil liability suit.

Civil liability refers to a person's degree of risk of being sued. Officers must face the unfortunate reality that being sued goes with wearing the uniform: "In the past few years, police litigation has skyrocketed in terms of both the number of lawsuits and the amount of money needed to defend these lawsuits (and to pay out large verdicts when they occur)" (Ramirez, 2006, p. 52).

Most civil lawsuits brought against law enforcement officers are based on Statute 42 of the U.S. Code, Section 1983, also called the Civil Rights Act. This act, passed in 1871, was designed to prevent the abuse of constitutional rights by officers who "under color of state law" denied defendants those rights. The Civil Rights Act states:

Every person who, under color of any statute, ordinance, regulation, custom, or usage, of any State or Territory, subjects, or causes to be subjected any citizen of the United States or other person within the jurisdiction thereof to the deprivation of any rights, privileges, or immunities secured by the Constitution and laws, shall be liable to the party injured in an action at law, suit in equity, or other proper proceeding for redress.

Basically, Section 1983 states that anyone who acts under the authority of law and who violates another person's constitutional rights can be sued.

Many aspects of police work (e.g., use of force, high-speed pursuits) leave officers and their departments vulnerable to possible lawsuits. Of particular relevance to criminal investigations are those constitutional protections involving searches and seizures, interrogations, and custody situations, which all carry with them the potential for lawsuits, as do failures to investigate or arrest.

Rossmo (2009) examined criminal investigative failures and asserts that the damage caused to society—to victims, to innocent people, and to the public at large—by such failures is significant. According to Rossmo, the reasons behind criminal investigative failure and faulty thinking can be grouped into three general categories:

- Cognitive biases—includes mental errors such as a mistaken eyewitness identification or the tunnel vision of an investigator who focuses only on the first most likely suspect to the exclusion of all other potential suspects.

- Organizational traps—includes organizational inertia and momentum which make it difficult for an investigator to abruptly change direction when new facts come to light; assumptions that gain credibility simply by the passage of time and not based on any supporting evidence; red herrings, or tips that misdirect the investigation; as well as ego, fatigue, and groupthink.

- Probability errors—includes uncertainty or ambiguity when discussing legal terms, computation mistakes made in evidence evaluation and testimony, errors in thinking, and coincidence.

Rossmo (2009) concludes: "Factors identified with cognitive and organizational failures (low information levels, limited resources, and pressure to obtain quick results) are all too common in such investigations. The potential benefits of advanced forensic techniques, comprehensive criminal databases, and highly skilled police personnel are undermined by the wrong mind-set and a limited organizational approach." Furthermore: "Like cascading failures in airplane crashes, an investigative failure often has more than one contributing factor." Rossmo warns investigators of three traps:

- One mistake, one coincidence, and one piece of bad luck can produce an investigative failure.

- Once one mistake has been made, the likelihood of further mistakes increases.

- Usually the biggest problem is refusing to acknowledge the original mistake.

Rossmo (2009) concludes: "Investigations should be led by the evidence, not by the suspects. Case conclusions should be deferred until sufficient information has been gathered, and tunnel vision should be avoided at all costs. Investigative managers must remain neutral and encourage open inquiries, discussion, and dissent. Assumptions, inference chains, and uncertainties need to be recognized and recorded."

Operations manuals and training are critically important in thwarting investigative failures and protecting departments against lawsuits (Cotton & Donlon-Cotton, 2007). Such manuals provide guidelines within which officers and investigators should operate. Manuals should be updated as case law changes and as new technologies become available.

Hess, Orthmann, and Cho (2015, p. 451) observe, "Investigative procedure is [one] area of police work commonly brought up in lawsuits. Almost every investigation gives officers discretion to decide what evidence should be included in prosecutor reports and warrant applications, and what evidence should be omitted." If investigators withhold **exculpatory evidence**, which is evidence favorable to the accused, the courts have deemed this to be a violation of a defendant's due process rights: "Leaving out exculpatory evidence may lead to liability for false arrest, malicious prosecution and illegal search and seizure claims. To support such liability claims, a plaintiff must show that the affiant knowingly and deliberately, or with reckless disregard for the truth, omitted facts that are material or necessary to a finding of probable cause" (*Franks v. Delaware*, 1978).

One of the best ways to avoid lawsuits or to defend yourself if sued is to keep complete, accurate records of all official actions you take. Hess, Orthmann, and Cho (2014, p. 536) offer suggestions to avoid lawsuits.

LO7 Describe some of the ways investigators can protect against civil lawsuits.

Protection against lawsuits includes

- Effective policies and procedures clearly communicated to all.
- Thorough and continuous training.
- Proper supervision and discipline.
- Accurate, thorough police reports.

Well-honed interpersonal communication skills are one way to mitigate liability risks and avoid lawsuits. Interpersonal communication techniques are discussed in Chapter 6.

Summary

A criminal investigation is the process of discovering, collecting, preparing, identifying, and presenting evidence to determine what happened and who is responsible. The primary goals of police investigation vary from department to department, but most investigations aim to

- Determine whether a crime has been committed.
- Legally obtain sufficient information and evidence to identify the responsible person.
- Arrest the suspect.
- Recover stolen property.
- Present the best possible case to the prosecutor.

Among the numerous functions performed by investigators are those of providing emergency assistance; securing the crime scene; photographing, videotaping, and sketching; taking notes and writing reports; drafting legal documents such as search warrants and subpoenas; searching for, obtaining, and processing physical and digital evidence; obtaining information from witnesses and suspects; conducting photographic and in-person lineups; identifying suspects; conducting raids, surveillances, stakeouts, and undercover assignments; and testifying in court.

All investigators—whether patrol officers or detectives—are more effective when they possess certain intellectual, psychological, and physical characteristics. Effective investigators obtain and retain information, apply technical knowledge, and remain open-minded, objective, and logical. They are well-organized and able to prioritize and manage cases effectively. They are also culturally adroit, that is, skilled in interacting across gender, ethnic, generational, social, and political group lines. They are emotionally well-balanced, detached, inquisitive, suspecting, discerning, self-disciplined, conscientious, and persevering. Further, they are physically fit and have good vision and hearing. Undercover officers must also "look the part."

The first officer to arrive at a crime scene is usually a patrol officer assigned to the area. In any preliminary investigation, it is critical to establish priorities. Emergencies are handled first to achieve scene security, next the crime scene is secured to protect the integrity of the investigation, and then the investigation can begin. Any suspect at the scene should be detained, questioned, and then either released r arrested, depending on circumstances. If a suspect has recently left the scene, officers obtain descriptions of the suspect, any vehicles, direction of travel, and any items taken and then dispatch this information immediately.

After emergencies are dealt with, the first and most important function is to protect the crime scene and evidence. All necessary measures to secure the crime scene should be taken—including locking, roping, barricading, and guarding—until the preliminary investigation is completed.

Once the scene is secured, the preliminary investigation is conducted, which includes questioning victims, witnesses, and suspects; conducting a neighborhood canvass; measuring, photographing, videotaping, and sketching the scene; searching for evidence; identifying, collecting, examining, and processing physical evidence; and recording all statements and observations in notes. Case screening involves the systematic evaluation of solvability factors, such as the existence of witnesses and physical evidence, to determine which cases have the greatest likelihood of being solved and, thus, should be assigned for further investigation.

Investigators must interrelate with uniformed patrol officers; dispatchers; the prosecutor's staff; the defense counsel; community corrections personnel; social services; physicians, the coroner, or medical examiner; laboratories; and citizens, including witnesses and victims. Criminal investigation is, indeed, a mutual effort.

Protection against lawsuits includes effective policies and procedures clearly communicated to all, thorough and continuous training, proper supervision and discipline, and accurate, thorough police reports.

Can You Define?

civil liability	data mining	investigate
community policing	deductive reasoning	leads
crime	elements of the crime	Locard's principle of exchange
crime mapping	exculpatory evidence	misdemeanor
criminal investigation	felony	modus operandi (MO)
criminalist	forensic science	ordinance
criminalistics	hot spots	*res gestae* statements
criminal statute	inductive reasoning	solvability factors
culturally adroit	intuition	

Checklist

Preliminary Investigation

- Was a log kept of all actions taken by officers?

- Were all emergencies attended to first? (first aid, detaining suspects, broadcasting information regarding suspects)

- Was the crime scene secured and the evidence protected?

- Were photographs or videotapes taken?

- Were measurements and sketches made?

- Was all evidence identified preserved, including digital evidence?

- Were witnesses interviewed as soon as possible and statements taken?

- How was the complaint received?

- What were the date and time it was received?

- What was the initial message received? (State the offense and location.)

- Where was the message received?

- Who was present at the time?

- Were any suspicious persons or vehicles observed while en route to the scene?

- What time did officers arrive at the scene?

- How light or dark was it?

- What were the weather conditions? Temperature?

- Were there other notable crime scene conditions?

- How did officers first enter the scene? Describe in detail the exact position of doors or windows—open, closed, locked, glass broken, ajar, pried, or smashed. Were the lights on or off? Shades up or down?

- Was the heating or air conditioning on or off? Was a television or radio on?

- Were dead or injured persons at the scene?

- What injuries to persons were observed? Was first aid administered?

- What type of crime was committed?

- Was the time the crime occurred estimated?

- Who was the first contact at the scene? (name, address, telephone number)

- Who was the victim? (name, address, telephone number)

- Was the victim able to give an account of the crime?

- What witnesses were at the scene? (names, addresses, telephone numbers)

- Were unusual noises heard—shots, cars, screams, loud language, prying, or breaking noises?

- Had clocks stopped?

- Were animals at the scene?

- Was an exact description of the suspect obtained? (physical description, jewelry worn, unusual voice or body odors; unusual marks, wounds, scratches, scars; nicknames used; clothing; cigarettes or cigars smoked; weapon used or carried; direction of leaving the scene)

- Was a vehicle involved? Make, model, color, direction, unusual marks?

- Were items taken from the scene? Exact description?

- What was done to protect the crime scene physically?

- What officers were present during the preliminary investigation?

- Were specialists called to assist? Who?

- Was the coroner or medical examiner notified?

- What evidence was discovered at the scene? How was it collected, identified, preserved? Were field tests used?

References

Alper, M., Durose, M. R., & Markman, J. (2018, May). *2018 update on prisoner recidivism: A 9-year follow-up period (2005–2014)*. Special Report. Washington, DC: Bureau of Justice Statistics. (NCJ 250975)

Boetig, B. P., & Mattocks, M. (2007, December). Selecting personnel for multi-agency task forces. *Law and Order*, pp. 51–54.

Brantner Smith, B. (2007, July). The "love/hate" relationship between cops and their dispatchers. *Police One*. Retrieved April 17, 2020, from policeone.com/police-products /communications/dispatch/articles/1271472-The-love-hate-relationship-between-cops-and-their-dispatchers/

Bumpas, S. (2006, July). Permission to be human. *9-1-1 Magazine*, pp. 20–43.

Cawley, D. F., Miron, H. J., Araujo, W. J., Wasserman, R., Mannello, T. A., & Huffman, Y. (1977, June). *Managing criminal investigations*. Washington, DC: U.S. Department of Justice. (NCJ 040305)

Community Policing Defined. (n.d.). Washington, DC: Office of Community Oriented Policing Services. (e030917193)

Cotton, M., & Donlon-Cotton, C. (2007, November–December). Operations manuals, training and liability. *Tactical Response*, pp. 18–20.

Coupe, R. T., Ariel, B., & Mueller-Johnson, K. (2019). *Crime solvability factors: Police resources and crime detection*. Cham, Switzerland: Springer International Publishing.

Donahue, G. (2007, May). Intelligent GIS. *9-1-1 Magazine*, pp. 32–35, 62.

Donlon-Cotton, C. (2007, March). Positive scene presentations. *Law and Order*, pp. 74–76.

Durose, M. R., & Burch, A. M. (2016, November). *Publicly funded forensic crime laboratories: Resources and services, 2014*. Washington, DC: Bureau of Justice Statistics. NCJ 250151

Eck, J. E., & Spelman, W. (1987). *Problem-solving: Problem-oriented policing in Newport News*. Washington, DC: The Police Executive Research Forum. (NCJ 111964)

Fantino, J. (2007, November). Forensic science: A fundamental perspective. *The Police Chief*, pp. 26–28.

Federal Bureau of Investigation. (2018). *Crime in the United States*. Washington, DC: Federal Bureau of Investigation, Uniform Crime Reports. Retrieved April 17, 2020, from ucr. fbi.gov/crime-in-the-u.s/2018/crime-in-the-u.s.-2018 /topic-pages/clearances

Garrett, R. (2007, October). Taming the beast: How to keep news-hungry media fed. *Law Enforcement Technology*, pp. 22–32.

Hess, K. M., Orthmann, C. H., & Cho, H. (2014). *Police operations* (6th ed.). Clifton Park, NJ: Delmar, Cengage Learning.

Hess, K. M., Orthmann, C. H., & Cho, H. L. (2015). *Introduction to law enforcement and criminal justice* (11th ed.). Stamford, CT: Cengage Learning.

Hickman, M. J., Hughes, K. A., Strom, K. J., & Ropero-Miller, J. D. (2007, June). *Medical examiners and coroners' offices, 2004*. Washington, DC: Bureau of Justice Statistics Special Report. (NCJ 216756)

Hunt, J. (2019, November). "From crime mapping to crime forecasting: The evolution of place-based policing." *NIJ Journal*, Issue 281. Retrieved April 17, 2020, from nij.ojp. gov/nij-journal/nij-journal-issue-281

International Association of Chiefs of Police (IACP). (1957). *The canons of police ethics*. Alexandria, VA: IACP.

Jang, H., Hoover, L. T., & Joo, H. J. (2010, December). An evaluation of CompStat's effect on crime: The Fort Worth experience. *Police Quarterly*, *13*(4), 387–412.

Jordan, S., Romashkan, I., & Werner, S. (2007, October). Launching a national strategy for enhancing response to victims. *The Police Chief*, pp. 44–50.

Langan, P. A., & Levin, D. J. (2002, June). *Recidivism of prisoners released in 1994*. Washington, DC: Bureau of Justice Statistics. (NCJ 193427)

Miller, L. S., Hess, K. M., & Orthmann, C. H. (2011). *The police in the community: Partnerships for problem solving* (6th ed.). Belmont, CA: Wadsworth Publishing Company.

Morgan, R. E., & Oudekerk, B. A. (2019, September). *Criminal victimizations, 2018*. Washington, DC: Bureau of Justice Statistics. (NCJ 253043)

Murphy, G. R., Wexler, C., Davies, H. J., & Plotkin, M. (2004, October). *Managing a multijurisdictional case: Identifying the lessons learned from the sniper investigation.* Washington, DC: Police Executive Research Forum.

National Institute of Justice. (2008, January). *Increasing efficiency in crime laboratories.* Retrieved April 17, 2020, from ojp.gov/pdffiles1/nij/220336.pdf

National Institute of Justice. (2010, August 11). *Backlogs of forensic DNA evidence.* Retrieved April 17, 2020, from nij.ojp.gov/topics/articles/backlogs-forensic-dna-evidence

National Institute of Justice. (2019, July 17). *Forensic DNA laboratory efficiency improvement and capacity enhancement program.* Retrieved April 17, 2020, from bja.ojp.gov/program/dna-cebr/overview

Nelson, M., Chase, R., & DePalma, L. (2013, December). *Making sense of DNA backlogs, 2012—myths vs. reality.* Special Report. Washington, DC: National Institute of Justice. (NCJ 243347)

Oetinger, T. (2007, October). Providing better service to victims of crime. *The Police Chief,* pp. 40–43.

Paris, C. (2007, March). Lights, camera, action. *Law Officer Magazine,* pp. 50–55.

Ramirez, E. P. (2006, August). Limiting SWAT liability. *Police,* pp. 52–57.

Rossmo, D. K. (2009, October). Failures in criminal investigation. *The Police Chief,* pp. 54–66.

Sonenshein, D. A., & Nilon, R. (2010). Eyewitness errors and wrongful convictions: Let's give science a chance. *Oregon Law Review, 89*(1), 263–304.

Stockton, D. (2006, September). Patrol investigators. *Law Officer Magazine,* p. 12.

U.S. Bureau of Labor Statistics. (n.d.). *Occupational outlook handbook.* Retrieved April 15, 2020, from bls.gov/ooh/protective-service/police-and-detectives.htm#tab-6

U.S. Department of Justice. (2019, December 20). *Forensic science.* Retrieved April 20, 2020, from justice.gov/olp/forensic-science

Wandrei, G. (2007, November). Instant access to vital information: The role of GIS. *Law Enforcement Technology,* pp. 56–61.

Cases Cited

Andrews v. State, 533 So. 2d 841 (Fla. Dist. Ct. App., 1988).

Franks v. Delaware, 438 U.S. 154, 165–166 (1978).

SECTION 2

Basic Investigative Responsibilities

As Berg (1999, p. 8) points out, "Police can learn a few lessons from legendary basketball coach John Wooden," who believed that constantly practicing, mastering, and executing the basics were the keys to a team's success. Berg contends,

> Officers, detectives, and sergeants should constantly evaluate their fundamentals. Are reported crimes being thoroughly investigated or merely reported? Are neighborhoods being canvassed for that one witness who may give us the little piece of information we need to identify the suspect? Have we searched thoroughly for evidence, including fingerprints, and have we protected evidence and gathered it in an expert manner? Are we completing well-written reports that contain all of the information that will make a subsequent follow-up successful? Are we doing a comprehensive job investigating at a crime scene or do we always expect the experts and the specialists to "figure it out"?

> Essentially, how well do our frontline patrol investigators, detectives, and sergeants execute the fundamentals of high-quality police work at the scene of a crime? As Coach Wooden taught us so many years ago, you don't get to cut the net down after the final game if you don't understand the most

basic fundamentals of the game and perform them consistently well. So, too, is it with frontline police work.

The basic investigative techniques introduced in Chapter 1 are central to the successful resolution of a crime. Investigators must be skilled in documenting the crime scene and any continuing investigation, including taking notes and photographs or videotaping and sketching (Chapter 2) and then casting this information into an effective report (Chapter 3). Investigators must also be skilled in searching (Chapter 4); obtaining and processing physical evidence (Chapter 5); obtaining information through interviews and interrogation (Chapter 6); and identifying and arresting suspects and conducting raids, surveillances, stakeouts, and undercover assignments (Chapter 7).

Although these techniques are discussed separately, they actually overlap and often occur simultaneously. For example, note taking occurs at almost every phase of the investigation, as does obtaining information. Further, the techniques require modification to suit specific crimes, as discussed in Sections 3, 4, and 5. Nonetheless, investigation of specific crimes must proceed from a base of significant responsibilities applicable to most investigations. This section provides that base.

Chapter 2
Documenting the Crime Scene: Note Taking, Photographing, and Sketching

Chapter Outline

Learning Objectives

L01   Explain why notes are important in an investigation.

L02   Identify thfe characteristics of effective notes.

L03   Summarize the purposes served by crime scene photography.

L04   Describe the minimum photographic equipment an investigator should have available and be skilled in using.

L05   Understand what should be photographed at a crime scene and in what sequence.

L06   Identify the various types of photography used in criminal investigations and the circumstances in which they are applied.

L07   Explain the specific criteria photographs must meet to be admissible in court.

L08   List the steps involved in making a rough sketch.

L09   Describe the requirements for a sketch or a scale drawing to be admissible in court.

Scott Olson/Getty Images News/Getty Images

Introduction

Police sergeant Drew Peterson had been flying under the radar until his fourth wife, Stacy, to whom he had been married just over four years, disappeared suddenly, leaving behind their two small children. Peterson seemed unconcerned at the time, claiming Stacy had simply left to start a new life somewhere else. However, suspicions of foul play began brewing when details of Peterson's past surfaced, particularly the untimely death of his third wife, Kathleen Savio, three years earlier. Savio had been found dead in her bathtub, five months after her divorce from Peterson, presumably from a fall, since the tub was dry and her hair was soaked with blood. A cursory assessment of the scene led investigators to conclude the death was a result of an accident, not murder.

The deputy coroner who initially examined Savio's body at the scene later testified that he had asked others present whether measures should be taken to preserve potential evidence. The officers had all replied, "No," so the suspicious-death protocol was not followed. When pressed to explain this lack of documentation, one investigator testified that there had been none of the typical signs of a struggle that he had witnessed at other murder scenes— no blood splattered everywhere, broken furniture, doors torn off their hinges, holes punched in walls, and so on. "When someone is fighting for their lives, it's an intense thing," the investigator stated under oath (Crime Scene Investigation Under Scrutiny, 2012). Because the death scene did not match the investigator's notion of what happens during a violent life-and-death struggle, he admitted he made only a superficial search of Savio's home. No evidence had been collected for a match against a possible suspect. When questioned about a partially full glass of orange juice found in the kitchen, the investigator acknowledged that it had not been analyzed for fingerprints, saliva, blood, or any other evidence to suggest someone other than Savio had touched it.

Following the disappearance of Stacy Peterson in 2007, Kathleen Savio's body was exhumed and a second autopsy revealed evidence of a struggle. Her death in 2004 was reclassified as a homicide, and Drew Peterson was charged with her murder. On September 6, 2012, he was convicted of killing his third wife, despite any physical evidence linking him to the murder. On February 21, 2013, Peterson was sentenced to 38 years in prison. Then in 2016, Peterson was found guilty of hiring someone to kill one of the prosecuting attorneys who helped convict him, a crime for which Peterson received an additional 40 years to the original sentence (Maple, 2018). Furthermore, Peterson's 2017 appeal to his murder conviction involving Savio was denied.

Meanwhile, Stacy has never been found, and Peterson has not been charged in that case, although many speculate that she became another victim of his violence. Which begs the question: had the Savio death scene been more thoroughly documented, would there have been another victim?

Documentation is vital throughout an investigation. Most people who go into law enforcement are amazed at the amount of paperwork and writing that is required— as much as 70% of an investigator's job is consumed by these functions. Notes are often used for the purpose of writing reports and, as such, are crucial pieces of an investigation. In addition, photography plays an important role in documenting evidence and presenting cases in court. Some larger departments have a photographic unit. Other departments rely on their investigators to perform this function. Often both photographs and sketches must accompany written reports to provide a clear picture of the crime scene. As indispensable products of a criminal investigation, photographs, sketches, and reports are given to the charging authority to determine if and what charges need to be considered.

Field Notes: The Basics

Note taking is not unique to the police profession. News reporters take notes to prepare stories; physicians record information furnished by patients to follow the progress of a case; lawyers and judges take notes to assist in interviewing witnesses and making decisions; and students take notes in class and as they read. Quite simply, notes are brief records of what is seen or heard.

> **LO1** Explain why notes are important in an investigation.
>
> Investigative notes are a permanent written record of the facts of a case to be used in further investigation, in writing reports, and in prosecuting the case.

Note taking and report writing are often regarded as unpleasant, boring tasks. Yet no duty is more important, as many officers have found, much to their embarrassment, when they did not take notes or took incomplete notes. Detailed notes can make or break a case. For example, when a defense attorney challenges in court the reliability or validity of various breath or blood measurements of alcohol content, the case often hinges on the thoroughness of an officer's written report. Accurate notes aid later recall and are used for preparing sketches and reports. Notes are important throughout an entire investigation.

When to Take Notes

Sometimes it is physically impossible to take notes immediately—for example, while driving a vehicle or in complete darkness. At other times, taking notes immediately could hinder obtaining information if it intimidates a witness or suspect. Whether to take out a notebook immediately in the presence of a person being questioned is a matter of personal insight and experience.

When people are excited, want to get their name in the newspaper, or want to get your attention, you can usually record information immediately. Most people are willing to give information if you are friendly and courteous and you explain the importance of the information. In such cases, no delay in taking notes is required.

On the other hand, reluctant witnesses and suspects may not talk if you record what they say. In such cases, obtain the information first and record it later. You must sense when it is best to delay writing notes.

Often, rookie officers are so focused on taking good notes that they fail to do well on building rapport with suspects, victims, and witnesses, which can lead to a failed interview. Note taking is supposed to benefit the investigation, but how information is obtained—whether the officers establish good rapport or not—can greatly influence investigative success. Specific methods of obtaining information from willing and unwilling people are discussed in Chapter 6.

If someone gives you an exact wording of what was said by a person committing a crime, have the witness initial that portion of your notes after reading it to help ensure its accuracy. If possible, have people who give you information take time to write a statement in their own handwriting. This avoids the possibility that they may later claim that they did not make the statement or were misunderstood or misquoted.

What to Record

Enter general information first: the time and date of the call, location, and arrival time at the scene. Police departments using centrally dispatched message centers may automatically record date, time, and case numbers. Even if this is done, make written notes of this initial information because digital records may not be kept for extended periods or may become unusable. The computerized records and notes corroborate each other.

Record all information that helps answer the questions Who? What? Where? When? How? and Why? As you take notes, ask yourself specific questions such as these:

- Who: are suspects? accomplices? Complete descriptions include gender, race, color, age, height, weight, hair (color, style, condition), eyes (color, size, glasses), nose (size, shape), ears (close to head or protruding), distinctive features (birthmarks, tattoos, scars, beard), clothing, voice (high or low, accent), and other distinctive characteristics such as walk.

- Who: were the victims? associates? was talked to? were witnesses? are children of those involved? saw or heard something of importance? discovered the crime? reported the incident? made the complaint? responded to the scene (e.g., EMS, fire department, coroner—important for contamination consideration)? investigated the incident? worked on the case? marked and received evidence? was notified? had a motive?

- What: type of crime was committed? are the elements of the crime? was the amount of damage or value of the property involved? happened (narrative of the actions of suspects, victims, and witnesses; combines information included under "How")? evidence was found? preventive measures had been taken (safes, locks, alarms, etc.)? knowledge, skill, or strength was needed to commit the crime? are possible motives? was said? did the police officers do? further information is needed? further action is needed?

- Where: did the incident happen? was evidence found? was it stored? do victims, witnesses, and suspects live? do suspects tend to spend a lot of time? were suspects arrested?

- When: did the incident happen? was it discovered? was it reported? did the police arrive on the scene? were suspects arrested?

- How: was the crime discovered? does this crime relate to other crimes? did the crime occur? was evidence found? was information obtained?

- Why: was the crime committed (was there intent? consent? motive?)? was certain property stolen? was a particular time selected?

Make notes that describe the physical scene, including general weather and lighting conditions. Witnesses may testify to observations that would have been impossible given the existing weather or lighting. Accurate notes on such conditions will refute false or incorrect testimony.

Record everything you observe in the overall scene: all services rendered, including first aid; description of the injured; location of wounds; who transported the victim and how, including ambulance and hospital information. If, at a later time, you wish to obtain medical records for sustained injuries related to the case, such hospital information will be useful. Record complete and accurate information regarding all photographs taken at the scene. As the search is conducted, record the location and description of evidence and its preservation. Record information to identify the type of crime and what was said and by whom. Include the name, address, and phone number of every person present at the scene and all witnesses.

The amount of notes taken depends on the type of offense, the conditions of the case, your attitude and ability, and the number of other officers assigned to the case. Make sure you take enough notes to completely describe what you observe and do during an investigation. This will provide a solid foundation for a detailed report and for court testimony. If in doubt about whether to include a specific detail, record it. If it catches your attention, document it. Take notes about everything you do in an official investigative capacity. Record all facts, regardless of where they may lead. Information establishing a suspect's innocence is as important as that establishing guilt:

> In most cases, there will be some evidence pointing to the suspect's guilt ("inculpatory") and other evidence that appears inconsistent with the suspect's guilt

("exculpatory").... When such evidentiary conflicts exist, the general rule is that *all* of the evidence, both inculpatory and exculpatory, should be reported to the prosecutor for evaluation. (Rutledge, 2007, p. 68)

This begins with including such information in the notes about a case.

Personal opinions should not be written in notes. It is acceptable to note someone's appearance, but such statements must be free from any attributed opinion. For example, it is fine to record: "John Doe (disheveled, ripped shirt) stated he did not see anything." It is not okay to record: "John Doe (lying) stated he did not see anything."

Do *not* jot down information unrelated to the investigation—for example, the phone number of a friend, an idea for a poem, or a doodle. If the defense attorney, judge, or jury see your notes, such irrelevant material will reflect poorly on your professionalism.

Where to Record Notes

Use a notebook to record all facts observed and learned during an investigation. Despite the availability of sophisticated recorders and computers, the notebook remains one of the simplest, most economical, and most basic investigative tools. Notes taken on scraps of paper, on the backs of envelopes, or on napkins are apt to be lost, and they reflect poorly on an officer's professionalism.

Divide the notebook into sections for easy reference. One section might contain frequently used telephone numbers. Another section might contain frequently needed addresses. This information can be a permanent part of the notebook. Identify the notebook with your name as well as the address and telephone number of your police department.

Opinions vary about whether it is better to use a loose-leaf notebook or separate spiral-bound notebooks for each case. The decision to use a loose-leaf or spiral-bound notebook is sometimes a matter of department policy. If you use a loose-leaf notebook, you can easily add paper for each case you are working on as the need arises, and you can keep it well organized. Most investigators favor the loose-leaf notebook because of its flexibility in arranging notes for reports and for testifying in court. However, use of a loose-leaf notebook opens the opportunity for challenge from the defense attorney that the officer has fabricated the notes, adding or deleting relevant pages. This can be countered by numbering each page, followed by the date and case number or by using a separate spiral notebook for each case.

Disadvantages of the latter approach are that the spiral notebook is often only partially used and, therefore, can be wasteful and may be bulky for storage. Further, if other notes are kept in the same notebook, they also will be subject to the scrutiny of the defense. A final disadvantage is that if you need a blank sheet of paper for some reason, you should not take it from a spiral notebook because most of these notebooks indicate on the cover how many pages they contain. The defense can only conjecture about loose-leaf pages that might have been removed, but missing pages from a spiral notebook can be construed as evidence that something has been removed.

In addition to the notebook, always carry pens and pencils. Use a pen for most notes because ink is permanent. You may want to use pencil for rough sketches that require minor corrections as you sketch.

How to Take Notes

Note taking is an acquired skill. Time does not permit a verbatim transcript. Learn to select key facts and record them in abbreviated form. Do not include words such as *a*, *and*, and *the* in your notes. Omit all other unnecessary words. For example, if a witness said, "I arrived here after having lunch at Harry's Cafe, a delightful little place over on the west side, at about 1:30, and I found my boss had been shot," you would record, "Witness arrived scene 1:30 (after lunch at Harry's Cafe) to find boss shot." You would not know at the time if the fact that she had lunch at Harry's Cafe was important, but it might be, so you would include it.

Whenever possible, use standard abbreviations such as *mph*, *DWI*, *Ave*. Do *not*, however, devise your own shorthand. For example, if you wrote, "Body removed by A. K.," the initials *A. K.* would be meaningless to others. If you become ill, injured, or deceased, others must be able to read and understand your notes. This is necessary to further the investigation, even though some question regarding admissibility in court may arise.

Some police departments use digital recorders extensively because of the definite advantage of recording exactly what was stated with no danger of misinterpreting, slanting, or misquoting. In fact, when taking a verbatim statement, the preferred method now is to make a digital audio recording, if reasonable for the situation. Witnesses', suspects', and victims' memories of the situation can change over time, and if their recollection of the events changes from what is documented in your report, the recorded statement provides supporting evidence. Even better is a video of a disheveled victim or an out-of-control suspect. A suspect can put on a suit and tie in court and appear quite civilized, but having a statement from the suspect when they are angry and swearing, drunk and disorderly, paints quite a different picture for the court. It is also more effective for juries to hear the voice of a victim in the immediate aftermath of an incident and the fear in that voice. The use of recording as an investigative technique is discussed in more detail in Chapter 6.

As valuable as digital recordings are, they do not replace the notebook. Despite their advantages, they also have serious disadvantages. The most serious is that they can malfunction and fail to record valuable information. Weak batteries or background noise can also distort the information recorded. In addition, transcribing recordings is time-consuming, expensive, and subject to error. Finally, the recordings themselves, not the transcription, are the original evidence and thus must be retained and kept for possible use in court.

Characteristics of Effective Notes

Effective notes are complete and describe the scene and the events well enough to enable a prosecutor, judge, or jury to visualize them.

> **LO2** Identify the characteristics of effective notes.
>
> Effective notes are complete, factual, accurate, specific, legible, clear, arranged in chronological order, and well-organized.

The basic purpose of notes is to record the *facts* of a case. Recall the discussion of the importance of objectivity in an investigation. Use this same objectivity in note taking. For example, you might include in your notes the *fact* that a suspect reached inside his jacket and your *inference* that he was reaching for a gun. Your *opinion* on the merits of gun-control laws, however, has no place in your notes. If you have a specific reason for including an opinion, clearly label the statement as an opinion. Normally, however, restrict your notes to the facts you observe and learn and the inferences you draw. If, for example, you see a person you consider to be nervous and you make a note to that effect ("The man appeared nervous"), you are recording an inference. If, on the other hand, you record specific observations such as, "The man kept looking over his shoulder, checking his watch, and wiping perspiration from his forehead," then you are recording facts on which you based your inference. These facts help support the inference that the man was nervous, as you may not remember six months or a year later why you thought that the man was nervous.

Record the facts accurately. An inaccurately recorded name can result in the loss of a witness or suspect. Inaccurate measurements can lead to wrong conclusions. Have people spell their names for you. Repeat spellings and numbers for verification. Recheck measurements. If you make an error, cross it out, make the correction, and initial it. Do *not* erase. Whether intentional or accidental, erasures raise credibility questions.

Be as specific as possible. Rather than writing *tall*, *fast*, or *far*, write *6´8˝*, *80 mph*, or *50 feet*. Little agreement may exist on what is tall, fast, or far.

Notes are usually taken rapidly, increasing the chance of errors. Take enough time to write legibly and clearly. Legibility and clarity are not synonymous. *Legibility* refers to the distinctness of your letters and numbers and is especially important when recording names, addresses, telephone numbers, license numbers, distances, and other specific facts. *Clarity*, on the other hand, refers to the distinctness of your statements. For example, lack of clarity is seen in a note that states, "When victim saw suspect he pulled gun." *Who* pulled the gun: the victim or the suspect? The same lack of clarity is seen in the statements "When suspect turned quickly I fired" (Did the suspect turn quickly, or did the officer fire quickly?) and "When the suspect came out of the house, I hit him with the spotlight." Make certain your notes are clear and can be interpreted only one way.

Effective notes are also arranged in chronological order and are well-organized. Make entries from each case on separate pages and number the pages. Keep the pages for each case together and record the case number on each page.

Retaining Notes

Some officers destroy all their field notes after they have written their reports, contending that notes simply duplicate what is in the report and may, in fact, contain information no longer pertinent when the report is written. Some police departments also have this as a policy. Be aware, however, that the defense attorney may ask for an officer's original notes regarding an investigation, with the strategic intent to imply that, in cases where officers have discarded their notes, the investigators may be trying to withhold or hide crucial facts or evidence to make the prosecution's case stronger. Thus, it is important to consider a method of retaining field notes in preparation for this defensive tactic. One common response to this potential challenge is for investigators to digitally record everything along with taking their field notes, helping to avoid any issues later if the field notes have been discarded.

If department policy is to keep the notes, place them in a secure location and under a filing system that makes them available months or even years later. While an investigation is open, many agencies require notes to be stored in an official police department case file or any secure location where they are available on short demand. Some departments keep notes with the original file in the official records department. Others permit an officer to keep the original notes and file only the report made from the notes. Wherever notes are filed, they must be secure.

No one filing system is best. Notes may be filed alphabetically by the victim's name, by case number, or in chronological order. Again, department policy may dictate which system is used, but if an investigator is allowed to choose his or her own method of organization, as long as the system is logical, the notes will be retrievable. Appeals have been granted as long as 20 years after convictions, with the defendant being granted a new trial. Because of this, many officers retain their notes indefinitely.

Digitization (scanning) of paper notes allows for the electronic storage of such documents that, previously, had to be stored in file cabinets, boxes, or other space-consuming containers. For large agencies that generate thousands of reports annually and must retain these documents for long periods of time, electronic storage is a welcome advancement. Again, department policy usually determines where and for how long notes are filed or retained.

Admissibility of Notes in Court

The use of notes in court is probably their most important legal application. They can help discredit a suspect's or a defense witness's testimony; support evidence already given by a prosecution witness, strengthening that testimony; and defend against false allegations by the suspect or defense witnesses. Notes give you an advantage because others rarely make written notes and, therefore, must testify from memory.

All officers who are present at the scene while the notes are being taken and who witness the writing and initial the notes at that time may use the notes during courtroom testimony. If you anticipate the need to have other investigators testify from a specific set of notes, be sure they do in fact witness the original note taking at the crime scene and provide their initials on the original notes. The admissibility of notes in court is presented in greater detail in the final chapter of this text.

In addition to accurate notes, photographs and video recordings provide vital and necessary means of documenting a crime scene.

Investigative Photography: An Overview

A picture is, indeed, worth a thousand words, and investigative photographs and videos are essential to proper crime scene documentation. The basic purpose of crime scene photography is to record the scene permanently. Photos and videos taken immediately, using proper techniques to reproduce the entire crime scene, provide a factual record of high evidentiary value. The time that elapses between the commission of a crime and when a suspect in that crime is brought to trial can stretch into months or years, with the condition of the crime scene and physical evidence deteriorating along the way. Photos and videos preserve the scene. Do not touch or move any evidence until pictures and videos have been taken of the general area and all evidence.

> **LO3** Summarize the purposes served by crime scene photography.
>
> Photographs and video recordings reproduce the crime scene in detail for presentation to the prosecution, defense, witnesses, judge, and jury in court and are used in investigating, prosecuting, and police training.

Although investigators take most crime scene photographs, photos may also be acquired from commercial or amateur photographers, attorneys, news media personnel, or the coroner's staff. Also, with today's technology and the prevalence of smart phones, a large percentage of the general population has access to a camera or video recorder at almost all times. For example, in an arson case at a church, photographs came from multiple outside sources. The pastor hired a photographer to take pictures for historical purposes and to assess damage, an insurance company photographer took pictures, a television news crew had taken live in-progress footage, and numerous bystanders with cell phones watched and recorded as the firefighters battled the blaze. These pictures, along with those taken by police personnel, provided an excellent record of the fire in progress, its point of origin, and the resulting damage.

Video is now well established as an investigative tool. Lightweight, handheld video recorders are easy to use at a crime scene and provide a high-quality digital format of crime scene images. Video can also be taken of witness testimony, depositions, evidence, lineups, and even trials.

Advantages and Disadvantages of Photographs

One advantage of photographs is that they can be taken immediately, an important factor in bad weather or when many people are present. For example, a picture of a footprint in the dirt outside a window broken during a burglary can be important if it rains before a casting can be made. The same is true when the large number of people present might alter the scene.

Another obvious advantage of crime scene photographs is that they accurately represent the crime scene in court. The effect of pictures on a jury cannot be overestimated. Photographs are highly effective visual aids that corroborate the facts presented.

Benefits of digital photography are numerous: the images are quickly adaptable as email attachments; most digital cameras record technical information about each photograph, such as the date and time and specific camera settings, in a text file associated with the image; the issue of image degradation, a common problem with film, is avoided; and the physical space required to file and store a large number of photographs is greatly reduced.

Although photographs of a crime scene accurately represent what was present, they include everything at the scene, both relevant and irrelevant. So much detail may distract viewers of photographs. It is important that investigators keep up with technology to ensure that the equipment they are using can capture discrete evidence, such as fingerprint outlines. However, obtaining and maintaining the most advanced equipment can be expensive, and not every department can justify the need for such expenses. Other disadvantages of photographs are that they do not show actual distances and may be distorted by technical errors in shooting.

Despite these disadvantages, photography is a valuable investigative technique, and photographic quality continues to improve as technology advances. Even the cameras currently available on most cell phones can often provide better quality images than could the more expensive, cumbersome cameras commonly used a decade ago.

The introduction of digital video technology into crime scene investigation has allowed investigators to compensate for some of the shortcomings of still photography.

Advantages and Disadvantages of Video

A video or DVD, played before a jury, can bring a crime scene to life and offers some distinct advantages over photographs, such as showing distance and including audio capability. Furthermore, a slow pan of a crime scene is more likely than is a series of photographs to capture all evidence, including that in the periphery of view, which might seem rather inconsequential at the time.

As part of the *CSI effect*, juries now expect to see video of a crime scene. Regrettably, many agencies, whether because of lack of funding or prioritization, fail to provide adequate training to those tasked with videotaping a crime scene, assuming that if officers are able to tape their cousin's wedding or their daughter's soccer game, they should be able to handle videotaping a crime scene.

The negative consequences of poor video can damage a case. Some common mistakes made by untrained crime scene videographers include shooting without planning ahead, not shooting enough, shooting too much (resulting in a boring presentation), poor focusing, overusing the zoom feature, making jerky camera movements, including unintentional audio, and failing to use a tripod. Proper training can help eliminate most, if not all, of these common videotaping errors and increase the video's documentation value.

A vast array of modern equipment has greatly enhanced the investigative usefulness of photography and videography.

Basic Photographic Equipment

Previous editions of this text discussed both film and digital photography. Indeed, film photography was, for more than a century, a fundamental technique in criminal investigation. The first time photographic evidence was used in a criminal case was in 1874 (*Udderzook v. Commonwealth*), and color photography gained prominence during the 1960s (Dutelle, 2010). Digital photography entered the scene during the 1990s, and by the mid-1990s, many criminal justice agencies had begun using this technology. Early digital equipment lacked the high-resolution capability found in film cameras used at the time—a capability necessary for identification, examination, and courtroom purposes—but advances in technology have since elevated digital image resolution to levels that match or exceed that available from film photography. Thus, by year-end 2009, all 50 state crime laboratories had officially converted from film to digital technology, making the processing of film and the submission of film as photographic evidence a thing of

The use of digital technology is becoming commonplace in criminal investigations. Digital cameras allow instant verification of a photo's quality, and most automatically stamp the date and time of the image capture on an attached text file.

David Clayton/Shutterstock.com

the past (Dutelle, 2010). Therefore, this section on photographic equipment no longer presents information on film photography.

Crime scene photography uses both common and special-function cameras and equipment, depending on the crime investigated and the investigator's preferences.

> **LO4** Describe the minimum photographic equipment an investigator should have available and be skilled in using.
>
> At a minimum, have available and be skilled in operating an instant-print camera, a point-and-shoot camera, a digital single-lens reflex (DSLR) camera, a cell phone camera, a fingerprint camera, and video equipment.

Investigators commonly have individual preferences about the equipment to use in a given situation, and agencies are well advised to purchase a variety of photographic equipment for different applications: "A garden-variety traffic accident investigation doesn't require a lot of photographic horsepower. . . . This is mostly point-and-shoot work, and the main concern is whether there's enough power in the camera's strobe to illuminate the scene at night. But if the same officer's next call is to take a report and document the injuries of a domestic violence victim at the hospital, that point-and-shoot camera may not be up to the task" (Dees, 2008, p. 68).

Video recording equipment has been used for some time to record in-station bookings, traffic stops, and field sobriety tests of suspected intoxicated drivers. Videotaping crime scenes and other steps taken throughout the investigative process, including victim and witness interviews and suspect interrogations, is now common.

The basic photographic equipment used in criminal investigations are summarized in Table 2.1.

Specialized cameras such as binocular cameras and trip cameras (cameras that set themselves off) are helpful in surveillance. Cameras can be hidden in many different objects (e.g., the "nanny" cam inside a stuffed animal), which can lend assistance in undercover investigations. Furthermore,

TABLE 2.1 **Common Types of Photographic Equipment Used in Criminal Investigations**		
Camera Type	**Features and Advantages**	**Disadvantages**
Instant-print cameras (in digital format)	■ Low cost per image ■ Immediate confirmation of quality and accuracy of the photo while still on scene, when it is possible to take another shot ■ Simple to operate, lessening the need for training ■ Good optics, resolution, and color ■ Can document small objects such as bullet holes	■ Significantly lower image quality and resolution than digital single-lens reflex (DSLR)
Point-and-shoot cameras (with fixed lens)	■ Relatively inexpensive and easy to use ■ Automatically adjust the shutter speed, aperture control, and other settings, lessening the likelihood of poor image quality resulting from operator error ■ Some models are ruggedized to be water-, shock-, and temperature-resistant, allowing for longer use ■ Adequate for many routine investigations, allowing them to be placed in every patrol car ■ Provide instant feedback regarding a photo's quality, allowing the officer to verify whether the shot contains what it was intended to capture, that the lighting is sufficient, and that the image is not blurry	■ Ruggedized models cost more
Digital single-lens reflex (DSLR) cameras	■ Offer significantly higher image quality and resolution than point-and-shoot cameras ■ Superior to point-and-shoots for taking photos at close range ■ With accessories, can be adapted to take better photos in more challenging situations ■ A zoom or telephoto lens can capture details from far away, if it is not possible to physically reach the location of piece of evidence ■ Wide-angle lenses enable officers to better document evidence in close quarters, such as bathrooms, vehicle interiors, and other small spaces	■ More difficult to use properly than point-and-shoots, thereby requiring more training in proper use ■ Generally, sometimes considerably, more expensive than point-and-shoots

(Continued)

TABLE 2.1 *(Continued)*

Camera Type	Features and Advantages	Disadvantages
Cellphone cameras	■ Convenient ■ Portable ■ Can navigate into small spaces ■ Requires minimal training for use ■ Can upload images quickly to social media	■ Limited battery life ■ May require additional features or equipment for optimal photos ■ Expensive ■ Photos can easily be deleted or lost ■ Limited manual camera control
Fingerprint cameras*	■ Specially constructed to take pictures of fingerprints without distortion ■ Provide their own light through four bulbs, one in each corner ■ Removing a bulb from any corner provides slanted lighting to show fingerprint ridge detail ■ Can also photograph trace evidence such as bloodstains and tool marks	■ Require an amount of training to use properly ■ Not easily portable

Video cameras	■ Video recording devices have become much less expensive, much more portable, and much easier to operate over the years
	■ Can be played back immediately
	■ Can eliminate a middle processing step in the chain of evidence
	■ Most can operate in quite limited light
	■ Permanently installed units can capture crimes actually being committed, such as bank robberies or shoplifting
	■ Can be used to record alleged bribery, payoffs, and narcotics buys, increasing the conviction rate
	■ Dash-mounted cameras in patrol vehicles offers many benefits:
	  • Most are designed to start 30 seconds before activation, allowing events that led up to the activation to be captured. Activation usually starts automatically with lights/sirens or officer can manually start.
	  • Provide real time data in many instances, including car accidents, high speed chases/vehicle pursuits, and field sobriety tests
	  • Provide community transparency
	  • Can be used for officer training using real life scenarios
		■ Limited field of vision
		■ Dash-cam:
		  • Must be turned on for proper use
		  • Privacy issues on private property

Body-worn cameras	■ Captures video from the officer's perspective ■ Constantly recording, even when not activated and, like a squad camera, can go back and record 30 seconds prior to an officer physically activating it ■ Can automatically start recording with a triggered event (weapon drawn, elevated heart rate, or even facial recognition)	■ Expensive ■ Require large data storage capacity ■ Privacy issues of recording inside people's homes ■ Only captures what is occurring in the direction the camera is facing ■ If officer is engaged in an altercation or while running, video may not be clear ■ Laws have not caught up with this technology, creating liability issues for officers and agencies

*Fingerprint cameras are becoming obsolete. Most agencies now use macro lenses on DSL cameras for trace evidence and prints. They may also use UV lens.

an increasing number of homeowners now have their own residential photographic equipment, such as doorbell cameras and exterior-facing security cameras, that can provide crucial evidence to police during a criminal investigation.

Accessories, depending on the camera(s) used, include an exposure meter, flash attachments and flood lamps, and high-intensity spotlights. Lighting equipment can also assist in illuminating the scene as officers search for minute evidence. Lenses and filters are available for different purposes. Normal lenses are best for evidence, but sometimes special lenses are needed. For example, a telephoto lens can capture a distant subject, whereas a wide-angle lens can cover an entire room in a single frame. Various filters can eliminate certain colors from a photograph. Lens care products and a soft bristled lens airbrush and lens cloth are also necessities.

Storage of photographic equipment is a concern, and cameras should be protected from contact with other items commonly used in criminal investigation. Dees (2008, p. 68) cautions, "One agency I know of went to considerable trouble and expense to make fitted cases for all of their crime scene investigation gear so officers could check it out of the station at the beginning of the watch and throw it in the trunk until needed. None of the gear ever got broken, but the cameras didn't work well once they had been coated inside and out with fingerprint powder."

Selection of a camera and accessories is determined by budget, local needs, and investigator preference. Sometimes investigators can borrow equipment from local schools or community organizations or share it with other agencies. In some communities, citizens lend special-purpose equipment to the police department.

A major advance is the ability of computer software to stitch together digital photos of 180 degrees or more to create one 360-degree photo—a panoramic view of a crime scene that is interactive, allowing viewers, including jury members, to walk through it as though they were there (Figure 2.1). This type of 360-degree photographic view is called **immersive imaging**. Crime Scene Virtual Tour (CSVT) software lets jurors virtually step into a crime scene. The software allows the scene to be viewed from any angle with zoom, pan, tilt, and rotate features. If a witness claims to have been standing at a certain place, an investigator can virtually go there to view that perspective (Fletcher, 2016).

This panoramic capability is also found on most cellular phones today, and several cell phone applications are available to enhance photos. However, investigators must know how to use and apply the proper photographing technique for the crime scene environment.

Training in and Using Investigative Photography

Investigators can master most photographic equipment by reading the accompanying manuals and practicing. Some equipment, however, requires special training. Photographic training includes instruction in operating all available photographic equipment; shooting techniques; anticipated problems; and identifying, filing, and maintaining continuity of photographic evidence. Learn the nomenclature and operation of your available photographic equipment. Sometimes camera and equipment manufacturers or outlets provide such training.

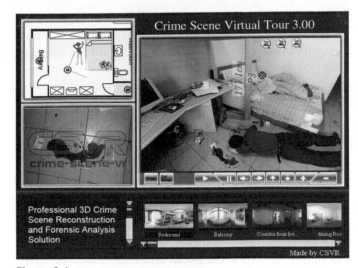

Figure 2.1
The Crime Scene Virtual Tour software program allows investigators to recreate the crime scene and to piece together better the events that occurred. These programs may also be presented during trial to help a jury visualize the crime scene.
© Crime Scene Virtual Tour

Professional commercial photographers in the community can sometimes assist in training or serve as consultants. They can provide information on photographic techniques and special problems such as lighting, close-ups, exposures, and use of filters. Training programs also include instructions on identifying and filing photographs and on establishing and maintaining the continuity of the chain of evidence.

As with other types of crime scene–processing techniques, proper training in the use of digital equipment is essential. Digital technology brings with it a new

Technology Innovations

3-D Crime Scene Mapping

Crime scene mapping technology is continuously evolving. Tripod-mounted scanners, such as the 3D DISTO developed by Leica Geosystems, Inc., use lasers to measure a room with an unprecedented degree of accuracy. For example, the 3D DISTO laser is accurate to within 1 mm at 10 meters away and to within 1/16″ at a 33′ distance. Multiple scans of the area are taken, replacing the traditional measurements taken by hand. The images are then uploaded to a software program which creates a virtual tour of the crime scene.

Source: https://shop.leica-geosystems.com/buy/3d-disto/3d-disto

language and application skill set for investigators to learn. Although an in-depth discussion of digital technology, capabilities, and applications is beyond the scope of this text, a few examples should make clear the critical need for investigators to be thoroughly trained in using digital equipment.

One of the most basic terms used when discussing digital photography is **resolution**, which refers to the fineness of image detail captured with a camera, displayed on a monitor, or printed on paper. High resolution produces a sharp image; low resolution, a blurrier image. Resolution is commonly quantified by pixels. A **pixel** is the smallest unit of a digital image, generally a dot within the image (just as traditional newsprint photos are made up of tiny dots); one **megapixel** is about a million dots. The more dots, the larger the image can be made without losing resolution quality. Digital cameras or other capture devices range in resolution from 2 megapixels to more than 50 megapixels, and camera companies are constantly striving to develop equipment with higher resolution capabilities. However, resolution of computer monitors and printers, referred to as *output devices*, are given in pixels per inch, or **PPI**. Both types of resolution must be factored in when taking digital photographs because both affect the final size and quality of the image. An image photographed with a high-resolution camera (the capture device), if printed on a low-resolution printer (the output device), will not show fine detail clearly. A low-resolution image, if enlarged too much, will also lose quality.

Myth The more megapixels a digital camera has, the better the pictures will be.

Fact Higher megapixel count does not necessarily equate to better photographs. Having more megapixels can help create larger prints but not necessarily better pictures. The camera is only as good as the person operating it. While a great deal of technology goes into a camera, the photographer must have the knowledge and training to make the most of that technology.

An understanding of resolution is critical for investigators who use digital cameras to document a crime scene because resolution affects every aspect of digital imaging. Improper choice of equipment or incorrect settings on it will produce low-quality results, which may have damaging consequences in the courtroom. Investigators must have hands-on training and practice with digital cameras. Good pictures can make a case. Pictures and videos are the only evidence that visually puts a jury at a crime scene.

The importance of understanding resolution, and the plethora of other digital terms and concepts too detailed to explore here, is brought into focus when one considers evidentiary standards and requirements surrounding this technology. For example, an investigator photographing latent prints at a crime scene must know that the FBI's Integrated Automated Fingerprint Identification System (IAFIS) requires a latent print to be photographed with a minimum resolution of 1,000 PPI (Dutelle, 2010). In effect, for digital images to have value in the courtroom, investigators must thoroughly understand their equipment and apply the technology properly. (Admissibility of photographs is examined shortly.)

What to Photograph or Videotape

Photographs of the crime scene should be taken as soon as possible to avoid losing or contaminating evidence. The most fragile areas of the crime scene should be the first areas photographed. Take sufficient photographs or videos to reconstruct the entire scene. This usually requires a series of shots, notably of the entrance point, the crime commission area, and the exit point. If possible, show the entire crime scene in a pictorial sequence. This helps relate the crime to other crimes.

Move the camera to cover the entire crime scene area, but plan a sequence of shots that least disturbs the scene. The initial photographs showing the entire crime scene should use a technique called **overlapping**. Photograph the scene clockwise and take the first picture with a specific object on the right. For the second photo, make sure that the same object is on the left side of the photograph. Continue in this way until you have covered the entire scene.

L05 Understand what should be photographed at a crime scene and in what sequence.

First, photograph the general area, then specific areas, and finally specific objects of evidence. Take exterior shots first because they are the most subject to alteration by weather and security violations.

This progression of shots or videos will reconstruct the commission of a crime:

1. Take *long-range* shots of the locality, points of ingress and egress, normal entry to the property and buildings, exterior of the buildings and grounds, and street signs or other identifiable structures that will establish location.

2. Take *medium-range* shots of the immediate crime scene and the location of objects of evidence within the area or room.

3. Take *close-range* shots of specific evidence such as hairs, fibers, footprints, and bloodstains. The entire surface of some objects may be photographed to show all the evidence; for example, a table surface may contain bloodstains, fingerprints, hairs, and fibers. It is especially important to take such close-range photographs of objects that will not be collected or taken for preservation as evidence.

Zoom lenses allow close shots without disturbing the crime scene, and close-ups are possible with macro lenses. Such close-range shots usually should include a **marker**, which is anything used in a photograph to show accurate or relative size. It is usually a ruler, but it can be some other object of a known size, such as a pen or pencil. An important point: Using a marker introduces something foreign to the crime scene. The same is true of chalk marks drawn around a body or placed on walls to illustrate bullet direction. Therefore, first take a picture of the scene or object without the marker, then add the marker and take a second photograph. If a marker is used, it should be preserved with the case evidence so that it can be presented in court if requested.

Different crimes require different types of photographs. In arson cases, photograph the point of origin and any incendiary devices. In burglaries, photograph the points of entry and exit, tool marks, fingerprints, and other trace evidence. In assaults, photograph injuries. In homicides or suicides, photograph the deceased, including pictures of the clothing worn; take a full-length picture showing height, position of the body and all extremities, and evidence near the body. Photograph injured parts of the body to show the location and extent of injuries or petechiae and any postmortem lividity (discussed in Chapter 8).

Photogrammetry can be used at most crime scenes. **Forensic photogrammetry** is the technique of extrapolating three-dimensional (3-D) measurements from two-dimensional (2-D) photographs. Photogrammetry can also automatically orient photographs taken from awkward angles and can correct for camera misalignment. Furthermore, this technique can cut in half the amount of time investigators spend performing on-site mapping of a crime scene. The major advantage is that images can be recorded quickly, reducing time spent at the crime scene.

Errors to Avoid

To obtain effective photographs and videos, be familiar with your equipment and check it before you use it. Unfamiliarity and lack of practice with photographic equipment increase the chance of error.

If something has been moved, do *not* put it back. It is virtually impossible to return an object to its original position. The item should still be photographed and noted that it is not believed to be in its original location. To minimize distortion or misrepresentation, maintain proper perspective and attempt to show the objects in a crime scene in their relative size and position. Take pictures from eye level, the height from which people normally observe objects. Make sure true north is known and notated on at least one reference image, to facilitate orientation of the scene. Do not video record or photograph members of the crime scene team; take photos before these individuals begin their work. Finally, when videotaping a crime scene, be sure to verbalize clearly and introduce what is being shown.

Checklists are important when it comes to crime scene photography and can help eliminate errors. A checklist for a DSLR camera might include such items as the following: Are there batteries in the camera? Is the memory medium loaded? Is the camera on? Is the lens cap removed? Are there spare batteries and memory media readily available?

Types of Investigative Photography

In addition to crime scene photography, certain other types of photography play vital roles in investigation.

> **LO6** Identify the various types of photography used in criminal investigations and the circumstances in which they are applied.
>
> Types of investigative photography include crime scene, surveillance, aerial, night, laboratory, mug shot, and lineup.

Surveillance Photography

Surveillance photography establishes the identity of a subject or records criminal behavior without the photographer's presence being known to the subject. The photographs or videos can help identify a suspect's associates, destroy an alibi, plan a raid, or develop a surveillance plan. Banks and stores frequently use surveillance cameras to help identify robbers and burglars. With a wellthought-out plan, surveillance cameras can potentially be a significant force multiplier for a police agency, regardless of size (Kanable, 2008).

Photographs during a stakeout are usually taken with a DSLR camera with several telephoto lenses. Sometimes infrared capability is used. It may be necessary to use a van—preferably borrowed because it is best to use a vehicle only once; a subject is more likely to notice and become suspicious of a vehicle that appears suddenly and is parked close by on a regular basis. An appliance repair van or any van that would commonly be seen in the area is desirable.

Concealing a camera can be a problem. You might use a bag, briefcase, suitcase, or coat pocket with an opening. You can also conceal the camera by using rooftops or windows of buildings or vehicles in the area. A camera kept away from a vehicle window is rarely seen by people outside the vehicle. Keep the camera on and adjusted to the required light so you can take pictures instantly.

Surveillance photography is often called **trap photography** because the photos prove that an incident occurred and can help identify suspects and weapons. These photos corroborate witness testimony and identification. The fact that the photos exist often induces guilty pleas without court appearances, thus saving investigators' time.

Often the recordings from security cameras leave much to be desired. Problems such as poor lighting conditions, blurry images, and low resolution can be overcome through the use of professional video and audio forensic tools such as dTective™ and dVeloper™, both available from Ocean Systems.

The Department of Justice and the International Association of Chiefs of Police (IACP) have developed four Regional Forensic Video Analysis Labs, located in Cincinnati, Ohio; Fort Worth, Texas; Raynham, Massachusetts; and Phoenix, Arizona. These labs are equipped with dTective™, currently in use by 90% of all agencies with video analysis capabilities: "Just as DNA has CODIS and fingerprints have AFIS, now forensic video evidence will have the Regional Forensic Video Analysis Labs—a national database of criminals caught on tape" (Heinecke, 2007, p. 87).

Surveillance photography can also be a crime prevention and detection tool. For example, the Newark, New Jersey, Police Department has video cameras mounted in six different areas of the two-square-mile downtown area. An officer observes what is taking place in each area from a central location. Burglaries and street robberies have decreased, and the police have successfully presented the videos as evidence in court.

Aerial Photography

Criminal investigations often make use of aerial photography. The FBI's *Handbook of Forensic Services* (2019, p. 54) notes that specially modified aircraft are capable of taking high-resolution vertical and oblique photographs, with ground resolution measurements of 4 inches or less, to help with crime scene documentation, tactical planning, special event mapping, construction planning and documentation, and geospatial intelligence (GEOINT) products. Aerial photography can be used to

cover extensive areas; for example, in following a bank robbery to show roads leading to and from the bank.

Aerial photography is also useful when police know that a crime is going to be committed but not when. Aerial photography shows routes to the scene as well as how to block escape routes and avoid detours during pursuit and where to set up roadblocks. It is essential in locating dead-end streets—information that can be very important if a chase ensues. Aerial pictures can help establish the location of a crime scene, especially in large rural areas or mountainous sectors. Aerial images are also used when executing search warrants, as they allow officers to see the entrances and exits to a house, where a suspect may run to, and, for large properties, all of the outbuildings. An unmanned aerial vehicle (UAV) might be used to provide aerial video in real time.

Geographical information systems (GIS) technology is now enhancing the aerial views of crimes scenes by providing infrastructure data and intelligence information about specific crime scenes, such as buildings and streets, to the investigator. With GIS, aerial images can be georeferenced to provide distance and area measurements, latitude/longitude location, and area-of-interest visualization. "Analysis of imagery and geospatial information can help visually depict geographically referenced activities on the earth" (FBI, 2019, p. 55), allowing investigators to more easily understand spatial relationships of land features, the overall topography of the land, and points of interest within a 360-degree view.

Aerial photographs are often available in commercial photographers' files, engineering offices, or highway-planning agencies, since the vast areas covered by highways and engineering projects usually require aerial mapping. Federal, state, county, and municipal agencies also may have aerial photos. If none are available, a local photographer can be hired to provide them. Many larger departments and county sheriff's offices have helicopters that may be available.

Investigators are increasingly making use of tools such as Google Maps, Google Earth, or Microsoft Bing Maps to view aerial imagery, 3-D buildings, maps, and terrain. The geographical content of these resources allows officers to obtain street views of property, learn what the property layout is, see a structure's proximity to neighboring structures, and give insight into what neighborhoods need to be canvassed after a criminal incident.

Aerial photos can be enlarged or presented on slides to show the relationships of streets and roads. For example, in the John F. Kennedy assassination investigation, the entire area was photographed, including all points from which shots might have been fired. More recently, software based on aerial photography was used by multiple jurisdictions involved in the Washington, DC, sniper investigation.

A high-tech application of aerial photography uses EagleView Reveal® Imagery, a unique, patented computer technology that integrates various aerial shots of a land-based artifact taken straight down (orthogonal) and from numerous angles (oblique). The result is a high-resolution 3-D image of the object, whether it be a landmark, a neighborhood, a bridge, a river, a house or any other structure, or geological feature, which investigators may view from multiple perspectives with the simple click of a mouse (Figures 2.2A and 2.2B). The software also features extreme zooming capabilities, allowing investigators to rotate and zoom in on a particular structure.

Figure 2.2A
Pictometry software with GIS overlays allows investigators to see as many as 12 different views of this geographic area.

Image courtesy of EagleView Technologies, Inc.

Figure 2.2B
This screen capture highlights some of the different functions available with Pictometry software, such as measuring distances and heights, and determining a precise geographic location with latitude/longitude coordinates.

Image courtesy of EagleView Technologies, Inc.

Night Photography

Taking pictures at night presents special problems, particularly that of illuminating a scene. Adequate light can be obtained by increasing exposure time, using a photoflash for small areas and a flash series for larger areas or using floodlights. Floodlights also aid in locating evidence and decrease the chance of evidence being accidentally destroyed.

Investigators can make the camera see as the photographer sees through camera position, time exposure, and supplemental lighting. State-of-the-art night-vision devices and cameras are dramatically better than earlier ones, with a range extending as far as a mile. Night-vision devices use image intensification and can be binoculars, weapon mounted, camera mounted, or head mounted.

Laboratory Photography

Not all investigative photography is done in the field. Sometimes objects are photographed in a laboratory with special equipment that is too large, delicate, or expensive to use in the field. For example, infrared film photographs can reveal the contents of unopened envelopes, bloodstains, alterations to documents, variations in types of ink, and residue near where a bullet has passed through clothing. X-ray cameras can detect loaded dice.

Microphotography takes pictures through a microscope and can help identify minute particles of evidence such as hairs or fibers. In contrast, **macrophotography** enlarges a subject. For example, a fingerprint or a tool mark can be greatly enlarged to show the details of ridges or striations.

Laser-beam photography can reveal evidence indiscernible to the naked eye. For example, it can reveal the outline of a footprint in a carpet, even though the fibers have returned to normal position.

Ultraviolet-light photography uses the low end of the color spectrum, which is invisible to human sight, to make visible impressions of bruises and injuries long after their actual occurrence. Bite marks, injuries caused by beatings, cigarette burns, neck strangulation marks, and other impressions left from intentional injuries can be reproduced and used as evidence in criminal cases by scanning the presumed area of injury with a fluorescent or blue light. The damage impression left by the injury is then photographed. In addition, the type of weapon used in committing a crime can often be determined by examining its impression, developed by using ultraviolet light.

Mug Shots

Although investigators seldom take **mug shots** themselves, these photographs, also called *booking photos*, are often significant in criminal investigations. Mug shots originated in nineteenth-century France when Alphonse Bertillon developed a method of identification that used an extensive system of measurements to describe people. The Bertillon identification system included a written description, the complete measurements of the person, and a photograph. The pictures of people in police custody were kept in department files for identification and became known as *mug shots*. Gathered in files and displayed in groups, they were called a **rogues' gallery**.

Opinions differ regarding the preferred poses for mug shots. Some agencies believe the front and profile of the head are sufficient; others prefer full-length, stand-up pictures. No matter what the pose, mug shots should include the facial features and the clothing worn at the time of arrest, because a defendant's appearance may change between the time of arrest and trial. Mug shots can be filed by age, sex, and height to make them more readily accessible for viewing. Mug shots are valuable resources for investigators to use to help identify suspicious persons and for crime victims to assist in identifying their attacker. Mug shots are also used for "wanted" circulars distributed to other police agencies and the public. A caution: some cases have been lost when an officer has shown a single photo to a victim or witness and asked, "Is this the person that . . . ?" This is not good investigative policing. The use of mug shots in suspect identification is discussed in Chapter 7.

Lineup Photographs

The computer's capacity to sort through a database of mug shots and bring up all the "hits" within specific categories can assist in generating photographic lineups. After entering characteristics of a known suspect, an officer can select 6 to 12 other "hits" to be used for presentation with the suspect's photo. In addition, videotapes or photographs of people included in lineups may be taken to establish the fairness of the lineup. Lineup identification are discussed in greater detail in Chapter 7.

Computer-Facilitated Lineups

Considering the weight given by the criminal justice system to eyewitness identification of suspects, it is imperative that lineup procedures be conducted according to best practices and not introduce bias at any point. But it is not enough to simply conduct a fair lineup; the identification process must be documented if it, as evidence, is to withstand scrutiny in court. eLineup is a product developed by investigators, prosecutors, and software engineers that guides lineup administrators step-by-step through the creation, presentation, and documentation of the lineup process. The program accesses a filler photo database to create an unbiased double-blind or blinded lineup. The eLineup software can be configured to run sequential or simultaneous photos lineups and is designed to adhere to a department's state and local laws. Furthermore, "eLineup automatically documents and records the entire lineup process. A complete video record is created showing exactly what the witness saw on screen and how they interacted with the software. Video of the witness is also included to see and hear the witness completing the photo lineup."

Source: https://elineup.org/Default.aspx

Identifying, Filing, and Maintaining Security of Evidence

Photographs must be properly identified, filed, and kept secure to be admissible as evidence.

Identifying

In the field notes, the photographs taken should be dated and numbered in sequence. Include the case number, type of offense, and subject of the picture. To further identify the photograph with the crime scene and the subject, record the photographer's name; the location and direction of the camera; lens type; approximate distance in feet to the subject; lighting; weather conditions; and a brief description of the scene in the picture.

Filing

File the images for easy reference. Pictures in the case file are available to others; therefore, it is usually best to put them in a special photograph file, cross-referenced by case number. For digital images, file them appropriately as evidence or within the department's internal secured hard drive, whatever department policy dictates.

Maintaining Security

Record the chain of custody of the photographs in the field notes or in a special file. Mark and identify the memory medium as it is removed from the camera. Each time the medium changes possession, record the name of the person accepting it.

Admissibility of Photographs in Court

Photographs must be taken under certain conditions and must meet specific criteria to be admissible in court.

> **LO7** Explain the specific criteria photographs must meet to be admissible in court.
>
> Rules of evidence dictate that photographs must be material, relevant, competent, accurate, free of distortion, and noninflammatory to be admissible in court.

A **material photograph** relates to a specific case and subject. Material evidence is relevant and forms a substantive part of the case presented or has a legitimate and effective influence on the decision of the case. A **relevant photograph** helps explain testimony. A **competent photograph** accurately represents what it purports to represent, is properly identified, and is properly placed in the chain of evidence and secured until court presentation.

Testimony reports the exact conditions under which the photographs were taken and the equipment used. Photographs must be accurate and free of distortion. If nothing has been removed from or added to the scene, the photograph will be accurate. Inaccuracies do not necessarily render the photograph inadmissible as evidence as long as they are fully explained and the court is not misled about what the picture represents.

Likewise, distortion will not necessarily disqualify a photograph as evidence if no attempt is made to misrepresent the photograph and if the distortion is adequately explained. For example, an amateur photographer may have taken the picture from an unusual camera height to produce a dramatic effect, not knowing the picture would later be useful as evidence in a criminal investigation.

Color distortion is a frequent objection. Because most objects have color, black-and-white photographs are technically distorted. Therefore, color photographs usually constitute better evidence. However, color can also be distorted by inadequate lighting or faulty processing. Nevertheless, the photograph can still be useful, especially if the object's shape is more important than its color.

Although color photographs are less distorted and are usually better evidence than black-and-white photographs, they have often been objected to as being inflammatory—for example, showing in gruesome, vivid color a badly beaten body. To be ruled inadmissible, color photographs must be judged by the court to be so inflammatory that they will unduly influence the jury. Sometimes taking both color and black-and-white pictures is advisable. The black-and-white pictures can be introduced as evidence; the color pictures can be used for investigatory purposes only.

Myth Photos do not lie.

Fact Digital alteration software is readily available and may be of particular concern if a victim or witness supplies photos to the police as evidence. All photographs should be authenticated by the photographer.

The transition from film to digital photography, and the ready availability of software that modifies, enhances, or otherwise alters digital images, has raised authenticity issues and concerns regarding such digital photographs' originality and integrity. However, "The legal requirements for the admissibility of digital images as evidence within court are the same as that for film images. The majority of legal challenges surrounding digital images have been concerned with processed images" (Dutelle, 2010, p. 63).

The FBI's Scientific Working Group on Imaging Technologies (SWGIT) was created in 1997 to provide leadership to the law enforcement community by developing guidelines for best practices regarding the use of imaging technologies within the criminal justice system. Although this group was defunded in 2015, the Forensic Photographic and Imaging Certification Board, part of the International Association for Identification

(IAI), continues to recognize SWGIT's best practices for recertification purposes, while also working to develop new best practices (International Association for Identification, 2016). Despite losing funding, SWGIT has striven to maintain an active presence both on the web and through social media, and many of their documents are still available at www.swgit.org. One document, *SWGIT Guidelines for the Forensic Imaging Practitioner*, provides guidelines for image processing and states that any changes to an image made through image processing are acceptable in forensic applications provided the following criteria are met:

- The original image is preserved.

- Processing steps are documented when appropriate (see SWGIT document "*Best Practices for Documenting Image Enhancement*") in a manner sufficient to permit a comparably trained person to understand the steps taken, the techniques used, and to extract comparable information from the image.

- The end result is presented as a processed or working copy of the image.

- The recommendations of this document are followed (IAI, 2016, p. 45).

To overcome defense challenges that a digital image was altered or otherwise tampered with, investigators must rigorously maintain the chain of custody and use techniques that safeguard the authenticity of their photographs. Several software programs have been developed that "watermark" or authenticate the original image, either at the point of capture (within the camera) or as it is downloaded from the camera to a computer. The programs then store the original image in a secure location and write-protect it, making it impossible to alter the original, yet still allowing copies to be manipulated for investigative purposes.

Crime Scene Sketches: An Overview

In addition to admissible photographs and videotapes, and after such images have been taken, investigators usually must prepare a crime scene sketch, particularly of serious crimes and crash scenes. An investigator's scene sketch can be more descriptive than hundreds of words and is often an extremely important investigative aid. The crime scene **sketch**

- Portrays the physical facts accurately

- Relates to the sequence of events at the scene

- Establishes the precise location and relationship of objects and evidence at the scene

- Helps create a mental picture of the scene for those not present

- Is a permanent record of the scene

- Is usually admissible in court

A crime scene sketch assists in interviewing and interrogating people, preparing the investigative report, and presenting the case in court. The sketch supplements photographs, notes, plaster casts, and other investigative techniques. Artistic ability is helpful but not essential in making crime scene sketches. Still, many police officers avoid making sketches. To overcome this hesitance, practice by drawing familiar scenes such as your home, office, or police station. Use graph paper to make sketching easier.

The most common types of sketches are those drawn at the crime scene, called *rough sketches*, and those completed later by an investigator or a drafter, called *scale* (or *finished*) *drawings*. Both describe the crime scene pictorially and show the precise location of objects and evidence.

The Rough Sketch

A **rough sketch** is the first pencil-drawn outline of a scene and the location of objects and evidence within this outline. It is not usually drawn to scale, although distances are measured and entered in the appropriate locations. It is better to include too much rather than too little, but do not include irrelevant objects that clutter and confuse the sketch.

The area to be sketched depends on the crime scene. If it involves a large area, make a sketch of nearby streets, vegetation, and entrance and exit paths. If the scene is inside a house or apartment building, show the scene's location in relation to the larger structure. If the scene involves only a single room, sketch only the immediate crime scene, including an outline of the room; entrances, exits, and windows; objects; and the evidence within it.

Do not overlook the possible availability of architectural drawings of the house or building. These are often on file with local engineering, assessing, or building departments, or with the architect who drew the original plans.

Sketching Materials

Materials for the rough sketch include paper, pencil, long steel measuring tape, carpenter-type ruler, straightedge, clipboard, compass, protractor, and thumbtacks. These items should be assembled and placed in their own kit or in the crime scene investigation kit.

Paper of any type will do, but plain white or graph paper is best. No lines interfere if you use plain white. On the other hand, graph paper provides distance ratios and allows for more accurate depictions of the relationships between objects and evidence at the scene. When sketching, use a hard lead pencil to avoid smudges. Keep two or three pencils on hand.

Use a 50- to 150-foot steel measuring tape for measuring long distances. Steel is preferable because it does not stretch and therefore is more accurate than cloth tape. Use a carpenter-type ruler to take short and close-quarter measurements and a straightedge to draw straight lines. A clipboard will give a firm, level drawing surface.

Use a compass to determine true north, especially in areas and buildings laid out in other than true directions. Use a protractor to find the proper angles when determining coordinates.

Thumbtacks are helpful to hold down one end of the tape when you measure. You can also use them to fasten paper to a drawing surface if no clipboard is available.

Steps in Sketching the Crime Scene

Once photographs have been taken and other priority steps in the preliminary investigation performed, you can begin sketching the crime scene. First, make an overall judgment of the scene. Remember not to move, remove, touch, or pick up anything until it has been photographed, located on the rough sketch, and described in detail in your notes. Then handle objects only in accordance with the techniques for preserving evidence.

> **LO8** List the steps involved in making a rough sketch.
>
> To sketch a crime scene
> - Observe and plan.
> - Measure distances and outline the area.
> - Plot objects and evidence within the outline.
> - Take notes and record details.
> - Identify the sketch with a legend and a scale.
> - Reassess the sketch.

Step One: Observe and Plan

Before starting to sketch, observe the scene as many times as you need to feel comfortable with it. Take in the entire scene mentally so you can recall it later. Plan in advance how to proceed in an organized way to avoid destruction of evidence. Ask yourself, "What is relevant to the crime? What should be included in the sketch?"

The size of the area determines how many sketches you make. For example, part of the crime may have taken place indoors and another part outdoors a considerable distance away. To include the entire area would make the scale too small. Therefore, make two sketches.

The overview also helps you determine where to start sketching and measuring. If the scene is a room, stand in the doorway and start the sketch there. Then continue clockwise or counterclockwise. The photographs, sketch, and search are all made in the same direction. Usually it does not matter which direction is selected, but try to use the one that is least disturbing to evidence.

Step Two: Measure Distances and Outline the Area

All measurements must be accurate. Do not estimate distances or use paces or shoe length measurement. Use conventional units of measurements such as inches, feet, or yards. Do not move any objects while measuring.

If another officer is helping you take measurements, reverse the ends of the tape so you both can observe the actual distance on the tape. Legally, it is *hearsay* for officers to testify to what they did not actually observe. If a third officer is taking notes, that officer can testify to only the measurements given by the other officers unless the third officer actually saw the tape measurement. However, all officers may testify from the same notes if they review and initial them as they are made.

Do not measure from movable objects. Use *fixed locations* such as walls, telephone poles, building corners, and curbs. Measure from wall to wall, not baseboard to baseboard. A note about using trees and other landscape-type objects as objects from which to measure: it is advised to not consider trees as "fixed" locations because they change with time and, in some cases, can be relocated on a property or removed and replaced by another tree. Going back to a crime scene years later, the defense may challenge these measurements. Therefore it is best to avoid any nonpermanent objects.

Once the outside measurements have been made, sketch the outline, maintaining some distance ratio. Use the longest measurement first and orient the sketch paper to this distance, positioning the sketch so *north is toward the top of the paper*. Place the outside limits in the sketch using dimension lines such as this:

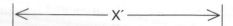

Determine the **scale** by taking the longest measurement at the scene and dividing it by the longest measurement of the paper used for sketching. For example, if your paper is 10 inches and the longest measurement at the scene is 100 feet, let 1 inch equal 10 feet. Use the largest, simplest scale possible. Table 2.2 presents suggested scales for sketches.

Graph paper makes it easier to draw to scale. Each square can equal 1 square foot or 1 square inch, depending on the size of the scene. The outline sketch of an outdoor scene might look like Figure 2.3, whereas the outline sketch of a room might look like Figure 2.4.

Figure 2.4 also includes locations and measurements of doors and windows. On the sketch, record these measurements and indicate whether the doors open in or out. To measure windows, use the width and height of the actual window opening; do not include the window frame.

Sketch the location of physical objects within the perimeter. Use approximate shapes for large objects and symbols for small ones. Place items of evidence in the sketch at the same time you place objects. Use numbers to designate objects and letters to designate evidence. Include such items as bullet entry or exit points, body, hair, gun, fibers, and bloodstains. Use exact measurements to show the location of evidence within the room and in relation to all other objects.

Opinions differ about whether to include the location of evidence in this sketch. If evidence is placed within the sketch, some courts have withheld introduction of the sketch until the evidence has been approved. If the evidence is placed only in the finished scale drawing, the sketch can be introduced and used by witnesses to corroborate their testimony.

While sketching, check measurements frequently. Make corrections if needed, but make no changes after leaving the scene. Measurements may or may not be placed in the sketch itself, depending on how many

TABLE 2.2 **Suggested Scales for Sketches**	
Indoor Areas	**Outdoor Areas**
1/2″ = 1′ (small rooms)	1/2″ = 10′ (large buildings and grounds)
1/4″ = 1′ (large rooms)	1/8″ = 10′ (large land areas)
1/8″ = 1′ (very large rooms)	

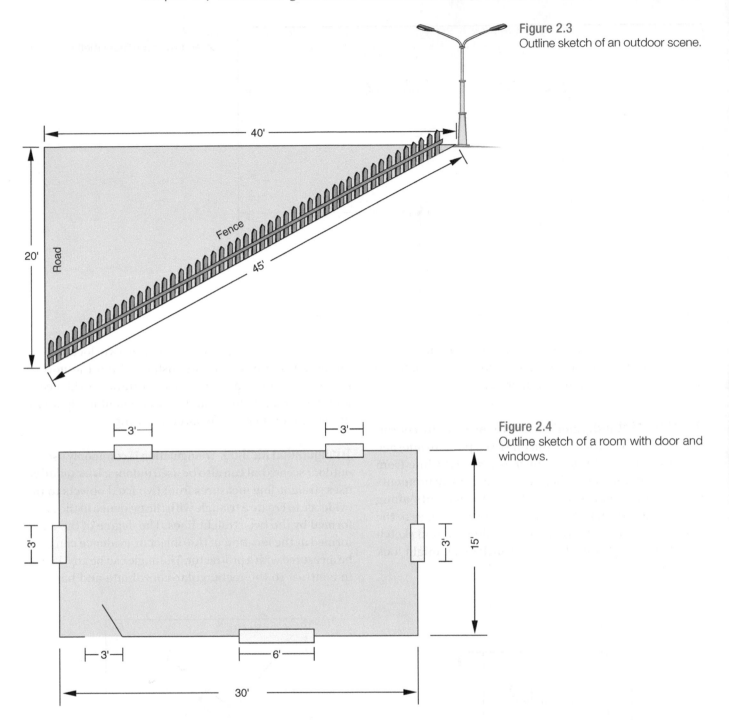

Figure 2.3
Outline sketch of an outdoor scene.

Figure 2.4
Outline sketch of a room with door and windows.

objects are located in the available space. Measurements can be placed in your notes and later entered in the scale drawing. As mentioned earlier in this chapter, software products allow laser measurements to be coupled with digital photographs of an area to create a virtual scene that can be rotated and zoomed in on.

Step Three: Plot Objects and Evidence

Plotting methods are used to locate objects and evidence on the sketch. These methods include the use of

rectangular coordinates, a baseline, triangulation, and compass points. A cross-projection sketch shows the floor and walls in the same plane. To plot objects and evidence accurately, determine fixed points from which to measure.

Rectangular-Coordinate Method. The rectangular-coordinate method is a common way to locate objects and evidence in a room. The **rectangular-coordinate method** uses two adjacent walls as fixed points from which distances are measured at right angles. Locate objects by

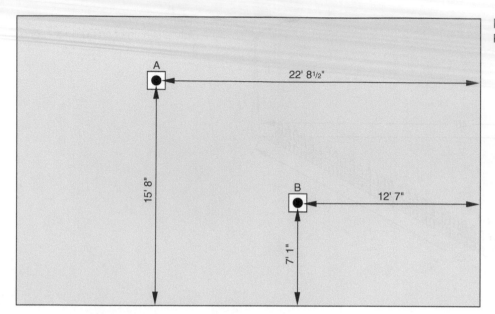

Figure 2.5
Rectangular-coordinate method.

measuring from one wall at right angles and then from the adjacent wall at right angles. This method is restricted to square or rectangular areas (Figure 2.5).

Baseline Method. Another way to measure by coordinates is to run a baseline from one fixed point to another. The **baseline method** establishes a straight line from one fixed point to another, from which measurements are taken at right angles. Take measurements along either side of the baseline to a point at right angles to the object to be located. An indoor baseline method sketch might look like Figure 2.6 or 2.7. Outdoors, it might look like Figure 2.8.

Sometimes the distance between two locations is important. For example, the distance from the normal route to a door might be very important if evidence is found in a room. The 34-foot measurement in Figure 2.8 illustrates this need in an outdoor setting.

Triangulation Method. Triangulation is commonly used in outdoor scenes but can also be used indoors. **Triangulation** uses straight-line measures from two fixed objects to the evidence to create a triangle with the evidence in the angle formed by the two straight lines. The degree of the angle formed at the location of the object or evidence can then be measured with a protractor. The angle can be any degree, in contrast to the rectangular-coordinate and baseline

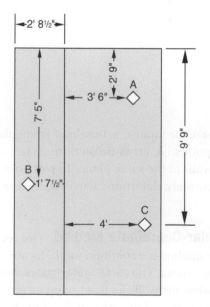

Figure 2.6
Center baseline method.

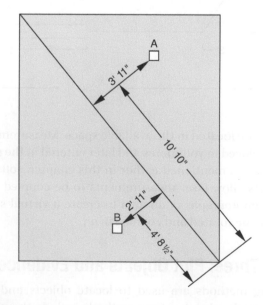

Figure 2.7
Diagonal baseline method.

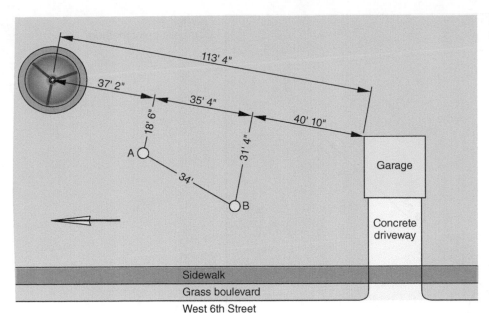

Figure 2.8
Outdoor baseline method.

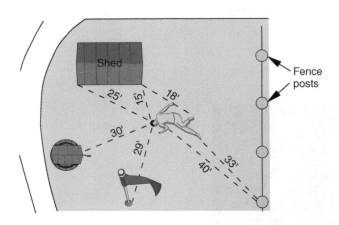

Figure 2.9
Triangulation method.

methods, in which the angle is always a right angle (90°). Triangulation is illustrated in Figure 2.9.

Always select the best possible fixed points, with emphasis on their permanence. Fixed points may be closet doors, electrical outlets, door jambs, or corners of a structure. It is sometimes impossible to get to the corners of a room for accurate measurements because of obstacles. Remember never to move potential evidence to get to a corner or object of permanence. Use what you can without disturbing the evidence, because it is impossible to move an item and place it back exactly where it was located.

Compass-Point Method. The **compass-point method** uses a protractor to measure the angle formed by two lines. In Figure 2.10, for example, Object *A* is located 10′7″ from origin *C* and at an angle of 59° from the vertical line through point *C*. Object *B* is 16′7″ from origin *C* at an angle of 47° from the vertical.

Cross-Projection Method. For some interior crime scenes, it is useful to show the relationship between evidence on the floors and the walls. This can be done by sketching the room as though the viewer is straight above it, looking down. In effect, the room is flattened out much like a box cut down at the four corners and opened flat. A **cross-projection sketch** presents the floor and walls as though they were one surface. Objects of evidence on both the floor and the walls can be measured to show their relationship on a single plane, as shown in Figure 2.11.

Step Four: Take Notes and Record Details

After you have completed your sketch, take careful notes regarding all relevant factors associated with the scene that are not sketchable, such as lighting conditions, weather conditions, colors, and people present.

Step Five: Identify the Scene

Prepare a **legend** containing the case number, type of crime, name of the victim or complainant, location, date, time, investigator, anyone assisting, scale of the sketch, direction of north, and name of the person making the sketch (see Figure 2.12).

Step Six: Reassess the Sketch

Before leaving the scene, make sure you have recorded everything you need on the sketch. Make sure nothing has been overlooked or incorrectly diagrammed. Once you have left, nothing should be added to the sketch.

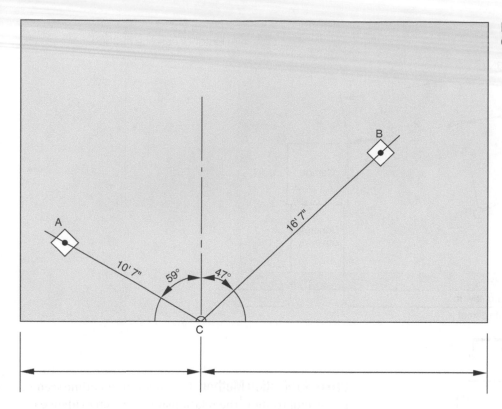

Figure 2.10
Compass-point method.

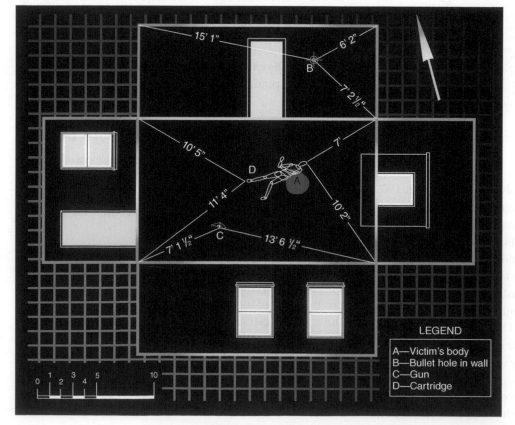

Figure 2.11
Cross-projection sketch.

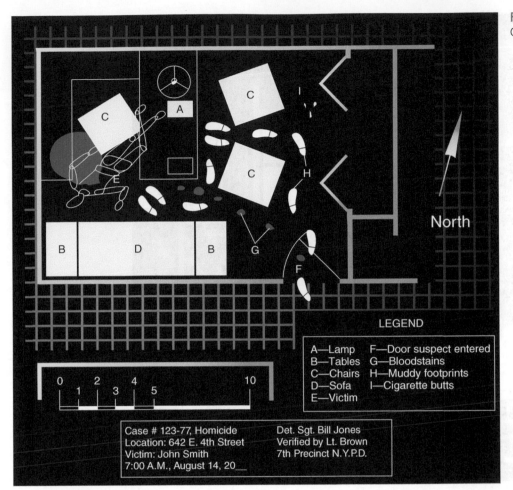

Figure 2.12
Completed crime scene sketch.

LEGEND

A—Lamp   F—Door suspect entered
B—Tables   G—Bloodstains
C—Chairs   H—Muddy footprints
D—Sofa   I—Cigarette butts
E—Victim

Case # 123-77, Homicide   Det. Sgt. Bill Jones
Location: 642 E. 4th Street   Verified by Lt. Brown
Victim: John Smith   7th Precinct N.Y.P.D.
7:00 A.M., August 14, 20___

Compare the scene with the sketch. Are all measurements included? Have all relevant notations been made? Have you missed anything? Figure 2.12 is a completed rough sketch of a crime scene.

Filing the Sketch

Place the rough sketch in a secure file. It is a permanent record for all future investigations of the crime. It may be used later to question witnesses or suspects and is the foundation for the finished scale drawing. The better the rough sketch is, the better the finished drawing will be.

Keep the rough sketch in its original form even after the scale drawing is completed because it may be needed for testifying. Otherwise, the defense may claim that changes were made in preparing the scale drawings.

The Finished Scale Drawing

Given a well-drawn rough sketch, the finished scale drawing can be completed. The **finished scale drawing** is done in ink on a good grade of paper and is drawn to scale, using exact measurements. The materials used for making scale drawings are listed in Table 2.3.

TABLE 2.3 **Materials for Making Scale Drawings**	
Materials	**Uses**
Drawing kit	Contains tools for finer drawing
Triangular scale rule	Accurate scaling
Templates (assorted shapes, sizes)	Curves, oddly shaped objects
Indelible ink	Permanency of finished drawing
Drafting table	Ease, perfection in drawing
T-square	Accurate, straight lines, right angles
Drafting paper	Higher-quality absorption of inks, better display

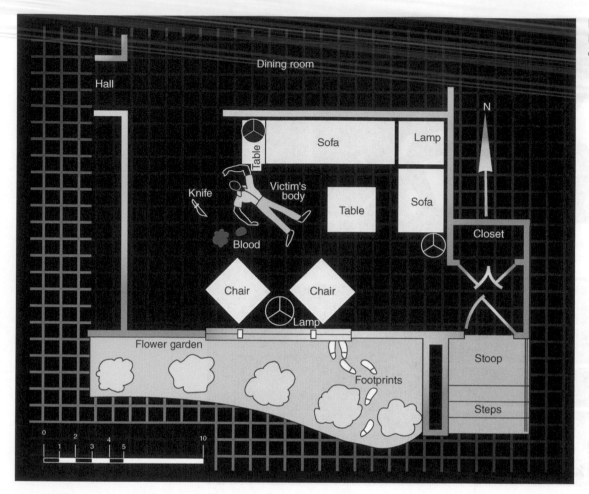

Figure 2.13
Finished scale
drawing.

The artistic refinements of the scale drawing do not permit it to be made at the crime scene. Instead, the scale drawing is made at the police station by the investigator or by a drafter. If anyone other than the investigator prepares the finished scale drawing, the investigator must review it carefully and sign it along with the drafter.

The finished drawing can be simple or complex, but it must represent the actual distances, objects, and evidence contained in the rough sketch. Color designations and plastic overlays to illustrate other phases of the investigation are often added. The drawing can be duplicated for other investigators and distributed to the prosecuting attorney. It is usually placed on white mounting board for display in court. A finished scale drawing is illustrated in Figure 2.13.

Computer-Assisted Drawing

As evidenced throughout this entire chapter, computer technology has enhanced many of the processes and procedures involved in crime scene documentation. In the fourth edition of this text (1990), computer-aided design (CAD) was highlighted as a technological advance, a cutting-edge tool for criminal investigators. Back then, cumbersome, confusing, and complicated CAD software made it challenging for even the most computer-savvy investigators to fully implement this technology. However, drawing software for investigators has improved significantly, and today a plethora of user-friendly CAD programs are available: FARO Zone 3D, Quick Scene, Virtual CRASH5, iWitness, ScenePD, SmartDraw, Leica Geosystems Incident Mapping Suite (IMS) Map360—and the list is sure to grow.

Benefits of CAD programs, alternately called computer-assisted drafting programs, include their accuracy, repeatability, and simplicity. In addition, the diagram files can be inserted into other documents, including final crime reports. Figure 2.14 compares a typical hand-drawn diagram with one drawn with a CAD software program.

Crime Zone, a popular forensic diagramming application, is easy to use and can create diagrams with great precision and attention to detail, giving the drawing greater credibility in court. Crime Zone's 3-D graphics

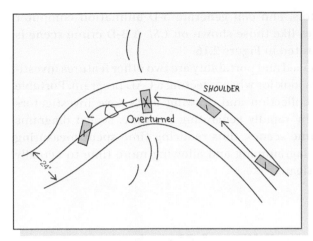

Typical hand-drawn diagram

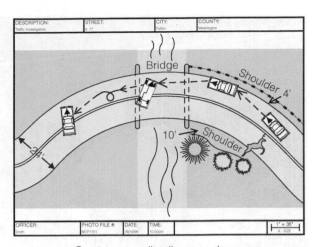

Courtroom-quality diagrams drawn
with the Crime Zone diagramming software

Figure 2.14
Comparison of a hand-drawn and computer-generated crime scene "sketch."
Source: Reprinted by permission of the CAD Zone, Inc.

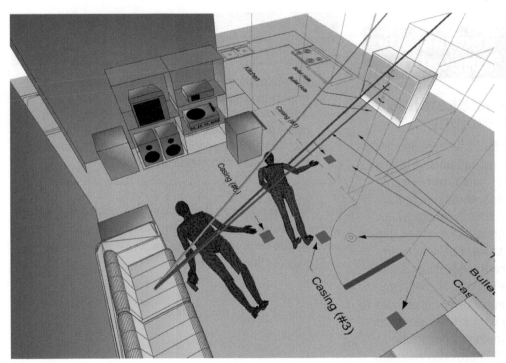

Figure 2.15
This is a 3-D re-creation of a homicide shooting, showing in detail the bullet trajectories and the final resting positions of the fatalities. The diagram contains both solid and "see-through" walls to display a more correct perspective. The diagram was created with The Crime Zone diagramming software, available from the CAD Zone, Inc.
Source: Image created by the CAD Zone, Inc.

have been used to diagram the trajectory of bullets, to document the scene of a carjacking, and to help a jury visualize the locations of witnesses, victims, and suspects at the scene of a shooting (Figure 2.15).

CAD software packages often contain different versions with features geared toward specific applications. For example, crash reconstruction programs generally include a linear momentum analysis feature, calculators for deriving acceleration and deceleration rates, and pre-drawn symbols of intersections and other driving- and road-related icons. In contrast, a crime scene investigation edition of the same general CAD package might offer a bloodstain-pattern analysis feature, ballistics data, and pre-drawn symbols of bodies or various weapons. The MapScenes software package has more than 7,000 pre-drawn shapes and

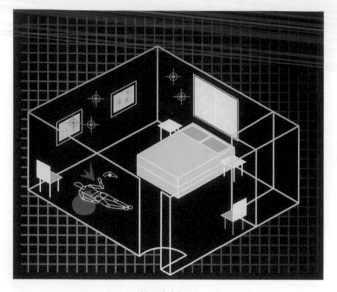

Homicide

Figure 2.16
3-D crime scene.
Source: Reprinted by permission of the CAD Zone, Inc.

symbols, and can generate 3-D animation computer movies like those shown on *CSI*. A 3-D crime scene is illustrated in Figure 2.16.

Speed and portability are two other features investigators look for when selecting a CAD program. Portable data collection and drawing units save investigators time by rapidly generating accurate, scaled diagrams at crime scenes, thus reducing time spent measuring and diagramming and allowing more time to actually investigate.

Admissibility of Sketches and Drawings in Court

As with all other evidence, the investigator must be prepared to testify about the information contained in the sketch, the conditions under which it was made, and the process used to construct it.

> **LO9** Describe the requirements for a sketch or a scale drawing to be admissible in court.
>
> An *admissible sketch* is drawn or personally witnessed by an investigator and accurately portrays a crime scene. A scale drawing also is admissible if the investigating officer drew it or approved it after it was drawn and if it accurately represents the rough sketch. The rough sketch must remain available as evidence.

Well-prepared sketches and drawings help judges, juries, witnesses, and other people visualize crime scenes. The responsibilities of an investigator in court are the focus of Chapter 21.

Technology Innovations

Creating Crime Scene Sketches with Laser Technology

In addition to the old-fashioned tape measure, today's diagramming tools include survey equipment, global position systems (GPSs), scanners, and lasers—equipment that can run from hundreds of dollars to hundreds of thousands of dollars. Laser Technology, Inc. (LTI) pioneered the first commercial laser speed gun and is continuously improving its laser devices to improve accuracy. One of LTI's recent innovations in the field of laser measurement is the TruPoint™ 200h, a hybrid laser that combines a traditional laser rangefinder (which uses pulse technology) with a laser distance meter (which uses phase technology). According to LTI's website, "The TruPoint™ 200h provides accurate long range outdoor measurements and high accuracy to short range indoor measurements, achieving millimeter to centimeter accuracy."

Source: https://www.lasertech.com/Laser-Technology-Breakthrough-Products.aspx

Summary

Investigative notes and reports are critical parts of a criminal investigation. Notes are a permanent written record of the facts of a case to be used in further investigation, in writing reports, and in prosecuting the case. Effective notes are complete, factual, accurate, specific, legible, clear, arranged in chronological order, and well-organized. If notes are retained, file them in a secure location readily accessible to investigators.

Photographs and video recordings reproduce the crime scene in detail for presentation to the prosecution, defense, witnesses, judge, and jury in court and are used in investigating, prosecuting, and police training. At a minimum, have available and be skilled in operating an instant-print camera, a point-and-shoot camera, a DSLR camera, a cellphone camera, a fingerprint camera, and video equipment.

Take photographs and videos of the entire crime scene before anything is disturbed. First, photograph the general area, then specific areas, and finally specific objects of evidence. Take exterior shots first because they are the most subject to alteration by weather and security violations. Categories of investigative photography include crime scene, surveillance, aerial, night, laboratory, mug shot, and lineup.

Rules of evidence dictate that photographs be material, relevant, competent, accurate, free of distortion, and noninflammatory to be admissible in court.

In addition to photographs, crime scene sketches are often used. The steps involved in sketching include (1) observing and planning, (2) measuring distances and outlining the general area, (3) plotting objects and evidence within the outline, (4) taking notes and recording details, (5) identifying the sketch with a legend and a scale, and (6) reassessing the sketch. An admissible sketch is drawn or personally witnessed by an investigator and accurately portrays a crime scene. A scale drawing also is admissible if the investigating officer drew it or approved it after it was drawn and if it accurately represents the rough sketch. The rough sketch must remain available as evidence.

Can You Define?

baseline method
compass-point method
competent photograph
cross-projection sketch
finished scale drawing
forensic photogrammetry
immersive imaging
laser-beam photography
legend
macrophotography

marker
material photograph
megapixel
microphotography
mug shots
overlapping
pixel
PPI
rectangular-coordinate method
relevant photograph

resolution
rogues' gallery
rough sketch
scale
sketch
trap photography
triangulation
ultraviolet-light photography

Checklists

Note Taking

- Is my notebook readily available?
- Does it contain an adequate supply of blank paper?
- Is it logically organized?
- Have I recorded all relevant information legibly?

- Have I identified each page of notes with case number and page number?
- Have I included sketches and diagrams wherever appropriate?
- Have I filed the notes securely?

Police Photography

- Have I photographed the entire scene and specific objects before moving anything?

- Have I included markers where needed to indicate size of evidence?

- Have I recorded equipment and techniques used, lighting conditions, and so on in my notes?

- Have I checked for other sources of available photographs?

- Do the photographs taken at the crime scene depict the scene as I saw it?

- Do they show the exact appearance and condition of the scene as it appeared on my arrival?

- Have exterior pictures been taken to show entrances to the scene, including windows, and the outside appearance of the crime scene?

- Have close-up shots been taken of the entry and exit points?

- Were aerial photos taken of the crime scene to show routes into and out of the scene area?

- Were interior pictures taken showing the entire layout of the facility in which the crime occurred?

- Do the photographs show the criminal act itself? For example, in a burglary, do the pictures show pry marks on the door, a broken window, or shattered glass on the ground or floor?

- Were detailed pictures taken of how the crime was committed? The tools with which it was committed? Any weapon used?

- Do photographs show the victim? Injuries? Were wounds, scratches, bruises, or other marks recorded in color as soon as possible after the commission of the crime? A day or two later as well?

- Were pictures taken of the deceased at the scene, including exact position, clothing worn, wounds?

- Were pictures taken at the autopsy?

- Do photographs show the damage to property?

- Were detailed pictures taken of all items of evidence before they were collected, showing exact condition and position at the scene?

- Was anything moved before the picture was taken? (If so, was it recorded in your notes?)

- Were photographs true and accurate representations of relevant material?

- Are laboratory photos available for scientific tests conducted?

- Were photographs taken of the suspect to show appearance and condition at the time of the crime, including close-ups of clothing worn?

- Were all pictures used for identifying suspects placed in special envelopes for later court testimony?

- If a lineup was conducted, were pictures taken of the lineup to show the people selected and their appearance in relation to each other?

- If a motor vehicle was involved, were detailed pictures taken of the vehicle's exterior and interior, color, license plate, and any damaged areas?

- What types of photographs are available? Moving pictures, black-and-white, color, videos?

- Are there crime-in-progress pictures from on-the-scene cameras such as bank surveillance cameras, or were pictures taken by media photographers?

- Have photographs been suitably mounted for presentation in court?

- Have all relevant notes been recorded in the notebook?

Sketches

- Is my sketching kit readily available?

- Is the kit completely equipped?

- Have I formed a plan for making the sketch?

- Have I selected the simplest, largest scale?

- Have I sketched the outline of the room or area first?

- Have I used the appropriate plotting method to locate objects and evidence?

- Have I then added objects and evidence, including measurements?

- Have I recorded in my notes information that cannot be sketched?

- Have I prepared a legend for the sketch that includes identifying information, the scale, and the direction of north?

- Have I reassessed the sketch and compared it with the scene?

- Have I kept the sketch secure?

- Have I prepared or had someone else prepare a finished scale drawing if needed?

References

Berg, G. R. (1999, March 31). Crime scene investigations—time to get back to the basics. *Law Enforcement News,* p. 8.

Crime scene investigation under scrutiny at Drew Peterson murder trial. (2012, August 7). *Associated Press,* as reported on Fox News. Retrieved April 26, 2021 from https://www.foxnews.com/us/crime-scene-investigation-under-scrutiny-at-drew-petersons-murder-trial

Dees, T. (2008, July). Digital cameras: 6 questions to ask before you buy. *Law Officer Magazine,* pp. 68–71.

Dutelle, A. (2010, June). Say goodbye to film: After 136 years, digital tech takes over. *Law Enforcement Technology,* pp. 60–66.

Federal Bureau of Investigation. (2019). *Handbook of forensic services.* Retrieved April 27, 2020, from www.fbi.gov/file-repository/handbook-of-forensic-services-pdf.pdf/view

Fletcher, M. (2016, November 25). *Crime scene virtual tour. Just on the spot.* Shanghai, China: Crime-Scene-VR.

Retrieved April 26, 2021 from https://silo.tips/download/crime-scene-virtual-tour-just-on-the-spot

Heinecke, J. (2007, April). Criminals caught on tape. *Law Enforcement Technology,* pp. 86–91.

International Association for Identification. (2016, July 6). "Section 5: Guidelines for image processing." *SWGIT guidelines for the forensic imaging practitioner.* Version 2.1 2010.01.15. Retrieved April 27, 2020, from theiai.org/docs/SWGIT_Guidelines.pdf

Kanable, R. (2008, February). Setting up surveillance downtown. *Law Enforcement Technology,* pp. 30–39.

Maple, T. (2018, April 5). "Where is Drew Peterson in 2018? His wives' murders are getting a renewed look." Retrieved April 20, 2020, from www.bustle.com/p/where-is-drew-peterson-in-2018-his-wives-murders-are-getting-a-renewed-look-8680565

Rutledge, D. (2007, December). Full disclosure. *Police,* pp. 68–71.

Case Cited

Udderzook v. Commonwealth, 76 Pa 340 (1874).

Chapter 3
Writing Effective Reports

Chapter Outline

The Importance of Reports

Uses of Reports

The Audience

Common Problems with Many Police Reports

The Well-Written Report: From Start to Finish

Recording and Dictating Reports

Computerized Report Writing

Evaluating Your Report

Citizen Online Report Writing

The Final Report

A Final Note on the Importance of Well-Written Reports

Learning Objectives

LO1   Explain why reports are important to an investigation.

LO2   List the ways in which reports are used.

LO3   Identify the various individuals who comprise your audience and may read your reports.

LO4   List the common problems that occur in many police reports.

LO5   Explain the difference between *content* and *form* in the context of report writing.

LO6   Identify the characteristics of effective investigative reports.

LO7   Differentiate between a fact, an inference, and an opinion.

LO8   Understand the benefits of well-written reports.

Introduction

Detective Christopher Hines has responded to a crime scene involving a serious assault in which the victim is unable to remember details of the attack. After booking the suspect, Hines contacts his sergeant, Olivia Quan, to review and sign the report, as department policy requires all reports to be reviewed and signed by an officer of sergeant rank or higher. Hines's report reads as follows:

I responded to an assault call around 2100 hours. As I approached the scene, I noticed a crowbar lying in the street. I also noticed a young man looking out of his window. The crowbar was identified, photographed, sketched, logged, and collected for evidence. I spoke with the man whom I saw in the window. He told me that he took a picture with his cell phone of the suspect running away. He agreed to let me see the photo. I immediately recognized the suspect from previous law enforcement contacts. I put an attempt to locate out on the suspect.

The witness stated he heard someone scream and went to the window to see if everything was ok. That is when he saw the victim laying in a pool of blood and the suspect running down the street. He took a photo with his cell phone and then called 911. He went out of his house and saw the suspect run into a house at the corner of the street.

I went to the house the witness described and knocked on the door. A woman answered. I saw the suspect inside. He was arrested without incident and confessed. I placed him in handcuffs and advised him he was under arrest. I read him his *Miranda* rights. He agreed to talk and told me about the assault. He hit the woman with the crow bar because he wanted her money. She fell to the ground. He grabbed her purse and ran back down the street toward his house, dropping the crowbar as he ran. He didn't know anyone saw him.

After reading the report, Quan and Hines have the following dialogue:

Sergeant:	How were you notified about the assault?
Detective:	I was notified by patrol officer, Tyus Jackson.
Sergeant:	You did not put that in your report. You state that you saw a crowbar lying in the street as you were driving up to the scene. It was 2100 hours. What was the lighting like?
Detective:	It was dark and there were no lights, just a little light coming from my headlights.
Sergeant:	You did not put that in your report. Your report states you observed a young male looking out a window of a nearby house.
Detective:	Yes.
Sergeant:	What was the address of that house? How far away was the residence from where the victim was found? What window was he looking out? Isn't he about 20 years old?
Detective:	He was in the window directly to the east of the front door at 1240 Pierce Street. He appeared to be on his cell phone. I don't know how old he is.
Sergeant:	None of that is in your report. Why did you ask to see his phone?
Detective:	He told me that he took a picture of the suspect running away. He agreed to let me see the photo. I immediately recognized the suspect from previous law enforcement contacts. I immediately put an attempt to locate out on the suspect. Detective Ramirez took a formal statement from the witness.
Sergeant:	Ok, you need to add some of that to your report. What made him look out the window?
Detective:	He heard a woman scream.
Sergeant:	Your report states he heard *someone* scream. Did the witness hear a *woman* scream?

Detective: Yes. He stated he heard a woman scream and went to the window to see if everything was okay. That is when he saw the victim laying in a pool of blood and the suspect running down the street. He took a photo with his cell phone and then called 911. He went out of his house and saw the suspect run into a blue and white house on the corner of Pierce Street and Grant Avenue.

Sergeant: You left out several of these details in your report. Why not write it exactly like you just told me? So you went to the house the witness described and knocked on the door. A woman answered and you saw the suspect inside. What was his demeanor?

Detective: He was sweating. He was pacing back and forth. I told him to come out. He was arrested without incident and confessed.

Sergeant: When you say he confessed, what do you mean?

Detective: I placed him in handcuffs and advised him he was under arrest. I read him his *Miranda* rights. He agreed to talk. He stated that he knew the victim from the neighborhood. He said he needed money. He saw her walking down the street, holding a purse. He grabbed a crowbar and ran out of his house. As he was getting close to her, she quickly turned and startled him. He hit her with the crowbar in the head and she fell to the ground. He picked up her purse, turned, and ran back down the street toward his house, dropping the crowbar as he ran. I located the victim's purse in the suspect's living room. He didn't know anyone saw him.

Sergeant: With the exception of the processing of the actual crime scene, several crucial details are missing from your report. I want you to rewrite this report detailing exactly what happened in chronological order. Begin by explaining why you were called to the scene. Include all the details we just discussed.

Given the totality of the circumstances, did this officer have a right to arrest the suspect? Yes. However, this report would crumble in court and fail judicial scrutiny. The lack of thoroughness not only could result in nonprosecution of the suspect but also could lead to civil liability of the officer and the department.

One of the most important skills patrol officers and investigators must develop is report writing. The remainder of this volume discusses in detail how evidence is located and processed; how witnesses, victims, suspects, and others are questioned; and how specific cases are investigated. Report writing is included here because the report captures the essentials of an investigation.

The Importance of Reports

Orlando W. Wilson & Roy C. McLaren wrote *Police Administration* half a century ago, but their words ring as true today as they did then: "Almost everything that a police officer does must be reduced to writing. What is written is often the determining factor in whether a suspect is arrested in the first place and, if he is arrested, whether he is convicted and sentenced. The contents of written reports, in fact, often have great bearing in life-and-death situations. To say that officers need to be proficient in report writing is an understatement" (1972, p. 482).

A considerable proportion of frontline officers' time is spent writing reports: "As first responders, we consistently spend more time writing reports than on any other single task in law enforcement. The only thing that beats it is probably driving around patrolling our zones" (Murgado, 2010).

The importance of well-written reports becomes obvious when you realize that your reports are *used*, not simply filed away. If investigative reports were not required for efficient law enforcement, you would not have to write them.

> **L01** Explain why reports are important to an investigation.
>
> Reports are permanent written records of important facts of a case to be used in the future and are a crucial and necessary cog in the wheel of justice.

Figure 3.1 shows the typical path of an investigative report. The number of times the report loops between the supervisor and the officer, or between the prosecutor and the officer, depends on how carefully (or carelessly) the officer constructs the report to begin with.

Most law enforcement officers submit their reports for prosecution with concern about the outcome but without much thought about the wheels they have started in motion.

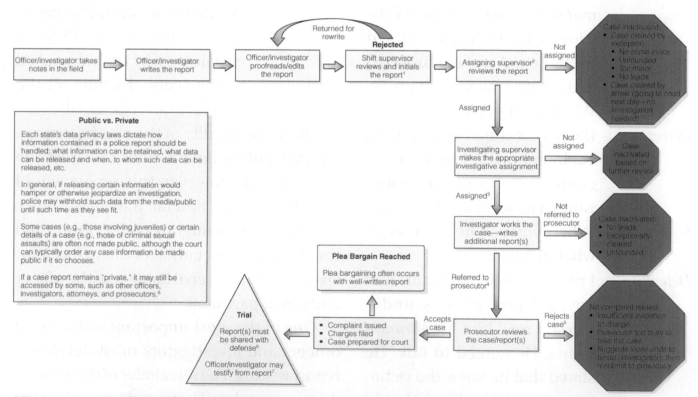

[1] Often the report is simply handwritten by the officer, given to the shift supervisor for a cursory review/initialing, and then sent off for transcription before going to an assigning supervisor.
[2] Assigning supervisor is typically of higher rank (lieutenant, captain, etc.).
[3] In smaller departments, the case may go to a generalized investigator. In larger departments, several investigative units may exist (homicide, arson, motor vehicle theft, etc.).
[4] Case can proceed to prosecutor with or without an arrest having been made.
[5] A rejection does not necessarily mean the case is not prosecutable at a later date. It means only that a complaint is not issued at that time.
[6] Who has access to the report(s) at trial varies by state. For example, in Minnesota, the judge and jury do not automatically receive the report(s).
[7] The report itself is not evidence, but any testimony the officer/investigator provides based on the content of a report becomes part of the trial record (testimonial evidence).
[8] Check your state's data privacy law. Laws vary from state to state regarding what can be retained, what must be released, and when information must be released. Consideration must also be given to whether or not release of information would hamper any ongoing investigations.

Figure 3.1

Typical path of an investigative report. Note: Because this process varies from department to department, this flowchart illustrates a generalized oversimplification of one way an investigative report might travel from origination to final disposition.

This is understandable, for they have done their jobs and many more cases wait to be investigated. But what happens when they have not really done their jobs? When their reports are distorted or incomplete (as many are) because of poor writing? The results cost the taxpayers in wasted personnel hours, and they breed disaster in the courtroom, if the case even makes it that far. Poor police report writing can jeopardize effective criminal prosecution.

The little things in a report can have major consequences for the **disposition** of a case, or how the case is disposed of, whether it be referred, closed (inactive), open (active), dismissed, pending further information, and so on. Consider this all-too-common example: in one criminal case, the reporting officer, using the passive voice, wrote, "The weapon was found in the bushes where the suspect had thrown it." He did not clarify this statement elsewhere in his report. Expectedly, the prosecuting attorney subpoenaed the reporting officer to testify at the preliminary hearing. Unfortunately, the reporting officer's testimony revealed that his partner, not he, had observed the suspect's action and had retrieved the weapon. The partner was unavailable to testify on short notice. Without her testimony, the necessary elements of the crime could not be established, and the case was dismissed, having to be refiled. The personnel hours expended at the time of the dismissal—by witnesses, clerks and clerical assistants, attorneys, and the judge—were virtually wasted because the whole process had to be repeated. The reporting officer could have avoided the problem at the outset through the use of the active voice, which would have provided clarification. Sadly, this basic writing error is not an isolated example; errors like these slip into the system daily, where they are often caught by defense attorneys who meticulously comb through reports, looking to exploit such defects. Such report writing errors result in delays in the judicial process and the depletion of dwindling budgets.

To better understand how to write effective reports, consider first how they may be used.

Uses of Reports

Reports are permanent records of all the important facts in a case. They are a stockpile of information to be drawn on by all individuals on a law enforcement team. They are an aid to individual law enforcement officers and investigators, supervisors, administrators, the courts, other governmental agencies, reporters, and private individuals. Further, a department's efficiency is directly related to the quality of its reports and reporting procedures.

Consider the case of an officer called to the scene of a hit-and-run. The initial accident report will be used to continue the investigation of the offense. If the offender is apprehended, the report will be used by the prosecuting attorneys in preparing the case, by the responding police officer when testifying in court, by the defense counsel in an effort to discredit the written account, by the judge in determining the facts of the case, and by the jury if a trial results. The report might also be used by the department in determining where dangerous intersections exist and in making future plans. In this scenario, the report may be given to the State Highway Department to determine if traffic control devices or a change in road design is needed. Also, in this scenario, the

Retrieving and recording information are essential steps in constructing a sound report. Improved technology in squad cars allows officers to take notes in the field and look up relevant information, thereby increasing the accuracy and effectiveness of their reports.

© Henry Cho

report may be requested by a private insurance company to proceed with civil litigation. Additionally, an officer's supervisor could use the report to evaluate the investigating officer's performance. If the officer failed to conduct a thorough investigation, this lack of thoroughness would show in the report. A well-written report can be used for many reasons.

> ### L02 List the ways in which reports are used.
>
> Reports are used to
> - Examine the past.
> - Provide a documented record of incidents.
> - Keep other police officers informed.
> - Continue investigations.
> - Prepare court cases.
> - Provide the courts with relevant facts.
> - Refresh a witness's memory about what he or she said occurred.
> - Refresh the investigating officer's memory during the trial.
> - Coordinate law enforcement activities.
> - Plan for future law enforcement services.
> - Identify hot spots or areas where administration should focus more resources to reduce crime.
> - Compile statistics on crime in a given jurisdiction.
> - Evaluate individual officer and department performance.
> - Investigate potentially illegal police practices such as racial profiling.
> - Provide information to insurance investigators.

Reports are critical in examining police performance and investigating potentially illegal police practices such as racial profiling. Many departments have begun voluntarily augmenting their traffic stop reports in an effort to shed light on allegations of racial profiling. Although some agencies are embracing the initiative as a way to seize control of their traffic data and build confidence in the fairness of their policing, other departments are opting out of the program, claiming that the more extensive reports add to their already excessive paperwork load. Critics of the program believe officers might be dissuaded from making legitimate traffic stops because of the undue amount of paperwork these will generate.

The various uses of reports make it obvious that they will be read by many different people for many different reasons. These people make up your audience.

The Audience

What you write may be read by other officers, your supervisor, lawyers, judges, jurors, social workers, city officials, insurance adjusters and investigators, civil rights groups, citizens, and the media—people from different backgrounds and fields who have varying degrees of familiarity with legal terms and police jargon. **Jargon** is the shorthand vocabulary and technical terminology specific to a particular profession or trade that allows colleagues within that area of work to communicate quickly and concisely. However, many in your audience will be from the "outside" and will be unfamiliar with police jargon. Certainly, most of your audience will not have been present at the crime scene. Therefore, you must communicate clearly to these numerous readers *what* happened, *when*, and *how*.

> ### L03 Identify the various individuals who comprise your audience and may read your reports.
>
> Reports are read by
> - Other officers.
> - Supervisors.
> - Attorneys and judges.
> - Jurors.
> - Social workers.
> - City officials.
> - Insurance adjusters and investigators.
> - Civil rights groups.
> - Citizens.
> - Media.

You should neither talk down to your audience nor try to make your report appear "more professional" by using bureaucratic, complicated language. Keep your reports straightforward and reader friendly, focusing on the need to *express* the facts of the case rather than on trying to *impress* the audience with your expansive vocabulary. Writing to impress rather than to express is a common problem with many investigative reports.

Common Problems with Many Police Reports

Writing effective investigation reports is a skill that must be learned and practiced just as any other skill necessary in police work, such as firearms use, self-defense techniques, and interview methods. Unfortunately, some departments have yet to develop a full appreciation of the benefits of well-written reports. In these agencies, reports are viewed as tedious time wasters that keep investigators from more significant tasks. Field training officers encourage new recruits to take report shortcuts, while administrators look the other way, happy to avoid the overtime that can occur with thorough, accurate, and complex reports. Amid such an environment, effective report writing skills are neither taught nor recognized as important and problems in the department's police reports abound.

LO4 List the common problems that occur in many police reports.

Among the common problems in police reports are

- Confusing or unclear sentences.
- Conclusions, assumptions, and opinions.
- Extreme wordiness and overuse of police jargon and abbreviations.
- Missing or incomplete information.
- Misspelled words and grammatical or mechanical errors.
- Referring to "above" information.

Having briefly looked at the "don'ts" of report writing, the discussion now turns to the "dos" and how to craft a well-written report.

The Well-Written Report: From Start to Finish

Myth Report writing is a talent—you are either born with it or you aren't.

Fact Report writing is a skill that takes time and practice to develop. It is *not* a talent—you are not expected to write entertaining literary masterpieces, full of insight and originality.

To write an effective report, you must organize your notes and adhere to some basic standards of written English regarding content and form.

Organizing Information

A cornerstone of good report writing is organization. Good reports do not just happen. The writer plans in advance in what order the information should be written. Too many officers simply sit down and start writing without giving any thought to how the report should flow, which results in more time spent rewriting and revising later. To use your time most efficiently, first make an informal outline. Next, list what you want to include under each heading in the outline. Review your notes and number each statement to match a heading in your outline. For example, if Section III.C of the outline is headed "Description of Suspect #2," write *III.C* in the margin wherever Suspect #2 is described in your notes.

List the facts of the investigation in **chronological order**, beginning with the response to the call and concluding with the end of the investigation. If the report is long (more than four pages), use headings to guide the reader—for example, "Initial Response," "Crime-Scene Conditions," "Photographs Taken," "Evidence," "Witnesses," and "Suspects." After you complete the outline and determine where each note fits, you are ready to begin writing.

Structuring the Narrative

Usually the **narrative**, the "story" of the case in chronological order, is structured as follows:

1. The opening paragraph of a police report states the time, date, type of incident, and how you became involved. This is where you identify yourself and your rank. For example, "On January 9, 2020, at 2046 hours, I, Sergeant Katsu Tanaka, was on patrol in the City of Hampton. I was dispatched to a report of a burglary occurring at . . . ."

2. The next paragraph contains what you were told by the victim or witness. For each person talked to, use a separate paragraph.

3. Next record what you did based on the information you received.

4. The final paragraph states the disposition of the case.

Steps 2 and 3 may be repeated several times in a report on a case where you talk to several witnesses and victims.

A Brief Look at Law Enforcement Report Forms.

Although this chapter focuses on writing narrative reports, many departments use box-style law enforcement report forms for certain offenses and incidents. Law enforcement

Test City	**INCIDENT**	Case Number: 11001234
Disposition: Cleared by Arrest		Title: Domestic Assault

Charges/Offenses: 609.2242.4, 609.78.2

Needs Follow-up: No **Investigation Needed:** No **Investigation Complete:** Yes **Citation Issued:** No **CAD #:**

Gang Related: No   **Incident Type:** Other   **How Initiated:** Dispatch

OFFICER INFORMATION

Name	Agency	Badge	Type
Billy Bob Testman	Test City	978675	Primary

EVENT DATES

Reported	On Scene	Cleared
2011-05-02 11:16	2011-05-02 11:16	2011-05-02 11:16

INCIDENT DETAILS

Address: 1234 American Boulevard; Test City, MN 55100 US

Location Type: RESIDENCE/HOME

Location Description:

Start Date: 2011-05-02 11:17   **End Date:** 2011-05-02 11:17

SYNOPSIS

On 04/30/11 at 0055 hours I and Officer Jones responded to 1223 American Blvd. in regards to a Domestic Assault. Upon arrival I observed the suspect John Jacob Johnson, DOB-01/01/80 physically assaulting his wife Mary Margaret Johnson, DOB-01/02/80.John was arrested without further incident and transported to jail. See Report.

Parties Involved

PERSON 001

Role(s): Suspect, Arrested

Last: Johnson	First: John	Middle: Jacob	Suffix:
Date of Birth: 1980-01-01	Age: 31	Is Juvenile: No	

Sex: Male	Height: 6-0	Weight: 200 lbs	Hair: Bald	Eyes: Brown
Race: Unknown	Ethnicity: Unknown	Build: Large	Complexion: Ruddy	

EMPLOYMENT INFORMATION

Name: Buy Things, Inc.	Type: RETAIL
Occupation: Sales	Shift:

CHARGES/ORDINANCES

Type: Statute	Chapter: 609	Section: 2242	Subdivision: 4	Citation #:
UOC: 1302B		Level: Felony		Enh. Factor: Previous Convictions

Description: Domestic Assault-Felony, two prior convictions with the same victim.

- -

Type: Statute	Chapter: 609	Section: 78	Subdivision: 2	Citation #:
UOC: 5399		Level: Gross Misdemeanor		Enh. Factor: Domestic

Test City (MN0190000)	Page 1 of 2	Creation: Mary B Cerkvenik 2011-05-02 11:36:00

Incident Report

Figure 3.2

An example of a law enforcement report form.

Source: Cho, H. L., Cho Research & Consulting, LLC.

(continued)

report forms vary greatly in format, and the example shown in Figure 3.2 is only one type of forms in use.

Hess and Orthmann (2019, p. iv) state, "Report forms . . . contain boxes or separate category sections, e.g., property loss section, for placement of descriptive information, addresses and phone numbers of those involved. It is unnecessary to repeat this information in the narrative *unless it is needed for clarity* because it tends

```
┌─────────────────────────────────────────────────────────────────────────┐
```

Test City

INCIDENT

Case Number: 11001234

Disposition: Cleared by Arrest

Title: Domestic Assault

Description: Emergency Telephone Calls/CommunicInterfere with 911 Call

PERSON 002

Role(s): Reporting Person, Victim

Last: Johnson	**First:** Mary	**Middle:** Margaret	**Suffix:**
Date of Birth: 1980-01-02	**Age:** 31	**Is Juvenile:** No	

Cell Phone: (555) 888-1111   **Description:**

Sex: Female	**Height:** 5	**Weight:** 100 lbs	**Hair:** Black	**Eyes:** Brown
Race: Unknown	**Ethnicity:** Unknown	**Build:** Small	**Complexion:** Fair	

EMPLOYMENT INFORMATION

Name: Flotech, Inc.   **Type:** Technology

Occupation: Software Engineer   **Shift:**

Vehicles Involved

VEHICLE 001

Role(s): Involved

Associated with: John Jacob Johnson (Owner), Mary Margaret Johnson (Owner)

Regular Passenger Automobile Plates	**Number:** 5589L	**Authority:** MINNESOTA	**Tab:** 144478 ()
Make: Chevrolet	**Model:** Malibu	**Year:** 2001	**Style:** Sedan
Primary Color: Blue	**Secondary Color:**	**VIN:** 145J45K719OPU77	
Odometer Reading: 85000	**Estimated Value:** 3000	**Keys Location:**	
Doors Locked: No	**Ignition Locked:** No	**Trunk Locked:** No	

PROPERTY INFORMATION

ID: 392   **Associated with:** Mary Margaret Johnson (Owner)

Description: Personal Data Device

Quantity: 1	**Unit Price:** 300	**Value:** 300.00	**Seized:** Yes	**Forfeiture:** No
Brand Name: Blueberry	**Model:** P45	**Code:**	**Color:** black	

Serial Number: 7844KK855Y2E   **Owner Applied Number:**

NARRATIVE

DOCUMENT APPROVAL HISTORY

Created By: Mary B Cerkvenik   **On:** 2011-05-02 11:36:00

Test City (MN0190000)   Page 2 of 2   Creation: Mary B Cerkvenik 2011-05-02 11:36:00

Incident Report

Figure 3.2
(continued)

to interrupt the flow of words and clutter the narrative." In contrast, narrative reports that do *not* use the box-style format include descriptive information, addresses, and phone numbers within the body of the narrative.

Read the following excerpt from a narrative report, noting the underlined descriptive information.

I talked to the victim, Beret LaFoure, <u>355 Rose St., Albany, New York, phone 612-555-9002</u>. LaFoure told me that her diamond ring was taken during the burglary. The ring was a <u>2-carat diamond stone, platinum setting, with the initials B.A.L. inside the band, valued at $11,500.00</u>.

If these data were, instead, to be formatted into a box-style report, the underlined descriptive information, address, and phone number would be deleted from the narrative *unless that information was needed for clarity*, as shown in the following excerpt:

> The victim, Beret LaFoure, told me that her diamond ring was taken during the burglary.

Characteristics of Effective Reports: Content and Form

In addition to a well-structured narrative, an effective report exhibits several other characteristics, which generally fall into one of two areas: **content**, or *what* is said, and **form**, or *how* it is written. The effective report writer attends to both content and form because they are equally important in a well-written report.

| LO5 | Explain the difference between content and form in the context of report writing. |

The *content* of an effective report is factual, accurate, objective, and complete. The *form* of a well-written report is concise, clear, grammatically and mechanically correct, and written in Standard English.

An effective report is also organized into paragraphs and written in the past tense, using the first person and active voice. Finally, a well-written report is audience-focused, legible, and submitted on time. Table 3.1 illustrates the differences between content and form as they relate to investigative reports.

| LO6 | Identify the characteristics of effective investigative reports. |

An effective report is factual, accurate, objective, complete, concise, clear, grammatically and mechanically correct, written in Standard English, organized into paragraphs, and written in the past tense; uses the first person and active voice; and is audience-focused and legible, leaving the reader with a positive impression of the writer's competence. A well-written report is also submitted on time.

Facts, opinions, and inferences were introduced in Chapter 1. Investigators *must* differentiate between these three types of statements: "The ability of investigators

TABLE 3.1 Investigative Reports: Content and Form Compared

Content—*What* Is Said	Form—*How* It Is Said
The elements of the crime	Word choice
Descriptions of suspects, victims, etc.	Sentence and paragraph length
Evidence collected	Spelling
Actions of victim, witnesses, suspects	Punctuation
Observations: weather, road conditions, smells, sounds, oddities, etc.	Grammar
	Mechanics

to explain both verbally and in writing how inferences (e.g., clues, evidence, etc.) lead them to draw logical and reasonable conclusions (e.g., probable cause, facts, etc.) remains a critical skill in investigative work" (Jetmore, 2007, p. 22).

Factual. The basic purpose of any investigation report is to record the facts. A *fact* is a statement that can be proven. (It may be proven false, but it is still classified as a factual statement.) The truthfulness or accuracy of facts will be discussed shortly. First, consider how to clearly distinguish between these three basic types of statements.

| LO7 | Differentiate between a fact, an inference, and an opinion. |

Fact:	A statement that can be proven.
Example:	The man has a bulge in his black leather jacket pocket.
Inference:	A conclusion based on reasoning.
Example:	The man is probably carrying a gun.
Opinion:	A personal belief.
Example:	Black leather jackets are cool.

A well-written report is factual. It does *not* contain opinions. You can discuss and debate facts and inferences logically and reasonably and come to some agreement about them. An *opinion*, however, reflects personal beliefs, on which there is seldom agreement. For example, how do you resolve the differences between two people arguing about whether pie tastes better than cake? You can't. It's simply a matter of personal preference.

Inferences (conclusions) can prove valuable in a report, provided they are based on sufficient evidence. Sometimes it is hard to distinguish between facts and inferences. One way to tell them apart is to ask the question, "Can the statement be simply proven true or false, or do I need other facts to make it reasonable?" For example, if you wanted to verify the statement, "The driver of the truck was drunk," you would need to supply several facts to support your inference. One such fact might be that he had a blood alcohol content higher than 0.08. Other facts might include your observations, such as his slurred speech, his red and watery eyes, five empty beer cans behind the driver's seat, and the strong odor of an alcoholic beverage on the driver's breath.

An *inference* is not really true or false; it is sound or unsound (believable or not believable). And the only way to make an inference sound (believable) is to provide facts to support it. One way to ensure that your inference is clearly an inference, instead of a fact, would be to use the word *apparently* or *appeared* (e.g., "The driver appeared to be under the influence of alcohol").

Inferences are also referred to as **conclusionary language**. Avoid conclusionary language by *showing*, not *telling*. For example, do not write, "The man *could not* walk a straight line." You do not know what another person can or cannot do, or may choose not to do. A more factual way to report this would be, "The man *did* not walk a straight line." Even better would be, "The man stepped 18 inches to the right of the line twice and 12 inches to the left of the line three times." Consider this account by Rutledge (2000, pp. 110–111):

> I once got into a drunk driving trial where, according to the arresting officer, the defendant had "repeatedly refused" to take a chemical test. The defendant was named Sanchez, and at trial he insisted, through a court interpreter, that he neither spoke nor understood any English. His defense that he couldn't possibly refuse an English-language request when he couldn't even understand it sold well with the jury, especially after the officer had to admit that he didn't recall exactly how or in what specific words the defendant had "refused" a test. The cop couldn't live with his conclusionary report. Neither could I. The defendant lived with it very comfortably, and he owed his acquittal directly to the same officer who had arrested him. Ironic?

We would have been much better off if the cop had never used the conclusionary word "refused," but had instead married the defendant to his own words! The report could have helped the prosecution, instead of the defense, if it had been written like this:

> *After I explained the need to take a chemical test, Sanchez said, in Spanish-accented English, "Screw you, cop. . . . I ain't taking no test, man. Why don't you take it yourself?" I told him he had to take a test or his license would be suspended. He said, "I don't need no license to drive, man. I know lots of people drive without a license. You ain't scared me, man, and I ain't taking no stupid test. I'll beat this thing."*

See the difference? Not a single conclusion or interpretation. The reader gets to "hear" the same things the writer heard. The officer could have lived with something like that—the defendant couldn't.

The following conclusionary statements can also jeopardize the effectiveness and value of investigative reports:

- "She *was belligerent* when asked about her involvement in the arson."
- "He *admitted* to breaking into the warehouse."
- "He *refused* to perform a field sobriety test."
- "She *waived* her rights per Miranda."
- "They *denied* any involvement in the attack."

Table 3.2 presents alternatives to conclusionary words and phrases that will make reports more factual and, thus, more effective and valuable.

Conclusionary language may also lead to inaccuracies in your report.

Accurate. To be useful, facts must be accurate. An effective report accurately records the correct time and date, correct names of all persons involved, correct phone numbers and addresses, and exact descriptions of the crime scene, property, vehicles, and suspects involved. Have people spell

TABLE 3.2 Avoiding Conclusionary Language

You Can't Live with These	So Use	You Can't Live with These	So Use
Indicated, refused, admitted, confessed, denied, consented, identified, waived, profanity, threatening, obscene, evasive, deceptive	A verbatim or approximate quotation of what was said	Angry, upset, nervous, excited, happy, unhappy, intentional, accidental, heard, saw, knew, thought	The source of your conclusions (when you're attributing them to someone else)
Assaulted, attacked, accosted, confrontation, escalated, struggle ensued, resisted, battered, intimidated, bullied, forced	A factual account of who did what	Matching the description, suspicious, furtive, strange, abnormal, typical, uncooperative, belligerent, combative, obnoxious, abusive, exigent	The reasons for your belief that these apply

Source: From Rutledge, D. (2000). *The new police report manual* (2nd ed.). Belmont, CA: Wadsworth Publishing Company. © 2000 Cengage Learning.

their names. Repeat spellings and numbers for verification. Recheck measurements. Be sure of the accuracy of your facts. An inaccurately recorded license number may result in losing a witness or suspect. Inaccurate measurement or recording of the distance and location of skid marks, bullet holes, or bodies may lead to wrong conclusions.

Myth A minor error on a report, such as a name misspelled or a transposed number in a suspect's address, will get a case thrown out.

Fact Courts have ruled that *minor* errors in police reports will *not* prevent prosecution. However, these are preventable errors and can complicate the investigation. Take measures to ensure accuracy in your notes and reports.

To be accurate, you must be specific. For example, it is better to say, "The car was traveling in excess of 90 mph" than to say, "The car was traveling fast." It is more accurate to describe a suspect as "approximately 6′ 6″" than to describe him as "tall."

You must have the facts in the case correct. If your report says four men were involved in a robbery but in reality, three men and a woman were involved, your report would be inaccurate. If you are unsure of the gender of the individuals involved in an incident, identify them as "people," "suspects," "witnesses," or whatever the case may be. If your facts come from the statement of a witness rather than from your own observation, say so in your report. It is also acceptable to state that you do not know something as fact. For example, "An unknown number of suspects were involved in this robbery" is far better than guessing how many suspects may have been involved.

Phrases such as "He saw what happened" or "He heard what happened" are conclusionary and may lead to inaccuracies in your report. People can be looking directly at something and not see it, either because they are simply not paying attention or because they have terrible vision. The same is true of hearing. Again, you do not know what another person sees or hears. Your report should say, "He *said* he saw what happened" or "He looked directly at the man committing the crime."

Another common conclusionary statement found in police reports is "The check was signed by John Doe." Unless you saw John Doe sign the check, the correct (accurate) statement would be "The check was signed John Doe." The little two-letter word *by* can create tremendous problems for you on the witness stand.

Vague, imprecise words have no place in police reports. The following words and phrases should *not* be used because they are not specific: *a few*, *several*, *many*, *frequently*, *often*. An exception to this is when you are directly quoting something that was said to you. Finally, instead of writing *contacted*, be specific by using *telephoned*, *visited*, *emailed*, *texted*, or whatever particular mode of communication was involved.

Another common mistake often found in police reports is using the phrase *the PC for the stop*, referring to *probable cause*. Probable cause is required only for an arrest. The standard required by the Fourth Amendment for a stop, or a detention, is the lesser threshold of reasonable suspicion. Police officers who write about "the PC for the stop" feed the confusion of legal standards that may already be cloudy to some prosecutors, the defense attorneys, and trial judges. Probable cause and reasonable suspicion are easily confused concepts among the general public. Leaving probable cause out of police reports is highly recommended because if the report goes before a jury, an officer does not want to face the struggle of defining the terms and explaining the differences in front of that jury.

Objective.   You have seen that reports must be factual. It is possible, however, to include only factual statements in a report and still not be objective. Being **objective** means being nonopinionated, fair, and impartial. Lack of objectivity can result from either of two things: poor word choice or omission of facts.

Word choice is an often overlooked—yet very important—aspect of report writing. Consider, for example, the difference in effect achieved by these three sentences:

The woman cried.

The woman wept.

The woman blubbered.

Although you want to be specific, you must also be aware of the effect of the words you use. Words that have little emotional effect, for example, *cried*, are called **denotative** words. The denotative meaning of a word is its *objective* meaning. In contrast, words that do have an emotional effect are called **connotative** words, for example, *wept*, *blubbered*. The connotative meaning of a word comprises its positive or negative overtones. In the three earlier sentences, only the first sentence is truly objective. The second sentence makes the reader feel sympathetic toward the woman. The third makes the reader unsympathetic.

Likewise, derogatory, biased terms referring to a person's race, ethnicity, religion, or sexual preference have no place in police reports. A defense attorney will certainly capitalize on words with emotional overtones and attempt to show bias. Even the use of *claimed* rather than *stated* can be used to advantage by a defense attorney, who might suggest that the officer's use of *claimed* implies the officer did not believe the statement.

Also, use the correct word. Do not confuse words that are similar, or you can be made to appear ridiculous. For example, this sentence in an officer's report would probably cast suspicion on the officer's intelligence: "During our training we spent four hours learning to resemble a firearm and the remainder of the time learning defective driving."

Keep to the facts. Include all facts, even those that may appear to be damaging to your case. Objectivity is attained by including both sides of the account. **Slanting**, that is, including only one side of a story or only facts that tend to prove or support the officer's theory, can also make a report nonobjective. A good report includes both sides of an incident when possible. Even when facts tend to go against your theory about what happened, you are obligated to include them. Omitting important facts is *not* objective. Recall from Chapter 1 the discussion of the legal and ethical importance of including both inculpatory and exculpatory statements and evidence in reports: "Due process disclosure of exculpatory evidence must be determined and made by the prosecutor, and 'tainted' evidence may still be fully admissible, or useful for limited purposes. Full reporting helps avoid civil liability, reversals of convictions, and miscarriage of justice" (Rutledge, 2007, p. 71).

Complete. Information kept in the reporting officer's head is of no value to anyone else involved in the case. Scarry (2007, p. 68) points out, "What officers write in their report stays with them forever." Conversely, if something is not documented in the report, the defense attorney can and will argue that it never happened. Consequently, every report should be a complete account of the details of the event. Scarry concludes, "When it comes to writing police reports, officers should always strive to document all injuries they receive during any incident, even if it's a minor injury; record any unusual statements germane to the event; and explain why the officers took certain actions, particularly with respect to the need to use force" (2007, p. 71).

An effective report contains answers to at least six basic questions: Who? What? When? Where? How? and Why? The *who, what, when,* and *where* questions should be answered by factual statements. The *how* and *why* statements may require inferences. When this is the case, clearly label the statements as inferences. This is especially true when answering the question of cause. To avoid slanting the report, record all possible causes no matter how implausible they may seem at the time.

If a form is used for your reports, all applicable blanks at the top of the form should be filled in. Certain agencies require a slash mark, the abbreviation *NA* (not applicable), or the abbreviation *UNK* (unknown) to be placed in any box that does not contain information. Before submitting a report, review it to make sure any blanks that were overlooked are filled in and the report is complete.

Each specific type of crime requires different information. Sections 3, 4, and 5 of this text discuss specific offenses and contain checklists outlining information that should be included in your report.

Concise. Being **concise** means making every word count without leaving out important facts. Avoid wordiness; length alone does not ensure quality. Some reports can be written in half a page; others require 12 or even 20 pages. No specific length can be prescribed, but strive to include all relevant information in as few words as possible.

You can reduce wordiness in two basic ways: (1) leave out unnecessary information and (2) use as few words as possible to record the necessary facts. For example, do not write, "The car was blue in color"; write "The car was blue." A phrase such as "information that is of a confidential nature" should be recognized as a wordy way of saying "confidential information."

Do not make the mistake of equating conciseness with brevity. Being brief is not the same as being concise. For example, compare

Brief	She drove a car.
Concise	She drove a dark blue 2018 Chevrolet Camaro.
Wordy	She drove a car that was a 2018 Chevrolet Camaro that was dark blue in color.

Avoiding wordiness does not mean eliminating details; it means eliminating empty words and phrases. Consider these examples of how to make wordy phrases more concise:

Wordy	Concise
made a note of the fact that	noted
square in shape	square
in the amount of	for
despite the fact that	although
for the purpose of determining	to determine

Table 3.3 lists more natural-sounding alternatives for wordy, artificial phrases.

TABLE 3.3 Artificial-Sounding vs. Natural-Sounding Words and Phrases

Artificial	Natural	Artificial	Natural
initiated	began	altercation	fight
commenced		mutual combat	
inaugurated		physical confrontation	
originated		exchange of physical blows	
presently	now	in reference to	about
currently		reference	
at the present		in regard to	
at the present time		regarding	
at this time		on the subject of	
due to the fact that	because, since	visually perceived	saw
considering that		visually noticed	
as a result of the fact that		observed	
in view of the fact that		viewed	
in light of the fact that			
made an effort	tried	related	said
made an attempt		stated	
endeavored		verbalized	
attempted		articulated	
maintained surveillance over	watched	informed	told
kept under observation		advised	
visually monitored		indicated	
		communicated verbally	
at this point	then	6' in height	6' tall/high
at this time		2' in width	2' wide
at which time		3' in length	3' long
at which point in time		8" in depth	8" deep
as of this date	yet	telephonically contacted	phoned
as of this time		reached via landline	
as of the present time		contacted by telephone	
alighted from	got out	verbal altercation	argument
exited		verbal dispute	
dismounted		verbal confrontation	
requested	asked	prior to	before
inquired		previous to	
queried		in advance of	
in order to	to	for the reason that	so
with the intention of		in order that	
with the objective to			

Clear. An investigation report should have only one interpretation. Two people should be able to read the report and come up with the same word-picture and understanding of the events. As one trainer puts it, "a good report should stand alone and is like a good joke—if you have to explain it, it sucks" (Bell and Razey, 2018). This is one reason why it is best practice, when possible, to utilize officers that speak the same language as the suspect during interviews or when filling out reports. Often this language ability will allow officers to understand slang, culture, and norms that make the narrative of the report more clear. Make certain your sentences can be read only one way. For example, consider the following unclear sentences:

- When completely plastered, officers who volunteer will paint the locker room.
- Miami police kill a man with a machete.
- Three cars were reported stolen by the Los Angeles police yesterday.
- Police begin campaign to run down jaywalkers.
- Squad helps dog bite victim.

Rewrite such sentences so that only one interpretation is possible. For example, the first sentence in the previous list might read, "Officers who volunteer will paint the locker room after it is completely plastered." The third sentence might read, "According to the Los Angeles police, three cars were reported stolen yesterday."

Follow these guidelines to make your reports clearer:

- *Use specific, concrete facts and details.* Compare the following statements and determine which is clearer:

  1. The car sped away and turned the corner.
  2. The gold 2014 Cadillac Escalade pulled away from the curb, accelerated to approximately 65 mph, and then turned off First Street onto Brooklyn Boulevard.

    The second statement is clearer because it contains concrete facts and details.

- Keep descriptive words and phrases as close as possible to the words they describe. Compare the following statements and determine which is clearer.

  1. He replaced the gun into the holster which he had just fired.
  2. He replaced the gun, which he had just fired, into the holster.

    The second statement is clearer because the phrase "which he had just fired" is placed close to the word it modifies (*gun*).

- *Use diagrams and sketches when a description is complex.* This is especially true in reports of crashes, homicides, and burglaries. The diagrams do not have to be artistic masterpieces. They should, however, be in approximate proportion and should help the reader follow the narrative portion of the report. As noted in Chapter 2, several software programs for computer-assisted diagrams are now readily available.

- *If a witness or victim has provided any written information, make sure it is clear and understood.* If it is not, make sure clarification and additional information is sought. For example, if a victim of a burglary hands you a sketch of their garage, make sure you know which direction is north. If the victim hands you a list of items stolen from their house and one of the items is "a set of Nike golf clubs," the officer should obtain more details such as whether the clubs were loose or contained within a golf club bag, color of the bag, if the clubs were for a left- or right-handed golfer, etc.

- *Do not use uncommon abbreviations.* Some abbreviations (such as *Mr., Dr., Ave., St., Feb., Aug., NY, CA*) are so commonly used that they require no explanation. Other abbreviations, however, are commonly used only in law enforcement. Do not use these in your reports because not all readers will understand them. Confusion can result if two people have different interpretations of an abbreviation. For example, what does "S.O.B." mean to you? To most people it has a negative meaning. But for people in the health field, it means "short of breath." Consider the following example as information that can be written in your notes but should *not* appear, as such, in a report: "Unk/W/F/, nfd, driving Fd/4DRed, nfd." Instead, write out, "I saw an unknown white female (no further description available) driving a red Ford 4-door (no further description available)." Use only abbreviations common to everyone.

- *Use short sentences, well organized into short paragraphs.* Short sentences are easier to read. Likewise, paragraphs should be relatively short, usually five to ten sentences. Each question to be answered in the report should have its own paragraph. The report should be organized logically. Most commonly, it begins with *when* and *where* and then tells *who* and *what*. The *what* should be in chronological order—that is, going from beginning to end without skipping back and forth.

Grammatically and Mechanically Correct. If you were to *hear* the words, "Your chances of being promoted are good if you can write effective reports," you would probably feel differently than if you were to *read* the same words written like this: "yur chances of bein promottid are gud if you kin rite afectiv riports." The **mechanics**—spelling, capitalization, and punctuation—involved in translating ideas and spoken words into written words are important. Mistakes in spelling, punctuation, capitalization, and grammar give the impression that the writer is careless, uneducated, or stupid—maybe all three!

Arp (2007, p. 101) contends, "Spelling is the most important part of writing. Even if the structure of your paragraph leaves a little to be desired, if you spell everything correctly, the reader will have some forgiveness. But not if your spelling is bad!" He points out that many officers make the mistake of using words that are too complicated: "A good rule to follow is that if you can't spell it, don't use it."

Most officers either type their reports or dictate them. If they dictate, they often do not need to spell the words out. For officers typing on computers, most have Internet access and can find a program online to check their spelling. Another option is to download an app to a smart phone to help with spelling.

Use caution when relying on grammar- and spell-checker programs to find mistakes in computerized documents. For example, if an investigator wrote that a victim of an assault was unable to be interviewed because "she had lapsed into a *comma*," or that a suspect had been restrained because "he was acting *erotically*," when what the writer meant to say was "coma" and "erratically," respectively, the computer program might not flag these words as they are spelled correctly, albeit used incorrectly. Allowing such errors to pass in a report may lead a reader to question the investigator's intelligence or attention to detail. Always thoroughly read your report before submitting it. It never hurts to ask a colleague to read it as well.

Written in Standard English.

People often disagree about what Standard English is. And the standards for spoken and written English differ. For example, if you were to *say*, "I'm gonna go walkin' in the mornin'," it would probably sound all right. People often drop the final "g" when they speak. In writing, however, this is not acceptable.

Just as there are rules for spelling, capitalization, and punctuation, there are rules for *what* words are used *when*. For example, it is standard to say "he doesn't" rather than "he don't," "I don't have any" rather than "I ain't got none," and "he and I are partners" rather than "him and me are partners."

Your experience with English will often tell you what is standard and what is not—especially if you have lived in surroundings in which Standard English is used. If you speak Standard English, you will probably also write in Standard English. But that is not always true.

Paragraphs.

As discussed earlier, in structuring the narrative and making your report clear, effective writers use paragraphs to guide the reader. Keep the paragraphs short (usually 100 words or less). Skip a line to indicate the beginning of a new paragraph. Discuss only one subject in each paragraph. Start a new paragraph when you change speakers, locations, time, or ideas—for example, when you go from observations to descriptions to statements.

Paragraphs are reader friendly, guiding the reader through your report. Most paragraphs should be 5–6 sentences, although they may be a single sentence or as many as 10–15 sentences on occasion.

Past Tense.

Write in the **past tense** throughout the report. Past-tense writing uses verbs that show that events have already occurred. Your report contains what *was* true at the time you took your notes. Use of present tense can cause tremendous problems later. For example, suppose you wrote, "John Doe *lives* at 100 South Street and *works* for Ace Trucking Company." One year later, you find yourself on the witness stand with a defense attorney asking you, "Now, Officer, your report says that John Doe lives at 100 South Street. Is that correct?" You may not know, and you would have to say so. The next question: "Now, Officer, your report says John Doe works for Ace Trucking Company. Is *that* correct?" Again, you may be uncertain and be forced into an "I don't know" response. Use of the past tense in your report avoids this problem.

First Person.

Use the first person to refer to yourself. **First person** in English uses the words *I, me, my, we, us,* and *our*. The sentence "*I* responded to the call" is written in the first person. This contrasts with "*This officer* responded to the call," which uses the third person. Whether you remember your English classes and discussions of first-, second-, and third-person singular and plural is irrelevant. Simply remember to refer to yourself as *I* rather than as *this officer*.

Active Voice.

A sentence may be either active or passive. This is an easy distinction to make if you think about what the words *active* and *passive* mean. (Forget about the term *voice*; it is a technical grammatical term you do not need to understand to write well.) In the **active voice** the subject of the sentence performs the actions—for example, "I wrote the report." This contrasts with the *passive* voice, in which the subject does nothing—for example: "The report was written by me." The report did not do anything. The problem with the passive voice is that often the *by* is left off—for example: "The report was written." Later, no one knows who did the writing. Passive voice results in a "whodunit" that can have serious consequences in court.

Statements are usually clearer in the active voice. Although most sentences should be in the active voice, a *passive* sentence is acceptable in the following situations:

1. If the doer of the action is unknown, unimportant, or obvious.

   EXAMPLE: "The gun had been fired three times." We don't know who fired it. This is better than "Someone had fired the gun three times."

   EXAMPLE: "The woman has been arrested four times." Who arrested her each time is not important.

   EXAMPLE: "Felix Umburger was paroled in April." *Who* is obviously the parole board.

2. When you want to call special attention to the receiver of the action rather than the doer.

   EXAMPLE: "Officer Morris was promoted after the examination." You want to call attention to Officer Morris, rather than to the person who promoted him.

3. When it would be unfair or embarrassing to be mentioned by name.

   EXAMPLE: "The program was postponed because the wrong film was sent."

   BETTER THAN: "The program was postponed because Sergeant Fairchild sent the wrong film."

   EXAMPLE: "Insufficient evidence was gathered at the crime scene."

   BETTER THAN: "Investigator Hanks gathered insufficient evidence at the crime scene."

Audience-Focused. Always consider who your audience is. Recall the diversity of possible readers of police reports. Given these varied backgrounds and individuals with limited familiarity with law enforcement terminology, the necessity for audience-focused reports becomes obvious. By keeping in mind this diverse audience, you will construct a reader-friendly report.

One way to be reader friendly is to be certain that the narrative portion of your report can stand alone. That calls for eliminating such phrases as *the above*. A reader-friendly report does not begin like this: "On the above date at the above time, I responded to the above address to investigate a burglary in progress."

Using such phrases presents two problems. First, if readers take time to look "above" to find the information, their train of thought is broken. It is difficult to find where to resume reading, and time is wasted. Second, if readers do *not* take time to look "above," important information is not conveyed, and it is very likely the reader, perhaps subconsciously, will be wondering what would have been found "above."

Using *the above* can also cause confusion. The cover page of the report often contains the dispatch time, and what might really be of importance is the time the burglary took place or the officer's arrival time, depending upon the circumstances. If information is important enough to refer to in your report, include it in the narrative. Do not take the lazy approach and ask your reader to search for the information "above."

Another way to write a reader-friendly report is to avoid police lingo and other bureaucratic language and use plain English rather than "Cop Speak." One of the most common mistakes officers make is failing to prepare their report so that civilian jurors or review board members (many of whom get their law enforcement "expertise" from watching television crime dramas) can clearly understand why the officers had to do what they did. Consider this example provided by Robinson (2006, p. 30):

> "Officer, would you read the marked section from your report?"
>
> "I attempted to apply an escort hold to the subject, but I noted resistive tension in his arm, so I applied pain compliance instead. The subject actively resisted, so I administered a focused knee strike to the lower abdominal area, and decentralized the subject."
>
> "In other words, Officer, you tried to grab my client's arm, and when he pulled away, you twisted his wrist, and then kicked him in the groin and threw him down on the pavement, is that about it?"
>
> "Well, I wouldn't put it in quite those words."
>
> "No, officer, I imagine you wouldn't. No further questions."

Robinson explains that the defense attorney made the jury think the officer tried to hide his use of force behind a smoke screen of clinical language and that he did so to minimize brutality. According to Robinson, law enforcement trainers use such jargon to make communication *within* the profession more concise and efficient. When it comes to this clinical-sounding terminology for use of force, they use it for two additional reasons: (1) to enable precise description and (2) to differentiate between trained techniques and "street-fighting." Under *Graham v. Connor* (1989), officers must use only that amount of force that is objectively reasonable under the circumstances. Referring to specific trained techniques such as an "escort hold" or "focused knee strike" in a report provides greater accuracy in documenting that an officer used appropriate force tactics during a given incident.

Robinson (2006, p. 32) does not suggest that officers abandon clinical-type descriptions but rather should describe their actions in everyday language: "For example, instead of saying, 'I decentralized the subject,' have the officer describe exactly what push-down technique was used to take Mr. Jones to the ground. 'I pulled him toward me and stabilized his forehead against my upper chest, by locking my arms around the back of his head and neck. Then I stepped back, and used my hands to direct him to the ground, while also verbally commanding him to get down.'" Robinson (2006, p. 32) concludes, "If officers learn to articulate their use of force in specific, everyday language, the reasonableness will become more apparent. A good report can make an excessive-force lawsuit less likely to be filed in the first place, and if it does go to court, less likely to be successful."

Legible and On Time. It does little good to learn to write well if no one can read your report or if it is turned in after it was needed. **Legibility** refers to the ease with which a handwritten or type-printed character is recognizable based on its appearance. Some people's handwriting is simply so sloppy or scribbly that it is difficult, if not impossible, to discern individual letters and words. In short, it is illegible. Similarly, some typefaces or fonts are visually challenging to read, so steer clear of those. Ideally, reports should be typed in a simple, common font (e.g., Times New Roman, Garamond), and in today's computer-driven world, most reports are generated this way. Sometimes, however, this is not practical or possible. In fact, a poorly typed report is often as difficult to read as an illegible one.

If you do not type your reports, and if you know that you have poor handwriting, you may want to print your reports by hand. A key factor in legibility is speed, and most officers need to slow their writing speed (Arp, 2007). A report that cannot be read is of little use to anyone. Whether your reports are typed, written, or printed, make certain that others can read them easily and that they are submitted on time.

Recording and Dictating Reports

Recording or dictating reports is common in some departments, and the demand for transcription services and software is increasing across the country (Lesney, Rose, & Aspland, 2008). Many departments are moving toward digital report recording because it is more efficient and less costly than the old-fashioned method of tape recording. Reports that need quick attention may be red-tagged, so that records personnel will type those cases first.

Recording or dictating reports shifts the bulk of writing time to the records division. Even with recording or dictating, however, officers must still take final responsibility for what is contained in the report. Do not assume that what you think you spoke into a dictation machine is what will end up on paper. Following are some humorous illustrations of how some dictated sentences can be misinterpreted:

- He called for a toe truck.
- Smith was arrested for a mister meaner.
- Jones was a drug attic.
- The victim was over rot.
- Johnson died of a harder tack.

If time and department procedures allow, officers should always read through their reports before submitting them for charging considerations.

Computerized Report Writing

How many times have you heard, "Great job. Now do it again"? This demoralizing phrase can deflate an officer who has gone to great lengths to ensure an accurate, complete report. Yet police officers often encounter this "do it again" hurdle when they write a report. Report writing is filled with redundancies—turning handwritten notes into typed reports, sometimes filling out numerous forms along the way, all involving the same basic information garnered from the initial note-taking event. Each transfer of data takes time from an investigator and introduces an opportunity for error—a transposed number or two, a misspelled name, a detail that gets overlooked and never makes it to the final report.

Computers have made significant contributions to efficiency in report writing. The hardware available for word processing has become smaller and faster. It is easier to use and much more portable. Most of today's officers use vehicle-mounted computers or portable laptops. Software has also kept pace, with software developments allowing faster, more efficient report writing. In addition to sophisticated spell- and grammar-checker programs (to be used with the caveats noted earlier in "Grammatically and Mechanically Correct"), other programs have been developed to help in the actual preparation of police reports: "Software selection is specific to each agency and their particular requirements, based on that agency's roles and responsibilities" (Brewer, 2007, p. 38). For example, an agency with a large marine section should have the ability to query a boat's hull identification number (HID) on the software's query mask (Brewer, 2007). Pen-based computers and laptops, which involve the use of a stylus to write on the screen, have also made report writing easier.

One advance is computer-assisted report entry (CARE). This live-entry system centers around a CARE operator who leads officers through preformatted screens and questions, allowing them to complete reports in minutes. The CARE system has reduced report-writing times and improved the quality, accuracy, and timeliness of police reports. In addition, Uniform Crime Reporting information is automatically aggregated.

Digital report writing software, such as that offered by Omnigo and Presynct, can greatly streamline the handling of data and workflow management. It is important to use "open" software programs and networks, which are nonproprietary and interface with myriad systems already in use. This technology also enables departments to file Uniform Crime Reports (UCR) and National Incident-Based Reporting System (NIBRS) data electronically.

Although computerized report writing has greatly increased officers' efficiency, it cannot correct sloppy data entry. Officers are responsible for the accuracy and clarity of the data. The accuracy and clarity of a report are often deciding factors in whether a case is prosecuted. Preparing for and presenting cases in court are discussed in Chapter 21.

Evaluating Your Report

Once you have written your report, evaluate it. Do not simply add the final period, staple the pages together, and turn it in. Reread it. Proofread it to look for mistakes in spelling, punctuation, and capitalization.

Also make certain it says what you want it to say and contains no content or composition errors. Ask yourself if the report is factual, accurate, objective, complete, concise, clear, grammatically and mechanically correct, written in Standard English, organized into paragraphs, written in the past tense, uses the first person and active voice, and is audience-focused and legible. For larger reports, ask a colleague whose writing you admire to read your report. It is very difficult to proofread your own writing.

Table 3.4 provides an evaluation checklist for investigative reports.

TABLE 3.4 **Evaluation Checklist for Reports**
Is the Report:
Factual?
Accurate?
Objective?
Complete?
Chronological?
Concise?
Clear?
Mechanically correct?
Grammatically correct?
Written in Standard English?
Organized into paragraphs?
Does the Report Use:
First person?
Active voice?
Past tense?
Are the Sentences Mechanically Correct in:
Spelling?
Capitalization?
Punctuation?
Abbreviations?
Is the Report Audience-Focused and Legible?
Does the Report Allow the Reader to Visualize What Happened?

Source: Adapted from Hess, K. M., and Orthmann, C. H. (2019). *For the record: Report writing in law enforcement* (6th ed., revised). Rosemount, MN: Innovative Systems-Publishers, Inc., p. 208. Used with permission.

Citizen Online Report Writing

Allowing citizens to file crime reports online has the potential to increase caseload processing efficiency, increase patrol office effectiveness, and ease reporting delays for those jurisdictions suffering from staffing shortages or unmanageable caseloads (Cartwright, 2008). Such reporting is used only for discovery crimes, not involvement crimes, and is most appropriate for property crimes where no suspect information is available. For example, the San Francisco Police Department allows citizens to file online police reports for harassing phone calls; lost property; vandalism and graffiti; vehicle tampering, including vandalism; vehicle burglary (property stolen from a vehicle); and theft, unless it involves a residential or

Paperless Reporting

As agencies look for ways to "do more with less," paperless reporting is becoming increasingly popular. In addition to reducing the money spent on office supplies and postage, paperless reporting increases efficiency by getting information where it needs to be more quickly. One such technology innovation is Presynct, a platform for field-based reporting. Presynct is a secure Web-based application for paperless management of the incident and investigative reporting processes from creation to archive that uses digital versions of existing forms so there is minimal training or behavior change required on the part of the users.

Presynct combines voice and text in one application that integrates with proprietary records management systems (RMS) or operates as a stand-alone document management system. Presynct allows departments to add e-forms that are agency specific and also allows for digital attachments so statements and photos can be attached to the report. All case files can be found in one convenient place.

Presynct enhances confidentiality by doing away with paper drafts, lost or broken tapes, and misplaced tape recorders. Turnaround time from incident to data sharing is instant instead of days or weeks. Dictated reports are typed by data entry staff, leaving officer time and resources more effectively utilized in the field. Authors can also type their own reports and skip the dictation and data entry step. Transcription can be securely outsourced without losing control and management of the workflow.

Encrypted voice recordings are created in Presynct with digital handheld recorders, computer workstations, or telephones and available immediately for typing or automatic speech recognition (ASR). Presynct electronically routes reports for author review and editing. Immediately on approval, reports are automatically routed for supervisor approval or rejection with comments. Workflow routing is configurable to five levels. Finalized reports are archived in a searchable database, and incident data is exported to the RMS.

Source: https://presynct.com/features-benefits/

commercial burglary or the stolen property is a passport, Social Security card, firearm, license plate, car or electric vehicle, including electric bikes, wheelchairs and Segways. Special applications can also be used, such as allowing private security guards to file shoplifting reports online (Cartwright, 2008).

In accessing the local department's website and pulling up the page with the crime report form, citizens are able to complete an online report with such required fields as name, address, type of incident or loss experienced, and so on. Before the citizen can submit the report, a warning appears stating the penalties for filing a false report. Gitmed (2007, p. 124) notes, "Trying to obtain police reports from tourists, who would rather get back to their vacations than deal with filing a report, and trying to obtain a copy of these reports for insurance purposes can be a logistical nightmare."

Benefits of citizen online reporting include a reduction in time and resources spent responding to and writing reports for minor incidents that often lack a suspect and are usually filed only for insurance purposes (Cartwright, 2008). These systems often allow the police department to email a copy of the report, once approved by the agency, back to the citizen for easier, more timely submission to their insurance company. Furthermore, such systems often meet Americans with Disabilities Act (ADA) requirements and can receive reports in multiple languages, features that help agencies overcome communication barriers and better serve segments of the population that have traditionally been less likely to report crime and victimization (Cartwright, 2008).

Once submitted, the report can be retrieved and proofed by a records clerk in the police department, who determines whether the report is valid and assigns a case number to those meeting the predetermined criteria. Some systems allow the report to be directly downloaded into the department's records management system.

The Final Report

The culmination of the preceding steps is the final, or prosecution, report, containing all essential information for bringing a case to trial. The final report will be examined more closely in Chapter 21, as part of preparing a case for court.

A Final Note on the Importance of Well-Written Reports

Given the many uses of reports and the number of individuals who rely on them, the importance of reports should now be clear. What is key here is to make these necessary documents as well-written as possible, thus maximizing the benefits they can provide. Well-written reports further the cause of justice and reflect positively on your education, your competence, and your professionalism. In fact: "Your reputation and that of your department often rest on your written words" (Arp, 2007, p. 100). Officers who report false information or selectively exclude from their reports any information favorable to the defendant may find themselves caught in a "Brady/Giglio" situation where their testimony is considered unreliable or impeachable by the court. The two cases that structure this credibility issue are *Brady v. Maryland* (1963), which requires any adverse disciplinary information about officers' integrity or honesty to be turned over to the defense by the law enforcement agency, and *Giglio v. United States* (1972), which affirmed *Brady* and extended the reach of impeachment evidence, particularly within the context of law enforcement officer testimony at a criminal trial. The combination of these two court decisions has caused many district attorneys to tell local police chiefs and sheriffs that they will not use an officer's reports or testimony if that officer has been disciplined for not being truthful. Such an officer is then considered ***Giglio*-impaired**, meaning there exists potential impeachment evidence that would render that officer's testimony in a case, or any future case, of marginal value. Consequently, an officer with compromised credibility and a proven record of dishonesty is essentially useless as a law enforcement officer. (The *Brady* and *Giglio* cases are discussed again in Chapter 21.) The slippery slope of compromised credibility often begins with the integrity of the written report.

A report written well the first time means less time spent rewriting it. A well-written report also keeps everyone involved in the case current and clear about the facts, which can lead to higher prosecution rates, more plea bargains, fewer trials, and an easing of caseloads on the court system. A well-written report can also save an investigator from spending an inordinate amount of time on the witness stand attempting to explain any omissions, errors, or points of confusion found in poorly written reports. All these benefits ultimately save the department time and expense. Jetmore (2008, p. 26) stresses,

> It's not just skillful investigation that brings the bad guy to justice . . . . It's the investigator's ability to prepare a report that will withstand minute scrutiny by judges, prosecutors, defense counsel, citizens and the media. The report's ability to hold up under scrutiny may determine whether the guilty go free or justice is rendered to the victim. Why? Because in a democracy, the police are rightly constrained by a legal framework that not only presumes innocence, but places strict legal limitations on every police contact, detainment, arrest and search of its citizens.

Swobodzinski (2007, p. 47) notes, "Your investigative report may be the one pivotal piece of documentation that makes a difference in the prosecution of a murderer or a serial rapist. You certainly don't want it to be the weakest link in the investigation and provide a gap for an offender to get away with their crime."

In today's litigious society, where anyone can sue anyone else for practically anything, law enforcement is not immune to becoming the target of a lawsuit. For this reason, well-written reports can reduce legal liability for both the officer and the department by clearly documenting the actions taken throughout the investigation.

A final benefit of well-written reports is to the writer, in that they can greatly enhance an officer's career by reflecting positively on the investigator's education, competence, and professionalism.

Figures 3.3 and 3.4 (provided by Detective Richard Gautsch) are examples of a poorly written and a well-written report, respectively.

L08 Understand the benefits of well-written reports.

A well-written report helps the criminal justice system operate more efficiently and effectively, saves the department time and expense, reduces liability for the department and the officer, and reflects positively on the investigator who wrote it.

Report of Officer Iam Clueless

This officer was working the middle shift to cover for Officer Johnson who had called in sick. While on routine patrol in the north shopping center at the above listed time I responded with lights and siren in accordance with our policy to a report of a robbery at Helen's Liquor Store. The perp had been arrested by officer Andrews driving northbound several blocks from the scene. When this officer arrived at the above listed address their were two men standing near the front door. The clerk was frightened bad and nearly out of control as he walked back into the store. He said he'd been ripped off by a man wearing orange colored coveralls, a blue baseball cap about 40 years old, 6', with big ears weighing about 200 pounds who pushed him against the wall and grabbed money from the till and a gun had been fired as he exited the front door. No one was hurt and this officer decided not to request an ambulance. The other witness followed us into the store and was obviously drunk and also adorned in coveralls orange in color and two sizes too big, which made him look sloppy. This witness proceeded to the main door and a piece was pointed out a short distance from the sidewalk where the perp must have thrown it. The clerk indicated that he new the guy and that there regular customers. This officer asked the clerk if he could make a positive identification of the party and he acknowledged in the affirmative. I new Officer Andrews was 10–12 with one and I asked him his ETA. He said he was waiting for a CSO to stand by for the hook, but there always late and we needed a new system for tows. He snapped your just gonna have to wait, I'll get there ASAP. He said he thought we were close enough in time to do a one on one showup and this officer concurred. When I first arrived at the scene, this officer was of the opinion that the man in the orange colored coveralls was acting strange and may have been thinking about booking on me. I contemplated cuffing him, but the PC was a little weak. I engaged the party in further conversation to ascertain weather he'd offer additional incriminating evidence or make a damaging utterance. Having recently attended training in the latest Miranda rulings, this officers surmised he was within his rights to converse with the subject since he wasn't in custody and he hadn't lawyered up. As I asked him questions, he became defensive and moved in a suspicious manner. It became evident that he had drug and alcohol problems and this officer made the decision to render the firearm safe and secure it in the trunk of my squad. On the arrival of Officer Andrews, the clerk shouted out the door that their brothers and of course he can identify him. Officer Andrews then rolled up and lowered his window. The clerk went hysterical and screamed that he owed him a hundred bucks. Both witnesses positively identified the suspect sitting in the back seat with a sour look. Officer Andrews gave the clerk back a hundred dollars and transported the suspect who was wearing orange colored coveralls and a blue hat to the PD for booking. He identified the defendant as Bart Jennings, 5-11-65. The suspect confessed in front of us and totally exonerated his brother. The clerk calmed down and asked when he'd get the gun back. I said that was up to the detectives and cleared the scene at 5624 Forest Street. This officer identified the witnesses as Stanley Jennings and Thomas Benson. See above for addresses and DOB's. END OF REPORT

Figure 3.3
Example of a poor police report.
Source: Courtesy of Detective Richard Gautsch. Reprinted with permission.

Report of Officer Gotta Clue

On 10-20-14 at 1900 hours, I was dispatched to Helen's Liquor Store (5624 Forest Street) regarding a robbery. I arrived at 1905 and saw the victim, Thomas Benson, and a witness, Stanley Jennings, standing outside the front door. Both men identified themselves with Minnesota driver's licenses. I followed Benson into the store.

Benson paced and his hands trembled as he spoke. He told me that at 1845 hours a customer pushed him against the wall, grabbed about $100 from the cash register, and ran from the store. The robber dropped a handgun outside the door as he left, and it fired. Benson described the man as white, about 40 years old, 6 feet tall, 200 pounds, with big ears. He wore orange coveralls and a blue baseball hat. Benson said he knew the man and could identify him.

As I spoke with Benson, S. Jennings came into the store and stood by the front door. He was wearing orange coveralls, swayed from side to side, and repeatedly moved his hands in and out of his pockets. His eyes were red and watery, and I smelled the odor of an alcoholic beverage on his breath. S. Jennings opened the door and pointed at a Colt 38 caliber revolver in the grass about 6 feet west of the sidewalk.

After marking the location of the revolver with an evidence tag, I placed the gun in the trunk of my squad for safety reasons.

At 1910 hours Officer Andrews contacted me by radio. He had detained Bart Jennings (5-11-65) several blocks north of Helen's Liquor Store. Andrews brought B. Jennings back to the liquor store at 1925 hours. B. Jennings was wearing orange coveralls, a blue baseball cap, and had big ears. He stayed in the back seat of the squad. (Please see Officer Andrews' arrest report.)

Benson ran toward the squad and shouted, "That's him, that's the creep. He owes me 100 bucks." He also told me that Stanley and Bart Jennings were brothers.

S. Jennings leaned against the front door of the store and said, "Yup, that's him."

B. Jennings shifted forward in his seat and stated, "I done it, but I didn't use no gun. It just fell out of my pocket. And Stan didn't know I was going to do it."

Officer Andrews transported B. Jennings to the Police Department. I told Benson and S. Jennings that a detective would contact them. I logged the gun into evidence.

Case referred to Investigations.

Figure 3.4
Example of a well-written police report.
Source: Courtesy of Detective Richard Gautsch. Reprinted with permission.

Summary

Reports are permanent written records of important facts of a case to be used in the future and are crucial and necessary cogs in the wheel of justice.

Reports are used to examine the past, provide a documented record of incidents, keep other police officers informed, continue investigations, prepare court cases, provide the courts with relevant facts, refresh a witness's memory about what he or she said occurred, refresh the investigating officer's memory during the trial, coordinate law enforcement activities, plan for future law enforcement services, identify hot spots or areas where administration should focus more resources to reduce crime, compile statistics on crime in a given jurisdiction, evaluate individual officer and department performance, investigate potentially illegal police practices such as racial profiling, and provide information to insurance investigators. Reports are read by other officers, supervisors, attorneys and judges, jurors, social workers, city officials, insurance adjusters and investigators, civil rights groups, citizens, and media. Among the common problems in police reports are

- Confusing or unclear sentences

- Conclusions, assumptions, and opinions

- Extreme wordiness and overuse of police jargon and abbreviations

- Missing or incomplete information

- Misspelled words and grammatical or mechanical errors

- Referring to "above" information

The effective report writer attends to both content and form because they are equally important in a well-written report. The *content* of an effective report is factual, accurate, objective, and complete. The *form* of a well-written report is concise, clear, grammatically and mechanically correct, and written in Standard English. An effective report is factual, accurate, objective, complete, concise, clear, grammatically and mechanically correct, written in Standard English, organized into paragraphs, and written in the past tense; uses the first person and active voice; and is audience-focused and legible, leaving the reader with a positive impression of the writer's competence. A well-written report is also submitted on time.

A fact is a statement that can be proven, an inference is a conclusion based on reasoning, and an opinion is a personal belief.

A well-written report helps the criminal justice system operate more efficiently and effectively, saves the department time and expense, reduces liability for the department and the officer, and reflects positively on the investigator who wrote it.

Can You Define?

active voice	denotative	legibility
chronological order	disposition	mechanics
concise	first person	narrative
conclusionary language	form	objective
connotative	*Giglio*-impaired	past tense
content	jargon	slanting

Checklist

Report Writing

- Have I made a rough outline and organized my notes?

- Have I included all relevant information?

- Have I included headings?

- Have I proofread the paper to spot content and composition errors?

- Have I submitted all required reports on time?

- Has all information, including exculpatory information, been submitted to the prosecuting attorney?

References

Arp, D., Jr. (2007, April). Effective written reports. *Law and Order*, pp. 100–102.

Bell, A., & Razey, B. (2018, January 15). "Back 2 basics: How to write a good police report." *In public safety*. Retrieved April 29, 2020, from inpublicsafety.com/2018/01 /back-2-basics-how-to-write-a-good-police-report/

Brewer, B. (2007, November). ABCs of mobile reporting. *Law and Order*, pp. 36–44.

Cartwright, A. (2008, November). Beyond the paper chase. *Law Enforcement Technology*, pp. 58–62.

Gitmed, W. (2007, August). Citizens reporting crimes online. *The Police Chief*, pp. 124–131.

Hess, K. M., & Orthmann, C. H. (2019). *For the record: Report writing in law enforcement* (6th ed., revised). Rosemount, MN: Innovative Systems – Publishers, Inc.

Jetmore, L. F. (2007, September). Hone your investigative skills. *Law Officer Magazine*, pp. 22–23.

Jetmore, L. F. (2008, February). Investigative report writing. *Law Officer Magazine*, pp. 26–30.

Lesney, T., Rose, M., & Aspland, M. (2008, June). Transcription outsourcing: A rapidly emerging trend in law enforcement. *The Police Chief*, pp. 76–80.

Murgado, A. (2010, November 22). How to master report writing. *Police*. Retrieved April 29, 2020, from www .policemag.com/340434/how-to-master-report-writing

Robinson, P. A. (2006, January/February). What you say is what they write: Everybody teaches report writing. *The Law Enforcement Trainer*, pp. 30–32.

Rutledge, D. (2000). *The new police report manual* (2nd ed.). Belmont, CA: Wadsworth Publishing Company.

Rutledge, D. (2007, December). Full disclosure. *Police*, pp. 68–71.

Scarry, L. L. (2007, February). Report writing. *Law Officer Magazine*, pp. 68–71.

Swobodzinski, K. (2007, February). The crime scene report. *Law Officer Magazine*, pp. 47–49.

Wilson, O. W., & McLaren, R. C. (1972). *Police administration* (2nd ed.). New York: McGraw-Hill.

Cases Cited

Brady v. Maryland, 373 U.S. 83 (1963).

Giglio v. United States, 405 U.S. 150 (1972).

Graham v. Connor, 490 U.S. 386 (1989).

Miranda v. Arizona, 384 U.S. 436 (1966).

Chapter 4
Searches

Chapter Outline

The Fourth Amendment: An Overview of Search and Seizure

Legal Searches

Conducting Investigatory Searches

Use of Dogs in a Search

Use of Technology in a Search

Search Warrant Checklist

A Reminder

Learning Objectives

LO1 Identify the constitutional amendment and the two key terms contained therein that restrict investigative searches and seizures.

LO2 Illustrate the progression of the common levels of proof required during various stages of the criminal investigative process.

LO3 Explain the conditions that justify a legal search.

LO4 Summarize the warrantless search precedents established by the *Randolph*, *Terry*, *Chimel*, *Riley*, *Carroll*, *Chambers*, *Quarles*, *King*, *Hester*, *Weeks*, and *Mapp* decisions.

LO5 Understand what the exclusionary rule is, how it affects investigators, and which cases made it applicable at the federal and state levels.

LO6 Diagram the different types of exterior search patterns commonly used at crime scenes.

LO7 Explain how interior crime scene searches are typically conducted.

LO8 Compare how a search of an arrested suspect differs from a search of a suspect who has not been arrested.

Introduction

A Hollywood legend is accused of sexually assaulting a woman at a prominent mansion, and the woman's lawyer believes footage from the numerous surveillance cameras on the premises will support his client's claims. A former Olympic gold medalist and reality television star is involved in a fatal car crash along the Pacific Coast Highway, and questions immediately surface about whether he was driving while distracted by cell phone use. Although evidence of criminal conduct can often be found by examining such things as surveillance tapes from private residences or cell phone records, investigators are not free to simply walk up and demand that citizens turn over such items simply because the government wishes to poke through the history of one's private activities in the search for clues.

One of the great legal authorities granted to law enforcement is the ability to search people and their private spaces and to seize people and their property.

Of course, this authority is not unlimited but, rather, is strictly regulated by an ever-growing body of constitutional and case law. Because this text is an overview of criminal investigation and not a police procedure book, per se, the beginning discussion covering the legal aspects of searches and seizures will be relatively brief, serving more as a review of fundamental law enforcement practices with which the criminal justice student should already be familiar, and highlighting specific aspects of criminal procedure and key terminology that are particularly germane to criminal investigations. The remainder of the chapter will explore the search function of investigators. The arrest function is discussed in Chapter 7.

The Fourth Amendment: An Overview of Search and Seizure

A **search** is an examination of a person, place, or vehicle for contraband, illicit or stolen property, or some evidence of a crime to be used in prosecuting a criminal action or offense and is, by its very nature, an intrusion into one's privacy. In fact, in *United States v. Jacobsen* (1984) the Supreme Court defined a search as "a governmental infringement of a legitimate expectation of privacy." A **seizure** is a taking by law enforcement or other government agent of contraband, evidence of a crime, or even a person (via arrest) into custody. The foundation of legal search and seizure rests in the Fourth Amendment to the U.S. Constitution, which states:

> *The right of the people to be secure in their persons, houses, papers, and effects, against unreasonable searches and seizures, shall not be violated, and no Warrants shall issue, but upon probable cause, supported by Oath or affirmation, and particularly describing the place to be searched, and the persons or things to be seized.*

LO1   Identify the constitutional amendment and the two key terms contained therein that restrict investigative searches and seizures.

The Fourth Amendment to the U.S. Constitution forbids *unreasonable* searches and seizures and requires that legal searches and seizures be based on *probable cause*.

The Fourth Amendment strikes a balance between individual liberties and the rights of society. It is an outgrowth of the desire of the founders of the United States to eliminate the offensive British practices that existed before the Revolutionary War, such as forcing the colonists to provide British soldiers housing and indiscriminately searching the homes of those suspected of disloyalty to the king. The Fourth Amendment meant to ensure that the new government would respect its citizens' dignity and privacy. The courts are bound by rules and can admit evidence only if it is obtained constitutionally. Thus, an understanding of the Fourth Amendment and its relevance for searches and seizures is critical for any investigator.

The Fourth Amendment contains two clauses of importance to search-and-seizure issues:

- The Reasonableness Clause: "The right of the people to be secure in their persons, houses, papers and effects, against *unreasonable* searches and seizures shall not be violated."

- The Warrant Clause: "[A]nd no Warrants shall issue but upon *probable cause*, supported by Oath or affirmation, and particularly describing the place to be searched, and the persons or things to be seized."

All officers must understand the legal concepts of *reasonableness* and *probable cause*.

Reasonableness

"The touchstone of the Fourth Amendment is reasonableness, and the reasonableness of a search is determined 'by assessing, on the one hand, the degree to which it intrudes upon an individual's privacy and, on the other, the degree to which it is needed for the promotion of legitimate governmental interests' " (*United States v. Knights*, 2001). In short, the Fourth Amendment prohibits "unreasonable" searches and seizure.

So what is *reasonable* or *unreasonable*? Considerable debate and a plethora of legal decisions have been generated in the pursuit of defining what is reasonable for the government to do. Case definitions for *reasonable* include the following:

- "What is reasonable depends upon a variety of considerations and circumstances. It is an elastic term which is of uncertain value in a definition" (*Sussex Land & Live Stock Co. v. Midwest Refining Co.*, 1923).

- "Not extreme. Not arbitrary, capricious or confiscatory" (*Public Service Comm'n v. Havemeyer*, 1936).

- "That which is fair, proper, just, moderate, suitable under the circumstances, fit and appropriate to the end in view, having the faculty of reason, rational, governed by reason not immoderate or excessive, honest, equitable, tolerable" (*Cass v. State*, 1933).

Simply stated, **reasonable** means sensible, rational, and justifiable. It is one of those terms the framers of the Constitution used to require interpretation and application of a law intended to meet the needs of the people, rather than providing such rigidity that a commonsense application could not be made. Thus a key consideration in determining whether a search or seizure is reasonable is the balance between individual rights and the needs of society, as stressed previously.

Probable Cause

"Probable cause [to arrest] exists where the facts and circumstances within the officers' knowledge, and of which they had reasonably trustworthy information, are sufficient in themselves to warrant a belief by a man of reasonable caution that a crime is being committed" (*Brinegar v. United States*, 1949).

In *Brinegar*, the Court referenced Chief Justice John Marshall's observation in *Locke v. United States* (1813) that probable cause "means less than evidence which would justify condemnation or conviction," then added, "[s]ince, Marshall's time, at any rate, it has come to mean more than bare suspicion."

Probable cause exists when facts and circumstances are sufficient in themselves to warrant a person of reasonable caution to believe that a crime has been or is being committed. Probable cause to search requires that a combination of facts makes it more likely than not that items

sought are where the police believe them to be. Probable cause is stronger than reasonable suspicion but less than the quantum of evidence—proof beyond a reasonable doubt—required for conviction (see Figure 4.1).

> **LO2** Illustrate the progression of the common levels of proof required during various stages of the criminal investigative process. Explain the conditions that justify a legal search.
>
> The escalating levels of proof required during various stages of the criminal investigative process are as follows: reasonable suspicion is required to stop a person; probable cause is required to conduct a search or arrest (seizure); and proof beyond a reasonable doubt is required to convict someone of a crime.

Smith v. United States (1949) defined probable cause as "The sum total of layers of information and the synthesis of what the police have heard, what they know and what they observe as trained officers. We [the Court] weigh not individual layers but the laminated total." This "laminated total" is more often referred to as the **totality of circumstances**, the principle on which a number of legal assessments are made, including probable cause. Totality of circumstances is not a mathematical formula for achieving a certain number of factors; rather, it looks at what factors exist to assess whether the sum total would lead a reasonable person to believe what the officers concluded. The more factors present, generally the more likely a finding of probable cause will be upheld. However, probable cause may also be developed with fewer factors if those factors are particularly strong. In factor assessment, quality and quantity are both important, but if one is lacking, the other can compensate.

Developing probable cause is an objective, fact-dependent, and contextual process. The same facts in one situation may not provide probable cause in a different situation. The Court has described probable cause as being a "fluid concept—turning on the assessment of probabilities in particular factual contexts—not readily, or even usefully, reduced to a neat set of legal rules" (*Illinois v. Gates*, 1983).

Probable cause must be established *before* a lawful search or arrest can be made. It is important to note that the terms used here are *arrest* and *search*, not *stop* and *frisk*. Facts and evidence obtained after a search or arrest cannot be used to establish probable cause. They can be used, however, to strengthen the case if probable cause was established before the arrest, making the arrest legal.

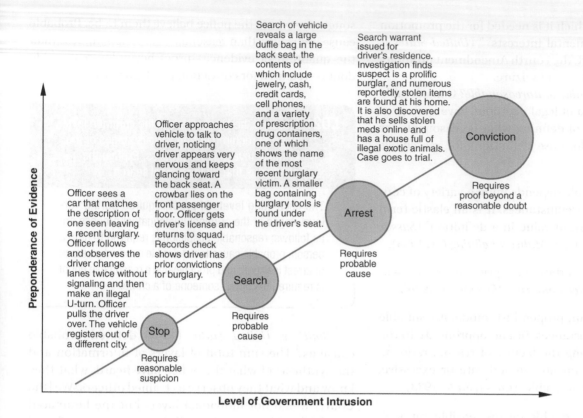

Figure 4.1
Standards of proof.

If probable cause is not present, police cannot act; if they do, negative consequences will ensue. Absent probable cause, seized evidence may be inadmissible in court, arrests determined illegal, and officers and others held liable for such illegality, as discussed later in the chapter. Probable cause and its establishment are key elements in motions to suppress in both warrant and warrantless situations.

A partial list of factors used to build probable cause includes flight, furtive movements, hiding, an attempt to destroy evidence, resistance to officers, evasive answers, unreasonable explanations, contraband or weapons in plain view, a criminal record, police training and experience, unusual or suspicious behavior, and information from informants and citizens. The more of these conditions exist, the stronger the probable cause.

The Supreme Court has established requirements for using informants in establishing probable cause. In *Aguilar v. Texas* (1964), the Court adopted a two-pronged test: (1) is the informant reliable/credible? and (2) is the information believable? This two-pronged approach was upheld in *Spinelli v. United States* (1969) when the Court ruled that the affidavit of the Federal Bureau of Investigation (FBI) for a warrant was insufficient to establish probable cause because there was not enough information to adequately assess the informant's reliability.

The Court abandoned this two-pronged approach in *Illinois v. Gates* (1983), where the Court ruled that probable cause is a practical concept that should not be weighed by scholars using tests, such as the *Aguilar-Spinelli* two-pronged test. Rather, the test for probable cause under the Fourth Amendment should be a totality-of-the-circumstances test that evaluates the sum total of factors that would lead a reasonable person to a course of action. However, federal courts are still guided by the two-pronged *Aguilar-Spinelli* test, and several states adhere to this more stringent requirement for establishing probable cause.

Having set the foundation for legal searches and seizures on the basic principles of reasonableness and probable cause, the remainder of the chapter will examine the important investigatory task of conducting searches.

Legal Searches

Because an investigative search is an intrusion into someone's privacy, it is strictly regulated by the Fourth Amendment to the U.S. Constitution. However, when and where there is no reasonable expectation of privacy, there exists no "search" to justify, and so no warrant is needed.

Myth Police always need a warrant to search for evidence.

Fact If there is no reasonable expectation of privacy, a search warrant is not needed.

The "reasonable expectation of privacy" implied in the Fourth Amendment was first explained by the Supreme Court in *Katz v. United States* (1967), when it held that what "a person knowingly exposes to the public, even in his own home or office, is not a subject of Fourth Amendment protection. . . . But what he seeks to preserve as private, even in an area accessible to the public, may be constitutionally protected." Thus, any action by the government that violates a person's reasonable expectation of privacy is considered a search. The courts have adopted guidelines to assure law enforcement personnel that if they adhere to certain rules, their searches or seizures will be reasonable, and thus legal.

LO3 Explain the conditions that justify a legal search.

A search can be justified and therefore considered legal if any of the following conditions are met:

- A search warrant has been issued.
- Consent is given.
- An officer stops a suspicious person and believes the person may be armed (frisk).
- It is incidental to a lawful arrest.
- The search is of a moveable vehicle (automobile exception).
- It is for inventory purposes.
- An emergency or exigent circumstance exists.
- It occurs at a point of entry into this country (border crossings, airports, ports).
- The search involves an officer using "plain sense" (sight, sound, smell, touch).
- It involves open fields, abandoned property, or a public place (i.e., there exists no reasonable expectation of privacy).

If any *one* of these *preconditions* exists, a search will be considered "reasonable" and therefore legal. However, states can impose further restrictions on police powers within their boundaries.

Search with a Warrant

Technically—according to the Fourth Amendment—all searches are to be conducted under the authority of a warrant. In 1948, the Supreme Court ruled in *Johnson v. United States* that without exigent circumstances, searches are presumptively unconstitutional if not authorized by a search warrant.

To obtain a valid search warrant, officers must appear before a judge and establish probable cause to believe that the location contains evidence of a crime, specifically describing the evidence sought. In addition to establishing probable cause for a search, the warrant must contain the reasons for requesting it, the name of the officer or officers presenting affidavits, what specifically is being sought, and the signature of the judge issuing it. The warrant must be based on the facts and sworn to by the officer(s) requesting the warrant. The address and description of the location must be given—for example, "100 S. Main Street," "the ABC Liquor Store," or "1234 Forest Drive, a private home." When officers use information from civilians on search warrant applications, they should state whether the civilian is an informant or citizen giving information as a civic duty. Figure 4.2 is an example of a search warrant. A search warrant can be issued to search for and seize

- Stolen or embezzled property
- Property designed or intended for use in committing a crime
- Property that indicates a crime has been committed or a particular person has committed a crime

A search conducted with a warrant must be limited to the specific area and specific items named in the warrant, in accordance with the **particularity requirement** (*Stanford v. Texas*, 1965). During a search conducted with a warrant, items not specified in the warrant may be seized if they are similar to the items described, if they are related to the particular crime described, if they are contraband, or if such unrelated, unspecified evidence is in plain view.

In *Groh v. Ramirez* (2004), the Supreme Court sent a message to law enforcement on the importance of paying attention to detail. In this case, police obtained a warrant to search a residence. Although the application

Figure 4.2
An example
of a search
warrant.

SEARCH WARRANT

STATE OF MINNESOTA, COUNTY OF ANY   **DISTRICT COURT**

TO: LILLIAN Y. BOARD, A MINNESOTA PEACE OFFICER, AND ALL OTHER OFFICERS ACTING UNDER HER DIRECTION AND CONTROL (A) PEACE OFFICERS(S) OF THE STATE OF MINNESOTA.

WHEREAS, Lillian Y. Board has this day on oath, made application to the said Court applying for issuance of a search warrant to search the following (property) (premises) (~~motor vehicles~~) (person):

- Residence located at 1234 Main Street, Anycity, Any County, Minnesota, and all garages and/or storage areas associated with that residence. 1234 Main Street is described as a blue two-story, single homestead, with a white front door.
- Person of John NMN Doe, date of birth: 01-30-1980.

located in Anycity, Any County, STATE OF MINNESOTA, for the following described property and things:

1. 40 inch sword with a white plastic handle and ornamental figurine.
2. 32 inch sword with a black fancy handle in a hard leather sheath
3. Set of three swords, all black, between 18 inches length and 36 inches in length.
4. Buck knives

WHEREAS, the application and supporting affidavit of Lillian Y. Board (was) (~~were~~) duly presented and read by the Court, and being fully advised of the premises.

NOW, THEREFORE, the Court finds that probable cause exists for the issuance of a search warrant upon the following grounds: (Strike inapplicable paragraphs)

1. The property above described was stolen or embezzled.
2. ~~The property above described was used as means of committing a crime.~~
3. The possession of the property above described constitutes a crime.
4. ~~The property above described is in the possession of a person with intent to use such property as a means of committing a crime.~~
5. The property above-described constitutes evidence which tends to show a crime has been committed, or tends to show that a particular person has committed a crime.

The Court further finds that probable cause exists to believe that the above-described property and things (are) (~~will be~~) at/in the above-described premises, and/or property and/or ~~motor vehicle,~~ and/or person.

~~The Court further finds that a nighttime search outside the hours of 7 a.m. and 8 p.m. is necessary to prevent the loss, destruction, or removal of the objects of said search, or to protect the searchers or the public.~~

~~The Court further finds that entry without announcement of authority or purpose is necessary (to prevent the loss, destruction, or removal of the objects of said search) [and] (to protect the safety of the peace officers).~~

NOW, THEREFORE, YOU, LILLIAN Y. BOARD, A MINNESOTA PEACE OFFICER, AND ALL OTHER OFFICERS ACTING UNDER YOUR DIRECTION AND CONTROL, THE PEACE OFFICER(S) AFORESAID, ARE HEREBY COMMANDED (~~TO ENTER WITHOUT ANNOUNCEMENT OF AUTHORITY AND PURPOSE~~) (BETWEEN THE HOURS OF 7 A.M. AND 8 P.M.) (~~AND A NIGHTTIME SEARCH OUTSIDE THOSE HOURS~~) TO SEARCH (THE DESCRIBED PREMISES) (~~THE DESCRIBED MOTOR VEHICLE~~) (THE DESCRIBED PERSONS) FOR THE ABOVE-DESCRIBED THINGS AND (TO RETAIN THEM IN CUSTODY SUBJECT TO COURT ORDER AND ACCORDING TO LAW) (~~DELIVER CUSTODY OF SAID PROPERTY AND THINGS TO _____~~).

                                        BY THE COURT:

Subscribed and sworn to before me this _____
day of _____, _____.   _____
                                            Judge of District Court

and affidavit described the items to be seized, the warrant did *not* contain such a description as required by the Fourth Amendment. The section that was to contain a list of *items* to be seized instead described the *place* to be searched. A judge reviewed and signed the warrant, which was then executed. The officer was sued for an alleged Fourth Amendment violation. The lower court agreed that a constitutional violation occurred and that any reasonable officer would have concluded that the warrant was invalid. The U.S. Supreme Court agreed: "It is incumbent upon the officer executing a search warrant to ensure the search is lawfully authorized and lawfully conducted."

Once a warrant is obtained, it should be executed promptly. In many states, the warrant is good for a set number of days (e.g., 7 or 10 days) and is to be executed during daytime hours, typically between 6 a.m. and 9 p.m. unless endorsed otherwise. A **nightcapped warrant** authorizes a search or arrest at any time, day or night. Nightcapped warrants can generally be served when a suspect is in any public area regardless of time. The court determines the legitimacy of a nightcapped warrant based on considerations such as safety of the public and those executing the warrants, or the prevention of the loss, destruction, or removal of evidence.

The Knock-and-Announce Rule. Usually the officer serving the warrant knocks on the particular door, states the purpose of the search, and gives a copy of the warrant to the person who has answered the knock. This procedure follows the "knock-and-announce" rule, which is based on English common law and ensures the right to privacy in one's home. The knock-and-announce rule requires officers serving a search warrant to knock, announce themselves, and wait a "reasonable length of time" before attempting entry. In *Wilson v. Arkansas* (1995), the Court made this centuries-old rule a constitutional mandate: "The underlying command of the Fourth Amendment is always that searches and seizures be reasonable, and that the common-law requirement that officers announce their identity and purpose before entering a house forms a part of the Fourth Amendment inquiry into the reasonableness of the officers' entry."

The knock-and-announce rule is intended (1) to protect citizens' right to privacy, (2) to reduce risk of possible violence to police and residence occupants, and (3) to prevent needless destruction of private property. "Most officers find it judicious to knock and announce their presence and intentions. 'Surprise' entries can lead to misunderstanding on the suspect's part, creating situations that can escalate into unnecessary violence" (Geoghegan, 2007, p. 99).

If officers attempting to serve a search warrant are not admitted by occupants following a knock-notice announcement, forcible entry may be made. In a unanimous ruling in *United States v. Banks* (2003), the Supreme Court upheld the forced entry into a suspected drug dealer's apartment 15 to 20 seconds after police knocked and announced themselves. This ruling strengthened police powers in cases where loss of evidence or physical danger were crucial factors and provides guidance to law enforcement officers and entry teams on how long they need to wait before forcing entry into a residence. However, unnecessary damage to the structure or any other private property may make the entry unreasonable and, thus, a violation of the Fourth Amendment, despite the entry itself being legal (*United States v. Ramirez*, 1998).

The courts have recognized that in some instances safe and effective law enforcement requires certain exceptions be made to the knock-and-announce rule. A **no-knock warrant** may be issued if evidence may be easily destroyed or if there is advance knowledge of explosives or other specific danger to an officer (*Richards v. Wisconsin*, 1997)—for example, if a suspect has a prior history of being armed, combative, or resistant to arrest.

In 2006 the Supreme Court ruled 5–4 in *Hudson v. Michigan* that the Constitution does not require the government to forfeit evidence gathered through illegal no-knock searches while executing a search warrant, stating, "Suppression of evidence has always been our last resort, not our first impulse. The exclusionary rule generates substantial social costs which sometimes include setting the guilty free and the dangerous at large." Writing for the Court's five-member conservative majority, Justice Samuel Alito said police blunders should not result in a "get-out-of-jail-free card" for defendants. The Court also referred to alternative remedies to police errors, such as internal discipline or civil lawsuits. Such alternatives, which allow the evidence to be admitted but sanction the officer, mirror the procedure used in the British system. Law enforcement agencies are cautioned, however, not to misinterpret the Court's ruling in *Hudson v. Michigan* as a license to freely disregard the procedure of knocking, announcing, and waiting a reasonable amount of time for a resident to answer the door before entering to execute a search warrant: "That interpretation is both wrong and dangerous. Failure to adhere to the requirements of the knock-and-announce rule can result in terrible tragedy and extremely expensive litigation" (Hilton, 2007, p. 38).

Video recording of knock-notice announcement and entry provides evidence of compliance with the rule as well as the amount of time officers waited before entry.

Anticipatory Search Warrants. In *United States v. Grubbs* (2006), the Supreme Court approved the use of an anticipatory search warrant. The Court defined an **anticipatory warrant** as one "based upon an affidavit showing probable cause that at some future time (but not presently) certain evidence of crime will be located at a specified place." The Court noted that, in a sense, all search warrants are anticipatory. Anticipatory warrants are constitutional if a proper showing is made that contraband or evidence will likely be found at the target location at a given time or when a specific triggering event occurs. The Court ruled that where a triggering condition was specified in the search warrant application or affidavit, the failure to include that triggering condition in the warrant did not undermine the warrant's validity. Anticipatory search warrants are rarely sought, and there must be substantial probable cause for the court to issue one.

Search with Consent

Officers can conduct a search without a warrant under certain circumstances, one of which occurs when consent to search is given. And as with a search warrant, searches conducted with consent have limitations. First, officers must convey a genuine *request* for permission to search, not simply state that they would like to conduct a search. Then, consent to search must be given freely and voluntarily, not in response to an officer's claim of lawful authority or to a request phrased as a command or threat. A genuine affirmative reply must also be given; a simple nodding of the head or opening of a door is not sufficient. Silence is *not* consent. The Supreme Court ruled in *Schneckloth v. Bustamonte* (1973) that it would use the totality-of-the-circumstances test to determine whether the consent was voluntary. This includes the characteristics of the subject, the environment (location, number of people and officers present, and time of day), the subject's actions or statements, and the officer's actions or statements. Even when police have an alternative justification for a search, such as a warrant, they may ask for consent to establish another layer of validation for their actions.

Officers should thoroughly document everything they say and do when asking for consent and while conducting the search. Such documentation might involve the audio or video recording of the consent to search. Some officers use a prepared consent form to be signed by the person giving consent. The person has the right to limit the area for which consent is given. Further, the person may revoke the consent at any time during the search. If this occurs, officers are obligated to discontinue the search.

If consent is given, the person granting it must be legally competent to do so. Searching without a warrant is allowed if consent is given by the actual property owner or, as set forth in *United States v. Matlock* (1974), by a person in charge of that property. In *Matlock* the Supreme Court held that if a third party has common authority over the premises of items to be searched, this individual could provide government officials with a valid consent. Furthermore, if the police believe the person giving consent has authority, they may act on this belief, even though it later turns out the person did not have authority (*Illinois v. Rodriguez*, 1990). Examples of relationships where third-party consent may be valid include the following:

- Parent/Child—A parent who owns a property can generally give consent to search the room and other belongings of a child living on those premises. However, if the child uses a given area of the premises exclusively, has sectioned it off, has furnished it with his or her own furniture, pays rent, or has otherwise established an expectation of privacy, the parent may not consent to a search of that area occupied by the child.

- Employer/Employee—In general, an employer may consent to a search of any part of the employer's premises used by an employee, including employee lockers. However, an employee's briefcase, purse, or other personal items stored in a locker, desk, or work area are protected under the Fourth Amendment, and a search of such personal articles should occur only with consent of the employee to whom they belong or after a lawful search warrant has been obtained. Recent court cases have held that the contents of electronic devices owned by the employer (computers, cell phones, etc.) are *not* shielded by employees' right to privacy. In *City of Ontario v. Quon* (2010), the Supreme Court unanimously upheld a city's search of its police officers' text messages, but noted that the search was reasonable under the Fourth Amendment *only* because it was motivated by a legitimate work-related purpose (in this case, an audit of employees' on-duty texting volume to determine whether a new department-wide service agreement was needed).

- Host/Guest—The host, owner, or primary occupant of the premises may consent to a search of the area in which a guest is staying. Any evidence found would be admissible against the guest. It should be noted, however, that this ability to grant consent exists only when *no* rent or occupancy payment has been made. The situations involving landlords and hotels, or other properties where an individual has paid to stay for a certain duration, will be discussed shortly.

- Spouses—If two people, such as husband and wife, have equal rights to occupy and use premises, either may give consent to a search.

If more than one person owns or occupies a building, only one need give permission. Thus if two people share an apartment, all that is required is the consent from one of them (*Wright v. United States*, 1938). However, consent may be given for only those areas commonly used, not private space of one or the other. Even spouses do not have totality in area of consent if one area is considered to be off-limits to one party.

In *Georgia v. Randolph* (2006), the Supreme Court addressed the issue of what happens when one occupant grants permission to search a private premise and another one withholds consent. In this case, Scott Randolph's estranged wife, Janet, gave police consent to search the marital residence for items of her husband's drug use after Randolph, who was also present, had unequivocally refused to give consent. The police went ahead and searched, finding evidence of cocaine possession, and

Scott Randolph was indicted. The trial court denied his motion to suppress the evidence as products of a warrantless search unauthorized by consent. The Georgia Court of Appeals, however, reversed. In affirming, the state supreme court created a "disputed permission rule" when it held that consent given by one occupant is invalid and nullified in the face of the refusal of another physically present occupant. In a 5–3 opinion, the court stated, "If any party who is present and has authority to object to the search does object to the search, the police may not conduct the search on the authority of that party who gave consent."

> **L04** Summarize the warrantless search precedents established by the *Randolph, Terry, Chimel, Riley, Carroll, Chambers, Quarles, King, Hester, Weeks,* and *Mapp* decisions.
>
> The Court ruled in *Georgia v. Randolph* that police may not legally search a home when one physically present resident consents but another physically present resident objects. The objection overrides the consent.

Randolph was modified in *Fernandez v. California* (2014), when the Court examined how the Fourth Amendment prohibition on warrantless searches applies when one cooccupant, who had previously refused consent to search, is no longer present and the co-occupant who is present consents to the search. In this case, police came to the apartment of robbery suspect Fernandez, and his girlfriend, with whom he shared the apartment, answered the door. Seeing the suspect inside, the officers requested permission to enter and search the residence, to which Fernandez refused. At that point Fernandez was arrested and removed from the apartment. Once the suspect was no longer on the premises, officers explained to the girlfriend that Fernandez was arrested for robbery and requested her consent to search the apartment, which she granted. At trial, Fernandez argued that, under *Randolph*, his objection to the search should have held even after he was involuntarily removed from the premises. The Court, however, noted that the ultimate rationale for searches under the Fourth Amendment is reasonableness and that it was reasonable, once the nonconsenting party was no longer present, for officers to conduct a warrantless search if the remaining co-occupant gives consent.

The bottom line, when it comes to shared property, is that a warrant or consent from *both* parties is always preferred. The law has been shifting in recent years, with conflicting legal case outcomes on who can give consent to search a shared property. Over the past few years, a trend has been noticed with the courts tending to sway away from single-party consent, often citing that officer presence is intimidating. Some criminal justice practitioners believe it is likely that law enforcement may soon be required to present a *Miranda*-type warning for consent searches.

Examples of instances when individuals *cannot* give valid consent to search include the following:

- Landlord/Tenant—A landlord, even though the legal owner, does not have authority to give consent to a search of a tenant's premises or a seizure of the tenant's property. Only the tenant may offer consent. This situation includes children (tenants) living at home but paying rent to their parent (landlords).

- Hotel Employee/Hotel Guest—The Supreme Court extended the principles governing a landlord's consent to a search of tenant's premises to include consent searches of hotel and motel rooms allowed by hotel/motel employees. In these searches, only the hotel guest can give consent.

- Rental Car Company/Driver—Rental car companies cannot give consent to search a rented vehicle, even if an unauthorized driver is the only person in possession of the vehicle. Drivers of rental cars, even those persons not listed on the rental agreement and who are, thus, considered "unauthorized" drivers, retain a reasonable expectation of privacy for possessions stored in the trunk.

In *Byrd v. United States* (2018), the U.S. Supreme Court held that officers conducted an illegal search when they stopped Byrd, who was driving a rental car, for a traffic violation and then proceeded to search the trunk of the car without his consent because he was not listed on the rental agreement. In this case, Terrence Byrd was driving a car that had been rented by a female friend. She did not list Byrd as an additional driver, and the rental agreement warned that allowing unauthorized drivers to operate the vehicle would violate the agreement. Nonetheless, she gave Byrd the keys to the rental car, he placed his personal belongings in the trunk of the car, and then drove off alone.

When state troopers later stopped Byrd for a traffic violation, they discovered that the vehicle was rented, that Byrd was not listed on the agreement as an authorized driver, and that Byrd had prior drug and weapons convictions. When Byrd stated he had a marijuana cigarette in the car, the troopers proceeded to search the entire vehicle, finding body armor and 49 bricks of heroin in the trunk. Byrd admitted that the drugs were his and that he planned to sell them, and the evidence was used to charge Byrd with federal drug and other crimes. While Byrd's attorneys argued the evidence was the fruit of an illegal search, two lower courts disagreed. Both the district court and the circuit appellate court denied Byrd's motion to suppress the evidence on the grounds that, because Byrd was not listed as an authorized driver on the rental agreement, he lacked a reasonable expectation of privacy in the vehicle and, therefore, the search of the trunk was lawful.

The U.S. Supreme Court, however, disagreed and overturned the rulings of the two lower courts, holding that "the mere fact that a driver in lawful possession or control of a rental car is not listed on the rental agreement will not defeat his or her otherwise reasonable expectation of privacy" (*Byrd v. United States*, 2018). Chief Justice Roberts stated, "One of the things that I think is very important in these types of cases is the ability to give clear guidance not only to the courts but to the police."

One form of consent with which officers should be familiar is the *consent once removed* exception to the search warrant requirement. Under this exception, officers can make a warrantless entry to arrest a suspect if consent to enter was given earlier to an undercover officer or informant.

Another form of consent pertinent to law enforcement is *implied consent*, which differs from the previously discussed expressed consent in that it is not directly communicated verbally or in writing but, rather, inferred by a person's actions or involvement in specific contexts. Implied consent often attaches at schools, airports, and national borders, contexts within which persons must consent to reasonable searches or, for security reasons, be denied access. Implied consent laws also apply to the operation of motor vehicles and state that anyone who drives on public roadways has agreed to submit their blood, breath, or urine to a test for drugs if they are stopped or arrested for suspicion of driving while impaired, that the test results can be used as evidence against the driver, and that failure to submit to such a test can lead to the loss of their driver's license, among other penalties. Searches at points of entry into the country are discussed shortly.

Patdown or Frisk during a "Stop"

Another exception to the warrant requirement is a stop-and-frisk situation. Two situations require police officers to stop and question individuals: (1) to investigate suspicious circumstances, and (2) to identify someone who looks like a suspect named in an arrest warrant or whose description has been broadcast in an all-points bulletin (APB).

The procedures for stopping and questioning suspects are regulated by the same justifications and limitations associated with lawful searches and seizures. If it is suspected that a person stopped for questioning may be armed, the officer is justified in conducting a through-the-clothes patdown for weapons. If the officer feels an object that may be a weapon, the officer may seize it.

The prime requisite for stopping, questioning, and possibly frisking someone is *reasonable suspicion*, a lesser standard than probable cause but equally difficult to define. A stop and a frisk are two separate actions, and each must be separately justified: "Just because a stop is permissible doesn't mean a frisk is permissible. In fact, in most stops, a non-consensual frisk would not be permitted because of the absence of reasonable suspicion of the presence of weapons" (Means, 2008, p. 23). The landmark decision in *Terry v. Ohio* (1968) established police officers' right to **patdown** or **frisk** a person they have stopped to question if they believe the person might be armed and dangerous.

> **LO4** Summarize the warrantless search precedents established by the *Randolph, Terry, Chimel, Riley, Carroll, Chambers, Quarles, King, Hester, Weeks,* and *Mapp* decisions.
>
> The *Terry* decision established that a patdown or frisk is a "protective search for weapons" and as such must be "confined to a scope reasonably designed to discover guns, knives, clubs and other hidden instruments for the assault of a police officer or others."

The Court warned that a patdown or frisk is "a serious intrusion upon the sanctity of the person which may inflict great indignity and arouse strong resentment, and it is not to be undertaken lightly." The "search" in a frisk is sometimes referred to as a *safety* search. Officers should know the limits of their authority to protect themselves, both physically and legally, so that they never are forced to choose between being safe and being sued (Rutledge, 2007b).

Terry has been further expanded in other cases. *Adams v. Williams* (1972) established that officers may stop and question individuals based on information received from informants. *United States v. Hensley* (1985) established that police officers may stop and question suspects when they believe they recognize them from "wanted" flyers issued by another police department.

When officers have reasonable suspicion to believe someone they have stopped to question may be armed and dangerous, they are legally justified in frisking that person for weapons, as established by the *Terry* decision.
© Henry Cho

Stop-and-frisk has been validated on the basis of furtive movements; inappropriate attire; carrying suspicious objects such as a television or a pillowcase; vague, nonspecific answers to routine questions; refusal to identify oneself; and appearing to be out of place. As established in *Alabama v. White* (1990), such a stop-and-frisk can also be made based on an anonymous tip, provided the tip predicts future activities the officer can corroborate, making it reasonable to think the informant has reliable knowledge about the suspect. However, in *Florida v. J. L.* (2000), the Court held that police could not stop and frisk someone based solely on an anonymous tip.

Usually during a **Terry stop**, law enforcement officers ask those they detain to identify themselves. *Hiibel v. Sixth Judicial District Court of Nevada, Humboldt County* (2004) ruled that state statutes requiring individuals to identify themselves as part of an investigative stop are constitutional and do not violate the Fourth or Fifth Amendments. However, the *Hiibel* ruling applies only if a state law requires people to provide their names to law enforcement officers.

In *United States v. Drayton* (2002), the Supreme Court ruled that law enforcement officers do not need to advise bus passengers of their right not to cooperate during a consensual bus interdiction. Vehicle stops as well as checkpoints for various purposes are discussed shortly.

Search Incident to Arrest

Every lawful arrest is accompanied by a search of the arrested person to protect the arresting officers and others and to prevent destruction of evidence. This search, unlike the "through-the-clothes" search called a frisk, involves going through the person's pockets, purses, bags, wallets, etc. Any weapon, dangerous substance, or evidence discovered in the search may be seized. However, as discussed shortly, some items, such as locked containers or cell phones, may be temporarily seized while a warrant is sought.

In *United States v. Johnson* (2019), the court clarified that the order or timing of these two actions—the search and the arrest—is irrelevant. Officers who have probable cause can either place the person under arrest and then conduct the search, or the search can be conducted prior to the arrest being made, as long

LO4   Summarize the warrantless search precedents established by the *Randolph, Terry, Chimel, Riley, Carroll, Chambers, Quarles, King, Hester, Weeks,* and *Mapp* decisions.

The *Chimel* decision established that a search incidental to a lawful arrest must be made simultaneously with the arrest and must be confined to the area within the suspect's immediate control.

as probable cause exists and the search and arrest are roughly contemporaneous.

Limitations on a search incidental to arrest are found in *Chimel v. California* (1969).

A person's **immediate control** encompasses the area within the person's reach. The Court noted that using an arrest to justify a thorough search would give police the power to conduct "general searches," which were declared unconstitutional nearly 200 years ago.

Myth Police can search a person only after they have arrested them.

Fact Several justifiable reasons exist that allow police to search a person prior to or without formally arresting them, such as through-the-clothes protective searches for weapons during stops and searches at points-of-entry into the country.

If law enforcement officers take luggage or other personal property, including cell phones or computers, into their exclusive control and there is no longer any danger that the arrestee might gain access to the property to seize a weapon or destroy evidence, a search of that property is no longer an incident of the arrest and a search warrant should be obtained. Given the proliferation of cell phones and wireless technology, electronic data searches have become a hot topic and an increasingly complicated territory for officers to navigate, particularly since the law has struggled to keep pace with the accelerated development and availability of such technology.

A recent Supreme Court ruling held unequivocally that an officer must obtain a search warrant to go through an arrested person's cell phone unless consent is given or exigent circumstance exists, although whatever is visible on the screen to the officer at the time of arrest is considered plain view. *Riley v. California* (2014) is considered a landmark decision regarding electronic data searches, with Chief Justice Roberts delivering the opinion of the unanimous Court, stating in part:

> Digital data stored on a cell phone cannot itself be used as a weapon to harm an arresting officer or to effectuate the arrestee's escape. Law enforcement officers remain free to examine the physical aspects of a phone to ensure that it will not be used as a weapon—say, to determine whether there is a razor blade hidden between the phone and its case. Once an officer has secured a phone and eliminated any potential physical threats, however, data on the phone can endanger no one....

We cannot deny that our decision today will have an impact on the ability of law enforcement to combat crime. Cell phones have become important tools in facilitating coordination and communication among members of criminal enterprises, and can provide valuable incriminating information about dangerous criminals. Privacy comes at a cost.

Our holding, of course, is not that the information on a cell phone is immune from search; it is instead that a warrant is generally required before such a search, even when a cell phone is seized incident to arrest....

Modern cell phones are not just another technological convenience. With all they contain and all they may reveal, they hold for many Americans "the privacies of life," ... The fact that technology now allows an individual to carry such information in his hand does not make the information any less worthy of the protection for which the Founders fought. Our answer to the question of what police must do before searching a cell phone seized incident to an arrest is accordingly simple—get a warrant.

LO4 Summarize the warrantless search precedents established by the *Randolph*, *Terry*, *Chimel*, *Riley*, *Carroll*, *Chambers*, *Quarles*, *King*, *Hester*, *Weeks*, and *Mapp* decisions.

The *Riley* decision established that a search of a cell phone seized incident to a lawful arrest, in the absence of consent or an emergency situation, requires a warrant.

The student is strongly encouraged to go online and read the Court's opinion of *Riley* in its entirety, for it went to great lengths to address many nuances of cell phone technology, including cloud computing, remote wiping, and data encryption, that complicate the job of the investigator in conducting legal searches and seizures. *Riley* also illustrates how the law must adapt to stay applicable to the changes in modern, daily life.

Maryland v. Buie (1990) expanded the area of a premises search following a lawful arrest to ensure officers' safety. In this case, the Supreme Court added authority for the police to search areas immediately adjoining the place of arrest. Such a **protective sweep**, or *Buie* sweep, is justified when reasonable suspicion exists that another person might be present who poses a danger to the arresting officers. The search must be confined to areas where a person might be hiding.

Previous editions of this text cited *New York v. Belton* (1981) as the landmark case regarding warrantless searches of vehicles incident to and contemporaneous with a lawful arrest. In *Belton*, the Supreme Court defined a bright-line rule: "When a policeman has made a lawful custodial arrest of the occupant of an automobile, he may, as a contemporaneous incident of that arrest, search the passenger compartment of that automobile. It follows from this conclusion that the police may also examine the contents of any containers found within the passenger compartment, for if the passenger compartment is within reach of the arrestee, so also will containers in it be within his reach." The caveat to this ruling was that a warrant was still needed to search any locked area of the vehicle or locked containers inside the vehicle, the rationale being that locked contents were not in the arrestee's immediate control and posed no threat to law enforcement.

However, *Belton* has since been limited by *Arizona v. Gant* (2009), in which the Supreme Court reduced law enforcement's authority to automatically search, as a matter of routine, the passenger compartment of a vehicle incident to arrest. In this case Rodney Gant was arrested in his driveway, after parking and exiting his vehicle, for driving with a suspended license. After getting out of his car, Gant was arrested immediately, handcuffed, and placed into the back of a patrol car. Officers then conducted a search, incident to Gant's arrest, of his vehicle and found a gun and a bag of cocaine in a jacket in the backseat. Gant was charged with and convicted of possession of narcotics for sale and possession of drug paraphernalia. He appealed on the basis that the warrantless search of his vehicle was a Fourth Amendment violation. The Arizona Supreme Court agreed that the warrantless search of Gant's vehicle was unreasonable not only because the scene was secure and Gant was in custody, unable to pose a threat to the officers or to destroy evidence, but also because Gant had been arrested for driving on a suspended driver's license and it was unreasonable for officers to believe that any evidence related to that offense would be found inside the vehicle. The U.S. Supreme Court affirmed this decision.

Gant provides an excellent example of why police officers must understand the rationale behind why they are permitted to perform certain actions. Officers must also be knowledgeable of the individual state statutes and department policies governing searches incident to arrest in their jurisdiction as some legislation may further restrict the scope of such searches (Jetmore, 2007a). It is important to understand that although *Gant* restricts searches incident to arrest, it has no impact on the other warrant exceptions, such as consent, the motor vehicle exception, and exigent circumstances (Myers, 2011).

Warrantless Searches of Moveable Vehicles

A vehicle stop is a seizure within the meaning of the Fourth Amendment and, therefore, must generally be supported by reasonable suspicion of wrongdoing. However, because of their *mobility* (the fact that they can be easily and quickly moved before a warrant can be obtained), a vehicle may need to be searched without a warrant. The justified warrantless search of a moveable vehicle is known as the automobile exception, the precedent for which was established in *Carroll v. United States* (1925).

> **LO4** Summarize the warrantless search precedents established by the *Randolph, Terry, Chimel, Riley, Carroll, Chambers, Quarles, King, Hester, Weeks,* and *Mapp* decisions.

The *Carroll* decision established that vehicles may be searched without a warrant if (1) there is probable cause for the search, and (2) the vehicle would be gone before a search warrant could be obtained.

After stopping a moving vehicle, if officers have probable cause, they may search the vehicle and any closed containers in it. It is worth noting that cell phones are *not* considered "containers" in the context of the vehicle exception and, therefore, may not be searched without a warrant (*United States v. Camou*, 2014). If probable cause does not exist, officers may be able to obtain voluntary consent to search the vehicle, including any closed containers (*Florida v. Jimeno*, 1991). The driver must be competent to give such consent, and silence is not consent. If at any time the driver rescinds consent, the search must cease.

Officers must also know their state's laws regarding full searches of vehicles pursuant to issuing a traffic citation, which may often seem contradictory. Although several states have statutes that authorize searches of vehicles following the issuance of a traffic citation, the policy in most states is to allow searches only after a driver has been arrested and is in custody. In *Knowles v. Iowa* (1998), the Supreme Court ruled that when an officer issues a citation instead of making an arrest, a full search of the driver's car violates the Fourth Amendment. The Court also made another point in *Knowles* when it ruled that a search incident to arrest can occur before the actual arrest, even if the crime of arrest is different from the crime for which probable cause first existed.

Pretext Stops. A **pretext stop** occurs when officers stop a vehicle for a relatively minor offense when the real motivation is to search for evidence of a more serious crime. In *Whren v. United States* (1996), plainclothes officers saw a truck wait at a stop sign for an unusually long time, turn suddenly without signaling, and then speed away. The officers pursued and stopped the vehicle. As they approached the truck, they saw the driver, Whren, holding bags of crack cocaine, and arrested him on federal drug charges. Whren argued that the police used the traffic stop as a pretext to uncover the drugs. The Court, however, held that as long as probable cause existed to believe a traffic violation occurred, stopping the motorist was reasonable: "Subjective intentions play no role in ordinary, probable-cause Fourth Amendment analysis."

An officer's ulterior motive for stopping a vehicle is not unconstitutional as long as legal justification exists for a valid traffic stop. In other words, any *pretext* is overridden by an officer's probable cause to believe the motorist is, or is about to be, engaged in criminal activity. Scarry (2007b, p. 86) notes, "State vehicle codes are written to provide law enforcement officers ample opportunity to establish probable cause to initiate a traffic stop when an individual is suspected of having committed, or about to commit, a crime other than the infraction of the vehicle code. They are invaluable tools."

Searches of Passengers in a Stopped Vehicle.

If there are passengers inside a private vehicle that is stopped, their rights may differ from those of the driver but they are all considered detained at the stop: "Passengers may be ordered out and kept from leaving. Passengers may be arrested for joint possession of contraband. And passengers' property and the vehicle may be searched incident to their arrest (passenger compartment), or with probable cause (any hiding place)" (Rutledge, 2007e, p. 71).

However, the Court has also ruled in *Wyoming v. Houghton* (1999) that an officer may search an automobile passenger's belongings simply because the officer suspects the driver has done something wrong. This "passenger property exception" ruling was intended to prevent drivers from claiming that illegal drugs or other contraband belonged to passengers, rather than themselves.

In *Brendlin v. California* (2007), the Supreme Court held that all passengers inside a vehicle during a traffic stop are "seized" just as the driver is. A logical outgrowth of this ruling followed in *Arizona v. Johnson* (2009), when the Court determined that an officer may frisk a passenger in a car that has been lawfully stopped for a traffic violation, if the officer has developed reasonable suspicion that the passenger is armed and dangerous.

Searches of Vehicles Incident to and Contemporaneous with Lawful Arrests. In *Thornton v. United States* (2004), the Supreme Court ruled that police can search the passenger compartment of a vehicle incident to arrest when the arrestee was approached after recently occupying that vehicle. However, officers must keep in mind the restrictions placed on vehicle searches via *Gant*—that the search of a vehicle incident to the driver's arrest is justified only when it is reasonable to believe evidence of the crime for which the driver was arrested will be found inside that vehicle.

Vehicle Inventory Searches. Unlike a search incidental to an arrest, a vehicle inventory search need not be made immediately.

> **LO4** Summarize the warrantless search precedents established by the *Randolph, Terry, Chimel, Riley, Carroll, Chambers, Quarles, King, Hester, Weeks,* and *Mapp* decisions.

Chambers v. Maroney (1970) established that a vehicle may be taken to headquarters to be searched for inventory purposes.

When police take custody of a vehicle (or other property), the courts have upheld their right to inventory such property for specific reasons:

- *To protect the owner's property.* This obligation may be legal or moral, but the courts have supported the police's responsibility to protect property taken into custody from unauthorized interference.

- *To protect the police from disputes and claims that the property was stolen or damaged.* Proper inventory at the time of custody provides an accurate record of the property's condition at the time it was seized.

- *To protect the police and the public from danger.* Custody of an automobile or a person subjects the police to conditions that require searching the person or the vehicle for objects such as bombs, chemicals, razor blades, and weapons that may harm the officers or the premises where the vehicle or person is taken.

- *To determine the owner's identity.* Identifying the owner may be associated with identifying the person under arrest, or it may help the police know to whom the property should be released.

The courts have held that each of these factors outweighs the privacy interests of property and therefore justifies an inventory search. The search must be reasonable.

To be correct in the inventory process, the police must show legal seizure and make a documented inventory according to the approved procedures established by department policy. Courts have emphasized that vehicle inventory searches are proper only if done following standardized procedures adopted by the law enforcement agency. In *United States v. Torres* (2016), a routine inventory search uncovered a handgun hidden inside the air filter compartment of the vehicle operated by Torres. The defense filed a motion to suppress the evidence, but the court concluded that the officer's search of the air filter compartment, as part of his duty to search "all containers" in accordance with police department policy, was appropriate. It was further held that the department's inventory search policy appeared reasonably designed to not only produce an inventory but to also ensure sufficient uniformity to protect the owners and occupants of impounded vehicles from the risk that officers would apply discretionary inventory searches only when they suspected such searches would uncover the fruits of criminal activity.

Although *inventory* and *search* are technically two different processes, in practice they may take place simultaneously. If property found during such an inventory is evidence of a crime, it is admissible in court. It is advisable, however, where a vehicle is no longer mobile or is in police custody, to obtain a search warrant so as not to jeopardize an otherwise perfectly valid case.

Vehicle Searches at Roadblocks and Checkpoints.

Roadblocks and checkpoints, while technically "seizures" because they involve an investigatory stop, are discussed here because their purpose also involves a search element. More than four decades ago, in *United States v. Martinez-Fuerte* (1976), the Supreme Court ruled that vehicle checkpoints at the country's borders were constitutional because they served a national interest and that this interest outweighed the checkpoint's minimal intrusion on driver privacy. In *Brown v. Texas* (1979), the Supreme Court created a *balancing test* (an evaluation of interests and factors) to determine the constitutionality of roadblocks. The *Brown* balancing test requires that courts evaluating the lawfulness of roadblocks consider three factors:

1. The gravity of the public concerns served by establishing the roadblock

2. The degree to which the roadblock is likely to succeed in serving the public interest

3. The severity with which the roadblock interferes with individual liberty

Michigan Department of State Police v. Sitz (1990) established that *sobriety checkpoints* to combat drunken driving

were reasonable under the *Brown* balancing test if they met certain guidelines. However, the Court ruled in *City of Indianapolis v. Edmond* (2000) that checkpoints for *drugs* are unconstitutional: "We cannot sanction stops justified only by the generalized and ever-present possibility that interrogation and inspection may reveal that any given motorist has committed some crime." Thus, vehicle checkpoints for general crime control are constitutionally unreasonable.

In *Illinois v. Lidster* (2004), the Court upheld the constitutionality of *informational checkpoints*. Justice Stephen Breyer explained, "The stop's primary law enforcement purpose was not to determine whether a vehicle's occupants were committing a crime, but to ask vehicle occupants, as members of the public, for their help in providing information about a crime in all likelihood committed by others. The police expected the information elicited to help them apprehend, not the vehicle's occupants, but other individuals."

This ruling was a victory for law enforcement. Another victory for law enforcement came in 2004 in *United States v. Flores-Montano*, in which the Supreme Court unanimously overturned a decision by a circuit court of appeals, ruling that privacy interests do not apply to vehicles crossing the border. Chief Justice William Rehnquist wrote, "Complex balancing tests to determine what is a 'routine' search of a vehicle ... have no place in border searches of vehicles. The government's interest in preventing the entry of unwanted persons and effects is at its zenith at the international border. Time and again, we have stated that searches made at the border ... are reasonable simply by virtue of the fact that they occur at the border."

Although the major cases governing warrantless searches of a vehicle have just been discussed, others may be encountered during an investigation. Table 4.1 summarizes the relevant court rulings related to vehicle searches.

Search When an Emergency or Exigent Circumstance Exists

In situations where police officers believe there is probable cause but have no time to secure a warrant—for example, if shots are being fired or a person is screaming—they may act on their own discretion. Imminent danger to public safety and medical emergencies are situations also classified as exigencies.

Most courts recognize certain conditions that must be met to support a warrantless entry under the **exigent circumstances** exception. For example, officers must believe a real emergency exists requiring immediate action to protect or preserve life or to prevent serious injury. Also, the emergency and the area entered or searched must have a connection.

TABLE 4.1 **Summary of Major Court Rulings Regarding Vehicle Searches**

Case Decision	Holding
Carroll v. United States (1925)	Automobiles may be searched without a warrant if (1) there is probable cause for the search and (2) the vehicle would be gone before a search warrant could be obtained.
Chambers v. Maroney (1970)	A vehicle may be taken to headquarters to be searched.
South Dakota v. Opperman (1976)	Warrantless routine inventory searches of automobiles impounded or otherwise in lawful police custody, pursuant to standard police procedures, are reasonable and not prohibited by the Fourth Amendment.
United States v. Ross (1982)	A search may be made when probable cause exists to believe that contraband or evidence is within the vehicle. This includes the trunk or closed containers in the vehicle.
Texas v. Brown (1983)	Contraband or evidence in plain view may be confiscated. Two conditions must exist: (1) the officer must be legally present and (2) there must be probable cause to believe that the object in plain view is contraband or the instrumentality of a crime.
Florida v. Wells (1990)	The contents of a lawfully impounded vehicle may be inventoried for purposes of property accountability, public safety and protection against later claims of damage or loss of property.
Florida v. Jimeno (1991)	A warrantless search may be made when consent is obtained from the owner or person in possession of the vehicle. The entire vehicle may be searched, including closed containers, unless the consenter has expressed limitation.
United States v. Ibarra (1991)	If there is no statutory authority to impound, the vehicle cannot be taken into custody legally; therefore, an inventory search under these circumstances would be inadmissible.
United States v. Bowhay (1993)	Because a department policy required officers to search everything, the officers had no discretion. Therefore, the presence of an investigative motive did not prohibit the inventory search.
Knowles v. Iowa (1998)	When an officer issues a citation instead of making an arrest, a full search of the driver's car violates the Fourth Amendment.
Wyoming v. Houghton (1999)	An officer may search an automobile passenger's belongings simply because the officer suspects the driver has done something wrong. This "passenger property exception" ruling was intended to prevent drivers from claiming that illegal drugs or other contraband belonged to passengers, rather than themselves.
Thornton v. United States (2004)	Police can search the passenger compartment of a vehicle incident to arrest when the arrestee was approached after recently occupying that vehicle.
Brendlin v. California (2007)	Officers must have a reasonable suspicion of criminal activity to stop a vehicle. If officers have no lawful basis for a traffic stop, anyone in the car—the driver or its passengers—may challenge the stop's constitutionality.
Arizona v. Gant (2009)	This case narrowed the previously allowed automatic searches of vehicles incident to the arrest of an occupant (*New York v. Belton*, 1981) to permit such a search only if the officer has a reasonable belief that the arrestee can gain access to the vehicle or that evidence of the crime of arrest will be found in the vehicle.
Arizona v. Johnson (2009)	During the course of a valid traffic stop, an officer may frisk a passenger if there is reasonable suspicion to believe the passenger is armed.
United States v. Jones (2012)	Attaching a GPS device to a vehicle is a search that requires a warrant.
Byrd v. United States (2018)	A driver in lawful possession of a rental car but who is not listed on the rental agreement retains a reasonable expectation of privacy under the Fourth Amendment.
Collins v. Virginia (2018)	The automobile exception does not allow for entry into a home or curtilage.
United States v. Camou (2018)	Cell phones located in vehicles are not "containers" and require a warrant to search.

In *Mincey v. Arizona* (1978), the Supreme Court stated that the Fourth Amendment does not require police officers to delay a search during an investigation if to do so would gravely endanger their lives or the lives of others. Once the danger has been eliminated, however, any further search should be conducted only after obtaining a search warrant.

In *Brigham City, Utah v. Stuart* (2006), the Supreme Court ruled that "law enforcement officers may enter a home without a warrant to render emergency assistance to an injured occupant or to protect an occupant from imminent injury," as occurred in this case, when officers entered a private home to stop a fight in progress and

LO4 Summarize the warrantless search precedents established by the *Randolph, Terry, Chimel, Riley, Carroll, Chambers, Quarles, King, Hester, Weeks,* and *Mapp* decisions.

A warrantless search in the absence of a lawful arrest or consent is justified only in emergencies or exigent circumstances where probable cause exists and the search must be conducted immediately (*New York v. Quarles*, 1984).

ended up making an arrest. The defendant argued that his conduct was not serious enough to justify the officers' intrusion into the home, and that evidence observed by officers should be suppressed as fruit of an illegal entry. The Supreme Court, however, disagreed and held the entry reasonable, noting "the role of a peace officer includes preventing violence and restoring order, not simply rendering first aid to casualties." The Court also stated, "Because the Fourth Amendment's ultimate touchstone is 'reasonableness,' the warrant requirement is subject to certain exceptions." Citing entry onto private property to fight a fire, or to engage in "hot pursuit" of a fleeing suspect, the Court held, "Thus the 'exigencies of the situation' may make the needs of law enforcement so compelling that a warrantless search is objectively reasonable under the Fourth Amendment."

In *Michigan v. Fisher* (2009), the Court further clarified when officers may enter a home under the exigent circumstances to the warrant requirement by specifically identifying the *emergency aid requirement*: "This 'emergency aid exception' does not depend on the officers' subjective intent or the seriousness of any crime they are investigating when the emergency arises. It requires only 'an objectively reasonable basis for believing' that 'a person within [the house] is in need of immediate aid'." This exception extends to suicidal persons and allows officers to make an immediate, warrantless entry to protect a person from him- or herself (Rutledge, 2010).

The imminent destruction of evidence as part of a narcotics investigation has been found to constitute an exigent circumstance in which warrantless entry into a residence is justified (*United States v. Iwai*, 2019). Although the district court ruled that the officers' warrantless entry into the defendant's home was presumptively unreasonable under the Fourth Amendment, consideration of the totality of the circumstances justified the entry because it was reasonable to conclude that the destruction of incriminating evidence was occurring.

One highly debated case that challenged warrantless search under exigent circumstances was *Kentucky v. King* (2011), which examined whether police are justified in entering and searching a structure if their actions had played a role in creating the exigency in the first place. In this case officers followed a suspected drug dealer to his apartment building but were just far enough behind as to not see which unit down a particular hallway the suspect entered. When the officers arrived at one doorway from which the smell of marijuana was coming, they knocked loudly and announced their presence. No one from inside the apartment opened the door, but officers immediately heard sounds from inside the apartment that they considered consistent with destroying evidence. Officers announced their intention to enter and then kicked in the door to investigate the situation. They found the suspect with others, and during a protective sweep of the apartment, observed drugs in plain view:

> In *King*, the Supreme Court recognized the danger in adopting a rule that would prevent the police from relying upon the exigent circumstances exception to prevent the destruction of evidence if their actions had played a role in creating the exigency. The Court noted that although a number of federal and state courts had considered this issue, they had employed multiple tests using different legal theories to decide such cases. In rejecting several of these tests due to their adoption of legal requirements that it characterized as "unsound," the Supreme Court reaffirmed the long-established legal principle that "warrantless searches are allowed when the circumstances make it reasonable, within the meaning of the Fourth Amendment, to dispense with the warrant requirement. (Pettry, 2012, p. 29)

LO4 Summarize the warrantless search precedents established by the *Randolph, Terry, Chimel, Riley, Carroll, Chambers, Quarles, King, Hester, Weeks,* and *Mapp* decisions.

The *King* decision established that officers may enter a home without a warrant in response to an emergency, which includes the imminent destruction of evidence, as long as the police, themselves, do not create the emergency through conduct that violates the Fourth Amendment.

Point-of-Entry Searches

Routine border searches of persons—citizens and noncitizens alike—and their personal belongings or vehicles can be made without probable cause, without a warrant, and without any articulable suspicion (*Boyd v. United States*, 1886; *Carroll v. United States*, 1925; *United States v. Ramsey*, 1977). Such searches are justified because they serve a compelling national security interest, namely stopping illegal immigrants and the flow of prohibited items into the country. The only limitation on a border search is the Fourth Amendment requirement that it be conducted reasonably. The *functional equivalent doctrine* establishes that routine border searches are constitutional at places other than actual borders where travelers frequently enter or leave the country, including international airports and shipping ports.

Plain-Sense Evidence

The limitations on searches are intended to protect the privacy rights of all citizens and to ensure due process of law. They are not intended to hamper investigations, nor do they preclude the use of evidence that is not concealed and is accidentally found through any of the officer's senses. The courts recognize that expecting officers to turn a blind eye to contraband or postpone acting on something they "sense" is illegal is unreasonable, essentially allowing that when officers have a legal right to be where they are, they have a right to see, hear, and smell—faculties that may be used to detect plain-sense evidence. The most common type of plain-sense evidence is that seen by an officer.

Plain-View Evidence. **Plain-view evidence** is unconcealed evidence that is seen by an officer engaged in a lawful activity. The plain-view doctrine permits the warrantless seizure of contraband or evidence of a crime, and allows its admissibility in court, provided the officers are legally allowed to be where they are. This doctrine puts few constraints on officers and often yields very productive results.

Although the Fourth Amendment prohibits unreasonable intrusions into a person's privacy, the precedent for plain-view evidence was established in *Katz v. United States* (1967) when the Supreme Court held, "The Fourth Amendment protects people, not *places*. What a person knowingly exposes to the public, even in his own home or office, is not a subject of Fourth Amendment protection." In both *Michigan v. Tyler* (1978) and *Mincey v. Arizona* (1978), the Court ruled that while officers are on the premises pursuing their legitimate emergency activities, any evidence in plain view may be seized.

Containers can be opened if their outward appearance reveals criminal contents, for example, a kit of burglar tools or a gun case (Rutledge, 2007c). By their nature, they do not support a reasonable expectation of privacy because their contents can be inferred from their appearance.

An officer cannot obtain a warrant and fail to mention a particular object and then use "plain view" to justify its seizure. If the officer is looking for it initially, it must be mentioned in the warrant. Plain-view evidence

itself is not sufficient to justify a warrantless seizure of evidence; probable cause must also exist.

Officers may seize any contraband they discover during a legal search. In *Boyd v. United States* (1886), Justice Joseph Bradley stated, "The search for and seizure of stolen or forfeited goods or goods liable to duties and concealed to avoid payment thereof, are totally different things from a search or a seizure of a man's private books and papers. In one case the government is entitled to the property, and in the other it is not."

Plain Feel/Touch. The "plain feel/touch" exception is an extension of the plain-view exception. If a police officer lawfully pats down a suspect's outer clothing and feels an object that he *immediately* identifies as contraband—in other words, **plain feel/touch evidence**—a warrantless seizure is justified because there is no invasion of the suspect's privacy beyond that already authorized by the officer's search for weapons (*Minnesota v. Dickerson*, 1993).

Plain Smell. Evidence may also be seized if an officer relies on a sense other than sight or touch. For example, a customs officer who smells marijuana coming from a package has probable cause to make an arrest under a "plain-smell" rationale (*United States v. Lueck*, 1982). Some odors, such as gasoline, are easily detectable to officers investigating an arson, while other odors are commonly detected by trained K-9s. "Merely smelling the air surrounding a suspect, his vehicle or some container does not constitute a search. If the odor reveals the presence of seizable objects, they may be seized" (Rutledge, 2007c, p. 71).

Plain Hearing. Officers or undercover agents can position themselves in accessible locations where they can overhear criminal conversation without any extraordinary listening devices (e.g., wiretaps or parabolic microphones). Anything overheard can be used as evidence.

Open Fields, Abandoned Property, and Public Places

Just as when a suspect reveals incriminating evidence by exposing it to an officer's senses, a search is considered justified and legal when a suspect casts off any expectation of privacy, such as leaving contraband exposed and untended in a public place. While it may seem to be a natural extension of the plain-view doctrine, the courts have tended to approach this area from a privacy perspective, ruling that anything held out to the public is not protected by the Fourth Amendment because no reasonable expectation of privacy or physical trespass exists.

LO4   Summarize the warrantless search precedents established by the *Randolph, Terry, Chimel, Riley, Carroll, Chambers, Quarles, King, Hester, Weeks,* and *Mapp* decisions.

The precedent case for search and seizure of abandoned property and open fields is *Hester v. United States* (1924), in which the Court held that "The special protection accorded by the Fourth Amendment to the people in their 'persons, houses, papers and effects,' is not extended to the open fields." This exception includes property disposed of in such a manner as to relinquish ordinary property rights.

Trash and garbage cans in alleys and on public sidewalks are often the depository for evidence of thefts, drug possession, and even homicides. In *California v. Greenwood* (1988), the Supreme Court ruled that containers left on public property are open to search by police without a warrant and that such a search does not constitute a violation of the Fourth Amendment or a reasonable expectation of privacy: "It is common knowledge that plastic garbage bags left on a public street are readily accessible to animals, children, scavengers, snoops and other members of the public," and therefore "no reasonable expectation of privacy" is violated by such a search. Searches of trash may also extend to the local landfill.

Trash pulls can yield valuable incriminating evidence that investigators may use to obtain a search warrant of a home. However, a single trash pull is rarely sufficient to justify a legally valid search warrant. Furthermore, "When applying for a search warrant based on a trash pull, investigators must establish probable cause that two separate elements exist: (1) that a crime has been committed and (2) that relevant evidence is likely located at the place to be searched" (Sanchez & Rubin, 2010, p. 12).

The most important factor in determining the legality of a warrantless trash inspection is the physical location of the retrieved trash. Police cannot trespass to gain access to the trash location, and, generally, the trash must not be located within the **curtilage**, which the Supreme Court has described as "the area to which extends the intimate activity associated with the sanctity of a man's home and the privacies of life." In other words, curtilage is that portion of a residence that is not open to the public. It is reserved for private owner or family use, and an expectation of privacy exists.

To more fully understand the profound privacy protections that attach to curtilage, consider *Collins v. Virginia* (2018). In this case, a community had been experiencing a string of traffic incidents involving an orange and black motorcycle with an extended frame. Investigators discovered that the motorcycle was likely stolen and in possession of Collins. A search on social media revealed photos of a similar motorcycle parked in Collins's driveway.

An officer went to Collins's residence and could see, from the street, what looked like a motorcycle under a tarp. Justifying his warrantless search as being based on the automobile exception and the potential mobility of the bike, the officer walked up the driveway, removed the tarp, ran the license plate and vehicle identification numbers, and confirmed that the motorcycle was, in fact, stolen. The officer replaced the tarp and returned to his squad to wait. When Collins returned, the officer arrested him.

The case escalated to the Virginia Supreme Court, which affirmed the lower courts' denials of a motion to suppress, citing the Fourth Amendment's automobile exception. The U.S. Supreme Court, however, reversed, holding that the automobile exception does not permit the warrantless entry of a home or its curtilage to search a vehicle therein. The scope of the automobile exception extends no further than the vehicle itself, and when an officer physically intrudes on the curtilage to gather evidence, a Fourth Amendment search has occurred and is presumptively unreasonable absent a warrant. The part of the driveway where the motorcycle was parked is curtilage.

The protections afforded to curtilage stand in stark contrast to sidewalks and alleys, which are used by the public. In *United States v. Dunn* (1987), the Court ruled, "We believe that curtilage questions should be resolved with particular reference to four factors: the proximity of the area claimed to be curtilage to the home, whether the area is included within an enclosure surrounding the home, the nature of the uses to which the area is put and the steps taken by the resident to protect the area from observation by people passing by."

Although trash or garbage containers within the curtilage of private property are generally considered off-limits to warrantless searches, the courts have allowed the warrantless seizure of trash from within the curtilage for very fact-specific instances (*United States v. Segura-Baltazar*, 2006). However, it remains prudent for investigators to consult with their agency's legal advisors or the local prosecutor before seizing trash from within a home's curtilage (Sanchez & Rubin, 2010).

Laws regulating how and when searches may be legally conducted are numerous and complex. It is critical that officers responsible for criminal investigations know these laws and operate within them. The penalty for not doing so is extreme—no evidence obtained during an illegal search will be allowed at a trial, as established by the exclusionary rule.

The Exclusionary Rule

Through the **exclusionary rule**, the courts enforce the prohibition against unreasonable searches set forth in the Fourth Amendment. In the early 1900s the federal courts declared that they would require evidence to be obtained in compliance with the constitutional standards set forth in the Fourth Amendment.

> **LO4/LO5** Understand what the exclusionary rule is, how it affects investigators, and which cases made it applicable at the federal and state levels.

> The exclusionary rule established that courts may not accept evidence obtained by unreasonable search and seizure, regardless of its relevance to a case. *Weeks v. United States* (1914) made the rule applicable at the federal level; *Mapp v. Ohio* (1961) made it applicable to *all* courts.

The exclusionary rule affects illegally seized evidence as well as evidence obtained as a result of the illegally seized evidence, referred to as *fruit of the poisonous tree*. The **"fruit-of-the-poisonous-tree" doctrine** established that evidence obtained as a result of an earlier illegality must be excluded from trial. The exclusionary rule may seem to favor criminals at the expense of law enforcement, but this was not the Court's intent. The Court recognized that important exceptions to this rule might occur. Four of the more important exceptions to the exclusionary rule are the inevitable discovery doctrine, the good faith doctrine, the independent source doctrine, and the attenuation doctrine.

The Inevitable Discovery Exception

In *Nix v. Williams* (1984), a defendant's right to counsel under the Sixth Amendment was violated, resulting in his making incriminating statements and leading the police to the body of his murder victim. Searchers who had been conducting an extensive, systematic search of the area then terminated their search. If the search had continued, the Court reasoned, the search party would inevitably have discovered the victim's body. The **inevitable discovery doctrine** established that if illegally obtained evidence would in all likelihood eventually have been discovered legally, it may be used.

The intent of the exclusionary rule, the Court said, was to deter police from violating citizens' constitutional rights. In the majority opinion, Chief Justice Warren E. Burger wrote, "Exclusion of physical evidence that would inevitably have been discovered adds nothing to either the integrity or fairness of a criminal trial."

The Good Faith Exception

In *United States v. Leon* (1984), police in Burbank, California, were investigating a drug trafficking operation and, following up on a tip from an unreliable informant, applied for and were issued an apparently valid search warrant. Their searches revealed large quantities of drugs and other evidence at various locations. The defendants challenged the sufficiency of the warrant and moved to suppress the evidence seized on the basis of the search warrant.

The district court held that the affidavit was insufficient to establish probable cause because of the informant's unreliability. The U.S. Court of Appeals affirmed the district court's action. Then the U.S. Supreme Court reviewed whether the exclusionary rule should be modified to allow the admission of evidence seized in *reasonably good faith*. The Court noted that the exclusionary rule is a *judicially created remedy* intended to serve as a deterrent rather than a guaranteed constitutional right. The **good faith doctrine** established that illegally obtained evidence may be admissible if the police were truly not aware they were violating a suspect's Fourth Amendment rights.

A decade later in *Arizona v. Evans* (1995), the Court reaffirmed the good faith exception, noting that the exclusionary rule does not require suppression of evidence seized in violation of the Fourth Amendment where the clerical errors of court employees caused officers to act on erroneous information. Scarry (2007a, p. 76) notes, "Courts know police officers can and will make reasonable mistakes. It's simply the nature of the job." Rutledge (2007a, p. 71) contends, "Objectively reasonable good faith may prevent suppression and liability in these kinds of cases: search warrants, misidentification, invalid statutes, arrest warrants and consent."

The Independent Source Doctrine

Another exception to the exclusionary rule arises when evidence that is first obtained during an unlawful search or seizure is later obtained through another (independent) constitutionally valid search or seizure. The rationale behind this exception is similar to that of the inevitable discovery doctrine in that if a second, lawful search can reveal the same evidence that the initial, illegal search did, there is no reason to exclude the evidence. Thus the **independent source doctrine** allows the admission of evidence initially discovered during an unlawful search if officers were later able to acquire the same evidence from a separate, wholly independent source, such as the execution of a valid search warrant (*Murray v. United States*, 1988).

The Attenuation Doctrine

Like the inevitable discovery doctrine and the independent source doctrine, the attenuation doctrine involves a causal relationship between the unconstitutional act and the discovery of evidence. One case that illustrates this exclusionary rule exception is *Utah v. Strieff* (2016), in which an officer made an illegal traffic stop of Strieff but then discovered during the stop that Strieff was subject to an outstanding, valid arrest warrant. The officer arrested Strieff and, during a search incident to that arrest, found incriminating evidence. Strieff sought to suppress the evidence as a product of an illegal stop, but the U.S. Supreme Court ruled that the evidence seized as part of the search incident to the arrest was admissible under the Fourth Amendment because the officer's discovery of the arrest warrant attenuated the connection between the unlawful stop and the evidence seized incident to arrest. In other words, no flagrant police misconduct led to the discovery of the evidence. Thus the **attenuation doctrine** allows for the admission of evidence when the connection between unconstitutional police conduct and the evidence is remote or has been interrupted (attenuated) by some intervening circumstance, so that the interest protected by the constitutional guarantee that has been violated would not be served by suppression of the evidence obtained.

Conducting Investigatory Searches

Having looked at the legal restrictions on searching, now consider how investigatory searches are actually conducted, beginning with the search of a crime scene.

The Crime Scene Search

A basic function of investigators is to conduct a thorough, legal search at the scene of a crime. Even though not initially visible, evidence in some form is present at most crime scenes. Although each crime scene is unique, certain general guidelines apply. The goal of any search during an investigation, at the crime scene or elsewhere, is to discover evidence that helps

- Establish that a crime *was* committed and *what* the specific crime was
- Establish *when* the crime was committed
- Confirm *where* the crime was committed (e.g., in a homicide, the crime may not have occurred where the body was found)
- Identify *who* committed the crime
- Explain *how* the crime was committed
- Suggest *why* the crime was committed

A successful crime scene search locates, identifies, and preserves all evidence present. Evidence found at a scene assists in re-creating a crime in much the same way that bricks, properly placed, result in constructing a building. A meticulous, properly conducted search usually results in the discovery of evidence. The security measures taken by the first officer at the scene determine whether evidence is discovered intact or after it has been altered or destroyed. During a search, do not change or contaminate physical evidence in any way, or it will be declared inadmissible. Maintain the chain of custody of evidence from the initial discovery to the time of the trial as discussed in the next chapter.

Organizing the Crime Scene Search. After emergencies have been attended to, the scene has been secured, witnesses have been located and separated for interviewing, and photographing and sketching have been completed, a search plan must be formulated. Also, a search headquarters needs to be established away from the scene to prevent destruction of evidence.

Organizing a search includes dividing the duties, selecting a search pattern, assigning personnel and equipment, and giving instructions. Proper organization results in a thorough search with no accidental destruction of evidence. However, even the best organized search may not yield evidence. Evidence may have been destroyed before the search or removed by the criminal. In a few rare instances, evidence is simply nonexistent.

In a single-investigator search, one officer conducts the physical search and describes, identifies, and preserves the evidence found. If two or more officers conduct the search, the highest-ranking officer on the scene usually assumes command. In accordance with department policy, the officer in charge assigns personnel based on their training. For example, if one officer has specialized training in photography, another in sketching, and a third in fingerprinting, they are assigned to their respective specialties. Someone is assigned to each function required in the search. Often two officers are assigned to take measurements to ensure accuracy. These same two officers can collect, identify, and preserve evidence as it is found. Evidence should never be removed from the scene without the search leader's permission.

The search leader also determines the number of personnel needed, the type of search best suited for the area, and the items most likely to be found. Personnel are assigned according to the selected search pattern. Search party members are given all known details of the crime and instructed on the type of evidence to seek and the members' specific responsibilities.

The search leader also determines whether anyone other than the person who committed the crime has entered the scene. If so, the person is asked to explain in detail any contacts with the scene that might have contaminated evidence. If no one has entered the scene between the time the crime was committed and when the police arrived, and if the scene was immediately secured, the scene is considered to be a **true**, or **uncontaminated, scene**; that is, no evidence has been introduced into it or taken from it except by the person or persons who committed the crime.

Physical Evidence. Knowing what to search for is indispensable to an effective crime scene search. *Physical evidence* is anything material and relevant to the crime being investigated. Physical evidence ranges in size from very large objects to minute substances. Understanding what types of evidence can be found at various types of crime scenes is important to the search. Not everything found at a scene is evidence. The elements of the crime help determine what will be useful as evidence. For example, a burglary requires an illegal entry; therefore, tool marks and broken glass in a door or window are evidence that help prove burglary.

A forcible rape requires a sexual act against a victim's will. Therefore, bruises, semen stains, or witnesses hearing screams would help establish evidence of that crime. Specific types of evidence to seek are discussed in Chapter 5 and throughout Sections 3, 4, and 5.

Besides knowing what types of evidence to search for, investigators must know where evidence is most likely to be found. For example, evidence is often found on or near the route used to and from a crime. A suspect may drop items used to commit a crime or leave shoe or tire prints. Evidence is also frequently found on or near a dead body.

The **"elephant-in-a-matchbox" doctrine** requires that searchers consider the probable size and shape of evidence they seek because, for example, large objects cannot be concealed in tiny areas. Ignoring this doctrine can result in a search that wastes resources, destroys potential evidence, and leaves a place in shambles. It may also result in violating the Fourth Amendment requirements on reasonable searches.

Search Patterns. All search patterns have a common denominator: they are designed to locate systematically any evidence at a crime scene or any other area where evidence might be found. Most patterns involve partitioning search areas into workable sizes. The search pattern should be adapted to the area involved, the personnel available, the time limits imposed by weather and light conditions, and the circumstances of the individual crime scene. Search patterns ensure thoroughness.

Exterior Searches. Exterior searches can cover small, large, or vast areas. Regardless of the dimensions, the area to be searched can be divided into subareas and diagrammed on paper. As each area is searched, check it off. Be certain sufficient light is available. A search conducted with inadequate light can destroy more evidence than it yields. If weather conditions are favorable, delay nighttime searches until daylight if feasible. If it is not feasible to wait for daylight, get spot lights. Most fire departments have large spot lights if the local police do not.

L06	Diagram the different types of exterior search patterns commonly used at crime scenes.

Exterior search patterns divide an area into lanes, strips, concentric circles, or zones.

The *lane-search pattern* partitions the area into lanes, or narrow strips, using stakes and string, as illustrated in Figure 4.3. An officer is assigned to each lane. Therefore, the number of lanes used depends on the number of officers available to search. These lanes can be imaginary. Officers' search widths vary from arm's length to shoulder-to-shoulder, either on foot or on their knees. Such searches use no string or cord to mark the lanes.

If only one officer is available for the search, the lane pattern can be adapted to what is commonly called the *strip-search pattern*, illustrated in Figure 4.4. For an extensive search, the lane pattern is often modified to form a grid, and the area is crisscrossed, as illustrated in Figure 4.5.

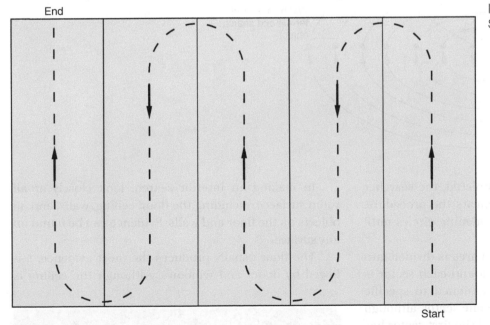

Figure 4.3
Lane-search pattern.

Figure 4.4
Strip-search pattern.

Another commonly used pattern is the *circle search*, which begins at the center of an area to be searched and spreads out in ever-widening concentric circles (Figure 4.6). A wooden stake with a long rope is driven into the ground at the center of the area to be searched. Knots are tied in the rope at selected regular intervals. The searcher circles around the stake in the area delineated by the first knot, searching the area within the

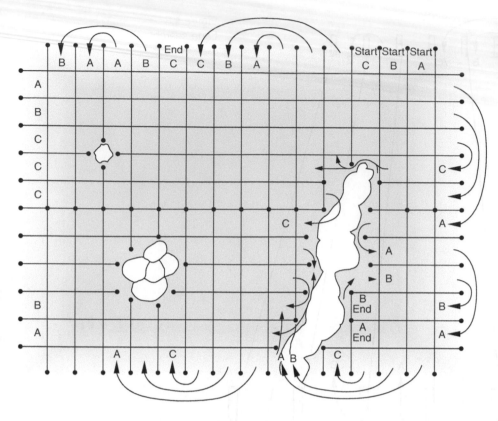

Figure 4.5
Grid-search pattern.

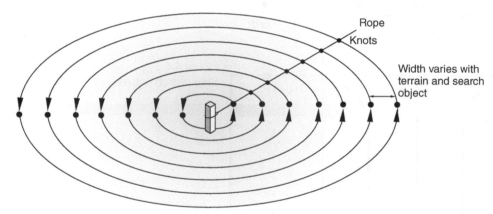

Figure 4.6
Circle-search pattern.

first circle. When this area is completed, the searcher moves to the second knot and repeats the procedure. The search is continued in ever-widening circles until the entire area is covered.

In the *zone* or sector search, an area is divided into equal sectors on a map of the area and each sector is identified. Search personnel are assigned to specific sectors and may search more than one sector, although personnel should not move on until the first sector has been thoroughly searched (Figure 4.7).

Interior Searches. Most searches are interior searches. The foregoing exterior search patterns can be adapted to an interior crime scene. Of prime concern is to search thoroughly without destroying evidence.

In making an interior search, look closely at all room surfaces, including the floor, ceiling, walls, and all objects on the floor and walls. Evidence can be found on any surface.

The floor usually produces the most evidence, followed by doors and windows. Although the ceiling is

L07 Explain how interior crime scene searches are typically conducted.

Interior searches go from the general to the specific, usually in a circular pattern, covering all surfaces of a search area. The floor should be searched first.

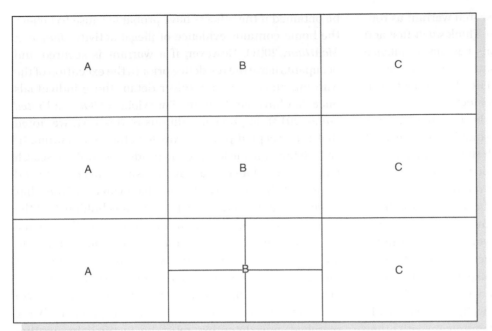

Figure 4.7
Zone- or sector-search pattern.

often missed in a search, it too can contain evidence such as stains or bullet holes. It can even contain such unlikely evidence as footprints. Footprints were found on the ceiling by an alert officer during a bank burglary investigation. Paperhangers had left wallpaper on the bank's floor during the night and had hung it on the ceiling early the next morning before the burglary was discovered. During the night, one burglar had stepped on the wallpaper, leaving a footprint that was transferred in a faint outline to the paper later placed on the ceiling.

An interior room search usually starts at the point of entry. The floor is searched first so no evidence is inadvertently destroyed during the remainder of the search. The lane- or zone-search patterns are adaptable to an interior floor search.

After the floor search, the walls—including doors and windows—and then the ceiling are searched, normally using a clockwise or counterclockwise pattern around the room. Because doors and windows are points of entry and exit, soil, fingerprints, glass fragments, and other evidence are often found there. Walls may contain marks, bloodstains, or trace evidence such as hairs or fibers.

After a room is searched in one direction, it is often searched in the opposite direction because lighting is different from different angles. The same general procedures are followed in searching closets, halls, or other rooms off the main room. The search is coordinated, and the location of all evidence is communicated to members of the search team.

General Guidelines. The precise search pattern used is immaterial as long as the search is systematic and covers the entire area. Assigning two officers to search the same area greatly increases the probability of discovering evidence. Finding evidence is no reason to stop a search. Continue searching until the entire area is covered. Schonely (2007, p. 60) notes, "Many officers search like it is a race and they are being timed to complete the task. These officers will miss many suspects over their careers. . . . Slowing down and being patient will allow your senses to work as you complete the search."

Building Searches

When executing a warrant to search a building, officers should first familiarize themselves with the location and the past record of the person living there. Check records for any previous police actions at that location. Decide on the least dangerous time of day for the suspect, the police, and the neighborhood. For example, the time of day when children come home from school would not be a good time to execute a high-risk warrant.

All officers who will be executing the warrant should meet to discuss a plan of action, including which positions they are all responsible for and how they should each approach. All available resources should be accessed during this planning stage, such as Google Maps or real estate information, to gain a thorough understanding of the targeted property's layout.

Do not treat the execution of a search warrant as routine. Plan for the worst-case scenario. Think *safety* first and last. In any high-risk warrant situations, have an ambulance on standby and near the area. For some warrants, the fire department may also be needed. Fire departments can often assist with safe entries and other locks.

Arrive safely. Turn off your vehicle's headlights, dome light, and brake lights (often times squad cars have a cut out switch for this) as you approach the building, as well as anything that may illuminate your location, such as the mobile data terminal (MDT) computer screen inside the squad. Once outside the squad car, stay away from other lights and use any available cover as you approach the building. Also consider radio volume, as the noise can notify suspects of police presence if radio volume is turned on high. Officers will often use ear microphones to keep radio noise minimized or will notify dispatch of entry times to avoid immediate welfare checks while positioning. Use hand signals to communicate with other officers at the scene.

Before entering the building, secure the outside perimeter and as many exits as possible—at a minimum, the front and rear doors. If possible, call for a backup before entering and search with a partner. Use extreme caution in the "fatal funnel," that zone that exists through a doorway, where officers are most vulnerable to attack by a suspect. Move through the fatal funnel rapidly and then, once clear, slow down to perform the search operations. Once inside the structure, wait for your vision to adjust to interior light conditions.

Keep light and weapons away from your body. Go quickly through doors into dark areas. When moving around objects, take quick peeks before proceeding. Avoid windows. Use light and cover to your advantage. Know where you are at all times and how to get back to where you were. Look for exits. If the entire building is to be searched, use a systematic approach. Secure each area as it is searched.

Sometimes when police search a suspect's home under authority of a search warrant, several people may be present, perhaps outnumbering the officers on the scene, creating problems of safety and control. Guidelines for this situation were established in *Michigan v. Summers* (1981) when the Supreme Court stated, "We hold that a warrant to search for contraband founded on probable cause carries with it the limited authority to detain the occupants of the premises while a proper search is conducted." The Court did not specify whether detained individuals could be handcuffed or for how long they could be detained.

Law enforcement officers may also require residents to remain outside their home until a search warrant can be obtained if the officers have probable cause to believe the home contains evidence of illegal activity (*Illinois v. McArthur*, 2001). However, if a warrant is secured and occupants leave the residence prior to the execution of the warrant, officers can no longer detain those individuals once they have left the immediate vicinity (*Bailey v. United States*, 2013). In previous editions of this text, we noted that the accepted practice was for officers to automatically detain anyone leaving the residence until the search had been concluded as a way to ensure officer safety and to protect the integrity of moveable evidence. *Bailey* has since altered this practice, with the Court holding that the rule from *Michigan v. Summers* no longer applies when a recent occupant of the premises is no longer immediately outside of the property being searched. The Court further noted that while arrests incident to the execution of a search warrant remain permissible under the Fourth Amendment, once a person leaves the premises being searched, any detention must be justified by another lawful means.

Vehicle Searches

Cars, aircraft, boats, motorcycles, buses, trucks, and vans can contain evidence of a crime. Again, the type of crime determines the area to be searched and the evidence to be sought. In a hit-and-run accident, the car's undercarriage can have hairs and fibers or the interior may reveal a hidden liquor bottle. In narcotics arrests, various types of drugs are often found in cars, planes, and boats. An ordinary vehicle has hundreds of places to hide drugs. In some cases, vehicles may have specially constructed compartments.

As with other types of searches, a vehicle search must be systematic and thorough. Evidence is more likely to be found if two officers conduct the search. First, remove all occupants from the car. Next, the vehicle should be thoroughly photographed, inside and out, before searching. Also remember to photograph all items of tangible (nonfiber) evidence as they are located during the search before moving them.

Begin the actual search outside, in the area surrounding the vehicle, for evidence related to the crime. Next, examine the vehicle's exterior for fingerprints, dents, scratches, or hairs and fibers. Examine the grill, front bumper, fender areas, and license plates. Open the hood and check the numerous recesses of the motor, radiator, battery, battery case, engine block, clutch and starter housings, ventilating ducts, air filter, body frame, and supports. Open the trunk and examine any clothing, rags, containers, tools, the spare tire well, and the trunk lid's interior.

A thorough search of a vehicle is needed to locate drugs or other contraband and evidence. Officers should take precautions to protect themselves while avoiding contamination of the scene.
Slava Dumchev/Shutterstock.com

Finally, search the vehicle's interior. If the vehicle search is to include hairs or fibers, vacuum the car before getting into it. Use a clean vacuum collection bag for each compartment of the vehicle; label and submit each collection package separately. Note that this step need not be performed on all vehicle searches. For example, if an investigator is looking for documents of a crime, stolen property, or narcotics, there would be no need to vacuum. Once vacuuming is completed (if warranted), continue searching the interior of the vehicle systematically, proceeding along one side from front to back and then returning along the other side from back to front. Examine ashtrays, the glove compartment, areas under the seats, and the window areas. Remove the seats and vacuum the floor. Hairs and fibers or traces of soil may be discovered that will connect a suspect with soil samples from the crime scene.

Use a flashlight and a mirror to examine the area behind the dashboard. Feeling by hand is not effective because of the numerous wires located there. Look for fingerprints in the obvious places: window and door handles, underside of the steering wheel, radio buttons, ashtrays, distributor cap, jack, rearview mirror, hood latches, and seat adjustment levers. Figure 4.8 illustrates the areas of vehicles that should be searched. The vehicle is divided into specific search areas to ensure order and thoroughness.

As in any other search, take precautions to prevent contaminating evidence. Be alert to what is an original part of the vehicle and what has been added. For example, compartments for concealing illegal drugs or other contraband are sometimes added. The systems and equipment of the vehicle should be validated. Is the exhaust real or phony? Check recesses and cup holders for hidden flip panels that may contain contraband or weapons. Check the headliner. In convertibles, check the boot.

Some officers use a wheeled platform that has dual periscopic mirrors and fluorescent lights and rolls easily under a vehicle, allowing them to view its underside. A handheld model is also available, allowing viewing of vehicle interiors, engine compartments, and tops of high-profile vehicles.

Suspect Searches

How a suspect should be searched depends on whether an arrest has been made. If you have reasonable suspicion to stop or probable cause to arrest a person, be cautious. Many officers are injured or killed because they fail to search a suspect. If a suspect is in a car, have him or her step out of the car, and be careful to protect yourself from a suddenly opened door.

Before conducting any search, ask the suspect if he or she has anything on them that could injure the officer, asking specifically about needles and blades. When possible, search a suspect while a cover officer observes. If arresting the suspect, first handcuff and then search. Every search should be done wearing protective gloves.

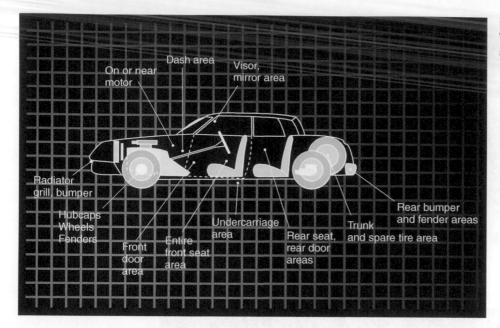

Figure 4.8
Vehicle areas that should be searched.

On or near motor

Dash area

Visor, mirror area

Radiator grill, bumper

Hubcaps Wheels Fenders

Front door area

Entire front seat area

Undercarriage area

Rear seat, rear door areas

Trunk and spare tire area

Rear bumper and fender areas

LO8 Compare how a search of an arrested suspect differs from a search of a suspect who has not been arrested.

If the suspect has not been arrested, confine your search to a patdown or frisk for weapons. If the suspect has been arrested, make a complete body search for weapons and evidence. In either event, always be on your guard.

If you arrest a suspect, conduct a complete body search for both weapons and evidence. Whether you use an against-the-wall spread-eagle search or a simple stand-up search, follow a methodical, exact procedure as determined by department policy. Regardless of whether an arrest has been made, respect the suspect's dignity while conducting the patdown or search, but keep your guard up.

Strip searches may be conducted only after an arrest and when the prisoner is in a secure facility. Such searches should be conducted in private by individuals of the same gender as the suspect and should follow written guidelines. Considerations in deciding when a strip search is necessary include the individual's past behavior, the possibility the person is concealing dangerous drugs or weapons, whether the person will be alone or with others in a cell, and how long the person will be in custody. Cavity searches go beyond the normal strip search and must follow very strict departmental guidelines.

Normally such searches should be conducted only by medical personnel and only under a court order.

A variety of factors may inhibit an officer's ability or desire to conduct a thorough search of a suspect. The presence of bodily fluids is one factor that may interfere with a complete search. The threat of contracting an infectious disease in the line of duty has led police to consider using special equipment when searching suspects. Goggles or face masks are pieces of equipment that reduce personal contact with blood and other body fluids, the main carriers of pathogens. Officers must also be alert to suspects who may spit on or bite them.

Another inhibitor to thorough searches is a concern over being accidentally poked by something sharp. When searching, officers should avoid putting their hands into suspects' pockets. They should use patting, rather than grabbing, motions to avoid being stuck by sharp objects such as hypodermic needles. Techniques for collecting evidence that may be contaminated with infectious disease material are discussed in the next chapter.

Weather can be another factor that compromises the thoroughness of a search. Driving rains, freezing or sweltering temperatures, blowing snow—all may entice an officer to hurry through a search. Weather may also complicate a suspect search because in colder climates, winter weather usually leads people to put on more layers of clothing. Street people and the homeless often wear several layers, which officers must carefully search through.

Dead Body Searches

Searching a dead body should be done only *after* the coroner or medical examiner has arrived or given permission. In one case, a well-meaning officer turned a body over to search for identification before the medical examiner arrived. This caused major problems in documenting the body's position.

Searching a dead body is unpleasant, even when the person has died recently. It is extremely unpleasant if the person has been dead for a long period. In some such cases, the body can be searched only in the coroner's examination room, where effective exhaust ventilation is available.

As with any other type of search, search of a dead body must be systematic and complete. It must also include the immediate area around and under the body. The search usually begins with the clothing, which is likely to reveal a wallet or personal identification papers as well as trace evidence. If the body is not fingerprinted at the scene, tie paper bags securely on the hands so that fingerprinting can be done at the coroner's laboratory. If possible, place the body in a body bag to ensure that no physical evidence is lost while it is being transported.

Search the area around and beneath where the body lay immediately after it is removed. A bullet may have passed through part of the body and lodged in the floor or the dirt beneath it. Trace evidence may have fallen from the body or clothing as the body was removed. Inventory and describe all items removed from the deceased. If there are bugs that are near or flying around the body, try to collect and preserve them, as such evidence can provide valuable information to an entomologist (e.g., the bug and its larvae can help determine the time and place of death). Forensic entomology is discussed further in Chapter 8.

Department policy determines the extent of a search at the scene. Normally a complete examination is delayed until the body is received by the coroner's office. The coroner may take fingernail scrapings, blood, and semen samples and possibly some body organs to establish poisoning or the path of a bullet or knife.

Once the body is taken to a funeral home, its organs and fluids will be contaminated by burial preparation. After the body is buried, it is a long, difficult legal process to exhume it for further examination. If the body is cremated, obviously no further examination is possible.

Underwater Searches

Underwater searches might involve victim, aircraft, firearm, or vehicle recovery. Underwater searches are affected by limited visibility, extreme water temperature, swift currents, and hazardous materials. When a victim is located, the first concern is whether it is a crime scene or an accident scene. The normal body position of a drowning victim is face down and in a semi-fetal position. If a victim found underwater has straight limbs and closed fists, this indicates the person may have been killed on land and rigor mortis had set in before the body was submerged.

Metal detectors are needed in most underwater searches—particularly pulse induction metal detectors, which are known for their deep-seeking capabilities. Advances in the technology have reduced power requirements, resulting in longer battery life and decreased weight.

Use of Dogs in a Search

Canines (K-9s) are a valuable force multiplier for law enforcement and can be trained to detect drugs and other chemicals, explosive devices, weapons, accelerants and igniters (in arson investigations), money, and cadavers. A keen sense of smell enables a dog to complete a building search in 10 minutes when it would otherwise take two or three officers an hour to conduct the same search. Dogs can track and capture suspects and are ideally suited to assist in searching large areas; areas with poor visibility, such as warehouses that may contain thousands of items; or any area with numerous hiding places. In addition, using dogs for such purposes lessens the physical risk to investigating officers.

The use of dogs to sniff out narcotics has been widely publicized. Because narcotics can be concealed in so many different ways, using dogs to locate them has greatly assisted law enforcement officers. Attempts to mask drug odors from dogs trained to sniff out drugs are futile because dogs can smell more than one odor simultaneously.

In *Illinois v. Caballes* (2005), the Supreme Court confirmed that a dog sniff was not a search under the Fourth Amendment, a ruling that reinforced law enforcement's ability to identify drug traffickers and users by using police K-9s in walk-around searches of vehicles stopped for traffic offenses. If, however, use of a drug-sniffing K-9 prolongs a stop, the dog sniff may become an illegal search. More recently, the Supreme Court unanimously held that a drug-detection K-9's alert to a vehicle's exterior can provide probable cause for an officer to perform a warrantless search of the vehicle's interior (*Florida v. Harris*, 2013).

In another K-9 search case, a divided Court ruled 5-4 in *Florida v. Jardines* (2013) that bringing a drug-sniffing dog onto the front porch of a home *does* constitute a search under the Fourth Amendment and, as such, requires a warrant. In this case, officers received a tip that Jardines was growing marijuana in his house. As two detectives and a trained narcotics detection K-9 stepped onto the porch and approached the front door, the dog alerted to the presence of drugs. The detectives used the dog's signal as probable cause to obtain and execute a search warrant, and Jardines was arrested and charged with trafficking cannabis. Jardines challenged that the dog's sniff on his porch was an illegal search and that any evidence obtained as a result of that search should be inadmissible as fruit of the poisonous tree. The Court agreed that the detectives had intruded into the curtilage of the home, which is a constitutionally protected area, when they used the dog to gather information to develop probable cause to search the home. In the Court's opinion, Justice Scalia wrote:

> . . . a police officer not armed with a warrant may approach a home and knock, precisely because that is "no more than any private citizen might do" (*Kentucky v. King*, 2011).

> But introducing a trained police dog to explore the area around the home in hopes of discovering incriminating evidence is something else. There is no customary invitation to do *that*. . . . To find a visitor knocking on the door is routine (even if sometimes unwelcome); to spot that same visitor exploring the front path with a metal detector, or marching his bloodhound into the garden before saying hello and asking permission, would inspire most if us to—well, call the police.

Prior to *Jardines*, officers could develop probable cause for a search warrant by using trained narcotics K-9s outside a residence. No longer is that allowed. The clear difference between *Jardines* and *Harris* is the location of the search and the suspect's expectation of privacy at each. The privacy one expects while driving a vehicle on a public road is quite different from the privacy expected inside one's own home.

More recently, the Seventh Circuit Court extended *Jardines* when it ruled in *United States v. Whitaker* (2016) that the use of a drug-detecting dog in the hallway outside of a suspect's apartment constituted a search under the Fourth Amendment and, as such, required a warrant. In this case, the court effectively equated the hallway outside of an apartment unit to the curtilage of a single-family dwelling.

Dogs have also been trained to detect explosives both before and after detonation. Their ability to detect explosives before detonation lessens the officer's risk and can help prevent crimes. A study by the Law Enforcement Assistance Administration and the Federal Aviation Authority demonstrated that dogs can locate explosives twice as often as people can. In the case of detonated explosives, dogs have helped locate bomb fragments hidden under piles of debris and at considerable distances from the detonation point.

As agents of the police, dogs are subject to the same legal limitations on searches that officers are. Court rulings appear to highlight the benefits of using K-9s to build probable cause to seize and arrest. In *United States v. Place* (1983), the Supreme Court ruled that exposing luggage located in a public place to a police K-9 sniff was not a search within the meaning of the Fourth Amendment. In essence, such a ruling concedes that the use of dogs may lead to the same end via less intrusive means, thus sparing law enforcement other time-consuming steps required to effect a legal search.

K-9s have also been used to seek and detain suspects. Courts have ruled that using K9s can enhance the safety of officers, bystanders, and suspects and that K-9s might be considered as less-lethal alternatives to deadly force. Guidelines for deploying K-9s are found in *Graham v. Connor* (1989). Before deploying a K-9, a handler should consider the totality of the circumstances and the available information, including the severity of the crime, whether the suspect poses an immediate threat to the safety of officers or others, and whether the suspect is actively resisting arrest or attempting to evade arrest by flight. Administrators and trainers should be familiar with case law pertaining to K-9s.

If a police department is not large enough to have or lacks sufficient need for a search dog and trained handler, learn where the nearest trained search dogs are and how they can be obtained if needed. Many major airports have dogs trained to locate explosives and may make these dogs available to police upon request.

Use of Technology in a Search

The rapid development of investigatory technology has presented a double-edged sword to law enforcement. While using technology can make investigations more efficient and effective, officers must take care not to overstep the privacy line that will likely put their case on shaky legal ground. For example, in *Kyllo v. United States* (2001), the Court held that thermal scanning of a private residence from outside the residence is a search under the Fourth Amendment and requires a search warrant.

In *United States v. Jones* (2012), the Court affirmed that attaching a global position system (GPS) device to a suspect's vehicle in an effort to obtain information is also a search under the Fourth Amendment and, as such, requires a warrant. In this case, investigators suspected Jones was involved in drug trafficking and placed a GPS device on his vehicle to monitor his movements. Although the officers had a search warrant to install and monitor the GPS, the specifics of the warrant were not followed. The device was left on and monitored after the warrant expired and was used to track the suspect outside the geographic boundaries set in the warrant. Consequently, the Court determined that the evidence obtained was acquired illegally since the search exceeded the scope allowed in the warrant. The Court did not rule on whether the installation and monitoring of the GPS device was reasonable or not, but focused instead on what actions constitute a "search" under the Fourth Amendment and remanded the case for further proceedings.

Cell phones have presented increasingly pervasive legal challenges to investigators. Because a large percentage of the population, worldwide, owns these phones, and because people tend to carry their phones with them wherever they go, day or night, these devices can present a wealth of data to investigators. However, because these phones also serve purposes that go far beyond the simple ability to make and receive phone calls, such as storing photos, facilitating the exchange of text messages, and providing users with myriad apps that contain sensitive personal information, in addition to being access-protected by a user's unique biometric data, these devices have come to be regarded by the courts as having a shield of privacy around them.

In *Carpenter v. United States* (2018), the FBI used cell phone data to track three individuals, one of whom was Timothy Carpenter, suspected of committing a series of armed robberies. At trial, Carpenter moved to suppress the cell phone evidence as the fruit of an illegal search. The district court denied the motion to suppress, and the Sixth Circuit affirmed. However, the Supreme Court granted certiorari and faced the question: "Does the warrantless search and seizure of cell phone records, including the location and movement of cell phone users, violate the privacy rights of the Fourth Amendment?" In a 5–4 decision, the Court held that, yes, the government's warrantless acquisition of Carpenter's cell-site records violated his Fourth Amendment right against unreasonable searches and seizures. It is worth noting that in *Carpenter*, the Court declined to extend the "third-party doctrine"—a doctrine where information disclosed to a third party carries no reasonable expectation of privacy—to cell-site location information, which implicates even greater privacy concerns than GPS tracking does.

Drones, or unmanned aerial vehicles (UAVs), are another emerging technology finding applications in law enforcement. Police drones can be used for search and rescue missions, surveillance, and documentation of crime scenes. UAVs can be equipped with a variety of equipment to enhance their utility, including video and audio recorders, live feed cameras, low visibility and infrared cameras, radar sensors, GPS, and thermal imaging devices (Kissiah, 2020). Because the federal government maintains full jurisdiction over the skies above the United States, law enforcement agencies throughout the country must apply to the Federal Aviation Administration (FAA) for permission to use police drones, and the FAA grants or denies such permission based solely on public safety concerns.

Once a law enforcement agency receives federal permission to use drones, regulation then shifts to state control, as the various civil rights and privacy laws that could potentially affect such usage are determined by policies, ordinances, and legislation created at the local city, county, and state levels. This has led to variability in restrictions across the country, with some police departments being required to get a warrant before using police drones or any kind of UAV for surveillance purposes and others not being required to do so (Kissiah, 2020). At the time of this writing, 14 states had laws requiring search warrants for the use of drones during criminal investigations. However, even in jurisdictions where warrants are not legally required, many police agencies have created their own internal regulations.

To date, the Supreme Court has not yet faced any cases challenging the constitutionality of police drone searches. However, legal precedents can inform law enforcement as to how the Court *might* apply Fourth Amendment privacy protections to cases involving searches facilitated by UAVs, including key cases discussed in this chapter, such as *Katz v. United States* (1967), *Kyllo v. United States* (2001), and *United States v. Jones* (2012) (Maciel, 2020). Furthermore, it can be anticipated that state drone statutes will also influence judges' perceptions of the types of police practices that warrant regulation by the Fourth Amendment, including how courts interpret what constitutes a reasonable expectation of privacy (Matiteyahu, 2015).

Automated license plate readers (ALPRs) were part of the court's focus in *United States v. Williams* (2015), a case in which an officer had received an alert from the squad's LPR system that a vehicle associated with a "wanted person" was nearby. After locating the car and pulling it over, the officer asked both men inside for identification. The driver, Hicks, was the actual subject of the alert, but the officer was also justified in asking for identification from the passenger, Williams, who was acting very nervous as he reached for his license. Williams was briefly handcuffed while the officer did a patdown for weapons, during which time the officer felt what he recognized to be a firearm in Williams's waistband. In addition to the firearm, the officer found a rock-like substance in Williams's pocket that was later identified as heroin. Williams was arrested and indicted for possessing a firearm as a felon.

Before trial, Williams moved to suppress the gun and heroin on the grounds that the officer lacked reasonable suspicion to stop the car and, therefore, the firearm and drugs were fruits of an illegal search. Williams's defense argued that a "police officer who receives an alert from an LPR system has no way of knowing the extent of the person's relationship to the vehicle." The appellate court, however, disagreed, saying the alert from the LPR was equivalent to information received from a flyer or bulletin, sources that officers commonly rely on and that courts have approved of, in providing articulable facts to support reasonable suspicion to justify the stop, check identification, pose questions to the individuals stopped, and detain the individuals briefly to obtain more information.

Facial recognition software databases are another emerging technology that has not yet been tested in the courts. However, the use of biometrics as a general investigative tool has begun to flow through the judicial system, with recent cases providing little definitive guidance. Some cases fall on the side of the defendant and privacy rights, while others have been deemed to justify the states' duty to protect public safety. *In re Search of a Residence in Oakland, California* (2019), officers investigating two people suspected of engaging in extortion sought a warrant for various electronic devices they believed would provide evidence of the crime. While the court agreed that probable cause existed to search the premises occupied by the suspects, the court also ruled that the warrant did "not establish

sufficient probable cause to compel any person who happens to be at the Subject Premises at the time of the subject to provide a finger, thumb, or other biometric feature to potentially unlock any unspecified digital device that may be seized during an otherwise lawful search." The court held that the use of such biometric features is "testimonial" and that the government's attempt to gain access to data that is "protected" on the digital devices by biometric locks infringes on the Fifth Amendment's privilege against self-incrimination and is, thus, unconstitutional. In conclusion the judge wrote:

> The challenge facing the courts is that technology is outpacing the law. In recognition of this reality, the United States Supreme Court recently instructed courts to adopt rules that "take account of more sophisticated systems that are already in use or in development." . . . Courts have an obligation to safeguard constitutional rights and cannot permit those rights to be diminished merely due to the advancement of technology . . . . Citizens do not contemplate waiving their civil rights when using new technology, and the Supreme Court has concluded that, to find otherwise, would leave individuals "at the mercy of advancing technology."

Complete chapters or entire books can and, indeed, have been devoted to the issue of privacy rights in the wake of advancing technology. With case law coming out faster than this text can be revised, students are strongly encouraged to continue monitoring legal developments delineating how law enforcement officers can and cannot apply technology in the course of their investigations. Here we have presented only a handful of cases to illustrate the spectrum of technologies finding their way into the courts. But it remains clear that this area of law will continue to develop and will affect many aspects of criminal investigation in the years to come.

Search Warrant Checklist

When analyzing a search issue today, investigators must be prepared to make several inquiries. First, does the action involve a physical intrusion on a person, house, paper, or effect to gather information? Second, is there a reasonable expectation of privacy in the area being infringed on? If the answer to either question is "yes," it can safely be stated that a search implicating the Fourth Amendment has occurred.

Having established that a search is implicated, investigators must obtain a warrant unless the search can be authorized by a recognized exception (Rutledge, 2008):

- Independent justification (consent, probation or parole, incident to arrest, officer safety, booking search, inventory).

- Exigent circumstances (rescue, protection of property, imminent destruction of evidence, fresh pursuit, escape prevention, public safety).

- Fleeing target (car, van, truck, RV, bus, boat, aircraft, etc.) with PC and lawful access.

- No search (plain sense, open fields, abandoned property, private-party delivery, controlled delivery, exposed characteristics).

The courts have also identified several "special needs" exceptions that do not fit into other categories, such as school searches, searches of highly regulated businesses (e.g., firearms dealers, pawn shops, law firms, financial institutions, clergy offices, and junkyards), employment and educational drug screening, and the immediate search for "evanescent" evidence (e.g., blood-alcohol content) (Rutledge, 2007d). Searches in these special categories require extra prudence and due diligence by investigators, whether because of an enhanced expectation of privacy, the

documentation of "privileged" communication or presence of other sensitive information, or for some other reason. For example, searches that involve evanescent, or short-lived, temporary, evidence of a crime, such as the blood-alcohol content (BAC) of one suspected of driving under the influence, became more complicated when the Supreme Court decided *Missouri v. McNeely* (2013), in which a divided Court held, in a 5–4 decision, that "In drunk-driving investigations, the natural dissipation of alcohol in the bloodstream does not constitute an exigency in every case sufficient to justify conducting a blood test without a warrant."

A Reminder

Jetmore (2007b, p. 26) stresses, "Ability to skillfully document in writing facts and circumstances that lead to logical inferences and reasonable conclusions remains a professional requirement in criminal investigation. Excellent investigative work is negated and the guilty may walk free if the legal framework on which it was based can't be adequately explained." The Fourth Amendment requires that officers' actions be *reasonable*: "Clearly outline in your report every detail known to you at the time so that a subsequent reviewing authority has the full situation in mind when deciding whether your actions were reasonable given the totality of the circumstances" (Jetmore, 2007b, p. 30).

Summary

The Fourth Amendment to the Constitution forbids unreasonable searches and seizures and requires that legal searches and seizures be based on probable cause. Therefore, investigators must know what constitutes a reasonable, legal search. The escalating levels of proof required during various stages of the criminal investigative process are as follows: reasonable suspicion is required to stop a person; probable cause is required to conduct a search or arrest (seizure); and proof beyond a reasonable doubt is required to convict someone of a crime.

A search can be justified and therefore considered legal if any of the following conditions are met: (1) a search warrant has been issued, (2) consent is given,

(3) an officer stops a suspicious person and believes the person may be armed (a frisk), (4) the search is incidental to a lawful arrest, (5) the search is of a moveable vehicle (the automobile exception), (6) it is for inventory purposes, (7) an emergency or exigent circumstance exists, (8) it occurs at a point of entry into this country (border crossings, airports, ports), (9) the search involves an officer using "plain sense" (sight, touch, sound, smell), or (10) it involves open fields, abandoned property, or a public place (i.e., there exists no reasonable expectation of privacy).

Each of these search situations has limitations, as set forth in case law. The Court ruled in *Georgia v. Randolph* that police may not legally search a home when one physically present resident consents but another physically present resident objects. The objection overrides the consent. The *Terry* decision established that a patdown or frisk is a "protective search for weapons" and as such must be "confined to a scope reasonably designed to discover guns, knives, clubs and other hidden instruments for the assault of a police officer or others."

The *Chimel* decision established that a search incidental to a lawful arrest must be made simultaneously with the arrest and must be confined to the area within the suspect's immediate control. The *Riley* decision established that a search of a cell phone seized incident to a lawful arrest, in the absence of consent or an emergency situation, requires a warrant.

The *Carroll* decision established that automobiles may be searched without a warrant if (1) there is probable cause for the search, and (2) the vehicle would be gone before a search warrant could be obtained. *Chambers v. Maroney* (1970) established that a vehicle may be taken to headquarters to be searched for inventory purposes.

A warrantless search in the absence of a lawful arrest or consent is justified only in emergencies or exigent circumstances where probable cause exists and the search must be conducted immediately (*New York v. Quarles*, 1984). The *King* decision established that officers may enter a home without a warrant in response to an emergency, which includes the imminent destruction of evidence, as long as the police, themselves, do not create the emergency through conduct that violates the Fourth Amendment.

The precedent case for search and seizure of abandoned property and open fields is *Hester v. United States* (1924), in which the Court held that "The special protection accorded by the Fourth Amendment to the people in their 'persons, houses, papers and effects,' is not extended to the open fields." This exception includes property disposed of in such a manner as to relinquish ordinary property rights.

If a search is *not* conducted legally, the evidence obtained is worthless. The exclusionary rule established that courts may not accept evidence obtained by unreasonable search and seizure, regardless of its relevance to a case. *Weeks v. United States* (1914) made the rule applicable at the federal level; *Mapp v. Ohio* (1961) made it applicable to all courts.

A successful crime scene search locates, identifies, and preserves all evidence present. Search patterns have been developed that help ensure a thorough search. Exterior search patterns divide an area into lanes, strips, concentric circles, or zones. Interior searches go from the general to the specific, usually in a circular pattern, covering all surfaces of a search area. The floor should be searched first.

If the suspect has not been arrested, confine your search to a patdown or frisk for weapons. If the suspect has been arrested, make a complete body search for weapons and evidence. In either event, always be on your guard.

Can You Define?

anticipatory warrant

attenuation doctrine

Buie sweep

curtilage

"elephant-in-a-matchbox" doctrine

exclusionary rule

exigent circumstances

frisk

"fruit-of-the-poisonous-tree"
   doctrine

good faith doctrine

immediate control

independent source doctrine

inevitable discovery doctrine

nightcapped warrant

no-knock warrant

particularity requirement

patdown

plain feel/touch evidence

plain-view evidence

pretext stop

probable cause

protective sweep

reasonable

search

seizure

Terry stop

totality of circumstances

true scene

uncontaminated scene

Checklist

The Search

- Is the search legal?

- Was a pattern followed?

- Was all evidence photographed, recorded in the notes, identified, and packaged properly?

- Was the search completed even if evidence was found early in the search?

- Were all suspects searched?

- Did more than one investigator search?

- Was plain-view evidence seized? If so, were the circumstances recorded?

References

Geoghegan, S. (2007, March–April). *Hudson v. Michigan* and forced entry. *Tactical Response*, pp. 96–99.

Hilton, A. M. (2007, August). Clearing up knock-and-announce confusion. *Police*, pp. 38–43.

Jetmore, L. F. (2007a, April). Searching without a warrant. *Law Officer Magazine*, pp. 26–31.

Jetmore, L. F. (2007b, March). Understanding probable cause. *Law Officer Magazine*, pp. 26–30.

Kissiah, M. (2020, May 14). *Police drones in law enforcement*. Retrieved May, 20, 2020, from www.einvestigator.com/the-use-of-drones-in-law-enforcement-and-private-investigation/

Maciel, S. A. (2020, Spring). Fourth Amendment considerations in the utilization of drones by law enforcement. *FAU Undergraduate Law Journal* *1*(1), 37–55. Retrieved May 20, 2020, from journals.flvc.org/FAU_UndergraduateLawJournal/article/view/121971/120755

Matiteyahu, T. (2015). Drone regulations and the Fourth Amendment rights: The interaction of state drone statutes and the reasonable expectation of privacy. *Columbia Journal of Law and Social Problems, 48*(2), 265–307. Retrieved May 20, 2020, from jlsp.law.columbia.edu/wp-content/uploads/sites/8/2017/03/48-Matiteyahu.pdf

Means, R. (2008, March). Frisk searches are not automatic, Part I. *Law and Order*, pp. 23–24.

Myers, K. A. (2011, April). Searches of motor vehicles incident to arrest in a post-*Gant* world. *FBI Law Enforcement Bulletin*, pp. 24–32.

Pettry, M. T. X. (2012, March). The exigent circumstances exception after *Kentucky v. King*. *FBI Law Enforcement Bulletin*, pp. 26–32.

Rutledge, D. (2007a, June). The "Good Faith" doctrine. *Police*, pp. 70–71.

Rutledge, D. (2007b, October). How to justify officer safety searches. *Police*, pp. 36–40.

Rutledge, D. (2007c, April). Plain sense seizure. *Police*, pp. 70–71.

Rutledge, D. (2007d, February). Search warrant exceptions. *Police*, pp. 54–56.

Rutledge, D. (2007e, September). Seizing and searching passengers. *Police*, pp. 70–71.

Rutledge, D. (2008, March). How to tell when you need a search warrant. *Police*, pp. 28–30.

Rutledge, D. (2010, February). The "Emergency Aid Doctrine." *Police*, pp. 60–63.

Sanchez, A. J., & Rubin, J. K. (2010, June). The use of garbage to establish probable cause for granting valid search warrants. *The Police Chief*, pp. 12–13.

Scarry, L. L. (2007a, October). Oops, wrong house. *Law Officer Magazine*, pp. 76–78.

Scarry, L. L. (2007b, August). Probable cause trumps pretext. *Law Officer Magazine*, pp. 82–86.

Schonely, J. H. (2007, August). Tactical search techniques. *Police*, pp. 60–62.

Cases Cited

Adams v. Williams, 407 U.S. 143 (1972).

Aguilar v. Texas, 378 U.S. 108 (1964).

Alabama v. White, 496 U.S. 325 (1990).

Arizona v. Evans, 514 U.S. 1 (1995).

Arizona v. Gant, 556 U.S. 332 (2009).

Arizona v. Johnson, 555 U.S. 323 (2009).

Bailey v. United States, 568 U.S. 186 (2013).

Boyd v. United States, 116 U.S. 616 (1886).

Brendlin v. California, 551 U.S. 249 (2007).

Brigham City, Utah v. Stuart, 547 U.S. 398 (2006).

Brinegar v. United States, 338 U.S. 160 (1949).

Brown v. Texas, 443 U.S. 47 (1979).

Byrd v. United States, 584 U.S. ___ (2018).

California v. Greenwood, 486 U.S. 35 (1988).

Carpenter v. United States, 585 U.S. ___ (2018).

Carroll v. United States, 267 U.S. 132 (1925).

Cass v. State, 124 Tex. Crim. 208, 61 S.W.2d 500 (1933).

Chambers v. Maroney, 399 U.S. 42 (1970).

Chimel v. California, 395 U.S. 752 (1969).

City of Indianapolis v. Edmond, 531 U.S. 32 (2000).

City of Ontario v. Quon, 560 U.S. 746 (2010).

Collins v. Virginia, 584 U.S. ___ (2018).

Fernandez v. California, 571 U.S. 292 (2014).

Florida v. Harris, 568 U.S. 237 (2013).

Florida v. Jardines, 569 U.S. 1 (2013).

Florida v. Jimeno, 500 U.S. 248 (1991).

Florida v. J. L., 529 U.S. 266 (2000).

Florida v. Wells, 495 U.S. 1 (1990).

Georgia v. Randolph, 547 U.S. 103 (2006).

Graham v. Connor, 490 U.S. 386 (1989).

Groh v. Ramirez, 540 U.S. 551 (2004).

Hester v. United States, 265 U.S. 57 (1924).

Hiibel v. Sixth Judicial District Court of Nevada, Humboldt County, 542 U.S. 177 (2004).

Hudson v. Michigan, 547 U.S. 586 (2006).

Illinois v. Caballes, 543 U.S. 405 (2005).

Illinois v. Gates, 462 U.S. 213 (1983).

Illinois v. Lidster, 540 U.S. 419 (2004).

Illinois v. McArthur, 531 U.S. 326 (2001).

Illinois v. Rodriguez, 497 U.S. 177 (1990).

In re Search of a Residence in Oakland, California, Case No. 19-mj-70053-KAW-1 (JD) (N.D. Cal. Dec. 10, 2019).

Johnson v. United States, 333 U.S. 10 (1948).

Katz v. United States, 389 U.S. 347 (1967).

Kentucky v. King, 563 U.S. 452 (2011).

Knowles v. Iowa, 525 U.S. 113 (1998).

Kyllo v. United States, 533 U.S. 27 (2001).

Locke v. United States, 11 U.S. (7 Cranch) 339 (1813).

Mapp v. Ohio, 367 U.S. 643 (1961).

Maryland v. Buie, 494 U.S. 325 (1990).

Michigan Department of State Police v. Sitz, 496 U.S. 444 (1990).

Michigan v. Fisher, 558 U.S. 45 (2009).

Michigan v. Summers, 452 U.S. 692 (1981).

Michigan v. Tyler, 436 U.S. 499 (1978).

Mincey v. Arizona, 437 U.S. 385 (1978).

Minnesota v. Dickerson, 508 U.S. 336 (1993).

Miranda v. Arizona, 384 U.S. 436 (1966).

Missouri v. McNeely, 569 U.S. 141 (2013).

Murray v. United States, 487 U.S. 533 (1988)

New York v. Belton, 453 U.S. 454 (1981).

New York v. Quarles, 467 U.S. 649 (1984).

Nix v. Williams, 467 U.S. 431 (1984).

Public Service Comm'n v. Havemeyer, 296 U.S. 506 (1936).

Richards v. Wisconsin, 520 U.S. 385 (1997).

Riley v. California, 573 U.S. 373 (2014).

Schneckloth v. Bustamonte, 412 U.S. 218 (1973).

Smith v. United States, 337 U.S. 137 (1949).

South Dakota v. Opperman, 428 U.S. 364 (1976).

Spinelli v. United States, 393 U.S. 410 (1969).

Stanford v. Texas, 379 U.S. 476 (1965).

Sussex Land & Live Stock Co. v. Midwest Refining Co., 294 F. 597 (8th Cir. Wyo. 1923).

Terry v. Ohio, 392 U.S. 1 (1968).

Texas v. Brown, 460 U.S. 730 (1983).

Thornton v. United States, 541 U.S. 615 (2004).

United States v. Banks, 540 U.S. 31 (2003).

United States v. Bowhay, 992 F.2d 229 (9th Cir. 1993).

United States v. Camou, 773 F.3d 932 (9th Cir. 2014).

United States v. Drayton, 536 U.S. 194 (2002).

United States v. Dunn, 480 U.S. 294 (1987).

United States v. Flores-Montano, 541 U.S. 149 (2004).

United States v. Grubbs, 547 U.S. 90 (2006).

United States v. Hensley, 469 U.S. 221 (1985).

United States v. Ibarra, 502 U.S. 1 (1991) (per curiam).

United States v. Iwai, 930 F.3d 1141 (2019).

United States v. Jacobsen, 466 U.S. 109 (1984).

United States v. Johnson, No. 17-10252 (9th Cir. 2019).

United States v. Jones, 565 U.S. 400 (2012).

United States v. Knights, 534 U.S. 112 (2001).

United States v. Leon, 468 U.S. 897 (1984).

United States v. Lueck, 678 F.2d 895, 903 (11th Cir. 1982).

United States v. Martinez-Fuerte, 428 U.S. 543 (1976).

United States v. Matlock, 415 U.S. 164 (1974).

United States v. Place, 462 U.S. 696 (1983).

United States v. Ramirez, 523 U.S. 65 (1998).

United States v. Ramsey, 431 U.S. 606 (1977).

United States v. Ross, 456 U.S. 798 (1982).

United States v. Segura-Baltazar, 448 F. 3d 1281 (11th Cir., 2006).

United States v. Torres, 828 F.3d 1113 (2016).

United States v. Whitaker, 820 F.3d 849 (2016).

United States v. Williams, 796 F.3d 951 (2015).

Utah v. Strieff, 579 U.S. ___ (2016).

Weeks v. United States, 232 U.S. 383 (1914).

Whren v. United States, 517 U.S. 806 (1996).

Wilson v. Arkansas, 514 U.S. 927 (1995).

Wright v. United States, 302 U.S. 583 (1938).

Wyoming v. Houghton, 526 U.S. 295 (1999).

Chapter 5
Forensics and Physical Evidence

Chapter Outline

Definitions

Crime Scene Investigators

Investigative Equipment

Crime Scene Integrity and Contamination of Evidence

Processing Evidence: Maintaining the Chain of Custody from Discovery to Disposal

Frequently Examined Evidence

Evidence Handling and Infectious Disease

Learning Objectives

LO1 Explain the requisite steps involved in processing physical evidence correctly, from its discovery to final disposition.

LO2 Identify the common errors in collecting evidence.

LO3 Understand the criteria required to ensure admissibility of evidence in court.

LO4 List the types of evidence most commonly found in criminal investigations.

LO5 Compare and contrast the determinations that can and cannot be made from fingerprint, DNA, blood, and hair evidence.

LO6 Describe special collection and processing considerations for the following types of evidence: shoe and tire prints and impressions, tools and tool marks, firearms and ammunition, glass, soils and minerals, safe insulation, ropes, strings, tapes, drugs, documents, laundry and dry-cleaning marks, paint, and skeletal remains.

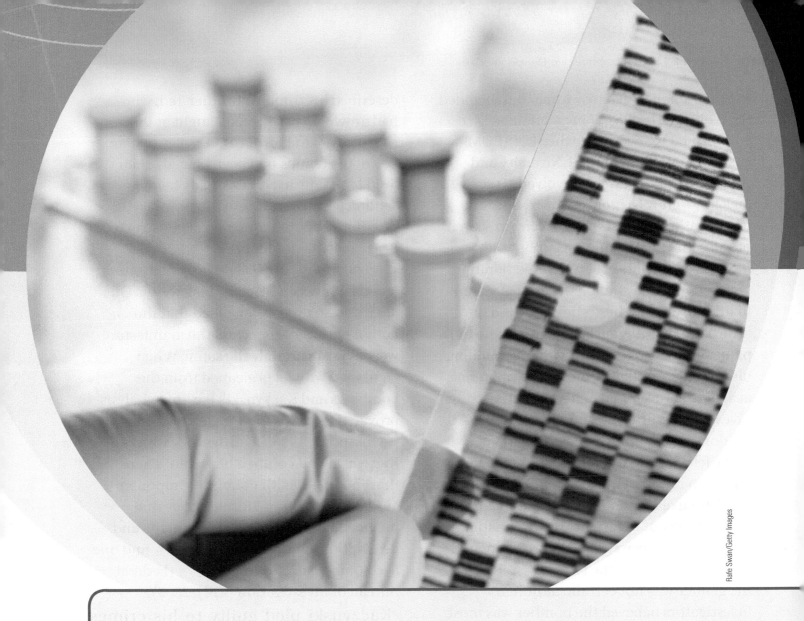

Introduction

Consider the following narrative the Federal Bureau of Investigation (FBI) offers in its history of the agency's most famous cases and criminals:

How do you catch a twisted genius who aspires to be the perfect, anonymous killer—who builds untraceable bombs and delivers them to random targets, who leaves false clues to throw off authorities, who lives like a recluse in the mountains of Montana and tells no one of his secret crimes?

That was the challenge the FBI and its investigative partners faced, who spent nearly two decades hunting down this ultimate lone-wolf bomber.

The man who the world would eventually know as Theodore Kaczynski came to our attention in 1978 with the explosion of his first, primitive homemade bomb at a Chicago university. Over the next 17 years, he mailed or hand delivered a series of increasingly sophisticated bombs that killed three Americans and injured 24 more. Along the way, he sowed fear and panic, even threatening to blow up airliners in flight.

In 1979, an FBI-led task force that included the ATF and U.S. Postal Inspection Service was formed to investigate the "UNABOM" case, code-named for the **UN**iversity and **A**irline **BOM**bing targets involved. The task force grew to more than 150 full-time investigators, analysts, and others. In search of clues, the team made every possible forensic examination of recovered bomb components and studied the lives of victims in minute detail. These efforts proved of little use in identifying the bomber, who took pains to leave no forensic evidence, building his bombs essentially from "scrap" materials available almost anywhere. And the victims, investigators later learned, were chosen randomly from library research.

We felt confident that the Unabomber had been raised in Chicago and later lived in the Salt Lake City and San Francisco areas. This turned out to be true. His occupation proved more elusive, with theories ranging from aircraft mechanic to scientist. Even the gender was not certain: although investigators believed the bomber was most likely male, they also investigated several female suspects.

The big break in the case came in 1995. The Unabomber sent us a 35,000-word essay claiming to explain his motives and views of the ills of modern society. After much debate about the wisdom of "giving in to terrorists," FBI Director Louis Freeh and Attorney General Janet Reno approved the task force's recommendation to publish the essay in hopes that a reader could identify the author.

After the manifesto appeared in *The Washington Post* and *The New York Times*, thousands of people suggested possible suspects. One stood out: David Kaczynski

described his troubled brother Ted, who had grown up in Chicago, taught at the University of California at Berkeley (where two of the bombs had been placed), then lived for a time in Salt Lake City before settling permanently into the primitive 10' × 14' cabin that the brothers had constructed near Lincoln, Montana.

Most importantly, David provided letters and documents written by his brother. Our linguistic analysis determined that the author of those papers and the manifesto were almost certainly the same. When combined with facts gleaned from the bombings and Kaczynski's life, that analysis provided the basis for a search warrant.

On April 3, 1996, investigators arrested Kaczynski and combed his cabin. There, they found a wealth of bomb components; 40,000 handwritten journal pages that included bomb-making experiments and descriptions of Unabomber crimes; and one live bomb, ready for mailing. (Federal Bureau of Investigation [FBI], 2008)

Kaczynski pled guilty to his crimes in January 1998 and is serving eight life sentences without the possibility of parole. He spends 23 hours each day alone in his cell at the United States Penitentiary Administrative Maximum Facility (ADX) in Florence, Colorado, a prison known as the "Alcatraz of the Rockies" (Worthen, 2019).

The National Institute of Justice (NIJ) defines **forensic science** as "the application of sciences such as physics, chemistry, biology, computer science and engineering to matters of law" (NIJ, n.d.). The American Academy of Forensic Sciences (AAFS) elaborates (n.d.):

The forensic sciences are used around the world to resolve civil disputes, to justly enforce criminal laws and government regulations, and to protect public health. Forensic scientists may be involved anytime an objective, scientific analysis is needed to find the truth and to seek justice in a legal proceeding. Early on, forensic science became identified with law enforcement and the prosecution of criminal cases—an image enhanced by books, television, and movies. This is misleading because forensic science is objective, unbiased, and applies equally to either side of any criminal, civil, or other legal matter.

Modern forensic science dates back to 1910 and the "exchange principle" set forth by French criminologist Dr. Edmond Locard. As explained in Chapter 1, *Locard's exchange principle* states that whenever two objects come in contact with each other (e.g., a criminal and an object or objects at a crime scene), there is always a transfer of information, however minute, between them. In other words, a criminal always removes something from the crime scene and leaves behind incriminating evidence. The remnants of this transfer are called **proxy data**, the evidence analyzed by forensic scientists to uncover the relationships between people, places, and objects.

A primary purpose of an investigation is to locate, identify, and preserve **evidence**—data on which a judgment or conclusion may be based. Evidence is used for determining the facts in a case, for later laboratory examination, and for direct presentation in court. **Best evidence**, in the legal sense, is the original evidence or highest available degree of proof that can be produced. Investigators should be cognizant throughout an investigation of the best-evidence rule, which stipulates that the original evidence is to be presented in court whenever possible. Other factors pertaining to admissibility of evidence will be discussed later in the chapter.

Students should also keep in mind that entire books have been written about the collection and analysis of the various types of evidence discussed in this chapter. Because of space constraints, this discussion will present merely an overview of the most common types of physical evidence investigators are likely to encounter and, where applicable, will refer the reader to other resources that provide a more detailed examination of specific types of evidence.

Definitions

Evidence is generally categorized as one of four types: testimonial, documentary, demonstrative, or physical. *Testimonial evidence* is information obtained through interviewing and interrogating individuals about what they saw (eyewitness evidence), heard (hearsay evidence), or know (character evidence). Testimonial evidence is the subject of Chapter 6. *Documentary evidence* typically includes written material (including emails and text messages), audio recordings, and videos.

Demonstrative evidence includes mockups and scale models of objects or places related to the crime scene and helps juries visualize more clearly what they are unable to view personally. Occasionally, however, juries are taken to the crime scene if the judge deems it vital to the fair processing of the case, but this is expensive and time-consuming. Most commonly, investigators deal with physical evidence. **Physical evidence** is anything real—that is, which has substance—that helps establish the facts of a case. It can be seen, touched, smelled, or tasted; is solid, semisolid, or liquid; and can be large or tiny. It may be at an immediate crime scene or miles away; it may also be on a suspect or a victim.

Some evidence ties one crime to a similar crime or connects one suspect with another. Evidence can also provide new leads when a case appears to be unsolvable. Further, evidence corroborates statements from witnesses to or victims of a crime. Convictions are not achieved from statements, admissions, or confessions alone. A crime must be proven by independent investigation and physical evidence.

For example, in a small western town, a six-year-old girl and her parents told police the girl had been sexually molested. The girl told police that a man had taken her to the desert, had shown her some "naughty" pictures that he burned, and had then molested her. Because it was difficult for the police to rely on the girl's statement, they needed physical evidence to corroborate her story. Fortunately, the girl remembered where the man had taken her and led the police there. They found remains of the burned pictures and confiscated them as evidence. The remains of one picture, showing the suspect with a naked young girl on his lap, were sufficient to identify him by the rings on his fingers. This physical evidence supporting the girl's testimony resulted in a charge of lewdness with a minor.

Physical evidence can be classified in different ways. One common classification is direct and indirect evidence. **Direct evidence** establishes proof of a fact without any other evidence. **Indirect evidence** merely *tends* to incriminate a person—for instance, a suspect's footprints found at the crime scene. Although the footprints do not directly prove the suspect committed the crime at issue, the prints do place the suspect at the scene of the crime. If the suspect states that he or she was never at the scene, that statement will prove to be untrue based on the indirect evidence. This helps build a case against the suspect and contributes to convictions based on circumstantial evidence. Indirect evidence is also called **circumstantial evidence**, or evidence from which inferences are drawn. A popular myth is that circumstantial evidence will not stand alone without other facts to support it; however,

indirect evidence combined with suspect interviews and testimonial evidence can often lead to convictions.

Extremely small items, such as hair or fibers, are a subset of direct evidence called **trace evidence**. Evidence established by law is called ***prima facie*** **evidence**. For example, 0.8% ethanol in the blood is direct or *prima facie* evidence of intoxication in some states. **Associative evidence** links a suspect with a crime. Associative evidence includes fingerprints, footprints, bloodstains, hairs, and fibers.

Corpus delicti evidence establishes that a crime has been committed. Contrary to popular belief, the **corpus delicti** ("body of the crime") in a murder case is not the dead body but the fact that death resulted from a criminal act. Corpus delicti evidence supports the elements of the crime. Pry marks on an entry door are corpus delicti evidence in a burglary.

Probative evidence is vital to the investigation or prosecution of a case, tending to prove or actually proving guilt or innocence. Also of extreme importance to the investigator is *exculpatory evidence*, discussed in Chapter 1, which is physical evidence that clears one of blame—for example, having a blood type different from that of blood found at a murder scene. **Material evidence** forms a substantive part of the case, or has a legitimate and effective influence on the decision of the case. **Relevant evidence** applies to the matter in question. **Competent evidence** has been properly collected, identified, and continuously secured.

Crime Scene Investigators

A crime scene investigator (CSI) is a specialist in organized scientific collection and processing of evidence. A CSI develops, processes, and packages all physical evidence found at the crime scene and transports it to the lab for forensic evaluation; attends and documents autopsies; and writes reports and testifies in court about the evidence. With advances in technology occurring continuously, it is imperative that CSIs keep up-to-date on training and the newest developments in forensic equipment and methodology. Although some law enforcement agencies hire civilians to handle crime scene processing and forensics and to work closely with investigators, it is more common that the CSI is a licensed peace officer with specialized training who is part of an investigative unit.

The public has become familiar with how CSIs operate through the popular television series *CSI: Crime Scene Investigation*, which first aired on CBS in October 2000 and since then has attracted millions of viewers and spawned dozens of other forensic drama television shows. Hollywood's depiction of CSI, however, has created a glamorized, impractical image of this field in the public's mind. This phenomenon has been called the **CSI effect**, which describes "the perception in the criminal justice system, popular media, and general population that consumption of crime-based television programming focusing on the forensic sciences has created a juror bias toward the requirement of forensic evidence at trial to justify a conviction" (Eatley, Hueston, & Price, 2016). In turn, these unreasonable expectations by the jurors increase the burden of proof faced by prosecutors and increase the chance of acquittal, allowing guilty defendants to go free in the absence of overwhelmingly supportive forensic evidence (Chin & Workewych, 2016).

Myth Most crimes are solved with DNA evidence.

Fact Most crimes are not solved at all, and of those that are, only a small percentage are solved through DNA.

This blurring of reality and fiction (the *CSI* effect) was the topic of a study published in the *National Institute of Justice Journal*, in which 1,000 jurors were surveyed about their expectations regarding forensic evidence before their participation in the trial process:

- 46% expected to see some kind of scientific evidence in *every* criminal case.

- 22% expected to see DNA evidence in *every* criminal case.

- 36% expected to see fingerprint evidence in *every* criminal case.

- 32% expected to see ballistic or other firearms laboratory evidence in *every* criminal case. (Shelton, 2008, p. 3)

The survey found that for all categories of evidence, *CSI* viewers had higher expectations for scientific evidence than did nonviewers. Fortunately, these expectations were not shown to translate into an actual prerequisite of jurors in finding defendants guilty. In other words, while the expectations were high, the *demand* that such evidence be presented in order to convict or acquit was not observed, leading researchers to relabel this phenomenon the *CSI myth* (Shelton, Barak, & Kim, 2011). In fact, several follow-up studies have bolstered this conclusion, finding support for the argument that if a *CSI* effect exists at all, it is likely negligible (Chin & Workewych, 2016). Results of

another study found that for those jurors who may have been under the influence of a limited *CSI* effect coming into trial, those biases were attenuated during actual deliberation (Klentz, Winters, & Chapman, 2020). In studying another component of the *CSI* effect—the impact such shows had on those who commit crimes—Vicary and Zaikman (2017) found that individuals who were highly involved, avid viewers of forensic crime dramas, when compared to those who were less involved, did possess more knowledge of forensic techniques that could help them prevent being caught for a crime.

While average citizens have become increasingly technologically sophisticated, their expanded familiarity with technology is more likely due to the general pervasiveness of and exposure to consumer-level technology, including the ability to scour the Internet for information pertaining to scientific evidence, than it is the result of watching certain television shows. This finding has led to the identification of a more general **tech effect**—a broad public awareness of and familiarity with the capabilities of modern technology—that is indirectly influencing juror expectations (Shelton et al., 2011).

Regardless of whether the crime scene is processed by a generalist investigator or a specialized CSI, the task is the same—to locate and properly process evidence at a crime scene. To accomplish this task, investigators must have the necessary tools and equipment.

Investigative Equipment

Although not all crime scenes require all items of equipment, you cannot predict the nature of the next committed crime or the equipment you will need. Therefore, you should have available at all times a crime scene investigation kit containing basic equipment. Check the kit's equipment after each use, replacing items as required.

Investigations can be simple or complex and can reveal little or much physical evidence. Consequently, the equipment needs of each investigation are different. Table 5.1, alphabetized for easy reference, contains the investigative equipment most often used.

Although the list may seem extensive, numerous other items are also often used in investigations: bags, binoculars, blankets, brushes, bullhorns, cable, capsules, chains, checklists, chemicals, chisels, coat hangers (to hang up wet or bloodstained clothing), combs, cotton, cutters, directories, drug kits, eyedroppers, files, fingernail clippers, fixatives, flares or fuses, flood lamps, forceps, forms, gas masks, generators, gloves, glue, guns, hammers, hatchets, levels, lights, magnets, manuals, maps, matches, metal detectors, moulages (for making impressions or casts), nails, padlocks, pails, plastic sheets, punches, putty, rags, receipts, rubber,

TABLE 5.1 **Equipment for Processing Evidence**

Item	Uses
Cameras* and memory cards	To photograph scene and evidence
Chalk and chalk line	To mark off search areas; to outline bodies or objects removed from the scene
Compass*	To obtain directions for report orientation and searches
Containers (Boxes, bags of all sizes and shapes; lightweight plastic or paper; telescoping or collapsible glass bottles and new paint containers)	To contain all types of evidence
Crayon or magic marker	To mark evidence
Envelopes, all sizes	To collect evidence
Evidence markers, alphas and numerics	To label/identify evidence
Fingerprint kit (Various developing powders, brushes, fingerprint camera, fingerprint cards, ink pads, spoons, iodine fumer tube, lifting tape)	To develop latent fingerprints
First-aid kit	To treat injured persons at the crime scene
Flashlight and batteries	To search dark areas, such as tunnels, holes, wells, windowless rooms; to search for latent fingerprints
Knife	To cut ropes, string, stakes, etc.
Labels, all sizes (Evidence labels; labels such as "do not touch," "do not open," "handle with care," "fragile")	To label evidence and to provide directions
Magnifier	To locate fingerprints and minute evidence
Measuring tape, steel	To measure long distances
Mirror with collapsible handle	To look in out-of-the-way locations for evidence
Notebook*	To record information
Paper* (Notebook, graph, scratch pads, wrapping)	To take notes, sketch scene, wrap evidence
Pencils* (At least two; sharpened)	To make sketches
Pens* (At least two; non-smudge type)	To take notes, make sketches
Picks (Door lock picks and ice picks)	To use as thumbtacks; to hold one end of a rope or tape
Plaster	To make casts of tire treads and footprints
Pliers	To pry and twist
Protractor	To measure angles
Pry bar	To get into spaces otherwise inaccessible
Rope (Fluorescent, lightweight, approximately 300 feet)	To protect the crime scene
Ruler, carpenter-type*	To measure short distances
Ruler, straightedge*	To measure small items/distances
Scissors	To cut tapes, reproduce size of objects in paper, cut first-aid gauze
Screwdrivers, standard and Phillips	To turn and pry
Scribe	To mark metal objects for evidence
Sketching supplies* (Ruler, pencil, graph paper, etc.)	To make sketches
Spatula	To dig; to stir

(Continued)

TABLE 5.1 *(Continued)*	
Sterile distilled water	To use with swabs
String	To tie objects and boxes containing evidence; to protect the crime scene; to mark off search areas
Swabs	To lift DNA evidence
Tags	To attach to items of evidence
Templates	To aid in sketching
Tongue depressors, wooden	To stir; to add reinforcements to plaster casts; to make side forms for casting; to lift objects without touching them
Tubes, glass, with stoppers	To contain evidence
Tweezers	To pick up evidence without contamination
Wrecking bar	To pry open doors, windows, entryways, or exits

*The use of these items has been discussed earlier in the text (see Chapter 2).

saws, scrapers, shovels, side cutters, solvent, sponges, sprays, stamps, syringes, tape, tape recorders, thermometers, tin snips, towels, transceivers (to communicate in large buildings, warehouses, apartment complexes, or open areas), vacuums, wax, wire, and wrenches. The blood-test kits, gun-residue kits, and other field-test kits described in Chapter 1 are also used.

More specialized equipment for investigation includes night-vision goggles, metal detectors, electronic tracking systems, digital voice recorders, camcorders, and much more, discussed throughout this section. Many departments are able to use forfeiture assets confiscated during drug busts and other law enforcement efforts to purchase specialized investigative equipment. Additional heavy-duty, less-portable types of equipment such as large pry bars or long ladders are frequently found on fire and rescue vehicles and can be used jointly by the police and fire departments.

Selecting Equipment

Survey the types of crimes and evidence most frequently found at crime scenes in your jurisdiction. Select equipment to process and preserve the evidence you are most likely to encounter. For example, because fingerprints are often found at crime scenes, fingerprint-processing equipment should be included in the basic kit. However, you would probably not need to take a shovel along to investigate a rape.

After the basic equipment needs are identified, select specific equipment that is frequently needed, lightweight, compact, high quality, versatile, and reasonably priced. For example, boxes should either nest or be collapsible. Containers should be lightweight and plastic. The lighter and smaller the equipment, the more items can be carried in the kit. Consider miniaturized electronic equipment rather than heavier, battery-operated items. Select equipment that accomplishes more than one function, such as a knife with many features or other multipurpose tools.

Equipment Containers

The equipment can be put into one container or divided into several containers, based on frequency of use. This is an administrative decision determined by each department's needs. Dividing equipment results in a compact, lightweight kit suitable for most crime scenes while ensuring availability of other equipment needed to investigate less-common cases.

Carriers or containers come in all shapes, sizes, colors, and designs. Briefcases, attaché cases, and transparent plastic bags are convenient to use. Some commercially produced kits include basic equipment. However, many departments prefer to design their own kits, adapted to their specific needs. The container should look professional, and a list of its contents should be attached to the outside or inside the cover.

Transporting Equipment

Crime scene investigative equipment is transported in a police vehicle, an investigator's vehicle, or a crime scene vehicle. The equipment can be transported in the trunk of a car, or a vehicle can be modified to carry it. For example, special racks can be put in the trunk, or the rear seat can be removed and special racks installed. Investigators are advised, when storing equipment in a car trunk, to organize items laterally instead of longitudinally, for if the car is involved in a high-speed rear-end collision, equipment oriented front-to-back can puncture through the back seat of the car or rupture the fuel tank.

A mobile crime lab is usually a commercially customized vehicle that provides compartments to hold equipment and countertops for processing evidence. However, some vehicles cannot go directly to some crime scenes, so the equipment must be transported from the vehicle in other containers. The most frequently used equipment should be in the most accessible locations in the vehicle. Substances that freeze or change consistency in temperature extremes should be protected.

All selected vehicles should be equipped with radio communication and be able to convey equipment to disaster scenes as well as crime scenes—to make them cost-effective. Cost reduction can be achieved if vehicles are shared by multiple jurisdictions. For example, cities or counties may partner to form a crime scene team that responds to serious crimes; this multijurisdictional approach shares costs for training, equipment, vehicles, and personnel expenses. Cost-effectiveness can be further enhanced if the vehicles are available as command posts, for stakeouts, and as personnel carriers.

Regardless of whether you work with a fully equipped mobile crime laboratory or a small, portable crime scene investigation kit, your knowledge and skills as an investigator are indispensable to a successful investigation. The most sophisticated, expensive investigative equipment available is only as effective as you are in using it.

Training in Equipment Use

The largest failure in gathering evidence is not the equipment available but lack of training in using it effectively. Each officer should understand the use and operation of each item of equipment in the kit. Expertise comes with training and experience. Periodic refresher sessions should be held to update personnel on new techniques, equipment, and administrative decisions. Investigators must also stay up-to-date on court decisions regarding the use of crime scene equipment and its reliability.

Once investigators have the proper equipment and are competent in using it, they are ready to begin finding and processing evidence. Before actually stepping into the crime scene to process evidence, however, it is vitally important that investigators protect the integrity of the scene to keep it from becoming contaminated.

Crime Scene Integrity and Contamination of Evidence

The value of evidence is directly affected by what happens to it immediately following the crime. Evidence in an unprotected crime scene will degrade, diminish, or disappear over time unless collected and preserved. Recalling Locard's principle of exchange, the very act of collecting evidence, no matter how carefully done, will result in a postcrime transfer of material. When anything is introduced to the scene that was not there originally, **contamination** has occurred. In fact, most contamination is caused by those who are investigating the crime scene (Warrington, 2014).

To minimize contamination of a crime scene and the evidence within, cordon off the area and keep all unnecessary people, including police officers, outside the scene perimeter. Law enforcement officers not assigned to the crime who walk through a scene out of curiosity can obliterate clues and add trace evidence.

Another important step to minimizing contamination is for all personnel processing the scene to wear protective clothing, including Tyvek® suits that cover the head, disposable gloves, and shoe booties. Such protective gear keeps fibers, hairs, dirt, and anything else present on the investigator's clothing from falling off and contaminating the crime scene.

Take extreme care to avoid **cross-contamination**, that is, allowing items of evidence to touch one another and thus exchange matter. When using the same tool for several tasks, be certain it is thoroughly cleaned after each use to prevent the transfer of material from one piece of evidence to another. Change gloves in between the handling of each piece of evidence. A common practice is to wear two pairs of gloves so that when the outer layer needs changing, it can be taken off quickly and fresh pair put back on, without the risk of contaminating the scene with an officer's bare hands (Warrington, 2014).

Bag items of evidence separately to prevent transfer of material between them. For example, in a sexual assault investigation, each item of clothing should be placed in its own bag to prevent fluids, fibers, or other trace evidence on that item from potentially mixing with those on other items. Finally, bag gloves and shoe coverings and submit them with the evidence, in the event that such protective gear has picked up any evidence. Gloves, booties, and any other clothing that has been in contact with bodily fluids should be bagged and labeled as a biohazard.

Make sure that evidence does not lose its value—its integrity—because of a contaminated crime scene.

Integrity of evidence refers to the requirement that any item introduced in court must be in the same condition as when it was found at the crime scene. This is documented by the **chain of evidence**, also called the **chain of custody**: documentation of what has happened to the evidence from the time it was discovered until it is needed in court, including every person who has had custody of the evidence and why.

The value of evidence may also be compromised by improper collection, handling, or identification. Therefore, investigators' evidence processing skills are extremely important.

Processing Evidence: Maintaining the Chain of Custody from Discovery to Disposal

Simply collecting physical evidence is not enough. To be of value, the evidence must be legally seized and properly and legally processed. Of importance at this point is processing evidence correctly.

> **LO1** Explain the requisite steps involved in processing physical evidence correctly, from its discovery to final disposition.
>
> Processing physical evidence correctly includes discovering or recognizing it; collecting, recording, and identifying it; packaging, conveying, and storing it; examining it; exhibiting it in court; and disposing of it when the case is closed.

Discovering or Recognizing Evidence

During a crime scene search, it is often difficult to determine immediately what is or might be evidence. Numerous objects are present, and not all are evidence.

> **LO1** Explain the requisite steps involved in processing physical evidence correctly, from its discovery to final disposition.
>
> To determine what is evidence, first consider the apparent crime. Then look for any objects unrelated or foreign to the scene, unusual in location or number, damaged or broken, or whose relation to other objects suggests a pattern that fits the crime.

Recall from Chapter 4 that evidence left out in the open, in plain view, that is immediately recognizable as relating to a crime, can be seized by officers engaged in a lawful activity. Also recall from Chapter 1 that investigators may discover exculpatory evidence, or evidence that is favorable to the accused. According to the Brady rule, which will be explored in greater depth in Chapter 21, law enforcement officers are required to gather all evidence that helps establish guilt *or* innocence. Officers must, however, be aware of the risks inherent in both over- and underdisclosure: "Over-disclosure could unnecessarily muddy the waters of the case and, in some cases, harm the reputation of a witness officer. Under-disclosure would deprive the original defendant of his constitutional right to a fair trial and could even lead to civil liability for law enforcement" (Means, 2008, p. 12). Investigators must use common sense in deciding what is or might be evidence.

The importance of physical evidence depends on its ability to establish that a crime was committed and to show how, when, and by whom. Logic and experience help investigators determine the relative value of physical evidence. Evidence in its original state is more valuable than altered or damaged evidence.

Probabilities play a large role in determining the value of evidence. Fingerprints and DNA, for example, provide positive identification. In contrast, blood type does *not* provide positive identification, but it can help eliminate a person as a suspect.

An object's individuality is also important. For example, a heel mark's value is directly proportional to the number of its specific features—such as brand name, number of nails, and individual wear patterns—that can be identified. Some objects have identification marks on them. Other evidence requires a comparison to be of value—a tire impression matching a tire, a bullet matching a specific revolver, a torn fragment of clothing matching a shirt.

A **standard of comparison** is an object, measure, or model with which evidence is compared to determine whether both came from the same source. Fingerprints are the most familiar example of evidence requiring a standard of comparison. A fingerprint found at a crime scene must be matched with a known print to be of value. Likewise, a piece of glass found in a suspect's coat pocket can be compared with glass collected from a window pane broken during a burglary.

Sometimes how an object fits with the surroundings determines whether it is likely to be evidence. For example, a man's wristwatch found in a women's locker room does not fit. The same wristwatch in a men's locker room is less likely to be evidence.

Sometimes, to detect evidence, the human eye needs assistance. Tools and techniques available to enhance evidence detection include forensic light sources (FLSs) and three-dimensional (3-D) technology.

FLSs, also called alternative light sources (ALSs), are becoming increasingly popular and easier to use. An FLS that works on the principle of ultraviolet fluorescence, infrared luminescence, or laser light can make evidence visible that is not otherwise detectable to the naked eye, such as latent prints, body fluids, and even altered signatures.

Ultraviolet (UV) light is the invisible energy at the violet end of the color spectrum that causes substances to emit visible light, commonly called *fluorescence*. Evidence that fluoresces, or glows, is easier to see— sometimes thousands of times easier. For some kinds

Technology Innovations

Crime-lite® XL Forensic Light Source

Portable forensic light sources have becoming increasingly prevalent in crime scene investigations, with new technology rolling out continuously. The Crime-lite XL, developed by Foster + Freeman, has been touted as the world's most powerful, handheld LED forensic light source. Equipped with 96 high-intensity LEDs, the Crime-lite XL offers shadow-free light beams in a range of wavelengths, including blue, blue/green, green, and orange, for either close-up examination or wide-area detection of even the most minute traces of blood, body fluids, fingerprints, hairs and fibers, bone and tooth fragments, explosive residues, and accelerants.

The Crime-lite XL emulates the power density of a forensic laser and enhances the visibility of evidence through various features such as anti-glare camera filters, narrowband "trimming filters" to reduce interference from background fluorescence, and anti-glare viewing goggles. The light can be powered by plugging in to a typical AC voltage outlet or by a pair of rechargeable lithium batteries carried inside an all-weather power pack weighing less than four pounds and worn across the investigator's shoulder. The batteries have a run-life of 44–270 minutes, depending on the intensity of the light beams used, and can be recharged in 22 minutes.

Source: http://ffsupport.co.uk/Brochures/Crimelite_XL.pdf.

of hard-to-see evidence—small amounts of semen, for instance, or fibers—an FLS is the only practical way to make the invisible visible. An inexpensive tool for investigators projects a filtered light beam onto evidence dusted with fluorescent powder, and a luminescent print appears immediately. A portable long-wave UV light source can illuminate latent prints on several types of objects. Evidence can also be brought back to a lab and exposed to superglue (cyanoacrylate), then stained or dusted, and viewed under a UV light source.

Lasers can also assist in investigations by helping to detect evidence such as body fluids, fibers, fingerprints, and various other materials containing chemicals that fluoresce under the high-energy beam of laser light (Geberth, 2010a). Thermal imaging is another common forensic light technique. In one case, a motorcyclist driving along a highway had shot a trucker. The crime scene was 1.5 miles long, and officers had 14 shell casings to locate. Using a thermal imager, they were able to recover all 14 casings.

The Law Enforcement Thermographers Association (LETA) has approved thermal imaging for search and rescue missions, fugitive searches, perimeter surveillance, vehicle pursuits, flight safety, marine and ground surveillance, structure profiles, disturbed surfaces, and hidden compartments. Police often use thermal imaging to detect heat generated by indoor marijuana-growing operations. However, recall from Chapter 4 that the Supreme Court has ruled that using thermal imaging to view inside a residence is a search under the Fourth Amendment and requires a search warrant.

Marking, Identifying, and Collecting Evidence

Once evidence is discovered, place an evidence marker next to it (these come in alpha and numeric versions, and some have a ruler on them for scale); record the item on an evidence log, listing the marker (letter or number) placed by it for identification; and then photograph and sketch it before collecting or otherwise moving it. Mark, log, photograph, and collect all objects that are or may be evidence, leaving the final decision regarding relevance to the prosecutor.

Collecting evidence requires judgment and care. Put liquids in bottles. Protect cartridges and spent bullets with cotton, and put them in small containers. Put other items in appropriate containers to preserve them for later packaging and transporting. The scene of a violent crime should be vacuumed with a machine that has a filter attachment. The vacuumed material can then be placed in an evidence bag and submitted to a crime laboratory.

Be sure to collect an adequate amount of the sample and to obtain standards of comparison, if necessary.

> **LO2** Identify the common errors in collecting evidence.
>
> Common errors in collecting evidence are (1) not collecting enough of the sample, (2) not obtaining standards of comparison, and (3) not maintaining the integrity of the evidence.

To simplify testimony in court, one officer usually collects evidence and another officer takes notes on the location, description, and condition of each item. The officer collecting evidence enters this information in personal notes or witnesses and initials the notes of the officer assigned to record information. All evidence is identified by the officer who collects it and by any other officer who takes initial custody of it.

> **LO1** Explain the requisite steps involved in processing physical evidence correctly, from its discovery to final disposition.
>
> Mark or identify each item of evidence in a way that can be recognized later. Indicate the date and case number as well as your personal identifying mark or initials.

Make your marking easily recognizable and as small as possible—to reduce the possibility of destroying part of the evidence. Mark all evidence as it is collected or received. Do not alter, change, or destroy evidence or reduce its value by the identification marking. Where and how to mark depends on the item. A pen is suitable for some objects. A stylus is used for those that require a more permanent mark that cannot be done with a pen, such as metal boxes, motor parts, and furniture. Other objects can be tagged, labeled, or placed in containers that are then marked and sealed.

> **LO1** Explain the requisite steps involved in processing physical evidence correctly, from its discovery to final disposition.
>
> Record in your notes the date and time of collection, where the evidence was found and by whom, the case number, a description of the item, and who took custody of it.

Evidence descriptions can be entered into the computer and cross-referenced to current cases in the local jurisdiction and the surrounding area.

Packaging and Preserving Evidence

Careful packaging maintains the evidence in its original state, preventing damage or contamination. Do not mix, or cross-contaminate, evidence. Package each item separately, keeping in mind the specific requirements for that type of evidence. Some evidence is placed in sterile containers. Other types, such as firing-pin impressions or markings on a fatal bullet, are packed to prevent breakage or wrapped in cotton to prevent damage to individual characteristics. Hairs, fibers, and other trace evidence are often placed in paper that is folded using a druggist fold so that the evidence cannot fall out.

> **LO1** Explain the requisite steps involved in processing physical evidence correctly, from its discovery to final disposition.
>
> Package each item separately in a durable container to maintain the integrity of evidence.

Packaging is extremely important. An investigator should have both plastic and paper forms of packaging available so items can be packed properly based on what the evidence is. Although sometimes plastic bags are used, few departments use plastic because it does not "breathe" and hence may cause condensation to form. This can impede laboratory examination of the evidence. Many departments use new brown-paper grocery bags, especially for clothing. Although boxes may be better in some respects and are preferable for handguns, they can be impractical to carry and difficult to find. You can usually find a supermarket open somewhere if you run out of bags. Be sure to provide a means of sealing whatever type of container is used to maintain the integrity of the evidence. Remember to put a biohazard sticker on or otherwise label packages holding items that contain bodily fluids. Some agencies also provide investigators with stickers to identify packages containing chemicals.

Preserve evidence on immovable items at the scene. Often some reproduction of the evidence is made. Fingerprints are developed, photographed, lifted, and later compared. Tool marks are reproduced through photography, modeling clay, moulage, silicone, and other impression-making materials. (These methods are acceptable in accordance with the best-evidence rule.) Specific requirements for the most frequently found evidence and best evidence are discussed later.

Submit movable items directly into evidence or send them to a laboratory for analysis. Sometimes an object is both evidence and a container of evidence. For example, a stolen laptop found in a suspect's car is evidence of theft, and the fingerprints of a second suspect found on the laptop are evidence that links that person to the theft.

Before packaging evidence for mailing to a laboratory, make sure it was legally obtained and has been properly identified and recorded in your notes. Submitting inadmissible evidence is costly and inefficient. Pack any bulky item in a sturdy box, seal the box with tape, and mark it "evidence." If any latent evidence such as a fingerprint is on the surface of the object be sure to state this clearly (Figure 5.1).

Place a transmittal letter to the laboratory in an envelope attached to the outside of the box. This letter should contain the name of the suspect and the victim, if any; what examinations are desired and which tests, if any, have already been done; and refer to any other pertinent correspondence or reports. Include a copy of the letter with the evidence, and mail the original separately. Retain a copy for your files. Figure 5.2 shows a sample letter.

Transporting Evidence

If the crime laboratory is nearby, an officer can deliver the evidence personally. However, even if the evidence is personally delivered, include with it a written request on department letterhead or a department form. Most laboratories have guidelines on this and provide forms that include boxes for all of the information they request.

> **LO1** Explain the requisite steps involved in processing physical evidence correctly, from its discovery to final disposition.
>
> Personal delivery, registered mail, insured parcel post, air express, FedEx, and United Parcel Service (UPS) are legal ways to transport evidence. Always specify that the person receiving the evidence is to sign for it.

How evidence should be transported depends on its size and type and the distance involved. Use the fastest method available. If the package is mailed, request a return receipt.

> **LO1** Explain the requisite steps involved in processing physical evidence correctly, from its discovery to final disposition.
>
> Package evidence properly to keep it in substantially the same condition in which it was found and store it securely. Document custody of the evidence at every stage.

Protecting, Storing, and Managing Evidence

Before, during, and after its examination, evidence must be securely protected, properly stored, and consistently managed. Securing, storing, and tracking evidence is no small task because each article must be accounted for at all times.

A major crime scene investigation might generate more than 200 pieces of evidence. The amount of property that must be tracked and stored in metropolitan departments is typically 100,000 to 400,000 or more items. To account for so many items accurately and to maintain the chain of custody, each item must be categorized and described, including ownership (rightful, seized, found, etc.). Its location should be documented, as should its disposition (returned, auctioned, burned, etc.).

All evidence received is recorded in a register, properly marked, and put in an appropriate storage place. An evidence custodian checks each piece of evidence to ensure that all forms are properly completed and that the evidence is the same as described in the forms. Strict checkout procedures ensure that the evidence is always accounted for. Everyone who takes evidence signs for it, giving the date, time, place it is to be taken, and purpose. When the evidence is returned, it is again signed for, dated, and examined to ensure it is in the same condition as when taken. Any change in condition is noted and explained.

Physical evidence is subject to chemical change, negligence, accident, intentional damage, theft, and alteration during handling. With proper storage, however, theft, loss, tampering, contamination, and deterioration may be prevented. The storage area must be secure, well organized, and free from pests, insects, and excessive heat or moisture. A proper storage area has ample space and is climate controlled, typically kept at 65°–75° F. Evidence is stored in vaults, property rooms, evidence rooms, evidence lockers, garages, or morgues or under special conditions such as refrigeration. At a crime scene, an officer's vehicle trunk can provide temporary storage.

Some evidence requires more care than others. For example, explosives or biohazardous material may pose a danger to property room managers, require special

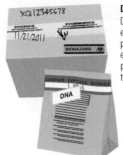

DNA/Biological Evidence

DNA and other forms of biological evidence should be collected and packaged dry using paper bags, envelopes, and boxes. Avoid using plastic or containers that hold moisture to prevent decomposition of the sample.

Latent Prints

Latent cards and lift tape are packaged in sealed envelopes. Paperwork, photographs, and information about where the prints were lifted should be included as well.

Controlled Substances/Narcotics

Items can vary in type and size: bongs, pipes, containers, cans, etc. Items can also include vegetation and organic substances. Nonorganic items should be packaged accordingly using bags or boxes to match their size. Items should be dry when packaged. Organic items should also be packaged using paper instead of plastic to avoid decomposition.

Ballistics/Tool Mark/Castings

Firearms should be packaged securely in an evidence gun box. Plastic zip ties should be used to secure the firearm in place. Firearms should only be packaged unloaded and with the safety on. Casings and loose ammunition should be packaged separately from the firearm.

Trace

There is a wide range of trace evidence. Depending on the evidence the proper packaging can differ. Trace evidence related to explosives is typically analyzed through the ATF and packaged using their specific guidelines. For residues use sterile absorbent materials such as swabs or gauzes. These items should be packaged in dry paper envelopes. Soil samples should be frozen or refrigerated, and collected in a plastic or glass container which should then be packaged in a Styrofoam container to maintain cold temperatures. Liquids should be packaged in glass vials and carefully secured and packaged in evidence boxes. Evidence related to arson that may have flammable chemicals should be packaged in appropriate containers such as lined metal cans.

Multimedia/Digital

Multimedia and digital evidence can include, but is not limited to, computer hard drives (external and internal), USB flash drives, various forms of memory cards, video game consoles with hard drives, cell phones, pad computers, digital cameras, etc. Evidence should be packaged securely in evidence boxes.

Sealing of Evidence

Proper sealing of evidence is imperative to prevent contamination and to maintain the integrity of the sample. Self-sealing evidence bags, evidence tape or heat sealing are all acceptable ways to seal evidence. Evidence tape must completely cover open seams and edges of the evidence bag. The sealer should initial or place another form of identification, such as a badge number, directly on or across the seal. If the evidence contains biohazardous material, a biohazard sticker should also be placed on the evidence.

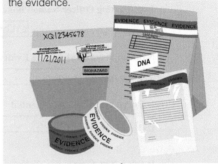

Evidence Submission

All chain of custody forms, related reports, invoices, and other required forms should be completed and attached with the evidence. If the evidence is to be mailed, the evidence should be safely packaged in a box that will ensure protection. An invoice and other required paperwork should be attached to the outside of this packaging. If necessary, the package should also be identified using markers or stickers to notify the receiver of the type of evidence contained or if the evidence is hazardous. The package should then be wrapped to cover the invoice and package.

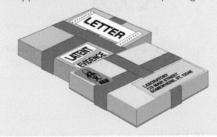

Figure 5.1
Evidence packaging.

Print Form

001-EV
Authorization: DAS 05/03/2010
Page 1 of 3 Pages

MINNESOTA BCA FORENSIC SCIENCE SERVICE
ANALYSIS REQUEST FORM

Bureau of Criminal Apprehension
Forensic Science Laboratory
1430 Maryland Avenue East
St. Paul, MN 55106
651-793-2900
Email: bca.lab@state.mn.us

Bureau of Criminal Apprehension
Forensic Science Laboratory
3700 N. Norris Court NW
Bemidji, MN 56601
218-755-6600

Please provide the following information, as well as the Submitting Agency Report, so we can effectively and efficiently process your case. If submitting by mail or delivery service, please mail each case separately. Please type or print clearly.

Submitting Agency: Anycity Police Department

Agency Case Number: 11-0011

Investigating Officer Name/Phone: Detective Christine Y. Lim

Investigating Officer Email: CYLIM@ci.anycity.mn.us

Name of Person Submitting Evidence: Detective Christine Y. Lim

Type of Offense: Burglary

If Burglary: **Residential**   ☒   **Commercial**   ☐

Date of Offense: 04/01/2011

Is this a New Case?   Yes   ☒   No   ☐

If No: Additional Item(s)   ☐   Resubmitted Item(s)   ☐

If Additional/Resubmitted – BCA Lab #

Requested Analysis *(please check)*:

Alcohol	☐	**Questioned Documents**	☐
Toxicology	☐	**Arson**	☐
Latent Prints	☒	**Trace**	☐
Firearms	☐	**Drug Chemistry**	☐
Nuclear DNA	☐	**Mitochondrial DNA**	☐

UNCONTROLLED COPY WHEN PRINTED
MN BCA Forensic Science Service

BCA

Figure 5.2
Bureau of Criminal Apprehension (a division of the Minnesota Department of Public Safety) evidence processing request.

Source: http://dps.mn.gov/divisions/bca/bca-divisions/forensic-science/Documents/Minnesota%20BCA%20Forensic%20Science%20Service%20Analysis%20Request%20Form.pdf

training in handling, and necessitate specialized facilities and features for safe storage. Electronic evidence, such as computers and digital storage media, must be kept away from strong magnets and other forces that may corrupt the data. Improperly sealed containers can allow liquid evidence to evaporate or moisture to enter; envelopes can split open; tags can fall off; writing on labels can become smudged, blurred, or faded to the point of illegibility. Therefore, use extreme care whenever handling evidence, keeping it away from moisture, heat sources, and any other factor that may degrade the integrity of the evidence.

Managing the growing mass of evidence is becoming increasingly challenging. Nationwide, law enforcement agencies are facing a rising need for more storage space

001-EV
Authorization: DAS 05/03/2010
Page 2 of 3 Pages

MINNESOTA BCA FORENSIC SCIENCE SERVICE
ANALYSIS REQUEST FORM - Continued

Drug Cases :

　　Possession　☐

　　Sale　☐

　　Search Warrant　☐

　　Manufacture　☐

For Marijuana Cases, Please Provide the Jury Court Date: _____
(Marijuana cases will not be accepted without a Jury Court Date)

Syringes are not accepted

Latent Print Cases:
Elimination Prints from All Principals　Yes ☒　No ☐

Major Case Prints (fingers/palms) for Crimes Against People　Yes ☒　No ☐

Is the Evidence Processed?　Yes ☐　No ☒

If Yes, what Type of Processing? _____

DNA Cases:
Known DNA Samples from All Principals　Yes ☐　No ☒

EACH ITEM MUST BE SEALED SEPARATELY. INITIALS MUST BE ON SEALS.

Principals Information

Victim(s) (Last Name, First Name, Middle Name)	Date of Birth (MM/DD/YYYY)	SID Number or N/A
Smith, Joseph Daniel	01/03/1980	N/A

UNCONTROLLED COPY WHEN PRINTED
MN BCA Forensic Science Service

Figure 5.2
(Continued)

to accommodate the seemingly exponential increase in the quantity of evidence they must store for longer periods, as scientific advances in DNA technology have caused many state legislatures to extend or eliminate their statutes of limitation.

Automated evidence storage can prevent many problems. Computer programs are available to help manage the property/evidence room. Many property control systems are using bar codes, which are extremely efficient and effective. At the time property is "booked," it is entered into a computer and given a bar code, which is affixed to the item. During any subsequent signing in or out of the property, the chain of custody is updated by scanning the item's evidence bar code into the log. Such a system provides an audit trail,

MINNESOTA BCA FORENSIC SCIENCE SERVICE
ANALYSIS REQUEST FORM - Continued

Suspect(s) *(Last Name, First Name, Middle Name)*	Date of Birth *(MM/DD/YYYY)*	SID Number or N/A
Unknown		

Elimination Principal(s) *(Last Name, First Name, Middle Name)*	Date of Birth *(MM/DD/YYYY)*	SID Number or N/A
Johnson, John Jacob	01/01/1980	N/A
Johnson, Mary Margaret	01/02/1980	N/A

Additional Information/Comments:

To Evidence Processing Personnel:

I would like to request that Anycity Police Department case File#11-0011, Burglary of a residence evidence items #1-3, which are the suspect's fingerprints that were lifted from the scene, be compared with the known prints of John Jacob Johnson DOB-01/01/80 item #1a, and Mary Margaret Johnson DOB-01/02/80 item #2a. Items #1-3 were submitted on 04/31/11.

Any questions, please contact me at 555-222-3333.

Thank You,

Detective Christine Y. Lim, Badge# 100
Anycity Police Department

Figure 5.2
(*Continued*)

helps with the inventory process, and prints management and audit reports and disposition logs.

Handheld computers and portable printers capable of generating bar-coded labels are making the task of tagging and securing evidence more manageable. Bar codes can also help reduce the time investigators need to spend collecting and recording evidence at complicated crime scenes, such as homicides or major traffic crashes.

More advanced evidence tracking systems include software that can integrate both physical and electronic evidence, allowing the attachment of electronic images (e.g., digital crime scene photos and images of the physical evidence itself) to individual case files. If investigators need to access the evidence, they can pull up the electronic version online rather than having to check the physical evidence out of the system. These systems usually include a digital signature feature to track who has accessed the evidence (Mitchell, 2009).

The consequences of mishandling such property can range from public embarrassment to financial liability, civil charges against the department, and the inadmissibility of key evidence. All too often defendants are found not guilty because evidence in the chain of custody is not documented and cannot be determined. Furthermore, officers may be held civilly or even criminally liable if a case is thrown out because their negligence has compromised the chain of custody. Mismanaged evidence compromises the case at hand and can have negative impacts on other cases as well, if defense attorneys are able to show prior instances of poor evidence management (Schreiber, 2009).

Exhibiting Evidence in Court

Evidence is of little value to a criminal case if it is inadmissible in court. Therefore, adherence to a strict protocol is essential to ensure that evidence may be used during a trial.

> **LO3** Understand the criteria required to ensure admissibility of evidence in court.
>
> To ensure admissibility of evidence in court, be able to (1) identify the evidence as that found at the crime scene, (2) describe exactly where it was found, (3) establish its custody from discovery to the present, and (4) voluntarily explain any changes that have occurred in the evidence.

Typically, the officer who will identify the evidence in court obtains it from the evidence custodian and delivers it to the prosecuting attorney, who takes it to the courtroom and introduces it at the proper time. The identifying officer uses the notes he or she made at the scene to lay the proper foundation for identifying the evidence.

In addition to the integrity of the evidence itself, consideration should be given to *how* evidence is presented in court. Evidence presented in a dirty, battered cardboard box creates a much different image than evidence presented in a clean, neatly labeled box. Simple details like this can make a difference in jury perception, which, right or wrong, influences the credibility of the prosecution's case.

Scientific evidence is commonly presented in court as part of either the prosecutor's or the defense's case and is frequently accompanied by expert testimony. When assessing the admissibility of expert opinions based on scientific evidence or knowledge, courts look to the rulings of the *Frye* and *Daubert* cases for guidance. The opinion in *Frye v. United States* (1923) reads, in part, "Just when a scientific principle or discovery crosses the line between the experimental and demonstrable stages is difficult to define. Somewhere in this twilight zone the evidential force of the principle must be recognized, and while courts will go a long way in admitting expert testimony deduced from a well-recognized scientific principle or discovery, the thing from which the deduction is made must be *sufficiently established to have gained general acceptance in the particular field* in which it belongs" [emphasis added].

The merits of *Frye* faced much debate, and the *Frye* test was effectively displaced when the Supreme Court, in *Daubert v. Merrell Dow Pharmaceuticals* (1993), held that the Federal Rules of Evidence, not *Frye*, provide the standard for admitting expert scientific testimony. Within the rules is specifically R.702, which speaks directly to expert testimony: "If scientific, technical, or other specialized knowledge will assist the trier of fact to understand the evidence or to determine a fact in issue, a witness qualified as an expert by knowledge, skill, experience, training, or education, may testify thereto in the form of an opinion or otherwise."

In its opinion summary the Supreme Court stated, "'General acceptance' is not a necessary precondition to the admissibility of scientific evidence under the Federal Rules of Evidence, but the Rules—especially R.702—do assign to the trial judge the task of ensuring that an expert's testimony both rests on a reliable foundation and is relevant to the task at hand. Pertinent evidence based on scientifically valid principles will satisfy those demands." This requirement that an expert's testimony be both *reliable* and *relevant* is known as the two-pronged **Daubert** standard.

Final Disposition of Evidence

Evidence must be legally disposed of to prevent major storage problems as well as pilferage or unauthorized conversion to personal use. State statutes and city ordinances specify *how* to dispose of evidence, but most do not specify *when* this should occur. Therefore, departments typically go by the statute of limitations for the type of case when deciding how long to hold items of evidence before disposing of them. Every criminal offense has a statute of limitations except homicide, and these statutes vary from state to state.

In cases involving suspects, arrests, plea bargains, or trials, evidence is held until the case is cleared, at which time personal property may be returned to the rightful owner. In cases in which prosecution is not anticipated, contraband items can be released at any time. In misdemeanor cases where there are no suspects or arrests after one year, the property can generally be returned to the owner, sold, or destroyed. Items of evidence may also be returned or otherwise disposed of because the cases have exceeded the statute of limitations. As a general rule, evidence for felony cases is held three to five years, and evidence in sexual assault cases is retained for five to ten years. However, when an appeal occurs or is anticipated or the case is a homicide, evidence must be maintained indefinitely. "More mandates are being placed on evidence with DNA implications, which sometimes must be saved for as long as the case remains open, or must remain available to convicted individuals during the terms of his or her incarceration" (Schreiber, 2009, p. 11).

Furthermore, guidelines for disposing of evidence are changing because of advancing forensic technologies, which are allowing cases to be solved many years after the commission of a crime.

LO1 Explain the requisite steps involved in processing physical evidence correctly, from its discovery to final disposition.

After a case is closed, evidence is returned to the owner, auctioned, destroyed, or retained for training purposes.

Evidence is either disposed of continuously, annually, or on a special date. Departments using computerized evidence management programs can generate routine inventory reports that show the status of each case and whether the related evidence must be maintained or can be disposed of. Departments without such a system must manually review the status of items and then either return them as evidence to storage or dispose of them. Witnessed affidavits of disposal list all items sold, destroyed, or returned. The affidavits include the date, type of disposition, location, and names of all witnesses to the disposition.

An innovative approach to disposing of evidence that is no longer needed is the online auction. Noting that, by statute, law enforcement agencies are legally required to auction all seized, found, and unclaimed personal property, a former police detective decided to reshape and consolidate the typical auctions taking place in the parking lots of thousands of local police departments across the nation. In 1999, he created PropertyRoom.com, an auction website designed to ease the burden on local agencies. According to the site, PropertyRoom.com handles everything, from asset pickup, to evaluating and assessing each item, posting it online for auction, and returning the proceeds back to the local community from which the asset had come. To date, PropertyRoom.com has provided online auction services to more than 4,100 law enforcement agencies and has returned more than $170 million in proceeds back to local communities.

Occasionally, evidence that is not returned or sold is retained by the department for training purposes. If property is unclaimed, training coordinators may see if there is use for it. For example, weapons are often disguised for concealment and can be used in use-of-force classes. Drug evidence can be shown to landlords as examples of what to look for if they suspect their tenants are involved in illegal narcotic activity.

Having explored the path evidence generally takes during the course of an investigation, the discussion now turns to the most common types of evidence encountered and how they are examined.

Frequently Examined Evidence

The laboratory analyzes evidence associated with the physical characteristics of suspects using biometrics. **Biometrics** is the statistical study of biological data and a means to positively identify an individual by measuring that person's unique physical or behavioral characteristics. Biometric identification technology ranges from fingerprints to techniques that recognize voices, hand geometry, facial characteristics, and even blood vessels in the iris of an eye. Fingerprints and iris recognition are considered most reliable, followed by facial and hand, with voice the least reliable.

The lab also analyzes the class and individual characteristics of objects providing evidence. **Class characteristics** are the features that place an item into a specific category. For example, the size and shape of a tool mark may indicate that the tool used was a screwdriver rather than a pry bar. **Individual characteristics** are the features that distinguish one item from another of the same type. For example, chips and wear patterns in the blade of a screwdriver may leave marks that are distinguishable from those of any other screwdriver.

Whether the examination is done in-house or by a public or private forensic lab, investigators are strongly urged to use a lab that is accredited. Studies have found that crime labs that have not participated in a forensic science accreditation program often provide results of dubious quality, exposing a law enforcement agency to liability and potentially threatening the careers of officers who relied on the services of such labs. A 2009 National Academy of Sciences study of forensic science found serious shortcomings in the way many crime labs operate, reporting high fragmentation in the field (Hansen, 2013):

- Of the 389 publicly funded forensics labs operating in the United States in 2005, 210 were state or regional labs, 84 were county labs, 62 were municipal labs, and 33 were federal labs. Some major cities and counties have their own labs, as do some big-city medical examiner offices.

- There is wide variability in forensic science disciplines, not only in techniques and methodologies but also in reliability, error rates, reporting, research, general acceptability, and published material.

- There is a dearth of peer-reviewed, published studies establishing the scientific bases and reliability of many forensic disciplines.

- Many labs are underfunded and understaffed, which contributes to case backlogs and likely makes it more difficult for lab workers to do as much as they could to inform investigations, provide strong evidence for prosecutions, and avoid errors.

- Most labs operate under the auspices of law enforcement agencies, making them susceptible to pressures—overt and otherwise—to produce the kinds of results that police and prosecutors are looking for.

- Rigorous and mandatory accreditation and certification programs are lacking, as are strong standards and protocols for analyzing and reporting on forensic evidence. Only a few states require crime labs to be accredited.

Fingerprints

At the end of each human finger, on the palm side, exists a unique arrangement of small lines called *friction ridges*, which provide just enough roughness to give fingers "traction" when holding or otherwise manipulating objects. Within these friction ridges lie sweat pores. When the sweat they produce mixes with body oils, dirt,

L04 List the types of evidence most commonly found in criminal investigations.

Frequently examined physical evidence includes fingerprints; voiceprints; language; DNA; blood and other body fluids; scent; hairs and fibers; shoe and tire prints and impressions; bite marks; tools and tool marks; firearms and ammunition; glass; soils and minerals; safe insulation; rope, strings, and tapes; drugs; documents; laundry and dry-cleaning marks; paint; skeletal remains; wood; digital evidence; and other types of evidence, including weapons of mass destruction.

or other matter, that substance will rub off on any surface the finger touches, leaving behind a print if the surface is relatively smooth. Such friction-ridge skin impressions, or fingerprints, have been used as a means of identification for thousands of years and in several cultures (Barnes, 2011). It is thought that fingerprints were used as proof of a person's identity in China perhaps as early as 300 B.C., in Japan as early as A.D. 702, and in the United States since 1902.

Sir Francis Galton, a cousin of Charles Darwin, took up the scientific study of friction-ridge skin and authored the first book on fingerprints (Galton, 1892), in which he established that friction-ridge skin was unique to each individual and persistent throughout a person's life. Because Galton was the one to first define and name specific print minutiae, the minutiae have become known as Galton details (Barnes, 2011).

The fact that a person's friction-ridge patterns are formed before birth and remain the same throughout that person's life is what makes these features useful in criminal investigations. The lines in the thumbprint raindrops made by a second grader in art class will be the same pattern the person's thumb will leave on the newspaper they read every morning before going to work years later. Besides remaining consistent over time, prints are useful because they are unique—no two people have the same friction-ridge pattern. Therefore, through friction-ridge analysis, a fingerprint can be a positive way to prove that a suspect was at a crime scene. The implications of finding identifiable prints at the scene vary with each case. For example, prints may not be important if the suspect had a legitimate reason for being there. Often, however, this is not the case.

Although many laypeople assume that identifiable fingerprints are almost always found at a crime scene, in many cases none are found. Even when they are, it is often difficult to locate the person who matches the prints. If a person's prints are not on file and there are no suspects, fingerprints are virtually worthless. Other times, however, fingerprints are the most important physical evidence in a case (Figure 5.3). Finding fingerprints at a crime scene requires training and experience. An excellent reference for more information on fingerprint identification is *The Fingerprint Sourcebook* (International Association for Identification, et al., 2011).

Fingerprints are of various types:

- **Latent fingerprints** are impressions transferred to a surface, either by sweat on the ridges of the fingers or because the fingers carry residue of oil, dirt, blood, or other substances. Latent prints are not readily seen but can be developed through powders or chemicals. They are normally left on nonporous surfaces.

- **Visible fingerprints** are made when fingers are dirty or stained. They occur primarily on glossy or light-colored surfaces and can be dusted and lifted.

- **Plastic fingerprints**, one form of visible print, are impressions left in soft substances such as putty, grease, tar, butter, or soft soap. These prints are photographed, not dusted.

Any hard, smooth, nonporous surface can contain latent fingerprints. Nonporous surfaces include light switches; window frames and moldings; enameled surfaces of walls, doors, and painted or varnished objects; wood; lamps; polished silver surfaces; and glass. Fingerprints often occur on documents, glass, metals, tools, and weapons used in a crime as well as on any objects picked up or touched by a suspect or any other person. Objects such as firearms, tools, small metal objects, bottles, glassware, documents, and other transportable items are submitted to a laboratory, where the prints are developed by experts.

Some porous materials also produce latent prints. For example, paper and cloth surfaces have developed excellent prints. Passing a flashlight at an oblique angle over a surface helps to locate possible prints. Latent prints have even been collected from human skin.

Begin the search for fingerprints by determining the entry and exit points and the route through a crime scene. Look in the obvious places as well as less-obvious places such as the underside of toilet seats and the back of car rearview mirrors. Examine objects that appear to have been moved. You may need to expose surfaces to lighting at different angles to see prints. Consider the nature of the crime and how it was probably committed. Prints found on large, immovable objects are processed at the scene by photographing or dusting with powder or chemicals.

Dusting Latent Fingerprints. Fingerprint dusting powders are available in various colors and chemical compositions to provide maximum development and contrasts. When dusting for fingerprints, use a powder that contrasts in color to the surface. Do not powder a print unless it is necessary, and do not powder a visible print until after you photograph it.

Spraggs (2007, p. 26) cautions, "The number one mistake officers make is over-processing the latent fingerprint. First rule: use less powder than you think you need." Another serious error, one that can negate the forensic integrity and evidentiary value of the print, is using a contaminated brush: "Although using fingerprint powder is quick and inexpensive, concerns have been raised recently concerning the possibility of contamination

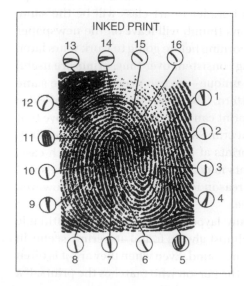

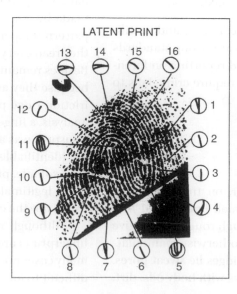

Figure 5.3
Three men checked into a motel at 11:00 p.m. Shortly after midnight, when a new desk clerk came on duty, the men went to the office and committed an armed robbery. Police investigating the scene went to the room occupied by the three men and found a latent fingerprint on an ashtray. The print was later matched to one of the suspects whose fingerprints were on file with the police department.

due to the transfer of DNA through the use of fingerprint brushes. . . . Crime scene examiners are being warned to be aware of this possibility" (Yamashita & French, 2011, pp. 7–14).

To dust for fingerprints, follow these steps:

1. Make sure the brush is clean and that you are wearing a clean pair of gloves. Roll the handle of the brush rapidly between your palms. This action will cause the bristles at the end of the brush to separate and fan out.

2. Shake the powder can to loosen the powder. Open the can and place a small amount of powder into the lid. Dip the brush into the powder contained in the lid, not directly into the can, so as to avoid contaminating the entire powder container. The remaining powder in the lid should be discarded before replacing the lid back on the can.

3. Apply the powder lightly to the print, following the contour lines of the ridges to bring out details.

4. Remove all excess powder with the brush.

5. Photograph.

Use a camel-hair brush for most surfaces. Use an aspirator for dusting ceilings and slanted or difficult areas. If in doubt about which powder or brush to use, test them on a similar area first.

A word of caution to crime scene examiners: concern exists surrounding the possibility of contamination and the transfer of DNA through improper use of fingerprint brushes (Yamashita & French, 2011). Investigators must take care to not inadvertently cross-contaminate samples when dusting prints that may be from different sources.

Learn to use the various materials by watching an experienced investigator demonstrate the correct powders, brushes, and techniques. Then practice placing latent prints on various surfaces and using different-colored powders to determine how well each adheres and how much color contrast it provides. Practice until you can recognize surfaces and select the appropriate powder.

When photographing developed latent prints, record the color of the powder used, the color of the surface, and the location of the prints. Place your identification, date, and case number on the back of the photograph and submit it to the crime laboratory. The laboratory will determine whether it is an identifiable print and whether it matches a known suspect or other people whose prints were submitted for elimination.

Lifting Prints. To lift fingerprints, use a commercially prepared lifter that has both a black-and-white background and a wide transparent lift tape. Use black lifters for light powders and light lifters for black powders.

To lift prints on doorknobs or rounded surfaces, use transparent tape so you can see any spots where the tape is not sticking. Put the tape over the dusted print. Do not use too much pressure. Work out any bubbles that appear under the tape by applying extra pressure. When you have lifted the print, transfer it to a fingerprint card.

Common errors in lifting prints include removing too much or too little powder from the ridges, allowing bubbles to develop under the tape, and failing to make two lifts when a second lift would be better than the first.

Chemical Development of Latent Fingerprints. Although powders are used to develop latent fingerprints on many surfaces, they are not recommended for unpainted wood, paper, cardboard, or other absorbent surfaces. Using powder on such surfaces will smudge any prints, destroying their value as evidence. For such surfaces, use a special chemical such as iodine, ninhydrin, or silver nitrate.

Use gloves and a holding device to avoid contaminating the evidence by inadvertently adding your own fingerprints. The chemicals can all be applied to the same specimen because each reacts differently with various types of materials. However, if *all* are used, the order must be iodine first, then ninhydrin, and finally silver nitrate.

In the *iodine method*, iodine crystals are placed in a fuming cabinet or a specially prepared fuming gun. The crystals are heated and vaporized, producing a violet fume that is absorbed by the oil in the fingerprints. The fingerprint ridges appear yellow-brown and must be photographed immediately because they fade quickly. Fuming cabinets and guns can be made or purchased from police supply houses.

The *ninhydrin method* develops amino acids. Ninhydrin (highly flammable) is available in spray cans or in a powder form from which a solution of the powder and acetone or ethyl alcohol is made. The evidence is then either sprayed or brushed with or dipped into the ninhydrin. Development of prints can be speeded up by applying heat from a fan, pressing iron, or oven. At room temperature, prints develop in a minimum of two hours; with a pressing iron, they develop almost immediately. Ninhydrin-developed prints do not fade immediately, but they eventually lose contrast. Therefore, photograph them soon after development.

The *silver nitrate method* develops sodium chloride in the fingerprint ridges into silver chloride that appears as a red-brown print. Because silver nitrate destroys oils and amino acids, it must be used *after* the iodine and ninhydrin methods. Immerse the specimen in a solution of 3%–10% silver nitrate and distilled water. Remove it immediately and hang it to dry. The prints can be developed more rapidly by applying light until they start to develop. They should be photographed immediately because they disappear after several hours.

Other Methods of Lifting Prints. Fingerprints may also be located and developed by using Magnabrush techniques, laser technology, gelatin lifters, and cyanoacrylate (superglue). Superglue fuming involves heating three or four drops of glue to generate fumes that adhere to fingerprints. The process can effectively develop prints on plastic, bank checks, counterfeit money, metal, and skin. Portable lasers are used to find and highlight fingerprints.

Photo Library/Getty Images

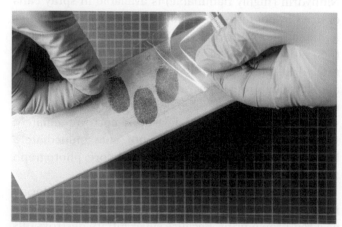

Lifting a print involves dusting powder onto a surface to reveal the print (top image) and then applying a lifter, typically a transparent adhesive tape, over the print. The next step is to transfer the lifted print on the tape to a print card (bottom image).

Sendo Serra/Shutterstock.com

They can detect fingerprints on the skin of a murder victim and trace a gunshot path.

Investigators can also use gelatin lifters to lift dusted prints or dust marks (footprints) from a wide variety of surfaces. Used in Europe for decades, the lifters are flexible and easily cut to suit specific needs. They can lift dust prints from any smooth surface—from tile floors to cardboard boxes. The high contrast of the black lifters allows investigators to see dust prints not visible to the naked eye, and the lifted prints photograph extremely well. In addition, the lifters can pick up particle samples such as hair or paint chips. In the laboratory, tweezers or a scalpel can remove the samples from the lifter without damaging the sampled material.

Elimination Prints. If fingerprint evidence is found, it is important to know whose prints "belong" at the scene. Prints of persons with reason to be at the scene are taken and used as **elimination prints**. For example, family members in a

Technology Innovations

Fingerprint Detection with Lumicyano™

Conventional fingerprinting methods that use dusting powders, developers, lifters, or vapors are beneficial in enhancing contrast but they may also alter the print or damage DNA in the sample and render additional testing worthless. In an effort to mitigate the detrimental impact on prints when they are subjected to multiple stages of testing, French researchers have developed an innovative method of detecting and enhancing prints that is faster and less expensive than traditional techniques. The method uses a product called Lumicyano™ to enhance the contrast of visible prints with a single step and, thereby, avoid the need to treat prints with toxic fumes or other chemicals that degrade the sample and compromise further testing for DNA. Lumicyano combines the common fuming ingredient of cyanoacrylate with a molecule of a small fluorescent colorant from the tetrazine family.

A study that compared Lumicyano to the conventional two-step cyanoacrylate fuming process found that Lumicyano detected fingerprints with equal or better sensitivity and ridge details than traditional fuming processes. Use of this technique helps preserve the integrity of prints, thus allowing investigators the option to conduct further testing for DNA (Prete et al., 2013).

home where a crime has occurred or employees of a business that has been robbed should be fingerprinted so that their fingerprints at the scene can be eliminated from suspicion.

Inked Prints. Most police departments have equipment for taking fingerprints. Standard procedure is to fingerprint all adults who have been arrested, either at the time of booking or at the time of release. These fingerprint records help ensure that the person arrested is identified correctly. Some departments have portable fingerprint kits in patrol vehicles that allow them to take inked prints and develop latent prints at crime scenes.

To take inked prints, start by rolling the right thumb and fingers on the ink pad in the order stated on the card. Then roll the left thumb and fingers in order. Use a complete roll—that is, go from one side to the other. Next, *press* the fingers and then the thumb of each hand on the spaces provided on the card. The card also has spaces for information about the person and the classification made by the fingerprint examiner. Learn to take inked fingerprints by having someone demonstrate.

Digital Fingerprinting. Advances in computer technology are allowing digital fingerprinting to replace inked printing. Latent fingerprints are scanned and converted into an electronic image or **inkless fingerprint** that is stored in a database for rapid retrieval. In this method, a suspect's hand is placed onto a glass platen, where a laser optically scans the prints and transfers them onto a fingerprint card. Benefits of using optical live-scan devices include rapid, accurate acquisition of a print; simple storage; easy retrieval; and quick transmittal to other officers and agencies.

Stored fingerprint information includes the person's gender, date of birth, classification formula, and each finger's ridge count. This Automated Fingerprint Identification System (AFIS) technology maps fingerprints and creates a spatial geometry of the minutiae of the print, which is changed into a binary code for the computer's searching algorithm. When queried, the system selects the cards within the range limitations for the entered classification formula. The capability of registering thousands of details makes it possible for the computer to complete a search in minutes that would take days manually. The search success rate has been as high as 98% in some departments with files under one million. Once the computer search finds a hit, a fingerprint expert then visually compares the prints.

If no match is found in local or state files, prints are submitted to the FBI Identification Division for a further search. This division has on file fingerprints of arrested people as well as of nearly 100 million other people such as aliens and individuals in government services, including the military. Given that approximately 35%–40% of crime scenes have latent prints, AFIS has provided a tremendous advance in crime fighting, first proving its value when it was used to solve the "Night Stalker" serial killer case in 1985.

The FBI's AFIS provides five major services to local, state, and federal law enforcement and criminal justice agencies:

- Ten print–based identification services (i.e., 10 rolled fingerprint impressions and 10 flat fingerprint impressions)

- Latent fingerprint services

- Subject search and criminal history services

- Document and image services

- Remote search services

One benefit of electronic fingerprinting systems is their increased speed and accuracy. Another major benefit of this technology is the ability to transmit the print image over wirelessly from one AFIS system to another or to computerized criminal records centers. This feature also allows international sharing of databases to help capture criminals who move from one country to another.

In September 2006, the FBI and the Department of Homeland Security merged their fingerprint databases into what is called the Integrated Automated Fingerprint Identification System, known as IAFIS. The merger of databases containing millions of fingerprints taken from convicted criminals and illegal immigrants marks an unprecedented interagency effort to capture more terrorists and solve more crimes. A fingerprint entered into IAFIS led to Lee Boyd Malvo, one of the two suspects in the Washington, DC, area sniper case. Malvo had been previously arrested by the Immigration and Naturalization Service (INS).

In 2011, the FBI upgraded its AFIS to **Advanced Fingerprint Information Technology (AFIT)**, an integrated system that can also incorporate additional biometric data such as latent palmprints and facial recognition technology. AFIT is part of the FBI's broader technology initiative called Next Generation Identification (NGI), which also includes an enhanced IAFIS repository. The new system reduces the time it takes to analyze fingerprints, from hours with AFIS to minutes with AFIT, and is more than 99% accurate, whereas the old system performed at a 92% accuracy rate.

Automated fingerprint identification systems are constantly being augmented with the introduction of new services and features and recently went mobile, allowing investigators in the field to take a live scan of a person's prints. The potential exists to adapt mobile fingerprint systems to quickly identify prints at crime scenes. The units will need to be modified to accommodate the scanning of crime scene prints, but this process could greatly reduce the important time frame of the first 24 hours after the commission of a crime, the period in which a suspect is most likely to be identified.

Despite the many benefits provided by automated fingerprint technology, these programs simply search the databases for possible matches. In the end, a human fingerprint examiner must determine the match. Furthermore, "Although automatic systems have improved significantly, the design of automated systems do not yet match the complex decision-making of a well-trained fingerprint expert as decisions are made to match individual fingerprints (especially latent prints)" (Moses, 2011, p. 31).

Fingerprint Patterns, Analysis, and Identification. Once a print has been captured, whether chemically developed, rolled in ink, or digitally scanned, the fingerprint patterns are analyzed for unique features that will, it is hoped, lead to identifying one individual. Fingerprint patterns are classified as *arched, looped,* or *whorled.* Variations of these configurations result in the nine basic fingerprint patterns illustrated in Figure 5.4. There are as many as 150 ridge characteristics in the average fingerprint, and examiners must typically match a minimum of 12–20

Technology Innovations

Mobile Fingerprint Readers

Mobile fingerprint readers are an investigative tool growing in popularity and usage among police departments nationwide and are carried by homicide detectives, coroner staff, motorcycle and foot patrol officers, and those patrolling on public transit buses or trains. DataWorks Plus has designed a variety of devices to enable officers in the field to identify individuals who either have no identification or who may be carrying fraudulent ID. The company's Evolution collection includes "all-in-one tablets, handheld smartphone devices, as well as separate RAPID-ID devices" that connect wirelessly to mobile data terminals. These products include "a patented light-emitting sensor with large fingerprint capture area." They offer "multimodal biometric identification by capturing fingerprints and/or irises and photos (for facial recognition), submitting to State or Federal databases, then returning results" to the device itself and/or MDT, typically within a few minutes. Furthermore, the technology allows officers to view associated record data, including NCIC, state arrest history, mugshots (when on file), and wants/warrants.

Source: http://dataworksplus.com/evolution.html

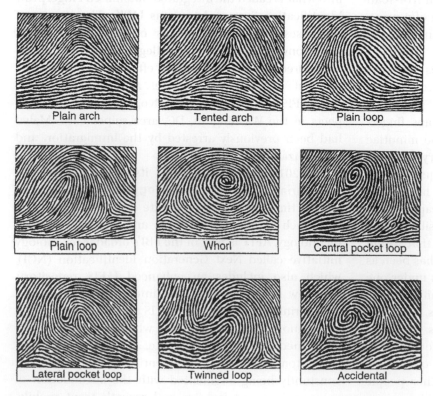

Figure 5.4
Nine basic fingerprint patterns.
Source: Courtesy of the FBI Law Enforcement Bulletin

Plain arch · Tented arch · Plain loop

Plain loop · Whorl · Central pocket loop

Lateral pocket loop · Twinned loop · Accidental

(as set by a department's or lab's standard operating procedures) characteristics on a single fingerprint for positive identification.

When using digital fingerprint images, the image quality becomes critical. As with rolled (inked) prints, smudges and distortions reduce the print's usefulness. Digital programs, if not up to standard, might also create artifacts or false minutiae in the image, which will impair an examiner's ability to analyze and match a print. Minimum standards have been established to ensure maximum usefulness of the prints they scan.

Usefulness of Fingerprints. Fingerprints are extremely valuable in criminal investigations.

> **L05** Compare and contrast the determinations that can and cannot be made from fingerprint, DNA, blood, and hair evidence.
>
> Fingerprints are *positive* evidence of a person's identity. They cannot, however, indicate a person's age, sex, or race.

Fingerprinting is increasingly being applied to homeland security efforts because fingerprints can be sent via communications systems across the country and around the globe and visually reproduced. Crime victims are identified by their prints to prove the corpus delicti. Courts, parole and probation officers, and prosecutors use fingerprints to positively identify people with multiple criminal records.

Fingerprints also aid in noncriminal investigations by helping to identify victims of mass disasters, missing persons, amnesia victims, and unconscious persons. Military agencies use fingerprints recorded at enlistment to identify those killed in combat. Hospitals use fingerprints or footprints to identify newborn babies. Furthermore, fingerprints are becoming widely used as identification for cashing checks and processing legal documents.

Admissibility in Court. To ensure admissibility in court, investigators should establish the probative value of the print; that is, either the defendant had claimed never being at the scene, or even if the defendant had legitimate access to the scene, that person did not have legitimate access to the object on which the print was found, or the print was found on the instrumentality of the crime. Investigators should also ensure admissibility by the testimony of the investigator who lifted the latent print, by the level of

expertise used by the fingerprint examiner, and by the testimony of the file supervisor who maintained the print.

As with digital photography, digital fingerprinting has faced authenticity and admissibility challenges in court. Despite attempts to create tracking software, to overcome such challenges, thus far no tool has been designed that will offer a secure chain of custody for digital prints.

Other Types of Prints. Suspects may leave palmprints, footprints, or even prints of lips, and these impressions can be photographed and developed just as fingerprints are. Palmprints contain many more friction-ridge landmarks than fingerprints have, thus giving print examiners more points of comparison when determining matches. Biometric databases are also beginning to store prints from the part of the hand called the *writer's edge*, the side of the hand, from the wrist up to the curled fifth, or "pinkie," finger that rests on the table or paper when someone is writing.

In one interesting case, a burglar shattered a restaurant's plate glass window. The police found no fingerprints around the window but did find footprints and a toe print on a piece of the broken glass. These were developed and lifted. Later, a 17-year-old was arrested for vagrancy. Learning that he often went barefoot, police also took his footprints and forwarded them to the FBI. They were identical to those on the plate glass window fragment. It was learned that the youth had taken off his shoes and put his socks on his hands to avoid leaving fingerprints at the crime scene. He was found guilty.

In another case, a string of peeping-Tom cases was solved because of three lip impressions left by the suspect on a windowpane. And in a case in Illinois, authorities matched lip prints on a piece of duct tape the suspect had held in his mouth while binding a victim.

Voiceprints

A **voiceprint** is a graphic record made by a sound spectrograph of the energy patterns emitted by speech. Like fingerprints, no two voiceprints are alike. Voice identification uses advanced computer systems and software to collect a speech sample and analyze how the person's words flow together, how they pause and breathe, and other unique patterns generated by each individual's mouth and larynx (Stern, 2015). Similar to the printout of a polygraph, a stylus produces jagged lines representing the frequency and intensity of the vocal sounds, which can later be compared against another voice sample provided by a suspect. Voiceprints can assist in identifying persons making bomb threats or hoax calls, obscene phone callers, kidnappers, terrorists, and others who use the phone in the commission of their criminal activities. A voiceprint captured during a phone call can be retained until a suspect is in custody. Then a sample of a suspect's voice can be taken and compared with the voiceprint evidence.

As with many other investigative techniques, advances in forensic audio analysis are giving investigators higher-quality data despite efforts of those being surveilled to distort their voices or conceal them with high levels of background noise. Use of adaptive digital filters can remove background noise and enhance speech and data from tapes. This technology can also analyze sounds other than voices, thus converting annoying background noise into isolated, distinguishable sounds that give clues about where the calls are originating.

The scientific community, while explicitly discrediting some voice analysis techniques, has not yet reached a consensus on the most effective method for identifying voices (Catanzaro, Tola, Hummel, & Viciano, 2017). Some researchers have highlighted limitations in the capacity of current technology to "see through" certain factors that might influence voice samples obtained from the same person but at different times, including stress, deception, intoxication, and illnesses (e.g., a severe cold) that impact breathing and speech, thus making comparison difficult (Hollien, 2012). Despite the growing popularity of voice analysis, most experts assert that the identity of a speaker can never be determined solely on voice alone. At most, analysts can say that two voices are compatible. Therefore, it is highly recommended that voiceprint results be used for investigative guidance only.

The use of voiceprints in criminal trials is controversial. In a number of cases, convictions obtained through voiceprints have been reversed because the voiceprints were not regarded as sufficiently reliable. Considering the current limitations of the science of voice identification, investigators are cautioned to not place too much reliance on the results of its application. As one renowned Italian forensic phoneticist once said, "In my opinion, nobody should be condemned because of a voice. . . . With voice, the likelihood of error is too high for a judge to ever be able to state that someone is guilty 'beyond any reasonable doubt'" (Catanzaro et al., 2017).

Language Analysis

An individual's communication, whether written or spoken, may provide clues about gender, age, race or ethnicity, or what part of the country (or world) the person grew up in or has spent recent time in. Language analysis may also provide insight into a person's educational level, political views, and religious orientation, which may in turn provide further evidence regarding a criminal motive. One area of language analysis involves *psycholinguistics*, the study of the mental processes involved in comprehending, producing, and acquiring language.

A useful and often overlooked type of evidence is the actual language used by victims, witnesses, and suspects at the crime scene. Analysis of such "excited utterances" can reveal the speaker's state of mind and may be admitted into testimony even if the person does not testify. To qualify for this exception to the hearsay rule, the victim or witness must have seen an exciting or startling event and made the statement while still under the stress of the event. This is similar to *res gestae* statements discussed in Chapter 1. To capture this type of evidence, many officers and investigators carry lightweight digital voice recorders with date- and time-stamp features.

Human DNA Profiling

Human cells contain discrete packs of information known as chromosomes, which are made of DNA. **DNA**, or *deoxyribonucleic acid*, is an organic substance contained in a cell's nucleus. The DNA double-helix strand is composed of building blocks called *nucleotides*, which consist of a base molecule connected to a molecule of sugar and a molecule of phosphoric acid. The four bases are adenine (A), guanine (G), cytosine (C), and thymine (T), which link to each other to form a chain millions of nucleotides long. Within this DNA chain are areas of *conserved regions*, where the A–G–C–T pattern is the same for every human, and *variable regions*, where the nucleotide sequence is distinct and different for every person, thereby determining a person's individual characteristics. This unique genetic code can be used to create a genetic fingerprint to positively identify a person. Except for identical (monozygotic) twins, no two individuals have the same DNA structure.

> **L05**   Compare and contrast the determinations that can and cannot be made from fingerprint, DNA, blood, and hair evidence.
>
> DNA can tell investigators the sample donor's gender, ethnicity, eye color, and hair color, and matching DNA to a known profile can provide positive identification of an individual.

The more officers know how to use DNA, the more powerful a tool it becomes. **DNA profiling** can be done on cells from almost any part of the body and is used in

Myth Identical twins have the same DNA.

Fact While identical (monozygotic) twins are born with identical DNA sequences, studies are beginning to suggest that random mutations that occur spontaneously over the course of one's lifespan may allow for the detection of these slight genetic divergences and variations over time (Drake, 2014).

paternity testing, immigration disputes, missing persons and unidentified body cases, and criminal and assailant identification. DNA analysis was used to identify many of the World Trade Center victims killed on September 11, 2001. DNA keeps its integrity in dried specimens for long periods and consequently can help resolve cold cases.

In the past, DNA evidence was usually collected only in violent crimes. In fact, the FBI laboratory does not accept cases involving property crimes such as theft, fraud, burglary, and automobile theft unless the cases involve more than $100,000. Part of the reason is that an average DNA case costs approximately $2,000 in forensic science, analytical time, and supplies. However, law enforcement agencies nationwide are beginning to recognize the value of using DNA technology to solve high-volume property crimes, such as burglary, despite the cost of such analysis (Wilson, McClure, & Weisburd, 2010).

For example, studies have found that habitual burglars commit an average of more than 120 high-volume offenses each year and they often escalate to more serious, violent crimes (Roman et al., 2008). Thus, identifying, apprehending, and prosecuting these offenders can have considerable payoff from a public safety standpoint. While the historical approach to property crimes was to conduct lab tests only if blood was found at the scene, the past decade has seen a rise in the volume of property crime evidence passing through labs because techniques are now able to yield results from previously unknown types of evidence, such as touch DNA (Roman et al., 2008).

Several NIJ studies have demonstrated that analyzing DNA from property crimes can be extraordinarily beneficial. For example, a 2008 DNA field experiment that compared burglary investigations using traditional methods, including fingerprint analysis, to burglary investigations that added DNA technology to traditional methods found:

- *Suspect identifications and arrests doubled.* Twice as many property crime suspects were identified and arrested when DNA evidence was collected (in addition to fingerprint evidence) compared to a traditional property crime investigation.

- *Cases accepted for prosecutions doubled.* More than twice as many cases were accepted for prosecution when DNA evidence was processed than when it was not.

- *The suspects arrested through DNA identifications were more dangerous.* DNA arrestees had double the number of prior arrests and double the prior convictions as those arrested through traditional investigations.

- *DNA was twice as effective in identifying suspects as fingerprints.* In cases where both fingerprint and biological evidence were collected, more suspects were identified via the FBI's Combined DNA Index System (CODIS) than were identified via the FBI's AFIS. (National Institute of Justice [NIJ], 2010)

Identifying, Collecting, and Preserving DNA Evidence. Considering the potential value of DNA evidence in a criminal case, investigators must understand and be trained in proper identification, collection, and preservation procedures for this type of evidence. "DNA testing for forensic analysis is only as effective as the sample collection methods. Improper sample collection, transport, and testing can lead to contaminated evidence and potentially invalidated results" (Puritan Medical Products, 2018). Table 5.2 lists possible items of crime scene evidence on which DNA might be located.

Often only a few cells are needed from which to obtain useful DNA information. Keep in mind that just because a stain is not visible does not mean there are not enough cells for DNA typing (NIJ, 2012b). Collection of DNA samples is often quite easy, with the bigger challenge becoming protecting against contamination. One of the easiest ways to collect a DNA sample from someone is to take a simple buccal swab of the suspect's mouth (Lindstrom, 2012, p. 9): "Buccal samples are collected by swabbing the inside of the person's mouth, thus removing epithelial cells from the inside of the cheek. These cells provide an excellent source of DNA, and the collection method does not require a specialized medical staff. This non-invasive procedure uses no needles, contains little biohazard waste, and permits sample retention at room temperature for many years."

When collecting DNA, officers should ensure the swabs are completely dry before packaging and during transport to prevent mold and other bacterial growth from contaminating the DNA sample (Puritan, 2018). Samples should never been stored or transported in plastic, as such containers have the potential to retain moisture which can degrade or destroy the integrity of the DNA sample. The recent development of specially designed collection tubes has made preserving DNA

TABLE 5.2 Identifying DNA Evidence

Evidence	Possible Location of DNA on the Evidence	Source of DNA
Bseball bat or similar weapon	Handle, end	Sweat, skin, blood, tissue
Hat, bandanna, or mask	Inside	Sweat, hair, dandruff
Eyeglasses	Nose or ear pieces, lens	Sweat, skin
Facial tissue, cotton swab	Surface area	Mucus, blood, sweat, semen, ear wax
Dirty laundry	Surface area	Blood, sweat, semen
Toothpick	Tips	Saliva
Used cigarette	Cigarette butt	Saliva
Stamp or envelope	Licked area	Saliva
Tape or ligature	Inside/outside surface	Sweat, tissue
Bottle, can, or glass	Sides, mouthpiece	Sweat, tissue
Used condom	Inside/outside surface	Semen, vaginal or rectal cells
Blanket, pillow, sheet	Surface area	Sweat, hair, semen, urine, saliva
"Through and through" bullet	Outside surface	Blood, tissue
Bite mark	Person's skin or clothing	Saliva
Fingernail, partial fingernail	Scrapings	Blood, sweat, tissue

Source: U.S. Department of Justice, National Institute of Justice, National Commission on the Future of DNA Evidence. (1999). *What every law enforcement officer should know about DNA evidence.* Washington, DC: Author.

samples more convenient and effective, as they incorporate air breathable Tyvek filters that allow swabs to dry while maintaining the integrity of the sample during transport. An added benefit of these new tubes is that they are designed to fit into traditional test tube racks, a feature that aids the laboratory analysts (Puritan, 2018).

States often produce their own handbooks to guide officers and investigators on the preferred methods of recognizing, collecting, and preserving physical evidence. The guidelines presented below are to help investigators avoid contaminating DNA evidence, and many have already been mentioned as standard best practices for evidence collection in general. These methods and standards, which are from the Wisconsin Department of Justice's *Physical Evidence Handbook* (2017, pp. 65–66), are similar to the protocols of many other states. We selected this checklist as an example because of its conciseness and its similarity to the streamlined checklist from the NIJ that had been presented in previous editions of this text (U.S. Department of Justice [DOJ], 1999). In noting the critical importance of preventing contamination of DNA evidence throughout all stages of a criminal investigation, starting with collection, the Wisconsin Department of Justice outlines the following precautions for officers to take:

- Wear proper protective clothing—gloves, mask/face shield, glasses.

- Do not handle any items without gloves. Change gloves after handling each item.

- Double glove if desired. May change only top gloves after each item collected.

- Avoid handling any item where the DNA may be deposited—you will wipe it off (even with gloves).

- Do NOT talk, cough, or sneeze on or near DNA evidence.

- Put each item of evidence in new paper bags or envelopes—one item per bag/envelope. This includes swab boxes (except for multiple swabs from the same item or area of an item if multiple areas were swabbed, which may be packaged together).

- Do NOT put your gloves in with the item of evidence. Dispose of them properly.

Note that the need to change gloves between the handling of different items of evidence is to avoid secondary transfer of DNA material. A **primary transfer** occurs when the DNA is initially deposited on an item by a victim, suspect, or other individual. This evidence is what the investigator needs to find and preserve. **Secondary transfer** is a form of evidence contamination in which DNA from the original object is moved to another object by an intermediate agent or vector, such as a hand or instrument. It is possible to continue spreading this matter multiple times to many other items, creating tertiary, quaternary, and even higher levels of transfer.

It is also important to not touch your face, nose, or mouth when collecting and packaging evidence, as that introduces contaminants onto your gloved hand which can be transferred to other items you touch (Taupin, 2016). Removing gloves after handling an item of evidence and donning a new pair before touching another item of evidence stops this secondary transfer of DNA from one object to another.

Investigators should also be aware that coughing, sneezing, or even talking close to items of evidence may place their own DNA, via primary transfer, on that item, thereby contaminating it. For this reason, the *Best Practices Manual for Evidence Collection, Handling, Storage, and Retention in Massachusetts* (Committee for Public Council Services Innocence Program, 2015) states, in addition to the guidelines outlined above by Wisconsin, that officers should avoid blowing into their gloves prior to putting them on in an effort to prevent the unintended contamination of the gloves with the officer's DNA.

Finally, if disposable tools and instruments are not available, all equipment must be cleaned thoroughly

before and after handling each sample to prevent secondary transfer of DNA during evidence collection. Guidelines for collecting and preserving DNA evidence are provided in Table 5.3.

Investigators should be aware that of the various forms of DNA evidence that may exist at a crime scene—blood, oral/saliva, worn (such as skin cells left on a hat brim or shirt collar), and touch—some types are more valuable than others when it comes to helping identify an offender: "Blood and saliva samples are significantly more likely to yield usable profiles when compared with samples consisting of cells from items that were touched or handled. . . . Whenever possible, evidence collectors would be well served to collect whole items rather than swab the evidence item for DNA, a practice that maximizes the probability of obtaining a DNA profile. For instance, items such as soda cans can be used to search for multiple types of DNA evidence (touch

TABLE 5.3 Collecting Evidence for DNA Analysis

DNA Collection and Analysis	DNA Sample Type	Collection Method	Proper Packaging and Storage of DNA Evidence	Investigation/ Disposition
Unknown or Questionable Samples	Any biological sample including liquid or dried blood, liquid or dried saliva, liquid or dried semen, on almost all surfaces; genital/vaginal/cervical/rectal/anal swabs; penile swabs, skin/tissue; fingernails; hair (head and pubic); skin cells on items such as cups, cigarettes, clothing; and liquid urine.	Liquid samples require about 3 drops; 1 cc or 1 ml. Swabbed samples require 2 swabs. Dried or stained samples must be about the size of a quarter or a dime. Other types are unpredictable because of variables such as age and concentration.	Wet samples should be dried if possible before collection to avoid bacterial contamination. If samples are collected wet, use items such as glass vials or plastic airtight bags until the items can be brought to an area where they can be dried for a sample. Dried samples should be collected in paper bags and kept free of moisture. The evidence should be sealed and signed by the collector. Proper evidence chain of custody and forms should be completed as well.	DNA evidence should be submitted for forensic analysis to the responsible investigating agency. The results of the evidence dictate the follow-up of the investigation and whether or not the evidence needs to be kept or destroyed.
Unidentified Individual	Blood, buccal (oral) swabs, hairs, bone, teeth, fingernails, skin, muscle, and tissue from internal organs.	Liquid samples require about 3 drops; 1 cc or 1 ml. Swabbed samples require 2 swabs. Dried or stained samples must be about the size of a quarter or a dime. Other types are unpredictable because of variables such as age and concentration.	Same process as above	DNA evidence should be submitted for forensic analysis to the responsible investigating agency. The results of the evidence dictate the follow-up of the investigation and whether or not the evidence needs to be kept or destroyed.

(Continued)

TABLE 5.3 *(Continued)*

DNA Collection and Analysis	DNA Sample Type	Collection Method	Proper Packaging and Storage of DNA Evidence	Investigation/ Disposition
Known Sample/ Identified Individual	Blood, buccal (oral) swabs, hair (head and pubic).	Liquid samples require about 3 drops; 1 cc or 1 ml. Swabbed samples require 2 swabs.	Same process as above	DNA evidence should be submitted for forensic analysis to the responsible investigating agency. The results of the evidence dictate the follow-up of the investigation and whether or not the evidence needs to be kept or destroyed.
No Conventional Reference Sample	Soiled clothing with deposited biological fluids including women's underwear, blood, saliva, and semen-stained items. Other clothing that has had contact with skin cell transfer such as a shirt collar, hat, or waistband. Bedding with biological stains or skin cell transfer, fingernail clippings, hair, cigarettes, toothbrushes, razors, combs, discarded tissues, gum, used condoms, feminine products, teeth.	Liquid samples require about 3 drops; 1 cc or 1 ml. Swabbed samples require 2 swabs. Dried or stained samples must be about the size of a quarter or a dime.	Same process as above	These samples are considered when samples are taken from reluctant individuals or those that are unavailable. The same investigation and disposition should be executed.
Known Transfused Sample	Liquid blood or stains on materials such as clothing or bedding. Oral, genital, rectal/anal swabs, and other items listed above depending on the investigation.	Liquid samples require about 3 drops; 1 cc or 1 ml. Swabbed samples require 2 swabs. Dried or stained samples must be about the size of a quarter or a dime.	Same process as above	These samples are considered after a victim has received a transfusion shortly before a blood sample is provided (such as in a homicide). The DNA analysis may identify the presence of more than one DNA. Typically the predominant DNA type is the result, but a combination of other DNA samples might be required for definitive results. The same investigation and disposition should be executed.
Relatives for Testing	Buccal swab, blood, tissue. These samples are typically taken from relatives for DNA comparison of samples taken from another category.	Liquid samples require about 3 drops; 1 cc or 1 ml. Swabbed samples require 2 swabs.	Same process as above	These samples are considered in cases such as identifying a body of a missing person. A person inherits DNA from each parent. It is common and possible to use DNA collected from relatives as reference samples. This comparison can establish a biological relationship with the family of a victim. The same investigation and disposition should be executed.
Paternity/Maternity Testing	Aborted fetal tissue, buccal swab, blood, tissue.	This form of collection would be done by a medical doctor, forensic pathologist, or private organization, not law enforcement.	These samples would be packaged and stored in a laboratory or medical facility.	These samples are considered to determine the paternity or maternity of a fetus or child. This might be the evidence used in sexual assault cases and incest cases that are criminal. If it is criminal, the investigation and disposition should be executed as cited earlier.

Source: Cho, H. L. Cho Research & Consulting, LLC (2020).

samples and cells left on the mouthpiece of the can) as well as for fingerprinting" (Roman et al., 2008, p. 44).

In some cases, DNA analysis has been rendered worthless by the defense's successful attack on the methods used to collect and store the evidence on which DNA analysis was performed. For example, in the O. J. Simpson double-murder trial, jurors disregarded DNA matches after questions were raised about how blood samples were collected, preserved, and examined.

DNA Testing. Because of the expense and time involved, three criteria must usually be met for a lab to accept DNA samples:

- Sufficient material must be submitted.

- Samples (exemplars) must be submitted from both the suspect and the victim.

- The evidence must be probative.

The FBI's *Handbook of Forensic Services* (2019, p. 28) explains two types of DNA used in DNA analysis:

Nuclear DNA (nDNA) is the most discriminating and is typically analyzed in evidence containing blood, semen, saliva, body tissues, bones, and hairs that have tissue at their root ends. The power of nDNA testing lies in the ability to exclude individuals from being the source of the DNA. . . .

Mitochondrial DNA (mtDNA) is typically analyzed in evidence containing naturally shed hairs, hair fragments, bones, and teeth. Typically, these items contain low concentrations of degraded DNA, making them unsuitable

for nDNA examinations. The high sensitivity of mtDNA analysis allows scientists to obtain information from old items of evidence associated with cold cases, samples from mass disasters, and small pieces of evidence containing little biological material.

Different methods of DNA analysis are available, but most crime labs' typing systems use the polymerase chain reaction (PCR), duplicating short segments of DNA. The short pieces of DNA that PCR targets are areas where the genetic code repeats, called short tandem repeats (STRs) (NIJ, 2012a). Each human chromosome contains hundreds of different types of STRs, with the number of repeats on each chromosome varying greatly among individuals. This variation creates a genetic uniqueness for every person that DNA analysts are able to profile.

Before PCR, the dominant technique for DNA analysis was restriction fragment length polymorphism (RFLP, pronounced *riff-lip*). Although many labs still use this method, a significant shortcoming is that it requires a large amount of intact DNA, whereas PCR needs only a tiny amount of DNA, even if degraded.

Another extremely useful forensic DNA analysis method examines a genetic marker called a single nucleotide polymorphism (SNP, pronounced *snip*) (Figure 5.5). A SNP is a one-base difference in the DNA sequence between individuals. Advancements continue to be made in DNA testing. The National Institute of Standards and Technology has developed a quality assurance standards kit for DNA typing that laboratories can use to assess the accuracy of their DNA testing procedures within a narrow margin of error.

Figure 5.5
DNA profiling process.
Source: Courtesy of Orchid Cellmark Inc.

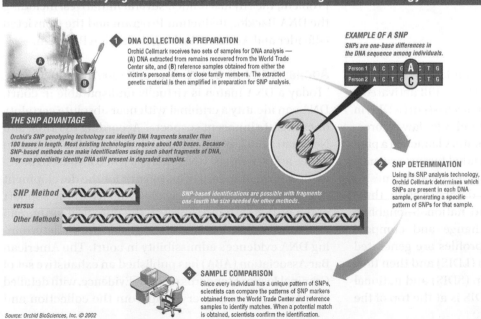

Identifying World Trade Center Victims Using SNP Technology

① DNA COLLECTION & PREPARATION
Orchid Cellmark receives two sets of samples for DNA analysis — (A) DNA extracted from remains recovered from the World Trade Center site, and (B) reference samples obtained from either the victim's personal items or close family members. The extracted genetic material is then amplified in preparation for SNP analysis.

EXAMPLE OF A SNP
SNPs are one-base differences in the DNA sequence among individuals.

Person 1 A C T G **A** C T G
Person 2 A C T G **C** C T G

THE SNP ADVANTAGE
Orchid's SNP genotyping technology can identify DNA fragments smaller than 100 bases in length. Most existing technologies require about 400 bases. Because SNP-based methods can make identifications using such short fragments of DNA, they can potentially identify DNA still present in degraded samples.

SNP Method
versus
Other Methods

SNP-based identifications are possible with fragments one-fourth the size needed for other methods.

② SNP DETERMINATION
Using its SNP analysis technology, Orchid Cellmark determines which SNPs are present in each DNA sample, generating a specific pattern of SNPs for that sample.

③ SAMPLE COMPARISON
Since every individual has a unique pattern of SNPs, scientists can compare the patterns of SNP markers obtained from the World Trade Center and reference samples to identify matches. When a potential match is obtained, scientists confirm the identification.

Source: Orchid BioSciences, Inc. © 2002

Snapshot® Forensic DNA Phenotyping System

By now, it is widely understood that DNA carries the genetic blueprint for each individual's physical characteristics. Snapshot® is a new technology developed by Parabon© Nanolabs, with funding support from the U.S. Department of Defense (DoD), that reads tens of thousands of genetic variants, or genotypes, from a DNA sample to predict what an unknown person's physical appearance, or phenotype, looks like. This forensic analysis is based on the knowledge that certain human traits, including eye color, hair color, skin color, freckling, and face shape, can be predicted from a DNA sample because these physical characteristics are largely determined by a person's genotype, with little influence from environmental factors. The Snapshot DNA phenotyping system is able to predict, with a certain measure of confidence, the physical appearance and ancestry of an unknown person from their DNA sample.

Furthermore, Snapshot is able to predict with high confidence which traits can be *excluded* from someone's physical appearance. According to the company's website, "Snapshot is ideal for generating investigative leads, narrowing suspect lists, and solving human remains cases, without wasting time and money chasing false leads."

In addition to DNA phenotyping, the Snapshot DNA analysis service can perform genetic genealogy to identify a subject by searching for relatives in public databases and building family trees. Snapshot can also determine kinship between DNA samples out to six degrees of relatedness.

Source: http://snapshot.parabon-nanolabs.com

DNA Databases. In October 1998, under the authority of the DNA Identification Act of 1994, the FBI activated a database called the National DNA Index System (NDIS) in an effort to establish a national DNA index for law enforcement purposes. In 1990, the FBI Laboratory launched a pilot project called the *CODIS*, which blended forensic science and computer technology to help solve violent crimes.

CODIS created a distributed database with three hierarchical tiers—local, state, and national—enabling participating laboratories to exchange and compare DNA profiles electronically. DNA profiles are generated at the local level DNA index system (LDIS) and then flow to the state level DNA index system (SDIS) and national level DNA index system (NDIS). NDIS is at the top of the

CODIS hierarchy. When CODIS was first implemented, it served 14 state and local laboratories. It has since grown to serve more than 190 public law enforcement laboratories across the United States and, internationally, more than 90 law enforcement laboratories in over 50 countries (FBI, *Combined*, n.d.).

The CODIS database is organized into two indexes: the forensic and offender indexes. The *forensic index* contains DNA profiles from crime scene evidence where the offender's identity is unknown. The *offender index* contains DNA profiles of individuals convicted of sex offenses and other violent crimes. Investigators can submit biological evidence from a crime scene to CODIS and cross-check it against existing profiles, generating investigative leads, and making links between crimes and offenders. As with IAFIS and fingerprint searches, all DNA hits identified by CODIS must be subsequently validated as a match by a qualified DNA analyst.

As of April 2020, the NDIS contained over 14,215,626 offender profiles, 3,965,672 arrestee profiles, and 1,018,442 forensic profiles. Also as of April 2020, CODIS had produced over 511,176 hits assisting in more than 500,108 investigations (FBI, 2020).

Backlog of DNA Awaiting Testing. Although crime laboratories have made great strides to increase their capacity to process samples, they continue to accumulate a backlog because the demand for DNA analysis continues to outpace existing capacity, as discussed in Chapter 1. The U.S. Government Accountability Office (2019) found that from 2011 to 2017, the reported number of backlogged requests for crime scene DNA analysis at state and local government labs increased by 85%, from approximately 91,000 in 2011 to about 169,000 in 2017. In an effort to reduce the backlog problem, the NIJ has funded several initiatives, including the DNA Backlog Reduction Program and the Convicted Offender and Arrestee Backlog Reduction Program.

Admissibility in Court. Spagnoli (2007, p. 42) asserts, "Today a DNA match is virtually undisputable in court. DNA can identify a criminal with near absolute certainty or exonerate innocent suspects." According to Prime and Newman (2007, p. 35), "Through partnerships between police and scientists, DNA analysis will continue to be regarded as the standard of excellence for the development of impartial, unbiased scientific evidence in the support of the justice system." However, the potential for human error and contamination is a critical factor in determining DNA evidence's admissibility in court. The American Bar Association (ABA) has published an exhaustive set of Criminal Justice Standards on DNA Evidence, with detailed standards covering everything from the collection and preservation of DNA evidence to testing of DNA, charging of persons by DNA profile, pretrial proceedings, trial, post-conviction, and the use of DNA databases (American Bar Association, 2007).

Exoneration of Incarcerated Individuals through DNA Evidence.

DNA evidence is used not only to convict people, but to exonerate those wrongfully convicted. Data provided by the Innocence Project, a group founded at the Cardozo School of Law at Yeshiva University in New York, reveals that as of May 2020, 367 people have been exonerated through DNA testing. The leading cause of wrongful conviction was eyewitness misidentification, which accounted for 69% of the 367 cases. The misapplication of forensic science contributed to 45% of wrongful convictions in the United States proven through DNA evidence (Innocence Project, n.d.). Noting that only a small percentage of criminal cases involve biological evidence suitable for DNA testing, and that such evidence is frequently destroyed or otherwise "lost" following a conviction, those whose guilty verdict was the result of such faulty "proof" face a great challenge in proving their innocence.

The growing awareness that DNA can help right a wrongful conviction has been one impetus for state legislators nationwide to adopt changes in criminal justice procedures, such as requiring that DNA evidence be maintained as long as an inmate remains incarcerated. A recommendation by the Technical Working Group on Biological Evidence Preservation (Ballou, 2013, p. 4) is that "Biological evidence should be preserved through, at a minimum, the period of incarceration in the following crime categories, as defined in NIBRS, regardless of whether or not a plea was obtained: homicides, sexual assault offenses, assaults, kidnapping/abductions, and robberies. For all other offenses, biological evidence may be disposed of upon receipt of authorizations."

Moral, Ethical, and Legal Issues.

As with many new technologies finding their way into criminal investigation, the use of DNA evidence faces the challenge of balancing individual privacy rights along with the greater public concern of preserving civil liberties against law enforcement's duty to protect public order and safety and to investigate crimes to bring wrongdoers to justice. In examining the current debates over the use of DNA in forensic investigations, Hodge (2018, pp. 48–49) states: "The use of DNA in forensics has a proven track record that has assisted both the prosecution and defense, but it is not without controversy. . . . [A]s new forensic applications are discovered, some raise difficult ethical and legal issues. Two of the most controversial new applications are familial DNA and forensic phenotyping."

For example, familial DNA searching (FDS) was used to solve the "Grim Sleeper" case in 2010, a case that had dogged police for more than two decades (Silverman, 2020). Lonnie Franklin's reign of terror began in 1985, and over the next 22 years, he raped and murdered a dozen women in California. Although investigators had ample DNA of the suspect from many of the crime scenes, they were unable to find a match in any of the state or national databases. The case finally broke when investigators ran a familial search of the suspect's DNA sample against the state's database of convicted felons. They got a partial match to Franklin's son, Christopher, who was in prison for a weapons violation (Zetter, 2010).

Because Christopher was too young to have committed the string of murders, investigators focused on Lonnie. The elder Franklin was placed on 24-hour surveillance, and an undercover officer posing as a waiter was able to obtain DNA from a pizza crust Franklin left on his plate at a restaurant. The DNA on that crust matched the samples obtained from the "Grim Sleeper" crime scenes. Lonnie Franklin was arrested in July 2010, found guilty on 10 counts of first-degree murder, and sentenced to death on August 10, 2016, in Los Angeles County. He died while on death row (Silverman, 2020).

Since the Grim Sleeper case in California, at least eight other states have enacted legislation regarding the specific protocols for the use of FDS, and agencies in other states have used the technology informally as part of their investigations (Gerber, 2016). Despite the growing popularity of such searches and supporters' argument that it is an innocuous way to generate leads to help solve cold cases, privacy advocates warn that these techniques could possibly constitute a violation of the Fourth Amendment's protection against unreasonable searches and seizures by using the DNA of innocent people related to a suspect (Hodge, 2018). Critics also voice concern that FDS will subject a disparate number of Hispanics and African Americans to such searches, because these minorities have historically been imprisoned at disproportionately higher rates than other racial groups: "For instance, one study demonstrated that while the overall rate of false identification is small, African-Americans have twice the chance of being incorrectly targeted for further investigation. The higher probability of being incorrectly targeted will lead to far more African-Americans suffering disproportionately from intrusions of privacy and police interrogations" (Hodge, 2018, p. 52).

Another controversial development in the use of DNA evidence is the sampling of people not yet convicted of a crime but who have been arrested and are awaiting trial. Such preconviction DNA sampling is generally done at the same time fingerprints are taken and involves a simple buccal swab of an arrestee. As of April 2020, 31 states had passed laws requiring DNA collection from certain felony arrestees, and many other states were considering such legislation (DNA Saves, n.d.). The DNA Fingerprint Act of 2005 authorizes the federal government to collect DNA samples from any adult who is arrested, facing charges, or convicted of a federal offense. The Act also authorizes the collection of DNA samples from any individual who is not a U.S. citizen and who is detained by federal agents (U.S. DOJ, 2020). On June 3, 2013, the U.S. Supreme Court upheld "Katie's Law," denying a challenge that laws that require DNA collection upon arrest were a violation of a suspect's Fourth Amendment rights. Several states do allow for the expungement of DNA evidence upon request if the arrestee meets certain criteria.

Several studies have demonstrated that collecting DNA upon arrest can save lives, money, and time by identifying repeat offenders earlier, before they continue a protracted pattern of crime (Wallentine, 2010). A study by the Denver, Colorado, District Attorney's Office examined the criminal history of five defendants and concluded that DNA collection upon arrest of these prolific offenders would have prevented 3 murders, 18 sexual assaults, 1 attempted sexual assault, 7 kidnappings, 4 robberies, 3 felony assaults, and 11 home invasions during the study period (Wallentine, 2010).

Skin-Associated Chemical Signatures

Bouslimani et al. (2016) have studied an emerging type of trace evidence—skin-associated lifestyle chemistries. The researchers suggest that the molecular signatures found on human hands are distinct and, when transferred to items held by those hands (e.g., cell phones, keys, pens, luggage or handbags), can provide insight to investigators regarding a person's habits. Analysis of these chemical signatures can reveal a lifestyle profile of an individual, and the chemical traces can often be detected up to 4 months after the item was held by those hands.

In their proof-of-principle study, the researchers note: "The external environment influences the chemical composition of the outermost layer of the skin. Our daily routines leave chemicals on skin surface originating from our surroundings and the human habitats to which we are exposed. Skin-associated chemicals also arise from personal habits including diet, exercise, clothes, medications, and personal care products. Together, these sources represent the vast majority of identifiable chemical entities on the human skin surface" (Bouslimani et al., 2016, p. 1). Using mass spectrometry to conduct molecular

and elemental analysis of chemical traces found on cell phones, the researchers were able to show that the chemical signatures recovered from the phones could identify molecular classes such as beauty and hygiene products, pesticides and insecticides, certain dietary items, and medications such as antidepressants, antifungal treatments, and topicals to treat skin inflammation.

These skin-associated chemical signatures, while not revealing the exact identity of an individual, can help investigators develop composite sketch of a suspect's lifestyle. Consider this scenario:

Imagine that an investigator at a crime scene finds a smashed cell phone near the body of a homicide victim. The phone, apparently dropped by the perpetrator, is rushed to a forensics laboratory where it undergoes what researchers describe as a "lifestyle chemistry analysis."

Using a mass spectrometer to analyze the molecules on the surface of the phone, laboratory scientists quickly discern that the perpetrator was likely a person who wears high-end cosmetics, suffers from a fungal infection, uses eye drops, and takes an antidepressant. Further analysis of the phone's surface reveals the person smokes, uses sunscreen and anti-mosquito sprays, and recently took an antihistamine. The person also drinks coffee, likes citrus fruit, and has a diet that involves a lot of chili peppers (NIJ, 2017).

Blood and Other Body Fluids

Blood is frequently analyzed for DNA, but it and other body fluids such as semen and urine can also provide other valuable evidence to investigators. Blood assists in establishing that a violent crime was committed, in re-creating the movements of a suspect or victim, and in eliminating suspects. Body fluids can be found on a suspect's or victim's clothing, on the floor or walls, on furniture, and on other objects. Some body fluids, such as semen and saliva, may be difficult to detect but, given their natural fluorescent property, will become visible under a variety of FLSs.

Blood is important as evidence in crimes of violence. Heelprints of shoes in blood splashes may be identifiable apart from the blood analysis. It is important to test the stain or sample to determine whether it is, in fact, human blood. In addition, because blood is so highly visible and recognizable, those who commit violent crimes usually attempt to remove blood from items. A number of reagents—including luminol, tetramethyl benzedrine, and phenolphthalein—can identify blood at a crime scene, and because crime laboratories are swamped with evidence to examine, such preliminary on-scene testing is important.

Luminol, for example, is an easy-to-apply water-based solution sprayed from a pump bottle over an area where blood traces are suspected. Luminol causes blood to fluoresce a pale blue color and can detect blood that has been diluted as much as 10,000 times. Another benefit to using luminol is that it does not harm DNA in blood, thus allowing the blood to be collected for further analysis. However, luminol can give false positive reactions and is only a presumptive positive test for blood. Luminol also reacts with bleach products and some metals or strong oxidizing agents. Consequently, if a surface was cleaned with bleach, it might react when sprayed with luminol.

Bloodstain pattern analysis (BPA) is the study of bloodstains to assist in establishing spatial and sequential events that occurred during, and sometimes after, the act of bloodshed (Christman, 2015). Bloodstains and spatter patterns are useful evidence because they are characteristics of certain physical forces and can help investigators determine how a criminal event played out. With a sufficient quantity of bloodstain evidence at a crime scene, investigators can analyze the size, shape, and distribution of these bloodstains to determine the location of people or objects at a crime scene; the movement of people or objects within the scene; areas of origin of bloodshed; type(s) of weapon(s) used and force levels involved; the minimum number of blows, shots, or

events; and whether the suspect may have been injured (Christman, 2015). Furthermore, blood-spatter patterns can help to determine a suspect's truthfulness. In many cases, suspects have claimed a death was accidental, but the location and angle of blood-spatter patterns refuted their statements.

Some blood evidence is easier to interpret than others: "Bloodstain pattern analysis can range from the simple to the complex. The trails of blood in a crime scene or cast-off blood patterns are reasonably straightforward and understandable. Determining areas of convergence and origin employing string methods or trigonometric methodologies are more complex and call for a trained specialist" (Geberth, 2015, p. 240).

As a general rule, the greater the amount of force applied to the source, the smaller the drops will be. In other words, as the force increases, the drop size decreases. Force levels are broken into three categories. The low velocity level produces drops of blood. Medium velocity spatter produces bloodstains 4–6 mm in diameter or larger. High velocity force produces a mist or spray-type pattern. Investigators or technicians must accurately measure, record, and photograph blood spatters at a crime scene to allow proper interpretation of the spatter data by expert bloodstain analysts.

Bloodstain pattern software has been a mainstay of criminal forensic analysis for several decades and has made bloodstain analysis faster, easier, and more accurate. Some programs can calculate bloodstain measurements for point of origin, letting investigators know, for

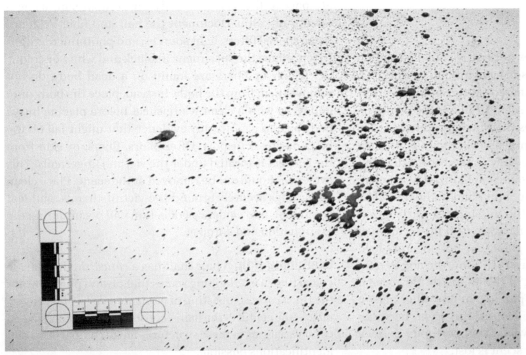

Blood pattern analysis can help investigators determine where the blood originated; the distance from there to where the blood came to rest; the type and direction of impact creating the blood stains; the type of object producing the blood spatter; and the position of the victim and the assailant during and after the bloodshed. Generally, the smaller the size of the blood spatters, the greater the energy used to create them.

Dan Christman

example, where a gunshot victim stood. Computer software is also available that takes bloodstain pattern data and converts them into a 3-D model of the crime scene, helping investigators reconstruct specific spatial and sequential events that occurred before and during the act of bloodshed.

Collect *liquid* blood with an eyedropper and put it in a test tube. Write the subject's name and other pertinent information on medical tape applied to the outside. Send by air express, priority mail, or registered mail. Scrape *dry* blood flakes into a pillbox or envelope, identified in the same way. Mark bloodstained clothing with a string tag or directly on the clothing. If the bloodstain is moist, air-dry the clothing or use an evidence drying chamber before packing.

> **LO5**   Compare and contrast the determinations that can and cannot be made from fingerprint, DNA, blood, and hair evidence.
>
> Blood can be identified as animal or human and is most useful in eliminating suspects. Age and race cannot be determined from blood samples, but DNA analysis of blood can provide positive identification.

In some cases, blood, without having DNA analysis performed on it, can help to infer race—for example, sickle-shaped red blood cells occur primarily in African Americans.

Scent

A type of evidence that does not receive much attention is scent evidence. Every person has a unique scent, which cannot be masked or eliminated, not even by the most potent perfume. A person's scent profile is the combination of sweat, oils, and gases their body produces. These smells, along with the skin cells everybody constantly sheds, are detectable to specially trained scent-discriminating dogs. Scents can also be categorized as primary and secondary. For example, in a child abduction case, a dog was given a shirt of the missing girl as the scent article and tracked this primary scent to the location of her body in a field. At this point, the investigators held off going to her body right away to allow the dog to refocus on the secondary scent of the abductor. However, if officers, search volunteers, parents, or any other person comes in contact with the victim, the scene becomes scent-contaminated and a valuable opportunity to track the perpetrator's secondary scent is lost.

Scent evidence can also be collected by placing a sterile gauze pad on another item of evidence. A Scent Transfer Unit uses a vacuum system to trap the scent on the gauze. If no scent article is available, the unit can be put in a closed room to vacuum the air for five minutes to try to capture a scent. These scent pads can be presented to a tracking dog or placed in a freezer for preservation.

Hairs and Fibers

Hairs and fibers are often difficult to locate without a careful search and strong lighting. FLSs are commonly used to locate hair and fiber evidence in carpets and bedding or on other surfaces. They are valuable evidence because they can place a suspect at a crime scene, especially in violent crimes in which interchange of hairs and fibers is likely to occur. The suspect can also take hairs and fibers from the scene.

Place hairs and fibers found at the crime scene in paper, using a druggist fold, or in a small box. Seal all edges and openings, and identify on the outside. If hairs and fibers are found on an object small enough to send to a laboratory, leave them on the object. Hairs and fibers often adhere to blood, flesh, or other materials. If the hairs are visible but are not adhering firmly to the object, record their location in your notes. Then place them in a pillbox or glass vial to send to a laboratory. Do not use plastic.

If you suspect that hairs are on an object, carefully wrap the object and send it intact to a laboratory. Attempt to obtain 25 to 50 full hairs from the appropriate part of the suspect's body for comparison, using a forceps or comb. Document the hair and fiber evidence using special filters, light sources, and photomicrographs to reproduce the specimens in black and white or color.

If hair or fibers are found on a dead body, do not remove them from the body. Instead, place the body onto and wrap with a clean white sheet before placing into a body bag, to capture any evidence that might fall off the body during transport. Often hairs, fibers, or skin from the suspect is located under the victim's fingernails. This evidence should not be removed at the scene. Place clean paper bags securely around the victim's hands, and feet if barefoot, and evidence collection will occur during the examination and autopsy.

Examining Hair. A hair shaft has a *cuticle* on the outside consisting of overlapping scales that always point toward the tip, a *cortex* consisting of elongated cells, and the *medulla*—the center of the hair—consisting of variably shaped cells. Variations in these structures make comparisons and identifications possible.

LO5 Compare and contrast the determinations that can and cannot be made from fingerprint, DNA, blood, and hair evidence.

Microscopic examination determines whether hair is animal or human. Many characteristics can be determined from human hair: the part of the body it came from; whether it was bleached or dyed, freshly cut, pulled out, or burned; and whether there is blood or semen on it. Race, sex, and age cannot be determined.

As with blood samples, it is extremely difficult to state that a hair came from a certain person, but it can usually be determined that a hair did *not* come from a certain person. Hair evidence is important because it does not deteriorate and is commonly left at a crime scene without a subject's knowledge. Laboratory examination does not destroy hair evidence as it does many other types of evidence. Hair evidence may be subjected to microscopic examination to determine type (e.g., facial or pubic), to biological examination to determine blood-type group, and to toxicological examination to determine the presence of drugs or poisons. Secondary ion mass spectrometry (SIMS) chemicals can distinguish trace hair samples using consumer chemicals as identifiers. Chemicals in hair conditioning products produce distinct chemical signatures, allowing the identification of hair samples. Although chemical colorants and other products commonly applied to hair can thwart microscopic analysis, SIMS is not affected by such substances and can capitalize on their presence to improve identification.

Examining Fibers. Fibers fall into four general groups: mineral, vegetable, animal, and synthetic. Mineral fibers most frequently submitted are glass and asbestos. Vegetable fibers include cotton, jute, manila, kapok, hemp, and many others. Animal fibers are primarily wool and silk. Synthetics include rayons, polyesters, nylons, and others. Each fiber has individual characteristics that can be analyzed chemically.

Fibers are actually more distinguishable than hairs are. Fiber examination can determine a fiber's thickness, the number of fibers per strand, and other characteristics that help identify clothing. Fibers can be tested for origin and color. Although often overlooked, fibers are the most frequently located microscopic evidence. They are often found in assaults, homicides, and rapes, where personal contact results in an exchange of clothing fibers. Fibers can be found under a suspect's or victim's fingernails. Burglaries can yield fibers at narrow entrance or exit points where clothing becomes snagged. Hit-and-run accidents often yield fibers adhering to vehicles' door handles, grilles, fenders, or undercarriages.

Advances in FLSs used to examine evidence have been particularly beneficial in the area of fiber evidence, where often only a strand or two is found.

Shoe and Tire Prints and Impressions

Shoe and tire prints and impressions are common evidence at crime scenes and, if collected, recorded, and analyzed properly, can yield valuable investigative data. Investigators should keep in mind that footprints can often be found on surfaces other than the floor, for example, on countertops, chairs, or even on victims, either on their clothing or as bruises (Nirenberg, 2016). Shoe footprints, in addition to providing unique wear patterns that can be compared with a suspect's shoes, can indicate whether a person was walking or running, was carrying something heavy, or was unfamiliar with the area or unsure of the terrain. Tire marks, which also commonly have unique wear patterns, can show the approximate speed and direction of travel and the manufacturer and year the tires were made. In the July 1999 slaying of a Yosemite Park naturalist, the killer left behind footprints and the distinctive tracks of his vehicle, which had a different brand of tire on every wheel.

If two-dimensional (2-D) shoe or tire prints are found on paper, cardboard, or other surface, photograph them and then submit the originals for laboratory examination. Use latent fingerprint lifters to lift shoe and tire tread impressions from smooth surfaces. Photograph with and without a marker before lifting the impression. The marker should contain a ruler, scale, or other standard measuring device. If no marker, per se, is used, photograph the impression with a ruler because a shoeprint can look larger or smaller than it is, depending on the camera angle. Never attempt to fit your shoe into or on top of the suspect's shoe print to determine size. This can destroy the shoe print and contaminate the evidence.

Regarding 2-D tire prints, unless the actual impression occurs on material small enough to be submitted to the lab, the only way to collect the evidence is to photograph the length of the impression with a long scale adjacent to it.

A relatively new technique in preserving shoe impression evidence involves a device called an electrostatic dust print lifter (EDPL). EDPL is used on dry-origin shoe impressions, which involve the transfer of dry residue on a shoe tread to another dry surface, such as a carpet or seat cushion. These impressions are very fragile and among the most difficult to locate. The lift must then be photographed, again with a marker or scale, before it can be analyzed, as the lift itself is extremely fragile.

Three-dimensional shoe and tire impressions should be photographed and then cast. When photographing shoe impressions in snow, mud, sand, or other substrate, it is imperative to use the proper scale in the proper plane, meaning the ruler should be in level with the bottom of the impression, not placed next to the impression on the top of the snow or soil surface: "Footwear examiners require 1:1, or life-sized, photographs of the impression to conduct a comparison with the known shoe. The distortion created by the placement of the scale above the impression may make this task very difficult, if not impossible" (Adair, 2009, p. 18). Also, when placing the scale next to and level with the bottom of the impression, take care not to allow snow or soil to fall into the impression. If no scale, marker, or ruler is available, place a common object, such as a dollar bill, next to the print and photograph it. Then submit the object as evidence if it is needed in court.

To **cast** is to make an impression. The word also refers to the impression that results. Some departments use plaster, whereas others prefer dental casting material because of its strength and durability and because it needs no reinforcement. Premeasured-mix kits are also available. The steps in making a plaster cast of a soil impression are as follows:

1. Build a retaining frame around the impression about two inches from its edges.

2. Coat the impression with five or six layers of alcohol and shellac or inexpensive hairspray, allowing each coat to dry before applying the next. Apply talcum powder to the last layer so the spray can easily be removed from the cast.

3. Rapidly mix the plaster following directions on the box.

4. Pour the plaster into the impression, using a spatula to cushion its fall and guide it into all areas of the impression. Fill the impression halfway.

5. Add wire or gauze to reinforce the impression.

6. Pour in more plaster until it overflows to the retaining frame.

7. Before the cast hardens, use a pencil or other pointed instrument to incise your initials, the case number, and the date on the back of the impression.

8. After the cast hardens, remove it and the retaining frame. Do not wash the cast; the laboratory does this.

9. Carefully wrap the cast in protective material to avoid breakage, and place it in a strong box to ship to the laboratory.

> **LO6** Describe special collection and processing considerations for the following types of evidence: shoe and tire prints and impressions, tools and tool marks, firearms and ammunition, glass, soils and minerals, safe insulation, ropes, strings, tapes, drugs, documents, laundry and dry-cleaning marks, paint, and skeletal remains.

After photographing, cast shoe or tire tread impressions found in dirt, sand, or snow.

Investigators must be aware that the typical techniques used to cast in soil or sand may actually damage impressions in snow. A primer or snow print wax should be applied prior to casting in snow to help prevent the casting material from leaking into the snow and damaging the print (Perin, 2014). Making a "dry cast" of an impression in snow requires particular attention to the moisture content of the casting material (too wet will collapse the fragile snow impressions) and allowing time for the dental stone powder to cool after mixing it with water, as this material heats up during the curing process. Pouring the casting material into the impression too soon will melt impression details (Perin, 2014). Once the cast is cured (the colder the temperature, the longer it takes to cure), lift it gently, place it in a safe storage container with the impression side up, and allow it to dry completely (usually about 24 hours) before packaging it to send to the laboratory. The laboratory compares the cast with manufacturers' shoe and tire tread files.

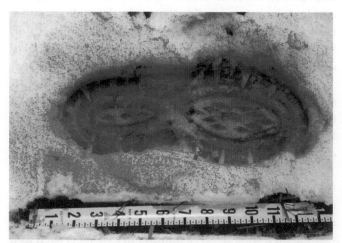

Shoes and boots can leave distinctive impressions that can be traced to an individual's personal possessions. Manufacturers can provide photographs of their specific lines of shoes and boots that can be compared with photographs taken at the scene.

County of Westchester, New York. Used with permission.

Several databases are available to help in the identification of shoe and tire prints. Previous editions of this text referenced the database of Scientific Working Group for Shoeprint and Tire Tread Evidence, which was operational from 2004 through 2013. However, in late 2014, the Footwear and Tire Subcommittee of Organization of Scientific Area Committees (OSAC) for Forensic Science, administered by the National Institute of Standards and Technology (NIST), was created. At that point, SWGTREAD opted to discontinue its operations and focus on supporting the subcommittee, with the latest versions of the SWGTREAD standards being recognized by the OSAC subcommittee as "best practices" in the field of forensic footwear and tire analysis. These standards were published on the subcommittee's newly created website Tread Forensics (treadforensics.com), a forum that went live in April 2017 and provides footwear and tire resources to the forensic community (Tread Forensics, 2019). The Footwear and Tire Subcommittee published their first official document in July 2019.

SoleMate® FPX is another footwear database containing information such as manufacturer, date of market release, images or offset prints of the sole, and pictorial images of the uppers of more than 31,000 sport, work, and casual shoes. SoleMate FPX is updated and distributed to subscribers four times a year (Foster and Freeman, n.d.). Similarly, Tire Guides, Inc., publishes several resources, including the *Tread Design Guide*, which can help investigators identify vehicle tire and tread pattern evidence.

Teeth, Bite Marks, and Lip Prints

Forensic odontology, a branch of forensic science that employs the skills of a dentist, involves the proper handling, examination, and evaluation of dental evidence to identify victims of mass disasters, remains of unidentified persons, and potential suspects in sexual assaults or child abuse. Dental evidence that might help investigators can include teeth, bite marks, and lip prints.

Teeth. Teeth are the most durable part of the human body, able to remain unchanged hundreds, if not thousands, of years after death (Balachander, Babu, Jimson, Priyadharsini, & Masthan, 2015). Like fingerprints or DNA, teeth are unique to an individual, and dental features such as tooth structure; differences in the shape, size, and color of teeth; wear patterns; presence of crowding or spacing; fillings and other restorations; and other anomalies can help investigators identify victims and suspects (Krishan, Kanchan, & Garg, 2015). Teeth can indicate not only a person's age, sex, and race or ethnicity, but they can often provide clues as to a person's occupation or behavioral habits: "Dressmakers or tailors keep needles between their teeth...; cobblers, carpenters and electricians hold nails between their incisors; ... Certain habits like pipe smoking, cigarette smoking and tobacco chewing can also leave their mark on the teeth (Krishan, Kanchan, & Garg, 2015).

Bite Marks. The marks teeth leave behind on skin or other tissue, as well as on food and other types of material, may also be of evidentiary value. Divakar (2017) defines a bite mark as "the physical alteration in or on a medium caused by the contact of teeth." Bites may occur during commission of a violent crime, inflicted by either the victim or the perpetrator. Bite marks may also be found in partially eaten food or other objects that had been placed inside a person's mouth.

Bite mark identification and analysis based on the "supposed" individuality of teeth has, until recently, been considered to be legally admissible in court. However, some forensic science disciplines, particularly those that rely on a degree of "pattern-matching," which bite mark analysis does, have been increasingly criticized as lacking the rigorous scientific foundation necessary to continue being admissible as trial evidence. Amidst intense scientific and legal scrutiny, some states have begun to disallow several of these disciplines, including forensic bite mark identification: "A number of DNA exonerations have occurred in recent years for individuals convicted based on erroneous bitemark identifications. . . . An important National Academies review found little scientific support for the field. The Texas Forensic Science Commission recently recommended a moratorium on the admission of bitemark expert testimony. The California Supreme Court has a case before it that could start a national dismantling of forensic odontology" (Saks et al., 2016, p. 538). The Texas decision resulted in the exoneration of Steven Chaney, who had served 25 years of a life sentence for double murder, his conviction based largely on bite mark evidence found on one of the murder victims (Resch, 2019).

Despite criticisms that label bite mark analysis a "pseudoscience," Souviron and Haller (2017, p. 617) assert: "Bitemark comparison, or matching or identification, is by no means the whole discipline of forensic odontology. There is valuable information that can and should be obtained from a bite mark, whether or not it can be, or is, used for comparison purposes." Therefore, it is important for investigators to know how to properly deal with bite mark evidence.

If the impression is visible, photograph it with a scale placed beside it and note the distance at which the photo was taken. Then swab the bite area for saliva, blood residue, DNA, and microorganisms. Finally, cast the bite impression in the same way as shoe and tire tread impressions. Dental impression material is again preferred because of its fine texture.

If a bite mark is too shallow to cast, photograph it (with a scale) and then "lift" it by placing tape over it and then transferring the tape to plastic to see the outline of the mark. A UV light or another FLS can be used to enhance the visibility of the bite mark, allowing photographs to see the deeper tissue damage and to capture the spacing, size, and shape of the teeth (Verma, Kumar, & Bhattacharya, 2013).

Lip Prints. Cheiloscopy, the study of lip prints, is a forensic investigation technique used to identify humans based on lips traces (Venkatesh & David, 2011). Edmond Locard was the first to suggest, in 1932, that lip prints could have evidentiary value in identifying individuals (Balanchander et al., 2015). Like fingers, a person's lips contain grooves and wrinkles that are unique to that individual, that are permanent, and that remain unchanged over time (Verma et al., 2015). In 1967, lip grooves were classified into four basic types: straight line, curved line, angled line, and sine shaped line (Divakar, 2017). Further classification of lip prints occurred in 1974 when it was recognized that these lines came together differently in each individual so as to create distinct patterns that could be identified as vertical, intersected, branched, or reticular (Verma et al., 2015). This taxonomy is similar to the way fingerprint patterns are classified (arched, looped, or whorled).

The lips contain sebaceous and sweat glands that produce secretions that can leave prints of these unique patterns of grooves and wrinkles on objects they come into contact with (Balanchander et al., 2015). Lip prints can be a useful forensic tool for determining personal identification because such prints are often found at crime scenes and, like fingerprints, are considered to be an important form of transfer evidence (Verma et al., 2015). These "latent" lip prints can be lifted using materials such as aluminum powder and magnetic bonds, techniques similar to those used in lifting fingerprints (Balanchander et al., 2015).

Tools and Tool Marks

Common tools such as hammers and screwdrivers are often used in crimes and cause little suspicion if found in someone's possession. Such tools are often found in a suspect's vehicle, on the person, or at the residence. If a tool is found at a crime scene, determine whether it belongs to the property owner. Broken tool pieces may be found at a crime scene, on a suspect, or on a suspect's property.

A **tool mark** is an impression left by a tool on a surface. For example, a screwdriver forced between a window and a sill may leave a mark the same depth and width as the screwdriver. The resiliency of the surface may cause explainable differences in mark dimensions and tool dimensions. If the screwdriver has a chipped head or other imperfections, it will leave impressions for

LO6 Describe special collection and processing considerations for the following types of evidence: shoe and tire prints and impressions, tools and tool marks, firearms and ammunition, glass, soils and minerals, safe insulation, ropes, strings, tapes, drugs, documents, laundry and dry-cleaning marks, paint, and skeletal remains.

Identify each suspect tool with a string tag, wrap it separately, and pack it in a strong box for transport to the laboratory.

later comparison. Tool marks are often found in burglaries, auto thefts, and larcenies in which objects are forced open.

A tool mark provides leads to the size and type of tool that made it. Examining a suspect tool determines, within limits, whether it could have made the mark in question. Even if you find a suspect tool, it is not always possible to match it to the tool mark, especially if the tool was damaged when the mark was made. However, residue from the forced surface may adhere to the tool, making a comparison possible.

Do not attempt to fit a suspected tool into a mark to see if it matches. This disturbs the mark, as well as any paint or other trace evidence on the suspect tool, making the tool inadmissible as evidence.

LO6 Describe special collection and processing considerations for the following types of evidence: shoe and tire prints and impressions, tools and tool marks, firearms and ammunition, glass, soils and minerals, safe insulation, ropes, strings, tapes, drugs, documents, laundry and dry-cleaning marks, paint, and skeletal remains.

Photograph tool marks and then either cast them or send the object on which they appear to a laboratory.

First, take mid-range photos to document the location of the tool or tool mark within the general crime scene. Then take close-ups first without and then with a marker to show actual size and detail.

After photographing tool marks, cast them. Casting of tool marks presents special problems because tool marks often are not on a horizontal surface. In such cases, construct a platform or bridge around the mark by taping tin or other pliable material to the surface. Plaster of Paris, plasticine, and waxes do not provide the detail necessary for tool striation marks. Better results are obtained from moulage, silicone, and other thermosetting materials.

Tool marks are easy to compare if a suspect tool has not been altered or damaged since it made the mark. If the tool is found, send it to the laboratory for several comparison standards. The material used for the standard should be as close as possible to the original material; ideally, a portion of the original material is used.

The tool mark found at the scene and the standard of comparison are placed under a microscope to make the striation marks appear as light and dark lines. The lines are then adjusted to see whether they match. Variations of approximately 10 degrees in angle are permissible. Roughly 60% of the lines should match in the comparison.

A specific mark may be similar to or found in the same relative location as tool marks found at other crimes. Evidence of the way a tool is applied—the angle,

> **L06** Describe special collection and processing considerations for the following types of evidence: shoe and tire prints and impressions, tools and tool marks, firearms and ammunition, glass, soils and minerals, safe insulation, ropes, strings, tapes, drugs, documents, laundry and dry-cleaning marks, paint, and skeletal remains.

A tool mark is compared with a standard-of-comparison impression rather than with the tool itself.

amount of pressure, and general use—can tie one crime to another. A tool mark also makes it easier to look for a specific type of tool. Possession of, or fingerprints on, such a tool can implicate a suspect.

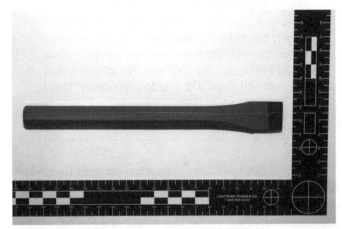
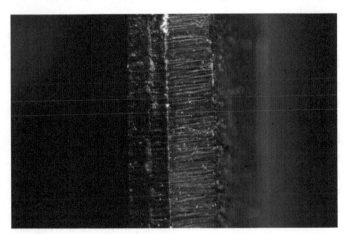

Tool mark comparison. A cold chisel and a magnified image of the tip of the chisel, showing the imperfections along the working surface. These imperfections are unique to this specific tool. Marks made with this chisel on a test surface can be compared with marks left at a crime scene. If found to be a reasonable match, such evidence can link the person in possession of the tool to the crime.

Ventura County Sheriff's Department Forensic Sciences Laboratory

This photomicrograph is a comparison of striated tool marks created using a lateral scraping motion with the tip of a cold chisel. The random imperfections present on the tip of the chisel create a unique, reproducible, three-dimensional contour pattern. The striated tool marks were made in sheet lead. Because the striations made in the test environment line up consistently with those found at the crime scene, this image depicts a positive identification.

Ventura County Sheriff's Department Forensic Sciences Laboratory

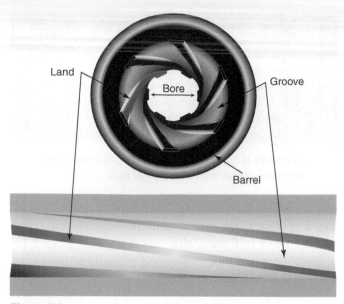

Figure 5.6
Features of a rifled firearm's barrel.

Firearms and Ammunition

Many violent crimes are committed with a firearm: a revolver, a pistol, a rifle, or a shotgun. Each firearm imparts a distinctive fingerprint, or ballistic signature, to every bullet and casing fired through it, which provides useful evidence to investigators. The broad definition of **ballistics** is that it is the study of the dynamics of projectiles, from propulsion through flight to impact; a narrower definition is that it is the study of the functioning of firearms.

The **bore** refers to the inside portion of a weapon's barrel, which is surrounded by raised ridges called *lands* and recessed areas called *grooves*. These lands and grooves comprise the **rifling**, the spiral pattern cut down the entire length of the firearm barrel that grips and spins the bullet as it passes through the bore, providing greater projectile control and accuracy (Figure 5.6). **Caliber** refers to the diameter of the bore as measured between lands, as well as the size of bullet intended for use with a specific weapon. As the bullet rotates through the barrel, it receives highly individualized and characteristic **striations**, or scratches, from the rifling, which provide valuable comparison evidence on recovered bullets. A fired bullet is marked only by the barrel, but a fired cartridge case is marked by several parts of the weapon when it is loaded, fired, and extracted.

When collecting a firearm found at a crime scene, do NOT put an object inside the barrel to pick it up. The object may scratch the inside of the barrel, affecting a ballistics test. Include the firearm make, caliber, model, type, serial number, and finish, along with any unusual characteristics in your notes.

A plethora of physical evidence can be obtained from gun-related crimes, including the actual firearms and spent bullets, shell casings, slugs, and shot pellets, as well as the fingerprints and DNA often located on these items. Ballistic evidence can help solve a crime even when the weapon is not recovered.

> **LO6** Describe special collection and processing considerations for the following types of evidence: shoe and tire prints and impressions, tools and tool marks, firearms and ammunition, glass, soils and minerals, safe insulation, ropes, strings, tapes, drugs, documents, laundry and dry-cleaning marks, paint, and skeletal remains.

Examine weapons for latent fingerprints. Photograph weapons and then identify them with string tags. Unload firearms and record their serial numbers on the string tags and in your notes. If the firearm is a revolver, take careful note of which chambers had ammunition in them and document the placement of the wheel. Label the packing container "Firearms." Identify bullets on the base, cartridges on the outside of the case near the bullet end, and cartridge cases on the inside near the open end. Put ammunition in cotton or soft paper and ship to a laboratory. Never send live ammunition through the mail; use a common carrier instead.

Gunpowder tests, shot pattern tests, and functional tests of a weapon can be made and compared. Defects acquired through use or neglect often permit positive identification of weapons. The rifling of a gun barrel, the gun's ejection and extraction mechanisms, and markings made by these mechanisms can also be compared. Class characteristics of a bullet caused by the firearm's barrel can help identify the weapon used. These class characteristics include the number of lands and grooves in the firearm's barrel and their height, width, and depth.

Gunshot residue (GSR) is another type of evidence investigators may seek in crimes involving firearms. Whenever a firearm is discharged, the gunpowder and primer combine to form a gaseous cloud or residue, sometimes referred to as a *plume*, that can reach as far as 5 feet from the weapon. This residue may settle on the hands, sleeves, face, and other parts of the shooter, as well as any other object or person within the residue fallout radius. Through various techniques, this residue may be detected and used as evidence.

Laboratory examination of GSR under a scanning electron microscope (SEM) is still considered a reliable analysis method, although enhancements in technology have been necessary to better detect, classify, and report on new types of lead-free ammunition (Geberth, 2010b). GSR can be collected by applying adhesive tape to a person's hands or clothing; a technician then runs the

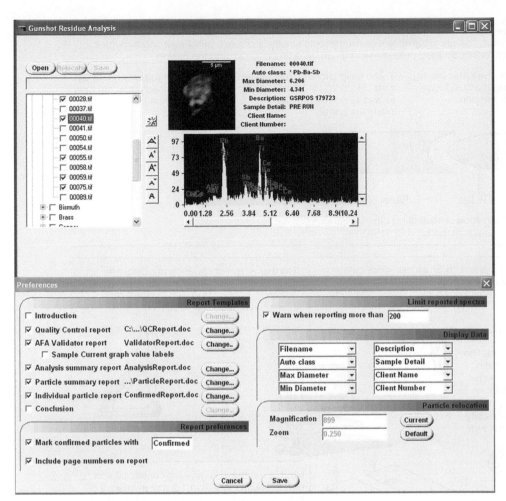

Software allows the automatic analysis of gunshot residue (GSR). This screen capture shows the results of GSR analysis with a scanning electron microscope (SEM, top image) and an X-ray beam (bottom image with spikes). Particles of interest can be isolated and relocated for further analysis.

Courtesy Aspex Corporation

sample through an analyzer to locate and identify specific residue particles and their composition.

Shooter identification kits are also available for conducting GSR tests in the field. These kits allow officers to quickly test multiple suspects and may be used by investigators in distinguishing between a suicide and a homicide, with the absence of GSR on a victim indicating homicide and an abundance of GSR suggesting suicide.

As with fingerprints and DNA, a national database of ballistic information has helped investigators link firearms with offenders. Before 2002, the ATF, with the Integrated Ballistics Identification System (IBIS) (originally called "CeaseFire"), and the FBI, with DrugFire, each collected ballistic data but kept their systems separate, because of incompatibility issues. Realizing the value in and need for a unified ballistic evidence system, the ATF created the National Integrated Ballistic Information Network (NIBIN), a grid that connects IBIS using departments across the country. NIBIN's database is continuously expanding and, at the time of this writing, holds more than 3.3 million images of cartridge casings or bullets either recovered from crime scenes or generated from test fires into shoot tanks using recovered firearms. NIBIN's database is responsible for at least 110,000 confirmed hits. Figure 5.7 illustrates how NIBIN uses ballistic signatures to help investigators solve crimes.

Glass

Glass can have great evidentiary value. Tiny pieces of glass can adhere to a suspect's shoes and clothing. Larger glass fragments are processed for fingerprints and can be fit back together to indicate the direction from which the glass was broken. The source of broken glass fragments also can often be determined.

LO6 Describe special collection and processing considerations for the following types of evidence: shoe and tire prints and impressions, tools and tool marks, firearms and ammunition, glass, soils and minerals, safe insulation, ropes, strings, tapes, drugs, documents, laundry and dry-cleaning marks, paint, and skeletal remains.

Label glass fragments using adhesive tape on each piece. Wrap each piece separately in cotton to avoid chipping, and place them in a strong box marked "Fragile" to send to the laboratory.

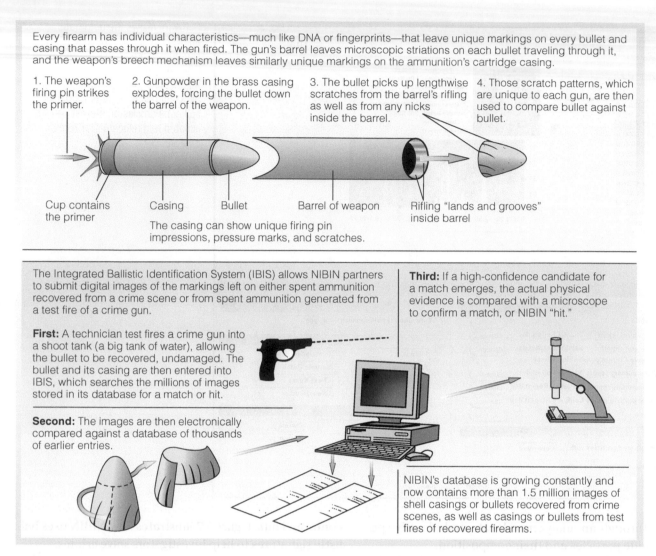

Every firearm has individual characteristics—much like DNA or fingerprints—that leave unique markings on every bullet and casing that passes through it when fired. The gun's barrel leaves microscopic striations on each bullet traveling through it, and the weapon's breech mechanism leaves similarly unique markings on the ammunition's cartridge casing.

1. The weapon's firing pin strikes the primer.

2. Gunpowder in the brass casing explodes, forcing the bullet down the barrel of the weapon.

3. The bullet picks up lengthwise scratches from the barrel's rifling as well as from any nicks inside the barrel.

4. Those scratch patterns, which are unique to each gun, are then used to compare bullet against bullet.

Cup contains the primer

Casing

Bullet

Barrel of weapon

Rifling "lands and grooves" inside barrel

The casing can show unique firing pin impressions, pressure marks, and scratches.

The Integrated Ballistic Identification System (IBIS) allows NIBIN partners to submit digital images of the markings left on either spent ammunition recovered from a crime scene or from spent ammunition generated from a test fire of a crime gun.

First: A technician test fires a crime gun into a shoot tank (a big tank of water), allowing the bullet to be recovered, undamaged. The bullet and its casing are then entered into IBIS, which searches the millions of images stored in its database for a match or hit.

Second: The images are then electronically compared against a database of thousands of earlier entries.

Third: If a high-confidence candidate for a match emerges, the actual physical evidence is compared with a microscope to confirm a match, or NIBIN "hit."

NIBIN's database is growing constantly and now contains more than 1.5 million images of shell casings or bullets recovered from crime scenes, as well as casings or bullets from test fires of recovered firearms.

Figure 5.7
Bullets and casings.

Source: Adapted from Cramer, T. (2009, December). Nab 'em with NIBIN: Ballistics imaging technology. *The Police Chief,* pp. 26–31. Copyright held by the International Association of Chiefs of Police, 515 North Washington Street, Alexandria, VA 22314 USA. Further reproduction without express written permission from IACP is strictly prohibited

Microscopic, spectrographic, and physical comparisons are made of the glass fragments. Microscopic examination of the edges of two pieces of glass can prove they were one piece at one time. Spectrographic analysis can determine the elements of the glass, even extremely small fragments. Submit for comparison pieces of glass at least the size of a half-dollar.

In general, high-velocity impacts are less likely to shatter glass than are low-velocity impacts. A bullet that does not shatter glass will generally leave a small, round entry hole and a larger, cone-shaped exit hole. The faster a bullet travels, the smaller the cracks and the tighter the entry point will be.

The sequence of bullets fired through a piece of glass can be determined from the pattern of cracks. The direction and angle of a bullet or bullets through glass can also be determined by assembling the fragments. When a bullet hits a glass surface, the glass bends, causing radial fractures on the side of the glass *opposite* the point of impact. This allows investigators to determine which side of a piece of glass has received an impact, because a blow causes the glass to compress on that side and to stretch on the opposite side. As the impact occurs, concentric fractures form around the point of impact and interconnect with radial cracks to form triangular pieces. The edge of each triangular piece has visible stress lines that reveal the direction of the blow. The lines on the side that was struck have almost parallel stress lines that tend to curve downward on the side of the glass opposite the blow (see Figure 5.8). Such an examination can establish whether a burglar broke out of or into a building.

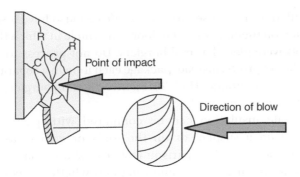

Figure 5.8
Glass cracks caused by blow.

In addition to concentric and radial fractures, investigators should look for *Wallner lines,* also called ridges, which are rib-shaped marks with a wavelike pattern and are almost always concave in the direction from which the crack was propagating. In low-velocity impact fractures, the ridges or Wallner lines on radial cracks nearest the point of impact are at right angles to the side opposite, or to the rear, of the impact, a phenomenon referred to as the "4R Rule" (*R*idges on *r*adial cracks are at *r*ight angles to the *r*ear). However, tempered glass, laminated glass, and small pieces of glass tightly held in a frame or window casing do not reliably demonstrate the fracture patterns just described.

Because larger glass fragments can be matched by fitting the pieces together, a slight mark put on the side of the glass that was facing out helps to reconstruct stress lines. To protect glass as evidence, put sharp points in putty, modeling clay, or some other soft substance.

The Glass Evidence Reference Database contains more than 700 glass samples from manufacturers, distributors, and vehicle junkyards and is a useful resource for investigators (Bowen & Schneider, 2007). Although it cannot determine the source of an unknown piece of glass, the database can assess the relative frequency that two glass samples from different sources would have the same elemental profile.

Soils and Minerals

Forensic geologists examine soils and minerals—substances such as mud, cement, plaster, ceramics, and insulation—found at a crime scene or on a victim, a suspect, clothing, vehicles, or other items. This circumstantial evidence can place a suspect at a crime scene or destroy an alibi.

Although most soil evidence is found outdoors, suspects can bring soil into structures from the outside. Soils found inside a structure are most valuable if brought there on a suspect's shoes or clothing from his or her area of residence. Because soils found in the victim's residence may have been brought there by the victim or by other persons not suspected in the crime, collect elimination samples of soil from the area around the scene. Because soil at a crime scene can change dramatically over time, soil samples must be collected as soon as possible (FBI, 2019).

Soils vary greatly in color, particle size, mineral content, and chemical composition. Some comparisons are visual; others are made through laboratory analysis. Both differences and similarities have value because

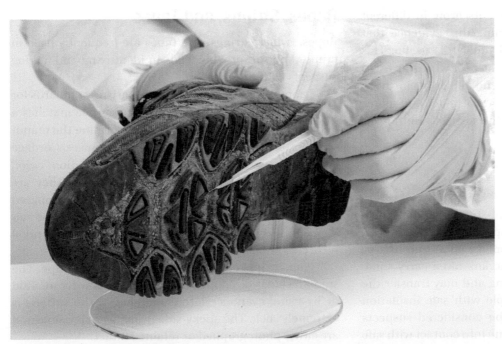

A forensic scientist collects soil evidence from the sole of a shoe.
Pablo Paul/Alamy Stock Photo

soils separated by only a few inches can be very different. Therefore, take sufficient samples (about one cup) directly from and around the suspected area at perhaps 5- to 100-foot intervals, depending on the scene. In addition, soil samples should only be packaged in glass vials or plastic locking bags, never envelopes.

> **LO6** Describe special collection and processing considerations for the following types of evidence: shoe and tire prints and impressions, tools and tool marks, firearms and ammunition, glass, soils and minerals, safe insulation, ropes, strings, tapes, drugs, documents, laundry and dry-cleaning marks, paint, and skeletal remains.

Put one pound of comparison soil into a container identified on the outside. Collect evidence soil the same way. Seal both containers to prevent loss, wrap them, and send them to a laboratory.

If soil evidence is in or on a suspect's clothing or shoes, or found on a tool at the scene, place the entire article with the soil intact in a paper bag and send it to the laboratory. If an object containing soil cannot be moved, use a spatula to scrape off or otherwise collect the soil. Then place the soil in a glass jar or plastic locking bag, properly marked and identified.

Chemical analysis of soil is expensive and not always satisfactory. Soil is generally examined by density, by X-ray diffraction (to determine mineral content), and by microscope.

Because varied species of plants grow in different sections of the country, examining dirt evidence that contains pollen and spores (palynology) is useful. This evidence can refute the alibi of a suspect who is arrested at a distance from a crime scene and denies having been there. Electron microscope detection of pollen and spores found at the crime scene and on the suspect's clothing or vehicle will refute the alibi.

Safe Insulation

Most safes are fire-resistant, sheet-steel boxes with thick insulation. If safes are pried, ripped, punched, drilled, or blown open, the insulation breaks apart and falls or disseminates into the room. Burglars often carry some of this insulation in their clothing and may transfer the particles to their vehicles. People with safe insulation in or on their clothing must be considered suspects because few people normally come into contact with safe

insulation. Tools used to open a safe can also have insulation on them, as may the floor of a vehicle in which the tools were placed after a burglary. Do not process tools for latent prints. Instead, package each item in a separate leakproof container (FBI, 2019). Investigating burglary is the focus of Chapter 13.

Safe insulation can be compared with particles found on a suspect or on the tools or vehicle used during a crime. Comparison tests can show what type of safe the insulation came from and whether it is the same insulation found at other burglaries. Insulation is also found on paint chips from safes. Always take standards of comparison if safe insulation is found at a crime scene. The FBI and other laboratories maintain files on safe insulations used by major safe companies. Home and building insulation materials are also on file. This information is available to all law enforcement agencies.

> **LO6** Describe special collection and processing considerations for the following types of evidence: shoe and tire prints and impressions, tools and tool marks, firearms and ammunition, glass, soils and minerals, safe insulation, ropes, strings, tapes, drugs, documents, laundry and dry-cleaning marks, paint, and skeletal remains.

Put samples of safe insulation in paper containers identified on the outside.

Ropes, Strings, and Tapes

Ropes, twines, strings, and tapes are frequently used in crimes and can provide leads in identifying and linking suspects with a crime.

Laboratories have various comparison standards for ropes, twines, and tapes. If a suspect sample matches a known sample, the laboratory can determine the manufacturer of the item and its most common uses. Cordage can be compared for composition, construction, color, and diameter. Rope ends can be matched if they are frayed. Likewise, pieces of torn tape can be compared with a suspect roll of tape. If the rope, string, or tape evidence must be cut during collection, label which end(s) were cut (FBI, 2019).

Fingerprints can occur on either side of a tape. The smooth side is developed by the normal powder method or by using cyanoacrylate (superglue) if the surface is extremely slick. The sticky-side prints will be visible and are either photographed or retained intact.

> **LO6** Describe special collection and processing considerations for the following types of evidence: shoe and tire prints and impressions, tools and tool marks, firearms and ammunition, glass, soils and minerals, safe insulation, ropes, strings, tapes, drugs, documents, laundry and dry-cleaning marks, paint, and skeletal remains.

Put labeled rope, twine, and string into a container. Put tapes on waxed paper or cellophane and then place them in a container.

Drugs

Drug identification kits can be used to make a preliminary analysis of a suspicious substance, but a full analysis must be done at a laboratory. One valuable reference is Ident-A-Drug, which contains codes imprinted on tablets and capsules, information on color and shape, the national drug code, and drug class (Bowen & Schneider, 2007). Other online resources include Pill Identifier (www.drugs .com/pill_identification.html) and RxList.com. If a drug is a prescription drug, verify the contents with the issuing pharmacist. Determine how much of the original prescription has been consumed.

> **LO6** Describe special collection and processing considerations for the following types of evidence: shoe and tire prints and impressions, tools and tool marks, firearms and ammunition, glass, soils and minerals, safe insulation, ropes, strings, tapes, drugs, documents, laundry and dry-cleaning marks, paint, and skeletal remains.

Put liquid drugs in a bottle and attach a label. Put powdered and solid drugs in a pillbox or powder box and identify them in the same way.

A portable, handheld electronic device called the Thermo Scientific™ TruNarc™ narcotics analyzer is helping investigators in the field detect, analyze, and identify a multitude of drugs and other substances quickly and accurately (PoliceOne, 2020). The device uses a spectroscopic laser light beam to measure the various vibrational modes of different molecules and read the characteristic signatures emitted from the specimen, allowing the device to match the wavelengths against an extensive library of substances. Because the technique uses light to interact with the chemical bonds of a substance, analysis does not require direct contact between the device and the sample being tested. This provides two major benefits. First, the analysis process does not consume, alter, or destroy any of the substances being analyzed, thereby preserving the original evidence. Second, because the light beam can "see" through translucent packaging material, analysis can often be done without removing the substance from its packaging, which enhances officer safety by preventing accidental exposure to potentially harmful matter. According to the manufacturer, the TruNarc is able to identify up to 324 prohibited substances in 30 seconds or less per sample and can scan for up to 500 total substances in a single, definitive test (PoliceOne, 2020). A detailed discussion of evidence in drug investigations is contained in Chapter 18.

Documents

Typing, handwriting, and printing can be examined. Typewriters and printers can be compared and paper identification attempted. Different types of writing instruments—pens, crayons, and pencils—and various types of inks can also be compared. Indented writings, obliterated or altered writings, used carbon paper, burned or charred paper, and shoeprint or tire tread impressions made on paper surfaces can all be examined in a laboratory. A document's age can also be determined.

> **LO6** Describe special collection and processing considerations for the following types of evidence: shoe and tire prints and impressions, tools and tool marks, firearms and ammunition, glass, soils and minerals, safe insulation, ropes, strings, tapes, drugs, documents, laundry and dry-cleaning marks, paint, and skeletal remains.

Do not touch documents with your bare hands. Place documents in a cellophane envelope and then in a manila envelope identified on the outside.

Standards of comparison are required for many document examinations. To obtain handwriting standards from a suspect, take samples until you believe he or she is writing normally. The suspect should not see the original document or copy. Tell the suspect what to write and remove each sample from sight after it is completed. Provide no instructions on spelling, punctuation, or wording. Use the same size and type of paper and writing materials as the original. Obtain right-handed and left-handed samples as well as samples written at different speeds. Samples of undicted writings, such as letters, are also helpful as standards. In forgery cases, include the genuine signatures as well as the forged ones.

A useful resource for investigators is the Forensic Information System for Handwriting (FISH), which is maintained by the U.S. Secret Service. This database merges federal and Interpol databases of genuine and counterfeit identification documents, such as passports, driver's licenses, and credit cards (Bowman & Schneider, 2007). Caution must be used in focusing solely on counterfeit documents, however, because in many cases criminals are able to use legitimate documents in illegal ways. For example, the terrorists involved in the 9/11 attacks breached the U.S. border through fraudulently obtained—but genuine—U.S. travel documents. As a result of that discovery, the U.S. Department of State's Bureau of Diplomatic Security (DS) stepped up its overseas investigations of visa fraud, and these investigations resulted in revocation of 1,680 visas and 512 arrests in 2006 alone (Griffin, 2007).

Passport and visa fraud continue to be challenges, as people constantly seek ways to circumvent our country's immigration policies. In late 2019, a 32-year-old California man plead guilty to his role in a multiyear, transnational visa fraud scheme to bring Armenian citizens into the United States, fraudulently claiming to the U.S. Citizenship and Immigration Services (USCIS) that the Armenians were members of performance groups and, thus, qualified for P-3 "Culturally Unique Artist" visas (U.S. DOJ, 2019). Todd J. Brown, Director of the Diplomatic Security Service (DSS) stated: "Deterring, detecting, and investigating U.S. passport and visa fraud is essential to safeguarding our national security."

To help identify and investigate other counterfeit or crime-related handwritten documents, the FBI maintains a national fraudulent check file, an anonymous letter file, a bank robbery note file, paper watermarks, safety paper, and checkwriter standards. Also, as in other areas of evidence examination, computer programs have been developed to analyze handwriting.

People often type anonymous or threatening letters, believing that typewritten materials are not as traceable as handwritten ones. However, some courts have held that typewriting can be compared more accurately than handwriting and almost as accurately as fingerprints. To collect typewriting standards, remove the ribbon from the suspected typewriter and send the ribbon to a laboratory. Use a different ribbon to take each sample. Take samples using light, medium, and heavy pressure. Submit one carbon-copy sample with the typewriter on stencil position. Do not send the typewriter to a laboratory, but hold it as evidence.

Given enough typing samples, it is often possible to determine the make and model of a machine. Typewriter standard files are available at the FBI laboratory. The information can greatly narrow the search for the actual machine. The most important comparison is between the suspect document and a specific typewriter.

With computerized word processing having almost exclusively replaced typewriters, the word-processing software program and the printer used become important evidence. Computer scanners and desktop publishing programs make producing fraudulent documents much easier. Collect as evidence the computer hard drive, printer, copier, scanner, or whichever devices were used to generate the document. Further complicating the collection of document evidence is technology that allows printing from a tablet or smartphone. When e-printing is involved, investigators must acquire not only the print source but the device from which the data was originally sent, necessitating forensic examination of the computer, tablet, or smartphone.

Computer-related document evidence may be contained on tapes, disks, thumb drives, or other portable storage devices not readily discernible and highly susceptible to destruction. In addition to information on tapes, disks, and portable media, evidence may take the form of data reports, programming, or other printed materials based on information from computer files. Investigators who handle computer tapes and disks should avoid contact with the recording surfaces. They should never write on computer disk labels with a ballpoint pen or pencil and should never use paper clips on or rubber bands around computer disks. To do so may destroy the data they contain. Computer tapes and disks taken as evidence should be stored vertically, at approximately 70 °F, and away from bright light, dust, and magnetic fields.

Photographs frequently are also valuable evidence, whether taken by an officer or by someone outside the department. Some researchers are focusing their efforts on techniques to enhance grainy, blurred, or poorly contrasted photographs by digitally converting them and subjecting them to software programs. Photographic images of injuries on human skin can be enhanced using reflective and fluorescent UV imaging.

Recall that the best-evidence rule stipulates that the original evidence is to be presented whenever possible. For example, a photograph or photocopy of a forged check is not admissible in court; the check itself is required.

When submitting any document evidence to a laboratory, clearly indicate which documents are original and which are comparison standards. Also indicate whether latent fingerprints are requested. Although original documents are needed for laboratory examinations and court exhibits, copies can be used for file searches. A photograph is superior to a photocopy.

Laundry and Dry-Cleaning Marks

Many launderers and dry cleaners use specific marking systems. The Laundry and Dry Cleaning National Association has files on such marking systems. Many police laboratories also maintain a file of visible and invisible laundry marks used by local establishments. Military clothing is marked with the wearer's serial number, name, and organization.

> **LO6** Describe special collection and processing considerations for the following types of evidence: shoe and tire prints and impressions, tools and tool marks, firearms and ammunition, glass, soils and minerals, safe insulation, ropes, strings, tapes, drugs, documents, laundry and dry-cleaning marks, paint, and skeletal remains.
>
> Use UV light to detect invisible laundry marks. Submit the entire garment to a laboratory, identified with a string tag or a marking directly on the garment.

Laundry and dry-cleaning marks are used to identify the dead and injured in mass disasters such as airplane crashes, fires, and floods and in other circumstances as well. For example, a dead baby was traced by a sheet's laundry marks. Clothing labels can also assist in locating the possible source of the clothing.

Paint

Paints are complex and are individual in color, composition, texture, and layer composition. The layer structure of a questioned paint sample can be compared with a known source from a suspect. The sequence, relative thickness, color, texture, number, and chemical composition of each of the layers can then be compared (FBI, 2019). The National Automotive Paint file, maintained by the FBI, contains more than 40,000 auto manufacturer paint samples, which can help identify the year, make, and color of a motor vehicle from a chip of paint left at the scene. The Paint Data Query (PDQ) database, developed by the Royal Canadian Mounted Police, can identify the make of a vehicle from samples of automotive paint, primers, and clear coat by matching the chemical

composition, physical attributes, and infrared spectrum (Lavine, White, Perera, Nishikda, & Allen, 2016). The PDQ database contains more than 21,000 automotive paint samples that correspond to more than 84,000 individual paint layers used on most domestic and foreign vehicles sold in North America.

> **LO6** Describe special collection and processing considerations for the following types of evidence: shoe and tire prints and impressions, tools and tool marks, firearms and ammunition, glass, soils and minerals, safe insulation, ropes, strings, tapes, drugs, documents, laundry and dry-cleaning marks, paint, and skeletal remains.
>
> In hit-and-run cases, collect paint samples from any area of the vehicle that had contact with the victim. Take paint samples down to the original metal to show the layer composition.

Use small boxes for submitting paint samples to the crime lab, putting samples from different parts of the vehicle in separate small boxes. If paint chips are on the clothing of the victim or suspect, send the entire article of clothing in a paper bag to the laboratory, properly labeled and identified. If an item itself cannot be submitted, it is standard to submit four samples, each at least the size of a nickel. Never collect and use transparent tape or plastic bags to secure the paint sample. Securing in an envelope or plastic container is acceptable.

Wood

Wood comparisons are made from items on a suspect, in a vehicle, or in or on clothing found at a crime scene. The origin is determined by the size or the fit of the fracture with an original piece of wood or by matching the sides or ends of pieces of wood. The type of wood is determined from its cellular elements. When handling wood evidence, if it is found wet, keep it wet; if it is dry, keep it dry.

Skeletal Remains

Laboratory examination can determine whether skeletal remains are animal or human.

Dental comparisons and X-rays of old fractures are other important identifying features or individual characteristics.

Forensic anthropology uses standard scientific techniques developed by physical anthropologists and

If adequate human skeletal remains are available, the sex, race, approximate age at death, approximate height, and approximate time since death can be determined.

archaeologists to identify human skeletal remains as they relate to a criminal case. Ongoing research at the Body Farm in Knoxville, Tennessee, is helping scientists observe the decomposition process of the human body following death and understand how exposure to various environmental conditions affects this process. Death investigations are the focus of Chapter 8.

Digital Evidence

The digital revolution and preponderance of electronic devices pervading everyday life, such as smartphones, computers, iPods, iPads, tablets, gaming systems, and global positioning systems (GPSs), have generated a new class of evidence and requirements for handling it: "The infusion of digital technology into contemporary society has had significant effects for everyday life and for everyday crimes" (Powell, Stratton, & Cameron, 2018, p. vi). The NIJ (2008, p. ix) has defined **digital evidence** as "information and data of value to an investigation that is stored on,

A forensic anthropologist examines a cranium exhumed from a mass grave. DNA samples from victims' remains are compared with the DNA samples taken from living family members in an effort to identify each victim.

Marco Di Lauro/Getty Images

received, or transmitted by an electronic device." Digital evidence may exist on myriad electronic devices, such as a computer hard drive (e.g., emails, browsing history), a cell phone, a CD, the flash card from a digital camera, the chat rooms or message boards of communication websites, and many others. "Given our current digital society, the concept of digital evidence is expansive in scope. The most obvious example is the wide range of devices that can contain digital evidence. Digital evidence examiners must be able to retrieve information from various models of cellular phones (e.g., Android, Apple, and Blackberry), desktops, laptops, tablets, external storage devices, GPS locators, and various other devices" (Goodison, Davis, & Jackson, 2015, p. 7).

Digital evidence may be found on the devices of both victims and suspects. "Digital evidence is commonly associated with electronic crime, or e-crime, such as child pornography or credit card fraud. However, digital evidence is now used to prosecute all types of crimes, not just e-crime" (Novak, Grier, & Gonzales, 2018, p. 1).

Learning about the suspects and their habits can help investigators zero in on particular devices: "The suspect's associates can often be counted on to reveal his or her habits, such as, 'He always has his thumb drive with him.' This can be especially crucial in cases of child pornography or intellectual property theft. Further, data recovered from devices such as in-vehicle GPS units and mobile phones can back up suspect patterns—or breaks in patterns" (Miller & Loving, 2009, p. 44).

Much of the information available about digital evidence relates to cell phones because of their pervasiveness in our modern society. As discussed in Chapter 4, these devices have undergone a revolution of capabilities during the twenty-first century and present new legal challenges to the courts. Industry surveys indicate that there are more wireless subscriptions in the United States than there are people (Goodison et al., 2015). Every cell phone leaves a digital trail. When the device is turned on, it transmits a registration signal to the closest cellular tower, and a record is made of that device's serial and phone number. Cell phone records are often very useful in establishing an accurate timeline surrounding a criminal event. Furthermore, GPS chips built into cell phones allow authorities to track criminals as well as people in need of help.

The first part of collecting evidence from a cell phone is the actual handling of the device. As with all other evidence, use gloves when handling cell phones. Also, do *not* change the condition of the evidence. This is one of the most basic rules of digital evidence collection: if the device is off, leave it off; if it's on, leave it on. Regardless of whether it is on or off, photograph the screen and then place the device in a Faraday bag or signal-blocking container, or wrap it in aluminum foil to prevent anyone from accessing the phone and altering the data contained on it: "The contents of smartphones can now be erased remotely. This means the phone could be in your patrol car on the way to the police department and your suspect can erase everything on it from a computer or another phone" (Kuzia, 2013). If the phone charger can be located, collect it and place it in the evidence bag with the phone, as it will be needed to keep the device powered up if it is on at the time of collection.

Investigators must know their state's laws regarding electronic searches: "Many states make it possible for officers to search a subject's cell phone incident to arrest; some require a search warrant. To obtain carrier data, however, investigators almost always need a court order" (Miller, 2008, p. 14). Each cell phone carrier stores and maintains subscriber records, which include such subscriber information as name, address, and birth date, as well as call-detail records containing data regarding incoming and outgoing phone numbers and the towers that transmitted these calls. Carriers have different lengths of time they hold onto records, ranging anywhere from six years to only a few days. Calldetail reports may be available for 45 days, whereas voicemail and text messages may be stored for a week or less (Miller, 2008).

If a warrant cannot be obtained within that time, a preservation order letter should be submitted to the carrier specifically documenting which cellular records you need preserved (Reiber, 2007). The records will be pulled and maintained for 90 days from the date the carrier receives the request to give investigators time to obtain a warrant, unless investigators "refresh" the preservation request for an additional 90 days.

Of course, in addition to cell phones, many more electronic devices exist that may hold critical digital evidence. As with any other type of evidence collection and examination, training is crucial: "From the perspective of a law enforcement department, the range of extraction modes that can be required to obtain digital evidence from different sources or types of devices means that its collection and use is truly a multifaceted challenge, potentially requiring building and maintaining a variety of quite different technical capabilities and expertise" (Goodison et al., 2015, p. 6). Many colleges and universities now offer undergraduate and graduate courses in digital forensics, with some courses available online. Several publications are also available as resources to investigators, such as *The Journal of Digital Forensic Practice*, which debuted in 2007. The National Institute of Justice has published *Investigative Uses of Technology: Devices Tools and Techniques* (2007), which presents detailed information regarding digital evidence. The investigation of computer crimes is the focus of Chapter 17.

Weapons of Mass Destruction

A weapon of mass destruction (WMD) is defined by U.S. law as any of the following:

- A destructive device, such as an explosive or incendiary bomb, rocket, or grenade;

- A weapon that is designed to cause death or serious injury through toxic or poisonous chemicals;

- A weapon that contains a biological agent or toxin; or

- A weapon that is designed to release dangerous levels of radiation or radioactivity

(FBI, "What we investigate," n.d.).

As implied by its name, a WMD is designed to produce widespread and substantial damage, disorder, and disruption to people and infrastructures. These weapons have come to be known by a variety of acronyms, including CBRN (chemical, biological, radiological, and nuclear) and CBRNE (chemical, biological, radiological, nuclear, and explosive).

In our post-9/11 world, the entire law enforcement profession has a heightened awareness of terrorists and the tools they use to paralyze people, not only psychologically through fear, but also perhaps physically through chemical agents. Although the methods to analyze and fingerprint the source of these weapons are currently insufficient, technology continues to advance in an effort to help investigators detect such threats in the field. For example, a handheld laser spectroscopy device, very similar to the one discussed in the section about drug evidence, can rapidly analyze the chemical composition of a substance in the field (Saito et al., 2018).

The Centers for Disease Control and Prevention (CDC) have certified laboratories around the country to analyze hazardous materials, including suspected WMDs. The response protocol may vary from jurisdiction to jurisdiction, but the following is an example of how the FBI would respond to a report of a suspicious white powder discovered in a letter delivered through the mail (FBI, 2004):

1. Specially trained FBI agents, local hazardous materials (hazmat) teams, and other first responders are **dispatched to the scene.** One of the onsite

agents **immediately contacts FBI Headquarters Counterterrorism**, which assembles a multi-agency team for threat assessment/response. The Headquarters team helps first responders address safety concerns, handle evidence properly, and develop an investigative plan.

2. The onsite team tests the material for radiation, volatile chemicals, pH, and other characteristics; wraps it in an airtight overpack and sends it to the nearest CDC-certified lab for more testing.

   ▪ If the field screen is negative, the team leaves the area.

   ▪ If it's positive, (1) the local area is shut down and tested by hazmat teams in protective suits and (2) people who had any contact with the powder are identified, decontaminated, and possibly examined at a hospital as a precaution.

3. **If a threat letter has been found**, the CDC-certified lab makes sure it's not contaminated, then **sends it to the FBI Laboratory** in Quantico, Virginia, to test for clues like fingerprints, hair samples, and—if the postage stamp/envelope has been licked—DNA. The letter's language and writing, which could provide important clues, are analyzed by the FBI Behavioral Science Unit.

4. Once lab tests determine definitively whether the powder is hazardous or not, the FBI works with the CDC and state and local health departments to **advise the public** whether the threat is real or a hoax.

5. The **evidence of the case is presented to the U.S. Attorney** to determine whether it should be prosecuted: If not, the case is closed. If so, a full investigation is begun. Even cases involving harmless substances, can, of course, be prosecuted because it's a violation of federal law even to threaten the use of a Weapon of Mass Destruction—including anthrax and other biological agents. The threat letters and substances collected during investigations are securely maintained as case evidence.

Investigating terrorism and other threats to homeland security is the focus of Chapter 20.

Other Types of Evidence

Prescription eyeglasses, broken buttons, glove prints, and other personal evidence found at a crime scene can also be examined and compared. Investigators should learn to read "product DNA," the printed code that appears on nearly every manufactured, mass-produced item, because it can provide valuable leads. For example, the numbers on a candy bar wrapper can tell investigators when that candy bar was made, packaged, shipped, and delivered and to what store. Other discarded items at a crime scene that may yield useful information include store and restaurant receipts, bank deposit slips, beverage containers, cigarette packages, and membership and check-cashing cards. If there is a problem processing any evidence, a laboratory can provide specific collecting and packaging instructions.

Evidence Handling and Infectious Disease

Throughout this chapter, you have looked at ways to collect evidence and keep it secure from contamination. As a final discussion in handling physical evidence, consider how to protect yourself from contamination through exposure to not only bloodborne pathogens such as the hepatitis B virus, the hepatitis C virus, and the human immunodeficiency virus (HIV), but to the novel coronavirus (COVID-19) and any other highly transmissible respiratory viruses that may arise in the future.

Investigators are likely to encounter crimes of violence involving the blood and other body fluids of people with infectious diseases. Police officers are likely to encounter these infectious body fluids during the search of crime scenes involving violence. Therefore, it is important to know the facts about these infectious agents.

AIDS is not spread through casual contact such as touching an infected person or sharing equipment. Nor is it spread through the air by coughing or sneezing. An important issue related to HIV/AIDS is people's confidentiality rights concerning their HIV status, including disclosure of such information in police reports. Investigators should be familiar with their jurisdiction's basic medical information confidentiality laws as well as any other specific laws pertaining to infectious diseases.

Chances are less than 1% that an officer will contract the AIDS virus on the job. Tuberculosis (TB), meningitis, and hepatitis pose greater threats. Tuberculosis is a relatively common disease, with the CDC estimating that nearly one-third of the world's population is infected with TB (OSHA, n.d.). TB is transmitted through the air by coughing, hacking, and wheezing. TB can also be transmitted through saliva, urine, blood, and other body fluids.

Meningitis, spread through the air, causes inflammation of the membranes that surround the brain. The hepatitis B virus, known today as HBV, is a bloodborne pathogen that can live outside the body longer than

HIV can. HBV is found in human blood, urine, semen, cerebrospinal fluid, vaginal secretions, and saliva. A safe, effective vaccine to prevent HBV is available, and the Occupational Safety and Health Administration (OSHA) now requires employers to offer and pay for a series of vaccinations to any employee who may be exposed to these pathogens during the course of their employment.

The novel coronavirus, also called COVID-19 or SARS-CoV-2, originated in China during 2019 and reached the United States by early 2020, bringing new threats to first responders and anyone interacting face-to-face with the public. Data show that the most common way the virus spreads is through person-to-person transmission. For example, when an infected person coughs, sneezes, shouts, sings, or even talks, respiratory droplets carrying the virus are expelled from that person and can become aerosolized, lingering in the air for a period of time. If another person breathes in these aerosols, that exposure can cause the other person to become infected. However, studies have also found that the virus can survive on surfaces for various lengths of time under certain conditions (Riddell, Goldie, Hill, Eagles, & Drew, 2020). Therefore, it is suggested that investigators handling evidence that may have been recently handled by a COVID-infected person wear, at minimum, disposable gloves and that they wash their hands immediately after collection of such evidence, taking extreme caution to not touch their eyes, nose, or mouth while gloved up and touching the evidence (Wyllie, 2020).

Use precautions when collecting blood evidence and other body fluids. *Universal precautions*, which is the protocol used by medical health professionals, dictates that public safety officials treat every individual as if he or she is infected and take precautions to minimize risks. *Consider all body secretions as potential health hazards.* If body fluids are present at a crime scene, even if dried, wear personal protective equipment (PPE), including latex gloves, goggles, and a face mask. Secure evidence in glass, metal, or plastic containers. Seal evidence bags with tape rather than staples. Do not allow hand-to-mouth or hand-to-face contact during collection. Do not eat, smoke, apply makeup, or drink at crime scenes because these activities may transfer contaminated body fluids to you. When finished, wash your hands thoroughly (20 to 30 seconds) with soap and water, as this simple task is considered the best way to protect against infection from dangerous pathogens.

While processing the crime scene, constantly be alert for sharp objects, such as hypodermic needles and syringes. If practical, use disposable items where blood is present so the items can be incinerated. All nondisposable items, such as cameras, tools, and notebooks, must be decontaminated using a bleach solution or rubbing alcohol. Even properly dried and packaged evidence is still potentially infectious. Therefore, place appropriate warnings on all items.

After processing, decontaminate the crime scene. If it is to be left for future decontamination, place biohazard warning signs and notify the cleaning team of possible contamination.

Further information on procedures for dealing with evidence with the potential to transmit an infectious disease can be obtained from the Centers for Disease Control and Prevention, Office of Genomics and Precision Public Health, 1600 Clifton Road N.E., Atlanta, GA 30333. 1-800-CDC-INFO. www.cdc.gov/genomics.

Summary

Criminal investigations rely heavily on various types of evidence. To be of value, evidence must be legally and properly seized and processed. Processing physical evidence includes discovering or recognizing it; collecting, recording, and identifying it; packaging, conveying, and storing it; examining it; exhibiting it in court; and disposing of it when the case is closed.

To determine what is evidence, first consider the apparent crime. Then look for any objects unrelated or foreign to the scene, unusual in their location or number, damaged or broken, or whose relation to other objects suggests a pattern that fits the crime. Common errors in collecting evidence are (1) not collecting enough of the sample, (2) not obtaining standards of comparison, and (3) not maintaining the integrity of the evidence.

Mark or identify each item of evidence in a way that can be recognized later. Indicate the date and case number as well as your personal identifying mark or initials. Record in your notes the date and time of collection, where the evidence was found and by whom, case number, description of the item, and who took custody of it. Package each item separately in durable containers to maintain the integrity of evidence. Personal delivery, registered mail, insured parcel post, air express, FedEx, and UPS are legal ways to transport evidence. Always specify that the person who receives the evidence is to sign for it.

Package evidence properly to keep it in substantially the same condition in which it was found and store it securely. Document custody of the evidence at every stage. To ensure admissibility of the evidence in court, be able to (1) identify the evidence as that found at the crime scene, (2) describe exactly where it was found, (3) establish its custody from discovery to the present, and (4) voluntarily explain any changes that have occurred in the evidence. After a case is closed, evidence is returned to the owner, auctioned, destroyed, or retained for training purposes.

Frequently examined physical evidence includes fingerprints; voiceprints; language; DNA; blood and other body fluids; scent; hairs and fibers; shoe and tire prints and impressions; bite marks; tools and tool marks; firearms and ammunition; glass; soils and minerals; safe insulation; rope, strings, and tapes; drugs; weapons of mass destruction; documents; digital evidence; laundry and dry-cleaning marks; paint; skeletal remains; wood; and many other types of evidence.

Fingerprints are *positive* evidence of a person's identity. They cannot, however, indicate a person's age, sex, or race. DNA can tell investigators the sample donor's gender, ethnicity, eye color, and hair color, and matching DNA to a known profile can provide positive identification of an individual. Blood can be identified as animal or human and is most useful in eliminating suspects. Age and race cannot be determined from blood samples, but DNA analysis of blood can provide positive identification. Microscopic examination determines whether hair is animal or human. Many characteristics can be determined from human hair: the part of the body it came from; whether it was bleached or dyed, freshly cut, pulled out, or burned; and whether there is blood or semen on it. Race, sex, and age cannot be determined.

Special collection and processing considerations are required depending on the type of evidence involved. After photographing, cast shoe or tire tread impressions found in dirt, sand, or snow. Identify each suspected tool with a string tag, wrap it separately, and pack it in a strong box to send to a laboratory. Photograph tool marks and then either cast them or send the object on which they appear to a laboratory. A tool mark is compared with a standard-of-comparison impression rather than with the tool itself.

Examine weapons for latent fingerprints. Photograph weapons and then identify them with string tags. Unload firearms and record their serial numbers on string tags and in your notes. If the firearm is a revolver, take careful note of which chambers had ammunition in them and document the placement of the wheel. Label the packing container "Firearms." Identify bullets on the base, cartridges on the outside of the case near the bullet end, and cartridge cases on the inside near the open end. Put ammunition in cotton or soft paper and ship to a laboratory. Never send live ammunition through the mail; use a common carrier instead.

Label glass fragments using adhesive tape on each piece. Wrap each piece separately in cotton to avoid chipping, and place them in a strong box marked "Fragile" to send to a laboratory. Put one pound of comparison soil into a container identified on the outside. Collect evidence soil the same way. Seal both containers to prevent loss, wrap them, and send them to a laboratory.

Put samples of safe insulation in paper containers identified on the outside. Put labeled rope, twine, and string in a container. Put tapes on waxed paper or cellophane and then place them in a container. Put liquid drugs in a bottle and attach a label. Put powdered and solid drugs in a pillbox or powder box and identify them in the same way.

Do not touch documents with your bare hands. Place documents in a cellophane envelope and then in a manila envelope identified on the outside. Use UV light to detect invisible laundry marks. Submit the entire garment to a laboratory, identified with a string tag or with a marking directly on the garment. In hit-and-run cases, collect paint samples from any area of the vehicle that had contact with the victim. Take paint samples down to the original metal to show the layer composition. If adequate human skeletal remains are available, the sex, race, approximate age at death, approximate height, and approximate time since death can be determined.

Can You Define?

Advanced Fingerprint Information Technology (AFIT)	bore	competent evidence
associative evidence	caliber	contamination
ballistics	cast	corpus delicti
best evidence	chain of custody	corpus delicti evidence
biometrics	chain of evidence	cross-contamination
bloodstain pattern analysis	circumstantial evidence	*CSI* effect
	class characteristics	*Daubert* standard

direct evidence

digital evidence

DNA

DNA profiling

elimination prints

evidence

forensic science

indirect evidence

individual characteristics

inkless fingerprint

integrity of evidence

latent fingerprints

material evidence

physical evidence

plastic fingerprints

prima facie evidence

primary transfer

probative evidence

proxy data

relevant evidence

rifling

secondary transfer

standard of comparison

striations

tech effect

tool mark

trace evidence

visible fingerprints

voiceprint

Checklist

Physical Evidence

- Was all physical evidence photographed before anything was moved?

- Was the physical evidence located in the crime scene sketch?

- Were relevant facts recorded in your notebook?

- Was the evidence properly identified, including the date, case number, your initials or mark, and a description of the evidence?

- Was the evidence properly packaged to avoid contamination or destruction?

- Were standards of comparison obtained if needed?

- Was the evidence sent in a way that kept it secure and provided a signed receipt, such as by registered mail?

- Was the evidence kept continuously secure until presented in court?

The following types of physical evidence are frequently found at a crime scene and should be searched for, depending on the type of crime committed:

- Blood

- Cigarettes, cigars, and smoking materials

- Clothing and fragments

- Containers and boxes

- Dirt and dust particles

- Documents and papers

- Fibers, ropes, and strings

- Fingernail scrapings

- Fingerprints, visible and latent

- Footprints

- Glass objects and fragments

- Greases, oils, salves, and emulsions

- Hairs, human and animal

- Inorganic materials

- Insulation from safes, buildings, and homes

- Metal objects and fragments

- Organic materials, plant and animal

- Paint and paint chips

- Palmprints

- Personal possessions

- Photographs

- Plastic impressions

- Soils

- Tires and tire tracks

- Tools and tool marks

- Weapons

- Wood chips or fragments

References

Adair, T. (2009, November). Capturing snow impressions. *Law and Order*, pp. 14–20.

American Academy of Forensic Sciences. (n.d.). *What is forensic science?* Colorado Springs, CO. Retrieved June 18, 2020, from aafs.org/Home/Resources/Students/What-is.aspx

American Bar Association. (2007, July). *ABA standards for criminal justice: DNA evidence* (3rd ed.). Washington, DC: Author.

Balanchander, N., Babu, N. A., Jimson, S., Priyadharsini, C., & Masthan, K. M. K. (2015, April). Evolution of forensic odontology: An overview. *Journal of Pharmacy and Bioallied Sciences 7*(Suppl 1): S1–S318. Retrieved June 7, 2020, from www.ncbi.nlm.nih.gov/pmc/articles/PMC4439663/

Ballou, S. (2013, April). *The biological evidence preservation handbook: Best practices for evidence handlers.* Gaithersburg, MD: National Institute of Standards and Technology, U.S. Department of Commerce. (NISTIR 7928)

Barnes, J. G. (2011, July). History. Chapter 1 in *Fingerprint sourcebook* by the International Association for Identification, et al. (NCJ 225321). Retrieved June 1, 2020, from nij.ojp.gov/library/publications/fingerprint-sourcebook

Bouslimani, A., Melnik, A. V., Xu, Z., Amir, A., da Silva, R. R., Wang, M., . . . Dorrestein, P. C. (2016, October 5). Lifestyle chemistries from phones for individual profiling. *Proceedings of the National Academy of Sciences of the United States of America.* Retrieved June 15, 2020, from www.pnas.org/content/pnas/early/2016/11/08/1610019113.full.pdf

Bowen, R., & Schneider, J. (2007, October). Forensic databases: Paint, shoe prints, and beyond. *NIJ Journal,* 258.

Catanzaro, M., Tola, E., Hummel, P; and Viciano, A. (2017, January 25). Voice analysis should be used with caution in court. *Scientific American.* Retrieved June 1, 2020, from www.scientificamerican.com/article/voice-analysis-should-be-used-with-caution-in-court/

Chin, J. M., & Workewych, L. (2016, March 21). *The CSI effect.* doi:10.2139.ssrn.2752445

Christman, D. (2015, February 25). *BPA for criminal investigation.* Document provided by author for use in this manuscript.

Committee for Public Council Services Innocence Program, et al. (2015, June). *Best Practices Manual for Evidence Collection, Handling, Storage, and Retention in Massachusetts.* Retrieved June 18, 2020, from www.publiccounsel.net/pc/wp-content/uploads/sites/4/2014/09/Best-Practices-Manual-for-Evidence-Collection-Handling-Storage-and-Retention-in-Massachusetts-FINAL-VERSION-2.pdf

Divakar, K. P. (2017, March). Forensic odontology: The new dimension in dental analysis. *International Journal of Biomedical Science 13*(1): 1–5. Retrieved June 9, 2020, from www.ncbi.nlm.nih.gov/pmc/articles/PMC5422639/

DNA Saves. (n.d.). Expanding the DNA database—Which method is right for your state? Retrieved June 6, 2020, from www.dnasaves.org/us-dna-laws/

Drake, N. (2014, December 4). DNA test that distinguishes identical twins may be used in court for first time. *Wired.* Retrieved June 18, 2020, from www.wired.com/2014/12/genetic-test-distinguishes-identical-twins-may-used-court-first-time/

Eatley, G., Hueston, H. H., & Price, K. (2016). A meta-analysis of the CSI effect: The impact of popular media on jurors' perception of forensic evidence. *Politics, Bureaucracy, & Justice 5*(2): 1–10. Retrieved June 10, 2020, from www.wtamu.edu/webres/File/Academics/College%20of%20Education%20and%20Social%20Sciences/Department%20of%20Political%20Science%20and%20Criminal%20Justice/PBJ/2018/5n2/5n2_01EPH.pdf

Federal Bureau of Investigation. (n.d.). *Combined DNA index system (CODIS).* Washington, DC: Author. Retrieved June 2, 2020, from www.fbi.gov/services/laboratory/biometric-analysis/codis

Federal Bureau of Investigation. (n.d.). What we investigate: Weapons of mass destruction. Washington, DC: Author. Retrieved June 15, 2020, from www.fbi.gov/investigate/wmd

Federal Bureau of Investigation. (2004, April 20). *FBI casework: Suspicious powders 101.* Washington, DC: Author. Retrieved June 15, 2020, from archives.fbi.gov/archives/news/stories/2004/april/powders_042004

Federal Bureau of Investigation. (2008, April 24). FBI history: The Unabomber. www.fbi.gov/history/famous-cases/unabomber

Federal Bureau of Investigation. (2019). *Handbook of forensic services.* Washington, DC: Author. Retrieved June 10, 2020, from www.fbi.gov/file-repository/handbook-of-forensic-services-pdf.pdf/view

Federal Bureau of Statistics. (n.d.). *CODIS – NDIS statistics.* Washington, DC: Author. Retrieved June 4, 2020, from www.fbi.gov/services/laboratory/biometric-analysis/codis/ndis-statistics

Foster and Freeman. (n.d.). "SoleMate FPX." Retrieved June 7, 2020, from www.fosterfreeman.com/latest-news/519-new-shoeprint-identification.html

Galton, F. (1892). *Finger prints.* New York: MacMillan.

Geberth, V. (2010a, September). Amazing advances in forensic science part 2: Advances in criminalistics. *Law and Order,* pp. 72–75.

Geberth, V. (2010b, October). Amazing advances in forensic science part 3: Firearms and ballistics. *Law and Order,* pp. 98–100.

Geberth, V. (2015). *Practical homicide investigations* (5th edition). Boca Raton, FL: CRC Press.

Goodison, S. E., Davis, R. C., & Jackson, B. A. (2015). *Digital evidence and the U.S. criminal justice system.* Santa Monica, CA: Rand Corporation. Retrieved June 15, 2020, from www.ncjrs.gov/pdffiles1/nij/grants/248770.pdf

Griffin, R. J. (2007, October). Operation triple X: Hitting hard at illegal document trade. *The Police Chief,* pp. 30–36.

Hansen, M. (2013, September 1). Crime labs under the microscope after a string of shoddy, suspect and fraudulent results. *ABA Journal*. Retrieved June 18, 2020, from www .abajournal.com/magazine/article/crime_labs_under_the_ microscope_after_a_string_of_shoddy_suspect_and_fraudu/

Hodge, S. D, Jr. (2018). Current controversies in the use of DNA in forensic investigations. *University of Baltimore Law Review 48*(1): 38–66. Retrieved June 6, 2020, from scholarworks.law.ubalt.edu/cgi/viewcontent .cgi?article=2042&context=ublr

Hollien, H. (2012, December). About forensic phonetics. *Linguistica 52*(1): 27.

Innocence Project. (n.d.). *DNA exonerations in the United States*. New York, NY: Author. Retrieved June 4, 2020, from www.innocenceproject.org /dna-exonerations-in-the-united-states/

International Association for Identification, et al. (2011, July). *The fingerprint sourcebook*. Washington, DC: National Institution of Justice. (NIJ 225320). Retrieved June 1, 2020, from nij.ojp.gov/library/publications /fingerprint-sourcebook

Klentz, B. A., Winters, G. M., & Chapman, J. E. (2020, January 7). The CSI effect and the impact of DNA evidence on mock jurors and jury deliberations. *Psychology, Crime & Law*. doi:10.1080/106831 6X.2019.1708353

Krishan, K., Kanchan, T., & Garg, A. K. (2015, July). Dental evidence in forensic identification: An overview, methodology, and present status. *The Open Dentistry Journal 9*: 250–256. Retrieved June 9, 2020, from www.ncbi .nlm.nih.gov/pmc/articles/PMC4541412/

Kuzia, G. (2013, April 18). Handling cell phones and their digital evidence. *Police Magazine*. Retrieved June 15, 2020, from www.policemag.com/374289 /handling-cell-phones-and-their-digital-evidence

Lavine, B. K., White, C., Perera, U., Nishikda, K., & Allen, M. (2016, May). Improving the PDQ database to enhance investigative lead information from automotive paints. Unpublished report made available electronically by the National Criminal Justice Reference Service. Retrieved May 5, 2021, from www.ojp.gov/pdffiles1/nij /grants/249893.pdf

Lindstrom, J. D. (2012, February). *A more efficient means to collect & process reference DNA samples*. Washington, DC: U.S. Department of Justice. Document No. 237764. Retrieved June 2, 2020, from www.ncjrs.gov/pdffiles1/nij /grants/237764.pdf

Means, R. (2008, February). Brady policy and officer credibility. *Law and Order*, pp. 12–14.

Miller, C. (2008, July). The other side of mobile forensics. *Law Enforcement Technology*, pp. 10–18.

Miller, C., & Loving, K. (2009, October). The crime scene evidence you're ignoring. *Law Enforcement Technology*, pp. 36–45.

Mitchell, B. (2009, August). Keeping track: Four common pitfalls in tracking and storing evidence. *Law Officer Magazine*, pp. 84–86.

Moses, K. R. (2011, July). Automated fingerprint identification system (AFIS). Chapter 6 in *Fingerprint sourcebook* by the International Association for Identification, et al. (NCJ 225326). Retrieved June 1, 2020, from nij.ojp.gov/library /publications/fingerprint-sourcebook

National Institute of Justice. (n.d.). *Forensic sciences*. Washington, DC: Author. Retrieved June 18, 2020, from nij. ojp.gov/topics/forensics

National Institute of Justice. (2007, October). *Investigative uses of technology: Devices, tools, and techniques*. Washington, DC: Author.

National Institute of Justice. (2008). *Electronic crime scene investigation: A guide for first responders* (2nd ed.). Washington, DC: U.S. Department of Justice. (NCJ 219941). Retrieved June 15, 2020, from www.ncjrs.gov/pdffiles1 /nij/219941.pdf

National Institute of Justice. (2010, July 23). *DNA and property crimes*. Washington, DC: Author. Retrieved February 24, 2015, from www.nij.gov/topics/forensics/evidence /dna /property-crime/pages/welcome.aspx

National Institute of Justice. (2012a, August 8). *DNA evidence: Basics of analyzing*. Retrieved June 2, 2020, from nij.ojp.gov /topics/articles/dna-evidence-basics-analyzing

National Institute of Justice. (2012b, August 8). *DNA evidence: Basics of identifying, gathering, and transporting*. Retrieved June 2, 2020, from nij.ojp.gov/topics/articles/dna-evidence -basics-identifying-gathering-and-transporting

National Institute of Justice. (2017, July 10). *Forensic identification using individual chemical signatures*. Washington, DC: Author. Retrieved June 15, 2020, from nij.ojp.gov/topics/articles/forensic-identification-using- individual-chemical-signatures

Nirenberg, M. (2016, January). Gait, footprints, and footwear: How forensic podiatry can identify criminals. *The Police Chief, 83*: web only. Retrieved June 6, 2020, from www .policechiefmagazine.org/gait-footprints-and-footwear -how-forensic-podiatry-can-identify-criminals/

Novak, M., Grier, J., & Gonzales, D. (2018, October 7). *New approaches to digital evidence acquisition and analysis*. Washington, DC: National Institute of Justice. (NCJ 250700). Retrieved June 15, 2020, from www.ncjrs.gov/pdffiles1 /nij/250700.pdf

Occupational Safety and Health Administration. (n.d.). Tuberculosis. Washington, DC: U.S. Department of Labor. Retrieved June 15, 2020, from www.osha.gov/SLTC /tuberculosis/

Perin, M. (2014, November 17). Casting in snow. *Officer.com*. Retrieved June 6, 2020, from www.officer.com/investigations /forensics/article/12007096/casting-in-snow

PoliceOne. (2020, January 24). How a new handheld tool is helping narcotics investigators in Kentucky. Retrieved June 9, 2020, from www.policeone.com/police-products /narcotics-identification/articles/how-a-new-handheld -tool-is-helping-narcotics-investigators-in-kentucky -hqDfk5LU02bwDGuq/

Powell, A., Stratton, G., & Cameron, R. (2018). *Digital criminology: Crime and justice in digital society*. New York, NY: Routledge.

Prete, C., Glamiche, L., Quenum-Possy-Berry, F., Allain, C., Thiburce, N., & Colard, T. (2013, December 10). Lumicyano™: A new fluorescent cyanoacrylate for a one-step luminescent latent fingermark development. *Forensic Science International, 233*(1–3): 104–112.

Prime, R. J., & Newman, J. (2007, November). The impact of DNA on policing: Past, present, and future. *The Police Chief*, pp. 30–35.

Puritan Medical Products. (2018, March 19). *Three key steps to effective DNA swab collection at crime scenes*. Retrieved June 2, 2020, from blog.puritanmedproducts.com/three-key-steps-to-effective-dna-swab-collection-at-crime-scenes

Reiber, L. (2007, June). Using cell phone records to solve crimes. *Law Officer Magazine*, pp. 40–41.

Resch, R. (2019, February). Report: Bitemark analysis debunked as pseudoscience. *Criminal Legal News 2*(2): 26. Retrieved June 9, 2020, from www.criminallegalnews.org/news/2019/jan/18/report-bitemark-analysis-debunked-pseudoscience/

Riddell, S., Goldie, S., Hill, A., Eagles, D., & Drew, T. W. (2020). The effect of temperature on persistence of SRS-CoV-2 on common surfaces. *Virology Journal, 17*(145). doi: 10.1186/s12985-020-01418-7

Roman, J. K., Reid, S., Reid, J., Chalfin, A., Adams, W., & Knight, C. (2008, April). *The DNA field experiment: Cost-effectiveness analysis of the use of DNA in the investigation of high-volume crimes*. Washington, DC: Urban Institute, Justice Policy Center. Retrieved June 18, 2020, from www.urban.org/sites/default/files/publication/31856/411697-The-DNA-Field-Experiment.PDF

Saito, M., Uchida, N., Furutani, S., Murahashi, M., Espulgar, W., Nagatani, N., . . . Tamiya, E. (2018, January 29). Field-deployable rapid multiple biosensing system for detection of chemical and biological warfare agents. *Microsystems & Nanoengineering 4*, 1783. doi:10.1038/micronano.2017.83

Saks, M. J., Albright, T., Bohan, T. L., Bierer, B. E., Bowers, C. M., Bush, M. A., . . . Zumwalt, R. E. (2016, December). Forensic bitemark identification: Weak foundations, exaggerated claims. *Journal of Law and the Biosciences 3*(3): 538–575. Retrieved June 9, 2020, from www.ncbi.nlm.nih.gov/pmc/articles/PMC5570687/

Schreiber, S. (2009, November). How clean is your (evidence) house? *Law Enforcement Technology*, pp. 8–13.

Shelton, D. E. (2008, March). The "CSI Effect": Does it really exist? *NIJ Journal, 259*: 1–8. (NCJ 221500)

Shelton, D. E., Barak, G., and Kim, Y. S. (2011, January 1). Studying juror expectations for scientific evidence: A new model for looking at the CSI myth. *Court Review: The Journal of the American Judges Association, 47*: 8–18.

Silverman, H. (2020, March 30). Convicted serial killer known as the "grim sleeper" found dead in prison cell. Retrieved June 6, 2020, from www.cnn.com/2020/03/30/us/grim-sleeper-dies-death-row/index.html

Souviron, R., & Haller, L. (2017, November 1). Bite mark evidence: Bite mark analysis is not the same as bite mark comparison or matching or identification. *Journal of Law and the Biosciences 4*(3): 617–622. Retrieved June 9, 2020, from academic.oup.com/jlb/article/4/3/617/4584307

Spagnoli, L. (2007, July). Beyond CODIS. *Law Enforcement Technology*, pp. 42–51.

Spraggs, D. (2007, February). How to lift fingerprints. *Police*, pp. 24–26.

Stern, J. (2015, April 9). Electronic voiceprints: The crime solving power of biometric forensics. *Forensic Focus*. Retrieved June 1, 2020, from www.forensicfocus.com/articles/electronic-voiceprints-the-crime-solving-power-of-biometric-forensics/

Taupin, J. M. (2016, Spring). Mechanisms of DNA transfer. *Evidence Technology Magazine*, pp. 30–31. Retrieved June 2, 2020, from www.nxtbook.com/nxtbooks/evidencetechnology/2016spring/

Tread Forensics. (2019). NIST OSAC footwear and tire subcommittee published first document. Retrieved June 7, 2020, from www.treadforensics.com/index.php

U.S. Department of Justice, National Institute of Justice, National Commission on the Future of DNA Evidence. (1999). *What every law enforcement officer should know about DNA evidence*. Washington, DC.

U.S. Department of Justice. (2019, November 1). Armenian citizen pleads guilty for his role in for-profit U.S. visa fraud scheme. Retrieved June 9, 2020, from www.uscis.gov/news/news-releases/armenian-citizen-pleads-guilty-his-role-profit-us-visa-fraud-scheme

U.S. Department of Justice. (2020, March 6). *Department of justice to publish final rule to comply fully with DNA fingerprint act of 2005*. Press release. Retrieved June 6, 2020, from www.justice.gov/opa/pr/department-justice-publish-final-rule-comply-fully-dna-fingerprint-act-2005-0

U.S. Government Accountability Office. (2019, March). *DNA evidence*. A report to Congressional requestors. Washington, DC: Author. Retrieved June 4, 2020, from www.gao.gov/assets/700/697768.pdf

Venkatesh, R, & David, M. P. (2011, July-December). Cheiloscopy: An aid for personal identification. *Journal of Forensic Dental Sciences 3*(2): 6770. Retrieved June 9, 2020, from www.ncbi.nlm.nih.gov/pmc/articles/PMC3296377/

Verma, A. K., Kumar, S., & Bhattacharya, S. (2013, May-August). Identification of a person with the help of bite mark analysis. *Journal of Oral Biology and Craniofacial Research 3*(2): 88–91. Retrieved June 9, 2020, from www.ncbi.nlm.nih.gov/pmc/articles/PMC3941620/

Verma, Y., Einstein, A., Gondhalekar, R., Verma, A. K., George, J., Chandra, S., . . . Samadi, F. M. (2015, January–June). A study of lip prints and its reliability as a forensic tool. *National Journal of Maxillofacial Surgery 6*(1): 25–30. Retrieved June 9, 2020, from www.ncbi.nlm.nih.gov/pmc/articles/PMC4668728/

Vicary, A., & Zaikman, Y. (2017). The CSI effect: An investigation into the relationship between watching crime shows and forensic knowledge. *North American Journal of Psychology 19*(1): 51–64.

Wallentine, K. (2010, January). Collection of DNA upon arrest: Expanding investigative frontiers. *The Police Chief*, pp. 12–13.

Warrington, D. (2014, January 4). Preventing crime scene contamination. *Forensic Magazine*. Retrieved February 23, 2015, from www.forensicmag.com/articles/2014/01/preventing-crime-scene-contamination

Wilson, D. B., McClure, D., & Weisburd, D. (2010, November). Does forensic DNA help to solve crime? The benefit of sophisticated answers to naïve questions. *Journal of Contemporary Criminal Justice, 26*(4): 458–469.

Wisconsin Department of Justice. (2017). *Physical evidence handbook* (9th edition). Madison, WI: Wisconsin State Crime Laboratories. Retrieved June 2, 2020, from wilenet.org/html/crime-lab/physevbook/index.html

Worthen, M. (2019, August 19). What is the Unabomber's life like now? *Biography*. Retrieved May 28, 2020, from www.biography.com/news/unabomber-ted-kaczynski-today

Wyllie, D. (2020, March 6). Coronavirus, infectious disease, and officer safety. *Police Magazine*. Retrieved June 15, 2020, from www.policemag.com/545596/coronavirus-infectious-disease-and-officer-safety

Yamashita, B., & French, M. (2011, March). Latent print development. *The Fingerprint Sourcebook*, by the International Association of Identification. Washington, DC: National Institute of Justice, Chapter 7. (NCJ 225320). Retrieved June 18, 2020, from www.ncjrs.gov/pdffiles1/nij/225327.pdf

Zetter, K. (2010, July 12). DNA sample from son led to arrest of accused "grim sleeper." *Wired*. Retrieved June 6, 2020, from www.wired.com/2010/07/dna-database/

Cases Cited

Daubert v. Merrell Dow Pharmaceuticals, Inc., 509 U.S. 579 (1993).

Frye v. United States, 54 App. D.C. 46, 293 F. 1013 (1923).

Additional Resource

Committee on Identifying the Needs of the Forensic Sciences Community and the National Research Council. (2009, August). *Strengthening forensic science in the United States: A path forward*. Washington, DC: The National Academies Press. (NIJ Document 228091). doi:10.17226/12589

Chapter 6
Obtaining Information and Intelligence

Learning Objectives

LO1   Identify the sources of information that are available to investigators.

LO2   Explain what the goal of interviewing and interrogation is.

LO3   Explain the different types of questions used during interviews and interrogations and how much reliance should be placed on each type.

LO4   Compare and contrast the approaches used to appeal to reluctant interviewees.

LO5   Describe how to conduct interviews when multiple people are at the scene.

LO6   State what the *Miranda* warning is and when it must be given.

LO7   Describe the various techniques used in an interrogation.

LO8   Explain what significance a confession has in an investigation.

LO9   Describe what a polygraph is, its role in investigation, and the acceptability of its results in court.

LO10   Differentiate between information and intelligence.

Introduction

On February 4, 2010, a California family of four went missing. On the surface, it looked as if Joseph and Summer McStay had packed up their two small boys, Gianni and Joseph Jr., and abandoned their home in San Diego for a new life in Mexico. Four days after they were last seen in the United States, their car was found parked near the Mexican border, and grainy video captured by a border surveillance camera showed four people resembling the family crossing into Tijuana, Mexico, on foot. A search of their home showed no signs of a struggle, yet there was food left out on the counter and the family dogs were in the backyard. Examination of their home computer revealed that someone had recently searched how to obtain passports to Mexico. While some authorities suspected foul play, there was little hard evidence to go on, and the case was classified as a missing-persons file.

More than three years passed, with no word from the family. Then in November 2013, a motorcyclist riding off-road in the Mohave Desert, 100 miles *north* of the McStays' home, found a human skull and contacted authorities. Four shallow graves were discovered nearby, and the identities of the bodies were confirmed through dental records. In the course of the ensuing murder investigation, numerous people connected to the family were interviewed by police, including Joseph's business partner, Chase Merritt, who it was known had met Joseph for a business lunch in Rancho Cucamonga the day the family disappeared.

A CNN Special Report, "Buried Secrets: Who Killed the McStay Family?," explored this murder mystery. In January 2014, CNN anchor Randi Kaye interviewed Merritt, with portions of that conversation available in the following transcript:

Kaye: "You took a polygraph test. What did it show?"

Merritt: "I don't know."

Kaye: "You passed the polygraph?"

Merritt: "Apparently, I mean I haven't, after I took the polygraph test, um, law enforcement has not contacted me at all since. So, I kind of simply assumed well apparently that, that resolved any issues that they may be looking at with me."

Kaye: "Did detectives ask if you killed Joseph McStay and his family?"

Merritt: "I don't recall them asking me that."

Kaye: "Nothing that direct?"

Merritt: "Hum?"

Kaye: "Nothing directly?"

Merritt: "No. I don't recall them being that direct." . . .

Kaye: "Were you surprised that the remains were found in this desert in Victorville?"

Merritt: "Yeah, actually, because I live in this area. Um . . ."

Kaye: "Near by."

Merritt: "Yeah, Probably um 20 miles or so."

Kaye: "So I mean, is this ever, I mean would you ever expect that this is how it would end in the desert like that?"

Merritt: "In the desert? I had no clue."

Kaye: "I mean in your gut, what did you think happened?"

Merritt: "I have absolutely no clue. I think that um, if I were to guess just like anyone else, I would think um, it was probably random ah because I honestly don't believe that family had anything to do with it." . . .

Kaye: "As far as you know, you were the last person or at least one of the last people to see him right?"

Merritt: "Yeah. Um. When he left Rancho Cucamonga nobody else, although I think somebody, there was another person or two that he talked to, I'm not sure."

Kaye: "But you were the last person he saw?"

Merritt: "I'm definitely the last person he saw." (McClish, 2014)

That conversation was analyzed by Mark McClish, a former federal law enforcement officer who now heads a company specializing in advanced interviewing techniques and statement analysis. According to McClish (2014), multiple statements made by Merritt during that interview indicate deception. Notably, Merritt states he does not recall being asked by police whether he killed the family, as if that is a question one gets asked so routinely you cannot possibly remember which times it comes up. Other telling aspects of Merritt's statements include his use of the deceptive phrase, "I have no clue," more than once; his answering a question with a question; stalling tactics through "um" and "ah;" and the changing of his language between past and present tense. McClish observes that the most revealing statement made by Merritt was his declaration that he was "definitely the last person [McStay] saw."

In November 2014, Merritt was arrested and charged with four counts of murder. In June 2019, Merritt was convicted, and in January 2020, he was sentenced to death. As of the time of this writing, there have not been any appeals. In this case, investigators faced challenges in obtaining information and intelligence because of the time that elapsed between when the family went missing and when their remains were found. As the San Bernardino County District Attorney Michael Ramos explains, "[W]itnesses forget, people forget the time frames, what occurred, etc." (Ramsay, Lipman, & Small, 2015).

Knowledge obtained through questioning and physical evidence are equally important. Physical evidence can provide a basis for questioning people about a crime, and questioning can provide leads for finding physical evidence. Although physical evidence is important by itself, supporting oral testimony adds considerable value when presented in court. Conversely, although a confession may appear conclusive, it cannot stand alone legally. It must be supported by physical evidence or other corroboration.

Sources of Information

In addition to physical evidence, three primary sources of information are available.

> **LO1** Identify the sources of information that are available to investigators.

Important sources of information include (1) reports, records, and databases, including those found on the Internet; (2) people who are not suspects in a crime but who know something about the crime or those involved; and (3) suspects in the crime.

Often these sources overlap. For example, information in a hotel's records may be supplemented by information supplied by the hotel manager or the doorkeeper.

Because so many informational sources exist in any given community, it is helpful to develop a **sources-of-information file**. Each time you locate someone who can provide important information on criminal activity in a community, make a card with information about this source or save the information electronically such as in a computer document or spreadsheet. For example, if a hotel manager provides useful information, make a card or computer entry with the manager's name, name of the hotel, address, telephone number, type of information provided, and other relevant information. File the card or save the information under *hotel*.

We have progressed from the agricultural age to the industrial age to the **information age**, a period in which knowledge and information are increasing exponentially, doubling every 2.5 years. Among the most important advances for law enforcement is the availability of computerized information. Such information has been in existence for several decades but not in individual squad cars or easily accessible by the average officer on the beat until relatively recently. Officers now receive information on stolen vehicles, individual arrest records, and the like within minutes.

Reports, Records, and Databases

Reports, records, and databases at the local, state, and federal levels assist in criminal investigations.

Local Resources. An important information source is the records and reports of your police department, including all preliminary reports, follow-up investigative reports, offense and arrest records, modus operandi files, fingerprint files, missing person's reports, gun registrations, and wanted bulletins. Closely examine a suspect's prior record and modus operandi. Examine all laboratory and coroner's reports associated with a case.

Also check records maintained by banks, loan and credit companies, delivery services, hospitals and clinics, hotels and motels, newspapers, city directories, street cross-directories, utility providers, personnel departments, pawnbrokers, storage companies, schools, and taxi or ridesharing companies. Neighboring law enforcement agencies, jails, probation files, court files, and social media websites are all valuable sources of information. Each time you locate a source whose records are helpful, add it to your sources-of-information file.

Inventory Tracking Systems. Automatic inventory tracking systems can be helpful if businesses believe their inventory is shrinking or they are losing tools and other equipment. Such tracking systems automatically generate reports on inventory and can capture transaction activity by department or other classifications.

Caller ID. The telephone number from which a call is placed can be recorded by a caller ID service, even if the call is not answered. Caller ID also provides the date and time of the call and can store numbers in its memory when more than one call is received.

In some criminal investigations, evidence has been obtained from telephones enabled with caller ID. For example, a person who committed a burglary first called the business or home to see if anyone was there, and the number the burglar called from was recorded on the office or home telephone's caller ID, providing a valuable lead to police in identifying and locating the suspect. Caller ID can be helpful in cases involving telephone threats, kidnappings, and the like.

Pen Registers. Pen registers are electronic devices that record all numbers dialed from specific phone lines. Title 18 of the U.S. Code defines a pen register as

> a device or process which records or decodes dialing, routing, addressing, or signaling information transmitted by an instrument or facility from which a wire or electronic communication is transmitted, provided, however, that such information shall not include the contents of any communication, but such term does not include any device or process used by a provider or customer of a wire or electronic communication service for billing, or recording as an incident to billing, for communications services provided by such provider or any device or process used by a provider or customer of a wire communication service for cost accounting or other like purposes in the ordinary course of its business.

This expanded definition was set forth in the USA PATRIOT Act.

Dialed Number Recorders (DNRs). A DNR can simultaneously monitor call activity on several lines and some have wiretapping capabilities. For each intercepted call, the DNR displays and prints a detailed call record. Once installed, the DNR is fully automatic and requires minimal attention.

State Resources. Investigators also use information from the state police, the Department of Motor Vehicles, the Department of Corrections, and the Parole Commission.

Federal Resources. Federal resources include the U.S. Post Office; U.S. Immigration and Customs Enforcement (ICE); the Social Security Administration; the Federal Bureau of Investigation (FBI); the Bureau of Alcohol, Tobacco, Firearms, and Explosives (ATF); the Drug Enforcement Administration (DEA); the Department of Homeland Security (DHS); and the U.S. Marshals.

The FBI's National Crime Information Center (NCIC) contains online databases on wanted and missing persons; victims; stolen guns, securities, articles, boats, license plates, and vehicles; criminal histories; foreign fugitives and deported felons; gang and terrorist members; and persons subject to protection orders. There is also a database for identity theft, the purpose of which allows law enforcement to "flag" stolen identities and identify imposters encountered by various authorities. The database contains passwords, fingerprints, and photographs, which are used to identify the victim or to distinguish someone who is fraudulently using the victim's identity.

The current generation, NCIC 2000, includes mug shots (e.g., of sexual offenders and persons on probation or parole or incarcerated in federal prisons) and other personal identifying images, such as scars and tattoos; images of vehicles; an enhanced name search (of all derivatives of a name, e.g., *Jeff, Geoff, Jeffrey*); automated single-finger fingerprint matching; and information linking. These provide the ability to associate logically related records across NCIC files for the same criminal or the same crime. For example, an inquiry on a gun could also retrieve a wanted person or a stolen vehicle. The NCIC 2000 system is continuously being enhanced, with recent improvements including the addition of a separate file for violent gangs and terrorists, continued development of the dental repository database, faster search and response capability, and the ability to add lost or stolen law enforcement credentials to the system. As this text goes to print, the FBI is preparing to roll out its next major upgrade, known as NCIC 3rd Generation, or the N3G Project, using input from "stakeholders to identify new functionalities to modernize and expand the capabilities of the existing NCIC system" (Federal Bureau of Investigation [FBI], 2017).

The Internet

The Internet is an extremely valuable source of information. Fast-breaking cases, such as a kidnapping, can be aided by an investigator's ability to distribute photographs and important details efficiently and quickly. Another resource is the website of the International Association of Chiefs of Police (www.theiacp.org). The FBI's website (www.fbi.gov) provides information about major investigations, wanted felons, various FBI programs and initiatives, and ways to contact FBI agents regarding various crimes.

The prevalence of smartphones has now placed a mobile computer with wireless connection to the Internet in the palm of nearly every officer. The myriad applications (apps) available to law enforcement are continuously growing. For example, the "US Cop" app includes a pill identifier and various legal databases. "PocketCop®" is another popular app that allows officers access to FBI databases, vehicle files, and much more to help investigators verify information they are being told while out in the field.

Victims, Complainants, and Witnesses

In addition to reports and records, databases, and other Internet resources, investigators obtain information from people associated with the investigation. Vast amounts of information come from people with direct or indirect knowledge of a crime. Although no one is legally required to provide information to the police except personal identification and accident information, citizens are responsible for cooperating with the police for their own and the community's best interests. Everyone is a potential crime victim and a potential source of information. Interview anyone other than a suspect who has information about a case. This includes victims, complainants, and witnesses.

A victim is a person injured by a crime. Frequently the victim is also the complainant and a witness. Victims are emotionally involved and may be experiencing anger, rage, and fear. Such personal involvement can cause them to exaggerate or distort what occurred. Victims may also make a **dying declaration**, a statement that can provide valuable information to investigators and usually qualifies as a hearsay exception, making it admissible as evidence.

A **complainant** is a person who requests that some action be taken. A complainant may also be the reporting party (RP), the individual who notified the police about a crime, but the RP is not always necessarily the complainant. For example, an overnight theft at a business might be discovered and called in to the police by the first employee who arrives in the morning, but the complainant might actually be the owner of the business. The complainant (or RP) is especially important in the initial stages of a case. Listen carefully to all details and determine the extent of the investigative problems involved: the type of crime, who committed it, what witnesses were present, the severity of any injuries, and any leads. Thank the complainant for contributing to the investigation.

A witness is a person who saw a crime or some part of it being committed. Good eyewitnesses are often the best source of information in a criminal investigation. Record the information a witness gives, including any details that can identify and locate a suspect or place the suspect at the crime scene. Although not always reliable, eyewitnesses' testimony remains a vital asset in investigating and prosecuting cases.

Sometimes a diligent search is needed to find witnesses. They may not want to get involved, or they may withhold information or provide it for ulterior motives. Make every effort to locate all witnesses. Check with the victim's friends and associates. Make public appeals for information online and on the radio and television.

Do not discount the tried-and-true method of posting flyers around town, asking for information. Although such requests are increasingly being sent through social media, not everyone has access to such technology. Putting up flyers at local establishments and on utility poles reaches people the investigator might not have otherwise had contact with. An informational checkpoint might also be used, as described in Chapter 4. Check the entire crime scene area. Conduct a neighborhood canvass to determine whether anyone saw or heard anything when the crime occurred.

The Neighborhood Canvass.

Often the best way to solve a crime is to go door to door in the area around the crime scene. Nyberg (2006, p. 36) says, "There's a sign mounted on the walls of our homicide office with wooden letters that read GOYAKOD.... It's a piece of advice on how to close cases. We would sit sometimes during meetings about our current cases, brainstorming ideas to generate leads. More often than not, someone would nod, smile, and say GOYAKOD, which stands for 'Get off your ass and knock on doors.' If any one phrase exemplifies what good police work is, that's it."

Knocking on doors is essential in a major criminal investigation. The area canvass is one of the first tasks an investigator should have on their lead sheet and, when done thoroughly and documented properly, can be a powerful investigative tool (Murgado, 2017). On the other hand, a canvass that is disorganized, conducted hastily, and documented poorly can seriously thwart the development of leads and negatively impact the resolution of a case (Boetig, 2010). Fundamentals of conducting a successful neighborhood canvass include:

- Identify one person to serve as canvass supervisor.

- Establish geographic boundaries for the canvass, recognizing the perimeter can be expanded or contracted as needed.

- Provide clear assignments and instructions to all canvass participants.

- Ask for the names of everyone who lives at, works at, visits, delivers to, or has access to the location.

- Interview everyone separately.

- Do not overlook or discount people who were not present at the time of the incident, as they may still be able to provide valuable information about local and neighborhood issues, past or recent suspicious activity, gossip and rumors, and what is considered "normal" in the area.

- Conduct a thorough, professional, well-documented canvass from start to finish, keeping in mind it is not a race.

Boetig (2010, p. 67) stresses, "[A]s the case develops, officers may not have another opportunity to speak to a certain person if he becomes a suspect and invokes certain constitutional rights. It is imperative for the first attempt to be done correctly."

The Knock and Talk.

Another practice used to obtain information from others is the "knock and talk," an investigative technique that takes place at a suspect's or witness's home and is generally considered by the courts to be a consensual encounter that, as such, does not violate the Fourth Amendment. In *United States v. Crapser* (2007), the Ninth District Court of Appeals set forth the general rule regarding knock-and-talk encounters that has become a firmly rooted notion in Fourth Amendment jurisprudence: "Absent express orders from the person in possession against any possible trespass, there is no rule of private or public conduct which makes it illegal per se, or a condemned invasion of the person's right of privacy, for anyone openly and peaceably, at high noon, to walk up the steps and knock on the front door of any man's 'castle' with the honest intent of asking questions of the occupant thereof—whether the questioner be a pollster, a salesman, or an officer of the law."

In Florida v. Jardines (2013), a case first discussed in Chapter 4, the Court held, "A police officer not armed with a warrant may approach a home and knock, precisely because that is no more than any private citizen might do." In *State v. Huddy* (2017), the court clarified, "An officer's implied right to knock and talk extends only to the entrance of the home that a reasonably respectful citizen unfamiliar with the home would believe is the appropriate door at which to knock." In most cases, the "appropriate" door is the front door. An officer who approaches a side door or the back door in an effort to conduct a knock-and-talk risks running afoul of the Fourth Amendment privacy protection that attach to the curtilage (Welty, 2018a).

It should be pointed out that the Court, in *Kentucky v. King* (2011), held that regardless of whether the person knocking is a private citizen or a law enforcement officer, the home's occupant is under no obligation to open the door or speak to whomever is knocking (Sikes, 2018). Furthermore, the fact that a homeowner does open the door does *not* mean that they have consented to an officer entering the home (Welty, 2018b). And it is this issue that has made the practice of knock and talk a somewhat controversial law enforcement tool, with some contending it is an unconstitutional effort by police to bypass the warrant requirement in order to gain information:

> No one doubts that the police may lawfully approach a home, stand on the threshold, and knock on the door in order to speak to the occupant. This is how some members of the Court define knock-and-talk. But, that is a "false generalization" of what a true knock-and-talk involves.
>
> In practice, the phrase "knock-and-talk" is a catch-all to explain different iterations of police activity, all of which share the same attribute: one or more law enforcement officers approach a targeted residence with a predetermined plan to circumvent the warrant requirement and convince the homeowner to let them inside using tactics designed to undermine, if not completely subjugate, the homeowner's free will. (Drake, 2014, p. 26)

Although the Supreme Court has upheld the constitutionality of knock and talks, lower courts are not always clear on what the limits are, if any, on knock-and-talk practices (Simon, 2019). In *Michigan v. Frederick* (2019), a case whose legal history dates back to 2012, the State of Michigan petitioned the Court in a bid to clarify law enforcement's knock-and-talk procedures. However certiorari was denied on October 7, 2019.

A Caution. Be aware that suspect and witness statements are not always reliable. Witnesses are often more confident in their knowledge of what happened than they are accurate. "The claim that eyewitness testimony is reliable and accurate is testable, and the research is clear that eyewitness identification is vulnerable to distortion without the witness's awareness. More specifically, the assumption that memory provides an accurate recording of experience, much like a video camera, is incorrect" (Chew, 2018). Adding to the ambiguity is the fact that many people see only a part of the commission of a crime but testify as though they witnessed the entire event.

Informants

An **informant** is anyone who can provide information about a case but who is not a complainant, witness, victim, or suspect. Informants may be interested citizens, individuals with criminal records, suspects with pending criminal records who are trying to work off cases against them, and people who seek to make money by providing information and assistance.

Informants are frequently given code names, and only the investigator knows their identity. In some instances, however, informants may not remain anonymous, and their identity might have to be revealed. Be extremely careful in using such contacts. Never make promises or deals you cannot legally fulfill. Many jurisdictions have policies regarding the use of juveniles as informants, specifying a certain minimum age for informants or requiring police to first get permission from a court, parent, or legal guardian.

Confidential Informants. Of importance to investigators is the *confidential informant* or CI, defined as "an individual requiring anonymity who provides useful information, directed assistance, or both, that enhances criminal investigations and furthers the mission of the agency, usually in exchange for financial or other consideration" (International Association of Chiefs of Police, 2017). Investigators' skill in recruiting, maintaining, and motivating CIs to supply information can greatly enhance their effectiveness in solving cases. CIs are usually recruited and managed in secret, making it hard to determine how many there are. Information from the Department of Justice (DOJ) indicates that the Drug Enforcement Administration (DEA) had more than 18,000 confidential sources between 2010 and 2015, and the FBI is said to maintain more than 15,000 secret informants (Devereaux, 2016).

Building trust is key in developing informants. A high level of trust in a CI can lead officers to regard that person "reliable." There is a legal difference between an informant and a **confidential (reliable) informant (CRI)** in that adding the credit of *reliable* means that a particular informant has previously provided information to the police that was corroborated and used. The status of being identified as a CRI might hold more weight with judges in cases where officers are seeking a search warrant based on information provided by an informant who has a record of being credible.

Establishing Reliability. The following steps are recommended to help investigators achieve the totality of circumstances necessary to establish probable cause:

1. Corroborate as much of the informant's information as possible.
2. Establish how, where, when, and under what circumstances the informant obtained the information.
3. Explain, without citing specific cases and names, how the informant's information has been used in prior criminal cases to achieve arrests, convictions, seizures, and so on.
4. Provide or disclose statements the informant has made.
5. If it is safe to do so, provide the informant's identity. (Law Officer, 2016)

Criteria for determining the reliability of an informant's information were discussed in Chapter 4. The Court ruled in *Alabama v. White* (1990), "An anonymous tip can provide the foundation for reasonable suspicion when the tip predicts future activities that the officer is able to corroborate, which makes it reasonable to think that the informant has inside knowledge about the suspect."

Suspects

A suspect is a person considered to be directly or indirectly connected with a crime, either by overt act or by planning or directing it. Do not overlook the suspect as a chief source of information. An individual can become a suspect either through information provided by citizens or by their own actions. Any suspicious individuals should be questioned. Complete a field interview card or create a field interview electronic document for any suspicious person you stop. This record places a person or vehicle in a specific place at a specific time and furnishes data for future investigative needs.

A person with a known modus operandi fitting a crime may be spotted at or near the crime scene. The person may be wanted for another crime or show an exaggerated concern for the police's presence, or the person may be in an illegal place at an illegal time—often the case with juveniles. When questioning occurs spontaneously on the street (referred to as a **field interview**), it is especially advantageous to officers to question someone suspected of involvement in a crime right after the crime has occurred.

Sometimes direct questioning of suspects is not the best way to obtain information. In cases in which direct contact would tip off the person, it is often better to use undercover or surveillance officers or various types of listening devices, as discussed in Chapter 7.

Investigative Questioning to Obtain Information: The Basics

Information is obtained continuously throughout an investigation. Some is volunteered, and some the police officer must really work for; some is useful and some worthless or even misleading. Most of an officer's time is spent meeting people and obtaining information from them, a process commonly referred to as either an *interview* or an *interrogation*.

An **interview** is questioning people who are not suspects in a crime but who know something about it or the people involved. An **interrogation** is questioning those suspected of direct or indirect involvement in a crime. Sometimes an interview turns into an interrogation, as facts become known and the person being questioned becomes a suspect.

> **L02** Explain what the goal of interviewing and interrogation is.
>
> The ultimate goal of interviewing and interrogating is to determine the truth—that is, to identify those responsible for a crime and to eliminate the innocent from suspicion.

Investigators must obtain all of the facts supporting the truth, whether they indicate a person's guilt or innocence. The best information either proves the elements of the crime (the corpus delicti) or provides leads.

Characteristics of an Effective Interviewer/Interrogator

Many of the emotional and intellectual traits of an investigator (discussed in Chapter 1) are especially valuable in communicating with others. Presenting a favorable appearance and personality and establishing rapport are more important than physical attributes. Sometimes, however, it is an advantage to be of the same race or gender as the person being questioned. Under some circumstances, it is better to not wear a uniform. Sometimes a suit or jeans and a sweater are more appropriate.

An effective interviewer/interrogator is

- *Adaptable and culturally adroit.* Your cultural and educational background and experience affect your ability to understand people from all walks of life; to meet them on their own level on varied subjects; and to adapt to their personalities, backgrounds, and lifestyles.

- *Self-controlled and patient.* Use self-control and patience to motivate people to talk. Be understanding yet detached, waiting for responses while patiently leading the conversation and probing for facts. Remain professional, recognizing that some people you interview may feel hostile toward you.

- *Confident and optimistic.* Do not assume that because the person you are questioning is a hardened criminal, has an attorney, is belligerent, or is better educated than you that no opportunity exists to obtain information. Show that you are in command, that you already know many answers, and that you want to corroborate what you know. If the conversation shifts away from the subject, steer the discussion back to the topic.

- *Objective.* Maintain your perspective on what is sought, avoiding preconceived ideas about the case. Be aware of any personal prejudices that can interfere with your questioning.

- *Sensitive to individual rights.* Maintain a balance between the rights of others and those of society. Naturally, suspects do not want to give information that conflicts with their self-interest or threatens their freedom. Moreover, many citizens want to stay out of other people's business. Use reason and patience to overcome this resistance to becoming involved.

- *Knowledgeable of the elements of the crime.* Know what information you need to prove the elements of the crime you are investigating. Phrase questions to elicit information related to these elements.

Enhancing Communication

Successful questioning requires two-way communication between the investigator and the person being questioned. There are several ways to improve communication, whether in interviewing or interrogating: prepare in advance; obtain the information as soon after the

incident as possible, but try to build some rapport before diving right in to what you are looking for; be considerate and friendly; use a private setting; eliminate physical barriers; sit rather than stand; encourage conversation; ask simple questions one at a time; listen and observe. If possible it helps to have facial tissue (Kleenex) easily accessible and if the interview/interrogation environment allows for it, offer a beverage. Something as simple as a glass of water can benefit communication.

Barriers to Communication

People often have reasons for not wanting to answer questions that police ask. Even though these reasons may have no logical basis, be aware of the common barriers to communication. One important barrier to communication between police and the public is the ingrained attitude that telling the truth to the police is wrong. The criminal element, those closely associated with crime, and even the police commonly use such terms as *fink*, *snitch*, and *rat*, which imply that giving information to the police is wrong, unsavory, or immoral.

Prejudices concerning a person's race, beliefs, religion, appearance, amount of education, economic status, sexual orientation, or place of upbringing can be barriers to communication. You may encounter prejudice because you are a police officer or because of your race, gender, or physical appearance. Equally important, prejudices you hold can interfere with your communication with some people and therefore with your investigation.

Building trust with citizens, including children, is important for law enforcement. The ability to communicate with individuals from diverse populations— various ages, ethnicities, socioeconomic groups, and so forth—is a critical skill for effective investigators.

U-T San Diego/ZUMA Press Inc/Alamy Stock Photo

Many departments are now training their officers to recognize their own implicit biases, which can also impede communication. Unlike explicit bias, which is a person's conscious awareness of the attitudes, beliefs, and stereotypes that form their worldview, **implicit bias** is comprised of subtle, largely unconscious or semiconscious attitudes that influence a person's behavior, judgments, and decisions (Dasgupta, 2013). As Mitchell and James (n.d.) observe: "Implicit bias is not denying or ignoring a prejudice, but being unaware that the prejudice or bias exists at all." Everyone has implicit biases, and these biases are expressed through a person's verbal and nonverbal communication, body language, and everyday interactions (Tyner, 2019).

One particularly damaging manifestation of implicit bias is the expression of microaggressions. A **microaggression** is a subtle condescending, hostile, or derogatory comment or action that, while not blatantly racist, conveys a negative message to a person that they are viewed as "less than" others (Clark, 2017). A study by researchers at Stanford University found that, on average, police officers spoke significantly less respectfully to black citizens than white citizens, disparities that can adversely affect the willingness of witnesses or suspects to cooperate with or provide information to the police (Voigt et al., 2017).

Fear is another barrier to communication. Some witnesses fear that criminals will harm them or their family if they testify, or victims may fear facing their attacker again in court. Some people fear the imposition on their time and the negative impact on their wages of having to go to court to testify.

People actually involved in a crime can be reluctant to talk for many reasons, the most important of which is self-preservation. Although suspects naturally do not want to implicate themselves, other factors may also cause them to not answer questions. Severe guilt feelings can preclude telling anyone about a crime. Fear of consequences can be so great that nothing will induce them to tell the truth. They may fear that if they are sent to prison they will be sexually assaulted or beaten, or they may fear that any accomplices they implicate will seek revenge.

As ethnic diversity increases and other languages proliferate, language barriers become an increasing challenge to law enforcement. Language barriers might be minimized or eliminated by seeking a mix of bilingual officers in hiring, training officers in conversational foreign languages, and matching officers to appropriate beats and assignments. One of the most common techniques used to help officers communicate with non–English-speaking people is to use the AT&T Language Line or an in-person interpreter.

Many aspects of intelligence interviews and interrogations are affected by cultural norms and expectations, and using interpreters who understand, firsthand, the intricacies of these norms and expectations can improve the effectiveness of investigative questioning. The High-Value Detainee Interrogation Group (HIG), an entity created in 2009 and comprised of intelligence professionals from the FBI, Central Intelligence Agency (CIA), and Department of Defense (DoD), reviewed the science of interrogation and found studies that showed that multilingual persons access some memories better in different languages (HIG, 2016). For example, Hispanic bilingual immigrants in the United States were found to be better able to access memories about their country of origin when asked in Spanish and, conversely, better able to remember occurrences from their time in the United States when asked in English.

Additional barriers to communication exist with individuals who are hearing impaired, who have Alzheimer's disease, or who are mentally disabled or suffer from a mental illness. Officers who know American Sign Language (ASL) can communicate with hearing impaired or deaf persons. This skill is also useful when silent communication between officers is necessary. However, the Americans with Disabilities Act (ADA) recommends it is always best to get an interpreter to help with interviews or interrogations involving the hearing impaired. If an interpreter is not available for the interview, the officer should write out everything that is discussed and retain the notes.

General Guidelines for Effective Questioning

Cases are more likely to be solved when investigators follow some general questioning guidelines, including the selection of the right type of questions, using repetition effectively, knowing how to question reluctant interviewees, and recognizing the importance of silence. Above all else, effective investigators follow two key rules: listen actively and observe.

How people act during questioning can tell as much as or more than their words. An effective investigator must be able to read and react to body language and nonverbal cues. Signs of unusual nervousness, odd expressions, rapid breathing, visible perspiration, or a highly agitated state are cause to question the person's truthfulness. Table 6.1 summarizes the guidelines for a successful questioning.

TABLE 6.1 **Interview/Interrogation Guidelines**
■ Ask one question at a time and keep your responses simple and direct.
■ Avoid questions that can be answered "yes" or "no"; a narrative account provides more information and may reveal inconsistencies in the person's story.
■ Be positive in your approach, but let the person save face if necessary so that you may obtain further information.
■ Observe the 80-20 talking rule, allowing the subject to talk for the majority (80%) of the time.
■ Give the person time to answer. Do not be uncomfortable with pauses in the interview. Often, guilty suspects are uncomfortable and feel a need to fill the silence because of their discomfort. This may cause them to provide more information that can be used against them throughout the interview or in later interviews.
■ Listen to answers, but at the same time anticipate your next question.
■ Watch your body language and tone of voice.
■ Start the conversation on neutral territory.
■ Digital recorders can be frightening. A technique commonly used is to tuck the recorder behind a portfolio or notepad. After a time, the interviewee often forgets that the recording device is there.
■ React to what you hear.
■ As you move into difficult territory, slow down.
■ Don't rush to fill silences. Again, allow the witness or suspect a chance to expose themselves through their words and actions.
■ Pose the toughest questions simply, directly, and with confidence.
■ No meltdowns. You must establish professional distance. Keep your role clear.

Selecting the Right Type of Question. An important difference exists between direct and indirect questions. A **direct question** is to the point, allowing little possibility of misinterpretation—for example, "What time did you and your husband leave the restaurant?" In contrast, an **indirect question** is disguised. For example, a question such as "How do you and your neighbor get along?" could elicit a variety of answers. Direct questions can be very useful in eliciting important details.

However, do not confuse a direct question with a **closed-ended question**, which requires only a "yes" or "no" or other short, simple answer. Closed-ended questions, such as "Do you get along well with your neighbor?" or "Did you go straight home after work?," should be avoided during interviews. In contrast, an **open-ended question** gives the victim, witness, or suspect the opportunity to provide a much fuller response, allowing the investigator greater insight into the person's knowledge and feelings. Examples include "What can you tell me about your relationship with your neighbor?" or "What did you do after work?" Open-ended questions often begin with "Why," "How," "Describe," "Explain," or "Tell me about." Studies have found that open-ended questions produce the most information from an interviewee, as much as nine times more information than closed yes-or-no questions (Snook, Luther, Quinlan, & Milne, 2012).

A **leading question** prompts or leads a person to a specific response and often implies an answer. For example, "How much did you drink before you went next door and assaulted your neighbor?" implies that the suspect had been drinking before the assault.

LO3 Explain the different types of questions used during interviews and interrogations and how much reliance should be placed on each type.

Ask direct questions and open-ended questions liberally. Asking leading questions can also be a useful interrogation technique. Use indirect questions and closed-ended questions sparingly.

Using Repetition. Anyone who watches detective shows has heard victims or suspects complain, "I've already told my story to the police." This is true to life. Individuals *are* asked to tell and retell their version of what happened and for very good reasons. Someone who is lying either will provide very inconsistent stories or will tell a story *exactly* the same way each time, as if it is well rehearsed. A truthful story, however, will contain the same facts but be phrased differently each time it is retold. After a person has told you what happened, guide the discussion to some other aspect of the case. Later, come back to the topic and ask the person to repeat the story. It is important to lock a suspect into a story so that you can go back and check facts later.

Repetition is an effective technique to obtain recall and to uncover lies. Often repeating what someone has told you helps the person provide additional information. Sometimes it also confuses the person being questioned, and if the original version was not true, another repetition will reveal this fact. If inconsistencies appear, go back over the information and attempt to account for them.

Interviewing Reluctant Subjects. Give reluctant subjects, whether victims or witnesses, confidence by demonstrating self-assurance. Give indifferent witnesses a sense of importance by explaining how the information will help a victim. Remind them that someday they may be victims themselves and would then want others to cooperate. Find a way to motivate every witness to talk with you and answer your questions.

Most people who are reluctant to be questioned respond to one of two approaches: logical or emotional. The *logical approach* is based on reason. Use logic to determine why the person refuses to cooperate. Explain the problems that result when people who know about a crime do not cooperate with investigators. The *emotional approach* addresses such negative feelings as hate, anger, greed, revenge, pride, and jealousy. You can increase these emotions or simply acknowledge them (e.g., "Anyone in your situation would respond the same way"). If such tactics do not work, warn the person of the serious consequences of withholding important information.

LO4	Compare and contrast the approaches used to appeal to reluctant interviewees.

Appeal to a reluctant subject's reason or emotions.

Whether to select a logical or an emotional approach depends on the person being interviewed, the type of investigation, and your personal preference.

Recognizing the Importance of Silence. With respect to investigative questioning, the adage "less is more" holds true. A best practice is to observe the 80-20 rule, where the interviewer talks for roughly 20% of the time, allowing the interviewee ample time to respond to a question (Snook et al., 2012). Silence can be an important tool in getting the subject to talk freely, possibly providing additional information the interviewer can dig deeper into.

Specific Questioning Techniques

Numerous techniques have been developed for questioning victims, witnesses, and suspects, including the Kinesic Method, the Scharff Technique, the Strategic Use of Evidence (SUE), the *Wicklander-Zulawski* (WZ) method, and Observing Rapport-Based Interview Techniques (ORBIT). This section will look briefly at the three techniques most often used by law enforcement in the United States: the Reid Technique, the PEACE Model, and the Cognitive Approach.

The Reid Technique. First introduced in the 1940s, this technique was developed by polygraph expert and former Chicago detective John Reid with the intention of reforming police interrogation practices, which had until that time frequently involved brutal tactics such as beatings to elicit information from subjects (Hager, 2017). Since then, the Reid Technique has been the standard for police interviewing and interrogation in the United States. The method, not surprisingly, utilizes principles from human psychology and skills Reid learned as a polygrapher. The three basic steps of this technique are:

1. The *factual analysis phase*—investigators collect evidence and testimony and use them to eliminate improbable subjects and develop possible suspects and leads.

2. The *Behavior Analysis Interview* (BAI)—investigators work to develop rapport with a subject and establish baseline behaviors, those specific, individual visual and verbal cues that are normal for the interviewee. Next, the interviewer asks behavior-provoking questions to see if the suspect deviates from their baseline behaviors. If the interviewer is reasonably certain, based on the behavioral analysis, that the interviewee has committed the crime in question, the interrogation phase begins.

3. The *interrogation*—investigators switch tactics, moving from an objective quest for information to a more adversarial method of questioning. Three basic strategies used in this phase are (1) telling the suspect that investigators know they committed the crime and interrupt any attempt by the suspect to deny their guilt, (2) steering the suspect toward a confession by offering a moral justification for committing the crime or other face-saving alternative ("minimization" of the crime), and (3) exaggerating the available evidence and the seriousness of the potential punishment ("maximization"), in an effort to break the suspect's resistance to confess. (Hood & Hoffman, 2019; Kozinski, 2018)

The Reid Technique places much emphasis on detecting verbal and nonverbal signs of deception, a skill many investigators believe they possess. However, one study put that confidence to the test when a psychologist recruited the best liars he could find—a group of prisoners inside a Massachusetts penitentiary:

> For a small fee he asked half to tell the truth of their crimes on video and the other half to lie, saying they had committed someone else's crime. He showed the videos to college students and police. Neither group did particularly well at truth detection (the average person is right about half the time), but the students performed better than the police. Yet the police felt more certain about their conclusions. "That's a bad combination," [the psychologist] says. "Their training makes them less accurate and more confident at the same time." (Starr, 2019)

According to the HIG, police are frequently taught to listen for verbal cues such as hesitations, pauses, speech errors, and changes in speech rate, and to watch for nonverbal cues such as gaze aversion, fidgeting, and grooming. However numerous studies have demonstrated that these cues are unreliable indicators of deception (HIG, 2016, p. 33): "Training to detect deception based on nonverbal cues does not help. A recent metaanalysis of 30 research studies showed that training on how to detect deception produced only modest improvements in accuracy of deception detection." Furthermore, cues to deception are likely to vary by culture.

Not surprisingly, a growing body of research suggests that the accusatorial and psychologically manipulative nature of the Reid Technique increases the likelihood of false confessions, a phenomenon that will be discussed in more depth shortly. To overcome the high potential for inaccuracies generated in such pressurized environments, a new questioning technique was developed—the PEACE Model.

The PEACE Model. An information gathering technique most associated with law enforcement in the United Kingdom but which is increasingly finding favor in the United States is the PEACE Model, which is an acronym for the five steps of the investigative interview process:

1. Preparation and planning
2. Engage and explain
3. Account clarification and challenge
4. Closure
5. Evaluation (Kelly & Meissner, 2017; Hood & Hoffman, 2019)

In contrast to the pressurized confession-seeking approach characteristic of the Reid Technique, the PEACE Model is a rapport-based approach to eliciting relevant, reliable, truthful, and accurate information from a subject (Kelly & Meissner, 2017). Under this model, interviewers are expected to be fair and open-minded. And while they ask open-ended, repetitive, and leading questions, share with suspects that police are in possession of evidence, and challenge subjects' accounts by pointing out contradictions and inconsistencies—interviewing and interrogating approaches common to other questioning techniques—investigators do not resort to threats and intimidation, nor do they minimize or maximize the crime as is commonly done when applying an accusatorial method (Hood & Hoffman, 2019). Finally, research has shown that the PEACE Model is effective not only with suspects but when questioning victims and witnesses as well (Howes, 2019).

The Cognitive Approach

The Cognitive Approach developed in the field of psychology during the late 1950s as a way of understanding how the human mind processes information and how thoughts affect behavior (McLeod, 2015). During the 1980s, the Cognitive Approach began to be applied to police interviews with victims and witnesses as a way to enhance the memories of interviewees. Although initially used only with victims and witnesses, studies have demonstrated that this approach is effective with suspects as well (HIG, 2016).

In acknowledging that interview style has important implications for how much information is received from subjects, the **cognitive interview** tries to get the interviewee to recall the scene mentally by using simple mnemonic techniques aimed at encouraging focused retrieval with minimal loss in accuracy. This approach is based on scientific principles of memory and cognition, social dynamics, and interpersonal communication (HIG, 2016). These techniques include allowing interviewees to do most of the talking (again, the 80-20 rule), asking open-ended questions, allowing ample time for answers, avoiding interruptions, and encouraging the person to report all details, no matter how trivial.

The cognitive interview method calls for using a secluded, quiet place free of distractions and encouraging a subject to speak slowly. The interviewer first helps the interviewee *reconstruct the circumstances* by asking, "How did you feel . . . ?" Have the interviewee describe the weather, the surroundings, objects, people, and smells. Interviewees are encouraged to *report everything*, even if they think something is unimportant. They might also be asked to *relate the events in a different order* or to *change perspectives.* What would another person present have seen? With victims and witnesses, the five steps used in a cognitive interview are (1) introduction, (2) open-ended narration, (3) follow-up questions, (4) review, and (5) closing (Hood & Hoffman, 2019).

The process changes slightly when using the cognitive interview with a suspect. Additional steps used with suspects are to have them draw or sketch the scene after their narration, have them tell their story backwards (the reverse-order technique) after the interviewer has asked follow-up questions, and challenging any inconsistencies or contradictions that arise between the two versions (chronological/forward and backward) of their narrative (Hood & Hoffman, 2019). The purpose of asking a suspect to recite their version of events in reverse order is that this exercise increases their cognitive load, or the mental effort required to "stick to the story." The premise here is that lying requires multitasking and, for that reason, is more difficult than truth-telling: "Liars must plan what they say, remember to play a role, and suppress the truth, as well as justify their deception, whereas truth telling requires none of these. . . . One way to increase cognitive load is to ask the subject to repeat their narrative in reverse order—that is, start with the last event and work backwards. This is difficult because memories are usually coded in a forward order sequence of events, and asking for a narrative backwards makes it more difficult to reconstruct the event. When study participants were asked to recall what they did on a recent Saturday night in reverse order, lies were detected with a higher accuracy (75%) than for the condition where a reverse-order account was not solicited (18%)" (HIG, 2016, pp. 35–36).

Among the drawbacks of the cognitive approach are the amount of time it takes and the need for a controlled environment. Nonetheless, the cognitive interview is especially effective for obtaining information from victims and witnesses who have difficulty remembering an event.

Recording and Videotaping Interviews and Interrogations

Many law enforcement agencies across the nation have implemented policies requiring the digital recording of all interviews of victims, witnesses, and suspects. Courts in Alaska and Minnesota have mandated recording all interrogations because of the exclusionary rule, and in 2019, Oklahoma became the twenty-fifth state to require

recording of certain suspect interrogations in their entirety (Bang, Stanton, Hemmens, & Stohr, 2018). Laws in other states vary as to whether suspects must consent to being recorded. Some agencies are video-recording interviews and confessions rather than simply audio-recording them.

Myth A person must always be informed and give consent if they are being video- or audio-recorded during a conversation with police.

Fact Federal law requires only one person to consent to the recording. Thus, a federal law enforcement officer does not have to tell a person that they are being recorded. State laws can be more restrictive and may require that both parties consent.

Recordings can benefit both the investigator and the person being interviewed or interrogated. For investigators, recordings provide a verbatim account directly from the source, verifying the accuracy of what the report says and alleviating any defense arguments about coercion, illegitimate handling of the suspect, and lack of *Miranda* rights being read. Recording interviews and interrogations frees investigators from having to scribble notes frantically, eyes down at their notepad, and lets them pay closer attention to the witness's or suspect's body language and nonverbal cues. Recordings also allow investigators the chance to review the conversation as often as needed. For those being interviewed or interrogated, the recordings ensure that detectives do not stray into third-degree tactics, take an unethical line of questioning, or engage in any conduct that violates the rights of those being questioned (Cleary, 2019).

Critics of mandatory recording policies voice concern that such techniques might deter confessions and cause some people to refuse to speak freely. However, a randomized field experiment found that video-recording, even when two-party consent is required and the suspect is fully aware of the recording taking place, does not inhibit suspects' willingness to talk nor does it adversely affect the confession-taking process (Kassin, Russano, Amrom, Hellgren, Kukucka, & Lawson, 2019). Interestingly, a similar concern was voiced when *Miranda* was decided. Yet, people continue to volunteer information despite being given a *Miranda* warning.

Technology Innovations

VALT

Police interview recording systems have been used for decades, and the technology continues to improve. For example, VALT (Video-Audio-Learning-Tool), developed by Intelligent Video Solutions (IVS), is a secure and reliable application that uses high-definition (HD) IP camera technology and recording software to capture police interviews and interrogations. The system replaces VHS and DVR technology, can store approximately 16,000 hours of HD video, and enables investigators to readily share video content electronically with other law enforcement agencies, prosecutors' offices, and others.

Metadata is attached to each police interview session, allowing users to tag specific points within the recording with searchable descriptions (e.g., suspect name, victim name, officer name, case number, etc.) or other "markers" to help users locate and jump to specific segments of a video. These recordings can be retrieved from a desktop computer, tablet, or any other network enabled device.

VALT can also be used in the field through the Beam application, which allows operators to create a mobile police interview recording system and capture police interviews using an iPad or iPhone. The VALT automatically syncs the video with the base server either over the department's secure network or when the officer returns to the department.

Source: Intelligent Video Solutions, LLC. ipivs.com/products/valt-software/

The Interview

Interviewing involves talking to people, questioning them, obtaining information, and reading between the lines. The main sources of information at the crime scene are the complainant, the victim, and witnesses. (These may be the same person.) Separate the witnesses as soon as possible and then obtain a complete account of the incident from each one.

L05 Describe how to conduct interviews when multiple people are at the scene.

Interview witnesses separately if possible. Interview the victim or complainant first, then eyewitnesses, and then people who did not actually see the crime but who have relevant information.

Finding, detaining, and separating witnesses are high priorities. Witnesses who are not immediately detained can drift off into the crowd or decide not to become involved. Sometimes witnesses leave the scene without realizing their importance to an investigation. Obtain the information as rapidly as possible. Identify all witnesses and check their names and addresses against their identification. Ask witnesses not to speak to one another or to compare stories until they have written down in their own words what happened or have verbally given their statement to the police.

If there are many witnesses, discuss the incident briefly with each. Then establish a priority for obtaining statements based on the witnesses' availability and the importance of their information.

In most cases, interview complainants first because they can often provide enough information to determine whether a crime has been committed and, if so, what type of crime. If department policy requires it, have complainants read and initial or sign the information you record during the interview.

Anyone who saw what happened, how it happened, or who made it happen is interviewed next. Such witnesses may be in a state of panic, frustration, or anger. In the presence of such emotions, remain calm and detached, yet show empathy and understanding—a difficult feat. If a witness truly is too upset to talk, or really needs or wants to get to the hospital to be with the victim, obtain a quick initial statement and demographic information so you can contact this person later. Occasionally witnesses will need some time to calm down and gather themselves before they can provide a coherent statement.

After interviewing witnesses, interview people who can furnish facts about what happened before or immediately after the crime or who have information about the suspect or the victim. Not all people with relevant information are at the crime scene. Some people in the general area may have seen or heard something of value. Even people miles away from the scene may have information about the crime or the person committing it. Explain to such individuals why you are questioning them, check their identification, and then proceed with your interview.

The main sources of immediate information away from the crime scene are neighbors, business associates, people in the general area such as motel and hotel personnel, and longtime residents. Longer-term contacts may include informants, missing witnesses, friends, and relatives. Appeals for public cooperation and reports from various agencies and organizations may also produce information. Record both positive and negative information. The fact that a witness did *not* see anyone enter a building may be as important as having seen someone.

Advance Planning

Many interviews, at least initial ones, are conducted in the field and allow no time for planning. If time permits, plan carefully for interviews. Review reports about the case before questioning people. Learn as much as possible about the person you are going to question before you begin the interview. Know which questions you need answers to, and have a plan of approach to the likely responses from those you are interviewing. This means anticipating how people may respond. A well-planned and prepared interview will mean greater success in obtaining information or getting a confession and prevents the need for a follow-up interview when an investigator has forgotten to ask something.

Selecting the Time and Place

Sometimes there is no time to decide when and where to conduct an interview. Arriving at a crime scene, you may be confronted with a victim or witness who immediately begins to supply pertinent information. Recall that these *res gestae* statements are extremely valuable. Therefore, record them as close to verbatim as possible.

After ensuring that the scene is safe and all emergencies, such as critical medical issues, have been handled, determine as soon as possible who the complainant is, where and how many witnesses exist, and whether the suspect has been apprehended. If more than one officer is present, the officer in charge decides who will be questioned and assigns personnel to do it.

Immediate contact with people who have information about a crime improves the chances of obtaining information. Although emotions may be running high, witnesses are usually best able to recall details immediately after an incident. They are also less likely to embellish or exaggerate their stories because others present can be asked to verify the information. Moreover, witnesses can be separated so they will have no opportunity to compare information. Finally, the reluctance to give the police information is usually not so strong immediately after a crime. Given time to reflect, witnesses may fear that they will have to testify in court, that cooperation will take them away from work and cost them financially, or that the criminal will retaliate.

Beginning the Interview

How an interview is started is extremely important. At this point, the interviewee and the interviewer size each other up. Mistakes in beginning the interview can establish insurmountable barriers. Make your initial contact friendly but professional. Begin by identifying yourself and showing your credentials. Then ask a general question about the person's knowledge of the crime.

Establishing Rapport

Rapport is probably the most critical factor in any interview. **Rapport** is an understanding between individuals created by genuine interest and concern. It requires empathy. *Empathy* means accurately perceiving and responding to another person's thoughts and feelings. This differs from *sympathy*, which is an involuntary emotion of feeling sorry for another person. Suggestions for developing rapport include introducing yourself by your first name, offering a tissue if the person is crying, giving them a bottle of water, and using a soft tone of voice if the person appears vulnerable.

People who are approached civilly may volunteer a surprising amount of useful information. Most people do not condone criminal behavior and will assist you. However, they often do not know what is important to a specific investigation. Provide every opportunity to establish rapport and to assist citizens in providing information.

Not everyone with information can provide it easily. People who are emotionally unstable, mentally deficient, have temporary loss of memory, or fear the police often cannot or will not be forthcoming. With them, establishing rapport is critical. If a person is deaf or speaks a foreign language, arrange for an interpreter. If a person appears unwilling to talk, find out why.

Careful listening enhances rapport. Do not indicate verbally or nonverbally that you consider a matter trivial or unimportant; people will sense if you are merely going through the motions. Take a personal interest. Discuss their family, their work, or their hobbies. Be empathetic and assure them that everything possible will be done but that you need their help.

Networking an Interview

Most people are familiar with the concept of a business or professional **network**—a body of personal contacts that can further one's career. In reality, networks can extend much farther than this. Networks also establish relationships between people and their beliefs. Networks produce a context in which to understand a person. These networks may be social, ethnic, cultural, business, professional/occupational, religious, or political. As American society becomes more diverse, officers will have to understand the networks in their jurisdictions.

Testimonial Hearsay

A recent development in interviewing individuals with knowledge of a crime has changed the timing of questioning in some situations, that is, those dealing with testimonial hearsay. **Testimonial hearsay** includes prior testimony as well as statements made as a result of police interrogation. Witness statements obtained through such "structured questioning" are inadmissible in a criminal trial unless the witness is unavailable to testify and was previously cross-examined by the defendant (*Crawford v. Washington*, 2004).

Police reports should differentiate between statements that resulted from structured questioning and those that did not. Officers should listen well, take good notes, and make it clear in the notes and report that they did not direct or extract the specific information. If an interview yields substantial information related to a case, a statement should be obtained.

Statements

A **statement** is a legal narrative description of events related to a crime. It is a formal, detailed account. It begins with an introduction that gives the place, time, date, and names of the people conducting and present at an interview. It should also include a case number in the event the statement gets misfiled. The name, address, and age of the person questioned are stated before the main body of the statement. Figure 6.1 shows a sample statement.

The body of the statement is the person's account of the incident. A clause at the end states that the information was given voluntarily. The person making the statement reads each page, makes any needed corrections, initials each correction, and then signs the statement.

Obtain statements in private, with no one other than police officers present, and allow no interruptions. However, other people will need to be called in to witness the signing of the statement.

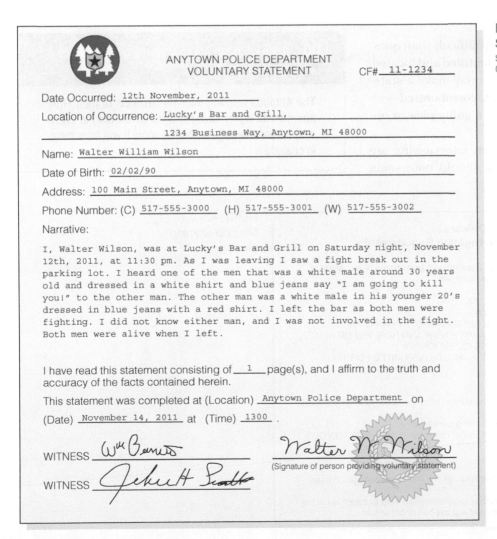

Figure 6.1
Sample voluntary statement.
Source: Drafted by Cho, H. Cho Research & Consulting, LLC. Copyright 2011.

Statements can be taken in several ways: prepared in longhand by the person interviewed, dictated to a typist in question-and-answer format, or digitally recorded for later typing and signing. A combination of questions and answers, with the answers in narrative form, is often the most effective format. However, a question-and-answer format is often challenged in court on grounds that questions guide and control the response. Another alternative is for you to write down the words of the person and have the person read and sign your notes. Also record the ending time. Beginning and ending times may be of great value in court testimony.

Closing the Interview

End each interview by thanking the person for cooperating. If you have established good rapport with the interviewee, that person will probably cooperate with you later if needed.

The Interrogation

Questioning suspects is usually more difficult than questioning witnesses or victims. Once identified and located, a person who *is* involved in a crime may make a statement, admission, or confession that, corroborated with independent evidence, can produce a guilty plea or obtain a conviction.

Many of the procedures used in interviewing are also used in interrogating, but you should note some important differences in how you question suspects. One of the most critical is ensuring that you do not violate suspects' constitutional rights, so that the information you obtain will be admissible in court. It is imperative that officers distinguish between questioning in a *Terry*-type stop/detention situation and a custodial situation requiring giving the *Miranda* warning.

The *Miranda* Warning

Before interrogating any suspect in custody about a crime, you must give the **Miranda warning**, as stipulated in *Miranda v. Arizona* (1966). In this decision, the Supreme Court ruled that suspects must be informed of their right to remain silent, to have an attorney present, and to have a state-appointed attorney if they cannot afford private counsel. Suspects must also be warned that anything they say may be used against them in court. It is highly recommended to read suspects their rights from a card (Figure 6.2).

L06 State what the *Miranda* warning is and when it must be given.

The *Miranda* warning informs suspects of their Fifth Amendment rights. Give the *Miranda* warning to every suspect you interrogate about a crime if you have them in custody.

Peace Officers
Constitutional Pre-Interrogation Requirements

The following warnings must be given prior to questioning a person who is in custody or is deprived of his freedom of action in any significant way:

THE CONSTITUTION REQUIRES I INFORM YOU THAT:
1. YOU HAVE THE RIGHT TO REMAIN SILENT.
2. ANYTHING YOU SAY CAN AND WILL BE USED AGAINST YOU IN COURT.
3. YOU HAVE THE RIGHT TO TALK TO A LAWYER NOW AND HAVE HIM OR HER PRESENT NOW OR AT ANY TIME DURING QUESTIONING.
4. IF YOU CANNOT AFFORD A LAWYER, ONE WILL BE APPOINTED FOR YOU WITHOUT COST.

Waiver of Rights
The suspect may waive his or her rights, but the burden is on the officer to show the waiver is made voluntarily, knowingly, and intelligently.
He or she must affirmatively respond to the following questions:
1. DO YOU UNDERSTAND EACH OF THESE RIGHTS I HAVE EXPLAINED TO YOU?
2. DO YOU WISH TO TALK TO US AT THIS TIME?

Election of Rights
A subject can avail him- or herself of his or her rights at any time and interrogation must then cease.
If a subject will not waive his or her rights or, during questioning, elects to assert his or her rights, no testimony of that fact may ever be used against him or her at trial.

FIGURE 6.2
Miranda warning.

Myth Arrested persons must be read their *Miranda* rights before the police can talk to them.

Fact A *Miranda* warning is required only when questioning a person about the crime and while they are in police custody (not free to leave).

The Fifth Amendment states, "No person shall be compelled in any criminal case to be a witness against himself." The *Miranda* decision established that this right must be made known to suspects in custody before any questioning about their criminal involvement can occur.

Thousands of words have been written for and against this decision. The general interpretation and application of the *Miranda* decision is that once you have reasonable grounds to believe a person has committed a crime and have taken that person into custody, that person's constitutional rights are in jeopardy unless the *Miranda* warning is given *before* any questioning about that crime occurs.

Many court cases illustrate the gray area that exists in determining when to give the warning. The terms most often used to describe when it should be given are **in custody** or **custodial arrest**. *In custody* generally refers to a point at which an officer has decided a suspect is not free to leave, there has been considerable deprivation of liberty, or the officer has arrested the suspect.

In *Oregon v. Mathiason* (1977), the Supreme Court defined **custodial interrogation** as questioning initiated by law enforcement officers after a person has been taken into custody or otherwise significantly deprived of freedom. If a suspect chooses to remain silent, ask no further questions. If the suspect requests counsel, ask no more questions until counsel is present.

The *Miranda* custody standard is no different for juveniles. In *Yarborough v. Alvarado* (2004), the Supreme Court held that a trial court need not consider age in determining whether a "reasonable person" is in custody for *Miranda* purposes.

Another *Miranda*-related concern, the "fruit-of-the-poisonous-tree" doctrine (Chapter 4), makes inadmissible any evidence obtained through an earlier violation of the defendant's constitutional rights (*Wong Sun v. United States*, 1963). That same consequence does *not* follow from a failure to follow the *Miranda* procedures. If officers learn about contraband or evidence from a statement that does not comply with *Miranda*, the contraband or evidence need not be suppressed as "poisonous fruit" of the inadmissible statement (*United States v. Patane*, 2004).

The *Miranda* warning does not have to be given in the exact form described in *Miranda* (Rutledge, 2010). In fact, a Florida court found that law enforcement agencies had 89 different versions of the warning. In *Florida v. Powell* (2010), the U.S. Supreme Court held that no exact wording is required to satisfy *Miranda*, as long as the four components of the warning are conveyed.

When *Miranda* Does Not Apply. The *Miranda* warning has never applied to voluntary or unsolicited, spontaneous statements, admissions, or confessions. Someone can approach a police officer and say, "I want to confess that I killed Vang Lee. I took a gun from my car and shot him." If this remark was unsolicited and completely voluntary, the police officer is under no obligation to interrupt the person giving the confession. In one instance, a person telephoned the police from out of state to voluntarily confess to a felony.

Miranda warnings are *not* required during identification procedures such as fingerprinting, taking voice or handwriting exemplars, or conducting a lineup or sobriety tests. They are *not* required during routine booking questions, during brief on-the-scene questioning, or during brief investigatory questioning during a temporary detention such as a *Terry* stop. A *Miranda* warning is also *not* required during roadside questioning following a routine traffic stop or other minor violation for which custody is not ordinarily imposed. *Miranda* warnings are not required by probation officers questioning those on probation for whom they are responsible. Finally, a warning is *not* required during questioning by a private citizen who is not an agent of the government.

Waiving the Rights. A suspect can waive the rights granted by *Miranda* but must do so intelligently and knowingly. A **waiver**, that is a giving up of a right, is accompanied by a written or witnessed oral statement that the waiver was voluntary (Figure 6.3).

Silence, in itself, is *not* a waiver. The suspect must articulate a waiver of rights. Therefore, many officers read the *Miranda* warning aloud from a printed card and then have the suspect read and sign the card (see Figure 6.3). The date and time are also recorded. If no card is available, a summary of the *Miranda* warning can be written, read, and signed. Police have the legal burden of proving that the suspect did waive their rights. The suspect retains the right to stop answering questions at any point, even when they originally waived the right to remain silent.

Officers should not just state the suspect waived their rights; it is important to state which specific rights were waived (Rutledge, 2007). The Fifth Amendment requires

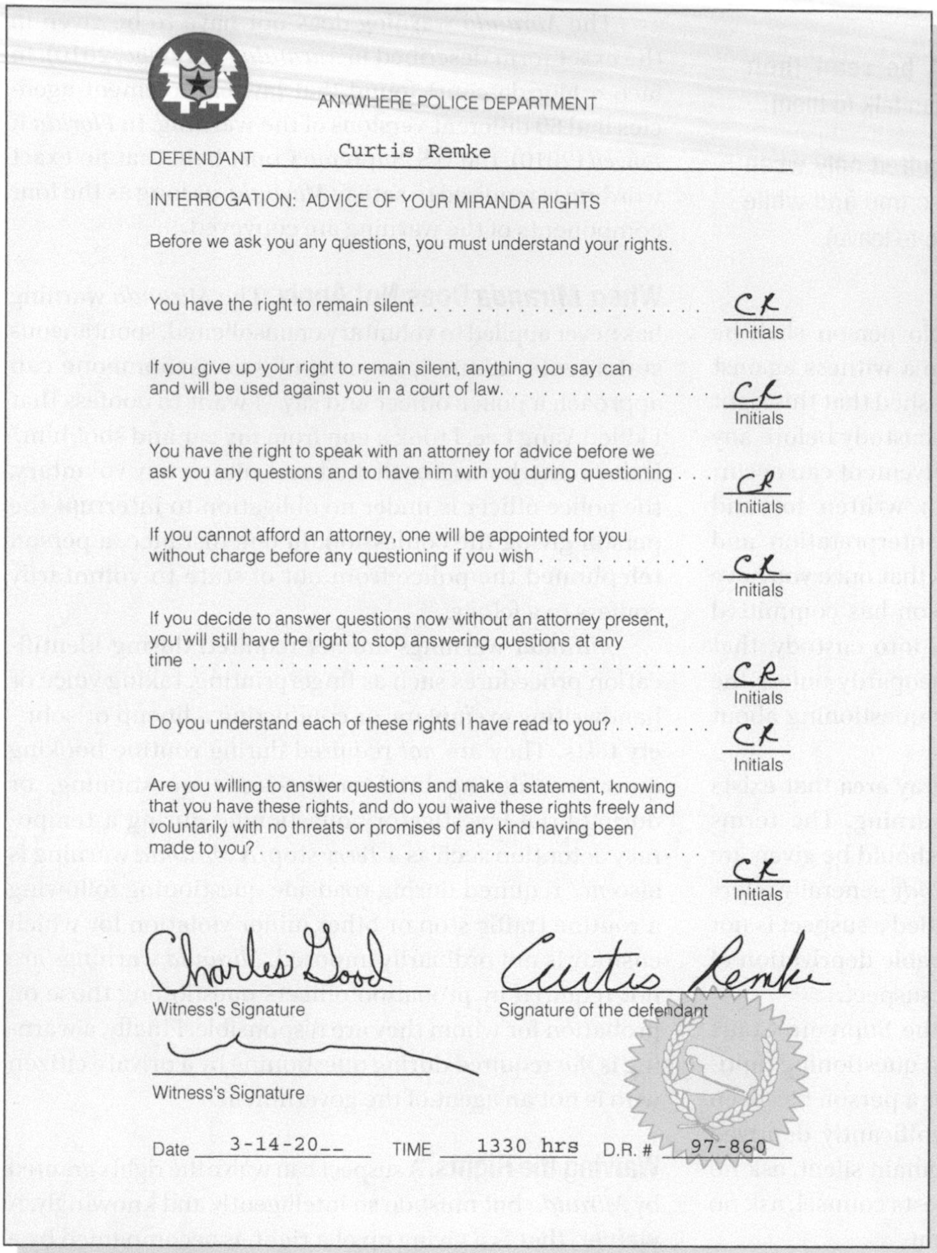

ANYWHERE POLICE DEPARTMENT

DEFENDANT _____ Curtis Remke _____

INTERROGATION: ADVICE OF YOUR MIRANDA RIGHTS

Before we ask you any questions, you must understand your rights.

You have the right to remain silent . . . . _CR_
                                                                    Initials

If you give up your right to remain silent, anything you say can
and will be used against you in a court of law . . . . _CR_
                                                                    Initials

You have the right to speak with an attorney for advice before we
ask you any questions and to have him with you during questioning . . . _CR_
                                                                    Initials

If you cannot afford an attorney, one will be appointed for you
without charge before any questioning if you wish . . . . _CR_
                                                                    Initials

If you decide to answer questions now without an attorney present,
you will still have the right to stop answering questions at any
time . . . . _CR_
                                                                    Initials

Do you understand each of these rights I have read to you? . . . . . . _CR_
                                                                    Initials

Are you willing to answer questions and make a statement, knowing
that you have these rights, and do you waive these rights freely and
voluntarily with no threats or promises of any kind having been
made to you? . . . . _CR_
                                                                    Initials

Charles Good   _Curtis Remke_
Witness's Signature   Signature of the defendant

_____
Witness's Signature

Date ___3-14-20__   TIME ___1330 hrs   D.R. # ___97-860

FIGURE 6.3
Miranda waiver form.
Source: Drafted by Cho, H. Cho Research & Consulting, LLC.
Copyright 2011.

that suspects do not have to incriminate themselves; the Sixth Amendment requires that suspects be provided a lawyer. The Sixth Amendment right to counsel applies only to the specific crime for which the person has been indicted or arraigned. This situation often occurs when detectives are investigating a cold case and want to question suspects who are incarcerated on a different charge.

The Effects of *Miranda*. The *Miranda* warning does not prevent suspects from talking. It simply requires that suspects be advised of and fully understand their constitutional rights. The basic intent of the *Miranda* decision is to guarantee the rights of the accused. The practical effect is to ensure that confessions are obtained without duress or coercion, thereby removing any inferences that third-degree tactics were used.

Several Court decisions relate to the *Miranda* warning. In *Edwards v. Arizona* (1981), the Supreme Court held that after a suspect has been read their *Miranda* rights and then invokes the right to remain silent and to have legal counsel, the suspect cannot be reapproached, either by the same or different officers, and cannot be questioned further until a lawyer is made available. The *Edwards* decision, however, has since been modified under *Shatzer*.

In *Maryland v. Shatzer* (2010), the Court effectively set an expiration date on the right-to-counsel invocation by announcing a "14-day break-in-custody" rule. This rule changed *Miranda* protocol under *Edwards* by allowing police to reinitiate contact with a suspect who had previously asserted the right to counsel if at least 14 days had passed since the original invocation of that right. In other words, as long as two weeks have passed and the suspect has been out of *Miranda*, or police custody for that time, having returned to "normal" life, even if that "normal" life is as an inmate behind bars, the suspect can be reapproached without violating *Edwards*.

According to the *Davis* rule, as established in *Davis v. United States* (1994), police are not required to resolve ambiguous statements made by suspects regarding the invocation of the right to an attorney. In this case, the suspect, who had waived his *Miranda* rights, said about an hour and a half into the interrogation, "Maybe I should talk to a lawyer," but then said, "No, I don't want a lawyer," so the questioning continued, and Davis provided incriminating statements. Finding that the statements were not an unambiguous invocation of the right to counsel, the Supreme Court upheld admission of Davis's statements and unanimously affirmed his conviction and sentence: "The suspect must unambiguously request counsel. He must articulate his desire to have counsel present sufficiently clearly that a reasonable police officer in the circumstances would understand the statement to be a request for an attorney. . . . We decline to adopt a rule requiring officers to ask clarifying questions. If the suspect's statement is not an unambiguous or unequivocal request for counsel, the officers have no obligation to stop questioning him."

Examples of specific language that does not require questioning to stop are:

- "I just don't think that I should say anything." (*Burket v. Angelone*, 2000)

- "I don't got nothing to say." (*United States v. Banks*, 2003)

- "Could I call my lawyer?" (*Dormire v. Wilkinson*, 2001)

In 1984, *Minnesota v. Murphy* established that probation officers do not need to give the *Miranda* warning, and *Berkemer v. McCarty* (1984) ruled that the *Miranda* warning is not required for traffic violations.

The Supreme Court ruled in *Illinois v. Perkins* (1990) that jailed suspects need not be told of their right to remain silent when they provide information to undercover agents. Justice Anthony Kennedy wrote that the intent of the *Miranda* decision was to ensure that police questioning of suspects in custody is not sufficiently coercive to make confessions involuntary. Suspects must be told of their rights not to incriminate themselves.

Miranda was *not* meant to protect suspects who boast about their criminal activities to individuals they believe to be cellmates.

***Miranda* Challenged.** The Supreme Court's ruling in *Dickerson v. United States* (2000) held that *Miranda* is a constitutional decision and therefore could not be overruled by an act of Congress. In declining to strike down *Miranda*, the Court said it found no compelling reason to overrule a 34-year-old decision that "has become embedded in routine police practice to the point where the warnings have become part of our national culture."

The "Question First" or "Beachheading" Technique

An interrogation technique commonly used in some departments is the "question first," or **beachheading**, technique: an officer questions a custodial suspect without giving the *Miranda* warnings and obtains incriminating statements; the officer then gives the warning, gets a waiver, and repeats the interrogation to obtain the same statement. The thinking behind this technique is that even though the first statement would be suppressed, the second, waived statement would be admissible. However, in *Missouri v. Seibert* (2004), the Supreme Court found this technique unconstitutional: "It is likely that if the interrogators employ the technique of withholding warnings until after interrogation succeeds in eliciting a confession, the warnings will be ineffective in preparing the suspect for successive interrogation, close in time and similar in content."

The Interplay of the Fourth and Fifth Amendments

Chapter 4 discussed how the Fourth Amendment restricts searches. This chapter discusses how the Fifth Amendment restricts confessions. Often the two amendments become intertwined, as seen in *New York v. Quarles* (1984), a case in which an exigent search resulted in a Fifth Amendment issue because of the statements elicited pursuant to the search. In *Quarles*, the Supreme Court ruled on the **public safety exception** to the *Miranda* warning requirement.

In 1980, two police officers were stopped by a young woman who told them she had been raped and gave them a description of her rapist, who, she stated, had just entered a nearby supermarket and was armed with a gun. The suspect, Benjamin Quarles, was located, and one officer ordered him to stop. Quarles ran, and the officer momentarily lost sight of him. When he was apprehended and frisked, he was wearing an empty shoulder holster. The officer asked Quarles where the gun was, and he nodded toward some cartons and said, "The gun is over there." The officer retrieved the gun, put Quarles under formal arrest, and read him his rights. Quarles waived his rights to remain silent and to speak with an attorney and answered questions.

At the trial, the court ruled pursuant to *Miranda* that the statement, "The gun is over there," and the subsequent discovery of the gun as a result of that statement were inadmissible. After reviewing the case, the Supreme Court ruled that the procedural safeguards that both deter a suspect from responding and increase the possibility of fewer convictions were deemed acceptable in *Miranda* to protect the Fifth Amendment privilege against self-incrimination. However, if *Miranda* warnings had deterred the response to the officer's question, the cost would have been more than just loss of evidence that might lead to a conviction. As long as the gun remained concealed in the store, it posed a danger to public safety.

The Court ruled that in this case the need to have the suspect talk (an exigent circumstance) took precedence over the requirement that the defendant be read his rights. The Court ruled that the material factor in applying this "public safety" exception is whether a public threat could possibly be removed by the suspect making a statement. In this case, the officer asked the question only to ensure his and the public's safety. He then gave the *Miranda* warning before continuing questioning.

The Fourth and Fifth Amendments also came into play in one case that was argued twice. The trials involved the same defendant (Robert Williams) but different prosecutors. In the first trial, *Brewer v. Williams* (1977), the issue revolved around information solicited from Williams without his being Mirandized. An arrest warrant was issued in Des Moines, Iowa, for Williams, an escapee from a mental institution wanted for murdering a little girl on Christmas Eve. Williams turned himself in to police in Davenport, Iowa. Des Moines police went to Davenport to transport Williams back to Des Moines, with all agreeing that Williams was not to be questioned on the way. However, one detective, knowing Williams was a psychiatric patient who possessed a strong religious faith, told Williams that he wanted him to think about where the little girl was buried. He could perhaps show them where the body was on the way back because it was sleeting and they might not be able to find it in the morning. The officer told Williams that the little girl who was snatched away on Christmas Eve needed a Christian burial (the Christian Burial Speech). Williams complied and showed the officers where he had buried the girl. "Although the lower courts admitted Williams's

damaging statements into evidence, the Supreme Court in *Brewer v. Williams* affirmed the court of appeals's decision that any statements made by Williams could not be admitted against him because the way they were elicited violated his constitutional right to counsel" (Harr, Hess, Orthmann, & Kingsbury, 2018, p. 235). The Court granted Williams a new trial.

At the second trial, in *Nix v. Williams* (1984), the Court allowed the body of the little girl to be admitted into evidence because a search party had been approaching the location of the burial site and would have discovered the body without Williams's help. This case established the *inevitable-discovery doctrine* discussed in Chapter 4.

Right to Counsel under the Fifth and Sixth Amendments

The Supreme Court concluded in *Miranda* that custodial interrogation creates an inherently coercive environment in which a person's Fifth Amendment privilege against compelled self-incrimination is jeopardized and that under such circumstances, procedural safeguards must be employed to protect that privilege: "The circumstances surrounding in-custody interrogation can operate very quickly to overbear the will of one merely made aware of his privilege by his interrogators. Therefore, the right to have counsel present at the interrogation is indispensable to the protection of the Fifth Amendment privilege under the system we delineate today. Our aim is to assure that the individual's right to choose between silence and speech remains unfettered throughout the interrogation process. ... Thus, the need for counsel to protect the Fifth Amendment privilege comprehends not merely a right to consult with counsel prior to questioning, but also to have counsel present during any questioning if the defendant so desires." The Sixth Amendment right to counsel, however, does not hinge on the issue of custody. The right to counsel under the Sixth Amendment does not apply until proceedings against a suspect have begun.

Fellers v. United States (2004) illustrates the difference between these two rights. Officers went to John Fellers's home to discuss his involvement in methamphetamine distribution. They told him a grand jury had indicted him and four others and had a federal warrant for his arrest. The officers did not advise Fellers of his *Miranda* rights and asked him no questions, but Fellers told them he knew the four others and had used methamphetamine with them. The officers transported Fellers to jail and advised him of his rights, which he waived. At trial, Fellers filed a motion to suppress all his statements, claiming they were obtained in violation of his rights.

The Supreme Court ruled in favor of Fellers, emphasizing that the Sixth Amendment right to counsel differs from the Fifth Amendment (*Miranda*) custodial-interrogation principle and applies even when the police do not question a defendant. The Court stated, "There is no question that the officers in this case deliberately elicited information from Fellers during the contact at his home."

Foreign Nationals, the Vienna Convention Treaty, and Diplomatic Immunity

Partly because of concern that foreign nationals charged with crimes in the United States will not fully understand their rights within the complex U.S. legal system, the Vienna Convention Treaty, signed in 1963, gives foreign nationals the right to contact their consulate in the event of their detention or arrest. Another treaty signed in 1972 provides diplomatic immunity for certain individuals. Officers who want to interrogate a person claiming diplomatic immunity should request the diplomatic identification and check the reverse of the card, where that individual's level of immunity will be stated. If officers have questions, they can call the Bureau of Diplomatic Security. A general guideline is to treat foreign nationals and diplomats as you would want Americans to be treated under similar circumstances abroad.

Selecting the Time and Place

Like interviews, interrogations are conducted as soon as possible after a crime. Selecting the right place to question suspects is critical because they are usually reluctant to talk to police. Most interrogations are conducted at police headquarters. However, if a suspect refuses to come to the station and evidence is insufficient for an arrest, the interrogation may take place at the crime scene, in a squad car, or at the suspect's home or place of work. If possible, suspects should be interrogated in an unfamiliar place, away from their friends and family.

Conduct interrogations in a place that is private and free from interruptions. Ideal conditions exist at the police station, where privacy and interruptions can be controlled. Visible movements or unusual noises distract a suspect undergoing questioning. Only the suspect, the suspect's attorney, and the interrogators should be in the room. Having two officers conduct the interrogation helps deflect false allegations or other untrue claims by the suspect. Allow no telephone calls and no distracting noises; allow no one to enter the room. Under these conditions, communication is more readily established.

Opinions differ about how interrogation rooms should be furnished. An austere, sparsely furnished room is generally less distracting; pictures can reduce the effectiveness of questioning. Many interrogation rooms have only two chairs: one for the investigator and one for the suspect. Some include a small, bare table. Some officers feel it is better *not* to have a desk or table between the officer and the suspect because the desk serves as a psychological protection to the suspect. Without it, the suspect tends to feel much more uncomfortable and vulnerable. Keep all notebooks, pencils, pens, and any objects of evidence to be used in the interrogation out of view, preferably in a drawer, until the appropriate time. A stark setting develops and maintains the suspect's absolute attention and allows total concentration on the conversation.

Other investigators, however, contend that such a setting is not conducive to good rapport. It may remind suspects of jail, and a fear of going to jail may keep them from talking. Instead, some investigators prefer a normally furnished room or office for interrogations. Doctors, lawyers, insurance investigators, and others have shown that a relaxed atmosphere encourages conversation. Even background music can reduce anxiety and dispel fear—major steps in getting subjects to talk.

Starting the Interrogation

Conducting the interrogation at the police station allows many options in timing and approach. A suspect can be brought to the interrogation room and left alone temporarily. Often the suspect has not yet met the investigator and is apprehensive about what the investigator is like, what will be asked, and what will happen. Provide time for the anxiety to increase, just as a football team sometimes takes a time-out before the opposing team attempts a critical field goal.

As you enter the room, show that you are in command, but do not display arrogance. The suspect is in an unfamiliar environment, is alone, does not know you, has been waiting, is apprehensive, and does not know what you will ask. At this point, select your interrogation technique, deciding whether to increase or decrease the suspect's anxiety. Some investigators accomplish their goals by friendliness, others by authoritarianism. Show your identification and introduce yourself to the suspect, state the purpose of the interrogation, and then give the *Miranda* warning. Avoid violating the suspect's personal zone. Try to stay two to six feet away when questioning.

Do not become so wrapped up in yourself and your quest for information that you overlook body language or **nonverbal communication** that may indicate deception, remorse, anger, or indifference. Research has shown that

10% of a message delivered is verbal and 90% is nonverbal. And while nonverbal cues, as discussed earlier, have not been scientifically validated as absolute indicators of deception, they can provide a useful guide as an investigator navigates the interrogation, and officers who can correctly interpret what they see arm themselves with a powerful tool.

Deception, for example, *may* be indicated by looking down, rolling the eyes upward, placing the hands over the eyes or mouth, or rubbing the hands around the mouth. Other possible indicators of deception include continual licking of the lips, twitching of the lips, intermittent coughs, rapid breathing, change in facial color, continuous swallowing, pulsating of the carotid artery in the neck, face flushing, tapping the fingers, and avoiding eye contact. Excessive protestations of innocence should also be considered suspect, for example, "To be perfectly honest," or "I swear on my father's grave."

Establishing Rapport

As with interviewing, specific approaches during interrogating may either encourage cooperation or induce silence and noncooperation. The techniques for establishing rapport during an interview also apply in an interrogation. You may decide to instill the fear that there will be serious consequences if the suspect fails to cooperate ("maximization" under the Reid Technique). You may downplay the moral consequences of the offense and skip over any legal consequences ("minimization"). You may choose to appeal to the suspect's conscience, emphasizing the importance of getting out of the present situation and starting over with a clean slate. Try any approach that shows the person that cooperation is more desirable than having you find out about the crime another way. Whichever approach is selected, however, be aware that several studies have found a positive correlation between an offender's willingness to provide information and an investigator who takes a humanitarian approach to questioning, treating the suspect with empathy and respect (Snook et al., 2012).

It is important to have some knowledge of the suspect's criminal history. If, for example, an officer is dealing with a first-time offender, a soft approach may go over better. If an officer is interrogating a person who has been in and out of prison several times, an authoritative approach might be the more effective way to go. It may also help rapport to gather some personal information about suspects, such as details regarding their family, kids, dogs, hobbies, where they grew up, and where they went to school. Taking the time to gather some background information before the interrogation could mean the difference between getting a confession or being told to get lost.

It also helps to know why the crime was committed. Some crimes are committed out of uncontrollable passion, panic, or fear without consideration of the consequences. Other crimes result from the demands of the moment; the presumed necessity of the crime appears to justify it. Some criminals' guilt becomes so overpowering that they turn themselves in to the police. Other criminals turn to drugs or alcohol or leave the area to start over somewhere else.

It takes skill to obtain information from those involved in crime, especially if they know the consequences can be severe. Suspects who understand there is no easy way out of a situation may become cooperative. At this point, offering alternatives may be successful. Because most people respond to hard evidence, show suspects the physical evidence against them. Acknowledge to the suspect that there is no completely agreeable solution, but point out that some alternatives may be more agreeable than others.

Make no promises, but remind the suspect that the court decides the sentence and is apt to be easier on those who cooperate. Also point out that family and friends are usually more understanding if people admit they are wrong and try to "go straight." And if the suspect will not provide the names of accomplices because they are friends, explain that such "friends" have put the suspect in the present predicament.

Approaches to Interrogation

As with interviews, interrogations can follow an emotional or a logical approach. An emotional approach is either empathetic (PEACE Model) or authoritarian (Reid Technique). After talking with the suspect, select the approach that seems to offer the best chance for obtaining information. Rapport has been stressed previously. Rationalization, projection, and minimization are among techniques commonly used in interrogation.

L07 Describe the various techniques used in an interrogation.

Interrogation techniques include inquiring directly or indirectly, forcing responses, deflating or inflating the ego, minimizing or maximizing the crime, projecting the blame, rationalizing, and combining approaches.

Inquiring Indirectly or Directly. Indirect inquiry draws out information without mentioning the main subject. For example, an indirect approach may be phrased, "Have you ever been in the vicinity of Elm Street? Grove Street? the intersection of Elm and Grove?" In contrast, a direct question would be, "Did you break into the house on the corner of Elm and Grove Streets on December 16th?"

Forcing Responses. A forced response is elicited by asking a question that will implicate the suspect, regardless of the answer given. For example, the question "What time did you arrive at the house?" implies that the suspect *did* arrive at the house at some time. Answering the question with a time forces the suspect to admit having been there. Of course, the suspect may simply state, "I never arrived there," or may refuse to answer at all.

Deflating or Inflating the Ego. Belittling a suspect is often effective. For example, you may tell a suspect, "We know you couldn't be directly involved in the burglary because you aren't smart enough to pull off a job like that. We thought you might know who did, though." Question the suspect's skill in committing a crime known to be his specialty (this is where having background information about the suspect's criminal history can help your interrogation). Suggest that the suspect's reputation is suffering because his latest burglaries have been bungled. The suspect may attempt—out of pride—to prove that it was a professional job.

The same results can be obtained by *inflating* suspects' egos, praising the skill shown in pulling off the job. Suspects may want to take the credit and admit their role in the crime.

Minimizing or Maximizing the Crime. Concentrate your efforts on the crime itself, ignoring for the moment the person committing it. Minimize the crime by calling it "the thing that happened" rather than using the word *crime.* Refer to stolen property as "the stuff that was taken." Do not use terms such as *robbery, homicide,* or *arson.* Use other, less threatening terms. For example, asking the suspect "to tell the truth" is much less threatening than asking someone "to confess." Overstating the severity of an offense can be as effective as understating it. Mentioning that the amount of stolen money was $5,000 rather than the actual $500 puts the suspect on the spot. Is a partner holding out? Is the victim lying about the losses? Will the suspect be found guilty of a felony because of such lies? Making the offense more serious than it actually is can induce suspects to provide facts implicating them in lesser offenses.

Projecting the Blame. Projecting blame onto others is another effective way to get suspects talking. When suspects feel as if others are at fault, they may be more willing to share information that will ultimately incriminate them. This is often seen in rape cases where the officer suggests that the woman "was asking for it" by the way she was dressed.

Rationalizing. Rationalizing is another technique that shifts fault away from a suspect. Even though the suspect committed the act, they may believe that there was a good reason to justify it. Skilled interrogators understand this psychology and convey empathy by saying they understand where the suspect is "coming from."

Combining Approaches. Having the suspect tell the story using different methods can reveal discrepancies. If an oral statement has been given, have the suspect put this information in writing and compare the two versions. Then give the story to two different investigators and have them compare the versions.

Using Persuasion during Interrogation

Sometimes investigators may obtain much better results using persuasive techniques: making sure the suspect is comfortable and has basic needs taken care of, such as being allowed to go to the restroom and to get a drink of water. Once the suspect has been made comfortable, begin by acknowledging that a problem exists but that before talking about it, the suspect needs to be informed of their rights. Then suggest that the suspect probably already knows all about these rights and ask the suspect to tell what they do know. Usually the suspect can paraphrase the *Miranda* warning, and you can then compliment them on that knowledge. This helps establish rapport. Next, encourage the suspect to tell their side of the story in detail, intervening only to give encouragement to continue talking. When the suspect has finished, review the account step by step.

Following this, begin a "virtual monologue about robbery" and how some people's desperate financial circumstances lead them into such a crime. The monologue describes how no one starts out planning a life of crime, but some, like an addict, fall into a criminal pattern that leads either to getting shot and killed or to spending a lifetime in prison. End the monologue by emphasizing that the inevitable result of this pattern of crime is life in prison or death.

Next, suggest that the suspect can avoid this fate only by breaking this pattern and that the first step is to admit that it exists. Add that a person's life should not be judged by one mistake, nor should that person's life be wasted by a refusal to admit that mistake. Following this monologue, begin to talk about the suspect's accomplices and how they are still free, enjoying the fruits of the crime.

Finally, talk about the suspect's previous encounters with the criminal justice system and how fairly it has treated the suspect. In the past, the suspect has probably always claimed to be not guilty. Judges are likely to go easier on suspects who indicate remorse for what they have done. This cannot happen unless the suspect first admits the crime. Point out that intelligent people recognize when it is in their best interest to admit a mistake.

Investigative Questionnaires. An alternative to a face-to-face interrogation is the Crime Questionnaire™ (CQ), a tool with 30 questions that test for truth and deception and can be used in conjunction with a polygraph or in situations

---

Technology Innovations

Virtual Interrogations

Virtual interrogation software allows officers the opportunity to fine-tune their interrogation skills on or off duty. For example, one product created by SIMmersion called the Hands-on Interview and Interrogation Training System (HIITS)™ provides training and practice exercises through which officers can learn and hone their investigative interview, interrogation, and confession-solicitation skills on a simulated suspect named "Jennifer":

As each conversation progresses, users will witness verbal, nonverbal, and paralinguistic cues that will help support their decisions whether to question Jennifer further or allow her to leave.

User will learn to build rapport with suspects, identify confession-solicitation themes, solicit an admissible confession, and use proper post-confession tecniques.

Variances in Jennifer's motivation, personality, and veracity will provide the user with hours of training. HIITS™ can strengthen the preparation and techniques of all personnel, ranging from novices to experienced investigators.

Source: SIMmersion™. "Hands-on Interview and Interrogation Training System." Columbia, MD. Retrieved April 26, 2021, from www.simmersion.com /Hands-on_Interview_and_Interrogation_Training_with_Jennifer_Lerner

---

where a polygraph cannot be used. A research study involving members of the American Polygraph Association found that the CQ correctly predicted results of an actual polygraph 85% of the time (Bassett, 2013). Formal training, however, is required to interpret these questionnaires; thus investigators must submit the questionnaire to the company that created it.

Ethics and the Use of Deception

Although law enforcement officers are expected to be honest, the Supreme Court has recognized that their duties may require limited officially sanctioned deception during a criminal investigation. Several cases support officer use of deception. The Supreme Court stated in *Sorrells v. United States* (1932), "Criminal activity is such that stealth and strategy are necessary weapons in the arsenal of the police officer." In *United States v. Russell* (1973), the Court said, "Nor will the mere fact of deceit defeat a prosecution, for there are circumstances when the use of deceit is the only practicable law enforcement technique available." *United States ex rel. Caminito v. Murphy* (1955) held that it is permissible to tell suspects that they have been identified by witnesses even though that is untrue. *Moore v. Hopper* (1974) allowed telling suspects that material evidence, such as a firearm used to commit a crime, has been found, when it has not. *Frazier v. Cupp* (1969) held that it is permissible to tell suspects that an accomplice has already confessed, when this is untrue.

Interrogatory deception may include claiming to possess evidence that does not really exist, making promises, misrepresenting the seriousness of the offense, and misrepresenting identity (e.g., pretending to be a cellmate or a reporter). Actually creating or forging false evidence, however, is unethical and illegal.

Television and movies often depict the good-cop/bad-cop method of interrogation, portraying one officer as very hostile and another one as trying to protect a suspect from the hostile officer. Routines such as this could be considered illegal if carried to an extreme.

Some interrogation techniques, such as coercive deception, even if not illegal, may be unethical. Critics of the use of deception by investigators during interrogations argue that such tactics are a form of coercion akin to police use of force in that both influence the way a suspect behaves (Hritz, 2017, p. 502): "[L]ies distort the suspect's estimates of the costs and benefits of confessing. For example, when a police officer lies about the presence of evidence, an innocent person may feel that it is necessary to confess to avoid conviction of a more serious offense. Therefore, lies allow police to make conditional offers that attempt to induce the suspect to confess based on false information about the suspect's legal situation."

In *People v. Thomas* (2014), the court recognized that highly coercive deception by police during an interrogation may infringe on a suspect's Fifth Amendment protection from self-incrimination, with such tactics being "of a kind sufficiently potent to nullify individual judgment in any ordinarily resolute person and . . . manifestly lethal to self-determination when deployed against defendant, an unsophisticated individual without experience in the criminal justice system." In this case, the court held that the defendant's "inculpating statements were . . . inadmissible as 'involuntarily made' . . . The various misrepresentations and false assurances used [by the interrogators] to elicit and shape defendant's admissions manifestly raised a substantial risk of false incrimination. . . . Indeed, there is not a single inculpatory fact in defendant's confession that was not suggested to him [by his interrogators]."

The use of deception in interrogation and the determination of ethical, professional behavior remain important issues.

Third-Degree Tactics

Considerable literature deals with the use of the third degree in police interrogations, although it is not known how widely these methods are used and how much of what is claimed is exaggeration. **Third degree** is the use of physical force, the threat of force, or other physical, mental, or psychological abuse to induce a suspect to confess to a crime. Third-degree tactics, which are illegal, include: striking or hitting a suspect; denying food, water, or sleep for abnormal time periods; not allowing a suspect to go to the restroom; having a number of officers ask questions in shifts for prolonged periods; and refusing normal privileges. Obtaining information by these methods is inexcusable, and any information so obtained, including confessions, is inadmissible in court.

The image of police brutality is difficult to offset when third-degree tactics are used. Such tactics create a loss of respect for the officer involved and for the entire department and the police profession. This conduct also puts the engaging officers and their departments at risk for criminal and civil lawsuits.

Although physical force is not permitted, this does not rule out physical contact. Placing a hand on a shoulder or touching a suspect's hand can help to establish rapport. Looking directly at a suspect while talking and continuing to do so during the conversation is not using physical force, even though it usually makes the suspect extremely uncomfortable.

If you give a suspect all the privileges you yourself have within the interrogation context, there is no cause for a charge of third-degree tactics. Allow the suspect the same breaks for meals, rest, and going to the restroom that you take. Law enforcement officers are obligated to protect both the public interest and individual rights. No situation excuses a deliberate violation of these rights.

Admissions and Confessions

When a suspect has become cooperative, you can increase the amount of conversation. Once rapport is established, listen for words indicating that the suspect is in some way connected with the crime, such as "I didn't do it, but I know who did." If the suspect is not implicated in the crime but has relevant information, attempt to obtain a statement. If the suspect is implicated, try to obtain an admission or confession. The format for obtaining admissions and confessions from suspects in criminal cases is fairly standard. However, state laws, rules, and procedures for taking admissions and confessions vary, so you need to know the rules and requirements of your jurisdiction.

An **admission** contains some information concerning the elements of a crime but falls short of a full confession (Figure 6.4). A **confession** is information supporting the elements of a crime given by a person involved in committing it. It can be oral or written and must be voluntary and not given in response to threats, promises, or rewards. It can be taken in question-and-answer form or in a narrative handwritten by the suspect or the interrogator (Figure 6.5).

The voluntary nature of the confession is essential. For example, Ernesto Miranda had an arrest record and was familiar with his rights; yet, his confession was ruled inadmissible because these rights had not been clearly stated to him. Although formal education is not required for making a confession, a suspect must be intelligent enough to understand fully everything stated.

In most states, oral confessions are admissible in court, but written confessions usually carry more weight. Put an oral confession into writing as soon as possible, even if the suspect refuses to sign it. Have the suspect repeat the confession in the presence of other witnesses to corroborate its content and voluntariness. In extremely important cases, the prosecutor often obtains the confession to ensure that it meets all legal requirements. Today most departments use digital recorders for oral confessions, and many states

ANYTOWN POLICE DEPARTMENT
ADMISSION   CF#___11-1234___

Date Occurred: _12th November, 2011_____

Location of Occurrence: _Lucky's Bar and Grill,_____

_____1234 Business Way, Anytown, MI 48000_____

Name: _Walter William Wilson_____

Date of Birth: _02/02/90_____

Address: _100 Main Street, Anytown, MI 48000_____

Phone Number: (C) _517-555-3000_ (H) _517-555-3001_ (W) _517-555-3002_

Narrative:

I, Walter Wilson, was at Lucky's Bar and Grill on Saturday night, November 12th, 2011 at 11:30 pm. I met a friend there named John Jacobs and we ate dinner and had some drinks. While we were leaving the bar a guy came up to us and said he wanted to fight with us. He was a white guy around 30 years old wearing blue jeans and a white shirt. We got into a verbal argument because he was drunk and said he was going to kill us. We both left shortly after. The man was alive when we left the bar.

I have read this statement consisting of __1__ page(s), and I affirm to the truth and accuracy of the facts contained herein.

This statement was completed at (Location) _Anytown Police Department_ on

(Date) _November 14, 2011_ at (Time) _1300_ .

WITNESS _Wm Bennett_____   _Walter W. Wilson_____
                                        (Signature of person providing voluntary statement)
WITNESS _Jehu H Scott_____

FIGURE 6.4
Sample admission.
Source: Drafted by Cho, H. Cho Research & Consulting, LLC. Copyright 2011.

---

require at least an audio recording. Of course, it is preferable to have both video and audio because if the confession is played in court, the jury can hear *and* see the suspect's anger, tears, or lack of compassion.

After obtaining a confession, you may also go with the suspect to the crime scene and reenact the crime before witnesses. Take pictures or films of this reenactment. Go over the confession and the pictures with the suspect to verify their accuracy. (Such confessions and reenactments can also be used for police training.)

Even though a confession is highly desirable and often referred to as the "gold standard" in evidence, it may not be true, it may later be denied, or there may be claims that it was involuntary. Some research has found that the incidence of false confessions is higher than many believe and can be exacerbated by certain interrogation tactics, such as "the sympathetic detective with a limited time offer" (Davis, Leo, & Follette, 2010).

A growing body of research suggests that accusatorial interrogation methods significantly increase the probability of a false confession (Kelly & Meissner, 2017). This is a primary reason why a number of scholars are calling for an end to confrontational models of interrogation, such as the Reid Technique (Kozinski, 2018). Data collected by The National Registry of Exonerations indicates that two groups are particularly vulnerable to making false confessions, particularly under the pressure of an accusatorial interrogation: juvenile suspects and those with mental disabilities (Gross & Possley, 2016). For example, of the 103 exonerees who reported a mental illness or an intellectual disability, 72 percent were found to have falsely confessed.

Your investigation will proceed in much the same way with or without a confession. However, a confession often provides additional leads. Although it cannot stand alone, it is an important part of the case.

L08 Explain what significance a confession has in an investigation.

A confession is only one part of an investigation. Corroborate it with independent evidence.

ANYTOWN POLICE DEPARTMENT
CONFESSION   CF#___11-1234___

Date Occurred: _12th November, 2011_

Location of Occurrence: _Lucky's Bar and Grill,_

1234 Business Way, Anytown, MI 48000

Name: _Walter William Wilson_

Date of Birth: _02/02/90_

Address: _100 Main Street, Anytown, MI 48000_

Phone Number: (C) _517-555-3000_ (H) _517-555-3001_ (W) _517-555-3002_

Narrative:

I, Walter Wilson, was at Lucky's Bar and Grill on Saturday night,
November 12th, 2011 at 11:30 pm. I met a friend there named John Jacobs
and we ate dinner and had some drinks. While we were leaving the bar a
guy came up to us in the parking lot and said he wanted to fight with us.
He was a white guy around 30 years old wearing blue jeans and a white
shirt. We got into a verbal argument because he was drunk and he said he
was going to kill us. I got angry at him because he was verbally
threatening me and my friend as well as being belligerent. He then
punched me in the face so I pulled out my pocket knife and stabbed him
three times in the stomach with it. I think he was dead in the parking
lot when we left.

I have read the ___1___ page(s) of this statement and the facts contained therein are
true and correct.

This statement was completed at (Location) _Anytown Police Department_ on

(Date) _November 14, 2011_ at (Time) _1300_ .

WITNESS _Wm Bennett_

WITNESS _Jekett Scott_

Walter W. Wilson
(Signature of person providing voluntary statement)

FIGURE 6.5
Sample confession.
Source: Drafted by Cho, H. Cho Research & Consulting, LLC.
Copyright 2011.

According to the *Bruton* rule, which resulted from *Bruton v. United States* (1968), a defendant's Sixth Amendment right to confront and cross-examine witnesses against him is violated if a confessing defendant's statement is used against a nonconfessing defendant at their joint trial (Rutledge, 2008). To avoid this situation, Rutledge (p. 63) suggests that if two suspects have waived *Miranda* but only one has confessed, bring the two together and ask the confessor to repeat his confession implicating the other suspect. If the nonconfessing suspect does not deny the allegations made by the suspect who confessed, this can be considered an adoptive admission by the nonconfessor: "An **adoptive admission** occurs when someone else makes a statement in a person's presence and under circumstances where it would be logical to expect the person to make a denial if the statement falsely implicated him, but he does not deny the allegations" (2008, p. 63).

Questioning Children and Juveniles

Special considerations exist when questioning children and juveniles. As in any interview, the first step is to build rapport. You might give the child a tour of the building and show them where the parent(s) will be waiting.

Interviews of child victims, particularly those involved in sex crimes investigations, can be extremely challenging, not only because of the very sensitive nature of the crime but also because the limited vocabulary of some children, especially very young ones, can present considerable communication barriers (Melinder, Magnusson, & Gilstrap, 2020). A recommendation is to begin by establishing what words a child uses to refer to the private parts of the body, possibly with the aid of a diagram or an anatomically correct doll. It is a good idea to have a specially trained investigator or social worker present to either assist or lead in the interview of youthful sex crime victims. The psychology of children can be entirely different than that of an adult, and the same techniques used on adults may not be effective on juveniles.

Investigators should obtain parental permission before questioning a juvenile, unless the situation warrants immediate questioning at the scene. Although getting a parent's permission is not required, and the courts have ruled in favor of law enforcement when it can be shown that a teen has an extensive criminal knowledge, it is considered a best practice to attempt to obtain parental permission to interview their child. Parents usually permit their juveniles to be questioned separately if the purpose is explained and you have valid reasons for doing so. Recognize, however, that overprotective parents can distract and interfere with an interview or interrogation. Some parents are actually more belligerent with the police than are their children, having had multiple negative encounters with the law themselves. And there are situations where it is best to not get the parents involved, such as when a parent may also be suspected of criminal activity. Often, however, parents can assist if the youth is uncooperative. They can ask questions and bring pressures to bear that you cannot. They know and understand the child and can probably sense when the child is lying. Decide whether to question a juvenile in front of the parents or separately after you determine their attitudes when you explain to them the reasons for the inquiry.

Often juveniles will not feel comfortable being honest if their parents are present. If you sense this is the case, advise the parents and request to speak with the juvenile separately. Topics of inquiry that can hinder a juvenile interview, if parents are present, include drugs and sex.

Your attitude toward youths will greatly influence how well you can communicate with them. Ask yourself whether you consider the youth a person who has a problem or a youth who *is* a problem.

Many juveniles put on airs and act tough in front of their friends. For example, in one case, a juvenile and some other youths were brought into a room for observation by witnesses. The suspect youth knew he was being watched and challenged his school principal by stating that he had a right to know who was looking at him and why. This 10-year-old boy wanted to impress his friends. A few days later, the boy's parents brought him to the police station at the officer's request. It took two questions to determine that the boy had set a fire that resulted in an $80,000 loss. After a third question, the youth admitted his guilt. Although he had acted like a big shot in front of his friends, his action weighed heavily on his conscience. The presence of the police and the knowledge that his parents were waiting in another room motivated him to cooperate.

Whenever feasible, an officer who is questioning a juvenile should be in plain clothes with their weapon out of plain sight. Also, officers should inform juveniles they can leave anytime, if it is the case and the juvenile is not in custody, and ask if they would like their parent present.

Finally, juveniles may have definite opinions about the police. Some dislike adults in general and the police in particular. Like adults, however, most do not dislike the police and will cooperate with them. Put yourself in their shoes; learn their attitudes and the reasons for them. Time and patience are your greatest allies when questioning juveniles. Explain why you are questioning them, and you will probably gain their confidence.

Do not underrate young people's intelligence or cleverness. They are often excellent observers with good memories. Talk to them as you would to an adult. Praise them and impress upon them their importance to the investigation. However, while investigators may ask juveniles to provide information about crimes to follow up on, a juvenile should never be used as an informant, even if parents know about it. Most agencies have agreement forms for informants to sign, yet even with parent's signature, using a juvenile as an informant is an extremely unwise decision.

If a juvenile confesses to a crime, bring in the parents and have the youth repeat the confession to them. The parents will see that the information is voluntary and not the police's account of what happened. Parents often provide additional information once they know the truth. For example, they may be alerted to stolen items at home and report them.

Investigators must understand that juveniles are afforded the same rights as adults and a *Miranda* warning is required when questioning a juvenile who is in custody about a crime they are suspected of committing. To counter the argument that officer presence scares juveniles, officers assigned to juvenile investigations or school resource officers often do not wear a uniform.

Evaluating and Corroborating Information

Do not accept information obtained from interviews and interrogations at face value because often the information provided to the police is only partially truthful. Verify all information. You cannot know the motives of all those who provide information. Do not assume that all information, even though volunteered, is truthful. Corroborate or disprove statements made during questioning.

To cross-check a story, review the report and the details of the offense. Determine the past record, family status, hobbies, and special interests of those questioned. If a person has a criminal record, determine their prior modus operandi. With such information, you can ask questions in a way that indicates you know what you are talking about and that deceptive answers will be uncovered.

A person who resorts to half-truths or lies usually ends up on the defensive and becomes entangled in deceit. Knowing the facts of a case allows you to neutralize deliberate lies. If discrepancies in statements occur, question the suspect again or use polygraph or psychological tests. Compare the replies of people questioned and assess whether they are consistent with the known facts. A person who is telling the truth can usually repeat the story the same way many times, although they may use different words and a different sequence in retelling it. Times and dates may be approximate, and the person may simply not be able to remember some things. In contrast, a person who is telling a fabricated story can usually repeat it word for word innumerable times. Dates and times are usually precise, and all details are remembered. However, it is often difficult to repeat lies consistently; each one sounds better than the previous one, and the story becomes distorted with mistakes and exaggerations. To break a pat story or one you suspect is rehearsed, ask questions that require slightly different answers and that will alter memorized responses.

Statement analysis is a technique used to determine whether a person's verbal or written statement is truthful or deceptive. According to McClish (2021), "A person cannot give a lengthy deceptive statement without revealing that it is a lie. This is because people's words will betray them." McClish's Statement Analysis® method incorporates examination of word definitions and rules of grammar to dissect elements of a statement and assess whether they indicate an attempt to deceive.

Scientific Aids to Obtaining and Evaluating Information

Many attempts have been made to determine the truth through scientific instruments. Even before instruments were developed, however, trials by ordeal and other tests relied on psychological and physiological principles. For example, it was common knowledge for centuries that when a person was lying or nervous, visible or measurable physiological changes occurred in the body. These include dryness of the mouth, shaking or trembling, perspiration, increased heartbeat, faster pulse, and rapid breathing. The ancient Chinese capitalized on the symptom of mouth dryness when they made a suspect chew rice. If the rice remained dry after being chewed, the suspect was assumed to be lying.

Science and technology have provided aids to help determine the reliability of information. Among them are the polygraph, the computerized voice stress analyzer (CVSA), hypnosis, and truth serums.

The Polygraph and Voice Stress Tests

As implied by the name, a **polygraph** (literally, "many writings") records several measurements on a visible graph. The polygraph scientifically measures respiration and depth of breathing, as well as changes in the skin's electrical resistance, blood pressure, and pulse rate. The same factors measured by the polygraph may be visible to a trained observer through such signs as flushing of the face, licking the lips, slight pulsing of the neck arteries, beads of perspiration, rapid breathing, and other signs of nervousness. A person does not actually have to respond verbally for a polygraph to work because the machine measures the mental and emotional responses regardless of whether the person answers questions.

Many law enforcement agencies use polygraphs in their investigations; however, the effectiveness of the polygraph has been questioned. Among polygraph supporters, opinions differ regarding its accuracy, which depends on the subject, the equipment, and the operator's training and experience. In some cases, the machine may fail to detect lies because the subject has taken drugs, makes deliberate muscular contractions, or has a psychopathic personality.

Technology Innovations

Statement Analysis

Software has been developed to analyze written statements and assist investigators in determining whether a subject is being truthful or deceptive. The Statement Analyzer is an online program capable of examining a statement up to 3,000 words long in as few as five seconds. The program flags keywords and provides a description of why those words were flagged; highlights deceptive language within a statement; points out sensitive areas within a statement that warrant further investigation; and indicates places where a subject may be withholding information.

SOURCE: http://0www.statementanalysis.com/analyzer/faq/

The subject must be physically, mentally, and emotionally fit for the examination. The examination must be voluntary and completed under conditions conducive to cooperation. A clear, concise summary of the test results is furnished only to authorized personnel.

Despite advances in technology, improved training of polygraph operators, and claims of 95% accuracy, polygraph results are not now accepted by the courts. The Supreme Court has said, "There is simply no consensus that polygraph evidence is reliable. To this day, the scientific community remains extremely polarized about the reliability of polygraph techniques.... There is simply no way to know in a particular case whether a polygraph examiner's conclusion is accurate, because certain doubts and uncertainties plague even the best polygraph exams" (*United States v. Scheffer*, 1998). Some authorities claim that the results violate hearsay rules because it is impossible to cross-examine a machine.

LO9 Describe what a polygraph is, its role in investigation, and the acceptability of its results in court.

The polygraph is an instrument used to verify the truth, not a substitute for investigating and questioning. Although the results are not presently admissible in court, any confession obtained as a result of a polygraph test is admissible.

The polygraph is sometimes useful to develop leads, verify statements, and crosscheck information. Moreover, it provides the police with a psychological advantage that may lead to a confession. Such confessions are admissible in court even though the test results are not. Even in jurisdictions in which the polygraph is not admissible in court, prosecuting attorneys often give weight to the findings of a polygraph examination in deciding whether to prosecute a case.

The normal procedure for setting up a polygraph test is for the police agency to request in writing that a polygraph test be conducted. The examiner reviews the complete case, including any statements made by the subject before the test. A pretest interview with the subject covers the information to be included in the test, a review of the questions to be asked, and an advisement of the suspect's constitutional rights.

The polygraph examiner will need some basic information before the test:

- The case facts—the precise criminal offense involved, the complete case file, and a summary of the evidence

- Information about the subject—complete name; date of birth; physical, mental, emotional, and psychological data, if known; and criminal history

The proper tests are then determined, and the questions prepared and reviewed with the subject. After the test is completed, the subject and the police are advised of the results in person or by letter. If the test indicates deception, an individual interrogation may follow. Any confessions that follow from such tests are almost universally accepted by the courts. The examiner's testimony is not conclusive evidence but rather opinion evidence regarding either guilt or innocence.

The psychological stress evaluator (PSE), which measured stress in the microtremors of the human voice, was introduced in the 1970s. A more recent version of this technology is the computer voice stress analyzer (CVSA). In the first decade of the twenty-first century, voice stress tests had not yet undergone peer-reviewed, independent research to demonstrate their degree of accuracy, and a study by the National Institute of Justice (NIJ) found that two of the most popular VSA programs used by agencies nationwide were "no better than flipping a coin" when it came to detecting deception (Damphouse, 2008). Since then, however, several studies have shown that refinements in the tools and the training can deliver better results in terms of identifying untruthful statements and that the accuracy of VSA technology depends on the algorithms used as well as the effectiveness of the examiners (Patil, Nayak, & Saxena, 2013). New methods, such as the Model for Voice and Effort (MoVE), are grounded on the principle that human respiration is the driving force behind both stress and speech. The MoVE framework

Computerized polygraphy eliminates most of the mechanical equipment, replacing it with a virtual graph on a computer monitor. The graph can be printed, if desired. In computerized polygraph systems, the software analyzes physiological changes and reports the probability that the person has answered the question truthfully.
Sproetniek/Getty Images

hypothesizes that the physiological, cognitive, and emotional loads a person experiences under stress translate into variances in voice production, which can be the key to understanding the underlying mechanisms of the dynamic between speech and stress (Van Puyvelde, Neyt, McGlone, & Pattyn, 2018).

Both the polygraph and the CVSA reduce investigative costs, focus on specific suspects, increase conviction rates (because many tests are followed by confessions), and eliminate suspects. Police agencies should not go on "fishing expeditions," however. Through normal investigative practices, the number of suspects should be narrowed to not more than two people before a polygraph examination or CVSA is used.

Hypnosis and Truth Serums

Like the polygraph, hypnosis and truth serums are supplementary tools to investigation. They are not used as shortcuts but rather in specific cases where the criteria for their use have been determined by thorough review. Cases that meet these criteria are normally crimes of violence or cases where loss of memory or ability to recall is involved and all other standard investigative efforts have been exhausted. Because of the restricted criteria, these techniques are used in a comparatively small number of cases.

Hypnosis. Hypnosis psychically induces a trancelike condition in which the person loses consciousness but responds to a hypnotist's suggestions. Hypnosis is used with crime victims and witnesses to crimes, not with suspects. It should be used only after careful consultation with the person to be hypnotized and after a detailed review of the case as well as of the subject's mental, physical, and emotional condition. Written consent from the subject and permission from the prosecutor's office should be obtained, and a lawyer should be present.

A professional should carefully analyze the subject and the case before hypnosis is conducted. The actual act of hypnotism and interrogation should be performed only by a psychiatrist, psychologist, or physician specifically trained in the techniques.

Courts have established guidelines for using testimony gained from hypnosis. The guidelines require that a trained professional perform it and that the professional be independent of, rather than responsible to, the prosecution. The number of people present should be restricted to the hypnotist and the coordinator from the police agency who has knowledge of the case, the hypnotized individual's legal representative, and perhaps an artist who can draw a sketch based on any descriptions of suspects. And although forensic hypnosis has finally been accepted as a valuable crime-fighting tool, many states remain reluctant to allow testimony elicited from hypnosis into court.

The session should be video recorded. Questions should relate only to what the witness states under hypnosis. The witness should not be prompted or induced in any way.

Truth Serums. Truth serums are fast-acting barbiturates of the type used to produce sleep at the approximate level of surgical anesthesia. Alcohol produces somewhat the same effects to a much lesser degree. The theory is that the drug removes people's inhibitions so that they are more likely to tell the truth. In the past, scopolamine and hyoscine were the most used drugs, but sodium amatol and sodium pentothal are more commonly used today.

Truth serums are not used extensively by the police because the accuracy of the information obtained with them is questionable. Truth serum is administered by a physician, preferably a psychiatrist, who remains to monitor the person's condition while the questions are asked. The drugs can cause serious side effects, so the subject must be monitored continually. Some patients also become violently excited. Moreover, individuals vary greatly in their response to truth serums. Some can withhold information even under the influence of a large dose of the serum.

The courts do not officially recognize truth serums or their reliability, nor do they admit the results as evidence.

Using Criminal Profilers

Television shows have popularized the use of profilers in criminal investigations. Profiling combines art and science, resting on the premise that careful analysis of the crime scene and the crime will yield clues about the type of person who would commit such a crime. Effective profiling relies on the profiler's ability to combine investigative experience, training in forensic and behavioral sciences, and information about the characteristics of known offenders.

Information versus Intelligence

Information is simply raw data that, by itself, is of limited value. But information that is analyzed, interpreted, evaluated, refined, and connected to other information becomes *intelligence*. The FBI defines intelligence as both a *product* of information analysis and refinement and a *process* through which information is identified, collected, and analyzed.

> **LO10** Differentiate between information and intelligence.

Information or raw data is not intelligence. Information plus analysis equals intelligence.

Criminal intelligence drives investigations. Although law enforcement officers and agencies may be very skilled at collecting information, such data in isolation does not help generate the intelligence often required to solve complex cases. An "Intelligence Toolbox" training program is offered through Michigan State University as a quick-start program to help state, local, and tribal law enforcement agencies understand the intelligence process, which involves planning and direction (what to collect), collection, processing/collation, analysis, dissemination, and feedback or reevaluation (Law Enforcement Forecasting Group, 2012). This process is illustrated in Figure 6.6.

Often during a criminal investigation, information or intelligence collected by one agency must be shared with other agencies in the effort to generate leads that help solve the crime.

Sharing Information and Intelligence

In the beginning of this chapter, the vast amount of information available on the Internet was discussed. The Internet allows information related to criminal investigations to be shared across jurisdictional lines as never before. Since September 11, 2001, the sharing of information has become increasingly important as the United States focuses on homeland security. The key to combating terrorism lies with the local police and the intelligence they can provide to federal authorities. The role of police in the "war on terrorism" is discussed in Chapter 20.

Substantial obstacles prevent police agencies from sharing information, including competing local systems, myriad interfaces involving records management systems (RMSs) and computer-aided dispatch (CAD) systems used by various agencies that often overlap and conflict with each other, incompatible data formats and platforms, debate over who controls the data, security questions, cost, and training time and resources (Hollywood & Winkelman, 2015). To overcome the obstacle of incompatible data formats and enable federal, state, and local justice and public safety agencies to exchange data in a common, replicable format, the Global Justice XML Data Model (GJXDM) was developed in 2001. The successor to GJXDM is the National Information Exchange Model (NIEM), a partnership between the U.S. Department of Justice (DOJ), the Department of Homeland Security (DHS), and the Department of Health and Human Services (HHS) designed to develop and support standards and processes to facilitate efficient information exchange across public and private organizations nationwide.

Collaboration between law enforcement agencies is often required for the successful investigation of a crime. Here an ATF and an FBI agent look at a nail found outside of a nightclub that was bombed the previous night. The explosion injured five people. A second bomb was found by police and was detonated at the site.
Tami Chappell/Reuters

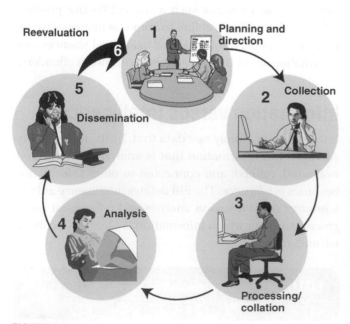

FIGURE 6.6
The intelligence process.

Source: *Intelligence-led policing: The new intelligence architecture.* Washington, DC: Bureau of Justice Assistance, September 2005, p. 6.

Another information sharing effort is the Regional Information Sharing Systems (RISS) Program, which was created more than 40 years ago and provides adaptive solutions and services to local, state, federal, and tribal criminal justice partners with the goals of facilitating information and intelligence sharing, supporting criminal investigations, and promoting officer safety (RISS, 2020). RISS is composed of six regional centers and the RISS Technology Support Center (RTSC). RISS works regionally and on a nationwide basis to respond to the unique crime problems of each region while strengthening the country's information sharing environment. More than 9,200 local, state, federal, and tribal law enforcement and public safety agencies are members of RISS. RISS is used and trusted by hundreds of thousands of law enforcement officers and criminal justice professionals in all 50 states, the District of Columbia, U.S. territories, England, New Zealand, and parts of Canada.

The National Data Exchange (N-DEx), developed by the Raytheon Corporation, is an unclassified national strategic investigative information sharing system that allows criminal justice agencies to search, link, analyze, and share local, state, tribal, and federal records (see Figure 6.7). The benefits to criminal investigators are numerous:

The N-DEx system provides detectives with immediate access to criminal justice records from thousands of agencies across the nation. Users can view incident reports, arrest reports, booking and incarceration reports, pre-trial investigations, and probation and parole records. The

N-DEx collaboration tool, which allows users to invite authorized members from other agencies to view and share information in a safe and secure online environment, enables users to team up with other investigators to quickly and securely share pertinent information, including images, videos, charts, graphs, notes, case reports, etc. Visualization tools graphically depict associations between people, places, things, and events on link-analysis charts or maps. With the subscription and notification feature, detectives are notified if other users are searching for the same criteria or if a new record related to one of their investigations enters the system (FBI, n.d.).

Although N-DEx is not an intelligence system, per se, and does not contain intelligence data, the information it can help investigators access is an extremely valuable resource to the intelligence community.

One of the most notable actions that resulted from the terrorist attacks of September 11, 2001, was the development and release of the National Criminal Intelligence Sharing Plan (NCISP) in 2003. The NCISP was the result of a partnership between the International Association of Chiefs of Police (IACP) and the U.S. Department of Justice and was designed to provide a path forward in improving the collection and analysis of information to create valuable and actionable intelligence products. Further, the NCISP highlighted that the sharing of intelligence products among state, local, tribal, and federal partners is critical in the prevention of terrorism and other criminal activity. The NCISP marked a transformation in

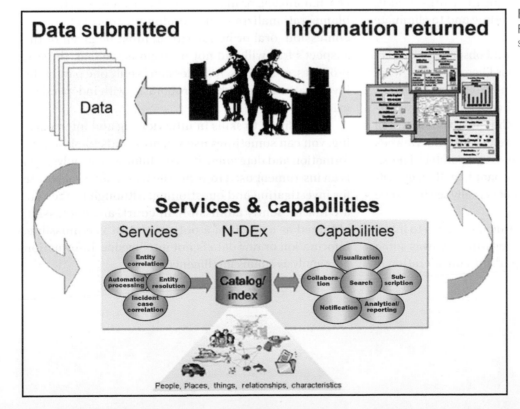

FIGURE 6.7
Flow of information in N-DEx.
Source: http://www.fbi.gov/about-us/cjis/n-dex/ndex_concept

American law enforcement, notably that every agency, regardless of size, has a stake in the development and sharing of criminal intelligence (DOJ, Bureau of Justice Assistance, 2013).

Fusion centers are another effective means for transforming information into intelligence and have been a worthy avenue by which to implement elements of the NCISP. A fusion center collects information from a variety of sources, including all levels of law enforcement, vets or assesses the information, analyzes it to identify trends or patterns in threats to public safety, and shares the information and intelligence with the necessary agencies (Serrao, 2012). Currently, 78 fusion centers of various sizes and capabilities exist across the country (McGhee, 2015). Fusion centers are discussed in greater depth in Chapter 20.

A natural outgrowth of these efforts to develop and share intelligence, particularly in our post-9/11 society, is the emergence of intelligence-led policing (ILP), a model that builds on community policing by combining problem-solving policing, information sharing, and police accountability with enhanced intelligence operations (LeCates, 2018). ILP has helped drive the concept of holistic investigations (DOJ, Bureau of Justice Assistance, 2012). Whereas criminal investigations have traditionally focused on a single crime or category of crimes, such as drugs, burglary, or homicide, law enforcement has long recognized that criminals often do not specialize, particularly if they are part of a gang or organized crime group. Given the increasing mobility of the public and the blurring of jurisdictional boundaries in some crimes, such as those involving the Internet, the need for law enforcement at all levels and in all areas of the country and, indeed, the world, to share information and intelligence has never been greater.

Summary

Most solved cases rely on both physical evidence and information obtained from a variety of sources. Important sources of information include (1) reports, records, and databases, including those found on the Internet; (2) people who are not suspects in the crime but who know something about the crime or those involved; and (3) suspects in the crime. The ultimate goal of interviewing and interrogating is to determine the truth—that is, to identify those responsible for a crime and to eliminate the innocent from suspicion.

To obtain information, listen and observe. Ask direct questions and open-ended questions liberally. Asking leading questions can also be a useful interrogation technique. Use indirect questions and closed-ended questions sparingly. Repetition is an effective technique to obtain recall and to uncover lies. Appeal to a reluctant interviewee's reason or emotions. Interview witnesses separately if possible. Interview the victim or complainant first, then eyewitnesses, and then people who did not actually see the crime but who have relevant information.

Although many of the same principles apply to interrogating and interviewing, interrogating involves some special considerations. One important consideration is when to give the *Miranda* warning, which informs suspects of their Fifth Amendment rights and must be given to any suspect who is interrogated about a crime while in custody. It is also important to conduct interrogations in a place that is private and free from interruptions. Interrogation techniques include inquiring directly or indirectly, forcing responses, deflating or inflating the ego, minimizing or maximizing the crime, projecting the blame, rationalizing, and combining approaches. Any confession, oral or handwritten, must be given of the suspect's free will and not in response to fear, threats, promises, or rewards. A confession is only one part of the investigation. It must be corroborated with independent evidence.

In addition to skills in interviewing and interrogating, you can sometimes use scientific aids to obtain information and determine its truthfulness. The polygraph is an instrument used to verify the truth, not a substitute for investigating and questioning. Although the results are not presently admissible in court, any confession obtained as a result of a polygraph test is admissible. Information or raw data is not intelligence. Information plus analysis equals intelligence.

Can You Define?

admission

adoptive admission

beachheading

closed-ended question

cognitive interview

complainant

confession

confidential (reliable) informant (CRI)

custodial arrest

custodial interrogation

direct question

dying declaration

field interview

implicit bias

in custody

indirect question

informant

information age

interrogation

interview

leading question

microaggression

Miranda warning

network

nonverbal communication

open-ended question

polygraph

public safety exception

rapport

sources-of-information file

statement

statement analysis

testimonial hearsay

third degree

waiver

Checklist

Obtaining Information

- Were the complainant, witnesses, victim, and informants questioned?

- Were all witnesses found?

- Was all information recorded accurately?

- Was the questioning conducted in an appropriate place? At an appropriate time?

- Was the *Miranda* warning given to all suspects before questioning about the crime(s)?

- Were the type of offense and offender considered in selecting the interviewing or interrogating techniques?

- Were answers obtained to the questions of who, what, where, when, why, and how?

- Were checks made of all available reports and records? The sources-of-information file? Field-identification cards? The NCIC? Other police agencies? Public and private agencies at the local, county, state, and national levels?

- Were CIs sought?

- Was a request for public assistance or an offer of a reward published?

- Is there a private number to call or a private post office box to write to that persons who have information about a crime can use?

- Was a polygraph used to check the validity of information given?

- Were all statements, admissions, and confessions rechecked against other verbal statements and against existing physical evidence?

- Were those providing information thanked for their help?

- Were all statements, admissions, and confessions properly and legally obtained? Recorded? Witnessed? Filed?

References

Bang, B. L., Stanton, D., Hemmens, C., & Stohr, M. K. (2018, January 10). Police recording of custodial interrogations: A state-by-state legal inquiry. *International Journal of Police Science & Management 20*(1). doi:10.1177/1461355717750172

Bassett, J. W. (2013, October 21). *Self portraits of innocence and guilt: An investigator's casebook.* Kindle version published by author.

Boetig, B. (2010, June). Fundamentals of a successful neighborhood canvass. *Law and Order,* pp. 66–70.

Chew, S. L. (2018, August 20). Myth: Eyewitness testimony is the best kind of evidence. Association for Psychological Science. Retrieved June 19, 2020, from www.psychologicalscience.org/teaching/myth-eyewitness-testimony-is-the-best-kind-of-evidence.html

Clark, A. (2017, August 24). The harmful effects of implicit racial bias in the police. Madison: WI: University of Madison-Wisconsin, Department of Sociology. Blog by Pamela Oliver. Retrieved June 19, 2020, from www .ssc.wisc.edu/soc/racepoliticsjustice/2017/08/24 /the-harmful-effects-of-implicit-racial-bias-in-the-police/

Cleary, H. (2019). Electronic recording of police interrogations. *VCU Scholars Compass*. Richmond, VA: Virginia Commonwealth University, Center for Public Policy. Retrieved June 25, 2020, from scholarscompass.vcu .edu/cgi/viewcontent.cgi?article=1005&context=resear ch-fellows

Damphouse, K. R. (2008, March). Voice stress analysis: Only 15 percent of lies about drug use detected in field test. *NIJ Journal, 259*: 8–13. (NCJ 221500)

Dasgupta, N. (2013). Implicit attitudes and beliefs adapt to situations: A decade of research on the malleability of implicit prejudice, stereotypes, and the self-concept. In *Advances in Experimental Social Psychology, 47*: 233–279. San Diego, CA: Academic Press.

Davis, D., Leo, R. A., & Follette, W. C. (2010, September). Selling confession: Setting the stage with the "Sympathetic Detective with a Limited-Time Offer." *Journal of Contemporary Criminal Justice, 26*(4): 441–457.

Department of Justice, Bureau of Justice Assistance. (2012, September 25). *Reducing crime through intelligence-led policing*. Washington, DC: Author. Retrieved June 29, 2020, from bja.ojp.gov/sites/g/files/xyckuh186/files /Publications/ReducingCrimeThroughILP.pdf

Department of Justice, Bureau of Justice Assistance. (2013, October). *National criminal intelligence sharing plan: Building a national capability for effective criminal intelligence development and the nationwide sharing of intelligence and information*. Washington, DC: Author. Retrieved June 29, 2020, from bja.ojp.gov/library /publications/national-criminal-intelligence-sharing -plan-building-national-capability

Devereaux, R. (2016, September 30). DEA's army of 18,000 informants pocketed $237 million over five years. *The Intercept*. Retrieved June 19, 2020, from theintercept .com/2016/09/30/deas-army-of-18000-informants -pocketed-237-million-over-five-years/

Drake, J. J. (2014, January). Knock and talk no more. *Maine Law Review 67*(1): 25–42. Retrieved June 19, 2020, from digitalcommons.mainelaw.maine.edu/cgi/viewcontent .cgi?article=1080&context=mlr

Federal Bureau of Investigation. (2017). NCIC turns 50: Centralized database continues to prove its value in fighting crime. Retrieved April 24, 2021, from www.fbi.gov /news/stories/ncic-turns-50

Federal Bureau of Justice. (n.d.). *National data exchange (N-DEx) system*. Washington, DC: Author. Retrieved June 29, 2020, from www.fbi.gov/services/cjis/ndex

Gross, S., & Possley, M. (2016, June 12). *For 50 years, you've had "the right to remain silent."* Ann Arbor, MI: University of Michigan Law School. Retrieved June 27, 2020, from www .law.umich.edu/special/exoneration/Pages/False -Confessions-.aspx

Hager, E. (2017, March 7). The seismic change in police interrogations. New York, NY: The Marshall Project. Retrieved June 26, 2020, from www .themarshallproject.org/2017/03/07/the-seismic -change-in-police-interrogations

Harr, J. S., Hess, K. M., Orthmann, C. H., & Kingsbury, J. (2018). *Constitutional law and the criminal justice system* (7th ed.). Boston, MA: Cengage Learning.

High-Value Detainee Interrogation Group (HIG). (2016, September). *Interrogation: A review of the science*. Washington, DC: Federal Bureau of Investigation. Retrieved June 27, 2020, from www.hsdl.org/?view&did=800243

Hollywood, J. S., & Winkelman, Z. (2015). *Improving information sharing across law enforcement: Why can't we know?* Santa Monica, CA: Rand. Retrieved June 29, 2020, from www.ncjrs.gov/pdffiles1/nij/grants/249187.pdf

Hood, M. B., & Hoffman, L. J. (2019, November 6). Current state of interview and interrogation. *FBI Law Enforcement Bulletin*. Retrieved June 27, 2020, from leb.fbi.gov/articles/featured-articles /current-state-of-interview-and-interrogation

Howes, L. M. (2019, May 16). Interpreted investigative interviews under the PEACE interview model: Police interviewers' perceptions of challenges and suggested solutions. *Police Practice and Research*. doi:10.1080/156142 63.2019.1617145

Hritz, A. C. (2017, January). Voluntariness with a vengeance: The coerciveness of police lies in interrogations. *Cornell Law Review 102*(2), Article 4: 487–511. Retrieved June 27, 2020, from scholarship.law.cornell.edu/clr/vol102/iss2/4

International Association of Chiefs of Police. (2017). *Confidential informants*. Alexandria, VA: Author. Retrieved June 19, 2020, from www.theiacp.org/sites/default/files /all/c/ConfidentialInformantsPaper2017.pdf

Kassin, S. M., Russano, M. B., Amrom, A. D., Hellgren, J., Kukucka, J., & Lawson, V. Z. (2019). Does video recording inhibit crime suspects? Evidence from a fully randomized field experiment. *Law and Human Behavior, 43*(1): 45–55. doi:10.1037/lhb0000319

Kelly, C. E., & Meissner, C. A. (2017). Interrogation and investigative interviewing in the United States: Research and practice. Chapter 21 in *International Developments and Practices in Investigative Interviewing and Interrogation* (Vol. 2: Suspects). Edited by D. Walsh, G. E. Oxburgh, A. D. Redlich, & T. Myklebust. New York, NY: Routledge.

Kozinski, W. (2018, April 14). The Reid interrogation technique and false confessions: A time for change. *Seattle Journal for Social Justice, 16*(2), Article 10: 311–345. Retrieved June 26, 2020, from digitalcommons.law.seattleu.edu/cgi /viewcontent.cgi?article=1905&context=sjsj

Law Enforcement Forecasting Group. (2012, June). *Increasing analytic capacity of state and local law enforcement agencies: Moving beyond data analysis to create a vision for change*. Washington, DC: Author. Retrieved June 29, 2020, from bja .ojp.gov/sites/g/files/xyckuh186/files/Publications /LEFGIncreasingAnalyticCapacity.pdf

Law Officer. (2016, January 8). Investigations: Establishing informant reliability. Retrieved

June 19, 2020, from www.lawofficer.com /investigations-establishing-informant-reliability/

LeCates, R. (2018, October 17). Intelligence-led policing: Changing the face of crime prevention. *Police Chief Online*. Retrieved May 5, 2021 from www.policechiefmagazine.org /changing-the-face-crime-prevention/?ref=4f1d967f817ac8 11b21c97eea171a4d4

McClish, M. (2014, December). The McStay family murders. *Statement Analysis*. Retrieved June 18, 2020, from www .statementanalysis.com/cases/mcstay-family/

McClish, M. (2021). Statement Analysis®: The most accurate way of detecting deception. Retrieved April 26, 2021, from www.statementanalysis.com/

McGhee, S. (2015, February). Impacting the evolution of information sharing in the post9/11 United States. *The Police Chief*, pp. 26–31.

McLeod, S. (2015). Cognitive psychology. *Simply Psychology*. Retrieved June 26, 2020, from www.simplypsychology.org /cognitive.html

Melinder, A., Magnusson, M., & Gilstrap, L. L. (2020). What is a child-appropriate interview? Interaction between child witnesses and police officers. *International Journal on Child Maltreatment*. doi:10.1007/s42448-020-00052-8

Mitchell, R. J., & James, L. (n.d.). Addressing the elephant in the room: The need to evaluate implicit bias training effectiveness for improving fairness in police officer decision-making. *Police Chief Magazine*. Retrieved June 19, 2020, from www.policechiefmagazine.org/addressing-the -elephant-in-the-room/?ref=805f2482a67f556b2215076044 6857c9

Murgado, A. (2017, November 3). How to conduct an area canvass. *Police Magazine*. Retrieved June 18, 2020, from www.policemag.com/342350 /how-to-conduct-an-area-canvass

Nyberg, R. (2006, July). Going door to door. *Police*, pp. 36–40.

Patil, V. P., Nayak, K. K., & Saxena, M. (2013). Voice stress detection. *International Journal of Electrical, Electronics, and Computer Engineering* 2(2): 148–154. ISSN No. (online) 2277-2626. doi:10.1.1.669.502

Ramsay, K., Lipman, M. D., & Small, J. (2015, February 10). Time is the enemy in solving the McStay family killings. *CNN Online*. Retrieved March 16, 2015, from www.cnn .com/2015/02/03/us/mcstay-family-chase-merritt/

Regional Information Sharing Systems Program (RISS). (2020). *About the RISS program*. Retrieved June 29, 2020, from www .riss.net/about-us/

Rutledge, D. (2007, March). Cold case interrogations. *Police*, pp. 70–72.

Rutledge, D. (2008, March). The *Bruton* rule. *Police*, pp. 61–63.

Rutledge, D. (2010, April). Miranda wording. *Police*, pp. 60–61.

Serrao, S. G. (2012, January/February). What's changed in law enforcement intelligence analysis since 9/11? *Public Safety IT*. Retrieved March 16, 2015, from www.hendonpub.com /resources/article_archive/results/details?id=1157

Sikes, S. K. (2018). Get off my porch: *United States v. Carloss* and the escalating dangers of "knock and talks." *Oklahoma Law Review 70*(2): 493–517. Retrieved June 19, 2020, from digitalcommons.law.ou.edu/cgi/viewcontent .cgi?article=1322&context=olr

Simon, J. (2019, July 31). *Michigan v. Frederick*: A chance to clarify law enforcement's knock-and-talk procedures. *University of Cincinnati Law Review*. Retrieved June 19, 2020, from uclawreview.org/2019/07/31/michigan-v-frederick -a-chance-to-clarify-law-enforcements-knock-and-talk -procedures/

Snook, B., Luther, K., Quinlan, H., & Milne, R. (2012, October). Let 'em talk! A field study of police questioning practices of suspects and accused persons. *Criminal Justice and Behavior 39*(10): 1328–1339. doi:10.1177/0093854812449216

Starr, D. (2019, June 13). This psychologist explains why people confess to crimes they didn't commit. *Science Magazine*. Retrieved June 26, 2020, from www.sciencemag.org /news/2019/06/psychologist-explains-why-people-confess -crimes-they-didn-t-commit

Tyner, A. R. (2019, August 26). Unconscious bias, implicit bias, and microaggressions: What can we do about them? Washington, DC: American Bar Association. Retrieved June 19, 2020, from www.americanbar.org /groups/gpsolo/publications/gp_solo/2019/july-august /unconscious-bias-implicit-bias-microaggressions-what- can-we-do-about-them/

Van Puyvelde, M., Neyt, X., McGlone, F., & Pattyn, N. (2018, November 20). Voice stress analysis: A new framework for voice and effort in human performance. *Frontiers in Psychology*. doi:10.3389/fpsyg.2018.01994

Voigt, R., Camp, N. P., Prabhakaran, V., Hamilton, W. L., Hetey, R. C., Griffiths, . . . Eberhardt, J. L. (2017, June 5). Language from police body camera footage shows racial disparities in officer respect. *Proceedings of the National Academy of Sciences of the United States of America*. doi:10.1073 /pnas.1702413114

Welty, J. (2018a, June 4). Even when the controlled buys happen at the back door, knock and talks must happen at the front door. Chapel Hill, NC: University of North Carolina School of Government. Retrieved June 18, 2020, from nccriminallaw.sog.unc.edu/9309-2/

Welty, J. (2018b, June 11). What everyone needs to know about knock and talks. Chapel Hill, NC: University of North Carolina School of Government. Retrieved June 19, 2020, nccriminallaw.sog.unc.edu /what-everyone-needs-to-know-about-knock-and-talks/

Cases Cited

Alabama v. White, 496 U.S. 325 (1990).

Berkemer v. McCarty, 468 U.S. 420 (1984).

Brewer v. Williams, 430 U.S. 387 (1977).

Bruton v. United States, 391 U.S. 123 (1968).

Burket v. Angelone, 208 F.3d 172 (4th Cir. 2000).

Crawford v. Washington, 541 U.S. 36 (2004).

Davis v. United States, 512 U.S. 452 (1994).

Dickerson v. United States, 530 U.S. 428 (2000).

Dormire v. Wilkinson, 249 F.3d. 801 (8th Cir. 2001).

Edwards v. Arizona, 451 U.S. 477 (1981).

Fellers v. United States, 540 U.S. 519 (2004).

Florida v. Jardines, 569 U.S. 1 (2013).

Florida v. Powell, 559 U.S. 50 (2010).

Frazier v. Cupp, 394 U.S. 731 (1969).

Illinois v. Perkins, 496 U.S. 292 (1990).

Kentucky v. King, 563 U.S. 452, 469 (2011).

Maryland v. Shatzer, 559 U.S. 98 (2010).

Michigan v. Frederick, 140 S.Ct. 114 (2019).

Minnesota v. Murphy, 465 U.S. 420 (1984).

Miranda v. Arizona, 384 U.S. 436 (1966).

Missouri v. Seibert, 542 U.S. 600 (2004).

Moore v. Hopper, 389 F. Supp. 931 (M.D. Ga. 1974).

New York v. Quarles, 467 U.S. 649 (1984).

Nix v. Williams, 467 U.S. 431 (1984).

Oregon v. Mathiason, 429 U.S. 492 (1977).

People v. Thomas, 22 N.Y. 3d 629 (N.Y. Court of Appeals 2014).

Sorrells v. United States, 287 U.S. 435 (1932).

State v. Huddy, 253 N.C. App. 148, 799 S.E.2d 650 (2017).

United States v. Banks, 540 U.S. 31 (2003).

United States ex rel. Caminito v. Murphy, 222 F.2d 698 (2nd Cir. 1955).

United States v. Crapser, 472 F.3d 1141 (9th Cir. 2007).

United States v. Patane, 542 U.S. 630 (2004).

United States v. Russell, 411 U.S. 423 (1973).

United States v. Scheffer, 523 U.S. 303 (1998).

Wong Sun v. United States, 371 U.S. 471 (1963).

Yarborough v. Alvarado, 541 U.S. 652 (2004).

Chapter 7
Identifying and Arresting Suspects

Learning Objectives

LO1 Explain what field identification is, when it is used, and the rights a suspect has during such an event.

LO2 Identify the various sources commonly accessed for help in developing a suspect.

LO3 Describe the basic techniques used to identify a suspect, including what each requires, when they are used, and what rights a suspect has during each.

LO4 Explain when surveillance is used, what its objectives are, and the basic types of surveillance commonly deployed in criminal investigation.

LO5 List the objectives of undercover assignments and the precautions officers working undercover should take.

LO6 Summarize the objectives of raids, what to consider before conducting a raid, and precautions to take when conducting a raid.

LO7 List the circumstances under which police officers are authorized to make an arrest.

LO8 Identify the elements that constitute an arrest having been made.

LO9 Explain how much force is justified when making an arrest.

Introduction

Monday, April 15, 2013, was a sunny spring day in Boston, a holiday—Patriots Day—a day to celebrate the free and passionately independent character of the city, and a day that attracted the world to its streets, year after year, in the spirit of friendly competition (Russell & Farragher, 2013):

> Hundreds of thousands of spectators lined the 26.2-mile course from Hopkinton to the Back Bay, many holding signs and offering cups of water to runners. In the city's favorite rite of spring, they cheered on friends, loved ones, and strangers trailing far behind the clusters of elite athletes.
>
> Few noticed the two young men, one in a black baseball cap, the other in a white hat turned backward, as they rounded the corner from Gloucester Street onto Boylston Street at 2:38 p.m. Each carried a bulky backpack. They strode toward the finish line where just a short time earlier the governor had hugged race organizers.
>
> Along the way, they put down their bags, paused several minutes, and left the scene....

The Marathon clock, showing the time since the start of the race, flashed 4:09:43. Some 5,700 runners were still on the course. The time was 2:49 P.M. For one final instant, everything was normal.

Then, two explosions ripped through the sidelines of the race, 12 seconds and 214 yards apart, setting in motion a series of extraordinary, unthinkable, indelible events and triggering the largest manhunt in New England history. . . .

In the immediate aftermath of the attack, which left 3 people dead and more than 140 injured, the 2 bombers, brothers Tamerlan and Dzhokhar Tsarnaev, slipped quietly back into the city and resumed their normal routines, seemingly unconcerned that thousands of investigators would soon be looking for them:

Within minutes of establishing the command post . . . , [police commissioner] Davis . . . issued the first order to collect video. Investigators, led by Boston Police Sergeant Detective Bill Perkins, began going after surveillance cameras from surrounding businesses. . . .

[L]aw enforcement analysts at FBI headquarters in Boston's Center Plaza got to work reviewing the torrent of videotapes of Boylston Street that were streaming in from businesses and ordinary spectators alike. Eventually, more than 100 analysts were painstakingly reviewing thousands of hours of surveillance and amateur videotape for anything suspicious. . . .

By early the next morning, hundreds of investigators had descended on the area, documenting evidence, labeling objects of interest, and combing the blast scene. And by Tuesday afternoon, 19-year-old Dzhokhar

was back on campus at the University of Massachusetts–Dartmouth, apparently unconcerned by any thought of being apprehended:

"I'm a stress-free kind of guy," he tweeted after midnight.

But back in Boston, investigators . . . had begun to see a pattern among the various videos, their attention drawn especially to two young men walking east along Boylston Street in the 12 minutes before the explosions.

Neither seemed particularly worried about hiding their appearance—the man in the white hat even turned his cap around backward, giving the cameras a full shot of his profile. Suspect number 2, as he became known, talks nonchalantly on his cellphone, then scarcely reacts at all when the first bomb goes off.

When Alben, of the State Police, saw the results of the analysts' work on Wednesday morning, he couldn't believe it: they had captured an image of the young man in a white hat dropping a backpack outside the Forum restaurant and then walking away.

"There was a eureka moment. . . . It was right there for you to see," said the colonel. "It was quite clear to me we had a breakthrough in the case." . . .

They had faces. Now they needed names. . . .

A key question, with game-changing consequences, was bearing down on the men in charge: to release the photos to the public or to hold them close?

The wrong move could be deadly. But with the bombers still at large, they had to decide soon. . . .

"There is a huge conundrum here that if you release the photos, if they haven't fled the Boston area they are going to flee,"

Alben said. "You would always prefer to identify them yourself. You always want to apprehend someone when you have control of the situation, not when someone has been tipped you're coming through the door." . . .

Sixty miles away at UMass Dartmouth, Dzhokhar Tsarnaev used his swipe card to enter his dorm at 4:02 P.M. He had one more hour of anonymity remaining. . . .

[Then] the FBI released images of the suspects . . . . [and] Dzhokhar's life as a "stress free kind of guy" who sold pot on the side to raise pocket money was about to end. By the time he arrived back in Cambridge sometime that night, his face would be known to millions, and tips about his identity would be pouring in to federal agents.

At trial in 2015, a jury found Tsarnaev guilty of all 30 charges against him. He received six death sentences and eleven concurrent life sentences, but an appellate court overturned the death sentences in July 2020. In March 2021 the U.S. Supreme Court agreed to reconsider reinstating the death sentences during its next term, which begins October 2021. Tsarnaev remains behind bars at the U.S. Penitentiary Florence-High in Colorado.

The classic question in detective stories is "Whodunit?" This question is also critical in criminal investigations. In some cases, the suspect is obvious. However, in most cases, there is no suspect initially. Although many crimes are witnessed, victims and witnesses may not recognize or be able to describe the suspect. Further, many crimes are not witnessed.

Recall from Chapter 1 that **solvability factors** are those elements of information that are crucial to resolving criminal investigations, one of the most important being whether a suspect can be named or at least described and located. However, even if a suspect is known or has confessed, you must prove the elements of the crime and establish evidence connecting the suspect with the criminal act. Some cases require that suspects be developed, located, identified, and then arrested. Others begin with an arrest and proceed to identification. No set sequence exists. Regardless of whether an arrest begins or ends an investigation, the arrest must be legal.

Identifying Suspects at the Scene

If a suspect is at the scene, you can use the person's driver's license, mobile identification technology, or field or show-up identification.

Identification by Driver's License

Technology has advanced by leaps and bounds since the first driver's license was issued more than 100 years ago. As an unfortunate consequence, today's driver's licenses and their rightful owners have fallen victim to theft, forgery, and counterfeiting. According to multiple reports, all 19 of the September 11, 2001, hijackers had used valid driver's licenses to pass through airport security. By some accounts, these 19 men held as many as 63 driver's licenses between them.

In an effort to make driver's licenses more secure, Congress passed the REAL ID Act of 2005, requiring states to take new steps to verify the identity of applicants before issuing driver's licenses and other ID cards. At the time this text goes to press, 95 million compliant

IDs have been issued throughout the country and 47 states and territories are deemed compliant, meaning they have implemented the procedures required by the Act to verify the identity of the drivers seeking licenses. In the meantime, bills continue to be introduced into Congress aimed at amending or repealing REAL ID.

Asking to see a suspect's driver's license is routine. However, often suspects do not carry identification or, if they do, it may be fake. Investigators need to determine whether licenses are legitimate as well as whether they belong to those using them. One aid in determining authenticity of driver's licenses is the *Drivers License Guide*, which contains information and graphics of more than 200 driver's licenses, as well as other documents commonly used for identification. If a hardcopy of this publication is not readily available, it may be accessed online.

Biometric Identification

Biometrics was introduced in Chapter 5 as a way to positively identify an individual. Common physiological or behavioral characteristics measured in biometric analysis include fingerprints, palm vein patterns, facial geometry, iris and retina patterns, and voice or speech prints, features that are well established, genetically determined, and distinctive for each individual.

Facial recognition software can help an officer positively identify an individual during a face-to-face interaction. Some police agencies use images from public sources, such as department of corrections databases or motor vehicle records, and others have arranged, through legal avenues, to have access to privately-owned image galleries, such as those maintained by sports venue security firms (Law Enforcement Imaging Technology Task Force, 2019). An image captured by an in-car or body-worn camera can be compared with images contained in these databases.

The Repository for Individuals of Special Concern (RISC), established in 2011 by the FBI as part of its Next Generation Identification (NGI) system, uses a mobile identification (ID) device to allow officers in the field to have on-scene access to a national database of wants and warrants including the National Sex Offender Registry, the Immigration Violator File (IVF), known or suspected terrorists, and other persons of special interest (Criminal Justice Information Services Division, 2020). This rapid search service boasts an average response time of 8 seconds and, as of January 2018, contained records of more than 2.7 million persons of concern (Mentalix, 2018).

Technology Innovations

FIVE-0 Fingerprint Scanner

Integrated Biometrics develops and manufactures seven FBI-certified fingerprint biometric scanners that use light emitting sensor (LES) technology that allows their devices to work in direct sunlight; on dry, dirty, or moist fingers; and under demanding conditions such as exposure to cold, heat, humidity, and abrasive materials such as dust and dirt. One of these scanners, the Five-0, is lightweight (6.76 oz.) and small enough to fit inside a shirt pocket, yet can provide complete mobile 10-finger enrollment, verification, and booking. It resists latent fingerprints and can run for hours using power provided by a smartphone, requiring no separate battery. The Five-0 saves time and improves officer safety by enrolling or confirming an individual's identity at the first point of contact since the device needs only a smartphone and cellular or Wi-Fi service to operate.

Source: Integrated Biometrics (2020). https://integratedbiometrics.com/

Field or Show-Up Identification

If a suspect is apprehended while committing a crime, you can have witnesses identify the suspect in the field. The same is generally true if the suspect is apprehended at or near the crime scene shortly after the commission of the crime. A field or show-up identification is an officer-arranged identification procedure in which the police bring a single person before a witness and ask the witness if they recognize that person as the suspect.

> **L01** Explain what field identification is, when it is used, and the rights a suspect has during such an event.

Field identification or **show-up identification** is on-the-scene identification of a suspect by a victim of or witness to a crime. Field or show-up identification must be made within a short time after the crime was committed.

The critical element in a field identification is *time*. Identification must occur very soon after the crime was committed (usually 15 to 20 minutes). If the suspect has fled but is apprehended within minutes, you can either return the suspect to the scene or take the witness to where the suspect was apprehended. It is usually preferable to take the witness to the suspect than to return the suspect to the crime scene. Although case law often defines the time and distance limits allowed for such procedures, officers typically adhere to a two-hour cutoff time following the commission of a crime in which to perform a show-up (National Academies of Science [NAS], 2014).

Whether the identification is made at or away from the scene, the victim or witness must identify the suspect as soon after the crime as possible so that details are still clear. However, a reasonable basis must exist for believing that immediate identification is required before using field identification.

LO1 Explain what field identification is, when it is used, and the rights a suspect has during such an event.

United States v. Ash, Jr. (1973) established that a suspect does not have the right to have counsel present at a field identification.

Read suspects the *Miranda* warning before questioning them about a crime. Suspects may refuse to answer questions and may demand a lawyer before any questioning occurs, but they do not have the right to have a lawyer present before field identification is made. Suspects may not even know such identification is occurring. Victims or witnesses may be positioned so they can see the suspect but the suspect cannot see them. Have the victim or witnesses put their positive identification in writing and sign and date it and then have it witnessed.

Show-up identifications have been attacked on the basis that the victim or witness is too emotionally upset at the time to make an accurate identification. While research about the reliability of the show-up procedure is scant, the few studies that have been done tend to show that this method of identification is highly suggestive and likely to result in innocent people being falsely identified as suspects (Sjöberg, 2016). One study found that a significant percentage of witnesses mistakenly identify the first "suspect" they are presented with at a show-up, and that the innocence risk (the probability that the "suspect" was more likely to be innocent than guilty) exceeds 50% after the witness was presented with a second show-up (Smith et al., 2014). Innocence risk continues to increase with each additional show-up, as do false positives.

Developing Suspects

If a suspect is not at the scene and not apprehended nearby, you must develop a suspect.

LO2 Identify the various sources commonly accessed for help in developing a suspect.

Suspects are developed through several means:

- Information provided by victims, witnesses, and other persons likely to know about the crime or the suspect
- Physical evidence left at the crime scene
- Informants
- Modus operandi information
- Psychological and geographic profiling
- Information in police files and the files of other agencies
- Tracking
- Other information aids, such as news media (TV, radio, newsprint) and social media requests to the public for information

---

Many sources are sometimes needed to develop a suspect. Most of these sources were introduced in the preceding chapter, including informants. At other times, the victim or witnesses provide the required information. Then your task is to corroborate the identification through associative evidence such as fingerprints or DNA analysis, shoe prints, personal belongings, and other such evidence left at the scene as described in Chapter 5. Police agencies also have automated fingerprint identification systems and computerized imaging systems to assist in identifying suspects.

Victims and Witnesses

Developing a suspect is much easier if the victim or witnesses can describe and identify the person who committed the crime. Rather than simply asking a witness to describe a suspect, ask specific questions about each item in Table 7.1. Also obtain information about how the suspect left the scene—on foot or in a vehicle.

Witnesses may not have observed the actual crime but may have seen a vehicle leaving the scene and can describe it and its occupants. They may have also captured a complete or partial license plate number. The prevalence of cell phones with cameras has enabled bystanders to collect value information that can help police develop criminal suspects. Identifying the car may lead to identifying the suspect. Officers should also check for video from another source near the crime scene.

TABLE 7.1 **Key Items in Suspect Identification**
Gender
Height
Weight
Build—stout, average, slim; stooped, square-shouldered
Age
Race
Face—long, round, square; fat, thin; pimples, acne, scars
Complexion—flushed, sallow; pale, fair, dark
Hair—color; thick, thin, partly bald, completely bald; straight, curly, wavy; long, short
Forehead—high, low; sloping, straight, bulging
Eyebrows—bushy, thin, average
Eyes—color; close together or wide-set; large, small; glasses or sunglasses
Nose—small, large; broad, narrow; crooked, straight; long, short
Ears—small, large; close to head or protruding; pierced
Mustache—color; short, long; thick, thin; pointed ends
Mouth—large, small; drooping, upturned
Lips—thick, thin
Teeth—missing, broken, prominent, gold, conspicuous dental work
Beard—color; straight, rounded; bushy, thin; long, short
Chin—square, round, broad; long, narrow; double, sagging
Neck—long, short; thick, thin
Distinctive marks—scars, moles, amputations, tattoos, birthmarks
Peculiarities—peculiar walk or talk, twitch, stutter, foreign accent, distinctive voice or dialect
Clothing—shabby or well dressed, monograms, association with an occupation or hobby, general description
Weapon (if any)—specific type, how carried, how displayed and when
Jewelry—any obvious rings, bracelets, necklaces, earrings, watches

Victims can provide information about who has a motive for the crime, who has the knowledge required to commit it, and who is not a likely suspect. For example, in an "inside" burglary, the employer may be able to provide important information about which employees may or may not be suspects.

Eyewitness identification is highly fallible because of factors such as poor visibility, brief duration, distance, the presence of distractions, and faulty memory (Albright, 2017). Because of such problems with witness identification, victim or eyewitness identification of a suspect should be corroborated by as much physical and circumstantial evidence as possible.

Booking Photos. If the victim or witness does not know the suspect but saw that person clearly, identification through booking photos (mug shots) may be attempted. However, this procedure, frequently depicted in television detective shows, is very time-consuming and is of value only if the suspect has a police record and has been photographed. Using facial recognition to scan the face of a suspect against a database of thousands of booking photos helps officers pare down a list of suspects or solve a case.

The Integrated Law Enforcement Face-Identification System (ILEFIS) deploys a three-dimensional system to match images from surveillance or still photographs to existing booking photos with a high degree of accuracy.

Composite Drawings and Sketches. If witnesses can provide adequate information, a composite image can be made of the person who committed the crime. Composite drawings are most commonly used to draw human faces or full bodies, but they can also be used for any inanimate object described by a witness—for example, vehicles, unusual marks or symbols, tattoos, or clothing.

Composite sketches can also be created using a computerized identification kit such as Identi-Kit®, although some training is required to use it. Identi-Kit Version 7.0 is a computerized version of the original Identi-Kit, developed in the late 1950s. The process starts with a police officer asking a series of initial questions, which creates a general likeness of a suspect based on a victim's or witness's description. After creating a general composite, officers can fine-tune the image of the criminal. Figure 7.1 illustrates how Identi-Kit helps develop suspects. Other software such as CompuSketch or SketchCop® FACETTE is also becoming more popular for drafting computer-generated composites.

Modus Operandi Information

A series of crimes often creates a recognizable modus operandi (MO). For instance, a forger may use the same or a very similar name on each forgery, or a burglar may take the same type of property. If a series of burglaries occurs at the same time of day, this may be the suspect's time away from a regular job. For example, if several burglaries are committed between 11 A.M. and 1 P.M. in one area of a community and all involve broken glass in a door, one may infer that the same individual committed the crimes. The probability of the burglaries being unrelated is low. One may further assume that the burglar would not commit armed robbery or other crimes unless surprised while committing a burglary.

Such assumptions are *not certainties*, however. Some criminals commit several types of crimes and may change the type according to need, opportunity, inability to

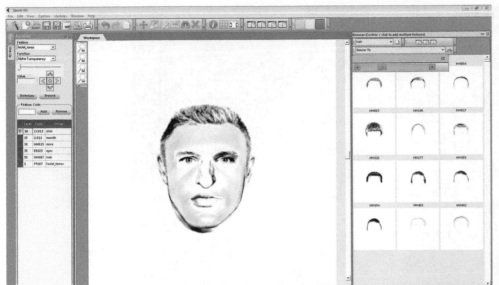

Figure 7.1
Computerized composite sketch applications, such as Identi-Kit®, help investigators work with victims and witnesses to generate more accurate images of suspects.
Source: © Identi-Kit Solutions. www.identikit.net

repeat certain types of crimes, or greater sophistication. For example, a narcotics user may commit larceny, burglary, or robbery to obtain money for drugs. A burglar may switch from targeting residences to engaging in shoplifting or may first steal checks and a check writer and then turn to forgery to cash the checks. Nonetheless, recognizable MOs can furnish important investigative leads.

Check the details of a specific crime against your department's MO files, as well as those of surrounding agencies, since criminals are often quite mobile. If no similar MO is listed, a new criminal may be starting activity in your area, or this may be the only crime the suspect intends to commit. In such cases, the suspect must be developed through sources other than MO information, such as information contained in a psychological or criminal profile.

Psychological or Criminal Profiling

One method of suspect identification is **psychological** or **criminal profiling**, which attempts to identify an individual's mental, emotional, and psychological characteristics. Profiles are developed primarily for violent acts such as homicides, sadistic crimes, sex crimes, arson without apparent motive, and crimes of serial or ritual sequence. The profile provides investigators with corroborative information about a known suspect or possible leads to an unknown suspect.

The psychological profile is determined by examining all data and evidence from a specific crime scene, including but not limited to crime scene photographs, detailed photos of bodily injuries to victims, photos of any mutilation evidence, information related to the condition of the victim's clothing or absence thereof, information regarding whether the crime scene was altered or unaltered, photos of the area beyond the immediate crime scene, available maps of the area, the medical examiner's report and opinion, and any other relevant information concerning the crime, particularly abnormalities such as multiple slashings, disembowelment, or dismembering of the body. Specific information is then categorized to produce predictive information regarding the suspect's likely age, sex, race, weight, and height; physical, mental, and psychological condition; area of residence; whether known to the victim; whether the suspect has a criminal record; and other details.

The psychological profile produced by experts in criminal behavior analysis can provide excellent leads for investigators. Investigators who desire such assistance may provide a complete crime report to the local office of the FBI. If the report is accepted, it is then forwarded to the National Center for the Analysis of Violent Crime (NCAVC), which provides behavioral-based investigative support to the FBI; national security agencies; and other federal, state, local, and international law enforcement agencies that are involved in the investigation of unusual or repetitive violent crimes, threats, terrorism, cybercrime, white-collar crime, and public corruption. The three units within the NCAVC are as follows (FBI, *National Center*, n.d.):

- Behavioral Analysis Unit (BAU)—East/West Regions: helps law enforcement agencies by providing "criminal investigative analysis" in which crimes are reviewed from both a behavioral and investigative perspective to assess the facts of a criminal act and interpret offender behavior, focusing on interaction with the victim.

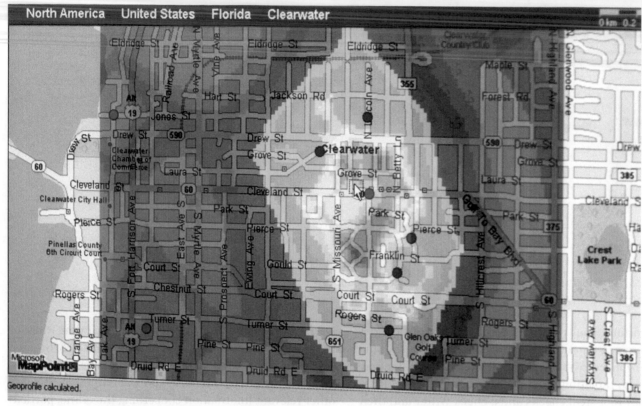

The Pinellas County (Florida) Sheriff's Office Crime Analysis Section uses geographic profiling software to help predict the general area in which an offender might reside or work. This tool applies the color spectrum to allow investigators to visualize areas of greatest (red) to least (purple) likelihood in their effort to focus resources most efficiently and effectively. In this map, the software has calculated that the suspect is most likely to live or work in the red-shaded area, with the likelihood diminishing as one moves out through the other "rings."

St Petersburg Times/ZUMA Press/Largo/Florida/USA/Newscom

- Child Abduction Serial Murder Investigative Resources Center (CASMIRC): provides investigative support to state and local law enforcement through the coordination and provision of federal resources, training, and application of other multidisciplinary expertise in cases involving child abductions, mysterious disappearances of children, child homicide, and serial murder across the nation.

- Violent Criminal Apprehension Program (VICAP): a nationwide data information center designed to collect, collate, and analyze crimes of violence, including solved and unsolved homicides or attempts, missing persons cases where foul play is strongly suspected, cases involving unidentified human remains where the manner of death is known or suspected to be homicide, and sexual assault cases.

In one criminal investigation, the FBI's Behavioral Analysis Unit advised a police department that the serial rapist they were seeking was probably a 25- to 35-year-old, divorced or separated white male, with a high school education who worked as a laborer, lived in the area of the rapes, and engaged in voyeurism. Based on this information, the agency developed a list of 40 suspects with

these characteristics. Using other information in the profile, they narrowed their investigation to one suspect and focused on him. Within a week, they had enough information to arrest him.

William Tafoya of the FBI developed a psychological profile of the Unabomber that many rejected. However, after the arrest of Theodore Kaczynski, Tafoya's assessment was observed to be much more accurate than many in the FBI had believed.

Psychological profiling is most often used in crimes against people in which a motive is unknown. The profile seeks to disclose a possible motive. Continued use of the technique has shown that the more information the police furnish the FBI, the greater the possibility of obtaining accurate leads. Reporting the unusual is extremely important. Psychological profiling can help both eliminate and develop suspects, thereby saving investigative time.

Despite its usefulness, profiling is not infallible. Investigators should not rely solely on a profile without supporting evidence. For example, in the Atlanta Olympic bombing case of 1996, the profile resulted in the arrest of the security guard, who was later cleared. In addition, the legitimate use of criminal profiling is sometimes confused with the illegal practice of racial profiling.

Racial Profiling

Racial targeting by law enforcement has been a fact of life for Black Americans for centuries, even before the designation of organized police forces in the United States, dating back to when the slave patrols kept watch over the Antebellum South (Harris, 2020). Fridell (2017, p.7) states: "The implicit association between African Americans and crime—'the Black-Crime implicit bias'— can lead individuals to be more likely to perceive ambiguous actions on the part of African Americans, versus Caucasians, as threatening." The persistent stereotyping that Blacks are dangerous criminals has, for generations, marked young men of color for different treatment by police, including more frequent stops, searches, and use of force—a phenomenon that became known as "Driving while Black." "Research demonstrates that implicit bias impacts policing . . . and all aspects of the criminal justice system, leading to higher rates of childhood suspension, expulsion, and arrest at school; disproportionate contact with the juvenile justice system; harsher charging decisions and disadvantaged plea negotiations; a greater likelihood of being denied bail and diversion; an increased risk of wrongful convictions and unfair sentences; and higher rates of probation and parole revocation (Taylor, 2019).

Racial profiling occurs when an officer focuses primarily on race, ethnicity, national origin, or religious appearance, to the exclusion of legitimate factors such as behavior, to decide which people are suspicious enough to warrant police stops, questioning, frisks, searches, and other routine police practices. Notice that using a reasonably detailed description that includes the race of a suspect who has been observed is *not* racial profiling (e.g., the suspect is a Black male, approximately 5′6″, wearing red shorts and red baseball cap). It is important to distinguish between *profiling* (legitimate) as a policing technique and the politically charged term *racial profiling* (not legitimate). Some have suggested replacing *racial profiling* with the term *biased-based policing* to emphasize this distinction.

The courts *have* ruled that race can be one factor among others to use in developing suspects. For example, airport security personnel are taught to watch for certain traits—young, African American male paying for a ticket in cash, no luggage, nervousness, and so on—to profile possible drug dealers and are frequently criticized for such profiling. In *United States v. Weaver* (1992), a Drug Enforcement Administration (DEA) agent stopped and questioned Arthur Weaver at a Kansas City airport "because he was 'roughly dressed,' young, Black, and on a direct flight from Los Angeles, a source city for drugs." Weaver was carrying illicit drugs but challenged the legality of the arrest. The Eighth Circuit Court of Appeals upheld the officer's conduct:

Facts are not to be ignored simply because they may be unpleasant—and the unpleasant fact in this case is that the [DEA agent] had knowledge, based upon his own experience and upon the intelligence reports he had received from Los Angeles authorities, that young, male members of the African-American Los Angeles gangs were flooding the Kansas City area with cocaine. To that extent then, race, when coupled with the other factors [the agent] relied upon, was a factor in the decision to approach and ultimately detain [the suspect]. We wish it were otherwise, but we take the facts as they are presented to us, not as we would wish them to be.

Bias-based policing in the United States has expanded over the years to include a broader population of individuals. The war on drugs in the 1980s, which placed the focus of attention on Blacks and Hispanics, grew to include the profiling of Middle Easterners following the terrorist attacks of 9/11 (Harris, 2020). The new war on terror led to a sharp increase in public support for the use of racial profiling by police to prevent another terror attack (Welch, 2019). The increased scrutiny on those of Middle Eastern descent created a new phenomenon known as "flying while Arab" and defined the terrorist profiling that ensued, in which a person was suspected of being involved in a terrorist act merely because of physical characteristics and behavioral cues (Smith & Mason, 2016).

The most recent wave of racial profiling arrived in the mid to late 2000s, amidst new political interest in suppressing illegal immigration to the United States. When Congress passed the Illegal Immigration Reform and Immigrant Responsibility Act in 1996, Section 287(g) of that law offered state and local police agencies the opportunity to become involved, voluntarily, in immigration enforcement. And while nearly all police departments either ignored the invitation or spoke out against it, approximately 80 agencies across the United States do operate under section 287(g), the vast majority of which operate only inside jails and focusing on those already arrested (Harris, 2020).

The *perception* of racial profiling may be bolstered by discussions of **pretextual traffic stops**, that is, stopping vehicles when the officer's intent (pretext) was not the real reason for the stop. For example, an officer may stop someone for a traffic violation when he really suspects that the person has drugs in the car, but he does not have reasonable suspicion to make the stop for drug possession. In *Whren v. United States* (1996), the Supreme Court affirmed that officers could stop vehicles to allay any suspicions even though they have no evidence of criminal behavior. The legality of the stop will be gauged by its objective reasonableness, as discussed in Chapter 6.

Shortly after September 11, 2001, the Supreme Court refused to hear the only remaining case previously docketed concerning an equal-protection claim in a case where police officers stopped persons based primarily on racial or ethnic descriptions. In *Brown v. City of Oneonta* (2001), a court of appeals for the Second Circuit held that where law enforcement officials have a description of a suspect that consists only of the suspect's race and gender, and lacking evidence of discriminatory intent, they can act on that description without violating the equal-protection clause of the Fourteenth Amendment. Subjecting officers to equal-protection scrutiny when they detain or arrest could hamper police work. Officers who fear personal liability from equal-protection violations might fail to act when they are expected to.

Geographic Profiling

Geographic profiling, introduced in Chapter 1, can also be helpful in developing and identifying suspects who commit multiple crimes (serial criminals). Geographic profiling is based on the fact that all people have a pattern to their lives, particularly in relation to the geographical areas they frequent. Serial criminals operate within a comfort zone—near to where they live but far enough away to remain anonymous and still feel comfortable because they know the area.

Using principles of environmental criminology theory, research data on offender spatial behavior, and mathematics, software has been developed that can create a two-dimensional geo-profile, which superimposes those locations where an offender suspect is most likely to live over a street map, giving investigators zones of addresses on which to focus their search for a suspect (Rossmo, 2013). A geographic profile can also help detectives prioritize areas for canvassing and determine placement of tools, such as license plate readers or pole cameras, to collect data about people or vehicles that pass through a specific area (Velarde, 2016).

Information in Police Files and Files of Other Agencies

Police records on solved crimes and on suspects involved in certain types of crimes often suggest leads. For example, in the "Son of Sam" case in New York City, one lead was provided by a woman who saw an illegally parked car that fit the description of the car reported as being used in the crimes. Police then checked all parking tickets issued on that date for that time and location. This, combined with other information, eventually led to the suspect.

Technology Innovations

CrimeStat®

CrimeStat®, developed by Ned Levine & Associates of Houston, Texas, is a spatial statistics program for analyzing crime incident locations. It provides statistical tools to aid law enforcement agencies and criminal justice researchers in their crime mapping efforts. CrimeStat IV (version 4.02), the most recent version of this software, is Windows-based and interfaces with most desktop GIS programs. Many police departments around the country use CrimeStat, as do criminal justice and other researchers. In addition to hot spot identification and analysis, the program includes features that plot crime incidents on a map, track offender behavior over time, and estimate a serial offender's likely residence given the distribution of incidents, assumptions about travel behavior, and the origin of offenders who committed crimes in the same locations (Levine, 2015).

Police files contain considerable information about people who have committed or are suspected of committing crimes. The files contain such information as their physical characteristics, date of birth, age, race, general build, kind of clothing usually worn, height, weight, hair color and style, facial features, unusual marks, scars, tattoos, deformities, abnormalities, alcohol or drug use, MO, and other information.

Field-interview (FI) cards that patrol officers file when they stop people under suspicious circumstances can also provide leads. Physical cards are becoming less common as various digital tools, such as e-briefing intel sheets, are being made available. One app for smartphones generates field-interview cards that allow officers to record personal information and bio-data for subjects; document gang affiliations, tattoos, and other identifying marks; record or check on the probation or parole status of subjects; capture vehicle information; capture and attach photos of evidence, tattoos, or people to case files; maintain an alphabetical list of subjects interviewed with photos; and email or print any FI cards from the officer's phone. Additional features include speech-to-text support; auto-calculation of a subject's age; and the retention of the officer's name, ID, and agency name.

An officer may not know of an actual crime committed at the time of a stop but may later learn that a business or residence in the area of the stop was burglarized at about the same time. Descriptions of vehicles in a high-crime area that do not fit the neighborhood also help to identify suspects. Chapter 6 discussed sources of information ranging from the local to the federal level, as well as the use of informants.

Tracking

Sometimes, knowledge of tracking is helpful in developing suspects. Forensic tracking is the science of locating, retaining, and interpreting footprint and tire tread impressions to solve criminal cases. Unfortunately tracking is becoming somewhat of a lost art: "'What we don't look for, we don't find' is a cliché that seems to apply to tracks. Footprints are truly 'the missed evidence' in many jurisdictions" (Hanratty, 2007, p. 50). Indeed, Hilderbrand (2013) echoes that the only footwear evidence that is not found is that which is not looked for.

Footprints can provide valuable clues. Footwear evidence can help investigators determine the number of suspects involved, their direction of travel when arriving at and leaving the scene, and their movements while on the scene (Hilderbrand, 2013). The length of stride and depth of impression of footprints can help determine the size or height of a person and whether that person was carrying a heavy load. To determine an individual's height from shoeprint length, "Measure the shoeprint length in inches and divide by two to get the height in feet. For example, a shoeprint that measures 12 inches in length will indicate a person six feet tall. This is a rough estimate for use at the scene to rule in or rule out possible suspects" (Hanratty, 2007, p. 47).

Gait analysis can also help investigators develop a suspect. One's gait is the manner in which the person walks or moves. Forensic podiatry involves the analysis and evaluation of evidence related to the human foot, including footprints, footwear, and gait. In one case involving the robbery of a jewelry store, a forensic podiatrist was able to compare the suspect's gait with surveillance video of the perpetrator and testify in court that the thief and the suspect were one and the same (Nirenberg, 2016). Video showing an offender walking or running away from a crime scene can indicate whether the person has unique gait characteristics, such as a limp, which can help investigators develop a suspect.

Tire prints can also provide information to investigators. For example, transfer of sticky soils is a good way to determine vehicle direction. Wet sand, mud, or clay will initially stick to tires. As the vehicle continues moving, this material will fall off the tires in the direction the vehicle is headed. If the tracks shine in grass, they are headed away from you. Tire tracks coming toward you will show faintly as an off color to the surrounding grass (Lee, 2007). Tire prints can also provide a clue as to the type of vehicle involved, helping investigators develop a suspect.

Tracking skill can be developed for impressions other than footprints and can provide many investigative leads. People hiding in outside areas may leave foot, knee, hand, heel, or body impressions. Broken tree branches provide evidence of when the branch was broken—the lighter the color of the break, the more recent it is. Recent overturning of a stone may be indicated by the dirt or by the moist side being on top.

Other Identification Aids

Visual aids such as media photos or video disseminated to the public may provide rapid identification of suspects. Yearbooks have also proved to be valuable in developing suspects. Currently one of the most effective ways to generate identification leads is through social media.

If a suspect or victim is deceased and the identity is unknown, dental and orthopedic records may help. Facial reconstruction is also used in many areas to identify unknown victims or suspects if sufficient skull and facial parts are available. Several states have implemented an innovative way to jump start a cold case—playing cards. In Minnesota, the Bureau of Criminal Apprehension (BCA) has partnered with the Department of Corrections (DOC) and law enforcement agencies throughout the state to create a deck of cold case playing cards, each card highlighting one of 52 violent unsolved homicide, missing person, and unidentified remains cases that have occurred in Minnesota in the past 50 years. The decks are distributed to every police department and sheriff's office in the state, as well as to county jail and state prison facilities. The cards have had limited success in generating new leads for cold cases (Minnesota Department of Public Safety, Bureau of Criminal Apprehension, 2015).

Locating Suspects

Many information sources used to develop a suspect can also help locate the suspect. If the suspect is local and frequents public places, the victim may see the suspect and call the police. In one instance, a rape victim saw the alleged rapist in a shopping center and remembered that she had seen him there just before her rape occurred. The investigator accompanied the victim to the shopping center for several evenings until the victim saw the suspect and identified him.

Telephoning other investigative agencies, inquiring around the neighborhood of the suspect's last known address or checking the address on a prison release form, questioning relatives, and checking with utility companies and numerous other contacts can help locate suspects.

Identifying Suspects

Time is of the essence in identifying a suspect. The amount of time it takes to identify a suspect is directly correlated with the length of time it takes to solve a crime. Several techniques are available to identify suspects.

> **LO3** Describe the basic techniques used to identify a suspect, including what each requires, when they are used, and what rights a suspect has during each.

Suspects can be identified through field or show-up identification, booking photos, field views, photographic identification, or live lineups.

Field identification and booking photos have been discussed previously.

Field Views

A field view can be used if investigators have reason to believe, through the course of developing a suspect, that an offender may frequently visit a particular location at a particular time, such as a gym or restaurant. During a field view, an investigator accompanies a victim or witness to such a site to observe the people in the hopes the offender might appear. It is important that the investigator not direct the victim's or witness's attention to any specific individual during a field view (NAS, 2014).

Photographic Identification

Often the victim or witnesses get a good look at the suspect and can make a positive identification. Two general types of photographic identification are the single confirmatory photo and the photo array.

A single confirmatory photograph can be shown to a witness to confirm or clarify the legal identity of a suspect. This method is generally limited to situations in which the offender is previously known to the witness. In some cases, the witness may only know the suspect by a nickname or street name, such as "Shorty." Investigators can display a single photo to a witness to establish or confirm Shorty's legal name.

> **LO3** Describe the basic techniques used to identify a suspect, including what each requires, when they are used, and what rights a suspect has during each.

Use photographic identification when you have a good idea of who committed a crime but the suspect is not in custody or when a fair live lineup cannot be conducted. Tell witnesses they need not identify anyone from the photographs.

A more common type of photographic identification is the photo array, a collection of photographs that includes the suspect plus at least five other nonsuspects, referred to as "fillers." Photographs can be obtained through surveillance, from booking photos, or from driver's license databases, and the fillers should be as similar in appearance to the suspect as possible. Characteristics to consider when selecting filler photos are gender, race, skin tone, facial hair, age, height, weight, and any distinctive features comparable to that of the suspect. The U.S. Department of Justice has set forth principles and procedures, based on the study of research and identification of best practices, for conducting photo arrays (U.S. Department of Justice, 2017). Much of what follows in this section is adapted from that document.

The photographs can be kept separate or mounted on a composite board. Write a number or code on the back of each photograph to identify the individual, but do not include any other information, especially that the person has a criminal record. Tell witnesses that they need not identify anyone from among the photographs and that it is as important to eliminate innocent people from suspicion as it is to identify the guilty.

When the officer presenting the photo array knows the identity of the suspect, this is referred to as a single-blind procedure. The National Academies of Science (NAS), however, has recommended a double-blind administration of the photo array as the best practice, meaning that the officer who is presenting the photos to the witness does not know which one is the suspect. Using the double-blind approach diminishes the likelihood of the investigator influencing, even unintentionally, a witness's selection of a suspect or affecting the witness's confidence in their choice (NAS, 2014). Any outside influence or suggestiveness during the identification process can lead to that identification being suppressed as evidence in court, impairing the prosecution's ability to prove the case beyond a reasonable doubt.

> **LO3** Describe the basic techniques used to identify a suspect, including what each requires, when they are used, and what rights a suspect has during each.
>
> A suspect does not have the right to a lawyer if a photographic lineup is used (*United States v. Ash, Jr.*, 1973).

If there are several witnesses, have each one view a separate set of pictures independently and in a different room, if other witnesses are viewing the photographs at the same time. Fillers should not be reused when photo arrays for different suspects are shown to the same witness. For each suspect, the investigator administering the procedure should use the same photo array for multiple witnesses but change the arrangement of the photos if possible (U.S. Department of Justice, 2017).

Photo arrays can be presented simultaneously or sequentially. A simultaneous array shows all of the photos to the witness at the same time. A sequential approach, in contrast, presents the photos one at a time to the witness, allowing a witness to decide about each photo before looking at the next, thereby reducing the tendency to compare photos. Research is mixed as to which photo array presentation method produces more accurate results (U.S. Department of Justice, 2017).

It is unwise to show a single photograph to a victim or witness to obtain identification. Such identification is almost always inadmissible as evidence because it allows a chance of mistaken identity and improperly suggests to the witness that the single person shown is the suspect sought. The Supreme Court decision in *Manson v. Brathwaite* (1977), however, did approve the showing of a single picture in specific circumstances. In this case, the witness who used a single photograph to positively identify suspect Manson as the man from whom he had purchased heroin was, in fact, Jimmy Glover, a specially trained, assigned, and experienced undercover narcotics officer. Manson argued that the showing of a single photograph to Glover was "impermissibly suggestive," and in most cases, the courts would likely agree. However, the Supreme Court, in their analysis, weighed the following facts of this case:

- ***The opportunity to view.*** Unlike many witnesses who view a crime from a distance or from behind some type of barrier, Glover stood face to face with the suspect.

- ***The degree of attention.*** Glover was not a casual or passing observer, as is so often the case with eyewitness identification, but rather was a trained police officer on duty.

- ***The accuracy of the description.*** Glover's description of the narcotics seller, given to a fellow officer within minutes after the transaction, was accurate enough to allow the other officer, who was familiar with many local drug dealers, to pull a photograph of the suspect from the police department's records division.

- ***The witness's level of certainty.*** Glover, in response to a question whether the photograph was that of the person from whom he made the purchase, testified: "There is no question whatsoever."

- ***The time between the crime and the confrontation.*** Glover's description of his vendor was given to the other officer within minutes of the crime. The photographic identification took place only two days later. There was not the passage of weeks or months between the crime and the viewing of the photograph, as is often the case with witness identification and during which time the witness's memory of specific identifying details may deteriorate.

The facts of this case highlight the high level of scrutiny with which the courts assess witness identification. The vast majority of the witnesses that investigators deal with will not be highly trained and experienced officers; therefore, it is essential that investigators not compromise the identification process by improperly showing only a single photograph to a witness.

If witnesses recognize a photograph in a simultaneous photo array, have them circle the photograph and then sign and date it. If witnesses identify a suspect during a sequential photo array, have them sign and date either the front or back of the photograph. If a witness fails to make an identification, record this in writing (U.S. Department of Justice, 2017).

The NAS recommends the video recording of eyewitness identification procedures as a best practice, both to be used in court and to protect those who administered the procedure against unfounded claims of misconduct. The recording can also serve to document, verbatim, the witness's level of confidence at the time of identification. New research has demonstrated that a witness's confidence during an initial identification is a reliable indicator of accuracy, often far more reliable than that same witness's confidence during a trial (Wixted & Wells, 2017). Such confidence statements support the criteria used by the Supreme Court in *Manson v.*

Brathwaite (1977) to assess the reliability of eyewitness identification.

After identification is made, review with the witness the conditions under which the suspect was seen, including lighting at the time and distance from the suspect. Also ask witnesses just how confident they are in their identification. Record their statements and the conditions of the identification and have the witnesses sign the documents.

Live Lineup Identification

Live lineup identification is commonly used when the suspect is in custody and there were witnesses to the crime. A live lineup involves the suspect and at least five fillers (although some have up to nine) either standing or sitting before the witness, who is usually behind a one-way mirror. Police have adopted lineup procedures to ensure accurate, fair identifications and to meet the standards established by Supreme Court decisions.

> **L03** Describe the basic techniques used to identify a suspect, including what each requires, when they are used, and what rights a suspect has during each.
>
> Use a live lineup when the suspect is in custody. Use at least six individuals (including the suspect) of the same gender and comparable race, height, weight, age, and general appearance. Ask all to perform the same actions or speak the same words. Instruct witnesses viewing the lineup that they need not make an identification.

Although the live lineup is often portrayed in TV shows and movies as "the" way witnesses identify suspects, they are not so common in real life. A representative survey of police departments nationwide found that only 21% reported the use of live lineups, compared to a 94% reported use of photo arrays (Police Executive Research Forum, 2013). Numerous studies have found that photo identification is more practical and more fair than live lineups (Fitzgerald, Price, & Valentine, 2018). Furthermore, it may not only be difficult to find suitable fillers for a live lineup in smaller jurisdictions, live lineups require significantly more time and labor on the part of investigators, making photo arrays a more reasonable and resource-conscious option (NAS, 2014).

However, when a live lineup is conducted for suspect identification, it has essentially the same requirements as photographic identification. The suspect must not be of a different race, exceptionally taller or shorter, have longer or shorter hair, or be dressed very differently from the others in the lineup. The suspect must not be handcuffed unless everyone in the lineup is handcuffed. Nor may the suspect be asked to step forward, turn a certain direction, or speak certain words unless everyone in the lineup is asked to do the same.

As with photographic identification, it is the best practice to conduct double-blind live lineups to keep the officer conducting the procedure from influencing the witness in any way (NAS, 2014; Charman & Quiroz, 2016). Live lineups may also be simultaneous or sequential. In the traditional simultaneous live lineup, the witness views all potential perpetrators at the same time and

This lineup, in which alleged rapist Ronald Cotton appears, shows seven individuals of comparable race, height, weight, age, and general appearance in accordance with lineup standards set by the U.S. Supreme Court. A rape victim incorrectly identified Cotton from this lineup as the man who had sexually assaulted her. Cotton spent 10 years behind bars for a crime he didn't commit, before the real rapist was identified and held accountable. In a later interview, following Cotton's exoneration, the victim recalled the lineup and identification process and stated, "I was certain, but I was wrong."

Courtesy Burlington Police Department, North Carolina

selects the suspect from the fillers. In contrast, during a sequential lineup, the witness views only one person at a time and must make a decision on each one—*yes*, this is the perpetrator, or *no*, this is not the right person—before moving on to the next one.

Some studies have shown that with simultaneous lineups, there is a tendency for the witness to compare one member with the others and make relative judgments, thereby selecting, through the process of elimination, the person who looks most like the perpetrator. The conclusion of these studies is that sequential lineups yield more accurate eyewitness identification. However, other studies have found that sequential lineups actually increase the risk of false identification (Mecklenburg, Larson, & Bailey, 2008). Despite the conflicting research, many departments have adopted the sequential double-blind lineup protocol (Charman & Quiroz, 2016).

If the suspect refuses to participate in the lineup or a lineup cannot be conducted fairly for some reason, simply photograph the suspect and each individual in the lineup separately and use photographic identification.

LO3 Describe the basic techniques used to identify a suspect, including what each requires, when they are used, and what rights a suspect has during each.

Suspects may refuse to participate in a lineup, but such refusals can be used against them in court (*Schmerber v. California*, 1966). Suspects have a Sixth Amendment right to have an attorney present during a lineup.

In *United States v. Wade* (1967), a robber forced a cashier and a bank official to place money in a pillowcase. The robber had a piece of tape on each side of his face. After obtaining the money, he left the bank and drove away with an accomplice who had been waiting outside in a car.

In March 1965, an indictment was returned against Wade and an accomplice for the bank robbery. He was arrested on April 2, 1965. Approximately two weeks later, an FBI agent put Wade in a lineup to be observed by two bank employees. Wade's counsel was not notified of the lineup. Each person in the lineup had strips of tape similar to those worn by the bank robber, and each was requested to say words allegedly spoken at the robbery. Both bank employees picked Wade out of the lineup as being the robber, and both employees again identified Wade in the courtroom.

The defense objected that the bank employees' courtroom identifications should be stricken because the original lineup had been conducted without the presence of Wade's counsel. The motion was denied, and Wade was found guilty. Counsel held that this violated his Fifth Amendment right against self-incrimination and his Sixth Amendment right to counsel being present at the lineup.

The *Wade* decision ruled, "Prior to having a suspect participate in a lineup, the officer must advise the suspect of his constitutional right to have his lawyer present during the lineup." Recall that this right to a lawyer does not apply to field identification or photographic identification. The Court held that a suspect has the right to have counsel present at the lineup because a lineup is held for identification by eyewitnesses and may involve vagaries leading to mistaken identification. The Court cited the many cases of mistaken identification and the improper manner in which the suspect may have been presented. The Court commented that neither the lineup nor anything that Wade was required to do in the lineup violated his privilege against self-incrimination.

The Court stated in *Schmerber v. California* (1966) that protection against self-incrimination involved disclosure of knowledge by the suspect. Both state and federal courts have held that compulsion to submit to photographs, fingerprinting, measurements, blood analysis, or samples of writing and speaking is not self-incrimination under the Fifth Amendment.

The ruling in *Gilbert v. California* (1967), a companion case to *Wade*, also held that ID evidence from a lineup conducted without counsel, after indictment and arraignment, was inadmissible at trial. This requirement of providing counsel to a suspect in a lineup that occurs after indictment or arraignment is known as the "Wade-Gilbert Rule." If suspects waive their right to counsel, get the waiver in writing. A waiver such as the one in Figure 7.2 can be used.

If a suspect chooses to have a lawyer, they may either select their own or ask you to obtain one. The lawyer may confer with the suspect in private before the lineup and may talk with witnesses observing the lineup, but witnesses are not obligated to talk with the lawyer. Witnesses may wear face covers to avoid recognition by the suspect. Usually the lineup room ensures viewers' anonymity.

Give witnesses clear instructions before the lineup. Tell them they need not identify anyone in the lineup and that they are not to confer with any other witnesses viewing the lineup. Tape record or videotape the proceedings and take a color photograph of the lineup to nullify any allegations by the defense counsel of unfair procedure. The form in Figure 7.3 provides additional evidence of the fairness and reliability of a lineup identification.

WAIVER OF RIGHT TO LEGAL COUNSEL AT LINEUP

Your Rights Are: The police are requesting you to personally appear in a lineup. There will be a number of other persons similar in physical characteristics with you. The purpose of the lineup is to permit witnesses to observe all persons in the lineup, to make an identification. You may be asked to perform certain actions such as speaking, walking or moving in a certain manner or to put on articles of clothing. You must appear in the lineup, but you have a right to have legal counsel of your choice present. If you do not have an attorney, one can be appointed for you by the court, and the lineup will not be held until your legal counsel is present. An attorney can help you defend against an identification made by witnesses at the lineup.

You have the right to waive legal counsel being present at the lineup.

WAIVER

I have read, or have had read to me, this statement of my rights and I understand these rights. I am willing to participate in a lineup in the absence of legal counsel. I fully understand and give my consent to what I am being asked to do. No promises or threats have been made to me, and no pressure of coercion has been used against me. I understand that I must appear in the lineup, but this consent is to the waiver of legal counsel being present at the lineup.

Signed _____   Place _____

Witness _____   Date _____

Witness _____   Time _____

Figure 7.2
Sample waiver.

Special Investigative Techniques Used to Identify and Arrest Suspects

"Follow that car!" "I think we're being tailed!" "I lost him!" "My cover's blown!" "We've been made!" "It's a raid!" Police officers, criminals, and the public are very aware of investigative practices such as observing suspects or their houses or apartments, following suspects, staking out locations, and conducting raids. Television shows and movies, however, usually depict the glamorous, dangerous sides of this facet of investigation. They seldom show the long hours of preparation or the days—even weeks—of tedious watchfulness frequently required.

Surveillance, undercover assignments, and raids are used only when other methods of continuing the investigation fail to produce results. These techniques are expensive and potentially dangerous and are not routinely used.

Surveillance

The covert, discreet observation of people or places is called **surveillance** ("to watch over").

LO4 Explain when surveillance is used, what its objectives are, and the basic types of surveillance commonly deployed in criminal investigation.

The objective of surveillance is to obtain information about people, their associates, and their activities that may help solve a criminal case or to protect witnesses.

Surveillance can aid an investigation in many ways by helping an investigator:

- Gain information required for building a criminal complaint
- Determine an informant's loyalty

Figure 7.3
Police report of lineup.

POLICE REPORT OF LINEUP
Boulder City Police

| Police Department |

Name of suspect ___John Vance___ Birth date ___2-14-1964___

Address ___1424 Colten Street, Boulder City___

Case Number ___6432___ Complainant or victim ___Thelma Crump___

Name of legal counsel ___John Simmons___ Present: Yes _X_ No ____

Was waiver signed: Yes _X_ No ____

Place of lineup ___Las Vegas, Nevada, Police Dept.___

Date of lineup ___5-12-20__ ___ Time of lineup ___1640___

Names of persons in lineup (left to right, facing the lineup)

	Name	Height	Weight	Birth date	Other
1.	Charles Upright	5-11	184	4-10-1966	
2.	Gary Starrick	5-10	178	2-14-1965	
3.	Jerry Stilter	5-11	190	10-11-1967	
4.	Ralph Barrett	5-10	185	12-24-1968	
5.	John Vance	5-10	183	2-14-1964	
6.	Christian Dolph	5-11	190	6-12-1964	
7.					
8.					
9.					
10.					

Subject identified by witness: Number ___5___ Name ___John Vance___

Recording taken of lineup: Yes _X_ No___ Photos taken of lineup: Yes _X_ No___

Persons present at lineup ___Thelma Crump   Alfred Nener___
___John Simmons   Emmanuel Sorstick___

Person conducting lineup ___Sgt. Lloyd Brenner, LVPD___

- Verify a witness's statement about a crime

- Gain information required for obtaining and executing a search or arrest warrant, such as who lives at a property, how many people are there, what the layout of the property is, and if dogs are present

- Gain information necessary for interrogating a suspect

- Identify a suspect's associates

- Observe members of terrorist organizations

- Find a person wanted for a crime

- Observe criminal activities in progress

- Make a legal arrest

- Apprehend a criminal in the act of committing a crime

- Prevent a crime

- Recover stolen property

- Protect witnesses

Whenever practical, it is prudent for investigators to drive around the property before conducting a search warrant or a raid of a house. Officers do not want any surprises. They do not want to encounter the local school bus, a dog in the yard, extra vehicles in the driveway, or a house cleaner inside. The best way to minimize or eliminate as many unknowns as possible is to drive through the neighborhood before executing the search warrant, whether it is a day or two before or only an hour before.

Because surveillance is a time-consuming, expensive operation that can raise questions of invasion of privacy, first exhaust all alternatives. Balance the rights of the individual against the need for public safety.

The Surveillant. The **surveillant** is the plainclothes investigator who makes the observation. Surveillants must be prepared for tedium. No other assignment requires as much patience and perseverance while demanding alertness and readiness to respond instantly. Surveillants must display ingenuity in devising a cover for the operation. Lack of resourcefulness in providing adequate answers at a moment's notice can jeopardize the entire case. The most successful surveillants do not attract attention but blend into the general populace. Multiple surveillants may also compose a surveillance team (ST). An effective ST requires everyone to be "on the same page," which calls for communication and briefings.

The Subject. The **subject**, also referred to as a target, is who or what is being observed. It can be a person, place, property, vehicle, group of people, organization, or object. People under surveillance are usually suspects in a crime or their associates. Surveillance of places generally involves a location where a crime is expected to be committed; the residence of a known criminal; a place suspected of harboring criminal activities such as illegal drug transactions, gambling, prostitution, or purchase of stolen goods or fencing operations; or the suspected headquarters of a terrorist organization.

Types of Surveillance. The type of surveillance used depends on the subject and the objective of the surveillance. In general, surveillance is either stationary or moving.

> **LO4** Explain when surveillance is used, what its objectives are, and the basic types of surveillance commonly deployed in criminal investigation.
>
> The types of surveillance include stationary (fixed, plant, or stakeout) and moving (tight or close, loose, rough, on foot, or by vehicle).

Stationary surveillance. Stationary, or **fixed surveillance**, also called a **plant** or **stakeout**, is used when you know or suspect that a person is at or will come to a known location, when you suspect that stolen goods are to be dropped, or when informants have told you that a crime is going to be committed. Such assignments are comparatively short. An outside surveillance simplifies planning. The observation may be from a car, van, or truck or by posting an officer

in an inconspicuous place with a view of the location. A "dummy" van or a borrowed business van and a disguise as a painter, carpenter, or service technician are often used. Take photographs and notes throughout the surveillance.

In longer surveillances, it is often necessary to photograph people who frequent a specific location, such as a store suspected of being a cover for a bookmaking operation or a hotel or motel that allows prostitution or gambling. If the subject of surveillance is a place rather than a person, obtain a copy of the building plan and personally visit the building in advance if possible. Know all entrances and exits, especially rear doors and fire escapes. To properly record what is observed, use closed-circuit camera equipment, movie or video cameras, binoculars with a camera attached, telephoto lenses, or infrared equipment for night viewing and photographing.

Lengthy fixed surveillance is often conducted from a room with an unobstructed view of the location, such as an apartment opposite the location being watched. Naturally, the surveillant must not be noticed entering the observation post.

Whether the stationary surveillance is short or long, have adequate communications such as radio, horn signals, or hand signals. Use simple hand signals such as pulling up the collar, buttoning the shirt, pulling down the brim on a hat, tying a shoelace, running the hand through the hair, or checking a wristwatch. If you use radio communications, find out whether the subject might be monitoring police radio frequencies and, if likely, establish a code.

Select the ST to fit the case and area, and have enough surveillants to cover the assignment. Scout the area in person or by studying maps. Sketch the immediate area to determine possible ways the subject could avoid observation or apprehension. Be aware of alleys, abnormal street conditions, one-way streets, barricades, parking ramps, and all other details. This is especially critical when the objective of the surveillance is to apprehend people committing a crime. In such cases, all members of the stakeout must know the signal for action and their specific assignments.

Moving surveillance. The subjects of moving surveillance are almost always people, although occasionally the subject may be a vehicle. The first step in planning such a surveillance is to obtain as much information about the subject as you can. View photographs and, if possible, personally observe the subjects. Memorize their physical descriptions and form a mental image of them. Concentrate on their appearance from behind, as this is the view you normally have while following them. Although subjects may alter their physical appearance, this usually presents no problem.

The major problem is to keep subjects under constant surveillance for the desired time. Know the subjects' habits, where they are likely to go, and whether they walk or drive. If they drive, find out what kind of vehicle(s) they use. Also find out who their associates are and whether they are likely to suspect that they are being observed.

Other problems of moving surveillance are losing the subject and having the subject recognize you as a surveillant. Sometimes it is not important if the subject knows of the surveillance. This is often true of material witnesses the police are protecting. It is also true of organized crime figures, who know they are under constant surveillance and expect this. In such instances, a **rough surveillance** or **open surveillance** is used. You need not take extraordinary means to remain undetected. The major problem of a rough surveillance is that it is liable to the charge of police harassment or invasion of privacy.

At other times, it is more important to remain undetected than to keep the subject under constant observation. In such cases, a **loose surveillance** is used. Maintain a safe distance one or two vehicles behind the subject and "hand off" the subject to another officer after taking one turn. If the subject is lost during surveillance, you can usually relocate the subject and resume the surveillance. A loose surveillance is often used when you need general information about the subject's activities or associates, for example, the simple need to place a subject at an address.

Often, however, it is extremely important not to lose the subject, and a very **close (tight) surveillance** is maintained. On a crowded street, this means staying within a few steps of the subject; on a less crowded street, it means keeping the subject in sight. A close surveillance is most commonly used when you know the subject is going to commit a crime, when you must know the subject's exact habits, or when knowledge of the subject's activities is important to another critical operation. Close surveillance is also best done with multiple officers, if the resources are available.

When surveilling a subject on foot, you can use numerous delaying tactics. You can cross to the other side of the street, talk to a person standing nearby, increase your distance from the subject, read a magazine or newspaper, buy a soda, tinker with the engine in your car, tie your shoe, look in windows or in parked cars, or stall in any other way.

If the subject turns a corner, do not follow closely. When you do turn the corner, if you find the subject waiting in a doorway, pass by without paying attention. Then try to resume the surveillance by guessing the subject's next move. This is often possible when you have advance information on the subject's habits.

If the subject enters a restaurant, you can either enter and take a seat on the side of the room opposite from the subject, making sure you are near the door so you can see the subject leave, or you can wait outside. If a subject enters a building that has numerous exits, follow at a safe distance, noticing all potential exits. If the subject takes an elevator, wait at the first floor until the subject returns, noticing the floors at which the elevator stops. If there is a stairway near the elevator, stand near the door so you can hear if the subject has gotten off the elevator and taken the stairs. Such stairs are seldom used, and when someone is going up or down, their footsteps echo and can easily be heard.

When surveilling a subject on the street, do not hesitate to pass the subject and enter a store yourself. The less obvious you are, the more successful you will be. Use the glass in doors and storefront windows to see behind you.

Subjects who suspect they are being followed use many tricks. They may turn corners suddenly and stand in a nearby doorway, go into a store and duck into a restroom, enter a dressing room, hide behind objects, or suddenly jump on a bus or into a taxi. They may do such things to determine *whether* they are being followed or to lose someone they *know* is following them. *It is usually better to lose subjects than to alert them to your presence or to allow them to identify you.*

Surveillants often believe they have been recognized when in fact they have not. However, if you are certain the subject knows you are following, stop the surveillance, but do not return to the police department right away because the subject may decide to tail *you*. A **tail** is a type of counter-surveillance when the watcher becomes the watched, as when the subject who was being surveilled by the investigator or undercover officer turns the tables and starts to follow the police.

If it is critical not to lose the subject, use more than one surveillant, preferably three. Surveillant A keeps a very close tail immediately behind the subject. Surveillant B follows behind Surveillant A and the subject. Surveillant C observes from across the street parallel with the other two. If the subject turns the corner, Surveillant A continues in the previous direction for a while, and Surveillant B or Surveillant C picks up the tail. Surveillant A then takes the position previously held by the surveillant who picked up the close tail.

When surveilling by vehicle, have descriptions of all vehicles the subject drives or rides in. A tracking device is sometimes useful in surveillance of vehicles. However, recall from Chapter 4 that attaching a GPS device to a suspect's vehicle in an effort to obtain information is a search under the Fourth Amendment and, as such, requires a warrant (*United States v. Jones*, 2012).

Your own vehicle should be inconspicuous. Obtain unregistered ("dead") plates for it from the motor vehicle authorities and change them frequently, or change your vehicle daily, perhaps using rental cars. Changing the number of occupants tends to confuse a suspicious subject, as does altering the headlight patterns of your vehicle during night surveillance. If surveillance is to be primarily at night, install a multiple contact switch to allow you to turn off either one of your headlights at will.

Like subjects being followed on foot, subjects being trailed by a vehicle often use tricks to determine whether they are being watched or to lose an identified surveillant. They may turn in the middle of the block, go through a red light, suddenly pull into a parking space, change traffic lanes rapidly, go down alleys, or go the wrong way down a one-way street. In such cases, if temporarily losing the subject causes no problem, stop the surveillance.

If it is critical not to lose the subject, use more than one vehicle for the surveillance. The ideal system uses four vehicles. Vehicle A drives ahead of the subject and observes through the rearview mirror. (This vehicle is not used if only three vehicles are available.) Vehicle B follows right behind the subject. Vehicles C and D follow on left and right parallel streets to pick up the surveillance if the subject turns in either direction.

Avoiding Detection. Criminals are often suspicious of stakeouts or of being followed and may send someone to scout the area to see whether anybody has staked out their residence or their vehicle. This person may stand on the corner near the residence or drive around the block several times to see if everything is clear. Criminals often watch the windows or roofs of buildings across the street for movements. When they leave their residences, they may have an accomplice trail behind to see if anyone is following. Anticipate and plan for such activities. Sometimes a counter-counter-surveillance is used if personnel are available.

Not every surveillance is successful. In some instances, the subject is lost or the surveillant is recognized, despite the best efforts to avoid either. Like any other investigative technique, failure results from unforeseen circumstances such as vehicle malfunction, illness of the surveillant, unexpected absence of the subject because of illness or emergency, abnormal weather conditions or terrain, and other factors beyond control. Usually, however, information and evidence obtained through surveillance are well worth the time and effort invested.

Surveillance Equipment. Surveillance equipment includes binoculars, telescopes, night-vision equipment, video systems, body wires, costumes, and disguises.

Surveillance systems have become extremely sophisticated. One system, for example, conceals a periscope in what looks like a standard air vent in the roof of a van. The periscope rotates 360 degrees and is undetectable. Remote motion detectors activate the system to videotape the area under surveillance. GPS technology, as already mentioned, can be used in surveillance operations but officers must understand the legal restrictions placed on such practices. In *United States v. Knotts* (1983), the Court ruled that installing and monitoring a beeper, or a radio transmitter, in a public location did not violate a suspect's rights.

Aerial Surveillance. Aerial surveillance may provide information about areas inaccessible to foot or vehicle surveillance. Communication between air surveillance and ground vehicles facilitates the operational movement in and around the target area. The aerial pilot should either be a police officer or be carefully selected by the police. The pilot should be familiar with the landmarks of the area because many such surveillances involve moving suspect vehicles.

Photographs taken from navigable air space, usually 1,000 feet, do not violate privacy regulations. In one aerial surveillance, officers viewed a partially covered greenhouse within the residential curtilage from a helicopter 400 feet above the greenhouse. The greenhouse, which contained marijuana plants, was located 10 to 20 feet behind the residence, a mobile home. A wire fence surrounded the entire property, and "Do Not Enter" signs were posted. Nonetheless, the court in *Florida v. Riley* (1989) approved the warrantless aerial surveillance, noting that there should be no reasonable expectation of privacy from the skies above.

Visual/Video Surveillance. Video images are often used as evidence in high-profile criminal investigations, with thousands of lesser crimes caught on video each year. High-crime areas, such as locations commonly used for illegal drug sales, are increasingly being monitored by 24-hour surveillance cameras mounted on utility poles, buildings, and other strategic vantage points. These cameras may have hardwired or wireless connections back to a viewing and recording station. Although there may or may not be someone actively supervising the output on the receiving end, the activity is recorded and can be accessed if an incident is reported. Many visual surveillance systems have night-vision or telephoto lenses, time-and-date generators, and printers that produce black-and-white or color photographic copies on site.

Although many cameras are overtly placed, sometimes officers want to conduct covert surveillance, disguising video systems in a variety of ways, such as in clocks, picture frames, exit signs, and domes. Such systems can record drug buys, money laundering, shoplifting, and bank robberies and are usually admissible in court. Remote network video cameras are available that can send video via commercial cellular telephone networks.

Automated license plate recognition (ALPR) technology can be used passively to record, with a time and location stamp, every license plate that passes in front of the camera. New artificial intelligence–driven technology allows ALPR software to be installed into security cameras that are already in place (Crandall, 2020). Recorded data can later be accessed and used to confirm alibis or place suspect vehicles in the area of a crime. In one case, ALPR information led investigators to a mail theft suspect (Wallentine, 2020). Facial recognition software can also be used in a similar fashion, as previously discussed.

Although a warrant is required to use surveillance when there exists an expectation of privacy, the courts have allowed law enforcement to protect certain investigative techniques, to protect information regarding sensitive equipment, or to protect surveillance locations. The courts have allowed warrantless surveillance if revealing the technique may endanger law enforcement officers' lives or the lives of those who allow their property to be used in such activity, or when the owners of property may no longer allow their property to be used for surveillance if the technique is revealed. The courts have also allowed warrantless surveillance if once a technique is revealed it will be of no further value to law enforcement or if revealing the technique might show criminals how to use the technique.

Visual or video surveillance is often used in conjunction with audio or electronic surveillance.

Audio or Electronic Surveillance.

In special instances, electronic devices are used in surveillance. Such electronic surveillance techniques include wiring a person who is going to be talking with a subject or entering a suspicious business establishment, **bugging** a subject's room or vehicle, or **wiretapping** a telephone.

The most common forms of lawfully authorized electronic surveillance available to law enforcement are pen registers, trap-and-trace devices, and content interceptions. Pen registers and trap-and-trace devices record dialing and signaling information used in processing and routing telephone communication, such as the signals that identify the dialed numbers of outgoing calls or the originating numbers of incoming calls.

Electronic surveillance and wiretapping are considered forms of search and are therefore permitted only with probable cause and a court order (*Katz v. United States*, 1967). In *Katz v. United States*, the Supreme Court

Technology Innovations

Through-the-Wall Surveillance

A potentially life-saving innovation is through-the-wall surveillance (TWS), which can detect motion through interior or exterior building walls. TWS technology can penetrate brick, reinforced concrete, concrete block, sheetrock, wood, plaster, fiberglass and common building materials, but not solid metal (e.g., it can "look" through rebar reinforced concrete but not a solid metal wall). It can be used, for example, to locate and track individuals inside a building during hostage rescue operations. Some TWS devices must be placed next to the structure; others can operate at a distance from it, enabling building searches from a vehicle or other safe cover.

Radar systems for TWS are handheld units placed against a barrier to "see" what's on the other side. One such device is the Range-R® Link by L3Harris CyTerra, which boasts many advantages, including being lightweight, compact, ergonomic, rugged, and easy to use. It has excellent penetration, can detect subtle movement, can filter out operator movement, requires no special tools for the battery compartment, and allows for simple battery change. It features an easy-to-use dimmer, an intuitive system control, and a remote display.

Source: U.S. Department of Homeland Security. (2014, May). Radar systems for through-the-wall surveillance. Washington, DC: Author. Retrieved July 26, 2020 from https://www.dhs.gov/sites/default/files/publications/Radar-TWS-SUM_0514-508.pdf

considered an appeal by Charles Katz, who had been convicted in California of violating gambling laws. Investigators had observed Katz for several days as he made telephone calls from a particular phone booth at the same time each day. Suspecting he was placing horse-racing bets, the investigators attached an electronic listening and recording device to the telephone booth and recorded Katz's illegal activities. The evidence was used in convicting Katz. The Supreme Court reversed the California decision, saying, "The Fourth Amendment protects people, not places. . . . Wherever a man may be, he is entitled to know that he will remain free from unreasonable searches and seizures." The investigators did have probable cause, but they erred in not presenting their information to a judge and obtaining prior approval for their actions.

The importance of electronic surveillance is recognized in the introduction to Title III of the Omnibus Crime

Control and Safe Streets Act of 1968, which authorized courtordered electronic surveillance of organized crime figures. The U.S. Congress stated, "Organized criminals make extensive use of wire and oral communications in their criminal activities. The interception of such communications to obtain evidence of the commission of crimes or to prevent their commission is an indispensable aid to law enforcement and the administration of justice."

Title III does not prohibit surreptitiously recording telephone conversations if one party consents. To avoid wiretaps, suspects often use "drop phones," prepaid cell phones that are disposed of regularly. Prepaid phone cards serve the same purpose and can be easily purchased in many places without a person having to produce identification.

Federal and state laws allow electronic surveillance (eavesdropping), provided it is authorized by a federal or state judge and specified procedures are followed. Advertisements in police magazines describe state-of-the-art surveillance systems that make undercover work more efficient and effective. Laser technology can direct a beam at the glass in a window with another beam modulated by sonic vibrations inside the room, bouncing the sound back to a receiver so officers can hear what is being said. Eavesdropping with "bugs" is now easier than ever. Criminals are using high-tech electronic countermeasures to detect such devices in a room before they hold a meeting or conversation there.

The courts have upheld the right of officers to tape conversations that occur inside their squad cars. In the case of *United States v. McKinnon* (1993), two suspects were stopped for a traffic violation and asked to sit in the patrol car while the officer conducted a consent search in the vehicle for drugs. While in the patrol car, the suspects made incriminating statements that were recorded without their knowledge. Although one defendant argued that the recording violated his right to privacy, the court disagreed, stating, "No reasonable expectation of privacy exists in the back seat of a patrol car."

The courts have also held that no expectation of privacy exists in prison cells or in interrogation rooms.

Surveillance and the Constitution. Throughout the discussion on surveillance, of most importance is the balance between acting without violating suspects' constitutional rights and the need for law enforcement to do its job of protecting society. The Court's desire to maintain this balance was seen in *Kyllo v. United States* (2001), introduced in Chapter 4. In this case, the Court held that thermal imaging of a house was a search and required a warrant. X-ray devices, like thermal imaging, require a warrant if they are to be used in a search capacity.

Technology Innovations

ShotSpotter Flex®

Acoustic surveillance systems, such as gunshot detection technology (GDT), help law enforcement respond more quickly to life-threatening emergencies by detecting and locating incidents in real time. In addition to such emergency response benefits, GDT is valuable in shooting investigations and prosecutions because the faster officers are able to arrive on scene, the more likely they are to apprehend any shooting suspects, locate pertinent evidence, and obtain relevant information from witnesses and victims.

One of the most well-known providers of GDT is ShotSpotter, and their leading product, ShotSpotter Flex®, is used by more than 100 jurisdictions throughout the country. Through the placement of outdoor acoustic sensors around a geographic area, ShotSpotter Flex can detect and locate, by triangulation, an incidence of gunfire to enable a fast and precise response to over 90% of gunfire incidents. This technology benefits investigators by providing precise data regarding the time and location of gunfire that results in injuries or homicides. Furthermore, GDT-generated data can be integrated with ballistics analyses to determine whether shell casings found at one crime scene are connected with guns used in other crimes (La Vigne, Thomson, Lawrence, & Goff, 2019). One study found that GDT improved the recovery of shell casings in gun-related homicides from 50% to 89% and in gun-related robberies from 12% to 41% (Lawrence, La Vigne, Goff & Thomson, 2019).

Police departments across the United States have put ShotSpotter to use. For example, the Denver, Colorado, Police Department has made 102 arrests and recovered 84 guns since implementing ShotSpotter in 2015 (Allen, 2018). In September 2019, investigators in Glendale, Arizona, used a combination of ShotSpotter and surveillance video to arrest a serial shooter who had fired more than 80 rounds from two different pistols over the course of several weeks (Crenshaw, 2019).

Source: ShotSpotter. Retrieved July 28, 2020, from https://www.shotspotter.com/results/

The courts have, thus far, held that the use of ALPR technology is not a search and requires no warrant, although legal challenges persist. In *United States v. Yang* (2020), investigators used data from an ALPR to hone in on Yang, who was suspected of mail theft. The defense moved to suppress the evidence seized from Yang's residence on the grounds that the use of the ALRP to monitor Yang's movement violated his Fourth Amendment right to privacy, citing *Carpenter v. United States* (2018) as the precedent. Recall from Chapter 4 that in *Carpenter*, the Supreme Court ruled that the warrantless procurement of cell phone records to track a robbery suspect was an unconstitutional violation of his Fourth Amendment right against unreasonable searches and seizures.

The facts in *Yang* were, however, different in that the vehicle being tracked was a rental and Yang had been more than a week late in returning it when the last episode of mail theft was documented. At that point, the rental car company considered the vehicle stolen and, in an effort to repossess it, attempted to remotely disable the vehicle by activating an onboard GPS unit. Investigators eventually learned that the vehicle was not at the location indicated and that the GPS unit was not functioning, having apparently been disabled by an unknown party. Finally, it was discovered that the credit card used to reserve the rental vehicle was stolen. With these facts, the Ninth Circuit Court of Appeals held that the defendant had no reasonable expectation of privacy in the location data of a rental vehicle he was no longer in lawful possession of.

Students are strongly encouraged to stay apprised of cases involving the use of technology and Fourth Amendment privacy rights, as this area of the law promises to evolve rapidly as new technology emerges.

Undercover Assignments

The nonuniformed or plainclothes investigator is in a good position to observe illegal activities and obtain evidence. For example, a male plainclothes officer may appear to accept the solicitations of a prostitute, or any plainclothes police officer may attempt to buy stolen goods or drugs or to place illegal bets. Many such activities require little more than simply "not smelling like the law." Unlike other forms of surveillance in which a prime objective is not to be observed, **undercover** (UC)

> **LO5** List the objectives of undercover assignments and the precautions officers working undercover should take.

The objective of an undercover assignment may be to gain a person's confidence or to infiltrate an organization or group by using an assumed identity and to thereby obtain information or evidence connecting the subject with criminal activity.

surveillants make personal contact with the subject using an assumed identity, or **cover**.

Undercover assignments can be designed to

- Obtain evidence for prosecution
- Obtain leads into criminal activities
- Check the reliability of witnesses or informants
- Gain information about premises for use in later conducting a raid or an arrest
- Check the security of a person in a highly sensitive position
- Obtain information on or evidence against subversive groups

Some UC assignments are relatively simple and are referred to as *ruses*. The two general types of ruses are (1) deception as to identity—for example, posing as a drug dealer or prostitute, and (2) deception as to purpose—for example, pretending to investigate a different person.

Many undercover assignments are more elaborate. Such UC assignments are frequently made when criminal activity is greatly suspected or even known but no legal evidence of it exists. Such assignments can be extremely dangerous and require careful planning and preparation.

The undercover agent selected must fit the assignment. Age, sex, race, general appearance, language facility, health, energy level, emotional stability, and intelligence are all important selection considerations. Undercover agents must be good actors—able to assume their roles totally. They must be intelligent and able to deal with any problems that arise, make quick decisions, improvise plans and actions, and work with the person or within the group or organization without arousing suspicion.

A good cover is essential. Rookies are often used because they are not yet known and because they have not been in law enforcement long enough to acquire expressions or mannerisms that hardened criminals recognize as "the law."

In addition to devising a good cover, the undercover agent learns everything possible about the subject, regardless of whether it is a person or an organization. If you are going to be working undercover, make plans for communicating with headquarters. Make telephone calls from a nontraceable phone, or mail letters to a fictitious friend's post office box. Have a plan for communicating emergency messages, and know what to do if the authorities move in on the subject when you are there. Have a plan for leaving the subject when you have acquired the desired information or evidence.

Because you might be arrested if the subject is arrested, learn ahead of time whether you are to "blow

An undercover narcotics investigator makes a drug buy. "Looking the part" is essential to a successful undercover operation.
Monkey Business Images/Shutterstock.com

your cover" or submit to arrest. In some instances, outside sources may interfere with the lawful arrest, posing great danger for an undercover agent whose identity has become known during the arrest. When the assignment is successfully completed, give the subject a plausible explanation for leaving because it may be necessary to reestablish the undercover contact later.

It is often better to use undercover agents than informants because the testimony of a reliable, trained investigator is less subject to a defense attorney's attack than is that of an informant.

The legality of placing an undercover officer in a high school to investigate student drug use was decided in *Gordon v. Warren Consolidated Board of Education* (1983). High school officials had put an undercover officer into classes. The claimants alleged deprivation of their civil rights, but the federal district court dismissed the case for failure to state a cause of action. On appeal, the Supreme Court affirmed the prior judgment, stating that the presence of the undercover officer did not constitute any more than a "chilling" effect on the First Amendment right because it did not disrupt classroom activities or education and had no tangible effect on inhibiting expression of particular views in the classroom.

Undercover officers posing as prison inmates can acquire key information from other inmates suspected of other crimes. They may also operate undercover online. As social media becomes more pervasive throughout our society, investigators are finding that undercover online surveillance can be a valuable tool in generating information about criminal activities. While there are certainly

legitimate reasons why police may create undercover social media accounts using false identities, such as tracking child predators, the practice remains largely unregulated by both law enforcement agencies and the courts (Murillo, Rosenberg, & Rebuck, 2018). The hazards of warrantless, unregulated "undercover friending," such as privacy violations, discrimination, and racial profiling, are of great concern to civil liberties groups (Bliss, 2019).

One survey, in which 50 Freedom of Information Act Requests were sent to police departments across the nation, asked about their policies surrounding the use of social media in investigative work. Forty-three departments responded, and the results showed that most departments' social media policies dealt only with employee conduct, such as posting inappropriate photos that reflected poorly on the agency, and did not address the use of social media in investigations. Only 13 of the departments that responded indicated they had internal rules governing the use of social media in undercover work, with four departments citing policies in which investigators must (1) request and receive supervisor permission before creating a social media account for undercover purposes and (2) keep a detailed log of all activity on the account (Bliss, 2019). As one sergeant with the Seattle, Washington, Police Department noted, undercover work should not be a broad data mining mission but, rather, a focused effort on a targeted individual and a clear objective in working toward a particular investigative outcome.

Facebook has implemented a policy that requires law enforcement agencies to use their real identity on the company's platform. And although, to date, the Supreme

Court has not ruled that online dragnet surveillance falls under the protections of the Fourth Amendment requiring a search warrant, this issue is working its way through the lower courts, where defendants are arguing that undercover surveillance constitutes a search comparable to the use of GPS trackers and cell phone records and, as such, is illegal unless conducted with a warrant (Bliss, 2019).

Grossi (2009, pp. 24–28) offers several suggestions to consider when working undercover:

- Adopt credible aliases. Keep your real first name and date of birth.

- Whether you're going to "carry" or not may be a matter of personal preference or an issue your agency addresses.

- Choose your clothing based on your assignment. The primary objective is to fit in with your target group.

- Avoid the draw of the street, which can be overwhelming and even addicting.

- Although many UC operations require you to appear alone, always have backup within eye or earshot, either via wire or through direct visual contact.

- Remember who you are. Nothing is worth compromising your integrity as a police officer.

It is vital that undercover investigators keep accurate notes during their investigation, yet they must not allow the subject to be aware of such documentation.

LO5 List the objectives of undercover assignments and the precautions officers working undercover should take.

Precautions for undercover agents:

- Write no notes the subject can read.
- Carry no identification other than the cover ID.
- Ensure that any communication with headquarters is covert.
- Use a burner cell phone with no tracking software.
- Do not suggest, plan, initiate, or participate in criminal activity.

The final precaution warrants particular notice because regardless of how well planned and executed an undercover operation is, if the suspect can prove the criminal action for which they were arrested resulted from a suggestion made by the undercover officer, the entire case may be jeopardized by a charge of entrapment.

Entrapment. The Supreme Court defined **entrapment** in *Sorrells v. United States* (1932) as "the conception and planning of an offense by an officer, and his procurement of its commission by one who would not have perpetrated it except for the trickery, persuasion or fraud of the officer." *Sorrells* also explained the need for trickery in obtaining evidence: "Society is at war with the criminal classes, and the courts have uniformly held that in waging this warfare the forces of prevention and detection may use traps, decoys and deception to obtain evidence of the commission of a crime." *Sorrells* concludes, "The fact that government agents merely afford opportunities or facilities for the commission of the offense does not constitute entrapment."

These Court rulings still stand. In *Sherman v. United States* (1958), the Court explained, "Entrapment occurs only when the criminal conduct was 'the product of the creative activity' of law enforcement officials. To determine whether entrapment has been established, a line must be drawn between the trap for the unwary innocent and the trap for the unwary criminal."

Sting Operations. Sting operations target specific crimes such as fencing and stolen property, drug dealing, sales of alcohol and tobacco to minors, prostitution, car theft, fraud and corruption, and child pornography (Newman, 2007). Because of the wide variety of illegal activity targeted by stings and the need to employ different techniques depending on the sting's immediate or long-term purposes, it is difficult to formulate a simple yet precise definition of a sting operation. However, as Newman (2007, p. 3) notes, "with some exceptions, all sting operations contain four basic elements:

1. An opportunity or enticement to commit a crime, either created or exploited by police.

2. A targeted likely offender or group of offenders for a particular crime type.

3. An undercover or hidden police officer or surrogate or some form of deception.

4. A 'gotcha' climax when the operation ends with arrests."

Benefits of sting operations include the facilitation of investigation and increased arrests, enhanced public relations and police image, enhanced police presence, improved collaboration between police and prosecutors, provision of an impressive conviction record, the possibility of success without convictions or arrests, and the necessary partnering with community and business organizations that improves community relations by recovering stolen property (Newman, 2007).

Stings also have their downside, including not reducing or preventing recurring crime problems, being expensive, being deemed unethical by some, and raising privacy and entrapment issues.

Raids

A police **raid** is a planned, organized operation based on the element of surprise. Consider all other alternatives before executing a raid.

> **LO6** Summarize the objectives of raids, what to consider before conducting a raid, and precautions to take when conducting a raid.
>
> The objectives of a raid are to recover stolen property, seize evidence, or arrest a suspect.

Sometimes all three objectives are accomplished in a single raid. The first consideration is whether there are alternatives to a raid. A second consideration is the legality of the raid.

> **LO6** Summarize the objectives of raids, what to consider before conducting a raid, and precautions to take when conducting a raid.
>
> A raid must be the result of a hot pursuit or be under the authority of a no-knock arrest or search warrant.

If you are in hot pursuit of a known felon and have no time to plan a raid, make sure enough personnel and weapons are available to reduce danger. Call for backup before starting the raid. If time permits, however, careful planning and preparation will enhance the likely success of the raid.

Planning, organizing, and executing a raid are somewhat similar to undertaking a small military attack on a specific target. Without careful planning, the results can be disastrous, as illustrated in the 1993 federal raid on the compound of the Branch Davidian cult in Waco, Texas, in which nearly 80 cult members were killed.

Planning a Raid. Begin planning a raid by gathering information on the premises to be raided, including the exact address and points of entry and exit for both the raiding party and the suspect. Obtain a picture or sketch of the building and study the room arrangement. Additional location information might be obtained from aerial photographs, surveillance photos, walking the neighborhood, the city planning department, the county tax information website, and online resources such as Google Earth. Does the location have surveillance? Animals? Dogs are often used both as a means of notifying the suspects of trespassers and as weapons.

Consider whether there will be other people or the possibility of other people in or at the location. Will these people include other possible suspects, associates, innocent bystanders, juveniles, and so forth? If children are known or suspected to reside at the location, try to arrange the raid time for when the children are away at school or, at the least, asleep, to help avoid hostage situations.

If time permits, also consider the surrounding area. Is it in a neighborhood with families? Schools, parks, and so on? Do people need to be evacuated or notified?

Next, study the suspect's background. What crimes has the suspect committed? What difficulties were encountered in making past arrests? Is the suspect a narcotics addict? An alcoholic? Likely to be armed? If so, what type of weapon is the suspect likely to wield?

Obtain the appropriate warrants. Most raids are planned and result from an arrest warrant. In such cases, the subject is usually living under circumstances that necessitate a raid to make an arrest. In addition, if the raid is conducted to obtain evidence or property, obtain an exact description of the property sought, its likely location on the premises, and a legal search warrant. Specify that you require a no-knock warrant to conduct the raid and perhaps a nighttime warrant to enhance the element of surprise.

Throughout the entire planning process, keep the raid plan as simple as possible. Because the subject may be extremely dangerous, intend to use adequate firepower and personnel. Determine the required weapons and equipment. Plan for enough personnel to minimize violence, overcome opposition through superiority of forces, and prevent the suspect's escape or destruction of evidence. Also anticipate that the suspect may have installed surreptitious surveillance devices or booby-trapped the premises to thwart intruders. Make sure all entrances and exits will be covered and that a communication system is established. Decide how to transport the raiding party to the scene and how to take the suspect or evidence and property away. Determine who will be in command during the raid.

Remember that other people may be in the vicinity of the raid. If possible, evacuate everyone from the area of the raid without making the suspect suspicious. It is not always possible to do this without losing the element of surprise vital to the success of the raid.

Executing a Raid. Surprise, shock, and speed are essential elements in a raid. A raid should occur only after a careful briefing of all members of the raiding party. Each participant must know the objective, who the suspect is or what evidence or property is sought, and the exact plan of the raid itself. Give each participant proper equipment such as body armor, weapons, radios, whistles, megaphones, and signal lights. Give each participant a specific assignment, and answer all questions about the raid before leaving the briefing. The raid commander directs the raid, giving the signal to begin and coordinating all assignments.

Decisions about the initial entry and control phase of a raid must be made rapidly, because control is usually established within the first 15 to 30 seconds of a successful raid. No two raids are executed in precisely the same manner. The immediate circumstances and events dictate what decisions and actions are made.

Handguns are still the most versatile weapon during a raid, but shotguns and other assault-type weapons are useful in the perimeter operations and to control arrested individuals. If guard animals are known to be inside the raid area, provide for their control. Special equipment such as sledgehammers or rams may help in breaking down fortified entrances. An ambulance should be on standby, or raid personnel should at least know the fastest route to the nearest hospital.

Because raids are highly visible, the public and the news media often take interest. Therefore, raids are likely to be the object of community praise or criticism. They are also often vital to successfully prosecuting a case.

> **LO6** Summarize the objectives of raids, what to consider before conducting a raid, and precautions to take when conducting a raid.

Precautions in conducting raids:

- Ensure that the raid is legal.
- Plan carefully.
- Assign adequate personnel and equipment.
- Thoroughly brief every member of the raiding party.
- Be aware of the possibility of surreptitious surveillance devices or booby traps at the raid site.

SWAT Teams. Many police agencies have developed tactical squads, sometimes called *special weapons and tactics (SWAT)* teams, to execute raids. These units, also called *paramilitary police units (PPUs)*, are thoroughly trained to search areas for criminals, handle sniper incidents and hostage situations, execute arrest and search warrants, and apprehend militants who have barricaded themselves inside a building or other location.

SWAT was born on August 1, 1966, in Austin, Texas, when Charles Whitman went on a 96-minute shooting spree from the top of a tower at the University of Texas, killing 15 people and wounding 31 before two Austin police officers were able to climb the tower and stop him. In the 1990s, two seemingly contradictory models of policing emerged: community-oriented policing (COP) and SWAT teams. COP is a philosophy that stresses community partnerships and proactive problem solving, in contrast to the militaristic, reactive approach used by SWAT teams to deal with high-risk situations. Such teams generally adhere to the approach used by General Colin Powell of being the "meanest dog in town." According to the Powell doctrine, force should be used sparingly, but if used, it should be used decisively. In most jurisdictions, both approaches are needed depending on specific circumstances, with community policing being the predominant approach, but with SWAT teams at the ready for emergency situations and to execute well-planned operations such as raids. A successful raid usually results in arrests.

Legal Arrests

Once a suspect has been located and identified, the next step is generally an arrest. An arrest is a type of seizure and, like a search, is restricted by the Fourth Amendment and requires probable cause. Just as state laws define and establish the elements of crimes, they also define arrest and establish who may make an arrest, for what offenses, and when. Most state laws define an **arrest** in general terms as "the taking of a person into custody in the manner authorized by law for the purpose of presenting that person before a magistrate to answer for the commission of a crime." An arrest may be made by a police officer or a private citizen. It may be made with or without a warrant, although a warrant is generally preferred because this places the burden of proving that the arrest was illegal on the defense.

> **LO7** List the circumstances under which police officers are authorized to make an arrest.

Police officers are authorized to make an arrest

- For any crime committed in their presence
- For a felony (or for a misdemeanor in some states) not committed in their presence if they have probable cause to believe the person committed the crime
- Under the authority of an arrest warrant

Most arrests are for misdemeanors such as disorderly conduct, drunkenness, traffic violations, minor larceny, minor drug offenses, simple assaults, nuisances, and other offenses of lesser severity. In most states, the police officer must *see* such offenses to make an arrest without a warrant. In *Atwater v. Lago Vista* (2001), the Supreme Court allowed personally observed probable cause to permit an arrest and custodial detention for a minor misdemeanor. In other words, warrantless arrests for nonjailable offenses such as failing to wear a seatbelt were held to be constitutional. *Atwater* authorized police to arrest drivers of vehicles for violations punishable by only a monetary fine, widening police authority in traffic-related stops. In many states, an arrest may also be made by a "private person" who witnesses a misdemeanor and then turns the suspect over to law enforcement authorities.

If you have probable cause to believe a suspect has committed a felony and there is no time to obtain an arrest warrant, you can make an arrest without the warrant. Facts gathered *after* the arrest to justify probable cause are *not* legally admissible as evidence of probable cause. They can, however, strengthen the case if probable cause was established *before* the arrest.

An arrest for a felony or gross misdemeanor can usually be made any time if there is an arrest warrant or if the arresting officer witnessed the crime. An arrest may be made only in the daytime if it is by warrant, unless a magistrate has endorsed the warrant with a written statement that the arrest may be made at night. This is commonly referred to as a *nightcap provision*. Nightcapped warrants were discussed in Chapter 4.

Officers are allowed to break an inner or outer door to make an arrest after identifying themselves, stating the purpose for entry, and demanding admittance. This is often necessary when officers are in plainclothes and hence not recognized as police. The courts have approved no-knock entries in cases in which the evidence would be immediately destroyed if police announced their intention to enter. Officers may break a window or door to leave a building if they are illegally detained inside. They may break a door or window to arrest a suspect who has escaped from custody. Finally, officers may break an automobile window if a suspect rolls up the windows and locks the doors to prevent an arrest. Officers should give proper notification of the reason for the arrest and the intent to break the window if the suspect does not voluntarily comply.

Officers can accomplish the physical act of arrest by taking hold of or controlling the person and stating, "You are under arrest for . . ." In most jurisdictions the arresting officer's authority must be stated, and the suspect must be told for what offense the arrest is being made. In some cases the apparent reason for the arrest turns out to be incorrect, with a different charge being brought. In *Devenpeck v. Alford* (2004), the Supreme Court ruled that an arrest is not rendered unlawful even if an arresting officer's probable cause for making it is not the same criminal offense for which the known facts provided probable cause. The Court held that although it is a "good police practice" to inform a person of the reason for his arrest at the time he is taken into custody, the Court has "never held that to be constitutionally required."

Arresting a suspect requires that the *Miranda* warning be given before any questioning *about a crime* can occur. It is important to understand that not all questioning requires *Miranda*. For example, police can ask demographic questions to determine a person's identity or inquire why they are in the area. Routine booking questions, such as name, address, and birthdate, do not require *Miranda*. The *Miranda* warning was discussed in Chapter 6 as an extension of the Fifth Amendment due process requirements that govern obtaining information legally. The point being made here is that *Miranda* is not invoked simply because an arrest has occurred. *Miranda* is required only for custodial interrogations; in other words, when questioning of a suspect takes place while that suspect is in police custody or is otherwise deprived of their freedom of action in any significant way. Sometimes a street officer will make a probable cause arrest and book the subject, and then an investigator will arrive, who then Mirandizes the arrestee does the questioning.

Myth Any time a person has been arrested, the police must give *Miranda* for the arrest to be legal.

Fact Mirandizing a suspect is required only when two elements exist together: (1) a suspect is in custody and not free to leave and (2) the police ask the suspect questions about a crime. If either of these elements is absent—no custody or no questions—*Miranda* is not required.

An arrest also starts the clock on the time limits within which a judge must review the case, usually within 48 hours (*County of Riverside v. McLaughlin*, 1991). Officers who postpone an arrest can conduct additional investigation before starting the *McLaughlin* clock and can bolster their probable cause for arrest as well.

In some departments, it is a common practice to take a suspect who is not under arrest to the department questioning. If bringing someone in for questioning a▓▓▓ to be an arrest without probable cause, even if t▓▓▓ ▓▓ not told they are under arrest, and even i▓▓▓▓▓▓▓ ▓ not personally consider them to be under ▓▓▓▓▓▓ courts are likely to rule that the officers have, in effect, made an illegal **de facto arrest**. As a result, the courts will suppress any evidence so obtained. At minimum, the Supreme Court has ruled four times that if police take someone involuntarily to a police facility for investigation, this will be considered a de facto arrest. The first case was *Davis v. Mississippi* (1969), followed by *Dunaway v. New York* (1979), then *Hayes v. Florida* (1985), and more recently by *Kaupp v. Texas* (2003). If you are going to question the suspect about a crime, read the *Miranda* warning first.

> **LO8** Identify the elements that constitute an arrest having been made.
>
> If your intent is to make an arrest and you inform the suspect of this intent and then restrict the suspect's right to go free, you have made an arrest.

Officers may also pursue a fleeing suspect to make a *Terry*-type stop that could escalate into an arrest. In *Illinois v. Wardlow* (2000), the Supreme Court ruled that a person's sudden flight upon seeing a police officer can be used to establish reasonable suspicion for a *Terry* stop.

Sometimes a suspect will refuse to identify themselves. Pursuant to the Supreme Court's opinion in *Hiibel v. Sixth Judicial District Court of Nevada* (2004), a state law requiring a subject to disclose their name during a *Terry* stop does not violate the Fourth Amendment's ban on unreasonable search and seizure nor does it violate a person's Fifth Amendment protection against self-incrimination. Laws that require people to identify themselves to police, known as *Hiibel* laws, vary from state to state, but there is currently no federal statute requiring someone to identify themselves to federal law enforcement officers (Immigrant Legal Resource Center, 2018). In the majority opinion in *Hiibel*, Justice Kennedy wrote:

> Asking questions is an essential part of police investigations.... Obtaining a suspect's name in the course of a *Terry* stop serves important government interests. Knowledge of identity may inform an officer that a suspect is wanted for another offense, or has a record of violence or mental disorder. On the other hand, knowing identity may help clear a suspect and allow the police to concentrate their efforts elsewhere.

If, during the *Terry* stop, an officer establishes probable cause to arrest, and if the suspect resists, the officer may use force, but use of force also leaves the officer open to civil liability.

Residential Entry after Outdoors Arrest

"Entry incident to outdoors arrest" is not a lawful way to get inside a residence (Rutledge, 2008, p. 60). Three separate Supreme Court cases have held such entries to be unconstitutional. In *James v. Louisiana* (1965), the defendant was lawfully arrested and then driven to his home more than two blocks away. Without a warrant, consent, or an emergency, the officers entered and searched Otis James's home, finding narcotics equipment and morphine. He was convicted, but on appeal, the Supreme Court held that the evidence was the result of an illegal entry and could not be used against him: "In the circumstances of this case, the search of the defendant's home cannot be regarded as incident to his arrest on a street corner more than two blocks away. A search can be 'incident to an arrest' only if it is substantially contemporaneous with the arrest and is confined to the immediate vicinity of the arrest" (*James v. Louisiana*, 1965).

In *Shipley v. California* (1969), officers had staked out a suspect in an armed robbery and arrested him when he got out of his car in front of his home. They took him inside and searched his home, finding the stolen jewelry. In this case, the Court also reversed Shipley's conviction: "The Constitution has never been construed by this Court to allow the police in the absence of an emergency to arrest a person outside his home and then take him inside for the purpose of conducting a warrantless search."

In the third case, *Vale v. Louisiana* (1970), police conducting surveillance on Donald Vale's home saw him walk outside and sell drugs to people who drove up and honked. They arrested Vale on the front steps of his house and then entered and searched the residence. In this case, the Court held, "If a search of a house is to be upheld as incident to arrest, that arrest must take place inside the house. Our past decisions make clear that only in a few specifically established and well-delineated situations may a warrantless search of a dwelling withstand constitutional scrutiny. We decline to hold that an arrest on the street can provide its own exigent circumstance so as to justify a warrantless search of the arrestee's house."

Police do, however, have a right to maintain control over suspects once they are arrested. Therefore, if a suspect is arrested outside their home and asks to go back inside quickly, whether to get an ID or a jacket, the suspect has given the police *implied consent* to accompany them inside the residence. Once inside, officers may seize any contraband or evidence they see in plain view.

Arresting a Group of Companions

In *Maryland v. Pringle* (2003), an officer stopped a car for speeding. The three male occupants consented to a search of the vehicle, which turned up more than $700 of rolledup cash and five bags of cocaine. All three denied any knowledge of the money and drugs, so the officer arrested all three, including Joseph Pringle. The Maryland state court held that absent specific facts establishing Pringle's control over the drugs, the officer's mere finding that it was in a car occupied by Pringle was insufficient to justify probable cause to arrest. On appeal, the Supreme Court reversed, concluding that the officer had sufficient probable cause to arrest Pringle based on the information known to him at the time of arrest.

Off-Duty Arrests

Every department needs a policy that allows off-duty officers to make arrests. A suggested policy for off-duty arrests requires officers to

- Be within the legal jurisdiction of their agency

- Not be personally involved

- Perceive an immediate need for preventing a crime or arresting a suspect

- Possess the proper identification

Unless all these conditions exist, officers should not make an arrest but should report the incident to their department for disposition. In fact, sometimes it is better for an off-duty officer to call the police and report the crime. Officers can make good eyewitnesses and add credibility to a case.

Some of the factors officers must consider when deciding whether to make an off-duty arrest include their personal safety and the safety of their families or other individuals they might be with, what weapons they have available, and the likelihood of a person fleeing and causing additional issues. Another important consideration is that, in the event they are unable to notify dispatch of what is occurring, any other responding officers may not recognize the presence of off-duty officer who is only trying to help. To avoid being confused with the suspect, an officer involved in an off-duty arrest should make sure dispatch notifies the responding officers that an off-duty officer is on scene and provide a description of that officer's clothing so as to be readily identifiable. Plainclothes officers can encounter similar issues when attempting to make an arrest.

Avoiding Civil Liability When Making Arrests

Officers should be aware of the situations in which they may find themselves named in a lawsuit and should be aware of case law in these areas. Officers leave themselves open to lawsuits in several areas related to arrests, including false arrests, excessive force, shootings, and wrongful death.

Wrongful Arrest

Police officers always face the possibility of wrongful arrest, also known as false arrest. Some officers carry insurance to protect themselves against such lawsuits. Most are idle threats, however.

A wrongful-arrest suit is a civil tort action that attempts to establish that an officer who claimed to have authority to make an arrest did not have probable cause at the time of arrest. The best protection is to be certain that probable cause to arrest does exist, to have an arrest warrant, or to obtain a conviction in court.

Even when the defendant is found not guilty of the particular offense, a basis for a wrongful-arrest suit is not automatically established. A court will consider the totality of the circumstances at the time of the arrest and will decide whether they would lead an ordinarily prudent person to perceive probable cause and take the same action.

As with stop-and-identify laws, laws determining the statute of limitations, or the time frame within which a claimant can file a civil rights lawsuit, for wrongful arrest varies by state, as well as by the type of offense for which the claimant was arrested. Police officers should know what the statute of limitations is for a claim for false arrest in their state. In *Wallace v. Kato* (2007), the Supreme Court ruled, in a 7–2 decision, that the correct starting point for a false-arrest claim, or when the clock starts ticking, is when a judge reviews the criminal charges against the defendants and binds them over for trial.

Police officers reduce the probability of valid wrongful-arrest actions by understanding the laws they enforce, the elements of each offense, and what probable cause is needed to prove each element. Police officers who honestly believe they have probable cause for an arrest can use the "good-faith" defense, as established in *Pierson v. Ray* (1967): "A policeman's lot is not so unhappy that he must choose between being charged with dereliction of duty if he does not arrest when he has probable cause, and being mulcted [penalized] in damages if he does. Although the matter is not entirely free from doubt, the same consideration would seem to require excusing him from liability for acting under a statute that he reasonably believed to be valid but that was later held unconstitutional on its face or as applied."

Use of Force

The most difficult lawsuits to handle are those dealing with use of force. While there is no single, universally agreed-upon definition of use of force, the International Association of Chiefs of Police (IACP) describes **force** as the "amount of effort required by police to compel compliance by an unwilling subject" (2001). Force is most often thought of as physical influence, but it need not necessarily be "hands on."

Physical force is not a necessary part of an arrest; in fact, most arrests are made without physical force. Data from the Public Police Conduct Survey, which surveys persons who have had police contact during the previous 12 months, including traffic stops, shows that in 2015, persons who had had contact with police had physical force used against them or threatened against them in 2.0% of all contacts (Davis, Whyde, & Langton, 2018). This is an increase from the 1.4% reported in 2008. The majority of those who reported the threat of force in 2015 (84%) perceived the action to be excessive.

The use of force by law enforcement has long been a topic of national discussion, but a number of high-profile cases in recent years involving allegations of excessive use of police force has heightened awareness of these incidents. A lack of nationwide statistics has hindered efforts to analyze such use-of-force incidents and to have an informed dialogue on how best to address the issue. To this end, the FBI launched a national use-of-force data collection initiative on January 1, 2019 (FBI, *National use-of-force*, n.d.). However, participation in the program is voluntary, and in 2019, only 5,043 out of 18,514 federal, state, local, and tribal law enforcement agencies throughout the country participated and provided use-of-force data.

Determining the Amount of Force to Use. No two situations are the same, and the amount of force to use varies depending on the situation. The landmark case on use of force is *Graham v. Connor* (1989), in which

the Supreme Court set parameters when stating, "Our Fourth Amendment jurisprudence has long recognized that the right to make an arrest or investigatory stop necessarily carries with it the right to use some degree of physical coercion or threat thereof to effect it." In *Graham*, the Court explained, "The reasonableness of a particular use of force must be judged from the perspective of a reasonable officer on the scene, rather than with the 20/20 vision of hindsight." Furthermore, the "calculus of reasonableness must embody allowance for the fact that police officers are often forced to make split-second judgments—in circumstances that are tense, uncertain, and rapidly evolving—about the amount of force that is necessary in a particular situation."

Reasonable force is the amount of force used by police measured by what a prudent individual would accept or use themselves in a similar situation. When making an arrest, officers may legally use that level of force reasonably necessary to gain control of the person or the situation. With actively combative subjects, that level of force might be considerable. The Constitution does not require officers to use the least amount of force possible in a given situation. It requires only that the force used be "objectively reasonable" (Federal Law Enforcement Training Center, n.d.; Thompson, 2015). The circumstances include when the officer believes deadly force is necessary to prevent the death or serious bodily injury to another. The takeaway is not that police cannot use force, but that it must be *reasonable* under the circumstances.

LO9 Explain how much force is justified when making an arrest.

When making an arrest, use only as much force as is reasonably necessary to overcome any resistance and gain compliance.

Officers should be aware of research findings regarding encounter characteristics and when force is most likely to be used. For example, some research has found that officers were significantly more likely to use higher levels of force with suspects encountered in disadvantaged neighborhoods and neighborhoods with higher homicide rates (Feldman, Gruskin, Coull, & Krieger, 2019). Other research suggest that disrespectful suspects are more likely to have their behavior reciprocated, and some researchers conclude that force is most likely to be used when suspects show signs of alcohol or drug intoxication or engage in hostile behavior (Bolger, 2015; Terrill, Paoline, & Ingram, 2011). Officers should be aware of this finding and not take any disrespect shown to them too personally or be goaded into using more force than necessary.

Most police departments know of officers who tend to become involved in resistance or violent situations more frequently than others do. In some instances, these officers' aggressive approach seems to trigger resistance. Officers and police departments who routinely engage in or condone a culture of violent interactions risk not only public exposure and civil liability, but will lose the trust of the community. In any situation that is *not* out of control when you arrive, give a friendly greeting and state who you are and your authority if you are not in uniform. Speak calmly and convey the impression that you are in control. Show your badge or identification and give your reason for the questioning. Ask for identification and listen to their side of the story. Then decide on the appropriate action: warn, release, issue a citation, or make an arrest.

Deciding how much force to use in making an arrest requires logic and good judgment. However, in the heat of the moment, police officers may use more force than intended. Courts and juries have usually excused force that is not blatantly unreasonable, recognizing that many factors are involved in such split-second decisions. However, some force exceeds that which is objectively reasonable.

Claims of Excessive Force.

Excessive force means more than ordinary force, going above and beyond what is required to control the situation or behavior of an individual. What is considered to be excessive force in one situation (using a nightstick on an arrestee who willingly places their hands behind their back) may be justified (reasonable) force in another situation (using a nightstick on a physically combative, actively resisting arrestee who is swinging a metal bar at the officer). Excessive force used by police can be criminal and may leave the enforcer and agency open to both civil liability and criminal charges.

In seeking to determine what constitutes "objective reasonableness," *Graham* established three factors to evaluate alleged cases of excessive force:

- The severity of the crime

- Whether the suspect posed an immediate threat to the officer or others

- Whether the suspect was actively resisting arrest or attempting to evade arrest by flight

Graham v. Connor further held that plaintiffs alleging excessive use of force need show only that the officer's actions were unreasonable under the standards of the Fourth Amendment.

In *Saucier v. Katz* (2001), the Supreme Court held, "The inquiry as to whether an arresting police officer is entitled to qualified immunity for the use of excessive force is distinct from the inquiry as to whether the use of force was objectively reasonable under Fourth Amendment excessive force analysis."

Use-of-Force Policies and Continuums.

The public is very aware of and sensitive to police use of force. The instantaneous decisions and actions by police officers at the scene are subject to long-term review by the public and the courts. Police departments must review their use-of-force policies to ensure that they are clear and in accordance with court decisions as well as effective in ensuring officer safety. Some departments have rephrased these policies, replacing "use-of-force" with "response-to-resistance," to better reflect the reasoning behind why an officer chooses a particular action or force option (Police Executive Research Forum, 2012).

Regardless of terminology, officers must know their department's policies regarding use of force as well as their department's use-of-force continuum, if it has one. Not all departments have the same continuum. For instance, in some agencies the TASER may be accepted for use at a lower level on the continuum compared with other departments that may have it on the higher end of a spectrum. Further, uses of force in making arrests should be critiqued, and complaints of excessive force should be thoroughly reviewed.

Although voluntary compliance is the "best" arrest, there are always situations that are not peaceful, when a subject resists and the officer must respond with physical force. Force continuums were developed in the 1960s to train officers in the proper use of force, in large part because the courts at the time offered little guidance on how the police could, or should, use force against a citizen (Police Executive Research Forum, 2016). During the past half-century, dozens of continuums have been developed, most of which are based on a subject's degree of resistance and specify what level of force is appropriate in response.

Traditionally, use-of-force continuums have been linear, going from no resistance or very minimal resistance by the subject to aggravated, life-threatening aggression, and with corresponding officer response progressing from mere officer presence and verbal commands all the way to—in the case of life-threatening resistance—deadly force. Note that the least amount of force relies on communication skills. Officers must develop the communication skills necessary to resolve conflicts, where possible, before physical force is necessary.

Critics of linear use-of-force continuums note that the continuums seem to imply that force events are predictable and escalate in an orderly step-like fashion, when this is not reality. However, even if officers are taught that they can skip steps and go up and down on the continuum, linear continuums are sometimes explained in court as calling for such an orderly progression, which can be misleading or confusing to juries. Furthermore, in many situations, multiple levels or types of force would all be reasonable, and it is often difficult if not impossible to ascertain which force option imposes a greater degree of control over the subject than any of the others.

In an attempt to address this situation, some departments shifted from linear to nonlinear models. One such circular model is a force wheel, with the spokes in the wheel representing a specific type of force, as shown in Figure 7.4. This continuum avoids the implied stepwise progression of linear models, but such models otherwise provide little guidance to officers' force decisions.

As mentioned, not all departments have use-of-force continuums, and many that have had such continuums are now choosing to abandon them. Some police agencies still use the continuums in training but have removed them from formal policy (Police Executive Research Forum, 2012). Several federal law enforcement training organizations, including the Federal Law Enforcement Training Center (FLETC), the FBI Academy, and the Drug Enforcement Administration (DEA) Academy, have eliminated continuums in their force training programs altogether (Ciminelli, 2014).

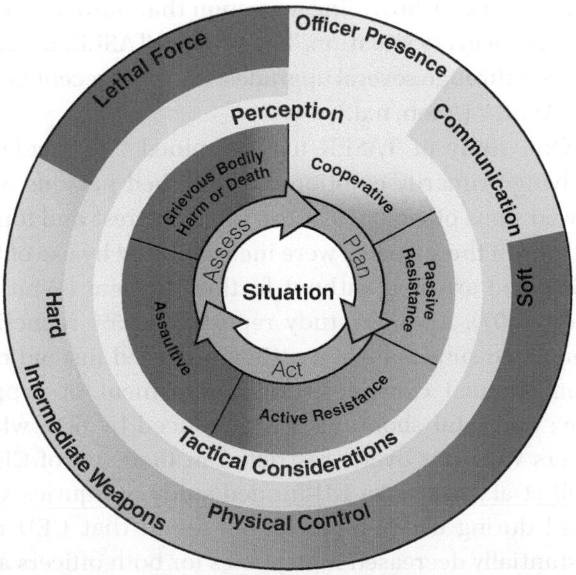

Those who oppose continuums cite several reasons for discontinuing their use. First, as mentioned, use-of-force situations are seldom as straightforward as the continuum. Second, officers might hesitate to react if they have to mentally consult the continuum before taking action. Third, it has been found that officers often try to match their reports to the continuum instead of writing out exactly what they recall.

Although many agencies still have use-of-force continuums, the trend is to find an alternative such as adopting a "force options" model. This type of model policy moves away from a two-dimensional diagram, focusing instead on the premise of objective reasonableness set forth in *Graham* (Flosi, 2012). In a force options model, the various types of force available to the officer are not ranked in any particular level, allowing the officer more flexibility and discretion to choose the force option that is most reasonable based on the immediate situation and totality of the facts known at that time.

Decision charts are also gaining popularity as police department re-engineer their use-of-force policies and training. One example of this kind of decision-making chart is used by the Philadelphia (Pennsylvania) Police Department. In its *Guiding Principles on Use of Force*, the Police Executive Research Forum (2016) calls for law enforcement agencies to discard use-of-force continuums and adopt a critical decision-making model (CDM), in which officers are trained to evaluate the totality of circumstances and find the most effective and safest response proportional to the threat: "[T]he CDM is anchored by the ideals of ethics, values, proportionality, and the sanctity of human life. Everything in the model flows from that principled core" (2016, p. 28).

Less-Lethal Weapons

Often when one thinks of a "weapon," a handgun is the first thing that comes to mind, and the intent when using the gun is to cause death, the most extreme use of force. But police have a variety of other weapons at their disposal when they must use lesser degrees of force to make an arrest. Whether they are called *less-than-lethal, less-lethal,* or *nonlethal weapons*, their intent is to avoid the use of deadly force. However, less-lethal does not mean *never* lethal, as fatalities can occur if munitions fired from such less-lethal weapons strike vital areas, such as the temple, throat, or upper abdomen (Haar, Iacopino, Ranadive, Dandu, & Weiser, 2017).

Figure 7.4

Circular use-of-force continuum of the Canadian Association of Chiefs of Police.

Source: From Ederheimer, J. A., & Fridell, L. A. (2005, April). *Chief concerns: Exploring the challenge of police use of force.* Washington, DC: Police Executive Research Forum, p. 50. Reprinted by permission

Myth Nonlethal weapons are those that cannot cause death.

Fact No weapon can ever be considered 100% nonlethal.

Discussing the use of nonlethal use-of-force options during an arrest, Ashley (2007) notes that such options are not only the most commonly used force options but are also the ones most likely to lead to officer injury or a lawsuit. Consider, for example, the commonly used restraint option of handcuffs: "Improper or sloppy use of handcuffs, and sometimes failure to use them at all, has probably gotten more officers hurt and killed than any other commonly used law enforcement tool" (Ashley, 2007, p. 72). In addition to restraints, the other basic ways to control a subject through less-lethal force include aerosols, impact munitions, conducted energy devices (CEDs), empty-hand control, and, of course, verbal management of the scene.

Restraints. The most commonly used restraint is handcuffs. Police officers are usually trained that the best way to transport a suspect under arrest is to place handcuffs on the person's wrists with the person's hands placed behind their back. Sometimes, when the handcuffs are removed, red marks, abrasions, bruising, numbness, and other injuries can be seen. Several courts have addressed the issue of whether tight handcuffs can constitute excessive force under the Fourth Amendment, but no general rule says handcuffs must be loose or at what level they become "too tight." Departments typically train officers to double-lock the cuff to prevent the cuffs from getting increasingly tighter if a suspect struggles in them. Double-locking keeps a routine arrest from progressing into a medical call (and a lawsuit) caused by cuffs that have cut off circulation to a suspect's hands.

Aerosols. While tear gas is one aerosol used for large-scale riot-control purposes, the most common aerosol used in the context of making an arrest is oleoresin capsicum (OC) spray, also referred to as *pepper spray*. Pepper spray has been used by police since the early 1990s and grew in popularity because it was cost effective, generally very safe, easy to use and train with, and effective most (81%) of the time (Ijames, 2007). The use of pepper spray began to wane when Conducted Energy Devices (CEDs) came on the market, which were found to be significantly more effective than pepper spray in subduing subjects and did not carry the same detrimental effects on the officer as did the deployment of OC spray (Haskins, 2019). Today, many police agencies have stopped issuing OC because of its limited effectiveness and potential safety risks to officers.

Impact Munitions. An impact munition, also called a kinetic impact projectile (KIP), is a projectile specially designed to cause nonlethal blunt trauma and incapacitation when it strikes a subject's body. For example, beanbag rounds or rubber bullets fired from a distance allow officers to control, without inflicting serious injury to, combative subjects without compromising their own safety. However, several studies have found evidence that these weapons can, in fact, be lethal at close range and are inherently inaccurate at longer ranges, making them a danger to bystanders and others not specifically targeted by officers (Haar, Iacopino, Ranadive, Dandu, & Weiser, 2017).

Conducted Energy Devices (CEDs). CEDs are also called Electronic Control Weapons (ECWs) or Conducted Electrical Weapons (CEWs). These handheld devices operate by delivering a burst of electricity to a subject. The hit of high voltage causes neuromuscular incapacitation (NMI) and, usually, immobilization, making it easier for officers to gain control of the subject (Haskins, 2019). Perhaps the best-known and most controversial less-lethal weapon is the TASER™, an acronym for Thomas A. Swift Electric Rifle, which is used by more than 15,000 law enforcement and military agencies worldwide (U.S. Department of Justice, Office of Community Oriented Policing Services, 2011). Axon, the company the manufactures the TASER, is continuously working to improve their technology, the goal being to protect life by providing a weapon that outperforms a handgun in every situation. The original TASER, the X26, has been through several upgrades, the most recent being the TASER 7 (Axon, n.d.).

One study of TASER use examined 243 incidents involving primarily emotionally disturbed persons who showed signs of violence at the time of arrest and found that 85% of the suspects were incapacitated by use of the TASER and arrested without further incident (White & Ready, 2007). Another study reported a 65% reduction in injury to subjects when a CED was used instead of a baton, manual control, or the deployment of pepper spray; and fatal shootings were reduced by 66% when officers were not overly restricted in their use of CEDs (Kroll et al., 2019). An NIJ-funded study of injuries sustained during use-of-force events found that CED use substantially decreased injury rates for both officers and offenders (Bulman, 2011).

Although the risk to the subject of electrocution is low, the possibility of death, while rare, does exist (Haskins, 2019). And while research to date has not provided any definitive evidence that CEDs, when deployed properly, cause any permanent cognitive or physical damage to subjects who lack predisposing factors, other harms may occur when a CED is deployed, including head trauma and bone breaks caused when a subject falls to the ground, puncture wounds and burns caused when the barbed probes (sometimes called darts) enter a suspect's skin, and eye injuries and blindness when a probe hits a subject's eye (Haskins, 2019; Kroll et al., 2019).

Criticism began to rise in the early 2000s about officers misusing CEDs, and a government-sponsored use-of-force study found that officers were, indeed, deploying their TASERs too early and too often during many encounters (Haskins, 2019). Federal courts began hearing more excessive force cases involving CEDs, and in 2016, the Fourth Circuit's decision in *Armstrong v. Village of Pinehurst* (2016) set a stricter constitutional standard for CED deployment. Noting that the deployment of a TASER is a serious use of force, the court ruled that using a CED to cause pain compliance on a uncooperative subject, in contrast to using a CED on a subject who poses an immediate physical threat to the officer or others, was an unjustified use of force:

> Force that imposes serious consequences requires significant circumscription. Our precedent, consequently, makes clear that tasers are proportional force *only* when deployed in response to a situation in which a reasonable officer would perceive some immediate danger that could be mitigated by using the taser. . . . And this conclusion, that taser use is unreasonable force in response to resistance that does not raise a risk of immediate danger, is consistent with our treatment of police officers' more traditional tools of compliance.

As with any other use of force, departments must have sound policies for the use of CEDs that address such issues as using the devices on high-risk individuals, limiting the number of applications or successive "stuns," and providing medical and mental health evaluations after exposure (Haskins, 2019). Furthermore, "the effectiveness and safety of CEDs are a function of the quality of training received by officers on the street" (Haskins, 2019). Recognizing this need, Cronin and Ederheimer (2006), with the collective efforts of the Police Executive Research Forum (PERF) and the Department of Justice (DOJ), developed *Conducted Energy Devices: Standards for Consistency and Guidance: The Creation of National CED Policy and Training Guidelines*. This document was updated five years later, again through the collaborative efforts of PERF and the DOJ, with the publication of *2011 Electronic Control Weapon Guidelines* (Office of Community Oriented Policing Services, 2011).

Technology Innovations

BolaWrap

One less-lethal option that has been referred to as "remote handcuffs" is the BolaWrap®, a hand-held device developed by Wrap Technologies that discharges an 8-foot bola-style Kevlar® tether at 513 feet per second to wrap and restrain a subject's legs or arms. Each tether has a 4-pronged hook on either end. The tether is contained in a cartridge that is powered by a partial charge .380 blank. The device can be effectively deployed from 10–25 feet away from the subject and features a green laser light for accurate targeting. The BolaWrap does not rely on pain compliance, provides a remote response to resistance that allows officers to remain a safe distance from the subject, and decreases the potential for injury to the subject, the officer, and any bystanders.

Source: https://wraptechnologies.com/faqs/?=undefined

Use of Deadly Force

From 2003 to 2014, the Bureau of Justice Statistics (BJS) administered the Arrest-Related Deaths (ARD) program to fulfill the data collection requirement of the Death in Custody Reporting Act (DICRA) of 2000. The goal of the ARD program was to document the number of persons who died during the process of arrest or while in the custody of state or local law enforcement officials nationwide, including deaths due to police use of lethal force or justifiable homicides, suicides, accidental deaths, and deaths from intoxication and medical conditions that occurred during interaction with state or local law enforcement.

In 2014, BJS suspended the ARD program after an assessment of the data collection method revealed serious shortcomings and that only about half of the estimated number of justifiable homicides in the United States were being captured. A redesign of the ARD launched in 2015, and using improved data collection methods, a potential 1,348 arrest-related deaths were identified for the period between June 1, 2015, and March 31, 2016 (Banks, Ruddle, Kennedy, & Planty, 2016). Extrapolating this data to a full calendar year led analysts to estimate that 1,900 arrest-related deaths occurred in 2015, the majority (64%) of which were homicides, the remainder being suicides and accidental deaths.

Police officers carry guns and are trained in using them. They also have department policy on deadly force as a guide. Unfortunately, the point of last resort may be immediate because many police situations rapidly deteriorate to the point of deadly force decision making. When such situations occur, they must be viewed from the perspectives of both the department's policies and the individual's situation.

Department policies on deadly force should be reviewed periodically in the light of the most recent Supreme Court decisions. Policies must be restrictive enough to limit unreasonable use of deadly force but not so restrictive that they fail to protect the lives of officers and members of the community.

Use of a deadly weapon is carefully defined by state laws and department policy. Such policies usually permit use of a gun or other weapon only in self-defense or if others are endangered by the suspect. Some policies also permit use of a deadly weapon to arrest a felony suspect, to prevent an escape, or to recapture a felon when all other means have failed. Warning shots are not usually recommended because they can ricochet, harming others, and can prompt sympathetic fire by other officers, if more than one officer is at the scene.

The landmark case on use of deadly force is the Supreme Court ruling in *Tennessee v. Garner* (1985), where the Court ruled, "It is not better that all felony suspects die than that they escape. Where the suspect poses no immediate threat to others, the harm resulting from failing to apprehend him does not justify the use of deadly force to do so. It is no doubt unfortunate when a suspect who is in sight escapes, but the fact that the police arrive a little late or are a little slower afoot does not always justify killing the suspect."

In this case, the Court banned law enforcement officers from shooting to kill fleeing felons unless an imminent danger to life exists. This ruling invalidated laws in almost half the states that allowed police officers to use deadly force to prevent the escape of a suspected felon. In this case, police shot and killed an unarmed 15-year-old boy who had stolen $10 and some jewelry from an unoccupied house. The Court ruled, "A police officer may not seize an unarmed, nondangerous suspect by shooting him dead."

The *Garner* decision did not take away police officers' right to use deadly force. The Court acknowledged legitimate situations in which deadly force is acceptable and necessary: "Where the officer has probable cause to believe that the suspect poses a threat of serious physical harm, either to the officer or to others, it is not constitutionally unreasonable to prevent escape by using deadly force. Thus, if the suspect threatened the officer with a weapon or there is probable cause to believe that he had committed a crime involving the infliction or threatened infliction of serious physical harm, deadly force may be used if necessary to prevent escape and if—where feasible—some warning has been given." In some deadly force incidents, officers have had suspects attempt to grab the officers' sidearms to use against them.

The "21-foot rule" in using deadly force states that a knife-wielding attacker could be as far away as 21 feet and still stab the officer before he could effectively fire his handgun (Irwin, 2007). This "rule" was based on a series of simple trials conducted in 1983 by a firearms instructor, and some contend the exercise was done merely to warn officers about maintaining a "safety zone" between themselves and offenders with edged weapons (Police Executive Research Forum, 2016). And while few departments formally train their officers in the "21-foot rule," many police chiefs acknowledge that it continues to be shared and perpetuated informally.

However, research by Lewinski and Fackler of the Force Science Research Center shows that officer reaction times are significantly longer than commonly believed, with the average officer requiring at least a full second to perceive the threat and then decide to react by drawing their weapon. This delay in reaction means that an attacker closing in at 14 feet per second could start out as far as 35 feet away from an officer and still reach that officer before the officer could fire a round. Furthermore: "It is extremely difficult to smoothly draw and accurately fire when under a life-threatening attack. So that means that we had better add another 10 feet to allow for the attacker to keep coming if we miss center mass or even if we hit him, even mortally wound him, but he doesn't go down. It's now the 45-foot rule" (Irwin, 2007, p. 83).

The Police Executive Research Forum has officially recommended discontinuing the outdated concept of using any fixed distance "rule," noting that over time this "safety zone" concept has become corrupted, in some cases coming to be thought of as a "kill zone" and leading some officers to believe they are automatically justified in shooting anyone with a knife who gets within 21 feet, 45 feet, or whatever the fixed distance is from the officer. In fact, PERF's research found examples of the "rule" being cited by officers or their defense attorneys to justify shootings of suspects with edged weapons (Police Executive Research Forum, 2016).

Everyone understands that force should be used as a last resort, and whether to use deadly force is a major and difficult decision for police officers. When it should be used is generally defined in state statutes.

"Ramming" in Pursuit as Use of Force. The intentional collision of a law enforcement officer's vehicle with another vehicle—ramming—constitutes a Fourth Amendment seizure and requires objective reasonableness at the time of the seizure. Ramming is viewed as deadly force by the courts. This issue was addressed in *Scott v. Harris* (2007), a case that resulted when Victor Harris ignored the blue lights and siren of Deputy Timothy Scott, who was trying to stop Harris for speeding. Harris led officers on a 6-minute, 10-mile chase at speeds exceeding 85 miles per hour on mostly two-lane roads. The Eleventh Circuit Court ruled that the facts and circumstances did not justify use of deadly force, focusing on Harris's "crime" as speeding. When the case reached the Supreme Court, it focused on the "relative culpability" in balancing the nature and quality of the intrusion against the importance of the government interest. The Court concluded that the motoring public in the area was innocent; Harris, however, was culpable because he, by initiating the chase, had placed himself and others in danger.

The case is significant in several respects: "First, the Court is willing to consider raw evidence (in this case, the recording of the chase) rather than reserving the factual determinations for the jury in a case where the objective recording eliminates any genuine issue of material facts. In addition, the Fourth Amendment does not require officers to abandon a pursuit when the pursued drives so recklessly as to endanger others" (Risher, 2007, p. 11). As shown in *Harris*, the court will consider two questions:

1. Whether a law enforcement officer's conduct is objectively reasonable under the Fourth Amendment when the officer makes a split-second decision to terminate a high-speed pursuit by bumping the fleeing suspect's vehicle with his push bumper because the suspect has demonstrated that he would continue to drive in a reckless and dangerous manner that put the lives of innocent persons at a serious risk of death.

2. Whether at the time of the incident the law was clearly established such that no court had ruled the Fourth Amendment is violated when a law enforcement officer used deadly force to protect the lives of innocent persons from the risk of dangerous and reckless vehicular flight.

An alternative to ramming that is not necessarily viewed as use of deadly force is the Precision Immobilization Technique, more commonly known as the PIT maneuver. PIT is a driving technique that trains police officers to end a pursuit quickly using tactics such as hitting the suspect vehicle at a specific location at slower speeds, which throws the suspect vehicle into a tailspin and brings it to a stop. Proper execution of the PIT maneuver requires specialized training and certification that not all police officers have completed. The goal of this method is to terminate a pursuit safely.

In-Custody Death: Excited Delirium. When a person suddenly dies in police custody, it is often labeled as a case of *excited delirium* (EXD). Excited delirium syndrome (ExDS) is characterized by bizarre and aggressive behavior, paranoia, panic, violence, hyperthermia, and unexpected physical strength (Mash, 2016).

ExDS is not a medical or psychiatric diagnosis but, rather, a set of symptoms and behaviors that make up a syndromal disorder (Takeuchi, Ahern, & Henderson, 2011).

Consider the following scenario involving a case of EXD (Wesley, 2011): Officers respond to a report of a naked man "acting strangely holding a bat," who has been screaming and breaking car windows. They find an obese man standing in the middle of the street, wielding a bat and screaming, "Make them stop!" Though the officers have him at gunpoint and order him to put down the bat, the subject does not obey the officers' commands. Several applications of a Taser fail to subdue the man, and it takes six officers 10 minutes of struggling to finally gain control over the subject. He is placed face down on the pavement with his hands cuffed behind his back and a flex cuff around his ankles. Suddenly, the subject becomes quiet and still, and an officer notices that the man has stopped breathing. Officers roll the man onto his back and, finding no pulse, start CPR and call for an ambulance. Efforts continue to resuscitate him, but the subject is pronounced dead when the ambulance arrives.

Takeuichi et al. (2011) observe: "While the contribution of restraint, struggle and the use of electrical conduction devices to the cause of death raises controversy, recent research points toward central nervous system dysfunction of dopamine signaling as a cause of the delirium and fatal autonomic dysfunction. Victims of EXD usually die from cardiopulmonary arrest, although the exact cause of such arrest is likely multifactorial and chronic." Mash (2016) adds: "Excited delirium is . . . controversial and highly debated precisely because the mechanism of lethality is unknown. However, molecular studies of the brain of autopsy victims who died in states of excited delirium reveal a loss of dopamine transporter function as a possible trigger of a lethal cascade of neural activities that progress to asphyxia and sudden cardiac arrest."

Officers recognizing such symptoms of EXD should immediately call for help. Because of the potential for lawsuits in such cases, it is imperative that officers know how to investigate such deaths immediately. Investigating in-custody deaths is discussed in Chapter 8.

Use of Force and the Mentally Ill. Dealing with people who are mentally ill or otherwise emotionally disturbed can present a use-of-force challenge. Use of less-lethal weapons may contain the situation or worsen it. Researchers Swartz and Lurigio (2007) studied the relationships among psychiatric disorders, substance use, and arrests for violent, nonviolent, and drug-related offenses and found that the statistical association between serious mental illness (SMI) and arrest across psychiatric diagnoses was substantially but only partially mediated by substance use. For nonviolent offenses and for drug-related offenses, the relationship between SMI and arrest was almost completely mediated by substance use, reduced to statistical nonsignificance: "These findings suggest that co-occurring substance use increases the chances a person with any SMI, not just schizophrenia, will be arrested for any offense, not just violent offenses, but that the magnitude of this relationship varies by offense type and, to a lesser extent, by disorder" (Swartz & Lurigio, 2007, p. 581).

In 2017, an estimated 11.2 million adults (4.5%) aged 18 or older had a severe mental illness (National Institute of Mental Health, 2019). That same year, nearly half (49.5%) of U.S. adolescents aged 13–18 were estimated to have had a mental disorder, and of those adolescents, an estimated 22.2% had a severe mental illness. The police are frequently called to respond to incidents involving individuals with mental health issues. Often these individuals have not been diagnosed and are not on proper medication, have stopped taking their prescribed medication, or are under the influence of another behavior altering drug. Research suggests that police often see the mentally ill as more dangerous than other suspects are. In fact, those with mental illness are often unfairly portrayed as violent.

One method used in responding to calls involving emotionally disturbed individuals is the deployment of a crisis intervention team (CIT). The Memphis, Tennessee, Police Department established training under the CIT model in 1998, stressing communication and de-escalation, and many departments across the country have since adopted the model. CIT officers are taught to recognize the various psychiatric syndromes, the biologic basis for severe mental illness, de-escalation of crisis situations, the law pertaining to the detention of the mentally ill, and access to emergency and nonemergency mental health services (Watson & Fulambarker, 2012).

Some contend that this should be standard training for *all* police officers, not just a specialized group because it is not plausible that there will be a CIT-trained officer available in every situation that calls for one. However, research has found that ongoing refresher courses are needed to maintain the skills acquired during initial CIT training, as a measurable decay was observed over time in officers' self-efficacy in responding to mental health crises as well as their perceptions of verbal de-escalation (Davidson, 2014).

Suicide by Police. When individuals who are mentally ill force police officers into shooting them, the question often arises, Is this a case of suicide by cop? *Suicide by police* is a phenomenon in which someone intentionally acts so threateningly toward officers as to force them to fire, accomplishing the subject's ultimate goal of dying, albeit not by their own hand. Sometimes it seems very implausible that a person really wants to die in what appears to be a suicide-by-cop situation. Such instances have been presented as "death by indifference." When it seems that suicide by cop is not probable, investigators should consider the possibility of death by indifference by an offender apathetic to their own fate.

When a law enforcement officer uses deadly force, a lawsuit will almost certainly follow. That underscores the criticality of use-of-force reports.

Use-of-Force Reports

As has been stressed, thorough, accurate, well-written reports are critical to the investigator. Litigation has prompted a push for precision in describing exactly what happened during the incident in a use-of-force report. Language intended to convey precision and professionalism may sound like euphemisms to a jury, as though the officer is being evasive. Therefore, officers need to articulate their use of force in everyday language to show the reasonableness of their actions (Grossi, 2008). For example, rather than writing "I decentralized the subject," an officer might write, "I used a push-in/pull-down technique to take Mr. Jones to the ground, while verbally commanding him to get down" (Robinson, 2006, p. 32). Using such language can reduce the likelihood of excessive-force lawsuits being filed in the first place, and, if the case does go to court, such reports make the prosecution's case less likely to be successful: "We have a duty to teach officers to use force effectively so they can survive on the street. If we don't also teach them to report it effectively, they may not survive in court" (Robinson, 2006, p. 32).

Summary

Developing, locating, identifying, and arresting suspects are primary responsibilities of investigators. Field identification or show-up identification is on-the-scene identification of a suspect by a victim of or witness to a crime. Field or show-up identification must be made within a short time after the crime was committed. *United States v. Ash, Jr.* (1973) established that a suspect does not have the right to have counsel present at a field identification.

If the suspect is not immediately identified, you must develop a suspect through information provided by victims, witnesses, and other people likely to know about the crime or the suspect; physical evidence at the crime scene; informants; modus operandi information; psychological and geographic profiling; information in police files and the files of other agencies; tracking; and other aids, such as news media (TV, radio, newsprint) and social media requests to the public for information.

Suspects can be identified through field or show-up identification, booking photos, field views, photographic identification, or live lineups. Use field identification when the suspect is arrested at or near the scene. Use booking photo identification if you believe the suspect has a police record. Use photographic identification when you have a good idea who committed the crime but the suspect is not in custody, or when a fair live lineup cannot be conducted. Tell witnesses they need not identify anyone from the photographs. A suspect does *not* have the right to a lawyer if a photographic lineup is used (*United States v. Ash, Jr.*, 1973).

Use a live lineup when the suspect is in custody. Use at least six people (including the suspect) of the same gender and comparable race, height, weight, age, and general appearance. Ask all to perform the same actions or speak the same words. Instruct witnesses viewing the lineup that they need not make an identification. Suspects may refuse to participate in a lineup, but such refusals may be used against them in court (*Schmerber v. California*, 1966). Suspects have a Sixth Amendment right to have an attorney present during a lineup.

Surveillance, undercover assignments, and raids are used only when normal methods of continuing the investigation fail to produce results. The objective of surveillance is to obtain information about people, their associates, and their activities that may help solve a criminal case or protect witnesses. The types of surveillance include stationary (fixed, plant, or stakeout) and moving (tight or close, loose, rough, on foot, or by vehicle). Electronic surveillance and wiretapping are considered forms of search and therefore are permitted only with probable cause and a court order (*Katz v. United States*, 1967).

The objective of an undercover assignment may be to gain a person's confidence or to infiltrate an organization or group by using an assumed identity and to thereby obtain information or evidence connecting the subject with criminal activity. Precautions for undercover agents are to write no notes the subject can read; carry no identification other than the cover ID; ensure that any communication with headquarters is covert; use a burner cell phone with no tracking software; and do not suggest, plan, initiate, or participate in any criminal activity.

The objectives of a raid are to recover stolen property, seize evidence, or arrest a suspect. To be legal, a raid must be the result of a hot pursuit or under authority of a no-knock arrest warrant or a search warrant. Precautions in conducting raids include ensuring that the raid is legal, planning carefully, assigning adequate personnel and equipment, thoroughly briefing every member of the raiding party, and being aware of the possibility of surreptitious surveillance devices or booby traps at the raid site.

An arrest may occur at any point during an investigation. Police officers are authorized to make an arrest (1) for any crime committed in their presence, (2) for a felony (or for a misdemeanor in some states) not committed in their presence if they have probable cause to believe the person committed the crime, or (3) under the authority of an arrest warrant. Probable cause for believing the suspect committed a crime must be established *before* a lawful arrest can be made. If your intent is to make an arrest and you inform the suspect of this intent and then restrict the suspect's right to go free, you have made an arrest. When making an arrest, use only as much force as is reasonably necessary to overcome any resistance and gain compliance.

Can You Define?

arrest

bugging

close surveillance

cover

criminal profiling

de facto arrest

entrapment

excessive force

field identification

fixed surveillance

force

geographic profiling

loose surveillance

open surveillance

plant

pretextual traffic stops

psychological profiling

racial profiling

raid

reasonable force

rough surveillance

show-up identification

solvability factors

stakeout

subject

surveillance

surveillant

tail

tight surveillance

undercover

wiretapping

Checklists

Identifying and Arresting Suspects

- Was a suspect observed by police on arrival at the scene?

- Was a suspect arrested at the scene?

- Was anyone observed at the scene by any other person?

- Was a neighborhood check made to determine suspicious people, vehicles, or noises?

- Was the complainant interviewed?

- Were statements taken from witnesses or people with information about the crime?

- Was a description of the suspect obtained?

- Was the description disseminated to other members of the local police force? To neighboring police departments?

- Was any associative evidence found at the scene or in the suspect's possession?

- Were informants checked?

- Were similar crimes committed in the area? In the community? In neighboring communities? In the state? Anywhere else in the nation?

- Were field-identification cards checked to determine who was in the area?

- Were MO files reviewed to determine who commits a similar type of crime? Are the suspects in or out of prison?

- Were traffic tickets checked to see whether any person or vehicle was in the area at the time of the crime? How does the vehicle or crime compare with the suspect vehicle or person?

- Where any surveillance videos available and checked in the vicinity of the crime?

- Have other agencies been checked?—Municipal? County? State? Federal? Fusion centers?

- How was the person identified? Field identification? Booking photos? Photographic identification? Lineup identification? Was it legal?

- Was the arrest legal?

Surveillance

- Is there any alternative to surveillance?

- What information is needed from the surveillance?

- What type of surveillance is needed?

- Have equipment and personnel needs for the surveillance area been determined?

- Are the required equipment and personnel available?

- Are proper forms available for recording necessary information during the surveillance?

- Are all signals preestablished?

Undercover Assignments

- Is there any alternative to undercover work?

- What information is needed from the assignment?

- Is adequate information about the subject available?

- Have you established a good cover?

- How will you communicate with headquarters?

- What are you to do if you are arrested?

- Do you have an alternative plan if the initial plan fails?

- Do you have a plausible explanation for leaving once the assignment is completed?

Raids

- Is there any alternative to a raid?

- Have appropriate warrants been obtained?

- Have the objectives of the raid been clearly specified?

- Has a pre-surveillance of the raid location been conducted?

- Are adequate personnel and equipment available?

- Has a briefing been held?

References

Albright, T. D. (2017, July 24). "Why eyewitnesses fail." *Proceedings of the National Academy of Sciences of the United States of America*, *114*(30):7758–7764. doi:10.1073 /pnas.1706891114

Allen, J. (2018, April 4). Denver police to test shotspotter system in 4 different neighborhoods with live gunfire. *The Denver Channel.com*. Retrieved July 28, 2020, from www .thedenverchannel.com/news/crime/denver-police-to -test-shotspotter-system-in-4-different-neighborhoods -with-live-gunfire

Ashley, S. (2007, February). What gets you sued gets you hurt. *Law Officer Magazine*, pp. 72–75.

Axon. (n.d.). Taser 7. Seattle, WA: Author. Retrieved August 3, 2020, from www.axon.com/products/taser-7

Banks, D., Ruddle, P., Kennedy, E., & Planty, M. G. (2016, December). *Arrest-related deaths program redesign study, 2015–16: Preliminary findings*. Washington, DC: Bureau of Justice Statistics. (NCJ 250112). Retrieved August 4, 2020, from www.bjs.gov/content/pub/pdf /ardprs1516pf.pdf

Bliss, K. (2019, March). Police use of "undercover friending" investigative technique unregulated. *Criminal Legal News*: 35. Retrieved July 27, 2020, from www.criminallegalnews .org/news/2019/feb/14/police-use-undercover-friending -investigative-technique-unregulated/

Bolger, P. (2015). Just following orders: A meta-analysis of the correlates of American police officer use of force decisions. *American Journal of Criminal Justice, 40*(3): 466–492. doi:10.1007/s12103-014-9278-y

Bulman, P. (2011, March). Police use of force: The impact of less-lethal weapons and tactics. *NIJ Journal*, 267, 4–11. (NCJ 233281)

Charman, S. D., & Quiroz, V. (2016). Blind sequential lineup administration reduces both false identifications and confidence in those false identifications. *Law and Human Behavior, 40*(5): 477–487. Retrieved July 23, 2020, from psycnet.apa.org/record/2016-25882-001

Ciminelli, M. L. (2014). *Legal implications of use-of-force continuums in police training*. Rochester, NY: Author. Retrieved July 28, 2020, from www.aele.org /Continuum2014.pdf

Crandall, S. (2020, April 29). How ALRPs can be a force multiplier for law enforcement in times of crisis. *Police1*. Retrieved July 25, 2020, from www.policeone.com/police -products/traffic-enforcement/license-plate-readers /articles/how-alprs-can-be-a-force-multiplier-for-law -enforcement-in-times-of-crisis-oo5ur6TA6Ez2RquU/

Crenshaw, Z. (2019, September 10). Shotspotter technology helps arrest serial shooter in Glendale. *ABC15.com*. Retrieved July 28, 2020, from www.abc15.com/news/region -west-valley/glendale/shotspotter-technology-helps-arrest -serial-shooter-in-glendale

Cronin, J. M., & Ederheimer, J. A. (2006, November). *Conducted energy devices: Development of standards for consistency and guidance*. Washington, DC: Police Executive Research Forum and the Department of Justice.

Davidson, M. L. (2016, February). A criminal justice system-wide response to mental illness: Evaluating the effectiveness of the Memphis crisis intervention team training curriculum among law enforcement and correctional officers. *Criminal Justice Policy Review, 27*(1). doi:10.1177/0887403414554997

Davis, E., Whyde, A., & Langton, L. (2018, October). *Contacts between police and the public, 2015*. Washington, DC: Bureau of Justice Statistics. (NCJ 251145) Retrieved July 28, 2020, from www.bjs.gov/content/pub/pdf/cpp15.pdf

Federal Bureau of Investigation. (n.d.). *National center for the analysis of violent crime.* Washington, DC: Author. Retrieved July 20, 2020, from www2.fbi.gov/hq/isd/cirg/ncavc.htm

Federal Bureau of Investigation. (n.d.). *National use-of-force data collection.* Washington, DC: Author. Retrieved July 28, 2020, from www.fbi.gov/services/cjis/ucr/use-of-force

Federal Bureau of Investigation. (n.d.). *Next generation identification (NGI).* Washington, DC: Author. Retrieved July 19, 2020, from www.fbi.gov/services/cjis/fingerprints-and-other-biometrics/ngi

Federal Law Enforcement Training Center. (n.d.). *Use of force: Myth and realities part 1* (MP3). Glynco, GA: Author. Retrieved July 28, 2020, from www.fletc.gov/audio/use-force-myths-and-realities-part-i-mp3

Feldman, J. M., Gruskin, S., Coull, B. A., & Krieger, N. (2019, March). Police-related deaths and neighborhood economic and racial/ethnic polarization, United States, 2015–2016. *American Journal of Public Health, 109*(3): 458–464. doi:10.2105/AJPH.2018.304851

Fitzgerald, R. J., Price, H. L., & Valentine, T. (2018). Eyewitness identification: Live, photo, and video lineups. *Psychology, Public Policy, and Law, 24*(3): 307–325. Retrieved July 23, 2020, from www.ncbi.nlm.nih.gov/pmc/articles/PMC6078069/

Flosi, Ed. (2012, May 10). Use of force: Downfalls of the continuum model. *PoliceOne.com*, May 30, 2012. Retrieved July 28, 2020, from www.policeone.com/use-of-force/articles/use-of-force-downfalls-of-the-continuum-model-dtXx4gU5SWkIvJwW/

Fridell, L. A. (2016). The science of implicit bias and implications for policing. In *Producing Bias-Free Policing: A Science-Based Approach.* Cham, Switzerland, Springer International Publishing. doi:10.1007/978-3-319-33175-1_2

Grossi, D. (2008, October). Tactics for survival writing. *Law Officer Magazine*, pp. 30–33.

Grossi, D. (2009, April). Going under. *Law Officer Magazine*, pp. 24–28.

Haar, R. J., Iacopino, V., Ranadive, N., Dandu, M., & Weiser, S. (2017). Death, injury, and disability from kinetic impact projectiles in crowd-control settings: A systematic review. *The BMJ*, 7(12). Retrieved July 29, 2020, from bmjopen.bmj.com/content/7/12/e018154.full

Hanratty, T. (2007, April). Walking in another's shoes. *Law Enforcement Technology*, pp. 42–51.

Harris, D. A. (2020, January 21). Racial profiling: Past, present, and future? *Criminal Justice 34*(4). Retrieved July 21, 2020, from www.americanbar.org/groups/criminal_justice/publications/criminal-justice-magazine/2020/winter/racial-profiling-past-present-and-future/

Haskins, P. A. (2019, May 1). Conducted energy devices: Policies on use evolve to reflect research and field deployment experience. *NIJ Journal*, Issue 281. Retrieved August 3, 2020, from nij.ojp.gov/topics/articles/conducted-energy-devices-policies-use-evolve-reflect-research-and-field-deployment

Hilderbrand, D. S. (2013). Footwear: The missing evidence (3rd ed.). Wildomar, CA: Staggs Publishing.

Ijames, S. (2007, November–December). Less-lethal technologies, part 2. *Tactical Response*, pp. 22–24.

Immigrant Legal Resource Center. (2018, February 1). *Chart of stop-and-identify state statutes.* San Francisco, CA: Author. Retrieved July 28, 2020, from www.ilrc.org/chart-stop-and-identify-state-statutes

International Association of the Chiefs of Police. (2001). *Police use of force in America.* Alexandria, VA: Author.

Irwin, B. (2007, October). Rethinking the 21-foot rule. *Police*, pp. 82–85.

Kroll, M. W., Brave, M. A., Pratt, H. M. O., Witte, K. K., Kunz, S. N., & Luceri, R. M. (2019, July 31). Benefits, risks, and myths of TASER® handheld electrical weapons. *Human Factors and Mechanical Engineering for Defense and Safety, 3*(7). doi:10.1007/s41314-019-0021-9

La Vigne, N. G., Thompson, P. S., Lawrence, D. S., & Goff, M. (2019, October). *Implementing gunshot detection technology.* Washington, DC: Urban Institute. Retrieved July 28, 2020, from www.nationalpublicsafetypartnership.org/clearinghouse/Content/ResourceDocuments/UI-Implementing%20Gunshot%20Detection%20Technology.pdf

Law Enforcement Imaging Technology Task Force. (2019, March). *Law enforcement facial recognition use case catalog.* Alexandria, VA: International Association of Chiefs of Police. Retrieved July 19, 2020, from www.theiacp.org/resources/document/law-enforcement-facial-recognition-use-case-catalog

Lawrence, D. S., La Vigne, N. G., Goff, M., & Thompson, P. S. (2019, January 2). Lessons learned implementing gunshot detection technology: Results of a process evaluation in three major cities. *Justice Evaluation Journal, 1*(2): 109–129. doi:10.1080/24751979.2018.1548254

Lee, B. (2007, October). Cuttin' sign: Ten tips for following the tracks. *Law Officer Magazine*, pp. 28–34.

Levine, N. (2015, January). *CrimeStat: A spatial statistics program for the analysis of crime incident locations* (v 4.02). Houston, TX: Ned Levine & Associates, and Washington, DC: National Institute of Justice. Retrieved July 21, 2020, from nij.ojp.gov/topics/articles/crimestat-spatial-statistics-program-analysis-crime-incident-locations

Mash, D. C. (2016, October). Excited delirium and sudden death: A syndromal disorder at the extreme end of the neuropsychiatric continuum. *Frontiers in Physiology, 7* (Article 435. Retrieved August 4, 2020, from www.ncbi.nlm.nih.gov/pmc/articles/PMC5061757/pdf/fphys-07-00435.pdf

Mecklenburg, S. H., Larson, M. R., & Bailey, P. J. (2008, October). Eyewitness identification: What chiefs need to know now. *The Police Chief*, pp. 68–81.

Mentalix. (2018, June 19). *RISC-y business: Why mobile ID matters.* Dallas, TX: Author. Retrieved July 19, 2020, from mentalix.com/risc-y-business-why-mobile-id-matters/

Minnesota Department of Public Safety, Bureau of Criminal Apprehension. (2015). *Cold case playing card initiative.* St. Paul, MN: Author. Retrieved July 22, 2020, from dps.mn.gov/divisions/bca/bca-divisions/investigations/Pages/cold-case-playing-card-initiative.aspx

Murillo, M., Rosenberg, L., & Rebuck, M. (2018, December 17). *Undercover policing in the age of social media*. New York, NY: NYU School of Law, Policing Project. Retrieved July 27, 2020, from www.policingproject.org/news-main /undercover-policing-social-media

National Academies of Science (NAS). (2014). *Identifying the culprit: Assessing eyewitness identification*. Washington, DC: National Academies Press.

National Institute of Mental Health. (2019, February). Mental Illness. Bethesda, MD: Author. Retrieved August 4, 2020, from www.nimh.nih.gov/health/statistics/mental-illness .shtml

Newman, G. R. (2007). *Sting operations*. Washington, DC: Office of Community Oriented Policing Services.

Nirenberg, M. (2016, January). Gait, footprints, and footwear: How forensic podiatry can identify criminals. *The Police Chief 83*: web only. Retrieved July 22, 2020, from www.policechiefmagazine.org/gait-footprints-and -footwear-how-forensic-podiatry-can-identify-criminals/

Office of Community Oriented Policing Services. (2011, March). *2011 electronic control weapon guidelines*. Washington, DC: Author. Retrieved August 4, 2020, from www.policeforum.org/assets/docs/Free_Online _Documents/Use_of_Force/electronic%20control%20 weapon%20guidelines%202011.pdf

Police Executive Research Forum. (2012, August). *An integrated approach to de-escalation and minimizing use of force*. (Critical Issues in Policing Series). Washington, DC: Author. Retrieved July 28, 2020, from www.policeforum.org /assets/docs/Critical_Issues_Series/an%20integrated%20 approach%20to%20de-escalation%20and%20 minimizing%20use%20of%20force%202012.pdf

Police Executive Research Forum. (2013, March 8). *A national survey of eyewitness identification processes in law enforcement agencies*. Washington, DC: Author. Retrieved July 24, 2020, from www.policeforum.org/assets/docs /Free_Online_Documents/Eyewitness_Identification /a%20national%20survey%20of%20eyewitness%20 identification%20procedures%20in%20law%20 enforcement%20agencies%202013.pdf

Police Executive Research Forum. (2016, March). *Guiding principles on use of force*. Washington, DC: Author. Retrieved July 24, 2020, from www.policeforum.org/assets /guidingprinciples1.pdf

Risher, J. (2007, July). U.S. Supreme Court decides "Ramming" case: Force was reasonable under the circumstances. *The Police Chief*, pp. 10–12.

Robinson, P. A. (2006, January/February). What you say is what they write: Everybody teaches report writing. *The Law Enforcement Trainer*, pp. 30–32.

Rossmo, D. K. (2013). Geographic profiling. In G. Bruinsma & D. L. Weisburd (Eds.), *Encyclopedia of criminology and criminal justice*, pp. 1934–1942. New York: Springer.

Russell, J., & Farragher, T. (2013, April 28). 102 Hours in pursuit of marathon suspects. *The Boston Globe*. Retrieved March 31, 2015, from www.bostonglobe.com/metro/2013/04/28 /bombreconstruct/VbSZhzHm35yR88EVmVdbDM /story.html

Rutledge, D. (2008, February). Residential entry after outdoor arrest. *Police*, pp. 60–62.

ShotSpotter. (2019). Flex: Proven crime-fighting tool disrupts gun violence cycle. Newark, CA: Author. Retrieved July 28, 2020, from www.shotspotter.com/law-enforcement-flex/

Sjöberg, M. P. (2016, January 28). The show-up identification procedure: A literature review. *Open Journal of Social Sciences 4*: 86–95. doi:10.4236/jss.2016.41012

Smith, A. L., & Mason, S. E. (2016). The age of racial profiling in the context of terrorism. *Modern Psychological Studies 21*(2), Article 10. Retrieved July 21, 2020, from scholar.utc .edu/mps/vol21/iss2/10

Smith, A. M., Bertrand, M., Lindsay, R. C. L., Kalmet, N., Grossman, D., & Provenzano, D. (2014). The impact of multiple show-ups on eyewitness decision-making and innocence risk. *Journal of Experimental Psychology: Applied, 20*(3), 247–259. doi:10.1037/xap0000018

Swartz, J., & Lurigio, A. J. (2007, October). Serious mental illness and arrest: The generalized mediating effect of substance use. *Crime & Delinquency, 53*(4), 581–604.

Takeuchi, A., Ahern, T. L., & Henderson, S. O. (2011, February). Excited delirium. *Western Journal of Emergency Medicine, XII*(1): 77–83. Retrieved August 4, 2020, from www.ncbi.nlm.nih.gov/pmc/articles/PMC3088378/pdf /wjem12_1p0077.pdf

Taylor, J. R. (2019, May 16). A history of tolerance for violence has laid the groundwork for injustice today. *Human Rights Magazine 44*(1). Retrieved July 21, 2020, from www.americanbar.org/groups/crsj/publications /human_rights_magazine_home/black-to-the-future /tolerance-for-violence/

Terrill, W., Paoline, E. A., III, & Ingram, J. (2011, May). *Final technical report draft: Assessing police use of force policy and outcomes*. Washington, DC: National Institute of Justice. Retrieved July 28, 2020, from www.ncjrs.gov/pdffiles1/nij /grants/237794.pdf

Thompson, R. M., III. (2015, October 30). *Police use of force: Rules, remedies, and reforms*. Washington, DC: Congressional Research Service. (R44256). Retrieved July 28, 2020, from fas.org/sgp/crs/misc/R44256.pdf

U.S. Department of Justice. (2017, January 6). *Eyewitness identification procedures for conducting photo arrays*. Washington, DC: Author. Retrieved July 23, 2020, from elineup.org/Laws/US_DOJ_Jan_2017_memo.pdf

U.S. Department of Justice, Office of Community Oriented Policing Services. (2011, March). *2011 Electronic control weapon guidelines*. Washington, DC: Author. Retrieved August 4, 2020, from www.policeforum.org/assets/docs /Free_Online_Documents/Use_of_Force/electronic%20 control%20weapon%20guidelines%202011.pdf

U.S. Department of Homeland Security. (2014, May). *Radar systems for through-the-wall surveillance*. Washington, DC: Author. Retrieved July 26, 2020, from www.dhs.gov/sites /default/files/publications/Radar-TWS-SUM_0514-508.pdf

Velarde, L. (2016, Fall). The use of geographic profiling in crime analysis. *Crime Mapping & Analysis News (Issue 5)*: 5–9. Retrieved July 20, 2020, from crimemapping.info /wp-content/uploads/2016/12/CMAN-Issue-5.pdf

Wallentine, K. (2020, June 2). Automated license plate reader information leads to mail "fishing" suspect. *Police1*. Retrieved July 25, 2020, from www.policeone.com/police -products/traffic-enforcement/license-plate-readers /articles/automated-license-plate-reader-information -leads-to-mail-fishing-suspect-LQbv8JAzRXpwpf8z/

Watson, A. C., & Fulambarker, A. J. (2012). The crisis intervention team model of police response to mental health crises: A primer for mental health practitioners. *Best Practices in Mental Health, 8*(2): 71. Retrieved August 4, 2020, from www.ncbi.nlm.nih.gov/pmc/articles /PMC3769782/

Welch, K. (2019, July). Race, ethnicity, and the war on terror. *Oxford Research Encyclopedias of Criminology and Criminal Justice.* New York, NY: Oxford University Press. Retrieved July 21, 2020, from oxfordre.com/criminology /view/10.1093/acrefore/9780190264079.001.0001 /acrefore-9780190264079-e-335

Wesley, K. (2011, February 1). Excited delirium strikes without warning. *Journal of Emergency Medical Services, 36*(Issue 2). Retrieved August 4, 2020, from www.jems.com/2011/02/01 /excited-delirium-strikes-witho/

White, M. D., & Ready, J. (2007, October). The TASER as a less lethal force alternative: Findings on use and effectiveness in a large metropolitan police agency. *Police Quarterly, 10*(2), 170.

Wixted, J. T., & Wells, G. L. (2017, May 1). The relationship between eyewitness confidence and identification accuracy: A new synthesis. *Psychological Science in the Public Interest, 18*(1): 10–65. doi:10.1177/1529100616686966

Cases Cited

Armstrong v. Village of Pinehurst, 810 F.3d 892 (2016).

Atwater v. Lago Vista, 532 U.S. 318 (2001).

Brown v. City of Oneonta, 221 F.3d 329 (2d Cir. 2000), cert denied 534 U.S. 816 (2001).

Carpenter v. United States, 585 US ___ (2018).

County of Riverside v. McLaughlin, 500 U.S. 44 (1991).

Davis v. Mississippi, 394 U.S. 721 (1969).

Devenpeck v. Alford, 543 U.S. 146 (2004).

Dunaway v. New York, 442 U.S. 200 (1979).

Florida v. Riley, 488 U.S. 445 (1989).

Gilbert v. California, 388 U.S. 263 (1967).

Gordon v. Warren Consolidated Board of Education, 706 F.2d 778 (1983).

Graham v. Connor, 490 U.S. 386 (1989).

Hayes v. Florida, 470 U.S. 811 (1985).

Hiibel v. Sixth Judicial District Court of Nevada, Humboldt County, 542 U.S. 177 (2004).

Illinois v. Wardlow, 528 U.S. 119 (2000).

James v. Louisiana, 382 U.S. 36 (1965).

Katz v. United States, 389 U.S. 347 (1967).

Kaupp v. Texas, 538 U.S. 626 (2003).

Kyllo v. United States, 533 U.S. 27 (2001).

Manson v. Brathwaite, 432 U.S. 98 (1977).

Maryland v. Pringle, 540 U.S. 366 (2003).

Pierson v. Ray, 386 U.S. 547 (1967).

Saucier v. Katz, 533 U.S. 194 (2001).

Schmerber v. California, 384 U.S. 757 (1966).

Scott v. Harris, 550 U.S. 372 (2007).

Sherman v. United States, 356 U.S. 369 (1958).

Shipley v. California, 395 U.S. 818 (1969).

Sorrells v. United States, 287 U.S. 435 (1932).

Tennessee v. Garner, 471 U.S. 1 (1985).

United States v. Ash, Jr., 413 U.S. 300 (1973).

United States v. Jones, 565 U.S. 400 (2012).

United States v. Knotts, 460 U.S. 276 (1983).

United States v. McKinnon, 985 F.2d 525 (11th Cir. 1993).

United States v. Wade, 388 U.S. 218 (1967).

United States v. Weaver, 966 F.2d 391 (8th Cir. 1992).

United States v. Yang, No. 18-10341 (9th Cir. 2020).

Vale v. Louisiana, 399 U.S. 30 (1970).

Wallace v. Kato, 549 U.S. 384 (2007).

Whren v. United States, 517 U.S. 806 (1996).

Investigating Violent Crimes

For more than eight decades, the Federal Bureau of Investigation (FBI) has collected crime data through its Uniform Crime Reporting (UCR) program and published its results in an annual report, Crime in the United States, to serve as a national barometer of crime in this country. Prior to 2011, the UCR used a Summary Reporting System (SRS) to collect statistics on eight types of serious crimes, previously called index offenses: murder, aggravated assault, forcible rape, robbery, burglary, larceny/theft, motor vehicle theft, and arson. A shortcoming of the SRS was that it used the hierarchy rule, meaning only the most serious offense was counted. For example, if an incident involved both an armed robbery and a homicide, only the homicide was recorded.

Recognizing that the SRS left a serious gap in the estimation of crime in the United States, the FBI developed the National Incident-Based Reporting System (NIBRS) to capture details on each single crime incident, as well as on separate offenses within the same incident. NIBRS also collects information on victims, known offenders, relationships between victims and offenders, arrestees, and property involved in the crimes. NIBRS is set to become the new standard in crime reporting by 2021, as the FBI phases out the SRS. Throughout these changes, however, Crime in the United States has maintained its separation of crimes into two broad categories—violent crime and property crime. This section looks at violent crime; property crime is the focus of Section 4.

According to the most recently available data, a violent crime occurred nationally every 26.2 seconds in 2018 (FBI, 2018a):

- 1 murder every 32.5 minutes

- 1 rape every 3.8 minutes

- 1 robbery every 1.9 minutes

- 1 aggravated assault every 39.2 seconds

FBI data also indicate that an estimated 1,206,836 violent crimes were committed in the United States in 2018, representing a decrease of 3.3% from the 2017 estimate. The five-year trend (2018 compared with 2014) indicated that violent crime increased 4.7%. However, for the 10-year period (2018 compared with 2009), violent crime was down 9%. As in previous years, aggravated assaults comprised the largest portion of violent crime in 2018 at 66.9%, followed by robbery (23.4%), rape (8.4%), and murder (1.3%). According to *Crime in the United States*, an estimated 368.9 violent crimes per 100,000 inhabitants occurred in 2018 (FBI, 2018b). Firearms were used in 72.7% of the nation's murders, in 38.5% of the robbery offenses, and in 26.1% of the aggravated assaults. (Weapons data are not collected for rape.)

The violent-crime rate in the United States has fluctuated over the past several decades. From its peak in 1994,

at roughly 1.86 million violent crimes (a rate of 713.6 violent crimes for every 100,000 people), to its lowest point in 2013 (1.16 million violent crimes and a rate of 367.9 per 100,000 people), it has trended up and down at various times between 2004 and 2018 (see Figure III.1). Caution must be used when interpreting such figures, however, as they do not include crime data for categories not included in the UCR program and thus underrepresent the true extent of violent crime.

Another measure of crime is achieved through the National Crime Victimization Survey (NCVS), which tallied more than 6.0 million crimes of violence and 3.3 million crime victims in 2018 (Morgan & Oudekerk, 2019). The overall violent-crime rate was 23.2 victimizations per 1,000 persons age 12 or older. Note the great difference between the findings of these two national measures of crime in the United States. It should also be noted that the NCVS does not collect data on murder.

Investigating violent crimes is made more difficult by the emotionalism usually encountered not only from the victim but also from the public. Generally, however, investigating violent crimes results in more and better information and evidence than investigating crimes against property, discussed in Section 4.

Although states vary in what elements must be proven in a given crime, some common elements exist, as shown in Figure III.2.

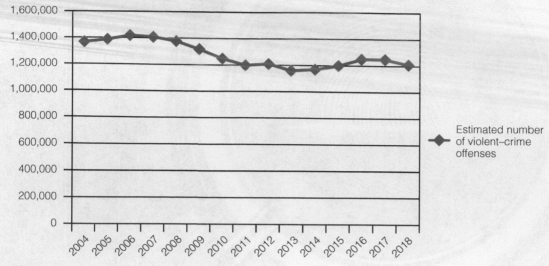

FIGURE III.1
Violent-crime offense figure, 15-year trend, 2004–2018.

Source: *Crime in the United States*—years 2004 through 2018.

Individual year data points available at www.fbi.gov/about-us/cjis/ucr/crime-in-the-u.s

In recent years, violent-crime investigations have been enhanced by the establishment of the Violent Crime Apprehension Program (VICAP) at the FBI National Police Academy in Quantico, Virginia. VICAP maintains a national data information center that collects, classifies, and analyzes violent crimes, including homicide and attempted homicide, sexual assaults, child abductions, missing persons, and unidentified deceased persons. VICAP analysts examine crime data and patterns to identify potential similarities among crimes, create investigative matrices, develop timelines, and identify homicide and sexual assault trends and patterns (FBI, n.d.). Information considered viable is published in the *FBI Law Enforcement Bulletin*. If the case merits interagency cooperation, a major case investigation team of investigators from all involved agencies may be formed.

Viability is determined by specialists at VICAP who review the information submitted and compare it with information received from other departments about similar cases and their modus operandi (MOs). This is especially important in serial killings and other major violent crimes in which the suspects have moved to other areas and committed similar crimes.

The chapters in this section of the book discuss specific considerations in investigating deaths/murder (Chapter 8); assault, domestic violence, stalking, and elder abuse (Chapter 9); sex offenses (Chapter 10); crimes against children (Chapter 11); and robbery (Chapter 12). In actuality, more than one offense can occur in a given case. For example, what begins as a robbery can progress to an assault, then a forcible rape, and finally a murder. Each offense must be proven separately.

References

Federal Bureau of Investigation. (n.d.). Privacy impact assessment violent criminal apprehension program (VICAP) July 18, 2003. Washington, DC: Author. Retrieved August 6, 2020, from www.fbi.gov/services/information-management/foipa /privacy-impact-assessments/vicap

Federal Bureau of Investigation. (2018a). 2018 crime clock statistics. Washington, DC: Author. Retrieved August 6, 2020, from ucr.fbi .gov/crime-in-the-u.s/2018/crime-in-the-u.s.-2018/topic-pages /crime-clock

Federal Bureau of Investigation. (2018b). Crime in the United States, 2018. Washington, DC: Author. Retrieved August 6, 2020, from ucr .fbi.gov/crime-in-the-u.s/2018/crime-in-the-u.s.-2018

Morgan, R. E., & Oudekerk, B. A. (2019, September). Criminal victimization, 2018. Washington, DC: Bureau of Justice Statistics. (NCJ 253043). Retrieved August 6, 2020, from www.bjs.gov /content/pub/pdf/cv18.pdf

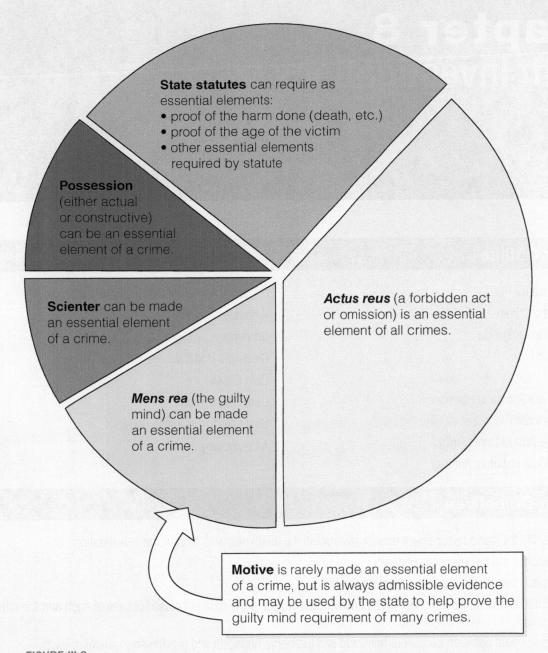

State statutes can require as essential elements:
• proof of the harm done (death, etc.)
• proof of the age of the victim
• other essential elements required by statute

Possession (either actual or constructive) can be an essential element of a crime.

Scienter can be made an essential element of a crime.

Actus reus (a forbidden act or omission) is an essential element of all crimes.

Mens rea (the guilty mind) can be made an essential element of a crime.

Motive is rarely made an essential element of a crime, but is always admissible evidence and may be used by the state to help prove the guilty mind requirement of many crimes.

FIGURE III.2
Elements that may be essential to the proof of a crime.

Source: Gardner, T. J., & Anderson, T. M. (2018). Criminal law (13th ed.). Wadsworth, a part of Cengage Learning, Inc.

Chapter 8
Death Investigations

Chapter Outline

Manners of Deaths

Elements of the Crime

Challenges in Investigation

Equivocal Death

Suicide

Preliminary Investigation of Homicide

The Homicide Victim

Estimating the Time of Death (ToD)

The Medical Examination or Autopsy

Unnatural Causes of Death and Method Used

Witnesses

Suspects

Clearing a Homicide

Cold Cases

Death Notification

Strategies for Reducing Homicide

A Case Study

Learning Objectives

LO1 Identify the basic requirement used to determine if a death warrants a homicide investigation.

LO2 Describe the five manners of death.

LO3 Explain the various classifications of homicides.

LO4 Compare and contrast murder and manslaughter, including the different classifications of each and the different elements that must be proven.

LO5 Differentiate between excusable homicide and justifiable homicide and provide an example of each.

LO6 Explain the significance of premeditation in a death investigation.

LO7 List the signs commonly looked for during the preliminary investigation of a homicide to determine that death has occurred.

LO8 List the various resources used to identify an unknown homicide victim.

LO9 Explain how these specific factors are used to estimate the ToD: body temperature, rigor mortis, postmortem lividity, eye appearance, and stomach contents.

LO10 Explain the effect water has on a dead body.

LO11 Describe the purpose of the medical examination or autopsy.

LO12 List the indicators investigators use to determine whether the following causes of unnatural death most likely indicate that the death was accidental, a suicide, or a homicide: gunshot wounds; stabbing and cutting wounds; blows from blunt objects; asphyxia; poisoning; burning; explosions, electrocution, and lightning; drugs; and vehicles.

LO13 Explain why determining a motive is important in homicide investigations.

LO14 Identify the similarities that exist between school and workplace mass murders.

Introduction

You arrive at the scene of a death in response to an emergency call and find the body of a 55-year-old white male crumpled at the bottom of a steep staircase—obviously dead. Did the victim trip and fall (accidental death)? Did he suffer a fatal heart attack at the top of the stairs and then fall (natural death)? Did he throw himself down the stairs to end some intense physical or mental suffering (suicide)? Or was he pushed (homicide)?

Only the fourth explanation involves a criminal action meriting an official police investigation. However, because the police must determine whether it actually was homicide, the other three possible explanations must be investigated.

Consider another scenario involving a death investigation: In April 2013, North Dakota college student Andrew Sadek found himself in legal trouble after selling a small amount of marijuana to a confidential informant. The deals took place on campus, making them serious felonies. In November of that year Sadek agreed to become a confidential informant himself, as part of an arrangement with authorities to keep the felonies off his record. Over the next three months, he completed three of the four required drug deals for the regional task force. On May 1, 2014, the security camera at his college dorm captured Sadek leaving early in the morning, and that was the last image anyone had of him, until his body was pulled from a river two months later. He had been shot in the head.

An autopsy concluded that Sadek died from the gunshot wound and that no drugs or alcohol were in his system at the time of his death. Still, investigators were left wondering whether the student was slain in a drug deal gone bad or if he killed himself. There were no clues as to how his body ended up in the river, and no weapon had been found. But it was determined that a gun that fires the same caliber bullet that killed Sadek was missing from his family's home (Nicholson, 2015).

LO1 Identify the basic requirement used to determine if a death warrants a homicide investigation.

A basic requirement in a homicide investigation is to establish whether death was caused by a criminal action.

Statistically, murder is the least significant of the violent crimes, with the FBI reporting 16,214 criminal homicides in the United States in 2018, an increase of 14.5% from 2017 (FBI, 2018). However, deaths reported as accidents or suicides may actually have been murder, and vice versa. It may be necessary to determine whether a death was a murder made to appear as a suicide to eliminate further investigation or a suicide made to appear as an accident to collect life insurance.

Manners of Deaths

The manner of death is defined as how the death came about. It is not to be confused with the *cause* of death or the *mechanism* of death. For example, a gunshot wound to a robbery victim's femoral artery:

Manner of death: homicide

Cause of death: gunshot wound

Mechanism of death: excessive blood loss

LO2 Describe the five manners of death.

The five manners of death are as follows:

- Natural
- Accidental
- Suicide
- Homicide (noncriminal or criminal)
- Undetermined ("could not be determined")

Natural Causes

Natural causes of death include heart attacks, strokes, fatal diseases, pneumonia, sudden crib deaths, and old age. Frequently, a person who dies of natural causes has been under a physician's care, and a death from natural causes is easily established. Sometimes, however, a death is made to look as though it resulted from natural causes. For example, drugs that simulate the effects of a heart attack may be used in a suicide or homicide.

Accidental Deaths

Among the causes of accidental death are falling; drowning; unintentionally taking too many pills or ingesting a poisonous substance; entanglement in industrial or farm machinery; or involvement in an automobile, boat, train, bus, or plane crash. Some people advocate that certain accidental deaths be investigated as criminal homicide—for example, fatal crashes. A homicide investigation can routinely involve 30 officers. A fatal-crash clearance is usually completed by just one or two officers.

As with natural deaths, an apparently accidental death can actually be a suicide or a homicide. For example, a person can jump or be pushed from a roof or in front of a vehicle or can voluntarily or involuntarily take an overdose of pills. Or a person may engage in autoerotic asphyxiation to achieve sexual gratification but may accidentally kill themselves in the process.

Suicide

Suicide—the intentional taking of one's own life—can be committed by shooting, stabbing, poisoning, burning, asphyxiating, or ingesting drugs or poisons. However, homicides are often made to look like suicides, and many suicides are made to look like accidents, usually for insurance purposes or to ease the family's suffering.

Although suicide is not a criminal offense, in most states it is a crime to *attempt* to commit suicide. This allows the state to take legal custody of such individuals for hospitalization or treatment. All states have a law or code that allows law enforcement officers and other qualified personnel to enforce a mandatory mental health hold for suicidal persons that require immediate evaluation for risk of being a danger to themselves or others.

It may also be a crime to help someone commit or attempt to commit suicide by either intentionally advising, encouraging, or actually assisting the victim in the act. The topic of assisted suicide is extremely controversial. The Supreme Court has found that there is no constitutional "right to die" and has left this decision to each individual state. One high-profile figure in this controversy is Jack Kevorkian, "Dr. Death," a pathologist-turned-assisted-suicide-crusader who facilitated more than 130 suicides during the 1990s. After being tried multiple times on assisted suicide charges, Kevorkian was eventually tried for murder, found guilty, and sent to prison in 1999. He was paroled in 2007 and died in June 2011.

Homicide

If another individual is the direct or indirect cause of the death, the death is classified as homicide. **Homicide** is the killing of one person by another. Homicide includes the taking of life by another person or by an agency, such as a government. It is either criminal or noncriminal, that is, felonious or nonfelonious. **Criminal homicide** is subdivided into murder and manslaughter, both of which are further subdivided. **Noncriminal homicide** is subdivided into excusable and justifiable homicide.

Thus, *murder* and *homicide* are not synonymous. All murders are homicides (and criminal), but not all homicides are murders (or criminal).

LO3 Explain the various classifications of homicides.

Classification of homicides:

- Criminal (felonious)
  - Murder (first, second, or third degree)
  - Manslaughter (voluntary or involuntary)
- Noncriminal (nonfelonious)
  - Excusable homicide
  - Justifiable homicide

Myth Murder and homicide are the same thing.

Fact Murder and homicide are not synonymous. All murders are homicides, but not all homicides are murders.

Criminal Homicide. The two classes of criminal homicide—murder and manslaughter—have several similarities but also important differences.

Murder, the killing of another human being with malice aforethought, is the most severe statutory crime, one of the few for which the penalty can be life imprisonment or death. (In some states, treason and ransom kidnapping carry a similarly severe penalty.) Some laws classify murder into first, second, or third degrees. **First-degree murder** requires *premeditation* (advanced planning) and the intent to cause death. Some statutes include in this classification any death that results during the commission of or the attempt to commit a felony such as rape or robbery. Also, in most states, the intentional killing of a law enforcement officer is classified as first-degree murder.

Second-degree murder includes the intent to cause death, but not premeditation. An example is a violent argument that ends in one person spontaneously killing the other. **Third-degree murder** involves neither premeditation nor intent. It results from an act that is imminently dangerous to others and shows a disregard for human life, such as shooting into a room where people are likely to be present or playing a practical joke that may result in someone's death.

Manslaughter is the unlawful killing of another person with no prior malice. It may be voluntary or involuntary. **Voluntary manslaughter** is the intentional causing of the death of another person in the heat of passion, that is, because of words or acts that provide adequate provocation. For example, the law generally recognizes such acts as adultery, seduction of a child, or rape of a close relative as outrageous enough to constitute adequate provocation. This provocation must result in intense passion that replaces reason and leads to the immediate act. The provocation, passion, and fatal act must occur in rapid succession and be directly, sequentially related; that is, the provocation must cause the passion that causes the fatal act.

Involuntary manslaughter is accidental homicide that results from extreme (culpable) negligence. Examples of involuntary manslaughter include handling a firearm negligently; leaving poison where children may take it; and operating an automobile, boat, or aircraft in a criminally negligent manner. Some states, such as California, have a third category of manslaughter: manslaughter with a motor vehicle.

LO4 Compare and contrast murder and manslaughter, including the different classifications of each and the different elements that must be proven.

Murder, the killing of another human with malice aforethought, is frequently classified as

- First degree—premeditated and intentional, or while committing or attempting to commit a felony

- Second degree—intentional but not premeditated

- Third degree—neither intentional nor premeditated, but the result of an imminently dangerous act

Manslaughter, the unlawful killing of another human with no prior malice, is classified as

- Voluntary—intentional homicide caused by intense passion resulting from adequate provocation

- Involuntary—unintentional homicide caused by criminal (culpable) negligence

---

Other acts that can be classified as involuntary manslaughter include shooting another person with a firearm or other dangerous weapon while mistakenly believing

that person to be an animal; setting a spring gun, pitfall, deadfall, snare, or other dangerous device designed to trap animals but capable of harming people; and negligently and intentionally allowing a known vicious animal to roam free.

Noncriminal Homicide. Although the term *homicide* is usually associated with crime, not all homicides are crimes.

LO5 Differentiate between excusable homicide and justifiable homicide and provide an example of each.

Excusable homicide is the unintentional, truly accidental killing of another person. **Justifiable homicide** is killing another person under authorization of the law.

Excusable homicide results from an act that normally would not cause death or from an act committed with ordinary caution that, because of the *victim's* negligence, results in death, as when a person runs in front of a moving car.

Justifiable homicide includes killing in self-defense or in the defense of another person if the victim's actions and capability present imminent danger of serious injury or death. Killing an enemy during wartime is also classified as justifiable homicide. This classification further includes capital punishment, death caused by a public officer while carrying out a court order, and deaths caused by police officers while attempting to prevent a dangerous felon's escape or to recapture a dangerous felon who has escaped or is resisting arrest. Officers need not risk their lives when faced with a shoot-or-be-shot situation.

Undetermined

A final classification of death is *undetermined*, or "could not be determined," which is used when there is either insufficient information available to determine with reasonable medical certainty that only one of the manners of death applies (natural, accidental, suicide, or homicide), or when equally compelling arguments can be made to support two or more manners of death. For example, a woman is found, deceased and with massive subdural hemorrhage, at the bottom of a staircase. Lacking any information on the events leading up to her death, it may be impossible to determine if the hemorrhage was due to an accidental fall or homicidal violence.

Elements of the Crime

Laws on criminal homicide vary significantly from state to state, but certain common elements are usually found in each, as summarized in Table 8.1. The degree eventually charged is decided by the prosecuting attorney based on the available evidence. For example, the only difference between first- and second-degree murder is the element of premeditation. If thorough investigation does not yield proof of premeditation, a charge of second-degree murder is made.

Causing the Death of Another Person

Usually the death of a person is not difficult to prove; a death certificate completed by a physician, coroner, or medical examiner (ME) suffices. If a death certificate is not available, the investigator must locate witnesses to testify that they saw the body of the person allegedly killed by the suspect. When insufficient remains exist to identify the body positively, death is proven by circumstantial evidence such as examination by a qualified pathologist or by other experts and their expert testimony regarding dental work, bone structure, and the like.

A more difficult portion of the element to prove is the cause of death. To show that the suspect's act caused the death, you must prove the cause of death and prove that the suspect, through direct action, inflicted injury sufficient to cause the death with some weapon or device. For example, if the cause of death was a fatal wound from a .22-caliber weapon, it is necessary to show that the suspect produced the cause of death. Did the suspect own such a weapon? Can witnesses testify that the suspect had such a weapon immediately before the fatal injury? Was the suspect seen actually committing the offense? Did the suspect admit the act by statement or confession? Was the suspect's DNA on the weapon? Did the suspect test positive for gunshot residue (GSR)? Did the suspect threaten the victim directly or through text messages, emails, or voicemails?

Premeditation

Premeditation is the consideration, planning, or preparation for an act, no matter how briefly, before committing it. Laws use such terms as *premeditated design to kill* or *malice aforethought*. Whatever the law's wording, it is necessary to prove some intention and plan to commit the crime before it was actually committed.

> **LO6** Explain the significance of premeditation in a death investigation.
>
> Premeditation—the consideration, planning, or preparation for an act, no matter how briefly, before committing it—is the element of first-degree murder that sets it apart from all other homicide classifications.

Were oral statements or threats made during a heated argument? Did the suspect buy or have a gun just before the crime was committed or travel a long distance

TABLE 8.1 **Degrees of Homicide**					
	Murder			Manslaughter	
Element to Be Proven	**First Degree**	**Second Degree**	**Third Degree**	**Voluntary**	**Involuntary**
Causing the death of another person	·	·	·	·	·
Premeditation	·				
Malicious intent	·	·			
Adequately provoked intent resulting from the heat of passion				·	
··While committing or attempting to commit a felony	·				
··While committing or attempting to commit a crime not a felony			·	·	
When forced or threatened				·	
Culpable negligence or depravity				·	
Negligence					·

** Indicates that starred elements other than causing the death of another person need not be proven.

to wait for the victim? Premeditation can be proved in many ways. Sometimes the time interval between thought and action is only a minute; other times, it may be hours, days, weeks, months, or even years.

Determine at what time before the killing the suspect considered, planned, threatened, or made some overt act to prepare to commit the murder. This may be established by statements from witnesses or from the victim before death, from evidence at the crime scene, or through a review of the suspect's criminal history and past statements.

Evidence of planning may also be found on suspects' electronic devices. For example, someone planning a murder might conduct an Internet search on ways to effect a death and make it look like an accident. There may be a search history for poisons, electrocution, falls, or similar methods that cause death.

Intent to Effect the Death of Another Person

Intent is a required element of most categories of criminal homicide. **Criminal intent** is purposely performing an unlawful act, knowing that act to be illegal. Evidence must show that the crime was intentional, not accidental. **Malicious intent**, an element of first- and second-degree murder, implies ill will, wickedness, or cruelty. How the act was committed shows the degree of intent. The type of weapon used, how and when it was acquired, and how the suspect and victim came together help prove the intent as well as the act that caused the death.

Intent and *premeditation* are not the same. Premeditation is not a requirement of intent. Most crimes of passion involve intent but not premeditation or malicious intent.

This element—intent—also applies to a death caused to someone other than the intended victim. For example, in one case a woman intended to kill her husband by placing poison in a bottle of whiskey he kept under the seat of the family car. Unknowingly, the husband offered a drink from the bottle to a friend, who died as a result. The wife was charged with first-degree murder and convicted, even though the person who died was not her intended victim. It was a reasonable consequence of her act.

An explosive that was set for one person may detonate prematurely and kill someone else. A person shooting at an intended victim may miss and kill an innocent bystander. Both of these would constitute first-degree murder.

Adequately Provoked Intent Resulting from Heat of Passion

This element is the alternative to premeditation. It assumes that the act was committed when the suspect suddenly became extremely emotional, thus precluding premeditation. **Heat of passion** results from extremely volatile arguments between two people, from seeing a wife or family member raped, from a sudden discovery of adultery, or from seeing a brutal assault being committed against a close friend or family member.

While Committing or Attempting to Commit a Felony

In some states, a charge of first-degree murder does not require that the murder was committed with premeditation if the victim died as a result of acts committed while the suspect was engaged in a felony such as rape, robbery, or arson. Proof of the elements of the felony must be established.

While Committing or Attempting to Commit a Crime Not a Felony

If a death results from an act committed by a suspect engaged in a nonfelonious crime such as purse snatching or petty theft, it can be charged as either third-degree murder or voluntary manslaughter, depending on the state in which the offense occurs.

Culpable Negligence or Depravity

The act and the way it is committed establish this element. The act must be so dangerous that any prudent person would see death of a person as a possible consequence. A person causing a death while depraved and committing acts evident of such depravity is guilty of third-degree murder.

Negligence

A fine line separates this element from the preceding element. Some states make no distinction, classifying both in a separate category of **criminal negligence**. Where separate categories exist, this lesser degree of negligence involves creating a situation that results in an unreasonable risk of death or great bodily harm.

Challenges in Investigation

Police have an obligation to act on behalf of the deceased and their families. They are expected to conduct a professional investigation to identify, arrest, and prosecute suspects. Among the numerous challenges officers encounter in homicide investigations are pressure by the media and the public, the difficulty in establishing homicide rather than suicide or an accidental or natural death, identifying the victim, and establishing the cause and time of death (ToD). Other challenges are obtaining witness cooperation and protecting the crime scene when emergency medical technicians (EMTs) are working on the victim(s), both of which will be further discussed shortly.

Homicides create high interest in the community, as evidenced by increased hits on newspaper websites and higher ratings for the news media. Indeed, the media have a special interest in police investigations of deaths—accidental or otherwise. Police officers who have dealt with the news media understand the important relationship between law enforcement and the media, as discussed in Chapter 1.

Police policies and guidelines should specify what information is to be released: the deceased's name, accused's name, and general identifying information; any details regarding formal charges; and general facts about the investigation that are not harmful to the continuing investigation.

Do not pose the accused for photographs, and do not permit the accused to talk to the press. If investigators have details known only to them and the accused, that information must not be released. Exercising good sense, getting to know the reporters personally, and refraining from giving off-the-record comments will prevent many problems. Departments that have media liaisons should use them for all press releases and conferences, which will help to establish a positive relationship with the media. Reporters have a right to be at the scene, and cooperation is the best policy—within the policies and guidelines of the department.

From time to time, public outrage over particular crimes places increased pressure on the police to solve murders. A more serious problem is the difficulty of establishing that a crime has, in fact, been committed. Search warrants can be issued if proof of a crime exists; however, such proof may not be legally available without a warrant. In addition, many perpetrators attempt to make the crime scene look as if a robbery or burglary has taken place. It can also be difficult to determine whether the death was homicide or suicide.

Equivocal Death

Equivocal death investigations are situations that are open to interpretation. The case may present as homicide, suicide, or accidental death. The facts may be intentionally vague or misleading as in staged crime scenes. A staged crime scene is one where a killer hopes to cover their tracks by making it look like the victim committed suicide, suffered a fatal accident, or died of natural causes. Inexperienced investigators who jump to the hasty conclusion that a man found hanging in his garage or the dead woman in the bathtub with slit wrists must have committed suicide may be allowing a perpetrator to get away with murder.

A distinction exists between posing and staging. *Posing* refers to positioning of the body only, whereas *staging* refers to manipulation of the scene around the body in addition to posing of the body. Staging is defined as any intentional actions taken by an offender to alter physical evidence at the crime scene to purposely mislead investigators and thwart the overall criminal justice process (Pettler, 2016). Most staging occurs after the crime, but it can also happen before a homicide (Bitton & Dayan, 2019). One study of homicides staged as suicides found that such scenes frequently involved firearms, hangings, or asphyxiations, and the offenders and victims usually knew each other, although not necessarily intimately (Ferguson & Petherick, 2016).

Staging does not include actions taken by nonsuspects upon discovering the victim, for example, when a husband discovers the naked body of his murdered wife and covers, dresses, or moves the body before the police arrive in an effort to spare the victim further insult and embarrassment. Emotionally distraught family members or friends may do things that unintentionally change the conditions of the crime scene, making it crucial for investigators to conduct initial interviews as soon as possible so as to learn from the survivors exactly what happened and what actions they may have carried out before the police arrived (Geberth, 2010).

A critical piece of the investigation is assessing the **victimology**—the collection of significant and relevant information related to a victim and that victim's lifestyle—because it helps investigators develop and ascertain suspects, motives, and risk factors: "Personality, employment, education, friends, habits, hobbies, marital status, relationships, dating history, sexuality, reputation, criminal record, history of alcohol or drugs, physical condition and neighborhood of residence are all pieces of the mosaic that comprise victimology" (Geberth, 2013). What was the victim's state of mind in the days leading up to the death? Had the victim made long-term plans, such as having purchased plane tickets for a vacation, prepaid membership dues, or begun a major house renovation project? Answers to these questions may not support an initial assessment of suicide. The prudent investigator approaches all equivocal death scenes as if they were homicides until forensic evaluation of evidence can point one way or the other—homicide or not.

Another equivocal death situation involves sudden, unexplained infant death (SUID), which is not to be confused with SIDS or sudden infant death syndrome. SIDS is the sudden death of a child under age one that remains unexplained even after a thorough investigation involving a complete autopsy, examination of the death scene, and review of the infant's clinical history. It is a "diagnosis of exclusion," when all other possible causes of death (disease, illness, abuse, etc.) have been explored and ruled out. SUID is a preinvestigative term. A SUID case, after a thorough investigation, may be classified as SIDS (approximately 85% of cases) or will identify another cause of death, such as homicide. Investigating SUID is covered in Chapter 11.

Sudden in-custody deaths (SICDs) present a tremendous challenge to investigators. These cases typically involve suspects who have been restrained for some time, during which they enter a state of medical crisis and die. Families of the deceased frequently file lawsuits claiming that police brutality caused the death, and the officers involved contend that the restrained person succumbed to some type of preexisting physical defect (weak heart, aneurysm, etc.) brought about by the subject's own state of agitation. Sometimes this state is referred to as *excited*

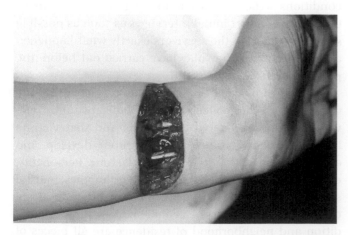

A slit wrist is often interpreted as a suicide indicator. Investigators should not automatically conclude that a person whose wrists are slit did, in fact, commit suicide.

© Dr. Lindsey Thomas

delirium (EXD), as discussed in Chapter 7, and the deaths that result are often complex and multifactorial. Recall from the previous chapter that victims of EXD usually die from either respiratory arrest and asphyxia or cardiac dysrhythmia, a disruption in the regular heartbeat, that eventually leads to heart failure and cardiac arrest (Takeuchi, Ahern, & Henderson, 2011). According to Ross and Hazlett (2018): "When a sudden arrest-related death occurs in police or in correctional custody, numerous questions will emerge as to the cause of death. Because these types of deaths involve a multitude of factors, classification of death may be listed as undetermined, an accident, natural, or a homicide."

Because police are involved in the death, a thorough but objective investigation is critical. Ideally, these cases are handled by an outside agency to lessen any suggestion of bias during the investigation. If the body is still at the scene, it should be photographed and documented in terms of its final position and location, and the amount and types of clothing worn. Request that the responding medical personnel take the decedent's core body temperature.

Hyperthermia and excessive sweating are hallmark characteristics of EXD. Medical literature presents considerable evidence that the symptom of "hot to the touch" is a critical warning sign that significantly increases the risk of sudden arrestee death due to EXD (Ross & Hazlett, 2018). Because of this finding, additional photographs should be taken of wet clothing, furniture, or sheets that indicate the person was perspiring.

Photographs that indicate drug use should also be taken, including any drugs found on the person and drug paraphernalia. Particular attention should be paid to the decedent's thumb. Investigators have noted that chronic crack users often use a lighter to heat up a crack pipe, and the repeated flicking of the lighter causes a callous to form on the pad of the thumb, a characteristic known as "crack thumb" (Peters & Brave, 2006).

A checklist for investigating SICDs is provided in Appendix A. As with SUID cases, in-custody deaths must be thoroughly investigated, beginning with a complete autopsy to determine whether a heart attack, stroke, or other physical condition caused the death. Autopsies of people who displayed signs of excited delirium and had been restrained at the time of, or just prior to, death have shown myocardial contraction bands and other heart abnormalities, which can help investigators assess whether the death caused by restraint was secondary to some other primary, chronic medical condition (Otahbachi, Cevik, Bagdure, & Nugent, 2010). Sometimes an equivocal death investigation reveals the cause to be suicide.

Suicide

Suicide often presents as a homicide. Investigators should keep in mind that more Americans die by suicide than by homicide. Often depression or schizophrenia is involved, and usually these people have made their intentions known to someone. Therefore, investigators should try to determine whether a suspected suicide victim was suffering from a mental illness or whether the victim had talked to anyone about committing suicide.

The reason for an apparent suicide must be determined. An act that appears to be too violent for suicide and is therefore a suspected homicide may actually be a natural death. Never exclude the possibility of death from natural causes in the initial phase of an investigation because of the presence of obvious marks of violence. The abnormal activity of a person suffering from an acutely painful attack can create the appearance of a struggle. The onset of more than 70 diseases can produce sudden death. People who experience such an attack may disarrange their clothing and sustain severe injury by falling. In one case, a man shot himself to relieve excruciating pain, and the autopsy showed that a ruptured aorta caused his death, not the gunshot. What appeared to be suicide was declared to be death by natural causes.

Check for weapons on or near the body, being aware that a weapon may be underneath the body and only noticeable after the body has been moved. In one case, investigators were called to a scene where a man had died from a gunshot wound to the head at close range. Seeing no weapon present, investigators began working the scene as a homicide. However, once the body was moved, a pistol was discovered beneath the body.

Learn whether the victim was left- or right-handed and see whether this fits with the method of committing suicide. Note lividity conditions and the body's location to determine how long the person has been dead and whether the body has been moved. Note the condition of rigor mortis. Are there "hesitation marks" indicating indecision before the final act? Do not assume that any blood on the victim is the victim's; it may be from a murderer. (These issues are discussed later in the chapter.)

When smaller-caliber weapons are fired, blood may not appear on the hands of the person firing the gun. In fact, in most suicide cases, blood does not appear on the hands. A test for GSR can help support the theory that the deceased fired the weapon. In more than 75% of suicide cases in which a gun is used, the gun is not found in the victim's hand but is near the body. If the victim is found clutching a weapon, ensure that the weapon in hand was the one used to cause the death. It might be that both the victim and an assailant were armed and that the death was not suicide. In a number of suicides, the victims have multiple wounds. If evidence surfaces after the initial investigation that proves a suicide was actually a homicide, the case should be reopened.

What appears to be a double suicide can also present problems. It may be a murder-suicide. Determine who died first or who inflicted the fatal wounds. Attempt to determine the motive. Search for a note. Look for signs of a violent struggle before death. Sometimes suicide is obvious, as when suspects kill themselves to avoid being captured by the police.

To gain a better understanding of the victim's frame of mind when the suicide occurred or to reveal that the act was perhaps not suicide at all, victimology is important. Investigators must examine the personality traits, character, and lifestyle of the victim, reconstructing as accurately as possible the days and hours preceding the victim's death. Were there any prior suicide attempts, a history of mental illness, or recent traumatic incidents? Were there any recent changes or conflicts in the victim's personal relationships? Was the victim being treated for a medical condition? Were any prescription drugs found at the scene? What was the cause of death?

Although some suicides occur without any outward warning, most people who are contemplating suicide do display noticeable warning signs, including these:

Behavior

- Increased use of alcohol or drugs
- Looking for a way to kill themselves, such as searching online for materials or means
- Withdrawing from activities
- Isolating from family and friends
- Sleeping too much or too little
- Visiting or calling people to say goodbye
- Giving away prized possessions
- Aggression
- Fatigue

Mood

- Depression
- Loss of interest

- Rage

- Irritability

- Humiliation

- Anxiety

Talking about

- Killing themselves

- Feeling hopeless

- Having no reason to live

- Being a burden to others

- Feeling trapped

- Unbearable pain (American Foundation for Suicide Prevention, 2020)

When investigating suspected suicides, attempt to find a note or letter, keeping in mind such a note might exist electronically in the form of a text message or email. However, lack of a note does not eliminate the possibility of suicide—a suicide note is left in only one fourth of the cases investigated. If you do find a note, have it compared with the deceased's handwriting. If the note exists in electronic form, have the device submitted for analysis. The time stamp of the note and prior activity, such as an online search for suicide methods, can provide valuable evidence to support either suicide or another cause of death.

Also look for videos describing the actions taken. Examine any pads of paper near the body for the presence of indentation remaining from writing on sheets of paper torn from the pad and destroyed. Look for manuals on how to commit suicide. Check on prior arrangements with an undertaker or other evidence of putting one's affairs in order. Preserve all evidence until the ME or coroner's office rules whether the death is a suicide.

Suicide by Police

Suicide by police was introduced in Chapter 7 and refers to a situation in which a person decides they want to die but do not want to pull the trigger. Such people may lack the constitution to take their own lives and choose, instead, the option of forcing a police officer to do it for them; or they may view suicide as socially or religiously unacceptable but believe that if they are killed by police, the stigma of suicide will be averted and society may see them as victims. Some insurance

policies will not pay if a person commits suicide, making suicide by cop an attractive option for those bent on killing themselves.

Often such cases involve a "man-with-a-gun" call. Arriving police are confronted with a person acting bizarrely and threatening to shoot themselves, a hostage, or the responding officers. In many instances, the gun is not loaded, is a fake, or is inoperative, but if it is pointed at the police, the police are forced to shoot. The actions of armed individuals who go out of their way to provoke a lethal response by police have led those in academia to refer to such suicide-by-cop incidents as "victim-precipitated."

When investigating a suspected case of suicide by cop, a critical element to determine is the probable motivation of the offender/victim. Suicide-by-cop offender profiles indicate that such subjects often have a poor self-image, feel a sense of guilt for harm they have caused, talk about death and express a desire to be with deceased loved ones, speak often of a higher being, are aggressively confrontational with police, and possess an unloaded or nonfunctioning (toy) gun. Other issues that may potentially indicate suicidal motivations include the following:

- Financial concerns

- Divorce or serious relationship issues

- Loss of a job or retirement

- Being investigated

- Health problems

The presence of such factors may help officers identify potential suicide-by-cop cases. Investigators must evaluate the totality of physical evidence and behavioral indicators to accurately assess whether the incident is one of suicide by cop, as no single piece of evidence, action, or behavior is usually sufficient to establish an offender's motivation.

Whatever the circumstances, a police officer who is forced to take a life may suffer emotionally. In some instances, officers who have taken a life end up taking their own.

Suicide of Police Officers

There is no question—police work is stressful. And it can take its toll in tragic ways. Although many consider police work to be a dangerous profession primarily because of the risk of encountering violent and armed individuals, more officers lose their lives to suicide than to homicide. According to a 2019 report by the Police Executive

Research Forum (PERF), the risk of suicide among police officers in the United States is 54% greater than among American workers in general—the highest risk of suicide among all professions. The suicide rate for police officers (17 per 100,000) also exceeds that for the general population (13 per 100,000) (Hilliard, 2019). Although the numbers of officer suicide deaths and line-of-duty deaths fluctuate from year to year, studies have shown one consistency: more officers die every year by their own hand than from injuries sustained on the job (Hilliard, 2019).

Various sources of information are available regarding police suicides. According to the National Study of Police Suicides (NSOPS), a survey conducted approximately every four years by the Badge of Life, there were 108 police suicides in 2016 (Clark & O'Hara, 2018). In 2017, there were 140 police suicides (Heyman, Dill, & Douglas, 2018). And in 2018, 167 police officers took their own lives (Hilliard, 2019). The profile of suicide cases recorded in 2016 shows the average age of officers who committed suicide was 42, the average time on the job was 17 years, 91% were male, and those between the ages of 40 and 44 with 15 to 19 years on the job were most at risk (Clark & O'Hara, 2018). The overwhelming majority (approximately 95%) of officer suicides involve a firearm (PERF, 2019).

Contributing factors in police suicides, as with other victims of suicide, are relationship problems and alcohol use and abuse. Other risk factors associated with suicidal ideation among police officers are organizational stress, shift work, and critical incident trauma (Chae & Boyle, 2013). Similar to the increased risk faced by military personnel who return to civilian life and succumb to suicide as a result of the traumatic experience of serving combat duty, police officers can suffer from post–traumatic stress disorder (PTSD) brought about by traumatic events they face on the job, such as seeing murdered children or other victims of brutal crimes, or being involved in a shooting. PTSD contributes to depression and various forms of addiction and can lead to suicide. While it is often unclear what the exact motivations underlying a police suicide are, it is commonly believed that the overwhelming majority occur from stresses officers experience from within the department, versus stress that comes from the street (Davis, 2014).

The public's image of the police, and indeed officers' image of themselves, is that of the strong protector of society. Yet police work forces officers to confront the dark side of human nature daily and may eventually cause officers to lose their faith in the goodness of humanity or in their abilities to make a positive impact on the lives of others. This sense of weakness and failure is so contradictory to the image of the police that some officers may simply see no other choice than to "take themselves out of the game."

When an officer commits suicide, the family—and sometimes the first officer on the scene—may attempt to make the death look accidental or like a homicide to avoid the dishonor associated with suicide or to ensure that the family can collect the life insurance. In fact, some research suggests that police suicides are underestimated, underreported, or misclassified as accidental deaths to protect the family or the agency from the stigma associated with suicide (Clark, White, & Violanti, 2012).

Any officer's death requires a thorough investigation. As with suspected suicide-by-cop incidents, investigation into the officer's prior mental/emotional status (presence of depression, PTSD), substance use or abuse, family situations (divorce, death of a spouse or child), financial status (large debts), and health (serious or chronic illness) provide critical insight into possible motivations for suicide. Being under an internal affairs investigation and facing the potential loss of one's identity as an officer is the most compelling reason for an officer to make a hasty decision to commit suicide.

Once forensic examination concludes that a death was caused by suicide, the investigation is over and the case closed. For those cases that are homicides, a thorough criminal investigation must be conducted.

Preliminary Investigation of Homicide

"The homicide crime scene is, without a doubt, the most important crime scene to which a police officer or investigator will be called upon to respond," says Geberth (2015, p. 1). He explains, "Because of the nature of the crime (death by violence or unnatural causes), the answer to 'What has occurred?' can be determined only after a careful and intelligent examination of the crime scene and after the professional and medical evaluation of the various bits and pieces of evidence gathered by the criminal investigator. These bits and pieces may be in the form of trace evidence found at the scene, statements taken from suspects, direct eyewitness accounts, or autopsy results."

The initial investigation of a homicide is basically the same as for any other crime, although it may require more flexibility, logic, and perseverance. The primary goals of the investigation are (1) to establish whether a human death was caused by the criminal act or omission of another, and (2) to determine who caused the death. *Death Investigation: A Guide for the Scene Investigator* (National Institute of Justice [NIJ], 2011) and *Promising Strategies for Strengthening Homicide*

Investigations (Bureau of Justice Assistance, 2018) are two valuable resources for homicide investigators.

The homicide case normally begins with a report of a missing person or the discovery of a body. The officer in the field seldom makes the initial discovery. The first notification is received by the police communications center or a dispatcher who records the date, time, and exact wording used. Because the original call is sometimes made anonymously by a suspect, a voice recording is made for comparison with later suspects.

In *Flippo v. West Virginia* (1999), the Supreme Court held that police may make warrantless entries onto premises where they reasonably believe a person is in need of immediate aid or may make a prompt warrantless search of a homicide scene for other victims or a killer on the premises. However, the Court specifically rejected the idea that there is any general "murder scene exception" to the search warrant requirement of the Fourth Amendment. The situation qualifies as simply an exigent circumstance.

As in any crime scene investigation, the first officer on the scene is extremely important. A meta-analysis of literature on how investigative techniques influence clearance rates found that homicide cases are more likely to be solved when the first responding officers:

- contact the homicide unit, medical examiner's office, and the crime lab;

- immediately secure the crime scene; and search for witnesses.

Furthermore, homicide cases are more likely to be cleared when

- detectives arrive within 30 minutes of crime-scene discovery;

- multiple detectives (minimum of three) are assigned to a case;

- computer database checks are run on all parties and evidence (victim, suspect, witnesses, and weapons); and

- thorough interviews are conducted with witnesses, family members, acquaintances, and neighbors of the witnesses.

(Davis, Jensen, & Kitchens, 2011)

As you enter the scene, it is important to introduce yourself, identify key personnel, and assess the safety of the scene. The first priority is to make sure the scene is safe and to protect yourself, others, and the victim from

further danger posed by a suspect who might still be on scene and able to cause more harm. Then, the second priority is to render aid to the victim, making sure an ambulance is en route.

If the suspect is still at the scene, priorities may differ slightly. An ideal outcome would be to take the suspects into custody and secure them after the victim has been attended to. However, if the suspect flees when you arrive, prioritize medical aid to the victim and others over pursuing the suspect. Normally, however, the suspect is not at the scene, and the victim is the first priority. If the victim is obviously dying, take a dying declaration.

The first officer on the scene determines the path to the victim that will least disturb evidence and sets up the taped-off restricted crime scene area. If the victim is obviously dead, the body remains at the scene until the preliminary investigation is complete. It is then taken to the morgue by the ME or coroner for postmortem examination or autopsy. Whenever possible, the ME or coroner should come to the scene to view the body and its surroundings before the deceased is removed.

Following the assessment of the victim, investigators must document everything they can about the scene. This includes detaining and identifying everyone present, obtaining brief statements from each, maintaining control of the scene and everyone present, listing all officers present upon the investigator's arrival and throughout the investigation, and recording the presence of all other personnel at the scene (medical personnel, coroner, and family members). A death scene checklist developed by the FBI can help ensure a thorough preliminary investigation. This checklist is reprinted in Appendix B.

Determining that Death Has Occurred

Medically, death is determined by the cessation of three vital functions: heartbeat, respiration, and brain activity. The first two signs are observable.

L07 List the signs commonly looked for during the preliminary investigation of a homicide to determine that death has occurred.

Signs of death include lack of breathing, lack of heartbeat, lack of flushing of the fingernail bed when pressure is applied to the nail and then released, and failure of the eyelids to close after being gently lifted.

Cessation of respiration is generally the first visible sign of death. However, in cases such as barbiturate overdoses, breathing can be so shallow that it is undetectable. Therefore, always check for a heartbeat and pulse. Except in some drug overdoses and with certain types of blindness, failure of the pupils to dilate in reaction to light is also a sign of death.

If the victim appears to have died at the moment of the officer's arrival or dies in the officer's presence, the officer should attempt resuscitation with the standard cardiopulmonary resuscitation methods.

Securing and Documenting the Scene

As with any other criminal investigation, the homicide scene must be secured, photographed, and sketched. Videotaping the crime scene can produce excellent results and is being done more frequently. All evidence must be obtained, identified, and properly preserved. Physical evidence can be found on the body, at the scene, or on the suspect.

If EMTs are actively working on a critically injured victim, investigators need to document the personnel who have entered the scene and may have contaminated it during their duty to administer aid. Do not overlook this aspect of the crime scene investigation, and take care to photograph or otherwise record the path taken by emergency personnel when approaching and removing the victim.

In violent homicides, the victim may grab the suspect's hair or shirt buttons or other parts of clothing or scratch and claw the suspect. A victim may leave injuries on the suspect, and traces of the suspect's flesh may be found under the victim's fingernails. Identify and preserve all belongings and evidence on or near the deceased. Carefully examine the location where the body was found even if it is not where death occurred.

Broken nails on a homicide victim may indicate a violent struggle occurred during the commission of the crime. In such cases, the suspect's DNA may be found underneath the victim's fingernails.
© Dr. Lindsey Thomas

Any of the various types of evidence discussed in Chapter 5 can be present at a homicide scene, but the most common evidence to search for, besides the body, are a weapon, blood or other body fluids, hairs, and fibers.

Collecting and Moving the Body

After the entire scene and the evidence have been photographed and sketched, move the body carefully. Lift it a few inches off the surface and slide a clean, white sheet under it to catch any evidence that may fall while transporting the body to the vehicle. Evidence on the body that falls off is much easier to see on a sheet. The sheet also absorbs moisture. Also, place clean brown paper bags on the victim's hands and feet and secure them for transport to preserve any evidence that may exist on such body parts. Itemize other possessions and send them along with the body to the morgue for later release to the family if they are not evidence.

The Focus of the Homicide Investigation

After priority matters are completed, the focus of the homicide investigation is to

- Identify the victim
- Establish the time of death
- Establish the cause of and the method used to produce death
- Develop a suspect

The preliminary investigation either accomplishes these things or provides leads that investigators can follow up.

The first 48 hours after a homicide is reported to the police are critical, and a prompt, effective response to a homicide call can greatly increase the probability of clearing the case. The types of tasks to conduct during these crucial hours will vary based on the facts of the case, environmental factors, and how many victims and crime scenes are involved. The Bureau of Justice Assistance (BJA) launched a Homicide Process Mapping initiative to identify best practices in navigating these first 48 hours after a homicide is reported. Figure 8.1 shows the process flow in the early stages of a homicide investigation and how critical tasks, techniques, and resources can most effectively be implemented or deployed within three distinct time intervals:

- Interval 1 (0–8 hours after the homicide is reported): managing the crime scene responsibly and effectively

- Interval 2 (8–24 hours after): investigation begins to focus on the suspect

- Interval 3 (24–48 hours after): the tasks seek to tie all the evidence together, develop new leads if no suspect has yet been identified, and establish a foundation for moving the investigation forward

A more detailed breakdown of the 80 separate tasks to be performed by those involved in the initial stages of a homicide investigation (e.g., patrol officers, homicide investigators, CSIs, intelligence analysts, supervisors, the medical examiner investigator, the Public Information Officer, etc.) can be found in the online document titled *Homicide Process Mapping*. As Carter (2013) observes, "The individual tasks . . . should not be viewed as sequential steps, per se, in the homicide investigation. Rather, the group of tasks within each time interval should be performed sometime within that noted interval. The key issue for a successful homicide investigation is not 'what' tasks are performed but 'how effectively' they are performed."

The Homicide Victim

In most crimes, the victim provides verbal details of what occurred. In homicides, the victim may be able to provide such information if witnesses or the police are present before death occurs. However, the information usually comes from the crime scene, witnesses, physical and circumstantial evidence, and the suspect.

Victims often know the persons who killed them, so information about the deceased can furnish leads to the suspect. Also, information about the victim's background can provide insight into whether the death was an accident, suicide, or homicide. Evidence on and around the victim's body can also provide important leads.

Obtain the victim's name, address, age, sex, nationality, and type and place of work. Also find out the names of family members, close friends, and known enemies and learn about the victim's habits. Inquire about the victim's romantic relationships. Ask about any religious, political, or business actions or remarks that might have enraged someone. Take the victim's fingerprints and determine whether any criminal history may lead to a suspect.

Interview personal contacts such as doctors, pastors, or counselors to learn about the victim's physical and emotional condition, especially if the manner of death has not yet been determined. The person's medical background may provide information about an extremely painful or terminal disease that could motivate suicide. Inquire about the victim's mental stability. Most suicide victims attempt to avoid inflicting severe pain on themselves when they take their lives, but this is not always true. One woman cut off both her feet before fatally stabbing herself in the chest. Some people set themselves on fire to commit suicide.

A history of domestic violence or intimate partner violence (IPV) can precede an intimate partner homicide (IPH). Many batterers eventually kill their intimate partner, and women who leave their batterers face a 75% greater risk of being killed by them than do women who stay. In some cases, batterers themselves become victims of homicide. In homicides where the victim-offender

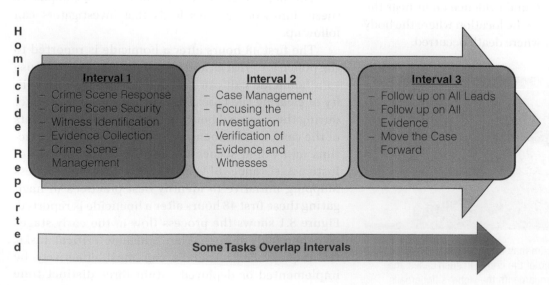

Figure 8.1

Functions of Each Time Interval in the First 48 Hours.

Source: Carter, D. L. (2013, September). Homicide process mapping: Best practices for increasing homicide clearances. Tallahassee, FL: Institute for Intergovernmental Research, p.33. Retrieved August 14, 2020, from www.iir.com/Documents/Homicide_Process_Mapping_September_email.pdf

relationship is known, 1 in 2 female murder victims and 1 in 13 male murder victims were killed by an intimate partner (Ertl, Sheats, Petrosky, Betz, Yuan, & Fowler, 2019). Data from the Violence Policy Center (2020) indicates that nearly two-thirds (65%) of all murder-suicides involve intimate partners and, of these, 96% of cases involved females killed by their partner. Many of these homicides occurred despite restraining orders on the battering partner.

Discovering the Victim

In some cases, nobody is present. It may have been burned, cut up beyond recognition, or dissolved in acid. Some states allow the use of circumstantial evidence to prove the corpus delicti when nobody can be found. In other cases, there is a body, but locating it is a challenge. It may have been weighted and sunk in a body of water or buried underground.

Technology Innovations

Using LABRADOR to Find Buried Remains

Breakthroughs are being made in discovering clandestine graves and determining time of death, based on the progressive breakdown of biological compounds, called *volatile organic chemicals (VOCs)*, found in the human body. Researchers at the University of Tennessee's Forensic Anthropology Center (aka the Body Farm) have isolated and identified 30 uniquely human VOCs that are specifically linked to decomposition in buried bodies. Not only is this finding useful in training cadaver dogs but it is being applied to portable technology. One handheld instrument is LABRADOR (Light-weight Analyzer for Buried Remains and Decomposition Odor Recognition), developed by Oak Ridge National Laboratory, a device used at the soil surface to detect VOCs emitted by decomposing human bodies buried up to 3.5 feet beneath the ground (Page, 2010): "According to the FBI, the average clandestine grave is about 2 to 2.5 feet deep. In the case of a corpse buried in roughly 18 inches of soil, it takes about 17 days for odors to first make their way to the surface."

When searching for human remains, investigators can use technologies such as ground-penetrating radar, magnetometers, metal detectors, and infrared thermography, which can distinguish between hidden new and old gravesites faster and more accurately than can other techniques. In addition, cadaver-search canines have proven effective. Dogs can be trained to detect human remains long after death, despite burial or attempted concealment. According to the Search Dog Organization of North America (SDONA, n.d.), human remains detection (HRD) dogs are specifically trained to locate the odor of decomposing human remains and to ignore live human scent, animal scent, and any other odor that is not indicative of human remains.

Identifying the Victim

Once a body is found, it must be identified.

> **LO8** List the various resources used to identify an unknown homicide victim.
>
> Homicide victims are identified by immediate family, relatives, friends, or acquaintances; personal effects, fingerprints, DNA analysis, and dental and skeletal studies; clothing and laundry marks; or through missing-persons files.

In many cases, identifying the deceased is no problem. The spouse, parents, a close friend, or a relative makes the identification. If possible, have several people identify the body, because people under stress make mistakes. In a number of cases, a homicide victim has been identified only to turn up later alive. Although personal identification by viewing the deceased is ideal, corroborate it with other evidence. Personal effects found on the victim assist in identification. However, such personal effects may not necessarily belong to the deceased. Therefore, check them carefully.

If identification cannot be made by relatives or acquaintances or by personal effects, the most positive identification is by fingerprint or DNA analysis. Comparative fingerprints are not always available, however, and blood type does not provide a positive identification, although it can prove that a body is *not* a specific person.

Investigations involving unidentified human remains often require the involvement of experts from a variety of scientific fields, and the earlier they are brought into the case, the better the chances of resolving it. In addition to the medical examiner, the team should consist of a forensic anthropologist (to provide information on gender, height, race, and age), a forensic odontologist (to provide an age range), a forensic osteologist (to determine if there is evidence of bone trauma), and a forensic entomologist (FE) (to provide information on the location and approximate time of death).

Scenes of mass disasters, such as those created by the September 11, 2001, terrorist attacks, present great forensic challenges. The Kinship and Data Analysis Panel (KADAP) report, *Lessons Learned from 9/11: DNA Identification in Mass Fatality Incidents* (NIJ, 2012, p. 1), states, "DNA analysis is the gold standard for identification of human remains from mass disasters. Particularly in the absence of traditional anthropological and other physical characteristics, forensic DNA typing allows for identification of any biological sample and the association of body parts, as long as sufficient DNA can be recovered from the samples. This is true even when the victim's remains are fragmented and the DNA is degraded." The bulk of the report is aimed to inform technicians who perform such DNA analysis.

Cases involving unidentified human remains can be extremely challenging for criminal investigators, and these cases often intersect with missing person cases. Considering that an estimated 4,400 unidentified human remains cases are opened every year in the United States, with about 1,000 of these cases remaining unidentified after a year and going into "cold case" status, and with approximately 100,000 missing-persons cases active on any given day, the need for a central repository for such case records became apparent. In July 2007, the NIJ launched a program to help law enforcement agencies, medical examiners, and others identify missing persons who have been murdered or have died of other causes. This program, the National Missing and Unidentified Persons System (NamUs), serves as a national information clearinghouse and resource center for missing, unidentified, and unclaimed person cases across the United States (www.namus.gov). NamUs is funded and administered by the NIJ, managed through a cooperative agreement with the UNT Health Science Center in Fort Worth, Texas, and provides resources at no cost to law enforcement, medical examiners, coroners, allied forensic professionals, and family members of missing persons.

For an unknown victim, record a complete description and take photographs if possible. Check these against missing-persons files. Circulate the description and photograph in the surrounding area. Check the victim's clothing for possible laundry marks or for labels that might indicate where the clothes were purchased. If there are leads as to whom the victim might be, you can attempt identification by comparing dental charts and X-rays of prior fractures; by examining signs of prior surgical procedures, such as scars; by comparing other characteristics such as birthmarks or moles; or through tattoos or piercings.

If the body is badly decomposed, the bones provide a basis for estimating height, gender, and approximate age as well as proof that the deceased was a human. Bones can show whether the victim suffered from certain diseases or infections, such as tuberculosis or syphilis; metabolic disorders, such as osteoporosis or rickets; or degenerative disorders, such as osteoarthritis (Cunha & Pinheiro, 2013), clues that may help investigators identify a body. Radiographs, or X-ray scans, can help with identification by revealing fractures, medical implants, or evidence of surgeries. Bone analysis can also shed light on the "timing" of a fracture and whether an injury occurred well before death or was part of the trauma that caused death (Morgan, Adlam, Robinson, Pakkal, & Rutty, 2014). Stress or fatigue fractures are often noted in athletes, ballet dancers, military recruits, and others who engage in repetitive physical activity, and the presence of such fractures may provide leads as to the victim's occupation or hobby (Cunha & Pinheiro, 2013).

In addition to identifying the victim, the homicide investigator must establish the approximate time of death, typically with the help of the ME or coroner.

Estimating the Time of Death (ToD)

In many homicides, there is a delay between the commission of the crime and the discovery of the body—sometimes only minutes, other times years. This period between death and corpse discovery is called the *postmortem interval (PMI)*. Understanding the processes that occur in a body during the PMI can help investigators estimate a time of death (ToD), also referred to as *time since death (TSD)*. Research facilities, such as the University of Tennessee's Body Farm outside of Knoxville, Tennessee, are allowing forensic scientists to study and document these processes under various environmental conditions in an effort to help investigators more accurately determine the time of death.

Noting that the determination of ToD is both an art and a science that requires medical examiners to apply several techniques and observations in order to calculate a best estimate, Rodgers (2015) states: "As a general rule, the sooner after death the body is examined, the more accurate this estimate will be. Unfortunately, the changes that a body undergoes after death occur in widely variable ways and with unpredictable time frames. There is no single factor that will accurately indicate the time of physiological death. It is always a best guess. But when the principles are properly applied, the medical examiner can often estimate the physiologic time of death with some degree of accuracy."

Myth Through modern forensic science, an exact time of death can be determined.

Fact There is no scientific way to determine the exact time of death. A thorough investigation will reveal a time frame, and the more information available, the narrower that time frame can be.

The ToD relates directly to whether the suspect could have been at the scene and to the sequence of multiple deaths. It is also important to the victim's family in settling insurance claims and Social Security and pension payments.

Both the investigator and the ME or coroner are responsible for estimating the time of death. Knowing how the professional examiner estimates time of death helps investigators to understand better what circumstances are important at the crime scene and alerts them to observe and record specific factors that aid in estimating the time of death, including environmental (or ambient) temperature. Some of these factors are available only to the first officers at the scene.

Without eyewitnesses, the time of death is seldom completely accurate. Normally, however, the time of death—if it has occurred within the past four days—can be determined to within four hours, depending on the examiner's expertise and the factors available for examination. Figure 8.2 shows the timing of various body changes after death.

Evidence found in and around the body, such as rigor mortis, water in the lungs, and decomposition levels, is known as *corporal evidence*. Information and details gathered from the vicinity of the body or general surroundings that can provide clues as to time of death, such as food left on the stove, uncollected mail, or the condition of pets found in the home, is called *environmental and associative evidence. Anamnestic evidence* is derived from evaluating the victim's ordinary habits, routines, and daily activities—were sleep patterns regular, appointments kept, correspondences answered or unanswered (*Standards Employed to Determine Time of Death,* n.d.).

L09 Explain how these specific factors are used to estimate the ToD: body temperature, rigor mortis, postmortem lividity, the eyes, and stomach contents.

Factors that help in estimating the time of death are body temperature, rigor mortis, postmortem lividity (livor), eye appearance, stomach contents, and stage of decomposition; evidence found in the vicinity of the body; and evidence suggesting a change in the victim's normal routine.

Recent Death

A time of death that is less than one-half hour before examination is normally the easiest determination to make. The body is still warm; mucous membranes are still moist but drying; blood is still moist but drying; the pupils have begun to dilate; and in fair-skinned people, the skin is becoming pale. This last characteristic of recent death becomes less discernible as skin pigmentation increases.

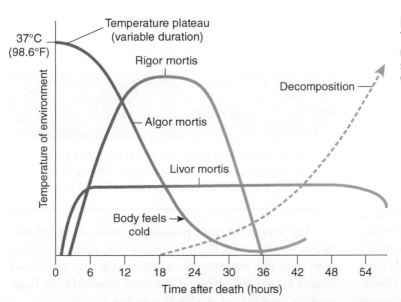

Figure 8.2
Timing of postmortem cooling, livor, rigor mortis, and putrefactive changes.
Source: Sopher, I. M. (1973, October). The law enforcement officer and the determination of the time of death. FBI Law Enforcement Bulletin.

Death that Occurred One-Half Hour to Four Days Prior

Generally, if the death occurred within the past four days but more than one-half hour ago, the mucous membranes and any blood from the wounds are dry, there are skin blisters and skin slippage, the body is slightly pink, body temperature has dropped, rigor mortis and postmortem lividity are present, and the pupils are restricted and cloudy.

Body Temperature. Though not an accurate measure of time of death, body temperature is helpful in conjunction with other factors. **Algor mortis** refers to the postmortem cooling process of the body and can be extremely helpful in homicide investigations. After death, the body tends to assume the temperature of its environment (the ambient temperature). Record the temperature of the surroundings and the amount of clothing on the body. Reach under the clothing to determine the body's warmth or coldness. Compare this with exposed parts of the body to determine whether the clothing is retaining body heat.

> **LO9** Explain how these specific factors are used to estimate the ToD: body temperature, rigor mortis, postmortem lividity, the eyes, and stomach contents.
>
> A general guideline regarding body cooling, barring extreme conditions, is that body temperature drops 2 to 3 degrees in the first hour after death and 1 to 1.5 degrees for each subsequent hour until 18 hours, when it tends to assume the same temperature as the environment in which it is found.

Some investigators use the formula of 1.5 degrees cooling per hour, assuming an internal temperature of 98.6° F and an environmental temperature of 70° to 75° F, with the rate of loss adjusted up and down depending on the actual environmental temperature and with the accuracy decreasing after 10 hours. The formula would be $98.5 - T / 1.5 = N$, where T equals rectal temperature in degrees Fahrenheit and N is the number of hours since death.

These times vary in abnormally hot or cold environments. Also, body temperature drops more slowly in large or obese people, if a high fever was present before death, if humidity prevents evaporation, or if strenuous physical activity occurred immediately before death.

Rigor Mortis. The body is limp after death until rigor mortis sets in. **Rigor mortis**, a Latin term that literally translates to "stiffness of death," is a stiffening of the joints of the body after death due to partial skeletal muscle contraction caused by chemical changes in muscle fibers. Onset may occur anywhere from 10 minutes to several

hours postmortem, depending on physical conditions concerning the body and the environment. Excitement, vigorous activity, heavy clothing, and abnormally high temperatures increase the rapidity of rigor; cold slows it. Babies and the aged have little rigor.

Rigor mortis is first noticed in smaller muscles, such as those of the face, and spreads to larger muscle groups throughout the body, reaching maximum rigor between 12 and 24 hours. The body can remain rigid for approximately three days, until the muscles themselves begin to decompose, although rigor generally begins to diminish after 36 hours postmortem.

> **LO9** Explain how these specific factors are used to estimate the ToD: body temperature, rigor mortis, postmortem lividity, the eyes, and stomach contents.
>
> Rigor mortis appears as a stiffening of muscles several hours after death, with maximum stiffness occurring 12 to 24 hours after death. Rigor then begins to disappear and is generally gone three days postmortem.

The degree of rigor mortis as an indicator of time of death is usually accurate to within four hours when used along with other factors, such as ambient temperature.

Postmortem Lividity. When the heart stops beating at death, the blood no longer circulates and gravity drains the blood to the body's lowest levels. This causes a dark blue or purple discoloration of the body called **postmortem lividity**, or **livor mortis**. Lividity is cherry red or a strong pink if death has been caused by carbon monoxide poisoning, and various other poisons give lividity other colors.

If a body is on its back, lividity appears in the lower portion of the back and legs. If facedown, it appears on the face, chest, stomach, and legs. If the body is on its side, lividity appears on the side on which the body is resting and if the body is upright, it appears in the buttocks and lower legs.

> **LO9** Explain how these specific factors are used to estimate the ToD: body temperature, rigor mortis, postmortem lividity, the eyes, and stomach contents.
>
> Postmortem lividity starts one-half to three hours after death and is congealed in the capillaries in four to five hours. Maximum lividity occurs within 10 to 12 hours.

Any part of the body pressing directly on a hard surface does not show lividity because the pressure of the body's weight prevents blood from entering the blood vessels in that area. If blood has been released from large wounds, very little if any lividity occurs.

Postmortem lividity and bruises appear similar, but they are easy to distinguish. When bruises are pressed with the thumb or fingers, they remain the same, whereas lividity turns white, or blanches, when pressure is applied. If the blood has already congealed, an incision reveals whether the blood is still in the vessels (lividity) or outside them (bruise). In addition, the color of a bruise varies, whereas the color of lividity is uniform.

> **L09** Explain how these specific factors are used to estimate the ToD: body temperature, rigor mortis, postmortem lividity, the eyes, and stomach contents.
>
> The location of lividity can indicate whether a body was moved after death.

Besides helping to establish time of death and sometimes the cause, lividity helps determine whether the body was moved after death occurred. Postmortem lividity in a body moved immediately after death would provide no clues. However, if the body was moved to a

different position after lividity had set in, lividity will occur in unlikely areas, indicating that the body was moved.

Examination of the Eyes. The appearance of the eyes also assists in estimating the time of death. Ocular changes that occur after death include a lessening of eye muscle tone and dilation of the pupils.

> **L09** Explain how these specific factors are used to estimate the ToD: body temperature, rigor mortis, postmortem lividity, the eyes, and stomach contents.
>
> A partial restriction of the pupil occurs in about seven hours. In 12 hours, the cornea appears cloudy.

The cornea clouds more rapidly if the eyes are open after death. During the medical examination, fluid can be withdrawn from the eyeball (or the spine) to determine the level of potassium, which tends to rise at a predictable rate after death.

Examination of Stomach Contents. Under normal circumstances, it takes four to six hours after eating for the

Postmortem lividity. When the heart stops beating at death, the blood no longer circulates and gravity drains the blood to the body's lowest levels. This results in a dark blue or purple discoloration. Areas of the body in hard contact with surfaces will often appear blanched because the pressure keeps blood from pooling there.
© Dr. Lindsey Thomas

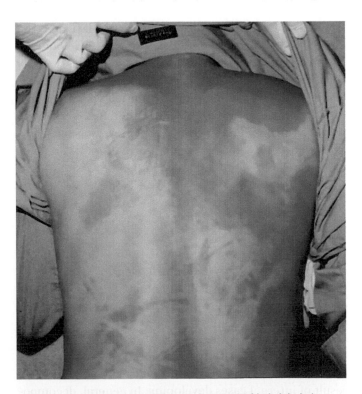

Carbon monoxide poisoning. When carbon monoxide is inhaled, it enters the bloodstream and displaces oxygen from the blood. Reddish lividity, as seen on the body in this photo, indicates carbon monoxide poisoning. This 35-year-old white male committed suicide by lying next to a running vehicle in a closed garage.
Courtesy of the Lakewood Police Department Crime Lab

stomach to empty its contents, although in some individuals, complete gastric emptying can occur as quickly as 2.5 hours after eating (Kaul, Kumar, Kaul, Chanana, & Kumar, 2017). Factors that affect the rate of digestion include the type and volume of food eaten, temperature, and individual metabolism and stress level.

Digestion processes effectively stop at the time of death. Thus, if a dead body is found with a full or partially full stomach, it is reasonable to conclude that death occurred shortly after the victim ate. Also, if the stomach is empty, death likely occurred at least four to six hours after the victim last ate, and if the small intestine is also empty, it is likely the victim died 12 or more hours after the last meal (Kaul et al., 2017). Although the stomach contents must be examined during the medical examination, the investigator can provide important information for the examiner, such as whether vomit was present near the body.

> **LO9** Explain how these specific factors are used to estimate the ToD: body temperature, rigor mortis, postmortem lividity, the eyes, and stomach contents.
>
> Determine when and what the victim last ate. If any vomit is present, preserve it as evidence and submit it for examination.

Attempt to find out when the victim last ate. The medical examiner can often determine how long the victim lived after eating because digestion is a fairly constant process, measurable in hours. If the victim has vomited, the stomach has been emptied which will distort the estimate of time of death; therefore, report the presence of any vomit near the body. Preserve such vomit as evidence, as it may provide information on drugs or poisons related to the cause of death.

Many Days after Death

It is more difficult to estimate the time of death if death occurred several days before discovery of the body. At this point, the cadaver is likely bloated, lividity is darkened, the abdomen is greenish, blisters are filled with gas, and a distinct odor is present.

The ME makes a rough estimate of time of death based on the body's state of decomposition. Decomposition is first observed as an extended stomach and abdomen, the result of internal gases developing. In general, decomposition is increased by higher temperatures and decreased by lower temperatures.

If the body is in a hot, moist location, a soapy appearance called **adipocere** develops. This takes as long as three months to develop fully. Attacks by insects, bacteria, animals, and birds also increase the decomposition rate. Complete dehydration of all body tissues results in **mummification**. A cadaver left in an extremely dry, hot area will mummify in about a year and will remain in this condition for several years if undisturbed by animals or insects.

Insects can detect newly dead body odors two miles away, and the presence on the body of insect eggs, their stage of development, and the life cycle of the species are valuable evidence. Blow flies, in particular, are often the first insects to find and lay eggs on a freshly deceased body, and the species-specific developmental rates of their larvae can provide information about the time of death (Ahmad, 2017; Heath, 2012). For this reason, investigators must collect and submit any insects on or flying near the body. A forensic entomologist can examine various types of insects to assist in estimating the time of death. Table 8.2 provides a checklist for investigators working a homicide where entomological evidence is found.

Because forensic entomology is an exact science, based on empirical data derived from laboratory studies, forensic entomologists can accurately estimate the PMI. Examination of insects is especially helpful when death occurred more than 72 hours prior to discovery (Sharma, Garg, & Gaur, 2015). Particular insects work or rest during the day or the night; therefore, the types of insects at the scene provide clues as to the timing of the body's deterioration.

Insect analysis can also provide additional information such as whether the body was moved and the location where the murder occurred. For example, in one case, a tiny piece of a crushed grasshopper was found at a murder scene and a fractured grasshopper leg was located inside the pant cuff of the perpetrator, allowing investigators to place the suspect at the scene.

It is possible to tie a suspect to the area in which a body is found by comparing entomological evidence on the body or commonly found in the area with insect parts smashed on the suspect's windshield, grille, or other vehicle parts. Such evidence was used when, in 2003, Vincent Brothers flew from his home in California to Ohio to "visit family" and then rented a car to drive back to California, where he murdered his wife, his mother-in-law, and his three children. His alibi was that he had been in Ohio at the time of the killings. At trial, a forensic entomologist testified that some of the insects found on Brothers's rental car and in the radiator were only found west of the Rocky Mountains (Winkley, 2015). That evidence combined with the mileage logged on the rental car helped convict Brothers and place him on death row.

TABLE 8.2	**Checklist: Entomological Evidence at a Homicide Scene**

Habitat

General—woods, a beach, a house, a roadside?

Vegetation—trees, grass, bush, shrubs?

Soil type—rocky, sandy, muddy?

Weather—at time of collection sunny, cloudy?

Temperature and possible humidity at time of collection?

Elevation and map coordinate of the death site?

Is the site in shade or direct sunlight?

Anything unusual, such as the possibility that the body may have been submerged in water at any time?

Remains

Presence, extent, and type of clothing

Is the body buried or covered? If so, how deep and with what (soil, leaves, cloth)?

What is the cause of death, if known? In particular, is there blood at the scene?

Are any other body fluids present?

Are there any wounds? If so, what kind?

Are drugs likely to be involved? This may affect the decomposition rate.

What position is the body in?

What direction is the body facing?

What is the state of decomposition?

Is a maggot mass present? How many? This will affect the temperature of the body.

What is the temperature of the center of the maggot mass(es)?

Is there any other meat or carrion around that also might attract insects?

Is there a possibility that death did not occur at the present site?

Source: Anderson, G. S. (no date). *Forensic entomology: The use of insects in death investigations.* Burnaby, B.C., Canada: Simon Fraser University. Retrieved September 7, 2020, from https://www.sfu.ca/~ganderso/forensicentomology.htm

Interestingly, a lack of insect evidence can also be used to eliminate suspects or, in the case of Kirstin Blaise Lobato, exonerate the wrongly convicted. Lobato, who served 16 years for a murder she did not commit, was set free after a new examination of the facts of the case proved there were no blow flies or eggs present on the victim, an indication that the body was discovered very shortly after death when Lobato was three hours away from the crime scene (Anderson, 2018).

Effects of Water

A body immersed in water may decompose rapidly, depending on the water temperature, salinity, mineral content, and effects of fish and other marine life. Keep in mind that injuries observed on a body are not necessarily part of the cause of death. A **postmortem artifact** is an injury occurring after death from another source. An example would be fish nibbling on the skin of a drowning victim or travel abrasions on the body's forehead, hands, knees, feet, or other exposed surfaces as the body is dragged against the bottom surface or propelled back and forth by a wave (Armstrong & Erskine, 2018). The injuries can look as if they were related to the homicide but may actually have occurred from an outside source after death.

LO10 Explain the effect water has on a dead body.

A dead body usually sinks in water and remains immersed for 8 to 10 days in warm water or 2 to 3 weeks in cold water. It then rises to the surface unless restricted. The outer skin loosens in five to six days, and the nails separate in two to three weeks.

As with insects found on bodies on land, diatoms and algal material can help forensic biologists determine the time of death for bodies found in water, as well as whether the person was drowned. Diatoms are tiny, single-celled aquatic organisms that live in both saltwater and freshwater environments. The composition of diatoms in one particular body of water or aquatic ecosystem is often unique and can be distinguished from other groups of diatoms from other locations. Thus, forensic biologists who collect diatoms from a suspect's shoes and match

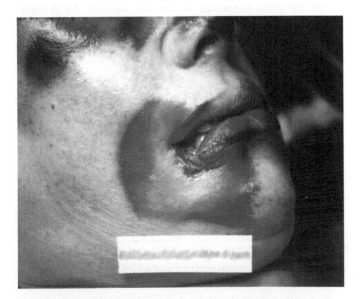

Postmortem artifact on a drowning victim. The damage to the flesh around the corner of the victim's lip and mouth occurred after death.
© Dr. Lindsey Thomas

them to the population of diatoms existing in a pond where a murder victim was found can help investigators place that suspect at the crime scene.

Factors Suggesting a Change in the Victim's Routine

Check telephone calls made to and by the victim. Have a forensic examination done of the victim's cell phone and computer, as information contained on these devices can provide useful insight into the victimology of the person. Check dates on mail and newspapers and expiration dates on food in the refrigerator. Determine who normally provides services to the victim, such as dentists, doctors, barbers, hairdressers, and clerks. Find out whether any appointments were not kept. Were any routines discontinued, such as playing cards or tennis, going to work on schedule or riding a particular bus? Was there food on the stove or the table? Was the stove on? Were the lights, television, radio, or stereo on or off? Were pets fed? Were dirty dishes on the counters or in the sink? Was this normal for the victim? Was a fire burning in the fireplace? Was the damper left open? Determining all such facts helps estimate the ToD and can corroborate the estimate based on physical findings.

The Medical Examination or Autopsy

After the preliminary investigation, the body is taken to the morgue for an autopsy, a term derived from the Greek *autopsia*, meaning "to see for oneself." Most large departments have medical examiners (MEs) and forensic pathologists on staff or available as consultants for autopsies. The medical or forensic pathologist assists investigations by relating the evidence to the autopsy findings. Studies have found that when investigators attend the postmortem exam, the odds of a homicide case being cleared increase by as much as 75% (Higginson, Eggins, & Mazerolle, 2017).

The main purpose of the coroner's or medical examiner's office is to determine the cause and manner of death. If no unnatural cause is found, no crime exists. Much of the evidence that leads the examiner to conclude that the death was murder also provides corroborating evidence for investigating and prosecuting the case; therefore, pathologists and investigators work together closely.

Certain types of death must be investigated. These include all violent deaths, whether homicide, suicide, or an accident; sudden deaths not caused by a recognizable disease; deaths under suspicious circumstances, including those of persons whose bodies will be cremated, dissected, buried at sea, or otherwise made unavailable for further examination; deaths (other than from disease) of inmates in prisons or public institutions; deaths caused by disease that may constitute a public threat; and deaths resulting from hazardous employment.

Before an autopsy, the body is kept intact. An investigator present at the autopsy records the location, date, time, names of those attending, and the name of the person who performs the autopsy. The body is weighed, measured, and photographed before the autopsy begins and is then periodically photographed as each stage is completed. Facial features and any marks, cuts, wounds, bruises, or unusual conditions, including bullet holes and separation points for any missing body parts, such as a leg or foot, are photographed close-up. The deceased, including clothing, is completely described. The clothing is tagged, marked for identification, and sent to the police laboratory for examination. Fingerprints are usually taken, even if the body has been personally identified.

L011 Describe the purpose of the medical examination or autopsy.

The medical examination provides legal evidence related to the cause and time of death and to the presence of drugs or alcohol.

After the autopsy is completed, the cause of death, if determined, is recorded. Deaths not recorded as natural, suicide, or accidental are recorded as either undetermined or homicide. Before making a final determination, the ME reads the police investigation reports to date. These reports indicate prior symptoms such as vomiting, a comatose state, partial paralysis, slow or rapid respiration, convulsions, and various colorations.

During the investigation, report everything relating to the cause of death to the pathologist. Likewise, information discovered by the pathologist is conveyed to the investigative team.

All states have passed laws mandating that before a body is cremated, the coroner must approve the cremation. Although an autopsy is not typically done in most cases of death, the body is examined and X-rays are usually taken. This law is intended to decrease the likelihood of a murder going unnoticed.

Exhuming a Body for Medical Examination

It is not common to exhume a body. Usually this is done to determine whether the cause of death stated on the death certificate is valid. It may also be done if the body is suspected of having been buried to conceal the cause of death or if the identity of the body is in question.

Exhuming a body requires adherence to strict legal procedures to prevent later civil action by relatives. First, obtain permission from the principal relatives. If they do not grant it, it is necessary to obtain a court order to proceed. Arrange to have the coroner or medical examiner, a police representative, a gravedigger, a cemetery official, and a family member present at the exhumation. Have the cemetery official or the person who placed the marker identify the grave. Photograph the general area, the specific grave with the marker, and the coffin before exhumation.

Present at the lid opening at the morgue are the coroner, police, family, undertaker, and pathologist. The body is then identified by the persons present if they knew the deceased, and the examination is conducted.

Unnatural Causes of Death and Method Used

As just discussed, in all cases of violent death, industrial or accidental death, or suicide, the medical examiner determines the cause of death. A number of deaths involve circumstances that are investigated by police and the medical examiner, even though many are not criminal homicides.

Among the most common causes of unnatural death are gunshot wounds; stabbing and cutting wounds; blows from blunt objects; asphyxia induced by choking, drowning, smothering, hanging, strangulation, gases, or poisons; poisoning and drug overdose; burning; explosions, electrocution, and lightning; drugs; and vehicles. Table 8.3 indicates the probability of a specific cause of death being the result of an accident, suicide, or homicide.

Gunshot Wounds

Most deaths caused by gunshot wounds result from discharges of handguns, rifles, or shotguns. Knowing the type of weapon is important for making comparison tests and locating unknown weapons. The major cause of death from gunshot wounds is internal hemorrhaging and shock. The size, number, and velocity of the ammunition used and the type of weapon determine the effect on the body, as does the point of impact. Even a relatively small caliber round can be fatal if it impacts the body at a vital area.

TABLE 8.3 **Cause of Death and the Likelihood It Resulted from Accident, Suicide, or Homicide**			
Cause of Death	**Accident**	**Suicide**	**Homicide**
Gunshot wound	·	·	·
Stabbing and cutting wounds	Rare	·	·
Blow from blunt object			
Fall	·	·	·
Hit-and-run vehicle	·	·	·
Asphyxia			
Choking	·		
Drowning	·	·	·
Hanging	Autoerotic	·	Rare
Smothering	·		Rare
Strangulation	Autoerotic	Rare	·
Poisoning and overdose	·	·	·
Burning	·		
Explosion	·		
Electric shock	·	Rare	
Lightning	·		

Shots fired from a large distance produce little or no powder tattooing or carbons on the skin around where the bullet entered the body, and it is difficult to determine the exact distance—even though the angle of trajectory can be determined from the bullet's path through the body. In the intermediate-distance range, tattooing appears on the clothing or the body when handguns are fired from as much as approximately two feet away. Powder tattooing results from both burned and unburned powder. By using test-firing pattern comparisons with the same weapon and ammunition, the actual firing distance can be determined. GSR evidence was discussed in Chapter 5.

If the muzzle of the weapon was in direct contact with the body, contact wounds will be evident. You may notice a muzzle impression on the skin and soot or powder fragments in the entrance area or around the wound. At the entry point, the hole is smaller than the bullet because the skin's elasticity closes the entry point slightly. Entrance wounds are normally round or oval with little bleeding. As the bullet passes through the skin, it leaves a gray to black abrasion collar around the edges of the entrance wound.

The exit wound is usually larger than the entrance wound, but this is not always the case. The exit wound also bleeds more profusely and has no abrasion collar. It is typically larger because gases build up in the body, especially from shots at close range, and tissues bunch up ahead of the bullet until reaching the outer skin. Elasticity then forces the skin outward until it breaks, permitting the bullet and the gases to pass through. The exit wound is generally jagged and torn. The difference between entrance and exit wounds is observable.

Shotgun wounds are distinctly different because numerous pellets penetrate the body. At close range these leave a much larger hole than does a bullet, and at farther range, they produce a discernible pellet pattern. Both the entrance and exit wounds are larger than those produced by single bullets.

Shotgun-wound patterns and the appearance of entrance and exit wounds from handguns and rifles help determine the distance from which the gun was fired. Contact wounds (fired at point-blank range) cause a large entrance wound with smudging around the edges. The principal damage is caused by the blasting and flame of the powder. Smudging around a wound can be wiped off, but the tattooing pattern cannot be eliminated. If the gun is more than 18 inches from the body when fired, no tattooing or smudging occurs.

In addition, a bullet or pellets from any weapon produce a track through the body that follows the angle between the weapon and the victim at the time of firing. The bullet's path or angle helps determine the angle at which the weapon was fired and therefore the suspect's possible location at the time of firing. This angle also helps differentiate between suicide and murder. Postmortem computerized tomography (PMCT) scans can also help investigators reconstruct bullet trajectories, further helping to establish the manner of death (Morgan et al., 2014).

When investigating gunshot deaths, determine whether the death was the result of the wound or from some other injury. Was the wound impossible for the victim to have produced? What is the approximate distance from which the weapon was fired? Were there one or more wounds? Examine the victim's hands to determine whether they fired the gun. What was the position of the body when found?

> **LO12** List the indicators investigators use to determine whether the following causes of unnatural death most likely indicate that the death was accidental, a suicide, or a homicide: gunshot wounds; stabbing and cutting wounds; blows from blunt objects; asphyxia; poisoning; burning; explosions, electrocution, and lightning; drugs; and vehicles.

Gunshot Wounds

- *Suicide indicators:*
  - Gun held against skin
  - Wound in mouth or in the right temple if victim is right-handed and the left temple if left-handed
  - Not shot through clothing, unless shot in the chest
  - Weapon present, especially if tightly held in hand
- *Homicide indicators:*
  - Gun fired from more than a few inches away
  - Angle or location that rules out self-infliction
  - Shot through clothing
  - No weapon present

The muzzle impression on the skin around the gunshot wound indicates the weapon was held in direct contact with the body. Gun powder residue on the victim's hand may support suicide, as would a wound occurring on the same side of the head as the victim's handedness (i.e., a right-handed victim would usually hold a gun to the right side of their own head).

D. Willoughby Custom Medical Stock Photo/Newscom

Stabbing and Cutting Wounds

Stabbing and cutting wounds differ in shape, size, and extent of external and internal bleeding. A knife is the most frequently used weapon. The weapon and wound can be different sizes, depending on the depth and severity of the wound and whether it is into or across the tissues and fibers.

Stab Wounds. Stab wounds are caused by thrusting actions. They vary in size in different areas of the body but are usually smaller than cutting wounds. A stab wound in a soft part of the body produces a larger hole than does one in the head or a bony area. Ice-pick wounds in a skull covered by a substantial amount of hair can easily be missed on initial examination.

The major damage in stab wounds is to internal tissues, followed by bleeding, primarily internal. The extent and rapidity of internal bleeding depends on the size of the blood vessels affected. In most cases, the cause of death is bleeding rather than damage to a vital organ. A stab wound can be deeper than the length of the weapon used because the force of the thrust on the softer tissues can compress the body's surface inward.

Even if a weapon is found, it can rarely be designated as the murder weapon unless part of it separates and remains in the body or it contains blood, tissue, and fibers from the deceased.

Most stabbing deaths are homicides. In homicides, stab wounds can be single or multiple and can be in several areas of the body if the victim attempted self-defense. **Defense wounds**—cuts on the hands, arms, and legs—result when the victim attempts to ward off the attacker.

Cutting Wounds. With cutting wounds, external bleeding is generally the cause of death. Cutting wounds are frequently the result of suicide. It is common in such cases to observe **hesitation wounds** in areas where the main wound occurs. These less severe, superficial cutting marks are caused by attempts to build up enough nerve to make the fatal wound.

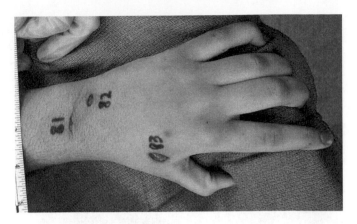

Defensive stab wounds on the hand of a homicide victim.
© Dr. Lindsey Thomas

Suicidal cutting wounds are made at an angle related to the hand that held the weapon, generally in a downward direction because of the natural pull of the arm as it is brought across the body.

Blows from Blunt Objects

Fatal injuries can result from hands and feet and blows with various blunt objects, including hammers, clubs, heavy objects, and rocks. It is often impossible to determine the specific type of weapon involved. If death by a blunt object is expected, officers should carefully note and examine all possible items near the scene. Any plausible item should be collected and examined for fibers, blood, and DNA.

The injuries can occur to any part of the body and can result in visible external bruises. The size of the bruise may not correspond to the size of the weapon because blood escapes into a larger area. Severe bruises are not often found in suicides.

In battered-child investigations, it has been found that death rarely results from a single blow or a single series of blows but, rather, from physical abuse over an extended period. An autopsy reveals prior broken bones or injuries. Death may also have been caused by starvation or other forms of neglect.

Falls can cause death or can be used to conceal the real cause of death. In some cases, the victim is taken to a staircase and pushed down after being severely beaten. Intoxication is often given as the reason for the fall, but this can easily be checked through blood tests.

Asphyxia

Asphyxiation results when the body tissues and the brain receive insufficient oxygen to support the red blood cells. An examination of blood cells shows this lack of oxygen. Discoloration occurs in all dead bodies, but in asphyxia deaths, it is usually more pronounced and varied because

---

LO12 List the indicators investigators use to determine whether the following causes of unnatural death most likely indicate that the death was accidental, a suicide, or a homicide: gunshot wounds; stabbing and cutting wounds; blows from blunt objects; asphyxia; poisoning; burning; explosions, electrocution, and lightning; drugs; and vehicles.

Stabbing and Cutting Wounds

- *Suicide indicators:*
  - Hesitation wounds
  - Wounds under clothing
  - Weapon present, especially if tightly clutched
  - Usually wounds at throat, wrists, or ankles
  - Seldom disfigurement
  - Body not moved
- *Homicide indicators:*
  - Defense wounds
  - Wounds through clothing
  - No weapon present
  - Usually injuries to vital organs
  - Disfigurement
  - Body moved

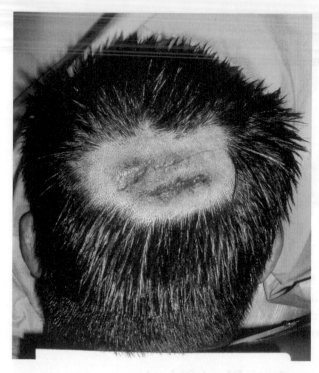

Lacerations caused by blunt force trauma on the head of a homicide victim.
© Dr. Lindsey Thomas

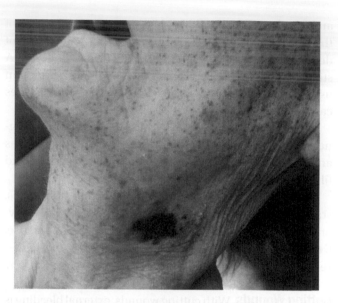

Petechiae—small spots or blotches caused by hemorrhaging—on the face or neck can be a sign of death by asphyxiation.
© Dr. Lindsey Thomas

of the lack of oxygen—especially in the blood vessels closest to the skin surface. It is most noticeable as a blue or purple color around the lips, fingernails, and toenails. Although you need not know the varied coloration produced by different causes and chemicals, be certain to record precise descriptions of coloration that can be interpreted by the medical examiner and related to probable cause of death.

Asphyxia deaths result from many causes, including choking, drowning, smothering, hanging, strangulation, swallowing of certain chemicals, poisoning, and overdosing on sleeping pills. Asphyxiation may also result from certain types of autoerotic behavior.

Choking. Foreign bodies in the throat cause choking, as do burial in grain or sand slides or rapid pneumonia in infants in cribs. Such deaths are almost always accidental.

Drowning. Most drownings are accidental. However, a smaller but still significant number are the result of suicidal or homicidal drowning (Armstrong & Erskine, 2018). In many cases where a body is retrieved from the water, the initial manner of death is undetermined, and a thorough investigation can shed light on how the drowning occurred, or whether a drowning even happened (Leth, 2019).

Bodies immersed in water for some time undergo changes, and several factors can alert an investigator to whether a drowning is a suicide, an accident, or a homicide (Armstrong & Erskine, 2011; Stevens, 2007):

- **Body placement.** In a drowning, most victims curl up in a semi-fetal position.

- **Lividity and rigor mortis.** Lividity, the position of rigor mortis, and blanching of the body can indicate if the person was dead before entering the water.

- **The victim's eyes.** The eyes of a drowning victim will glisten for a short time when they are brought up but then quickly dry out. If examination shows that part of the eye looks dry immediately after being pulled from the water, the victim likely died on land.

Homicide is rarely proven unless witnesses are present. If a dead body is placed in water to make it appear as though death was caused by drowning, a medical examination can determine whether the person was dead when immersed. If accidental or suicide, diatoms and algal material will be found in lungs. In a homicide, diatoms or algae may be found on the mouth or lips but not in the lungs. However, if the victim was killed by drowning, these organisms would be sucked into the lungs as the person struggled to escape and surface, similar to what happens to someone who accidentally drowns.

Not all persons who drown will have water in their lungs. There is a scenario known as *dry drowning*. Two theories exist as to what causes dry drowning, both of which may be correct. The first theory is that a sudden rush of water into the throat causes the airway to snap shut, a condition called *laryngospasm*. No water enters the lungs, but no air enters either, so the victim dies of asphyxiation. The second theory is that the shock to a body when it suddenly enters extremely cold water causes the heart to stop abruptly.

Smothering. Smothering is an uncommon means of homicide, despite many fictional depictions of this method. Intoxicated persons, the elderly, and infants are most likely to be victims of smothering, usually by the hands or a pillow. Often, however, such deaths are accidental. For example, an infant weak from disease may turn over, face downward, or become tangled in bedclothes and accidentally suffocate.

Hanging. Hangings are normally suicides, but homicides have been made to appear as suicides. Some hangings result from experimentation to achieve sexual satisfaction, as discussed later. In suicides, the pressure on the neck is usually generated by standing on a chair or stool and kicking the support away, jumping off, or simply letting the body hang against the noose. (A body need not be completely suspended to result in death by hanging.) Although it is commonly thought that death results from a broken neck, it is usually the result of a broken trachea or a complete constriction of the air supply.

In hangings, the ligature marks start from the area of the neck below the chin and travel upward to the point just below the ears. The ligature marks form an inverted V across the back of the neck, which indicates the death was likely a suicide and not a homicide by strangulation, as strangulations do not typically leave an inverted V mark. Observe the condition and angle of these marks and save the entire rope, including the knot, as evidence.

Strangulation. Strangulation by rope, hands, wire, or scarf produces the same effect as hanging. In both, the cause of death is total constriction of air. In contrast to hangings, however, the ligature marks caused by strangulation are normally evenly grooved and are horizontal around the neck. In cases of manual strangulation, marks often remain from the hand pressure.

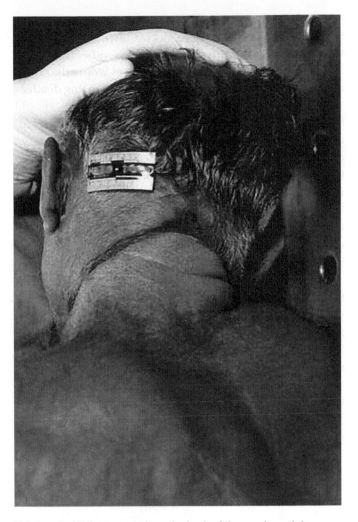

This inverted V ligature mark on the back of the man's neck is indicative of suicidal hanging.
© Dr. Lindsey Thomas

> **LO12** List the indicators investigators use to determine whether the following causes of unnatural death most likely indicate that the death was accidental, a suicide, or a homicide: gunshot wounds; stabbing and cutting wounds; blows from blunt objects; asphyxia; poisoning; burning; explosions, electrocution, and lightning; drugs; and vehicles.

In asphyxiation deaths, most cases of choking, drowning, and smothering are accidental; most cases of hanging are suicides; most cases of strangulation are homicide.

Poisons, Chemicals, and Overdoses of Sleeping Pills. Asphyxiating chemicals, including ammonia and chloroform, can cause irritation severe enough to totally constrict the breathing passages. Ingestion of certain chemicals and drugs can also cause constriction and blockage of the airways. Examination of the air passages indicates paralysis.

Asphyxiation can occur by breathing carbon monoxide (CO), a method chosen by some to commit suicide. Accidental carbon monoxide poisoning can occur from improperly installed or malfunctioning gas appliances, such as furnaces, water heaters, and clothes dryers. Using charcoal grills indoors or burning wood in an improperly vented fireplace can also lead to CO poisoning.

Autoerotic Fatalities. In **autoerotic asphyxiation**, the victim has sought to intensify sexual gratification by placing a rope or other ligature around the neck and causing just enough constriction to create *hypoxia*, or a deficiency of oxygen in the bloodstream that results in semiconsciousness. Such experimentation may be successful a number of times, but then results in total unconsciousness rather than semiconsciousness. In such a case, the body goes limp in the noose, and the body's weight tightens the noose, causing death.

Although not common, autoerotic fatalities should be recognized by police officers. In these instances, suicides are in fact tragic accidents that occurred during dangerous autoerotic acts. Such deaths are classified into three categories: suffocation, strangulation, and chemical asphyxia—the most common of which is strangulation resulting from suspension of the body. In such cases, the body is usually touching the ground and the victim is often bound. Analysis will show, however, that the binding could have been done by the victim.

Dake (2015) notes that an important clue that a death might be the result of an autoerotic episode is that the victim is often found nude or with exposed genitals. However, investigators must also recognize that not all dead bodies found nude or with exposed genitals are victims of autoerotic death, nor are all victims of autoerotic death found nude or with exposed genitals. Other indicators of accidental death during autoerotic practices include:

- Evidence of solo sexual activity

- Mirrors placed to observe the ritual

- Evidence of masturbation and presence of such items as tissues or towels for cleanup

- Lubricants

- Presence of sexual fantasy aids or sexually stimulating paraphernalia (vibrators, dildos, sex aids, and pornographic magazines)

- Presence of bondage (of genitals, arms, legs, or entire body)

- Protective padding around ropes, cuffs, etc.

- Covering of face (mask, panty hose, duct tape)

- Gags

- Cross dressing

- Foreign body inserted into the anus

- Other masochistic behavior

- Evidence of repetitive behavior

- Video recording

Investigators should recognize that these types of deaths are ones in which the body is commonly moved

and signs of autoerotic asphyxiation are hidden because, often, the person who finds the victim is embarrassed or does not want to bring shame to the victim. Consequently, the scene is altered in an effort to protect either the victim's dignity or that of the person who discovered the victim.

There is limited clinical or forensic information about other autoerotic fatalities, but in several documented cases, an act of risky solitary sexual behavior went further than anticipated, leading to accidental death. Such fatalities have involved electrocution, crushing, sepsis following perforation of the bowel, and accidental self-impalement. Such accidental fatalities can easily be misinterpreted as suicide.

Poisoning

Poisoning, one of the oldest methods of murder, can occur from an overwhelming dose that causes immediate death or from small doses that accumulate over time and cause death. Poisons can be injected into the blood or muscles, inhaled as gases, absorbed through the skin surface, taken in foods or liquids, or inserted into the rectum or vagina.

Poisoning can be accomplished with any one of thousands of substances, but some are more common than others. Traditional poisons such as arsenic, cyanide, and pesticides (e.g., parathion and strychnine) are still used but narcotics have become the more commonly detected substance in poisoning victims (Finnberg et al., 2013). Experts in **toxicology** (the study of poisons) can determine the type of poison, the amount ingested, the approximate time ingested, and the effect on the body.

Detecting poisoning is a challenge, and determining whether the victim died by accidental, suicidal, or homicidal poisoning can be an even greater challenge. One difficulty is that many of the signs and symptoms of poisoning appear similar to those caused by natural disease, making it hard to detect or diagnose the true cause of death, particularly if the crime occurs in a hospital setting (Finnberg et al., 2013).

An overdose death is not necessarily a suicide. It might have been accidental—a result of the person's not knowing when medication was last taken or being in a semistupor and taking more pills than intended. Or it may have been a homicide, if a perpetrator placed a poison in with the regular medication or switched medications entirely. If a prescription bottle is found, use the date when the prescription was filled and dosing instructions to calculate how much medication should remain in the bottle. Confirm with the issuing pharmacist whether it was a legal prescription, how many pills were prescribed, and the date the prescription was last filled.

Family members might be able to state whether the person regularly took their medication as prescribed as well as provide information as to what over-the-counter and "street medications" (i.e., illegal narcotics) the person routinely took. All pills and medications should be collected at the scene. Preserve all evidence until the coroner's office rules on the manner of death. Other important evidence includes the medicine cabinet's contents, any excretions or vomit at the scene, and any food the victim recently ate.

Investigators should ask several specific questions to help determine if a homicidal poisoning has occurred:

- Did the death occur suddenly in a normally healthy person?

- Did the person seem to be suffering from a natural disease but normal treatment methods failed to cure the ailment?

- Did the person suffer cyclical reoccurrence of the illness, for example, getting sick at home, getting better in a medical facility, and then getting sick at home again?

- Were there signs of violence or trauma to the victim that could explain the death?

- Did the symptoms appear in a common group of people at the same time, indicating that those other than the target were exposed to the poison?

- Did a caregiver or another individual close to the victim interfere with the victim receiving proper and timely medical attention?

- Did a caregiver or another individual close to the victim prevent family and friends from seeing or talking to the victim during the illness?

- Did the caregiver or another individual close to the victim have access to restricted drugs or other chemicals?

- Does the caregiver or another individual close to the victim indicate an unusual knowledge about poisons?

- Does the caregiver or another individual close to the victim seem anxious to dispose of any medication, food, or liquid the victim may have consumed?

- Does anyone close to the victim insist no autopsy be performed or that rapid cremation occur?

(Demirci & Dogan, 2011)

In the case of child poisonings, was the victim preceded in death by any other children in the family? If a child is poisoned by accidentally ingesting cleaning fluid, detergents, pills, or other such substances, the parents are sometimes charged with manslaughter or negligent homicide.

Burning

Most deaths by burning are accidental. However, a death resulting from burns received in a fire caused by arson is classified as homicide. Moreover, people sometimes try to disguise homicide by burning the victim's body. Even in the most destructive fires, however, considerable information is available from an autopsy because bones are not easily burned. Even in extreme heat, enough blood usually remains to enable a carbon monoxide analysis to determine whether the victim was alive at the time of the fire. In extremely hot fires, however, the heat may cause the skin to break open, and the resulting wounds may appear to be knife or other wounds inflicted by an assailant before the fire.

Explosions, Electrocution, and Lightning

Explosives can cause death from the direct tearing force of the blast, from a shock wave, or from the victim being blown off the top of a structure or against an object with enough force to cause death. Such deaths are usually accidental.

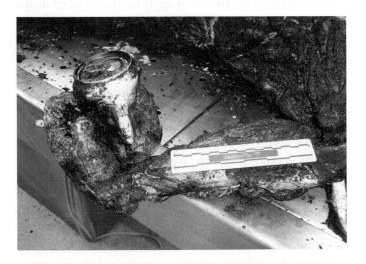

A charred human arm, with a beer can still in hand. In this case, a victim was found lying on a couch, with his hand still wrapped around a beer can. An investigator would need to determine if the victim was so intoxicated that he did not wake when his house accidentally caught fire, or whether the victim had been killed prior to the fire and then the perpetrator staged the scene to look as if the victim had been drinking and smoking and had passed out, perhaps setting the house on fire with a cigarette.

© Dr. Lindsey Thomas

Electrocution paralyzes the heart muscle, causing rapid death. Nearly all electrocution deaths are accidental (except, of course, in capital punishment cases). High-voltage lines and lightning are the main causes. Lightning leaves linear stripes on the body, turns the skin blue, and burns the skin, especially at the lightning bolt's entry and exit points.

LO12 List the indicators investigators use to determine whether the following causes of unnatural death most likely indicate that the death was accidental, a suicide, or a homicide: gunshot wounds; stabbing and cutting wounds; blows from blunt objects; asphyxia; poisoning; burning; explosions, electrocution, and lightning; drugs; and vehicles.

Poisoning deaths can be accidental, suicide, or homicide. Most deaths caused by burning, explosions, electrocution, and lightning are accidental, although burning is sometimes used in an attempt to disguise homicide.

Drugs

Many studies have documented the relationship between drugs and homicide and the prominent role drugs play in homicide events. The same techniques used in general death investigations also apply to drug-related death investigations. Look for evidence of alcohol use or consumption of drugs (pill bottles or paraphernalia). Alcohol mixed with certain drugs can pose a particularly lethal combination.

In 2020, opioids were the main driver of drug overdose deaths. Data from the Centers for Disease Control and Prevention (CDC) indicate that opioid-related deaths in 2018 were nearly six times higher than the number of opioid-involved overdose deaths in 1999, and deaths from prescription opioids were more than four times higher in 2018 than 1999 (CDC, 2020).

Recent legislation has focused on holding responsible those who supplied opioids or other drugs to victims of overdose deaths. For example, in Cincinnati, Ohio, prosecutors are being more aggressive in bringing manslaughter charges against people who provide heroin that results in a death, with sentences of up to 11 years in prison if convicted (Grasha & DeMio, 2018). And in March 2018, a 36-year-old Wareham, Massachusetts, drug dealer because the first person to be convicted of manslaughter related to an overdose death (Shepard, 2018).

Drug-related homicides also include deadly disputes involving individuals high on drugs (no organized drug or gang affiliation); deaths caused during the commission of economically motivated crimes, such as robbery, in the offender's effort to get money to buy drugs; and homicides associated with the systemic violence surrounding the drug business itself. This third category includes hits on traffickers, dealers, or buyers (may be gang related); assassinations of law enforcement officers or others fighting drug trafficking; and the killing of innocent bystanders in drug-related disputes.

Drug trafficking operations commonly cross jurisdictional boundaries, a factor that severely impedes the progress of an investigator working a drug trafficking homicide. To better address this challenge, some areas have developed a Violent Offenders Task Force (VOTF). VOTF groups can be multijurisdictional or within one law enforcement agency, and they tend to work the most serious crimes when it is suspected that a narcotics dealer or gang member is a suspect. Typically, they assist the homicide detectives and work robberies, rape, and serious assaults. Investigating drug offenses is discussed in greater detail in Chapter 18.

Vehicles

According to the National Highway Traffic Safety Administration (NHTSA), motor vehicle traffic crashes caused 36,560 fatalities and more than 2 million injuries during 2018, and alcohol-related fatalities accounted for nearly one-third (29%) of overall vehicle-related deaths (NHTSA, 2020). Vehicular homicide can result from reckless driving, driving under the influence, or other circumstances where a driver's failure to obey the rules of the road, either intentionally or negligently, leads to the death of another person. Aggressive driving and road rage can escalate to a case of vehicular homicide: in fact, the only difference between a vehicular homicide and other homicides is the use of a motor vehicle as a weapon rather than a gun or knife.

When a traffic crash results in a fatality, all vehicles involved must be thoroughly examined. Document the condition of the vehicles through photographs and written observations. Also of extreme importance are weather, lighting conditions, and road conditions at the time of the incident. An accident reconstruction expert must be brought in to help the investigator make sense of skid marks, impact dynamics, and other factors present at the scene.

If the driver or drivers are still at the scene, obtain evidence for a toxicology examination to determine whether there were any drugs in the person's system at the time of the incident. Toxicology evidence is also necessary for the victim, even if that person wasn't driving a car, because their condition before the incident may have played a role. Officers must be aware that the law is evolving in this area of investigation, and the concept of implied consent is being challenged in courts. In many states, officers are required to obtain a court order (i.e., a warrant) before they can collect toxicology evidence.

In *Missouri v. McNeely* (2013), the U.S. Supreme Court ruled against law enforcement, with Justice Sotomayor writing for the majority: "We hold that in drunk-driving investigations, the natural dissipation of alcohol in the bloodstream does not constitute an exigency in every case sufficient to justify conducting a blood test without a warrant." *McNeely* does not invalidate existing implied consent laws but, rather, requires that a warrant be obtained if a person revokes their "implied" consent. Further, if an officer deems that a mandatory nonconsensual blood draw is necessary and a search warrant is not obtained, that officer must be able to articulate the exigent circumstances that made the blood draw *reasonable* (Oh, 2013).

The issue in *State v. Brooks* (2013) was whether police violated Brooks's Fourth Amendment rights when they took blood and urine samples from him, without a search warrant, on three separate occasions over a six-month period in which Brooks was stopped for suspicion of driving while impaired. On each occasion, when Brooks was told that, under the state's implied consent laws, refusing the DWI test was a crime, Brooks consulted with his attorney and then agreed to the chemical test. And in each of the three separate incidents, the State of Minnesota charged Brooks with two counts of first-degree driving while impaired. Brooks moved to suppress the results of the blood and urine tests in each of the three cases because, under *McNeely*, the warrantless searches of his blood and urine could not be upheld solely because of the exigency created by the dissipation of alcohol in the body. While the court agreed on that fact, it also ruled that since Brooks had consented to the searches at issue, which were valid incident to Brooks's lawful arrests, warrants were unnecessary and the searches were constitutional.

The 2019 case of *Mitchell v. Wisconsin* centered on the constitutionality of a warrantless blood draw from an unconscious individual suspected of drunk driving. Under Wisconsin's implied consent law, a driver consents to a blood draw if incapacitated. Mitchell argued, however, that under the *McNeely* standards, there was no exigency and, therefore, police needed a warrant before conducting a blood draw. The defense further challenged the warrantless blood draw by claiming that the speed with which an electronic warrant could be obtained meant officers would have been able to get their evidence before any significant decrease in Mitchell's system *if* they had bothered to ask for an e-warrant. The Supreme Court disagreed, and in a 5–4 decision held that the proper, and higher, standard by which to judge the facts of this case was *Schmerber* (discussed in Chapter 7):

> BAC tests are Fourth Amendment searches.... A warrant is normally required for a lawful search, but there are well-defined exceptions to this rule, including the "exigent circumstances" exception, which allows warrantless searches "to prevent the imminent destruction of evidence."... In *McNeely,* this Court held that the fleeting nature of blood-alcohol evidence alone was not enough to bring BAC testing within the exigency exception.... But in Schmerber v. California,... the dissipation of BAC did justify a blood test of a drunk driver whose accident gave police other pressing duties, for then the *further* delay caused by a warrant application would indeed have threatened the destruction of evidence. Like *Schmerber,* unconscious-driver cases will involve a heightened degree of urgency for several reasons....
>
> *Schmerber* demonstrates that an exigency exists when (1) BAC evidence is dissipating and (2) some other factor creates pressing health, safety, or law enforcement needs that would take priority over a warrant application. Because both conditions are met when a drunk-driving suspect is unconscious, *Schmerber* controls. A driver's unconsciousness does not just create pressing needs; it is *itself* a medical emergency....
>
> Like *Schmerber*, this case sits much higher than *McNeely* on the exigency spectrum. *McNeely* was about the minimum degree of urgency common to all drunk-driving cases. In *Schmerber*, a car accident heightened that urgency. And here Mitchell's medical condition did just the same....
>
> A driver so drunk as to lose consciousness is quite likely to crash, especially if he passes out before managing to park. And then the accident might give officers a slew of urgent tasks beyond that of securing (and working around) medical care for the suspect. Police may have to ensure that others who are injured receive prompt medical attention; they may have to provide first aid themselves until medical personnel arrive at the scene. In some cases, they may have to deal with fatalities.... This is just the kind of scenario for which the exigency rule was born—just the kind of grim dilemma it lives to dissolve.

The Supreme Court vacated and remanded the case back to the state for further proceedings, effectively allowing the lower court's decision to stand. There will undoubtedly be more challenges to the warrant exception by implied consent in coming years, and investigators are urged to stay current with this area of constitutional law.

If the case is one of hit-and-run, physical evidence left at the scene, such as paint, metal shavings, tire impressions, and glass, can help link a suspect and a vehicle to the crime. Evidence to look for on the suspect's vehicle includes hairs, fibers, blood, and other biological fluids from the victim. The vehicle may contain evidence of the impact. Evidence of fresh paint jobs or recent repairs warrants further investigation.

After the victim has been identified, the time of death has been estimated, and the cause of and method used to produce death have been established, the homicide investigation turns to developing a suspect. Witnesses can be a vital source of information in this endeavor.

Witnesses

In violent criminal deaths, struggles often create noise and attract the attention of neighbors or passersby. Witnesses may know and name a suspect, or they may have seen the suspect or vehicle. Often, however, there are no witnesses, and information must be sought from family members, neighbors, and associates. Conducting a neighborhood canvass is a critical step in a thorough homicide investigation and was discussed in detail in Chapter 6.

Many jurisdictions have recognized the value of homicide hotlines and other venues for obtaining vital leads from citizens. Crime Stoppers, the brainchild of an Albuquerque detective who was seeking leads on the murder of a local college student, has been fielding anonymous tips pertaining to homicides and other crimes since it began in September 1976. Since then, and as of July 20, 2020, tips from the public have helped solve 16,324 homicides (www.crimestoppersusa.org). A new smartphone app called P3 allows the public to share information anonymously with local Crime Stoppers programs, law enforcement agencies, and schools (see Figure 8.3).

Suspects

If the suspect is arrested at the crime scene, follow the procedures described in Chapter 1. If the suspect is known but is not at the scene, immediately disseminate the description to other investigators, field officers, and police agencies.

If the suspect is not known, identification becomes a priority. Often, several suspects are identified and eventually eliminated as information and evidence are obtained and the list is reduced to one or two prime suspects. In major cases, any number of suspects may be developed from information at the scene, from informants, and from intelligence files.

Discovering a motive is not a specific requirement in the investigation, but motive is so closely tied to intent and to developing a suspect that it should be determined. Also attempt to establish the victim-offender relationship (VOR) and understand the difference between *expressive* and *instrumental* violence. **Expressive violence** is that stemming from hurt feelings, anger, or rage, such as when the jealous lover stabs her ex-boyfriend while he's on a date with his new girlfriend. In these cases, the VOR is close and established. **Instrumental violence** is goal-directed predatory behavior used to exert control—for example, the carjacker who shoots his victim before stealing the vehicle.

The VOR in events involving instrumental violence may or may not be close, with such events commonly occurring between strangers who have no preestablished relationship. A prevalent theory regarding VOR and risk of instrumental versus expressive violence is that a close relationship (spouse/lover, family member, close personal friend) may protect a person from certain types of instrumental violence (e.g., robbery) because they have someone to watch out for them, but it may also make them more vulnerable to expressive violence.

Homicides are committed for many reasons. Common types of criminal homicide include the anger killing, the love-triangle killing, the revenge or jealousy killing, killing for profit, random killing, murder-suicide, the sex-and-sadism killing, and felony murder. Anger killings often begin as assaults. The possibility of killing for profit almost always exists. Thus, it is always critical to determine who would stand to profit from the victim's death.

Some homicides are contracted or hired. This is frequently the case in murders of organized crime figures.

> **LO13** Explain why determining a motive is important in homicide investigations.
>
> Determine a motive for a killing because it provides leads to suspects and strong circumstantial evidence against a suspect.

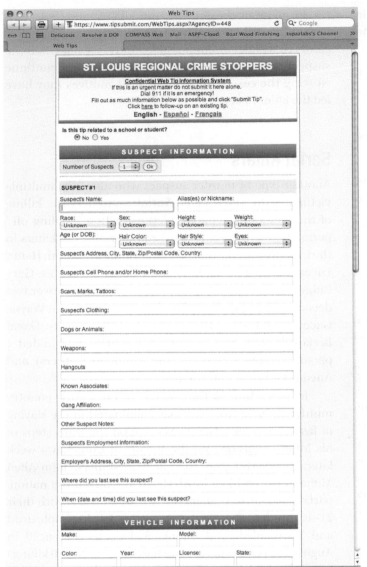

Figure 8.3
St. Louis (Missouri) Regional Crime Stoppers online homicide tip site.
Source: © St. Louis Regional Crime Stoppers and © The Crime Report.

Mass Murderers

The Federal Bureau of Investigation defines a **mass murder** as "a number of murders (four or more) occurring during the same incident, with no distinctive time period between the murders" (National Center for the Analysis of Violent Crime, 2008). Following the 2012 Sandy Hook Elementary massacre in Newtown, Connecticut, in which 26 people were killed, 20 of whom were children, Congress amended the definition of a "mass killing" and lowered the casualty threshold to "3 or more killings in a single incident (Investigative Assistance for Violent Crimes Act of 2012, 2013). Mass shootings are a subtype of "mass murders" or "mass killings" that denote use of a firearm during the incident.

Recent years have seen several highly publicized cases of mass familicides, particularly parents killing their children—the Fresno, California, man who murdered nine of his children; the Texas mom who methodically drowned her five kids. Without a doubt, the terrorist attacks of September 11, 2001, were the most horrific mass murder events ever witnessed by contemporary Americans in their homeland. Mass shootings continue to claim lives across the country:

- 2012 Aurora, Colorado, movie theater shooting (12 fatalities and 58 injuries)

- 2013 Washington Navy Yard shooting (12 fatalities, 8 injuries)

- 2016 Pulse Nightclub shooting in Orlando, Florida, that left 49 victims dead

- 2017 killing of 58 people at an outdoor concert in Las Vegas, Nevada, by a sniper who fired more than 1,000 rounds on the crowd below from his 32nd floor hotel room

- 2017 shooting at the First Baptist Church in Sutherland Springs, Texas, where 26 people died and 20 others were wounded

- 2018 shooting at Marjory Stoneman Douglas High School in Parkland, Florida, in which 17 people were killed

- 2018 Santa Fe High School shooting in New Mexico in which 10 people died and 13 were injured

- 2018 shooting at the Tree of Life synagogue in Pittsburg, Pennsylvania, that killed 11 and wounded 6

- 2018 shooting at a Thousand Oaks, California, bar where 12 people died and more than 10 were injured

- 2019 shooting at an El Paso, Texas, Walmart that left 22 people dead and 26 more injured

The tremendous publicity such events receive leaves many American citizens feeling like such an event could happen just about anywhere and anytime.

Felony-related mass murder, such as the killing of eyewitnesses during a robbery or a group of participants at a drug buy, increased during the last part of the twentieth century. Frequently these killers unleash their murderous fury on total strangers. School shootings resulting in multiple deaths have occurred throughout the United States, and many of the shooters have, themselves, been youths who had attended the targeted school. It is important to realize that school violence almost never occurs without warning, with most school shooters dropping hints about their intentions.

Workplace violence may also result in multiple homicides: "The perpetrators are frequently loners with poor social skills, often obsessed with violence and weapons. The targets include authority figures and peers who are in conflict with the perpetrators. The perpetrators often bring an arsenal of weapons and kill all who get in their way" (Hess, Orthmann, & Cho, 2014, p. 277). As with school shootings, workplace violence may sometimes be anticipated by noting personality changes in the potential shooter as well as the occurrence of certain precipitating events, such as a missed promotion or a termination. Other triggers include divorce and severe financial troubles.

LO14 Identify the similarities that exist between school and workplace mass murders.

Similarities between school and workplace murders include the perpetrators' profiles, the targets, the means, and the motivation.

In many of these cases, the killers take their own lives at the end of the shooting rampage, leaving investigators to wonder about possible motives. Even when the suspect is known and deceased, investigators continue working the case to determine what motives may have led the killer to act.

Serial Killers

Another type of murder suspect who also kills multiple victims is the serial killer. **Serial murder** is the killing of three or more separate victims, with a "cooling off" period between the killings. A number of serial killers in the United States have received national attention: Henry Lucas, who confessed to 188 murders in 24 states; Gary Ridgway, the Green River strangler, 48 murders over two decades; Theodore (Ted) Bundy, 40 murders; John Wayne Gacey, 33 murders; Jeffrey Dahmer, 16 murders; David Berkowitz, the "Son of Sam," 6 murders (he blinded 1 person, paralyzed another, and wounded 7 others); and Aileen Wuornos, 7 murders.

In 1997, Andrew Cunanan went on a cross-country murder spree of five men that culminated in the slaying of fashion designer Gianni Versace on the front steps of his Miami mansion and the suicide of Cunanan a week later. The Washington, DC, "Beltway snipers," John Allen Muhammad and Lee Boyd Malvo, terrorized the nation, particularly citizens along the Northeast coast, with their 21-day random shooting rampage that left 10 people dead and 3 wounded. And Dennis Rader was sentenced in August 2005 to 10 consecutive life terms for the 10 killings he confessed to as the BTK (Bind, Torture, Kill) serial killer.

Investigating a murder committed by a serial killer may initially seem the same as investigating any other homicide. As a case is investigated, however, and if no suspect can be developed, the investigator should consider reporting the crime to the FBI's National Center for the Analysis of Violent Crime (NCAVC) at Quantico, Virginia. NCAVC provides a profiling program as well as research and development, training, and the Violent Criminal Apprehension Program (VICAP). Police departments investigating cases they believe involve serial murder can submit their cases to VICAP. Other cases with similar MO submitted by other agencies are then compared, and information is furnished to the submitting agencies. As the Henry Lucas cases illustrate—where murders were committed in 24 states—VICAP is an important resource in investigating and prosecuting this type of killer. If VICAP determines that a serial murderer is probably involved, a multijurisdictional major crime investigation team may be assembled to handle the case.

In some cases, where media coverage leads to an avalanche of citizen tips to authorities, investigators find themselves overwhelmed by the flood of potentially useful, but more often useless, information.

Because of improved information sharing, interjurisdictional communication, and media coverage, some homicide investigations that begin as single-incident investigations may now have the potential to develop into serial killing investigations. For example, Donald Blom, who confessed to abducting and murdering 19-year-old Katie Poirier in Minnesota, is a possible suspect in several other unsolved disappearances and murders around the state and in neighboring states. Cary Stayner, a handyman convicted of the murder of a national park tourist, is suspected of three other killings. Authorities speculate that if Stayner's last victim had not put up such a struggle, leaving behind a small but invaluable collection of physical evidence, Stayner's first three victims—and potentially more in the future—may have forever remained untraceable and unconnected to him.

DNA evidence obtained in any homicide can provide valuable leads for investigators, and the importance of such evidence is magnified greatly in serial killings, even if investigators are at first unaware of any links to other crimes. Police officers who understand the psychology underlying serial killings will be more effective in investigating the murders and in interviewing the murderers. Serial killers generally select strangers as their victims, although by the time the actual murder occurs, they may have become quite familiar with them.

Rader, the BTK serial killer, divulged in court how he selected victims as he played out his sexual fantasies. During his self-described "trolling phase," Rader would look for several potential victims, referring to them as "projects," and begin stalking them. Multiple projects were selected so if one didn't work out, he'd have some "backups." Over time, Rader explained, he'd start really honing in on one person to become *the* victim.

The acts of serial killers are typically considered in discussions of homicides, and, indeed, the very term used to describe this group of offenders focuses on the killing part of the crime. However, to the perpetrator, the actual homicide is more of an incidental event.

These killers are often quite intelligent and very much in touch with reality, which partially explains their success in eluding capture. When interviewing serial killers, any attempts to evoke sympathy for the victims or surviving relatives will probably be futile. Appeals to their ego, on the other hand, may succeed. It is also important not to display shock at the atrocities that may have been committed because this is often what serial murderers want.

The acts of serial murderers seem incomprehensible to "normal" people. For example, in 1991, the killing and mutilation of 16 young men and boys by Dahmer made national headlines. When police entered Dahmer's stench-filled apartment, they found body parts of 11 males—painted human skulls, severed heads, and body parts in cold storage and torsos disintegrating in an acid-filled vat. Dahmer's murders can also be classified as lust murders.

Lust Murderers

A **lust murder** is a sex-related homicide involving a sadistic, deviant assault. In lust murder, the killer depersonalizes the victim, sexually mutilates the body, and may displace body parts. Two types of lust murderers are often described—organized and disorganized. *Organized offenders* are usually of above-average intelligence, methodical, and cunning. They are socially skilled and trick their victims into situations in which they can torture and then murder them. In contrast, the *disorganized offender* is usually of below-average intelligence, has no car, and is a loner who acts on impulse.

Both the organized and the disorganized offenders usually murder victims from their own geographic area, and the murders involve fantasy, ritual, fetishes, and symbolism. They also both usually leave some sort of physical evidence.

Clearing a Homicide

No other crime is measured as accurately and precisely as homicide. Homicides continue to receive the most attention by police because they are considered the most serious crime and are complex cases to investigate. Nonetheless, a significant proportion of these violent crimes go unsolved or without an arrest being made. The term used to define the quantity of cases removed from active investigation is the **clearance rate**, which is the ratio of crimes resolved to the number of crimes reported. *Cleared, closed,* and *solved* are often used interchangeably. The FBI uses the term *cleared*.

A case can be cleared by arrest or by exceptional means. *Crime in the United States* (FBI, 2018) explains, "In certain situations, elements beyond law enforcement's control prevent the agency from arresting and formally charging the offender. When this occurs, the agency can clear the offenses *exceptionally*." To do so, law enforcement agencies must have identified the offender; gathered enough evidence to support an arrest, make a charge, and turn over the offender to the court for prosecution; identified the offender's exact location so that the suspect could be taken into custody immediately; and encountered a circumstance outside the control of law enforcement that prohibits the officers from arresting, charging, and prosecuting the offender. The FBI clarifies, "Examples of exceptional clearance include, but are not limited to, the death of the offender (e.g., suicide or justifiably killed by law enforcement or citizen); the victim's refusal to cooperate with the prosecution after the offender has been identified; or the denial of extradition because the offender committed a crime in another jurisdiction and is being prosecuted for that offense."

The Declining Clearance Rate for Homicide

Although the national clearance rate for homicide is the highest of all the serious offenses, homicide clearances have declined dramatically over the past several decades. The Criminal Justice Information Services (CJIS) Division of the FBI, which tracks and estimates the homicide clearance rate in the United States, found that in the mid-1960s, roughly 90% of homicides in this nation were cleared through the arrest of offenders, and that that rate has steadily dropped, reaching an estimated reported 61% in 2017 (Murder Accountability Project, 2019). FBI data shows 62.3% of murder and nonnegligent manslaughter cases were cleared by arrest or exceptional means in 2018 (FBI, 2018). A review of the FBI's Supplemental Homicide Report (SHR) by the nonprofit Murder Accountability Project (MAP) found that this alarming 40-year decline in law enforcement's ability to clear murders has been driven entirely by declining homicide clearance rates for African Americans (MAP, 2019). The review also found that the reported homicide clearance rates for whites (which includes ethnic Hispanics), Asians, and Native Americans actually improved slightly from 1976 to 2017.

A critical factor in clearing homicides is time, as cases become harder to solve the longer it takes to make an arrest. As time passes, offenders can gain physical distance from the scene, witnesses forget vital information, and evidence becomes lost or contaminated (Regoeczi, Jarvis, & Riedel, 2008). Criminologists and law enforcement practitioners have identified other potential causes of declining homicide clearance rates, including the following:

- higher legal standards for charging suspects with murder

- the expense associated with homicide investigations and the inability of many poorer jurisdictions to dedicate the needed resources to these cases

- public distrust of the police and an unwillingness to help with cases

- a growing number of immigrants from countries where residents fear and do not trust the local police

- the growth of "Thug Culture" and "Stop Snitchin" campaigns

- the paradigm shift in the 1980s which moved the focus to preventing, instead of solving, crimes
  (Kaste, 2015)

Witness cooperation, or the lack thereof, and a lack of cooperation from other departments appear to be significant roadblocks to homicide clearances (Carter & Carter, 2015). Authors of one study suggest that the proliferation of gangs and drugs in certain jurisdictions has led to "police devaluation," where community members distrust law enforcement to effectively resolve crime in their neighborhoods. Finally, higher standards of evidence needed to convict defendants and an expansion of the legal protections and rights afforded suspects have contributed to diminished clearance rates for homicide.

Aspects of the Offense Associated with Likelihood of Clearing a Case

Different theories exist as to which aspects of a homicide are most likely to result in the case being cleared. Some focus heavily on the race and socioeconomic status of the victim. For example, a theory posited by Black (1976) held that the vertical location (i.e., social status) of a victim influenced the amount of legal resources deployed to solve the crime.

More recent studies have examined the neighborhood context in which homicide investigations took place and found that homicides occurring in neighborhoods with larger Black and Latino populations were less likely to be cleared, in part because of lower citizen cooperation rates with police (Petersen, 2017; Fagan & Geller, 2018). Other research finds that communities with low collective efficacy and social cohesion—those in which residents are unwilling to intervene to help other residents or exert any level of informal social control—tend to have lower homicide clearance rates (Kirk & Matsuda, 2011; Mancik, Parker, & Williams, 2018). These results suggest that neighborhood demographics and social and structural organizational features of neighborhoods may play a significant role, perhaps more than the victim's race, in explaining homicide clearance rates.

Other research has identified several aspects of the crime itself that are associated with the likelihood of clearing the case:

- ***Homicide circumstances.*** Several studies report that felony-related homicides are more difficult to clear than are homicides resulting from other circumstances.

- ***Weapons.*** Homicides committed with weapons that bring the offender and victim into contact with one another (such as a knife) increase the likelihood of closing the case.

- ***Location.*** Among the more consistent findings concerning homicide clearance is the greater likelihood of clearance for cases occurring in residences.

(Regoeczi et al., 2008)

Much of the empirical evidence supports the hypothesis that homicide clearance rates are most affected by random circumstances and factors beyond investigators' control, such as those just identified (Roberts, 2014). However, other research has shown that clearance rates may also be affected by actions taken by officers and investigators.

Law Enforcement Actions Affecting Clearance

Numerous studies have examined if and how specific investigative actions affect clearance rates, and many have found affirmative evidence that the tactics and strategies police departments implement within their investigative units can improve homicide clearance rates (Braga & Dusseault, 2018; Pizarro, Terrill, & LoFaso, 2020). For example, when the Boston Police Department (BPD) designed an intervention to enhance their homicide criminal investigative processes and practices, they noticed a 10% increase in their yearly homicide clearance rate (Braga & Dusseault, 2018). Specific actions taken by the BPD included the following:

- Increasing the number of investigative personnel dedicated to homicide cases

- Increasing the number of computer database searches done in real time and pursuing analyses to generate investigative leads

- Improving the collection and testing of physical evidence

- Increasing efforts to interview witnesses after leaving the scene

The final recommendation by the researchers was that departments engage in a problem-oriented policing approach and that "investigators need to adopt a business model that leads to the construction of a robust 'information chain' from witness statements and physical evidence that enhances their ability to hold offenders accountable" (Braga & Dusseault, 2018).

Research by criminologists David L. Carter and Jeremy G. Carter (2015) examined seven geographically representative law enforcement agencies across the country in an effort to identify strategies and tactics that increase homicide clearance rates. Their study found the following best practices adopted by those departments with high homicide clearance rates:

- A strong community policing presence and solid community relationships

- The ability to network and collaborate with external agencies and other law enforcement agencies

- Effective use of crime analysis and intelligence analysis

- Embracing an innovative culture focused on competence and capability to include staffing, training, and the development of expertise (e.g., collective digital evidence)

One of the more interesting findings of the study was that agencies with higher homicide clearance rates viewed patrol officers as partners in the investigation, encouraging them to take a more active role and perform a variety of tasks associated with the investigation (Carter & Carter, 2015).

Many departments use a homicide case review solvability chart to determine which cases to focus on. Such tools can provide support for requesting additional resources. Appendix C shows an example of a solvability chart.

The 10 Most Common Errors in Death Investigations

Investigator error can have a substantial deleterious effect on homicide clearances. Geberth (2015) lists the 10 most common errors in death investigations:

1. Improper response to the scene
2. Failure to protect the crime scene
3. Not handling suspicious deaths as homicides
4. Responding with a preconceived notion
5. Failure to take sufficient photos
6. Failure to manage the process (maintaining the chain of custody and proper documentation)

7. Failure to evaluate victimology
8. Failure to conduct an effective canvass
9. Failure to work as a team
10. Command interference or inappropriate action

Consider the following scenario (adapted from Geberth, 2007):

A call comes in to 911 that a man has fallen out of a window and is lying in an alleyway; the caller thinks the man might be dead. Uniformed officers respond to the address and find a large crowd gathered around a lifeless body. The officers radio for an ambulance and request detectives, telling the crowd to disperse. "There's nothing to see here, folks. Move along." A man with an open bottle of whiskey is slumped against the building and refuses to leave. He's staring at the body and telling officers, in slurred speech, that the man lying on the ground is his roommate. The officers, thinking the drunk simply wants to indulge an urge to stare at a dead body, tell the inebriated man to get lost before they arrest him for public intoxication. He reluctantly gets to his feet and shuffles away as the ambulance pulls up. An EMT pronounces the victim dead.

Several minutes later, two detectives arrive and begin to canvass the street and building for witnesses. They manage to get one woman to open her door and talk to them. She lives on the fourth floor in the unit across the hall from the victim and acknowledges that she heard the victim and another man shouting at each other earlier in the evening in the victim's apartment. The other man had left abruptly and appeared drunk, as she watched him from the peep hole in her front door. Detectives think it is possible an altercation and assault occurred in the victim's apartment, culminating with the drunken man tossing his friend out of the window.

The problem: this area is now a possible crime scene, yet none of it—the victim's apartment, the building itself, or the street below where the body was found—has been secured, most of the witnesses were told to leave without any contact information collected, and the likely assailant has also been chased away by the uniformed officers.

Impact of Unsolved Homicides

When homicides go unsolved, they not only deny justice to victims and their grieving families but they can also fuel a cycle of more homicides and continued decline in homicide clearance rates. Fagan and Geller (2018,

p. 283) note: "It is worrisome that the same neighborhood conditions that elevate murder and other violent crime rates seem to also reduce citizen cooperation with police, a problematic intersection that compounds each of these processes. When homicides remain unsolved, the killer is free to kill again, compounding the alienation from police and skewing the racial distribution of homicide clearance rates." Because successful homicide investigations lead to higher homicide clearance rates, and because such investigations rely heavily on information provided by not only witnesses to the crime itself but by other residents who live in the crime area, a reluctance on the part of witnesses and local citizens to cooperate with a homicide investigation will very likely hamper a successful resolution to the case and, consequently, drive the clearance rate down (Carter & Carter, 2015).

As David Kennedy, director of the National Network for Safe Communities at John Jay College of Criminal Justice, has said: "Low clearance rates mean people have low confidence in the police, which leads to reluctance to cooperate, which leads to low clearance rates. At the same time, low clearance rates mean that there isn't legal accountability for serious violence, which leads people to take things into their own hands, which leads to high levels of violence and low clearance rates. It's a spiral of decline" (Mirabile, 2017).

Cold Cases

Despite the relatively high clearance rate of homicides, nearly 40% go unsolved. Unsolved crimes become cold cases. At any given time, a large metropolitan jurisdiction may have thousands of cold homicide cases on its shelves. One study identified with confidence more than 230,355 unresolved homicides throughout the United States for the period 1980–2014, and estimated another 12,000 unresolved homicides for 2015 and 2016 combined, noting the high homicide rates for those two years, bringing the figure closer to 242,000 as of 2017 (Stein, Kimmerle, Adcock, & Martin, 2017). The researchers note that of the estimated 40,000 unidentified dead in the country, many could have died as the result of homicide, which would bring the number of unresolved homicides even higher.

An NIJ working group formed in 2015 to examine the state of cold case investigations in the United States and develop a best practices guide for implementing and sustaining a cold case unit notes: "No universal definition of a cold case currently exists. Some jurisdictions consider a case to be cold when investigative leads have seemingly been exhausted. Others consider the length of time that has elapsed since the crime occurred—for example, one, three, or five years.... Some agencies never really regard a case as cold; rather, an investigator is simply assigned to the case, working on it when time allows until it is solved or until he or she retires or is transferred to another position" (Barcus, Heurich, Ritter, Schwarting, & Walton, 2019, p. 2). The working definition developed by the NIJ Cold Case Working Group is as follows: a **cold case** is "a case, such as a violent crime, missing person, or unidentified person, that has remained unsolved for at least three years and has the potential to be solved through newly acquired information or advanced technologies to analyze evidence" (Barcus et al., 2019, p. 2).

Many departments have created cold case squads dedicated to handling these challenging cases. Other departments do not have a designated unit but, rather, use individual investigators to handle individual cold cases. The NIJ Cold Case Working Group recommends that investigators assigned to cold cases have at least five years of investigative experience, given the complex nature of these cases, and that they receive specific training in how to approach unresolved case investigations (Barcus et al., 2019). In addition, at least two full-time investigators should be assigned to each cold case investigation to allow for continuity of operations should one investigator need to leave the case, and to ensure transparency, officer safety, and the ability to handle multiple tasks at the same time, such interviewing victims or testifying in court.

Although the mantra for fresh homicide investigations is typically "time is of the essence"—assuming that if after 72 hours no suspect has been found, the case is unlikely to be solved—cold case squads use the passing of time to their advantage. Different squads use different criteria in deciding which cases to reinvestigate, but in general, the presence of well-preserved physical evidence and the ability to identify and locate original witnesses raise the priority level of a case. Involving a prosecutor early in the case selection process will help identify cases that have the most potential for a quick resolution. Factors to consider when deciding which cold cases to pursue include:

- Prosecution considerations (e.g., statute of limitations, chain of custody, key witness availability, and factual analysis of the case)

- Database hits

- New information

- Evidence that could provide investigative leads if analyzed/reanalyzed

- Named suspects

- Persons of interest

- Previously issued or recalled warrants

- Interest and communication from the community or other stakeholders

(Barcus et al., 2019)

A cold case investigation begins with the examination of work conducted by the original investigators, and one of the first tasks is usually to locate and re-interview witnesses. Over time, witnesses who were once uncooperative, either feeling too threatened or intimidated to get involved or still in shock from what they saw, may no longer be afraid to talk to the police; people who had once had a relationship with the suspect but no longer do may decide to come forward with incriminating information.

In addition to getting information from witnesses, investigators may generate leads by having physical evidence reexamined. Advances in technology during the past decade, particularly DNA analysis techniques, are helping to crack once unsolvable cases. If fingerprint, DNA, or other evidence in a cold homicide case had been previously examined but not entered into a national database, such as the Automated Fingerprint Information Technology (AFIT) system, the Combined DNA Index System (CODIS), or VICAP, that information should certainly be entered now. Besides national forensic evidence databases, cold case investigators have several other resources they should tap for help, including the media, the public, and the inmate population.

Cold case investigators also need to work closely with prosecutors to ensure that their efforts will meet the requirements to get a case to court. Figure 8.4 is a checklist of the criteria used by the Kansas City (Missouri) Police Department in determining which cold case homicides to reopen. Appendix D provides the Las Vegas Metropolitan Police Department Cold Case Solvability Criteria.

Volunteer Cold Case Squads

Some jurisdictions have tapped into the resources of retired law enforcement officers to staff their cold case squads. The first all-volunteer retired law enforcement cold case squad in the country is the "Cold Case Cowboys," who first came together in Roseburg, Oregon, in December of 2002. It wasn't until they had solved their first case—a 35-year-old unresolved murder—that they received their moniker by the local media, mainly because of how they all dressed: Wrangler jeans, western shirts, cowboy hats, and boots (Mains, 2014). According to their official website (www.thecoldcasecowboys.com), they have helped similar volunteer cold case squads form in other jurisdictions throughout the country.

Figure 8.4

Kansas City (Missouri) Police Department cold case solvability checklist.

Source: Reprinted by permission of the Kansas City Police Department.

Offense Number _____

Victim _____

Date of Crime _____

Evidence	Yes	Pt.	No	Unk	N/A
1. Fingerprints recovered?		2			
2. Prints checked through AFIS?		–			
3. Any prints AFIS quality?		3			
4. Prints available on possible suspect?		2			
5. Trace evidence recovered for DNA analysis?		4			
6. DNA analysis requested?		–			
7. DNA profile obtained from analysis?		3			
8. DNA sample obtained from suspects?		2			
9. Murder weapon recovered?		4			
10. Projectiles/casings recovered?		2			
11. Checked through NIBIN System?		–			
12. NIBIN identification made?		2			
13. Victim's property taken in crime?		2			
14. Stolen property entered in NCIC?		4			

Witness(es)	Yes	Pt.	No	Unk	N/A
15. Eyewitness(es) to the crime?		3			
16. Cooperative witness(es)?		2			
17. Hostile witness(es)?		1			
18. Good witness(es) developed in canvass?		2			

Suspect(s)	Yes	Pt.	No	Unk	N/A
19. Suspect(s) named by witness(es)?		4			
20. Does eyewitness(es) know suspect(s)?		2			
21. Suspect(s) developed in investigation?		2			
22. Can witness(es) identify suspect(s)?		2			
23. Is suspect(s) still in Kansas City?		2			

Total solvability points (50 possible)	

Detective _____   Date _____

Benefits of a Cold Case Unit

In today's climate of budget tightening, it may be difficult for police executives, elected officials, and other policymakers who make funding decisions to understand the benefits of a dedicated cold case unit. Indeed, "Measuring the successes of a cold case unit is difficult because they are often intangible and not easily quantified. Although the community may not comprehend the complexities of a case, knowledge of ongoing activity in an investigation may still afford public reassurance and may therefore be some level of success. Other, less apparent benefits . . . may include enhanced perceptions of 'justice, integrity, fear reduction, citizen satisfaction, protection and help for those who cannot protect or help themselves'" (Barcus et al., 2019, p. 11).

Noting that every unresolved case represents a person, as well as their family, friends, and community, the NIJ Cold Case Working Group asserts: "Creating and maintaining a cold case unit demonstrates an agency's commitment to victims and the community by solving crimes, holding offenders accountable, and ensuring public safety. Doing so reinforces a community's confidence in its police and the criminal justice system (Barcus

et al., 2019, p. 1). Charles Heurich, a senior scientist with the Office of Investigative and Forensic Sciences at the National Institute of Justice and a member of the Cold Case Working Group puts it more succinctly: "If we don't solve [cold cases], the number of unsolved crimes will just go up and then there will be thousands of cases—more and more, committed by people who continue to offend if they are not dead or incarcerated" (Barcus et al., 2019, p. 77).

Cold cases are, without a doubt, one of the most challenging tasks a homicide investigator may face. Another difficult responsibility is that of making a death notification.

Death Notification

Departments may use a police dispatcher, a police chaplain, or an officer to perform death notifications, but such messages should be delivered by a two-person team. Generally, if the police chaplain or a pastor from the deceased's religious faith accompanies the officer, the chaplain or the pastor performs the initial notification and the officer fills in the details. If the relative is in another community or state or is out of the country, ask police of that jurisdiction to make the notification, using the telephone to make the actual notification only as a last resort.

Officers must be prepared for a wide range of emotional and physical reactions people may have upon hearing of a death. They may collapse or suffer another reaction that requires first aid. They may become aggressive or even violent and require physical restraint. Having two officers perform death notifications will afford better control of such reactions. Furthermore, if two or more survivors are to be notified at the same location, it may be advisable to do the notifications separately, particularly if one or more individuals will be asked to provide investigative information. Because some homicides are committed by the survivor receiving the notification, officers should be sure to observe and later record how the survivor reacted.

The FBI, through a cooperative agreement with Penn State University, has developed a training course for law enforcement officers on how to offer death notifications. The course is available online (www.deathnotification. psu.edu) and those who successfully pass the assessment will receive a certificate of completion. The general recommendations are to:

- Make the notification in pairs, and have only one person do the speaking.

- Avoid words such as *passed* or *expired*. Be prepared to say *dead* or *died* numerous times.

- Use the deceased's name.

- Be familiar with local regulations regarding viewing the body.

- Follow up with the next of kin within 24 hours.

In today's environment, where social media is pervasive, it is critical that death notifications be done promptly, before family members learn about it from an outside source. Finally, if local regulations allow viewing of the body, it should take place at the hospital or the morgue. Viewing a body at the scene may compromise the investigation.

Notifying the family of an officer who has been killed is even more difficult. Departments should develop a protocol for handling these notifications, including having officers fill out a questionnaire covering several points:

- Who should be notified after a line-of-duty death? Include address and relationship to officer.

- Are there any special circumstances to be aware of, such as a survivor's heart condition?

- Is there a clergy preference?

- Is there a family friend who can provide support?

Strategies for Reducing Homicide

Traditionally, police have treated homicide as a crime relatively immune from police suppression efforts, a crime over which they had little control. Two trends are changing this reactive view. The first trend is crime analysis showing that homicide is greatest for young people in core, inner-city neighborhoods and is often related to drugs, guns, and gangs. The second trend is the emergence of community policing and a problem-solving approach to crime. In this approach, homicide is viewed as part of a larger, more general problem—violence. Results of numerous studies of police departments across the country that have implemented community policing support the theory that greater community involvement and a shift in policing philosophy to one that emphasizes proactive problem solving can reduce overall levels of violence within a community.

Thus, the conventional wisdom about homicide has changed in some departments from viewing it as a series of unconnected, uncontrollable episodes to seeing it as part of the larger, general problem of violence, which can be addressed proactively. This change in perspective allows departments to develop strategies to reduce homicides in their jurisdictions. One strategy being used is CompStat, which uses computer software to perform statistical analysis of crime data and target geographic areas throughout the city that have high levels of violent crime. By focusing resources and efforts on those areas, law enforcement is able to effect greater change and have a more positive impact. Other departments are implementing early intervention programs to keep small issues from growing into bigger, more violent events.

A Case Study

Nyberg (2007) presents the following case study: "The Moonberry Pond Murder" of James Mixon. James Mixon was a 46-year-old unemployed plumber and a drunk who ran afoul of everyone he met. Ruth and Jason Brunson also did not fit in with mainstream society, choosing instead to live with their 4-year-old daughter, Muffin, in a tent next to a pond in a remote part of Dade County, Florida. They had swung a deal with the state: they could camp on that small piece of land, on a road that led to an antenna housing, in exchange for guarding the road and stopping people who tried to drive up to the little fenced structure. One day Mixon showed up, and they figured he was harmless so they let him stay. He could be useful by catching fish from the pond, gathering firewood, and helping with other chores. Muffin spent her time with her beloved kitten Moonberry. She also named all the critters around the campsite, including a young alligator she named "Tater the Gator."

One day a man looking for a place to dump some junk found Mixon's shirtless body in a small clearing not far from the campsite, shot multiple times in the head. The investigators who were searching the area came across the Brunson's campsite—the couple cooperated in turning over their Ruger .357 and providing fingerprints and handwriting samples.

A detective interviewed Ruth Brunson, who was very cooperative while her daughter played next to her. Whenever Muffin would get a little loud, Ruth would gently shush her and resume the interview. At one point, however, when the detective asked, "Was there anything that caused you to decide he [Mixon] shouldn't stay?" Muffin spoke up and said, "He was mean to Moonberry." At this, her mother exploded with "QUIET! You shut up when Mommy is talking!" Ruth's outburst was so markedly different from her previous demeanor than it struck the investigator as odd.

The investigators took the gun, the handwriting sample, and the fingerprints and let the Brunsons go. Four days later, they got two calls and two hits. The handwriting on the bill of sale for the gun the Brunsons claimed to have purchased from Mixon was not a match for Mixon's but,

rather, closely resembled Jason Brunson's. And ballistics showed that the bullets taken from Mixon's head matched Brunson's Ruger .357. Investigators called the Brunsons in and questioned them separately. Under pressure, Ruth confessed, surprising the investigators, one of whom had assumed the husband was the killer. This tendency to assume a male is more likely than a woman to commit a violent crime is sometimes referred to as "gender prejudice." But what had happened was that Mixon, in a typical drunken act of meanness, had grabbed Muffin's beloved Moonberry and thrown the kitten into the pond, where Tater devoured it. A few days later, when Mixon was again drunk and unguarded, Ruth saw an opportunity to avenge Moonberry. She took Mixon to help gather firewood and, once far enough away from camp, she shot him while he was turned away from her.

Lessons learned by the Miami-Dade homicide unit:

- Work as a team—having two interviews going at the same time led to success.

- Avoid gender prejudice—women can kill, too.

- Stay attuned to subtle clues—Ruth's outburst at Muffin was a telltale clue.

Summary

Homicide investigations are challenging and frequently require all investigative techniques and skills. A basic requirement in a homicide investigation is to establish whether death was caused by a criminal action. The five basic manners of death are death by natural causes, accidental death, suicide, homicide, and undetermined. Although technically you are concerned only with homicide, you frequently do not know at the start of an investigation what type of death has occurred; therefore, any of the types of death may require investigation.

Homicide—the killing of one person by another—is classified as criminal (felonious) or noncriminal (nonfelonious). Criminal homicide includes murder and manslaughter. Noncriminal homicide includes excusable homicide and justifiable homicide. Murder, the killing of another human with malice aforethought, is frequently classified into three degrees:

- First degree—premeditated and intentional, or while committing or attempting to commit a felony

- Second degree—intentional but not premeditated

- Third degree—neither intentional nor premeditated, but the result of an imminently dangerous act

Manslaughter, the unlawful killing of another human with no prior malice, is classified as

- Voluntary—intentional homicide caused by intense passion resulting from adequate provocation

- Involuntary—unintentional homicide caused by criminal (culpable) negligence

Excusable homicide is the unintentional, truly accidental killing of another person. Justifiable homicide is killing another person under authorization of the law. Premeditation—the consideration, planning, or preparation for an act, no matter how briefly, before committing it—is the essential element of first-degree murder that sets it apart from all other homicide classifications.

Signs of death include lack of breathing, lack of heartbeat, lack of flushing of the fingernail bed when pressure is applied and then released, and failure of the eyelids to close after being gently lifted. Homicide victims are identified by immediate family, relatives, friends, or acquaintances; personal effects, fingerprints, DNA analysis, and dental and skeletal studies; clothing and laundry marks; or through missing-persons files.

Factors that help in estimating the time of death are body temperature, rigor mortis, postmortem lividity (livor), eye appearance, stomach contents, and stage of decomposition; evidence found in the vicinity of the body; and evidence suggesting a change in the victim's normal routine. A general guideline regarding body cooling, barring extreme conditions, is that body temperature drops 2 to 3 degrees in the first hour after death and 1 to 1.5 degrees for each subsequent hour until 18 hours. Rigor mortis appears as a stiffening of muscles several hours after death, with maximum stiffness occurring 12 to 24 hours after death. Rigor then begins to disappear and is generally gone three days postmortem. Postmortem lividity starts one-half to three hours after death and is congealed in the capillaries in four to five hours. Maximum lividity occurs within 10 to 12 hours. The location of lividity can indicate whether a body was moved after death. A partial constriction of the pupil occurs in about seven hours. In 12 hours, the cornea appears cloudy. Determine when and what the victim last ate. If any vomit is present, preserve it as evidence and submit it for examination. A dead body usually sinks in water and remains immersed for 8 to 10 days in warm water or 2 to 3 weeks in cold water. It then rises to the surface unless restricted. The outer skin loosens in five to six days, and the nails separate in two to three weeks.

The medical examiner provides legal evidence related to the cause and time of death and to the presence of alcohol or drugs.

Among the most common causes of unnatural death are gunshot wounds; stabbing and cutting wounds; blows from blunt objects; asphyxia induced by choking, drowning, smothering, hanging, strangulation, gases, or poisons; poisoning and drug overdoses; burning; explosions, electrocution, and lightning; drugs; and vehicles. In the case of a gunshot wound, suicide may be indicated if the wound shows gun contact against the skin; the wound is in the mouth or in the right temple if victim is right-handed and the left temple if left-handed; the shot did not go through clothing, unless the person was shot in the chest; or the weapon is present, especially if tightly held in hand. Homicide may be indicated if the gun was fired from more than a few inches away or from an angle or location that rules out self-infliction, if the victim was shot through clothing, or if there is no weapon present.

Stabbing and cutting wounds may be the result of suicide if the body shows hesitation wounds; if the wounds appear under clothing or on the throat, wrists, or ankles; if the weapon is present; if there is a lack of disfigurement; or if the body has not been moved. Defense wounds, wounds through clothing or to vital organs, the absence of a weapon, disfigurement, and signs that the body has been moved indicate homicide. In asphyxiation deaths, most cases of choking, drowning, and smothering are accidental; most cases of hanging are suicides; most cases of strangulation are homicides. Poisoning deaths can be accidental, suicide, or homicide. Most deaths caused by burning, explosions, electrocution, and lightning are accidental, although burning is sometimes used in an attempt to disguise homicide.

Determine a motive for the killing because it provides leads to a suspect and strong circumstantial evidence against a suspect. Similarities between school and workplace murders include the perpetrators' profiles, the targets, the means, and the motivation.

Can You Define?

adipocere	heat of passion	postmortem artifact
algor mortis	hesitation wounds	postmortem lividity
asphyxiation	homicide	premeditation
autoerotic asphyxiation	instrumental violence	rigor mortis
clearance rate	involuntary manslaughter	second-degree murder
cold case	justifiable homicide	serial murder
criminal homicide	livor mortis	suicide
criminal intent	lust murder	suicide by police
criminal negligence	malicious intent	third-degree murder
defense wounds	manslaughter	toxicology
equivocal death	mass murder	victimology
excusable homicide	mummification	voluntary manslaughter
expressive violence	murder	
first-degree murder	noncriminal homicide	

Checklist

Homicide

- How were the police notified? By whom? Date? Time?
- Was the victim alive or dead when the police arrived?
- Was medical help provided?
- If the victim was hospitalized, who attended the victim at the hospital? Are reports available?
- Was there a dying declaration?
- What was the condition of the body? Rigor mortis? Postmortem lividity?
- How was the victim identified?
- Has the cause of death been determined?
- Was the ME notified? Are the reports available?
- Was the evidence technician team notified?
- Was the crime scene protected?
- Were arrangements made to handle the news media?
- Are all the elements of the offense present?
- What types of evidence were found at the scene?
- How was the ToD estimated?
- Was the complainant interviewed? Witnesses? Suspects? Victim, if alive when police arrived?
- What leads exist?
- Was a description of the suspect obtained? Was it disseminated?
- Was a search or arrest warrant necessary?
- Was all evidence properly collected, identified, and preserved?
- Were photographs taken of the scene? Of the victim? Of the evidence?
- Were sketches or maps of the scene made?

Applications

Read the following and then answer the questions:

A. Jessi Girard, an 18-year-old high school girl, got into an argument with her boyfriend, Treyvon Green. At 3 a.m. following the evening of their argument, Jessi went to Treyvon's home to return a jacket he had given her, along with a few other personal items she no longer wanted, as they reminded her of him. Treyvon stated that after receiving the items, he went to his room, went to sleep, and woke up around 8 a.m. When he looked out his window, he saw Jessi's car parked out front.

Looking into the car, he discovered Jessi sitting up behind the steering wheel, shot through the chest, a .22 revolver lying beside her on the front seat. She was dead—apparently a suicide. The revolver had been a gift to Jessi from her father. Treyvon called the police to report the shooting.

Jessi had been shot once. The bullet entered just below the right breast, traveled across the front of her body, and lodged near her heart. The ME theorized that she did not die immediately. When found, she was sitting upright in the car, her head tilted slightly backward, her right hand high on the steering wheel, and her left hand hanging limp at her left side.

When questioned, Treyvon steadfastly denied any knowledge of the shooting. Jessi's clothing, the bullet from her body, and the gun were sent to the FBI laboratory for examination. An examination of her shirt where the bullet entered failed to reveal any powder residues. The bullet removed from her body was identified as having been fired from the gun found beside her body.

Questions

1. Is the shooting likely to be a suicide or a homicide? What facts support this?

2. How should the investigation proceed?

B. Ten-year-old Denise was playing in a school playground with her 9-year-old stepbrother, Jeremy. A car pulled up to the curb next to the lot, and the man driving the car motioned for Denise and Jeremy to come over. When the man asked where they lived, Denise described their house. The man then asked Denise to take him to her house so he could use the phone to report a crime he had just witnessed, saying he would bring her right back to the playground afterward. Denise got into the car with the man, and they drove away. When they did not return after an hour, Jeremy went into the school and told a teacher what had happened. Denise did not return home that evening. The next day the police received a report that a body had been found near a lake about a mile away from the school playground. It was Denise, who had been stabbed to death with a pocketknife.

Questions

1. What steps should be taken immediately?

2. Where would you expect to find leads?

3. What evidence would you expect to find?

4. Specifically, how would you investigate this murder?

References

Ahmad, Z. (2017, June 20). Corpse's time of death estimated by profiling blow fly eggs. *Science Magazine*. Retrieved August 18, 2020, from www.sciencemag.org/news/2017/06/corpse-s-time-death-estimated-profiling-blow-fly-eggs

American Foundation for Suicide Prevention. (2020). *Risk factors and warning signs*. New York: Author. Retrieved September 6, 2020, from afsp.org/risk-factors-and-warning-signs#warning-sign--mood

Anderson, G. (2018, December 9). How forensic blow flies helped solve a gruesome Vegas murder case. *The Conversation*. Retrieved August 18, 2020, from theconversation.com/how-the-absence-of-blow-flies-overturned-a-wrongful-conviction-107865

Armstrong, E. J., & Erskine, K. L. (2011). *Water-related death investigation: Practical methods and forensic applications*. Boca Raton, FL: CRC Press.

Armstrong, E. J., & Erskine, K. L. (2018, March 7). Investigation of drowning deaths: A practical review. *Academic Forensic Pathology, 8*(1). doi:10.23907/2018.002

Barcus, J., Heurich, C., Ritter, N., Schwarting, D. E., & Walton, R. (2019, July). N*ational best practices for implementing and sustaining a cold case investigation unit*. Washington, DC: National Institute of Justice. (NCJ 252016). Retrieved August 21, 2020, from www.ncjrs.gov/pdffiles1/nij/252016.pdf

Bitton, Y., & Dayan, H. (2019, September). "The perfect murder": An exploratory study of staged murder scenes and concealed femicide. *The British Journal of Criminology, 59*(5): 1054–1075. doi:10.1093/bjc/azz015

Black, D. J. (1976). *The behavior of law*. New York: Academic Press.

Braga, A. A., & Dusseault, D. (2018). Can homicide detectives improve homicide clearance rates? *Crime & Delinquency, 64*(3): 283–315. doi:10.1177/0011128716679164

Bureau of Justice Assistance. (2018, October). *Promising strategies for strengthening homicide investigations*. Washington, DC: Police Executive Research Forum. Retrieved August 12, 2020, from www.policeforum.org/assets/homicideinvestigations.pdf

Carter, D. L. (2013, September). *Homicide process mapping: Best practices for increasing homicide clearances*. Tallahassee, FL: Institute for Intergovernmental Research. Retrieved August 14, 2020, from www.iir.com/Documents/Homicide_Process_Mapping_September_email.pdf

Carter, D. L., & Carter, J. G. (2015, May 16). Effective police homicide investigations: Evidence from seven cities with high clearance rates. *Homicide Studies*. doi:10.1177/1088767915576996

Centers for Disease Control and Prevention. (2020, March 19). *Opioid overdose*. Atlanta, GA: Author. Retrieved August 19, 2020, from www.cdc.gov/drugoverdose/data/index.html

Chae, M. H., & Boyle, D. J. (2013, March). Police suicide: Prevalence, risk, and protective factors. *Policing: An International Journal, 36*(1): 91–118. doi:10.1108/13639511311302498

Clark, D. W., White, E. K., & Violanti, J. M. (2012, May). Law enforcement suicide: Current knowledge and future directions. *The Police Chief*, pp. 48–51.

Clark, R., & O'Hara, A. (2018). *2016 Police suicides: The NSOPS study*. Middlebury, CT: Badge of Life Police Mental Health Foundation. Retrieved August 12, 2020, from shadowsofthebadge.org/police-suicide

Cunha, E., & Pinheiro, J. (2013, December). Bone pathology and antemortem trauma. *Encyclopedia of Forensic Sciences* (2nd Ed.): pp. 76–82. Waltham, MA: Academic Press. Retrieved August 17, 2020, from www.researchgate.net/publication/282365085_Bone_Pathology_and_Antemortem_Trauma

Dake, D. (2015, January 11). Autoerotic fatalities—asphyxia. *Coroner Talk* podcast. Retrieved August 19, 2020, from coronertalk.com/23

Davis, K. (2014, February). The sad incidence of police suicide. *Law Enforcement Technology*, pp. 23–24.

Davis, R. C., Jensen, C., & Kitchens, K. E. (2011). *Cold-case investigations: An analysis of current practices and factors associated with successful outcomes*. Santa Monica, CA: Rand Corporation. (NCJ 237558). Retrieved August 12, 2020, from www.ncjrs.gov/pdffiles1/nij/grants/237558.pdf

Demirci, S., & Dogan, K. H. (2011). Death scene investigation from the viewpoint of forensic medicine expert. Chapter 2 in *Forensic Medicine: From Old Problems to New Challenges* (Ed. D. N. Vieira). London, UK: IntechOpen Limited. Retrieved August 19, 2020, from www.intechopen.com/books/forensic-medicine-from-old-problems-to-new-challenges

Ertl, A., Sheats, K. J., Petrosky, E., Betz, C. J., Yuan, K., & Fowler, K. A. (2019, October 4). Surveillance for violent deaths—national violent death reporting system, 32 states, 2016. *MMWR. Surveillance Summaries, 68*(9): 1–36. Retrieved August 15, 2020, from www.cdc.gov/mmwr/volumes/68/ss/ss6809a1.htm#contribAff

Fagan, J. A., & Geller, A. (2018, Fall). Police, race, and the production of capital homicides. *Berkeley Journal of Criminal Law, 23*(2): 261–313. Retrieved August

20, 2020, from scholarship.law.columbia.edu /faculty_scholarship/2509

Federal Bureau of Investigation. (2018). *Crime in the United States 2018*. Washington, DC: Author. Retrieved August 20, 2020, from ucr.fbi.gov/crime-in-the-u.s/2018 /crime-in-the-u.s.-2018/topic-pages/clearances

Ferguson, C., & Petherick, W. (2016). Getting away with murder: An examination of detected homicides staged as suicides. *Homicide Studies, 20*(1). doi:10.1177/1088767914553099

Finnberg, A., Junuzovic, M., Dragovic, L., Ortiz-Reyes, R., Hamel, M., Davis, J., & Eriksson, A. (2013, March). Homicide by poisoning. *The American Journal of Forensic Medicine and Pathology, 34*(1): 38–42. doi:10.1097 /PAF.0b013e31823d2977

Geberth, V. (2007, November). 10 most common errors in death investigations, part 1. *Law and Order*, pp. 84–89.

Geberth, V. (2010, February). Frequency of body posing in homicides. *Law and Order*, pp. 29–31.

Geberth, V. J. (2013, January). The seven major mistakes in suicide investigation. *Law and Order*, pp. 54–57. Retrieved August 11, 2020, from view.officeapps.live.com/op/view .aspx?src=http%3A%2F%2Fwww.practicalhomicide .com%2FResearch%2F7mistakes.docx

Geberth, V. J. (2015). *Practical homicide investigation: Tactics, procedures, and forensic techniques* (5th ed.). Boca Raton, FL: CRC Press.

Grasha, K., & DeMio, T. (2018, September 8). Manslaughter charges filed in heroin overdose deaths of 2 women. *The Cincinnati Enquirer*. Retrieved August 19, 2020, from www.cincinnati.com/story/news/crime/crime-and -courts/2018/09/07/manslaughter-charges-filed-heroin -overdose-deaths-2-women/1224037002/

Hawes, A., & Mileusnic-Polchan, D. (2019, February). Medical examiners and "manner of death": How is a suicide determination made? *Tennessee Bar Journal, 55*(2). Retrieved August 11, 2020, from www.tba.org/index .cfm?pg=LawBlog&blAction=showEntry&blogEntry=33465

Heath, A. C. G. (2012, February 6). Beneficial aspects of blowflies (Diptera: Calliphoridae). *New Zealand Entomologist, 7*(3): 343–348. Retrieved August 18, 2020, from www.tandfonline.com/doi/abs/10.1080/00779962.19 82.9722422

Hess, K. M., Orthmann, C. H., & Cho, H. (2014). *Police operations: Theory and practice* (6th ed.). Clifton Park, NY: Cengage Learning.

Heyman, M., Dill, J., & Douglas, R. (2018, April). *The Ruderman white paper on mental health and suicide of first responders*. Boston, MA: Ruderman Family Foundation. Retrieved August 12, 2020, from rudermanfoundation.org/white _papers/police-officers-and-firefighters-are-more-likely-to -die-by-suicide-than-in-line-of-duty/

Higginson, A., Eggins, E., & Mazerolle, L. (2017, October). Police techniques for investigating serious violent crime: A systematic review. *Trends & Issues in Crime and Criminal Justice, 539*. Retrieved September 6, 2020, from www.researchgate.net/publication/320557831_Police _techniques_for_investigating_serious_violent_crime_A _systematic_review

Hilliard, J. (2019, September 14). *New study shows police at highest risk for suicide of any profession*. Orlando, FL: Addiction Center. Retrieved August 12, 2020, from www.addictioncenter.com/news/2019/09 /police-at-highest-risk-for-suicide-than-any-profession/

Kaste, M. (2015, March 30). Open cases: Why one-third of murders in America go unresolved. *NPR*. Retrieved August 20, 2020, from www.npr.org/2015/03/30/395069137/open -cases-why-one-third-of-murders-in-america-go-unresolved

Kaul, M., Kumar, K., Kaul, A. K., Chanana, A., & Kumar, A. (2017, October). Digestive status of stomach contents—An indicator of time since death. *IOSR Journal of Dental and Medical Sciences, 16*(10): 26–35. Retrieved August 17, 2020, from www.iosrjournals.org/iosr-jdms/papers/Vol16 -issue10/Version-10/G1610102635.pdf

Kirk, D. S., & Matsuda, M. (2011). Legal cynicism, collective efficacy, and the ecology of arrest. *Criminology, 49*(2): 443–472. Retrieved August 20, 2020, from liberalarts .utexas.edu/_files/kirkds/KirkMatsuda_Criminology _Published2011.pdf

Leth, P. M. (2019, June). Homicide by drowning. *Forensic Science, Medicine, and Pathology, 15*(2): 233–238. doi:10.1007/s12024-018-0065-9

Mains, K. L. (2014, August 26). AISOCC partners up with the "cold case cowboys." The American Investigative Society of Cold Cases. Retrieved August 21, 2020, from aisocc.wordpress.com/2014/08/26 /aisocc-partners-up-with-the-cold-case-cowboys/

Mancik, A. M., Parker, K. F., & Williams, K. R. (2018). Neighborhood context and homicide clearance: Estimating the effects of collective efficacy. *Homicide Studies, 22*(2): 188–213. doi:10.1177/1088767918755419

Mirabile, F. (2017, June 26). When police fail to solve homicides, families carry the weight. *The Trace*. Retrieved August 20, 2020, from www.thetrace.org/2017/06 /police-fail-solve-homicides-families-carry-weight/

Morgan, B., Adlam, D., Robinson, C., Pakkal, M., & Rutty, G. N. (2014, April). Adult post-mortem imaging in traumatic and cardiorespiratory death and its relation to clinical radiological imaging. *The British Journal of Radiology, 87*(1036): 20130662. doi:10.1259/bjr.20130662

Murder Accountability Project. (2019, February 18). Black murders accounted for all of America's clearance decline. Alexandria, VA: Author. Retrieved August 20, 2020, from www.murderdata.org/2019/02/black-murders-account-for -all-of.html

National Center for the Analysis of Violent Crime. (2008). *Serial murder: multi-disciplinary perspectives for investigators*. (NCJ 223848). Quantico, VA: Author. Retrieved May 14, 2021, from www.ojp.gov/ncjrs/virtual-library/abstracts /serial-murder-multi-disciplinary-perspectives-investigators

National Highway Traffic Safety Administration. (2020, June). *State alcohol-impaired-driving estimates*. Washington, DC: Author. (DOT HS 812 917). Retrieved August 19, 2020, from crashstats.nhtsa.dot.gov/Api/Public /ViewPublication/812917

National Institute of Justice. (2011, June). *Death investigation: A guide for the scene investigator*. Washington, DC: Author. (NCJ 234457). Retrieved August 12, 2020, from www.ncjrs .gov/pdffiles1/nij/234457.pdf

National Institute of Justice. (2012). *Lessons learned from 9/11: DNA identification in mass fatality incidents.* Createspace Independent Publisher. (NCJ 214781)

Nicholson, B. (2015, April 8). Student's mystery death raises doubts on drug informer use. *Associated Press.* Retrieved September 7, 2020, from apnews.com /b307300e761e4d88b8aeef4a28850007

Nyberg, R. (2007, January). The Moonberry Pond murder. *Police,* pp. 38–41.

Oh, M. J. (2013, August). *Missouri v. McNeely:* What does this mean for DUI enforcement? *The Police Chief,* pp. 16–17.

Otahbachi, M., Cevik, C., Bagdure, S., & Nugent, K. (2010, June). Excited delirium, restraints, and unexpected death: A review of pathogenesis. *American Journal of Forensic Medicine and Pathology, 31*(2): 107–112.

Page, D. (2010, June 10). LABRADOR: New alpha dog in human remains detection? *Forensic Magazine.* Retrieved April 6, 2015, from www.forensicmag.com/articles/2010/06 /labrador-new-alpha-dog-human-remains-detection# .UqOVtOJDB0Q

Peters, J. G., & Brave, M. (2006, September/October). Sudden death, "excited" delirium, and issues of force: Part IV. *Police and Security News, 22*(5): 1–4. Retrieved August 12, 2020, from www.ipicd.com/uploads/1/3/0/0/130090143 /suddendeathpartiv--psn--0906.pdf

Petersen, N. (2017). Neighbourhood context and unsolved murders: The social ecology of homicide investigations. *Policing and Society, 27*(4): 372–392. Retrieved August 20, 2020, from www.tandfonline.com/doi /full/10.1080/10439463.2015.1063629?src=recsys&

Pettler, L. G. (2016). *Crime scene staging dynamics in homicide cases.* Boca Raton, FL: CRC Press.

Pizarro, J. M., Terrill, W., & LoFaso, C. A. (2020). The impact of investigation strategies and tactics on homicide clearance. *Homicide Studies, 24*(1): 3–24. doi:10.1177/1088767918816741

Police Executive Research Forum. (2019, October). *An occupational risk: What every police agency should do to prevent suicide among its officers.* Washington, DC: Author. Retrieved August 12, 2020, from www.policeforum.org /assets/PreventOfficerSuicide.pdf

Regoeczi, W., Jarvis, J., & Riedel, M. (2008, May). Clearing murders: Is it about time? *Journal of Research in Crime and Delinquency, 45*(2): 142–162.

Roberts, A. (2014, June). Adjusting rates of homicide clearance by arrest for investigation difficulty: Modeling incident- and jurisdiction-level obstacles. *Homicide Studies, 19*(3). doi:10.1177/1088767914536984.

Rodgers, G. (2015, February 15). Determining time of death. *Coroner Talk* podcast. Retrieved August 17, 2020, from coronertalk.com/28

Ross, D. L., & Hazlett, M. H. (2018). Assessing the symptoms associated with excited delirium syndrome and the use of conducted energy weapons. *Forensic Research & Criminology International Journal, 6*(3): 187–196. doi:10.15406/frcij.2018.06.00206

Search Dog Organization of North America. (n.d.). Human remains detection. Bloomington, IL: Author. Retrieved August 16, 2020, from www.sdona.org/human-remains -detection-hrd.html#:~:text=HRD%20dogs%20are%20 trained%20to%20specifically%20find%20the,scent%20 sources%2C%20and%20natural%20or%20man-made%20 disaster%20events.

Sharma, R., Garg, R. K., & Gaur, J. R. (2015, March). Various methods for the estimation of the post mortem interval from Calliphoridae: A review. *Egyptian Journal of Forensic Science, 5*(1): 1–12. doi:10.1016/j.ejfs.2013.04.002

Shepard, C. (2018, March 31). Wareham drug dealer convicted of manslaughter in overdose death. *The Enterprise.* Retrieved August 19, 2020, from wareham.wickedlocal .com/news/20180330/wareham-drug-dealer-convicted-of -manslaughter-in-overdose-death

Standards Employed to Determine Time of Death. (n.d.). Edited by Jeff Kercheval. Retrieved August 17, 2020, from www .peachschools.org/userfiles/192/Classes/12724/date .pdf?id=15291

Stein, S. L., Kimmerle, E., Adcock, J. M., & Martin, S. (2017, May). Cold cases: An exploratory study into the status of unresolved homicides in the USA. *Investigative Sciences Journal, 9*(2). Retrieved August 21, 2020, from cmr-journal .org/index.php/ISJ/article/view/17644

Takeuchi, A., Ahern, T. L., & Henderson, S. O. (2011, February). Excited delirium. *Western Journal of Emergency Medicine, XII*(1): 77–83. Retrieved August 4, 2020, from www .ncbi.nlm.nih.gov/pmc/articles/PMC3088378/pdf /wjem12_1p0077.pdf

Violence Policy Center. (2020). *American roulette: Murder-suicide in the United States* (7th ed.). Washington, DC: Author. Retrieved August 16, 2020, from vpc.org/studies /amroul2020.pdf

Winkley, L. (2015, January 10). How insects help solve murders. *The San Diego Union-Tribune.* Retrieved August 18, 2020, from www.sandiegouniontribune.com/sdut -forensic-entomology-bugs-murders-2015jan10-story .html#:~:text=Forensic%20entomology%2C%20the%20 study%20of,homicide%20detectives'%20most%20 mysterious%20cases.

Cases Cited

Flippo v. West Virginia, 528 U.S. 11 (1999).

Missouri v. McNeely, 133 S.Ct. 1552 (2013).

Mitchell v. Wisconsin, 139 S.Ct. 2525 (2019).

Schmerber v. California, 384 U.S. 757 (1966).

State v. Brooks, 838 N.W.2d 563 (2013).

Chapter 9
Assault, Domestic Violence, Stalking, and Elder Abuse

Chapter Outline

Assault: An Overview

Classification

Elements of the Crime

Special Challenges in Investigation

The Preliminary Investigation

Investigating Domestic Violence

Investigating Stalking

Investigating Elder Abuse

Learning Objectives

LO1 Define assault.

LO2 Explain how simple assault differs from aggravated assault.

LO3 Identify the elements of simple assault, aggravated (felonious) assault, and attempted assault.

LO4 List the factors investigators must address to prove the elements of both simple and aggravated assault.

LO5 Define the categories of assault that are identified as separate crimes to aid in data collection.

Introduction

Shortly before 6:30 a.m. on June 8, 2014, actress Sandra Bullock woke to the sound of something, or someone, banging inside her Hollywood Hills home. As she went to shut her bedroom security door, she saw him—her "husband," or so he claimed to be, standing in the hallway. But she had never laid eyes on him before. With her bedroom door locked, she quickly dialed 911 and waited. Minutes later, Los Angeles police officers arrived at the house and, with guns drawn, entered to find Joshua James Corbett, 39, inside. In a search warrant later drawn up to gather more evidence, responding officers describe how, when they searched Corbett following his on-scene arrest, they found photos of Bullock in his pockets, a notebook, a letter portraying himself as the love of her life, and a concealed weapon permit from Utah. "Sandy. I'm sorry. Please don't press charges," he is reported as shouting as officers removed him from the property.

Although he was unarmed when he broke into the actress's mansion, the search of his home uncovered a cache of illegal weapons, including two automatic rifles. He was charged with 19 felonies, including weapons violations and stalking. Evidence used to support the charge of stalking included the letter found on him at the time of his arrest, in which his obsession with the actress was revealed: "I love you and Louie [her son] and only want to be a part of your lifes [sic] I miss you very much and think of you every moment of every day," Corbett wrote, adding, "you are my wife by law, the law of God and belong to me. . . . Always and Love forever." The letter was signed "your Husband, Joshua James Corbett." The notebook in his possession also "exhibited stalking, obsessive and fixated behavior" regarding Bullock and her son, wrote one of the detectives in the search warrant affidavit (Winton & Mather, 2014).

Despite the elaborate fence, security system, and multiple surveillance cameras installed to protect Bullock's estate, Corbett was able to scale a gate and force open a sun room door to gain entry. His actions, he told investigators, were intended not to scare her but rather "to show . . . security that her residence was not impervious and she was in danger," the affidavit said.

A common misperception is that only celebrities are stalked, but the reality is that more than 3 million people—regular citizens—are stalked every year (Catalano, 2012). Stalking often co-occurs with domestic violence, which was once viewed as a private family matter but has become a priority in many departments, partly because such violence may end in homicide. Psychological assaults or stalking behaviors have been law enforcement concerns since 1990, and with the increasing population of senior citizens, elder abuse is also a growing police concern.

Assault: An Overview

Two people have a violent argument and hurl insults at each other. A bouncer physically ejects a belligerent drunk from a bar. A mob enforcer breaks all the fingers of a man who is past due on a gambling debt. An angry wife hurls a frying pan, striking her husband in the back. A teacher slaps a disrespectful student. A group of teenagers mugs an old man. A jealous lover stabs a rival with a knife. Each of these scenarios has one thing in common—each is an assault.

Some assaults take place very publicly, often with victims and witnesses who are willing to press charges and testify in court. Others take place behind closed doors in the privacy of the home. The court has defined assault as "an intentional, unlawful act of injury to another by force, or force directed toward another person, under circumstances that create fear of imminent peril, coupled with an apparent ability to execute the attempt, if not prevented. The intention to harm is of the essence. Mere words, although provoking or insulting, are not sufficient" (*Naler v. State*, 1933).

> **L01** Define assault.
>
> **Assault** is unlawfully threatening to harm another person, actually harming another person, or attempting unsuccessfully to do so.

Assaults range from violent threats to brutal gangland beatings, from a shove to a stabbing. Many assaults arise from domestic conflicts, often during periods of heavy drinking or while under the influence of illegal narcotics by one or both parties. Some result from long-developing ill feelings that suddenly erupt into open violence. Some result from an argument such as a barroom dispute that ends in a brawl. Assaults often are connected with robberies.

In many states, the term *assault* formerly referred to threats of or attempts to cause bodily harm, whereas **battery** referred to the actual carrying out of such threats. Actual physical contact is not required for assault. The threat or fear of an assault along with the ability to commit the act is sufficient.

In most revised state statutes, the term *assault* is synonymous with *battery*, or the two terms have been joined in a single crime termed *assault*. Some states, however, still have separate statutory offenses of assault and battery. Where one statute remains, battery includes the lesser crime of assault.

Classification

Assaults are classified as either simple or aggravated (felonious).

> **LO2** Explain how simple assault differs from aggravated assault.

> **Simple assault** is intentionally causing another person to fear immediate bodily harm or death or intentionally inflicting or attempting to inflict bodily harm on the person. **Aggravated** or **felonious assault** is an unlawful attack by one person on another to inflict severe bodily injury.

Simple assault is usually a misdemeanor. It does not involve a deadly weapon, and the injuries sustained, if any, are neither severe nor permanent. Aggravated assault, on the other hand, is a felony. Nationally, it is the most frequently occurring of the serious violent crimes. Aggravated or felonious assault is sometimes further classified as assault with a deadly weapon or assault with intent to commit murder. National Crime Victimization Survey (NCVS) data indicate an overall victimization rate for violent crimes of 23.2 per 1,000 persons age 12 or older in 2018, a decline of 71% since 1993 (Morgan & Oudekerk, 2019). The victimization rate in 2018 was 14.6 for simple assault and 3.8 for aggravated assault. Data from the Federal Bureau of Investigation (FBI) show 807,410 aggravated assaults in 2018, at an estimated rate of 246.8 offenses per 100,000 inhabitants and a frequency of one aggravated assault every 39.2 seconds (FBI, 2018a). In general, the more serious the assault, the more likely it was to be reported to police. According to the NCVS, 43% of assaults were reported to the police in 2018, but when these assaults were separated by degree of seriousness, it

was found that 38.4% of simple assaults were reported, compared to 60.5% of aggravated assaults (Morgan & Oudekerk, 2019). The clearance rate for aggravated assault was 52.5% in 2018.

Legal Force

Physical force may be used legally in certain instances, without it constituting an *assault*. In specified instances, teachers, people operating public conveyances, and law enforcement officers can legally use reasonable physical force.

Teachers have the authority of *in loco parentis* ("in the place of the parent") in many states and are allowed to use minimum force to maintain discipline, stop fights on school property, or prevent destruction of school property. Bus drivers, train conductors, airplane pilots, and ship captains have the authority to use force to stop misconduct by passengers. Law enforcement officers may use as much force as reasonably needed to overcome resistance to a lawful arrest. Force used in self-defense is also justifiable.

Elements of the Crime

The elements of the crime of assault are not as straight-forward as with most other crimes and vary significantly from state to state.

Simple Assault

Most state statutes have common elements for simple assault.

> **LO3** Identify the elements of simple assault, aggravated (felonious) assault, and attempted assault.

> The elements of the crime of simple assault are
> - Intent to do bodily harm to another
> - Present ability to commit the act
> - Commission of an overt act toward carrying out the intention

Intent to Do Bodily Harm to Another. Evidence of specific *intent* to commit bodily injury must be present. Injury that is caused accidentally is not assault. A suspect's words and actions or any injuries inflicted on a victim imply this intent. The injury must be to another person; injury to property or self-inflicted injury—no matter how serious—is not assault.

The bodily harm or injury in simple assault need not cause severe physical pain or disability. The degree of force necessary in simple assault ranges from a shove or a slap to slightly less than that required for the great bodily harm that distinguishes aggravated assault.

Present Ability to Commit the Act.

The suspect must have been physically able to commit the act at the time. A suspect who hurled a knife at a victim who was obviously out of range would not have had the ability to hit the target. Although this action may have caused fear in the victim, and the suspect could be charged with a different crime if the requisite elements are present, it could not qualify as an element of simple assault.

Commission of an Overt Act.

An overt act, more than a threat or gesture, must have been completed. If the suspect was in range to strike the victim, even if someone intervened, an assault can be proven. Intentionally pushing, shoving, or physically preventing someone from entering or leaving property is often determined to be simple assault.

Aggravated Assault

Aggravated assault includes the three elements of simple assault plus an element relating to the severity of the attack. Aggravated assault is usually committed with a weapon or by some means likely to produce great bodily harm or death.

> **LO3** Identify the elements of simple assault, aggravated (felonious) assault, and attempted assault.
>
> An additional element of aggravated assault is that the intentionally inflicted bodily injury must have resulted in one of the following:
>
> - A high probability of death
> - Serious, permanent disfigurement
> - Permanent or protracted loss or impairment of the function of any body member or organ or other severe bodily harm

As with simple assault, the act must be intentional—not accidental.

High Probability of Death.

An assault is considered aggravated if it is committed by any means so severe that a reasonable person feels it would result in a high probability of death. Examples include a blow sufficient to cause unconsciousness or coma, a gunshot or knife wound that causes heavy bleeding, or burns inflicted over most of a person's body.

Serious, Permanent Disfigurement.

Permanent disfigurement includes such things as losing an ear, eye, or part of the nose, or permanent scarring of the face or other parts of the body that are normally visible. It cannot be a temporary injury that will eventually heal and not be evident.

Loss or Impairment of Body Members or Organs.

Regardless of the body part affected, a charge of aggravated assault is supported by the loss or permanent impairment of body members or organs, or maiming. "Maiming signifies to cripple or mutilate in any way which deprives the use of any limb or member of the body, to seriously wound or disfigure or disable" (*Shackleford v. Commonwealth*, 1945).

Only one of these additional elements is needed to show aggravated assault, although two or all three are sometimes present. Some states do not require permanent or protracted injury or loss if the weapon used in the assault is a dangerous weapon that causes fear of immediate harm or death.

Attempted Assault

Attempted aggravated assault is also a crime in many states. If the suspect intended to assault someone but was prevented from doing so for some reason, it is still a punishable offense categorized as "unlawful attempt to commit assault."

> **LO3** Identify the elements of simple assault, aggravated (felonious) assault, and attempted assault.
>
> Attempted assault requires proof of intent along with some overt act toward committing the crime.

Intent or preparation is not enough to prove attempted assault. For example, a suspect must have done more than obtain a weapon or make a plan or even arrange to go to the scene. Rather, the suspect must actually have gone there and have had the weapon in possession when the effort was aborted.

A person who intends to rob a grocery store and whose gun accidentally discharges while the person is in the store has indeed committed an overt act. However, if the gun discharges while the person is driving to the store, there is no overt act to support an attempted assault charge. Likewise, if a potential rapist approaches a woman and has raised his arm to strike her when he is apprehended, an overt act toward an assault has been committed. But if the man is apprehended while still lurking behind a bush, reasonable doubt could exist.

Special Challenges in Investigation

Sometimes in an assault investigation it is difficult to distinguish the victim from the suspect or to know who started a fight. Both parties may claim the other person struck the first blow. In such cases, both may be charged with disturbing the peace or disorderly conduct, depending on the state and statute, until officers can obtain more information. It is also necessary to determine whether the altercation is a civil or a criminal matter. A person who accidentally injures someone is not guilty of a criminal offense but may be sued in civil court by the victim.

It is sometimes difficult, especially in cases of spouse and child beating, to obtain a complaint from the victim. If it is simple assault, which is a misdemeanor, you must see the offense committed or obtain a complaint and arrest warrant or have the victim make a citizen's arrest. Some states, such as Pennsylvania, have given the same right of arrest for domestic assaults that exists for felony arrest—police can arrest without victim complaint and without actually witnessing the assault, as discussed later in the chapter.

Patrol officers usually make the first contact with the complainant or assault victim. Police on regular patrol sometimes observe an assault occurring. Usually, however, they are sent to the assault scene by the dispatcher. Assault calls are potentially dangerous for the police. The FBI reports that in 2018, 58.866 officers were assaulted while performing their duties, at a rate of 10.8 per 100 officers, with the largest %age (31.0) being assaulted while responding to disturbance calls (family quarrels, bar fights, etc.) (FBI, 2018c). Furthermore, more police officers are killed while investigating disturbance calls than in responding to robbery and burglary. Officers may arrive at the point of most heated emotions and in the middle of a situation that stems from a deep-rooted problem entirely unknown to them. Their first act is to stop any assaultive action by disarming, separating, or arresting the people involved. This reduces the possibility of further conflict.

Officers should be on their guard and not take sides in any dispute. If people are injured, first aid must be administered or emergency personnel summoned to the scene. The first officer on the scene should determine whether more help is needed and whether a description of the suspect must be broadcast.

In most assault cases, arriving police officers find that the assault has been completed. However, verbal abuse and considerable confusion may still exist. Interview the victim as soon as possible to obtain details about the injury, the degree of pain, medical assistance rendered, and other facts related to the severity of the attack. The extent and nature of the injury determines the degree of assault to be charged. Further facts supporting the severity of the attack are obtained by noting what treatment the victim requires and by talking to medical personnel.

The victim frequently knows who committed the assault, either by name or by an association that can be checked. Determine the reason for the assault. Find out what actions the victim and assailant took before, during, and after the assault. If the victim of an aggravated assault is severely injured and indicates by words, gestures, or appearance that death may be imminent, obtain a dying declaration.

If the suspect is at the scene, an arrest should be made if the situation warrants, or the victim may make a citizen's arrest. If the suspect is known but is not at the scene, the suspect's description should be broadcast and the investigation begun.

The Preliminary Investigation

At a minimum, an officer arriving on the scene of an assault should

- Have backup either present or on the way until the scene is secure

- Provide medical aid to injured people

- Separate suspects and victims

- Protect the crime scene

- Give the *Miranda* warning if applicable

- Obtain preliminary statements

- Photograph evidence

- Collect and preserve evidence

- Reconstruct the crime

Proving the Elements of Assault

An assault that involves no dangerous weapon and results in no serious injury is a relatively minor crime. In contrast, aggravated assault is an extremely serious crime.

> **L04** List the factors investigators must address to prove the elements of both simple and aggravated assault.

> To prove the elements of assault, establish the intent to cause injury, the severity of the injury inflicted, and whether a dangerous weapon was used.

Establish intent by determining the events that led up to the assault. Record the suspect's exact words and actions, and take statements from the victim and any witnesses.

Establish the severity of the assault by taking photographs and describing all injuries in your notes. Describe the size, location, number, color, depth, and amount of bleeding of any injuries. Some bruises do not become visible for several hours or even a day or two. Assault victims should be advised of this and told that additional photographs should be taken. Obtain an oral or written statement from a qualified medical person regarding the severity and permanence of the injuries and any impairment of bodily functioning. If injuries are severe enough to warrant hospitalization, attempt to obtain medical records documenting the injuries. Investigators should be aware that some states require a court order in order to obtain medical records, and other states require only a subpoena.

Determine the means of attack and the exact weapon used. Was it hands, fists, feet, a gun, or a knife?

Evidence in Assault Investigations

Corroborate the victim's information with physical evidence. Physical evidence in an assault case includes photographs of injuries, clothing of the victim or suspect, weapons, broken objects, bloodstains, hairs, fibers, and other signs of an altercation.

Two important pieces of evidence are photographs of injuries and the weapon used in the assault. If the hands, fists, or feet were used, examine them for cuts and bruises and photograph any injuries. Obtain fingernail scrapings from both the victim and the suspect, but make sure search warrants or court orders are sought first, if needed, before seizing DNA or other biological evidence.

Take as evidence any weapons found at the scene. The victim's clothing may contain evidence such as bullet holes or tears made by a knife or other cutting instrument. Clothing may also contain biological evidence such as blood, saliva, semen, and skin cells. If the victim believes the suspect touched with their skin any of the victim's clothing, that clothing can be examined for touch DNA.

If you suspect that alcohol or drug use may have contributed to the assault, arrange for the appropriate urine, blood, and breath tests (again, obtaining the requisite warrants beforehand). Photograph and make notes regarding evidence that indicates the intensity of the assault—for example, overturned furniture, broken objects, torn-up sod, and bent shrubs.

Reflective ultraviolet photography can allow investigators to document injuries on flesh as long as nine months after they have visibly healed. It can also reveal pattern injuries—that is, injuries that have a recognizable shape—including cigarette burns, whip or belt marks, bruising, contusions, abrasions, injury margins from immersion burns, bite marks, and scratches.

L05 Define the categories of assault that are identified as separate crimes to aid in data collection.

For data collection, special categories of assault are domestic violence, stalking, and elder abuse.

Investigating Domestic Violence

Domestic violence has deep roots in the patriarchal systems the colonists brought with them when they settled in the New World. At the time, however, such violence was perceived not as a crime but as a man's duty, for he, as head of the family and the authority figure in the home, was expected to keep control over his wife and children and was allowed to use any means necessary to achieve order. In the case of *State v. Rhodes* (1868), the North Carolina Supreme Court ruled that although a husband had the right to whip his wife, if the switch was thicker than the thumb, it was considered abuse. This Rule of Thumb standard, adopted by most state courts across the nation during the colonial period, was derived from English common law and permitted men to use any instrument to physically enforce family obedience as long as the object was no larger than the thickness of the man's thumb.

The use of force was an acceptable male privilege, and domestic violence was considered a family matter to be handled privately. The police were rarely, if ever, summoned to intervene. But times have changed, and now law enforcement regards domestic violence as an offense appropriate for criminal justice intervention. For example, during the period of 2006–2015, the domestic violence offender was arrested or charged in about two out of every five victimizations reported to police, either during the initial response or during follow-up (Reaves, 2018).

L05 Define the categories of assault that are identified as separate crimes to aid in data collection.

Domestic violence is a pattern of behaviors involving physical, sexual, economic, and emotional abuse, alone or in combination, to establish and maintain power and control over another person within a household or family environment.

Domestic violence is found at all socioeconomic levels across all racial demographics. Domestic violence, also sometimes called family violence, is abuse that occurs between family members or persons who live together, regardless of generation. It may be violence directed by a parent toward a child, by a child toward a parent, by a grandchild toward a grandparent, or by a child against another child, but it perhaps most commonly thought of as abuse by one partner against another. This last type of violence is known as **intimate partner violence (IPV)**, first discussed in Chapter 8, as this type of chronic abuse can lead to homicide. The Centers for Disease Control and Prevention (CDC) defines IPV to include physical violence, sexual violence, stalking, and psychological aggression (including coercive tactics) by a current or former intimate partner (i.e., spouse, boyfriend/girlfriend, dating partner, or ongoing sexual partner) (2018) (See Table 9.1).

An intimate partner is defined as "a person with whom one has a close personal relationship that may be characterized by the partners' emotional connectedness, regular contact, ongoing physical contact and sexual behavior, identity as a couple, and familiarity and knowledge about each other's lives. The relationship need not involve all of these dimensions" (Breiding, Basile, Smith, Black, & Mahendra, 2015). Intimate partners can be of the same or opposite sex, may or may not be cohabitating, and the relationships include current or former

- spouses (married spouses, common-law spouses, civil union spouses, domestic partners),
- boyfriends/girlfriends,
- dating partners, or
- ongoing sexual partners.

If the victim and the perpetrator have a child in common and a previous relationship but no current relationship, then by definition they fit into the category of former intimate partner. States differ as to what constitutes a common-law marriage (Breiding et al., 2015). Investigators will need to know what qualifies as a common-law marriage in their state.

The Office for Victims of Crime (OVC) reports that rates of intimate partner violence decreased during the 20-year period from 1995–2005, going from a rate of 15.5 to 5.4 per 1,000 women and from 2.8 to 0.5 per 1,000 men (Office for Victims of Crime, 2018). The OVC also cautions, however, that these victimizations remain highly underreported due to the personal nature of IPV. Data from the *National Crime Victimization Survey* indicate that in 2018, there were 1,333,050 reported incidents of domestic violence,

TABLE 9.1 Types of Intimate Partner Violence

Type	Definition	Actions Included	Additional Aspects/Criteria of the Crime
Physical Violence	The intentional use of physical force with the potential for causing death, disability, injury, or harm.	■ Scratching ■ Pushing ■ Shoving ■ Throwing ■ Grabbing ■ Biting ■ Choking ■ Shaking ■ Hair-pulling ■ Slapping ■ Punching ■ Hitting ■ Burning ■ Use of a weapon (gun, knife, or other object) ■ Use of restraints ■ Use of one's body, size, or strength against another person	Physical violence also includes coercing other people to commit any of the acts listed.

(Continued)

TABLE 9.1 *(Continued)*

Type	Definition	Actions Included	Additional Aspects/Criteria of the Crime
Sexual Violence	A sexual act that is committed or attempted by another person without freely given consent of the victim or against someone who is unable to consent or refuse.	■ Completed or attempted forced penetration of a victim ■ Completed or attempted alcohol/drug-facilitated penetration of a victim ■ Completed or attempted forced acts in which a victim is made to penetrate a perpetrator or someone else ■ Completed or attempted alcohol/drug-facilitated acts in which a victim is made to penetrate a perpetrator or someone else ■ Non-physically forced penetration which occurs after a person is pressured verbally or through intimidation or misuse of authority to consent or acquiesce ■ Unwanted sexual contact ■ Non-contact unwanted sexual experiences	Tactics or methods used to perpetrate sexual violence include, but are not limited to: ■ Use or threat of physical force to gain the victim's compliance with a sexual act (e.g., pinning the victim down, assaulting the victim) ■ Administering alcohol or drugs to gain the victim's compliance with a sexual act (e.g., spiking a drink, "roofie-ing") ■ Taking advantage of a victim who is unable to provide consent due to intoxication or incapacitation from voluntary consumption of alcohol, recreational drugs, or medication ■ Exploitation of vulnerability (e.g., immigration status, disability, age, undisclosed sexual orientation) ■ Intimidation ■ Misuse of authority (e.g., using one's position of doesn't love them enough) ■ False promises (e.g., marriage) ■ Nonphysical threats, such as threatening to break up or spread rumors ■ Grooming or other tactics to gain a child's trust ■ Control of a person's sexual behavior/sexuality through threats, reprisals, threats to transmit STDs, threat to force pregnancy, etc.
Stalking	A pattern of repeated, unwanted attention and contact that causes fear or concern for one's own safety or the safety of someone else (e.g., family member, close friend).	■ Repeated and unwanted phone calls, voice/text messages, and hang-ups ■ Repeated and unwanted emails, instant messages, or messages through websites (e.g., Facebook) ■ Leaving cards, letters, flowers, or presents when the victim doesn't want them ■ Watching or following from a distance ■ Spying with a listening device, camera, or GPS device ■ Approaching or showing up in places (e.g., home, work, school) when the victim does not want to see them ■ Leaving strange or potentially threatening items for the victim to find	Criteria for stalking victimization: The victim must have experienced multiple stalking tactics or a single stalking tactic multiple times by the same perpetrator and: ■ Felt fearful* or ■ Believed that they or someone close to them would be harmed or killed as a result of the perpetrator's behavior

TABLE 9.1 *(Continued)*

Type	Definition	Actions Included	Additional Aspects/Criteria of the Crime
		<ul><li>Sneaking into the victim's home or car and doing things to scare the victim by letting them know they (the perpetrator) had been there</li><li>Damaging the victim's personal property, pets, or belongings</li><li>Harming or threatening to harm the victim's pet(s)</li><li>Making threats to physically harm the victim</li></ul>	
Psychological Aggression	Use of verbal and non-verbal communication with the intent to: (a) Harm another person mentally or emotionally, and/or (b) Exert control over another person	<ul><li>Expressive aggression (e.g., name-calling, humiliating)</li><li>Coercive control (e.g., limiting access to money, family, friends; excessive monitoring of a person's whereabouts; making threats to self-harm)</li><li>Threats of physical or sexual violence with words or gestures (e.g., "I'll kill you," brandishing a weapon) if the victim doesn't do what the perpetrator wants</li><li>Control of reproductive or sexual health (e.g., refusal to use birth control; forced pregnancy termination)</li><li>Exploitation of a victim's vulnerability (e.g., immigration status, disability)</li><li>Exploitation of perpetrator's vulnerability (e.g., telling a victim, "If you call police, I could be deported.")</li><li>Gaslighting (i.e., mind games)—presenting false information to a victim with the intent of making them doubt their own memories and perceptions</li></ul>	Psychologically aggressive acts, while often not perceived by the victim as aggression because they are covert and manipulative in nature, are an essential component of IPV for a number of reasons: <ul><li>They often co-occur with other forms of IPV</li><li>They often precede physical and sexual violence</li><li>They can significantly influence the impact of other forms of IPV</li><li>Research suggests the impact is every bit as significant as that of physical violence by an intimate partner</li></ul>

Adapted from: Breiding, M. J., Basile, K. C., Smith, S. G., Black, M. C., & Mahendra, R. (2015). *Intimate partner violence surveillance: Uniform definitions and recommended data elements* (Version 2.0). Atlanta, GA: Centers for Disease Control and Prevention, pp.11–15. Retrieved August 22, 2020, from www.cdc.gov/violenceprevention/pdf/ipv/intimatepartnerviolence.pdf

847,230 of which were classified as IPV incidents (Morgan & Oudekerk, 2019). These incidents of domestic violence involved a reported 559,820 individual victims, meaning many victims experienced multiple episodes of violence.

Despite the criminalization of such assaults, domestic violence remains a persistent problem for thousands of households across the country, partly because the abusive behavior is part of the family dynamic, tightly woven into the fabric of family relationships and passed from generation to generation through a cycle of violence.

The Cycle of Violence

Domestic violence is commonly thought of as occurring in a three-phase cycle: (1) the tension-building stage, (2) the acute battering episode, and (3) the honeymoon. This **cycle of violence**, which typically increases in both frequency and severity, is illustrated in Figure 9.1. This pattern of abuse often becomes a vicious intergenerational cycle because research has found that children who witness abuse or are abused themselves are more likely to abuse a spouse or child when they become adults. Crimes against children are the focus of Chapter 11.

Victimology

Fear is one reason domestic violence goes unreported. Many women do not report domestic assaults because of threats such as "I'll take the kids and you'll never see them again" or "I'll kill you if you call the police." In many instances the wife fails to report the abuse (and to leave the relationship) because she has no work skills and no independent income, because of the stigma and embarrassment associated with the offense, or because she has one or more children to support. Some victims choose to stay with their batterers for fear that leaving would further enrage their partners.

On average, victims of domestic violence make seven attempts to leave the abusive relationship before finally breaking free for good (Barrie, Shaver, Lewis, Gibson, & McAdoo, 2020). Nearly half of all domestic violence victims intentionally prolong their abusive relationships and delay leaving because they fear for the safety of any pets they must leave behind, and roughly 70% of domestic violence survivors report that their abuser had injured or threatened the family pet (Tricarico, 2020). Pets are an important source of comfort and emotional support for domestic violence victims, yet few shelters across the country offer safe housing services for pets (Arkow, 2014). This is beginning to change, however, as more communities recognize the need to add pet accommodations to domestic violence shelters so that abused women no longer need to make the difficult choice of staying with their batterer, leaving but giving up their pet to a shelter, or living in their car with the animal that gives them so much comfort (Tricarico, 2020).

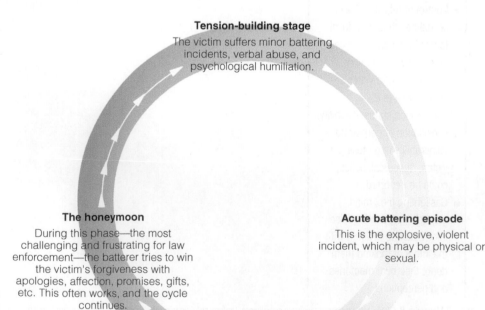

Tension-building stage
The victim suffers minor battering incidents, verbal abuse, and psychological humiliation.

The honeymoon
During this phase—the most challenging and frustrating for law enforcement—the batterer tries to win the victim's forgiveness with apologies, affection, promises, gifts, etc. This often works, and the cycle continues.

Acute battering episode
This is the explosive, violent incident, which may be physical or sexual.

Figure 9.1
Three-phase cycle of abuse.

Source: From Hess, K. M., & Orthmann, C. H. (2014). *Police operations: Theory and practice* (6th ed). Clifton Park, NY: Delmar, Cengage Learning. Reproduced by permission. www.cengage.com/permissions

Domestic abuse in families from diverse ethnic or cultural backgrounds also commonly goes unreported. For example, female abuse victims of Asian descent are reluctant to notify the police because they do not want to bring shame on their family or community.

Myth If the abuse was really that bad, the victim would just leave or they would call the police and make sure their abuser was sent to prison.

Fact Just because a victim does not leave does not mean that the situation is okay or that the victim wants to be abused. In fact, the most dangerous time for an abuse victim is when they try to leave. Most times, the victim does not want the batterer to be arrested and locked up; the victim just wants the abuse to stop.

Statistics document that many batterers eventually kill their intimate. One study found that in as many as 50% of domestic violence–related homicides, police had previously been called to respond to a domestic incident between the two parties (Kanable, 2010). In some instances, the male batterer becomes the victim of homicide. In such cases, the defense often attributes the murder to the "battered-woman syndrome," which is based on the concept of duress and results from a cycle of violence.

Women as Abusers

Although most abuse victims are women, women also perpetrate abuse. One study found that women who were the sole abusers in the relationship were more likely to use nonphysical tactics, such as emotional, verbal, and psychological abuse, in their commission of domestic violence (Taylor, 2014). These women berate and belittle their partners in an effort to manipulate or control them, and there is often no true "cycle of violence" with this type of abuse; the violence may stay in a state of "tension-building" where there is constant verbal abuse and psychological humiliation, but there is often no honeymoon stage or period of remorse.

Some women do commit physical abuse against their partner. An estimated 14.0% of men, or one in seven, experience physical violence by their intimate partner at some point during their lifetimes, and 5% of these

male IPV victims are killed by their abusers (Huecker & Smock, 2020). In the past, studies had found that women who assaulted their male partners were more likely to avoid arrest. However, more recent research shows a shift in arrest patterns.

While men were still identified as the primary aggressors and, consequently, were arrested in higher *numbers* of domestic violence incidents, women were arrested at a higher *rate* proportionate to the number of incidents in which they were involved. "During the 6-year tracking period, women were arrested every 3 incidents in which they were deemed perpetrators (in 32% of incidents), but men were only arrested in about every 10 incidents (in 11% of incidents)" (Hester, 2012). This increase was attributed to several factors, including the move in many states to implement statutes regarding mandatory arrest of perpetrators of domestic violence and a changing attitude among police officers to recognize that violence by women should not be minimized. Indeed, this study found that "the police appeared more ready to arrest women despite patterns of violent behavior that were less intense or severe than the patterns exhibited by men" (Hester, 2012).

Although women were found to have used a wide range of violent and aggressive behaviors, their motives rarely appeared to be to invoke fear or to manipulate and control their partners. The majority of women who used physical violence against a partner did so in self-defense (Hester, 2012). A smaller number of women used physical violence to decrease further future victimization. And while such "retaliatory violence" cannot simply be excused, when it is taken out of the context of an ongoing pattern of abuse by a male partner, it contributes to the result of the study: that women were three times more likely than men to be arrested in domestic violence incidents.

Although it is common for battered women to feel shame at being victims of domestic abuse, the stigma for battered men is even greater. Many reports of husband abuse go unreported because these men anticipate an unsympathetic or incredulous reaction from responding officers. Indeed, the misperception persists that women who commit violence against men have been driven to it through years of victimization at the hands of these men (the battered-woman syndrome), and thus, the men "have it coming." However, officers responding to a domestic violence call must not assume the male is always the perpetrator and the female always the victim.

Because male victims have historically been less likely to seek medical care, the prevalence of domestic violence against men may be underreported. The reporting of male domestic violence victimization varies depending on the seriousness of the injury. From

2006–2015, police were notified in 77% of cases where a serious injury occurred, in 57% of cases involving a minor injury, and less than half the time (49%) when no physical injury occurred (Reaves, 2017).

Same-Sex Domestic Violence

Traditionally the issue of gay and lesbian domestic violence was ignored and its extent undocumented. The fact that law enforcement once considered abuse within a heterosexual couple's relationship a private, personal matter makes understandable the lack of police concern regarding violence between homosexual partners. However, studies have found that the dynamics of same-sex domestic violence are, in many respects, quite similar to those of opposite-sex domestic violence. The cause is cyclical, escalates over time, and maintains a commonality in characteristics of batterers.

While data regarding the national prevalence of IPV among lesbian, gay, bisexual, transgender, and queer couples are limited, the overall rates of domestic violence occurring in LGBTQ relationships are thought to be similar to, or slightly higher than, the rates for heterosexual women—approximately 25% (Huecker & Smock, 2020). However, variations in rates are seen when examining the various subpopulations of the LGBTQ cohort. Researchers have found that, in general, females living with female partners experience less domestic violence than females living with males, males living with male partners report a higher number of domestic violence cases than do males living with female partners, and transgender individuals have a higher risk of domestic violence than either lesbian or gay couples, being approximately two times more likely to experience physical violence by an intimate partner (Huecker & Smock, 2020).

A report by the CDC shows that individuals who self-identify as lesbian, gay, and bisexual have an equal or higher prevalence of experiencing IPV, sexual assault, and stalking as compared to self-identified heterosexuals (Walters, Chen, & Breiding, 2013). More than 4 in 10 lesbian women (43.8%) and more than 1 in 4 gay men (26.0%) have experienced some form of IPV, whether physical violence, rape, and/or stalking, at some point in their lifetime (Breiding, Chen, & Black, 2014).

Lesbian, gay, bisexual, transgender, and queer victims may be reluctant to report domestic violence. One reason is because of previous encounters with police in which the victims had experienced homophobia and stigma, generating a learned anticipation of rejection and a general pessimistic view of a potential police response to a report of IPV involving a LGBTQ victim (Finneran

& Stephenson, 2013). While little empirical data exist to support unfair or homophobic treatment of LGBTQ victims by the police, some evidence exists to show that lesbian women often do anticipate homophobia and stigma by police officers during a police response, which has been demonstrated to lower their willingness to contact the police when experiencing IPV (Finneran & Shephenson, 2013). Another part of the challenge may be that support services, such as shelters, support groups, and hotlines, are not regularly available to members of the LGBTQ community, resulting in isolated and unsupported victims (Benavides, Berry, & Mangus, 2019).

When the Abuser Is a Police Officer

Knowing the seriousness of the crime and the damage it causes to victims and families does not make officers immune from committing domestic violence themselves. In fact, research suggests that domestic abuse may occur more often in police families than among the general public.

When the abuser is a police officer, special challenges exist. Few professions are characterized by the fierce loyalty to one's coworkers that prevails in law enforcement. This allegiance is put to the test when responding to a domestic violence call at an officer's home. In the past, responding officers would simply separate the parties and persuade the battered spouse to give the abuser time to cool off, explaining away the violence as the result of a stressful job and convincing the spouse that an arrest would only jeopardize the security of the entire family. Typically, no official report would be filed about the incident, and the abuse would be allowed to go on. Sometimes the abuse continues to escalate until the officer kills their spouse and then, commonly, themselves. In many, if not most, of these cases, the officer's service weapon is used in the crime.

Spurred by research that showed how domestic abuse can evolve to domestic homicide, particularly when a firearm is available to the abuser, a federal law was passed in 1996 prohibiting anyone, including a police officer, who has been convicted of a qualifying misdemeanor domestic violence offense from owning or using a firearm or possessing ammunition. This law, known as the Lautenberg Act (18 U.S.C. § 922 (g)(9)), amended the Gun Control Act of 1968, which barred only those convicted of a felony offense from owning or using a firearm. This law also puts another wrinkle in the issue of police-involved domestic violence because an officer who is unable to carry a gun is unlikely to find or retain a job.

Types of Weapons Used

Little research has thus far been devoted to the dynamics of weapon use in domestic violence incidence. What is known, however, is that the presence of external weapons (e.g., knives and guns) increases the dangerousness of domestic violence incidence to both victims and responding officers (Lee, Zhang, & Hoover, 2013; Folkes, Hilton, & Harris, 2013). One study of weapon use in domestic violence cases found that the majority of cases (60%) involved bodily weapons (e.g., hands, fists, and feet) (Lee et al., 2013). The other 40% of domestic violence cases involved external weapons: 4% involved guns, 7% involved knives, and in the remainder of cases, the type of weapon given in the police report was simply "other," a category that includes ash trays, baseball bats, bleach, bricks, cell phones, chairs, shoes, umbrellas, and so forth.

Another study of domestic violence reports similar results, with 78% of incidents involving the use of bodily weapons and 22% involving external weapons, the majority of which were not firearms (Sorenson, 2017). Nearly 80% of the cases involving a gun were male-on-female. While much attention is given to the role guns play in domestic violence homicides, nonfatal uses of firearms are more prevalent and have a greater impact on domestic violence victims (Zeoli, 2017). When a gun is brandished, the purpose in most cases (66%) is to threaten the intimate partner. In roughly 15% of cases involving a gun, the weapon is used to hit or pistol whip the victim, shoot at but miss the victim, or directly shoot the victim (Sorenson, 2017). Table 9.2 shows weapon use among domestic violence offenders.

Data from the National Crime Victimization Survey (NCVS) show that from 2006–2015, of all nonfatal domestic violence victimizations reported to the police, 20% involved an offender with a weapon (Reaves, 2017). And while these victimizations were far outnumbered by those in which the offender had no external weapon, they were more likely to be reported to the police than victimizations where no external weapon was used. Furthermore, in nonfatal domestic violence cases where the offender used a weapon, the victim was more likely to sign a criminal complaint and the offender was more likely to be arrested or charged for the crime (Reaves, 2017).

Predictors and Precipitators of Domestic Violence

Research has attempted to identify factors that predict or precipitate episodes of domestic violence, both for victimization and perpetration. While the myriad theories about why domestic violence exists and persists are beyond the scope of this text, it is important for investigators to be aware that certain risk factors are commonly present for those who experience domestic violence. These factors, when identified, can help investigators intervene more effectively to document the case, address the specific elements of the crime, hold offenders accountable, and help victims recover.

As mentioned, one well-documented predictor of the likelihood of family abuse is a history of family violence. Numerous studies support the finding that children who are exposed to domestic violence have an increased likelihood of becoming either a victim or perpetrator of violence later in life, perpetuating an intergenerational cycle of violence (Hart & Klein, 2013). One study found gender-specific risks related to witnessing domestic violence as a child in that such exposure doubled the risk of becoming a victim of domestic violence in adulthood for females and doubled the risk of committing domestic violence as an adult for men.

It is often said that the best predictor of future behavior is past behavior. Perpetrators of domestic violence are no different. There is much consensus in the research that domestic violence perpetrators who come to the attention of law enforcement often have a prior criminal history for a variety of nonviolent and violent offenses

TABLE 9.2 Weapon Use in Domestic Violence Cases	
Weapon Use	**All Cases**
TOTAL	**100%**
Primary weapon used during the incident	**26.0%**
Firearm	2.0%
Knife/sharp object	5.8%
Hard object/wall	5.7%
Blunt object	7.1%
Other weapon*	3.1%
Unknown weapon	2.3%
Defendant did not use a weapon**	**74.0%**

*Includes flammable items, ropes, telephone cords, belts, and other items.

**Defendant may have used hands, fists, or feet as a personal weapon.

Source: Adapted from Sorenson, S. B. (2017, March 1). Guns in intimate partner violence: Comparing incidents by type of weapon. Journal of Women's Health, 26(3): 249–258.

Lee, J., Zhang, Y., & Hoover, L. T. (2013). Profiling weapon use in domestic violence: Multilevel analysis of situational and neighborhood factors. Victims & Offenders, 8(2): 164–184.

Folkes, S. E. F., Hilton, N. Z., & Harris, G. T. (2013). Weapon use increases the severity of domestic violence but neither weapon use nor firearm access increases the risk or severity of recidivism. Journal of Interpersonal Violence, 28(6): 1143–1156.

Zeoli, A. M. (2017, September). Non-fatal firearm uses in domestic violence. Minneapolis, MN: The Battered Women's Justice Project.

(Hart & Klein, 2013). A meta-analysis of male domestic abusers found that IPV offenders who had even one prior arrest for any crime, not just domestic violence, were more than seven times more likely to be re-arrested than those without prior records (Hart & Klein, 2013).

In many cases, victims have made prior reports not for domestic assault but for other crimes, which are referred to as **indicator crimes**. Indicator crimes are offenses that, in situations involving the same victim and suspect, can establish a pattern of events indicative of an abusive relationship. These crimes can range from harassing phone calls to hit-and-run.

Animal cruelty is another predictor of abusive or violent behavior. Results of numerous studies have demonstrated a link between animal abuse and domestic violence, with some research going beyond the surface correlation to explore deeper aspects of the abusive psyche. As mentioned, many victims of IPV delay leaving the abusive situation because they fear any pet left behind will become a target of the abuser's violence, and data show this fear is warranted.

One study of men incarcerated for IPV and/or who admitted to committing IPV in a previous relationship found that 81% reported committing animal cruelty in their lifetime and 52% reported abusing and/or killing a pet during a relationship conflict. Childhood animal cruelty (CAC) was found to be significantly correlated to increased use of psychological abuse and sexual coercion in the context of intimate relationships and was also significantly associated with both threats to, and actual commission of, animal abuse during relationship conflicts (Haden, McDonald, Booth, Ascione, & Blakelock, 2018). Another study of men arrested for domestic violence found that 41% admitted having committed at least one act of animal abuse since age 18, compared to a 1.5% occurrence rate reported by men in the general population (Febres et al., 2014).

Other risk factors for domestic violence include unemployment of the batterer and estrangement, where the victim has moved out of the previously shared residence. Although not a predictor or precipitator of domestic violence, the presence of firearms can drastically change the complexion of domestic violence and make responding to such calls exponentially more dangerous for officers.

The Police Response

Response to such calls may be initiated by the dispatcher, who can save hours of legwork by exploring with the victim their frame of mind and that of the potential attacker. From that point on, responding officers' actions are critical.

The availability of computers in patrol vehicles and use of real-time response software enable a premise and individual records check as part of the preliminary investigation. This may include previous calls for service from the complainant's residence, complaints of illegal activities at this address, open warrants for involved parties, and background information on the victim or alleged assailant. This information enhances the safety of the officers and helps them better assess the situation upon arrival at the scene.

As this is an investigation text, not a police operations text, we will not go into the details about how to respond to the potentially dangerous domestic violence call other than to emphasize the strong recommendation to always arrive on scene with backup (minimum of two officers, ideally four), separate the parties involved for interviews, impound all firearms or other weapons at the scene if the laws and policies in your area permit, and never drop your guard (Wyllie, 2019).

Evidence in Domestic Violence Cases

Nelson (2013) notes that when a first-responding officer performs only a basic, cursory investigation of a domestic violence incident, prosecutors file criminal charges only 30% of the time. Take the time to do a thorough investigation, beginning with gathering evidence of the offense. A complete investigation should include the following evidence:

- 911 tapes

- Body-worn camera videos of responding officers

- Photographs of the victim, suspect, and scene

- Formal recorded statements from the victim, suspect, and all witnesses, including children

- Interviews of the neighbors, friends, and families of the victim and suspect

- Physical evidence

- DNA evidence

- Forensic examination results

- The suspect's prior record, including prior incidents of domestic violence

- Follow-up photographs to show bruising that may appear after several days

- Medical reports, including photos, scans, and diagnoses

- Jail calls placed by the suspect following arrest

- Digital recordings and communications, such as emails, texts, and social media posts

- Any other evidence to corroborate the charges

(National District Attorneys Association, 2017; Nelson, 2013; IACP, 2019)

One of the most important kinds of evidence in domestic violence investigations is photographs, which can increase the likelihood of prosecution by 58%–62% (Nelson, 2013). Take photos showing how the suspects and victims appeared when police arrived, including injuries, being aware that some bruises do not become visible until well after the battering episode. Take photos of the scene, including any weapons present, as well as any damaged clothing or other property.

Take statements from the suspect and the victim somewhere away from others at the scene and separated from each other. Tailor the questions to the victim's emotional and physical state. Ask the victim whether the suspect had used intimidation in an attempt to keep the police from being called or any other help summoned, and ask if there had been any previous stalking or threatening behaviors by the suspect or any other unwanted contact. Have both the victim and the suspect sign and date their statements so they cannot change their story later or say they don't remember what happened.

Witness statements, including those from children who were present during the incident, are important evidence in domestic violence cases. Statements from multiple witnesses not only help investigators determine the truth when the offender and victim tell conflicting versions of the event, but including more than one witness statement in a domestic violence report improves the likelihood of prosecution by 66%–70% (Nelson, 2013). Children in the home might be able to point out evidence of previous violence, such as dents in the drywall, broken glass, or other items the abuser used on the victim. Consequently, investigators working domestic violence cases need to be proficient in interviewing children. Neighbors might be able to describe specific arguments or threats they overheard, or might know that one partner had moved out of the home but has been seen sitting in their car across the street for long periods of time on multiple occasions, staring at the victim's house. Have witnesses sign and date their statements.

Recall that IPV includes not only physical violence but also sexual violence, stalking, and psychological aggression, each of which constitutes a separate crime. Because domestic abuse often co-occurs with other crimes, investigators should also look for evidence of child, elder, and animal abuse if the circumstances warrant. One study found that an estimated 10%–20% of all children in the country, while not direct victims of child abuse, have been exposed to IPV (Rydström, Edhborg, Jakobsson, & Kabir, 2019). In some states, this exposure constitutes child endangerment, yet child endangerment charges are rarely included as part of domestic abuse investigations (Nelson, 2013). Other crimes often go undetected during the investigation of domestic violence, such as weapons violations, property crimes, violations of court orders, and gang violence (IACP, 2019). Nelson (2013) stresses the importance of listing multiple crimes in the written report, if viable charges can be proven, because an investigation that recommends a single misdemeanor charge has little chance of being prosecuted or leading to a conviction. On the other hand, if the investigator's report supports evidence that more than one crime occurred, the chance of prosecution increases 260%–300%, and the likelihood of conviction rises 140%–150% (Nelson, 2013).

The importance of the incident report should not be overlooked. The better the report, the better the chance of obtaining a conviction. Describe completely any injuries and the victim's physical condition. Some departments have a supplemental report form to document evidence in domestic violence cases. In addition, the report should be submitted as soon after the incident as possible. A report that gets to the prosecutor more than 10 days after the incident lowers the chance of conviction by 25%. After 30 days, the likelihood drops to 50% (Nelson, 2013).

Explain to the victim that an *order of protection* may be obtained from a court to help prevent future assaults and increases the chance of prosecution and conviction, as discussed shortly. Many agencies also provide cards with a list of resources available to help victims of domestic violence.

To Arrest or Not?

Basically, any evidence that would lead an officer to make an arrest in any other situation also applies to spousal situations. All states permit an arrest based on probable cause. Many states now mandate police to make an arrest in domestic violence incidents if there is a protective or restraining order against the attacker, and some require an arrest even though no such order exists. The arrest of a domestic violence suspect raises greatly both the likelihood of prosecution (92%–96% increase) and the conviction rate (76%–80% increase) (Nelson, 2013).

Many departments have a mandatory arrest policy for domestic abuse, requiring the officer to make an arrest if there is probable cause, even without a signed complaint by the victim. Some states have legislated that police must have and implement such a policy. This philosophy was largely the result of the Minneapolis Domestic Violence Experiment (MDVE) conducted by Sherman and Berk in the early 1980s, which concluded that arrest was a more effective deterrent to repeat offenses than was advising or sending the suspect away. This report, sometimes summarized as "arrest works best," helped create a nationwide pro-arrest sentiment in domestic violence situations. However, "It may be premature to conclude that arrest is always the best way for police to handle domestic violence, or that all suspects in such situations should be arrested. A number of factors suggest a cautious interpretation of the finding" (Sherman & Berk, 1984, pp. 6–7).

Indeed, since that time, numerous other studies have found that alternatives to arrest may be better in specific circumstances, for example, when the batterer is employed and arrest would cause serious negative repercussions for the batterer as well as the family. In such instances, it is presumed the abuser has a higher stake in conformity and an alternative remedy can be more effective in breaking the abusive cycle.

Sherman (1995, p. 207) has asserted that arrest can backfire, and mandatory arrest laws can actually compound the domestic violence problem rather than alleviate it. Research has shown that many women, faced with the certain arrest of their abuser should they report it to police, consider the costs to be too high, citing a fear that the abuser's retaliation will worsen, the police may mistakenly arrest her as the aggressor, or that the abuser's arrest could deprive the victim and the family of the support they need (Novisky & Peralta, 2015). Indeed, the passage of mandatory arrest laws has led to an increase in the number of women arrested for domestic violence, in many cases because they had used violence in self-defense against their abuser and the police had no policy to address battered-spouse syndrome (National District Attorneys Association, 2017).

Other studies are shedding light on the fact that, in some jurisdictions where mandatory arrest laws have been enacted, responding officers are choosing to exceptionally clear cases of IPV to circumvent such laws, particularly when they assess that the seriousness of the offense is low (Hirschel & Faggiani, 2012). Nonetheless, researchers continue to reexamine whether arrest is the best response to domestic violence.

Officers should not base their decisions regarding arrest on their perception of the willingness of the victim or witnesses to testify, and victims should never be put in the position of stating to officers whether they want the abuse suspect to be arrested (IACP, 2019). Furthermore, the victim need not sign a complaint.

Departments vary in their policies regarding mutual abuse. Some departments require the responding officer to determine who the primary physical aggressor was and then arrest that person, whereas other agencies have a dual arrest policy. Dual arrest policies, which gained use following passage of pro-arrest laws, allow officers to circumvent the primary aggressor assessment and arrest both parties when injuries to both sides are observed. Critics of dual arrest policies have argued that they result in more arrests than are necessary because officers find it easier to simply arrest both parties than try to determine who the primary aggressor was, even if only one party shows injury. A dual arrest policy does not preclude the single arrest of the primary aggressor only, if the officer is able to make that determination. Factors to consider in making this assessment include

- Prior domestic violence involving either person

- The relative seriousness of the injuries inflicted upon each person involved

- The potential for future injury

- Whether one of the alleged batteries was committed in self-defense

- Any other factor that helps the officer decide which person was the primary physical aggressor

Police Nonresponse

One reason officers are criticized for not responding to domestic violence incidents is that they commonly receive calls from uninvolved third parties. For example, an apartment tenant calls to say the couple across the hall is shouting at each other and it sounds like things are being thrown and glass is breaking. When officers arrive, the couple may be embarrassed or angry because this is how they argue. They see no reason to involve the law and are irritated at the interference of neighbors and police. In other cases, a spouse may falsely report a domestic violence incident just to see the other party punished or the threat of punishment inflicted.

Several studies have examined whether the police response to domestic violence calls does receive a lower priority than other crime calls. The results generally show an increasingly high priority being placed on such calls.

Effectiveness of Various Interventions

Studies have found that the pattern of chronic abuse and victimization tends to follow individuals throughout multiple intimate relationships. A significant percentage of domestic abusers victimize multiple partners over their offending career, and a significant percentage of abuse victims are battered by different intimate partners over their lifespan (Barrie et al., 2020). For these individuals caught up in this ongoing series of violent relationships, effective intervention is crucial to breaking the abuse cycle.

Increasing numbers of departments throughout the United States are adopting a "zero-tolerance" approach to domestic violence, which appears to be highly successful. Although many departments view arrests as a critical part of a zero-tolerance stance, some researchers contend that it is not the arrest itself but what happens *after* the arrest that ultimately determines the effectiveness of the response.

Specialized domestic violence units hold promise because effectively dealing with domestic violence requires more than just effective investigation. Domestic violence is a community problem that requires a community solution. Specialized units often consist of a detective who jointly works cases with a deputy sheriff in the county. Whenever a patrol officer takes a report, the domestic violence unit follows up to ensure proper procedures have been followed.

Specialized domestic violence courts (DVCs), in step with the broader national trend that has given rise to "problem-solving courts," are another approach to addressing the domestic violence problem. While more than 200 such courts exist across the United States, they differ widely in their goals, policies, and adherence to evidence-based principles, making it difficult for researchers to study their effectiveness. Some data show that specialized DVCs do a better job than generalized courts of linking victims to victim resources, yet few studies have been able to demonstrate the ability of DVCs to reduce offender recidivism by any significant level. While DVCs have been found to increase the conviction rate of male offenders, but not of female offenders, as well as increase the likelihood of these men receiving a jail or prison sentence, DVCs were seen to produce only a modest positive impact on recidivism rates among convicted offenders (Cissner, Labriola, & Rempel, 2015). Again, the general theory is that effective interventions must do more than simply arrest, convict, and sentence offenders—they need to prioritize offender rehabilitation and implement evidence-based treatment practices.

In some jurisdictions, arrested abusers are required to participate in a batterer intervention program (BIP), a counseling and treatment alternative to sending these offenders to jail. The most common BIP used throughout the country is based on the Duluth Model, founded on the feminist theory that domestic violence is the result of a patriarchal ideology in which men are encouraged and expected to control their partners. The Duluth Model BIP seeks to enlighten abusive men by exploring their attitudes about control and teaching them strategies to better interact with their partners. However, research to date has failed to provide evidence that the treatment approach used in the Duluth Model has any significant effect on lowering recidivism among domestic violence offenders (Miller, Drake, & Nafziger, 2013).

Other BIPs are based on cognitive-behavioral modification to correct faulty thinking patterns, group practice models that seek to root out the multiple causes of battering and customize treatment to fit the offender's needs, and group therapy BIPs that take the controversial position that spouses are equal participants in creating disturbances in relationships. Some studies suggest that perhaps the most significant factor in the rehabilitation of a batterer is the offender's **stake in conformity**, a constellation of variables that, in effect, comprise "what an offender has to lose," such as marital status, residential stability, or employment. As with arrest research findings, results of studies that have examined the effectiveness of BIPs are mixed. What is known, however, is that batterers are a diverse group; approximately 20% of batterers do not benefit from treatment of any kind, are least likely to complete a BIP, and are most likely to continue their abusive behavior; and there is no "one size fits all" batterer intervention program (Ferraro, 2017).

Some jurisdictions have implemented intervention programs that draw on the cultural strengths of the community. In New Mexico, for example, domestic violence in Indian Country had become a significant problem, and the traditional route of incarceration was not having positive results. A sergeant with the local sheriff's department, himself a Navajo, suggested an intervention program built on a fundamental aspect of Native American communities—the clan and the wisdom of elders. The elders' knowledge and experience in resolving conflicts through peacemaking is what makes this unique intensive intervention program a success in Indian Country.

As important as intervention programs aimed at batterers are, of equal importance are efforts to help victims. It is fairly common for abuse victims who have filed a report and begun the process of pressing charges to change their minds and want to drop charges, whether out of guilt for having "turned" on their partner; out of worry that, because they are financially dependent on their abuser, conviction and imprisonment will lead to loss of income and medical insurance for the family; out of loyalty because they have patched things up with their abuser (the honeymoon phase has set in); or out of fear because the batterer threatens or tries to intimidate them into dropping the charges.

Some departments are taking an approach called **cocooning**, based on the idea that victims of violence need to surround themselves with others who are aware of the situation and can be an extra set of eyes and ears, a layer of protection to alert authorities if the victim is unable to call for help. A similar approach is to have a victim chose a **proximity informant**, someone who can keep tabs on the victim's normal schedule and who can establish a routine of contact with the victim, with the same principle being to serve as a lifeline to police if something seems wrong or "off" ("Police Improve Response to Domestic Violence," 2015). Another service being offered to some victims of domestic violence is the distribution of free cell phones, preloaded with a specific number of minutes and preprogrammed with the numbers of the police department and various victim service agencies.

Restraining Orders

Domestic violence victims themselves are taking a more active role in preventing recurring assaults by obtaining restraining orders. A **restraining order (RO)**, alternately called an order for protection or civil protective order, is a court-issued document that aims to restrict an alleged abuser's behavior and protect the intended victim. A provision of the Violence Against Women Act (VAWA) of 1994 assigns **full faith and credit** to valid orders of protection, meaning that an order issued anywhere in the country is legally binding and enforceable nationwide.

Restraining orders typically take several weeks to obtain, but if the victim is in immediate life-threatening danger, an emergency protective order (EPO) can generally be issued within 24 hours. Obtaining an EPO significantly increases the likelihood of prosecution (by 85%–89%) and raises conviction rates by 100% (Nelson, 2013). A court hearing is usually conducted before a restraining order is issued, allowing a judge time to review the facts of the case provided by the victim on the request form and to hear from the abuser, if they appear at the hearing. If an order of protection is granted, it may contain a variety of conditions regarding the abuser's personal conduct, use of alcohol, child custody or visitation, child or spousal support, a stay-away order, a move-out order, and a ban on the possession or use of firearms.

This final condition poses a problem for officers who have a restraining order filed against them, as they are prohibited from possessing a weapon even while on duty. Some restraining orders automatically expire after a specified time limit, unless renewed, but others are valid indefinitely unless a request is made for dismissal and a court grants such dismissal.

Although abuse victims are certainly encouraged to protect themselves, they cannot rely solely on a piece of paper for security. In fact, some studies have found that women who seek restraining orders are well aware of their potential ineffectiveness, and one study found that nearly 50% of IPV victims who obtain protective orders are stalked by their abusers (Hawkins, 2010).

Legislation

In addition to mandatory arrest laws, other laws address issues concerning convicted domestic abusers. One such statute already discussed is the Lautenberg Amendment to the Crime Control Bill of 1968, which prohibits individuals convicted of misdemeanor crimes involving domestic violence from owning or possessing a firearm. This retroactive statute is a problem for law enforcement officers, for if convicted of domestic violence, they will lose their jobs.

Avoiding Lawsuits

Failure to respond appropriately to domestic violence can result in serious financial liability to local governments. More and more, victims of domestic violence are suing local governments for failure to protect them. Perhaps the most well-known case is that of Tracy Thurman in Torrington, Connecticut. The police department was ordered to pay almost $1 million because they failed to protect Tracy from her husband, who had a history of battering her (*Thurman v. City of Torrington*, 1984).

Considerable confusion persists with regard to violations of protective orders, police duty to protect, and mandatory arrest statutes. Without question, states vary greatly in the types of legislation they have passed regarding domestic violence. Even in the presence of such laws, courts have excused law enforcement's noncompliance with mandatory arrest statutes, ruling that officers must be allowed to exercise the "deep-rooted" and "well

Technology Innovations

Monitoring Offenders with GPS

Several jurisdictions, including some in Vermont, Massachusetts, Illinois, and Washington, D.C., have implemented programs whereby certain domestic violence offenders are required to wear a global positioning system (GPS) monitoring device. Connecticut, for example, has placed such monitoring ankle bracelets on 168 high-risk offenders in designated test areas. The victim is issued a corresponding GPS device that signals an alert if the offender gets within 5,000 feet. If an offender comes within 2,500 feet, not only is the victim alerted but so are the police, who are directed to respond to the victim's home (Merritt, 2013).

Tennessee has followed in the footsteps of Connecticut, using GPS to monitor defendants charged with IPV as a condition of their pretrial release, as this time frame has been shown to be one of the most dangerous periods for victims of domestic abuse. An evaluation of the GPS monitoring pilot program found that victims who carried a GPS device were, indeed, less likely to be revictimized by their abuser (Barrie et al., 2020).

unwanted attention and contact that causes fear or concern for one's own safety or the safety of someone else, such as a family member or close friend.

Stalking may co-occur with IPV, as many studies have documented. Individuals who are stalked by a prior intimate partner are at a higher risk for violence than are other stalking victims (Gerbrandij, Rosenfeld, Nijdam-Jones, & Galietta, 2018). One study found that approximately 3.9% of women in the United States have experienced rape *and* stalking in the same relationship during their lifetime, 8.7% of U.S. women have experienced physical violence *and* stalking in the same relationship, and 1.7% of U.S. men have experienced physical violence *and* stalking in the same relationship (Breiding, Chen, & Black, 2014).

L05 Define the categories of assault that are identified as separate crimes to aid in data collection.

Although legal definitions vary among jurisdictions, **stalking** is generally defined as a pattern of repeated and unwanted attention and contact that causes fear or concern for one's own safety or the safety of someone else. The elements of the crime differ by state.

established tradition of police discretion" (*Castle Rock v. Gonzalez*, 2005). However, officers abusing discretionary powers by choosing to act or failing to take action may result in civil or criminal liability.

To reduce lawsuits, departments should have a pro-arrest policy if officers have probable cause to believe a domestic assault has occurred. They should train officers in this pro-arrest policy and require them to document why an arrest has or has not been made. Some agencies have a domestic violence checklist for patrol officers and detectives to complete during an investigation. Appendix E provides an example of one such checklist prepared by the International Association of Chiefs of Police (IACP, 2017) and highlights common investigative procedures. Use of such a checklist can help ensure that the department's domestic violence response protocol is followed and perhaps mitigate exposure to liability.

Investigating Stalking

Closely related to investigating domestic violence cases is the challenge of investigating stalking cases. Recall from Table 9.1 that stalking is a pattern of repeated and

The question often arises: What is the difference between *harassment* and *stalking*? Some would argue that there is no difference and that the terms are, for all practical purposes, synonymous. Laws have been passed against both, making them both proscribed, prosecutable conduct. And in some jurisdictions, the acts are combined into a solitary piece of legislation, further blurring any discernible legal distinction. Indeed, stalking is often categorized as a type of harassment (whereas harassment is not often considered stalking), and many commonalities exist between them: both involve continued, systematic unwelcome behavior directed at the victim, and both make the victim feel threatened. However, a nuanced difference is that stalking involves *obsessive* attention directed toward the victim by the perpetrator. Stalking also includes an element of *recurrent* or *escalating fear* felt by the victim caused by a *series of acts* that occur over time, acts that are not illegal when taken individually, such as sending love notes or flowers, sending texts or phone calls, or waiting for someone outside of their place of work. But when those behaviors repeatedly breach a victim's personal boundaries and lead the recipient to fear for their safety, they become criminal in the form of stalking. Furthermore, while stalking generally

Myth You can't be stalked by someone you are still in a relationship with, whether that is a dating or marriage partner.

Fact If your current partner tracks your every move or follows you around in a way that causes you fear, that is stalking.

involves a series of actions over time, harassment can often exist as a single occurrence.

According to the National Center for Injury Prevention and Control and the CDC, nearly 1 in 6 women (16%, or 19.1 million) and approximately 1 in 17 men (5.8%, or nearly 6.4 million) in the United States have been victims of stalking at some point in their lives (Smith et al., 2018). Data from the NCVS indicate that an estimated 3.3 million people age 18 and older are stalked every year (Catalano, 2012). Many of these victims obtain protective orders, yet such orders are generally much less effective for stalking victims than for other types of victims (Hawkins, 2010).

Stalking can lead to homicide. In fact, as Roberts (2017) asserts: "Stalking is one of the few crimes where early intervention can prevent violence and death." Statistics on **femicide**, the murder of a woman, reveal that the majority of femicide victims had been stalked by the person who killed them. One study found that 76% of women who were killed by their current or former intimate partner had been stalked by their killer within the year preceding the murder, and 85% of women who were victims of *attempted* murder by a current or former partner had also been victims of stalking by such partners in the 12 months leading up to the attempt (Garcia, 2010). More than half (54%) of these victims had reported the stalking to the police before they were murdered by their stalkers.

Types of Stalking

Stalkers are typically categorized as a certain typology, usually based on the relationship between the stalker and the victim. One system of stalking typologies involves the three categories of intimate or former intimate, acquaintance, and stranger stalking.

In *intimate or former intimate stalking*, the stalker and victim may be married or divorced, current or former cohabitants, serious or casual sexual partners, or former sexual partners. This is the most common relationship involved in stalking cases. In *acquaintance stalking*, the stalker and victim know each other casually.

They may be neighbors or coworkers. They might even have dated once or twice but were not sexual partners. In *stranger stalking*, the stalker and victim do not know each other at all. The most current data available from the Supplemental Victimization Survey (SVS) of the NCVS show that nearly 70% of victims were stalked by someone they knew, whether a former or current intimate, or someone known in another capacity (e.g., friend, roommate, neighbor, acquaintance, relative, or known from work or school) (Catalano, 2012).

Davis (2016) presents a different set of typologies for stalkers, also including three varieties: the simple obsessional, the love obsessional, and the erotomanic. *Simple obsessional* stalkers are the basic equivalent of the aforementioned intimate stalkers but also include acquaintance stalkers. These cases are the most common type and most often occur in the context of domestic violence. *Love obsessional* stalkers have no prior relationship with their victim but become fixated on that person, often a celebrity, believing they belong together. *Erotomanic* stalkers, the rarest of the three types, believe that their victim is in love with them.

Cyberstalking

The growing prevalence of technology has allowed for the spread of cyberstalking, which, in previous editions of this text, was simply defined as preying on a victim via computer. However, the problem has grown in such scope and severity that more elaborate and specific definitions are now used. The Department of Justice has defined **cyberstalking** as the repeated use of the Internet, email, or other digital electronic communications devices to stalk another person. Approximately 40% of Americans have personally experienced online harassment, and 7% report being the victim of online stalking (Duggan, 2017). Like other forms of stalking, cyberstalking can turn violent.

Sextortion is a form of harassment and online child sexual exploitation and, as such, will be discussed in greater detail in Chapter 11 (Crimes against Children). It is mentioned here simply because, while there are no laws that specifically define the federal offense of sextortion, this crime does fall under the federal cyberstalking law (FBI, 2018b).

Cyberbullying

Cyberbullying, like cyberstalking, uses technology to carry out the offense remotely and anonymously. The National Conference of State Legislatures (NCSL) defines **cyberbullying** as "the willful and repeated use of cell phones, computers, and other electronic communication devices to harass and threaten others" (NCSL, 2010). Cyberbullying is essentially cyberstalking or cyberharassment involving minors. As such, the techniques and processes used to investigate both cyberstalking and cyberbullying are the same and rely heavily on forensic digital analysis to help recreate the events and actions that occurred during the episode of offending. Children who previously had to worry only about the bully on the playground or the one lurking behind a fence on the walk to school now face the threat of being harassed and bullied in their own homes or anywhere they go with their mobile devices.

Results from the Youth Risk Behavior Surveillance Survey (YRBSS) show that 15.7% of students in the United States were electronically bullied during 2019, either through email, chat rooms, instant messaging, websites, or texting, with females more likely to experience cyberbullying (20.4%) than males (10.9%) (Basile et al., 2020). Kids who are cyberbullied, much like those who are bullied in the traditional face-to-face way, are more likely to use alcohol and drugs, skip school, receive poor grades, have lower self-esteem, and have more health problems (U.S. Department of Health and Human Services, n.d.). As with cyberstalking, the perception of anonymity afforded by online activity is thought to be one reason cyberbullying is on the rise. This trend has also led to the coining of a new term, **cybersuicide**: a completed or attempted suicide influenced or mediated by the Internet. Headline-making news stories about teens who have committed cybersuicide allegedly in the wake of being cyberbullied—including the 2006 suicide of 13-year-old Megan Meier and the 2016 suicide of 18-year-old Brandy Vela—have also brought increased pressure on legislators and authorities to address this problem.

Legislation and Department Policies

The first antistalking laws were passed in 1990 in California. Since 1999, all 50 states and the District of Columbia have enacted general antistalking laws and have expanded their legislation to include either cyberstalking or cyberharassment offenses. Fourteen states classify stalking as a felony upon the first offense; 35 states classify it as a felony upon the second offense or when it involves aggravating factors such as possession of a deadly weapon or violation of a court order or condition of probation or parole (Klein, Salomon, Huntington, Dubois, & Lang, 2012). Additional aggravating factors include a victim younger than 16 or the same victim as in prior incidents. Forty-eight states have enacted some form of legislation to address cyberbullying (Clement, 2020). Title 18, §875 of the U.S. Code makes it a federal offense

to transmit, electronically or otherwise, any threatening communication in interstate or foreign commerce, with such acts punishable by fine, imprisonment for as long as five years, or both.

Antistalking laws describe specific threatening conduct and hold the suspect responsible for proving that their actions were not intended to frighten or intimidate the victim. Thus, intent on the part of the suspect and fear on the part of the victim are two common elements of the crime of stalking (Roberts, 2017). Most stalking laws require proof of a credible threat made by the perpetrator against the victim or the victim's family. The other necessary element of stalking is a proven course of conduct (multiple acts or incidents and a continuity between them).

Although legislation makes stalking a specific crime and empowers law enforcement to combat the offense, a great deal of variation and subjectivity exists among the states' legal definitions of stalking. Many officers are unaware of antistalking legislation in their state. And many officers do not know about their own department's policy on stalking.

The Police Response

The traditional law enforcement response to stalkers has been to encourage victims to obtain court-issued restraining orders. Unfortunately, such orders are often ineffective, as demonstrated when one offender dramatically stabbed his wife to death and "knifed" the court order to her chest. Research has also found that women who are stalked after obtaining a restraining order have higher levels of fear of future harm and believed the orders were not as effective as they had anticipated. Furthermore, the stalking that occurred after the issuance of such protective orders was associated with more violence, "suggesting those who stalk are more violent and more resistant to court intervention" (Hawkins, 2010, p. 6). Because of this proven ineffectiveness of restraining orders, the perceived inability of criminal justice to effectively handle stalkers, and victims' fear of antagonizing and angering their stalkers, more than half of all stalking incidents go unreported. One study found that only 37% of male stalking victimizations and 41% of female stalking victimization are reported to law enforcement (Baum, Catalano, Rand, & Rose, 2009).

Although it has been shown that stalking often co-occurs with domestic violence, research has also found that police are not fully identifying stalking cases from among reported domestic violence cases. Results from one study shows that for every incident identified by police as stalking, another 21 stalking cases go unidentified (Klein et al., 2012). The study also found both short- and long-term ramifications concerning the proper identification of a domestic violence case as involving stalking, versus another domestic violence charge such as assault or violation of a protective order.

Since misidentification of stalking compromises the entire criminal justice response to it, the proper identification of stalking cases is a first step to effectively responding to such crimes. Yet law enforcement faces a challenge in addressing and investigating stalking incidents because of the lack of clear definitions of stalking or of the elements constituting the offense. Other investigative challenges and barriers presented in stalking cases include:

- The complex and varied nature of stalking behaviors

- The lack of a standard psychological profile of stalkers to assist investigators

- The tendency of law enforcement to focus more on the violence, when domestic abuse co-occurs with stalking, and exclude stalking behaviors in the investigation

- Jurisdictional challenges when stalkers in one area target victims in another jurisdiction

- The fact that stalkers are not easily deterred

- The difficulty in ensuring the victim's safety

> (Boehnlein, Kretschmar, Regoeczi, & Smialak, 2020; Lynch & Logan, 2015; Backes, Fedina, & Holmes, 2020; Dreke, Johnson, & Landhuis, 2020; Stalking Prevention, Awareness, and Resource Center, 2020)

One tool that may help investigators more effectively assess whether an incident is a potential case of stalking is a screening questionnaire such as that in Figure 9.2. This instrument was developed by a working group comprised of representatives from the Office on Violence against Women (OVW), the Bureau of Justice Statistics (BJS), and the Census Bureau, after consulting with researchers, law enforcement, prosecutors, and victim advocates—all experts in the areas of stalking and violence against women. The screening questionnaire was developed as part of the Supplemental Victimization Survey (SVS), an add-on to the NCVS, and intentionally does not mention "stalking" in its title or any of the questions so as to avoid biasing any responses from participants. To be counted as a stalking victim, a respondent must state that they experienced all of the following:

- At least one of the harassing behaviors in the stalking screener [Figure 9.2]

- Harassing behavior more than one time on separate days

- At least one of multiple harassing contacts during the 12 months prior to the interview

- Fear for their own or a family member's safety or experience of another crime committed by the offender that would make a reasonable person fearful

> (Catalano, 2012)

Because stalking is defined as a "course of conduct" or series of acts, documenting those acts is a crucial part of an investigation. Any of the following acts may become part of a stalking investigation:

- Violations of protective orders

- Domestic violence

- Assault

- Sexual assault

- Attempted murder

- Child abuse

- Hate crimes

- Harassment

- Vandalism

- Home invasion

- Trespass

- Kidnapping

- Burglary

- Theft

- Identity theft

- Wiretapping or utility theft

> (Roberts, 2017)

The more thorough the history, in terms of the frequency and nature of the acts, the stronger the case. Thus, victim input is not only encouraged but is essential to establishing historical evidence. Victims must be instructed on how to preserve and document each threatening act, including harassing phone calls, texts, emails, and letters; acts of vandalism; threats made through third parties; sending of unwanted "gifts;" and any other incident that establishes the pattern of

Screener questions for stalking behaviors

Now, I would like to ask you some questions about any unwanted contacts or harassing behavior you may have experienced that frightened, concerned, angered, or annoyed you. Please include acts committed by strangers, casual acquaintances, friends, relatives, and even spouses and partners. I want to remind you that the information you provide is confidential.

1. Not including bill collectors, telephone solicitors, or other sales people, has anyone, male or female, EVER — frightened, concerned, angered, or annoyed you by …

a. making unwanted phone calls to you or leaving messages?

b. sending unsolicited or unwanted letters, e-mails, or other forms of written correspondence or communication?

c. following you or spying on you?

d. waiting outside or inside places for you such as your home, school, workplace, or recreation place?

e. showing up at places where you were even though he or she had no business being there?

f. leaving unwanted items, presents, or flowers?

g. posting information or spreading rumors about you on the Internet, in a public place, or by word of mouth?

h. none

Actions that would cause a reasonable person to feel fear

1. In order to frighten or intimidate you, did this person attack or attempt to attack...

a. a child

b. another family member

c. a friend or coworker

d. a pet

2. During the last 12 months, did this person attack or attempt to attack you by...

a. hitting, slapping, or knocking you down

b. choking or strangling you

c. raping or sexually assaulting you

d. attacking you with a weapon

e. chasing or dragging with a car

f. attacking you in some other way

3. Other than the attacks or attempted attacks you just told me about, during the last 12 months, did this person threaten to...

a. kill you

b. rape or sexually assault you

c. harm you with a weapon

d. hit, slap, or harm you in some other way

e. harm or kidnap a child

f. harm another family member

g. harm a friend or co-worker

h. harm a pet

i. harm or kill himself/herself

4. What were you most afraid of happening as these unwanted contacts or behaviors were occurring?

a. death

b. physical/bodily harm

c. harm or kidnap respondent's child

d. harm current partner/boyfriend/ girlfriend

e. harm other family members

f. don't know what would happen

Questions used to measure fear

1. How did the behavior of (this person/these persons) make you feel when it FIRST started? Anything else?

a. anxious/concerned

b. annoyed/angry

c. frightened

d. depressed

e. helpless

f. sick

g. suicidal

h. some other way—specify

2. How did you feel as the behavior progressed? Anything else?

a. no change in feelings

b. anxious/concerned

c. annoyed/angry

d. frightened

e. depressed

f. helpless

g. sick

h. suicidal

i. some other way—specify

Figure 9.2
Screening questionnaire for stalking behaviors.

Source: https://www.bjs.gov/content/pub/pdf/svus_rev.pdf, p.7

conduct (Roberts, 2017; Stalking Prevention, Awareness, and Resource Center, 2020). All threatening electronic communications should be saved, a hard copy printed, and a screenshot or photo of the screen taken if possible. In the meantime, victims should obtain an unidentified phone number or a new email address or change their user name if the harassment involves cyberstalking. An important role of the investigator is to support and assist the victim in gathering evidence while helping suggest ways to keep themselves safe until the stalker can be stopped.

Also, because the crime is partially defined by the victim's reaction, victims must be instructed on how to document, either in writing or with a video or audio recording, their emotional and physical reactions to each stalking act. This "stalking log" must include dates, times, and locations, and should be recorded immediately, even if the victim does not intend to move forward with charges. This log could be an important component in applying for and receiving an order for protection or used in divorce or child custody proceedings. Figure 9.3 shows an example of what such a log might look like.

An important consideration for a victim to keep in mind when creating such a log is that, since it could be introduced as evidence if the case proceeds to court or could be otherwise inadvertently shared with the offender, it should not contain any information the victim does not want the alleged stalker to see (Stalking Prevention, Awareness, and Resource Center, 2018). Other documentation to include with the log is a photograph of the stalker, if available, copies of any orders for protection, and copies of police reports. The victim should be instructed to secure the log someplace safe and share the location of the log only with someone they trust completely.

When cyberstalking is involved, investigators should conduct a technology risk assessment with the victim that considers the number of computers, cell phones, and other electronic devices in the home and who has access to these devices (Roberts, 2017). Challenges and complications in investigating cyberstalking include the volatility of electronic evidence; the unwillingness of some Internet service providers (ISPs) to give law enforcement access to subscribers' records; and the increased ability to communicate anonymously through Internet tools, such as remailers that strip identifying information from email headers and erase transactional data from servers that would otherwise be used to trace a message's author. Another complication during stalking investigations, particularly those involving cyberstalking where an offender can be many miles away from the victim, is the fact that the crimes occurred at several locations across different jurisdictions, necessitating a joint effort with other law enforcement agencies.

An effective stalking investigation requires gathering information not only from the victim but also from witnesses and other sources, including the suspect. Information from multiple sources helps investigators and prosecutors create the "big picture" and put the stalking behavior into context (Roberts, 2017). Witnesses can help corroborate the victim's statements as well as help investigators assess the credibility and overall capability of the stalker to actually carry out their expressed intent to cause harm. Elements to consider include the target, the stalker's motivation, the stalker's ability to follow through on threats, the stalker's personal background, and the victim-offender relationship (VOR).

Evaluating the potential for violence is an important part of a stalking investigation because stalking behavior can, and in some cases does, elevate to homicide. The FBI's National Center for the Analysis of Violent Crime (NCAVC) is a valuable resource in helping stalking investigators assess an offender's potential for violence. The NCAVC stresses the need to consider a stalker's behavior

Date	Time	Description of the Act	Location of the Act	My emotional and physical reaction to this act	If any witnesses to the act, record name and phone number	If police were called, document responding officer (name and badge #) and Report #

Figure 9.3
Stalking log.

in its totality by considering specific actions and other factors, including

- Threats to kill

- Access to or recent acquisition of weapons

- Violations of protective orders

- Prior physical violence against the victim or others, including pets

- Substance abuse

- Location of violence (private versus public setting)

- Status of the victim-offender relationship

- Surveillance of the victim and "chance" meetings

- Mental illness

- Prior intimacy between victim and offender

- Fantasy—homicidal or suicidal ideation

- Obsessive jealousy

- Desperation

- Blaming the victim for personal problems

- Loss of power or control

Officers should interview the suspect and attempt to get a statement, documenting all reactions. Roberts (2017) notes: "Stalkers want to talk about their victims and explain away what they are doing to convince others they are 'right' in their behaviors." Investigators should conduct the interview in the stalker's home, if possible, and remain observant, noting the kind of vehicle the stalker drives and what kind of phone, computers, or cameras are visible (Roberts, 2017). Record the conversation(s) if possible, and include this information in the official report.

The follow-up investigation may involve taking additional statements from witnesses; corroborating the suspect's alibi, if one was provided; surveilling the suspect; and applying for a search warrant. Items to include when seeking a warrant for a suspect's residence or vehicle are photos of the victim; images or maps pertaining to the victim's home, work, or school; logs or diaries kept by the suspect that detail thoughts or fantasies; print material related to stalking; computers, laptops, and other portable digital devices, including SIM cards and memory cards, that may contain evidence linking the suspect to the victim; digital evidence such as Internet bookmarks and browser histories that may indicate searches related

to the victim or stalking in general; devices or tools used in stalking (e.g., binoculars, cameras, and night vision); and any personal items that once belonged to the victim (Roberts, 2017).

If the investigation leads to probable cause, the suspect should be arrested. If a suspect cannot be taken immediately into custody, a BOLO (Be On the Lookout) alert should be issued containing applicable arrest warrant data, and the victim should be advised (Roberts, 2017).

Investigating Elder Abuse

A final area to examine in the investigation of assault and family violence is elder abuse. In 2010, there were 40.3 million people over the age of 65 living in the United States. The U.S. Census Bureau projects that by 2030, more than 72 million people will be older than age 65, and by 2050, that number will climb to nearly 84 million. The number of people in the oldest old-age group, those aged 85 and older, is projected to grow from 5.9 million in 2012 to 8.9 million in 2030, and then doubling over the next 20 years to a projected 18 million (4.5% of the U.S. population) by 2050 (Ortman, Velkoff, & Hogan, 2014). As the U.S. population ages, a growing concern in law enforcement is elder abuse, a term for which no universally accepted definition currently exists. Furthermore, no consensus exists on the age at which one qualifies as an "elder," with some entities setting 60 years old as the age at which one becomes "an elderly person," while others set this threshold at age 65.

The Department of Health and Human Services has a fairly comprehensive definition of elder abuse as "physical, sexual, or psychological abuse, as well as neglect, abandonments, and financial exploitation of an elderly person by another person or entity, that occurs in any setting (e.g., home, community, or facility), either in a relationship where there is an expectation of trust and/ or when an elderly person is targeted based on age or disability" (Connolly, Brandl, & Breckman, 2014). The CDC's current definition of elder abuse is an "intentional act or failure to act by a caregiver or another person in a relationship involving an expectation of trust that causes or creates a serious risk of harm to an older adult" (Hall, Karch, & Crosby, 2016). This text defines **elder abuse** as intentional or neglectful acts by a caregiver or other trusted individual that lead to, or may lead to, harm of a vulnerable elderly person. This definition—one characterized by multiple *acts*—speaks to the ongoing or chronic nature of abuse and neglect which, from an investigative standpoint, presents different challenges from those encountered during a singular event, such as that encountered when an elderly person, who has no history of abuse or neglect, goes missing.

> **L05** Define the categories of assault that are identified as separate crimes to aid in data collection.
>
> Elder abuse includes the physical, sexual, and emotional abuse; financial exploitation; and general neglect of an elderly person.

Certainly, when an elderly person strays from their familiar and safe environment, they are placed at risk of being victimized. And the longer they are unaccounted for, the greater their risk. For this reason, many states have enacted **silver alert** programs, also called a Code Silver, which are public notification systems similar to amber alerts for missing children but that aim to recover missing seniors (Stringfellow, 2018). Twenty-seven states have a silver alert program, and nine other states have a similar program that goes by another name (e.g., Golden Alert, Missing Senior Alert). Six states have no alert system in place for seniors, and the remaining eight states have broad-reaching missing persons alert systems.

When a senior goes missing and is then victimized, this is not elder abuse. Elder abuse is a recurring pattern of mistreatment, neglect, and/or exploitation. Elder abuse is not a specific crime category in many states, which makes its frequency data difficult to obtain. Elder abuse is typically included in the assault, battery, or murder category, which does great injustice to creating an effective response to this ongoing offense. Although incidents of burglaries, robberies, motor vehicle thefts, assaults, rapes, and homicides of the elderly are relatively well documented in official reports, or at least at rates comparable to those documenting offenses against other age groups, cases of elder abuse typically involve the types of victimization that occur outside the spotlight focused on by the FBI, in the shadowy fringes of crime collection.

Types of Elder Abuse

The National Center on Elder Abuse (NCEA) identifies the following types of elder abuse:

- Physical abuse—use of physical force to threaten or physically injure an elderly person

- Sexual abuse—sexual contact this is forced, tricked, threatened, or otherwise coerced upon an elderly person, including anyone who is unable to give consent

- Neglect—a caregiver's failure or refusal to provide for a vulnerable elderly person's safety, physical, or emotional needs

- Emotional/psychological abuse—verbal attacks, threats, rejection, isolation, or belittling acts that cause or could cause mental anguish, pain, or distress to an elderly person

- Financial abuse, neglect, and exploitation—theft, fraud, misuse or neglect of authority, and use of undue influence as a level to gain control over an elderly person's money or property

- Abandonment—desertion of a frail or vulnerable elderly person by anyone with a duty of care

- Self-neglect—an inability to understand the consequences of one's own actions or inaction, which leads to, or may lead to, harm or endangerment

(NCEA, 2016)

Prevalence and Nature of Elder Abuse

Elder abuse has been called a "hidden" or "silent" crime because a large percentage of cases go unreported; thus, determining the prevalence of elder abuse is challenging due to incomplete data, a problem compounded by a reluctance to report the crime—similar to the situation with domestic assault. Further complicating the picture is the inconsistency among researchers and others in selecting an age threshold at which a person is considered an "elder," as well as the different research methods and operational definitions used. Nonetheless, in general, researchers estimate the prevalence of elder abuse among Americans age 65 and older to be around 10% (Lach & Pillemer, 2015; Office for Victims of Crime, 2017). As many as 5 million older Americans are estimated to suffer some type of elder abuse each year, but only 1 out of every 25 elder abuse cases are reported to authorities (National Council on Aging [NCOA], n.d.; NCEA, n.d.-b).

The nature of elderly victimization differs somewhat from the types of crimes experienced by those in other age groups. For example, one study found that while the rates of nonfatal violence and property crimes were lower against the elderly than against younger persons, people age 65 and older experienced more incidents of identity theft (5.0%) than persons age 16 to 24 (3.8%). Still, the rates of identity theft victimization for the elderly fell significantly below those for people aged 25 to 49 (7.9%) and aged 50 to 64 (7.8%) (Morgan & Mason, 2014).

Perpetrators of elder abuse can be men or women and of any age, race, or socioeconomic status. However, they generally fall into three broad categories: family members, hired caregivers, and professional con artists. The majority of elder abuse is committed by family members, although the victim-offender relationship does vary somewhat by type of crime (Office for Victims of Crime, 2017). For example, the majority (57%) of physical abuse against elderly victims is perpetrated by a spouse or intimate partner; most emotional sexual abuse is committed by either a spouse, partner, or acquaintance; and most neglect is perpetrated by a child or grandchild (Office for Victims of Crime 2017).

Risk Factors for Elder Abuse

Elder abuse can occur in private homes and assisted living facilities and affects seniors of all races, cultures, and socioeconomic statuses. Available data indicate that older women are more likely than older men to be victimized (NCEA, 2016; Lachs & Pillemer, 2015). Other factors that place an elderly person at higher risk of elder abuse include:

- Social isolation

- Mental or cognitive impairment (e.g., dementia, Alzheimer's)

- Functional impairment, physical disability, and poor physical health

- Physical, mental, emotional, of financial dependence

- Burnout of the caregiver

- Lack of access to support and other resources

- Living with a large number of people other than a spouse

- Having a lower income

- Mental health and substance abuse issues

- Experience of previous domestic violence and a perpetuation of the cycle of violence

This last factor supports the theory that domestic violence is a learned problem-solving behavior transmitted from one generation to the next. Research has shown that childhood emotional and sexual abuse is associated with a greater risk of elder victimization (Kong & Easton, 2018).

Fewer studies have examined the risk factors associated with committing elder abuse, but from the data that does exist, perpetrators are most likely to:

- Be adult children or spouses

- Be male

- Have a history of past or current substance abuse

- Have mental or physical health problems

- Have a history of trouble with the police

- Be socially isolated

- Be unemployed or have financial problems

- Be experiencing major stress

(CDC, 2020; Lachs & Pillemer, 2015; NCEA, 2016; NCOA, n.d.)

The Police Response

It cannot always be assumed that a broken bone in an elderly person or an unwise financial investment is the direct results of elder abuse or exploitation. Older people have weaker muscles and bones. They fall and bruise. They make bad choices on how to invest their money. But when these unfortunate events become a matter of routine, they may warrant further investigation.

Controversy exists about the role of law enforcement in dealing with elder abuse, especially in identifying "hard-to-detect" cases. Some departments believe this is the responsibility of social services, rather than law enforcement. Other departments feel they are in an ideal position to learn from and to assist social services in dealing with cases of elder abuse. In fact, some jurisdictions have designated a specialized Vulnerable Persons Unit to investigate and prosecute those who abuse, neglect, or exploit children and adults living in a private residence.

Many of the same skills used in dealing with domestic violence and child abuse are applicable in an elder abuse investigation. Investigators should observe the general condition of the residence when arriving to investigate an elder abuse complaint. Once inside, investigators should carefully observe the general conditions (sights *and* smells) and interview the alleged victim, paying particular attention to nonverbal cues, such as an unwillingness to make eye contact. Also observe the behaviors of any other persons present and assess their willingness or reluctance to let the elderly person speak freely.

Some elderly individuals are physically incapable of providing information or may be suffering from conditions such as senility or Alzheimer's disease that might cause others not to believe their statements. In other cases, victims may fear further abuse or loss of the care of the only provider they have, or they may be embarrassed that their child could mistreat them. If the abuser is a family member, which data suggest is more often the case than not, an elderly victim may often choose to suffer in silence rather than report conduct that will get a family member in trouble. Persons of older generations and from other cultures often consider such abuse to be a private family matter, something that is not talked about and is certainly never reported to the police. Such cultural and generational attitudes present considerable challenges to those investigating these crimes.

When interviewing an elderly person, use patience and allow them ample time to respond following these do's and don't's:

- DO speak slowly and use short sentences.

- DO ask open-ended questions.

- DO ask about only one thing at a time.

- DO speak with them at eye level (people who feel vulnerable may be intimidated by authority, and standing over them only exacerbates their anxiety).

- DON'T correct them. Record their response as it is given.

- DO believe someone when they say they have been abused or mistreated.

(University of Southern California [USC], n.d.)

Some general questions to gets answers to, regardless of the type of abuse being investigated, provide insight into the level of care needed and include:

- Who prepares your food?

- Does someone help you with your medication?

- How do you get to appointments?

- Who takes care of your checkbook and paying your bills?

- Do you feel safe where you live?

(USC, n.d.)

Beyond the basic inquiries, there are some specific indicators investigators should be aware of, questions to have answered, and evidence to collect when approaching possible cases of elder abuse and neglect.

Physical Elder Abuse—Indicators, Questions, and Evidence. One critical aspect of an investigation of physical elder abuse is to determine if bruising is the result of an accident or of abuse. Abuse indicators—known as forensic markers—can help distinguish between injuries caused by mistreatment and those that are the result of accidents, illnesses, or aging (McNamee & Murphy, 2006). Researchers have found that accidental bruising occurs in predictable locations in older adults, with 90% of all bruises found on the extremities; accidental bruises are rarely, if ever, seen on the ears, neck, genitals, buttocks, or soles of the feet (McNamee & Murphy, 2006). Indicators of physical abuse of an elderly person include[1]:

- Injury incompatible with the given explanation

- Burns (possibly caused by cigarettes, acids, or friction from ropes)

- Cuts, pinch marks, scratches, lacerations, or puncture wounds

- Bruises, welts, or discolorations

- Dehydration or other malnourishment without illness-related causes

- Unexplained loss of weight

- Pallor, sunken eyes, or cheeks

- Eye injury

- Soiled clothing or bedding

- Lack of bandages on injuries or stitches where needed, or evidence of unset bone fractures

- Injuries hidden under the breasts or on other areas of the body normally covered by clothing

- Hoarse voice and difficulty breathing (possible signs of strangulation)

- Choking on food (sign of force-feeding)

- Frequent use of the emergency room or clinic

---

[1]Content in this section, including the indicator lists, is a amalgamation from several sources unless otherwise cited: NCOA, n.d., NCEA, n.d.-b, NCEA, 2016; CDC, 2020; USC, n.d.

If injuries are observed, document the victim's, caretaker's, and any witnesses' accounts as to how and when the injuries occurred. Other questions to ask when investigating possible physical abuse of an elderly person include:

- Has anyone at home ever hurt you?

- Has anyone ever scolded or threatened you?

- Are you afraid of anyone at home?

- Has anyone ever touched you without your consent?

- Has anyone ever made you do things you didn't want to?

(Aravanis, 1992)

In any physical abuse case, regardless of the age of the victim, photographs of injuries must be taken, both during the initial response and then several days later. When taking photos, look for the appearance of other bruises or injuries at various stages of healing, which would indicate an ongoing pattern of abuse. If the victim is hospitalized, obtain a statement from the attending physician regarding the type and severity of any injuries (Albrecht, 2008). Other items to photograph include medication containers; refrigerator contents; and the victim's living quarters and bedroom, including the sheets (USC, n.d.). Note the presence of any locks on the outside of any doors. This goes for investigations of any type of elder abuse.

Sexual Elder Abuse—Indicators, Questions, and Evidence.
Some indicators of sexual abuse of an elderly person are behavioral or otherwise visible to an investigator, including:

- Difficulty walking or sitting

- Fear of or unusual behavior around the caregiver or others nearby

- Depression or social withdrawal

- Extreme agitation or panic attacks

- Suicide attempts

- Torn, stained, or bloodied clothing, undergarments, and bedding

Physical indicators of sexual elder abuse that might not be obvious and may require a medical examination include:

- Bruises or injuries around the inner thighs, the buttocks, the genital area, or breasts

- Unexplained genital infections or sexually transmitted diseases

- Unexplained vaginal or anal bleeding, pain, or irritation

When questioning an elderly victim of sexual abuse, ask for details in a sensitive but nonjudgmental way and use direct, short questions. Ask for the victim's and caregiver's accounts as to how and when the injuries occurred. In addition to those questions listed previously for physical abuse victims, questions an investigator should seek answers to pertaining to possible sexual abuse include:

- Is the elderly victim physically and mentally able to resist unwanted contact?

- Is the victim able to walk? Run? Or are they bed-bound?

- Does the victim have the capacity to consent to a sexual assault exam? If not, ask the health care power of attorney, if the victim has one.

- If the abuser is unknown to the victim, ask who had unsupervised access to the victim, perhaps someone who bathed and clothed the elder.

- Does the victim have difficulty urinating, defecating, walking, or sitting?

(USC, n.d.)

Evidence in an elder sexual abuse case are photographs of bruising and injuries as listed above; torn, stained, or bloodied clothing, undergarments, or bedsheets; and medical reports.

Elder Neglect—Indicators, Questions, and Evidence.
Elder neglect occurs when any of the basic necessities—nutrition, hygiene, shelter, clothing, safety, and necessary medical care—are withheld. Indicators that an elderly person is suffering from caregiver neglect include:

- Bedsores

- Poor hygiene

- Unchanged diapers

- Unattended medical needs, such as untreated injuries or unfilled prescriptions

- Lack of medical aids (glasses, dentures, hearing aids, medication), assistive medical devices (wheelchairs, walkers, canes, scooters), or incontinence supplies

- Unusual weight loss, malnutrition, or dehydration

- An unsupervised person with dementia

- A bed-bound elder left without care

Bedsores, also called pressure sores or, in medical terms, *decubitus ulcers*, are a telltale indicator of neglect and are caused by immobility. When a person lies in one position and place over a lengthy period of time, the continuous pressure where the body meets a surface reduces blood flow to that area of the body, causing the tissue to die and an open sore to form. Body parts where bedsores are commonly noted are the buttocks, hips, heels, shoulder blades, and ears.

Questions the investigator needs to seek answers to in suspected cases of elder neglect include:

- Is the victim often alone?

- Does the caregiver isolate the elder?

- Are prescriptions current and are medications being taken properly?

- Is the elder eating regularly? Do they require help at mealtime?

- Has anyone ever failed to help the elder take care of themselves when they needed help?

- How does the victim's living area compare to the rest of the house in terms of cleanliness, safety, and accessibility concerns?

In neglect cases, the investigator should document the scene by taking comprehensive video of the kitchen, bathrooms, bedrooms, and other living areas (Albrecht, 2008). Bedsores and other injuries should be photographed and their severity assessed, after consulting with a physician. Bedsore severity ranges from Stage I (mild redness but no open sore) to Stage IV (extremely severe open sore that reaches bone or cartilage) (USC, n.d.).

Emotional or Psychological Elder Abuse— Indicators, Questions, and Evidence.
Emotional or psychological elder abuse often co-occurs with other forms of abuse. Studies have also found that, among all the forms of elder abuse, emotional or psychological elder abuse is most often associated with a high risk of morbidity and mortality, as well as an increased risk of dementia and suicide (Ilie et al., 2017). Indicators that an elderly person might be a victim of emotional or psychological abuse include:

- Unusual changes in behavior or sleep

- Unexplained withdrawal from normal activities

- A sudden change in alertness

- Unusual depression

- Anxiety or fear

- Nervousness around the caregiver or other residents

- Strained or tense relationships between the victim and others in the residence

- Frequent arguments with the caregiver

In additional to verbal assaults, harassment, intimidation, belittling, humiliation, and general mental cruelty, emotional or psychological abuse also involves a denial of rights—rights to socialize, to have free access to regular items around the home, to go outside, or to enjoy any forms of entertainment (Oregon Department of Human Services, 2012). To assess whether the elder is being deprived of social interactions, ask the victim whether they have any family or friends, how often they get to see or communicate with family and friends, and how often they would *like* to visit or talk to family and friends. Ask: Is there anything that you wish was different? The investigator should also seek answers to the following questions regarding possible emotional or psychological abuse of an elderly person:

- Is the victim withdrawn or nonresponsive around the caregiver or other residents in the home or facility?

- Does the victim seem upset, agitated, or fearful in the presence of the caregiver or others in the residence?

- Does the victim seem fearful of saying or doing something wrong?

- Does the victim report being able to freely come and go from the residence? Or make phone calls or watch the television whenever they want?

This type of abuse, while more common than physical elder abuse, is often difficult to prove, and many state statutes do not criminalize emotional abuse. Evidence in emotional or psychological abuse cases may be difficult to collect, aside from victim and witness statements. However, the fact that emotional abuse often co-occurs with neglect or physical abuse informs investigators to be alert for evidence of those crimes when handling an emotional abuse case.

Interviews with neighbors, family members, and friends of the elderly victim may expose a pattern of ongoing denial of rights by the caretaker to the victim. One study found that abuser characteristics were more predictive of emotional or psychological abuse than were victim vulnerabilities, a result that suggests investigators pay special attention to the suspected perpetrator's temper control capacity and any negative attitudes expressed toward the victim (Liu, Conrad, Beach, Iris, & Schiamberg, 2017).

Financial Elder Abuse, Neglect, and Exploitation— Indicators, Questions, and Evidence. Financial abuse and exploitation of the elderly is an area of growing concern. Elderly financial abuse crimes generally fall into two categories: (1) fraud committed by strangers, who are often professional con artists and scammers, and (2) exploitation by relatives, caregivers, and close trusted friends.

Listed among the types of fraud commonly committed against the elderly by strangers are prize and sweepstakes scams, charitable contribution fraud, home and automobile repair scams, travel fraud, telemarketing fraud, mail fraud, fraudulent funeral plans, false health remedies and "miracle cures," and face-to-face contacts that give an offender a chance to steal from or otherwise scam the elderly victim, such as posing as a utility worker to gain access to the home to commit a robbery. Another common scam is the "grandparent" scam, where the elderly victim is called and told their grandchild is in jail and needs their grandparent to wire money immediately (National Adult Protective Services Association, 2020).

Common scams by "professionals" that target the elderly include predatory lending, investment fraud, securities schemes, annuity sales, Medicare scams, bogus or unnecessary duplicates of health and life insurance policies, identity theft, and Internet phishing, such as sending false emails about bank accounts or credit cards. Investigating fraud and white-collar crime are discussed in detail in Chapter 14.

This discussion focuses more on the second category of financial elder abuse—the victimization endured at the hands of trusted family members or others with whom the victim has an ongoing relationship. This type of financial exploitation, which is often even more unsettling than falling victim to a smooth-talking scam artist, can occur when a relative or caregiver borrows money without repaying; withholds medical care or other services to conserve funds; sells the elder's possessions without permission; signs or cashes pension or Social Security checks without permission; misuses the elder's automated teller machine (ATM) or credit cards; forces the elder to sign over property; or simply takes away the elder's money, property, or valuables (National Adult Protective Services Association, 2020). Other opportunities for exploitation occur with financial and legal arrangements such as joint bank accounts, deed or title transfers, powers of attorney and durable powers of attorney, and living trusts and wills.

Indicators of financial abuse or exploitation of an elderly person include:

- Sudden changes in financial situations
- Sudden changes to wills, trusts, or deeds
- Unusual bank withdrawals
- ATM withdrawals by an elderly person who has never used a debit or ATM card
- Checks written as "loans" or "gifts"
- Suspicious signatures or outright forgery on checks
- Loss of property
- Uncharacteristic purchases by the individual or caregiver
- New joint account suddenly opened up
- New credit cards showing up in the elder's name
- New powers of attorney the elderly person does not understand
- Sudden appearance of credit card balances
- Sudden nonsufficient fund activity
- Closing CDs or other savings accounts without regard to penalties
- Uncharacteristic attempts to wire large sums of money
- Bank and credit card statements that no longer go to the customer's home
- Failure to pay bills or keep appointments
- New "best friends" or romantic partners wanting to "help" the elderly victim with finances

Making poor financial decisions is not a crime. The challenge for an investigator is to distinguish between unwise, but legitimate, financial transactions and exploitative transactions that benefit not the victim but the perpetrator. Therefore, the key when investigating elder financial abuse and exploitation is to examine the elder's established financial patterns. Questions the investigator should seek answers to include:

- What is the victim's general understanding of their financial situation?
- Has the victim ever signed any documents that they didn't understand?
- Has a caregiver or other trusted person ever taken something from the victim without asking?

- Who pays the victim's bills?

- Who cashes the victim's social security checks?

- Who has access to or authorization to use the victim's bank account or credit cards?

- Is the caregiver compensated and, if so, how?

- Does the victim have a durable power of attorney and, if so, can you see it? Who is named as having power of attorney for the elder? **Take a copy or a picture of this document.**

- Is the older adult's money being used for their care?

Evidence in financial abuse cases includes credit card and bank statements, new credit card applications, power of attorney documents, annuity or investment account information, and any signs that recent unauthorized changes were made to the elder's will, trusts, or deeds. Also recognize that other types of elder abuse may co-occur with financial exploitation, so explore and document any indicators of other types of abuse.

Elder Abuse in Long-Term Care Facilities

Elder abuse in long-term care facilities has been a concern for decades. Data indicate that the prevalence of elder abuse in nursing homes and other long-term care facilities is high, with more than 4 in 10 (44%) elders reporting they had been abused themselves and nearly all residents (95%) stating they had been neglected or witnessed another elderly resident being neglected (NCEA, 2012). In addition, one study found that more than half of nursing home staff admitting to either physically abusing, mentally abusing, or neglecting their older patients during the past year. Another study found that elders in long-term care facilities are more likely to be victimized by other residents than by staff (Rosen et al., 2016).

Reducing Elder Abuse

With U.S. population projected to grow older over the next several decades, efforts to prevent and reduce elder abuse could have not only a substantial public health impact but also significantly reduce the number of cases needing criminal investigation. Because social isolation is one of the greatest contributors to elder abuse, encouraging seniors to remain connected and active in their communities can have a considerable positive effect on lowering the incidents of maltreatment of the elderly.

The National Center on Elder Abuse (n.d.-a) notes that prevention strategies can take many forms and provides the following examples:

- Abuse Registries & Criminal Background Checks—lists perpetrators of substantiated incidents of elder abuse and, in many instances, prohibits such individuals from working with certain populations or in certain settings, such as a nursing home. Registries allow these individuals to be flagged during a background check when applying for jobs.

- Addressing Ageism—like racism with skin color and sexism with gender, ageism is used to stereotype and discriminate against people because they are old. Ageism entails prejudices and actions against older people that result in older adults being socially marginalized and devalued. It is argued that a lack of honor and respect of older individuals results in permissive attitudes of, and societal blindness to, disrespect and even violence against older adults.

- Advance Planning Tools—tools for elders to reduce confusion and clarify their wishes in the event they become unable to do so themselves. These tools can also be used to protect against financial exploitation, as well as the possibility of abuse or neglect. Among these tools are:

  - Advance directives

  - Living wills

  - Limited powers of attorney and identified proxies for both health care and for finances

- Public Awareness—communication tools for promoting or improving health and well-being. Changes in services, technology, regulations, and policy are often also necessary to completely address a health or social problem.

Investigators working elder abuse cases can strive to ensure that seniors in their community know about the services and resource centers in their neighborhoods and whether any prevention strategies specifically targeting elder abuse have been implemented.

One approach to reducing elderly victimization is Triad, a cooperative effort of the International Association of Chiefs of Police (IACP), AARP (formerly the American Association of Retired Persons), and the National Sheriffs' Association (NSA). These three organizations are working together to design programs to reduce victimization of the elderly, assist those who have been victimized, and generally enhance law enforcement services to older adults and the community at large. AARP is another resource to tap when trying to reduce the occurrence of elder abuse. The AARP website (www.aarp.org) posts numerous articles about how to protect against financial exploitation and what to do if nursing home or other caregiver problems exist, along with various other links to resources able to assist elderly victims.

Summary

Assault is unlawfully threatening to harm another person, actually harming another person, or attempting unsuccessfully to do so. *Simple assault* is intentionally causing another to fear immediate bodily harm or death or intentionally inflicting or attempting to inflict bodily harm on the person. *Aggravated assault*, or *felonious assault*, is an unlawful attack by one person on another to inflict severe bodily injury.

The elements of the crime of simple assault are (1) intent to do bodily harm to another, (2) present ability to commit the act, and (3) commission of an overt act toward carrying out the intent. An additional element in the crime of aggravated assault is that the intentionally inflicted bodily injury results in (1) a high probability of death; (2) serious, permanent disfigurement; or (3) permanent or protracted loss or impairment of the function of any body member or organ or other severe bodily harm. Attempted assault requires proof of intent and an overt act toward committing the crime. To prove the elements of assault, establish the intent to cause injury, the severity of the injury inflicted, and whether a dangerous weapon was used.

For data collection, special categories of assault are domestic violence, stalking, and elder abuse. Domestic violence is a pattern of behaviors involving physical, sexual, economic, and emotional abuse, alone or in combination, often by an intimate partner and often to establish and maintain power and control over another person within a household or family environment.

Although legal definitions vary among jurisdictions, *stalking* is generally defined as the willful or intentional commission of a series of acts that would cause a reasonable person to fear death or serious bodily injury and that, in fact, does place the victim in fear of death or serious bodily injury. *Elder abuse* is the physical, sexual, and emotional abuse; financial exploitation; and general neglect of an elderly person.

Can You Define?

aggravated assault

assault

battery

cocooning

cyberbullying

cyberstalking

cybersuicide

cycle of violence

domestic violence

elder abuse

felonious assault

femicide

full faith and credit

indicator crimes

in loco parentis

intimate partner violence (IPV)

proximity informant

restraining order (RO)

silver alert

simple assault

stake in conformity

stalking

Checklist

Assault

- Is the assault legal or justifiable?

- Are the elements of the crime of assault present?

- Who committed the assault?

- Is the suspect still at the scene?

- Who signed the complaint? Who made the arrest?

- Has the victim given a recorded statement, either written, audio, or video? Have witnesses done so?

- Are injuries visible?

- Have photographs been taken of injuries? In color?

- Has the victim received medical attention?

- If medical attention was received, has a report on the nature of the injuries been received? Did the victim grant permission?

- What words did the assailant use to show intent to do bodily harm?

- Was a dangerous weapon involved?

- Has a complete report been made?

- If the assault is severe enough to be aggravated assault, what injuries or weapons support such a charge?

- If the victim died as a result of the attack, was a dying declaration taken?

- Was it necessary and legal to make an arrest at the scene? Away from the scene?

- How was the suspect identified?

Application

Read the following and then answer the questions:

Wade was drinking beer with friends in a local park at about 9:00 p.m. It was dark. He knew Ahmad was at the other end of the park and that Ahmad had been seeing Wade's girlfriend, Yasmin. Yasmin was with Wade, trying to talk him out of doing anything to Ahmad. Wade said he was going to find Ahmad and "pound him into the ground. When I get through with him, they'll have to take him to the hospital."

Wade left the group and Yasmin then, telling them to wait for him. Ahmad was found later that night two blocks from the park, lying unconscious on a boulevard next to the curb. His clothes were torn, and his left arm was cut. When he regained consciousness, he told police he was walking home from the park when someone jumped out from some bushes, grabbed him from behind, beat him with fists, and then hit him over the head with something. He did not see his assailant.

Wade was arrested because a person at the park overheard his threats.

Questions

1. What is the probability that Wade committed the assault?

2. Did he have the intent? Did he have the present ability to commit the act?

3. Did he commit the act? Should he have been arrested?

4. What evidence would you try to collect to support the assault charge?

References

Albrecht, L. (2008, April). Elder abuse investigations. *Law Officer Magazine*, pp. 44–46.

Aravanis, S. C. (1992). *Diagnostic and treatment guidelines on elder abuse and neglect.* Chicago, IL: American Medical Association, 1992.

Arkow, P. (2014, Summer). Form of emotional blackmail: Animal abuse as a risk factor for domestic violence. *Family & Intimate Partner Violence Quarterly, 7*(1), 7–13.

Backes, B. L., Fedina, L., & Holmes, J. L. (2020, February 21). The criminal justice system response to intimate partner stalking: A systematic review of quantitative and qualitative research. *Journal of Family Violence.* doi:10.1007/s10896-020-00139-3

Barrie, J., Shaver, N., Lewis, D., Gibson, T., & McAdoo, M. (2020, January). *Improving victim safety with global positioning system (GPS) monitoring as a condition of release for defendants accused of domestic violence.* Nashville, TN: Tennessee Advisory Commission on Intergovernmental Relations. Retrieved August 31, 2020, from www.tn.gov/content/dam/tn/tacir/2020publications/2020GPSmonitoring.pdf

Basile, K. C., Clayton, H. B., DeGue, S., Gilford, J. W., Vagi, K. J., Suarez, N. A., . . . & Lowry, R. (2020, August 21). Interpersonal violence victimization among high school students—youth risk behavior survey, United States, 2019. *Morbidity and Mortality Weekly Report (MMWR), 69*(Suppl-1): 28–37. Retrieved August 31, 2020, from www.cdc.gov/mmwr/volumes/69/su/pdfs/su6901a4-H.pdf

Baum, K., Catalano, S., Rand, M., & Rose, K. (2009, January). *Stalking victimization in the United States.* Washington, DC: Bureau of Justice Statistics Special Report, National Crime Victimization Survey. (NCJ 224527)

Benavides, M. O., Berry, O. O., & Mangus, M. (2019). *Guide to treating LGBTQ patients who have experienced intimate partner violence.* Washington, DC: American Psychiatric Association Publishing. Retrieved August 24, 2020, from www.psychiatry.org/psychiatrists/cultural-competency/education/intimate-partner-violence/lgbtq

Boehnlein, T., Kretschmar, J., Regoeczi, W., & Smialak, J. (2020, March 13). Responding to stalking victims: Perceptions, barriers, and directions for future research. *Journal of Family Violence.* doi:10.1007/s10896-020-00147-3

Breiding, M. J., Basile, K. C., Smith, S. G., Black, M. C., & Mahendra, R. (2015). *Intimate partner violence surveillance: Uniform definitions and recommended data elements* (Version 2.0). Atlanta, GA: Centers for Disease Control and Prevention. Retrieved August 22, 2020, from www.cdc.gov/violenceprevention/pdf/ipv/intimatepartnerviolence.pdf

Breiding, M. J., Chen, J., & Black, M. C. (2014, February). *Intimate partner violence in the United States—2010.* Atlanta, GA: National Center for Injury Prevention and Control, Centers for Disease Control and Prevention.

Catalano, S. (2012, September). *Stalking victims in the United States—revised.* Special Report. Washington, DC: U.S. Department of Justice, Bureau of Justice Statistics. (NCJ 224527)

Centers for Disease Control and Prevention. (2018, October 23). *Intimate partner violence.* Atlanta, GA. Retrieved August 24, 2020, from www.cdc.gov/violenceprevention/intimatepartnerviolence/index.html

Centers for Disease Control and Prevention. (2020, May 13). *Elder abuse.* Atlanta, GA: Author. Retrieved September 2, 2020, from www.cdc.gov/violenceprevention/elderabuse/index.html

Cissner, A. B., Labriola, M., & Rempel, M. (2015). Domestic violence courts: A multisite test of whether and how they change offender outcomes. *Violence Against Women, 21*(9): 1102–1122. doi:10.1177/1077801215589231

Clement, J. (2020, March 27). U.S. states with state cyberbullying laws as of November 2018. *Statista.* Retrieved August 31, 2020, from www.statista.com/statistics/291082/us-states-with-state-cyber-bullying-laws-policy/#statisticContainer

Connolly, M. T., Brandl, B., & Breckman, R. (2014). *The elder justice roadmap: A stakeholder initiative to respond to an emerging health, justice, financial and social crisis.* Washington, DC: Department of Health and Human Services. Retrieved September 2, 2020, from www.justice.gov/file/852856/download

Davis, J. A. (2016, June 14). Stalking crimes and victim protection. *Psychology Today.* Retrieved September 5, 2020, from www.psychologytoday.com/us/blog/crimes-and-misdemeanors/201606/stalking-crimes-and-victim-protection

Dreke, R. J., Johnson, L., & Landhuis, J. (2020). Challenges with and recommendations for intimate partner stalking policy and practice: A practitioner perspective. *Journal of Family Violence.* doi:10.1007/s10896-020-00147-3

Duggan, M. (2017, July 11). *Online harassment 2017.* Washington, DC: Pew Research Center. Retrieved August 31, 2020, from www.pewresearch.org/internet/2017/07/11/online-harassment-2017/

Febres, J., Brasfield, H., Shorey, R. C., Elmquist, J., Ninnemann, A., Schonbrun, Y. C., & Stuart, G. L. (2014). Adulthood animal abuse among men arrested for domestic violence. *Violence Against Women, 20*(9): 1059–1077. doi:10.1177/1077801214549641

Federal Bureau of Investigation. (2018a). *Crime in the United States 2018.* Washington, DC: Author. Retrieved August 22, 2020, from ucr.fbi.gov/crime-in-the-u.s/2018/crime-in-the-u.s.-2018/topic-pages/aggravated-assault

Federal Bureau of Investigation. (2018b). *Cyberstalking: Two federal cases illustrate the consequences of sextortion.* Washington, DC: Author. Retrieved August 31, 2020, from www.fbi.gov/news/stories/sentences-in-separate-cyberstalking-cases-103018

Federal Bureau of Investigation. (2018c). *Law enforcement officers killed & assaulted, 2018.* Washington, DC: Author. Retrieved August 22, 2020, from ucr.fbi.gov/leoka/2018/topic-pages/officers-assaulted

Ferraro, K. J. (2017, December). *Current research on batterer intervention programs and implications for policy.* Minneapolis, MN: The Battered Women's Justice Project. Retrieved August 31, 2020, from www.bwjp.org/assets /batterer-intervention-paper-final-2018.pdf

Finneran, C., & Stephenson, R. (2013, August). Gay and bisexual men's perceptions of police helpfulness in response to male-male intimate partner violence. *The Western Journal of Emergency Medicine, 14*(4): 354–362. Retrieved August 24, 2020, from www.ncbi.nlm.nih.gov /pmc/articles/PMC3735383/

Folkes, S. E. F., Hilton, N. Z., & Harris, G. T. (2013). Weapon use increases the severity of domestic violence but neither weapon use nor firearm access increases the risk or severity of recidivism. *Journal of Interpersonal Violence, 28*(6): 1143–1156. doi:10.1177/0886260512468232

Garcia, M. M. (2010, June). Voices from the field: Stalking. *NIJ Journal, 266,* 14–15.

Gerbrandij, J., Rosenfeld, B., Nijdam-Jones, A., & Galietta, M. (2018). Evaluating risk assessment instruments for intimate partner stalking and intimate partner violence. *Journal of Threat Assessment and Management, 5*(2): 103–118. doi:10.1037/tam0000101

Haden, S. C., McDonald, S. E., Booth, L. J., Ascione, F. R., & Blakelock, H. (2018). An exploratory study of domestic violence: Perpetrators' reports of violence against animals. *Anthrozoös, 31*(3): 337–352. doi:10.1080/08927936.2018.1455459

Hall, J., Karch, D. L., & Crosby, A. (2016). *Elder abuse surveillance: Uniform definitions and recommended core data elements* (Version 1.0). Atlanta, GA: Centers for Disease Control and Prevention. Retrieved September 2, 2020, from www.cdc.gov/violenceprevention/pdf/ea_book _revised_2016.pdf

Hart, B. J., & Klein, A. R. (2013, December). *Practical implications of current intimate partner violence research for victim advocates and service providers.* Washington, DC: U.S. Department of Justice. (NCJ 244348). Retrieved August 25, 2020, from www.ncjrs.gov/pdffiles1/nij/grants/244348.pdf

Hawkins, N. (2010, June). Perspectives on civil protective orders in domestic violence cases: The rural and urban divide. *NIJ Journal, 266,* 4–8.

Hester, M. (2012). Portrayal of women as intimate partner domestic violence perpetrators. *Violence Against Women, 18*(9):1067–1082. doi:10.1177/1077801212461428.

Hirschel, D., & Faggiani, D. (2012, December).When an arrest is not an arrest: Exceptionally cleared cases of intimate partner violence. *Police Quarterly, 15*(4), 358–385.

Huecker, M. R., & Smock, W. (2020, January). *Domestic violence.* Treasure Island, FL: StatPearls Publishing. Retrieved August 23, 2020, from www.ncbi.nlm.nih.gov/books /NBK499891/

Ilie, A. C., Pîslaru, A. I., Alexa, I. D., Pancu, A., Gavrilovici, O., & Dronic, A. (2017, June). The psychological abuse of the elderly: A silent factor of cardiac decompensation. *Maedica, 12*(2): 119–122. Retrieved September 4, 2020, from www.ncbi.nlm.nih.gov/pmc /articles/PMC5649032/

International Association of Chiefs of Police. (2019, April). *Domestic violence.* Alexandria, VA: Author. Retrieved August 25, 2020, from www.theiacp.org/sites/default /files/2019-04/Domestic%20Violence%20Paper%20-%20 2019_0.pdf

Kanable, R. (2010, March). Learning to read the danger signs. *Law Enforcement Technology,* pp. 8–14.

Klein, A., Salomon, A., Huntington, N., Dubois, J., & Lang, D. (2012, September 18). *A statewide study of stalking and its criminal justice response in Rhode Island, 2001–2005.* Ann Arbor, MI: Inter-University Consortium for Political and Social Research. doi:10.3886 /ICPSR25961.v1

Kong, J., & Easton, S. D. (2018, July). Re-experiencing violence across the life course: Histories of childhood maltreatment and elder abuse victimization. *The Journals of Gerontology, Series B, 74*(5): 853–857. doi:10.1093 /geronb/gby035

Lachs, M. S., & Pillemer, K. A. (2015, November 12). Elder abuse. *New England Journal of Medicine, 373:* 1947–1956. Retrieved September 2, 2020, from www.nejm.org/doi /full/10.1056/NEJMra1404688

Lee, J., Zhang, Y., & Hoover, L. T. (2013). Profiling weapon use in domestic violence: Multilevel analysis of situational and neighborhood factors. *Victims & Offenders, 8*(2): 164–184. doi:10.1080/15564886.2012.749123

Liu, P., Conrad, K. J., Beach, S. R., Iris, M., & Schiamberg, L. B. (2017, July). The importance of investigating abuser characteristics in elder emotional/psychological abuse: Results from adult protective services data. *The Journals of Gerontology, Series B, 74*(5): 897–907. doi:10.1093/geronb /gbx064

Lynch, K. R., & Logan, T. K. (2015). Police officers' attitudes and challenges with charging stalking. *Violence and Victims, 30*(6): 1037–1048. Retrieved September 1, 2020, from pubmed.ncbi.nlm.nih.gov/26440289/

McNamee, C. C., & Murphy, M. B. (2006, November). Elder abuse in the United States. *NIJ Journal, 255,* 16–21.

Merritt, G. (2013, September 4). GPS ankle bracelets reduce domestic violence injuries in Connecticut. *The Connecticut Mirror.* Retrieved September 5, 2020, from ctmirror .org/2013/09/04/gps-ankle-bracelets-reduce-domestic -violence-injuries-connecticut/

Miller, M., Drake, E., & Nafziger, M. (2013, January). *What works to reduce recidivism by domestic violence offenders?* Olympia, WA: Washington State Institute for Public Policy. (Doc. No. 13-01-1201)

Morgan, R. E., & Mason, B. J. (2014, November). *Crimes against the elderly, 2003–2013.* Washington, DC: U.S. Department of Justice, Bureau of Justice Statistics. (NCJ 248339)

Morgan, R. E., & Oudekerk, B. A. (2019, September). *Criminal victimization, 2018.* Washington, DC: Bureau of Justice Statistics. (NCJ 253043). Retrieved August 22, 2020, from www.bjs.gov/content/pub/pdf/cv18.pdf

National Adult Protective Services Association. (2020). *Elder financial exploitation.* Washington, DC: Author. Retrieved September 5, 2020, from www.napsa-now.org /get-informed/exploitation-resources/

National Center on Elder Abuse. (n.d.-a). *Prevention strategies.* Washington, DC: Author. Retrieved September 5, 2020, from ncea.acl.gov/What-We-Do/Practice/Prevention -Strategies.aspx

National Center on Elder Abuse. (n.d.-b). *Statistics and data.* Washington, DC: Author. Retrieved September 2, 2020, from ncea.acl.gov/About-Us/What-We-Do/Research /Statistics-and-Data.aspx

National Center on Elder Abuse. (2012). *Abuse of residents in long-term care facilities.* Washington, DC: Author. Retrieved September 5, 2020, from ncea.acl.gov/NCEA/media/docs /Abuse-of-Residents-of-Long-Term-Care-Facilities-(2012)_1.pdf

National Center on Elder Abuse. (2016). *Why should I care about elder abuse?* Washington, DC: Author. Retrieved September 2, 2020, from eldermistreatment.usc.edu/wp -content/uploads/2016/10/NCEA-WhyCare_print.pdf

National Center on Elder Abuse. (2017). *The facts of elder abuse.* Washington, DC: Author. Retrieved September 2, 2020, from ncea.acl.gov/NCEA/media/Publication/NCEA _TheFactsofEA_2019_5.pdf

National Conference of State Legislatures. (2010, December 14). *Cyberbullying.* Washington, DC: Author. Retrieved September 5, 2020, from www.ncsl.org/research /education/cyberbullying.aspx

National Council on Aging. (n.d.). *Elder abuse facts.* Arlington, VA: Author. Retrieved September 2, 2020, from www.ncoa .org/public-policy-action/elder-justice/elder-abuse-facts/

National District Attorneys Association. (2017, March 16). *National domestic violence prosecution best practices guide.* White Paper. Alexandria, VA: Author. Retrieved August 26, 2020, from www.ncdsv.org/NDAA_National-DV -Prosecution-Best-Practices-Guide_3-16-2017.pdf

Nelson, E. L. (2013). Police controlled antecedents which significantly elevate prosecution and conviction rates in domestic violence cases. *Criminology & Criminal Justice, 13*(5): 526–551. doi:10.1177/1748895812462594

Novisky, M. A., & Peralta, R. L. (2015). When women tell: Intimate partner violence and the factors related to police notification. *Violence Against Women, 21*(1): 65–86. doi:10.1177/1077801214564078

Office for Victims of Crime. (2017). Elder victimization. *2017 National Crime Victims' Rights Week Resource Guide.* Washington, DC: Author. Retrieved September 2, 2020, from www.ncjrs.gov/ovc_archives/ncvrw/2017 /images/en_artwork/Fact_Sheets/2017NCVRW _ElderVictimization_508.pdf

Office for Victims of Crime. (2018). Intimate partner violence fact sheet. *2018 National Crime Victims' Rights Week Resource Guide.* Washington, DC: Author. Retrieved August 23, 2020, from ovc.ojp.gov/sites/g/files/xyckuh226/files /ncvrw2018/fact_sheet.html

Oregon Department of Human Services. (2012, April 6). Emotional abuse guidelines. Salem, OR: Author. Retrieved September 4, 2020, from www.dhs.state.or.us/spd/tools /cm/aps/community/emot_abuse.pdf

Ortman, J. M., Velkoff, V. A., & Hogan, H. (2014, May). *An aging nation: The older population in the United States.* Washington,

DC: U.S. Census Bureau. Retrieved September 5, 2020, from www.census.gov/prod/2014pubs/p25-1140.pdf

Police improve response to domestic violence, but abuse often remains the "Hidden Crime." *Subject to Debate, 29*(1), January/February 2015. Retrieved September 5, 2020, from www.policeforum.org/assets/docs/Subject_to_Debate /Debate2015/debate_2015_janfeb.pdf

Reaves, B. A. (2017, May). *Police response to domestic violence, 2006–2015.* Washington, DC: Bureau of Justice Statistics. (NCJ 250231). Retrieved August 22, 2020, from www.bjs .gov/content/pub/pdf/prdv0615.pdf

Roberts, E. (2017, August 23). Part II: Stalking evidence: What to look for and how to get it admitted. *Battered Women's Justice Project Webinar Series Part II: Investigating & Prosecuting Stalking* (PowerPoint). Washington, DC: Office for Victims of Crime. Retrieved September 1, 2020, from www.bwjp.org/assets/documents/pdfs/webinars/8-23-17 -webinar0ppt.pdf

Rosen, T., Lachs, M., Teresi, J., Eimicke, J., Van Haitsma, K., & Pillemer, K. (2016). Staff-reported strategies for prevention and management of resident-to-resident elder mistreatment in long-term care facilities. *Journal of Elder Abuse & Neglect, 28*(1): 1–13. doi:10.1080/08946566.2015.1029659

Rydström, L., Edhborg, M., Jakobsson, L. R., & Kabir, Z. N. (2019). Young witnesses of intimate partner violence: Screening and intervention. *Global Health Action, 12*(1). doi: 10.1080/16549716.2019.1638054

Sherman, L. W. (1995). Domestic violence and defiance theory: Understanding why arrest can backfire. In D. Chappell & S. Egger (Eds.), *Australian violence, contemporary perspectives II* (pp. 207–220). Canberra: Australian Institute of Criminology.

Sherman, L. W., & Berk, R. A. (1984, April). *The Minneapolis domestic violence experiment.* Washington, DC: Police Foundation Reports.

Smith, S. G., Zhang, X., Basile, K. C., Merrick, M. T., Wang, J., Kresnow, M., & Chen, J. (2018, November). *The national intimate partner and sexual violence survey (NISVS): 2015 data brief—updated release.* Atlanta, GA: National Center for Injury Prevention and Control, Centers for Disease Control and Prevention. Retrieved August 31, 2020, from www.cdc.gov/violenceprevention/pdf/2015data -brief508.pdf

Sorenson, S. B. (2017, March 1). Guns in intimate partner violence: Comparing incidents by type of weapon. *Journal of Women's Health, 26*(3): 249–258. doi:10.1089 /jwh.2016.5832

Stalking Prevention, Awareness, and Resource Center. (2018). Stalking incident and behavior log. Washington, DC: Author. Retrieved September 1, 2020, from www .stalkingawareness.org/wp-content/uploads/2018/07 /SPARC_StalkingLogInstructions_2018_FINAL.pdf

Stalking Prevention, Awareness, and Resource Center. (2020). *Prosecutor's guide to stalking.* Washington, DC: Author. Retrieved September 1, 2020, from www.stalkingawareness .org/wp-content/uploads/2020/01/SPA-19.005 -Prosecutors-Guide-to-Stalking-00000002.pdf

Stringfellow, A. (2018, April 25). What is a code silver? How it works, state information, and more. Boston, MA: SeniorLink (Blog). Retrieved September 2, 2020, from www.seniorlink.com/blog/silver-alerts

Taylor, K. (2014). *Exposing the abusive female*. Orange County, CA: Author.

Tricarico, E. (2020, January). A refuge from violence—for pets and people. *dvm360, 51*(1): 1, 14, 16. Retrieved August 22, 2020, from www.dvm360.com/view/refuge-violence-pets-and-people

U.S. Department of Health and Human Services. (n.d.). *What is cyberbullying?* Washington, DC: Author. Retrieved September 5, 2020 from www.stopbullying.gov/cyberbullying/what-is-it

University of Southern California. (n.d.). *Elder abuse guide for law enforcement*. Portland, OR: East Bank Communications Group. Retrieved September 2, 2020, from eagle.usc.edu/

Walters, M. L., Chen, J., & Breiding, M. J. (2013, January). *The National Intimate Partner and Sexual Violence Survey (NISVS): 2010 Findings on victimization by sexual orientation*. Atlanta, GA: National Center for Injury Prevention and Control, Centers for Disease Control and Prevention.

Winton, R., & Mather, K. (2014, July 16). Sandra Bullock stalking case sparks concerns on celebrity safety. *LA Times*. Retrieved September 5, 2020, from www.latimes.com/local/lanow/la-me-ln-sandra-bullock-stalking-case-sparks-concern-on-celebrity-safety-20140716-story.html

Wyllie, D. (2019, February 15). 11 tips for responding to domestic violence calls. *Police Magazine* online. Retrieved August 25, 2020, from www.policemag.com/504864/11-tips-for-responding-to-domestic-violence-calls

Zeoli, A. M. (2017, September). *Non-fatal firearm uses in domestic violence*. Minneapolis, MN: The Battered Women's Justice Project. Retrieved August 25, 2020, from vaw.msu.edu/wp-content/uploads/2018/06/nonfatal-gun-dv-zeoli-1-1.pdf

Cases Cited

Castle Rock v. Gonzalez, 545 U.S. 748 (2005).

Naler v. State, 25 Ala. App. 486 (1933).

Shackleford v. Commonwealth, 183 Va. 423, 426, 32 S.E. 2d 682 (1945).

State v. Rhodes, 61 N.C. 453 (1868).

Thurman v. City of Torrington, 595 F. Supp. 1521 (D. Conn. 1984).

Chapter 10
Sex Offenses

Chapter Outline

Investigating Obscene Telephone Calls and Texts

Investigating Prostitution

Investigating Human Trafficking

Classification of Sex Offenses

Rape/Sexual Assault

The Police Response

The Victim's Medical Examination

Blind Reporting

Interviewing the Victim

Follow-Up Investigation

Interviewing Witnesses

Sex Offenders

Taking a Suspect into Custody and Interrogation

Coordination with Other Agencies

Prosecution of Rape and Statutory Charges

Civil Commitment of Sex Offenders after Sentences Served

Sex Offender Registry and Notification

Learning Objectives

LO1 Identify the key distinction between human trafficking and human smuggling.

LO2 Differentiate between the two typical classifications of rape.

LO3 List the elements of sexual assault.

LO4 List what modus operandi factors are important in investigating a sexual assault.

LO5 Identify the type of evidence often obtained in sex offense investigations.

LO6 Identify what evidence to seek in date rape investigations.

LO7 Explain what blind reporting is and what its advantages are in sexual assault investigations.

LO8 Identify the three federal statutes that form the basis for sex offender registries.

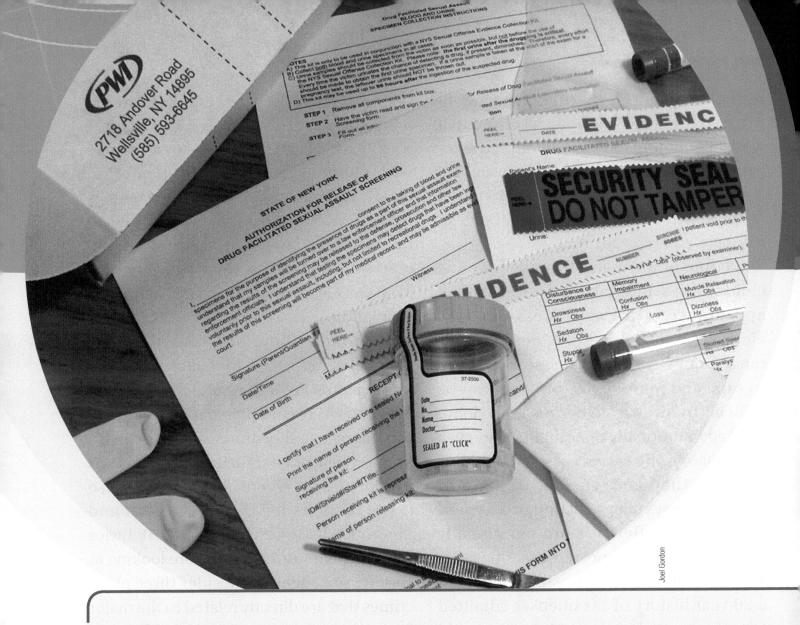

Joel Gordon

Introduction

It was a typical March day on a Florida beach—spring breakers in bikinis and swim trunks, loud music, and drinking—everyone having fun in the sun. At one point, a group of people begins to gather around a woman in a beach chair. She appears semiconscious, and the crowd has grown, not because anyone is worried about her but because she is being sexually assaulted by two young men. The other beachgoers simply stand around and watch. The assault may have gone undetected and unpunished had it not been captured on video by a cell phone, video that only came to light following a shooting a week later at a spring-break beach house party. The sheriff who was part of the investigation described the footage, which shows several men surrounding an incapacitated women on a beach chair, as "very, very graphic," calling it the "most disgusting, sickening thing" he had ever seen. During the follow-up with the victim, she told police she did not remember the incident well enough to report it, adding she suspected she may have been drugged prior to the assault. The sheriff's department released the video "to show the crowd that was surrounding the incident and to show people, not only was it a horrible event, but it was witnessed by so many people who did absolutely nothing to stop or call police" (Associated Press, 2015).

People of any age—from very young children to senior citizens, regardless of appearance or attractiveness—may be victims of sexual assault. Sex offenses range from **voyeurism** (the peeping Tom) to rape and murder. Sex offenses can be difficult to investigate because the victim is often emotionally distraught. Moreover, investigating officers may be uncomfortable because they lack special training in interviewing sex offense victims or offenders.

Some sex offenders are emotionally disturbed and feel no remorse for their actions. For example, a 38-year-old man with a 20-year history of sex offenses admitted to a prison psychiatrist that even he could

not remember how many rapes and sexual assaults he had committed. The suspect also talked freely about his sexual exploits with children and showed no emotion at all. A **pedophile**—a person who is sexually attracted to young children—can be extremely dangerous, as can a **sadist**, a person who derives sexual gratification from causing pain to others, often through mutilation.

Although some sex offenders are emotionally disturbed, the fact remains that most victims know their attacker and that most attacks occur not in dark alleys but in living rooms and bedrooms. Research also shows evidence that sexual assault is common in relationships where physical abuse also exists (Centers for Disease Control and Prevention [CDC], 2018; Engel, 2020; Taylor & Gaskin-Laniyan, 2007). Before looking at specific sex offenses, consider three other crimes that are directly related to the major focus of this chapter—sexual assault.

Investigating Obscene Telephone Calls and Texts

Obscene phone calls or text messages are not only harassing invasions of privacy but can also be stressful and frightening. Many people, including juveniles, are victims of obscene or harassing texting, which may include threats or obscene pictures and may be random or intentional. **Sexting** is the act of sending, receiving, or forwarding sexually explicit pictures or messages via email or text message. If the photo contains sexual images of a minor, the person sending the photo could be investigated for distribution of child pornography and, if convicted, may be required to register as a sex offender. Sexting can lead to serious issues because the original message is often shared through additional text messages, email, and social media. The publicized cases of several tragic

suicides in recent years have drawn attention to the bullying and torment victims often endure following an act of sexting.

Sextortion, a relatively newly defined offense, is a serious crime that occurs when an offender threatens to distribute a victim's private and sensitive material unless the victim provides images of a sexual nature, sexual favors, or money (Federal Bureau of Investigation [FBI], 2015). Offenders may also threaten to harm the victim's friends or relatives by using information obtained from the victim's electronic devices unless demands are met. Online perpetrators gain victims' trust by pretending to be someone they are not. Offenders often lurk in chat rooms and record young people who post or livestream sexually explicit images and videos of themselves, or they may hack into victims' electronic devices using malware to gain access to files and surreptitiously control victims' web cameras and microphones. Sextortion involving children is discussed further in Chapter 11.

Making obscene telephone calls is a crime. Recall that this is a frequent form of harassing stalking behavior. Police departments receive complaints of many types of harassment calls that are not of a sexual nature and have established procedures for investigating such calls. The same procedures apply to phone calls with sexual implications.

In most obscene phone calls, the callers want to remain anonymous, using the phone as a barrier between themselves and their victims. The callers receive sexual or psychological gratification from making contact with victims, even from a distance. Calls involving sexual connotations are threatening to the victims because they have no way of knowing the caller's true intent. Although such calls may be made randomly, the caller knows the victim in many cases.

If the victim wants to press charges, the first step is to make a police report. The next contact may be the phone company. The front section of most telephone directories and the websites of phone companies provide information about what constitutes a violation of the law and phone company regulations as well as instructions about what to do if a person receives obscene or harassing calls (stay calm, do not respond, and quietly hang up the phone; if the calls persist, call the phone company).

Caller ID may discourage obscene calls, although a caller may still be able to block their name, phone number, or both, or use an untraceable phone or app to hide identifying information. Furthermore, "phone spoofing," in which suspects cover or alter the source of their phone number information by using other existing ones, can provide another challenge in locating a suspect in police investigations. Victims may sign an affidavit allowing police to put a trap and trace on their phone which helps identify incoming phone numbers.

Police can use legal resources to identify service providers to a certain phone number, information that can be used to retrieve further suspect information. Police also have access to where calls were made from, how many times a number was called, and the duration of each call. Phone numbers that are not assigned to certain individuals, such as pay-as-you-go phones, cannot necessarily be traced to a specific person.

Investigating Prostitution

The U.S. Department of Justice (2014) defines **prostitution** as "a sexual act or contact with another person in return for giving or receiving a fee or a thing of value." Prostitution exacerbates community issues such as public health and safety by contributing to the spread of venereal disease and HIV, and with profits often going to organized crime. Of special concern to law enforcement officers is the practice of enticing very young girls into prostitution. Legislation—for example, the Mann Act—attempts to prevent such actions. Section 2423 of the Act prohibits "coercion or enticement of minor females and the taking of male or female persons across the state line for immoral purposes."

Studies show that many women enter prostitution as minors. One study of 60 prostitutes in Seattle, Washington, found that all of them had begun prostituting between the ages of 12 and 14 (Farley, 2018). Factors that lead women into prostitution, and which tragically keep many of them trapped there, include poverty; lack of educational or legitimate employment opportunities; and prior physical, sexual, or emotional victimization. One of the most commonly recognized precursors to prostitution is childhood abuse, with some experts calling childhood sexual abuse a type of "boot camp" for later prostitution (Farley, 2018).

Prostitutes experience extremely high rates of physical and sexual violence, victimizations that some call part of the job description for prostitution (Farley, 2020). Prostitutes are also at increased risk of fatal victimization, and their homicides are known to be particularly difficult to investigate (Chan & Beauregard, 2019). According to Salfati and Sorochinski (2019): "Sex workers as a group are one of the more common targets in serial homicide, yet the most likely to go unsolved. Part of the reason for this is the difficulty in linking individual crime scenes to a series, especially in those series where offenders not only target sex worker victims but also target non–sex worker victims."

A longitudinal study spanning more than three decades found that the general profile of an offender who murdered a prostitute was a male in his early 30s who committed the homicide against a female of similar age range and most commonly used an edged weapon, firearm, or personal weapon (Chan & Beauregard, 2019). Another study, this one of serial prostitute murderers, showed that the time of the first murder in their series:

- 25.9% of offenders were married

- 40.7% lived as dependents of either family members or intimate partners

- 14.8% were homeless

- 51.8% had a high school diploma or higher educational level, with 40.7% having some college education

- 22.2% had prior military service

- 70.4% were employed either part- or full-time at the time of the first homicide

- 92.6% had a prior arrest record

- 11.1% were formally diagnosed by a mental health professional with a psychiatric disorder

(Morton, Tillman, & Gaines, 2015)

In this study, offenders ranged in age from 21 to 43 years old, and the racial make-up was 55.6% Black, 33.3% white, 7.4% Hispanic, and 3.7% other (Morton et al., 2015). Most of the murders (34.4%) occurred at the offenders' residences, followed by outdoor public areas (26.0%) and the offenders' vehicles (17.5%). The most common cause of death (63.0%) was strangulation, followed by blunt force trauma (17.5%). The majority (82.5%) of victims' bodies were disposed at outdoor public areas. It is hoped that such knowledge might help detectives identify suspects and conduct their investigations more efficiently and thoroughly.

In some cases, the women involved are trafficked, presenting another challenge to law enforcement.

Investigating Human Trafficking

The Thirteenth Amendment to the U.S. Constitution, ratified in 1865, states, "Neither slavery nor involuntary servitude, except as a punishment for crime whereof the party shall have been duly convicted, shall exist within the United States, or any place subject to their jurisdiction." But it has yet to be abolished in this country. **Human trafficking**, also called *trafficking in persons (TIP)*, is a modern form of slavery, the two most severe types of which are:

- *Commercial sex trafficking* in which a commercial sex act is induced by force, fraud, or coercion, or in which the person induced to perform such an act has not attained 18 years of age. For cases in which the sex trafficking involves a minor, it is not necessary to prove force, fraud, or coercion.

- *Labor trafficking*, which involves the recruitment, harboring, transportation, provision, or obtaining of a person for labor or services through the use of force, fraud, or coercion for the purpose of subjecting that person to involuntary servitude, forced labor, peonage, debt bondage, or slavery. (U.S. Department of State, 2020, p. 10)

A person can be a victim of both sex trafficking and labor trafficking.

It is important to recognize that the defining element of human trafficking is *exploitation*, not *movement*, although movement can occur. A person may be considered a trafficking victim regardless of whether they were born into a state of servitude, were transported to the exploitative situation, were exploited in their hometown, previously consented to work for a trafficker, or participated in a crime as a direct result of being trafficked. The central element is the traffickers' aim to exploit and enslave their victims through coercion and deception. Figure 10.1 illustrates three elements of trafficking.

| **Myth** | Trafficking requires the crossing of international borders. |
| **Fact** | Trafficking victims can be enslaved in their own country, including the United States. |

Human trafficking, a multibillion-dollar global industry, is one of the world's fastest growing and most profitable criminal activities, operating on the same scale as the illegal trade of arms and drugs. Sex trafficking occurs in communities throughout the country, regardless of cultural composition or level of affluence: "No community is immune from being affected by the exploitation of human beings for commercial sexual activity" (U.S. Department of Justice, 2016).

The International Labor Organization (ILO) estimates that 3.8 million adults and 1.0 million children across the globe were victims of commercial sexual exploitation in 2016, the vast majority (99%) of which were women and girls (International Labour Organization and Walk Free Foundation, 2017). Data regarding the full scope of human trafficking in the United States is difficult to come by, in large part because of the hidden and complex nature of the crime, yet most sources believe it to be trending upward. The U.S. National Human Trafficking Hotline reported a nearly 20 percent increase in contacts from trafficking victims and survivors from 2018 to 2019 and identified 11,500 trafficking situations in 2019 (Polaris Project, 2019). Of those situations, 8,248 cases involved sex trafficking alone, with 14,597 individual victims and survivors identified. Another 505 situations involved both sex and labor trafficking, with 1,048 individual victims

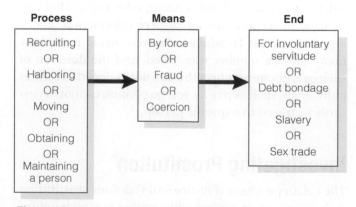

Figure 10.1
Three elements of trafficking.

Source: Reprinted from *The crime of human trafficking: A law enforcement guide to identification and investigation.* www.theiacp.org/documents/pdfs/rcd/completehtguide.pdf. Copyright held by the International Association of Chiefs of Police, 515 North Washington Street, Alexandria, VA 22314 USA. Further reproduction without express written permission from IACP is strictly prohibited.

and survivors identified. The average age of victims at the time their sex trafficking began was 17. It is worth noting that, with the exception of situations involving children, the Hotline will not contact law enforcement without the victim's consent. The sex trafficking of children is discussed further in Chapter 11.

The Trafficking Victims Protection Act (TVPA), signed into law in October 2000 and reauthorized in 2003, 2005, 2008, 2013, and 2017, was passed to (1) address the problem of trafficking in persons and (2) provide for protection and assistance for victims, prosecution of offenders, and prevention efforts internationally. While the U.S. Department of Justice (DOJ) has long enforced criminal laws against involuntary servitude and slavery, the enactment of the TVPA was a turning point that set forth a strategy often referred to as the "3P" paradigm: the *prosecution* of traffickers, the *protection* of victims, and the *prevention* of the crime. Partnerships, considered a fourth "P," between federal, state, local, and tribal agencies are the most effective ways to investigate human trafficking. The FBI operates Child Exploitation and Human Trafficking Task Forces in nearly every FBI field office in the country, with their goal being to recover victims and investigate traffickers at the state and federal level (FBI, n.d.).

Between January 2008 and June 2010, federally funded human trafficking task forces opened 2,515 suspected incidents for investigation, 82% of which were classified as suspected sex trafficking cases (Banks & Kyckelhahn, 2011). Investigations confirmed and identified 460 sex trafficking victims and 63 labor trafficking victims. More than half (53.9%) of the sex trafficking victims were age 17 or younger, the great majority (93.9%) were female, and most (75%) were U.S. citizens or U.S. nationals (Table 10.1).

TABLE 10.1 Victim Characteristics in Cases Confirmed to Be Human Trafficking by High Data Quality Task Forces, by Type of Trafficking

Victim Characteristic	Total[a]	Sex Trafficking	Labor Trafficking
Sex			
Male	49	27	20
Female	477	432	43
Age			
17 or younger	257	248	6
18–24	159	142	17
25–34	68	46	22
35 or older	27	12	15
Unknown	16	12	3
Race/Hispanic origin			
White[b]	106	102	1
Black/African American[b]	167	161	6
Hispanic/Latino origin	129	95	34
Asian[b, c]	26	17	9
Other[b, d]	35	23	11
Unknown	63	61	2
Citizenship			
U.S. Citizen/U.S. National	346	345	1
Permanent U.S. resident[e]	6	6	0
Undocumented alien[f]	101	64	36
Qualified alien[e]	19	1	15
Temporary worker	2	0	2
Unknown	50	41	9
Number of victims identified	527	460	63

Note: Analysis restricted to cases opened and observed between January 2008 and June 2010 in high data quality task forces.

[a]Includes cases of unknown trafficking type.

[b]Excludes persons of Hispanic or Latino origin.

[c]Asian may include Native Hawaiian and other Pacific Islanders or persons of East Asian or Southeast Asian descent.

[d]Includes persons of two or more races.

[e]Permanent residents and qualified aliens are legal residents in the United States but do not have citizenship.

[f]Undocumented aliens reside in the United States illegally.

Source: Banks, D., & Kyckelhahn, T. (2011, April). *Characteristics of suspected human trafficking incidents, 2008–2010.* Washington, DC: Bureau of Justice Statistics, Special Report. (NCJ 233732). Retrieved September 10, 2020, from www.bjs.gov/content/pub/pdf/cshti0810.pdf, p. 6, Table 5.

TABLE 10.2 Characteristics of Human-Trafficking Defendants in Cases Charged in U.S. District Court, 2015

Characteristic	Total Number	Total Percent	Peonage, slavery, forced labor, and sex trafficking Number	Peonage, slavery, forced labor, and sex trafficking Percent	Production of child pornography Number	Production of child pornography Percent	Transportation for illegal sex activity Number	Transportation for illegal sex activity Percent
Number of defendants	964	100%	283	100%	370	100%	311	100%
Sex								
Male	849	88.3%	215	76.0%	341	92.4%	293	94.5%
Female	113	11.7	68	24.0	28	7.6	17	5.5
Race/Hispanic origin[a]								
White	515	56.9%	53	20.4%	271	77.0%	191	65.2%
Black	219	24.2	157	60.4	29	8.2	33	11.3
Hispanic	157	17.3	46	17.7	47	13.4	64	21.8
American Indian or Alaska Native	6	0.7	1	0.4	3	0.9	2	0.7
Asian, Native Hawaiian, or Other Pacifc Islander	8	0.9	3	1.2	2	0.6	3	1.0
Age								
17 or younger	1	0.1%	1	0.4%	0	0.0%	0	0.0%
18–19	22	2.3	14	4.9	5	1.4	3	1.0
20–24	151	15.7	69	24.4	43	11.6	39	12.6
25–29	214	22.2	88	31.1	66	17.8	60	19.4
30–34	146	15.2	42	14.8	62	16.8	42	13.5
35–39	127	13.2	31	11.0	53	14.3	43	13.9
40–44	100	10.4	17	6.0	49	13.2	34	11.0
45–49	71	7.4	6	2.1	34	9.2	31	10.0
50–54	54	5.6	7	2.5	29	7.8	18	5.8
55–59	39	4.0	4	1.4	14	3.8	21	6.8
60–64	19	2.0	2	0.7	8	2.2	9	2.9
65 or older	19	2.0	2	0.7	7	1.9	10	3.2
Median age	33 years		27 years		35 years		35 years	
Citizenship								
U.S. citizen	896	93.9%	256	92.1%	355	96.5%	285	92.5%
Legal alien	28	2.9	13	4.7	6	1.6	9	2.9
Illegal alien	30	3.1	9	3.2	7	1.9	14	4.5
Education level								
Less than high school	182	22.2%	91	38.4%	52	16.5%	39	14.7%
High school graduate	283	34.6	77	32.5	121	38.4	85	32.0
Some college	242	29.6	58	24.5	89	28.3	95	35.7
College graduate	111	13.6	11	4.6	53	16.8	47	17.7
Marital status								
Single	418	49.9%	154	65.8%	142	43.2%	122	44.4%
Married or cohabitating	231	27.6	50	21.4	93	28.3	88	32.0
Divorced or separated	189	22.6	30	12.8	94	28.6	65	23.6
Criminal record[b]								
No prior convictions	477	49.5%	84	29.7%	209	56.5%	184	59.4%
Prior misdemeanor only	189	19.6	69	24.4	70	18.9	50	16.1
Prior felony conviction	297	30.8	130	45.9	91	24.6	76	24.5

Note: The unit of count was a defendant interviewed, investigated, or supervised by federal pretrial services. Percentages are based on nonmissing records. Data were missing for sex (2), race/Hispanic origin (59), age (1), citizenship (10), education level (146), marital status (126), and prior conviction (1).

[a]Excludes persons of Hispanic or Latino origin, unless specifed.

[b]Includes both federal and state convictions.

Source: Motivans, M., & Snyder, H. N. (2018, June). Federal prosecution of human-trafficking cases, 2015. Washington, DC: Bureau of Justice Statistics, Special Report. (NCJ 251390). Retrieved September 10, 2020 from https://www.bjs.gov/content/pub/pdf/fphtc15.pdf

In addition to being aware of the characteristics of victims of sex trafficking, investigators may also benefit from knowing about the characteristics of human trafficking defendants (Table 10.2). The majority (88.3%) of human trafficking defendants were male, white (56.9%), single (49.9%), U.S. citizens (93.3%), with no prior convictions (49.5%). The median age was 33 years (Motivans & Snyder, 2018).

Trafficking versus Smuggling

Confusion often exists regarding the differences between trafficking and smuggling, and some incorrectly consider them to be synonymous. But several key differences are noted between these two distinct and separate crimes, as shown in Table 10.3. It is important for investigators to recognize that a smuggling incident can turn into a human trafficking incident. For example, if a man initially consents to being smuggled illegally across a country's borders and pays for this service but then, after entering the destination country, is told he owes more money and is forced to work 18 hours a day in a warehouse until his debt is paid, he has now become a victim of human trafficking.

> **LO1** Identify the key distinction between human trafficking and human smuggling.
>
> The key distinction between human trafficking and smuggling lies in the individual's freedom of choice.

Victimology

No single profile of "the human trafficking victim" exists. Human trafficking victims come from all walks of life and are enslaved in many different settings.

Victims can be anyone, regardless of race, color, national origin, disability, religion, age, gender, sexual orientation, gender identity, socioeconomic status, or citizenship status. While there is no defining characteristic that all victims share, traffickers frequently prey on individuals who are poor, vulnerable, living in an unsafe situation, or are in search of a better life. These victims are deceived by false promises of love, a good job, or a stable life and lured into situations where they are forced to work under deplorable conditions with little to no pay. Whether made to work in agriculture, a factory, or a strip club, forced into commercial sex, or abused in a home as a domestic servant, federal law recognizes these people as victims of human trafficking.

The cases tell stories of a single trafficker who works alone to deceive and prey on victims; of families that have been in the business of human trafficking for generations; and of front businesses that appear legitimate at first glance but disguise human trafficking. Prosecutors have successfully demonstrated that someone can be enslaved without chains and that traffickers often go beyond physical abuse and use extreme forms of psychological abuse that exploit vulnerabilities to maintain control over victims and prevent them from escaping. To achieve their ends, traffickers instill fear of arrest or deportation, use threats of harm to a family member, perpetuate shame or guilt about what is happening, and warn of financial ruin. These experiences are traumatizing and

TABLE 10.3 Human Trafficking versus Human Smuggling

Key Feature	Human Trafficking	Human Smuggling
Voluntariness	Involuntary—Victims are forced, coerced, or defrauded into trafficking.	Voluntary—Individuals consent to be smuggled.
Nature of the crime	Trafficking is a crime committed against an individual person.	Smuggling is a crime committed against a border or country.
Physical movement	Not required. Trafficking can be domestic or transnational.	Requires an illegal border crossing. Smuggling is always transnational.
Citizenship	Victims can be U.S. citizens or foreign nationals.	Those being smuggled are always foreign nationals.
Basis of action	Exploitation-based. No benefit to the victim.	Service- and transportation-based. Transactional. A foreign national pays a fee for the service of being transported over a border illegally.

Sources: Adapted from:

Administration for Children and Families. (2017, November 21). *Fact sheet: Human trafficking.* Washington, DC: Author. Retrieved September 10, 2020, from www.acf.hhs.gov/sites/default/files/otip/fact_sheet_human_trafficking_fy18.pdf

Human Smuggling and Trafficking Center. (2016, June 15). *Human trafficking vs. human smuggling.* Washington, DC: Author. Retrieved September 10, 2020, from ctip.defense.gov/Portals/12/Documents/HSTC_Human%20Trafficking%20vs.%20Human%20Smuggling%20Fact%20Sheet.pdf?ver=2016-07-14-145555-320 often result in psychological dissociation, distrust, and gaps in the victim's memory that make recounting a clear and complete story difficult. In addition, traffickers sometimes promote drug dependencies among their victims, keeping the victims reliant on the trafficker for access to the substances that fuel addiction.

(President's Interagency Task Force to Monitor and Combat Trafficking in Persons, 2014, p. 6)

The common denominator among trafficking victims is vulnerability, and in the United States, some of the most vulnerable populations include recent migrants and undocumented workers; runaways, "throw-aways," homeless youth, and those involved in the child welfare system; individuals with substance abuse or addiction issues; individuals with mental health concerns; and those living in or near poverty (Polaris Project, 2019; Office for Victims of Justice Training and Technical Assistance Center, n.d.)

Challenges to Investigation

While movement is not a requirement of this crime, it is true that many instances of human trafficking involve transporting victims across international borders, leading to considerable jurisdictional and investigatory challenges for law enforcement. However, much of the human trafficking problem in the United States involves people who were either born here or are here with valid purpose and have since become ensnared in trafficking. Regardless of whether they have crossed the border illegally or not, a significant challenge is identifying victims and perpetrators of human trafficking.

Indicators of Human Trafficking. Law enforcement professionals often must rely on their instincts to notice "red flags" that might indicate someone is a victim or perpetrator of human trafficking because the settings and locations where such activity occurs do not always appear suspicious (Office for Victims, n.d.). Red flags that may suggest an individual is a victim of human trafficking include:

- A person whose movement and activities appear to be closely controlled or monitored by another

- A person who works excessive hours but receives little or no pay. This person may be told that payment is on its way or that their pay is being used for expenses, like housing or food.

- A person who works excessive hours and is fearful of discussing working conditions or is unaware that unsafe conditions are unlawful

- A person who has little or no idea where they are geographically located and is always transported to and from the worksite

- An able-bodied person who never leaves home without an escort

- A person who is fearful of discussing their relationship to a person who appears to have physical control over them

- Groups of workers who are transported in and out of labor locations covertly and under controlled conditions

- Foreign national adults or minors who are not in possession of their documents, particularly if they say that someone else has them

- A person with unexplained physical injuries or signs of abuse

- Unusual activity at a residential home or business, such as many different cars coming and going late at night

- A minor engaged in commercial sexual activities

- A minor or young adult who expresses interest in or is in an intimate relationship with a much older individual

- Frequenting Internet chat rooms or sites known for recruitment

- Going on unexplained shopping trips or having expensive clothing, jewelry, or a cell phone

- Using language from "the life" among peers, or referring to a boyfriend as "daddy"

- Inconsistencies in their story about where they stay or who is their guardian

- Constant communication with multiple men; evidence in phone of names with monetary amounts

- Reluctance to explain a tattoo

- Keeping late nights or unusual hours; vagueness regarding whereabouts

Keep in mind that not all indicators are present in every case of human trafficking, and the presence of any one or combination of the indicators is not necessarily proof of human trafficking.

Recognizing Traffickers. Recognizing individuals who perpetrate human trafficking is also a challenge for law enforcement. Human traffickers can be U.S. citizens or foreign nationals; males or females; individuals, business owners, gangs, or criminal enterprises; and family members, intimate partners, long-time friends, acquaintances, or strangers to their victims. Many human traffickers share ethnic or cultural backgrounds with their victims, enabling the traffickers to better understand, gain the trust of, and ultimately exploit their victims. Investigators should be aware of the tactics commonly used by traffickers to control of their victims, such as:

- Using or threatening to use violence

- Withholding basic necessities such as water, food, or sleep

- Threatening deportation

- Restricting contact with family and friends

- Making false promises

(Hammond-Deckard, 2014)

Overlap with Other Crimes. Human trafficking often intersects with other crimes, including:

- Adult and child pornography

- Arms trafficking (as "expendable" carriers)

- Assault

- Criminal street gang activities

- Domestic violence

- Drug trafficking (as human "vessels")

- Immigration violations and visa fraud

- Incest

- Kidnapping

- Money laundering

- Organized crime

- Petty theft

- Prostitution

- Sexual assault

- Traffic violations

- Workplace violations

(Office for Victims, n.d.)

Investigators should be ever mindful that victims of human trafficking are frequently forced by their captors to commit other crimes. There has been more than one case involving trafficking victims who are forced to commit commercial sex acts but then are arrested and prosecuted for prostitution or prostitution-related activity. However, failing to recognize such "criminals" as victims is truly a missed opportunity in the effort to combat human trafficking and may actually deepen the bond between the victim and their trafficker. Adults who are forced into commercial sexual activities are not criminals and should not be treated as such, even if they appear to be willing participants at first (Hammond-Deckard, 2014).

Gaining Victim and Witness Cooperation. Gaining victim cooperation is a challenge in many investigations, but it can be particularly difficult with victims of human trafficking. One reason is the formation of a trauma bond that a sex trafficking victim makes with the person who is exploiting them, a phenomenon commonly referred to as the *Stockholm Syndrome*. A **trauma bond** is a dysfunctional attachment formed in the presence of danger, shame, or exploitation (Gorbett & Anderson, 2018).

Some research has found that the trauma bonding experienced by adolescents who are commercially sexually exploited is different from other types of trauma bonding (Sanchez, Speck, & Patrician, 2019). This discovery has led to a refinement in terminology and the recognition of *trauma-coercive bonding* or *trauma-coercive attachment*, a long process in which victims of sex trafficking develop a powerful emotional dependency on their abusers and lose their sense of self (Doychak & Raghavan, 2020). The trauma experienced by human trafficking victims can be so deep and damaging that many may not even identify themselves as victims or ask for help (Hammond-Deckard, 2014).

Another reason it is often difficult to get victims and witnesses to cooperate in trafficking investigations and prosecutions is because they may be in the United States illegally. A partial solution is available in the form of "T visas," a limited visa option that helps overcome the reluctance of those who are here illegally by allowing them to remain in the country to testify against human traffickers and their criminal endeavors. The U.S. Citizenship and Immigration Services (CIS) website states: "T nonimmigrant status is a temporary immigration benefit that enables certain victims of a severe form of human trafficking to remain in the United States for up to 4 years if they have assisted law enforcement in an investigation or prosecution of human trafficking. T nonimmigrant status is also available for certain qualifying family members of trafficking victims" (2018).

Interviewing Survivors of Human Trafficking

A critical part of a successful trafficking investigation hinges on the interview with a suspected victim. Building rapport is the first step in interviewing sex trafficking survivors, and any approach should be a gradual and nonthreatening process. Understand that it may take several interviews for the survivor to finally open up about their experience. Use trauma-informed techniques during questioning which apply compassionate, victim-centered practices to avoid retraumatizing the trafficking survivor (Milam, Borrello, & Pooler, 2017; International Association of Chiefs of Police, 2020). For example, instead of saying, "Start at the beginning and tell me how you ended up as a prostitute," ask, "Where would you like to start?" If a survivor shows bonding with their trafficker and uses words such as "my boyfriend," use that language in your questioning instead of "your abuser" or "the man who made you have sex with other men." Do not be surprised if a survivor:

- Denies they are or ever were a victim

- Is fearful of what will happen to them

- Is fearful of you and what you will do to them

- Is distracted, angry, reluctant, or concerned about their own needs

- Has fears about their safety and privacy, particularly if the interview is in front of others

> (Office for Victims of Justice Training and Technical Assistance Center, n.d.)

Be aware that the survivor may have unmet medical needs, including lack of food or sleep, and give the victim some control in the situation (breaks, water, where they sit). When obtaining preliminary information, use a conversational approach instead of a rapid series of questions and avoid physical contact with the survivor. As with any victim interview, asking open-ended questions may elicit more information from trafficking survivors than yes or no questions.

Developing an Effective Response to Human Trafficking

While many officers may never encounter a case of human trafficking during their career, no jurisdiction is immune to the potential for this crime. The Polaris Project, named after the North Star, which guided slaves to freedom in the United States, operates the National Human Trafficking Resource Center hotline and reports that in 2019 the hotline received reports of human trafficking cases from all 50 states and Washington, D.C. (2019).

As mentioned, partnerships are crucial in responding effectively to the crime of human trafficking. The DOJ, Department of Homeland Security (DHS), and Department of Labor (DOL) have collaborated in developing high-impact human trafficking investigations through the formation of antitrafficking coordination teams (ACTeams), developed regional strategic plans, implemented coordinated strategies, and disseminated ACTeams operations guides (U.S. DHS, 2016). Data shows that in those jurisdictions where ACTeams were convened, the number of human trafficking cases filed, defendants charged, and defendants convicted increased significantly compared to jurisdictions without ACTeams. Local agencies may find the assistance of these resources invaluable in conducting human trafficking investigations.

Classification of Sex Offenses

While many investigators may never work a human trafficking case involving commercial sexual exploitation, there is a high likelihood they will need to investigate other sex offenses during their career. Sex crimes are sometimes classified according to whether they involve physical aggression and a victim—for example, rape—or are victimless acts between consenting adults, such as consensual sodomy. The former are most frequently reported to police and investigated. The latter are often simply offensive to others and are seldom reported or investigated.

Sex offenses include bigamy, child molestation, incest, indecent exposure, prostitution, sodomy, and rape (*sexual assault*). **Bigamy** is marrying another person when one or both parties are already married. **Child molestation** is usually a felony and includes lewd and lascivious acts, indecent exposure, incest, or statutory rape involving a child, male or female, under age 14. This is a difficult charge to prove because children frequently are not believed. Moreover, parents are often reluctant to bring charges in such cases. (This offense is discussed in depth in the next chapter.)

Incest is sexual intercourse between family members or close relatives, including children related by adoption. **Indecent exposure** is revealing one's genitals to another person to such an extent as to shock the other's sense of decency. It is not necessary to prove intent. The offense is a misdemeanor, although repeated offenses can be charged as a felony in many states. Ordinarily, **exhibitionists**—those who expose themselves—are not dangerous but may become so if they are humiliated or abused.

Sodomy is any form of anal or oral copulation. Although commonly thought of as being performed by homosexual males, sodomy can occur between a male and female, between two females, or between a human and an animal (bestiality). Oral or anal penetration must be proven. Both parties are guilty if the act is voluntary. When sodomy is a private act between consenting adults, it is difficult to obtain sufficient evidence for prosecution. In some states, sodomy between consenting adults is no longer a crime. Such acts between adults and juveniles remain crimes, however.

While state statutes vary considerably in the wording of their definitions, **rape**—or sexual assault—is broadly defined as nonconsensual sexual intercourse or sexual penetration of one person by another. Rape is usually considered the most serious crime after murder and carries a heavy penalty in most states. It is now viewed as a violent assault rather than a type of deviance.

Terminology commonly used when investigating sex offenses includes:

- **Cunnilingus.** Sexual activity involving oral contact with the female genitals.

- **Digital penetration.** The act of using fingers (digits) to penetrate or manipulate sexual organs that include the penis, vagina, and anus.

- **Fellatio.** Sexual activity involving oral contact with the male genitals.

- **Intimate parts.** Usually refers to the primary genital areas, groin, inner thighs, buttocks, and breasts.

- **Oral copulation.** The same as cunnilingus and fellatio; the act of joining the mouth of one person with the sex organ of another person.

- **Penetration.** Any intrusion, however slight, of any part of a person's body or any object manipulated or inserted by a person into the genital or anal openings of another's body, including sexual intercourse in its ordinary meaning.

- **Sadomasochistic abuse.** Fettering, binding, or otherwise physically restraining; whipping; or torturing for sexual gratification.

- **Sexual contact.** Includes any act committed without the complainant's consent for the suspect's sexual or aggressive satisfaction, such as touching the complainant's intimate parts, forcing another person to touch one's intimate parts, or forcing another person to touch the complainant's intimate parts. In any of these cases, the body area may be clothed or unclothed.

- **Sexual penetration.** Includes sexual intercourse, cunnilingus, fellatio, anal intercourse, or any other intrusion, no matter how slight, into the victim's genital, oral, or anal openings by the suspect's body or by an object. An emission of semen is not required. Any act of sexual penetration by the suspect without the affirmative, freely given permission of the victim to the specific act of penetration constitutes the crime of sexual assault.

- **Sexually explicit conduct.** Any type of sexual intercourse between persons of the same or opposite sex, bestiality, sadomasochistic abuse, lewd exhibition, or mutual masturbation.

Rape/Sexual Assault

Laws regarding rape and sexual assault vary widely by state, with some states using only one term or the other; some defining both rape and sexual assault as separate, distinct acts; some using a different term altogether, such as "unlawful sexual conduct" or "sexual battery"; and some defining varying degrees of the crime (similar to degrees of murder). Investigators must know the laws of their state and what the specific elements of the crime are if they are to effectively build a case for prosecution. In this chapter, the words *rape* and *sexual assault* are used synonymously and interchangeably. Although males report a significant number of rapes every year, women are by far the predominant victims. In view of that, this discussion assumes that the victim is usually female and the suspect male. Rape is often classified as either forcible or statutory.

> ## LO2 Differentiate between the two typical classifications of rape.
>
> **Forcible rape** is sexual intercourse against a person's will by the use or threat of force. **Statutory rape** is sexual intercourse with a minor, with or without consent.

A distinction is made in the research literature between forcible rape and two other kinds of rape: drug- or alcohol-facilitated rape and incapacitated rape. In a *drug-facilitated* or *alcohol-facilitated rape*, the perpetrator deliberately drugs the victim or tries to get the victim drunk and then commits the rape. An *incapacitated rape* (IR) refers to attempted or completed penetration that occurs while a victim is incapacitated because of consumption of alcohol or other drugs (Carey, Durney, Shepardson, & Carey, 2015). Either of these two types of sexual assault may also be called *date rape*, which is discussed shortly.

National estimates present a murky view of the number of sexual assault victims. The victimization figures reported by different sources seldom concur, a situation that is recognized as occurring with other types of offenses besides rape. Specifically, the FBI's Uniform Crime Reports (UCR) capture only those incidents reported to police, whereas the National Crime Victimization Study (NCVS) captures both reported and unreported events. A more troublesome complication is that some of the reporting instruments capture data pertaining only to sexual assaults of females. For example, until 2013, the UCR Program employed the legacy definition of rape, which is "the carnal knowledge of a female forcibly and against her will." A revised definition removes the term *forcible* and now classifies rape as "penetration, no matter how slight, of the vagina or anus with any body part or object, or oral penetration by a sex organ of another person, without the consent of the victim." This revised definition broadens the scope of the previously narrow (legacy) definition by capturing gender neutrality, the penetration of any bodily orifice, penetration by any object or body part, and offenses in which physical force is not involved (*Reporting Rape in 2013*, 2014). Prior to 2014, UCR reports included only the legacy definition of rape, and as of 2017, the UCR statistics represent solely the revised definition.

According to the UCR, an estimated 139,380 rapes were reported to law enforcement in 2018 (FBI, 2018). The NCVS, however, indicates that 734,630 sexual assaults occurred in 2018, evidence of the serious underreporting of these crimes to law enforcement (Morgan &

Oudekerk, 2019). The CDC's National Intimate Partner and Sexual Violence Survey (NISVS) showed that approximately one in five women (21.3% or an estimated 25.5 million) in the United States reported a completed or attempted rape at some point in their lifetime, and 1.2% of women (roughly 1.5 million) reported a completed or attempted rape in the 12 months preceding the survey (Smith et al., 2018). This same survey revealed that approximately 2.6% of men (an estimated 2.8 million) experienced completed or attempted rape victimization at some point in their lifetime.

Of those individuals who had experienced completed or attempted rape victimization during their lifetime, 43.2% of females reported that their first victimization occurred prior to age 18, and 51.3% of males first experienced such victimization prior to age 18. An estimated 3.2 million females (12.7% of all female victims) and 738,000 males (26% of all male victims) first became sexual assault victims at age 10 or younger (Smith et al., 2018)

Results of large-scale national studies indicate that most sexual assault victims do not report the crime to police and as many as 95% of such assaults go undocumented (Lonsway & Archambault, 2010). Indeed, data from NCVS reveals that only 24.9% of sexual assaults were reported to the police in 2018 (Morgan & Oudekerk, 2019). A variety of reasons are given for the nonreporting of sex crimes, including ambiguity about what illicit sexual conduct is; fear of reprisal from the offender; not wanting to get the offender in trouble; belief that police would not or could not do anything to help; believing the crime to be a personal issue or too trivial to report; feelings of embarrassment and stigma; not wanting others to know; and criminal justice concerns when the victim's drug or alcohol use was involved (Cohn, Zinzow, Resnick, & Kilpatrick, 2013; Kimble & Chettiar, 2018).

Police officers are often asked whether it is better for a victim to resist or to submit to a sexual attack. Does resistance increase the attacker's violence? It is a difficult question to answer because researchers have arrived at different conclusions. Some results indicate that resisting reduces the likelihood of continued assault; other results indicate that it makes the attacker more violent. Some people who have been sexually assaulted reported that they fought back only after they had already been harmed, which would appear to preclude that resisting caused increased violence. It has been found that people who have been attacked previously are more apt to resist.

One study pointed out that in no other crime are victims expected to resist or not to resist their assailants. Everyone has a right to defend themselves, but whether it is more harmful to the victim to choose to defend is not possible to state. This must be an individual decision. Some police departments do not give advice on this question because of the possibility of lawsuits.

More emphasis should be placed on the attacker's behavior than on that of the victim. Increasing the penalty where the attacker uses extreme violence may help reduce the severity of the attacks, although this is problematic because of the emotional status and possible mental instability of this type of criminal.

Elements of the Crime of Rape

Although rape is defined in various ways by state laws, certain elements of the offense are fairly universal.

> **LO3** List the elements of sexual assault.
>
> The elements of the crime of rape or sexual assault include
>
> - Penetration, no matter how slight, of
>   - the victim's genital or anal openings by an object or any part of another person's body, including sexual intercourse in its ordinary meaning, or
>   - the victim's mouth by a sex organ of another person
> - without the consent of the victim.

Previous editions of this text listed "with a female other than the spouse" and "by force" as two of the requisite factors of the crime of sexual assault. However, marriage status, gender, and use of force are no longer relevant factors in the contemporary definition of rape. In fact, all 50 states have enacted laws against marital rape.

Penetration, No Matter How Slight. *Penetration*, no matter how slight, has replaced *sexual intercourse* as the first defining element of rape. Penetration includes any intrusion of the victim's sexual organs (penis, vagina) or anus by any object (inanimate or the suspect's body part) or any intrusion of the victim's mouth by the suspect's sex organ. This element includes sexual intercourse and does not require that a complete sex act accompanied by ejaculation occurred. An emission of semen is not required. Any act of sexual penetration by the suspect without the affirmative, freely given permission of the victim to the specific act of penetration constitutes the crime of sexual assault.

Committed Without the Consent of the Victim. A crucial element in sexual assault is the victim's lack of consent. A lack of consent can include the victim's inability to say "no" to intercourse due to the effects of drugs or alcohol, mental illness, emotional disturbance, or unconsciousness. By the same token, consent given because of fear or panic, or by a child is *not* considered true consent. One recent legal case highlights the difficulty this element presents when the sexual activity occurs between spouses, one of whom has dementia.

Challenges to Investigation

Sexual assaults are among the most difficult and challenging cases to investigate, as evidenced by the low clearance rate (33.4%) for forcible rape in 2018 (FBI, 2018). Special challenges to investigating rape include the sensitive nature of the offense, social attitudes regarding the act, and the victim's horror or embarrassment. A rape investigation requires great sensitivity and compassion on the part of the investigator.

> **Myth** Not saying "no" is the same as saying "yes."
>
> **Fact** There are many reasons why one partner may be unable to actively refuse consent to a sexual encounter, such as being under the influence of drugs or because of a cognitive or mental impairment. If consent is not expressly given by both partners, the act is considered a sexual assault.

Immediate reporting increases the chances of obtaining physical evidence. Unfortunately, many victims of sexual assault delay in reporting, if they choose to report at all. They often feel the urge to shower immediately, and they frequently need some time to process the attack before making the decision to call the police. This delay in reporting increases the challenge to investigators because it allows for contamination and diminishes, if not effectively eliminates, and any physical evidence, particularly biological evidence such as semen, blood, or hairs, that could be used to identify an unknown assailant or build a case for prosecution.

The Police Response

The initial call concerning a rape (or other sexual offense) is normally taken by the dispatcher, communications officer, or complaint clerk. The person taking the call immediately dispatches a patrol unit because rape is a felony and because it is a crime in which the offender may be known or close to the scene. The person taking the call then tells the victim to wait for the police to arrive if they are at a safe location and to not alter their physical appearance or touch anything at the scene. It is especially important to stress to the victim that, no matter how strong the urge to wash away any lingering presence of their attacker, they should *not* shower or douche before having a medical exam, as such activity will destroy or eliminate evidence that could be crucial in identifying and prosecuting the suspect. The victim is asked whether they can identify or describe the suspect, whether serious injuries were sustained during the assault, and whether medical assistance is needed immediately. As with any violent crime, early response is critical in apprehending the suspect and in reducing the victim's anxiety.

The first officers to arrive can make or break a rape case depending on how they approach the victim. All police officers should have special training in handling sexual assault victims. Whenever possible, an officer without such training should not be assigned to this kind of case.

As soon as you arrive at the scene, announce yourself clearly to allay fears the victim may have that the suspect is returning. Explain to the victim what is being done for their safety. If the rape has just occurred, if there are serious injuries, or if it appears the victim is in shock, call for an ambulance.

Protect the crime scene and broadcast a description of the assailant, means and direction of flight, and the time and exact location of the assault. Ascertain how the offender gained access to the victim because this helps investigators determine the scope of the crime scene and, if multiple scenes are involved, which might be primary versus secondary scenes. Establish a command post away from the scene to divert attention from the address of the victim and to preserve the scene. Conduct the preliminary investigation as described in Chapter 1. At a minimum, officers on the scene should:

- Record their arrival time.

- Determine the victim's location and condition.

- Request an ambulance if needed.

- Obtain identification of the suspect if possible.

- Determine whether the suspect is at the scene.

- Protect the crime scene.

- Identify and separate witnesses. Obtain valid identification from them and then obtain preliminary statements.

- Initiate crime broadcast if applicable.

- Log the identification of all people on the scene, including medical personnel.

Recognize the possibility that emergency medical personnel or other responders who must enter the scene before it is secure may leave behind contaminating hairs, fibers, and other evidence that could be mixed with that left by the suspect. Thus, documenting who was present allows investigators to request hair, DNA, or other biological samples from such individuals at a later date.

Information to Obtain

If a suspect is arrested at or near the scene, conduct a field identification. If much time has elapsed between the offense and the report, use other means of identification. If the victim knows the assailant, obtain the suspect's name, address, complete description, and the nature of the relationship with victim. Then obtain arrest and search warrants. If the suspect is unknown to the victim, check modus operandi (MO) files and have the victim look at photo files on sex offenders.

These MO factors are manifested in the offender's behavior and should be asked about when interviewing victims, as discussed shortly.

> **LO4** List what modus operandi factors are important in investigating a sexual assault.

MO factors important in investigating sex offenses include type of offense, words spoken, use of a weapon, actual method of attack, time of day, type of location, and victim's age and gender.

The victim may be unable to describe the suspect because of stress or darkness or because the perpetrator wore a mask or other identity-concealing clothing. A time lapse before reporting the offense can occur because of the victim's embarrassment, confusion, or shock or because the victim was taken to a remote area, giving the suspect time to escape.

If emergency medical personnel were on scene before the police, ask if they noticed any suspicious person or vehicle when they arrived or noticed any distinctive odors or sounds. Such evidence can help investigators identify a suspect.

Physical Evidence

Sometimes it is difficult to determine whether an assault or homicide is a sex-related crime. Evidence of sexual activity observable at the crime scene or on the victim's body includes torn or no clothing, seminal fluid on or near the body, bloodstains, condoms or condom wrappers, genital bruising or injury, and sexually suggestive positioning of the body (if the case is a homicide). Refer to Table 5.3 regarding how to collect, package, and store various types of evidence containing potential DNA.

Because biological evidence deteriorates rapidly, obtain it as soon as possible. Some police departments have rape kits that contain the equipment needed to collect, label, and preserve evidence. However, it is best practice to take a victim of a sexual assault directly to a hospital for an examination and collection of evidence.

Do not place sole focus on obtaining DNA evidence, because in a case of "he said, she said," there will be DNA evidence present, but its presence alone will not prove a sexual assault. In many other cases, no suspect DNA is found. Therefore, investigators should not overlook the importance of non-DNA evidence: "A wealth of other forensic evidence may be invaluable in sexual assault investigations; some examples are trace evidence (e.g., hairs, fibers, glass, paint, or soil), toxicology, cellphone and digital forensics, and impression and pattern evidence (e.g., fingerprints, shoe prints, tire marks, and handwriting) (Waltke et al., 2018). Research has found that, in addition to bodily fluids, fingerprints and hairs are the most common types of physical evidence located, collected, and examined in sexual assault cases (Johnson, Peterson, Sommers, & Baskin, 2012).

As in any crime, fingerprint evidence can be instrumental when trying to place a suspect at a crime scene. In certain cases of sexual assault, chemical analysis of condom lubricants may provide valuable evidence, given that many assailants are serial perpetrators and routinely use condoms to avoid leaving their DNA. Toxicology results can also be critical in cases involving drug-facilitated sexual assault as a way to counter a suspect's claim that the sex was consensual (Waltke et al., 2018).

LO5 Identify the type of evidence often obtained in sex offense investigations.

Evidence in a rape case that shows the amount of force that occurred, establishes that a sex act was performed, and links the act with the suspect includes stained or torn clothing; bedsheets, comforters, and other linens; condoms or condom wrappers; scratches, bruises, or cuts; evidence of a struggle; semen; and bloodstains. Other evidence to collect includes fingerprints, trace evidence (hairs, fibers, glass, paint, soil), toxicology, cell phone and digital forensics, and impression and pattern evidence.

Do not allow family members access to the scene, for even if they are not considered perpetrators of the crime, their presence may jeopardize the investigation by contaminating or destroying evidence.

Photograph all injuries to the victim except those in the genital area—the hospital staff will take these. Examine the scene for other physical evidence such as a weapon, stains, or personal objects the suspect may have left behind. Examine washcloths or towels the suspect may have used. Photograph any signs of a struggle such as broken objects, overturned furniture, or, if outdoors, disturbed vegetation.

If the assault occurred outdoors, take soil and vegetation samples for comparison. If the assault occurred in a vehicle, vacuum the car seats and interior to obtain soil, hairs, and other fibers. Examine the seats for blood and semen stains. DNA analysis has become increasingly important in sexual assault cases.

If a suspect is apprehended, photograph any injuries, marks, or scratches on the suspect's body and give the appropriate tests to determine whether the suspect is intoxicated or on drugs. Obtain any clothing or possessions of the suspect that might connect them the assault. Obtain a warrant or court order to collect blood, hair, and DNA samples from the suspect and, if necessary, get a warrant to search the suspect's vehicle, home, or office. Such searches may reveal items associated with perversion or weapons of the type used in the assault.

Investigating Date Rape

A particularly difficult type of sexual assault is **date rape**, sometimes called *acquaintance rape*, in which the victim knows the suspect. Although the phrase "date rape" is commonly used, the perpetrator of the crime might not be on an actual date or in a relationship with the victim. The suspect might be someone the victim knows well, someone known through mutual friends, or someone the victim just met (Office on Women's Health, 2019). Drugs, including alcohol, are often used to make committing the rape or sexual assault easier, which is why most experts prefer the term *drug-facilitated sexual assault* (DFSA). "Date rape" drugs include alcohol, marijuana, cocaine, prescription drugs, and over-the-counter drugs, such as antidepressants and sleep aids. Aside from alcohol, the three most common date rape drugs are Rohypnol, ketamine, and gamma hydroxybutyric acid (GHB), which as a group are sometimes referred to as "club drugs." Ecstasy (MDMA) is another drug sometimes associated with cases of DFSA:

> Date rape drugs can be put into a drink without you knowing. Drugs or alcohol can make a person confused about what is happening, less able to defend themselves against unwanted sexual contact, or unable to remember what happened. . . .
>
> Some date rape drugs look like regular drinks or other drugs you may be used to seeing. . . . Often date rape drugs have no color, no smell, and no taste when added to a drink or food. . . .
>
> Drugs such as Rohypnol, GHB, GBL, and ketamine, are very powerful. They can affect you very quickly, and you might not know that something is wrong. The length of time that the effects last varies. It depends on how much of the drug is in your body and if the drug is mixed with other drugs or alcohol. Alcohol can make the effects of drugs even stronger and can cause serious health problems—even death.

> (Office on Women's Health, 2019)

LO6 Identify what evidence to seek in date rape investigations.

Additional evidence in date rape cases may include the presence of alcohol, drugs, or both in the victim's system.

One study that examined trends in the toxicology findings of DFSA cases over the past 20 years found that alcohol intoxication combined with voluntary drug use presented the greatest risk factor for DFSA, and that covert drink-spiking is less common than many thought (Anderson, Flynn, & Pilgrim, 2017).

The oldest drug used to commit DFSA is **Rohypnol**, a Schedule IV drug under the Controlled Substances Act which is illegal to manufacture, sell, possess, or use in the United States, and is as much as 10 times more powerful than Valium and Halcion in producing a slowing of physical and mental responses, muscle reflexes, and amnesia (Drug Enforcement Administration [DEA], 2020d). Legal in other countries throughout Europe and in Mexico, and commonly prescribed to treat insomnia, it is manufactured in pill form and dissolves in liquids.

In 1997, Rohypnol was reformulated to include a safety feature—a dye in the core of the pill that, when dissolved in light-colored drinks, turns the liquid blue. Generic forms of the drug, however, may not change colors when added to liquids. Rohypnol can cause many problems: amnesia or the loss of memory concerning events that happened while under the influence of the drug, sleepiness, muscle relaxation, loss of muscle control or coordination, decreased anxiety, slurred speech, weakness, headaches, respiratory depression, confusion, and impaired mental functioning and judgment (DEA, 2020d).

Ketamine is a clear liquid or white powder that can cause hallucination, lost sense of time and identity, distorted perceptions of sight and sound, feeling disconnected or out of control, impaired motor function and immobility, depressed breathing, nausea and vomiting, cognitive difficulties, unconsciousness, and amnesia. Ketamine is classified as a Scheduled III non-narcotic drug under the Controlled Substances Act and is legal in the United States as an injectable, short-acting anesthetic commonly used by veterinarians (DEA, 2020c). However, using it to facilitate sexual assault is clearly illegal, and assailants are often able to obtain the drug from diverted or stolen inventory from veterinary clinics or through smugglers bringing the drug in from Mexico.

GHB is usually sold as a liquid or a white powder. In liquid form, it is clear, colorless, and slightly salty tasting. It is an FDA-approved prescription medication to treat narcolepsy, and analogues of it, such as GBL, are sold legally as industrial solvents. These drugs are also sold illegally to supplement body building, help with fat loss, improve eyesight, reverse hair loss, and treat drug addiction. Because GHB can also increase libido, suggestibility, and passivity, in addition to causing hallucinations and amnesia, it is sometimes used to commit DFSA (DEA, 2020b).

Another date rape drug is Ecstasy, or MDMA (3,4 methylenedioxymethamphetamine), a Schedule I drug under the Controlled Substances Act with no currently accepted medical use in the United States (DEA, 2020a). Typically synthesized in clandestine labs, various forms of this drug include an odorless, colorless liquid, a white powder, and a pill.

Ecstasy is a stimulant with psychedelic effects that can last from four to six hours. It is usually taken orally in pill form. Its psychological effects include confusion, depression, anxiety, sleeplessness, drug craving, and paranoia. Adverse physical effects include muscle tension, involuntary teeth clenching, nausea, blurred vision, faintness, tremors, rapid eye movement, and sweating or chills. Although the main reason this drug is taken is to promote feelings of euphoria, closeness, and sexuality, MDMA presents a heightened risk for DFSA because many Ecstasy tablets have been found to contain other harmful drugs, such as ketamine, cocaine, and methamphetamine (DEA, 2020a).

Acknowledging the severe and dangerous nature of such drug-facilitated sexual assaults, the Drug-Induced Rape Prevention and Punishment Act was signed in 1996, allowing courts to impose prison sentences of as long as 20 years on anyone who distributes a controlled substance, such as Rohypnol, to another person with the intent to commit a crime of violence, including rape. Given that the distribution of a controlled substance is already a federal crime, the act does not federalize any new conduct but does establish the basis for harsher penalties under federal law if the distribution facilitates a violent crime.

Officers investigating a sexual assault where the victim cannot give much information about the crime should suspect a date rape drug is involved. Therefore, in addition to following the usual protocol for investigating sexual assault, officers should inform emergency medical technicians and emergency room (ER) personnel that a date rape drug is suspected. Blood and urine tests may show the presence of a specific drug.

The Victim's Medical Examination

Many rape victims choose not to go to the police immediately following their attack. Such victims, however, must be strongly encouraged to seek prompt medical attention and to allow for the collection of evidence at a medical examination in case they later decide to proceed with an investigation. The medical examination can establish injuries, determine whether intercourse occurred, and protect against venereal disease and pregnancy. Some hospitals provide drugs at the initial examination to lessen the possibility of pregnancy. Further examination for venereal disease is also conducted. If a potential suspect is apprehended at or near the scene, it is advisable to get consent from that individual to undergo a medical examination. It may be necessary to seek and obtain a warrant for a suspect medical exam.

Although each hospital has its own procedures, ER doctors and nurses are trained to observe and treat trauma; therefore, they can provide counseling and support services to the victim during this initial critical phase. Good examination-stage care promotes later cooperation from the victim.

Many hospitals have formed specially trained units of physicians and nurses to deal specifically with sexual assaults. These units may be on-call if an incident occurs and none of the team members are already on duty. One initiative that has been shown to enhance both the rape victim's recovery and the investigation's success, thereby increasing prosecution rates, is the Sexual Assault Nurse Examiners (SANE) program. A SANE is a Registered Nurse (RN) who has received special training to be able to provide comprehensive care to sexual assault victims, including conducting forensic examinations and providing expert testimony if a case goes to trial (RAINN, 2020). SANE teams use specialized equipment such as a colposcope, a lighted magnifying tool fitted with a camera to detect and document small cuts, bruises, and other injuries sustained during a sexual assault (Paul, 2020).

The hospital or health care professional obtains medical-legal evidence that includes a detailed report of an examination of the victim for trauma, injuries, and intercourse. The report contains precise descriptions of all bruises, scratches, cuts, and other injuries; the examiner's findings and prescribed treatment; the victim's statements; documentation of the presence or absence of semen; documentation of the presence of drugs in the victim's system; the specific diagnosis of trauma; and any other specific medical facts concerning the victim's condition. The report should contain no conclusions about whether the woman was raped because this is a legal matter for the court to decide. However, in some states, hospitals are required by law to report suspected rape cases to the police.

Most hospitals have a sexual assault and vaginal kit in the examination room with the proper forms and tests for semen. Tests can be made of the vagina, anus, or mouth, depending on the type of assault. After the examination, these kits are given to the police at the victim's request and sent to a crime laboratory for analysis.

The victim should be asked to sign a release form that authorizes the medical facility to provide police a copy of the examination record. Hospital reports may be introduced as evidence even if a police officer was not present during the examination. Also ask the hospital and the victim for the clothing the victim was wearing at the time of the assault if it was not obtained earlier.

Since 2005, these tests have been available at no cost to the victim. In jurisdictions with victim compensation laws, the victim pays for the medical examination at the time it is conducted but is then reimbursed, whereas other jurisdictions bill directly to the state or local government for the cost of the exam. Before 2005, it was common practice to link victim reimbursement to an obligation for the victim to cooperate with the police investigation. In other words, if a victim declined to make a formal police report and press charges, they often were not reimbursed for the cost of the medical exam. In addition, much of the evidence from these exams was routinely disposed of after only a few months, making it nearly impossible for a victim to decide at a later date, once the raw horror of the attack had subsided, to go to the police and have the rape investigated. The reasoning behind this process was that medical exams were expensive to conduct and were considered another ordeal for the victim to endure, and if the victim was unwilling to report the crime or participate in the investigation, why make jurisdictions foot the bill and store evidence that would never be used to prosecute the offender? However, in the immediate aftermath of a sexual assault, victims are often scared, ashamed, and profoundly confused, unsure of whom to trust or to confide in about the attack. In the midst of this turmoil, well-meaning friends and family members may try to insist that the victim report the rape to the police. But this intense pressure to take immediate action or make the perceived "now-or-never" decision to report the rape often leads the victim to say "no" (Lonsway & Archambault, 2010).

The consequences of such scenarios playing out hundreds of thousands of times, year after year, have fostered a dire situation in which rape remains a seriously underreported and reoccurring crime, with unprosecuted offenders free to commit more sexual assaults: "Obviously, if the crime is not reported, no time-sensitive evidence is collected from the victim, suspect, or crime scene. No information is documented by law enforcement, so there is little or no opportunity to prosecute the crime. . . . No investigation occurs, and, as a result, perpetrators are free to offend again. Nothing changes for the next victim, so the cycle repeats" (Lonsway & Archambault, 2010, p. 51).

The significance of this cycle is illustrated in a study of 1,882 men, with an average age of 26.5 years and demographically representative of the general male population in the United States (Lisak & Miller, 2002). In this sample of men, 120 (6.4%) admitted to engaging in acts that met the legal definition of rape against women they knew, yet none of them had had their offenses reported to law enforcement. Furthermore, nearly two-thirds (63.3%) of these men who had committed a sexual assault had done so more than once. In fact, this group was responsible for 439 rapes, which averages to nearly 6 rapes per undetected rapist. The percentage of sexual assaults committed by this small

cohort of serial sex offenders (4% of the original sample group) was calculated to be 91%.

A similar study of newly enlisted male military personnel found that 13% of the men had committed or attempted a rape and that 95% of the rapes involved serial rapists (McWhorter, Stander, Merrill, Thomsen, & Milner, 2009). One study of single versus recurrent rape victims suggests that when a victim fails to report a sexual assault, the offender may "learn" that he (or she) can get away with this type of victimization in the future by selecting the same victim (Fisher, B. S., Daigle, L. E., & Cullen, F. T. (2010, February). What distinguishes single from recurrent sexual victims? The role of lifestyle-routine activities and first-incident characteristics. Justice Quarterly, 27(1), 102–129).

In an effort to diminish this cycle and hold more sex offenders accountable by increasing the victim report rate, a change was needed in how sexual assault victims were treated following their attack. In 2005, when the Violence Against Women Act (VAWA) of 1994 was reauthorized (it has since been reauthorized in 2013 and again in 2019), it included a provision aimed at ensuring that all victims of sexual assault could receive a forensic medical exam at no cost, regardless of their decision to report the crime to the police or participate in the investigation. This provision reduces pressure on rape victims to jump right into the criminal justice process immediately following their attack, yet encourages them to seek a prompt medical examination that not only addresses injuries sustained but allows the collection of crucial forensic evidence, should the victim later change their mind and decide to press charges.

The take-away for investigators working sex offenses is that a softer response is often needed for victims of this crime compared with other crimes. For many rape victims, an aggressive response by law enforcement can backfire and damage the chances of bringing the perpetrator to justice. Many departments are implementing a reporting procedure for victims of sexual assault known as *blind reporting*.

Blind Reporting

Rape victims may feel foolish, hurt, ashamed, vulnerable, and frightened. Furthermore, the prospect of reliving the entire experience by having the police ask detailed and personal questions is more than many victims can bear, particularly immediately after the incident. However, given time, victims may come to trust others enough to recount the attack, even hoping to prevent the same assailant from attacking others.

L07 Explain what blind reporting is and what its advantages are in sexual assault investigations.

Blind reporting allows sexual assault victims to retain their anonymity and confidentiality while sharing critical information with law enforcement. It also permits victims to gather legal information from law enforcement without having to commit immediately to an investigation.

Blind reporting procedures dovetail well with procedures for collecting crucial medical-legal evidence from sexual assault victims as set forth in VAWA 2019. The success of blind reporting hinges on whether trust can be established between the victim and the investigator. Six steps law enforcement agencies can take to develop an effective blind reporting system are as follows:

1. Establish and uphold a policy of victim confidentiality.

2. Allow victims to disclose as much or as little information as they wish.

3. Accept the information whenever victims might offer it—a delay of disclosure is not an indicator of the validity of the statement.

4. Develop procedures and forms to facilitate anonymous information from third parties (e.g., examiners).

5. Clarify options with victims for future contact—where, how, and under what circumstances they may be contacted by the law enforcement agency.

6. Maintain blind reports in separate files from official complaints to prevent inappropriate use.

The legal acceptability of blind reporting varies from state to state, and even from county to county. In jurisdictions where prosecutors accept blind report records, such records become the "founding document" in the formal sexual assault investigation should the victim decide to file a complaint and proceed with a full investigation.

Some agencies have established a protocol that enhances efforts to protect the identity of rape victims. For example, because the Open Records Act allows public access to public records, some departments have implemented a way to shield the identity of sexual assault victims from the media by assigning victims a pseudonym that appears in the report. The victim's identifying information is maintained in a separate document that is protected from release, as is any information regarding the location of the offense, if it occurred within the victim's home.

Interviewing the Victim

Rape is typically a horrifying, violent experience of violation to the victim. Reporting it to the police is frequently a courageous act because the victim knows that they will be forced to relive the experience through numerous retellings and that their word may be doubted. In addition, rape is humiliating and can involve numerous undesirable repercussions such as ostracism by friends and family, hospitalization, pregnancy, venereal disease, and HIV infection. At the time of the interview, the rape victim may be hysterical or unusually calm. Remember: rape is a crime of aggression and hostility and is usually conducted violently. Attempt to establish rapport by using sympathetic body language and explaining the necessity for asking sensitive questions.

Attempt to reinforce the victim's emotional well-being, but also obtain the facts. The pressure and stress caused by rape can make victims uncooperative. Rape victims sometimes complain that investigative personnel question the complaint's validity even before hearing the facts; are rude and overly aggressive; fail to explain the procedures used in the investigation; ask highly personal questions too early in the interview; or have or express unsympathetic or negative attitudes about the victim's personal appearance, clothing, or actions, implying that the victim may be partly responsible for the crime.

Both uniformed and investigative personnel, male and female, can help the victim cooperate if they are understanding and supportive. Such an approach contributes to the victim's psychological well-being and helps obtain information and evidence required to apprehend and prosecute the offender. Some departments require that two investigators or a victim's advocate be present when a rape victim is interviewed. Some departments also have a specialized sexual assault investigative unit comprising specially trained investigators who focus on this type of crime. Despite the existence of such units, patrol officers are usually the first responding officer to an in-progress incident or assault that just occurred, and they must be cognizant of the special approach needed for these types of victimizations.

Although some police feel that professional medical personnel should obtain the personal details of a sexual attack, this is shirking responsibility. Deal with the victim's emotional and psychological needs completely while investigating the case and preserving evidence.

Whether the investigator's gender affects the victim's cooperation is debatable. Some believe that a female investigator should interview female victims, and male investigators should interview male victims. Insensitive actions by a male investigator may reinforce a female victim's image of male aggressiveness and result in refusal to answer questions. In fact, the mere involvement of a male officer, despite his every intention of helping the victim, may hinder the investigation if the victim has become so distrusting of men. Furthermore, if a male detective interviews a female victim, or a female detective interviews a male victim, one or both parties might be highly uncomfortable discussing the details of the assault and the victim's sexual history, which is an important part of the investigation.

However, how much victims cooperate usually depends less on the interviewer's gender than on their attitude, patience, understanding, competence, and ability to establish rapport. Treat the victim with care, concern, and understanding. Assume that the sexual assault is real unless facts ultimately prove otherwise.

The interview location is also important. The police station may be unsatisfactory. The victim's home may be ideal—if the rape did not occur there. Tell the victim you must ask questions about the incident and ask where they would be most comfortable talking about it. If the victim is hospitalized, consult with the medical staff about when you can question them.

No matter where the interview is conducted, do it privately. Although the victim should be allowed to have a relative or friend nearby to talk to, it is better to be alone with the victim when specific questions are asked. If the victim insists on having someone with her, discuss with this person the procedure to be followed. Explain that the person's presence is important to the victim for reassurance and security but that the person must allow the victim to talk freely and not interrupt.

The victim's family and friends can considerably influence whether the victim relates the entire story. A wide range of emotions can occur from mothers, fathers, husbands, wives, or other family members. They may be silent, hysterical, or angry to the point that they have every intention of killing the perpetrator if they find them. Sometimes such anger is turned against the victim.

Make a complete report of the victim's appearance and behavior: presence of liquor or drugs; bruises, scratches, or marks; manner of speech; emotional condition; appearance of clothes or hair; color of face; smeared makeup; torn clothes; and stains. Take photographs to supplement your notes.

The needed initial information includes the victim's name, age, home address, work address, telephone number(s), and any prior relationship with the offender, if the offender is known. At a *later* interview, investigators should obtain additional information about the victim, some of which is particularly useful when the suspect is unknown and it is suspected that the suspect chose the victim on purpose, including the following:

- Background check of the victim
- Children and their ages
- Educational level of the victim
- Family, parents, and the nature of the victim's relationship with them
- Fears
- Financial status, past and present
- Friends and enemies
- Hobbies
- Marital status
- Medical history, physical and mental
- Occupation, past and present
- Personal habits
- Physical description, including attire at the time of the incident
- Recent changes in lifestyle
- Recent court actions
- Reputation on the job and in the neighborhood
- Residence, past and present
- Social habits
- Use of alcohol and drugs

However, most of these issues need not be addressed during the initial interview. The main question to assess at the initial interview is: what happened? Did a crime occur and, if so, what crime? Obtain a detailed account of the crime, including the suspect's actions and statements, special characteristics or oddities, and any unusual sexual behaviors. Determine exactly where and how the attack occurred, what happened before and after the attack, and whether the victim can give any motive for the attack. Explain what you need to know and why, the procedures you will follow, and how important the victim's cooperation is. Use open-ended questions such as, "Take your time and tell me exactly what happened."

Determine the exact details of resistance, even if not required by law. Was there any unconsciousness, paralysis, or fainting? Was there penetration? Who did the victim first talk to after the assault? How soon was the report made, and if there was a delay, what was the reason?

Establish lack of consent. Obtain the names of any witnesses. Determine where the victim was before the attack and whether someone might have seen and followed them. The suspect's description can then be used at that location to see whether anyone there can identify them. Obtain as much information as possible about the suspect: voice, mannerisms, clothing, actions, and general appearance.

It is important to obtain as many details as possible even though they may appear insignificant at the time. How the initial contact was made; attempts at concealment; the suspect's voice, appearance, and exact words; unusual behavior, including unusual sexual acts performed—all these can be helpful in identifying and prosecuting the offender.

Establishing the Behavioral Profile in Sex Offense Cases

Because rapists are generally recidivists (about 70% of them commit more than one rape), the details and MOs of offenses in another area of the same city or another community might be identical to the present case. For this reason, the usefulness of behavioral profiling becomes apparent, and interviews with victims should focus on the *offender*'s behavior.

Several specific areas should be covered in the behavior-oriented interview of rape victims, embodied in three essential basic steps: (1) carefully interview the victim about the rapist's *behavior*, (2) analyze that behavior to ascertain the *motivation* underlying the assault, and (3) compile a *profile* of the individual likely to have committed the crime.

The three types of rapist behavior of concern to investigators are physical (use of force), verbal, and sexual. First, ascertain the method of approach. Three common approaches are the "con" approach, in which the offender is initially friendly, even charming, and dupes the victim; the "blitz" approach, in which the offender directly physically assaults the victim, frequently gagging, binding, or blindfolding the victim; and the "surprise" approach, in which the offender hides in the back seat of a car, in shrubbery or behind a wall or waits until the victim is sleeping.

After determining the approach, you should determine how the perpetrator maintained control. Four common methods of control are (1) mere presence, (2) verbal threats, (3) display of a weapon, and (4) use of physical force.

If the rapist used physical force, it is important to determine the amount of force because this gives insight into the offender's motivations. Four levels of physical force may be used: (1) *minimal*, perhaps slapping; (2) *moderate*, repeated hitting; (3) *excessive*, beating resulting in bruises and cuts; and (4) *brutal*, sadistic torture. This last type of offender is typically extremely profane, abusive, and aggressive, and the victim may require hospitalization or die.

In addition to the offender's sexual behavior, investigators should inquire about the offender's verbal behavior. Themes in rapists' conversations include threats, orders, personal inquiries of the victim, personal revelations, obscene names, racial epithets, and inquiries about the victim's sexual enjoyment. Also ask about the *victim*'s verbal behavior. Did the offender demand that the victim say certain words or demand that she beg, plead, or scream? Such demands also shed insight into the offender's motivation.

Specifically ask victims about any change in the offender's behavior during the course of the assault, whether verbal, physical, or sexual. Such changes can indicate weakness or fear if the offender lessens his efforts, or anger and hostility if he suddenly increases his efforts.

A further area of inquiry relates to the offender's experience level. Did he take actions to protect his identity, to destroy or remove evidence, or to make certain he had an escape route? The novice rapist may take minimal or obvious actions to protect his identity—for example, wearing a ski mask and gloves, changing his voice tone, affecting an accent, ordering the victim not to look at him, or blindfolding and binding the victim. These are common precautions a person not knowledgeable about acid phosphatase tests of hair and fiber evidence would be expected to take. In contrast, the experienced rapist may walk through the residence or prepare an escape route, disable the phone, order the victim to shower or douche, bring bindings or gags, wear surgical gloves, or take or force the victim to wash items the rapist touched or ejaculated on, such as bedding and the victim's clothing.

Also determine whether any items other than those of evidentiary value were taken by the offender. Of interest are items of value as well as items of a personal nature. It is important to determine whether items were taken and why. Again, such information may provide insight into the offender's motivation.

Ending the Victim Interview

End the interview with an explanation of available victim assistance programs, such as Sexual Offense Services (SOS). Arrange for a relative, friend, or staff member from a rape crisis center to help the victim. If the victim refuses to be questioned, is incapable of answering questions because of shock or injuries, or begins the interview but then breaks down emotionally, terminate the interview for the time being, but return later.

Explain to the victim what will happen next in the criminal justice system. Give the victim the case number and a phone number to call at the police department if any other details are remembered or if questions arise.

Follow-Up Investigation

After the preliminary investigation, medical examination, and initial interview are completed, conduct a follow-up investigation. Interview the victim again in two to five days to obtain further information and to compare the statements made after time has elapsed. Following that interview, determine whether the crime scene or evidence has been altered or contaminated and interview all possible witnesses to the offense.

Many prosecutors discourage conducting follow-up interviews with sexual assault victims, contending that the only thing these interviews accomplish is to provide the defense with inconsistent statements. Instead, these prosecutors argue, the victim should be interviewed by the on-the-scene officer and then formally interviewed by the investigator. Sexual assault investigators should be cognizant of this hazard of inconsistent statements and be familiar with the practices and preferences of prosecutors in their jurisdiction.

Interviewing Witnesses

Locate witnesses as soon as possible, and obtain their names, addresses, and phone numbers. Canvass the neighborhood for possible witnesses. Even though witnesses may not have seen the incident, they may be able to describe the suspect or his vehicle. They may have heard screams or statements made by the victim or the offender.

Determine whether a relationship exists between the witness and the victim or offender. Determine exactly what the witness saw and heard. Did the witness see the victim before, during, or after the assault? Did the witness see the victim with the suspect? How did the witness happen to be in the vicinity where the offense occurred? Interview acquaintances and individuals known to the victim because many victims know their rapists.

Sex Offenders

Suspects fall into two general classifications: those who know the victim and those who are known sex offenders. In the first category are friends of the victim, people who have daily contact with the victim's relatives, those who make deliveries to the victim's residence or business, and neighbors. In the second category are those on file in police records as having committed prior sex offenses. Known offenders with prior arrests are prime suspects because rehabilitation is often unsuccessful.

Some sexual assault offenders are sadistic and commit physical abuses in hostile, vicious manners that result in injury or even death. Others seek to control their victims through threats and physical strength but do not cause permanent physical injuries. Still others act out aggression and hatred in short attacks on women selected as random targets.

Sexual sadists become more sexually excited the more the victim suffers. The pleasure of complete domination over another person is the essence of the sadistic drive. Most sadists are cunning and deceitful and feel no remorse or compassion. They feel superior to society, especially the law. They often use pliers, electric cattle prods, whips, fire, bondage, amputation, and objects inserted into the vagina or anus. They may keep diaries, audiotapes, sexual devices and devices to torture victims, photographs of victims, and other incriminating evidence—all items to be included in a search warrant.

Rapists are often categorized as motivated by either power or anger. Each category is further divided into two subcategories (Table 10.4). However, many rapists are opportunist sexual predators who rape not because they are driven by anger or power issues but simply because they can. They want sex, and they will take it if the opportunity presents itself.

No personality or physical type can be automatically eliminated as a sex offender. Sex offenders include those who are married, have families and good jobs, are college educated, and are active churchgoers.

The Significance of Fantasy in Sexual Assaults

Because fantasy is strongly associated with sexual assault, search warrant applications should include a list of the materials officers would expect to recover from an offender who indulged in sexual fantasies, such as sadistic pornography, drawings, videotapes, women's lingerie and clothing, and fantasy stories featuring sexual sadism. The warrant should also include whips, chains, handcuffs, and other sex toys.

TABLE 10.4 **Profiles of Rapists**				
	Power Rapists		**Anger Rapists**	
	Manhood Reassurance	**Manhood Assertion**	**Retaliatory/ Punishment**	**Excitation/Sadism**
Purpose	Confirm manhood to self	Express manhood to victim	Punish women for real or imagined wrongs	Obtain
Preassault behavior	Fantasizes about successful sexual relationships; plans attack	Seldom preplanned; crime of opportunity	Spontaneous act in response to a significant stressor	Violent fantasies; careful planning
Victim selection	Observes (prowler, window peeker)	By chance	Spontaneous	Cruises
Victim characteristics	Same race; meek, nonassertive	Same age and race	Resembles female in his life	Same age and race
Location of approach	Inside victim's residence	Singles bars	Near his residence or job	Any location
Type of approach	Stealth; hand over mouth	Smooth talker; con	Blitz; immediate excessive use of force	Brandish a weapon
Weapon	Of opportunity (if used)	Of opportunity (if used)	Of opportunity (if used)	Of choice or planned
Time of day	Nighttime	Nighttime	Anytime	Anytime
Sexual acts	Normal	Self-satisfying; vaginal/penile intercourse; vaginal/anal intercourse; fellatio; spends long time	Violent, painful sex acts; degrading, humiliating acts; spends short time	Experimental sex; inserts objects into body cavities; spends long time
Sexual dysfunction	Erection problems; premature ejaculation	Retarded ejaculation	—	—
Other behaviors	Relatively nonviolent	Tears clothing off	Profanity; injury provoking; assaultive	Excessive, brutal force; bondage; torture; cuts clothing off; protects identity (mask, gloves); most likely to kill
Postassault behavior	Likely to apologize; takes personal items; keeps a diary	Likely to threaten; takes items as trophies; boasts of conquests	Leaves abruptly; may or may not threaten	Straightens scene; shows no remorse

Source: Bradway, W. C. (1990, September). Stages of a sexual assault. *Law and Order*, pp. 119–123. Reprinted by permission of the publisher.

Sexual sadists may be obsessed with keeping trophies and recordings of the assaults. Therefore, officers should include the following items in search warrant applications:

- Photographs
- Written documentation
- Newspaper articles
- Computers
- Cellular phones
- Video or audio tapes
- Items the victim knows were taken

Taking a Suspect into Custody and Interrogation

If a suspect is apprehended at the scene, record any spontaneous statements made by the suspect and photograph him. If more than one suspect is present, separate them. Do not allow communication among suspects, victims, and witnesses. Remove the suspect(s) from the scene as soon as possible.

When interrogating sex offenders, obtain as much information as possible, yet remain nonjudgmental. The suspect should be the last person interviewed. This allows the interviewer to have all information possible by the time of the suspect interview: facts about the victim, the type of offense, and the location of the crime;

statements from witnesses, neighbors, and informants; and information about the suspect's background.

As in most interrogation situations, building rapport is the first step. Suggest to the suspect that you understand what they are going through. Ask about family, job, and interests. Assess the suspect's character. After rapport is established, ask the suspect to tell their side of the story from beginning to end and do not interrupt. Show interest in what is being said and keep the suspect talking. The interrogator's approach should be one of "you tell me what happened and I will understand," even though that may not be the investigator's actual feelings.

The objective is to obtain the truth and the information necessary for proving guilt or innocence. To help accomplish this goal, attempt to gain the suspect's confidence. Many suspects feel they can justify their actions by putting some blame on the victim—for example, "She came on to me."

During the interrogation, remember that the seriousness of the charge to be brought will be based on the information you obtain. All elements of the charged offense must be proven, so keep the possible charges in mind and prepare questions to elicit supporting information.

Research has attempted to shed light on why some sex offenders choose to confess in full, confess partially, or not confess, in an effort to make police interrogation more effective. Several studies have found that sex offenders are less likely, in general, to confess their crimes during interrogation than are nonsexual offenders, with one hypothesis being that the humiliation experienced by sex offenders contributes to their reluctance to admit their actions (Beauregard & Mieczkowski, 2012). Other avenues of study have shown that different patterns of confession are often noticed when separating child molesters from rapists, meaning the interrogation techniques used for one class of offenders may not be as effective with the other group. For example, with child molesters, characteristics associated with an increased likelihood of confession include the offender's age at the time of the offense and feelings of guilt after the assault, whereas attributes associated with the decision for a rapist to confess were the offender's personality profile and whether there was a relationship with the victim (Beauregard & Mieczkowski, 2012). Thus the researchers suggest that interrogation tactics that attempt to appeal to a rapist's feelings of guilt or sense of remorse are unlikely to be effective.

Coordination with Other Agencies

A rape case often involves cooperation with medical personnel, social workers, rape crisis center personnel, and the news media. The public and the news media can greatly influence the prosecution of a rape case. Medical and hospital personnel influence the victim's attitude and cooperation in obtaining facts for medical reports and the necessary evidence for use in court. Rape crisis centers can provide various kinds of support to victims and encourage them to sign a complaint.

Prosecution of Rape and Statutory Charges

Few criminal cases are as difficult to prosecute as rape, at least under older laws. Despite changes in the law, it is virtually impossible to obtain a conviction on the victim's testimony alone. Factors that strengthen the prosecutor's case include medical evidence, physical evidence such as torn clothing, evidence of injuries, and a complaint reported reasonably close to the time of the assault. The more evidence, the stronger the case.

Defendants usually want a jury trial because of present laws and attitudes regarding rape, and because the defendant is not required to testify. However, the victim must relate a very difficult ordeal and be subjected to cross-examination that can make *him* or *her* appear to be the one on trial.

Juries tend to be unsympathetic with a victim who was drinking heavily, hitchhiking, or using drugs, or who left a bar with a stranger or engaged in other socially "unacceptable" actions. Many newer laws make it very explicit that such conditions are not to be considered during the trial. Newer laws also state that the victim's testimony need not be corroborated and that testimony about the degree of resistance—although it may be admitted—is not required.

Some victims decide not to prosecute because of pressure from family or friends, fear of reprisal, shame, fear of going to court, or emotional or mental disturbance. Sometimes the prosecuting attorney refuses to take the case to court because the case is weak and thus has little chance of conviction. For example, there may not be enough physical evidence to corroborate the victim's complaint, the victim may be a known prostitute or a girlfriend of the rapist, or she may be pregnant because of prior sexual relations with the assailant. At other times, the report is unfounded and unsubstantiated by the evidence.

In 1975, Congress adopted Rules 412, 413, 414, and 415 into the Federal Rules of Evidence. Referred to as "rape shield" laws, this legislation limited a sexual assault defendant's ability to attack an alleged victim's character and credibility by restricting the information that could be presented in court pertaining to the victim's past sexual behavior or reputation. These changes in the law were meant to overcome the reluctance of rape victims to report sexual assault, as many preferred to suffer in silence rather than endure public humiliation from having their sexual past brought up at a trial (Bishop, 2018). Enactment of rape shield laws means that juries are not allowed to:

- Presume that a victim who consented to sexual intercourse with other persons would be likely to have consented with the defendant

- Use the victim's prior sexual conduct to determine credibility

- Subject the victim's testimony to any greater test of credibility than in any other crime

Some have argued, however, that victims' characters are being judged even before a case has a chance to go to trial. These critics contend that victim characteristics and credibility issues frequently prevent sexual assault cases from ever reaching court by negatively affecting prosecutors' charging decisions in sexual assault cases. Testimony about the victim's previous sexual conduct is not admissible unless (1) the victim has had prior sexual relations with the defendant, (2) there is evidence of venereal disease or pregnancy resulting from the assault, (3) circumstances suggest that consent occurred within the calendar year, or (4) the victim has not told the truth or has filed a false report.

False Reports

Women make false reports of sexual assault for a number of reasons, including getting revenge on lovers who have jilted them, covering up a pregnancy, or getting attention. They may also file a false report as a way of defending against a lapse in judgment, a common scenario when a woman in a committed relationship goes out with friends, gets intoxicated, and ends up having consensual sex with someone, only to realize the mistake at a later time. Such circumstances need to be ruled out when investigating a reported sexual assault. The credibility of rape reports is probably questioned more frequently than that of any other felony report. A polygraph can help determine the truth of the complainant's statements. If the evidence of a false report is overwhelming, include all the facts in your closeout report.

If the victim admits orally or in writing that her story was false, close the case. When the victim's credibility is in serious doubt because of contradictory evidence, the investigating officer's superior or the prosecutor can close the case.

Civil Commitment of Sex Offenders after Sentences Served

Although studies have found that those convicted of sex offenses have a relatively low recidivism rate and are much less likely to reoffend compared to those convicted of other offenses, concern persists that sex offenders are a unique class of extremely dangerous career criminals with a high propensity to repeat acts of predatory sexual violence (Alper & Durose, 2019; Sawyer, 2019; Lave & Zimring, 2018). These concerns about sexually violent predators (SVPs), though unsupported by empirical data, have fostered strong public support for harsh, lengthy criminal sanctions and long-term social control policies, such as civil commitment, for those convicted of sex offenses (Hanson, Harris, Letourneau, Helmus, & Thornton, 2018).

Several actuarial-based, empirically validated tools have been developed to assess the risk of sex offender recidivism. Offenders whose scores place them at an elevated actuarial risk of reoffending may be selected for civil commitment, an involuntary post-sentence detention aimed at preventing further offenses (The Crime Report Staff, 2018). Legislation providing for sex offender civil commitment (SOCC) exists in 20 states and the federal government, amid widespread controversy. Such legislation acknowledges that although sex offenders may have paid a debt to society by spending time behind bars, often little if anything is accomplished during this incarceration to address and treat the disorders that lead offenders to commit sexual assault.

Although critics of involuntary civil commitment contend that these acts violate offenders' civil rights, the Supreme Court has upheld the constitutionality of at least one state's civil commitment law. In *Kansas v. Hendricks* (1997), the Court upheld Kansas's Sexually Violent Predator Act, which establishes procedures by which that state may civilly commit to a mental hospital people likely to commit predatory acts of sexual violence because of a mental abnormality or personality disorder. However, in *Kansas v. Crane* (2002), the Supreme Court began refining its 1997 ruling in *Hendricks*, adding a new limitation on such civil commitments, saying that there must be "proof of [an offender's] serious difficulty in controlling [his] behavior."

More recently, Minnesota's SVP law survived a constitutionality challenge when the Eighth Circuit Court of Appeals held, in *Karsjens v. Piper* (2018), that "the services and protections provided to those committed under the MCTA [Minnesota Civil Commitment and Treatment Act] were rationally related to the state's interest of protecting its citizens" (Kingston & Prabhu, 2018). The Supreme Court denied certiorari on this case. Despite the view apparent in these court rulings that the indeterminate lifetime civil commitment of sex offenders fulfills a necessary public safety objective, research results continue to challenge the perception that sex offenders, as a group, are violent predators destined to continue a lengthy trajectory of sexual assaults unless strict social control mechanisms are in place (Lave & Zimring, 2018; Mercado, Jeglic, Markus, Hanson, & Levenson, 2011).

Sex Offender Registry and Notification

In addition to civil commitment programs, jurisdictions have passed legislation authorizing sexual offender registries and community notification policies designed to inform the public when such offenders move into their neighborhoods and to assist law enforcement in keeping track of these individuals (Figure 10.2).

Figure 10.2
Sex offender registries vary from state to state, but most contain similar information. Many can be found on a state's website, such as this one taken from the Georgia Bureau of Investigation. A disclaimer, shown in red at the bottom of the screen, is important to protect the offender's rights. Without such a disclaimer, the registry could be declared unconstitutional.

Georgia Bureau of Investigation

The first sex offender registry was created in California in 1947, before it was legally required. By 1996, all states had enacted laws requiring sex offenders to register within their states to help law enforcement agencies manage offenders released from secure confinement.

> **LO8** Identify the three federal statutes that form the basis for sex offender registries.
>
> The evolution of sex offender registries can be traced to a trilogy of federal statutes: the Jacob Wetterling Act, Megan's Law, and the Pam Lychner Act.

The first act was named for 11-year-old Jacob Wetterling, who was abducted in October 1989 near his home in rural Minnesota and whose disappearance went unsolved for 27 years. The case broke in 2016 when Daniel Heinrich, a local man who had been interviewed several times during the interim and considered a suspect not only in the Wetterling case but in other child molestation cases, admitted to kidnapping, sexually assaulting, and murdering Jacob. Heinrich eventually led investigators to the place where he buried Jacob's body. The Jacob Wetterling Crimes against Children and Sexually Violent Offender Registration Act was enacted as part of President Bill Clinton's 1994 Crime Act. It required states to establish registration systems for convicted child molesters and other sexually violent offenders. States could release the information to the public, but they were not required to do so.

The second act was named for 7-year-old Megan Kanka, raped and murdered by a convicted sex offender who lived across the street from Megan's family with two other released sex offenders. Megan's Law, signed by President Clinton in 1996, amends the Jacob Wetterling Act in two ways: (1) it requires states to release any relevant information about registered sex offenders necessary to maintain and protect public safety and (2) it allows disclosure of information collected under a state registration program for any purpose permitted under the laws of the state.

The third law in the federal trilogy was named for a victims' rights advocate killed in a plane crash in July 1996. Officially called the Pam Lychner Sexual Offender Tracking and Identification Act, it directed the FBI to establish a national sex offender database. Initially called the National Sex Offender Public Registry (NSOPR), this public safety resource was renamed to the Dru Sjodin National Sex Offender Public Website (NSOPW) in 2006 by the Adam Walsh Child Protection and Safety Act in honor of the 22-year-old college student, Dru Sjodin, who was kidnapped from a parking lot in Grand Forks, North

Dakota, and murdered by a sex offender who was registered in Minnesota:

> Title 1 of the Adam Walsh Child Protection and Safety Act of 2006 established a comprehensive, national sex offender registration system called the Sex Offender Registration and Notification Act (SORNA). SORNA aims to close potential gaps and loopholes that existed under prior laws, and to strengthen the nationwide network of sex offender registrations.
>
> Sex offender registration and notification programs are important for public safety purposes. Sex offender registration is a system for monitoring and tracking sex offenders following their release into the community. The registration provides important information about convicted sex offenders to local and federal authorities and the public, such as offender's name, current location, and past offenses. Currently, the means of public notification includes sex offender websites in all states, the District of Columbia, and some territories. Some states involve other forms of notice. . . .
>
> It is a federal crime for an individual to knowingly fail to register or update his or her registration as required pursuant to the Sex Offender Registration and Notification Act (SORNA). For example, a sex offender is required to update their registration in each jurisdiction they reside, are employed, or attend school. Offenders convicted of this crime face statutory penalties.

(U.S. Department of Justice, 2020)

Many arguments exist both for and against sex offender registries and notification laws. People who advocate sex offender registration and notification cite the significant number of sex offenders under community supervision, the fear of recidivism, and the protection of children and their families. Critics contend that the registries violate the civil rights of offenders who have served their time and provide a false sense of security for the community because many sexual assaults are committed by first-time offenders who are, for obvious reasons, not identified on any registry. Furthermore, many offenders fail to register; failure to register is a crime in all 50 states and federally. The challenge is to balance the communities' rights to access public information with the protections provided to convicted offenders.

In an effort to thwart those sex offenders who meet the legal criteria for required registration but fail to register, some jurisdictions are tracking such offenders through the use of global positioning systems (GPSs) or other electronic monitoring devices. A GPS has several key benefits, including the deterrent it provides against repeat offending and the higher level of protection offered to the public by ensuring a subject does not enter proscribed areas such as an elementary school or victim's neighborhood without enforcement agencies being immediately notified. Another effort to track released sex offenders is to screen them against motor vehicle databases when they apply for or renew a driver's license.

The three basic objections to notification laws center around punishment, privacy, and due process issues. Some offenders claim that registration subjects them to additional punishment. However, in April 1998 the Supreme Court rejected constitutional challenges that claimed that the laws' notification requirements represented an unconstitutional added punishment. Another concern of opponents is that notification will lead to harassment of offenders and increased acts of vigilantism. Sometimes the stigma placed on sex offenders is too great a burden to handle. A convicted child molester in Maine shot himself to death, saying in a tape-recorded message that he feared living in a world "with no forgiveness."

It appears that sex offender registration and notification have more supporters than opponents. Internet access is quickly revolutionizing the way the public keeps informed of the whereabouts of convicted sex offenders. In many jurisdictions, residents are now able to access a registry online, enter their zip codes, and obtain information on sex offenders living in their area.

Summary

The key distinction between human trafficking and smuggling lies in the individual's freedom of choice. *Forcible rape* is sexual intercourse against a person's will by the use or threat of force. *Statutory rape* is sexual intercourse with a minor, with or without consent. The elements of the crime of rape or sexual assault include penetration, no matter how slight, of the victim's genital or anal openings by an object or any part of another person's body, including sexual intercourse in its ordinary meaning, or penetration of the victim's mouth by a sex organ of another person, without the consent of the victim.

MO factors important in investigating sex offenses include type of offense, words spoken, use of a weapon, actual method of attack, time of day, type of location, and the victim's age and gender.

Evidence in a rape case that shows the amount of force that occurred, establishes that a sex act was performed, and links the act with the suspect includes stained or torn clothing; bedsheets, comforters, and other linens; condoms or condom wrappers; scratches, bruises, or cuts; evidence of a struggle; semen; and bloodstains. Other evidence to collect includes fingerprints, trace evidence (hairs, fibers, glass, paint, soil), toxicology, cell phone and digital forensics, and impression and pattern evidence. Additional evidence in date rape cases may include the presence of alcohol, drugs, or both in the victim's system.

Many departments have implemented a procedure known as blind reporting, which allows sexual assault victims to retain their anonymity and confidentiality while sharing critical information with law enforcement. It also permits victims to gather legal information from law enforcement without having to commit immediately to an investigation. The evolution of sex offender registries can be traced to a trilogy of federal statutes: the Jacob Wetterling Act, Megan's Law, and the Pam Lychner Act.

Can You Define?

bigamy	incest	sadomasochistic abuse
blind reporting	indecent exposure	sexting
child molestation	intimate parts	sextortion
cunnilingus	oral copulation	sexual contact
date rape	pedophile	sexually explicit conduct
digital penetration	penetration	sexual penetration
exhibitionists	prostitution	sodomy
fellatio	rape	statutory rape
forcible rape	Rohypnol	trauma bond
human trafficking	sadist	voyeurism

Checklist

Sexual Assault

- What specific sex offense was committed?

- Are all the elements of the crime present?

- Who is the victim? Were there any injuries? Were they described and photographed?

- Were there any witnesses?

- Was the surrounding area canvassed to locate possible leads?

- Is there a suspect? A description of a suspect?

- Has there been a relationship between the suspect and the victim?

- What evidence was obtained at the scene?

- Was evidence submitted to the crime laboratory? Were reports received?

- Was the victim taken to the hospital for a medical examination?

- What evidence was obtained at the hospital? Is a medical report available?

- Was the victim interviewed? Will they sign a complaint?

- Was the victim reinterviewed two to five days after the assault?

- Was a background check made of the victim?

- If the suspect is known, was a criminal background check made of him or her?

- Were other police agencies in the area notified and queried?

- Were field interrogation cards, MO files, and other intelligence files checked?

- Have patrol divisions been checked for leads on cars or people in the area?

- Has a sexual assault or rape crisis center been contacted for help?

Application

Read the following and then answer the questions:

Several young people in a car wave down a police car and tell the officers that screams are coming from the south end of a nearby park. At about the same time, the police dispatcher receives a call from a resident who says she hears screams and cries for help but cannot tell exactly what part of the park they are coming from. The officers talk to the juveniles, get their names and a description of the area, and then head for the park without red lights and siren to avoid warning the attacker. Arriving at the south end of the park, the officers see a man running from some bushes. He is wearing a dark jacket and is bareheaded. One officer goes to find the victim; the other attempts to follow the fleeing man. At the scene, the officer observes a woman with torn clothing and a cut on the side of her head. She is unable to speak coherently, but she has obviously been assaulted. They call for an ambulance and additional officers to respond. The juveniles have followed the squad car to the scene and crowd around the victim to offer help. The officer chasing the suspect has lost him and has returned to the scene.

Several minutes later the ambulance arrives. The victim is loaded inside, and one officer follows the ambulance to the hospital. The other officer stays on the scene until more officers arrive, who are able to help secure the area. A search is conducted, during which branches are found to be broken from some of the bushes. Officers also find an article of clothing from the victim and a switchblade knife on the ground. They secure the scene by posting several of the juveniles around the area until further help arrives.

Questions

1. Should red lights and siren have been used in going to the scene?

2. Was it correct for the officers to split up as they did?

3. Evaluate the effectiveness of the officers' actions after arriving at the scene.

References

Administration for Children and Families. (2017, November 21). *Fact sheet: Human trafficking.* Washington, DC: Author. Retrieved September 10, 2020, from www.acf.hhs.gov/sites /default/files/otip/fact_sheet_human_trafficking_fy18.pdf

Alper, M., & Durose, M. R. (2019, May). *Recidivism of sex offenders released from state prison: A 9-year follow-up (2005–14).* Washington, DC: Bureau of Justice Statistics. Special Report. (NCJ 251773). Retrieved September 16, 2020, from www.bjs.gov/content/pub/pdf/rsorsp9yfu0514.pdf

Anderson, L. J., Flynn, A., & Pilgrim, J. L. (2017, April). A global epidemiological perspective on the toxicology of drug-facilitated sexual assault: A systematic review. *Journal of Forensic and Legal Medicine, 47*: 46–54. doi:10.1016 /j.jflm.2017.02.005

Associated Press. (2015, April 12). College students suspended after charges in beach sexual assault. *Associated Press.* Retrieved September 5, 2020, from www.wsj.com/articles /college-students-suspended-after-charges-in-beach -sexual-assault-1428895024

Banks, D., & Kyckelhahn, T. (2011, April). *Characteristics of suspected human trafficking incidents, 2008–2010.* Washington, DC: Bureau of Justice Statistics, Special Report. (NCJ 233732). Retrieved September 10, 2020, from www.bjs.gov/content/pub/pdf/cshti0810.pdf

Beauregard, E., & Mieczkowski, T. (2012, June). From police interrogation to prison: Which sex offender characteristics predict confession? *Police Quarterly, 15*(2), pp. 197–214.

Bishop, K. (2018, April 15). A reflection on the history of sexual assault laws in the United States. *The Arkansas Journal of Social Change and Public Service.* Retrieved September 16, 2020, from ualr.edu/socialchange/2018/04/15 /reflection-history-sexual-assault-laws-united-states/

Carey, K. B., Durney, S. E., Shepardson, R. L., & Carey, M. P. (2015, November). Precollege predictors of incapacitated rape among female students in their first year of college. *Journal of Studies on Alcohol and Drugs, 76*(6): 829–837. doi:10.15288/jsad.2015.76.829

Centers for Disease Control and Prevention. (2018, October 23). *Intimate partner violence.* Atlanta, GA. Retrieved August 24, 2020, from www.cdc.gov/violenceprevention /intimatepartnerviolence/index.html

Chan, H. C. O., & Beauregard, E. (2019, January). Prostitute homicides: A 37-year exploratory study of the offender, victim, and offense characteristics. *Forensic Science International, 294*: 196–203. doi:10.1016 /j.forsciint.2018.11.022

Cohn, A. M., Zinzow, H. M., Resnick, H. S., & Kilpatrick, D. G. (2013). Correlates of reasons for not reporting rape to police: Results from a national telephone household probability sample of women with forcible or drug-or-alcohol facilitated/incapacitated rape. *Journal of Interpersonal Violence, 28*(3): 455–473. doi:10.1177/0886260512455515

Doychak, K., & Raghavan, C. (2020). "No voice or vote": Trauma-coerced attachment in victims of sex trafficking. *Journal of Human Trafficking, 6*(3): 339–357. doi:10.1080 /23322705.2018.1518625

Drug Enforcement Administration (2020a). *Ecstasy/MDMA fact sheet.* Washington, DC: Author. Retrieved September 11, 2020, from www.dea.gov/sites/default/files/2020-06 /Ecstasy-MDMA-2020_0.pdf

Drug Enforcement Administration (2020b). *GHB fact sheet.* Washington, DC: Author. Retrieved September 11, 2020, from www.dea.gov/sites/default/files/2020-06/GHB -2020_0.pdf

Drug Enforcement Administration (2020c). *Ketamine fact sheet.* Washington, DC: Author. Retrieved September 11, 2020, from www.dea.gov/sites/default/files/2020-06 /Ketamine-2020.pdf

Drug Enforcement Administration (2020d). *Rohypnol fact sheet.* Washington, DC: Author. Retrieved September 11, 2020, from www.dea.gov/sites/default/files/2020-06 /Rohypnol-2020.pdf

Engel, B. (2020, March 3). Intimate partner sexual assault. *Psychology Today.* Retrieved September 8, 2020, from www.psychologytoday.com/us/blog/the -compassion-chronicles/202003/intimate -partner-sexual-assault

Farley, M. (2018, January). Risks of prostitution: When the person is the product. *Journal of the Association for Consumer Research, 3*(1). doi:10.1086/695670

Farley, M. (2020, Spring). Very inconvenient truths: Sex buyers, sexual coercion, and prostitution-harm-denial. *Logos: A Journal of Modern Society & Culture.* Retrieved September 8, 2020, from logosjournal.com/2016/farley-2/

Federal Bureau of Investigation. (n.d.). *Human trafficking.* Washington, DC: Author. Retrieved September 9, 2020, from www.fbi.gov/investigate/violent-crime /human-trafficking

Federal Bureau of Investigation. (2015, July 7). *What is sextortion?* Washington, DC: Author. Retrieved September 8, 2020, from www.youtube.com/watch?v=ctHCpay_onI

Federal Bureau of Investigation. (2018). *Crime in the United States, 2018.* Washington, DC: Author. Retrieved September 11, 2020, from ucr.fbi.gov/crime-in-the-u.s/2018 /crime-in-the-u.s.-2018/

Fisher, B. S., Daigle, L. E., & Cullen, F. T. (2010, February). What distinguishes single from recurrent sexual victims? The role of lifestyle-routine activities and first-incident characteristics. *Justice Quarterly*, 27(1), 102–129.

Gorbett, L., & Anderson, L. (2018, May 2). *Breaking the bond: Trauma bonds and the intersection of domestic violence, sexual assault, and trafficking.* Texas Association against Sexual Assault Conference, PowerPoint presentation. Retrieved September 10, 2020, from taasaconference.org/ wp-content/uploads/2018/06/37 -Breaking-the-Bond-TAASA-Conf-05-2018.pdf

Hammond-Deckard, L. S. (2014, July). Human trafficking 101 for law enforcement. *The Police Chief, 81.* Web only. Retrieved September 10, 2020, from www.policechiefmagazine.org /human-trafficking-101-for-law-enforcement1/

Hanson, R. K., Harris, A. J. R., Letourneau, E., Helmus, L. M., & Thornton, D. (2018). Reductions in risk based on time offense-free in the community: Once a sexual offender, not always a sexual offender. *Psychology, Public Policy, and Law, 24*(1): 48–63. Retrieved September 16, 2020, from www.apa .org/pubs/journals/features/law-law0000135.pdf

Human Smuggling and Trafficking Center. (2016, June 15). *Human trafficking vs. human smuggling.* Washington, DC: Author. Retrieved September 10, 2020, from ctip. defense.gov/Portals/12/Documents/HSTC_Human%20 Trafficking%20vs.%20Human%20Smuggling%20Fact%20 Sheet.pdf?ver=2016-07-14-145555-320

International Association of Chiefs of Police. (2020, June 5). *Successful trauma informed victim interviewing.* Alexandria, VA: Author. Retrieved September 11, 2020, from www.theiacp.org/resources/document /successful-trauma-informed-victim-interviewing

International Labour Organization and Walk Free Foundation. (2017). *Global estimates of modern slavery: Forced labour and forced marriage.* Geneva, Switzerland: Authors. Retrieved September 9, 2020, from www.ilo.org/wcmsp5 /groups/public/---dgreports/---dcomm/documents /publication/wcms_575479.pdf

Johnson, D., Peterson, J., Sommers, I., & Baskin, D. (2012). Use of forensic science in investigating crimes of sexual violence: Contrasting its theoretical potential with empirical realities. *Violence against Women, 18*(2): 193–222. doi:10.1177/1077801212440157

Kimble, C., & Chettiar, I. M. (2018, October 4). Sexual assault remains dramatically underreported. New York, NY: Brennan Center for Justice. Retrieved September 11, 2020, from www.brennancenter.org/our-work/analysis-opinion /sexual-assault-remains-dramatically-underreported

Kingston, A., & Prabhu, M. (2018, March). Constitutionality of involuntary commitment of sex offenders to state offender programs. *The Journal of the American Academy of Psychiatry and the Law, 46*(1): 105–107. Retrieved September 16, 2020, from jaapl.org/content/46/1/105

Lave, T. R., & Zimring, F. (2018). Assessing the real risk of sexually violent predators: Doctor Padilla's dangerous data. *American Criminal Law Review, 55.* Retrieved September 16, 2020, from repository.law.miami.edu/cgi/viewcontent .cgi?article=1577&context=fac_articles

Lisak, D., & Miller, P. M. (2002). Repeat rape and multiple offending among undetected rapists. *Violence and Victims, 17*(1), 73–84. Retrieved September 16, 2020, from sites.oxy.edu/clint/evolution/articles /RepeatRapeinUndetectedRapists.pdf

Lonsway, K. A., & Archambault, J. (2010, September). The earthquake in sexual assault response: Police leadership can increase victim reporting to hold more perpetrators accountable. *The Police Chief,* pp. 50–56.

McWhorter, S. K., Stander, V. A., Merrill, L. L., Thomsen, C. J., & Milner, J. S. (2009). Reports of rape reperpetration by newly enlisted male navy personnel. *Violence and Victims, 24*(2), 204–218. doi:10.1891/0886-6708.24.2.204

Mercado, C. C., Jeglic, E., Markus, K., Hanson, R. K., & Levenson, J. (2011, January). *Sex offender management, treatment, and civil commitment: An evidence based analysis aimed at reducing sexual violence.* New York, NY: John Jay College of Criminal Justice. Retrieved September 16, 2020, from www.ncjrs.gov/pdffiles1/nij/grants/243551.pdf

Milam, M., Borrello, N., & Pooler, J. (2017, November). The survivor-centered, trauma-informed approach. *United States Attorneys' Bulletin*: 39–43. Retrieved September 11, 2020, from www.nationalpublicsafetypartnership.org /clearinghouse/Content/ResourceDocuments/The%20 Survivor-Centered,%20Trauma-Informed%20Approach.pdf

Morgan, R. E., & Oudekerk, B. A. (2019, September). *Criminal victimization, 2018.* Washington, DC: Bureau of Justice Statistics. (NCJ 253043). Retrieved September 11, 2020, from www.bjs.gov/content/pub/pdf/cv18.pdf

Morton, R. J., Tillman, J. M., & Gaines, S. J. (2015). *Serial murder: Pathways for investigations*. Washington, DC: Federal Bureau of Investigation. Retrieved September 8, 2020, from www.fbi.gov/file-repository/serialmurder -pathwaysforinvestigations-1.pdf/view

Motivans, M., & Snyder, H. N. (2018, June). *Federal prosecution of human-trafficking cases, 2015*. Washington, DC: Bureau of Justice Statistics, Special Report. (NCJ 251390). Retrieved September 10, 2020, from www.bjs.gov/content/pub/pdf /fphtc15.pdf

Office for Victims of Justice Training and Technical Assistance Center. (n.d.). *Human trafficking task force e-guide*. Washington, DC: Author. Retrieved September 10, 2020, from www.ovcttac.gov/taskforceguide/eguide/

Office on Women's Health. (2019, April 26). *Date rape drugs*. Washington, DC: Author. Retrieved September 11, 2020, from www.womenshealth.gov/a-z-topics/date-rape-drugs

Paul, A. (2020, February 5). New equipment at crisis center of Tampa Bay changing lives of sexual assault victims. Tampa, FL: Crisis Center of Tampa Bay. Retrieved September 11, 2020, from www.crisiscenter.com/new-equipment -at-crisis-center-of-tampa-bay-changing-lives-of-sexual -assault-victims/

Polaris Project. (2019). *Myths, facts, and statistics*. Washington, DC: Author. Retrieved September 9, 2020, from polarisproject.org/myths-facts-and-statistics/

President's Interagency Task Force to Monitor and Combat Trafficking in Persons. (2014, January). *Federal strategic action plan on services for victims of human trafficking in the United States 2013–2017*. Washington, DC: Author. Retrieved September 10, 2020, from ovc.ojp .gov/sites/g/files/xyckuh226/files/media/document /FederalHumanTraffickingStrategicPlan.pdf

RAINN. (2020). *What is a SANE/SART?* Washington, DC: Author. Retrieved September 11, 2020, from www.rainn.org /articles/what-sanesart#:~:text=A%20Sexual%20Assault%20 Nurse%20Examiner,a%20case%20goes%20to%20trial.

Reporting rape in 2013: Summary Reporting System (SRS) user manual and technical specification. (2014, April 9). Washington, DC: U.S. Department of Justice, Federal Bureau of Investigation, Criminal Justice Information Services (CJIS) Division. Retrieved September 16, 2020, from ucr.fbi.gov/recent-program-updates /reporting-rape-in-2013-revised

Salfati, C. G., & Sorochinski, M. (2019, July). MATCH: A new approach for differentiating & linking series of sex worker homicides and sexual assaults. *International Journal of Offender Therapy and Comparative Criminology, 63*(9): 1794–1824. doi:10.1177/0306624X19839279

Sanchez, R. V., Speck, P. M., & Patrician, P. A. (2019, May-June). A concept analysis of trauma coercive bonding in the commercial sexual exploitation of children. *Journal of Pediatric Nursing, 46*: 48–54. doi:10.1016/j. pedn.2019.02.030

Sawyer, W. (2019, June 6). *BJS fuels myths about sex offense recidivism, contradicting its own new data*. Northampton, MA: Prison Policy Initiative. Retrieved September 16, 2020, from www.prisonpolicy.org/blog/2019/06/06/sexoffenses/

Smith, S. G., Zhang, X., Basile, K. C., Merrick, M. T., Wang, J., Kresnow, M; & Chen, J. (2018, November). *The national intimate partner and sexual violence survey (NISVS): 2015 data brief—updated release*. Atlanta, GA: National Center for Injury Prevention and Control, Centers for Disease Control and Prevention. Retrieved August 31, 2020, from www.cdc. gov/violenceprevention/pdf/2015data-brief508.pdf

Taylor, L. R., & Gaskin-Laniyan, N. (2007, January). Sexual assault in abusive relationships. *NIJ Journal, 256*, 12–14.

The Crime Report Staff. (2018, August 3). Did California authorities suppress research on sexually violent predators? *The Crime Report*. New York, NY: Center for Crime, Media, and Justice at John Jay College of Criminal Justice. Retrieved September 16, 2020, from thecrimereport .org/2018/08/03/did-california-authorities-suppress -research-on-sexually-violent-predators/

U.S. Citizenship and Immigration Services. (2018, May 08). *Victims of human trafficking: T nonimmigrant status*. Washington, DC: Author. Retrieved September 10, 2020, from www.uscis.gov/humanitarian /victims-of-human-trafficking-and-other-crimes /victims-of-human-trafficking-t-nonimmigrant-status

U.S. Department of Homeland Security. (2016, October 21). *Anti-trafficking coordination teams*. Washington, DC: Author. Retrieved September 11, 2020, from www.dhs .gov/sites/default/files/publications/ICE%20-%20Anti -Trafficking%20Coordination%20Teams.pdf

U.S. Department of Justice. (2014, June 18). *Model state provisions on pimping, pandering, and prostitution*. Washington, DC: Author. Retrieved September 7, 2020, from www.justice.gov/olp/model-state-provisions -pimping-pandering-and-prostitution

U.S. Department of Justice. (2016, August 10). *Human trafficking*. Washington, DC: Author. Retrieved September 9, 2020, from www.justice.gov/usao-ri/human-trafficking

U.S. Department of Justice. (2020, May 28). *Sex offender registration and notification act (SORNA)*. Washington, DC: Author. Retrieved September 16, 2020, from www.justice.gov/criminal-ceos /sex-offender-registration-and-notification-act-sorna

U.S. Department of State. (2020, June). *Trafficking in persons report*. Washington, DC: Author. Retrieved September 9, 2020, from www.state.gov/wp-content/uploads/2020/06/2020 -TIP-Report-Complete-062420-FINAL.pdf

Waltke, H., LaPorte, G., Weiss, D., Schwarting, D; Nguyen, M., & Scott, F. (2018, April). Sexual assault cases: Exploring the importance of non-DNA forensic evidence. *National Institute of Justice Journal*, No. 279. Retrieved September 11, 2020, from nij.ojp.gov/topics/articles/sexual-assault-cases -exploring-importance-non-dna-forensic-evidence

Cases Cited

Kansas v. Crane, 534 U.S. 407 (2002).

Kansas v. Hendricks, 521 U.S. 346 (1997).

Karsjens v. Piper, 336 F.Supp.3d 974 (2018).

Chapter 11
Crimes Against Children

Chapter Outline

Learning Objectives

LO1   Define the four common types of maltreatment.

LO2   Identify the most common form of child maltreatment.

LO3   List the possible effects of child abuse and neglect.

LO4   Identify the three components typically included in child abuse/neglect laws.

LO5   Explain when a child should be taken into protective custody.

LO6   List the factors investigators should consider when interviewing child victims.

LO7   Identify the sources that generally report most cases of child neglect or abuse.

LO8   Identify the various physical and behavioral indicators common in neglect and abuse cases.

LO9   Name the 1984 federal act that prohibits child pornography.

LO010   Identify the most common type of child abduction.

LO011   Describe the AMBER Alert program.

Introduction

On Thursday, August 22, 2002, 21-year-old Michelle Knight left her cousin's house in Cleveland and wasn't seen again for 11 years. She had been offered a ride by Ariel Castro, a man whose daughter Knight knew, and then lured into his home with the offer of a puppy for her son. Instead, she found herself restrained with extension cords and locked away from the world. Eight months later, on April 21, 2003, Amanda Berry disappeared a day before her 17th birthday. She was walking home after work when Castro pulled up and offered her a ride. He lured her into his home by saying his daughter, whom Berry knew, was inside. She, too, became his long-term captive. Nearly a year after that, on April 2, 2004, 14-year-old Gina DeJesus went missing on her walk home from school. Once again, it was Castro who had driven up and offered DeJesus, who was friends with one of his daughters, a ride. After getting the young girl to his home, he trapped her in his basement by telling her the door was an exit. No AMBER Alert was issued following DeJesus's disappearance because no one witnessed her abduction.

Three young women, all taken separately, all of whom had a connection to their abductor (through knowing one of his daughters), and all held captive together close to where they had disappeared. During the decade in which the three women were imprisoned by Castro, enduring repeated sexual, physical, and psychological abuse, police had been dispatched to the property several times following reports from neighbors about strange sights and sounds at the house. Yet knocks on the door went unanswered and the police had left.

On May 6, 2013, after Castro had left the house, Berry realized he had neglected to lock an interior door that kept the women from reaching the outer doors to the home and the free world beyond. She spotted a neighbor through the screen and screamed for help. In the 911 call, she is recorded saying, "I've been kidnapped, and I've been missing for 10 years, and I'm here. I'm free now." Responding officers found not only the three women but also a six-year-old girl inside the house, Berry's daughter fathered by Castro during her captivity. Castro was arrested that day and later pleaded guilty to 937 of the 977 charges against him, although he continued to maintain that he was "a good person" and "not a monster." He was sentenced to life in prison plus 1,000 years, and one month into his sentence he committed suicide.

Law enforcement agencies are charged with investigating all crimes, but their responsibility is especially great where crimes against children are involved. Children need the protection of the law to a greater degree than do other members of society because they are so vulnerable, especially if the offense is committed by one or both parents. Even after the offense is committed, the child may still be in danger of further victimization.

The victim's age is one of the essential components in determining whether the crime is one against a child. State statutes differ in their definitions of **minor**, with the most common specifying under the age of 16 or 18. When classifying crimes against children, several state statutes are applicable, including offenses of physical assault, sexual assault, incest, sexual seduction, indecent exposure, lewdness, and molestation. Federal law defines a minor as a child under the age of 18 unless specified otherwise.

Crimes against children that officers may find themselves investigating include maltreatment (neglect and abuse), sexual exploitation (pornography and prostitution), trafficking, and abduction.

Maltreatment of Children: Neglect and Abuse

Throughout history, children have endured physical violence. Infants have been killed as a form of birth control, to avoid the dishonor of illegitimacy, as a means of power, and as a method of disposing of physically or cognitively disabled children. In ancient Greece, a child was the absolute property of the father. The father would raise the first son and expose subsequent children to the elements. Under Roman law, the father had the power of life and death (*patria potestas*) over his children and could kill, mutilate, sell, or offer them as a sacrifice.

During the industrial, urban, and machine age, the exploitation of child labor was common. Children of all ages worked 16 hours a day, often with irons and chains on their ankles to keep them from running away. They were starved, beaten, and dehumanized, and many died from exposure in the workplace, from occupational diseases, or from suicide.

Karmen (2013, p. 231) notes, "For centuries, parents were permitted to beat their children as they saw fit in the name of imposing discipline. Legal notions of progeny as the property of their parents as well as religious traditions (such as 'honor thy father and mother' and 'spare the rod and spoil the child') legitimized corporal punishment of youngsters as a necessary, even essential, technique of child rearing. Only if permanent injury or death resulted were adults in danger of being held responsible for going too far, a problem labeled cruelty to children."

Just as domestic violence used to be considered a family matter, so was mistreating children considered a family matter. Now both are considered crimes, and they must be thoroughly investigated. And like domestic violence, crimes against children are underreported. It is estimated that for every report of abuse the police and child protective services (CPS) receive, there are 10 unreported cases.

Literally, **maltreatment** means to treat roughly or abuse. Maltreatment exists in many forms and along a continuum of severity and chronicity. Definitions of the various types of maltreatment vary from state to state and even locality to locality, but all are based on minimum standards set by federal law. The federal Child Abuse Prevention and Treatment Act (CAPTA) (42 U.S.C. §5106g), as amended by the Keeping Children and Families Safe Act of 2003, defines child abuse and neglect as follows:

- Any recent act or failure to act on the part of a parent or caretaker which results in death, serious physical or emotional harm, sexual abuse or exploitation; or

- An act or failure to act that presents an imminent risk of serious harm.

LO1 Define the four common types of maltreatment.

> The four common types of maltreatment are neglect, physical abuse, emotional abuse, and sexual abuse.

These forms of maltreatment may be found separately or in combination.

Neglect

Neglect is the failure to meet a child's basic needs, including housing, food, clothing, education, and access to medical care. Parental inaction is the essence of neglect.

LO2 Identify the most common form of child maltreatment.

> Neglect is the most common form of child maltreatment and may be fatal.

Often the families from which neglected children come are poor and disorganized. They have no set routine for family activity. The children roam the streets at all hours. They commonly have a record of truancy with the local school and are continually referred to juvenile court for loitering and curfew violations. The family unit is often fragmented by death, divorce, or the incarceration or desertion of parents.

Broken homes—homes perhaps in which a single parent is struggling to survive and make ends meet, or those families otherwise mired in dysfunction, even if both parents are present—often deprive children of affection, recognition, and a sense of belonging unless a strong parent can overcome these responses and provide direction. If a child's protective shield is shattered, the child may lose respect for moral and ethical standards. The broken or dysfunctional home, in and of itself, does not cause delinquency, but it can nullify or even destroy the resources youths need to handle emotional problems constructively. Children from such homes may suffer serious damage to their personalities. They may develop aggressive attitudes and strike out. They may think that punishment is better than no recognition. Even when marriages are intact, both parents often work. Consequently, many parents spend little time in the home interacting with or supervising their children.

Neglected children are often unkempt, bathing infrequently and wearing the same clothes day after day. They may be malnourished and physically weak, leaving them vulnerable to further victimization. They are often deprived of routine medical and dental care and may present numerous chronic health problems for which treatment is readily available but which they are not given.

Entering the arena of possible child neglect are cases in which parents willingly and knowingly choose to withhold medical treatment for their children, often because of religious beliefs. Such cases span the range of not vaccinating children to comply with local school district requirements to refusing life-saving cancer treatment. And while a parent typically has the option to seek treatment for medical conditions as they see fit, more states are intervening in cases where an illness or disease will be terminal without conventional medication or medical attention. In many jurisdictions the parents face involuntary manslaughter charges when the lack of medical care leads to a child's death.

Physical Abuse

Physical abuse refers to beating, whipping, burning, or otherwise inflicting physical harm upon a child. Physical abuse has been identified as the biggest single cause of death of young children. As our society becomes increasingly diverse, the likelihood increases that officers may encounter cultural or religious practices that, while sanctioned in some areas of the world, constitute abuse in this country. Certainly some cultures still consider **corporal punishment**, or the intentional infliction of pain or injury, an acceptable way for parents to correct or discipline their children. Indeed, the legitimacy of spanking as a disciplinary tactic continues to be debated among parents, psychologists, and criminal justice practitioners. A more extreme cultural practice that officers may encounter is **female genital mutilation (FGM)**, a procedure that involves partial or total removal of the external female genitalia, or other injury to the female genital organs for nonmedical reasons.

The World Health Organization (WHO) asserts, "FGM is recognized internationally as a violation of the human rights of girls and women. It reflects deep-rooted inequality between the sexes, and constitutes an extreme form of discrimination against women. It is nearly always carried out on minors and is a violation of the rights of children. The practice also violates a person's rights to health, security and physical integrity, the right to be free from torture and cruel, inhuman or degrading treatment, and the right to life when the procedure results in death" (World Health Organization, 2020). In December 2012, the United Nations General Assembly adopted a resolution on the elimination of female genital mutilation.

Although FGM is not prevalent among children born in the United States, investigators of sex crimes against children need to be aware of the procedures involved and its practice in foreign countries, particularly throughout Africa and the Middle East. Investigators may also find such information useful when investigating human trafficking crimes or when dealing with immigrant families.

Emotional Abuse

Emotional abuse is psychological or social abuse and refers to causing fear or feelings of unworthiness in children by such means as name calling, locking them in closets, ignoring them, constantly belittling or insulting them, threatening violence (even without acting on the threats), or exposing them to harmful psychological situations such as allowing them to witness the physical or psychological abuse of another. It is often more difficult to detect than physical abuse because the damage to the child's mental well-being occurs internally. However, such abuse often manifests, over time, in maladaptive behavior by the child such as a lack of confidence, persistent negative self-talk ("I'm dumb" or "I'm not worth it"), depression, aggression, being fearful of the parent, emotional immaturity, and inability to make friends.

Sexual Abuse

Sexual abuse includes sexually molesting a child, performing sexual acts with a child, and statutory rape and seduction. Some cultures sanction sexual relationships between adults and children, but such acts are illegal in this country.

Sexual seduction means ordinary sexual intercourse, anal intercourse, cunnilingus, or fellatio committed by a nonminor with a consenting minor. **Lewdness** means touching a minor to arouse, appeal to, or gratify the perpetrator's sexual desires. The touching may be done by the perpetrator or by the minor under the perpetrator's direction. **Molestation** is a broader term, referring to any act motivated by unnatural or abnormal sexual interest in minors that would reasonably be expected to disturb, irritate, or offend the victim. Molestation may or may not involve touching of the victim.

Legislatures in a number of states are attempting to broaden penalties to make them match the severity of the offense, especially if the victim is very young. There is also a concerted effort to expand the offenses to make genders equal, recognizing that victims and offenders may be male or female. The age of the offender as well as the type of crime are both considered. Illinois, for example, has consolidated nine sex offenses into four but provides for 24 combinations of charges.

The Extent of the Problem

According to the Administration for Children and Families (2020), one child is abused or neglected every 46.5 seconds. The National Child Abuse and Neglect Data System (NCANDS) is a federally sponsored effort that collects and analyzes data on child abuse and neglect and prepares an annual report, *Child Maltreatment*, released each spring. According to the most recent report (Administration for Children and Families [ACF], 2020), CPS agencies received an estimated 4.3 million referrals involving the alleged mistreatment of approximately 7.8 million children during federal fiscal year 2018. Of these, 2.4 million referrals were screened in for further investigation and an estimated 678,000 children were determined to be victims of abuse or neglect, a rate of 9.2 victims per 1,000 children in the U.S. population. Generally speaking, the youngest children are the most vulnerable to maltreatment, and the rate of victimization decreases as children age. Among the children confirmed as victims by CPS agencies in 2018:

- Victims in their first year of life had the highest rate of victimization at 26.7 per 1,000 children of the same age in the national population.

- The victimization rate for girls was 9.6 per 1,000 girls in the population, which was higher than boys at 8.7 per 1,000 boys in the population.

- In terms of pure numbers, the majority of victims were White (44.3%), followed by Hispanic (22.4%) and African American (20.5%).

- American Indian or Alaska Native children had the highest rate of victimization at 15.2 per 1,000 children in the population of the same race or ethnicity; African American children had the second highest rate at 14.0 per 1,000 children of the same race or ethnicity; White children had a victimization rate of 8.2 per 1,000; and Hispanic children had a victimization rate of 8.1 per 1,000.

(Administration for Children and Families, 2020)

As in prior years, neglect was the most common form of child maltreatment (60.8% of confirmed cases). Physical and sexual abuse, regardless of the age of the victim, are also classified as violent crimes.

Youth as Victims of Violent Crime

According to data from the most recent National Survey of Children's Exposure to Violence (NatSCEV II), more than half (57.7%) of youth surveyed reported at least one exposure to violence—physical assault, sexual victimization, maltreatment, or property victimization—during the previous year, either directly as victims or indirectly as witnesses (Finkelhor, Turner, Shattuck, Hamby, & Kracke, 2015). Furthermore, the survey revealed that during the previous 12 months

- Two in five children and adolescents (41.2%) had been physically assaulted at least once.

- One in eighteen youths (5.6%) had been exposed to sexual victimization during the previous year, and 2.2% had experienced sexual assault in the previous year.

- One in seven youths (13.8%) reported exposure to maltreatment during the previous year, including physical abuse, emotional abuse, and neglect.

- Nearly one-quarter (24.1%) of youth had experienced property victimization.

- Approximately one in twelve youths (8.2%) had witnessed one family member assault another, and one in six youths (16.9%) had been exposed to community violence.

- Bullying-type victimizations were also common, with one in seven youths (13.7%) being physically intimidated within the past year and more than one-third (36.5%) being victims of relational aggression (i.e., emotional bullying) within the past year.

These violent crimes are investigated using the procedures described in the preceding chapters but taking into consideration the age of the victims.

When the violence is severe enough, death can occur. Child fatalities are the most tragic consequence of maltreatment. CPS investigations determined that in 2018, 1,770 child fatalities resulted from abuse and neglect, a rate of 2.39 victims per 100,000 children in the U.S. population:

- The majority (70.6%) of all child fatality victims were younger than three years old.

- Although girls were maltreated at a higher rate, as previously mentioned, boys died at a higher rate as a result of the maltreatment. The child fatality rate for boys was 2.87 per 100,000 boys in the population, compared with 2.19 per 100,000 girls in the population.

- The majority of child fatalities from maltreatment were of White children (40.1%), followed by African American children (32.8%), and Hispanic children (14.4%).

- Four out of five (80.3%) child fatalities involved parents acting alone, together, or with other individuals. Fewer than fifteen percent (14.6%) of fatalities did not have a parental relationship to their perpetrator.

- One out of eleven (8.1%) child fatalities was attributed to medical neglect.

- Nearly three out of four (72.8%) child fatalities involved some degree of neglect.

- Almost half (46.1%) of child fatalities had suffered physical abuse either exclusively or in combination with other maltreatment types.

(Administration for Children and Families, 2020)

The rate of child abuse and neglect fatalities has fluctuated during the last several years, influenced in part by which states report data as well as by the U.S. Census Bureau's child population estimates: "Some States that reported an increase in child fatalities from 2012 to 2013 attributed it to improvements in reporting after the passage of the Child and Family Services Improvement and Innovation Act (P.L. 112–34), which passed in 2010. Most data on child fatalities come from State child welfare agencies. However, States may also draw on other data sources, including health departments, vital statistics departments, medical examiners' offices, law enforcement, and fatality review teams. This coordination of data collection contributes to better estimates" (Child Welfare Information Gateway, 2020, p. 2).

However, many researchers and practitioners believe child fatalities are underreported, perhaps by 50% to 60%. Reasons include variation among reporting requirements and definitions of child abuse and neglect, variation in death investigative systems and in training for investigators, variation in state child fatality review processes, and the amount of time it may take to establish the cause of death.

The Effects of Child Abuse and Neglect

The effects of child abuse and neglect can be devastating.

> **LO3**   List the possible effects of child abuse and neglect.
>
> Child abuse and neglect can result in serious and permanent physical, mental, and emotional damage, as well as in future violent and criminal behavior.

Physical damage may involve the brain, vital organs, eyes, ears, arms, or legs. Severe abuse may also cause severe mental illness, restricted language ability, restricted perceptual and motor-skill development, arrested physical development, blindness, deafness, loss of limbs, or even death.

Emotional damage may include impaired self-concept as well as increased levels of aggression, anxiety, and tendency toward self-destructiveness. These self-destructive tendencies can cause children to act out antisocial behavior in the family, the school, and the community at large. Such self-destructiveness can also manifest itself in risky behavior that endangers youths' health and safety.

Research has examined the potential correlation between childhood maltreatment and the likelihood of criminality and arrest later in life. Some studies have found that offenders who were physically abused or neglected as children had higher rates of violent, property, and total offending than did nonabused offenders (Cuevas, Finkelhor, Shattuck, Turner, & Hamby, 2013). These children were also at increased risk for myriad negative outcomes related to their emotional development and mental health, including learning disabilities, difficulties in relating to peers, depression, anxiety, oppositional defiant disorder, conduct disorder, aggression, and post–traumatic stress disorder (PTSD). Furthermore, as these children matured to adulthood, they continued to be at elevated risk for substance abuse, psychiatric disorders, serious medical illnesses, and lower economic productivity (Petersen, Joseph, & Feit, 2013). In contrast, other studies have concluded that physical abuse alone was *not* associated with future violent delinquency but that a history of sexual abuse and neglect was a significant predictor of violent delinquency (Yun, Ball, & Lim, 2011).

Another likely effect of child abuse is that as an adult, the former victim frequently becomes a perpetrator of child abuse, thereby creating a vicious cycle sometimes called the *intergenerational transmission of violence.* Research shows that a child's history of physical abuse predisposes that child to violence in later years. Victims of neglect are also likely to engage in later violent criminal behavior.

Risk Factors for Child Maltreatment

Parents or caretakers commit most emotional and physical child abuse. The causes of such abuse often center on a cycle of abuse passed from one generation to the next. Certain risk factors have been found to contribute to increased chance of child maltreatment, including

- Children younger than four years of age

- Special needs that may increase caregiver burden (e.g., disabilities, mental retardation, mental health issues, and chronic physical illnesses)

- Parents' lack of understanding of children's needs, child development, and parenting skills

- Parents' history of child maltreatment in family of origin

- Substance abuse and/or mental health issues, including depression in the family

- Parental characteristics such as young age, low education, single parenthood, large number of dependent children, and low income

- Nonbiological, transient caregivers in the home (e.g., mother's male partner)

- Parental thoughts and emotions that tend to support or justify maltreatment behaviors

- Social isolation

- Family disorganization, dissolution, and violence, including intimate partner violence

- Parenting stress, poor parent-child relationships, and negative interactions

- Community violence

- Concentrated neighborhood disadvantage (e.g., high poverty and residential instability, high unemployment rates, and high density of alcohol outlets) and poor social connections

(Centers for Disease Control and Prevention, 2020)

Before looking at investigating cases of child maltreatment, consider the laws under which investigators must operate.

Child Abuse and Neglect Laws

A complicating factor in investigating child abuse is the perceived ambiguity of what it is. Is spanking a child abuse? Belittling a child? Sending a child to bed without dinner? Is it neglectful when a parent leaves a young child home alone for half an hour? An hour? Eight hours? At what point does this behavior constitute child neglect and endangerment? To address and reduce some of this ambiguity, laws regarding child abuse and neglect have been passed at both federal and state levels.

> **LO4** Identify the three components typically included in child abuse/neglect laws.

Typically child abuse and neglect laws have three components: (1) criminal definitions and penalties, (2) a mandate to report suspected cases, and (3) civil process for removing the child from the abusive or neglectful environment.

Federal Legislation

In 1974, the federal government passed CAPTA. It was amended in 1978 under Public Law 95-266 and again in 2003 as the Keeping Children and Families Safe Act (P.L. 108-36), as mentioned at the beginning of the chapter. This act has been amended several times; most recently certain provisions of the act were amended on January 7, 2019, by the Victims of Child Abuse Act Reauthorization Act of 2018 (P.L. 115-424). The law states, in part, that the crimes of child abuse and neglect include "any recent act . . . on the part of a parent or caregiver that results in . . . serious physical or emotional harm."

Nonetheless, federal courts have also ruled that parents are free to strike children because "the custody, care and nurture of the child resides first in the parents" (*Prince v. Massachusetts,* 1944). This fundamental right to "nurture" has been supplanted by the Supreme Court with the "care, custody and management" of one's child (*Santosky v. Kramer,* 1982). This shift from "nurture" to "management" could herald a return to older laws, such as the one expressed in *People v. Green* (1909): "The parent is the sole judge of the necessity for the exercise of disciplinary right and of the nature of the correction to be given." The court needs to determine only whether "the punishment inflicted went beyond the legitimate exercise of parental authority."

Current laws often protect parents, and convictions for child abuse are difficult to obtain because of circumstantial evidence, the lack of witnesses, the husband-wife privilege, and the fact that an adult's testimony often is enough to establish reasonable doubt. All too often, the court determines punishment to be reasonable, never reexamining the age-old presumption that hitting children is permissible.

The courts' role is to decide when and to what degree physical punishment steps beyond "the legitimate exercise of parental authority" or what constitutes "excessive punishment." The courts always begin with the presumption that parents have a legal right to use force against their own children. In *Green*, 70 marks from a whipping was held to be excessive and unreasonable, even though the parent claimed he was not criminally liable because there was no permanent injury and he had acted in good faith. But the assumption remained that the parent had an unquestionable right "to administer such reasonable and timely punishment as may be necessary to correct growing faults in young children."

A determination of "reasonableness" was made in *Ingraham v. Wright* (1977) regarding the use of physical punishment of students by teachers, after one student was beaten by 20 strokes with a wooden paddle and another was beaten by 50 strokes. The Florida statute specified that the punishment was not to be "degrading or unduly severe." In September 2014, professional football player Adrian Peterson was indicted in Texas on felony child-abuse charges for using a wooden switch to discipline his then-4-year-old son, corporal punishment that left cuts and bruises on the boy's back, thigh, buttocks, and genitals. Peterson pleaded no contest to a reduced charge of misdemeanor reckless assault, but four years later, he was still using corporal punishment occasionally to discipline his children, according to a friend (Bieler, 2018).

CAPTA and the Keeping Children and Families Safe Act set forth a minimum definition of child abuse and neglect; identified the federal government's role in supporting research, evaluation, technical assistance, and data collection activities; and provided federal funding to states in their efforts to prevent, assess, investigate, and prosecute child maltreatment as well as treat those who perpetrate this crime. In 2000, Congress passed the Child Abuse Prevention and Enforcement Act making more funds available for child abuse and neglect enforcement and prevention initiatives.

In 2004, President George W. Bush signed the Unborn Victims of Violence Act, or Laci and Conner's Law. This law amended the U.S. Code and the Uniform Code of Military Justice to punish separately the harming of a child in utero. The punishment is the same as provided under federal law for conduct causing the injury to, or death of, the unborn child's mother, but the imposition of the death penalty is prohibited. This separate offense does not require proof that the person who committed the offense knew or should have known that the victim was pregnant or that the accused intended to harm the unborn child.

In 2006, the Adam Walsh Child Protection and Safety Act, first discussed in Chapter 10, was signed into law, aimed at tracking sex crime offenders and subjecting them to stiff, mandatory minimum sentences. The act, named for the 6-year-old son of John and Reve Walsh who was abducted and murdered in Florida in 1981, expands previous sex registry requirements, setting forth strict guidelines for states, territories, and tribal nations to develop and maintain a jurisdiction-wide sex offender registry. Failure to comply with the guidelines can result in a reduction in the amount of federal funds received by a jurisdiction.

State Laws

Since the 1960s, every state has enacted child abuse and neglect laws. On the whole, states offer a bit more protection to children by statute than does the federal

government. Legal definitions vary from state to state. California, for example, declares it illegal for anyone to willfully cause or permit any child to suffer or for any person to inflict unjustifiable physical or mental suffering on a child or to cause the child to "be placed in such situations that its person or health is endangered" (California Penal Codes, Sec. 273A).

Alaska defines abuse broadly: "The infliction, by other than accidental means, of physical harm upon the body of a child." Other state statutes are much less broad. For example, Maryland's statute states that a person is not guilty of child abuse if the defendant's intentions were good, but their judgment was bad. The defendant in *Worthen v. State* (1979) admitted he had punished his 2-year-old stepdaughter because she was throwing a temper tantrum, "but sought to explain as not having exceeded the bounds of parental propriety." The jury found him guilty of assault and battery for the multiple contusions about the girl's face, ribs, buttocks, and legs, but the appellate court ordered a new trial because the trial court in its jury instructions had omitted the defense of good intentions and also the defense that the stepfather had not exceeded the bounds of parental authority. What is "reasonable" varies from state to state, from one judge or court to another, and from jury to jury.

Case Processing

Most child abuse and neglect cases enter the child welfare system through CPS agencies (ACF, 2020). *CPS* generally refers to services provided by an agency authorized to act on behalf of a child when parents are unable or unwilling to do so. CPS may provide protective custody of a child outside the home or provide protective supervision of the child within the family unit at any point until a case is closed or dismissed. The specific options once a case enters formal court processing are the focus. Frequently a formal investigation is required.

Challenges in Investigating Child Maltreatment Cases

Many prosecutors, at all levels of the judiciary system, perceive crimes against children as among the most difficult to prosecute and for which to obtain convictions. Therefore, to most effectively prosecute the guilty and protect the innocent, officers interviewing child witnesses and victims should have specialized training themselves or should interview alongside a licensed professional with specialized training.

Regardless of whether crimes against children are handled by generalists or specialists within the department, certain challenges are unique to these investigations and include the need to protect the child from further harm, the possibility of parental involvement, the need to collaborate with other agencies, the difficulty of interviewing children, and credibility concerns. The challenges presented by technology and online predation of children will be discussed later in the chapter.

Protecting the Child

When child abuse is reported, investigators may initiate an investigation on their own, or they may investigate jointly with social services. Regardless of the source of the report, and regardless of whether the investigation is a single or joint effort, the primary responsibility of the investigator assigned to the case is the immediate protection of the child.

> **L05** Explain when a child should be taken into protective custody.
>
> If the possibility of present or continued danger to the child exists, the child must be removed into protective custody.

Under welfare regulations and codes, an officer may take a child into temporary custody without a warrant if there is an emergency or if the officer has reason to believe that leaving the child in the present situation would subject the child to further abuse or harm. **Temporary custody without hearing** usually means for 48 hours. Factors that would justify placing a child in protective custody include the following:

- The child's age or physical or mental condition makes the child incapable of self-protection.

- The home's physical environment poses an immediate threat to the child.

- The child needs immediate medical or psychiatric care, and the parents refuse to obtain it.

- The parents cannot or will not provide for the child's basic needs.

- Maltreatment in the home could permanently damage the child physically or emotionally.

- The parents may abandon the child.

Consultation with local welfare authorities is sometimes needed before police officials ask the court for a hearing to remove a child from the parents' custody or for protective custody in an authorized facility. Because police rarely have such facilities, the child should be taken to the nearest welfare facility or to a foster home as soon as possible, as stipulated by the juvenile court. The parents or legal guardians of the child must be notified as soon as possible.

The Need to Involve Other Agencies: The Multidisciplinary Team Approach

Another challenge facing law enforcement is the need to collaborate with various social services, child welfare, and health agencies to more effectively handle child abuse cases. Traditionally, law enforcement and social service agencies have worked fairly independently on child abuse cases, with each conducting its own separate interviews and investigations. Many police departments have seen no need to collaborate with social services unless their investigation determines a need to remove the child from parental custody. However, it is increasingly evident that this lack of communication and coordination among these agencies has led to numerous cases "falling through the cracks" of the disjointed system, sometimes with devastating results.

A multidisciplinary team (MDT) consists of professionals from CPS and law enforcement as well as psychologists, psychiatrists, medical doctors, prosecutors, and victims' advocates, all working together to create an effective response to reports of child abuse and neglect. It is important to understand, however, that the various roles of these team members overlap with and influence each other but may also potentially interfere with one another. For example, while the primary responsibility of CPS is to ensure a child's safety, law enforcement's role is to determine if a criminal investigation is warranted and what charges to bring. Because CPS investigations generally have stricter timelines than those of law enforcement, this accelerated schedule can impede evidence collection and derail successful prosecution if law enforcement is not afforded the time to adequately investigate for criminality (MacLeod, 2016).

A coordinated response can minimize the likelihood of conflicts between agencies with different philosophies and mandates. Joint investigations often result in more victim corroborations and perpetrator confessions than do independent investigations. In addition, referral agencies provide support and assistance to families and victims experiencing child abuse or neglect. A collaborative, community-based approach to problems associated with children and youths should result in identifying, developing, and implementing more effective, multiagency solutions.

Several national programs can assist in investigating abandoned or abducted children, such as the National Children Identification Program, which distributes fingerprint and DNA (cheek swab) collection kits to parents. This identifying information can be provided to law enforcement authorities if a child abduction occurs or a child runs away.

Other technological developments allow police to communicate more effectively with organizations such as the media in cases involving child abductions—cases where speed of information dissemination is critical.

Difficulty in Interviewing Children

When children are very young, a limited vocabulary can pose a severe challenge to investigators. Unfortunately, by the time children are old enough to possess the words or other skills needed to communicate and describe their abusive experiences, they have also developed the ability to feel such shame, embarrassment, and fear over these events that they might resist talking about them.

Interviewing a child abuse victim takes special understanding, skill, and practice. Children often have difficulty talking about abuse, and often they have been instructed not to tell anyone about it. They may have been threatened by the abuser, or they may have a close relationship with the abuser and not want anything bad to happen to that person. Keep in mind that you are a stranger to them and may be asking for information about someone they trust, such as a parent.

> **LO6** List the factors investigators should consider when interviewing child victims.
>
> When interviewing children, officers should consider the child's age, ability to describe what happened, and the potential for retaliation by the suspect against a child who "tells."

Another difficulty in interviewing children is their short attention spans. Questions should be brief and understandable, a skill that often proves difficult and requires training and practice. Interviewers who are excellent with adults may not be so successful with children.

Investigators may consider inviting a social service professional to help conduct the interview because they often have more formal training and experience in interviewing children at their level and may, therefore, be better able to establish rapport. More specific guidelines for interviewing abused children are discussed in detail shortly.

Credibility Concerns

Assessing the credibility of people reporting child abuse is a constant challenge for investigators. As repulsive as society finds child abuse, particularly sexual abuse, investigators must exercise great care to protect the innocent and falsely accused. No other crime is so fraught with stigma. Consequently, accusations of this type can be difficult to dispel even if false.

Because of the "loaded" nature of child sexual abuse allegations, parents who are divorcing may be tempted to use such claims as ammunition against their soon-to-be ex-spouse. For investigators, sorting through details of such allegations to determine their credibility can be extremely challenging. Occasionally, the credibility of the child victim is challenged. However, investigators must approach each case and each victim with an open mind, aware that in most child abuse cases, children tell the truth to the best of their ability.

People who work with child abuse cases point out that children will frequently lie to get out of trouble, but they seldom lie to get into trouble. Although most child abuse reports are valid, investigators must use caution to weed out those cases reported by a habitual liar or by a child who is telling a story to offset other misdeeds they have committed. A child's motivation for lying may be revenge, efforts to avoid school or parental disapproval, efforts to cover up for other disapproved behavior, or, in the case of sexual abuse, an attempt to explain a pregnancy or to obtain an abortion at state expense.

The Initial Report

According to the NCANDS, 67.3% of the child maltreatment reports in 2018 came from "professional" sources, such as child day care providers and medical personnel, with the top three report sources being law enforcement and legal personnel (18.7%), teachers and other education personnel (20.5%), and social services staff (10.7%) (ACF, 2020). The remainder of the reports were submitted by "nonprofessional" sources, such as friends, neighbors, parents and relatives, clergy members, sports coaches, camp counselors, and anonymous sources.

Most reports of child neglect or abuse are made by third parties such as teachers, physicians, neighbors, siblings, or parents. Seldom does the victim report the offense.

In most states, certain individuals who work with or treat children are required by law to report cases of suspected neglect or abuse. These **mandated reporters** include teachers, school authorities, childcare personnel, camp personnel, clergy, physicians, dentists, chiropractors, nurses, psychologists, medical assistants, attorneys, and social workers. Such a report may be made to social services or CPS, the juvenile court, or the local police or sheriff's department. It may be made verbally, but it should also be put in writing as soon as possible after the initial verbal report is made. Some states have special forms for child abuse cases. These forms are sent to a central location, thereby helping prevent child abusers from taking the child to different doctors or hospitals for treatment and thus avoiding the suspicion that would accompany multiple incidents involving the same child.

Child neglect and abuse reports should contain the name, age, and address of the child victim; the name and address of the child's parents or others responsible for the child's care; the name and address of the person suspected of the abuse; the nature and extent of the neglect or abuse; and any evidence of this or previous neglect or abuse. These reports are confidential.

In most states, action must be taken on a report within a specified time, frequently three days. If, in the judgment of the person receiving the report, it is necessary to remove the child from present custody, this is discussed with the responsible agency, such as CPS or the juvenile court. If the situation is deemed life-threatening, the police may temporarily remove the child. No matter who receives the report or whether the child must be removed from the situation, it is the responsibility of the law enforcement agency to investigate the charge.

The Police Response

As noted, as with domestic violence, child abuse and neglect were traditionally viewed as family matters—a social issue regulated by child protection agencies. It was not a crime. Currently, child abuse is viewed as a crime and within the jurisdiction of the criminal justice system. Therefore, it needs to be investigated by trained criminal investigators.

The investigator must talk with people who know the child and obtain background information about the child. For example, does the child have behavior problems? Is the child generally truthful?

If interviews are conducted with the parents, every attempt should be made to conduct the interviews in private, away from the child and the other parent. Explain why the interview is necessary. Be direct, honest, understanding, and professional. Do not accuse, demand, give personal opinions about the situation, request information from the parents unrelated to the matter under discussion, make judgments, place blame, or reveal the source of your information. If the parents are suspects, provide them the due process rights granted by the Fourth and Fifth Amendments, including the *Miranda* warning.

Interviewing Abused Children

Interviewing children requires special skills and, as discussed, coordination among members of a multidisciplinary team. Before the interview, obtain relevant background information from the parents or guardian and anyone else involved in the case, including caseworkers, counselors, and physicians. Also review the incident report.

Often several interviews are necessary to get a complete statement without overwhelming the child. While it is true that some children need more time to develop trust and become comfortable with an interviewer, research has clearly demonstrated the risks associated with repeated questioning and duplicative interviews: "Multiple, nonduplicative interviews are most effective when the interviewer uses best practices in forensic interviewing; adapts the interview structure to the developmental, cultural, and emotional needs of the child; and avoids suggestive and coercive approaches" (Newlin et al., 2015). When multiple interviews will be necessary, keep the initial interview brief, merely to establish the facts supporting probable cause, and conduct a second interview later.

Numerous forensic interviewing protocols have been developed, and in-depth discussion of them is beyond the scope of this text. However, a criminal investigator who receives specialized training in conducting forensic interviews of child abuse victims should be familiar with the different models used in the United States and understand that the most effective interviewers commonly receive training in multiple protocols so as to be able to apply a blended approach that best meets the circumstances, the needs of the child being interviewed, and the particular laws of their jurisdiction. The models most often used in the United States are:

- The National Institute of Child Health and Human Development (NICHD) Investigative Interview Protocol

- The CornerHouse RATAC (Rapport, Anatomy ID, Touch Inquiry, Abuse Scenario, and Closure) Forensic Interview Protocol

- The National Children's Advocacy Center (NCAC) Child Forensic Interview Structure

- The ChildFirst/Finding Words Forensic Interview Protocol

- The Step-Wise Interview

Generally, it is best to conduct the interview in private in the child's or a friend's home or in a small room at a hospital or the police station. An interview room in a police station can be converted into a friendly environment for youngsters with the addition of some simple toys or coloring books. If practical, a school can also be a good place to conduct a child interview. If the interview is to take place at the child's home, it might be best not to wear a uniform, especially if the child thinks they are to blame. The uniform could be too intimidating and frighten the child into thinking that they are going to be arrested. Casual, comfortable clothes are usually best.

Regardless of whether the interview is conducted at the child's home, at school, or at the police station, it is usually not advisable to have a family member present—but if the child so desires, the wish should be respected. The family member should be seated out of the child's view to avoid influencing the interview. However, if a parent is suspected of being the offender, neither parent should be present.

The investigator should record the time the interview begins and ends. The recommended protocol is to videotape the interview, which can be used later by other officers, prosecutors, and the courts, thus eliminating the need to requestion the victim. To obtain the most thorough and accurate account of the abuse possible, investigators should be proficient in cognitive interview techniques, discussed in Chapter 6.

When conducting an interview with a child, investigators must maintain rapport. The gender of the interviewer generally does not matter—the ability to elicit accurate information is the key quality. The interviewer should sit next to the child and speak in a friendly voice, without talking down to the child. It may help to play a game with the child or to get down on the floor at the child's level to get attention and to encourage the child to talk naturally. Allow the child freedom to do other things during the interview, such as moving around the room or playing with toys, but do not allow distractions from the outside.

Learn about the child's abilities and interests by asking questions about everyday activities, such as school and household chores. Ask about the child's siblings, pets, friends, and favorite games or television shows. It may help to share personal information when appropriate, such as about your own children or pets. Evaluate the child's cognitive level by asking if they can read, write, count, or tell time. Does the child know their birth date? Can the child recount past events (yesterday, holidays)? Does the child know about various body parts and their functions? Assess the child's maturity level by asking about chores and responsibilities—making his or her own breakfast, walking the dog, and so on. Does the child enjoy any privileges (staying home alone, going places on their own)?

Make the child feel comfortable, and keep in mind that questioning children is apt to be more of a sharing experience than a formal interview. Because young children have a short attention span, fact-finding interviews should last no more than 15 or 20 minutes. Questions should pertain to what happened; who did it; when it happened; where it happened; and whether force, threats, or enticements were involved. Ask simple, direct, open-ended questions. Avoid asking "why" questions, because they tend to sound accusatory. To alleviate the anxiety, fear, or reluctance found in children who have been instructed or threatened not to tell by the offender (*especially* if a parent), try statements such as, "It's not bad to tell what happened," "You won't get in trouble," "You can help your dad/mom/friend by telling what happened," and "It wasn't your fault." Never threaten or try to force a reluctant child to talk because such pressure will likely lead a child to "clam up" and may cause further trauma.

It is extremely important not to put words into a child's mouth. When the child answers your questions, be certain you understand the meaning of their words. A child may think "sex" is kissing or hugging or touching. If the child uses a word, learn what the word really means to the child to get to the truth and avoid later embarrassment in court. Furthermore, investigators should not correct the child's definition of the word and should refer to whatever word the child has used when discussing the topic.

In child interviews, it is also very important to establish who lives with the child. The people who live with the child have had the most exposure to the child and should be interviewed. Before that, however, have the child describe the relationship with that person. A parental friend may be called an "uncle" when, in reality, there is no family connection. Also, siblings may have nicknames that the interviewer may not know but which might prove important during the investigation. In sum, arriving at a working vocabulary—names of body parts, what certain people in the family (or close to the family) are called, words used to describe certain actions—is essential to conducting an effective interview with children.

In the case of sexual abuse of young children, it may be helpful to use drawings or anatomical dolls to assist the child in describing exactly what happened and the positions of the child and the abuser when the offense took place. Controversy exists, however, about whether such dolls help or hinder interview progress. Nonetheless, legislation in 10 states allows child witnesses to use dolls or diagrams as a testimonial aid, and in at least 15 states, appellate courts have upheld their usage during trial (National District Attorneys Association, 2014).

Some techniques, such as the NICHD Investigative Interview Protocol, generally do not make use of anatomical dolls, whereas in other techniques, including the RATAC and ChildFirst®/Finding Words protocols, interviewers are encouraged to use dolls under proper circumstances (Toth, 2011). Anatomical dolls can help the interviewer establish the names a child victim uses for various body parts and to follow a line of questioning regarding "good touch/bad touch." If such aids are used, several important guidelines should be adhered to:

- Interviewers should have specific training in the use of anatomical dolls and be aware of what is legally acceptable in their own jurisdictions.

- Introduce the dolls only *after* the child has verbally indicated abuse happened.

- Introduce the dolls as something to help "show" what happened, not toys to be played with.

- Use dolls only if needed to assist the child in communicating details of what happened and only later in the interview, if the child is unable or unwilling to communicate verbally (or in writing) and/or when the child's verbal description is limited or unclear.

- Use the dolls only if developmentally appropriate. Be extremely cautious using the dolls with preschoolers. An accurate portrayal of what happened using the assistance of dolls requires the child to have both understanding of the symbolic nature of the dolls (i.e., the developmental capability to understand the abstract notion that the dolls represent him/herself and/or the suspect), as well as the ability for dual representation (i.e., the ability to use them symbolically to communicate events).

- Present the dolls fully clothed.

- Use reputable professionally produced dolls with culturally appropriate features such as similar skin-tones and hair color, as well as developmentally appropriate physical characteristics.

- When the child has finished demonstrating with the dolls, they should be put away.

(American Professional Society on the Abuse of Children, 2012)

During the interview, do not try to extract promises from the child regarding testifying in court, because an undue emphasis on a trial may frighten the child, causing nightmares and apprehension. Investigators should avoid asking leading questions, repeated interviews, and confusing questions.

After the interview is completed, give the parents simple, straightforward information about what will happen next in the criminal justice system and approximately when, the likelihood of trial, and so on. Enlist their cooperation. Let them know who to contact for status reports or in an emergency; express appreciation and understanding for the efforts they are making by reporting and following through on the process. Answer any questions the child or parents have.

Anatomical dolls are sometimes used to diagnose and treat sexual abuse victims. The dolls enable victims (generally children) to better express thoughts and actions by "acting out" their trauma. These adolescent dolls feature a male or female sex organ, breasts, ears, mouth, navel, jointed legs, and individual fingers.

© Cynthia Harnest/www.teach-a-bodies.com

One final note: exact notes are critical in interviews of child sexual abuse victims because such cases are an exception to the hearsay rule, meaning an officer *may* testify in court about the victim's statements. Therefore, officers should be meticulous in recording all statements verbatim. The child may not be able to repeat the statements because of fear or anxiety. For this reason, as well as others mentioned earlier, interviews should be videotaped whenever possible.

Sample Protocol

The following excerpt from the Boulder City (Nevada) Police Department's protocol for investigating reports of sexual and physical abuse of children is typical.

It is the policy to *team* investigate all abuse allegations.

When a report comes in, a juvenile officer is immediately assigned all abuse cases. This officer is responsible for maintaining a 72-hour time frame. Contact is made as soon as possible.

The investigative process includes the following:

- The investigator contacts Nevada Welfare, and together they contact the victim at a location where the victim can be interviewed briefly, and not in the presence of the alleged perpetrator of the crime.

- During the initial interview the juvenile officer tries to determine if the report is a substantiated abuse, unsubstantiated, or unfounded.

- If the report is substantiated, the juvenile officer or Nevada State Welfare removes the child from the home and places the child into protective custody. If the juvenile officer and Nevada State Welfare investigator determine the child is not in danger of any abuse, the child can be allowed to remain in his/her home environment.

- If the report is unsubstantiated, the child is left in the home.

- If the report is unfounded, the reason for the false report is also investigated to identify other problems.

- If the case is substantiated abuse, the victim is housed at Child Haven, and there is a detention hearing at 9:00 a.m. the following working day.

An in-depth interview is conducted with the victim by the juvenile officer and the Nevada State Welfare investigator. Several aids are used, depending on the child's age and mental abilities: structured and unstructured play therapy, picture drawings, and use of anatomical dolls.

The juvenile officer also contacts the accused person and interviews him/her about the specific allegations, makes a report or statement relevant to the interview, and makes these reports available to Nevada State Welfare and/or Clark County Juvenile Court. Nevada State Welfare is encouraged to attend these interviews, and a team approach is used during this phase of the investigation also.

The juvenile officer also interviews other people, including witnesses or victims—anyone who might have information about the case. The officer prepares an affidavit and presents the case to the district attorney's office to determine whether the case is suitable for prosecution. If so, a complaint is issued, and a warrant or summons is issued for the accused. Once a warrant is obtained, the investigating officer locates and arrests or causes the accused person to be arrested.

Investigators must know their own state laws, as well as federal statutes and the possibility of dual prosecution.

Evidence

All the investigator's observations pertaining to the victim's physical and emotional condition must be recorded in detail. Evidence in child neglect or abuse cases includes the surroundings, the home conditions, clothing, bruises or other body injuries, the medical examination report, and other observations.

Photographs may be the best way to document child abuse and neglect where it is necessary to show injury to the child or the home environment conditions. Pictures should be taken immediately because children's injuries heal quickly and home conditions can be changed rapidly. Pictures in both color and black and white should be taken, showing bruises, burns, cuts, or any injury requiring medical treatment. These photographs should be done with a scale to show the size of the bruises, cuts, and so on, and should be witnessed by people who can later testify about the location and extent of the injuries, including medical personnel who examined the child. Explain the need for the pictures to the child to avoid further fear or excitement. All procedures for photography at a crime scene (discussed in Chapter 2) should be followed.

Additional types of evidence that may be obtained in sexual assault cases include photographs, torn clothing, ropes or tapes, and trace evidence such as the hair of the offender and the victim and, in some instances, semen. Researchers Walsh, Jones, Cross, and Lippert (2010, p. 438) note: "Child sexual abuse is distinct from other types of crimes because multiple forms of

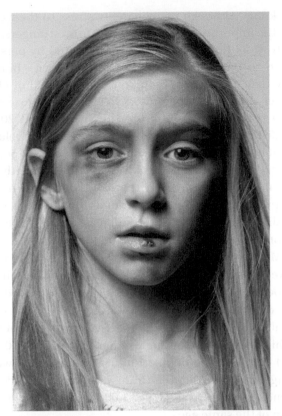

Injuries caused by abuse are best documented through photographs. Some of this girl's injuries will heal quite rapidly; thus, the severity of the battering will become less evident over time and must be captured as soon after the assault as possible. Be sure to photograph all injuries.

Peter Dazeley/Getty Images

convincing evidence are often lacking. As such, prosecutors must rely heavily on children's reports of the crime. . . . Whether and how well children provide useable testimony depends on their understanding and memory of the abuse, their ability to verbally describe what happened, and their concerns about the consequences." Although disclosures and detailed testimony from sexual abuse victims are more likely to be obtained from older children than younger ones, other useful evidence may be available to investigators, such as medical evidence, physical or material evidence; unusual psychological symptoms suffered by the victim, such as severe nightmares; atypical or non–age appropriate sexualized behavior by the victim; eyewitness accounts; witness testimony that corroborates aspects of the victim's testimony; offender confessions; and additional complaints against the offender that support the actions disclosed by the victim (Walsh et al., 2010).

Caution: The lists of indicators in this section are not exhaustive; many other indicators exist. In addition, the presence of one or more of these indicators does not prove that neglect or abuse exists. All factors and conditions of each specific case must be considered before you make a decision.

> **LO8** Identify the various physical and behavioral indicators common in neglect and abuse cases.
>
> Indicators of neglect or abuse may be physical or behavioral or both. Parental indicators may also be present.

Neglect Indicators

The *physical* indicators of child neglect may include frequent hunger, poor hygiene, inappropriate dress, wearing the same clothes for multiple days or wearing clothes that look like they have not been washed, consistent lack of supervision (especially in dangerous activities or for long periods), unattended physical problems or medical needs, and abandonment. Such indicators often appear in families where the parents are drug addicts. The *behavioral* indicators may include begging, stealing (e.g., food), extending school days by arriving early or leaving late, constant fatigue, listlessness or falling asleep in school, poor performance in school, truancy, alcohol or drug abuse, aggressive behavior, delinquency, and stating that no one is at home to care for them.

Emotional Abuse Indicators

Physical indicators of emotional abuse may include speech disorders, lags in physical development, and general failure to thrive.

Behavioral indicators may include habit disorders such as sucking, biting, and rocking back and forth and conduct disorders such as antisocial, destructive behavior; being physically or emotionally abusive toward others, including other children; and being persistently disruptive in social settings, including school. Other possible symptoms are sleep disorders, inhibitions in play, obsessions, compulsions, phobias, hypochondria, behavioral extremes, and attempted suicide.

Physical Abuse Indicators

Physical indicators of physical abuse include unexplained bruises or welts, burns, fractures, lacerations, and abrasions. These may be in various stages of healing. One obvious and important indicator of physical abuse is bruising.

Behavioral indicators include being wary of adults, being apprehensive when other children cry, extreme aggressiveness or extreme withdrawal, being frightened of parents, and being afraid to go home. Behavioral indicators in infants include the lack of crying for "normal" reasons such as when hungry, in need of a diaper change, and being too hot or too cold. In essence, they have learned that crying is unlikely to get the attention of their caregiver.

Parental indicators may include contradictory explanations for a child's injury; attempts to conceal a child's injury or to protect the identity of the person responsible; routine use of harsh, unreasonable discipline inappropriate to the child's age or transgressions; and poor impulse control.

Sexual Abuse Indicators

Physical indicators of sexual abuse include difficulty urinating and irritation, bruising, frequent urinary tract or bladder infections without explanation, or tearing around the genital or rectal areas. In young girls, frequent yeast infections without explanation are indicators. Venereal disease and pregnancy, especially in preteens, are also indicators.

Behavioral indicators of sexual abuse may include unwillingness to change clothes for or to participate in physical education classes; withdrawal, fantasy, or infantile behavior; bizarre sexual behavior, sexual sophistication beyond the child's age or unusual behavior or knowledge of sex; poor peer relationships; delinquency or running away; and reports of being sexually assaulted.

Parental indicators may include jealousy and over-protectiveness of a child. Incest incidents are insidious, commonly beginning with the parent fondling and caressing the child between the ages of three and six months and then progressing over a long period, increasing in intensity of contact until the child is capable of full participation, usually between the ages of eight and ten. A parent may hesitate to report a spouse who is sexually abusing their child for fear of destroying the marriage or for fear of retaliation. Intrafamily sex may be viewed as preferable to extramarital sex.

The Child Abuse Suspect

A major concern in these types of cases involves the frequency with which children are abused by people

they know. Although many parents stress to their children the importance of staying away from strangers, the sad truth is that most abuse is committed by persons known to the child. Data from the Children's Bureau show that the overwhelming majority (77.5%) of child neglect and abuse perpetrators in 2018 were those who had a parental relationship to the victim (ACF, 2020). At a distant second were perpetrators who were related to, but were not parents of, their victims (6.4% of perpetrators), and 4.2% had a multiple relationship with the victim. The remainder of perpetrators consisted of day care providers, foster parents, friends or neighbors, legal guardians, group home and residential facility staff, and persons classified as "other" or "unknown."

More than four-fifths (83.3%) of perpetrators were between the ages of 18 and 44 years. However, minors (perpetrators younger than 18 years) accounted for 1.9% of all perpetrators. Analysis of perpetrator data revealed that those in the 25- to 34-year age bracket had the highest rate of child abuse and neglect, at 5.0 per 1,000 adults in the population of the same age, while young adults in the 18- to 24-year bracket had the second highest rate at 2.8 per 1,000 adults in the population of the same age.

More than one-half (53.8%) of perpetrators were women and 45.3% of perpetrators were men; 0.9% were of unknown sex. The racial distributions of perpetrators were similar to the race of their victims.

The Parent as Suspect

As noted, research indicates child abuse is more often perpetrated by a parent than a nonparent. Sexual abuse of one or more children in a family is one of the most common child sexual abuse problems, but it is not often reported. Because of the difficulties in detecting it, it is the least known to the public. The harm to the child from continued, close sexual relationships with a family member may be accompanied by shame, fear, or even guilt. Additional conflict may be created by admonitions of secrecy.

Myth Teenage parents have the highest rate of child abuse and neglect.

Fact Young adults (those between the ages of 25 and 34) abuse children at a higher rate than any other age group.

Although girls are more frequently victims, if a girl is sexually abused by a family member, a boy in the same family may also be a victim. Incest usually involves children under age 11 and becomes a repeated activity, escalating in both severity and frequency. Courts have ruled that the spousal immunity rules do not apply to child sexual abuse cases. One spouse may be forced to testify against the other in court.

Investigators must be aware of unusual situations involving psychiatric or medical conditions that may lead to injuries in children and, consequently, cast suspicion on parents or caregivers as having been abusive.

Munchausen Syndrome and Munchausen by Proxy Syndrome.

Munchausen syndrome involves self-induced or self-inflicted injuries. If a child's injuries appear to be self-induced or self-inflicted, the child may be seeking attention or sympathy or may be avoiding something. Parents—usually the mother—may inflict injuries on their children for basically the same reasons. **Munchausen by proxy syndrome (MBPS)**, alternately called Munchausen syndrome by proxy (MSBP), is a form of child abuse in which a parent or adult caregiver deliberately provides false medical histories, manufactures symptoms and evidence of an illness, or causes real symptoms to create medical distress in a child (Kaneshiro, 2019). MBPS is usually done so the child will be treated by a physician and the abuser may gain the attention or sympathy of family, friends, and others.

MBPS allegations frequently come from an anonymous source or a health care professional. An unknown percentage of the anonymous calls come from health care professionals concerned with liability issues. One of the most logical first steps is to contact the primary-care physician. Early contact should be made with a childcare agency to coordinate issues regarding the child's safety when the investigation becomes known to the parent. MBPS should be considered as a possible motive in any questionable or unexplained death of a child.

Investigators assigned to work child abuse cases should investigate cases of MBPS as they do similar cases of abuse. In general, however, when confronted with possible cases of MBPS, investigators should:

- Obtain a court order to review the victim's medical records

- Determine from contact with medical personnel the reporting parent's concerns and reactions to the child's medical treatment

- Compile a complete family history

- Interview family members, neighbors, and babysitters

- Consider using video surveillance in the hospital

- Use a search warrant for the family's residence when collecting evidence

Offenders often have a medical background or have been around the medical profession in some way.

Whereas MBPS is a disorder that clearly results in a form of child abuse, another disorder whose symptoms closely resemble child abuse and for which parents are often mistakenly accused of abuse is osteogenesis imperfecta.

Osteogenesis Imperfecta.

Osteogenesis imperfecta (OI), or brittle bone disease, is a genetic disorder characterized by bones that break easily, often from little or no apparent cause. However, child abuse may also result in broken bones. Consequently, improper diagnosis of OI can lead to the parents of children with the disease being wrongly accused of child abuse. The U.S. Osteogenesis Imperfecta Foundation (OIF) states, "When a child has osteogenesis imperfecta, fractures may occur during ordinary activities, such as changing a diaper or burping the baby, or when an infant tries to crawl or pull to a stand. There may be no obvious indication that a fracture has occurred, other than the child crying or refusing to put weight on a limb" (2019).

The most routine childcare activities, performed by the most careful and loving parents, can easily and spontaneously break the bones of a child with OI and, in some severe cases, the condition may be lethal. Milder forms of OI are more likely to be misinterpreted as child abuse and, thus, more likely to lead to false accusations against caretakers (Christian, 2015). Furthermore, roughly one-fourth of all children born with OI have no family history of the disorder (OIF, 2019). Types of fractures that are typically observed in both child abuse and OI include fractures in multiple stages of healing, rib fractures, spiral fractures and fractures for which there is no adequate explanation of trauma (Marchiori, 2014; Flaherty, Perez-Rossello, Levine, & Hennrikus, 2014; Pandya, Baldwin, Kamath, Wenger, & Hosalkar, 2011).

During the 1940s, advances in diagnostic X-ray technology allowed physicians to detect patterns of healed fractures in their young patients. In 1946, Dr. John Caffey, a pediatric radiologist, suggested that multiple fractures in the long bones of infants had "traumatic origin," perhaps willfully inflicted by parents. Two decades later,

Dr. C. H. Kempe and his associates coined the phrase *battered child syndrome* based on clinical evidence of maltreatment, notably the presence of multiple fractures in various stages of healing. "Battered child syndrome describes nonaccidental trauma to children, representing a major cause of morbidity and mortality during childhood. The abuse usually is inflicted by boyfriends, step-parents, baby sitters, and others responsible for the child's care. Abuse is more common among stepchildren, handicapped, and first-born children. Most victims are younger than 2 years of age, with a reported average age of 16 months" (Marchiori, 2014). In 1964, individual states began enacting mandatory child abuse laws using Dr. Kempe's definition of a battered child, and by 1966 all 50 states had enacted such legislation.

The similarities between OI and child abuse symptoms can easily confuse investigators and anger parents wrongly accused of abuse. For example, in addition to displaying different types of fractures in various stages of healing, a child with OI often bruises easily. Furthermore, many children with OI are of shorter stature than average, a condition often mistaken as indicative of neglect (OIF, 2019). When these symptoms are detected, how do investigators determine whether the suspected abuse case is actually OI? First, a medical professional experienced in diagnosing OI should evaluate the child. Genetic counseling may also reveal a previously unrecognized family history of mild OI. Investigators should also look for inconsistencies between the explanation for the injury given by the child or parent and the diagnosis provided by the treating physicians and other medical personnel. Parents may also try to conceal child abuse by frequently changing doctors or hospitals, thus avoiding a buildup of incriminating records at any one office or facility. Keep in mind also that the presence of OI does not automatically preclude the existence of child abuse.

Sudden Infant Death Syndrome.

Another tragic condition that takes the lives of young victims and for which parents may become suspected of child abuse is **sudden infant death syndrome (SIDS)**, briefly introduced in Chapter 8. SIDS is a diagnosis by exclusion and is the most frequently determined cause of sudden unexplained infant death (SUID). A thorough death scene evaluation is a critical component of a potential SIDS death investigation. Officers responding to a call of an "infant not breathing" must observe several elements, including the infant's position when found, body temperature, presence or absence of rigor mortis, the condition of the crib and surrounding area, the presence of bedding and other objects in the crib, the type of bed or crib, any unusual or dangerous items in the room, any medications being given to the baby, room temperature, air quality, type of heating or cooling system used, and the caregiver's response (Adams, Good, & Defranco, 2009; Sidebotham, Marshall, & Garstang, 2018). They should also inquire as to any other children in the home, their welfare, and who will be looking after them.

Officers may also observe certain bodily appearances in the victim that typically occur in SIDS cases resulting from the death process, including discoloration of the skin, frothy drainage from the mouth or nose, and cooling rigor mortis that takes place quickly, usually in about three hours in infants. Studies suggest that two common bacteria might also play a role in SIDS, a discovery that may influence what additional tests are conducted during the autopsies of these young victims (Highet, Berry, Bettelheim, & Goldwater, 2014). At minimum, a complete autopsy with a radiographic skeletal survey and toxicology studies should be conducted (Adams, Owens, & Small, 2010).

The Centers for Disease Control and Prevention (CDC) has created the Sudden Unexplained Infant Death Investigation Reporting Form (SUIDIRF) to establish a protocol for the investigation of all sudden, unexplained infant deaths and to help investigative agencies better understand the circumstances and factors contributing to unexplained infant deaths. The form is available on the CDC website (www.cdc.gov/sids/pdf/SUIDI_Fill_508.pdf).

Table 11.1 compares the characteristic features of SIDS with child abuse, and Table 11.2 summarizes the characteristics of MBPS, OI, and SIDS.

Investigating Child Fatalities.

Investigating the death of a child can be one of the most difficult tasks an investigator ever encounters. Tough questions must be asked to grieving parents or caregivers so the investigator may determine whether the fatality resulted from an unknown medical condition, an accident, or a criminal act. Many child fatalities are first reported as natural deaths or accidents (Walsh, 2005; Hanzlick, Jentzen, & Clark, 2007). The following checklists of potential witnesses and other information sources will assist investigators working a child fatality case (Walsh, 2005). Potential witnesses include the following people:

- Parents—including current and former stepparents and parents' significant others

- Siblings

- Family members

TABLE 11.1 Comparison of Sudden Infant Death Syndrome (SIDS) and Child Abuse Characteristics

Characteristic/Feature	SIDS	Child Abuse/Neglect
Age typically affected	May occur from birth to 24 months but is most common from two to four months of age. Ninety percent of all cases occur by six months of age.	May occur at any time, but one-third of abused children are under four years old, and one-fifth of abused children are between four and seven years of age. Children younger than one year old have the highest rate of victimization, with victimization rate generally decreasing with age.
External signs of injury?	Not usually	Yes—distinguishable and visible signs
Signs of malnourishment?	Not usually; appears well-developed	Common
Do siblings show any symptoms?	Not usually; siblings appear normal and healthy	May show patterns of injuries
Parents' account of investigated event	Placed healthy baby to sleep in the crib and later found infant lifeless	May sound suspicious or may not account for all injuries to the child
Annual number of deaths in the United States	2,000–2,500 infants	Approximately 1,500 children; more than 46% are infants (less than one year old)
Noteworthy trends	Number and rate of SIDS cases has dropped dramatically since 1992. SIDS tends to occur more often in winter months, peaking in January.	The number and rate of child fatalities has been increasing over the past five years.

Source: Adapted from Adams S. M., Good, M. W., & Defranco, G. M. (2009, May 15). Sudden infant death syndrome. *American Family Physician, 79*(10), 870–874; Administration for Children and Families (2015). *Child maltreatment 2013*. Washington, DC: Author; PubMed Health Online. (2015, April 2). *Sudden infant death syndrome*. Bethesda, MD: Author. Retrieved October 12, 2020, from www.nlm.nih.gov/medlineplus/suddeninfantdeathsyndrome.html

TABLE 11.2 Comparison of the Characteristics of Munchausen by Proxy Syndrome (MBPS), Osteogenesis Imperfecta (OI), and Sudden Infant Death Syndrome (SIDS)

Characteristic/Feature	MBPS[a]	OI[b]	SIDS[c]
Age of child affected	Any age, although occurs more often in preschool-aged children	Any age	Typically occurs in newborn to 24 months but is most frequent from two to four months
Number of children who die every year in the United States due to it	Unknown	Unknown	2,000–2,500
External signs of injury (parent-inflicted)	Occasionally	Not usually	Not usually
Is it child abuse?	Yes	No	No

[a] Kaneshiro, N. K. (2019, August 7). *Munchhausen syndrome by proxy*. Bethesda, MD: National Institutes of Health, MedlinePlus. Retrieved September 25, 2020, from medlineplus.gov/ency/article/001555.htm

[b] Osteogenesis Imperfecta Foundation. (n.d.). *U.S. osteogenesis imperfecta foundation: "Child Abuse Issues."* Gaithersburg, MD: Author. Retrieved October 12, 2020, from oif.org/wp-content/uploads/2019/08/Child_Abuse__Child_Abuse_Issues.pdf; Osteogenesis Imperfecta Foundation. (n.d.). Child abuse or osteogenesis imperfecta? Gaithersburg, MD: Author. Retrieved October 12, 2020, from oif.org/wp-content/uploads/2019/08/Child_Abuse__Child_Abuse_or_Ostegenesis_Imperfecta.pdf

[c] PubMed Health Online. (2015, April 2). *Sudden infant death syndrome*. Bethesda, MD: Author. Retrieved October 12, 2020, from www.nlm.nih.gov/medlineplus/suddeninfantdeathsyndrome.htm

- Caretakers—babysitters, childcare employees
- Teachers—day care, preschool, school, church
- Neighbors—current and previous
- Friends of the child

- First responders—police and emergency medical technicians
- Emergency room personnel—physicians and nurses
- Medical providers who have seen the child previously, including school nurses

- Agency personnel—CPS, day care licensing, law enforcement personnel who have had prior contact with the family or child

Other potential information sources include the following:

- CPS records—for the deceased child, siblings, other children that the child's caretakers have had contact with

- Law enforcement records—criminal history, victim or suspect history, calls for service

- Medical records for the deceased child and siblings—birth, prenatal care, pediatrician, medical, emergency room

- 9-1-1 calls

- Emergency medical services (EMS) reports

- Telephone calls or other communications made or received by the suspect around the time of the child's death—including cell phones, emails, voicemails, messages on social media accounts

- Autopsy results

- If the child's family or suspect has previously lived in another community, check there for potential witnesses and other agency records that may document a history of abuse or neglect.

Walsh (2005, p. 25) provides the following tips and reminders for investigators working possible child fatality cases:

- An unreasonable delay in seeking medical attention is often a "red flag" that the child's injuries may have been caused by abuse.

- 9-1-1 call records often contain important information about how a child's injuries were initially reported.

- Treat cases involving severe injury as potential child fatalities because it is not uncommon for severely injured children to die days or weeks after the original injury.

- Delayed deaths often involve more than one crime scene. Examine the place where the injury occurred, the hospital where the child died, and any private vehicle used to transport the child to the hospital.

- There is no substitute for a timely, professional crime-scene search, including evidence collection, documentation, and photo-documentation.

- Coordinate and communicate with CPS investigators in child fatality cases. They have a legitimate role in the investigation and can often provide important information about the child and family involved.

Successful child fatality investigations hinge on three factors: effectively conducted, well-documented interviews of witnesses; thorough background checks on every witness and suspect involved in the case; and competent interrogation of the suspect(s) (Walsh, 2005). A final word of caution: do not automatically exclude children as potential suspects. Children have been known to inflict severe injuries on other children.

Child/Peer Suspects

A particular challenge to investigators is presented when the abuse is perpetrated by a child's peer or sibling. Many adults tend to downplay the severity of assault by one child on another unless severe injury results. But the toll inflicted by repeated physical, emotional, or sexual abuse is no less damaging to the victim just because their abuser is a minor. Research that examined how much, or how little, child victimization is made known to police, school, and medical authorities found that authorities were least likely to know about peer or sibling assault or dating violence (16.9% and 15.2% of victimizations, respectively) and were only slightly more likely to know about bullying (22.2%) (Finkelhor, Ormrod, Turner, & Hamby, 2012). Sexual abuse by a peer was made known to authorities in fewer than half (42.4%) of the cases.

Bullying, like other forms of behavior, occurs along a continuum from very mild, relatively benign deeds to more serious, even life-threatening acts, but in general it is "repeated, intentional aggression, perpetrated by a more powerful individual or group against a less powerful victim" (Shetgiri, 2013). Bullies harm in three basic ways:

- Physically (hitting, kicking, spitting, pushing, taking personal belongings)

- Verbally (taunting, malicious teasing, name calling, making threats)

- Psychologically (spreading rumors, manipulating social relationships, or engaging in social exclusion, extortion, or intimidation)

The key elements of bullying are

1. a physical, verbal, or psychological attack or intimidation;

2. an actual or perceived power imbalance between the perpetrator(s) or victim(s);

3. intent to cause fear, and/or harm to the victim; and

4. it is repeated and produces the desired effect.

(Shetgiri, 2013)

The spread of technology and social media has led to a fourth variant known as *cyberbullying*, or bullying through electronic means such as cell phones or computers (investigating cyberbullying was discussed in Chapter 9). Research has found that boys tend to be more involved in the physical and verbal forms of bullying, whereas girls are more involved in the relational and psychological forms (Wang, Iannotti, & Nansel, 2009). Bullying is significantly associated with suicidal ideation and suicide attempts among both victims and perpetrators of bullying, and the risks are generally higher for girls than for boys (Shetgiri, 2013). Some research indicates that bully-victims—those who bully others *and* are bullied themselves—may be at the highest risk for serious consequences, including perpetrating school shootings, compared with bullies, victims, and children uninvolved in bullying (Shetgiri, 2013).

When discussing child perpetrators of crimes against children, the offense most likely to come to the attention of authorities appears to be sexual assault, and even that is significantly underreported: "Authorities are far more likely to know about sexual offenses that adults commit than those that youth commit. This may be because adult sexual offenses are seen as more criminal, whereas peer allegiances may inhibit reporting of sexual crimes by younger perpetrators" (Finkelhor et al., 2012, p. 5). Juvenile sex offenders (JSOs) will be discussed shortly.

The Nonparent Suspect

Perpetrators other than parents have included babysitters, camp counselors, school personnel, clergy, and others. Habitual child sex abusers, whether they operate as loners or as part of a sex ring, have been classified into three types. First is the **misoped**, the person who hates children, has sex with them, and then brutally murders them. The second type is the **hebephile**, a person who selects high school–age youths as sex victims. The third and most common habitual child sex abuser is the **pedophile**, sometimes referred to as a **chicken hawk**, an adult who has either heterosexual or homosexual preferences for young boys or girls of a specific, limited age range.

The Pedophile

People who have normal behavior patterns in all other areas of life may have very abnormal sexual behavior patterns. Child sexual abusers may commit only one offense in their lifetimes, or they may commit hundreds. Surveys indicate that 35% to 50% of offenders know their victims. Some studies indicate an even higher percentage. Therefore, the investigator of a child sexual crime may not be looking for an unknown suspect or stranger.

There is no specific demographic for a child predator. Although pedophiles are typically male, this is not always the case. Women are also involved in the sexual abuse of children. Pedophiles come from all walks of life and range from professionals, to persons who are in a position of authority, to persons with an extensive criminal history.

Pedophilia is a sex offense in all states. Rarely deviating from the preferred age range, the pedophile is an expert in selecting and enticing young people. The pedophile frequently selects children who stand apart from other children, who are runaways, or who crave attention and love. Although some pedophiles are child rapists, most rarely use force, relying instead on befriending the victims and gaining their confidence and friendship. Pedophiles may become involved in activities or programs that interest the type of victims they want to attract and that provide them with easy access to these children. Pedophiles may also use drugs or alcohol as a means of seduction, reducing the child's inhibitions.

The Federal Bureau of Investigation (FBI) Behavioral Science Services Unit identifies and categorizes two types of child predators based on their descriptive types. Table 11.3 describes these two typologies, known as *situational* and *preferential*.

Pedophiles may obtain, collect, and maintain photographs of the children with whom they are or have been involved. Many pedophiles maintain diaries of their sexual encounters with children. Pedophiles may collect books, magazines, newspapers, and other writings on the subject of sexual activities with children. They may also collect addresses, phone numbers, or lists of people who have similar sexual interests. Pedophiles also locate and attract victims through the computer, as discussed shortly. In addition, many pedophiles are members of sex rings.

Child Sexual Abuse Rings

Adults (at least 10 to 15 years older than the victims) are usually the dominant leaders, organizers, and operators of sex rings. The adult leader selectively gathers young

TABLE 11.3 **Child Molester Typologies**

Child Molester Typologies	Victim Profile	Offender Profile-Methodology	Threat Level
Situational	The victim is often a relative, neighbor, friend or someone under the trusted care or authority of the offender. The victim might not have definite characteristics that attract the offender. The victim in this category may also only be a few years younger than the offender and perhaps becomes a victim in a social setting such as a party.	This offender can range from a one-time act to a long pattern of child sexual abuse. Typically they have a limited number of victims and may abuse out of opportunity. This offender may abuse children for other reasons than genuine sexual attraction.	There are fewer documented cases involving situational molesters because there are fewer victim-offender ratios. This is in addition to the less predictable behavior of this type of offender. The threat of offending and recidivism is lower than with the preferential molester.
Preferential	The victim is more likely unknown to the offender. The offender may meet the child at a random location that typically attracts children or through an online Internet forum. The child may have other issues in their life that the offender can exploit to gain trust. The victim is typically a specific gender or age range depending on what the offender is attracted to.	Often older, they look to "groom" a child and build a relationship. They have a definite sexual preference for children and are sexually attracted to them. A common form of building relationships can be through providing attention and tangible gifts. This type of offender is more apt to engage in highly predictable behavior and high-risk activities to locate and seduce victims. The preferential molester is more commonly identified as a pedophile.	Of the two types, the preferential is more dangerous. This is because those that fit under this category have a consistent need to fulfill their sexual desires and they will not stop pursuing them. Although statistically smaller in number than situational offenders, they have the potential to molest a larger number of victims.

Source: Table created by Cho, H. Cho Research & Consulting, LLC.

people together for sexual purposes. The involvement varies, with the longest periods occurring when prepubescent children are involved. Most cases involve male ringleaders, but some involve a female as well, usually a husband-wife pair.

Many ringleaders use their occupation as the major access route to the child victims. The adult has a legitimate role as an authority figure in the lives of the children selected for the ring or is able to survey vulnerable children through access to family records or history.

Sometimes rings are formed by an adult targeting a specific child, who then uses the child's associations and peer pressure to bring other children into the group. The initial child may be a relative or previously unknown. One common technique is to post a notice on a store bulletin board requesting girls to help with housework.

The adult's status in the neighborhood sometimes helps legitimize their presence with the children and their parents and permits unquestioned movement of young people into the offender's home. Such an offender often is well-liked by his neighbors.

Investigators should be aware of three types of sex rings: solo, transition, and syndicated. The organization of *solo sex rings* is primarily by the age of the child—for example, toddlers (ages 2 to 5), prepubescent (6 to 12),

or pubescent (13 to 17). This type of offender prefers to have multiple children as sex objects, in contrast to the offender who seeks one child at a time.

Pedophiles have a strong need to communicate with others about their interest in children. In *transition sex rings*, experiences are exchanged, whereas in solo rings, the pedophile keeps their activities and photographs totally secret. In transition rings, photographs of children as well as sexual services may be traded and sold. The trading of pornography appears to be the first move of the victim into the "possession" of other pedophiles. The photographs are traded, and victims may be tested by other offenders and eventually traded for their sexual services.

The third type of ring is the *syndicated sex ring*, a well-structured organization that recruits children, produces pornography, delivers direct sexual services, and establishes an extensive network of customers. Syndicated rings have involved a Boy Scout troop, a boys' farm operated by a minister, and a national boy prostitution ring.

Ritualistic Abuse by Cults

Certain cults are also involved in the sexual abuse of children. *Cults* are groups that use rituals or ceremonial acts to draw their members together into a certain belief system. When the rituals of a group involve crimes, including child sexual abuse, they become a problem for law enforcement. Crimes associated with cults are discussed in Chapter 19.

Juvenile Sex Offenders

A significant number of child sex crimes are committed by other children. Youths aged 17 or younger account for more than one-third (35.6%) of those known to police to have committed sex offenses against minors (Allardyce & Yates, 2018). Many people think such crimes cannot occur because they often view children as not being sexually capable. Some child sex offenders were molested themselves: "Strong evidence indicates that sexual victimization plays a disproportionate role in the development of sexually abusive behavior in adolescents" (Leversee, 2015). When investigators receive reports of children committing sex crimes against other children, they must not automatically dismiss them as fantasy and must thoroughly investigate all such reports.

JSOs differ in fundamental ways from adult sex offenders in that they reoffend less frequently and generally respond better to treatment than do adult sex offenders (Lobanov-Rostovsky, 2015). And just as there is no "typical" adult sex offender, there is no "typical" youth who commits a sex crime. Research on JSOs has, however, revealed several salient distinctions between juveniles who commit sex offenses against minors and adults who commit the same type of offense. For example, juveniles who commit sex offenses against other children are more likely than adult sex offenders to:

- Offend in groups

- Offend against acquaintances

- Commit their offense in a school

- Have a male victim

- Target young victims (those under age 12)

(Finkelhor, Ormrod, & Chaffin, 2009)

A small percentage (12.5%) of JSOs are younger than 12, the age at which the number of youths coming to the attention of police for sex offenses increases sharply. Early adolescence (ages 12 to 14) is the peak age for offenses against younger children, whereas offenses against teenagers surge during mid- to lateadolescence. Females constitute 7% of juveniles who commit sex offenses and are, as a group, typically younger than their male counterparts (Finkelhor et al., 2009). In 2018, juvenile courts processed 8,000 cases of rape and another 7,800 cases involving other violent sex offenses committed by persons under age 18. Of the 8,000 rape cases, 4,800 (60%) involved a perpetrator younger than 16; of the 7,800 other violent sex offenses, more than 5,100 (72%) involved a perpetrator younger than 16 (Hockenberry & Puzzanchera, 2020).

Victimology

People involved in intervening, investigating, or prosecuting child abuse cases must recognize that a bond often exists between the offender and the victim. In child sexual abuse cases, many victims find themselves willing to trade sex for attention, affection, and other benefits.

Children and teens often make the perfect victims because they are often naïve and trusting, are curious about sex, and often desire material things—things that perpetrators may promise in exchange for the child's participation in sex activities. And teens are particularly at risk because they are more likely to engage in communication revolving around sex and relationships. Furthermore, children and teens are not generally viewed as credible witnesses or victims.

Pedophile ring operators are, by definition, skilled at gaining the continued cooperation and control of their victims through well-planned seduction. These operators are skilled at recognizing and then *temporarily* filling the emotional and physical needs of children. They know how to listen to children—an ability many parents lack. These operators are willing to spend all the time it takes to seduce a child.

This positive offender-victim bond must not be misinterpreted as consent, complicity, or guilt. Police investigators, in particular, must be sensitive to this problem.

Commercial Sexual Exploitation of Children

The commercial sex trafficking and exploitation of children was introduced in Chapter 10. **Exploitation** refers to taking unfair advantage of children or using them illegally. This includes using children in pornography and prostitution. At the federal level, child abuse statutes pertain mainly to exploitation, but they also set forth important definitions that apply to any type of child abuse. Public Law 95-225 (1978) defines **sexual exploitation** as follows: "Any person who employs, uses, persuades, induces, entices, or coerces any minor to engage or assist in engaging in any sexually explicit conduct for the purpose of producing any visual or print medium, knowing that such visual or print medium will be transported interstate or in foreign commerce or mailed, is guilty of sexual exploitation. Further, any parent or legal guardian who knowingly permits such conduct, having control and custody of the child, is also subject to prosecution."

Commercial sexual exploitation of children (CSEC) is "a range of crimes and activities involving the sexual abuse or exploitation of a child for the financial benefit of any person or in exchange for anything of value (including monetary and non-monetary benefits) given or received by any person" (Office of Juvenile Justice and Delinquency Prevention [OJJDP], n.d.). The Justice Department reports that this type of crime is increasing at an alarming rate, and as many as 300,000 children in the United States are at risk for sexual exploitation every year (Adams et al., 2010). Research shows that the majority of child sexual exploiters are men aged 20 to 65, the average age that a child first falls victim to CSEC is between 13 and 14 years old, and one of the pressures driving the average age of victims down is exploiters' attempts to ensnare children who are less likely to already be infected with HIV or AIDS (Adams et al., 2010).

The 2016 National Child Exploitation Threat Assessment—which is based on a comprehensive survey of more than 1,000 federal, state, local, and tribal investigators; law enforcement managers; prosecutors; analysts; forensic examiners; victim service providers; and DOJ grant recipients—focuses on five areas of CSEC:

- child pornography
- "sextortion" and the livestreaming of child sexual abuse
- commercial sex trafficking and prostitution of children
- child sex tourism
- sex offender registry violations

Pornography

According to the Child Protection Act of 1984, child pornography is highly developed into an organized, multimillion-dollar industry producing and distributing pornographic materials nationally, exploiting thousands of children, including runaways and homeless youths. The act states that such exploitation is harmful to the physiological, emotional, and mental health of the individual and to society. Many states have passed similarly worded statutes and have increased penalties for sexual abuse and the production and distribution of child-pornographic materials.

> **LO9** Name the 1984 federal act that prohibits child pornography.
>
> The Child Protection Act (1984) prohibits child pornography and greatly increases the penalties for adults who engage in it.

Although adult pornography has always been objectionable to many people, it has not resulted in the aggressive public and legislative action that child pornography has received. In 1977, Congress passed the Protection of Children against Sexual Exploitation Act. This and other federal and state laws have prohibited commercial and noncommercial distribution of pornographic materials and more recently have made it a violation of law to *possess* such materials.

The basis for these laws has been the acceptance of a relationship between child-pornographic materials and child sexual abuse offenders and offenses. In many cases, arrested pedophiles have had in their possession child-pornographic literature used to lower their selected victims' inhibitions. It is often necessary to obtain search warrants for the suspect's premises to obtain these materials. It is necessary in the investigation to gain as much evidence as possible, because the problems of child testimony in court are well-established.

An emerging challenge in the area of child pornography is **sexting** (introduced in Chapter 10), which is the sending, receiving, or forwarding of nude images or sexually explicit material via email or text message. Often the persons taking and sending the photos of themselves are minors. In fact, various studies indicate that between 20% and 30% of all teens have sent and/or received a sext (Lohmann, 2012). And although the original transmission may be voluntary by the "victims," in the sense that they purposefully sent the images and intended for the recipient to receive and view the photos, once an image is online, it is often passed along to other parties indiscriminately. The possession of such images, regardless of the device involved (computer, cell phone, etc.) and the age of the person in possession of the images, constitutes engagement in child pornography. Many state laws require those found guilty of sexting to register as sex offenders and to complete sex offender treatment. As with other crimes, laws concerning sexting tend to lag behind technology. Where specific laws pertaining to sexting may not exist, the act is usually prosecuted under the general umbrella of child pornography laws.

Law enforcement is aware of hundreds of thousands of people trafficking in child pornography on the Internet, and this exploding multibillion-dollar market must be continuously supplied with fresh content. This means thousands of new images are posted every week, involving the continued sexual assault and exploitation of children, with research indicating that the victims are getting younger and being exposed to increasingly brutal and sadistic abuse. Unlike the traditional production of child pornography, where the producer and the victim are in the same physical location, the online exploitation of children allows the producer of this explicit content to be located anywhere in the world.

Newsgroups are believed to be the largest single forum for child pornography on the Internet. Although hundreds of thousands of legitimate bulletin boards are used for common interest and posting discussion, predators often prefer to exploit such newsgroups because these forums are free and not policed or controlled, except by the Internet service provider (ISP), which has discretion on hosting them.

In May 2020, a bill titled the Invest in Child Safety Act (H.R.6752/ S.3629- 116th Congress) was introduced to combat online child exploitation by providing $5 billion in funding to enforce child exploitation laws, investigate those who create and share child pornography online, and fund initiatives aimed at preventing children from becoming victims (Eggerton, 2020). At the time this text went to press, the bill had not moved beyond the first stage of the legislative process.

Sextortion and Livestreaming of Child Sexual Abuse

The 2016 National Child Exploitation Threat Assessment states: "Sextortion and live-streaming of child sexual abuse are extensions of the child pornography threat and involves offenders using Internet and cell phone technologies, such as mobile cameras, texting, social media, and mobile apps to interact with minors for the purpose of sexually exploiting them. Modern technology allows offenders' access to an unlimited global population of minors they may seek to contact, groom, entice, coerce, lure, trick, or extort into producing and transmitting sexually explicit content" (U.S. Department of Justice [DOJ], 2016).

Sextortion, which was introduced in Chapter 10, is by far the most significantly growing threat to children, with more than 60% of survey respondents indicating this type of online enticement of minors was increasing:

> Sextortion cases tend to have more minor victims per offender than all other child sexual exploitation offenses. Unfortunately, it is becoming common for investigations to reveal that a single sextortion offender has been communicating with hundreds of potential victims. Forensic examinations of sextortion offenders' digital media commonly reveal thousands of organized folders containing videos and documentation of their contact with countless minors, often around the world. . . .
>
> Many sextortion offenders purport to be like-aged peers to gain a child's trust and groom them to produce child pornography online. Offenders also routinely trick victims by representing themselves online as either the same sex as the victim, or as the opposite sex. Sextortion offenders typically threaten minors ages 10–17, the typical age range for juvenile Internet users, but increasingly it has been observed where the offender manipulates the victim to abuse younger siblings or friends, extending the threat to even younger and more vulnerable victims.
>
> (U.S. Department of Justice, 2016)

Livestreaming of child sexual abuse is also on the rise and occurs on online chat rooms, social media platforms, and communication apps that have video chat features. Viewers of livestreaming child sexual abuse can be passive (i.e., they pay to only watch) or active, in which they can communicate with the child, the sexual abuser, and/or the facilitator of the child sexual abuse. Active viewers can request that specific physical acts, such as choking, and/or sexual acts be performed on or by the child (Europol, 2018). In August 2019, a 42-year-old Illinois man was sentenced to more than 33 years in federal prison and a lifetime term of supervised release for livestreaming the sexual abuse of a child. Evidence presented at sentencing showed that the victim was under the age of 12 and the offender had been providing care to the child when the abuse occurred (Brannan, 2019).

Commercial Sex Trafficking and Prostitution of Children

According to the U.S. Department of Justice (DOJ): "Child sex trafficking, which is also referred to as child prostitution or CSEC, and includes survival sex, refers to the recruitment, harboring, transportation, provision, obtaining, patronizing, or soliciting of a minor for the purpose of a commercial sex act. Child sex trafficking does not require proof that the victim was subjected to force, fraud, or coercion, nor does it require that the victim was moved across state lines" (2016). Sex traffickers target young children because they are vulnerable, gullible, and in demand. The average age of entry into child sex trafficking is 17, although there are known cases of infants and toddlers being forced into prostitution (Polaris Project, 2019).

The prostitution of juveniles occurs in a variety of contexts. Both international rings and interstate crime operations traffic young girls to faraway places, promising them employment and money. Runaways and homeless youths are recruited by pimps or engage in "survival sex." Drug dealers get youths addicted and then force them to prostitute themselves to receive drugs or have a place to stay. Some parents have advertised and prostituted their children over the Internet.

The big question is often: Are these young prostitutes offenders or victims? Indeed, child sex trafficking victims are often not recognized as victims and may be arrested and jailed. But as the DOJ (2020) notes:

> The term prostitution can delude or confuse one's understanding of this form of child sexual exploitation. It is important to emphasize that the children involved are victims. Pimps and traffickers manipulate children by using physical, emotional, and psychological abuse to keep them trapped in a life of prostitution. It is not uncommon for traffickers to beat, rape, or torture their victims.

The method by which most traffickers identify, recruit, market, and maintain their victims results in a unique combination of sustained violent criminal behavior with reluctant victims and witnesses. In fact, an FBI analysis of more than 500 subjects of child sex trafficking investigations showed that approximately 60% had violent criminal arrest histories (including assault/battery, weapons offenses, kidnapping, and murder) and 24% had documented gang affiliations (U.S. DOJ, 2016). The National Child Exploitation Threat Assessment found a growing concern across the country regarding an increase in the volume of cases involving gang-led or gang-directed sex trafficking of minors operations.

Every region of the country is susceptible to the child sex trafficking threat. High profile, large scale events, such as major sporting events and large cultural or political events, have become lucrative opportunities for traffickers as such events receive substantial media attention and attract spectators from across the country. The considerable influx of tourists into the host city during such events creates an atmosphere where criminal enterprises engaged in sex trafficking can better blend into the crowd and capitalize financially. Victims commonly disclose traveling to these locations specifically for these events. The DOJ (2016) notes:

> Child sex trafficking investigations present unique challenges to law enforcement and require a robust multijurisdictional response, with multiple agencies playing a critical role in ensuring the protection of victims and effective prosecution of offenders. . . . Although interviews of sex trafficking victims frequently identify traffickers and other accomplices, some child victims may resist identifying their traffickers because of fear or other means of manipulation that the pimp has exercised over them. Furthermore, the victim may only know their traffickers' street name and cannot fully identify their traffickers. . . . The dangers faced by these children—from the traffickers, their associates, and from customers—are severe. These children become hardened by the treacherous street environment in which they must learn to survive. As such, they do not always outwardly present as sympathetic victims. These child victims also need specialized services that are not widely available given they often have illnesses, drug addictions, physical and sexual trauma, lack of viable family and community ties, and total dependence—physical and psychological—on their abusers.

Child Sex Tourism

Child sex tourism refers to U.S. citizens traveling abroad to sexually exploit foreign minors. This activity is a federal crime even if the minor is of legal age or if the sex act is not considered a crime according to the destination country's laws.

> Traditionally, popular destinations have high levels of poverty, a large population of at risk children, legalized adult prostitution, or ineffective law enforcement. Countries that are well-documented destinations (commonly referred to as "hotspots") include Thailand, Cambodia, the Philippines, Mexico, Costa Rica, Panama, Nicaragua, and Brazil.

(U.S. Department of Justice, 2016)

Sex Offender Registry Violations

According to the DOJ (2016), the number of sex offenders in the United States with an obligation to register has been estimated at more than 843,000. A sex offender's failure to register as required is often a deliberate decision to avoid being connected to new criminal activity, including sexual offenses against children. The Sex Offender Registration and Notification Act (SORNA), which was discussed in Chapter 10, created a comprehensive national system for the registration of both federal and nonfederal sex offenders and requires offenders to register where they live, work, and attend school, locations that are often in different jurisdictions. Similarly, investigations of noncompliance often involve multiple jurisdictions. An offender may have been convicted and required to register in one or more states, only to move to another state that does not comply with registration requirements. Therefore, effective coordination between all law enforcement agencies is required if registration of sex offenders is to actually improve public safety.

Online Child Sexual Abuse

Whether it is referred to as Internet sex crimes, online-facilitated sex crimes, technology-facilitated sexual exploitation, or some other term, the online sexual abuse and exploitation of children is a subcategory of sex crimes against children made possible by the expansion of the Internet and the creation of a global forum in which sex offenders can access potential victims, distribute or trade child pornography, network with other child abuse perpetrators, promote child sexual tourism, and traffic children. All of the services the Internet provides—email, the World Wide Web, instant messaging—can be used to facilitate crimes against children.

Technology has blurred the line between online and offline child sexual exploitation and has also given rise to new terminology used in the investigation of crimes involving the Internet (Greijer & Doek, 2016; Mitchell, Jones, Finkelhor, & Wolak, 2014):

- *Sexual solicitations* include requests to engage in sexual activities or sexual talk, or give personal sexual information that were unwanted or, whether wanted or not, made by an adult.

- *Aggressive sexual solicitations* are acts that involve offline contact with the solicitor through mail, by telephone, or in person, or any attempts or requests for offline contact.

- *Distressing sexual solicitations* were incidents where youth rated themselves as being very or extremely upset or afraid as a result of the episode.

Researchers found that in 2010, approximately 9% (1 in 11) of youth Internet users had received an unwanted sexual solicitation during the previous year, which was a decline from 19% reported in 2000 (Mitchell et al., 2014).

The National Online Juvenile Victimization (N-JOV) Study, a longitudinal study that began in 2009 and is currently collecting its fourth wave of data, categorizes Internet sex crimes against minors into three mutually exclusive groups: (1) Internet crimes against identified victims involving Internet-related sexual assaults and other sex crimes, such as the production of child pornography committed against identified victims; (2) Internet solicitations unknowingly to undercover law enforcement officers posing as minors that involved no identified victims; and (3) the possession, distribution, or trading of Internet child pornography (CP) by offenders who did not use the Internet to sexually exploit identified victims or unknowingly solicit undercover investigators. Figure 11.1 illustrates the categories and the data reported in NJOV-3.

Trends observed in analyzing the three N-JOV datasets available to date show that arrests for technology-facilitated child sexual exploitation crimes increased substantially between 2000 and 2009 and that proactive investigations of online child pornography trading generated significantly more arrests in 2009 (Wolak, Finkelhor, & Mitchell, 2012). Furthermore, of the cases that began with investigations of possession of child pornography in 2009, 1 in 10 led to the arrest of offenders who had molested children, and 1 in 5 caught molesters or offenders with past arrests for sex crimes against children (Wolak, 2011).

Online predators use the Internet in many ways, and it has quickly become the preferred method for child predators to use because of the ease of access to their prey and the anonymity and safety it affords in soliciting and grooming juveniles online. The grooming process often begins with an offender joining a chat room intended for children or teens and engaging potential victims in dialogue. After the initial contact, the offender will build rapport and trust with the child victim. The offender usually likes to make the child victim feel important, and offenders often seek children with problems at home. Over time, the child's inhibitions become lowered, which eventually leads to some level of victimization.

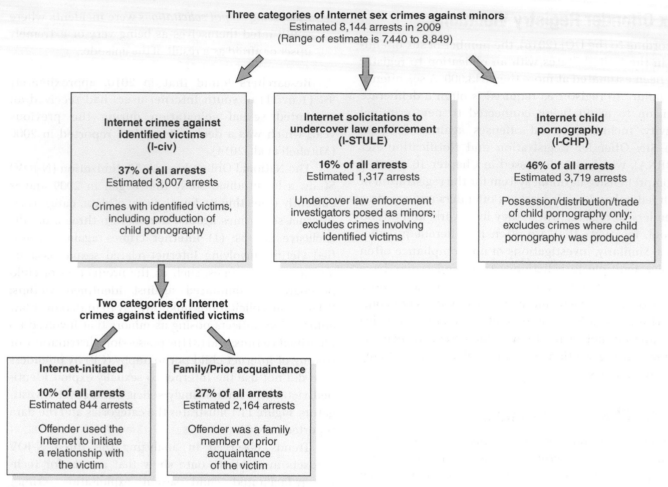

Three categories of Internet sex crimes against minors
Estimated 8,144 arrests in 2009
(Range of estimate is 7,440 to 8,849)

Internet crimes against identified victims (I-civ)

37% of all arrests
Estimated 3,007 arrests

Crimes with identified victims, including production of child pornography

Internet solicitations to undercover law enforcement (I-STULE)

16% of all arrests
Estimated 1,317 arrests

Undercover law enforcement investigators posed as minors; excludes crimes involving identified victims

Internet child pornography (I-CHP)

46% of all arrests
Estimated 3,719 arrests

Possession/distribution/trade of child pornography only; excludes crimes where child pornography was produced

Two categories of Internet crimes against identified victims

Internet-initiated

10% of all arrests
Estimated 844 arrests

Offender used the Internet to initiate a relationship with the victim

Family/Prior acquaintance

27% of all arrests
Estimated 2,164 arrests

Offender was a family member or prior acquaintance of the victim

Figure 11.1
Categories of Internet sex crimes against minors.

Source: Wolak, J., Finkelhor, D., & Mitchell, K. J. (2012, April). *Trends in law enforcement responses to technology-facilitated child sexual exploitation crimes: The third National Juvenile Online Victimization study (NJOV3).* Durham, NH: University of New Hampshire, Crimes against Children Research Center. Retrieved October 6, 2020, from scholars.unh.edu/ccrc/45/

The anonymity afforded by the Internet makes sex offenders more difficult to locate, and taking their activities to the Dark Internet emboldens them to commit more egregious offenses than they would perhaps commit on traditional Internet platforms. Investigations show that offenders often gather in online communities where trading of these images is just one component of a larger relationship that is premised on a shared sexual interest in children: "In closed and highly protected online spaces, online communities dedicated to the sexual abuse of children have proliferated. Hand-picked members normalize each other's sexual interest in children and encourage each other to act on their deviant sexual interests" (U.S. DOJ, 2016).

The challenge of controlling and investigating online sexual abuse of children is multifactorial and includes the decentralized structure of the Internet, immense volume of Internet activity, technological ability and expertise of offenders, jurisdictional uncertainties,

differences and discrepancies in legislation between jurisdictions, and a lack of monitoring and regulation of online activities. An additional challenge to investigators lies in the nontraditional skills often required to sift through the technical evidence involved in cybercrimes, including the need to identify the Internet Protocol (IP) address and where it is located. IP tracing technologies can provide valuable tools to identify the source of Internet communications. Helpful clues to the location of a suspect can be found by analyzing email header information, which reveals the IP address of the system the email came from. Once the IP address is obtained, investigators can easily identify the location with an IP tracing tool. Investigating cybercrime and other crimes that use the computer is the topic of Chapter 17.

The Child Protection and Sexual Predator Punishment Act, passed in 1998, imposes tougher penalties for sex crimes against children, particularly those facilitated by the use of the Internet. The Act prohibits contacting a minor via the Internet to engage in illegal sexual activity and punishes those who knowingly send obscenity to children.

Models to Combat Child Sexual Exploitation

Three law enforcement approaches have emerged as models to combat child sexual exploitation: special task forces, strike forces, and law enforcement networks.

Special task forces are useful in jurisdictions with a steady load of child sexual exploitation cases. In addition to a steady caseload, the model includes a centralized location, a standing team of experts, specialized staffing, victim services, and a multijurisdictional (federal, state, local) approach. In a *strike force* model, no core is dedicated exclusively to the problem. Rather, team members come together from individual agencies in response to a particular case. Under a *law enforcement network* model, law enforcement officers, prosecutors, victims' services providers, social service agents, and others come together proactively to focus on education, recruitment, building resources, and establishing personal contacts. This model has no dedicated resources and, over time, may evolve into a task force or strike force if needed.

Federal Initiatives to Protect Children Online

Several initiatives are aimed at protecting children in cyberspace. The Office of Juvenile Justice and Delinquency Prevention (OJJDP) of the U.S. Department of Justice funds the Internet Crimes against Children (ICAC) task force, which seeks to protect children online. Established in September 1998, this program helps state and local law enforcement agencies develop effective responses to online enticement and child pornography cases, including community education, forensic, investigative, and victim service components.

Project Safe Childhood (PSC) was designed and sponsored by the U.S. Department of Justice to empower federal, state, and local law enforcement officers with tools needed to investigate cybercrimes against children. Since 1998, 61 federally funded ICAC task forces, consisting of more than 3,500 affiliated state and local organizations, have been created across the country. During fiscal year 2019, ICAC task force programs conducted more than 81,000 investigations and 85,700 forensic exams, efforts that led to the arrests of more than 9,500 individuals. The ICAC program also trained over 39,570 law enforcement personnel, over 3,770 prosecutors, and more than 13,120 other professionals working in the ICAC field (OJJDP, 2020).

The National Center for Missing and Exploited Children (NCMEC) has a congressionally mandated CyberTipline (www.cybertipline.com), a reporting mechanism for child sexual exploitation that serves as the national clearinghouse for child pornography cases across the country. The CyberTipline maintains a 24-hour-a-day number (1-800-THE-LOST) that receives leads in five basic areas: (1) possession, manufacture, and distribution of child pornography; (2) online enticement of children for sexual acts; (3) child prostitution; (4) child sex tourism; and (5) child sexual molestation outside the family. In 2019, the CyberTipline received 16.9 million reports which included 69.1 million images, videos, and other files related to child sexual exploitation (NCMEC, 2020a).

In June 2008, the FBI, in partnership with NCMEC, began Operation Rescue Me, an aggressive program that uses image analysis to identify child victims depicted in child sexual exploitation material. Analysts focus on items visible in the backgrounds of child pornography images and videos to answer several basic questions in an effort to identify and rescue victimized children:

- Are useful clues visible in the background? (e.g., What's on the walls? Are distinct clothes or commercial labels visible?)

- Can a time frame be determined? (e.g., season, time of day, passage of time)

- Is the physical location identifiable? (e.g., country, state, hotel room)

- Finally, who are the children in the photos/videos?

Candidate images and videos for Operation Rescue Me arise from new child pornography series discovered by FBI field investigations, from forensic exams, or from nominations by NCMEC. In October 2012, the FBI's Crimes Against Children (CAC) program and the Innocent Images National Initiative (IINI) merged to form the Violent Crimes Against Children (VCAC) program in the Criminal Investigative Division. The VCAC continues the efforts of its predecessors by providing centralized coordination and analysis of case information on a national and international scale, requiring close cooperationnot only among FBI field offices and legal attachés but also with state, local, and international governments. From 2001 to 2013, the efforts of the VCAC generated more than 16,000 informations and indictments, led to nearly 24,000 arrests, and helped secure approximately 17,000 convictions.

International Initiatives

In 1996 the First World Congress against Commercial Exploitation of Children convened in Stockholm, Sweden. This congress adopted a Declaration and Agenda for Action calling on states to, among other things:

- Accord high priority to action against the commercial exploitation of children and allocate adequate resources to the effort

- Promote stronger cooperation between states and all sectors of society and strengthen the role of families

- Criminalize the CSEC

- Condemn and penalize the offenders while ensuring that child victims are not penalized

- Review and revise laws, policies, programs, and practices

- Enforce laws, policies, and programs

INTERPOL has established a Standing Working Party (SWP) on offenses against minors that seeks to improve international cooperation in preventing and combating child pornography and other forms of child sexual exploitation. The group meets twice a year to produce best-practices reports.

The Violent Crimes Against Children International Task Force (VCACITF), formerly known as the Innocent Images International Task Force, is a select unit of international law enforcement experts who collaborate to create and deliver a comprehensive global response to crimes against children. The VCACITF became operational on October 6, 2004, and serves as the largest task force of its kind in the world.

Project Spade was an international investigation that began in October 2010 in Toronto, Canada, and quickly spread to more than 50 other countries when it was discovered that the man at the center, Brian Way, had created a global network to generate, collect, and distribute child pornography. Officers executing a search warrant of Way's home and business seized roughly 1,000 items of evidence, including computers, servers, DVD burners, video editing software, and hundreds of movies (Payne, 2013). Way's customer records helped investigators orchestrate a worldwide sting that resulted in the arrests of 348 people, including 76 Americans, and the rescue of 386 children (Payne, 2013). The suspects included school teachers, doctors and nurses, police officers, clergymen, and many other people who volunteered with children in some capacity. In 2017, a former junior-college chemistry teacher and soccer coach from Quebec became the fourth person known to have committed suicide after being identified in connection with Project Spade (Mathieu, 2017).

Sex Offender Reactions to Being Caught

When a child pornography and sex ring is discovered, certain reactions by the offenders are fairly predictable. The intensity of these reactions may depend on how much the offenders have to lose by their identification and conviction.

Usually a sex offender's first reaction to discovery is complete denial. The offenders may act shocked, surprised, or even indignant about an allegation of sexual activity with children. This denial frequently is aided by their friends, neighbors, relatives, and coworkers, who insist that such upstanding people could not have done what is alleged.

If the evidence rules out total denial, offenders may switch to a slightly different tactic, attempting to minimize what they have done in both quantity and quality. Sex offenders are often knowledgeable about the law and might admit to acts that are lesser offenses or misdemeanors.

Either as part of the effort to minimize or as a separate reaction, sex offenders typically attempt to justify their behavior. They might claim that they care for these children more than their parents do and that what the offender is doing is beneficial to the children. They may claim to have been under tremendous stress, to have a drinking problem, or not to have known how young a certain victim was. The efforts to justify their behavior often center on blaming the victim. Offenders may claim that they were seduced by the victims, that the victims initiated the sexual activity, or that the victims were promiscuous or even prostitutes. When various reactions do not result in termination of the investigation or prosecution, sex offenders may claim to be sick and unable to control themselves.

Missing Children: Runaway or Abducted?

Another major challenge facing law enforcement involves cases of missing children. Missing children are often included in discussions of sexual victimization because missing children and sexually exploited children are distinct yet overlapping populations (Fernandes-Alcantara, 2014). The term *missing child* is defined under the Missing Children's Assistance Act, passed in 1984, as an individual under age 18 whose whereabouts are unknown to that individual's legal custodian (42 U.S.C. §5772). This act required that the OJJDP conduct periodic national incidence studies to determine the actual number of children reported missing and the number of missing children who are recovered for a given year. To that end, the OJJDP established the National Incidence Studies of Missing, Abducted, Runaway, and Thrownaway Children (NISMART). Results of the third run of this survey (NISMART-3) were released in 2017, with encouraging data that showed the rate of children missing to their caretakers in 2013 was 32% lower than the rate found in the NISMART–2 report from 1999 (Sedlak, Finkelhor, & Brick, 2017). However, despite the Act's mandate and the efforts of the NISMART survey, the actual number of children who are currently missing or exploited remains largely unknown (Fernandes-Alcantara, 2014).

NCMEC is a private, nonprofit organization established in 1984 to spearhead national efforts to locate and recover missing children and raise public awareness about ways to prevent child abduction, molestation, and sexual exploitation. From its inception through September 2020, NCMEC had received more than 5 million calls and had helped law enforcement recover more than 334,000 children (NCMEC, 2020a). In 2019, the FBI's National Crime Information Center (NCIC) received 421,394 entries for missing persons under the age of 18. It must be noted, however, that this number reflects the number of *reports* of missing children, not the number of children who go missing in a certain year, and when some children run away multiple times in 1 year and are reported missing each time, these cases skew the data (www.missingkids.org/footer/media /keyfacts).

When children go missing, the question often asked is: Did they leave on their own accord (run away) or were they taken against their will (abducted)? Reports from numerous sources indicate that the vast majority of missing children are runaways, not abductions. Of the more than 29,000 cases of missing children with which NCMEC assisted law enforcement and families in 2019,

91% involved endangered runaways, 4% were family abductions, and less than 1% were nonfamily abductions (NCMEC, 2020a). Data from NISMART-3 reflect similar findings (Sedlak et al., 2017).

Myth Most missing children have been abducted by strangers.

Fact Most missing children are runaways. Of those missing children who have been abducted, most are taken by a family member.

Runaway and Thrownaway Children

While no standard definition exists, a runaway is generally considered to be a minor who has left the care and control of their legal guardian without the guardian's consent and without intent to return. Sometimes a time frame is attached (e.g., missing for 24 hours, or gone overnight); other times, a child is considered a runaway if they do not return "within a reasonable period of time." A thrownaway, in contrast, is a minor who is told by a parent or other adult caregiver to leave the house without any alternative care arrangements having been made and is prevented from returning home. Although laws vary by state, most states do not consider running away from home to be illegal, and a few states classify it as a status offense. It is, however, illegal to harbor a runaway, and even well-meaning individuals who provide temporary shelter to a runaway child and who do not notify the police and parents can face criminal charges.

Assessing the true number of runaway children is difficult, partly because of the transient nature of this group and because they often do not run to shelters where such counts are often taken. Data from the most recent NISMART study (NISMART-3) estimate that 413,000 youth under age 18 left home (runaways) or were asked to leave home (thrownaways or push outs) in 2013 (Sedlak et al., 2017). Data from the *Juvenile Offenders and Victims: 2014 National Report* show that, of all the runaway cases processed by juvenile courts in the United States in 2010, 58% involved females and the peak age for runaways was 16 (Sickmund & Puzzanchera, 2014). The report also noted that the runaway case rate had decreased between 1995 and 2010 for all but black youth, with the runaway case rate for black youth more than three times the rate for White youth. More than half of all runaways return home within a week (Child Find of America, n.d.).

Many runaways and thrownaways are insecure, depressed, unhappy, and impulsive with low self-esteem. They commonly report conflict with and alienation from parents, rejection and hostile control, and lack of warmth, affection, and parental support. Although there is no "typical" runaway and the reasons given for leaving home are often multifaceted, the NCMEC (2020c) has identified several factors that increase a youth's risk of running away, including:

- A previous missing incident

- Involvement with drugs and/or alcohol

- Untreated or undiagnosed mental illness

- Suicidal or self-harm tendencies

- Gang involvement

- Pregnancy

- Online enticement

The NCMEC notes that of all the cases handled in 2019, 87% of missing children had at least one reported risk factor and 62% had two or more risk factors. The risk also increases for youth living in the foster care system, particularly those who have had multiple placements. Data show that the likelihood of running away increases as the number of state care placements rises, and that the highest risk of running is observed for those aged 15 when they first enter foster care (NCMEC, 2020d).

While risk factors contribute to youths running away in the first place, being a runaway also exposes youth to further risks, as they are more likely to engage in substance use and delinquent behavior, become teenage parents, drop out of school, suffer from sexually transmitted diseases, meet the criteria for mental illness, and have an increased risk of being sexual exploited and trafficked (U.S. DOJ, 2019). According to the NCMEC (2020b), one in six runaways in 2019 were likely victims of child sex trafficking.

Considerations about whether youths are missing voluntarily include resources available to them to satisfy basic needs, such as food and shelter, access to money or credit cards, skills to obtain a job, and access to a vehicle or public transportation. Another indicator that the absence is voluntary is that items such as clothing and treasured personal possessions are missing. Sometimes, information can be obtained by examining the teenager's computer, emails, texts, and social media accounts. Officers should also find out if the missing child has a cell phone and, if so, where it is. If it was left behind, officers

should collect it as evidence and conduct a forensic examination for possible helpful information. If the cell phone is gone from the home and presumed to be with the child, immediate attempts should be made to track the location of the phone.

Sometimes a note is left confirming that the youth has indeed run away, but often there is no note. In other cases, evidence indicates that the child has not run away but, rather, has been abducted.

Abducted Children

Abducted children are sometimes kidnapped. **Kidnapping** is taking someone away by force, often for ransom. Child kidnapping is especially traumatic for the parents and for those called upon to investigate. A highly publicized child kidnapping case in 1989 involved the abduction of 11-year-old Jacob Wetterling, who was taken at gunpoint from near his home in Minnesota by a masked man. No ransom was demanded, and despite national publicity and a nationwide search, nearly three decades passed before Jacob's abductor and murderer was identified, captured, and sentenced, and Jacob's remains were located.

Another high-profile case, in which the victim was eventually rescued alive, was that of 11-year-old Jaycee Dugard, kidnapped and held prisoner for more than 18 years by Phillip and Nancy Garrido, a husband and wife. During her time in captivity, Jaycee was repeatedly sexually assaulted and gave birth to two daughters, the first when Dugard was only 14 years old. More recently, 13-year-old Jayme Closs was kidnapped and her parents murdered in October 2018 by 22-year-old Jake Patterson, who told detectives he had been thinking about "taking a girl" for two years before he abducted Jayme (Mark, 2019). Jayme escaped after 88 days in captivity.

Some child kidnappings are committed by a parent who has lost custody of the child in divorce proceedings. In such cases, ransom is not demanded. Rather, the parent committing the kidnapping may take on a new identity and move to another part of the country. Childless couples have also been known to kidnap babies or young children to raise as their own.

LO10 Identify the most common type of child abduction.

The most frequent type of child abduction is parental abduction.

In some cases, parents are simply poorly educated about the law, not knowing it to be a crime to abscond with their children. Other risk factors or warning signs of a possible parental abduction include prior threats of abduction or a history of hiding the child or withholding visitation; a parent's lack of emotional or financial ties to the area where the child is living; signs that a parent has liquidated assets, borrowed money, or made maximum withdrawals of funds against credit cards; and various forms of mental illness in a parent.

Officers called to investigate a case in which a parent is suspected of abducting their child must be aware of special caveats in their state's laws regarding parental rights. In some states, if the noncustodial parent returns the child within 24 hours, there essentially is no crime.

Regardless of whether the investigator knows whether the child is a runaway or has been abducted, specific investigative steps should be taken.

Investigating a Missing-Child Report

The U.S. Department of Justice and the NCMEC have collaborated to create an Investigative Officer Checklist to facilitate effective communication and documentation of valuable information in response to reports of endangered missing or abducted children (see amber-ic. org/resources/checklists/). The NCMEC has also created *Missing and Abducted Children: A Law-Enforcement Guide to Case Investigation and Program Management* (2011), which outlines a standard of practice for law enforcement officers handling missing-child cases, whether runaways, thrownaways, family or nonfamily abductions, or when the circumstances of the disappearance are unknown. The guide was authored by a team of professionals from local, state, and federal agencies and describes—step-by-step with definitive checklists—the investigative process required for each of these types of cases and offers a wealth of resources to assist an investigator. The discussion that follows contains excerpts and highlights from the fourth edition of this guide.

The first responder conducts the preliminary investigation. Interview the parent(s) or person who made the initial report, verify that the child is in fact missing, and verify the child's custody status. Conduct a search to include all surrounding areas, including vehicles and other places of concealment, treating the area as a crime scene. Based on the circumstances of the child's disappearance, officers should consider using canine units, using forced entry into abandoned cars, sealing off any apartment complex where the child was last

seen, and considering use of search-and-rescue organizations, fire departments, military units, and scout groups and other volunteers for a large-scale search.

Officers should evaluate the contents and appearance of the child's room and determine whether any of the child's personal items are missing, including electronic devices. Obtain photographs and videotapes of the missing child. Prepare reports. Enter the missing child into the NCIC Missing Persons File and report it to NCMEC. Interview other family members and friends and associates of the child and of the family to determine when each last saw the child and what they think happened to the child. Ensure that everyone at the scene is identified and interviewed separately.

As time permits, prepare and update bulletins for local law enforcement agencies, state missing children's clearinghouses, the FBI, and other appropriate agencies. Also prepare a flyer or bulletin with the child's photograph and descriptive information and distribute it in appropriate geographic regions. Secure the child's latest medical and dental records. Establish a telephone hotline for tips and leads. Although the initial steps in the response are extensive, time-consuming, and labor intensive, the preliminary investigation should be commenced as soon as possible after the original missing-child report is received.

If the preliminary investigation does not resolve the situation, a follow-up investigation must be conducted. Responsibilities of the investigative officer are many:

- Obtain a briefing from the first responding officer and other on-scene personnel.

- Verify all information developed during the preliminary investigation.

- Obtain a brief, recent history of family dynamics.

- Correct and investigate the reasons for any conflicting information offered by witnesses and others submitting information.

- Develop an investigation plan for follow-up.

Investigators should also be aware of legislation pertaining to the length of time that passes between when a child goes missing and when a report is made. Caylee's Law, legislation named after Florida toddler Caylee Anthony who went missing and whose remains were found roughly six months after she was last seen, calls for a parent or guardian to be charged with a felony for not immediately reporting their child's disappearance.

Caylee's mother, Casey Anthony, failed to report her daughter missing for more than a month. Caylee's body was found several months later near her home. After giving several fabricated explanations, Casey admitted knowing about Caylee's death and disposing of the body. Although Casey was acquitted of first-degree murder and related felony charges, she was convicted on four misdemeanor counts of providing false information to the police. Several states have enacted or are considering such legislation, but these laws have faced numerous challenges in state courts for violating a person's Fifth Amendment protection against self-incrimination.

Runaways. If it is determined—either through a note or other evidence—that the child has run away, investigators (in addition to doing the investigative steps already described) should initially check agency records for recent contact with the child (arrests, other activities). Review school records and interview teachers, other school personnel, and classmates and check the contents of the school locker.

Investigators should also consider several criteria to determine whether the runaway child is endangered:

- Is the missing child younger than 13 years of age?

- Is the missing child believed to be out of the physical or geographic zone of safety for their age and developmental stage?

- Is the missing child mentally incapacitated?

- Is the missing child drug dependent—on a prescribed medication or an illegal substance—and is the dependency life-threatening?

- Was the missing child absent from home for more than 24 hours before being reported to police?

- Is the missing child believed to be in a life-threatening situation?

- Is the missing child believed to be in the company of adults who could endanger their welfare?

- Is the child's absence inconsistent with their established patterns of behavior and the deviation not readily explained?

- Are there other circumstances involved in the disappearance that would cause a reasonable person to conclude that the child should be considered at risk?

Any child who fits any of these criteria should be categorized as an endangered runaway, and efforts to locate the child should be immediately put into effect.

Abductions. For officers considering criminal charges against a parent who has abducted their child, several questions are pertinent:

- Is there sufficient documentation to demonstrate parentage and the individual's right to physical custody or access?

- Can the suspect-parent actually be identified as the abductor?

- A vacation or change of address is not necessarily illegal. Can it be clearly established that the intent of the move was to unlawfully deny access to the complainant?

- If removal from the state is an element of the offense, can it be proven that the child has been physically taken across the state line?

- Can it be demonstrated that the suspect-parent is responsible for the removal?

- Have mitigating factors (such as domestic violence and abuse) been evaluated that, by statute, could undermine the filing of a charge?

- If an accomplice was involved, can it be proven that they had sufficient personal knowledge of the legal custody issues to form criminal intent?

- If the accomplice was the abductor, can the suspect-parent's complicity be demonstrated? How can they be directly implicated?

If the situation warrants, officers should use the federal Unlawful Flight to Avoid Prosecution (UFAP) statute. Although UFAP warrants are not required for out-of-state arrests, they can be very helpful.

The investigation becomes exponentially more complicated when the suspect-parent leaves the country with the child. As soon as investigators determine that a child may have been taken to a foreign country, the parent or guardian still in the United States should immediately contact the U.S. Department of State to discuss the filing of an application invoking the Hague Convention or actions to be taken under the International Parental Kidnapping Crime Act. The Hague Convention is an international treaty calling for the prompt return of an abducted child, usually to the country of their residence. Rapid action is necessary because after a child has been in another country for one year, the treaty is no longer binding. One helpful resource in such circumstances is *A Law Enforcement Guide on International Parental Kidnapping* (OJJDP, 2018).

Because of the seriousness of missing-child cases and the critical need for a prompt response, investigators are strongly advised to seek the assistance of national resources and specialized services. One such resource used in all 50 states is the AMBER Alert plan.

The AMBER Alert Plan

America's Missing: Broadcast Emergency Response (AMBER) Alert is a voluntary partnership between law enforcement and broadcasters to activate an urgent bulletin in the most serious child abduction cases. The AMBER Alert was created in the Dallas–Fort Worth region in 1996 in response to the death of nine-year-old Amber Hagerman, who was abducted while riding her bicycle in Arlington, Texas, and then brutally murdered. AMBER Alerts are emergency messages broadcast when a law enforcement agency determines that a child has been abducted and is in imminent danger. The broadcasts include information that could assist in the child's recovery, including a physical description of the child and abductor. The OJJDP (2019) states: "The goal of an AMBER Alert is to instantly galvanize the community to assist in the search for and safe recovery of an abducted child. AMBER Alerts are activated in the most serious child abduction cases. The alerts are broadcast through radio, TV, road signs, cell phones, and other data-enabled devices. The AMBER Alert system is being used in all 50 states, the District of Columbia, Puerto Rico, the U.S. Virgin Islands, areas within Indian Country, and internationally across 27 countries." In most departments, the public information officer (PIO) is the communication cornerstone of this network and is the primary point of contact with the media.

> **LO11** Describe the AMBER Alert program.
>
> The National AMBER Alert Network Act of 2002 encouraged development of a nationwide alert system for abducted children. In 2019, DOJ issued a second edition of a guide on best practices for law enforcement and its partners in preparing for, and responding to, AMBER alerts.

According to AMBER Alert's home page, the program is a proven success and, as of May 2020, has helped rescue 988 children nationwide. The AMBER Alert system has been expanded to cell phone customers. As of January 1, 2013, AMBER Alerts can be automatically sent through the Wireless Emergency Alerts (WEA) program to millions of subscribers who have WEA-enabled devices, and as of May 2020, 66 children have been rescued because of WEAs.

A law enforcement agency can activate an AMBER Alert only if the circumstances surrounding a child's disappearance meet local or state criteria. The AMBER Alert criteria recommended by the U.S. Department of Justice are as follows:

1. Law enforcement officials must have a reasonable belief that an abduction of a child aged 17 or younger has occurred.

2. Law enforcement officials must believe that the child is in imminent danger of serious bodily injury or death.

3. Enough descriptive information must exist about the victim and the abductor for law enforcement to issue an AMBER Alert.

4. The child's name and other critical data elements—including the child abduction (CA) and AMBER Alert (AA) flags—must have been entered into the NCIC system.

The AMBER Alert program has evolved to include other agencies, organizations, and companies with the capability of expanding notification of recent child abductions to a much wider audience. These new participants, called AMBER Alert Secondary Distributors (AASD), include a variety of interests and industries and use different technologies to reach the public, but they all meet the following requirements:

- These distributors must have the capability to redistribute AMBER Alert messages to a geographically targeted audience as defined by the activating law enforcement agencies.

- They must redistribute the AMBER Alert at no charge to law enforcement or the public.

AMBER Alert Secondary Distribution Partners include:

- Federal law enforcement agencies (e.g., FBI, ICE, TSA, DEA)

- Additional resources for law enforcement (e.g., RISS, LEO)

- Wireless carriers

- Internet Service Providers, websites, and social media platforms (e.g., Google, Facebook, Bing)

- Apps (e.g., iTunes, Waze, Uber)

- Digital signs (e.g., digital billboard displays, Walgreens)

- Trucking industry

- Other organizations (e.g., Choice Hotels, OnStar, Time Warner Cable, Jump2Go)

(Office of Justice Programs, n.d.)

The first three hours after an abduction are critical, as a nationwide study found in cases when a child is killed during an abduction, 46.8% will die within an hour of the abduction and 76.2% will be dead within three hours of the abduction. After 24 hours, the child was dead in 88.5% of the cases (Brown, Keppel, Skeen, & Weis, 2006). Research has shown that the killer is statistically just as likely to be a friend or acquaintance as to be a stranger.

A Child Abduction Response Team

Because of the time-sensitive nature of child abductions, departments should consider establishing a child abduction response team (CART). The mission of a CART is to bring expert resources to child abduction cases quickly. The team typically consists of seasoned, experienced officers from around the region, each with a preplanned response related to that officer's field of expertise. Such teams might also include mounted patrols, all-terrain vehicles (ATVs), helicopters, and K-9s—whatever resources are readily available.

Additional Resources Available

One valuable resource in missing-children cases is the Missing and Exploited Children's Program. This program provides direct services through NCMEC, the Association of Missing and Exploited Children's Organizations (AMECO), and Health Opportunities for People Everywhere (Project HOPE). Services include the operation of a toll-free, 24-hour telephone hotline, and a CyberTipline to receive information about missing or exploited children, and the provision of mentoring and support programs for parents going through the trauma of having a missing child. The program also provides training and technical assistance to law enforcement, and it conducts research.

The Help Offering Parents Empowerment (Team HOPE) project, established in 1998, helps families of missing children handle the day-to-day issues of coping. Team HOPE links victim-parents with experienced and trained parent volunteers who have gone through the experience of having a missing child. Because they speak from firsthand experience, these volunteers provide compassion, counsel, and support in ways no other community agency can.

Having looked at the various incidents involving children as victims of crime, consider next their role in presenting a case in court. This discussion will be expanded in Chapter 21.

Children as Witnesses in Court

With the increase in criminal cases involving physical and sexual abuse of children, the problems associated with children providing testimony in court have increased proportionately. Court procedures and legal practices that benefit the child witness may not be balanced with the rights of the accused, and vice versa. To resolve some of these problems, the courts have changed a number of rules and procedures:

- Some courts give preference to these cases by placing them ahead of other cases on the docket.

- Some courts permit videotaping child interviews and then providing access to the tapes to numerous individuals to spare the child the added trauma of multiple interviews.

- Courts are limiting privileges for repeated medical and psychological examinations of children.

- To reduce the number of times the child must face the accused, the courts are allowing testimony concerning observations of the child by another person who is not a witness, allowing the child to remain in another room during the trial, or using a videotape of the child's testimony as evidence.

- Some courts remove the accused from the courtroom during the child's testimony.

Many of these changes in rules and procedures are being challenged. Sixth Amendment issues arise concerning the right to confront witnesses. In *Coy v. Iowa* (1988), the Supreme Court ruled that a protective screen violated the Sixth Amendment, but Justice Sandra Day O'Connor opined that the *Coy* decision did not rule out using videotapes or closed-circuit television (CCTV). In *Maryland v. Craig* (1990), the Supreme Court carved out an exception to the Sixth Amendment by stating that alleged child abuse victims could testify by CCTV if the court was satisfied through testimony that face-to-face confrontation would traumatize the victim.

Despite some courts' stance that children should be made to testify in court as any other victim or witness, some studies have provided evidence that courtroom testimony is not always the best way to elicit accurate information from children. If children will be testifying in court, several courtroom preparation techniques might improve their testimony and place them more at ease, such as giving them a tour of the courtroom, making available coloring or activity books depicting courtrooms and trials, or showing them videotapes about the court process.

Preventing Crimes against Children

Child abusers can be of any race, age, gender, or occupation; they can be someone close or a complete stranger. Signs that a child may be at risk of victimization, particularly by online predators, include the following:

- The child spends an inordinate amount of time online.

- The child minimizes a computer screen or turns the monitor off when a parent comes by.

- The child receives phone calls from unknown persons or gifts through the mail.

- The child experiences mood swings or behavioral changes.

- The child uses online accounts that belong to other people.

- The child hesitates or outright refuses to allow a parent to look at the contents of their cell phones, social media accounts, or other digital devices such as iPads and flash drives.

Often, children are unaware of the behaviors and activities they engage in that place them at risk. Crimes against children may be prevented by educating them about potential danger and by keeping the channels of communication open. When given adequate information, children can avoid dangerous situations and better protect themselves against such predators.

Digital technology is allowing police to become more effective in preventing and handling crimes against children. For example, some law enforcement departments are teaming up with schools and the community to create digital files of local children in a step toward discouraging child abduction. Such files contain digitized photographs, fingerprints, and other personal information of area students and, because of their digital nature, can be dispatched within minutes to any law enforcement agency, business, or other organization involved in the search for a missing child.

Technology Innovations

Bark

As children spend more time online, their chance of encountering a child predator or experiencing online abuse increases. And for parents, it is often unrealistic, if not impossible, to read every text message, post, and email their children send or receive. Bark, an award-winning dashboard created by and for parents in collaboration with child psychologists, youth advisors, digital media experts, and law enforcement professionals, helps families manage and protect their children's online lives.

The Bark dashboard monitors more than 30 of the most popular apps and social media platforms, including text messaging and email. If the Bark algorithms detect potential threats or risks, an automatic alert is sent to the child's parent or caregiver along with expert recommendations on how to discuss digital dangers and other sensitive online issues with their children. Alerts commonly involve communications pertaining to sex, depression, bullying, profanity, and violence. Parents note that it helps them monitor their children's digital communication without feeling like they are snooping.

According to its website, Bark analyzed more than 2.1 billion messages in 2020, including texts, email, YouTube, and more than 30 apps and social media platforms, and found:

- 88.5% of tweens and 94.1% of teens expressed or experienced violent subject matter/thoughts.
- 45.5% of tweens and 66.3% of teens engaged in conversations about depression.
- 76.7% of tweens and 82.0% of teens experienced cyberbullying as a bully, victim, or witness.
- 78.0% of tweens and 91.1% of teens engaged in conversations surrounding drugs/alcohol.
- 41.4% of tweens and 66.6% of teens were involved in a self-harm/suicidal situation.
- 70.9% of tweens and 87.9% of teens encountered nudity or content of a sexual nature.

Source: https://www.bark.us/#how

Summary

Crimes against children include maltreatment (neglect and abuse), sexual exploitation (pornography and prostitution), trafficking, and abduction. The four common types of maltreatment are neglect, physical abuse, emotional abuse, and sexual abuse. Neglect is the most common form of child maltreatment and may be fatal. Child abuse and neglect can result in serious and permanent physical, mental, and emotional damage, as well as in future violent and criminal behavior.

Typically child abuse and neglect laws have three components: (1) criminal definitions and penalties, (2) a mandate to report suspected cases, and (3) civil process for removing the child from the abusive or neglectful environment. If the possibility of present or continued danger to the child exists, the child must be removed into protective custody.

When interviewing children, officers should consider the child's age, ability to describe what happened, and the potential for retaliation by the suspect against a child who "tells." Most reports of child neglect or abuse are made by third parties such as teachers, physicians, neighbors, siblings, or parents. Seldom does the victim report the offense. Evidence or indicators of neglect or abuse may be physical, behavioral, or both. Parental indicators may also be present.

The Child Protection Act (1984) prohibits child pornography and greatly increases the penalties for adults who engage in it. Sex offenders' reactions to being discovered usually begin with complete denial and then progress to minimizing the acts, justifying the acts, and blaming the victims. If all else fails, they may claim to be sick.

A special challenge in cases where a child is reported missing is to determine whether the child has run away or been abducted. The most frequent type of child abduction is parental abduction. The National AMBER Alert Network Act of 2002 encouraged development of a nationwide alert system for abducted children. In 2019, DOJ issued a second edition of a guide on best practices for law enforcement and its partners in preparing for, and responding to, AMBER alerts.

Can You Define?

bullying	mandated reporters	physical abuse
chicken hawk	minor	sexting
corporal punishment	misoped	sexual abuse
emotional abuse	molestation	sexual exploitation
exploitation	Munchausen syndrome	sexual seduction
female genital mutilation (FGM)	Munchausen by proxy syndrome (MBPS)	sudden infant death syndrome (SIDS)
hebephile		
kidnapping	neglect	temporary custody without hearing
lewdness	osteogenesis imperfecta (OI)	
maltreatment	pedophile	

Checklist

Crimes Against Children

- What statute has been violated, if any?

- What are the elements of the offense charged?

- Who is the suspect, or are there multiple suspects?

- Who reported the crime?

- Are there witnesses to the offense?

- What evidence is needed to prove the elements of the offense charged?

- Is there physical evidence?

- Has physical evidence been submitted for laboratory examination?

- Who has been interviewed?

- Are written statements available?

- Would a polygraph be of any assistance in examining the victim? The suspect?

- Is there probable cause to obtain a search warrant?

- What items should you include in the search?

- Is the victim able to provide specific dates and times?

- Is the victim able to provide details of what happened?

- What physical and behavioral indicators are present in this case?

- Were photographs taken of the victim's injuries?

- Is the victim in danger of continued abuse?

- Is it necessary to remove the victim into protective custody?

- Has the local welfare agency been notified? Was there a joint investigation to avoid duplication of effort?

- Is there a file on known sexual offenders in the community?

- Is a child sexual abuse ring involved in the offense?

- Could the offense have been prevented? How?

Applications

Read the following and then answer the questions:

A. A police officer receives an anonymous call reporting sexual abuse of a 10-year-old female. The caller states that the abusers are the father and brother of the girl and provides all three names and their address. When the officer requests more details, the caller hangs up. You are assigned the case and initiate the investigation by contacting the alleged victim at school. She is reluctant to talk to you at first but eventually admits that both her father and brother have been having sex with her for almost a year. You then question the suspects and obtain written statements in which they admit the sexual abuse.

Questions

1. Should the investigation have been initiated on the basis of the anonymous caller?

2. What type of crime has been committed?

3. Was it appropriate to make the initial contact with the victim at her school?

4. Who should be present at the victim's initial interview?

5. What should be done with the victim after obtaining the facts?

6. What would be the basis for an affidavit for an arrest warrant?

B. A police officer receives an anonymous phone call stating that a child is being sexually assaulted at a specific address. The officer goes to the address—an apartment—and through an open door sees a child lying on the floor, apparently unconscious. The officer enters the apartment and, while checking the child for injuries, notices blood on the child's face and clothing. The child regains consciousness, and the officer asks, "Did your dad do this?" The child answers, "Yes." The officer then goes into another room and finds the father in bed, intoxicated. The officer rouses the father and places him under arrest.

Questions

1. Was the officer authorized to enter the apartment on the basis of the initial information?

2. Was the officer authorized to enter without a warrant?

3. Should the officer have asked whether the father had injured the child? If not, how should the question have been phrased?

4. Was an arrest of the father justified without a warrant?

5. What should be done with the victim?

C. A woman living in another state telephones the police department and identifies herself as the ex-wife of a man she believes is performing illegal sexual acts with the daughter of his current girlfriend. The man resides in the police department's jurisdiction. The woman says the acts have been witnessed by her sons, who have been in the area visiting their father. The sons told her that the father goes into the bathroom and bedroom with his girlfriend's 8-year-old daughter and closes the door. They also have seen the father making suggestive advances to the girl and taking her into the shower with him. The girl has told the woman's sons that the father does "naughty" things to her. The woman's sons are currently at home with her, but she is worried about the little girl.

Questions

1. Should an investigation be initiated based on this thirdhand information?

2. If the report is founded, what type of crime is being committed?

3. Who has jurisdiction to investigate?

4. What actions would be necessary in the noninitiating state?

5. Where should the initial contact with the alleged victim be made?

D. A reliable informant has told police that a man has been molesting children in his garage. Police establish a surveillance of the suspect and see him invite a juvenile into his car. They follow the car and see it pull into the driveway of the man's residence. The man and the boy then go into the house. The officers follow and knock on the front door but receive no answer. They knock again and loudly state their purpose. Continuing to receive no answer, they enter the house through the unlocked front door, talk to the boy and based on what he says, arrest the suspect.

Questions

1. Did the officers violate the suspect's right to privacy and domestic security?

2. Does the emergency doctrine apply?

3. What should be done with the victim?

4. Was the arrest legal?

Note: In each of the preceding cases, the information is initially received not from the victim but from third parties. This is usually the case in child abuse offenses.

References

Adams, S. M., Good, M. W., & Defranco, G. M. (2009, May 15). Sudden infant death syndrome. *American Family Physician, 79*(10), 870–874.

Adams, W., Owens, C., & Small, K. (2010, July). *Effects of federal legislation on the commercial sexual exploitation of children.* Washington, DC: Office of Juvenile Justice and Delinquency Prevention. (NCJ 228631)

Administration for Children and Families. (2020). *Child maltreatment 2018.* Washington, DC: Author. Retrieved September 21, 2020, from www.acf.hhs.gov/sites/default/files/cb/cm2018.pdf

Allardyce, S., & Yates, P. (2018). *Working with children and young people who have displayed harmful sexual behaviour.* Edinburgh, Scotland: Dunedin Academic Press.

American Professional Society on the Abuse of Children. (2012). *Forensic interviewing in cases of suspected child abuse.* Columbus, OH: Author. Retrieved September 23, 2020, from depts.washington.edu/hcsats/PDF/guidelines/Forensic%20Interviewing%20in%20Cases%20of%20Suspected%20Child%20Abuse.pdf

Bieler, D. (2018, November 21). Adrian Peterson says he still uses a belt and switch to punish son. *The Washington Post.* Retrieved September 22, 2020, from www.washingtonpost.com/sports/2018/11/22/adrian-peterson-says-he-still-uses-belt-switch-punish-his-son/

Brannan, D. (2019, August 5). Alton man sentenced to 33 years in prison for live streaming sexual abuse of a child. *Riverbender.com.* Retrieved October 1, 2020, from www.riverbender.com/articles/details/alton-man-sentenced-to-33-years-in-prison-for-live-streaming-sexual-abuse-of-a-child-36575.cfm

Brown, K. M., Keppel, R. D., Skeen, M. E., & Weis, J. G. (2006, May). *Investigative case management for missing children homicides: Report II.* Olympia, WA: Office of the Attorney General, State of Washington, and U.S. Department of Justice's Office of Juvenile Justice and Delinquency Prevention. (NCJ 218936)

Centers for Disease Control and Prevention. (2020, March 5). *Child abuse and neglect: Risk and protective factors.* Atlanta, GA: Author. Retrieved September 22, 2020, from www.cdc.gov/violenceprevention/childabuseandneglect/riskprotectivefactors.html

Child Find of America. (n.d.). *Facts and stats on missing children.* New Paltz, NY: Author. Retrieved October 8, 2020, from childfindofamerica.org/resources/facts-and-stats-missing-children/

Child Welfare Information Gateway. (2020, March). *Child abuse and neglect fatalities 2018: Statistics and interventions.* Washington, DC: U.S. Department of Health and Human Services, Children's Bureau. Retrieved September 22, 2020, from www.childwelfare.gov/pubPDFs/fatality.pdf

Christian, C. W. (2015, May). The evaluation of suspected child physical abuse. *Pediatrics, 135*(5): e1337–e1354. doi:10.1542/peds.2015-0356

Cuevas, C. A., Finkelhor, D., Shattuck, A., Turner, H., & Hamby, S. (2013, October). *Children's exposure to violence and the intersection between delinquency and victimization.* Washington, DC: Office of Juvenile Justice and Delinquency Prevention. (NCJ 240555)

Eggerton, J. (2020, May 10). New bill would attack child porn. *Broadcasting + Cable.* Retrieved October 1, 2020, from www.nexttv.com/news/new-bill-would-attack-child-porn

Europol. (2018). *Internet organised crime threat assessment (IOCTA) 2018.* The Hague, Netherlands: Author. Retrieved October 1, 2020, from www.europol.europa.eu/activities-services/main-reports/internet-organised-crime-threat-assessment-iocta-2018

Fernandes-Alcantara, A. L. (2014, August 1). *Missing and exploited children: Background, policies, and issues.* Washington, DC: Congressional Research Service. (RL 34050). Retrieved April 21, 2015, from www.fas.org/sgp/crs/misc/RL34050.pdf

Finkelhor, D., Ormrod, R., & Chaffin, M. (2009, December). *Juveniles who commit sex offenses against minors.* Washington, DC: Office of Juvenile Justice and Delinquency Prevention. (NCJ 227763). Retrieved May 26, 2021, from www.ojp.gov/pdffiles1/ojjdp/227763.pdf

Finkelhor, D., Ormrod, R., Turner, H., & Hamby, S. (2012, April). *Child and youth victimization known to police, school, and medical authorities.* Washington, DC: Office of Juvenile Justice and Delinquency Prevention. (NCJ 235394)

Finkelhor, D., Turner, H., Shattuck, A., Hamby, S., & Kracke, K. (2015, September). *Children's exposure to violence, crime, and abuse: An update.* Washington, DC: Office of Juvenile Justice and Delinquency Prevention. Retrieved September 20, 2020, from ojjdp.ojp.gov/sites/g/files/xyckuh176/files/pubs/248547.pdf

Flaherty, E. G., Perez-Rossello, J. M., Levine, M. A., & Hennrikus, W. L. (2014, February). Evaluating children with fractures for child physical abuse. *Pediatrics, 133*(2): e477–e489. Retrieved September 28, 2020, from ohioaap.org/wp-content/uploads/2016/08/e477.full_.pdf

Greijer, S., & Doek, J. (2016, June). *Terminology guidelines for the protection of children from sexual exploitation and sexual abuse.* Bangkok, Thailand: ECPAT International. Retrieved October 5, 2020, from www.interpol.int/en/Crimes/Crimes-against-children/Appropriate-terminology

Hanzlick, R. L., Jentzen, J. M., & Clark, S. C. (2007, January). *Sudden, unexplained infant death investigation: Guidelines for the scene investigator.* Atlanta, GA: Centers for Disease Control and Prevention. Retrieved September 28, 2020, from www.cdc.gov/sids/pdf/508suidiguidelinessingles_tag508.pdf

Highet, A. R., Berry, A. M., Bettelheim, K. A., & Goldwater, P.N. (2014, July). Gut microbiome in sudden infant death syndrome (SIDS) differs from that in healthy comparison babies and offers an explanation for the risk factor of prone position. *International Journal of Medical Microbiology, 304*(5-6): 735–741. Retrieved September 28, 2020, from www.sciencedirect.com/science/article/abs/pii/S1438422114000587

Hockenberry, S., & Puzzanchera, C. (2020). *Juvenile court statistics 2018.* Pittsburgh, PA: National Center for Juvenile Justice. Retrieved September 30, 2020, from ojjdp.ojp.gov/sites/g/files/xyckuh176/files/media/document/juvenile-court-statistics-2018.pdf

Kaneshiro, N. K. (2019, August 7). *Munchhausen syndrome by proxy.* Bethesda, MA: National Institutes of Health, MedlinePlus. Retrieved September 25, 2020, from medlineplus.gov/ency/article/001555.htm

Karmen, A. (2013). *Crime victims: An introduction to victimology,* 8th ed. Belmont, CA: Wadsworth, Cengage Learning.

Leversee, T. (2015, July). Etiology and typologies of juveniles who have committed sexual offenses. *Sex Offender Management Assessment and Planning Initiative* (Research Brief). Washington, DC: Office of Sex Offender Sentencing, Monitoring, Apprehending, Registering, and Tracking. Retrieved September 30, 2020, from smart.ojp.gov/sites/g/files/xyckuh231/files/media/document/juvenileetiologyandtypology.pdf

Lobanov-Rostovsky, C. (2015, July). Recidivism of juveniles who commit sexual offenses. *Sex Offender Management Assessment and Planning Initiative* (Research Brief). Washington, DC: Office of Sex Offender Sentencing, Monitoring, Apprehending, Registering, and Tracking. Retrieved September 30, 2020, from smart.ojp.gov/sites/g/files/xyckuh231/files/media/document/juvenilerecidivism.pdf

Lohmann, R. C. (2012, July 20). The dangers of teen sexting. *Psychology Today* online. Retrieved October 12, 2020, from www.psychologytoday.com/blog/teen-angst/201207/the-dangers-teen-sexting

MacLeod, K. J. (2016). Working with the multidisciplinary team. Chapter 3 in *Forensic Interviews Regarding Child Sexual Abuse: A Guide to Evidence-Based Practice,* W. T. O'Donohue & M. Fanetti (Eds.). Switzerland: Springer International Publishing.

Marchiori, D. M. (2014). Trauma. Chapter 10 in *Clinical Imaging* (3rd ed.). Maryland Heights, MO: Mosby. Retrieved September 28, 2020, from www.sciencedirect.com/topics/medicine-and-dentistry/battered-child-syndrome

Mark, M. (2019, December 21). The man who kidnapped Jayme Closs told police he'd been thinking of kidnapping a girl for 2 years and that "if it wasn't Jayme, it would probably be someone else." *Insider.* Retrieved October 10, 2020, from www.insider.com/jayme-closs-kidnapper-jake-patterson-police-interview-2019-12

Mathieu, I. (2017, September 22). Former teacher is fourth known person involved with child-porn case to have taken his own life. *The Globe and Mail.* Retrieved October 6, 2020, from www.theglobeandmail.com/news/national/man-poisons-himself-after-being-sentenced-in-child-pornography-case/article36374086/

Missing and Abducted Children: A Law Enforcement Guide to Case Investigation and Program Management, 4th ed.

(2011). Findlay, P., & Lowery, R. G., Jr. (Eds.). Alexandria, VA: National Center for Missing and Exploited Children.

Mitchell, K. J., Jones, L., Finkelhor, D., & Wolak, J. (2014, February). *Trends in unwanted sexual solicitations: Findings from the youth Internet safety studies.* Durham, NC: University of New Hampshire, Crimes against Children Research Center. Retrieved October 5, 2020, from www.unh.edu/ccrc/pdf/Sexual%20Solicitation%201%20of%204%20YISS%20Bulletins%20Feb%202014.pdf?kbid=62750

National Center for Missing and Exploited Children. (2020a). *About NCMEC.* Alexandria, VA: Author. Retrieved October 8, 2020, from www.missingkids.org/footer/media/keyfacts

National Center for Missing and Exploited Children. (2020b). *Child sex trafficking.* Alexandria, VA: Author. Retrieved October 8, 2020, from www.missingkids.org/theissues/trafficking

National Center for Missing and Exploited Children. (2020c). *Endangered runaways.* Alexandria, VA: Author. Retrieved October 8, 2020, from www.missingkids.org/theissues/runaways

National Center for Missing and Exploited Children. (2020d). *Our work.* Alexandria, VA: Author. Retrieved October 8, 2020, from www.missingkids.org/ourwork/ncmecdata

National District Attorneys Association. (2014, November). *State statute series: Anatomical dolls and diagrams.* Arlington, VA: Author. Retrieved September 23, 2020, from ndaa.org/wp-content/uploads/Anatomical_Dolls_11_7_2014.pdf

Newlin, C., Steele, L. C., Chamberlin, A., Anderson, J., Kenniston, J., Russell, A., . . . & Vaughan-Eden, V. (2015, September). *Child forensic interviewing: Best practices.* Washington, DC: Office of Juvenile Justice and Delinquency Prevention. (NCJ 248749). Retrieved September 24, 2020, from ojjdp.ojp.gov/sites/g/files/xyckuh176/files/pubs/248749.pdf

Office of Justice Programs. (n.d.). *AMBER alert secondary distribution program.* Washington, DC: Author. Retrieved October 11, 2020, from amberalert.ojp.gov/sites/g/files/xyckuh201/files/media/document/amber_alert_secondary_distribution_program_summary.pdf

Office of Juvenile Justice and Delinquency Prevention. (n.d.). *Commercial sexual exploitation of children.* Washington, DC: Author. Retrieved May 26, 2021, from ojjdp.ojp.gov/programs/commercial-sexual-exploitation-children

Office of Juvenile Justice and Delinquency Prevention. (2018, July). *A law enforcement guide on international parental kidnapping.* Washington, DC: Author. (NCJ 250606) Retrieved October 8, 2020, from ojjdp.ojp.gov/sites/g/files/xyckuh176/files/pubs/250606.pdf#:~:text=%20%20%20Title%20%20%20A%20Law,Created%20Date%20%20%206%2F20%2F2018%209%3A47%3A25%20AM%20

Office of Juvenile Justice and Delinquency Prevention. (2019, April). *AMBER alert best practices* (2nd ed.). (NCJ 252759). Washington, DC: Author. Retrieved October 10, 2020, from ojjdp.ojp.gov/sites/g/files/xyckuh176/files/pubs/252759.pdf

Office of Juvenile Justice and Delinquency Prevention. (2020). *Internet crimes against children task force program.* Washington, DC: Author. Retrieved October 5, 2020, from ojjdp.ojp.gov/programs/internet-crimes-against-children-task-force-program

Osteogenesis Imperfecta Foundation. (2019) *Child abuse or osteogenesis imperfecta?* Gaithersburg, MD: Author. Retrieved September 28, 2020, from oif.org/wp-content/uploads/2019/08/Child_Abuse__Child_Abuse_or_Ostegenesis_Imperfecta.pdf

Pandya, N. K., Baldwin, K., Kamath, A. F., Wenger, D. R., & Hosalkar, H. S. (2011, March). Unexplained fractures: Child abuse or bone disease? A systematic review. *Clinical Orthopaedics and Related Research, 469*(3): 805–812. doi:10.1007/s11999-010-1578-z

Payne, W. (2013, November 15). Youth baseball coach is first American out of 76 identified as pedophile trapped in global sting that rescued 400 children. *Daily Mail* online. Retrieved October 12, 2020, from www.dailymail.co.uk/news/article-2507696/David-Scott-Engle-American-identified-pedophile-Project-Spade-bust.html

Petersen, A., Joseph, J., & Feit, M. (Eds.). (2013). New directions in child abuse and neglect research. Washington, DC: National Academies Press. Retrieved September 22, 2020, from www.ncbi.nlm.nih.gov/books/NBK195985/pdf/Bookshelf_NBK195985.pdf

Polaris Project. (2019). *Myths, facts, and statistics.* Washington, DC: Author. Retrieved September 9, 2020, from polarisproject.org/myths-facts-and-statistics/

Sedlak, A. J., Finkelhor, D., & Brick, J. M. (2017, June). *National estimates of missing children: Updated findings from a survey of parents and other primary caretakers.* Washington, DC: Office of Juvenile Justice and Delinquency Prevention, Juvenile Justice Bulletin. (NCJ 250089). Retrieved October 10, 2020, from ojjdp.ojp.gov/sites/g/files/xyckuh176/files/pubs/250089.pdf

Shetgiri, R. (2013). Bullying and victimization among children. *Advances in Pediatrics, 60*(1): 33–51. Retrieved September 28, 2020, from www.ncbi.nlm.nih.gov/pmc/articles/PMC3766526/

Sickmund, M., & Puzzanchera, C. (2014, December). *Juvenile offenders and victims: 2014 national report.* Pittsburgh, PA: National Center for Juvenile Justice. Retrieved October 10, 2020, from www.ojjdp.gov/ojstatbb/nr2014/downloads/NR2014.pdf

Sidebotham, P., Marshall, D., & Garstang, J. (2018, May). Responding to unexpected child deaths. Chapter 5 in *SIDS sudden infant and early childhood death: The past, the present and the future.* Adelaide, AU: University of Adelaide Press. Retrieved September 28, 2020, from www.ncbi.nlm.nih.gov/books/NBK513395/

Toth, P. (2011, Northern Spring/Southern Autumn). Comparing the NICHD and RATAC child forensic interview approaches—Do the differences matter? *The Link* newsletter of the International Society for Prevention of Child Abuse and Neglect (ISPCAN). Retrieved September 24, 2020, from www.ispcan.org/wp-content/uploads/ispcan/link/ispcan_link_20.1.pdf

U.S. Department of Justice. (2016, April). *The national strategy for child exploitation prevention and interdiction. A report to Congress.* Washington, DC: Author. Retrieved October 1, 2020, from www.justice.gov/psc/file/842411/download

U.S. Department of Justice. (2019, November 26). *The invisible faces of runaway and homeless youth.* Washington, DC: Author. Retrieved October 8, 2020, from www.ojp.gov/news/ojp-blogs/2019/invisible-faces-runaway-and-homeless-youth

U.S. Department of Justice. (2020, May 28). *Child sex trafficking.* Washington, DC: Author. Retrieved October 5, 2020, from www.justice.gov/criminal-ceos/child-sex-trafficking

Walsh, B. (2005, August). *Investigating child fatalities.* Washington, DC: Office of Juvenile Justice and Delinquency Prevention.

Walsh, W. A., Jones, L. M., Cross, T. P., & Lippert, T. (2010, July). Prosecuting child sexual abuse: The importance of evidence types. *Crime and Delinquency, 56*(3), 436–454.

Wang, J., Iannotti, R. J., & Nansel, T. R. (2009, October). School bullying among US adolescents: Physical, verbal, relational and cyber. *Journal of Adolescent Health, 45*(4), 368–375.

Wolak, J. (2011, November). *What we know (and don't know) about Internet sex offenders.* (PowerPoint from the ATSA 30th Annual Research and Treatment Conference, Toronto, Canada, November 2–5, 2011). Durham, NC: University of New Hampshire, Crimes against Children Research Center. Retrieved October 5, 2020, from www.atsa.com/sites/default/files/ConfHO2011Wolak.pdf

Wolak, J., Finkelhor, D., & Mitchell, K. J. (2012). *Trends in law enforcement responses to technology-facilitated child sexual exploitation crimes: The third national juvenile online victimization study (NJOV3).* Durham, NC: University of New Hampshire, Crimes against Children Research Center. Retrieved October 6, 2020, from scholars.unh.edu/ccrc/45/

World Health Organization. (2020, February 3). *Female genital mutilation.* Geneva, Switzerland: Author. Retrieved September 17, 2020, from www.who.int/news-room/fact-sheets/detail/female-genital-mutilation

Yun, I., Ball, J., & Lim, H. (2011, January). Disentangling the relationship between child maltreatment and violent delinquency: Using a nationally representative sample. *Journal of Interpersonal Violence, 26*(1), 88–110.

Cases Cited

Coy v. Iowa, 487 U.S. 1012 (1988).

Ingraham v. Wright, 430 U.S. 651 (1977).

Maryland v. Craig, 497 U.S. 836 (1990).

People v. Green, 155 Mich. 524, 532, 119 N.W. 1087 (1909).

Prince v. Massachusetts, 321 U.S. 158 (1944).

Santosky v. Kramer, 455 U.S. 745 (1982).

Worthen v. State, 42 Md. App. 20, 399 A.2d 272 (1979).

Chapter 12
Robbery

Learning Objectives

LO1   Define robbery.

LO2   Explain how robberies are classified.

LO3   Describe what a home invasion is.

LO4   Define carjacking.

LO5   Identify with what types of robbery the FBI and state officials become involved.

LO6   List the elements of the crime of robbery.

LO7   Identify what factors to consider in responding to a robbery-in-progress call.

LO8   Explain what special challenges are posed by a robbery investigation.

LO9   Explain how to prove each element of robbery.

LO10   List what modus operandi information to obtain in a robbery case.

LO11   Identify the types of physical evidence that can link a suspect with a robbery.

Introduction

Robbery has plagued the human race throughout history. During the 1930s, John Dillinger, America's number-one desperado, captured the attention of citizens and law enforcement officers alike. This notorious bank robber's tools of the trade were a Thompson submachine gun and a revolver. Although admired by many for his daring and cast as a folk hero, Dillinger gunned down 10 men. "Pretty Boy" Floyd began his criminal career by robbing a local post office of $350 in pennies. Like Dillinger, he also killed 10 people. Bonnie Parker and Clyde Barrow's murder and robbery spree through Missouri, Texas, and Oklahoma is also legendary.

On February 28, 1997, two heavily armed men wearing full body armor robbed a branch of the Bank of America in North Hollywood, California, and, as they fled the building, were met by dozens of Los Angeles Police Department officers. The ensuing gun battle, which some likened to a war zone, lasted 44 minutes and ended with injuries to 11 officers and 7 civilians and the deaths of both suspects.

The preceding are vivid examples of the violent nature of many robberies. Robbery is one of the three most violent crimes against the person. Only homicide and rape are considered more traumatic to a victim. According to the Federal Bureau of Investigation's Uniform Crime Reports (UCR), there were an estimated 282,061 robberies in the nation in 2018, a 12% decrease from the 2017 estimate (Federal Bureau of Investigation [FBI], 2018b). Data from the National Crime Victimization Survey (NCVS) report a higher incidence of robberies—573,100 in 2018 at a rate of 2.1 per 1,000 households (Morgan & Oudekerk, 2019). Such differences underscore the need to recognize how crime data are gathered and to view such statistics with caution.

In 2018, robbery accounted for 23.4% of all violent crimes and had a reported clearance rate of 30.4% (FBI, 2018b). Other facts about robbery reported in *Crime in the United States 2018* include:

- By location type, most robberies (36.9%) were committed on streets or highways (see Figure 12.1).

- The average dollar value of property stolen per robbery offense was $2,119. By location type, residences had the highest average dollar value taken— $4,600 per offense.

- An estimated $598 million in losses were attributed to robberies during 2018.

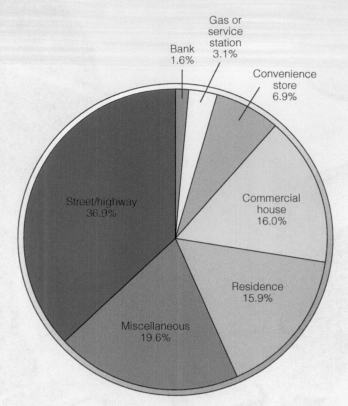

Figure 12.1
Robbery locations, percent distribution*, 2018.
*Due to rounding, the percentages may not add to 100.0.
Source: https://ucr.fbi.gov/crime-in-the-u.s/2018/crime-in-the-u.s.-2018/topic-pages/robbery

- Firearms were used in 38.2% of robberies for which the UCR program received data.

Armed robbery is a serious and dangerous crime and poses a definite hazard to law enforcement officers. Off-duty officers have been killed trying to intervene in these crimes. It is important that officers have a well thought out plan that follows their department's policy on how to respond if witnessing a robbery or attempted robbery when off duty.

Robbery: An Overview

Robbery takes many forms, from the daring exploits of criminals such as Dillinger to purse snatchings and muggings. Whatever the form, the potential for violence exists.

> ### L01   Define robbery.
>
> **Robbery** is the felonious taking of another's property, either directly from the person or in that person's presence, through force or intimidation.

To compel compliance from the victim, most robbers carry a weapon or other threatening item and make an *oral demand* for the desired money or property. The overt display of a weapon, or an indication by the robber that a weapon is concealed in a jacket pocket, usually keeps the victim from trying to fight off the robber. Therefore, little direct personal contact occurs between the robber and the victim, which reduces the probability of physical evidence remaining at the crime scene.

Some robbers present a *note* rather than speaking. The robber may or may not ask for the note to be returned. It is important evidence if left behind.

Despite the inherent danger to the victim during a robbery, most robberies do not result in personal injury, the theory being that the threat of force or the presence of a weapon reduces the likelihood of the victim resisting. Confronted with threatening statements, a threatening note, or a visible weapon, most robbery victims obey the robber's demands. Sometimes, however, a violent physical act is performed against the victim early in the robbery, either by original intent or because of unexpected circumstances or resistance. Such cases involve additional charges of aggravated assault or, in the case of death, murder. Violence against the victim also occurs in muggings and purse snatchings in which the victim is struck with a weapon, club, or the fists or is knocked down. Older people are often injured by the fall resulting from such violent acts. Any such violent contact increases the probability of hair, fibers, scratches, or other evidence being found on the victim or the suspect. According to the UCR, the use of violence during robberies has increased during the past 10 years, but such violence is not nearly as frequent as the public might expect.

Hostages are held in some robberies and are used as collateral or protection by robbers. If materials are used to restrain hostages, such as rope or tape, such items may provide useful evidence to investigators. Presence of such items can also provide modus operandi (MO) information about the suspect and be used to link separate robberies to the same offender. Bank robberies and hostage situations are discussed later in this chapter.

Robbers use various ruses to get themselves into position for the crime. They may loiter, pose as salespeople, or feign business, watching for an opportune moment to make their demands. Once the opportunity presents itself, robbers act quickly and decisively. A particularly brazen type of robbery is called **apple picking**, in which a suspect snatches an iPhone, iPad, or other mobile device directly from the hands of its user. Data from the Federal Communications Commission (FCC) indicates that nearly one in three robberies in the United States involves the theft of a mobile phone (Hill, 2013). One apple picker confided to a journalist that he targets older women, whom he is confident cannot run fast enough after him to catch him, and people who seem oblivious to their surroundings because they are talking on their cell phones or texting (Rosen & Patel, 2013). This offender's favorite time of day to "apple pick" was late afternoon when people were getting off work, the sidewalks were crowded and it was easy to blend in, and everyone seemed to be walking while on their phones, their guards dropped.

Beyond the obvious loss of the property from an apple picking event comes a more serious level of crime—identity theft. If you are using your phone when someone steals it, it is like standing with the bank vault open. No security password is required to get in because the system was already unlocked: "Now they have access to your email, your personal photos, videos, contacts, everything. They can even reset your password" (Rosen & Patel, 2013). Many phones and portable digital devices now use biometrics as a way to unlock and access stored information, and with the installation of "kill switch" software, these devices can be remotely wiped of all sensitive data if they are stolen, a feature that helps to not only prevent identity theft but also the theft of the phone to begin with (New York Office of the Attorney General, 2014; Tsukayama, 2014). Despite this technology, thieves and hackers continue efforts to thwart kill switches, and phones are often shipped overseas where they can be reset and used or disassembled for parts (CBS Local, 2018)

Another type of robbery gaining momentum, in which the victim willingly meets with the offender, is the **robbery-by-appointment**, also called buy-and-sell robberies. Many offenders find their victims through popular online classified ad sites such as Craigslist or Facebook Marketplace. These cases generally arise when an item—for example, a bike—is posted for sale in the paper or online and a buyer agrees to meet the seller somewhere in person to complete the transaction. But one of the parties arrives at the meeting with the ulterior motive of robbing the other. Either the seller has no intention of parting with the bike, if there even *is* a bike, and takes the money from the buyer, or the buyer does not intend to pay for the bike and takes it by force from the seller. Often there is an assault during the exchange, and several highly publicized murders have occurred after unwitting victims walked into a trap set by someone pretending to be buying or selling something.

Most robberies are committed by men. Robbers are usually serial criminals and may commit 15 to 25 robberies or more before being apprehended. People who commit robberies are often egotistical and prone to boasting of their crimes. Because of this, informants can provide excellent leads in robbery cases.

The most frequent victims of robberies are drug houses, liquor stores, fast-food establishments, jewelry stores, convenience stores, motels, gambling houses, and private residences. The elderly are frequently robbery victims of purse snatchings and snatches of packages committed by amateurs or juveniles. Consider several characteristics typical of robberies:

- They are committed by strangers rather than acquaintances.

- They are committed with the use of stolen cars, stolen motor-vehicle license plates, or both.

- They are committed by two or more people working together.

- The offender lives within 100 miles of the robbery.

- Robberies committed by a lone perpetrator tend to involve lone victims and are apt to be crimes of opportunity (spur of the moment).

- Youths committing robberies tend to operate in groups and to use strong-arm tactics more frequently than do adults.

- Less physical evidence is normally found after robberies than in other violent crimes.

- They take much less time than other crimes.

- Middle-aged and older people tend to be the victims.

In confrontational robberies, regardless of the offender's weapon, victims who defend themselves in some way are less likely to lose property than are victims who take no actions. However, victims who defend themselves against armed offenders are more likely to be injured than are those who take no actions during the crime.

Classification

Robberies are classified into four categories, each committed by different types of people using different techniques.

> **L02** Explain how robberies are classified.
>
> Robberies are classified as residential, commercial, street, or vehicle driver.

Residential Robberies

Residential robberies include those that occur in an inhabited housing structure, which can include a house, mobile home, hotel or motel room, houseboat, or other structure if it is considered one's residence. These robberies are less frequent than the other types but are dangerous and traumatic because they tend to involve entire families.

Entrance is frequently gained by knocking on the door and then forcing entrance when the occupant appears. Most residential robberies occur in the early evening when people are apt to be home. Victims are frequently bound and gagged or even tortured as the robber attempts to learn the location of valuables. In some cases, people are robbed because they arrive home to discover a burglary in progress. The burglar is thus "forced," by circumstances, to become a robber.

A type of residential robber challenging police departments across the country is the *home invader*, who usually targets a resident, not a residence. Home invaders often target women, senior citizens, immigrants, or drug dealers—people they consider either too vulnerable to fight back or who possess enough cash and contraband to be worth the risk.

> **L03** Describe what a home invasion is.
>
> A **home invasion** is a forced entry into an occupied dwelling to commit a violent crime, whether robbery, sexual assault, murder, or some combination of violent offenses.

Home invaders know that many immigrant families distrust banks and keep large amounts of cash and jewelry in their homes. This type of crime is growing in popularity and is increasing even in rural areas. Some states have passed or are considering legislation that makes home invasion deaths a capital crime.

Commercial Robberies

Convenience stores, loan companies, jewelry stores, liquor stores, gas stations, and bars are especially susceptible to robbery, and robberies at such locations are often carried out rapidly and frequently involve injury. Drugstores are apt to be targets of robberies to obtain narcotics as well as cash. Commercial houses, such as hotels and motels, can become targets of robbery if employees at such locations have information that a guest has a large amount of jewelry or money in their room.

Data from the U.S. Department of Justice indicate that, between 2005 and 2009, approximately 70% of workplace homicides were committed by robbers (Harrell, 2011). And data from the U.S. Bureau of Labor Statistics (2018) show that robbery was the motive in one-third of all work-related homicides of men in 2016.

Commercial robberies occur most frequently toward the end of the week between 6 p.m. and 4 a.m. Stores with poor visibility from the street and few employees on duty are the most likely targets. Many stores now keep only a limited amount of cash on hand during high-risk times. Stores also attempt to deter robbers by using surveillance cameras, alarm systems, security guards, and guard dogs.

Many commercial robberies are committed by individuals with criminal records and, because of the offenders' experience, such robberies are usually better planned than street or vehicle-driver robberies are. Also, because those who commit commercial robberies tend to be recidivists, their MOs should be compared with those of past robberies. For example, some robbers prefer to hit businesses first thing the morning—known as a **morning glory robbery**—catching arriving employees off guard and forcing their way into the premises to take cash or property. Other robbers prefer to strike at the end of the business day—the **closing robbery**—when the potential cash on site is highest or when employees are perhaps more distracted and less vigilant, their thoughts focused on going home or, at least, leaving work. Both the morning glory and closing types of robberies require preplanning and knowledge by the suspect of the business's opening and closing procedures.

Convenience store robberies are often committed by persons under the influence of drugs and/or alcohol who are robbing to obtain money to purchase more drugs and/or alcohol. Convenience stores that are robbed once are likely to be robbed again. In fact, about 8% of convenience stores account for more than 50% of these robberies. To thwart such robbery attempts, some businesses have mounted drop safes on the premises to limit access to deposited contents and installed alarm buttons that alert directly to local law enforcement.

Several factors put late-night retail workers at higher risk of becoming a target for robbery, including:

- The exchange of money
- Solo work and isolated work sites
- The sale of alcohol
- Poorly lit stores and parking areas
- Lack of staff training in recognizing and managing escalating hostile and aggressive behavior (National Institute for Occupational Safety and Health, 2018; Occupational Safety and Health Administration, 2009)

The Occupational Safety and Health Administration (OSHA) and the National Institute for Occupational Safety and Health (NIOSH) recommend taking several actions to deter workplace violence and the potential for robbery in late-night retail establishments:

- Keep the cash-register cash balance low.
- Provide good lighting outside and inside the store.
- Elevate the cash-register area so the clerk has better viewing ability and is in sight of passersby.
- Keep windows from being covered by signs or displays.
- Place silent panic alarms at cash points.

The OSHA and NIOSH websites are good resources for suggestions on post-incident response.

Street Robberies

Street robberies are most frequently committed on public streets and sidewalks and in alleys and parking lots, during the evening or nighttime and often in dimly lit areas. Most are committed with a weapon, but some are strong-arm robberies, in which physical force is the weapon. Both the victim and the robber are usually on foot.

Speed and surprise typify street robberies, which are often crimes of opportunity with little or no advance planning. Because such robberies happen so fast, the victim is often unable to identify the robber. Sometimes the victim is approached from behind and never sees the attacker. Because most street robberies yield little money, the robber often commits several robberies in one night.

In areas with large influxes of diverse groups of immigrants, especially undocumented ones, special problems occur. In Yonkers, New York, for example, numerous illegal immigrants from Mexico, Central America, and South America are preyed upon by robbers. Because of their illegal status, few of these immigrants have Social Security numbers. Without these, they are unable to open bank accounts or be paid by check. Therefore, they tend to carry large amounts of cash, sometimes their entire savings. Compounding the problem of investigating such crimes are the language barrier, fear and mistrust of police, fear of deportation, and lack of understanding of the justice system.

Vehicle-Driver Robberies

Drivers of taxis, limousines, ride-share vehicles (e.g., Uber, Lyft), buses, trucks, delivery and messenger vehicles, armored trucks, and personal cars are frequent targets of robbers. In fact, taxi, limo, and ride-share drivers are considered to have one of the most dangerous professions in the country due to their risk of being targets for robbery (NIOSH, 2018; Chaumont Menendez, Socias-Morales, & Daus, 2017). Taxi and rideshare drivers are vulnerable because they are often alone while cruising for fares, work early mornings and late nights when fewer witnesses are likely to be present to assist or identify attackers, are dispatched to addresses in high-crime locations, and may carry a lot of cash. Some taxi companies have taken preventive steps such as placing protective shields between the passenger and driver and reducing the amount of cash that drivers carry. Many cabs are now equipped with credit card scanners to further limit the amount of cash onboard, and some larger cab companies have equipped their fleet with onboard cameras, particularly those vehicles frequenting high-crime areas. Ride-sharing services, such as Uber and Lyft, have e-pay systems that avoid cash transactions entirely.

In an effort to reduce the amount of cash mass transit drivers possess, buses in many cities require passengers to have the exact change or to purchase tokens or passes at a central hub or satellite transit stations. Most modes of public transit, such as subways, light rail, and buses have installed security cameras to further deter criminal activity on board. Delivery vehicle drivers may be robbed of their merchandise as they arrive for a delivery, or the robbers may wait until after the delivery and take the cash. Many food delivery companies are now requiring customers to pay via credit card when placing the order, either online or by phone, which is also curbing the number of robberies involving delivery drivers.

Armored-car robberies are of special concern because they are usually well planned by professional, heavily armed robbers and involve large amounts of money. According to the FBI, in 2018 there were 34 armored carrier incidents involving a total of 67 known perpetrators (FBI, 2018b). A firearm was used in 21 of the 34 incidents, and acts of violence were reported in 15 of the 34 incidents, resulting in 6 injuries (3 employees, 1 perpetrator, 2 guards) and 2 deaths (1 employee and 1 perpetrator). One approach to this problem is to develop an intelligence network between the police department and the armored-car industry.

Drivers of personal cars are often approached in parking lots or while stopped at red lights in less-traveled areas. These robberies are generally committed by teenagers. Drivers who pick up hitchhikers leave themselves open to robbery, assault, and auto theft. Some robbers force people off roads or set up fake accidents or injuries to lure motorists into stopping. A combination of street and vehicle-driver robbery that has increased drastically over the past few years is carjacking.

Carjacking

Although not a "new" crime, carjacking had been included in the general category of "auto theft" before the 1990s and has since then been recognized as a growing threat. Initially, the more expensive vehicles were targeted, but this trend now covers all types of motor vehicles. Carjackings often occur at gas stations, automatic teller machines (ATMs), car washes, parking lots, shopping centers, convenience stores, restaurants, mass transit stations, and intersections requiring drivers to come to a stop. An estimated 38,000 carjacking incidents occurred annually from 1993 to 2002, according to the most recent government data available (Klaus, 2004). Carjackings have resulted in car thefts, injuries, and deaths.

LO4 Define carjacking.

Carjacking, a category of robbery, is the taking of a motor vehicle by force or threat of force. The FBI may investigate the crime.

The force may consist of use of a handgun, simulated handgun, club, machete, axe, knife, or fists. According to one survey, nearly three in four carjackings (74%) involved the use of a weapon (Klaus, 2004). The federal carjacking statute provides that a person possessing a firearm who takes a motor vehicle from the person or presence of another by force and violence or by intimidation shall (1) be imprisoned not more than 15 years; (2) if serious bodily injury results, be imprisoned not more than 25 years; and (3) if death results, be imprisoned for any number of years up to life.

Nearly every major city has experienced armed carjacking offenses in sufficiently substantial numbers that the UCR may soon be required to use carjacking as a designation rather than report these crimes without uniformity as armed robbery, auto theft, or some other offense.

Carjackers use many ruses to engage a victim. Some stage accidents (e.g., the bump and rob). Some pretend to be injured or have car trouble to get a driver to pull over and get out of their vehicle to help, only then pulling a weapon on the good Samaritan victim driver as a way to seize the car. Others wait for their victims at workplace parking lots, residential driveways, gas stations, car washes, or other locations where a victim is in close proximity to their vehicle, perhaps having left the keys inside. Once the target car is seized, it is then used as in the conventional crime of vehicle theft: for resale, resale of parts, joyriding, or committing another crime.

The motivation for carjacking is not clear because the vehicles are taken under so many different circumstances and for so many different reasons. One theory for the sudden increase is that the increased use of alarms and protective devices on vehicles, especially on more expensive ones, makes it more difficult to steal a vehicle by traditional means. Car operators are easy prey compared with convenience stores or other commercial establishments that may have surveillance cameras and other security measures in effect. Another theory suggests that status is involved: a criminal who carjacks a vehicle achieves higher status in the criminal subculture than does one who steals it in the conventional manner. And some police officers believe that the crime is becoming a fad among certain groups of young people as a way to enhance their image with their cohorts.

Carjackings have become a serious problem for police, who investigate them in the same way as other armed robberies. Publication of prevention techniques has become standard policy for police agencies in an effort to prevent property losses, injuries, and deaths. Some agencies use decoys in an effort to apprehend carjackers. The U.S. Department of State (2002) provides this set of guidelines to those reporting a carjacking:

Sometimes a robber will stage an auto accident or other incident to gain access to a victim. Other times, a robber will wait in a parking lot for an unsuspecting driver to return to their vehicle. Once the driver's vehicle is unlocked, the robber assaults the driver, takes the keys, and drives away in the victim's car.

Photo Courtesy of Reed Ketterling and Jordan Oliver

- Describe the event. What time of day did it occur? Where did it happen? How did it happen? Who was involved?

- Describe the attacker(s). Without staring, try to note height, weight, scars or other marks, hair and eye color, the presence of facial hair, build (slender, large) and complexion (dark, fair).

- Describe the attacker's vehicle. If possible, get the vehicle license number, color, make, model, and year, as well as any marks (scratches, dents, damage) and personal decorations (stickers, colored wheels).

- The golden rule for descriptions is to give only that information you absolutely remember. If you are not sure, don't guess!

In October 1992 Congress passed, and President George H. W. Bush signed, the Anti Car Theft Act, making armed carjacking a federal offense. Under this law, automakers must engrave a 17-digit vehicle identification number on 24 parts of every new car.

Bank Robbery

"Robbery in progress!" The call could mean a possible shootout or a hostage situation. Bank robbery is both a federal and a state offense. U.S. Code Title 18, Section 2113, defines the elements of the federal crime of bank robbery. This statute applies to robbery, burglary, or larceny from any member bank of the Federal Reserve system, any bank insured by the Federal Deposit Insurance Corporation (FDIC), any bank organized and operated under the laws of the United States, any federal savings and loan association, or any federal credit union. The number of bank robberies has increased with the number of branch banks, many of which are housed in storefront offices and outlying shopping centers, thus providing quick entrance to and exit from the robbery scene.

> **LO5** Identify with what types of robbery the FBI and state officials become involved.
>
> Bank robberies are within the jurisdictions of the FBI, the state, and the community in which the crime occurred and are jointly investigated.

In 2018, a reported 3,658 bank robberies occurred throughout the United States, with an average value of $4,303 per incident, for a total loss of more than $15.7 million (FBI, 2018b). The highest number of reported incidents occurred on Fridays between 3 and 6 p.m., and the most common modus operandi used was a demand note (60.9%), followed by the threat of a weapon (44.7%) and an oral demand (42.1%). A firearm was used in only 18.3% of reported incidents (FBI, 2018a). Many have theorized that the national opioid crisis may be a contributing factor in what motivates bank robbers. Data from the FBI indicate that of those persons involved in bank robberies, 35.4% were found to be narcotics users (FBI, 2018a).

Bank robberies are committed by rank amateurs as well as by habitual criminals. Amateurs are usually more dangerous because they are not as familiar with weapons and often are nervous and fearful. Weisel (2007, p. 14) points out:

> To a great extent, robbers can be classified as amateur or professional based on known characteristics of the robbery—the number of offenders, use of weapons and disguises, efforts to defeat security, timing of the robbery, target selection, and means of getaway.

> Bank robberies by amateurs are less successful: nearly one-third of all bank robberies by unarmed solitary offenders fail. Takeover robberies—those involving multiple armed offenders—are less common but more lucrative: losses in takeover robberies are 10 times greater than average. . . .

> Amateur bank robbers seek different targets from professionals and commit their offenses at different times. Solitary offenders tend to rob banks around midday, when branches are full of customers; professionals, on the other hand, prefer to operate when there are fewer customers, such as at opening time, which increases their control of the crime scene.

Takeover robbery—the type commonly portrayed in movies in which multiple perpetrators, heavily armed and wearing masks or disguises, conduct a hostile and violent takeover of a bank lobby, ordering patrons to the floor and often jumping over teller counters to demand money at gunpoint—are rare, accounting for approximately 5.7% of incidents in 2018 (FBI, 2018a). But because they generally involve seasoned professional thieves working in teams, takeovers can present considerable challenges for investigators. Table 12.1 summarizes the differences between the amateur and the professional bank robber.

Bank robbers often act alone inside the bank, but most have a getaway car with lookouts posted nearby. These individuals pose additional problems for the approaching police. The robbery car often has stolen plates or is itself stolen. Robbers use this "hot" car to leave the robbery scene and to transport them and their loot to a "cold" car left a distance from the robbery. Even if only one robber has been reported at the scene, an armed accomplice may be nearby.

TABLE 12.1 Distinguishing Professional and Amateur Bank Robbers*

	Professional	Amateur
Offenders	Multiple offenders with division of labor	Solitary offender
	Shows evidence of planning	Drug or alcohol use likely
	May be older	No prior bank crime
	Prior bank robbery convictions	Lives near bank target
	Travels further to rob banks	
Violence	Aggressive takeover, with loud verbal demands	Note passed to teller or simple verbal demand
	Visible weapons, especially guns	Waits in line
	Intimidation, physical or verbal threats	No weapon
Defeat Security	Uses a disguise	
	Disables or obscures surveillance cameras	
	Demands that dye packs be left out, alarms not be activated, or police not be called	
Robbery Success	Hits multiple teller windows	Single teller window victimized
	Larger amounts stolen	Lower amounts stolen
	Lower percentage of money recovered	Higher percentage of money recovered
	More successful robberies	More failed robberies
	Fewer cases directly cleared	Shorter time from offense to case clearance, including more same-day arrests
	Longer time from offense to case clearance	Direct case clearance more likely
Robbery Timing	Targets banks when few customers are present, such as at opening time	Targets banks when numerous customers are present, such as around midday
	Targets banks early in the week	Targets banks near closing or on Friday
Target Selection	Previous robbery	Previous robbery
	Busy road near intersection	Heavy pedestrian traffic or adjacent to dense multi-family residences
	Multidirectional traffic	Parcels without barriers
	Corner locations, multiple vehicle exits	Parcels with egress obscured
Getaway	Via car	On foot or bicycle

*This table is not prescriptive because it generalizes about bank robberies. Some factors will not fit your local pattern, and there will be exceptions that fit no category. The reader is encouraged to use the table as a starting point to separate and categorize local robberies.

Source: Weisel, D. L. (2007, March). *Bank robbery*. Washington, DC: Office of Community Oriented Policing Services.

Adding clerks is not necessarily a deterrent because a person with a gun has the advantage regardless of the number of clerks. Adding bulletproof glass around the cashier may increase the incidence of hostage taking. This problem has been reduced in some banks by enclosing and securing the bank's administrative areas. Video recording devices in banks can provide valuable information, including suspect description and MO. Problems arise when robbers conceal or disable the surveillance cameras. Other issues can result from improper usage, poor placement, inadequate lighting, and inferior video quality.

Other deterrents to bank robberies involve the use of bait money and dye packs, which, along with alarms

and security cameras, are required by federal banking regulations for federally insured financial institutions. **Bait money** is U.S. currency with recorded serial numbers placed at each teller position. Approximately 40% of victim institutions of bank crime in 2018 used bait money as a security measure (FBI, 2018a). A **dye pack** is a bundle of currency containing a colored dye and tear gas. Taken during a robbery, it is activated when the robber crosses an electromagnetic field at the facility's exit, releasing the brightly colored dye that stains the money and emits a cloud of colored smoke.

In an effort to generate leads in unsolved bank robberies, the FBI launched a "Wanted Bank Robbers" website in 2012 that enlists the public's help in identifying

Myth In most bank robberies, the suspect uses a gun and takes hostages.

Fact Unlike what is seen on TV, most bank robberies are done with a written or oral demand, occasionally producing or implying a weapon. In fact, many experienced robbers know that a note is very effective when combined with a threatened but unseen (and truly not carried) weapon, because, in many jurisdictions, being caught with a weapon often doubles the length of the sentence—an unnecessary risk when a note and hand in the pocket will do. Hostages are seldom taken, and most bank robberies are over within a few minutes.

suspects. The site, bankrobbers.fbi.gov, features a gallery of suspect images captured from surveillance video and a national map that plots robbery locations. Users can search by name, location, or other factors. Search results deliver a Wanted by the FBI poster that contains more images, a suspect's full description, and a brief narrative of the crime. In 2016, the FBI launched a mobile Bank Robbers app to make it easier for the public, financial institutions, law enforcement agencies, and others to view photos and information about bank robberies in different areas of the country. The app works with bankrobbers.fbi.gov and can be downloaded for free from Apple's app store or Google Play (FBI, 2016).

Robberies at ATMs

Robberies at ATMs are also of concern. Since their introduction in the United States during the late 1960s, ATMs have revolutionized the banking industry, facilitating billions of dollars in transactions every year (McRobbie, 2015). Brazen robbers wait nearby for people either on foot or in their vehicles to approach the ATM for a

Myth Entering your PIN in reverse at an ATM will send an automatic alert to local police that you are being forced to withdraw money against your will.

Fact Emergency-PIN technologies, such as reverse-PIN alerts, have never been installed on any ATMs in the United States.

withdrawal. These types of robberies tend to occur after dark in poorly lit areas but can occur any time of the day. The most common ATM robbery pattern involves a lone, armed offender against a lone victim.

Robbery versus Burglary versus Larceny

The general public tends to use the term *robbery* interchangeably with *burglary, larceny*, and *theft*. However, robbery, burglary, and larceny/theft are three distinct crimes, with specific elements that distinguish them from each other.

Recall the definition of robbery—the felonious taking of another's property, either directly from the person or in that person's presence, through force or intimidation. A burglary, by contrast, is an unlawful entry of a structure to commit a crime. Robbery differs from burglary in that robbers confront their victims whereas burglars seek to remain unseen. Robbery is a crime against a person, burglary is a crime against property. If the victim appears while the crime is occurring, the burglary turns into a robbery. Burglary is the topic of Chapter 13.

Larceny/theft is the unlawful taking of property from the possession of another. Like burglary, it is a crime against property but it does not require unlawful entry. In other words, the thief can be on the premises legally, such as an employee at work or a shopper in a store, but then unlawfully takes something that does not belong to them. Although there may be contact between the victim and the suspect, larceny/theft differs from robbery in that no force or threat of force is involved. Shoplifting is a common example of larceny/theft. Larceny/theft is the topic of Chapter 14.

So while a businessman might say that his store was robbed in the middle of the night, the accurate statement would be that it was burglarized. A woman may have money taken from her purse at work while she is busy waiting on customers and say that she was robbed but, legally, the crime was larceny. Such thefts are not robbery because the necessary elements are not present.

Elements of the Crime: Robbery

State statutes define *robbery* precisely. Some states have only one degree of robbery. Others have robbery in the first, second, and third degree. Still others have designated simple and aggravated robbery, with aggravated robbery involving the presence of a deadly weapon and/or the actual injury of the victim. Despite having different categories or degrees of robbery, most state statutes contain common elements.

LO6 List the elements of the crime of robbery.

The elements of the crime of robbery are

- the wrongful taking of personal property,
- from the person or in the person's presence,
- against the person's will by force or threat of force.

Wrongful Taking of Personal Property

Various statutes use phrases such as *unlawful taking*, *felonious taking*, and *knowing he or she is not entitled thereto*. Intent is an element of the crime in some, but not all, states. To take "wrongfully," the robber must have no legal right to the property. Moreover, property must be *personal property*, as distinguished from real property.

From the Person or in the Presence of the Person

In most cases, *in the presence of a person* means that the victim sees the robber take the property. This is not always the case, however, because the victim may be locked in a separate room. For example, robbers often take victims to a separate room such as a restroom or a bank vault while they search for the desired items or cash. Such actions do not remove the crime "from the presence of the person" as long as the separation from the property is the direct result of force or threats of force used by the robber.

Against the Person's Will by Use of Force or Threat of Force

This essential element clearly separates robbery from burglary and larceny. As noted, most robberies are committed with a weapon or other dangerous device or by indicating that one is present. The threat of force is generally sufficient to deter resistance. It can be immediate or threatened in the future. It can be directed at the victim, the victim's family, or a person who is with the victim.

Responding to a Robbery-in-Progress Call

A robbery-in-progress call involves an all-units response, with units close to the scene going there directly while other units cover the area near the scene, looking for a possible getaway vehicle. Other cars go to checkpoints such as bridges, converging highways, freeway entry and exit ramps, dead-end streets, and alleys.

Officers should observe all vehicles as they approach a robbery scene. Whether to use red lights and sirens depends on the information received from dispatch. It is often best to arrive quietly to prevent the taking of hostages. If shooting is occurring, using lights and siren may cause the robber to leave before police arrive. Officers must defer to their department's policies and procedures or state laws when determining the proper response to an in-progress robbery.

Police response time can be reduced if the robbed business or residence has an alarm system connected to the police department or a private alarm agency. Silent alarms can provide an early response, and audible alarms sometimes prevent a robbery. The "lag time"—that is, the elapsed time between the commission of a robbery and the time the police are notified—is usually much longer than the actual police response time.

LO7 Identify what factors to consider in responding to a robbery-in-progress call.

When responding to a robbery-in-progress call

- Proceed as rapidly as possible, keeping department policy and procedure in mind, but use extreme caution.
- Assume that the robber is at the scene, unless otherwise advised.
- Be prepared for gunfire.
- Look for and immobilize any getaway vehicle you discover.
- Look for accomplices fleeing the area or attempting to hide.
- Avoid a hostage situation if possible.
- Make an immediate arrest if the suspect is at the scene.

Officers should guard against the dangers inherent in stereotyping when responding to robberies in progress. For example, an officer responding to a robbery alarm at a convenience store, expecting to see a young male running from the scene, sees a young female walking calmly from the store, and after she passes the officer (who is ignoring her), she shoots him in the back because she was the robber. (This scenario could apply to an elderly person, a disabled person, or other assumed nonsuspect.)

Upon arrival at a robbery scene, attempt to locate any vehicle that the suspects might use, even if you have no description of it. It will probably be within a block of the crime scene, and its engine may be running. It generally has a person in it (the "wheelman," or lookout) waiting for the robber to return. If the vehicle is identified through prior information and is unoccupied, find a remote location and conduct surveillance on it. If an accomplice is waiting in the car, proceed with caution.

If police could check every license plate within the containment circle to see whether it was on a stolen car, and then accumulate that information, they might identify serial robbers.

Decide whether to enter the robbery location immediately or to wait until sufficient personnel are in position. Department policy determines whether it is an immediate or a timed response. Too early an entry increases the chances of a hostage situation or of having to use weapons. The general rule is to avoid a confrontation if it will create a worse situation than the robbery itself.

If you arrive at the robbery scene and find a suspect there with the victim, surround the building and order the suspect to come out. Get other people in the area to leave because of possible gunfire. Know the operational limitations imposed by the number of officers and the amount of equipment available at the scene. Take advantage of vehicles and buildings in the area for cover.

Technology Innovations

Automatic License Plate Recognition

Considering that more than 70% of crimes in the United States involve a vehicle, automatic license plate recognition (ALPR) can be of great assistance to investigators in a variety of cases, including in identifying a stolen vehicle that might be serving as a getaway car for a robbery. One of the most common solutions used by law enforcement is Leonardo's ELSAG ALPR system, a mobile license plate reader able to read up to 900 plates per minute, night or day, and in all weather conditions. Moreover, the system can read plates from all 50 U.S. states as well as those from most foreign countries.

Source: www.leonardocompany-us.com/lpr

Because the robber is committing a violent crime and is usually armed, expect that the robber may use a weapon against the police and that a hostage may be taken.

Hostage Situations

Hostage negotiation, which can be a long and stressful process, is a difficult job. A former FBI hostage negotiator states, "The first task of a negotiator is to bring down the emotions. We use a diagram in training that looks like a child's teeter-totter. On one side you have 'emotions,' and on the other side you have 'rational thinking.' When emotions go up, rational thinking goes down" (Shaw, 2016). The priorities in a hostage situation are to (1) preserve life, (2) apprehend the hostage taker, and (3) recover or protect property. Accomplishing these priorities requires specialized training in hostage situations. It also requires that the media be dealt with effectively.

In general, direct assault should be considered only if there has already been a killing or if further negotiations would be useless. Hostage situations may last for less than an hour or for more than 40 hours; the average length is approximately 12 hours.

However, this approach may result in conflict within the department between special weapons and tactics (SWAT) teams and crisis negotiation teams (CNTs). SWAT teams are action oriented, whereas CNTs are communication oriented. Both types of teams have a common goal but use a different approach. In reality, to successfully resolve a hostage situation, both teams must often work together. A successful hostage-incident outcome is not possible without a well-coordinated strategy.

Negotiators' biggest task is to convince subjects that no harm will come to them if they cooperate with the negotiation: "Are SWAT guys with big guns out there?" the subject may be very anxious to know. Assure the subject, "Sure, but they do what I tell them."

The need for negotiation is based on the principle that the main priority is to preserve life—that of the hostages or the hostage takers, as well as of police or innocent bystanders. SWAT teams or expert sharpshooters are often at or near the scene but do not participate in negotiations and in some cases are not visible except as a last resort. Figure 12.2 illustrates the typical emotions hostage takers experience during negotiations.

Usually you do not need to rush into the scene immediately and proceed with direct contact. In a few cases, it may be better to not do anything and allow the hostage taker resolve the situation. To its advantage, passage of time can

Elapsed Time in Hours

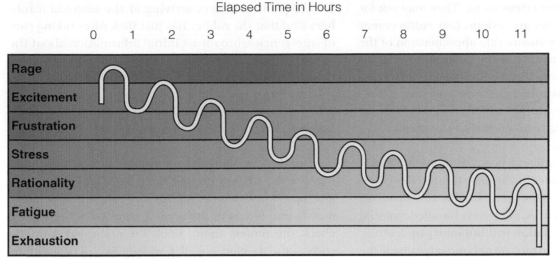

Figure 12.2
Timeline pattern for emotions of hostage takers during negotiations.

Source: Strentz, T. (1995, March). The cyclic crisis negotiations time line. *Law and Order*, p. 73. Reprinted by permission of the publisher.

- Provide the opportunity for face-to-face contact with the hostage taker

- Allow the negotiator to attempt to establish a trustful rapport

- Permit mental, emotional, and physical fatigue to operate against the hostage taker

- Increase the hostage taker's needs for food, water, sleep, and elimination

- Increase the possibility of the hostage taker's reducing demands to reasonable compliance levels

- Allow hostage-escape possibilities to occur

- Provide for more rational thinking, in contrast to the emotionalism usually present during the initial stage of the crime

- Lessen the hostage taker's anxiety and reduce their adrenalin flow, allowing more rational negotiations

- Allow for important intelligence gathering concerning the hostage taker, hostages, layout, protection barriers, and needed police reinforcement

A disadvantage of the passage of time is that it could possibly foster the *Stockholm syndrome*, by which hostages begin to identify with their captors and sympathize with them. The **Stockholm syndrome** occurs when hostages report that they have no ill feelings toward the hostage takers and, further, that they feared the police more than they feared their captors.

The negotiator should have street knowledge and experience with hostage incidents. Sometimes the first officers at the scene have established rapport with the hostage taker, and the negotiator only advises. In some cases, a trained clinical psychologist may be called to the scene, not as a negotiator but as a consultant regarding possible behavioral deviations of the hostage taker.

Face-to-face negotiations are ideal because they provide the best opportunity for gathering knowledge about and personally observing the hostage taker's reactions. Such contact should be undertaken only if circumstances indicate that the negotiator will not be in danger. An alternative is telephone contact, allowing for personal conversation and establishing rapport without the dangers of face-to-face contact. Use of a bullhorn is not the personal type of communication desired—nonetheless, it may be the only available method of communication.

Negotiable items may include food and drink (but not liquor, unless it is known that liquor would lessen the hostage taker's anxieties rather than increase them), money, media access, and reduced penalties. Transportation is generally not negotiable because of the difficulty in monitoring and controlling the situation. Police departments should establish policies regarding hostage negotiations in advance. In general, nothing should be granted to a hostage taker unless something is received in return. Complicating the situation may be that the hostage taker is alcohol or drug impaired.

When criminals caught in the act of robbery take hostages, it is usually a spontaneous reaction to being cornered, and they know what to expect from the police. They generally desire media attention or want to escape safely from the crime scene. They may ask for more money to prove they are serious. Law enforcement response will invariably ensure safe apprehension of the criminal in return for release of the hostages. There are other types of hostage situations—for instance, involving terrorists, mentally disturbed persons, and prisoners—but the motives of the hostage taker and guidelines for action require handling consistent with the characteristics of those situations.

Most instances involving negotiations lend themselves to general guidelines but are also unique. Decisions have to be made based on the immediate factors involved. In the vast majority of cases, effectively handled negotiations can resolve the situation without injury or death.

If a robber emerges on request or is already outside the building, they should be immediately arrested. The victim and any witnesses should make a field identification, and then the suspect should be removed from the scene.

A wounded suspect presents an especially dangerous situation. Officers should be alert to the possibility that a suspect is feigning more serious injury than exists to draw them off guard and get them close enough to be shot. Suspects should be covered at all times and immobilized with handcuffs as soon as possible. If a suspect is seriously injured, an armed escort should accompany the robber in the ambulance and take a dying declaration if necessary. If the suspect is killed, the coroner or medical examiner is notified.

The Preliminary Investigation and Special Challenges

As a violent crime, robbery introduces challenges that require special attention from the dispatcher, patrol officers, investigators, and police administrators. Three major problems occur in dealing with robberies: (1) they are usually not reported until the offenders have left the scene; (2) the rapidity of the crime makes it difficult to obtain good descriptions or positive identification from victims and witnesses; and (3) the items taken, usually currency, are difficult to identify.

> **LO8** Explain what special challenges are posed by a robbery investigation.

> The lag time in reporting a robbery, the speed of its occurrence, the traumatizing effect on victims and witnesses, and the nature of stolen items pose special challenges for investigators.

Frequently, officers arriving at the scene of a robbery find that the robber has just fled. After taking care of emergencies, broadcast initial information about the suspect, the getaway vehicle, and the direction of travel. Follow-up vehicles dispatched to the general area of the robbery can then attempt to apprehend the escaping robbers. Early information helps determine how far the suspect may have traveled and the most likely escape routes.

Conduct an immediate canvass of the neighborhood because the suspect may be hiding in a parked car, in a gas station restroom, or on the roof of a building. Check motels and hotels in the area. If another city is nearby, check the motels there. Look for discarded property such as the weapon, a wallet, money bag, or other items taken from victims, as stolen purses and wallets are usually discarded within minutes of the robbery. However, stolen jewelry or cash usually cannot be recovered unless an arrest is made immediately after the crime. In cases where jewelry or other high value tangible items are taken, officers should check with local pawn shops, resale stores, and online sale sites, such as Facebook Marketplace, Craigslist, and eBay.

Robbery usually leaves victims and witnesses feeling vulnerable and fearful, making it difficult for them to give accurate descriptions and details of what occurred. Be patient. Witnesses to a robbery suffer varying degrees of trauma even though they have not lost any property. They may have had to lie on the floor or been placed in a locked room or a bank vault, possibly fearing that the robber would return and kill them. Their ability to recall precise details is further impaired by the suddenness of the crime.

Proving the Elements of the Offense

Know the *elements of robbery* in your jurisdiction so you can determine whether a robbery has in fact been committed. Each element must be proven separately. Proving only some of the elements is not sufficient. Most state statutes have at least three elements for the crime of robbery.

Was Personal Property Wrongfully Taken?

Taking of property necessitates proving that it was carried away from the lawful owner or possessor to permanently deprive the owner of the property. Prove that the robber had no legal right to the property taken.

LO9 Explain how to prove each element of robbery.

Determine the legal owner of the property taken. Describe completely the property and its value.

Who is the legal owner? Take statements from the victim to show legal possession and control of the property before and during the robbery.

Was property taken or intended to be taken? Obtain a complete description of the property and its value, including marks, serial numbers, operation identification number (if available), color, size, and any other identifying characteristics.

Obtain proof of what was lost and its value. In a bank robbery, the bank manager or auditor can give an accurate accounting of the money taken. In a store robbery, any responsible employee can help determine the loss. Cash-register receipts, sales receipts, quotations of retail and wholesale prices, reasonable estimates by people in the same business, or the estimate of an independent appraiser can help determine the amount of the loss. In robberies of the person, the victim determines the loss. Some robbery victims claim to have lost more or less than was actually taken, thus complicating the case.

Was Property Taken from the Person or in the Person's Presence?

From the person or in the presence of the person necessitates proving that the property was under the victim's control before the robbery and was removed from the victim's control by the robber's direct actions.

LO9 Explain how to prove each element of robbery.

Record the exact words, gestures, motions, or actions the robber used to gain control of the property.

Answer such questions as these: Where was the property before it was taken? Where was the victim?

Against the Person's Will by Force or the Threat of Force?

By force or the threat of force may be the most difficult element to establish. If the victim perceived a threat, it is real.

LO9 Explain how to prove each element of robbery.

Obtain a complete description of the robber's words, actions, and any weapon used or threatened to be used.

If nothing was said, find out what gestures, motions, or other actions compelled the victim to give up the property.

The force need not be directly against the robbery victim. For example, a woman may receive a call at work, telling her that her husband is a hostage and will be killed unless she brings money to a certain location, or the robber may grab a friend of the victim or a customer in a store and direct the victim to hand over money to protect the person being held from harm.

Record in your notes descriptions of any injuries to the victim or witnesses. Photograph the injuries, if possible, and have injured victims and witnesses examined by a doctor, emergency room personnel, or ambulance paramedics.

The Complete Investigation

Most robberies are solved through prompt actions by the victim, witnesses, and the police patrolling the immediate area or by police at checkpoints. In many cases, however, a robbery investigation takes weeks or even months. Begin your investigation with a follow-up canvass of the area in which the robbery occurred, seeking witnesses who may not have been identified immediately following the crime. Check for surveillance video from locations adjacent to the crime scene. Check car rental agencies if no vehicle was reported stolen. Check airports, bus, and train stations and taxi companies for possible links.

Recheck all information and physical descriptions. Have a sketch of the suspect prepared and circulate it. Recognize that many robbers tend to stay relatively close to their home. Thus, successful investigations often involve speaking to employees of nearby businesses and sharing descriptions of suspects. Surveillance videos should also be reviewed to determine if the suspect appeared to be familiar with the store layout and area.

Alert your informants to listen for word of the robbery. Check with known "fences." A **fence** is the go-between who receives stolen goods for resale. Check local pawn shops, resale stores, and online resources like Craigslist, Facebook Marketplace, OfferUP, and eBay. Check MO files. Where applicable, check police field-interview/contact forms and communications records relating to recent citizen calls complaining about suspicious people or vehicles in the area of the robbery. If video or still images of the robbery are available, feed them into investigative networks that reach other law enforcement officers, jail staff, and, if warranted, the media.

Prepare your report carefully and thoroughly and circulate it to any officers who may assist. Even if you do not apprehend your suspect, the suspect may be apprehended during a future robbery, and their MO and other evidence may implicate them in the robbery you investigated.

Identifying the Suspect

The various techniques used in suspect identification (discussed in Chapter 7) are relevant at this point. At minimum, obtain information about the suspect's general appearance, clothing, disguises, weapon, and vehicle.

If the suspect is apprehended within a short time (20 minutes or so), they may be taken back to the scene for identification by the victim. Preferably, the victim may be taken to where the suspect is being held. Several people should be in the area of the suspect to witness that the victim makes any identification without assistance from the police. Photo lineups may be used if no suspect is arrested at or near the scene of the crime. Photo lineups should include five other people in addition to the suspect. A person who has been arrested does not have the right to refuse to have a photo taken.

Eyewitness identification is affected by many factors: the distance between the witness and the suspect at the time of the robbery; the time of day, lighting, and weather conditions; the amount of violence involved; whether the witness had ever seen or knew the suspect; and the time it took for the crime to be committed.

Disguises. To conceal their identities, many robbers use ski masks, nylon stockings pulled over their heads, or paper sacks with eyeholes. Other disguises include wigs, dyed hair, sideburns, scarves, various types of false noses or ears, and makeup to alter appearance. Gauze is sometimes used to distort the shape of the cheeks or mouth and tape is used to simulate cuts or to cover scars.

Clothing also can serve as a disguise. False heels and soles can increase height. Collars can be pulled up and hats pulled down. Recall the earlier statistic that most bank robberies occur at the counter on Friday afternoons between 3 p.m. and 6 p.m. (FBI, 2018a). In northern latitudes in particular, winter months provide early darkness, facilitating easy use of winter weather gear for disguises. Various types of uniforms that fit in with the area of the robbery scene, such as delivery uniforms or work clothes, have also been used. Clothing and disguises may be discarded by the robber upon leaving the scene and are valuable evidence if recovered because they may provide DNA evidence.

Weapons. Pistols, revolvers, and automatic weapons are frequently used in robberies. Sawed-off shotguns, rifles, air guns, various types of imitation guns, knives, razors and other cutting and stabbing instruments, explosives, tear gas, and various acids have also been used, or their use implied. Such weapons and devices are often found on or near the suspect when arrested, but many are hidden in the vehicle used or are thrown away during the escape. Robbery victims are the most likely of all victims of violent crime to face an armed offender.

Vehicles. Most vehicles used in robberies are inconspicuous, popular makes that attract no attention and are stolen just before the robbery. Some robbers leave the scene on foot and then take buses or taxis or commandeer vehicles, sometimes at gunpoint.

Establishing the Modus Operandi

Even if the suspect is apprehended at the scene, the MO can help link the suspect with other robberies.

> **L010** List what modus operandi information to obtain in a robbery case.

Important MO information includes the following:

- Type of robbery
- Time (day and hour)
- Method of attack (real or threatened)
- Weapon
- Number of robbers
- Voice and words
- Vehicle used
- Peculiarities
- Object sought

Finding that an MO matches a previous robbery does not necessarily mean that the same robber committed the crime. For example, in one instance three masked gunmen robbed a midwestern bank of more than $45,000 and escaped in a stolen car. The MO matched a similar robbery in the same town a few weeks earlier in which $30,000 was obtained. The three gunmen were identified and arrested the next day, and more than $41,000 of the loot was recovered. One gunman told the FBI agent that he planned the robbery after reading about the successful bank robbery that three other masked gunmen had pulled off. The FBI agent smiled and informed the robber that the perpetrators had been arrested shortly after the robbery. Aghast, the copycat robber bemoaned the fact that he had seen no publicity on the arrest.

Physical Evidence

Physical evidence at a robbery scene is usually minimal. Sometimes, however, the robbery occurs where a surveillance camera is operating. A copy of the surveillance footage should be immediately obtained for evidence.

> **LO11** Identify the types of physical evidence that can link a suspect with a robbery.
>
> Physical evidence that can connect a suspect with a robbery includes fingerprints, DNA, shoe prints, tire prints, tools, restraining devices, discarded garments, fibers and hairs, a note, and the stolen property. Do not overlook items such as cigarette butts, soda cans or bottles, and discarded chewing gum as these can provide valuable DNA evidence.

Fingerprints may be found at the scene if the suspect handled any objects, on the holdup note if one was left behind, on the getaway car, or on recovered property. They might also be found on pieces of tape used as restraints, which in themselves are valuable as evidence.

In one residential robbery, the criminal forced entrance into a home, bound and gagged the residents, stole several items of value and then left. As he backed up to turn his car around, he inadvertently left the impression of the vehicle's license plate clearly imprinted on a snow bank. He was apprehended within hours of the robbery.

Mapping Robbery

Because robbery is inherently serial, mapping has proven successful. The Charlotte-Mecklenburg (North Carolina) Police Department used mapping to address an increase in robbery victimization among Charlotte's growing Hispanic population.

Officers used the Global Information Software (GIS) mapping capabilities in the department's Crime Analysis Unit to map all robbery incidents with Hispanic victims citywide. Overlaying the maps revealed a close correlation between Hispanic robbery incidents and areas of high concentrations of Hispanic residents. Mapping narrowed the problem to robberies of Hispanic victims in the apartment complexes where they lived. It then identified a particular complex, the Park Apartments, that was a hot spot for the robberies. This complex consisted of 51 buildings with approximately 2,000 residents. Hispanics constituted 49% of the complex population but 64% of its robbery victims. The analysis then identified a number of factors that increased the risk of robbery, including the fact that victims often carried large sums of money instead of using banks, that poor lighting and poor security made robberies easy to commit, and that partly because of language barriers the police had done little community outreach.

In cooperation with complex managers, police officers addressed the identified physical factors. In addition to improving lighting, they restricted access to the apartment grounds and to the high-risk laundry area. An enforcement component with the department's robbery unit worked to arrest several suspects. Officers also built relationships with the residents to increase their willingness to report crime.

False Robbery Reports

Investigators need to rule out the probability that a robbery report is false. Among the indicators of a false robbery report are the following:

- An unusual delay in reporting the offense

- An amount of the loss not fitting the victim's apparent financial status

- A lack of correspondence with the physical evidence

- Improbable events

- An exceptionally detailed or exceptionally vague description of offender

- A lack of cooperation

- Inconsistencies in accounts of the event

Reasons that people file false robbery reports are numerous and varied. A search of recent news reports indicates motives ranging from gambling problems and financial hardships, to attempts to cover up a drug deal gone bad, to a college student who feared admitting to her parents she had lost her wallet.

Summary

Robbery is the felonious taking of another's property, either directly from the person or in that person's presence, through force or intimidation. Robberies are classified as residential, commercial, street, or vehicle driver.

A home invasion is a forced entry into an occupied dwelling to commit a violent crime, whether robbery, sexual assault, murder, or some combination of violent offenses. Another category of robbery is carjacking—the taking of a motor vehicle by force or threat of force. The FBI may investigate the crime.

Bank robberies are within the jurisdictions of the FBI, the state, and the community in which the crime occurred and are jointly investigated. The elements of robbery are (1) the wrongful taking of personal property, (2) from the person or in the person's presence, (3) against the person's will by force or threat of force.

When responding to a robbery-in-progress call, proceed as rapidly as possible, keeping department policy and procedure in mind, but use extreme caution. Assume that the robber is at the scene unless otherwise advised, and be prepared for gunfire. Look for any getaway vehicle you discover. Look for accomplices fleeing the area or attempting to hide. Avoid a hostage situation if possible, and make an immediate arrest if the suspect is at the scene. The lag time in reporting a robbery, the speed of its occurrence, the traumatizing effect on victims and witnesses, and the nature of stolen items pose special challenges for investigators.

To prove that personal property was wrongfully taken, determine the legal owner of the property and describe the property and its value. To prove that it was taken from the person or in the person's presence, record the exact words, gestures, motions, or actions the robber used to gain control of the property. To prove that the removal was against the victim's will by force or threat of force, obtain a complete description of the robber's words, actions, and any weapon the robber used or threatened to be used.

Important MO information includes type of robbery, time (day and hour), method of attack (real or threatened), weapon, number of robbers, voice and words, vehicle used, any peculiarities, and object sought. Physical evidence that can connect a suspect with a robbery includes fingerprints, DNA, shoe prints, tire prints, tools, restraining devices, discarded garments, fibers and hairs, a note, and the stolen property. Do not overlook items such as cigarette butts, soda cans or bottles, and discarded chewing gum as these can provide valuable DNA evidence.

Can You Define?

apple picking	fence	Stockholm syndrome
bait money	home invasion	takeover robbery
carjacking	morning glory robbery	
closing robbery	robbery	
dye pack	robbery-by-appointment	

Checklist

Robbery

- Are maps and pictures on file of banks and other places that handle large amounts of cash? Are there plans for police response in the event that these facilities are robbed?

- Was the place that was robbed protected by an alarm? Was the alarm working?

- Was the place that was robbed covered by a surveillance camera? Was the camera working? Was video immediately removed, saved, and processed?

- Was surveillance video from properties adjacent to the crime scene sought?

- What procedure did police use in responding to the call? Did they enter directly? To avoid a hostage situation, did they wait until the robber had left?

- Did police interview separately everyone in the robbed place? Did they obtain statements from each?

- Are all elements of the crime of robbery present?

- How was the robber dressed? Was a disguise used?

- What were the robber's exact words and actions?

- What type of weapon or threat did the robber use?

- Was anybody injured or killed?

- Was there a getaway car? Description? Direction of travel? A second person in the car?

- Was a general description of people and vehicles involved quickly broadcast to other police agencies?

- Did police secure and photograph the scene?

- What property was taken in the robbery? What was its value?

- Who is the legal owner?

- If a bank was robbed, were the FBI and state officials notified?

- If the suspect was arrested, how was identification made?

- If money or property was recovered, was it properly processed?

Application

Read the following account of an actual robbery investigation. As you read, list the steps the investigators took. Review the list and determine whether they took all necessary steps. (Adapted from a report by Captain R. J. Eagan, New Haven, Connecticut.)

On December 16, close to midnight, a woman looked in the window of the grocery store owned by Efimy Romanow at 187 Ashmun Street, New Haven, Connecticut, and saw Romanow lying behind the counter with his cell phone in his right hand. Thinking Romanow was sick, the woman notified a neighbor, Thomas Kelly, who went to the store and then called an ambulance. Romanow was pronounced dead on arrival at the hospital.

Autopsy revealed he had been shot near the heart. The bullet was removed and turned over to detectives, who immediately began an investigation. Officers protected the crime scene and made a thorough search for possible prints and other evidence. They found a small amount of money in the cash register. At the hospital, $15.50 was found in Romanow's pockets, and $313 in bills was found in his right shoe. A thorough check of neighborhood homes was made without result. One report received was that two white men were seen leaving the store before Romanow's body was discovered.

About 7 a.m., December 17, Mrs. Marion Lang, who lived directly opposite the store but was not home when the officers first went there, was contacted. She stated that at about 11:10 p.m. she had heard loud talking in the street, including the remark, "Damn it, he is shot, let's get out of here." She had not looked out the window, so she was unable to describe the people she had heard talking.

The investigation continued without any leads until 9:25 p.m., December 17, when a phone call was received from George M. Proctor, owner of a drugstore on a street parallel to Ashmun Street and one block away. He had just overheard a woman talking in his store say, "I will not stand for her taking my man away. I know who shot the store owner on Ashmun. It was Scotty and Almeda over on Dixwell." Mr. Proctor did not know the woman he had overheard.

Two detectives were assigned to this lead, and they began a search. A few hours later, they learned that Scotty and Almeda were in a room at 55 Dixwell Avenue. Arriving with several uniformed officers, they entered and found Francis Scott and Henry Almeda in bed with their clothes on. Both had previous records and were well known to the local police. The detectives took the two men to the police station for questioning and then returned to the room. Their search revealed five .32 caliber bullets at the top of a window casing where plaster had been broken up.

They also received information that Scott and Almeda had earlier visited Julia Redmond, who had a room in the same house. They asked Ms. Redmond if Scott and Almeda had left anything there. She responded, "They put something under the mattress." Turning over the mattress, the detectives found a .32 caliber Harrington and Richardson revolver, serial number 430-087. Ms. Redmond said, "That belongs to Scott and Almeda."

The detectives returned to the police station and searched the stolen gun files. They discovered that this gun had been reported stolen in a burglary at the home of Geoffrey Harrell, 46 Webster Street, in November. Both suspects were questioned during the night and denied any part in the shooting.

The questioning resumed on the morning of December 18 at 9:00 a.m. At 3:45 p.m. that day, Almeda broke and made a confession in which he involved Scott.

Almeda's statement was read to Scott with Almeda present. When Almeda identified the confession and stated it was true, Scott also admitted his part in the shooting.

When Almeda was shown the .32 caliber H&R revolver, he identified it as the gun used in shooting Romanow. He explained that they had to shoot Romanow because he refused to give up his money and placed himself between them and the door. In order to get out, he shot Romanow. Both stated that they had no car and that no one else was involved.

A preliminary examination of the bullet taken from Romanow's body did not satisfy the detectives that the bullet had been fired from the gun in their possession, even though it had been identified by both Almeda and Scott as the one used.

A detective sent the gun and bullet to the FBI Technical Laboratory in Washington, D.C., where a ballistics comparison established that the gun furnished for examination was not the gun that fired the fatal bullet. A search of the Technical Laboratory files revealed that the gun matched a bullet furnished by the same department as evidence in a robbery of Levine's Liquor Store on December 1 of that year. One shot had been fired, striking a chair and deflecting into a pile of trash in the rear of the store. Detectives had recovered the bullet after sifting through the trash.

When confronted with this information, Scott and Almeda admitted that they had committed this robbery and shooting while masked. They also admitted that they had stolen an automobile to use that night and that they had burglarized Harrell's home in November, when they took the gun.

The detectives conducted an extensive search for the gun used in killing Romanow. They cut a hole in the bottom of the floor of the room occupied by Scott and Almeda and even had the sewer department clean out 15 sewer catch basins in the area of the crime, but no weapon was discovered.

Both Almeda and Scott were indicted by the grand jury for first-degree murder. They were scheduled for trial February 13. The night before the trial was to begin, they told their lawyers that a third man had furnished the gun and driven the getaway car. In a conference with the state attorney and detectives, the lawyers identified the third man as William Sutton. Within half an hour, Sutton was apprehended and brought to the state attorney's office where, in the presence of Scott and Almeda, their statements were read to Sutton. He admitted participating in the crime.

This new turn in the case also revealed that the gun used in the killing was loaned to Sutton by John Foy. The morning after the shooting, Sutton brought the gun back to Foy and left it with him. A short time later Sutton returned and asked for the gun. He had decided he should get rid of it because it was hot. Sutton then took the cylinder from the gun while Foy broke the rest of it into small parts, which he threw in various places. Foy, who admitted he knew the gun was to be used in a robbery, was charged with conspiracy.

Sutton, Almeda, and Scott pled guilty to second-degree murder and received life sentences in the Connecticut State Prison. Foy received a one-year jail sentence.

Questions

1. List the steps the investigators followed.
2. Did they omit any necessary steps?
3. What comparison evidence was helpful in the case?
4. How did law enforcement agencies cooperate?
5. What interrogation techniques did they use?
6. How important was citizen information?

References

CBS Local (2018, January 31). Despite anti-theft features, thieves still seek out iPhones. Retrieved October 13, 2020, from cbslocal.com/2018/01/31 /despite-anti-theft-features-thieves-seek-out-iphones/

Chaumont Menendez, C. K., Socias-Morales, C., & Daus, M. W. (2017, August). Workrelated violent deaths in the US taxi and limousine industry 2003 to 2103. *Journal of Occupational and Environmental Medicine, 59*(8): 768–774. doi:10.1097/JOM.0000000000001071

Federal Bureau of Investigation. (2016). *FBI releases new bank robbers mobile app*. Washington, DC: Author. Retrieved October 20, 2020, from www.fbi.gov/news/stories /fbi-releases-new-bank-robbers-mobile-app

Federal Bureau of Investigation. (2018a). *Bank crime statistics (BCS), federally insured financial institutions, January 1, 2018–December 31, 2018*. Washington, DC: Author. Retrieved October 20, 2020, from www.fbi.gov/file -repository/bank-crime-statistics-2018.pdf/view

Federal Bureau of Investigation. (2018b). *Crime in the United States, 2018*. Washington, DC: Author. Retrieved October 12, 2020, from ucr.fbi.gov/crime-in-the-u.s/2018/crime-in-the-u.s.-2018/topic-pages/robbery

Harrell, E. (2011, March). *Workplace violence, 1993–2009*. Washington, DC: Bureau of Justice Statistics. (NCJ 233231). Retrieved October 13, 2020, from www.bjs.gov/content/pub/pdf/wv09.pdf

Hill, D. (2013, November 4). iPhone, iPad thefts so widespread it's coined a new term, "Apple Picking." *Los Angeles Daily News*. Retrieved April 22, 2015, from www.dailynews.com/technology/20131104/iphone-ipad-thefts-so-widespread-its-coined-a-new-term-apple-picking

Klaus, P. (2004, July). *Carjacking, 1993–2002*. Washington, DC: Bureau of Justice Statistics, Crime Data Brief. (NCJ 205123)

McRobbie, L. R. (2015, January 8). The ATM is dead. Long live the ATM! *Smithsonian Magazine*. Retrieved October 20, 2020, from www.smithsonianmag.com/history/atm-dead-long-live-atm-180953838/

Morgan, R. E., & Oudekerk, B. A. (2019, September). *Criminal victimization, 2018*. Washington, DC: Bureau of Justice Statistics. (NCJ 253043). Retrieved October 12, 2020, from www.bjs.gov/content/pub/pdf/cv18.pdf

National Institute for Occupational Safety and Health. (2018, May 21). *Young retail workers*. Atlanta, GA: Centers for Disease Control and Prevention. Retrieved October 14, 2020, from www.cdc.gov/niosh/topics/retail/violence.html

New York Office of the Attorney General. (2014). *Secure our smartphones initiative: One year later*. New York, NY: Author. Retrieved October 13, 2020, from ag.ny.gov/pdfs/SOS%201%20YEAR%20REPORT.pdf

Occupational Safety and Health Administration. (2009). *Recommendations for workplace violence prevention programs in late-night retail establishments*. Washington, DC: Author. (OSHA 3153-12R). Retrieved October 14, 2020, from www.osha.gov/Publications/osha3153.pdf

Rosen, J., & Patel, A. (2013, February 20). "Apple picking" thieves snatch iPhones. *Today.com*. Retrieved October 21, 2020, from www.today.com/news/apple-picking-thieves-snatch-iphones-1C8441809

Shaw, K. (2016, August 25). I was a crisis negotiator for 23 years. Here's what it's like to talk down an armed hostage taker. *The Trace*. Retrieved October 21, 2020, from www.thetrace.org/2016/08/crisis-negotiator-armed-hostage-taker/

Tsukayama, H. (2014, August 27). The smartphone "kill switch," explained. *The Washington Post*. Retrieved October 13, 2020, from www.washingtonpost.com/news/the-switch/wp/2014/08/27/the-smartphone-kill-switch-explained/

U.S. Bureau of Labor Statistics. (2018, January 23). There were 500 workplace homicides in the United States in 2016. *TED: The Economics Daily*. Retrieved October 14, 2020, from www.bls.gov/opub/ted/2018/there-were-500-workplace-homicides-in-the-united-states-in-2016.htm

U.S. Department of State. (2002, August). *Carjacking—Don't be a victim*. Washington, DC: Author. Retrieved October 21, 2020, from 2009-2017.state.gov/documents/organization/19697.pdf

Weisel, D. L. (2007, March). *Bank robbery*. Washington, DC: Office of Community Oriented Policing Services.

Investigating Crimes Against Property

Most of the crimes discussed in this section do not involve the use of force or violence against people and therefore are often not considered as serious as assault, robbery, rape, or murder. However, according to various official reports, crimes against property occur much more frequently than do crimes against persons. Federal Bureau of Investigation (FBI) statistics report an estimated 7,196,045 property crimes in the nation during 2018 (Federal Bureau of Investigation [FBI], 2018b). The 2-year trend showed that the number of property crimes declined 6.3% from 2017 to 2018, and the 10-year trend showed property crimes decreased 22.9% between 2009 and 2018. The downward trend of property crimes is illustrated in Figure IV.1.

The rate of property offenses in 2018 was 2,199.5 per 100,000 inhabitants. More than two-thirds (72.5%) of all property crimes were larceny/theft (the focus of Chapter 14). Property crimes accounted for an estimated $16.4 billion in losses in 2018. According to the FBI (2018a), a crime against property occurred every 4.4 seconds in the United States in 2018:

- One larceny/theft every 6.1 seconds

- One burglary every 25.7 seconds

- One motor vehicle theft every 42.2 seconds

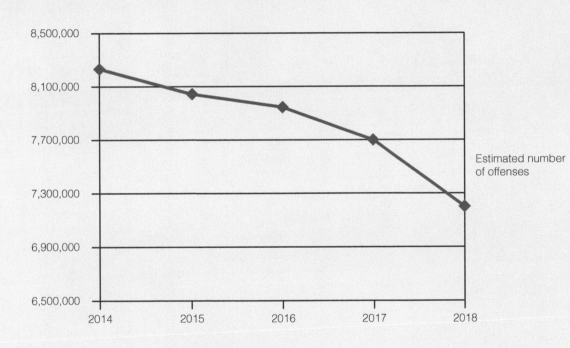

Figure IV.1
Property Crime Offenses,
Five-Year Trend, 2014–2018.

Source: Federal Bureau of Investigation. (2018). *Crime in the United States 2018*. Washington, DC: Author. ucr.fbi.gov/crime-in-the-u.s/2018 /crime-in-the-u.s.-2018/topic-pages/property-crime

Estimated number
of offenses

Victimization figures from the National Crime Victimization Survey (NCVS) are higher, showing that 9,080,490 property crimes occurred in 2018 (Morgan & Oudekerk, 2019). The property crime rate was 108.2 per 1,000 households. According to the NCVS, only about 38.7% of property crimes were reported to police in 2018.

Many property crimes are difficult to investigate because there is little evidence and there are usually no eyewitnesses. Physical evidence in property crimes is often similar to that found in violent crimes: Fingerprints, footprints, tire impressions, hair, fibers, broken glass, and personal objects left at the crime scene. Other important evidence in crimes against property includes tools, tool fragments, tool marks, safe insulation, disturbance of paint, and evidence of forcible entry.

Despite the possibility that touch DNA or other biological evidence may be left at the scene, unless it was a particularly severe crime resulting in significant monetary loss, such evidence will likely not be processed. For example, a rock suspected of being used to break a car window, through which some personal items were stolen, may have fingerprints on it, but because the crime is minor and the time and cost required to process that evidence is excessive in relation to the severity of the offense, most agencies would choose to not process that evidence.

The modus operandi of a property crime often takes on added importance because there are no other significant leads. In addition, crimes against property tend to occur in series, so solving one crime may lead to solving an entire series of similar crimes.

The chapters in this section discuss specific considerations in investigating burglary (Chapter 13); larceny/theft, fraud, and white-collar crime (Chapter 14); motor vehicle theft (Chapter 15); and arson, bombs, and explosives (Chapter 16).

References

Federal Bureau of Investigation. (2018a). *2018 Crime Clock.* Washington, DC: Author. Retrieved October 22, 2020, from ucr.fbi.gov/crime-in-the-u.s/2018/crime-in-the-u.s.-2018/topic-pages/crime-clock

Federal Bureau of Investigation. (2018b). *Crime in the United States 2018.* Washington, DC: Author. Retrieved October 22, 2020, from ucr.fbi.gov/crime-in-the-u.s/2018/crime-in-the-u.s.-2018/

Morgan, R. E., & Oudekerk, B. A. (2019, September). *Criminal Victimization,* 2018. Washington, DC: Bureau of Justice Statistics Bulletin. (NCJ 253043). Retrieved October 22, 2020, from www.bjs.gov/content/pub/pdf/cv18.pdf

Chapter 13
Burglary

Learning Objectives

LO1   Define burglary.

LO2   Explain the basic differences between burglary and robbery.

LO3   Identify the two basic classifications of burglary.

LO4   List the three elements generally present in laws defining burglary.

LO5   Identify what additional elements can be included in burglary.

LO6   Explain how the severity of a burglary is determined.

LO7   List the elements of the crime of possession of burglary tools.

LO8   List the common burglary tools.

LO9   Describe how to proceed to a burglary scene and what to do on arrival.

LO10   Identify the most frequent means of entry to commit burglary.

LO11   Describe the various methods used to break into safes.

LO12   List the types of physical evidence often found at a burglary scene.

LO13   Identify the modus operandi factors to consider when investigating a burglary.

LO14   List the sources investigators should check when searching for stolen property.

LO15   Identify the elements of the offense of receiving stolen goods.

Introduction

Burglary is a crime that affects essentially every community in the United States. And while the lone burglar is common and certainly capable of causing a sizeable loss, in many cases, these crimes are carried out by organized groups. Countless media reports illustrate how jurisdictions across the country are victimized by burglary rings. For example, five men arrested in May 2020 for running a burglary ring in Southern California were charged with stealing $1.9 million in cash, guns, jewelry, and designer purses from 44 different homes between August 2019 and February 2020 (Navarro, 2020). In four of the burglaries, investigators discovered that the residents had actually been in the home at the time of the crime.

In Central Texas, seven people, including a former probation officer, were indicted in August 2020 for their part in a multicounty burglary ring that netted more than $130,000 in stolen property, which included vehicles, trailers, welders, tires, and equipment (Shaw, 2020). One of the lead investigators, noting that the crimes were usually committed to get money to buy drugs, stated, "These are tools what people use to make a living. It's their livelihood and so all of the sudden they've lost it and this scum-bag is out there trying to sell it for ten cents on the dollar so he can get some more meth." Indeed, many investigators acknowledge that when it comes to burglaries, most of the time drugs are involved.

In Bibb County, Georgia, a months-long investigation into a series of business burglaries led to the arrest in April 2020 of four individuals accused of being involved in a burglary ring that, in many instances, breached the exterior walls of the victimized business with either a sledgehammer or a concrete saw (WGXA Digital Staff, 2020). Bolt cutters, crow bars, and other pry tools were also used to gain entrance to the businesses. When investigators executed several search warrants, they located not only the items used to break into the businesses but also many items fitting the descriptions of those taken from the burglarized businesses, including cash, clothing, cigarettes, guns, vehicles, TVs, and other electronic devices.

Finally, in Green Island, New York, a 23-year-old paraplegic with no prior criminal record was arrested in April 2020 for masterminding a multistate crime ring that specialized in stealing and selling thermostats and circuit breakers (Barnes, 2020). An investigation had begun five months earlier after a local HVAC business reported that $200,000 worth of equipment was ordered using stolen credit cards and then disappeared after delivery. Investigators eventually uncovered a crime ring that operated across seven states and committed not only burglary and theft but also robbery: "One of their victims was a California man who flew into Albany [New York] and drove to Newburgh, where he believed he would be picking up circuit breakers to ship home but was instead robbed at gunpoint of $12,000 cash, credit cards and a Rolex watch."

The word *burglar* comes from the German words *burg*, meaning "house," and *laron*, meaning "thief," thus the meaning "house thief." The Federal Bureau of Investigation's (FBI) Uniform Crime Reports (UCR) defines **burglary** as "the unlawful entry of a structure to commit a felony or theft, even though no force was used to gain entry." All such attempts also count as burglaries. The common-law definition of *burglary* (originating in sixteenth-century England) required that the breaking and entering be committed during the nighttime or "between sunset and sunrise." Many changes have been made in burglary statutes since that time, including eliminating the requirement that it occur at night.

> **LO1** Define burglary.
>
> Burglary is the unlawful entry of a structure to commit a crime.

Burglary is reported by frequency and by the value of the property stolen and recovered. This is because many burglaries yield low losses, although a single burglary can yield a high loss. According to the FBI, an estimated 1,230,149 burglary offenses occurred throughout the nation during 2018, a decrease of 28.2% from 2014 (Federal Bureau of Investigation [FBI], 2018b). Burglary offenses made up 17.1% of all property crimes reported in 2018. Of these, law enforcement cleared 13.9% by arrest or exceptional means (FBI, 2018b). Burglary offenses cost victims an estimated $3.4 billion in lost property, with the average dollar loss per burglary being $2,799.

Despite a brief increase in burglaries from 2010 to 2012, the overall trend in burglary rates has been downward over the past 30 years. Security systems and video recording motion alerts have contributed greatly to decreasing the number of burglaries. Other reasons for the decline include improvements in lock technology and the growing use of private security. More than 1 million private police and security guards work in residential communities, and empirical evidence suggests the presence of these patrols has a general deterrent effect on property offenders (Sparrow, 2014; Zimmerman, 2014; Hazbun, 2019; Blackstone, Hakim, & Meehan, 2020).

The public regards burglary as a major crime problem. Many people fear arriving at home or at work and confronting a burglar, a situation that can develop into an assault and robbery. Moreover, it is traumatic for people to realize they have been doubly victimized when someone has invaded the privacy of their home or business and stolen their possessions. Although the items taken may be covered by insurance, some may be irreplaceable because of their sentimental value.

Burglary versus Robbery

Recall from Chapter 12 that a burglar, in contrast to a robber, seeks to avoid contact with people near the scene or on the premises.

> **LO2** Explain the basic differences between burglary and robbery.
>
> Burglary differs from robbery in that burglars are covert, seeking to remain unseen, whereas robbers confront their victims directly. Burglary is a crime against property; robbery is a crime against a person.

Most burglaries occur in unoccupied homes and businesses; therefore, few witnesses exist, and few alarms are given to provide advance notice to the police. The best chances of apprehending a burglar in the act are when a silent alarm is tripped, a surveillance camera records the crime, a witness hears or sees suspicious activities and reports them immediately to the police, or alert patrol officers observe a burglary in progress. However, most burglaries are not solved at the crime scene but through subsequent investigation.

Classification

> **LO3** Identify the two basic classifications of burglary.
>
> Burglaries are classified as residential or commercial.

Residential Burglaries

A **residential burglary** occurs in buildings, structures, or attachments that are used as or are suitable for dwellings, even though they may be unoccupied at the time of the burglary. Residential units include private homes, tenements, mobile homes, cabins, apartments, rooms within a house leased by a renter, houseboats used as dwellings, and any other structure suitable for and used as a dwelling. Nearly two-thirds of all burglaries are residential burglaries (65.5% in 2018 according to the FBI). Of these, more than half took place during the day. The FBI's 2018 "Crime Clock" estimates that a home is burglarized every 25.7 seconds (FBI, 2018a).

Myth Most residential burglaries occur at night, under cover of darkness.

Fact More residential burglaries occur during the day, when people are at work or school, than at night. In 2018, 218,028 burglaries were categorized as residential nighttime offenses, and 346,312 were residential daytime burglaries (FBI, 2018b).

Residential burglaries are often committed by one or more juveniles or young adults who live in the same community. The targets are cash; items to convert to personal use; items to "fence" or sell, such as televisions, radios, and other small electronics; computers and other digital devices; guns; jewelry; tools; and other small household goods. Residential burglaries typically occur during weekdays when most people are away from their homes, either at work or at school.

Burglary at Single-Family House Construction Sites

Amateur opportunists and professional thieves alike take advantage of unprotected construction sites. With copper and other scrap metal prices on the rise, construction sites have become an increasingly attractive target for burglars. The stolen metals are typically sold at junkyards and refineries. Until recently it was difficult for investigators to track stolen metals because the materials were often immediately melted down and there were few or no requirements for the seller to provide any identification or information. However, because of the rise in these types of crimes, businesses that buy these items have begun implementing higher standards of acceptance, including requiring the seller to provide positive identification and proof of where they obtained the products. Some states have now mandated these standards as law.

The primary responsibility for preventing such losses is with the builder. However, the police response might include enhancing natural surveillance and disrupting the stolen goods market. Responses that have met with limited success include patrolling construction sites, surveillance and the installation of pole cameras, "baiting" thieves, and sting operations.

Commercial Burglaries

A **commercial burglary**, also referred to as a *nonresidential burglary*, is one that involves churches, schools, barns, public buildings, shops, offices, stores, factories, warehouses, pharmacies, veterinary clinics, stables, ships, or railroad cars. Most commercial burglaries are committed in service stations, stores, schools, manufacturing plants, warehouses, and office buildings. Burglars often specialize in one type of facility. Businesses located in out-of-the-way places are more susceptible to burglary because of a lack of police coverage and street lighting and because there are usually few witnesses to observe wrongdoing and notify the police. Businesses in high-poverty, rundown neighborhoods are also at high risk of burglary.

In contrast to residential burglaries, most nonresidential burglaries take place after-hours, either at night or on weekends, whenever the establishment is closed. For example, in 2018, approximately 190,000 nonresidential burglaries occurred at night, compared to roughly 150,000 daytime nonresidential burglaries. Businesses where drugs and chemicals used to manufacture drugs are kept on-site are becoming increasingly popular targets for burglars. For example, ketamine, a common anesthetic used in veterinary settings, is a drug used recreationally to produce hallucinogens and also to facilitate date rape. Prescription pain medication sold at pharmacies is another attractive target for burglars because of the high demand on the black market for such drugs.

Commercial burglaries are often committed by two or more people, depending on the type of premises, size, location, and the planned burglary attack. Sometimes a lookout is used who acts like a drunk, works on a stalled car, or walks an animal near the location. The building is "cased" in advance to learn about security devices, opening and closing times, employee habits, people in the neighborhood, and the presence of a private security officer. Casing is also done by obtaining information from an employee or by posing as a worker, repairperson, or salesperson to gain ostensibly legitimate entrance.

Elements of the Crime: Burglary

Although burglary laws vary from state to state, statutes of all states include three key elements.

Elements of the crime of burglary include

- entering a structure,
- without the consent of the person in possession,
- with the intent to commit a crime therein.

Entering a Structure

Paths of entry may be through an open door, window, or transom; a ventilation shaft; a hole in a wall; or a tunnel. Means of entry can be by jimmying a door or window, reaching through an open door or window with a long stick or pole, using a celluloid strip to open a door lock, climbing a ladder or stairs outside a building, descending through a skylight, hiding in an entryway, or breaking a window and taking items from the window display (called **smash and grab**). Entry also includes remaining in a store until after closing time and then committing a burglary.

Some state laws include vehicles, trailers, and railroad cars as structures.

Without the Consent of the Person in Possession

To constitute burglary, the entry must be illegal and must be done without permission of a person having lawful authority, that is, the property owner, the legal agent

Many burglars use force to enter a structure, and a surprising number of intruders gain access to a residence through the front door.

Ace Stock Limited/Alamy Stock Photo

of such person, or the person in physical control of the property, such as a renter or part-owner.

Entering a *public* place is done with consent unless consent has been expressly withdrawn. The hours for legal entry usually are posted on public buildings; for example, "Open Weekdays 9 a.m. to 5 p.m." Entrance at any other time is without consent. If a specific individual is restricted from entering a public place during its open hours, that individual must be notified orally or in writing that consent has been withdrawn.

With Intent to Commit a Crime

Regardless of whether the burglary is planned well in advance or committed on the spur of the moment, intent must be shown. When the first two elements are present, the third is often presumed present; that is, if a person enters a structure without the owner's consent, the presumption is that it is to commit a crime, usually larceny or a sex offense.

Additional Elements

Three additional elements are found in the laws of some states.

Elements of burglary can also include breaking into the dwelling of another during the nighttime.

Breaking Into. Actual "breaking" is a matter of interpretation. Any force used during a burglary to enter or leave the structure, even if a door or window is partly opened or closed, constitutes breaking. Entrance through trick or ruse or through threats to or collusion with any person residing in the building is also considered breaking.

Breaking and entering is strong **presumptive evidence** that a crime is intended; that is, it provides a reasonable basis for belief. Some laws include such wording as this: "Every person who shall unlawfully break and enter a building or dwelling or other structure shall be deemed to have broken and entered or entered the same with intent to commit grand or petit larceny or a felony therein, unless such unlawful breaking and entering shall be explained by testimony satisfactory to the jury to have been made without criminal intent." This, in effect, places the burden of proof on the defendant.

The Dwelling of Another. Some states still require that the structure broken into be a dwelling, that is, a structure suitable for sheltering people. This remnant from common law restricts burglary to residential burglaries.

During the Nighttime. Common law also specified that burglary occur under the cover of darkness, an element still retained in some state statutes. *Nighttime* is defined as the period from sunset to sunrise as specified by official weather charts.

Establishing the Severity of the Burglary

Most burglary laws increase the crime's severity if the burglar possesses a weapon or an explosive. Obtain the weapon and connect it with the burglar if possible. Check with the National Crime Information Center (NCIC) to see if the weapon is connected to any other criminal incidents. If the weapon is stolen, a separate felony charge of theft or illegal possession of a weapon can be made. Another element present in some statutes concerns whether the premises are occupied at the time of the offense, even though no contact is made with the occupant. An example is the "cat burglar" who sneaks into a house to steal a purse or phone left on the counter, while the homeowner is fast asleep. In some states, this type of burglary is treated with an enhanced level of severity.

> **LO6** Explain how the severity of a burglary is determined.
>
> A burglary's severity is determined by (1) the presence of dangerous devices in the burglar's possession, (2) the value of the property stolen, and (3) whether the premise is occupied.

If other crimes are committed along with the burglary or if the burglary is to commit another crime such as rape, the additional crime is separate and must be proven separately.

Elements of the Crime: Possession of Burglary Tools

A companion crime to burglary is possession of burglary tools, an offense separate from burglary. The charge of possession of burglary tools can be made even if a burglary has not been committed if circumstances indicate that the tools were intended for use in a burglary.

> **LO7** List the elements of the crime of possession of burglary tools.
>
> Elements of the crime of possessing burglary tools include
>
> - possessing any device, explosive, or other instrumentality,
> - with intent to use or permit its use to commit burglary.

Burglary tools include nitroglycerin or other explosives and any engine, machine, tool, implement, chemical, or substance designed for the cutting, burning, or prying open of buildings or protective containers.

A person with a large number of automobile keys probably intends to use them to open varied makes and models of vehicle doors. Portable key cutters, codes, and key blanks such as those used in hardware stores and key-making shops are also classified as burglary tools, as are *slam pullers*, devices that look like oversized screwdrivers and are inserted in car locks to force them open. A bump key is another burglary tool. **Lock bumping** is a lock picking technique used on standard pin tumbler locks in which the **bump key** (a generic key) is used along with another mechanism to apply force to open the lock. Lock bumping is an easy, quiet method used by thieves to commit burglaries and other crimes.

Many other tools used in burglaries are commonly obtained in hardware stores. These include pry bars, screwdrivers, bolt cutters, extension cords, pipe wrenches, channel locks, and tire irons. Lock picks and tension wrenches, lever-type wrenches, warded pass keys, pick guns, cylinder drill jigs, and various types of metal blades to open car doors can also be used as burglary tools.

> **LO8** List the common burglary tools.
>
> Common burglary tools include explosives, portable key cutters, key blanks, slam pullers, bump keys, lock picks, pry bars, screwdrivers, wrenches, bolt cutters, extension cords, pipe wrenches, channel locks, tire irons, and metal blades—basically any assortment of tools, devices, or chemicals to cut, burn, or pry open buildings or protective containers.

Because many people, especially mechanics and carpenters, have tools that might be used in a burglary in their car or on their person, circumstances must clearly show intent to use or allow their use in committing a crime.

The Burglar

The burglar is often portrayed as a masked person with a bag loaded with silverware and candlesticks over his shoulder. In reality, burglars fit no set image; they are of all sizes, ages, races, and occupations. They are either amateurs or longtime professionals whose sole income is derived from burglaries. Most amateur burglars are between the ages of 15 and 25; most professionals are 25 to 55. The amateur is usually an unskilled, "infancy-level" burglar who steals televisions; cash; cell phones, tablets, and other electronic devices; and other portable property and who learns through trial and error. In contrast, the professional burglar usually steals furs, jewelry, and more valuable items and has been carefully trained by other professional burglars.

Even though amateurs gain experience in burglaries, they are apt to make a mistake eventually and be captured by the police while committing a burglary. If caught and sentenced to prison, amateur burglars gain the opportunity to learn more about the "trade" from the professionals while behind bars.

Professional burglars may have lookouts who are in communication through two-way radios. A getaway vehicle is usually close to the burglary site, and the lookout monitors police radio frequencies.

Although most burglars' motives are monetary or drug related, sometimes the excitement of committing burglary and evading detection is equally or more important. One burglar said it was a "thrill" not to know what was waiting for him and whether he would get away with the crime.

Responding to a Burglary Call

Although officers should always follow department policy and procedure for responding to in-progress burglaries and after-the-fact burglaries, several common practices and techniques exist in most departments' response protocol. On the way to the burglary scene, watch for anyone fleeing the area, suspicious-looking people still at the scene, and suspicious automobiles. Do not use a siren on the way to the scene. Cut your flashing lights some distance from the scene, and do not use a spotlight or flashlight to determine the address. Park several doors away from the address of

the call, turn the radio down, and close car doors quietly. Approach the immediate area with low-tone conversation and avoid jangling keys or coins or flashing lights. Keep in mind that a suspect may still be on scene even if the reporting party believes the burglar is gone.

L09 Describe how to proceed to a burglary scene and what to do on arrival.

Proceed to a burglary scene quietly. Be observant and cautious at the scene.

The first two officers arriving place themselves at diagonally opposed corners of the building. This places each out of the other's line of fire but in position to protect each other. Search the premises inside and outside for the burglar. Use maximum cover and caution in going around corners. In a dark room, use a flashlight rather than room lights to prevent silhouettes. Hold the flashlight in front of you at a 45-degree angle. Have your gun drawn and in the low ready position.

Be alert for the possible presence of explosives at a burglary scene. If a bomb threat is connected with a burglary, notify the FBI. If explosives are actually detonated, notify the Bureau of Alcohol, Tobacco, Firearms, and Explosives (ATF) Division of the Department of Homeland Security. To dispose of explosives at the scene or in the suspect's possession, call the bomb squad of the nearest large metropolitan area or the explosives ordnance unit of the closest military installation. If an explosion has already occurred at the burglary scene, intentionally or accidentally, it may leave behind potentially valuable evidence. Collecting and handling such evidence is discussed shortly.

False Burglar Alarms

False burglar alarms from personal residential and commercial security systems are a huge problem for law enforcement agencies. Data from the Urban Institute indicates that between 90% and 99% of all burglar alarm activations are false (Schaenman, Horvath, & Hatry, 2012). False alarms are typically caused by user error, although occasionally they occur because of faulty equipment.

The growing problem of false alarms has led many departments to implement policies on how to handle such nuisance calls. Some law enforcement agencies have implemented a **verified response policy**, meaning that they will not respond to a burglary alarm unless criminal activity is first confirmed through either an on-site security officer; verbal communication with a resident or employee on-site, either via the phone or through an intercom integrated into the security system; or some other method of electronic surveillance, such as closed-circuit television. An aggressive form of verified response is Enhanced Call Verification (ECV), which requires that a minimum of two phone calls be made from the alarm monitoring center, to assess whether user error activated the alarm. Only then will a law enforcement response be activated. Case studies have found that departments can significantly decrease (by 90% to 95%) false alarm dispatches by implementing ECV policies, leaving officers available for higher priority duties (Schaenman et al., 2012).

Another approach that departments are taking is to use an escalating series of fines and fees for police dispatch when the alarm turns out to be false. For chronic abusers, alarm response by police is suspended entirely. False alarms are a waste of time for responding officers, and, more important, they may cause officers to be caught off guard when a genuine alarm occurs.

The Preliminary Investigation

Although burglary is a very basic crime to investigate, many investigators cut corners or simply skip the necessary steps of a preliminary investigation because, with a national clearance rate of less than 13%, such cases are perceived as being high-time investments for low-result rewards. Yet, for this very reason, the preliminary investigation is of utmost importance.

If no suspect is found at the scene of a burglary, conduct the preliminary investigation as described in Chapter 1. Obtain detailed information about the type of structure burglarized, the means of entry, the time and date, the whereabouts of the owner, other persons recently on the premises, the property taken, and the modus operandi (MO).

Determine who the occupants are and where they were at the time of the burglary. Were they on the premises? If not, when did they leave? Were the doors and windows locked? Who had keys? What visitors had recently been there? Obtain descriptions of salespeople, agents, service installers, or maintenance workers on the premises recently. Was the burglar familiar with the premises? Could the location of the stolen items be known only to a person who worked on the premises; that is, was it an inside job?

Obtain a complete list of the property taken and an estimate of the value from the victim. Find out where the property was obtained and where it was stored. Where

and when did the owner last see it? What type of property was *not* stolen? Log articles with serial numbers into the NCIC.

Interview witnesses. In many burglaries, there is a connection between the victim and the suspect. The suspect may have recently performed work, made a delivery, or attended a party in the home. Conduct a neighborhood canvass to see whether anyone saw anything and to alert neighbors.

Search for physical evidence, including latent fingerprints, items left on the premises by the burglar, or tool marks on doors or windows. Without physical evidence, there is little chance of charging anyone. It is especially important to search for prints at the scene and to obtain elimination prints of those with normal access to it.

An important point to remember is that concern should be shown for the victim. Surveys indicate that victims' impressions of the police are related to how professionally investigators conduct the crime scene investigation. If officers are thorough, courteous, considerate, concerned, and conscientious about keeping the victims informed of the progress of the investigation, victims generally express favorable opinions of the investigators. Let victims know how they can help in the investigation, and put them in touch with any victim assistance programs that are available. Solving the crime is the first priority for the police, but the victims' feelings must be considered as well. Victims may feel devastated, violated, angry, or completely dejected. Investigators must keep these feelings in mind while conducting interviews with victims.

Preliminary Investigation of Residential Burglaries

The preliminary investigation of a residential burglary should include the following steps as a minimum:

- Make contact with the resident(s).

- Establish points and methods of entry and exit.

- Collect and preserve evidence.

- Determine the type and amount of loss, with complete descriptions.

- Describe the MO.

- Check for recent callers such as friends of children, salespeople, and maintenance people.

- Canvass the neighborhood for witnesses, evidence, discarded stolen articles, and so on.

- Check for possible surveillance cameras.

Interviews of burglars have revealed that they prefer middle- to upper-class homes on corner lots that allow them to see people approaching from a maximum of directions. Burglars may knock on doors before entering to determine whether a dog is inside and may to pretend to be delivering a package should someone answer the door.

When processing the crime scene in a residential burglary, process the exit as well as the entry area. When looking for fingerprints, check the inside of drawers that have been ransacked, smooth glass objects, papers strewn on the floor, countertops, and clocks. The same procedures are followed if the burglary has occurred in a multiple-dwelling or a commercial-lodging establishment such as an apartment building or a hotel.

Preliminary Investigation of Commercial Burglaries

Preliminary investigation of a commercial burglary (e.g., a market, shop, office, or liquor store) should minimally include the following steps:

- Contact the owner.

- Protect the scene from intrusion by the owner, the public, and others.

- Establish the point and method of entry and exit.

- Locate, collect, and preserve possible evidence.

- Narrow the time frame of the crime.

- Determine the type and amount of loss.

- Determine who closed the establishment, who was present at the time of the crime, and who had keys to the establishment.

- Describe the MO.

- Identify employees' friends, maintenance people, and any possible disgruntled employees or customers.

- Collect and review any surveillance videos.

- Rule out a faked or staged burglary for insurance purposes.

Fake Burglaries

Do not overlook the possibility of faked burglaries, especially in commercial burglaries where the owner appears to be in financial difficulty. Check the owner's financial status.

So-called combination safe jobs, in which the safe is opened by the combination without the use of external force, are usually the result of the combination being found on the premises, the safe being carelessly left open or improperly locked, a dishonest present or former employee using the combination or selling it to the burglar, or the employer faking a burglary to cover a shortage of funds.

Myth Because burglaries are a relatively minor offense, compared to violent crimes, they are much easier to solve.

Fact Most burglary investigations do not produce any information or evidence about the crime, making them quite difficult to solve. Of the eight major crime categories tracked by the FBI, burglaries have the second lowest clearance rate after motor vehicle theft. Only 13.9% of burglaries were cleared in 2018.

Determining Entry into Structures

Burglary is a crime of opportunity and concealment. Entry is made in areas of a structure not normally observed, under the cover of darkness, in covered entryways, through windows screened by shrubbery or trees, or through ruse and trickery. Sometimes, however, the burglar breaks a shop window, removes some items on display, and rapidly escapes by jumping into a nearby vehicle driven by an accomplice.

LO10 Identify the most frequent means of entry to commit burglary.

Jimmying is the most common method of entry to commit burglary.

Almost every means imaginable has been used by burglars to gain entry, including tunneling; chopping holes in walls, floors, and ceilings; and using fire escapes. Tool marks, disturbed paint, footprints and fingerprints, broken glass, or forced locks help determine how the burglar gained entry.

Some burglars have keys made. For example, some people leave their car at a repair shop along with their full set of keys—an open invitation to make a duplicate house or office key. At other times, burglars hide inside a building until after closing. In such cases, they often leave behind evidence such as matches, cigarette butts, or candy wrappers because their wait is often lengthy.

The **hit-and-run burglary**, also called *smash and grab*, in which the burglar smashes a window to steal merchandise, is most frequently committed by younger, inexperienced burglars. Jewelry and furs are common targets. Cigarettes, e-cigarettes, and cash smash-and-grabs are common at gas stations and convenience stores.

In recent years, enterprising burglars have taken advantage of the prevalence of electric garage door openers. Using "code grabbers," burglars can record and replicate the electronic signal emitted from an automatic garage door opener. When a person leaves the house and activates the garage door opener, the burglar is able to capture the signal from as far as several hundred yards away and reopen the door once the resident is safely out of sight. Some burglars are bold enough to back their own car into the garage, load it up with stolen items, and drive away, leaving no sign of forced entry. To combat the code-grabbing technique to gain entrance into homes, a device called a "code rotator" is available. Each time an automatic door opener is used, the internal code rotates to a new one, rendering a code grabber useless. Many newly manufactured garage doors have this rolling-code technology built in.

Determining Entry into Safes and Vaults

Safes are usually considered a good way to protect valuables, but most older safes provide little more than fire protection. Unless they are carried away or demolished by a burglar or lost in a fire, safes last many years; therefore, many old safes are still in use.

A **safe** is a semiportable strongbox with a combination lock. The size of the safe or lock does not necessarily correlate with its security. A **vault** is a stationary room of reinforced concrete, often steel lined, with a combination lock. Both safes and vaults are common targets of burglars.

> **LO11** Describe the various methods used to break into safes.
>
> Safes and vaults are entered illegally by punching, peeling, chopping, pulling or dragging, blowing, and burning. Sometimes burglars simply haul the safes away.

In **punching**, the dial is sheared from the safe door by a downward blow with a sledge or by holding a chisel to the dial and using a sledge to knock it off, exposing the safe mechanism spindle. Sometimes a tire inner tube, or similar material, will be placed over the safe's dial to deaden the noise. Punching is most successful in attacking older-model fire-resistant safes and is less successful on newer models that have tapered spindles that will jam when someone attempts to punch them.

In **peeling**, the burglar drills a hole in a corner of the safe and then makes this hole successively larger by using other drills until the narrow end of a jimmy can be inserted in the hole to pry the door partially open. The burglar then uses the larger end of the jimmy to complete the job. Although slow, this method is less noisy than others.

In **chopping**, the burglar uses a sledge and chisels or a heavy chopping instrument, such as an axe, to chop a hole in the bottom of the safe large enough to remove the contents. This technique is also called a *rip* or *peel*, and all three terms are used to describe the opening by physical force of a hole, which is expanded until it is big enough to fit a hand inside the safe. A chop/rip/peel is commonly used on fire-resistant safes (sometimes after an unsuccessful punch).

In **pulling**, also called **dragging**, the burglar inserts a V plate over the dial, with the V in place behind the dial. The burglar then tightens the screw bolts one at a time until the dial and the spindle are pulled out. This method, the opposite of punching, works on many older safes but not on newer ones.

In **blowing**, the burglar drills a hole in the safe near the locking bar area or pushes cotton into an area of the safe door crack and puts nitroglycerin on the cotton. The burglar then places a primer cap against the cotton, tapes it in place, and runs a wire to a protected area. Mattresses and blankets are often used to soften the blast. The burglar ignites the nitroglycerin, which blows the safe open. This dangerous, noisy method requires experience and is rarely used.

The process of **burning** often uses a "burning bar," a portable safecracking tool that burns a hole into the safe to gain entry. This hole may be burned near the safe's locking mechanism, or the safe may be tipped over and the hole burned through the bottom. An arc-air burning tool can punch a hole completely through a 1-inch steel plate in about 10 seconds.

Some burglars prefer a site of their own choosing at which to employ one or more of these methods. So, they steal the entire safe, haul it away in a truck, and open it when they get there.

The preceding methods are used on older safes still found in many smaller stores. Often the safe can be entered in less than 15 minutes. Modern safes, however, do not have spindles and cannot be punched, peeled, or pulled. Safes of newer steel alloys are highly resistant to burning and drilling.

Obtaining Physical Evidence

Most burglars are convicted on circumstantial evidence. Any physical evidence at the burglary scene is of utmost importance.

> **LO12** List the types of physical evidence often found at a burglary scene.
>
> Physical evidence at a burglary scene includes fingerprints, footprints, tire prints, tools, tool marks, broken glass, paint chips, safe insulation, explosives residue, personal possessions, and DNA.

The competent, professional burglar will wear gloves to avoid leaving fingerprints and palmprints. However, an offender's inexperience and haste could result in such prints being scattered throughout the crime scene. Therefore, process the scene for prints, particularly at the entry point. Any and all prints obtained should be submitted to the FBI's Next Generation Identification (NGI) system, which replaced the Integrated Automated Fingerprint Identification System (IAFIS) in September 2014. Because burglars tend to be recidivists, a hit from one burglary case will likely help investigators clear many other burglary cases.

Shoe impressions and footprints may be visible inside or outside the structure and should be cast following the guidelines in Chapter 5. Similarly, any tire impressions located around the burglary scene should be cast as possible evidence.

Tools and tool marks are especially important items of evidence. Pry bars, augers, picks, and screwdrivers are commonly used to commit burglary. Locksmith tools can also be used and are illegal to possess unless one is a licensed locksmith. Burglars often have a "tool of choice" to gain entry, and this same tool, used over and over at different crime scenes, will leave behind characteristic striation marks that can connect one burglary to another. Tools used to pry open a door or window always leave a mark behind (recall Locard's principle of exchange discussed in Chapter 1). If the frame is made of wood, striation marks may be visible and can be cast. Before casting an impression in wood, however, spray the surface with a silicone oil-based release agent to ensure that the silicone casting material, once cured, does not stick to the wood and pull out wood fibers when the cast is removed.

Do not overlook a "tool of opportunity." Items such as bricks and large rocks or other objects in the landscaping are sometimes used when the burglary is not well-planned.

Be alert to the variety of containers used to carry burglary tools—handbags, suitcases, garbage bags, musical-instrument cases, and packages that appear to contain merchandise. Tools can also be concealed under coats, inside pant legs, or under car seats. Tools found on the premises are sometimes left there by the burglar to avoid being caught with burglary tools in possession and to thwart efforts to link multiple burglaries to one offender.

Broken glass and paint chips are common items of evidence at burglary scenes. An offender who smashes a window to gain entry to a building may unwittingly carry away tiny fragments of glass on their clothing or the soles of their shoes. Samples of glass or chipped paint collected at the scene can be matched to glass and paint fragments detected on the suspect, helping to establish the offender's presence at the crime scene.

Evidence at the scene of a safe burglary may also include safe insulation. As with glass and paint fragments, the burglar often has some of this insulation on their clothing, either in pants, coat or jacket pockets, or in the nail holes of shoes. Take comparison standards of safe insulation to be matched with particles found on the suspect, on tools the suspect used, or in the vehicle used during the crime. In some cases, safe insulation can also be matched with a series of burglaries.

In a western city, police officers noticed what they believed was safe insulation on the steps of a cabin occupied by a known burglar. They obtained a warrant and searched the premises for evidence of a burglary. The substance found on the steps and some burglary tools found inside the home were mailed to a laboratory, where the substance was confirmed as safe insulation. The suspect was arrested and convicted of burglary. On appeal, the courts held that such knowledge by the officers was in effect an extension of the laboratory and was therefore probable cause even without the laboratory examination. The verification by the laboratory only strengthened the probable cause, and the charge of burglary was sustained.

Sometimes explosives are encountered at a burglary scene. Use extreme caution in handling and preserving such evidence. If an explosion has already occurred at the burglary scene, intentionally or accidentally, identify and preserve fragments from the explosive device and send them to a crime laboratory.

DNA is also becoming important in burglary investigations. If a burglar gets cut breaking into a structure, they may leave blood behind that can be analyzed for DNA, perhaps linking the burglary to others. Touch or trace DNA can be obtained from surfaces at the scene, such as when a nervous and perspiring suspect presses their face against a window or a burglar with a cold sneezes on a counter. These types of actions, and the trace evidence they leave behind, are now receiving recognition among investigators and helping solve some difficult burglary cases.

Critics argue that DNA analysis is too expensive to use in an attempt to solve a burglary that, on average, involves a loss amount less than that of the analysis. However, the National Institute of Justice (NIJ) has advocated collecting DNA evidence in "minor" crime investigations as a way to yield major public safety benefits, noting the high recidivism rates of property crime offenders, that their crimes and violence often escalate, and that many property crime cases go unsolved (Wilson, McClure, & Weisburd, 2010; Ritter, 2008). Recall from Chapter 5 the study that showed how DNA analysis can more than double the identification rate of suspects, leading to a doubling of the arrest and prosecution rates of burglary suspects (Roman et al., 2008). Another study found that DNA analysis helps identify serial burglars, the arrest of whom can significantly reduce an area's burglary rate by taking repeat offenders off the streets, thereby saving communities millions of dollars in investigative resources and lost personal property (Geoghegan, 2009).

Despite the potential benefits of DNA analysis, many forensic laboratories have backlogs extending several months, and much of the caseload involves higher priority evidence from violent crimes. Thus, processing such evidence from property crimes is currently impractical for many jurisdictions. If, however, the cost of such analysis is reduced in the future and the process becomes simplified, more burglary investigations may rely on DNA evidence.

Modus Operandi Factors

Effective MO files are essential in investigating burglaries because most burglars commit a series of burglaries. Look for patterns in the location, day of week, time of day, type of property stolen, and method of entry and exit. The burglar may commit vandalism, ransack, write with lipstick on mirrors, take only cash or jewelry, drink liquor from the scene, or eat from the refrigerator. Such peculiarities can tie several burglaries to one suspect.

LO13 Identify the modus operandi factors to consider when investigating a burglary.

> Important MO factors include the time, type of victim, type of premises, point and means of entry, type of property taken, and any peculiarities of the offense.

Suspects often commit burglaries on only a certain day of the week, perhaps related to their day off from a regular job. The time of the burglary should be as accurate as possible, but when victims are gone on vacation, this is not easy to determine. Knowing the time also helps in checking alibis, interviewing witnesses, and, in some states, determining the degree of the burglary.

Determine any peculiarities of the offense, including oddities of the suspect. What method of search was used? Was anything else done besides committing the burglary? Did the burglar stake out the home earlier by posing as a delivery or maintenance person? Did neighbors see such activities? Determine any trademarks of the burglar. Some burglars take such pride in their professionalism that they leave a calling card of some type to let the police know whose work it is.

Check the MO with local files. Talk to other officers, inquire at other agencies within a 100-mile radius, and discuss the case at area investigation meetings. Other officers may have encountered a similar MO.

Effective Case Management

Because burglary is predominantly a serial crime, the serial burglar should be the primary target of the burglary unit. This requires effective case management, including an effective system for prioritizing cases. Profiling and mapping may be of considerable help.

Using the computer's search capabilities, information retrieval is fast and simple, and investigations can proceed on information that in the past would have taken hundreds of hours to retrieve, if indeed it could have been retrieved at all.

Effective case management also recognizes the mobility of burglars and makes assignments on the MO rather than on the geographic area—for example, burglaries involving forcible entry, daytime burglaries involving no force, and nighttime residential burglaries. All information should be shared with the drug enforcement unit because many burglaries are drug related.

A new investigative management tool to help deal with the rise in narcotics and other prescription drug thefts from pharmacies is a national database called Rx Pattern Analysis Tracking Robberies and Other Losses (RxPATROL). According to the program's website (RxPATROL, n.d.), which is updated regularly, RxPATROL is "designed to collect, collate, analyze and disseminate pharmacy theft intelligence to law enforcement throughout the nation." Pharmacies provide data directly to RxPATROL in the aftermath of a theft involving controlled substances, including any video or still photos captured. An analyst at RxPATROL uses an incident analysis software platform to evaluate the data, identify trends, and provide intelligence to the respective law enforcement agencies for action as they deem appropriate. Analysis provided by RxPATROL has helped several law enforcement agencies successfully apprehend and prosecute those involved in controlled substance pharmacy crime. As of October 26, 2020, the system had 14,333 registered users and had logged 10,871 incidents in its database, of which 2,559 were burglaries and 5,104 were robberies.

Recovering Stolen Property

Stolen property is disposed of in several ways. Because many people are looking for a bargain, thieves can often sell the property on the streets, thus avoiding a record of the sale but also risking being reported to the police by someone who sees the transaction. Other common forums for disposing of stolen property include pawnshops and Internet auction sites, the latter being popular because the seller can remain anonymous.

In the case of property being sold to pawnshops or secondhand stores or left at a store on consignment for sale, most states and communities have statutes or ordinances requiring a permanent record of the transaction. The seller must be given a receipt describing the property purchased and the amount paid, with the seller's name and address. A copy of the transaction is often sent to the police department of the community listed as the seller's home address. If the property is identified as stolen, the police contact the shop owner and, upon proof that the property is stolen, can recover it. Shop records are open to police inspection at all times. Information in these records can lead to the arrest of the seller as the person who committed the burglary. LeadsOnline.com is a technology service that helps make connections between law enforcement, missing items, and people who can serve as "witnesses." LeadsOnline provides documentation and

reporting services for secondhand dealers, pawnshops, gold buyers, scrap metal dealers, and pharmacies—businesses where stolen items either originate or end up.

Informants can often locate stolen property because they usually know who is active in the area. Surveillance of pawnshops also is often productive. Circulate a list of the stolen property to all establishments that might deal in such merchandise in your own community and surrounding communities. If the property is extremely valuable, enter it into the FBI's NCIC files.

> **LO14** List the sources investigators should check when searching for stolen property.
>
> Check with pawnshops, secondhand stores, flea markets, online auction sites, and informants for leads in recovering stolen property.

As with so many other types of crimes and evidence, national database and tracking tools are being implemented to help law enforcement find and recover stolen goods. For example, ScrapTheftAlert.com is a website that allows law enforcement to alert the scrap industry to materials thefts. A search of the active alerts reveals a variety of open cases involving automobile catalytic converters stolen in Las Vegas, Nevada; steel shipping carts missing from Elmhurst, Illinois; brass propeller shaft nuts taken from Richmond, British Columbia; fire hydrant valve extensions stolen in Detroit, Michigan; and copper fittings, couplings, and adapters missing in Minneapolis, Minnesota.

When you recover stolen property, record the date on which the property was recovered, where it was recovered, who turned it in, and the circumstances surrounding the recovery. List the names and addresses of anyone present at the time of recovery. Mark the property as evidence and take it into custody. In some states, it is legal to return the property as long as its identification is recorded and a photograph is taken. There is no reason the original property must be produced in court unless it was an instrument that caused death or serious injury.

Recovering stolen property and returning it to the rightful owner is aided by Operation Identification programs. In such programs, homeowners mark all easily stolen property with a personal identification number (PIN). The numbers are recorded and placed in a secure location.

Elements of the Crime: Receiving Stolen Goods

A go-between who receives stolen goods for resale is referred to as a *fence*.

> **LO15** Identify the elements of the offense of receiving stolen goods.
>
> The elements of the offense of receiving stolen goods are
>
> - receiving, buying, or concealing stolen or illegally obtained goods,
> - knowing them to be stolen or otherwise illegally obtained.

Receiving stolen property for resale is a crime, as is concealing stolen property, even though not purchased. A burglar does not have to personally sell goods to a fence. An "innocent" third party can sell the property for the burglar, but it is still an offense if the buyer knows the property was stolen.

It is difficult to prove that a buyer knew the purchased goods were stolen. The property must be found in the receiver's possession and identified as the stolen property by the owner's testimony, marks, serial numbers, or other positive identification. Knowing can then be proved by the very low price paid for the goods in comparison with the true value.

Usually evidence of the sale is provided through an informant who either made the sale or knows who did. The property may have been resold, and the person buying the item may be the informant who identifies the receiver of stolen goods. This person assists the police in making another sale or identifying property in the receiver's possession.

The receiver of stolen goods is often discovered when the person who stole the property is arrested and identifies the receiver. It is necessary to show that the receiver could not legitimately own the item unless they had bought it from a thief. Show that it was not purchased through a normal business transaction. The character of the person selling the property or any indication that the property was being concealed is evidence. Evidence that markings or serial numbers have been altered or removed indicates concealment and intent to deprive the rightful owner of the property. The seller can testify to conversations with the receiver about the property and the fact that it was stolen. The receiver's records may not show the transaction, which would be evidence of intent to conceal. The charge of receiving stolen goods can be used when possession of stolen items can be shown but there is not sufficient evidence to prove theft.

One indicator of fencing activity is an operation that makes merchandise available to retailers at extremely low wholesale prices provided they pay cash. Another possible indicator is a small local outlet that offers significant savings to customers, conducts a large volume of business over a short period, and then closes suddenly. Sales from fenced goods amount to tens of billions of dollars annually.

Sting Operations

Many cities have established sting operations, in which the police legally establish a fencing operation. A suitable shop is set up as a front for the operation. Normally, secondhand stores, repair shops, salvage dealers, appliance dealers, or pawnshops make good front operations. The store is stocked with items to support the type of business selected.

Word is spread through informants and the underworld that the business will "buy anything." Attractive prices are paid to get the business started. All transactions between the fence and the seller of stolen goods are recorded by closed-circuit television. The camera is usually focused on an area in which a calendar and clock are clearly visible to establish the date and time of each transaction. A parking lot surveillance camera shows the vehicle used to transport the property and its license number.

When an item is presented at the counter, the seller, the amount paid for the property, and the buyer are recorded. The property is then dusted for fingerprints to further prove the seller's possession. The stolen goods are checked through normal police channels to determine where they were stolen.

The shop is run for two to three months and then discontinued. Arrest warrants are then issued for those implicated during the store's operation.

Preventing Burglary

Research shows that premises that are burglarized are likely to be burglarized again: "A critical and consistent feature of repeat victimization [RV] is that repeat offenses occur quickly—many repeats occur within a week of the initial offense, and some even occur within 24 hours. An early study of RV showed the highest risk of a repeat burglary was during the first week after an initial burglary. . . . 60% of repeat burglaries occurred within one month of the initial offense; about 10% occurred during the second month" (Weisel, 2005, p. 2). Not only is the home that was burglarized at increased risk of being targeted again but research has shown that the other homes on that street and on nearby streets are also at elevated risk of burglary in the following one to two weeks (National Institute of Justice, 2014; Chainey & da Silva, 2016).

When asking the question of how to prevent burglary, many find it useful to ask, instead, what leads a burglar to choose this target at this time? What opportunities are at play? Indeed, the study of burglary and related crime rates has historically focused on the offender, and approaches such as rational choice theory are attempts to model human decision making in the context of criminal behavior: "Rational choice proposes that offenders' behavior seeks to obtain a benefit, and that they make their decisions on the basis of a judgment made after estimating their opportunities to commit a crime successfully, the risk of being caught, and the benefits they hope to obtain" (Miro, 2014).

Newer theories have taken the topic of opportunity and shifted the focus toward the victims and particular times and places. For example, criminal opportunity plays a relevant role in the focus on routine activities. The **routine activity theory** proposes that crime results from the simultaneous existence of three elements: (1) the presence of likely or motivated offenders, (2) the presence of suitable targets, and (3) an absence of guardians to prevent the crime. This theory acknowledges the role, however indirect, of victims in their own victimization and suggests that certain locations may be more susceptible to burglary at certain times because of the routine absence of residents (e.g., a neighborhood where most households consist of married couples who both work outside of the home and school-aged children who are gone for much of the day). Miro (2014) observes:

> Routine activity theory suggests that crime rates may rise or fall without any change in the number of criminals. In fact, the rise in availability of suitable targets or the diminished effectiveness of guardians, or changes in society's routine activities, may increase the probability that these elements converge in space and time and therefore increase opportunities for crime. One of the other most powerful ideas in routine activity theory is precisely that opportunities are not uniformly distributed in society, nor are they infinite. Instead, there is a limited number of available targets that the criminal may find attractive.

Although routine activity theory has faced much criticism related to its ethical and methodological foundation, in particular its tendency to "blame the victim," many critics reluctantly recognize "its capacity to express and explain the need to look at crime, in order to prevent it, by paying attention to the way in which daily life unfolds in different places" (Miro, 2014).

Officers who work with burglary victims can help them avoid future burglaries by conducting a security check of the premises and "hardening" the target. **Target hardening**, also called **crime prevention through environmental design (CPTED)**, involves altering physical characteristics of the property to make it less attractive to criminals. CPTED measures include the following:

- Eliminating bushes or other obstructions to windows—dense shrubbery next to windows and doors provides concealment to burglars and increases the attractiveness of the target. High privacy fences around homes also give cover to people attempting to break in.

- Installing adequate indoor and outdoor lighting—inadequate lighting increases the attractiveness of a property to burglars.

- Installing a burglar alarm and placing exterior signage to visibly indicate the presence of such an alarm—one study that examined the decision-making processes of 422 randomly selected, incarcerated male and female burglars found that most burglars try to determine if an alarm is present before attempting a burglary. Of those burglars who determined that an alarm was present after initiating a burglary, approximately half discontinued their attempt. (Kuhns, Blevins, & Lee, 2012)

Other measures that deter burglaries include the following:

- Installing adequate locks, striker plates, and doorframes
- Providing clearly visible addresses
- Securing any skylights or air vents larger than 96 square inches
- Installing burglarproof sidelight window glass beside doors
- Keeping dogs on the premises

Officers can also assist their jurisdiction in reducing burglaries by having input into building codes that would require adequate locks, lighting, and other security measures to deter burglaries.

Summary

Burglary is the unlawful entry of a structure to commit a crime. It differs from robbery in that burglars are covert, seeking to remain unseen, whereas robbers confront their victims directly. Burglary is a crime against property; robbery is a crime against a person.

Burglaries are classified as residential or commercial. The primary elements of the crime of burglary are (1) entering a structure, (2) without the consent of the person in possession, (3) with the intent to commit a crime therein. Elements of burglary can also include (1) breaking into (2) the dwelling of another (3) during the nighttime. A burglary's severity is determined by (1) the presence of dangerous devices in the burglar's possession, (2) the value of the stolen property, and (3) whether the premise is occupied.

The elements of the crime of possessing burglary tools include (1) possessing any device, explosive, or other instrumentality (2) with intent to use or permit its use to commit burglary. Common burglary tools include explosives, portable key cutters, key blanks, slam pullers, bump keys, lock picks, pry bars, screwdrivers, wrenches, bolt cutters, extension cords, pipe wrenches, channel locks, tire irons, and metal blades—basically any assortment of tools, devices, or chemicals to cut, burn, or pry open buildings or protective containers.

When responding to a burglary call, proceed to the scene quietly. Be observant and cautious at the scene. Jimmying is the most common method of entry to commit burglary. Safes and vaults are entered illegally by punching, peeling, chopping, pulling or dragging, blowing, and burning. Sometimes burglars simply haul the safes away.

Physical evidence at a burglary scene includes fingerprints, footprints, tire prints, tools, tool marks, broken glass, paint chips, safe insulation, explosives residue, personal possessions, and DNA. Important MO factors include the time, the type of victim, type of premises, point and means of entry, type of property taken, and any peculiarities of the offense.

Check with pawnshops, secondhand stores, flea markets, online auction sites, and informants for leads in recovering stolen property. The elements of the offense of receiving stolen goods are (1) receiving, buying, or concealing stolen or illegally obtained goods and (2) knowing them to be stolen or otherwise illegally obtained.

Can You Define?

blowing (a safe)	dragging (a safe)	residential burglary
bump key	hit-and-run burglary	routine activity theory
burglary	lock bumping	safe
burning (a safe)	peeling (a safe)	smash and grab
chopping (a safe)	presumptive evidence	target hardening
commercial burglary	pulling (a safe)	vault
crime prevention through environmental design (CPTED)	punching (a safe)	verified response policy

Checklist

Burglary

- Was a thorough preliminary investigation conducted?

- What is the address and description of the structure burglarized?

- What time and date did the burglary occur?

- What means was used to enter? Was it forcible?

- Who is the rightful owner? Was consent given for the entry?

- What visitors had recently been on the premises?

- Was the burglar familiar with the premises?

- What was taken (complete description and value of each item)?

- Where was the property located, and when was it last seen by the owner?

- What was not taken?

- What pattern of search did the burglar use?

- What was the burglar's MO?

- What physical evidence was found at the scene?

- Did any witnesses see or hear anything suspicious at the time of the burglary?

- Does the owner have any idea who might have committed the burglary?

- Have the MO files been checked?

- Have neighboring communities been informed of the burglary?

- Have you checked with fences, pawnshop owners, and secondhand stores for the stolen property? Have you circulated a list to the owners of such businesses?

- Might this be a fake burglary?

Application

Read this account of a criminal investigation and evaluate its effectiveness:

> In a California city, two custodians showing up for work were met at the door of the restaurant they were to clean by two armed men. One janitor was taken inside; the other escaped and notified the police. When the police arrived, both suspects were outside the building in different areas and claimed they knew nothing of a crime being committed. Inside, the one janitor was tied up in the kitchen, unharmed. The safe had been punched open. A substance believed to be safe insulation, along with paint chips, was found on the pants and shoes of both suspects. Both janitors made a positive field identification of the two suspects. Laboratory analysis of the substance found in the suspects' clothing and shoes matched a comparison sample of the safe insulation, and the paint chips matched the top two layers of paint on the safe. The men were charged with burglary.

Questions

1. Was it legal to take the men into custody?

2. Was field identification appropriate?

3. Were the men arrested on scene for probable cause?

4. Was a warrant issued for the clothes, or was consent given?

5. Was it legal to submit the safe insulation and paint chips for laboratory analysis?

6. Was the charge correct? If not, what is (are) the correct charge(s)?

7. What additional evidence should have been located and seized?

References

Barnes, S. (2020, May 6). Sheriff: Multistate crime ring busted in Green Island. *Times Union*. Retrieved October 22, 2020, from www.timesunion.com/news/article/Sheriff-Multistate-crime-ring-busted-in-Green-15241603.php

Blackstone, E., Hakim, S., & Meehan, B. (2020, September). Burglary reduction and improved police performance through private alarm response. *International Review of Law and Economics, 63*. doi:10.1016/j.irle.2020.105930

Chainey, S. P., & da Silva, B. F. A. (2016). Examining the extent of repeat and near repeat victimisation of domestic burglaries in Belo Horizonte, Brazil. *Crime Science, 5*(1). doi:10.1186/s40163-016-0049-6

Federal Bureau of Investigation. (2018a). *2018 Crime Clock*. Washington, DC: Author. Retrieved October 23, 2020, from ucr.fbi.gov/crime-in-the-u.s/2018/crime-in-the-u.s.-2018/topic-pages/crime-clock

Federal Bureau of Investigation. (2018b). *Crime in the United States 2018*. Washington, DC: Author. Retrieved October 22, 2020, from ucr.fbi.gov/crime-in-the-u.s/2018/crime-in-the-u.s.-2018/

Geoghegan, S. (2009, June). Forensic DNA. *Law and Order*, pp. 49–53.

Hazbun, C. (2019, July 24). *How security guards prevent and deter crime*. Long Beach, CA: Ecamsecure. Retrieved October 22, 2020, from www.ecamsecure.com/blog/security-guards/how-security-guards-prevent-crime/

Kuhns, J. B., Blevins, K. R., & Lee, S. (2012, December). *Understanding decisions to burglarize from the offender's perspective*. Charlotte, NC: The University of North Carolina at Charlotte Department of Criminal Justice and Criminology. Retrieved October 23, 2020, from www.researchgate.net/publication/268444817_Understanding_Decisions_to_Burglarize_from_the_Offender's_Perspective

Miro, F. (2014). Routine activity theory. In *The Encyclopedia of Theoretical Criminology*. Hoboken, NJ: John Wiley & Sons. Retrieved October 23, 2020, from onlinelibrary.wiley.com/doi/epdf/10.1002/9781118517390.wbetc198

Morgan, R. E., & Oudekerk, B. A. (2019, September). *Criminal victimization, 2018*. Washington, DC: Bureau of Justice Statistics. Retrieved October 23, 2020, from www.bjs.gov /content/pub/pdf/cv18.pdf

National Institute of Justice. (2014, June 8). *Translating "Near Repeat" theory into a geospatial police strategy*. Washington, DC: Author. Retrieved October 23, 2020, from nij.ojp.gov /topics/articles/translating-near-repeat-theory-geospatial -police-strategy#citation--0

Navarro, H. (2020, May 18). 5 arrested in burglary ring that netted $1.9 million in cash, designer watches. *NBCLosAngeles.com*. Retrieved October 22, 2020, from www.nbclosangeles.com/news/local/burglary-ring-orange -san-bernardino-millions-arrests/2364957/

Ritter, N. (2008, October). DNA solves property crimes (but are we ready for that?). *NIJ Journal*, 261, 2–12. (NCJ 224084)

Roman, J. K., Reid, S., Reid, J., Chalfin, A., Adams, W., & Knight, C. (2008, April). *The DNA field experiment: Cost-effectiveness analysis of the use of DNA in the investigation of high-volume crimes*. Washington, DC: Urban Institute, Justice Policy Center Accessed June 18, 2020, from www.urban.org/sites /default/files/publication/31856/411697-The-DNA-Field -Experiment.PDF

RxPATROL. (n.d.). RxPATROL statistics. Retrieved October 24, 2020, from www.rxpatrol.com/

Schaenman, P., Horvath, A., & Hatry, H. (2012, November). *Opportunities for police cost savings without sacrificing service quality: Reducing false alarms*. Washington, DC: Urban Institute. Retrieved October 22, 2020, from www .urban.org/sites/default/files/publication/23221/412729 -opportunities-for-police-cost-savings-without-sacrificing -service-quality-reducing-false-alarms_1.pdf

Shaw, R. (2020, February 17). 02.19.20: Central Texas burglary ring arrests. *KWTX.com*. Retrieved October 22, 2020, from www.kwtx.com/content/misc/Ex-probation-officer -arrested-one-on-the-run-in-multi-county-burglary -investigation-567949111.html

Sparrow, M. K. (2014, September). Managing the boundaries between public and private policing. *New Perspectives in Policing*. Washington, DC: National Institute of Justice. (NCJ 247182). Retrieved October 22, 2020, from www.ncjrs.gov /pdffiles1/nij/247182.pdf

Weisel, D. L. (2005). *Analyzing repeat victimization*. Washington, DC: Center for Problem-Oriented Policing, Tool Guide No.4.

WGXA Digital Staff. (2020, April 30). Bibb country burglary ring bust recovers stolen electronics, vehicles, cash, and guns. *WGXA.TV*. Retrieved October 22, 2020, from wgxa .tv/news/local/bibb-county-burglary-ring-bust-recovers -stolen-electronics-vehicles-cash-and-guns

Wilson, D. B., McClure, D., & Weisburd, D. (2010, November). Does forensic DNA help to solve crime? The benefit of sophisticated answers to naïve questions. *Journal of Contemporary Criminal Justice*, 26(4), 458–469.

Zimmerman, P. R. (2014, March). The deterrence of crime through private security efforts: Theory and evidence. *International Review of Law and Economics, 37*: 66–75. doi:10.1016/j.irle.2013.06.003

Chapter 14
Larceny/Theft, Fraud, and White-Collar Crime

Chapter Outline

Larceny/Theft: An Overview

Classification of Larceny/Theft

Elements of the Crime: Larceny/Theft

Found Property

The Preliminary Investigation

Types of Larceny/Theft

Proving the Elements of the Crime of Larceny/Theft

Fraud

White-Collar Crime

A Final Note about Jurisdiction

Learning Objectives

LO1   Explain how larceny differs from burglary and robbery.

LO2   Explain the two major categories of larceny.

LO3   Identify the elements of larceny/theft.

LO4   List the common types of larceny.

LO5   Identify the elements of the crime of larceny by shoplifting.

LO6   Explain how ORC differs from shoplifting.

LO7   Explain how fraud differs from larceny/theft.

LO8   List the common means of committing fraud.

LO9   Identify the elements of the crime of larceny by debit or credit card.

LO10   List the offenses that are often included in the crime category of white-collar or economic crime.

LO11   Explain the FBI's two-pronged approach to investigating money laundering.

Jochen Tack/Alamy Stock Photo

Introduction

Frank Abagnale is a world-renowned, highly respected authority on check fraud, forgery, and embezzlement, who has, for more than three decades, served as an advisor to and instructor for the FBI. Born in 1948 in Bronxville, New York, he honed his skill and expertise on these subject matters early in life, when, at age 16, he became a pilot for Pan Am Airlines using a pilot's ID and FAA license he had forged himself. By the time he had turned 19, he was working as a pediatrician in an Atlanta hospital, and a year later, armed with a forged Harvard law degree, he had found a job as an attorney in New Orleans. For more than five years, Abagnale was one of the world's most prolific and versatile con artists, a notorious globetrotting master of impersonation, fraud, and forgery, having cashed an estimated $2.5 million in fraudulent checks in every state in the Union as well as 26 foreign countries.

He was finally arrested at age 21 in France and served time in France, Sweden, and the United States before being granted parole at age 26. The deal: he had to teach the FBI the tricks of his trade. Ever since, he has worked tirelessly to help law enforcement agencies, financial institutions, and corporations stay informed about the evolving counterfeiting, forgery, and embezzlement techniques and technology used by modern-day fraudsters. His best-selling book, *Catch Me If You Can*, was turned into film in 2002, directed by Steven Spielberg and starring Leonardo DiCaprio as Abagnale. He also cohosts an AARP podcast, *The Perfect Scam*, to share victims' stories and provide tips on how to protect against becoming a victim of fraud.

Larceny/theft is one of the eight Index crimes reported in the Federal Bureau of Investigation's (FBI) Uniform Crime Reports (UCRs). Although fraud, white-collar crime, and environmental crime are not Index crimes, they are so closely related to larceny/theft that they are included in this chapter. Furthermore, they all have elements in common and are investigated in similar ways.

Some states eliminate the distinctions between larceny, fraud, and white-collar crimes, combining them into the single crime of *theft*. However, because many states have separate offenses, this chapter discusses them separately. The distinction may be unimportant in your jurisdiction.

Larceny/Theft: An Overview

Larceny/theft is the unlawful taking, carrying, leading, or driving away of property from the possession of another. Larceny is committed through the cunning, skill, and criminal design of the professional thief or as a crime of opportunity committed by the rank amateur. The FBI notes, "These crimes are characterized by deceit, concealment, or violation of trust, and are not dependent upon the application or threat of physical force or violence" (Federal Bureau of Investigation [FBI], 2011). The adage that "there is a little larceny in everyone" has considerable truth. Although some thefts result from revenge or spite, the motive for most larcenies is the same for the professional and the amateur thief—monetary gain: either actual cash or articles that can be converted to cash or personal use.

| **LO1** | Explain how larceny differs from burglary and robbery. |

> Both larceny and burglary are crimes against property, but larceny, unlike burglary, does not involve illegally entering a structure. Larceny differs from robbery in that no force or threat of force is involved.

Reported larceny/thefts exceed the combined total of all other Index crimes. Data from the FBI indicate that an estimated 72.5% of all property crimes in 2018 were larceny/thefts (FBI, 2018b). An estimated 5.2 million thefts occurred nationwide, a 5.4% decrease from 2017 and a 17.7% decrease from 2009. The FBI's *Crime Clock* (2018a) reports that one larceny/theft occurred every 6.1 seconds in 2018. The National Crime Victimization Survey (NCVS) reported 10,329,210 thefts in 2018, a rate of 82.7 per 1,000 households (Morgan & Oudekerk, 2019). Only 23.7% of theft victimizations were reported to police in 2018 (Morgan & Oudekerk, 2019). The average value of property stolen was $1,153 per offense, for an estimated $6.0 billion in lost property in 2018. Nationwide, law enforcement cleared 18.9% of all reported larceny/thefts in 2018 (FBI, 2018b).

Classification of Larceny/Theft

Most statutes have two major categories of larceny/theft based on the total value of the property stolen.

| **LO2** | Explain the two major categories of larceny. |

> The categories of larceny/theft are **grand larceny**, a felony; and **petty larceny**, a misdemeanor. Which category the crime falls under is based on the value of the property stolen.

In many states, the amount of theft that predicates grand larceny is $400 or more; any lesser amount is petty (petit) larceny. Check the laws in your jurisdiction for the dollar value that distinguishes petty and grand larceny. It is important to know whether the crime is a misdemeanor or a felony before proceeding with the investigation.

Elements of the Crime: Larceny/Theft

The crime of larceny/theft takes many forms, but the basic elements of the offense are similar in the statutes of every state.

> **LO3** Identify the elements of larceny/theft.
>
> The elements of the crime of larceny/theft are
>
> - The felonious stealing, taking, carrying, leading, or driving away,
> - of another's personal goods, property, or services,
> - valued above (grand) or below (petty) a specified amount,
> - with the intent to permanently deprive the owner of the property or goods.

Felonious Stealing, Taking, Carrying, Leading, or Driving Away

This element requires an unlawful, wrongful, or felonious removal of the property; that is, the property is removed by any manner of stealing. Taking items such as fuel and electricity is also included in this element. Withholding property is a form of larceny by a failure to ever return, or properly account for, the property or to deliver the property to the rightful owner when it is due. Failure to pay a debt is *not* larceny; civil remedies are sought for this type of conduct.

The Personal Goods, Property, or Services of Another

Goods or *property* refers to all forms of tangible property, real or personal. It includes valuable documents; electricity, gas, water, and heat supplied by municipalities or public utility companies; and domestic animals such as cats, dogs, and livestock. It also includes property in which the accused has a co-ownership, lien, pledge, bailment, lease, or other subordinate interest. Larceny laws also cover cases in which the property of a partnership is converted to one partner's personal use adverse to the other partner's rights, except when the accused and the victim are husband and wife.

Services are a type of intangible property that others must pay to access or use. For example, the chair lift at a ski resort requires a lift ticket to use. Movie theaters require movie goers to purchase a ticket if they wish to view the "property." Using the chair lift or getting in to see a movie without first purchasing the ticket is an illegal taking or theft of that service.

In the definition of larceny/theft, *another* refers to an individual, a government, a corporation, or an organization. This element refers to the true owner or the one authorized to control the property or service. Care assignment, personal custody, or some degree of legal control is evidence of possession. In numerous cases, ownership has been questioned. Ownership usually designates the true owner or the person who has superior rights at the time of the theft. The owner must support the charge of larceny; otherwise, there is no prosecution.

Of a Value Above or Below a Specified Amount

Value determines whether the offense is grand or petty larceny. *Value* refers to the market value at the time of the theft. Value is determined by replacement cost, legitimate market value, value listed in government property catalogs, fair market value, or reasonable estimates.

If the property is restored to the owner, value means the cost-equivalent of the property's use or the damage it sustained, whichever is greater, during the time the owner was deprived of its possession. However, this cannot exceed the original value declared.

If several items are stolen in a single crime, the value of *all* items combined determines the value of the loss, even if the property belonged to more than one owner. Identical items stolen from different larceny locations are not combined but are treated as separate offenses.

With the Intent to Permanently Deprive the Owner of the Property or Goods

Intent either exists at the time the property was taken or is formed afterward. The person may have intended only to borrow the property but then decided to keep it permanently. Intent is usually the most difficult element to prove. Establish ownership through documents of purchase, statements describing how the property was possessed, the length of time of possession, and details of the delegation of care and control to another by the true owner.

In an effort to prevent theft, many companies hire security personnel to monitor surveillance cameras located both inside and outside the premises.

Motortion Films/Shutterstock.com

Because of its frequency, much police time is devoted to larceny, and individual merchants and private security forces are also involved. Millions of dollars in losses go unreported each month. Those that are reported are usually for collecting insurance rather than in the hope of recovering the property or clearing the case.

Found Property

In most states, keeping or selling property lost by the owner is a form of theft. Although the finder has possession of the property, it is not legal possession. Thieves apprehended with stolen property often claim to have found it—an invalid excuse. A reasonable effort must be made to find the owner of the property—for example, by making inquiries, advertising in a newspaper, or posting a notice online. The owner, if located, must pay the cost of such inquiries before the property is returned. If the owner is not located after reasonable attempts are made to do so and after a time specified by law, the finder of the property can legally retain possession of it.

The Preliminary Investigation

Investigating larceny/theft is similar to investigating a burglary, except that in a larceny/theft, even less physical evidence is available because no illegal or forcible entry occurred. Physical evidence might include empty cartons or containers, empty hangers, objects left at the scene, footprints, and fingerprints.

Do not give the complainant or victim the impression that the investigation of the reported theft is unimportant. If there is little hope of recovering the property or finding the thief, inform the complainant of this, but only after you obtain all the facts.

Types of Larceny/Theft

The UCR for 2018 indicates the relative frequency of each type of larceny (Figure 14.1). The growing problem of identity theft is discussed later in the chapter.

> **LO4** List the common types of larceny.
>
> Common types of larceny are pocket picking and purse snatching; cell phone theft; bicycle theft; theft from motor vehicles; mail theft; retail shrinkage, including employee theft, shoplifting, and organized retail crime (ORC); jewelry theft; art theft; numismatic theft, including coins, metals, and paper money; agricultural theft; fish and wildlife theft; and cargo theft.

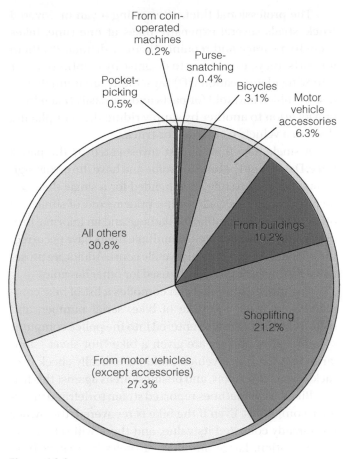

Figure 14.1
Relative frequency of different types of larceny/theft.

*Due to rounding, the percentages may not add to 100.0.

Source: Crime in the United States, 2018. U.S. Department of Justice—Federal Bureau of Investigation, 2018. ucr.fbi.gov/crime-in-the-u.s/2018/crime-in-the-u.s.-2018/topic-pages/larceny-theft

Pickpockets and Purse Snatchers

Pickpockets are difficult to apprehend because the victim must identify the thief. This proves challenging, if not impossible, unless the thief is observed by someone else, is caught in the act, or the crime was captured on surveillance video. The purse opener and purse snatcher are modern versions of the pickpocket. These thieves use force if necessary but generally rely instead on their skills of deviousness and stealth to avoid the use of force and evade identification. These types of thefts are sometimes called *distraction thefts* because of how the offender gains access to the victim's property. The two necessary elements of this crime are a distraction followed by an extraction, the actual theft. Lost wallets and purses, often the work of the pickpocket, are often not reported as thefts because the victims do not realize that theft has occurred.

Sporting events, New Year's Eve parties, parades, rock concerts, fairs and festivals, public transportation, and commuter trains present ideal situations for the pickpocket, full of potential victims in tight, distracted crowds.

Behavior that may indicate a pickpocket at work is "looping," in which a suspect exits at one train or bus door and reboards at another. Another common tactic is for pickpockets to immerse themselves in a crowd getting onto a bus or train and take advantage of the jostling body contact that almost always occurs during a boarding rush. Watch for "passengers" who join the crowd rushing toward the vehicle doorway but then, at the last minute, fail to board.

Purse snatching may be a larceny/theft or a robbery depending on whether force or threat of force is used. There are two distinct types of purse snatches. One type occurs when a victim is seated at a bus stop, outdoor restaurant, gambling casino, or similar public place and sets a purse, bag, or like item on the seat or floor and a thief grabs the property and runs off with it. Because this act lacks the element of use of force, it qualifies as a larceny/theft. The other type occurs when a victim is clutching a bag or purse tightly, has a purse strap over her shoulder, or has used some similar means of securing the property and force is used by the thief to seize it, qualifying the act as a robbery. As a general rule, investigators should determine whether the victim experienced any sensation of force being used because any force, no matter how slight, would satisfy the element of robbery. The statement of the victim on this point will be a critical factor for the prosecutor to determine whether to charge robbery or larceny/theft.

Obtain from the victim a description of what was stolen and its value. Ask if the victim recalls being jostled or distracted momentarily, and, if so, obtain complete details. Keep careful records of pickpockets and purse snatchers, as often they are caught.

Cell Phone Theft

According to the most recent available data from the Federal Communications Commission (2018), more than 3 million Americans were victims of smartphone theft in 2018. Theft of cell phones was introduced in Chapter 12 because of the often confrontational nature of this type of crime, as when a suspect brazenly swipes a phone from the hands of a user (apple picking). However, cell phones can also be stolen from cars, desks, lockers, backpacks, tables—any place the device is set down or stored out of sight from its owner. According to one report, the great majority (69.1%) of phones are simply misplaced, with no active "theft" from a person having occurred—the finder simply keeps the phone (Prey, 2018). The next more common ways phones are lost are from pickpockets (11.0%), home invasions (7.6%), and robbery (6.8%). Car break-ins and business break-ins each account for roughly 2.8% of cell phone thefts.

Depending on how new it is, a stolen cell phone can fetch between $100 and $300 if sold domestically and even more if sold overseas (Randhawa & Richey, 2020; Schulte, 2018).

As discussed in Chapter 12, the development of "kill switch" technology, allowing users to remotely deactivate their devices and turn them into virtual "bricks," appears to be having a positive impact on the smartphone theft epidemic, with jurisdictions in both the United States and the United Kingdom reporting significant decreases in smartphone thefts since newer devices incorporating this feature have hit the market. For example, New York City reported a 16% drop in general cell phone thefts and a 25% decrease in iPhone-specific crimes from January 2013 to December 2014, and San Francisco reported a 27% decrease in cell phone robberies and a 40% drop in iPhone thefts over the same period (Mlot, 2015). Similarly, officials in London report that, since September 2013—which was when Apple launched its new Activation Lock Feature with iOS7 that requires an Apple ID and password to reactive a device after it has been remotely wiped—the number of cell phones stolen has been reduced by half, resulting in 20,000 fewer victims each year.

Bicycle Theft

As bicycles have increased in popularity, so has bicycle theft. According to the website of Project 529™, which acquired the National Bike Registry in 2017 and merged it with its 529 Garage™ anti-theft bicycle service, more than 2 million bicycles, worth an estimated $500 million, are stolen each year in the United States (Project529, n.d.). Many stolen bikes are involved in secondary crimes, serving as modern "getaway vehicles" for criminals. Experienced thieves can steal a locked bike in less than 20 seconds. And although nearly 50% of all stolen bicycles are recovered every year by law enforcement, only 5% are returned to their owners because most bikes are unregistered.

Bicycles are most frequently stolen from schoolyards, college campuses, sidewalk parking racks, driveways, and residential yards. Juveniles are responsible for most thefts, although some professional bike theft rings operate interstate, even exporting stolen bicycles out of the country. Stolen bikes are used for transportation; are sold on the street, at flea markets, or to bike stores; and are disposed of through fences. On the street, the value of a stolen bicycle is approximately 5% to 10% of the bicycle's original retail value, with an inverse relationship between value and percentage worth on the street (Project529, n.d.). In other words, less expensive bikes are resold for a higher percentage of their original price than are top-of-the-line bikes. In some bicycle thefts, the crime is grand larceny because of the high value of the stolen bike.

The professional thief, often using a van or covered truck, steals several expensive bikes at one time, takes them to a garage and repaints them or dismantles them for parts. Bicycles are easy to disguise by painting over or removing identification (ID) tags. Many are immediately disassembled and sold for parts and are easily taken from one location to another by simply riding them or placing them in a vehicle trunk, van, or truck.

A single bike theft is best investigated by the patrol force. Determine the bicycle's value and have the owner sign a complaint. A juvenile apprehended for a single theft can be prosecuted, especially with a prior record of similar or other offenses. Restitution for damage and an informal probation are usually initiated. If multiple thefts have occurred, the offender usually goes to juvenile court. Adults are prosecuted by the same procedures used for other larcenies.

The investigative division compiles a list of bike complaints organized by make of bike, serial number, and color. Bike thefts are also entered into the police computer system. Patrol officers are given a bike "hot sheet" similar to that for stolen vehicles and periodically check bike racks at parks, schools, and business areas against this list.

Bikes are sometimes reported stolen to defraud insurance companies. Even if the bike is recovered, the owner has already collected its value, and there will seldom be a prosecution. Large numbers of thefts in a short time may indicate an interstate ring has moved into the community. These rings use covered trucks to transport bicycles from the area, making recovery almost impossible. However, when interstate or international bicycle theft rings attempt to dispose of their stolen inventory, their activity may become identifiable. Identification of bicycles is difficult because of failure to have a registration system or to use one that exists; the complex method of providing serial numbers; and the fact that stolen bikes are often altered, dismantled, repainted, and resold.

Theft from Motor Vehicles

One of the most common complaints received by police departments involves theft from a parked motor vehicle. According to FBI data, more than 1.1 million incidents, or more than one-quarter (27.3%) of all reported larceny/thefts in 2018, were from motor vehicles, with an average loss value of $994 per theft; another 6.3% were thefts of motor vehicle accessories (FBI, 2018b). In Washington, D.C., an average of 80 items were reported stolen each day in 2018 from parked cars, and the annual loss included nearly 6,000 stolen purses and handbags (MacFarlane, Yarborough, Jones, & Piper, 2019).

A type of theft increasing in popularity among teens and young adults is called **car shopping**—the theft of

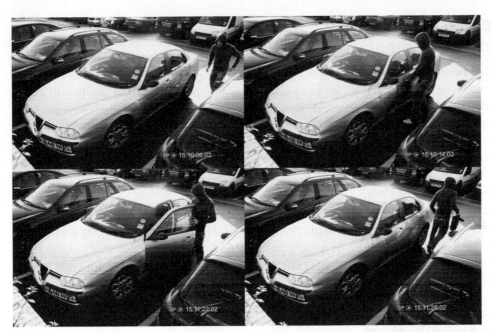

Closed-circuit video surveillance captures footage of a thief stealing from a parked car.
Image Source/Alamy Stock Photo

items from unlocked cars. Because stealth and speed are critical features of this type of crime, offenders do not want to call attention to the sound of breaking glass, take the time to force open a car door, or carry around tools needed to forcibly enter a vehicle. They target unlocked cars and small, portable valuables, such as loose change, CDs, sunglasses, chargers, dash-mounted GPS devices, and other vehicle-related accessories. Theft of motor vehicles themselves is the topic of Chapter 15.

Mail Theft

In the quest for new and easier ways to steal money, thieves may target sites used daily as repositories for hundreds of thousands of dollars, sites often left unsupervised for hours—mailboxes. More than 523 million pieces of mail travel across the country every day (United States Postal Service [USPS], 2014). On certain days of the month, with tremendous predictability, many households receive government assistance checks. Other mailboxes hold numerous applications for credit cards or the actual cards themselves, which thieves can take and use to commit identity theft.

Mailboxes are used to receive money as well as to submit payments. Millions of people leave their bills, accompanied by checks, for pickup in their mailboxes. Thieves known as **flaggers** go around neighborhoods targeting mailboxes with their flags up, searching for envelopes containing checks and other forms of payment. Thieves may also raid the large blue mailboxes used by people who may not trust leaving their own flag

up. Thieves also steal mail from postal trucks, apartment mailbox panels, co-op mailing racks, and neighborhood delivery and collection box units, looking for checks, credit card applications, bank account statements, greeting cards (which often contain checks, cash, or gift cards), and tax returns (for useful banking information). Mail carriers have also been known to steal items from the mail.

Once thieves have checks, they may call the bank posing as a legitimate business to confirm that the funds are available, or they may simply go ahead and alter the checks, assuming the checks will clear. The thieves protect the check signer's signature using a "liquid skin" coating and then use another solution to strip off the remaining ink, thus enabling them to rewrite the check payable to another source and for another amount.

Mail theft is a felony-level federal offense and is investigated by the U.S. Postal Service (USPS) Postal Inspectors. Postal Inspectors are federal law enforcement agents who investigate and enforce more than 200 federal postal-related laws. In Fiscal Year 2018, USPS Postal Inspectors initiated 1,356 investigations of mail theft by nonemployees, 2,487 arrests were made in connection to mail theft investigations, and 2,101 convictions were obtained relating to theft and possession of stolen mail (United States Postal Inspection Service, 2018). The U.S. Postal Inspection Service also maintains a state-of-the-art National Forensic Laboratory in Dulles, Virginia, staffed by highly trained forensic scientists and technical specialists who play a key role in identifying, apprehending, prosecuting, and convicting individuals responsible for postal-related criminal offenses.

Retail Shrinkage: Employee Theft, Shoplifting, and Organized Retail Crime

Shrinkage refers to the unexplained or unauthorized loss of inventory, merchandise, cash, or any other asset from a retail establishment due to employee theft, shoplifting, ORC, administrative errors, and vendor fraud. The *National Retail Security Survey*, an ongoing collaborative effort between the National Retail Federation (NRF) and the University of Florida that began in 1991, reports that U.S. retailers lost $48.9 billion, or 1.44% of sales, in 2016 (Hollinger & Moraca, 2018). The greatest source of shrinkage was shoplifting and ORC (36.5%), followed by employee theft (30.0%). Other losses were from administrative errors (21.3% of shrinkage) and vendor fraud (5.4% of shrinkage). The survey also found that ORC was gaining more awareness within the retail industry.

Employee Theft. Although many assume that the vast majority of a retail company's shrinkage is caused by external actors who shoplift, a significant proportion of retail losses every year are internal, committed by employees. In 2016, dishonest employees accounted for an average loss of $1,922.80 per act, an amount nearly $400 higher than the previous two years (Hollinger & Moraca, 2018). According to one survey, three-fourths of employees admitted to having stolen from their employer at least once, and 37.5% said they had stolen at least twice from their employer (Statistic Brain Research Institute, 2018; Boehmer, 2016). Common rationalizations given for employee theft include, "Businesses don't have feelings. They didn't get hurt." or "If my company is going to cut my benefits, mistreat me, or not give me the raise I deserve, then it owes me." (Wilkie, 2019; Boehmer, 2016).

Red flags that put an employee at higher risk for committing theft from their employer or that might indicate active theft is occurring include:

- Living beyond their means

- Financial difficulties

- Recent divorce or family problems

- Negative performance evaluations

- Fear of job loss

- An unusually close association with a vendor or customer

- Excessive control issues or unwillingness to share duties

- A general "wheeler-dealer" attitude involving shrewd or unscrupulous behavior

(Association of Certified Fraud Examiners, 2018; Wilkie, 2019; Pofeldt, 2017)

One recommendation for reducing employee theft is to keep the more expensive items under security lock and to have frank discussions with employees regarding the problem. Employees who are aware of management's policy regarding employee theft are less likely to steal. Some companies attempt to eliminate potential employee thieves by informing job applicants that a drug test is required, even if it is not. This announcement alone may weed out applicants who have a drug habit and therefore are more prone to steal to support it.

Shoplifting. Shoplifting, also known as *boosting*, involves taking items from retail stores without paying for them. It is usually committed by potential customers in the store during normal business hours. Shoplifting does *not* include thefts from warehouses or factories, or thefts by employees.

Shoplifting has increased with modern merchandising techniques that display goods for sale, remove barriers between customers and merchandise, and permit potential buyers to pick up and handle goods. Most items shoplifted are taken from the main floor, where it is easier to leave the store. Shoplifting is rising at many retail chains, and a contributing cause is the sputtering economy. In the past, much of shoplifting was done to support a drug habit, but in the current economy, everyday items, such as groceries, are being stolen.

Security technology is being employed to limit losses caused by shoplifting. For example, electronic article surveillance (EAS) uses small security tags applied to high-theft merchandise that alert retailers when shoplifters try to take stolen items through electronic sensors at exit doors. Systems using radio frequency identification (RFID) are also becoming more popular among retailers.

Closed-circuit television (CCTV) has become a standard security tool to curb shoplifting and help in the apprehension and prosecution processes. Despite advancing technology, the apprehension rate for shoplifters remains extremely low compared with the total number of shoplifting offenses committed.

Most apprehensions are by private security officers or loss prevention (LP) personnel working for department stores and shopping centers or by floorwalkers or supervisory personnel. A store that detects and apprehends a shoplifter can take several courses of action. Managers sometimes call the police for the chastening effect it will have on the shoplifter, particularly if the suspect is a juvenile, but if the property is recovered, store management often declines to sign a formal complaint. If a complaint is signed, the decision to press formal criminal charges rests solely with the county, state, or federal attorney who would prosecute the case. Another avenue may be civil litigation. However, this route can be relatively expensive when compared with the value of the item(s) shoplifted. Also, a store may opt to not pursue civil remedies if restitution is not ordered in a criminal case.

If a complaint is made by a merchant or merchant's employee, officers may arrest a suspected shoplifter without a warrant if reasonable cause exists for believing that the person has attempted or actually committed shoplifting. Police cannot request or encourage store personnel to question suspects because this effectively makes the store personnel an agent of the officer. Under such circumstances, the suspect would be entitled to *Miranda* and all other legal rights. Stores may have policies and procedures that direct LP personnel to question suspects. The LP officer's report can and should accompany the police officer's report if the case proceeds civilly or criminally.

Elements of Larceny by Shoplifting.

The elements of shoplifting are very similar to those required for general larceny.

LO5	Identify the elements of the crime of larceny by shoplifting.

The elements of larceny by shoplifting are

- Intentionally taking or carrying away, transferring, stealing, concealing, or retaining possession of merchandise or altering the price of the merchandise, without the consent of the merchant;

- with intent to permanently deprive the merchant of possession or of the full purchase price.

Altering the price of an item is considered larceny.

Early laws required that a shoplifter leave a store before an apprehension could be made. However, many laws have been changed to permit apprehension after the suspect has passed the last cashier's counter in the store for the particular level or department. The farther the suspect is from the normal place of payment, the greater the degree of intent shown to permanently deprive the merchant of the item. Corporate policies vary on the point at which they consider an act to be one of shoplifting.

Because intent is absent, it is not a crime for a person to walk out of a store after simply forgetting to pay for an item. This is a common problem for individuals who suffer from Alzheimer's disease and some other types of mental impairment. Such people may forget that they have picked up an item, may forget to pay for it, or may honestly believe that they have paid for it when they have not. Such incidents require officers to exhibit

patience and excellent communication skills in resolving the situation.

Because shoplifting can be either petty or grand larceny, a misdemeanor or a felony, the value of the property must be established. If the shoplifter is placed under arrest, the stolen item should be recovered and retained as evidence. Whether the individual is prosecuted depends on the individual's attitude, the policy of the store and the police department, the value of the property taken, and how many of the legal requirements for prosecution are fulfilled. Evidence to support shoplifting or altering a price requires an eyewitness or proof that the item could not have been removed except by the person charged. The property must be carried away or removed but not necessarily to outside the store. The manager or clerk should identify the property and show proof of the store's ownership.

Proving the intent to permanently deprive is the most difficult problem in investigating shoplifting. This intent is shown by the shoplifter's actions from the time the item was stolen until the arrest was made. Stores are legally within their rights to recover items taken from a store if there is no proof of purchase. This does not mean the person is guilty of shoplifting. It may be impossible to prove intent to steal.

If a store manager wants to prosecute, review the store's reports to determine whether a crime has been committed. If it has, place the shoplifter under arrest, search them for additional property, and take them to the police station for processing. Officers should also check the items the suspect is currently wearing, as accessories, jackets, and shoes are often stolen by wearing them out of the store. The store personnel making the arrest must sign a complaint. Most shoplifters never reach the stage of arrest and release to the police. When it does occur, encourage store cooperation because good arrests by store personnel aid convictions and can deter shoplifting in the particular store.

Overcrowded courts have become a problem to retailers who want to prosecute for shoplifting. Prosecutors have difficulty obtaining convictions. Many states have passed statutes providing for civil fines instead of or in combination with criminal penalties. Retailers are dissatisfied with criminal prosecution because of the delays, low conviction rate, and lack of restitution for the lost property. The civil approach permits the retailer to sue in small claims court, even in cases in which the offender is not convicted of a crime. Penalties under civil action range from $50 to $500, or in some cases actual damages plus five times the value.

In addition to contributing to the trade in and abuse of drugs, shoplifting has been recognized as a way for terrorist and organized crime (OC) groups to generate revenue.

Organized Retail Crime. Organized Retail Crime (ORC), alternately called *organized retail theft*, is an umbrella term used to describe large-scale retail theft and fraud activity by organized groups of **boosters**, or professional shoplifters, and includes a variety of retail crimes such as gift card fraud, receipt fraud, ticket switching, and cargo theft, among others (Finklea, 2012). The sources of such illegally obtained merchandise, cargo, cash, or cash equivalents (e.g., gift cards) include not only retailers but manufacturers and distributors as well.

LO6 Explain how ORC differs from shoplifting.

The fundamental difference between ORC and shoplifting is that amateur shoplifters tend to steal merchandise for their own personal use, whereas boosters are professional thieves who steal products from retail establishments and other venues and resell them to fences The fences, in turn, sell the boosted goods at a variety of venues—online marketplaces, pawnshops, swap meets, and flea markets—for a fraction of the retail cost.

Although ORC is not a federal crime, Congress has defined it for data collection purposes and, through the Violence against Women and Department of Justice Reauthorization Act of 2005, directed the Attorney General and FBI to establish both a task force to combat it as well as a clearinghouse within the private sector to facilitate information sharing between retailers and law enforcement. Federal legislation defines organized retail crime as

- violating a state ban against shoplifting or retail merchandise theft—if the quantities of items stolen are of the amount that would not normally be purchased for personal use or consumption—and stealing for the purposes of reselling the items or reentering them into commerce;

- receiving, possessing, concealing, bartering, selling, transporting, or disposing of any property that is known to have been taken in the violation outlined above; or

- coordinating, organizing, or recruiting persons to undertake either of the two violations outlined above.

(P.L. 109-162, §1105, codified at 28 U.S.C. §509 note)

The FBI considers ORC a "gateway crime" that often leads investigators to major crime rings that are using the illicit revenue generated by retail theft to fund other illegal enterprises, such as organized crime activities, health care fraud, and terrorism (FBI, 2011). According to the *Organized Retail Crime Survey*, 97% of all retailers reported being victims of organized retail crime activity in 2019 (National Retail Federation, 2019). The FBI has estimated U.S. retailers lose $30 billion annually to ORC (FBI, *Organized Crime*, n.d.).

ORC is a relatively low-risk, high-reward crime. The thefts usually involve specific small, high-priced items that have a high resale value on the black market. According to the *2019 Organized Retail Crime Survey*, the top stolen items by OCR gangs are designer clothes, infant formula, razors, designer handbags, laundry detergent, denim pants, energy drinks, allergy medicine, high-end liquor, teeth whitening strips, pain relievers, cigarettes, deodorant, laptops/tables, and weight loss pills (National Retail Federation, 2019). Once an item is boosted, it can be converted into cash by being:

- Fenced at a physical location (e.g., pawnshop, flea market) for roughly 30% of the original retail value

- e-fenced (listed and sold online through auction sites or other Web pages) for as much as 70% of retail value. More than half (51%) of retailers have found their stolen merchandise or gift cards being sold online.

- Fraudulently refunded by returning the merchandise to a retail store for 100% of the retail value plus tax (if applicable)

(NRF, 2019; Finklea, 2012)

One sophisticated and prolific Middle Eastern ORC ring is estimated to have stolen and fenced $10 million worth of merchandise each year from 2008 to 2012 before a multiagency investigation between the FBI, the Houston Police Department, and the Harris County Sheriff's Office, with assistance from victim merchants, shut them down (FBI, 2013). The local ringleader, Sameh Khaled Danhach, a native of Lebanon and a legal permanent resident of the United States, recruited boosters from among undocumented Mexican, Central American, and South American aliens residing in the United States. Members of this crew would travel around Texas and other states, often in cars rented by Danhach or his associates, boosting merchandise from retailers and pharmacies. When authorities executed a search warrant of Danhach's Houston warehouse in March 2012, they found more than $300,000 worth of stolen over-the-counter medications, shampoos, and baby formula, among other items, as well as financial ledgers documenting that from August 2011 to January 2012, Danhach had paid $1.8 million for stolen merchandise and sold it for $2.8 million—netting $1 million profit over six months.

A Web-based national database called the Law Enforcement Retail Partnership Network, or LERPnet, is a public to private partnership between the NRF, the Retail Industry Leaders Association, and the FBI. The latest version of the technology, LERPnet 2.0, provides a data sharing platform for reporting and analyzing retail crime. Through an annual subscription, retailers are allowed to share information with each other and with law enforcement, enabling them to track incidents and assist in the effort to apprehend members of criminal networks.

Jewelry Theft

According to the FBI, the jewelry industry loses more than $100 million each year to jewelry and gem theft. Most often stolen by sophisticated professional thieves, jewelry is also the target of armed robbers and burglars. Jewel thieves know the value of jewels, that they are extremely difficult to identify once removed from their settings, and that the rewards are higher for the amount of risk involved than in other types of larceny. Thieves also have ready outlets for disposition.

Most jewelry thefts are from vehicles owned by jewelry salespeople, who typically carry thousands of dollars in jewels, and from private individuals known to be careless about the security of their jewelry. Jewel thieves also operate in stores, distracting the salesperson and then substituting a cheap facsimile for expensive jewelry. Jewel thieves tend to operate interstate and to use locally known fences. Thieves use many ingenious methods to steal and hide jewelry.

The Jeweler's Security Alliance (JSA) published an alert in July 2005 to inform retail jewelry shop owners of a new trend in jewel theft—burglars entering a store overnight via the roof with the intention of carrying out an armed robbery when employees arrive at work the next morning (recall the *morning glory robbery* discussion from Chapter 12).

Because jewel thieves operate interstate, the FBI becomes involved. The local FBI office maintains files of known jewel thieves and their last known operations; their pictures, descriptions, and modus operandi (MOs); and information about whether they are in or out of prison. Therefore, investigators should always inform the FBI of jewel thefts, even without immediate evidence of interstate operation.

Since 1992, the FBI's Jewelry and Gem (JAG) Program has helped local law enforcement investigators by providing a sophisticated and multijurisdictional response to these types of thefts (FBI, *Jewelry*, n.d.). FBI jurisdiction is attained under several sections of Title 18 of the U.S. Code, two of which are Sections 2314 and 2315, known collectively as the Interstate Transportation of Stolen Property (ITSP). These two statutes "prohibit the transportation in interstate or foreign commerce of any goods of the value of $5,000 or more where the goods are known to have been stolen, converted or taken by fraud. These statutes also prohibit the receipt and sale of such known stolen goods." Mailing packages that contain illegally obtained jewels to another state also constitutes interstate operation.

Investigating jewelry theft is the same as for any other larceny. To obtain physical evidence, search the crime scene as you would in a burglary. Obtain the names of people in neighboring rooms at motels and hotels. Interview employees and other possible witnesses. Review the victim's account of the theft. Obtain a complete description of the jewelry, the value of each item, and the amount of insurance carried. Contact informants and have them be on the alert for information about the thieves and the location of the stolen items.

Art Theft

The FBI reports that the theft, fraud, looting, and trafficking across state and international lines of art and cultural property results in billions of dollars in losses every year (FBI, *Art Theft*, n.d.). This offense usually comes to the attention of law enforcement through an art gallery's report of a burglary or theft. In other instances, art objects are recovered during the investigation of another crime, or the theft is reported by another police agency. The stolen objects are frequently held for a long time and are then sold or moved coast-to-coast or internationally for disposition.

Art theft is an international problem. To cope with the problems resulting from the interstate and international nature of these thefts, the FBI created the National Stolen Art File (NSAF) in 1979. Administered through the FBI's Criminal Investigative Division, Violent Crimes and Major Offenders Section, Major Theft/Transportation Crimes Unit, the NSAF provides a computerized index of stolen art and cultural property as reported to the FBI by law enforcement agencies throughout the United States and internationally. For an object to be eligible for entry into the NSAF, it must meet these criteria:

- The object must be uniquely identifiable and have historical or artistic significance. This includes fine arts, decorative arts, antiquities, Asian art, Islamic art, Native American art, ethnographic objects, archaeological material, textiles, books and manuscripts, clocks and watches, coins, stamps, musical instruments, and scientific instruments.

- The object must be valued at least $2,000, or less if associated with a major crime.

- The request must come through a law enforcement agency accompanied by a physical description of the object, a photograph of the object if available, and a copy of any police reports or other information relevant to the investigation.

Thefts of valuable art should be reported to the FBI and to the International Criminal Police Organization (INTERPOL), which also has an international stolen art file.

Few police officers have training in identifying art, so they should conduct only the normal burglary, theft, or fraud investigation. Then an authenticity check of the art object should be conducted by the FBI and national art dealers. People who own art objects rarely have adequate descriptions or photos of each piece and the pieces rarely have identification numbers. Investigators should submit to the FBI all known information concerning the theft and a photograph of the art if available.

The FBI's Art Crime Team (ACT) consists of 20 special agents working in major art markets around the country, and supported by three special trial attorneys for prosecutions. The field agents are art savvy and can tell a Monet from a Manet; know the dealers, appraisers, collectors, curators, and auction houses; are well versed in the art markets; and are knowledgeable about the unique laws that apply. Art theft cases the FBI has handled in recent years include:

- January 2004: The return of a Civil War sword stolen from the U.S. Naval Academy Museum in 1931.

- February 2005: The return of eight ancient stone seals looted from Iraq during the aftermath of Saddam Hussein's fall.

- June 2009: The return of more than 1,500 stolen Italian artifacts discovered in a deceased Chicago man's home, including a 1662 doctoral diploma; a book preface written by Benito Mussolini; various manuscripts and writings by kings, emperors, and popes; thousands of books dating from the 17th and 18th centuries; and numerous religious artifacts and relics, including a shoe worn by a clergyman and about 100 terra cotta heads given as offerings to the Roman Catholic Church.

- July 2012: The recovery of a rare first edition of the *Book of Mormon*, printed in 1830 and valued at $100,000.

- October 2016: The arrest of a man who stole at least 40 pieces of art in Maryland from an art collector and dealer and transported them across state lines to sell them. The 42-year-old man admitted to stealing paintings, sculptures, and etchings between June and November 2014. In June 2017, he was sentenced to 12 months in prison and ordered to pay $92,240 in restitution.

Numismatic Theft: Coins, Metals, and Paper Money

Coin collections are typically stolen during commercial and residential burglaries. Obtain the exact description of the coins, the condition, any defects, scratches, dye breaks, how they were jacketed, and any other identifying information. The condition of coins determines their value; a coin in mint condition may be worth twice the value of a coin in poor condition. Stolen coins may be taken from one coast to the other for disposition. Large coin shows are held throughout the year in larger cities, usually at convention centers or hotels. If interstate transportation is suspected, notify the FBI.

Metals such as gold, copper, silver, bronze, and aluminum are valuable. Copper is obtained from electrical and telephone lines or from storage yards of these companies. Copper thieves have posed as utility or construction workers, outfitted in hard hats and reflective vests as they strip spools of wire from light poles or construction sites. Thieves have been known to cut down telephone lines and to strip electrical lines in remote areas.

Thieves may also take advantage of natural disaster sites. For example, following Hurricane Katrina, an Energy Department inspection reported that the tons of scrap copper that should have been found throughout the wreckage of buildings and fallen power lines across Louisiana and other affected areas of the Gulf Coast had "simply vanished" (Johnson, 2007). Everyday, common metal items, such as aluminum siding, air conditioning units, copper piping, manhole covers, bronze grave markers, and household appliances, are commonly involved in theft.

As mentioned in Chapter 13, data sharing platforms, such as ScrapTheftAlert, help facilitate communication between law enforcement and the scrap metal industry in an effort to detect and prosecute the resale of stolen materials such as copper, brass, and other base and semi-precious metals. Many states have passed legislation requiring the implementation of statewide databases, similar to the automated pawn system, requiring documentation for transactions involving the purchase or sale of scrap metal.

Agricultural Theft

In certain areas of the country, agricultural theft is an increasing problem that requires investigation. Agricultural theft rings are targeting a variety of items, including ginseng in Michigan, irrigation valves in Washington, anhydrous ammonia fertilizer in Minnesota and Ohio, Japanese radishes in Hawaii, and nuts and citrus in California. Such crimes have also targeted timber, cactus, livestock, farm equipment, and chemicals.

Timber Theft. The U.S. Forestry Service estimates $100 million in lumber is stolen annually through illegal logging. Tree "rustlers" harvest burls, the large gnarly root at the base of walnut trees. Burls can weigh as much as 2,000 pounds and are used to make fine woodwork. Tree "tippers" harvest the tips of pine trees to make into wreaths.

A timber theft crime scene will usually contain traceable evidence, such as tire tracks, stumps, and other items the thief may have discarded or accidentally left behind. As part of a stolen timber investigation, investigators should know how the timber might be used. For example, Douglas fir is harvested for firewood, and cedar for shake shingles and fence posts. Investigators can then contact area mills and timber buyers to obtain information that might help them apprehend the thief.

Cactus. As communities have cropped up in the desert Southwest, the demand for landscape cactus has soared and poachers have found a lucrative business in stealing these prickly plants. The theft of cactus has become such a problem in some areas of Arizona, Texas, and other Western states that special police units have been formed to crack down on the crime. Some jurisdictions, such as Lake Mead, Nevada, have gone as far as to implant computer ID chips in certain species of cactus to be able to track them if they go missing.

As with a timber theft, a cactus theft crime scene will likely contain tire tracks, shoe imprints, and perhaps residue from tools and equipment used to harvest the plants. Soil and sand samples from the crime scene may be linked to a particular vehicle used by the thieves or to transplanted cactuses at residences or commercial businesses.

Livestock. Just as in the days of the Wild West, cattle rustlers are still around, stealing millions of dollars worth of cattle annually and showing no signs of stopping. Most livestock is stolen from the open range and consequently may go undetected for weeks or even months. Cattle are usually stolen at night and are fairly easy to lure away because they are herd animals—once

rustlers get one animal to come, the rest soon follow. Cattle rustlers are almost always armed because they often slaughter the animals on the spot, butcher them, and load them into refrigerated trucks. Detectives may need the help of stock auctioneers, slaughterhouses, feedlot operators, and livestock associations when investigating these crimes.

Evidence in such cases again includes shoe and tire impressions, soil samples, broken fences, and perhaps forged bills of sale. Livestock branding, a practice dating back to 2700 BC, can also provide valuable evidence in cattle thefts. Brands, both hot irons and freeze brands, are unique identifying symbols placed on each animal of a specific ranch's herd. Brands are registered through a state's brand inspection office, which is generally under the jurisdiction of the state's department of agriculture. To the experienced livestock person, brands are a readable language, read from left to right, top to bottom, and outside to inside (Figure 14.2). In addition to branding, cattle are also ear marked and wattle marked, commonly with a knife, according to branding protocol. These cuts are further means of identification.

Horse rustling is another problem, with more than 50,000 horses stolen annually. Like cattle, horses are herd

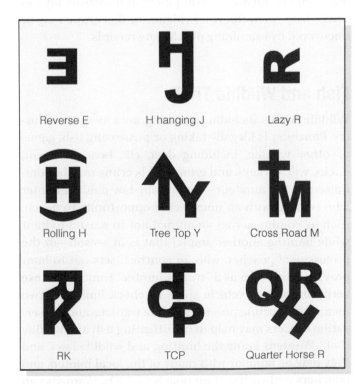

Figure 14.2
Cattle branding irons. Brands are composed of capital letters of the alphabet, numerals, pictures, and characters such as slashes, circles, crosses, and bars, with many combinations and adaptations. Letters can be used singly, joined, or in combinations. They can be upright, lying down ("lazy"), or reversed.

animals and are fairly easy to steal once rustlers have lured one animal away. Sometimes after the desired horses are loaded onto a truck, the rustlers break down the fence and scatter the remaining horses. Owners may then think the horses broke out themselves, and those not recovered are simply lost. Most stolen horses are slaughtered, and the meat is sold in Europe and Japan. The United States is the world's leading exporter of horsemeat, which in many countries is considered better than our best steaks.

As with cattle, horses are branded, with various breeds being marked in specific locations. In addition, thoroughbreds have registration numbers tattooed under the upper lip.

Brand altering is a common method used by livestock thieves to disguise the stolen animals, although with well-chosen and well-designed brands, such alterations are very difficult to make appear original. To foil brand-altering rustlers, DNA analysis is now being used to identify stolen cattle.

Farm Equipment and Chemicals. Farm equipment and chemicals are also targets for thieves. Because of their expense, pesticides and herbicides are especially attractive. Farmers themselves may be the thieves, or they may buy their chemicals and equipment at unreasonably low prices from such thieves. Evidence of this crime may be uncovered by examining purchasing records.

Fish and Wildlife Theft

Wildlife crimes, including poaching, are a lucrative industry. **Poaching** is illegally taking or possessing fish, game, or other wildlife, including deer, elk, bear, pheasant, ducks, wild turkeys, and grouse. This crime may be committed by the amateur—the usually law-abiding hunter who is faced with an unexpected opportunity to poach, such as coming across an animal not in season to hunt while hunting another animal that is in season—or the professional poacher, who, in contrast, sets out to hunt prey illegally, often as a "trophy hunter." Hunting-license verifications and vehicle stops to check limits are two means of detecting poachers. Game wardens and conservation officers may help in investigating fish and wildlife theft. Wardens know the hunting and wildlife laws, and they may be familiar with many of the local hunters and poachers and with certain poachers' MOs. Wardens can also help gather evidence.

Theft of fish and other wildlife is not merely a domestic problem. The illegal wildlife trade is global in scope, involves hundreds of millions of plant and animal specimens, and is estimated to generate between $5 billion and $20 billion each year for traffickers (Rosen & Smith, 2010). Experts hypothesize that the international wildlife trade is one of the world's largest illegitimate businesses, after the drug trade. Since 2000, more than 1.48 billion live animals have been imported into the United States, most having been captured in Southeast Asia (Rosen & Smith, 2010). Another hot zone for wildlife smuggling is the southern border of the United States, as many of the illegal animals imported as exotic pets come from Latin America (Deines, 2017). Animals are also captured and killed to be mounted as trophies or for their various body parts, including meat; skins, pelts, and furs; bones and teeth; tusks; horns; musk pods; gall bladders and other organs; and scales.

Wildlife trafficking poses not only conservation and environmental problems by threatening biodiversity and introducing invasive species, but also presents potential health threats to humans and native animal populations by allowing infectious agents to migrate to new regions of the world. Furthermore, wildlife smuggling poses a transnational security threat, as numerous sources have found links between some organized crime syndicates, insurgent groups, and foreign military units and various aspects of international wildlife trafficking (Wyler & Sheikh, 2013). A global black market for threatened and endangered species has billions of dollars changing hands and presents a serious threat to the political and economic stability in certain regions of the world, such as Central Africa. In addition, evidence supports a link between some militarized gangs of poachers and terrorist groups such as Al-Shabaab (Aldred, 2013).

The U.S. government stepped up its efforts against wildlife trafficking when, on July 1, 2013, President Barack Obama issued Executive Order 13648 on Combating Wildlife Trafficking, identifying wildlife trafficking as an escalating "international crisis," one that is in the U.S. interest to address because of its role in "contributing to the illegal economy, fueling instability, and undermining security." This landmark executive order led to the creation in 2014 of the National Strategy for Combating Wildlife Trafficking, which set forth a three-pronged approach with the strategic priorities of: (1) strengthening enforcement; (2) reducing demand; and (3) expanding international cooperation and commitment. It also created the Task Force on Wildlife Trafficking, bringing together 17 federal departments and agencies to implement the National Strategy's approach in an effort to deprive criminals of key sources of financing and reduce the criminal threat posed to U.S. citizens (U.S. Department of State, 2019). On October 7, 2016, Obama signed into law the Eliminate, Neutralize, and Disrupt (END) Wildlife Trafficking Act, again recognizing that such trafficking posed a serious transnational crime that threatened security, economic prosperity, the rule of law, long-standing conservation efforts, and human health.

Another entity responsible for developing and implementing anti–wildlife trafficking policies around the world is the U.S. Department of State's Bureau of International Narcotics and Law Enforcement Affairs (INL), which takes a criminal-justice approach to wildlife trafficking, focusing efforts around halting poaching, trafficking, and demand (U.S. Department of State, n.d.). INL efforts include:

1. Strengthening legislative frameworks of partner nations to ensure effective laws are in place to deter, investigate, prosecute, and sanction wildlife criminals

2. Enhancing investigative and law enforcement functions of our foreign enforcement partners, including support for park rangers

3. Developing capacities to prosecute and adjudicate wildlife crimes and related corruption worldwide

4. Supporting cross-border regional and global law enforcement communication and cooperation

Cargo Theft

Nearly everything we wear, eat, and use at home or work has, at some point, been on the back of a truck. The amount of cargo crisscrossing our country is mind-boggling and critical to daily life. The increasing popularity of cargo theft is the result of two primary features: it is low risk (few thieves are apprehended, prosecuted, or incarcerated), and it is extremely profitable (Tabor, 2018). The FBI reports that cargo theft caused $33 billion in losses in 2018 (FBI, 2018b). Like ORC, cargo theft is considered a gateway crime by the FBI: "In many instances, a cargo theft investigation will turn into a case involving organized crime, public corruption, health care fraud, insurance fraud, drug trafficking, money laundering, or possibly even terrorism" (FBI, 2010).

The illegal or unauthorized removal of cargo from the supply chain is called **leakage**, a concept similar to that of shrinkage. Cargo theft can occur from an 18-wheel trailer, a shipping container left on a dock or placed on a railway, or in a warehouse. Although some cargo thieves will take whatever commodity crosses their path, many groups steal to order. Items often sought by cargo thieves include designer clothing, handbags, and fragrances, high-end electronics, tobacco, and alcohol. A majority of retailers surveyed (73%) report having been a victim of

cargo theft in the past year (National Retail Federation, 2019). The majority of thefts occurred while the cargo was en route from the distribution center to the store, with the second most common point of leakage occurring between the manufacturer and the distribution center (59.0%). Other points of cargo theft occurred at the distribution center, after items arrived at the store, and when the merchandise was being shipped from one store to another (National Retail Federation, 2019).

Methods used to steal cargo vary, and such crimes are generally extremely difficult to detect after they occur. In some cases, thieves break the locking mechanism off the back door of a trailer or container or drill out a rivet holding the door in place, empty the cargo, and then shut the door again, sometimes taking the time to replace the rivet or otherwise visually disguise the theft so that nothing looks amiss to a passing security guard. Other times, the driver is hijacked en route. These "driver give-ups" typically happen close to major interstate corridors (Bibb, 2005).

A large portion of cargo theft occurs from commercial truck stops. Thieves know that truck drivers usually cannot offload their cargo over a weekend; thus, drivers who stop on a Friday evening are likely to drop their trailer and take only the tractor for transportation until Monday morning. Unsupervised trailers are more vulnerable to theft. Other times, thieves wait at truck stops and, knowing that many drivers simply leave their truck running for the few minutes it takes them to grab some food or use a restroom, get in and drive the entire rig away (Tabor, 2018).

Not uncommon are drivers who are part of the theft crew itself. For example, South American crews operating along the East Coast, primarily in New York and New Jersey, commit "leakage theft," where one member works as a truck driver, picks up a legitimate load from a marine terminal or distribution center and then diverts the cargo before delivery. The thieves enter the container or trailer, leaving the manifested seal intact, take out a portion of the load and then close the container. When the load is delivered, it appears to be short-shipped, that is, that the mistake was made by the shipper.

Although arresting thieves is still a goal, many agencies, including the FBI, are now focusing on finding the source—the organized crime groups and their front businesses. Cargo theft offenses are often part of larger criminal schemes and have been found to be components of organized crime rings, drug trafficking, and funding for terrorism (FBI, 2019). Certain nontraditional OC groups, such as those from Cuba and South America (Ecuador, Peru, etc.), engage in cargo theft nationwide and are fairly sophisticated. These groups typically work in cells or crews of three or four, occasionally more, and lack the typical hierarchy found in more traditional OC groups, such as the Mafia, aka La Cosa Nostra. The MOs do not vary much by group, except for the Asian and street gangs in Southern California, which tend to be quite violent and will use guns to conduct armed hijackings.

Numerous challenges face cargo theft investigators, not the least of which is the lack of respect or seriousness historically given to the issue. Although this crime has traditionally been categorized in the UCR simply as theft, a provision in the law reauthorizing the USA PATRIOT Act may help overcome this challenge by designating a UCR code specifically for cargo theft and requiring the establishment of a national cargo theft database.

Another investigative challenge centers on the mobile nature of the crime. Numerous jurisdictions around the country, particularly those close to major seaports and cargo distribution hubs, have developed cargo theft task forces to increase their effectiveness in conducting investigations. The success of these units has demonstrated that the surveillance and investigative abilities of a multijurisdictional team surpass those of any single agency.

Cargo theft investigations typically start simultaneously at two immediate locations—the place where the theft occurred and the area where the stolen cargo may be headed. Investigators who handle cargo theft do, over time, develop a good feel for which groups target certain types of loads and where they may go to off-load the stolen cargo. However, it is imperative that law enforcement agencies in the jurisdiction where the theft occurred be notified about the theft as quickly as possible because the chance of recovering the cargo decreases considerably after 48 hours (Cornell, 2017). A valuable resource that reaches not only law enforcement agencies but also private sector personnel and others who have experience with domestic and international cargo theft is CargoNet, with a command center that operates 24/7/365 (CargoNet, n.d.).

Having looked at the various types of larceny/theft, consider next how the crimes can be proved.

Proving the Elements of the Crime of Larceny/Theft

To prove the felonious stealing, taking, carrying, leading, or driving away of property, you must gather enough evidence to prove that the property is missing—not simply misplaced. Obtain proof of ownership through bills of sale or receipts or through evidence that the owner had custody or possession of or responsibility for the item.

Determine the item's value by ascertaining its replacement cost or legitimate market value or by obtaining reasonable estimates. The owner can testify to the actual value if they are familiar with the specific item and its quality and condition at the time of the theft. People with business knowledge of similar items can help determine value. If certain items obviously exceed the petty larceny limitation, it is not necessary to know their exact value. Take statements from the owner regarding where the property was located and what security was provided. Also obtain evidence that the owner no longer possesses the property.

Intent to permanently deprive the owner of the property is shown by the suspect's selling, concealing, hiding, or pawning the property or converting it to personal use. In shoplifting cases and related thefts, tampering with security devices can also demonstrate intent to permanently deprive the owner of the property. Intent is proven by a motive of revenge, possession under circumstances of concealment, denial of possession where possession is proven, or flight from normal residence.

Fraud

Fraud is a general term used for deceit, trickery, and cheating as well as to describe the activity of individuals who pretend to be what they are not. Legally, however, fraud has a narrower meaning. **Fraud** is an intentional deception to cause a person to give up property or some lawful right.

> **L07** Explain how fraud differs from larceny/theft.
>
> Fraud differs from larceny/theft in that fraud uses deceit rather than stealth to obtain goods illegally.

Advances in technology and, in particular, the proliferation of electronic commerce have given innovative criminals yet another way to commit fraud. Use of computers to commit fraud is discussed in Chapter 17.

Fraud victims are in a good position to provide information regarding suspects because they have had firsthand dealings with the suspects.

Investigators may find themselves working a case with the FBI if the matter involves fraud, theft, or embezzlement within or against the national or international financial community. The priority problem areas of this category of crime identified by the FBI's Financial Crimes Section (FCS) include corporate fraud, health care fraud, mortgage fraud, identity theft, insurance fraud, and money laundering. One unit of the FCS, the Economic Crimes Unit, investigates significant frauds targeted against individuals, businesses, and industries such as corporate fraud, securities and commodities fraud, telemarketing fraud, insurance fraud not related to health care, Ponzi schemes, advance fee schemes, and pyramid schemes. A **Ponzi scheme**—named after Charles Ponzi, whose pyramid-type fraud scheme during the 1920s led to a major federal investigation—involves using capital from new investors to pay off earlier investors. This scheme requires an ever-expanding base of new investors to support the financial obligations to the existing "higher ups"—hence the pyramidal shape used to depict such structures.

Because fraud often involves use of interstate communications devices (e.g., phones, computers), the mail system, or financial and banking institutions, many, if not most, types of fraud fall under the jurisdiction of the FBI. However, if the value amount involved does not meet or exceed a minimum monetary threshold, the federal government may opt not to become involved in the case, leaving local jurisdictions to deal with many of these types of crimes. Even if these crimes are investigated and prosecuted at the federal level, the victims typically call the local police first.

L08   List the common means of committing fraud.

Fraud includes confidence games, real estate and mortgage fraud, insurance fraud, health care fraud, mass marketing fraud, mail fraud, and fraud committed through counterfeiting or the use of checks or debit/credit cards. An increasingly serious and pervasive type of fraud is identity theft.

Confidence Games

Confidence games have separated people from their money for centuries; in fact, con games were known as early as 100 BC. Changing times require changing techniques, but four basic elements are always present: (1) locating a mark from whom to obtain money, (2) selecting the game, (3) conducting it, and then (4) leaving the area as rapidly as possible.

A **confidence game** obtains money or property by a trick, device, or swindle that takes advantage of a victim's trust in the swindler. The confidence game purports to offer a get-rich-quick scheme. The victim is sworn to secrecy and told that telling anyone could cause the deal

to fall through or the profits to be divided among more people. The game may require the victim to do something dishonest or unethical, thus making the victim less apt to report the swindle to the police. It is often conducted away from the victim's hometown so the victim cannot obtain advice from friends.

A particular type of person is needed to make the con game work. Con artists develop cunning, guile, and skills through their own systems of learning and education. They are taught by older people in the "trade," usually starting as the "number two" or "straight man." As they gain experience, they work their way up until they are the "number one" in a swindle of their own. Con artists understand human nature, are extremely convincing, lack conscience, have an uncanny ability to select the right victim, and have no mercy for their victims, often extracting the life savings of elderly people.

Two basic approaches are used in con games: the short con and the long con. **Short-con games** take the victims for whatever money they have with them at the time of the action. For example, three-card monte, similar to the old shell game, entices victims to bet on whether they can select one card from among three. "Huge Duke" involves betting on a stacked poker hand, with the victim dealing the final hand. "The Wipe" involves tying money into a handkerchief for safekeeping and then switching it with one containing newspaper bits. **Long-con games** are usually for higher stakes. For example, in "The Wire," the original long-con game, the victim is enticed to bet on horse races, convinced through an elaborate telegraph office setup that the manager can beat the bookmaker by delaying the results of the race long enough to let the victim and other cohorts in the scheme make bets. After allowing the victim to win a few games at low stakes, the "big bet" is made in which the victim may lose thousands of dollars.

When investigating con-game fraud, obtain a complete description of the confidence artists and the type of fraud, trick, or false pretense they used, as well as the exact amount of money involved.

Because the victim usually sees and talks with the con artists, it is often easy to identify them, but unless the police are notified quickly, the suspects will be gone from the area. Obtain descriptions of the perpetrators and their MO. Keep this information on file for future reference.

The FBI maintains a confidence artist file to assist in locating such suspects, as well as a general appearance file of con artists (even if photographs are not available). The FBI assists in investigating violations that occur on interstate conveyances such as planes, boats, and trains. It also assists if there is evidence that radio, television, or telegraph was used in committing the crime or if a money order was sent to a person in another state. If the swindle exceeds $5,000, the FBI has jurisdiction under the Interstate Transportation of Stolen Property Act. (Many con games exceed this amount.) Postal authorities may assist investigators in cases in which con artists use the mails to execute their crimes.

Most states include con games in statutes relating to larceny by trick and to obtaining money under false pretenses. Check the statutes in your jurisdiction for the specific elements that must be proven.

Online auction websites are becoming used more frequently to conduct scams. For example, one of the most common scams perpetrated on Craigslist, a free online bazaar used by about 60 million people each month, is the sale of fake or cancelled tickets to concerts, sporting events, and even airline flights (Sraders, 2020). Also trending are online penny auction sites. While, domestically, states are trying to make these sites illegal, many originate from outside the country, making them extremely difficult, if not impossible, to regulate or eradicate.

Other scams that investigators may be summoned to examine include:

- *Easy-credit scams.* Con artists target people who seek to repair damaged credit ratings by offering credit cards in exchange for advanced payments or deposits.

- *Bogus prize offers.* Mail, email, or phone announcements proclaim, "You're a big winner!" The winner is instructed to wire money to cover taxes or fees to receive the "grand prize."

- *Phony home repairs.* Workers knock on a door and explain that they are finishing several jobs (roofing, siding, driveways) in the neighborhood. They have leftover material and can offer to fix anything at a great discount. They may take a deposit or the entire payment and never return to complete the job, or they may begin the work and then claim the job is more involved than they had thought and state they will need additional payment to finish the job.

- *Travel scams.* Victims are promised an exciting, free vacation in an exotic location but must first provide a credit card number for "verification."

- *Cyber-scams.* The Internet offers numerous sites to sell or trade merchandise, and con artists are taking advantage of this lucrative virtual swap shop to sell defective or nonexistent products. One of the latest scams involves criminals using legitimate crowdfunding sites like GoFundMe, Kickstarter, and Indiegogo to create bogus stories and fraudulent business ventures in an attempt to get people to donate money to their "cause."

Although it may be hard to believe that people would fall for some of these scams, con artists are extremely well versed and tend to target more typically vulnerable and trusting victims, such as the elderly.

Real Estate and Mortgage Fraud

In many areas of the country, real estate scams, such as phantom down payments and "flipping," are costing lenders and homebuyers tremendous amounts of money. According to the FBI, each mortgage fraud scheme uses "some type of material misstatement, misrepresentation, or omission relating to a real estate transaction which is relied on by one or more parties to the transaction" (FBI, 2011). Common mortgage fraud schemes include equity skimming, illegal property flipping, air loans, foreclosure rescue schemes, loan modification, builder bailouts, inflated appraisals, nominee loans/straw buyers, and silent seconds.

Common equity skimming schemes involve use of corporate shell companies, corporate identity theft, and bankruptcy/foreclosure to dupe homeowners and investors. In **property flipping**, the offender buys a property near its estimated market value, artificially inflates the property value through a false appraisal, and then resells (flips) the property, often within days of the original purchase, for a greatly increased price. This process can be repeated several times with a single property through the help of the flipper's associates, ultimately leading to foreclosure by the victim lenders. Many deals rely on fraudulent appraisals inflating the property's value. Although flipping per se is not illegal, it often involves mortgage fraud, which is illegal.

Air loans involve a nonexistent property loan where there is usually no collateral. For example, a broker invents borrowers and properties, establishes accounts for payments, and maintains custodial accounts for escrows. Foreclosure rescue schemes involve perpetrators identifying homeowners at risk of foreclosure or already in foreclosure and misleading them into believing they can save their homes in exchange for a transfer of the deed and up-front fees. The perpetrator then either remortgages the property or pockets the fees.

Loan modification scams purport to help homeowners who are delinquent in their mortgage payments and on the verge of losing their home renegotiate the terms of their loan with the lender. However, the scammers demand large up-front fees and either negotiate unfavorable terms or do not negotiate at all, with the result being that the homeowners ultimately lose their homes. This scheme is similar to a foreclosure rescue scam. In a builder bailout, a builder who is facing severe losses resulting from rising inventory and declining demand for newly constructed homes finds "buyers" to obtain loans for the properties, who then allow the properties to go into foreclosure.

Inflated appraisals, as the name suggests, involve an appraiser acting in collusion with a borrower and providing a misleading appraisal report to the lender. Nominee loans or straw buyers conceal the identity of the borrower through use of a nominee who allows the borrower to use the nominee's name and credit history to apply for a loan. In the silent second, the buyer of a property borrows the down payment from the seller through the issuance of a nondisclosed second mortgage. The primary lender believes the borrower has invested their own money as the down payment, when in fact, it is borrowed.

Insurance Fraud

Insurance is one of the largest industries in the United States, with thousands of companies collecting nearly $1 trillion in premiums every year (FBI, 2011). The most prevalent type of insurance fraud involves premium diversion by insurance agents and brokers, where customers' payments are pocketed for personal gain instead of being sent to the policy underwriter. Scams run by unauthorized, unregistered, and unlicensed agents are also common and involve collecting premiums for nonexistent policies. The scam lasts as long as customers have no claims. Once claims start to be filed, the fraudster closes up shop and relocates. These fraudulent operations take advantage of individuals who seek high-risk lines of insurance for which few legitimate providers exist.

Another type of insurance fraud involves worker's compensation, in which the con operator collects a premium without providing any legitimate protection against claims. This type of fraud can leave injured victims and families of deceased victims with little or no coverage to pay their medical bills.

Insurance companies are duty-bound to hold customer premiums secure until a claim is made. However, when the economy takes a downturn and finances become strained, some insurance executives fraudulently dip into this premium pool to cover their own company's operating expenses. This illegal act leads to further illegal acts because accounting documents and financial statements must be doctored to cover up the misuse of customer premiums (FBI, 2011).

The FBI has investigated and shut down several highly profitable insurance fraud schemes. For example, in fiscal year 2011, the agency investigated 140 insurance fraud cases, which led to 19 indictments/informations, 13 arrests, and the convictions of 21 insurance fraud criminals, as well as generating $87.6 million in restitution (FBI, 2011). More recent data from the Coalition Against Insurance Fraud (2020), however, indicates that prosecutions for insurance fraud are at an all-time low, with prosecutions in January 2020 down 25% from 2015 levels, raising questions and concerns over how hard federal prosecutors are pursuing these crimes.

Although the FBI has focused its efforts on higher priority white-collar crime matters, insurance fraud investigations continue to be addressed using liaison efforts in conjunction with other federal, state, and local law enforcement. Insurance fraud investigations often require the collaborative efforts of the FBI, National Association of Insurance Commissioners (NAIC), International Association of Insurance Fraud Agencies (IAIFA), state fraud bureaus, and state insurance regulators. In addition to traditional investigation methods, the FBI uses covert undercover investigations to apprehend fraudsters.

Health Care Fraud

As with insurance fraud, health care fraud adds billions of dollars each year to U.S. health care costs. The FBI (2018d) describes health care related fraud as any scheme that attempts to defraud private or government health care programs, usually involving health care providers, companies, or individuals. Such schemes include offers for fake insurance cards; health insurance marketplace assistance; stolen health information; or medications, supplements, weight loss products, or diversion/pill mill practices. Health care scams are often initiated through spam email, Internet advertisements, links in forums or social media, and fraudulent websites.

Noting that Medicare and Medicaid are the most visible programs affected by such fraud, the FBI reports, "Estimates of fraudulent billings to health care programs, both public and private, are estimated between 3% and 10% of total health care expenditures. The fraud schemes are not specific to any general area, but are found throughout the entire country" (FBI, 2011). The FBI expects health care fraud to continue rising as people live longer. One of the most serious trends observed involves the increased number of medical professionals willing to risk patient harm in their fraud schemes, which can include unnecessary surgeries, dilution of cancer and other lifesaving drugs, and fraudulent lab tests.

Mass Marketing Fraud

The FBI considers mass marketing fraud as a general term to include frauds that exploit mass-communication media, such as telemarketing, mass mailings, and the Internet (FBI, 2011). Although these fraud schemes take a variety of forms, they have in common the use of false or deceptive representations to induce potential victims to make advance fee-type payments to fraud perpetrators.

One such fraud that has been around for decades is the Nigerian letter fraud, referred to as 4-1-9 Fraud by INTERPOL. Victims are contacted regarding substantial sums of money held in foreign accounts and are asked for their "assistance" in paying various fees to secure the funds transfer to the United States in exchange for a portion of the total proceeds. Alternatively, victims are asked to act as a U.S. agent in securing the release of such funds and are provided with counterfeit instruments that are to be cashed to pay any required fees, only to discover they must reimburse their financial institution for cashing a counterfeit instrument.

In 2016, a Canadian couple was extradited to the United States and sentenced for taking part in a mass marketing scheme that targeted hundreds of victims across the United States and brought in more than $110,000 (U.S. Attorney's Office, 2016). The couple, along with others, mailed hundreds of letters and checks to people across the country falsely stating that the letter recipient had been selected to act as a "secret shopper" at Walmart and MoneyGram. To participate in this opportunity, the victim simply needed to deposit into their own bank account the check that came with the letter and then immediately wire most of those proceeds at MoneyGram counters located inside Walmart stores. The balance of the checks would serve as the payment for the secret shoppers. The problem, however, was that the checks sent with the letters were bogus, and the banks were holding victims responsible for funds they withdrew and wired to the scammers in Canada. One of the fraudsters admitted in his plea agreement that he targeted more than 500 victims and intended to cause losses of approximately $1.9 million.

Telemarketing fraud and other types of fraud using the telephone have proliferated, and the victims are predominantly the elderly. In one such scam, a "representative" informs potential victims that they have won a sweepstakes prize and that the company needs their name, address, and Social Security number to process the award. The company then uses the Social Security number for fraudulent purposes. Other scams simply involve informing the "winner," aka victim, that they must first pay a service fee or tax for their prize and that once the payment has been received, the prize will be shipped. Of course, it never is.

Frauds involving cell phones and personal communication services (PCSs) are growing problems. One prevalent form of high-tech fraud is cloning, or "grabbing." Individuals obtain legitimate account information by theft from an owner carrier or by on-the-air interception. The thief then programs the account number into a cell or PCS phone, creating a clone of the legitimate phone. Other telephone scams include:

- **Slamming** is the illegal practice of switching a consumer's traditional wireline telephone company for local, local toll, or long-distance service without permission.

- **Cramming** involves a third party placing unauthorized charges on a consumer's wired, wireless, or bundled services telephone bill.

- **Gouging** refers to companies charging undisclosed fees for use or equipment. Most recent cases involve being billed for cable equipment or hidden fees for use.

- **Fluffing** occurs when rates are increased without notification.

Caller ID can both enhance and *hinder* fraud investigations. It can identify perpetrators of fraud, but it can also pose a danger to officers who work undercover. They may be exposed by having their phone numbers revealed to the criminals they call.

Mail Fraud

Mail fraud involves perpetuating scams through the mail—for example, bogus sweepstakes entries and notices. If mail fraud is suspected, police officers should contact the postal inspector through their local post office. Postal authorities can assist in investigating if the scheme uses the mail to obtain victims or to transport profits from crime.

Counterfeiting

Counterfeiting of money generally comes to the attention of the police through a retailer or a bank. The U.S. Secret Service publishes pamphlets on identifying counterfeit money. The most common denominations of counterfeit money are $10, $20, $50, and $100. The $100 bill shares the same watermark and weight as the $5 bill, making it appealing to counterfeiters, who will wash the lower denomination bill and reprint it to be of much higher value. The paper of authentic bills has red and blue fibers embedded in it, and the bills have intaglio (incised) printing. The portrait is detailed and lifelike; the U.S. Treasury seal is clear and distinct on sawtooth points; the borders are clear and unbroken; and serial numbers are distinct, evenly spaced, and the same color as the Treasury seal. INTERPOL's Counterfeits and Security Documents Branch (CSDB) has established programs that provide forensic support, operational assistance, and technical databases to help federal and local investigators in counterfeit currency cases.

If a bill is suspect, give a receipt to the retailer or bank and turn the bill over to the nearest Secret Service office to determine its authenticity. Obtain details of how the bill came into the complainant's possession as well as an accurate description of the bill passer.

A felt-tip highlighting marker can instantly detect even the finest-quality counterfeit money with a single stroke. With the felt-tip marker, a dot or short line is made on the suspected bill. If the dot or line remains gold, the bill is authentic; if it turns black, the bill needs scrutiny.

Counterfeit Identification Documents.
It is fairly easy for a perpetrator to make fake identification documents, a crime that can yield a large profit. Consider a situation in which a woman enters the United States illegally and purchases a fake Social Security card for $300. A month later she rents an apartment in Los Angeles and, together with other illegally entered persons, starts a business making fraudulent documents. Their business brings in $5,000 a week.

In November 2011, a sweep involving more than 300 federal, state, and local law enforcement officers, executing dozens of arrest and search warrants, netted more than two dozen suspects in a massive fraudulent document manufacturing network headquartered in Los Angeles, California, with operations in Illinois, Texas, and Mexico. The ring allegedly manufactured raw materials that were then used to manufacture false documents on a large scale, included United States Permanent Resident cards, Social Security cards, Mexican Consular Identification cards, and driver's licenses for 40 of the 50 states. During the investigation, evidence was developed showing that the fraudulent documents were used not only by illegal aliens to gain employment and other residency-related benefits but that the false documents were instrumental in supporting other criminal endeavors such as credit and bank fraud, tax fraud, identity theft, and pharmaceutical diversion schemes (FBI, Los Angeles Division, 2011). Document and benefit fraud is also often linked to human trafficking, money laundering, and drug crimes.

Commercial Counterfeiting.
Currency is not the only item targeted for counterfeiting. Commercial counterfeiting includes trademark counterfeiting and copyright pirating. *Trademark counterfeiting* is the illegal production of cheap "knock-offs" of well-known pricier products, such as Rolex watches, Gucci handbags, or Mont Blanc fountain pens. *Copyright pirating* is making—for trade or sale—unauthorized copies of copyrighted material, including print and sound media. In contrast to trademark counterfeiting, where products are sold far below the retail value of their legitimate counterparts, pirated music or movies impose much steeper prices on the consumer. It is also a felony in most states to pirate sound recordings, and nearly every state has some type of law related to pirated recordings. Despite the illegalities of this business, the practice continues, particularly on the Internet, as discussed in Chapter 17.

Check Fraud

Losses from bad-check operations cannot be determined exactly because no single clearinghouse gathers statistics on this offense. Estimates range from $815 million to $5– $10 billion annually.

Checks used to defraud include personal, business, payroll, counter, draft, and universal checks, as well as money orders. Fraudulent checks are made to appear genuine in many ways. The check blank can be similar to the one normally used and difficult to detect. In fact, many fraudulent and forged checks are written on stolen check blanks. Handwriting is practiced to look authentic. Various stamps, check writers, date stamps, and cancellation stamps are placed on the front and back of the check to give it a genuine appearance.

In some cases, the checks are not stolen but handed over willingly to thieves—for a price. The checking account owner benefits by being paid more money than is actually in the account, while the thief is allowed to cash checks or purchase merchandise for a few days before the bank is notified of the check "theft."

Common types of check fraud are issuing insufficient-fund or worthless checks and committing forgery. The *insufficient-* or *nonsufficient-fund check* falls into one of two categories: (1) accidental, in which people carelessly overdraw their checking account and are generally not prosecuted unless they do so habitually, or (2) intentional, in which professionals open a checking account with a small deposit, planning to write checks well in excess of the amount deposited. This is intent to defraud—a prosecutable offense. A variation of this second category of check fraud is the **bustout**, a fraud scheme designed to generate cash or credit in which the perpetrator first deposits a fictitious check that appears to be genuinely drawn on a real account into a checking or credit card account at a financial institution. Immediately afterward, the subject withdraws funds from the account into which the fictitious check was deposited. Once the fraudulent nature of the check is discovered and the check is dishonored by the institution, the account has been "busted." On May 14, 2014, law enforcement authorities arrested 12 people and were seeking three others who were accused of participating in a large-scale bustout scheme that victimized major financial institutions across Southern California and cost banks at least $15 million (FBI, Los Angeles Division, 2014).

Most bad checks are not written with intent to defraud. They may have been mistakenly drawn against the wrong bank, the account balance may have been less than the writer thought, two or more people may have used the same account without knowing the actual balance, or the bank may have made an error.

Issuing a worthless check occurs when the issuer does not intend the check to be paid. Proof of intent is shown if the issuer has no account or has insufficient funds or credit or both. A worthless check is normally prosecuted the same as one for insufficient funds. Obtain the check as well as statements from the person who accepted it, any other witnesses and bank representatives. Also obtain a signed complaint.

Another way to commit check fraud is to use the stolen routing and account numbers to print or order checks under the name that matches the identification card held by the suspect. The suspect can then take these checks and cash them wherever they can. Oftentimes, suspects use business account information, and it can take a considerable length of time for the business to catch the unauthorized charges from their accounts. This type of theft has become a growing problem for payroll check cashing businesses, and suspects arrested for these offenses often face identity theft and check fraud charges.

Forgery is signing someone else's name to a document with the intent to defraud. This includes actually signing the name as well as using a rubber stamp or a check writing machine. To prosecute, obtain the forged check or document, statements from the person whose name is forged, any witnesses to the transaction, and the testimony of a handwriting expert if necessary. Blank checks are often obtained through burglaries or office thefts committed by professionals. The check is authentic and therefore easier to cash once the endorsement is forged. It is also forgery to alter the amount on a check or to change the name of the payee. The person who initially draws the check must testify as to the authorized amount and payee. Additionally, it is forgery to change a name on a charge account slip.

Investigating bad or fraudulent checks requires precise details about the check and the entire transaction. The check itself is the main evidence. Carefully examine the front and back of the check and note peculiarities. Describe the check: type, firm name, and whether it is personal, payroll, federal, or state. Was it written in pencil or ink or typed? Were any special stamps used? Was anything altered: the payee, the date, the amount? Was the signature forged? Were there erasures or misspellings? Were local names and addresses used? Put the check in a protective polyethylene envelope or plastic container so it can also be processed for fingerprints.

Where was the check passed? Who took it? Were there other witnesses? If so, obtain their names and addresses. If currency was given, what were the denominations? Obtain an exact description of the check passer. Was the suspect known to the person taking the check? Had they ever done business with the store before? What identification was used: driver's license, Social Security card, bank identification card, credit card? Was the suspect alone? If with others, what did they look like? What approach was used? What words were spoken? If the check passer used a car, did anyone notice what it looked like or the license number?

Professional check passers who write several checks in a city in a short time and then move to another city or state often use the same technique. The FBI's National Fraudulent Check File helps identify such people and often shows a pattern of travel. The FBI maintains other files that assist in tracing bad-check writers. These include files on check-writer standards, watermarks, confidence operators, safety paper standards, rubber stamps, anonymous letters, and typewriter standards.

Debit and Credit Card Fraud

A *debit card*, sometimes called a *check card*, refers to a card presented to a merchant exactly as a credit card would be, with the amount instantly credited before verification of the existence of funds is established. A *credit card* refers to any credit plate, charge plate, courtesy card, or other identification card or device used to obtain a cash advance, a loan, or credit, or to purchase or lease property or services on the issuer's credit or that of the holder. The **holder** is the person to whom such a card is issued and who agrees to pay obligations arising from its use.

Use of debit and credit cards, referred to by the Department of Justice as *access devices*, has become a way of life in the United States. The cards have also opened a new avenue for criminals to obtain goods and services by theft and fraud, essentially leaving check fraud to become a dying crime as more people switch from paper to plastic to complete their transactions. Losses from debit and credit card fraud are in the billions annually. Despite such losses, these cards, like checks, reduce cash thefts from individuals and reduce the amount of cash-on-hand in places such as filling stations, as well as the amount of cash transferred to banks from businesses. Use of these cards also aids in identifying criminals who have the cards in their possession, more so than does cash, which is not as easily identifiable.

Because credit card fraud is often spread throughout several jurisdictions, many police departments place low priority on this type of offense. Further complicating this crime, many businesses accept credit card phone purchases. Fraudulent orders are placed, and if the victims do not review their bills, the fraud can go completely undetected: "Perhaps the biggest problem for police is that people rarely report check and card fraud to them. In one recent study, only one in four incidents of check and card fraud were reported to the police" (Newman & Herbert, 2020).

Most people involved in credit card fraud are also involved in other types of crimes. The credit cards are obtained principally by muggers, robbers, burglars, pickpockets, purse snatchers, thieves, and prostitutes. They can also be obtained through fraudulent application or by manufacturing counterfeit cards.

Credit cards can be stolen by mailbox thieves who may have been tipped off by a postal employee, by someone at apartment boxes, or by dishonest employees of the card manufacturer. Cards from the manufacturer are desirable because they are unsigned. Criminals can sign their holder's name in their own handwriting. These cards also provide more time for use before the theft is discovered. For the same reasons, these cards are more valuable for resale to other fraudulent users. To take maximum advantage without being detected, the criminal obtains the card by fraud, theft, or reproduction; uses it for a short time; and then disposes of it.

LO9 Identify the elements of the crime of larceny by debit or credit card.

The elements of the crime of larceny by debit or credit card include:

- Use of any counterfeit, fictitious, altered, forged, lost, stolen, or fraudulently obtained credit or debit card, or card number
- To intentionally obtain money, goods, or services.

Previous editions of this text noted that, to use another person's debit or credit card illegally, the criminal had to either forge the cardholder's signature on sales slips or alter the signature on the card, the latter being made difficult by colored or symbol undertones that indicate when erasures and alterations are attempted. However, the increased prevalence with which credit and debit cards are used to make online and telephone purchases has negated the need to prove a physical signature occurred as part of the crime. Furthermore, many retailers no longer require a signature for credit or debit card purchases under a certain amount.

The criminal must also operate under the floor-release limit to avoid having a clerk check the card's validity. The **floor-release limit** is the maximum dollar amount that may be paid with a charge card without getting authorization from the central office unless the business assumes liability for any loss. The limit is set by each company and is subject to change. It can be $50 or $100; in some gas stations, it is only $10. **Zero floor release** means that all credit card transactions must be checked. A suspicious merchant usually runs a check regardless of the amount of credit requested. Often, the criminal is asked for additional identification, which is difficult to produce unless other identification was also obtained in the theft.

Credit cards are attractive to criminals who operate interstate. Such criminals know that few companies will pay the witness fees for out-of-state prosecutions and that extradition is difficult to obtain unless the losses are great.

Many laws cover larceny or fraudulent use of credit cards. Possessing a forged credit card or one signed by a person other than the cardholder is the basis for a charge of possession of a forged instrument. Possessing two such cards is the basis for presuming intent to defraud. Illegally making or embossing a credit card or changing the expiration date or account number also subjects the person to a charge of intent to defraud. In most jurisdictions, it is not necessary to prove that the person possessing the card signed it. People who have machinery or devices to counterfeit or forge credit cards can be charged with possession of forgery devices.

It is larceny to fail to return a found credit card or to keep one sent by mistake if the finder or recipient uses the card. Airline tickets bought with a stolen or forged credit card are also stolen property. The degree of larceny, petty or grand, is determined by the ticket's value. It is also larceny to misrepresent credit information or identity to obtain a credit card. If a person sells their credit card to someone who uses it and the original cardholder then refuses to pay, the cardholder can be charged with larceny.

Some merchants and businesspeople commit credit card fraud themselves. For example, a merchant may direct an employee to make more than one authorized record of charge per sale and then forward the charges for payment or raise the amount on the credit card charge slip. This is larceny, with the degree determined by the difference between the actual charge and that forwarded for payment. It is also forgery because a document was altered. It is an attempt to commit larceny if such actions are not completed because of intervening circumstances, such as the cardholder becoming suspicious.

Most large credit card issuers assign personnel to work with local police in cases of credit card larceny. These people can be contacted for help or for information on the system used to manufacture and issue the cards.

When investigating credit card fraud, obtain samples of handwriting from sales slips signed by the suspect. If a card is obtained by false credit application, handwriting is available on the credit application form. If the card is used for a car rental, other information about the rented vehicle is available. Gas stations often record the state and license number of vehicles they service. Driver's licenses are used for identification. If a suspect is arrested, obtain a warrant to search the suspect's vehicle and residence for copies of sales slips or tickets obtained with the card, even though it has been discarded or sold.

Examine credit cards for alteration of the signature panel; the numbers or name can be shortened by using a razor blade to shave them off. New numbers can be entered to defeat the "hot card" list. Merchandise on sales slips found in the criminal's possession can provide further proof of illegal use.

As serious as credit card fraud is, it can have an even graver consequence—identity theft.

Identity Theft and Fraud

A type of theft that can wreak enormous havoc on a person's credit and financial security, as well as their emotional well-being, is **identity theft**, the stealing of personal, private, or financial information, data collectively referred to as personally identifiable information (PII). Identity theft is what happens when a data breach occurs and consumers' PII is illegally obtained. If this stolen information is used fraudulently, the theft becomes **identity fraud,** the unauthorized use or attempted use of PII to commit theft or fraud. Identity fraud is more damaging than identity theft (Skiba, 2020). Nonetheless, the two terms are often used synonymously. The Federal Trade Commission (FTC) states: "Under federal law, identity theft occurs when someone uses or attempts to use the sensitive personal information of another person to commit fraud. A wide range of sensitive personal information can be used to commit identity theft, including a person's name, address, date of birth, Social Security number (SSN), driver's license number, credit card and bank account numbers, phone numbers, and even biometric data like fingerprints and iris scans" (Federal Trade Commission [FTC], 2013, p. 4).

Identity theft, perhaps the defining crime of the information age, was the top consumer complaint received by the FTC in 2019, with more than 650,000 complaints reported (FTC, 2020). Approximately 14.4 million people were victims of identity theft in the United States in 2018, a decrease from 16.7 million people in 2017 (Marchini & Pascual, 2019). However, despite the fewer cases, identity fraud victims in 2018 bore a heavier financial burden: 3.3 million people (23% of identity fraud victims) were responsible for some of the liability of the fraud committed against them, nearly three times as many as in 2016. Most identity theft incidents (85%) involve the fraudulent use of existing account information, such as credit card or bank account information (Harrell, 2019).

Identity theft became a federal crime in the United States in 1998 with the passage of the Identity Theft and Assumption Deterrence Act. Before this act, no nationally accepted definition of *identity theft* existed, a factor that complicated the investigation and prosecution of these offenses. However, this act defined identity theft broadly, making it easier for prosecutors to conduct their cases. Most states have passed identity theft legislation, but the laws vary from state to state.

One difficulty in defining identity theft has been the considerable number of different crimes that it may involve, including check fraud, credit cards, check cards, immigration fraud, counterfeiting, forgery, terrorism using false or stolen identities, theft of various kinds (pickpocketing, robbery, burglary, or mugging), and postal fraud. In fact, identity theft is unique in that it is a crime in itself and is an MO to commit other crimes. A challenge for investigators, therefore, may be deciding what offense to accuse a suspect of involvement in.

Myth Identity theft and fraud is rare and, if it does happen, is easy to get fixed with minimal financial or emotional impact.

Fact In 2016, an estimated 26 million people age 16 or older in the United States (10% of people in this population) had been victims of identity theft during the prior 12 months (Harrell, 2019). About two-thirds of the identity-theft victims reported a direct financial loss resulting from the incident. Victims who experienced only the misuse of personal information for fraudulent purposes lost an average of $3,530, with a median of $1,900. While more than half (55%) of victims were able to resolve their problems in 1 day, 16% reported taking 8 to 30 days to resolve the issue, and another 9% spent a month or longer resolving problems caused by identity theft. For nearly 8% (7.8%) of victims, the problems were not resolved at all (Harrell, 2019). Furthermore, approximately 10% of identity-theft victims said they experienced severe emotional distress due to the incident. More than one-third (36%) of those who spent 6 months or longer resolving financial and credit problems caused by the identity theft experienced severe emotional distress. Studies have found that serious negative physical and mental health consequences are associated with identity theft victimization (Burnes, DeLiema, & Langton, 2020).

When President George W. Bush signed the Identity Theft Penalty Enhancement Act in 2004, he stressed, "The crime of identity theft undermines the basic trust on which our economy depends. When a person takes out an insurance policy, or makes an online purchase, or opens a savings account, he or she must have confidence that personal financial information will be protected and treated with care. Identity theft harms not only its direct victims, but also many businesses and customers whose confidence is shaken. Like other forms of stealing, identity theft leaves the victim poor and feeling terribly violated" (Office of the Press Secretary, 2004).

Identity theft is especially prevalent on college campuses. Identity thieves know this and hang around campus post office boxes to gain access to applications and fill them in themselves. Complicating the problem is the fact that there are more than 200 valid forms of ID or driver's licenses issued in the United States.

Identity theft has proliferated as use of the Internet has grown. The FTC notes that thieves steal identities through dumpster diving, skimming (using a special storage device when processing a card), completing a change of address form to divert billing statements to another location, "old-fashioned" stealing, and phishing. Phishing involves tricking consumers into replying to an email or accessing a website that appears to be associated with a legitimate business but is actually a carefully concocted hoax intended to strip consumers of personal identifying information that can be used for criminal purposes, such as identity theft and fraud. Figure 14.3 shows the four types of identity theft, based on the combinations of commitment and motive.

Identity theft and fraud can be committed by a lone actor, a small group, or a large ring. One case of a solo fraudster occurred in Georgia, when the FBI discovered a 43-year-old man had devised an elaborate scheme to steal the identities of multiple people:

> The headquarters of a large national bank had detected fraud on an account and sent word to an Atlanta branch to be on alert: If an individual comes in to pick up the new debit card linked to that account, call the Atlanta Police Department. An alert bank employee did just that when Khoi Nguyen came in to the branch to claim the debit card. Officers arrived quickly to ask Nguyen about his identity and the name on the bank account. Upon questioning, Nguyen produced a Department of Defense identification badge and claimed to be in law enforcement.
>
> The police weren't buying it, so they called the FBI to investigate Nguyen for impersonating a federal law enforcement officer. It was soon discovered that he was not only impersonating a government official but more than a dozen different people in a sophisticated identity theft scheme.
>
> "In his bag at arrest were 20 cellular phones, 13 different identifications, a number of credit cards, and about $11,000 in cash," said Special Agent Marcus Brackman, who worked the case out of the FBI's Atlanta Field Office.
>
> Brackman said that Nguyen had some technical skills and likely purchased the stolen personal information he used to create fake documents and open fraudulent financial accounts off encrypted websites. "Criminals can buy identities for 50 cents on the dark web," Brackman explained.
>
> (FBI, 2019)

In another case, four "U.S. citizens who lived in San Diego, California, but carried out their crimes from across the Mexican border in Tijuana, hacked the computer servers of major U.S. mortgage brokers" multiple times between 2011 and 2014 (FBI, 2018c). The hackers

	Financial Gain	Concealment
High commitment (substantial planning)	*Organized:* A fraud ring systematically steals personal information and uses it to generate bank accounts, obtain credit cards, etc. *Individual:* The offender sets up a look-alike Internet Web site for a major company; spams consumers, luring them to the site by saying their account information is needed to clear up a serious problem; steals the personal/financial information the consumer provides; and uses it to commit identity theft.	*Organized:* Terrorists obtain false visas and passports to avoid being traced after committing terrorist acts. *Individual:* The offender assumes another's name to cover up past crimes and avoid capture over many years.
Low commitment (opportunistic)	An apartment manager uses personal information from rental applications to open credit card accounts.	The offender uses another's name and ID when stopped or arrested by police.

Figure 14.3
There are four types of identity theft, based on the combinations of commitment and motive. Any single case could reflect aspects of more than one type.

Source: Washington, DC: Office of Community Oriented Policing Services, Problem-Oriented Guides for Police, Problem-Specific Guides Series No.25 Newman, G. R. (2004, July 26). *Identity theft.* p.15.

stole "detailed loan application information from thousands of customers and then used the victims' Social Security numbers, addresses, dates of birth, and driver's license numbers to open unauthorized lines of credit and take over and drain victims' retirement accounts." The hackers also used the victims' PII to commit extensive credit fraud, setting up bogus lines of credit and retail credit card accounts to which they charged thousands of dollars for goods and services. The resale of goods brought in money which was used mostly to buy drugs.

The chief hacker in the group, John Baden, infiltrated mortgage companies using a common hacking technique known as *fuzzing*, which works by overloading a web server with massive amounts of data that can lead to the server revealing security loopholes. Once the group had access to victims' information, they took control by contacting the companies managing the victims' brokerage accounts, providing the victims' personal information to change passwords and contact information, and then transferring out funds from these accounts—sometimes up to $30,000 at a time. The more than 25,000 victims stretched from California to Florida, and one individual lost nearly $1 million in the scheme:

"The damage crimes like these have on victims, the economy, and society in general are significant," said Special Agent Chris Christopherson, who investigated the case from the FBI's San Diego Division. "Individuals had their finances wrecked and their credit destroyed, through no fault of their own. For many of them," he added, "the impacts are still being felt." . . .

The FBI was alerted to the fraud by a financial institution that noticed irregularities, and about the same time, FBI cyber investigators detected that many victims had a "common point of compromise," Christopherson said. "They had all recently applied to the same mortgage company."

Armed with that information, investigators worked backward from the mortgage company, eventually identifying the hack—and the hackers. By that time, Baden was hiding in Mexico. In 2014, he was named to the San Diego FBI's Most Wanted Cyber Fugitives list, and the reward offered in the case eventually led to his capture in Mexico, Christopherson said. All four subjects pleaded guilty to their roles in the fraud scheme. . . .

But even years after the crimes were committed, Christopherson said, "the court was still receiving victim impact statements." Many victims were unable to get jobs or be approved for mortgages or car loans because their credit had been ruined by the fraudsters. (FBI, 2018c)

Sometimes identity theft and related financial crimes involve dozens of criminal coconspirators, as was the case in Newark, New Jersey, where in February 2014, the leader of a fraud ring comprised of 54 other individuals was sentenced to 144 months in prison for directing the large-scale, sophisticated criminal enterprise:

Sang-Hyun Park, a/k/a "Jimmy," 48, of Palisades Park, New Jersey, previously pleaded guilty before then-U.S. Magistrate Judge Patty Shwartz to a five-count information charging him with conspiracy to unlawfully produce identification documents and false identification documents (count one); conspiracy to commit wire fraud affecting financial institutions and bank fraud (count two); aggravated identity theft (count three); money laundering (count four); and conspiracy to defraud the Internal Revenue Service (count five). . . .

"Sang-Hyun Park presided over a criminal enterprise that was extraordinary in its scope and complexity," U.S. Attorney Fishman said. "The crimes for which he was sentenced today put us all at risk, not just because of the cost to our financial institutions, but also because of the threat posed by fake identification documents. Fortunately, the law enforcement agents and prosecutors who target identity theft and organized crime were just as patient and painstaking as the defendants who designed and executed this scheme, Mr. Park today joins dozens of his criminal conspirators in federal prison." . . .

Park defrauded various credit card companies, banks, and lenders out of $4 million. He and his conspirators also claimed more than $182,000 in tax refunds from the IRS through the filing of false and fictitious tax returns and accompanying documents.

In addition to the prison term, Judge Hayden sentenced Park to five years of supervised release and ordered to pay restitution of $4,774,116. He will also be deported upon his release from prison.

(FBI, Newark Division, 2014)

An effective police response to an investigation of identity theft will very likely require a multijurisdictional approach. The investigation begins with the victim reporting the theft to police per the provisions of the 2003 Fair and Accurate Credit Transactions Act (FACT Act). This federal law provides new rights and remedies to identity theft victims, but with a catch—the victim must first file a police report. Although this would appear to be common sense by the victim, the act was intended primarily to serve as an impetus to law enforcement in developing identity theft prevention and investigation

policies and protocols. To comply with the FACT Act, agencies must now have personnel trained in completing identity theft crime reports; investigating identity theft crimes, including the collection of evidence; and preparing identity theft cases for possible prosecution.

The FTC's recommended protocol for victims of identity theft is to complete a 6-page Identity Theft Affidavit (available online at ftc.gov/idtheft) to pair with an official police report to create an Identity Theft Report, which is generally more detailed than a typical police report and contains information specific enough for a credit reporting agency (CRA) or creditor to determine the legitimacy of the identity theft claims (FTC, 2013). Jurisdictions vary in their response to preparing and providing identity theft reports to victims—some states require police to write reports for identity theft crimes, others refuse to take reports from identity theft victims, and still others may allow officers to take the report but prohibit releasing copies of the official report to the victim. The FTC has prepared an open memo to law enforcement, explaining what an "Identity Theft Report" is and emphasizing its importance in helping identity theft victims recover from this crime (FTC, n.d.). Once a victim has a police report proving that they have suffered a theft of identity, the lengthy, difficult process of repairing the victim's damaged credit becomes somewhat easier through use of certain privileges not available to other consumers, such as blocking fraudulent trade lines on credit reports and obtaining the suspect's credit application.

Databases that investigators should search include the Financial Crimes Database, which includes information on stolen U.S. mail as well as stolen and fraudulently used checks and credit, automated teller machine (ATM), and debit cards. The FTC's Identity Theft Data Clearinghouse is a national identity theft database containing more than one million victim complaints, allowing investigators to search for information on identity theft victims and suspects across the country. Financial Crimes Enforcement Network (FinCEN) is another valuable resource for investigators because it links approximately three dozen independent databases in three main areas: law enforcement, finance, and commerce. Yet another valuable database is the FBI's National Crime Information Center (NCIC) Identity Theft File, which became operational in April 2005 and is designed to aid both police officers and crime victims.

With authorization from the victim, an investigator can get the victim's identity theft–related transaction records from creditors without first obtaining a subpoena, under the 2003 amendments to the Fair Credit Reporting Act, Section 609(e). A Request Letter template for law enforcement officers to use when requesting documents pertaining to an identity theft investigation is available from the FTC (Appendix F).

In addition to victim interviews, investigators should also seek information from informants. Other possible sources of informants include peripheral players in the identity theft, such as store employees who sold to suspects they knew were using stolen identities. Investigators should recognize the tools of the identity thief's trade, including blank checks, laminating machines, laptop computers, typewriters, color scanners and copiers, and **skimming** devices, through which a user can swipe a credit card and retrieve information from the card's magnetic strip.

Because the average American possesses 20 IDs in various forms—credit cards, bank accounts, personal identification numbers (PINs), Social Security numbers,

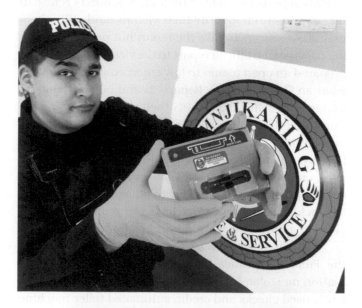

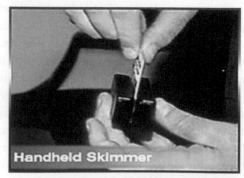

First Nation Mnjikaning Police Const. John Sahanatien displays a card skimmer, a device that houses a magnetic strip that copies account information, allowing criminals to steal personal information from a variety of types of credit and debit cards (top image).
Frank Matys/www.orilliatoday.com

Another much smaller handheld card-skimming device, this one is only the size of a pager (bottom image). These tiny devices can be easily concealed and carried, making it easy for a perpetrator to steal card information.
Courtesy Officer Jason Valdez and the Madera Tribune

driver's licenses, username/password combinations—the key to stopping identity theft may be biometrics, which relies on unique biological properties to positively identify an individual. Biometric identifiers include fingerprints, voiceprints, retinal scans, and facial recognition—IDs that are extremely difficult to steal or forge.

The Identity Theft and Assumption Deterrence Act allows prison sentences as long as 25 years for those convicted of the offense of identity theft and enables victims to seek restitution for identifiable losses and for expenses related to restoring their credit rating.

In May 2006 the President's Task Force on Identity Theft was established, cochaired by the attorney general and the chair of the FTC. The task force's mission is to provide a coordinated approach among government agencies to combat identity theft. It is also beneficial for law enforcement to form partnerships with the FTC, the National White Collar Crime Commission (NW3C), the Postal Inspection Service, the Secret Service, and the FBI.

Just as identity theft can overlap with and include other crimes such as credit card fraud and counterfeiting, identity theft can also be classified as white-collar crime.

White-Collar Crime

White-collar crime, also called **economic** or **corporate crime**, involves illegal, prohibited, and demonstrably harmful acts characterized by fraud, concealment, or a violation of private or public trust, committed by individuals or organizations in the conduct of their legitimate occupational roles or organizational functions, and directed toward financial advantage or to maintain and extend power and privilege (Simpson & Yeager, 2015; Friedrichs, 2020). White-collar crime is neither street crime nor conventional crime and does not depend on the actual or threatened use of physical force or violence. Many instances of larceny/theft and fraud can also be classified as white-collar crime. In some cases, perpetrators of white-collar crime do not "look like" criminals—they are often highly educated, socially accepted people who hold high-level positions of trust within a company. Because of such positions, high-level company executives are able to commit crimes involving millions of dollars.

White-collar crime makes headlines: the frauds and crooked accounting involved in the Enron and WorldCom bankruptcies; the scandals involving Tyco International and Adelphia Communications; and the ImClone stock debacle that sent the all-things-domestic guru Martha Stewart to a minimum-security women's prison in West Virginia known as "Camp Cupcake" for five months. With

CEOs pocketing millions, even billions, of dollars, investors and pensioners lost everything. This is probably the ultimate white-collar crime, perhaps better termed *corporate terrorism.* The American Society of Industrial Security (ASIS) Standing Committee on White-Collar Crime has changed its name to the Economic Crime Committee.

Much white-collar crime is never reported because it involves top-level executives of organizations that do not want their reputations damaged. White-collar crimes may be committed by individuals against other individuals such as family members, lawyers, real estate agents, insurance agents, and physicians. These crimes may be committed against organizations by insiders such as business partners, office managers, computer programmers, and senior executives. White-collar crimes may also be committed by individuals with no relationship to the victim, such as corporate spies, forgers, counterfeiters, computer hackers, and information pirates. Differences exist in how to define *white-collar crime* and what types of other crimes should fall within this classification.

LO10 List the offenses that are often included in the crime category of white-collar or economic crime.

White-collar or economic crime includes (1) securities and commodities fraud; (2) insurance fraud; (3) health care and medical fraud; (4) telemarketing fraud; (5) credit card and check fraud; (6) consumer fraud, illegal competition, and deceptive practices; (7) bankruptcy fraud; (8) computer-related fraud; (9) bank fraud, embezzlement, and pilferage; (10) bribes, kickbacks, and payoffs; (11) money laundering; (12) election law violations; (13) corruption of public officials; (14) copyright violations; (15) computer crimes; (16) environmental crimes; and (17) receiving stolen property.

Although traditionally law enforcement and the general public have focused on street crimes rather than white-collar crime, several studies show that this is no longer the case. In fact, survey research conducted over the past few decades has shown that Americans view white-collar crimes as serious and believe "upperworld" offenders should be punished (Cullen, Chouhy, & Jonson, 2019; Michel, 2018). The most recent *National Public Survey on White Collar Crime* (Huff, Desilets, & Kane, 2010) found that survey respondents viewed white-collar crime as slightly more serious than traditional crime types, and offenses committed at the organizational level were viewed more harshly than those committed by individuals.

Crimes committed by those in a position of trust were seen as more troubling than those committed by lower-status individuals, and the majority of respondents believed that white-collar crime contributes to the nation's economic struggles. Another survey found nearly three-fourths (74%) of respondents agreed or strongly agreed that white-collar crime is a considerable problem and is not being adequately addressed by legislators (Dearden, 2017).

Myth White-collar criminals receive lenient sentences due to the nonviolent nature of their crimes.

Fact Sentences are given at the judge's discretion within the law, and factors that may increase the penalties include the number of victims involved; the extent of harm to victims; the degree of sophistication used to execute or conceal the crimes; the leadership or supervisory role the offender played in the crime; whether the offender held a public position of trust; and if the offender obstructed or impeded the administration of justice. Therefore, some white-collar criminals receive more lenient punishments than others. Bernie Madoff, for example, received a sentence of 150 years in federal prison and forfeiture of more than $17 billion for his decades-long fraud scheme that bilked thousands of investors out of billions of dollars. Data from the U.S. Sentencing Commission shows the following federal court counts for various economic crimes:

- In FY2018, 494 individuals were sentenced in the federal system for tax fraud. The average sentence was 16 months, and 65% of offenders were sentenced to prison.

- In FY2018, 435 individuals were sentenced for health care fraud. The average sentence was 30 months, and 73.4% were sentenced to prison.

- In FY2019, 990 individuals were convicted of money laundering. The average sentence was 70 months, and 91.1% were sentenced to prison.
(U.S. Sentencing Commission, 2020)

Investigate these crimes as you would any larceny or fraud case. Whether they are felonies or misdemeanors depends not only on the value but also the number of victims involved.

White-collar crimes can be committed by any employee within a business or organization. However, low-level employees usually do not have the opportunity to steal large amounts from their employers. Most often, low-level employees' crimes consist of pilferage. Many employees do not see taking office supplies or placing personal long-distance phone calls from a work phone as dishonest. However, they would not think of doing the same thing in a place where they did not work. Over time, the losses from pilferage are often much more than what a high-level employee might embezzle.

Most law enforcement agencies are equipped to investigate basic white-collar crime, such as fraud, but when a case becomes too complex or the scale too large, additional resources should be sought. The NW3C links criminal justice agencies across international borders and bridges the gap between local and state criminal justice agencies. This center provides assistance in preventing, investigating, and prosecuting economic crime.

Corporate Fraud

Corporate fraud has gained national attention in recent years and is one of the highest priorities of the FBI's Financial Crimes Section. Despite all the media coverage and heightened scrutiny of business practices in corporations nationwide, the FBI anticipates no reduction in the number of such cases in the foreseeable future. FBI investigations show that corporate fraud involves such activities as falsification of financial information ("cooking the books"); self-dealing by corporate insiders, including insider trading and kickbacks; and obstruction of justice designed to conceal criminal conduct (FBI, 2011). Many cases of corporate fraud involve securities and commodities.

The highly publicized Enron scandal involved numerous illegal practices committed over several years by high-ranking company executives who sought to hide Enron's growing debt and keep perceived stock market value high. The deception and fraud began to receive notice when, in October 2001, the company made public the fact that it was actually worth $1.2 billion less than previously reported. This announcement set off an investigation by the Securities and Exchange Commission (SEC), which uncovered a tangled conspiracy between Enron executives, investment banking partners, and members of Enron's accounting firm to commit securities fraud, wire fraud, mail fraud, money laundering, and insider trading.

Other notable corporate fraud cases have included WorldCom and ImClone, companies both charged with securities fraud and other illegal accounting practices. These types of corporate fraud are generally discovered during routine auditing procedures and are often jointly investigated by the SEC and the FBI. In the WorldCom case, the company and its executives were also investigated by two congressional committees.

Money Laundering

Money laundering is converting illegally earned (dirty) cash to one or more alternative (clean) forms to conceal its illegal origin and true ownership. Drug traffickers and other racketeers who accumulate large cash inventories face serious risks of confiscation and punishment if considerable, unexplained cash hoards are discovered. For these criminals to fully benefit from their illicit activities, they must first convert those cash proceeds to an alternative medium—one that is both easier than cash to use in everyday commerce and avoids pointing, even indirectly, to the illegal activity that generated it.

Federal laws that drive the need for money laundering include the Bank Secrecy Act (BSA) of 1970, the first major piece of legislation to address the problem and require the reporting of certain cash transactions. Specific sections of this act include:

- 31 U.S.C. § 5313: Requires U.S. banks and other financial institutions to report cash transactions exceeding $10,000.

- 31 U.S.C. § 5324: Prohibits intentionally dividing cash sums exceeding $10,000 into smaller amounts to evade detection by ducking in under the required reporting threshold.

Other federal laws pertaining to money laundering include:

- 18 U.S.C. § 982: Allows the seizure of all property or money associated with a money laundering scheme and the forfeiture of such assets to the federal government.

- 18 U.S.C. § 1951 (The Hobbs Act): Addresses government corruption and makes illegal the act of extortion, through the actual or threatened use of violence or fear, exercised by someone in a position of authority or official capacity, for the purpose of personal gain.

- 26 U.S.C. § 7201 and § 7206(1): Prohibits the filing of a false federal income tax return or the commission of tax evasion through failure to report income.

- 26 U.S.C. § 60501: Requires all entities (individuals or organizations) engaged in commerce to report all cash transactions exceeding $10,000.

- The Money Laundering Control Act of 1986.

- The Anti-Drug Abuse Act of 1988.

- The 2001 USA PATRIOT (Providing Appropriate Tools Required to Intercept and Obstruct Terrorism) Act, which created a new money laundering statute, 18 U.S.C. § 5316, to deal with bulk cash smuggling.

The basic process of laundering money begins with **placement** of the funds into the legitimate U.S. market. Common methods of placement include creating shell corporations or fake cash-intensive businesses and **smurfing**, more technically known as **structuring**, whereby large amounts of cash are broken into increments less than $10,000, to avoid federal reporting requirements, and deposited into various bank accounts.

The second step in the laundering process is **layering**, where the money is cleaned by moving it around through a series of elaborate transactions, often involving offshore bank accounts and international business companies (IBCs). These multiple, complex transactions aim to obscure the connection between the money and the criminal group and to continue until the organization feels confident the money is adequately clean.

The third and final step in the money laundering cycle is **integration**, where criminals reclaim their money through seemingly legitimate business transactions. For example, the launderer creates a bogus export company in a free trade zone and a bogus import company owned through an IBC in a different country. A trading relationship is established where the exporter sends nonexistent goods or goods invoiced at greatly inflated prices to the importer, who pays the exporter in cleaned money, thus completing the laundry cycle.

A variety of businesses are used in laundering money. The amount of money laundered through these types of businesses and financial institutions across the country has been estimated at hundreds of billions of dollars and, despite efforts to curb such criminal practices, many expect money laundering to continue to increase with both domestic and international enforcement challenges given the ever-expanding potential of the Internet.

As part of the Money Laundering and Financial Crimes Strategy Act of 1998, High Intensity Financial Crimes Areas (HIFCA) were designated to help focus law enforcement efforts in those parts of the country where money laundering and related financial crimes were most prevalent.

Investigating money laundering usually uses white-collar–crime investigative techniques such as financial auditing and accounting, undercover operations (perhaps through sting operations), and electronic surveillance.

L011 Explain the FBI's two-pronged approach to investigating money laundering.

The FBI's proactive, two-pronged approach to investigating money laundering includes:

1. Investigating the underlying criminal activity. If there is no criminal activity, or specified unlawful activity that generates illicit proceeds, then there can be no money laundering.

2. A parallel financial investigation to uncover the financial infrastructure of the criminal organization. This involves following the money, discerning how it flows through an organization, and identifying what steps are taken to conceal, disguise, or hide the proceeds.

(FBI, 2011)

Investigators should routinely monitor the anti–money laundering initiatives of other countries. The Financial Action Task Force (FATF), of which the United States is a member, is an international assembly of more than 200 countries and jurisdictions, as well as two regional organizations, deemed to have strong anti–money laundering controls. Although FATF has no enforcement authority, its value lies in information sharing and promoting cooperation among nations. FATF's member-country websites are resources for information on current methods and trends in money laundering and the investigative techniques used to uncover them.

Investigators should carefully scrutinize the business activity of the suspected launderer, paying particular attention to such cash-intensive businesses as restaurants and bars, import/export companies, and diamond and fine jewelry businesses. Furthermore, know your community and the surrounding area.

Embezzlement

Embezzlement is the fraudulent appropriation of property by a person to whom it has been entrusted. The property is then used by the embezzler or another person contrary to the terms of the trust. The owner retains title to the property during the trust period. The property so entrusted may be real or personal property. Even though the title remains with the owner, the embezzler usually has control through appointment as agent, servant, bailee, or trustee. Because of the relationship between owner and embezzler, the embezzler has custody of the property. Most embezzlements involve employees. Most bank losses are from embezzlement, often involving large sums of money.

Businesses, industries, and other financial institutions besides banks are also victims of embezzlement. Embezzlement includes committing petty theft over time; "kiting" accounts receivable, in which a check is written on an account that does not have enough funds to cover the check amount; overextending credit and cash returns; falsifying accounts payable records; and falsifying information put into computers—a highly sophisticated crime. (Computer-related crimes are discussed in Chapter 17.)

Bank embezzlements often start small and gradually increase. Surprisingly, many embezzlements are committed not for the embezzler's benefit but as provision of unauthorized credit extensions to customers. As the amount increases, the employee is afraid to make the error known to the employer and attempts to cover the losses. In other cases, the employee uses funds to start other businesses, fully intending to replace the borrowed funds, but the businesses often fail. Other motives for embezzlement are to cover gambling debts, to support a drug habit, to make home improvements, to meet heavy medical expenses, or to get even with the employer for real or imagined grievances.

Embezzlement losses may be discovered by accident, by careful audit, by inspection of records or property, by the embezzler's abnormal behavior, by a sudden increase in the embezzler's standard of living, or by the embezzler's disappearance from employment. Bank embezzlement is jointly investigated by the local police and the FBI. However, the prosecution rate is low because of adverse publicity for both the individual and the company. Often the employee has been trusted for many years, and sympathy overrules justice.

Because police training rarely includes accounting courses, investigating embezzlement cases often requires help from professional accountants. In embezzlement cases, prove fraudulent intent to convert property contrary to the terms of a trust by establishing *how* and when the property was converted, *what* the exact amount was, and *who* did the converting. Establish that a financial loss did in fact occur. Determine the amount of the loss. Describe the property accurately if it is not money. Describe and prove the method of obtaining the property. Establish the nature of the trust. Seize all relevant books and financial records as evidence. It is often necessary to determine the motive to prove fraudulent intent.

Environmental Crime

Our environment—air, land, and water—has become a casualty in the battle among companies. Investigating environmental crime is a new area of specialization that mixes elements of law, public health, and science. Environmental crime is considered within the larger realm of white-collar crime because the motive behind these offenses is almost always an economic one. And contrary to what many believe, environmental crime is not victimless—the victims are our children and our children's children. Environmental crime is far-reaching and pervasive, and its consequences are often hidden for years or even decades.

INTERPOL entered the fight against environmental crime in 1992 when its general assembly adopted a resolution authorizing the creation of the Environmental Crimes Committee, with an initial participation of approximately 40 countries from all regions of the world. In 2012, during the First International Chiefs of Environmental Compliance and Enforcement Summit, 230 delegates from 70 countries and international bodies gathered to address the rising global concern over environmental crimes.

The most common environmental crimes prosecuted in the United States involve illegal waste disposal or dumping. Hazardous wastes are the most frequently involved substances in such offenses. Other substances often involved include used tires and waste oil. Collecting and processing evidence in these cases often require special training and equipment. Many law enforcement officers lack the scientific background needed to put together an environmental pollution case or to deal safely with the illegal disposal of hazardous waste. Indeed, walking into a hazardous waste site without proper protective gear or skills for handling the material may be just as deadly as facing an armed robber in a dark alley.

Furthermore, most officers have little or no idea of the existence of the complex array of environmental control laws with all their exceptions, changes, and omissions. For example, Congress and administrative agencies are continuously amending environmental laws and regulations to increase punishments for environmental criminal offenses, in many cases making them felonies rather than misdemeanors. Acts that have been amended to convert misdemeanor offenses into felonies include the

- Comprehensive Environmental Response, Compensation and Liability Act (CERCLA), also called Superfund, of 1980

- Resource Conservation and Recovery Act (RCRA) of 1976

- Federal Water Pollution Control Act (FWPCA), also known as the Clean Water Act (CWA), of 1972

- Clean Air Act (CAA) of 1970

- Federal Insecticide, Fungicide, and Rodenticide Act (FIFRA) of 1996

In 1990 the Pollution Prosecution Act was enacted, making enforcement of environmental crimes a new concern for law enforcement. Violations of various environmental crime acts call for penalties of as much as $25,000 per day for noncompliance or imprisonment for as long as 10 years. For some large corporations that engage in widespread, long-term improper disposal practices, the financial ramifications of criminal prosecution can be staggering. For example, in 2013, Walmart Stores Inc. pleaded guilty to six counts of violating the Clean Water Act by illegally handling and disposing of hazardous materials at its retail stores across the United States. The corporation also pleaded guilty to violating the Federal Insecticide, Fungicide, and Rodenticide Act (FIFRA) by failing to properly handle pesticides that had been returned by customers at its stores across the country: "As a result of the three criminal cases brought by the Justice Department, as well as a related civil case filed by the U.S. Environmental Protection Agency (EPA), Walmart will pay approximately $81.6 million for its unlawful conduct. Coupled with previous actions brought by the states of California and Missouri for the same conduct, Walmart will pay a combined total of more than $110 million to resolve cases alleging violations of federal and state environmental laws" (FBI, San Francisco Division, 2013).

Signs of Possible Environmental Violations. The Environmental Protection Agency (EPA) provides a list of some signs of possible environmental violations, including:

- Containers or drums that appear to be abandoned, especially if they are corroded or leaking

- Dead fish in streams or waterways, especially if the water appears to contain foreign substances (such as detergent, bleach, or chemicals) or has a strange color

- Dead animals alongside a riverbank or in a field

- Discolored or stressed, dying plant life

- Foul-smelling or oddly colored discharges onto the ground or into a stream or waterway

- Visible sheen on the ground or in the water

- Foul-smelling or strange-looking emissions into the air

- Stains around drains, sinks, toilets, or other wastewater outlets

- Pipes or valves that appear to allow the bypass of wastewater treatment systems

- Pipes or valves that would allow for discharge from a plant that appear hidden

- Building demolition that may involve illegal removal of asbestos or other hazardous materials
  (Environmental Protection Agency [EPA], 2017)

The EPA also recommends that investigators be aware of "odd activities" such as a truck dumping materials into a manhole or sewer drain or unloading drums at odd hours or in odd places. Also suspicious is a person burying drums on business or residential property. If any of the preceding is observed, law enforcement officers should investigate.

Investigating Possible Environmental Crimes. Local law enforcement plays an important role in protecting the environment. However, several challenges presented by environmental crimes investigations are understanding the numerous laws regarding what constitutes environmental crime, the fact that it is often considered a civil matter, and collaborating with civil regulatory agencies. In addition, the absence of credible legal threats or consequences increases the risk of corporate environmental crimes (Simpson et al., 2013).

Civil regulatory agencies are knowledgeable in these laws and have the resources to document evidence of a violation. For these reasons, in addition to the safety issues, many investigators find it beneficial to seek assistance from an environmental regulatory agency. Collaboration with specially equipped environmental labs, rather than crime labs, may also be necessary.

Some jurisdictions have designated specially trained law enforcement officers to investigate environmental crimes. Although many such officers are derisively being called "the garbage police," some agencies' sanitation police are gaining respect and recognition for their efforts in keeping cities clean and free of environmental wrongdoings. Massachusetts is one of several states that have created an environmental crimes strike force, an interagency law enforcement initiative that combines the technical, investigative, and legal resources necessary to detect, investigate, and prosecute environmental crimes.

Environmental hazards once common in industry, in America and abroad, include lead, asbestos, and chlorofluorocarbons (CFCs)—all of which have become regulated under various environmental laws. For example, when Freon, a brand name the public generally equates with the broader class of CFCs, was shown to contribute to the global problem of ozone depletion, countries from around the world gathered to find a solution. Through an international agreement signed by more than 160 countries at the 1987 Montreal Convention, the United States agreed to completely phase out CFC production by the year 2000. However, continued demand for CFCs and dwindling supplies have created an enormous black market.

The criminal enforcement program of the EPA investigates and assists in the prosecution of knowing or negligent environmental violations. In 2017, cases resulted in a total of 153 years of incarceration for individual defendants, plus fines of $2,829,202,563 for individual and corporate defendants, with an additional $3,092,631 in court ordered environmental projects and $147,520,585 in restitution. The write-ups below summarize information contained in public press releases from the EPA (2017):

Case 1: On February 23, 2017, Wood Group PSN Inc. (Wood Group), was ordered to pay $9.5 million in two separate cases involving conduct in the Gulf of Mexico. In the first case, investigators found that, from April 2011 to July 2014, Wood Group employees failed to inspect and maintain facilities they had contracts with and falsified reports to the government. The company admitted to 87 violations on offshore platforms and was ordered to pay $7 million for falsely reporting that personnel had performed safety inspections at offshore facilities in the Gulf of Mexico.

The second case stemmed from an explosion on an offshore oil production platform that resulted in the deaths of three construction workers and serious burns and injuries to others. Wood Group was convicted of violating the Clean Water Act and ordered to pay $1.8 million for negligently discharging oil into the Gulf of Mexico and another $700,000 in community service.

Case 2: On January 18, 2017, a Cedar Falls, Iowa man was sentenced to two years in federal prison for knowingly storing hazardous waste without a permit. Richard Delp's company, Cedar Valley Electroplating (CVE), was a large quantity hazardous waste generator, producing more than 1,000 kilograms of hazardous waste per month. Neither Delp nor CVE had a permit to treat, store, or dispose of hazardous waste under federal law. Delp closed CVE in 2011, leaving behind hundreds of gallons of corrosive and toxic chemicals and wastes inside and outside the building. Delp was convicted of violating RCRA and ordered to make nearly $800,000 in restitution to EPA's Superfund to pay for clean-up costs.

Case 3: In a FIFRA violation, case, a New Jersey swimming pool and spa chemicals company and its

president were sentenced on March 2, 2017, for convictions related to customs and import violations. Mark Epstein was sentenced to eight months in prison and four months of home confinement and ordered to pay $500,000 in restitution and forfeiture for his role in an elaborate rebate scheme which involved false statements, inflated payments, and rebates. Alden Leeds, Inc., was ordered to pay $2.25 million restitution and placed on three years' probation.

Epstein and Alden Leeds, Inc. had an agreement with a middleman to establish two prices for imported swimming pool sanitizing agents from China—an "actual price" that the company was paying and a higher "invoice price" that would be used for documentation at U.S. Customs. On August 21, 2015, the middleman in the scheme, Caiwei Sheng, was sentenced to a prison term of 12 months and ordered to pay restitution of $100,000.

Many of the problems associated with investigating environmental crime are similar to investigating other crimes that have become more prevalent in the 21st century. Definitions of environmental crimes vary from state to state. Statistics are not uniformly compiled. The suspects are often otherwise upstanding businesspeople who often do not feel they are committing crimes.

Premeditation or malice is not required to prove an environmental crime. All that must be proved is that an act that violated the law was done knowingly rather than by mistake. For example, the owner of a company makes a conscious decision to dump hazardous materials into a waterway or unload a truck full of construction and demolition debris, referred to by environmental investigators more simply as C&D debris, in a remote location off a desolate road under cover of darkness. Evidence of "knowing" may include tire tracks in remote locations and documented "after hours" activities, for it may be concluded that such "detours" are made to illegally dump and are not accidental.

As in any other crime, there must be a victim. Officers should determine who owns the property. Most judges do not like to see *State of X v. X* unless the state actually owns the property. In addition, officers should conduct a standard administrative interview, obtaining such information as name, date of birth, address, and whatever information is routinely asked *before* giving the *Miranda* warning if an interrogation is to take place.

Of special concern in environmental crime investigations is the search warrant. Investigators must know what substances they may seek and how they should collect such samples to avoid becoming contaminated. Again, regulatory personnel may provide assistance.

Through criminal prosecution of environmental crimes, local prosecutors have a crucial function and can assume the role of protector of the public health. Often, such prosecution is most successful using **parallel proceedings**, that is, pursuing civil and criminal sanctions at the same time.

A Final Note about Jurisdiction

A recurring theme throughout this chapter has been the interjurisdictional nature of many types of theft and fraud. Sometimes a single crime will violate local, state, and federal laws. Investigators must be aware that even though a crime may fall under federal jurisdiction, such as a theft of federally insured monies, that fact alone does not dictate whether another agency will assume responsibility for the investigation. Other factors, including the monetary value of the loss, will play a role in determining who is assigned the case. The amounts of these thresholds vary with the crime. Some crimes have no monetary threshold that must be exceeded before the federal government gains jurisdiction. Another factor that may impact jurisdiction is if there is a known suspect and, if so, what that suspect's criminal history is.

The FBI's website (www.fbi.gov/investigate) lists the agency's national security and criminal priorities, many of which were covered in this chapter, and provides additional details on which cases the federal government is more likely to become involved with. Furthermore, although INTERPOL offers a variety of support services to police agencies across the globe, such as training, communication, and database services, in many cases, this agency will not take an active role in investigations.

Summary

Larceny/theft is the unlawful taking, carrying, leading, or driving away of property from another's possession. Larceny is synonymous with theft. Both larceny and burglary are crimes against property, but larceny, unlike burglary, does not involve illegally entering a structure. Larceny differs from robbery in that no force or threat of force is involved. The categories of larceny/theft are grand larceny, a felony; and petty larceny, a misdemeanor. Which category the crime falls under is based on the value of the property stolen.

The elements of the crime of larceny/theft are (1) the felonious stealing, taking, carrying, leading, or driving away (2) of another's personal goods, property, or services, (3) valued above (grand) or below (petty) a specified amount (4) with the intent to permanently deprive the owner of the property or goods.

Common types of larceny are pocket picking and purse snatching; cell phone theft; bicycle theft; theft from motor vehicles; mail theft; retail shrinkage, including employee theft, shoplifting, and organized retail crime; jewelry theft; art theft; numismatic theft, including coins, metals, and paper money; agricultural theft; fish and wildlife theft; and cargo theft.

The elements of larceny by shoplifting are (1) intentionally taking or carrying away, transferring, stealing, concealing, or retaining possession of merchandise or altering the price of the merchandise; (2) without the consent of the merchant; (3) with intent to permanently deprive the merchant of possession or of the full purchase price. Federal legislation defines organized retail crime as violating a state ban against shoplifting or retail merchandise theft—if the quantities of items stolen are of the amount that would not normally be purchased for personal use or consumption—and stealing for the purposes of reselling the items or reentering them into commerce; receiving, possessing, concealing, bartering, selling, transporting, or disposing of any property that is known to have been taken in the violation outlined above; or coordinating, organizing, or recruiting persons to undertake either of the two violations outlined above.

Fraud is intentional deception to cause a person to give up property or some lawful right. It differs from theft in that fraud uses deceit rather than stealth to obtain goods illegally. Fraud includes confidence games, real estate and mortgage fraud, insurance fraud, health care fraud, mass marketing fraud, mail fraud, and fraud committed through counterfeiting or the use of checks or debit/credit cards. An increasingly serious and pervasive type of fraud is identity theft.

Elements of the crime of larceny by debit and credit card include (1) use of any counterfeit, fictitious, altered, forged, lost, stolen, or fraudulently obtained credit or debit card, or card number, (2) to intentionally obtain money, goods, or services.

White-collar or economic crime includes (1) securities and commodities fraud; (2) insurance fraud; (3) health care and medical fraud; (4) telemarketing fraud; (5) credit card and check fraud; (6) consumer fraud, illegal competition, and deceptive practices; (7) bankruptcy fraud; (8) computer-related fraud;

(9) bank fraud, embezzlement, and pilferage; (10) bribes, kickbacks, and payoffs; (11) money laundering; (12) election law violations; (13) corruption of public officials; (14) copyright violations; (15) computer crimes; (16) environmental crimes; and (17) receiving stolen property. The FBI's proactive two-pronged approach to investigating money laundering includes (1) investigating the underlying criminal activity (in simple terms, if there is no criminal activity, or specified unlawful activity that generates illicit proceeds, then there can be no money laundering) and (2) a parallel financial investigation to uncover the financial infrastructure of the criminal organization. This involves following the money, discerning how it flows through an organization, and identifying what steps are taken to conceal, disguise, or hide the proceeds.

Can You Define?

boosters	gouging	petty larceny
bustout	grand larceny	placement
car shopping	holder	poaching
confidence game	identity fraud	Ponzi scheme
corporate crime	identity theft	property flipping
cramming	integration	short-con games
economic crime	larceny/theft	shrinkage
embezzlement	layering	skimming
flaggers	leakage	slamming
floor-release limit	long-con games	smurfing
fluffing	money laundering	structuring
forgery	organized retail crime (ORC)	white-collar crime
fraud	parallel proceedings	zero floor release

Checklist

Larceny

- What are the name, address, and phone number of the complainant or the person reporting the crime?

- What are the name, address, and phone number of the victim if different from the complainant?

- Has the victim made previous theft complaints? If so, obtain all details.

- What were the date and time the crime was reported and the date and time the crime was committed, if known?

- Who owns the property or has title to it or right of possession?

- Will the owner or person in control or possession sign the complaint?

- Who discovered the loss? Was this the logical person to discover it?

- Where was the item at the time of the theft? Was this the usual place for the item, or had it been recently transferred there?

- When was the item last seen?

- Has the area been searched to determine whether the property might have been misplaced?

- What security precautions had been taken? Were these normal?

- Exactly what property was taken? Obtain a complete description of each item, including number, color, size, serial numbers, and other identifying marks.

- What was the value of the items? How was the value determined: estimated original price, replacement price, or estimated market value?

- How easily could the items be sold? Are there likely markets or buyers?

- Were online sale sites checked?

- Were there any witnesses to the theft or people who might provide leads?

- Who had access to the property before and during the time of the theft?

- Who were absentee employees?

- Could it be a case of employee theft?

- Who are possible suspects and why? What might be the motive?

Application

Read the following and then answer the questions:

A cash box was left on top of a desk at a university office. Some students had registered early that day, so there was about $600 in the box. The box was closed but not locked. The office manager went to lunch, leaving a college student in charge. The student took a phone call in the dean's office, and the box was out of her sight for about five minutes. Later she heard a noise in the hallway outside the office. She went out to see what had happened and discovered that a student had been accidentally pushed through a glass door across the hallway from the main office. She observed the scene in the hallway for about five minutes and then went back to the registration office, where she did not notice anything out of order.

After a half hour, the office manager returned from lunch and helped register two students at the front counter. When she went to the cash box to make change, she found that the $600 was missing. She immediately notified the administrator's office, and a controller was sent over to the registration office. The controller conducted a brief investigation and then notified the police. You are the investigator arriving at the registration office.

Questions

1. What procedure would you use upon arrival?

2. What crime was committed?

3. What steps would you take to investigate?

4. What evidence is likely to be located?

5. What questions would you ask?

6. What is the probability of solving the case?

References

Aldred, J. (2013, December 16). 2013 in review: The year wildlife crime became an international security issue. *The Guardian.* Retrieved November 17, 2020, from www.theguardian.com/environment/2013 /dec/16/2013-review-wildlife-crime-natural-world

Association of Certified Fraud Examiners. (2018). *Report to the nations: 2018 global study on occupational fraud and abuse.* Austin, TX: Author. Retrieved October 28, 2020, from s3-us-west-2.amazonaws.com/acfepublic/2018-report -to-the-nations.pdf

Bibb, T. (2005, August 11). Marion County [Florida] Sheriff's Office, Author interview.

Boehmer, M. (2016, June 2). *25 jaw dropping stats about employee fraud.* Portland, OR: SheerID, Inc. Retrieved October 28, 2020, from www.sheerid .com/blog/25-jaw-dropping-stats-about-employee -fraud/#:~:text=Employee%20Theft%20Statistics%3A,to%20 theft%20or%20fraud%20%E2%80%93%207%25&text =Percent%20of%20employees%20who%20have%20 stolen%20at%20least%20twice%20from,caused%20by%20 employee%20theft%20%E2%80%93%2033%25

Burnes, D., DeLiema, M., & Langton, L. (2020, March 17). Risk and protective factors of identity theft victimization in the United States. *Preventive Medicine Reports, 17*: 101058. Retrieved November 12, 2020, from www.ncbi.nlm.nih.gov /pmc/articles/PMC7013169/#b0085

CargoNet. (n.d.) *About cargonet.* Jersey City, NJ: Author. Retrieved November 8, 2020, from www.cargonet.com/

Coalition Against Insurance Fraud. (2020). *Fraud stats.* Washington, DC: Author. Retrieved November 10, 2020, from insurancefraud.org/fraud-stats/

Cornell, S. (2017). *How to run a successful cargo investigation.* Dallas, TX: International Supply Chain Protection Organization. Retrieved November 8, 2020, from www.iscpo.org/site/how-to-run-a-successful-cargo -investigation/

Cullen, F. T., Chouhy, C., & Jonson, C. L. (2019). Public opinion about white-collar crime. Chapter 14 in *The handbook of white-collar crime,* M. L. Rorie (Ed.). Hoboken, NJ: John Wiley & Sons.

Dearden, T. E. (2017, May 2). An assessment of adults' views on white-collar crime. *Journal of Financial Crime, 24*(2): 309–321. doi:10.1108/JFC-05-2016-0040

Deines, T. (2017, March 14). Illegal wildlife trade booming across U.S.-Mexico border. *National Geographic.* Retrieved November 4, 2020, from www.nationalgeographic.com /news/2017/03/wildlife-watch-wildlife-trafficking-reptiles -mexico-united-states/

Environmental Protection Agency. (2017, February 1). *Criminal enforcement: Signs of environmental violations.* Washington, DC: Author. Retrieved November 17, 2020,

from www2.epa.gov/enforcement/criminal-enforcement
-signs-environmental-violations

Federal Bureau of Investigation. (n.d.). *Art theft program.* Washington, DC: Author. Retrieved November 6, 2020, from www.fbi.gov/investigate/violent-crime/art-theft

Federal Bureau of Investigation. (n.d.). *Jewelry and gem theft.* Washington, DC: Author. Retrieved November 6, 2020, from www.fbi.gov/investigate/violent-crime/jewelry-gem-theft

Federal Bureau of Investigation. (n.d.). *Organized crime.* Washington, DC: Author. Retrieved October 28, 2020, from www.fbi.gov/investigate/organized-crime

Federal Bureau of Investigation. (2010, November 12). *Inside cargo theft: A growing, multi-billion dollar problem.* Washington, DC: Author. Retrieved November 17, 2020, from archives.fbi.gov/archives/news/stories/2010/november/cargo_111210

Federal Bureau of Investigation. (2011). *Financial crimes report to the public: Fiscal years 2010–2011.* Washington, DC: Author. Retrieved November 9, 2020, from www.fbi.gov/stats-services/publications/financial-crimes-report-2010-2011

Federal Bureau of Investigation. (2013, March 12). *Organized retail theft: Major middle eastern crime ring dismantled.* Washington, DC: Author. Retrieved November 17, 2020, from www.fbi.gov/news/stories/major-middle-eastern-crime-ring-dismantled

Federal Bureau of Investigation. (2018a). *2018 Crime Clock.* Washington, DC: Author. Retrieved October 22, 2020, from ucr.fbi.gov/crime-in-the-u.s/2018/crime-in-the-u.s.-2018/topic-pages/crime-clock

Federal Bureau of Investigation. (2018b). *Crime in the United States 2018.* Washington, DC: Author. Retrieved October 22, 2020, from ucr.fbi.gov/crime-in-the-u.s/2018/crime-in-the-u.s.-2018/

Federal Bureau of Investigation. (2018c). *Stolen identities: Hackers infiltrated mortgage company computers to steal customer information.* Washington, DC: Author. Retrieved November 10, 2020, from www.fbi.gov/news/stories/hackers-sentenced-in-identity-theft-case-032918

Federal Bureau of Investigation. (2018d). *2018 internet crime report.* Washington, DC: Author. Retrieved November 10, 2020, from pdf.ic3.gov/2018_IC3Report.pdf

Federal Bureau of Investigation. (2019, August 19). *A thief by many names: Atlanta man sentenced for aggravated identity theft.* Washington, DC: Author. Retrieved November 10, 2020, from www.fbi.gov/news/stories/atlanta-man-sentenced-for-aggravated-identity-theft-081919

Federal Bureau of Investigation, Los Angeles Division. (2011, November 3). *More than two dozen identified in massive fraudulent document manufacturing operation in Los Angeles.* Los Angeles, CA: Author. Retrieved November 10, 2020, from archives.fbi.gov/archives/losangeles/press-releases/2011/more-than-two-dozen-identified-in-massive-fraudulent-document-manufacturing-operation-in-los-angeles

Federal Bureau of Investigation, Los Angeles Division. (2014, May 14). *Fifteen charged in bustout scheme that cost victim banks more than $15 million.* Los Angeles, CA: Author. Retrieved November 17, 2020, from www.fbi.gov/losangeles/press-releases/2014/fifteen-charged-in-bustout-scheme-that-cost-victim-banks-more-than-15-million

Federal Bureau of Investigation, Newark Division. (2014, February 11). *Leader of large-scale identity theft ring sentenced to 12 years in prison for his role in fraud enterprise.* Retrieved November 10, 2020, from archives.fbi.gov/archives/newark/press-releases/2014/leader-of-large-scale-identity-theft-ring-sentenced-to-12-years-in-prison-for-his-role-in-fraud-enterprise

Federal Bureau of Investigation, San Francisco Division. (2013, May 28). *Walmart pleads guilty to federal environmental crimes, admits civil violations, and will pay more than $81 million.* San Francisco, CA: Author. Retrieved November 17, 2020, from www.fbi.gov/sanfrancisco/press-releases/2013/walmart-pleads-guilty-to-federal-environmental-crimes-admits-civil-violations-and-will-pay-more-than-81-million

Federal Communications Commission. (2018, December 9). *Technological advisory council (TAC) mobile device theft prevention (MDTP) working group (Version 1.0).* Washington, DC: Author. Retrieved November 19, 2020, from transition.fcc.gov/bureaus/oet/tac/tacdocs/reports/2018/11.30.18-MDTP-WG-Report-and-Recommendations.pdf

Federal Trade Commission. (n.d.). *Memo from FTC to law enforcement.* Washington, DC: Author. Retrieved November 11, 2020, from www.consumer.ftc.gov/articles/pdf-0088-ftc-memo-law-enforcement.pdf

Federal Trade Commission. (2013, September). *Guide for assisting identity theft victims.* Washington, DC: Author. Retrieved November 10, 2020, from www.consumer.ftc.gov/articles/pdf-0119-guide-assisting-id-theft-victims.pdf

Federal Trade Commission. (2020). *All identity theft reports.* Washington, DC: Author. Retrieved November 10, 2020, from public.tableau.com/profile/federal.trade.commission#!/vizhome/FraudandIDTheftMaps/IDTheftbyState

Finklea, K. M. (2012, December 11). *Organized retail crime.* Washington, DC: Congressional Research Service. (R41118) Retrieved November 17, 2020, from fas.org/sgp/crs/misc/R41118.pdf

Friedrichs, D. O. (2020). White collar crime: Definitional debates and the case for a typological approach. In Rorie, M. L. (Ed.), *The handbook of white collar crime* (pp. 16–31). Hoboken, NJ: Wiley Blackwell.

Harrell, E. (2019, January). *Victims of identity theft, 2016.* Washington, DC: Bureau of Justice Statistics. (NCJ 251147). Retrieved November 10, 2020, from www.bjs.gov/content/pub/pdf/vit16.pdf

Hollinger, R., & Moraca, B. (2018). *2017 National retail security survey: Final report.* Washington, DC: National Retail Federation. Retrieved October 28, 2020, from cdn.nrf.com/sites/default/files/2018-10/NRSS-Industry-Research-Survey-2017.pdf

Huff, R., Desilets, C., & Kanes, J. (2010, December). National public survey on whitecollar crime. Washington, DC: Bureau of Justice Assistance. (NCJ 233013)

Johnson, K. (2007, October 29). Copper is hot loot and quick cash for some thieves. *USA Today.* Retrieved November 19,

2020, from usatoday30.usatoday.com/news/nation/2007-10-29-arizonacopper_N.htm

MacFarlane, S., Yarborough, R., Jones, S., & Piper. J. (2019, May 21). Average of more than 80 items per day stolen from cars in DC in 2018. *NBCWashington.com*. Retrieved October 28, 2020, from www.nbcwashington.com/news/local/more-than-80-items-per-day-stolen-from-cars-in-dc-in-2018/159963/

Marchini, K., & Pascual, A. (2019, March 6). 2019 identity fraud study: Fraudsters seek new targets and victims bear the brunt. Livonia, MI: Escalent. Retrieved November 10, 2020, from www.javelinstrategy.com/coverage-area/2019-identity-fraud-report-fraudsters-seek-new-targets-and-victims-bear-brunt

Michel, C. (2018). Public knowledge about white-collar crime. *Criminology & Criminal Justice*. doi:10.1093/acrefore/9780190264079.013.496

Mlot, S. (2015, February 11). Cell phone kill switches prompt "dramatic" drop in thefts. *PCMagazine*. Retrieved October 26, 2020, from www.pcmag.com/news/cell-phone-kill-switches-prompt-dramatic-drop-in-thefts

Morgan, R. E., & Oudekerk, B. A. (2019, September). *Criminal victimization, 2018*. Washington, DC: Bureau of Justice Statistics Bulletin. (NCJ 253043). Retrieved November 6, 2020, from www.bjs.gov/content/pub/pdf/cv18.pdf

National Retail Federation. (2019). *2019 Organized retail crime survey*. Washington, DC: Author. Retrieved November 6, 2020, from cdn.nrf.com/sites/default/files/2019-12/NRF%20ORC%20Survey%202019.pdf

Newman, G. R., & Herbert, J. (2020). *Check and card fraud* (2nd Ed.). Tempe, AZ: ASU Center for Problem-Oriented Policing. Retrieved November 10, 2020, from popcenter.asu.edu/content/check-and-card-fraud-2nd-ed

Office of the Press Secretary. (2004, July 15). *President Bush signs identity theft penalty enhancement act*. Washington, DC: Author. Retrieved June 10, 2021, from georgewbush-whitehouse.archives.gov/news/releases/2004/07/text/20040715-3.html

Pofeldt, E. (2017, September 13). This crime in the workplace is costing US businesses $50 billion a year. CNBC.com. Retrieved October 28, 2020, from www.cnbc.com/2017/09/12/workplace-crime-costs-us-businesses-50-billion-a-year.html

Prey. (2018). *Mobile theft and loss report*. San Francisco, CA: Author. Retrieved October 26, 2020, from preyproject.com/uploads/2019/02/Mobile-Theft-Loss-Report-2018.pdf

Project529. (n.d.). *Our story*. Portland, OR: Author. Retrieved October 6, 2020, from project529.com/garage/

Randhawa, P. J., & Richey, E. (2020, February 6). Stolen phones keep getting sold to recycling kiosks. *5 on Your Side*. Retrieved October 26, 2020, from www.ksdk.com/article/news/investigations/phone-thieves-using-recycling-kiosks-quick-cash/63-406e74e8-2a7f-4606-880d-62c631c2e81b

Rosen, G. E., & Smith, K. F. (2010, August). Summarizing the evidence on the international trade in illegal wildlife. *EcoHealth, 7*: 24–32. doi:10.1007/s10393-010-0317-y

Schulte, S. (2018, June 15). Where do stolen smartphones go? *ABC7News.com*. Retrieved October 26, 2020, from abc7news.com/where-do-stolen-smartphones-go/3607823/

Simpson, S. S., Gibbs, C., Rorie, M., Slocum, L. A., Cohen, M. A., & Vandenbergh, M. (2013, Winter). An empirical assessment of corporate environmental crime-control strategies. *The Journal of Criminal Law and Criminology, 103*(1): 231–278. Retrieved November 17, 2020, from www.jstor.org/stable/24615613?seq=1

Simpson, S. S., & Yeager, P. C. (2015, March). *Building a comprehensive white-collar violations data system, final technical report*. Unpublished report funded by the U.S. Department of Justice. Retrieved November 13, 2020, from www.ncjrs.gov/pdffiles1/bjs/grants/248667.pdf

Sraders, A. (2020, February 18). Top 7 Craigslist scams. *The Street*. Retrieved November 9, 2020, from www.thestreet.com/personal-finance/craigslist-scams-14707309

Statistic Brain Research Institute. (2018). *Employee theft statistics*. Los Angeles, CA: Author. Retrieved October 28, 2020, from www.statisticbrain.com/employee-theft-statistics/

Tabor, J. (2018, March 28). In-transit cargo crime impacting the retail supply chain. *Loss Prevention Magazine*. Retrieved November 7, 2020, from losspreventionmedia.com/in-transit-cargo-theft-impacting-the-retail-supply-chain/

U.S. Attorney's Office, Central District of California. (2016, December 6). *Canadian couple sentenced to federal prison in "secret shopper" mass marketing scam that bilked victims across United States*. Los Angeles, CA: Author. Retrieved November 10, 2020, from www.justice.gov/usao-cdca/pr/canadian-couple-sentenced-federal-prison-secret-shopper-mass-marketing-scam-bilked

U.S. Department of State. (n.d.). *Environmental crime and wildlife trafficking*. Washington, DC: Author. Retrieved November 4, 2020, from 2009-2017.state.gov/j/inl/focus/combatting/environment/index.htm

U.S. Department of State. (2019, November 7). *2019 END wildlife trafficking report*. Washington, DC: Author. Retrieved November 4, 2020, from www.state.gov/2019-end-wildlife-trafficking-report/#:~:text=The%20Task%20Force%20on%20Wildlife,the%20%E2%80%9CNational%20Strategy%E2%80%9D).

U.S. Postal Inspection Service. (2018). *Annual report FY 2013*. Washington, DC: Author. Retrieved October 28, 2020, from www.uspis.gov/wp-content/uploads/2019/05/2018-AR.pdf

U.S. Sentencing Commission. (2020). *Quick facts*. Washington, DC: Author. Retrieved November 13, 2020, from www.ussc.gov/research/quick-facts

Wilkie, D. (2019, March 4). *Why is workplace theft on the rise?* Alexandria, VA: Society for Human Resource Management. Retrieved October 28, 2020, from www.shrm.org/resourcesandtools/hr-topics/employee-relations/pages/workplace-theft-on-the-rise-.aspx

Wyler, L. S., & Sheikh, P. A. (2013, July 23). *International illegal trade in wildlife: Threats and U.S. policy*. Washington, DC: Congressional Research Service. (RL34395). Retrieved November 19, 2020, from fas.org/sgp/crs/misc/RL34395.pdf

Chapter 15
Motor Vehicle Theft

Chapter Outline

Motor Vehicle Identification

Classification of Motor Vehicle Theft

Elements of the Crime: Unauthorized Use of a Motor Vehicle

Motor Vehicle Embezzlement

The Preliminary Investigation

Insurance Fraud

Vehicle Cloning

Cooperating Agencies in Motor Vehicle Theft

Recognizing a Stolen Motor Vehicle or an Unauthorized Driver

Recovering an Abandoned or Stolen Motor Vehicle

Combating Motor Vehicle Theft

Preventing Auto Theft

Thefts of Trucks, Construction Vehicles, Aircraft, and Other Motorized Vehicles

Learning Objectives

LO1 Explain what a VIN is and why it is important.

LO2 List the major categories of motor vehicle theft.

LO3 Identify the elements of the crime of unauthorized use of a motor vehicle.

LO4 Name the act that made interstate transportation of a stolen motor vehicle a federal crime.

LO5 Explain what embezzlement of a motor vehicle is.

LO6 List ways to improve effectiveness in recognizing stolen vehicles.

Introduction

In February 2014, a 10-month investigation in the northeast region of the United States culminated with the arrest and charging of 32 people—6 of whom were fugitives—for their involvement in an auto-theft ring that targeted and shipped luxury SUVs—primarily those made by Land Rover, BMW, and Mercedes Benz—to West Africa. Seven of those captured in the sweep face charges including racketeering, money laundering, fencing, and leading an auto-theft trafficking network. More than 160 cars were recovered in the investigation, 27 of which were carjacked. The remaining SUVs had been stolen off car carriers, at car washes, at airports, and from affluent neighborhoods where residents, living under a false sense of security, often left their cars unlocked, sometimes with the keys inside. Most of the thefts occurred in the New York City metropolitan area.

According to investigators, the stolen vehicles would first be taken to underground garages or other secure locations to "cool off" while ring members determined whether any tracking devices were attached. Once the vehicles were cool enough to be safe, "wheel men" would move them to different sites where fences would pay anywhere from $4,000 to $8,000 per car. The vehicles would then be transferred to "shippers," who would load them into shipping containers headed for ports in New Jersey and New York, where they would then be placed on a shipping vessel bound for Africa. Some of the stolen cars sold for as much as $100,000. Investigators did not believe any port employees were involved in the scheme, since the stolen vehicles were loaded into the shipping containers off site and were already accompanied by false documentation before they arrived at the port (Associated Press, 2014).

It is not unusual for an American family to finance or own more than $40,000 in motor vehicles. Yet the motor vehicle, even though highly vulnerable, is the least protected of all property subject to theft. The vehicle, its accessories, and the property inside are all targets for thieves.

Most people use motor vehicles to travel to work and for pleasure. Thousands of recreational vehicles are also targets for theft and burglary. Aircraft and watercraft thefts add to the problems facing police investigators.

According to the FBI Crime Clock, a car is stolen every 42.2 seconds in the United States (Federal Bureau of Investigation [FBI],

2018a). In 2018, 748,841 motor vehicles were reported stolen nationwide, at a theft rate of about 228.9 motor vehicles stolen for every 100,000 inhabitants (FBI, 2018b). The estimated number of motor vehicle thefts decreased 3.1% in 2018 when compared with the 2017 estimates, but rose 9.0% when compared with the 2014 estimates and dropped 5.9% when compared with the 2009 estimates (FBI, 2018b). The estimated cost of motor vehicle theft in 2018 was $6.3 billion, with the average value of a stolen vehicle placed at $8,407. Automobiles represented 74.9% of all motor vehicles stolen. Only 14.2% of thefts were cleared by arrest. Table 15.1 lists the most commonly stolen vehicles in the United States in 2018.

TABLE 15.1	National Insurance Crime Bureau's (NICB) Top 10 Stolen Autos in the United States, 2019		
Rank	Vehicle	Thefts	Most Frequent Vehicle Year Stolen
1	Ford Pickup (Full Size)	38,938	2006
2	Honda Civic	33,220	2000
3	Chevrolet Pickup (Full Size)	32,583	2004
4	Honda Accord	30,745	1997
5	Toyota Camry	15,656	2007
6	Nissan Altima	13,355	2015
7	Toyota Corolla	12,137	2018
8	Dodge Pickup (Full Size)	11,292	2001
9	GMC Pickup (Full Size)	11,164	2018
10	Honda CR-V	10,094	2001

Source: National Insurance Crime Bureau. (2019). *Hot wheels 2019*. Des Plaines, IL: Author. Retrieved June 14, 2021, from www.nicb.org/HotWheels2019

According to the Rocky Mountain Insurance Information Association (RMIIA), the top 10 metro areas with the highest auto-theft rates in 2016 were: (1) Albuquerque, New Mexico; (2) Pueblo, Colorado; (3) Bakersfield, California; (4) Modesto, California; (5) Riverside/San Bernardino/Ontario, California; (6) Anchorage, Alaska; (7) Merced, California; (8) San Francisco/Oakland/Hayward, California; (9) Fresno, California; and (10) Billings, Montana.

Myth New luxury cars are most at risk of being stolen.

Fact The most commonly stolen vehicles are consistently more than 10 years old and were never considered "high-end" luxury cars, even when new.

Motor Vehicle Identification

Given the millions of motor vehicles operating on our roads, an identification system is imperative. The most important means of vehicle identification is the **vehicle identification number (VIN)**.

L01 Explain what a VIN is and why it is important.

The VIN is the primary nonduplicated, serialized number assigned by a manufacturer to each vehicle made. This number—critical in motor vehicle theft investigation—identifies the specific vehicle in question.

VINs for vehicles manufactured prior to 1981 had anywhere from 11 to 17 numbers and letters, whereas all automobiles manufactured since 1981 contain a series of 17 numbers and letters (Montoya, 2019).

The Motor Vehicle Theft Law Enforcement Act of 1984 requires manufacturers to place the 17-digit VIN on 14 specified component parts including the engine, the transmission, both front fenders, the hood, both front doors, both bumpers, both rear quarter panels, both rear doors and the deck, lid, tailgate, or hatchback. In most late-model cars, the VIN is located on the left instrumentation or dash plate by the window, on the driver's door or post, or on the firewall.

A fictional example of a VIN would be "1F1CY62X1YK555888," where:

1 = nation of origin (1, 4, 5 = United States; 2 = Canada; 3 = Mexico; and J = Japan)

F = manufacturer symbol (A = Audi, B = BMW, H = Honda, etc.)

1 = make

C = restraint

Y = car line

62 = body type

X = engine symbol

1 = check digit

Y = model year

K = assembly plant

555888 = sequential production number

The VIN of a vehicle is the automotive equivalent of human DNA; no two VINs are identical. The VIN allows investigators to trace a vehicle from the factory to the scrap yard. Some manufacturers position the label in plain view; others hide it. Investigators must be aware that the location of the VIN can vary among vehicles. Car thieves frequently attempt to change or replace VINs to conceal vehicles' true identities. Decoding VINs can aid in investigating auto theft, cloning, and chop shop operations, to be discussed shortly. Manufacturers also use numbers to identify engines and various vehicle components.

Classification of Motor Vehicle Theft

Motor vehicle thefts are often classified by the thief's motive or purpose, but it may be impossible to determine the motive for thefts that end in the vehicle's being abandoned.

> **LO2** List the major categories of motor vehicle theft.
>
> Classifications of motor vehicle theft based on the offenders' motive include the following:
>
> - Joyriding
> - Transportation
> - Commission of another crime
> - Gang initiation
> - Stripping for parts and accessories
> - Reselling for profit

Joyriding

Joyriding is simply taking a vehicle for fun, often driving recklessly and without regard for any damage caused to the vehicle itself or other property, and then abandoning it. The joyrider and the person stealing for transportation are sometimes grouped together, but there is an important distinction between them. The joyrider is generally a younger person who steals for thrills and excitement.

Joyriders look for cars with keys in the ignition that can be started and driven away rapidly. These crimes of opportunity sometimes arise when a driver has left their vehicle running and unattended, with the doors unlocked, as often occurs in cold weather to warm up the car before driving it. The vehicle is taken for a comparatively short time and then abandoned near the location of the theft or near the joyrider's destination. A vehicle taken to another community is generally left there, and another vehicle is then stolen for the return trip. Police officers are often the ones who discover the crime of motor vehicle theft, such as when they find a car parked in an odd place and contact the registered owner, who only then realizes that the vehicle has been stolen.

Stolen vehicles are often found where young people congregate: fast-food places, malls, and athletic events. Several vehicle thefts within a short time may follow a pattern, providing clues for investigators. For example, most cars stolen by the same individual or group in a short period are the same make, entered in the same manner, and stolen and dropped off in the same general area. Juvenile informants can be extremely helpful in investigating such auto thefts.

Motor vehicle thefts by juveniles are often not regarded seriously by the courts, even though they account for most vehicle thefts and can cause injury or death to others. It is not unusual for juveniles to be involved in as many as a hundred car thefts before apprehension. Vehicle theft by juveniles is a serious problem, and in some states joyriding is a separate offense.

Transportation

Theft of a motor vehicle for transportation can involve a joyrider but is more apt to involve a transient, a hitchhiker, or a runaway. The objective is to travel from one point to another at no cost. These offenders are generally older than joyriders. Late fall and winter are peak periods for this type of theft.

A vehicle stolen for transportation is kept longer than one stolen for joyriding. Frequently it is operated until it runs out of gas or stops running. It is then abandoned (often to avoid suspicion) and another vehicle is stolen. The license plates may be changed, or a plate may be stolen and put on the rear of the vehicle. Sometimes the car thief removes the plates and displays a temporary tag.

Commission of Another Crime

Automobiles are used in most serious crimes. Robberies of banks, bank messengers, payroll offices, businesses, and service stations, as well as criminal escapes, almost always involve a getaway in a stolen vehicle. Vehicles provide both rapid transportation and a means to transport the loot. Other crimes frequently committed while using stolen vehicles include rapes, kidnappings, burglaries, larcenies to obtain gas, and assaults of police officers attempting to apprehend a suspect. Records indicate that many habitual criminals have stolen at least one car in their criminal careers. Some began as car thieves.

Stolen cars are used in committing other crimes to escape detection at the crime scene and to avoid being identified by witnesses. Therefore, the criminal normally uses the stolen vehicle only briefly. In fact, a stolen vehicle report may not yet have been made when the crime is committed. Stolen plates are often used to cause confusion in identification. The vehicle used in committing the crime—the "hot" car—is usually soon abandoned for a "cold" car—a vehicle used to escape from the crime scene vicinity.

Myth Motor vehicle theft is a nonviolent, "single victim" crime.

Fact Many stolen cars are involved in a secondary crime such as robbery or drug trafficking. A stolen car also has a higher likelihood of being involved in an accident. Thus, a stolen car can be very dangerous and can have negative impacts on not only the owner but also on the community.

Stolen vehicles played a major role in the search for serial killer Andrew Cunanan. Authorities were able to re-create the route taken by Cunanan in his cross-country killing spree by locating one victim's vehicle in the vicinity of the next victim's body. Cunanan's homicidal rampage began in late April 1997 in Minnesota with the killing of two men. Cunanan then stole the Jeep Grand Cherokee of one of the victims, and police later discovered this vehicle near the home of a third victim in Chicago. The Chicago victim's Lexus was reported missing and was later found in New Jersey at the murder scene of Cunanan's fourth victim. In continuing the pattern, the fourth victim's pickup truck was stolen and later turned up in a Miami Beach parking ramp, several blocks from where fashion designer Gianni Versace was murdered in front of his home by Cunanan, who, days later, then killed himself as authorities were closing in on his hiding place.

A stolen motor vehicle driven by a criminal is 150–200 times more likely to be in an accident than is a vehicle driven by a noncriminal; therefore, regard as suspicious any damaged abandoned vehicles you observe. Conditions contributing to this high accident rate include operating the vehicle on unfamiliar streets and roads, driving at high speeds in an attempt to escape police pursuit, testing the vehicle's speed, unfamiliarity with the vehicle, and use of drugs. A criminal apprehended with a stolen vehicle after committing another major crime is often charged with both crimes but, during plea bargaining, the lesser crime of auto theft is often dismissed.

Gang Initiation

Occasionally a vehicle is stolen as part of a gang initiation or "putting in work" for the gang. As noted in the court transcript of *The People v. Gregory Shelton* (2011): "[A gang expert] explained that 'to put in work for the gang' means doing something for the benefit of the gang. The gang would consider itself benefited if a gang member shoots or kills a member of another gang or if a gang member commits a robbery, by way of an example. It is very important 'to put in work for the gang' because this is what makes a gang's reputation."

Stripping for Parts and Accessories

Many vehicles are stolen by juveniles and young adults who strip them for parts and accessories to sell: transmissions, rear ends, motors, and wheels. Batteries, radiators, and heaters are sold to wrecking yards, used-car lots, and auto repair shops. Expensive accessories such as GPS devices, radar detectors, car speakers, and XM radio units also are removed for resale. The stripped vehicle is often crushed for scrap metal. The profit is extremely high. Sometimes thieves steal specific items for friends, other vehicle owners, or themselves. These are often parts that are impossible to buy or are very expensive.

Catalytic converter thefts have been on the rise. Metals such as platinum, palladium, and rhodium are found inside catalytic converters and, as precious metals rise in value, so do the converters. Scrap yards buy these converters, which are relatively easy for thieves to cut out of vehicles, for approximately $100 to $150.

Airbag Theft. The National Insurance Crime Bureau (NICB) reports that airbags are a primary accessory on the black market for stolen vehicle parts. A new airbag retails for approximately $1,000. Unscrupulous collision repair shops may replace a deployed airbag with a stolen one and charge the customer or the customer's insurer the full price (which constitutes insurance fraud). Insurance statistics show that approximately 50,000 airbags are stolen each year, resulting in an annual loss of more than $50 million to vehicle owners and their insurers (National Insurance Crime Bureau [NICB], *Airbag*, n.d.).

Stealing for Chop Shops. A **chop shop** is a business, usually a body shop, that disassembles stolen autos and sells the parts. The chop shop deals with car thieves who steal the cars specifically for them, often on demand, stealing the exact make, model, and color. The vehicle may triple in value when sold for parts. There is no waiting period and no tax to the customer. The cars are dismantled, and the parts are cataloged. In some cities, this business is so big that organized crime has been heavily involved and network organizations dispose of the stolen parts. Auto parts are also sought outside the United States.

The chop shop may also deal directly with the owner of a vehicle who wants to dispose of it for insurance purposes because of dissatisfaction with its performance. The owner leaves the vehicle registration with the chop shop. The shop returns the registration to the owner after the vehicle is dismantled and crushed. The insurance company has no chance of recovery.

Reselling

Auto thefts are also committed by professional thieves who take an unattended vehicle, with or without the keys, and simply drive it away. Or they may go to a used car lot, posing as a buyer, and drive the vehicle away on a no-return test-drive. Another method is to answer an ad in the paper for a particular car, try it out, and then never return it. This gives the thief time to escape because the owner gave permission to take the vehicle—which makes the case one of embezzlement.

Recovering a vehicle stolen by professionals requires a specialized knowledge of investigative techniques and often depends on a reliable informant to get started. Moreover, such thieves are difficult to detect and prosecute. As specialists in automobiles, the thieves know how to steal cars and how to alter them or the documents needed to make them eligible for resale. The professional is rarely the actual thief; rather, the professional hires others to steal cars and bring them to a specified location, usually a garage, for making the necessary alterations.

Alterations include repainting, changing seat covers, repairing existing damage, and altering the engine number. The car is also completely searched to eliminate any items that connect it with the former owner. The VIN is almost always altered or replaced. The most common method of changing the VIN is to buy a similar vehicle from a salvage lot and then remove and replace the entire dash, making the change undetectable. If the VIN is not located on the dash, the car thief has a much more difficult time. In some cases, the VIN plate itself is removed and carefully altered, or the car thief can make embossed tape with a handheld tape-numbering device and place it over the regular VIN plate. Unless the inside of the car is investigated, a false VIN plate is not usually detected.

After all number changes on the motor and the VIN plate are completed, the vehicle is prepared for resale with stolen or forged titles, fictitious bills of sale, or titles received with salvage vehicles bought by the thieves. When the mechanical alterations and paperwork are completed, the vehicle is registered through the department of motor vehicles (DMV) and resold, usually at a public car auction, to a used-car dealer or a private individual.

Many stolen cars are exported for resale in other countries, the most common destinations being Central and South America. Hundreds of thousands of vehicles are estimated to be illegally exported each year. One international car-theft ring was indicted by a federal grand jury for illegally obtaining vehicles from Reno, Nevada, car dealers and transporting them to the Port of Long Beach in California, where the cars were loaded onto freighters and shipped to China to be sold at three to four times their original price. The ring members then reported the cars stolen to police and insurance companies for reimbursement of their losses. Charges against ring members included making false statements on loan and credit applications, mail fraud, interstate and foreign transportation of stolen property, aiding and abetting, and attempting to evade financial reporting requirements. The FBI estimated that the scheme involved total losses of as much as $6 million.

Elements of the Crime: Unauthorized Use of a Motor Vehicle

Prosecution for auto theft requires proof that the thief intended to permanently deprive the owner of the vehicle, which is often difficult or impossible to establish. Consequently, most car thieves are prosecuted for unauthorized use of a motor vehicle rather than for auto theft.

> **LO3** Identify the elements of the crime of unauthorized use of a motor vehicle.
>
> The elements of the crime of unauthorized use of a motor vehicle are the following:
> - Intentionally taking or driving away
> - a motor vehicle
> - without the consent of the owner or the owner's authorized agent.

Intentionally Taking or Driving Away

Intent is often described in state laws as "with intent to permanently or temporarily deprive the owner of title or possession" or "with intent to steal." Intent can be inferred from the act of taking or driving, being observed taking or driving, or being apprehended while taking or driving. Laws often include as culpable any person who voluntarily rides in a vehicle knowing it is stolen.

A Motor Vehicle

Motor vehicle is not restricted to automobiles. It includes any self-propelled device for moving people or property or pulling implements, whether operated on land, on water, or in the air. Thus, *motor vehicles* include automobiles, trucks, buses, motorcycles, motor scooters, mopeds, snowmobiles, vans, all-terrain vehicles (ATVs), golf carts, self-propelled watercraft, and aircraft. Homemade motor vehicles are also included.

Without the Consent of the Owner or the Owner's Authorized Agent

Legitimate ownership of motor vehicles exists when the vehicle is in the factory being manufactured, when it is being sold by an authorized dealership, or when it is owned by a private person, company, or corporation. *Owner* and *true owner* are not necessarily the same. For example, the true owner can be a lending agency that retains title until the loan is paid.

Usually the owner or the owner's authorized agent reports the theft. Thus, it can be determined immediately whether consent was given. Previous consent is not a defense, although it may be considered.

If you stop a suspicious vehicle and the driver does not have proof of ownership, check the registration with the state DMV to determine who the legal owner is. If that person is not the driver, check with the legal owner to determine whether the driver has permission to use the vehicle.

Interstate Transportation

In 1919 the need for federal control of motor vehicle theft was recognized, and Congress approved the National Motor Vehicle Theft Act, commonly known as the Dyer Act.

> **LO4** Name the act that made interstate transportation of a stolen motor vehicle a federal crime.
>
> The **Dyer Act** made interstate transportation of a stolen motor vehicle a federal crime and allowed for federal help in prosecuting such cases.

The act was amended in 1945 to include aircraft and is now called the *Interstate Transportation of Stolen Motor Vehicles Act*. Since the Dyer Act was passed, more than 300,000 vehicles have been recovered and more than 100,000 criminals have been convicted in interstate car-theft cases. Cars and airplanes are not the only vehicles subject to interstate transportation laws. In 2012, three members of an organized crime ring involving ATVs were convicted and sentenced in Louisiana for their participation in the theft and interstate transportation of 60 ATVs valued at approximately $363,000. One defendant received five years' probation; one was sentenced to prison for 39 months, followed by three years of supervised release; and the third defendant received a sentence of 57 months in prison, followed by three years of supervised release. All three defendants were ordered to pay restitution of $309,933.78, each (FBI, New Orleans Division, 2012).

The elements of the crime of interstate transportation of a motor vehicle are as follows:

- The motor vehicle was stolen.

- It was transported in interstate or foreign commerce.

- The person transporting or causing it to be transported knew it was stolen.

- The person receiving, concealing, selling, or bartering it knew it was stolen.

The vehicle thief may be prosecuted in any state through which the stolen vehicle passed. Prosecution is normally in the state in which the vehicle was stolen, but sometimes it is in the state in which the person was arrested.

Intent is not required. The stolen vehicle could accidentally be driven over the state line or forced to detour into another state. If the vehicle is transported by train or truck through another state, prosecution is also possible.

The Anti Car Theft Act of 1992 provides tougher legislation against auto theft, previously a low-profile crime. The penalty for importing or exporting stolen vehicles was increased from 5 to 10 years, as was the penalty for interstate transportation of stolen vehicles. The act empowers U.S. Customs with new authority to check for stolen vehicles and provides funds to states that participate in the National Motor Vehicle Title Information System. The act also made armed carjacking a federal offense.

Motor Vehicle Embezzlement

This most frequently occurs when a new- or used-car agency permits a prospective buyer to try out a vehicle for a specific time. The person decides to convert the vehicle to personal use and does not return it. This is fraudulent appropriation of property. Motor vehicle embezzlement can also occur under rental or lease agreements or when private persons let someone test-drive a vehicle that is for sale.

Motor vehicle embezzlement exists if the person who took the vehicle initially had consent and then exceeded the terms of that consent.

The Preliminary Investigation

When a motor vehicle theft is reported, initial information obtained by police includes the time, date, and location of the theft; the make, model, and color of the vehicle; the state of issue of the license plate; license plate number; direction of travel; description of any suspect; and the complainant's present location. Officers should also ask about any unique features of the vehicle, such as OnStar, GPS location services, or remote disabling features, as several newer models of certain makes feature disabling devices and car-finder apps. In addition, any noticeable after-market vehicle features should be noted, such as rims, low-profile accessories, spoilers, wraps, or paint designs.

The complainant is asked to remain at their present location, and a police officer is dispatched to obtain further information and to complete the proper complaint form.

False motor vehicle theft reports are often filed when a car has been taken by a family member or misplaced in a parking lot, when the driver wants to cover up an accident or crime committed with the vehicle, or when the driver wants to provide an alibi for being late for some commitment. It is also possible that the vehicle has been reclaimed or repossessed ("repo'ed") by a loan company—a civil matter. Another civil matter is a situation in which someone lends a vehicle to another person and then the borrower fails to return the vehicle when the owner wants it back. This does not necessarily constitute a theft of motor vehicle; depending on the circumstances, such a scenario is often a civil matter.

If a vehicle is found with accident damage, it is necessary to determine whether the damage occurred before or after the report. Vehicles involved in a hit-and-run incident are sometimes abandoned by the driver and then reported as stolen. Drunk drivers may also report their cars stolen if they crash while driving under the influence and then leave the scene of the crash. Younger people sometimes report a car stolen if they crash and are afraid to tell their parents.

A preliminary description is provided to patrol officers, who are told that the theft has not been verified; therefore, no all-points bulletin is issued. During this time, patrol officers are alerted, but they make no move if they see the stolen vehicle because the report has not been validated. The officer in the field obtains information to determine the validity of the theft charge: the circumstances surrounding the alleged theft, identification of characteristics of the stolen vehicle, any details of items in the car, and any possible suspects. Interviews with witnesses are another crucial aspect of the preliminary investigation. Frequent false reports impair cooperation from other agencies, especially when the errors should have been detected by the investigating officers.

Recovered vehicles must be examined for usable latent prints, DNA, and other physical evidence. DNA samples may be recovered from the steering wheel, the shifter, the turn signal device, window roll down features, radio controls, and the rear-view mirror. Suspect DNA is also frequently found on items left behind in the car, such as cigarette butts, bottles, cans, and other trash. DNA has even been recovered from the inside of a glove inadvertently left behind in a stolen vehicle.

Computerized police files can assist in searching for suspects. Investigators can enter data concerning past suspects and other individuals in vehicles, types of vehicles stolen, the manner in which vehicles were entered or stolen, the types of locations from which they were stolen (apartment complexes, private residences, or commercial parking lots, for example), where vehicles were abandoned, and where vehicles were if the suspects were arrested in them.

Investigators must be familiar with the tools and methods commonly used to commit vehicle theft, including car openers, rake and pick guns, tryout keys, impact tools, keyway decoders, modified vise grips, tubular pick locks, modified screwdrivers, and hot wiring, as these provide valuable evidence in proving the crime.

Insurance Fraud

Vehicle insurance fraud is a major economic crime that affects every premium payer through increased insurance rates. Many police departments inadvertently facilitate insurance fraud by allowing car-theft reports to be phoned in or by taking them "over the counter" at the police station and then never investigating the reports. The primary reason the auto theft is reported is often for insurance purposes. To avoid this situation, law enforcement agencies should investigate all auto-theft reports and should not discount the possibility that the "victim" is actually committing insurance fraud.

For example, a luxury car stolen from a suburban mall parking lot was found four days later on fire on a rural road. The case seemed routine until a detective began an investigation to eliminate the car's reported owner. The detective found that there were three pending lawsuits against the "victim," who had filed for bankruptcy shortly after the lawsuits and months before the car was stolen. He had filed an affidavit claiming he no longer owned the car because he had sold it six months before. Investigation revealed that the buyer was a friend who let the car be transferred into his name so it would not be involved in the bankruptcy proceedings. This was a clear case of filing false information with the police. Further, after a fire investigator and a mechanic inspected the car, they reported that the lab tests showed ongoing engine failure. The victim wanted the insurance company to pay for a replacement vehicle—an obvious case of fraud.

Vehicle Cloning

The NICB describes vehicle **cloning** as a crime in which stolen vehicles assume the identity of legally owned, or "non-stolen," vehicles of a similar make and model. Criminals apply counterfeit labels, plates, stickers, and titles to these stolen cars, making them appear legitimate. The non-stolen vehicles can be actively registered or titled in another state or country, resulting in multiple vehicles having the same VIN being simultaneously registered or titled—but, of course, only the non-stolen vehicles are legitimate. The rest are fakes, or clones.

The first step in the cloning process is to copy a VIN from a legally owned car. Then the criminal steals a vehicle similar to the one from which the VIN had been lifted. The stolen vehicle's legitimate VIN is replaced with a counterfeit one, making the stolen vehicle a clone of the legally owned original vehicle. The criminal then creates counterfeit ownership documents and sells the stolen vehicle to an innocent buyer (FBI, 2009; Wagschal, Benitez, & Khoury, 2015; Sullivan; 2019).

The NICB notes that vehicle cloning is a relatively easy crime to commit, especially by organized rings of professional vehicle thieves and fraud artists. The cost to clone a vehicle is often less than $2,000, but the profit can be tens of thousands of dollars once the clone is sold (NICB, 2015). Luxury cars are often targeted for cloning because they yield higher returns.

Compounding the cloning problem is that many cloned vehicles are used for illegal operations, such as trafficking drugs or smuggling illegal aliens. For example, in December 2015 Laredo, Texas, Sector Border Patrol agents arrested a male subject attempting to smuggle illegal immigrants while using a cloned Border Patrol Tahoe (U.S Customs and Border Protection, 2017).

Cooperating Agencies in Motor Vehicle Theft

Police most frequently use state DMVs to check owners' registrations. They also use them to compare the driver of a vehicle with the registered owner. When vehicle registration and driver's registration checks are completed, further checks can be made in the FBI's National Crime Information Center (NCIC) files to determine whether the vehicle is stolen and whether the driver has a criminal record.

The FBI assists local and state authorities who notify the bureau that a stolen motor vehicle or aircraft has been transported interstate—which places it within the provisions of the Interstate Transportation of Stolen Motor Vehicles Act. The FBI works with local authorities to find the vehicle and the person who stole it. The FBI can also examine suspicious documents relating to false sales or registrations. In addition to information on stolen vehicles, the bureau's NCIC contains information on stolen auto accessories.

The Department of Justice is responsible for maintaining the National Motor Vehicle Title Information System (NMVTIS), which was created under the Anti Car Theft Act of 1992 and reauthorized in 1996. This database, operated by the American Association of Motor Vehicle Administrators, is designed to prevent and help investigate various types of automobile theft and fraud by providing an electronic means for verifying and exchanging title, brand, theft, and other data among state motor vehicle titling agencies, law enforcement officials, consumers, and other authorized users of the system.

In 1992, the National Auto Theft Bureau was incorporated into the NICB, a nonprofit organization supported and maintained by hundreds of automobile insurance companies. The organization helps law enforcement agencies reduce and prevent auto thefts and investigate questionable or fraudulent vehicle fires and thefts.

The NICB also disseminates reports on stolen vehicles to law enforcement agencies and serves as a clearinghouse for information on stolen vehicles. Computer files are maintained for several million wanted or stolen cars, listed by make, engine number, VIN, and component part number. This information is available free upon request to law enforcement agencies. The NICB can also trace cars from the factory to the owner. Its staff of specialists and technicians are experts in identifying stolen cars and restoring mutilated, changed, or defaced numbers. They also restore altered or obliterated VINs.

The NICB publishes and distributes to police agencies an annual *Passenger Vehicle Identification Manual*.

This publication describes the location of identifying numbers, gives license plate reproductions, and provides a short legal digest of each state's motor vehicle laws.

Recognizing a Stolen Motor Vehicle or an Unauthorized Driver

As with other crimes, a suspicious nature and an alert mind help an officer detect motor vehicle thefts. Detection is sometimes improved by an instinct developed through training, observation, and experience. Police officers develop individual techniques for recognizing stolen cars. No absolute, single peculiarity identifies a stolen car or a car thief, but either one can draw the attention of an observant officer.

> **LO6** List ways to improve effectiveness in recognizing stolen vehicles.

To improve your ability to recognize stolen vehicles

- Keep a list of stolen vehicles, or a "**hot sheet**," in your car.

- Develop a checking system for rapidly determining whether a suspicious vehicle is stolen.

- Learn the common characteristics of stolen vehicles and car thieves.

- Keep up to date with the most frequently stolen vehicles and the areas from which they are most often stolen.

- Take time to check suspicious persons and vehicles.

- Learn how to question suspicious drivers and occupants.

A *potential car thief on foot* usually appears nervous. They may be looking into cars on the street or in parking lots, trying door handles, and carrying some sort of entry tool. Observe such an individual from a distance until an overt act is committed.

Characteristics of a driver of a stolen vehicle include making sudden jerks or stops, driving without lights or excessively fast or slow, wearing gloves in hot weather, and attempting to avoid or outrun a squad car. Any unusual or inappropriate driving behavior may be suspicious. In addition, car theft is considered by some crime experts to be a gateway crime, the point where juvenile delinquents escalate the severity of their criminal activity. Juveniles account for approximately 16% of stolen vehicles, and in

2018, more than 2,700 persons under age 15 were arrested for motor vehicle theft, so it makes sense for officers to take a second glance at drivers who appear unusually youthful (FBI, 2018b).

Characteristics of a stolen vehicle include having one license plate when two are required, two when one is required, or no plates displayed at all. Double or triple plates with one on top of the other can indicate lack of time to take off the original plates. A set of old plates with new screws, wired-on plates, altered numbers, dirty plates on a clean car or clean plates on a dirty car, differing front and rear plate numbers, plates bent to conceal a number, upside-down or hanging plates, and homemade cardboard plates are all suspicious. Expired registration tabs are worth a closer look. Observe whether the trunk lid has been pried or whether side windows or door locks are broken. Look for evidence of a broken steering column or of tampering with the ignition switch. Abandoned vehicles are also suspicious.

When *questioning drivers and any occupants of cars* you have stopped on suspicion of motor vehicle theft, observe their behavior. Watch for signs of nervousness, hesitancy in answers, over-politeness, and indications that the driver does not know the vehicle. Request the driver's license and the vehicle registration papers for identification. Examine the driver's license and ask for the driver's birth date. The driver will probably not know the correct date unless it is their license. Compare the description on the license with the person. Compare the state of issuance of the license with the car's license plates. Ask the driver to sign their name and compare the signature with that on the driver's license.

Ask the driver the year, make, and model of the car and compare the answers with the registration papers. Ask the mileage. The driver of a stolen car rarely knows the mileage, whereas the owner or regular driver knows within a reasonable number of miles. Ask the driver to describe the contents of the car's trunk and glove compartment.

Check inside the vehicle for an extra set of license plates, bullet holes or other damage, bloodstains, and service stickers showing where and when the car was last serviced. Inspect the VIN plate for alterations. A roll of adhesive tape can indicate it was used to tape windows before breaking them. Wire or coat hangers bent straight to open doors, rubber gloves, jumper cables, or tools for breaking into a car are also alerting signals.

Parked cars may have been stolen if debris under the car indicates it has been in the same place for a long time. Check with neighbors to determine how long the vehicle has been parked there. The neighborhood canvass is one of the most effective techniques in investigating abandoned cars. Residential security and doorbell cameras can also provide valuable information. Check for illegal entrance, for open car windows in inclement weather, and for dirty vehicles indicating lack of care. A citation under the wiper can indicate when the car was abandoned. Keys left in the ignition and lack of license plates are also grounds for checking.

A warm or running motor and firearms or valuables left in the car may indicate that the thief has temporarily parked the car and intends to return. Stake out stolen vehicles (identified by license number or description) because the thief may return. Consider partially immobilizing the vehicle to prevent an attempted escape.

Recovering an Abandoned or Stolen Motor Vehicle

Most motor vehicle thefts are local problems involving locally stolen and recovered vehicles. Data from the FBI indicates that only 57.2% of stolen vehicles are ever recovered, many of them with damage (NICB, *Vehicle,* n.d.). Stolen vehicles are recovered when patrol officers observe a vehicle that is listed on a hot sheet, a suspicious vehicle or driver, an apparently abandoned vehicle, or when private citizens report an abandoned vehicle.

Although patrol units are responsible for most of the stolen vehicles recovered, investigative personnel play a major role in furnishing information to the uniformed patrol in all areas of motor vehicle theft.

The initial patrol officer at the scene examines recovered and abandoned vehicles unless there is reason to believe the vehicle was involved in a serious crime. Investigators assigned to such a crime may want to look for specific items in the vehicle that might not be known to the patrol officers. In these cases, the vehicle is protected until the specialists arrive.

Once recovery and impound reports have been completed, the car is removed from the hot sheet and the owner is notified of the recovery. A vehicle recovery report should be completed and filed.

If a crime has recently been committed in the area or if the vehicle's position and location suggest that the suspect may return, drive by and arrange for a stakeout. If the car is locked and the keys are gone, if heavy rain or fog exists and the windshield-wiper marks indicate they were recently used, or if no dry spot appears under the car, the vehicle was probably used recently and the driver may return. Round rain spots on the vehicle mean that it has been parked for a longer period than if there are elongated raindrops, which indicate recent movement. If it has been snowing but the car shows no accumulation, that also indicates recent movement. A quick check of heat remaining on the hood, radiator, or exhaust pipe also indicates whether the car was recently parked. Consider attempting to apprehend the criminal on return to the vehicle.

However, if a car has a flat tire, is up on blocks, or is covered with snow or fallen leaves, it is probably abandoned and can be immediately processed at the scene, the police station, or a storage location. Consider the possibility that the vehicle was used in committing another crime such as robbery, burglary, murder, hijacking, or abduction or kidnapping. Search the vehicle's exterior first and then the interior as described in Chapter 4. Many car thieves have been located through items left in a vehicle.

If you suspect the vehicle was used in another crime, have it impounded to be processed (it should not be driven until processing is complete). After processing, notify the rightful owner.

Technology is facilitating the recovery of stolen vehicles. LoJack has developed a system that places a homing device in an obscure place on a vehicle. If the vehicle is reported stolen, the device is activated and a tracker picks up a signal that is displayed on a lighted compass. An illuminated strength meter tells operators when they are nearing the stolen vehicle. The display also shows the model and color of the car. The LoJack website reports that the radio frequency–based system is used in more than 30 countries, has been installed in more than 9 million vehicles worldwide, and has helped track and recover billions of dollars' worth of vehicles around the world. The tracking technology has shown a consistently high 90% recovery rate. Furthermore, locating even one vehicle with the tracking system on it can lead investigators to other stolen assets.

The system is not without its drawbacks, however. First, the lag time between a car theft and its report may be hours or even days. Second, there are some dead spots—locations where transmitted radio signals will not be detected. Third, some departments hesitate to become a partner with a private company. Finally, some departments worry that the public will perceive them to be focused on preventing car theft from the more affluent members of the community—those who can afford the nearly $700 auto recovery system.

Other systems also are available, some of which activate automatically. If someone drives off in the car without deactivating the system, an alarm is sent to the tracking center. Such systems might, however, result in false alarms and pose as great a problem as false burglar alarms. Other systems provide a personal alert service that allows motorists to signal authorities in case of emergencies. One system allows controllers to shut off a stolen car's engine by remote control if police tracking the car believe it would be safe to do so. The OnStar system, for example, not only uses GPS to pinpoint a stolen vehicle's location, helping authorities quickly recover it, but can also send a slowdown signal to a stolen vehicle, thereby reducing the dangers of high-speed pursuits, and can deploy an ignition block signal, preventing a car thief from restarting a stolen vehicle.

Combating Motor Vehicle Theft

Police departments are using several strategies to combat rising auto-theft levels:

- Setting up sting operations—for example, a body shop that buys stolen vehicles—and using bait cars

- Providing officers with auto-theft training

- Coordinating efforts across jurisdictional lines

- Instituting anti–car-theft campaigns

- Increasing penalties for stealing vehicles

In areas where police have made special efforts to educate the public and to assign extra squads to patrol high–auto-theft areas, auto theft has significantly decreased.

New York City has instituted the Combat Auto Theft (CAT) program, which has been highly successful. Participating car owners sign a form indicating that they do not normally operate their automobiles between 1 a.m. and 5 a.m., the peak auto-theft hours. They also sign a consent form that authorizes the police to stop their vehicle during these hours without probable cause. Owners are given a CAT program decal to affix prominently on the inside of the car's rear window. Officers may stop any car having the decal, without probable cause, if they see it traveling on city streets between 1 a.m. and 5 a.m. (New York City Police Department, n.d).

Virginia's Help Eliminate Auto Theft (HEAT) program, which began in 1992 and is a cooperative effort between the Virginia Department of State Police, Virginia Department of Motor Vehicles, and local law enforcement agencies throughout the Commonwealth, offers up to $25,000 for tips that lead to the arrest of those suspected of auto theft, theft of vehicle parts, or chop shop operations. Tips called in to the program's toll-free number or submitted online are monitored by the Virginia State Police Criminal Investigation Section. In 2017, a reported 1,100 arrests were made for motor vehicle theft in Virginia and of those arrested, 184 were under the age of 17. That same year, the value of reported stolen motor vehicles totaled $86 million (Virginia State Police, 2017).

The increased use of alarms and protective devices may partly account for the rise in armed carjackings, as explained in Chapter 12. Unwilling to give up their lucrative "trade," car thieves may use force against a vehicle operator to gain control of the vehicle rather than risk being thwarted by antitheft devices. Whereas carjacking is treated as quite a severe crime, regular unarmed auto theft remains a relatively minor offense and, from a criminal perspective, a safe crime to commit.

License Plates

Something as low-tech as a license plate can often be used to identify and capture auto thieves as well as other criminals, considering that roughly 70% of crimes involve the use of a motor vehicle. Automated license plate readers (ALPRs) are being used in patrol cars across the country, and the technology is capable of scanning 3,600 vehicles per hour (Dees, 2019).

Routine Activities and Motor Vehicle Theft

The routine activity approach to crime suggests that the daily, routine activities of populations influence the availability of targets of crime. The existence of potential offenders, suitable targets, and lack of guardianship explains variation in the rate of motor vehicle theft. Research indicates that city blocks with bars have almost twice as many auto thefts as do city blocks without bars and that blocks adjacent to high schools have higher levels of auto theft than do blocks that are not near high schools. In addition, parking lots with attendants have lower rates of auto theft than do similar lots with no attendants on duty. Such findings might be used in designing auto-theft prevention programs such as using bait cars.

Bait Cars. The basic idea of a **bait car** is simple: a model of vehicle with a high theft rate is selected and placed in a high crime area. Officers then simply sit back and wait for the vehicle to be stolen.

Plate Hunter™ Mobile ALPR

Leonardo has developed the Plate Hunter™ Mobile ALPR—a tool that provides real-time knowledge and post-action criminal intelligence to law enforcement, thereby increasing officers' day-to-day productivity and safety. According to the company's website: "More than 70% of crimes in the U.S. involve a vehicle. Having technology that's able to read up to 900 plates per minute, [our] ALPR camera helps officers to quickly identify criminals and keep your community safe." ALPR technology can be used in numerous crime and situation deployments beyond the recovery of stolen vehicles, including:

- Removing suspended and revoked drivers from the road before they cause an accident

- Assisting with AMBER or Silver Alerts and missions related to missing and exploited children or vulnerable adults

- Safe school initiatives such as perimeter security and school bus safety

- Developing and maintaining Sexual Predators Hot Lists

- Drug interdiction

- Highway and traffic safety

- Terrorist interdiction and homeland security initiatives

- Gang and racketeering interdiction

- Collection of unpaid taxes, fines, and fees

Source: https://www.leonardocompany-us.com/lpr/alpr-products/mobile-alpr
www.leonardocompany-us.com/lpr/who-we-serve/alpr-law-enforcement

In California, the nation's "car-theft capital," bait cars are used extensively. The Los Angeles Sheriff's Department's Taskforce for Regional Auto-theft Prevention (TRAP) uses a traditional, watch-and-wait method of bait vehicles. In California, car theft is classified as a nonviolent felony, typically earning the perpetrator just 120 to 150 days in jail, and it isn't subject to California's three-strikes rule. Most of the offenders arrested have prior histories and consider jail time to be like going away to school to catch up on the latest techniques from colleagues.

Bait cars can be enhanced using **telematic technology**, which transfers data between a remote vehicle and a host computer. The data are transferred using the Internet and wireless technology as well as a global positioning system (GPS). A small radio transceiver called a vehicle locator unit (VLU) is hidden in the bait vehicle. The VLU transmits a silent homing signal, revealing the vehicle's location to an officer's remote control unit (RCU), a handheld two-way radio equipped with a keypad from which commands are entered, activating the tracking transmitter and controlling the bait vehicle's engine, door locks, flashers, and horn. The car is tracked by satellite and located. Mapping software can display the location, direction, and speed of the vehicle. When an officer catches up with the thief, they can remotely kill the stolen car's engine and lock the car's door.

Border Area Auto Theft

According to the NICB, many of the top metropolitan areas for vehicle theft are in or near ports or the Mexican or Canadian borders. Actually, there is no international border for this highly mobile crime. Particularly hard hit by auto theft are California, Texas, Florida, Washington, and Georgia, which the FBI ranks as the leading car-theft states in the nation (FBI, 2018b).

The Arizona law enforcement community has created programs to encourage binational cooperation. At the center of this effort is Policia Internacional Sonora y Arizona (PISA), a cross-border networking group that began more than 20 years ago when a few Arizona and Sonora (Mexico) officers gathered informally over breakfast. The group now has hundreds of members throughout the border region. Relationships established at these conferences create personal connections that could not be made any other way.

In 2003, Arizona established a Border Auto Theft Information Center (BATIC), a toll-free, long-distance telephone line that Sonoran police can use to seek and share information about vehicles recovered in or stolen from Mexico. The program averages about 50 calls a day from Mexican law enforcement officers.

Theft of Patrol Cars

Police vehicles are also vulnerable to thieves. Just as border area auto theft presents unique challenges, so does the theft of police vehicles. About the only police vehicle that appears to be immune from theft is a K-9 vehicle. A stolen unit driven by a fleeing felon might run down civilians, practically guaranteeing that the department will be sued. In addition, police cars grant the drivers access to high-security areas, so terrorists would jump at the chance to obtain one.

Most reports of stolen police vehicles involve suspects who get into a unit an officer has left unattended, usually to take a report or chase a suspect. Many officers need to keep their vehicles running almost nonstop through a shift. Turning the engine off drains the car's battery quickly because of the power demands of emergency lights, communications systems, laptops, and other devices. Turning off the engine also powers down those instruments, requiring inconvenient rebooting.

Technology offers some answers here. One solution is a brake-light kill switch. With the brake lights cut off, the car will not come out of park even when running. This solution works only with later-model vehicles that require the driver to step on the brake before the transmission can shift out of park.

Another solution is a secure-idle system in which an officer presses a button, places the transmission in park, turns the key to the normal off position, and removes the key. The engine keeps running and all accessories remain on. However, any unauthorized attempt to step on the brake or move the shift lever out of park cuts all electrical power. It can also trigger an optional alarm. The system is deactivated by putting the key back into the ignition and turning it to the on position.

Preventing Auto Theft

Effective preventive measures could eliminate many motor vehicle thefts. Vehicle theft requires both desire and opportunity, and it is often difficult to know which comes first. An unlocked automobile with keys in the ignition is a temptation. A parked vehicle with the motor running is also extremely inviting. Many juveniles take cars under such conditions and then boast of their ability to steal. Numerous motor vehicle thefts can be prevented by effective educational campaigns and by installing antitheft devices in vehicles during manufacture.

Educate motor vehicle owners about the importance of removing their keys from the ignition and locking their vehicles when parked. Public education campaigns might include distributing dashboard stickers with the reminder "Have you removed your keys from the ignition?" or "Don't forget to take your keys and lock your car."

To deter theft, some automakers have developed ignition systems and keys that use microchips with electronic codes embedded in them. However, car thieves have been able to duplicate these antitheft keys by using code grabbers similar to the devices used to duplicate codes that open garage doors. In response, as with garage door makers, some auto manufacturers are now using rolling codes and encrypted systems that use randomly generated codes to defeat thieves. They have also developed a buzzer system that warns the driver that the keys are still in the vehicle. Keyless entry and ignition systems are additional technologies designed to make it harder for thieves to break into vehicles to steal them. **Immobilizer** systems, in which the engine recognizes only the preprogrammed key(s) assigned to the car, are a further safety device to prevent auto theft.

The NICB website suggests a four-layered approach to combat auto theft:

1. *Common sense.* Remove keys, close windows, and lock doors. Park in well-lit areas. Do not leave the car running and unattended, especially with small children inside.

2. *Visible and audible warning devices.* Use steering wheel locks, wheel locks, theft deterrent decals, identification markers such as the VIN etched in the window, and audible alarms.

3. *Immobilizing devices.* Use cut-off switches, kill switches, smart keys, and fuel disablers.

4. Tracing devices. Give police the vehicle location.

(NICB, *Vehicle,* n.d.)

Thefts of Trucks, Construction Vehicles, Aircraft, and Other Motorized Vehicles

Investigating thefts of trucks and trailers, construction vehicles and equipment, recreational vehicles, motorized boats, snowmobiles, motorcycles, motor scooters, mopeds, and aircraft is similar to investigating auto thefts.

Trucks and Trailers

Usually trucks and trailers are stolen by professional thieves, although they are also stolen for parts. A "fingerman" often provides information to the thief. In most cases, the fingerman is an employee of the company that owns the truck. A "spotter" locates the truck after getting information from the fingerman and then follows the truck to the point where

Layer 4:
Tracing Devices

Layer 3:
Immobilizing Devices

Layer 2:
Visible and Audible
Warning Devices

Layer 1:
Common Sense

The National Insurance Crime Bureau's suggested four-layered approach to combat auto theft.

it is to be stolen. A driver experienced in operating the targeted vehicle then commits the actual theft.

Truck trailers are usually stolen by simply backing up a tractor to the trailer and hauling it away. The trailer's cargo is generally the target.

Stolen trucks and trailers are identified much as passenger vehicles are—by the manufacturer or through the *Commercial Vehicle Identification Manual* published by the NICB.

Construction Vehicles and Heavy Equipment

According to the National Equipment Register (NER), heavy equipment theft is a growing problem, with approximately 11,493 heavy equipment thefts reported in 2015, including backhoes, bulldozers, and dump trucks. Most of the thefts were committed by organized crime rings, which often had targeted equipment shopping lists. Many of the rings are international, filling equipment needs in underdeveloped countries (National Equipment Register, 2016).

National surveys suggest that the total cost of heavy equipment theft could be as much as $1 billion each year in the United States alone. More worrisome is the low recovery rate of stolen heavy equipment; the recovery rate in 2015 was only 22%. Adding to the problem is that product identification numbers (PINs) are nonstandard, vary dramatically in format among manufacturers, and may be located in numerous, often hard-to-find locations.

The NICB website notes that rubber-tired equipment is most likely to be stolen because it can be driven away under its own power. The most popular targets in 2015 were riding lawn mowers and garden tractors, followed by loaders and tractors (NER, 2016). Most vulnerable are less-secure construction sites on weekends. The stolen vehicles usually stay intact.

When the NER was launched in 2002, a significant step was taken toward reducing the ongoing problem of heavy equipment theft. According to the NER, heavy equipment is often stolen by organized crime rings and has a high benefit-to-risk ratio. Heavy equipment has little physical machine or site security, is valuable and easy to sell, and is often transported to a port or across the border before the theft is even discovered and reported.

The NER has registered more than 114,789 theft reports and provides access to more than 12 million equipment ownership records. The NER provides law enforcement officers with expert, free assistance in investigating and prosecuting equipment theft, including:

- 24/7 access to specialist NER operators who will offer expert advice on equipment identification, PIN locations, and other identification techniques

- 24/7 searches of the NER database online via a toll-free number (866-FIND-PIN)

- 24/7 access to millions of ownership records through NER operators

- Additional online investigation tools such as PIN location information

- Local and national training programs

Many construction companies have formed protection programs, have identified their equipment with special markings, and have offered rewards for information about thefts. Local construction firms can also provide information about possible outlets for stolen parts.

The NER recommends that site security be enhanced by posting "no trespassing" signs and using fencing, gates, locks, and good lighting. Vehicle security can be enhanced by marking, anchoring, and immobilizing equipment. Equipment not being used should be arranged in a way so that a missing unit would be obvious. Equipment should not be left on a trailer unattended.

The NER has a pocket-sized reference, *Law Enforcement Identification Guide for Construction and Agricultural Equipment*, which includes theft indicators, commonly stolen equipment, location of PIN numbers, and other useful items for investigators. The NER offers the following "red flags" as theft indicators, cautioning that legitimate explanations might exist for any of the indicators.

Transport

- Equipment being transported late at night or on weekends or holidays. Equipment theft most often happens at those times.

- Hauled equipment that is being moved in a hurry and therefore lacks the proper tie-downs, over-width/overweight signs, or lights

- Equipment being hauled on trucks not designed to haul such equipment

- Equipment being hauled with buckets in the up position or booms not lowered

- New equipment on old transport

- Labels/markings on a piece of equipment that do not match those of the unit carrying or hauling it

Use and Location

- Equipment in an unsecured location that has not been moved for some time—either by repeat observation or the age of the tracks leading to the equipment

- Type of equipment that does not suit the location or use—such as construction equipment on a farm or in a residential area with no building activity

Equipment and Markings

- Equipment with missing PIN plates. Manufacturers generally use mounting techniques that make it unlikely for a PIN plate to fall off during normal use.

- Equipment that has been entirely repainted or that has decals removed or painted over

- Manufacturer decals or model number stickers that do not match the piece of equipment to which they are affixed

- A commercially manufactured trailer with registration plates reflecting a homemade trailer (certain states only)

Price

- Equipment that is being offered, or has been purchased, at a price well below market value

When looking for "red flags," focus on the 10 most commonly stolen types of equipment, which account for 90% of all stolen equipment reported to the NER (2016):

- Mowers, riding or garden tractors (44%)

- Loaders, which includes skid steers, backhoes, and wheel loaders (17%)

- Tractors, which includes compact, utility, and agricultural tractors (12%)

- Utility vehicles (7%)

- Excavators (3%)

- Fork lifts (3%)

- Generators, compressors, welders (2%)

- Bulldozers (1%)

- Brush chipper (1%)

- Trencher (1%)

Recreational Vehicles

More than 450 makes and models of recreational vehicles (RVs) are marketed in the United States. Because there are so many makes and models, contact the manufacturer for any special numbers not readily visible. Recreational vehicles are also targets for vehicle burglaries because many contain CB radios, televisions, DVDs, and appliances. Many false theft claims are made because of the high cost of operating these vehicles.

Motorized Boats and Jet Skis

In 2019, a total of 4,240 watercraft thefts occurred, with 1,745 (41%) having been recovered as of March 10, 2020 (Moss, 2020). The highest number of watercraft thefts in 2019 took place in Florida (22%), and the holiday with the most watercraft thefts in 2019 was Independence Day. Since 1972 many states have required licensing boats, including an identification number on the boat's hull. Most such identification numbers are 10 to 13 digits. The first several digits are the manufacturer's number. This is followed by 4 or 5 identification digits and several certification digits.

Boat owners should record the specifics and effects of the boat by inventorying all electronics and other gear, including the trailer, and taking detailed photographs to document their property. To prevent boat theft, owners should place hardened steel locks on props, outboards, and outdrives; install stainless steel locking hasps or bars on cabin doors and hatch boards; install a fuel or electrical cutoff device; install an alarm system; keep curtains drawn; do not leave keys "hidden" on board; stow the vessel in a place with good lighting; and, whenever possible and practical, remove valuable equipment and store it at home. BoatUS (the Boat Owners Association of the United States) notes: "If you have a small outboard engine, it's much safer in your garage than hanging on your boat's transom. The more stuff you take off, the less attractive your boat will be to a thief" (Boat Owners Association of the United States, 2019). In addition, boat owners are encouraged to prominently display stickers announcing the presence of antitheft device because, as with home security systems, thieves are more inclined to pass up a well-guarded boat for one that seems less well protected. Finally, since most boats are stolen while on their trailer, owners should take steps to secure the trailer, either parking it so that the hitch faces away from the street, chaining it to a permanent object such as a tree or a sturdy post, removing two of the tires and storing them securely inside, or removing the license plate and lights because "the last thing a thief wants is a traffic stop" (Boat Owners Association of the United States, 2019). The same precautions apply to Jet Skis.

Because boats also are the objects of many fraudulent insurance claims, investigators should determine whether the theft claim is legitimate.

Snowmobiles

From January 1, 2018 to December 31, 2019, 949 snowmobiles were reported stolen in the United States, with slightly more thefts reported in 2019 (478) than in 2018 (471). Averaged out, there are 475 snowmobiles reported stolen every year (Buysse, 2020). The majority of thefts (about 58%) occur during the winter months, from December to March. Snowmobiles are easy to steal because they can be transported inside vans and trucks. Most major snowmobile manufacturers use chassis and engine numbers that aid in identification.

A popular snowmobile resort in Lanaudière, Quebec, reduced snowmobile theft by more than 50% through the joint efforts of tourism operators and law enforcement.

Tourism operators invested heavily in video surveillance and alarm equipment at restaurants, lodges, hotels, motels, and other tourist-oriented businesses. Police involvement was stepped up as well, with local law enforcement waging a deliberate war on snowmobile thieves, making the region known as a bad place to steal snowmobiles, trucks, and trailers.

Motorcycles, Motor Scooters, and Mopeds

Many motorcycles cost $20,000 or more. In 2018, 41,674 motorcycles were reported stolen to law enforcement (Jalowiecki, 2019). Motorcycles, motor scooters, and mopeds are easy to steal because they lack security devices and are often left unprotected. The lock number is easily identified, and substitute keys can be made. These cycles can be driven away or loaded onto trailers or into vans and transported, perhaps several at a time. A professional thief takes only 20 seconds to steal a motorcycle.

Identifying motorcycles is difficult because of the many types and the fact that parts are not readily identifiable. However, identification numbers can often be obtained through the NICB, local dealers, and manufacturers. Even so, the recovery rate for motorcycles is generally significantly lower than that for vehicles (Jalowiecki, 2019).

The NICB offers the following prevention suggestions: lock your motorcycle, even when it is stored in a garage; be wary of used cycles titled or registered as an "assembled vehicle"; be wary of cloned motorcycles; and obtain an expert appraisal or insurance policy pre-inspection before purchasing and insuring a used cycle.

Aircraft

Yet another area of motor vehicle theft that may be investigated, although relatively rare, is theft of aircraft. Nonetheless, aircraft theft, although infrequent, is a high-value theft. Such thefts are jointly investigated by the FBI and the Federal Aviation Administration (FAA). Many stolen aircraft are used in narcotics smuggling, so that the plane can be sacrificed at no cost if there is danger of apprehension.

Aircraft identification consists of a highly visible *N* identification number painted on the fuselage. Many aircraft parts, including the engine, radio equipment, landing gear, and tires, also have individual serial numbers. Aircraft identification can be verified through the manufacturer.

Since the September 11, 2001, attacks on the World Trade Center and the Pentagon, security of aircraft has become more of a priority. The Aircraft Owners and Pilots Association (AOPA) sponsors an Airport Watch, similar to a community's Neighborhood Watch, with America's pilots and aircraft owners banding together to protect our small airports. Everyone is encouraged to get to know one another and to report anything that appears to be suspicious. Chapter 20 discusses in depth the investigation of terrorist activity.

Summary

Motor vehicle thefts take much investigative time, but they can provide important information on other crimes under investigation. The VIN is the primary nonduplicated, serialized number assigned by a manufacturer to each vehicle made. This number—critical in motor vehicle theft investigation—identifies the specific vehicle in question.

Classifications of motor vehicle theft based on the offender's motive include (1) joyriding, (2) transportation, (3) commission of another crime, (4) gang initiation, (5) stripping for parts and accessories, and (6) reselling for profit.

Although referred to as "motor vehicle theft," most of these crimes are prosecuted as "unauthorized use of a motor vehicle" because a charge of theft requires proof that the thief intended to deprive the owner of the vehicle permanently, which is often difficult or impossible to establish. The elements of the crime of unauthorized use of a motor vehicle are (1) intentionally taking or driving away (2) a motor vehicle (3) without the consent of the owner or the owner's authorized agent.

The Dyer Act made interstate transportation of a stolen motor vehicle a federal crime and allowed for federal help in prosecuting such cases. Motor vehicle embezzlement exists if the person who took the vehicle initially had consent and then exceeded the terms of that consent.

To improve your ability to recognize stolen vehicles, keep a list of stolen vehicles, or a "hot sheet," in your car; develop a checking system for rapidly determining whether a suspicious vehicle is stolen; learn the common characteristics of stolen vehicles and car thieves; keep up-to-date with the most frequently stolen vehicles and the areas from which they are most often stolen; take time to check suspicious persons and vehicles; and learn how to question suspicious drivers and occupants.

Can You Define?

bait car
chop shop
cloning
Dyer Act
hot sheet

immobilizer
joyriding
motor vehicle
telematic technology
vehicle identification number (VIN)

Checklist

Motor Vehicle Theft

- Description of vehicle: year, make, model, color, body type?

- Anything unusual about the vehicle, such as color combination, after-market items or accessories, or damage?

- Identification of vehicle: VIN, engine number, license number by state and year, registered owner and legal owner, address, telephone number?

- What were the circumstances of the theft: date and time reported stolen, location of theft? Were doors locked? Was the key in the ignition?

- Was the vehicle equipped with OnStar, LoJack, or other locator system?

- Was the vehicle insured and by whom?

- Was the vehicle mortgaged and by whom? Are payments current?

- Is there a chance the vehicle was repossessed by the loan company?

- Did anyone have permission to use the vehicle? Have they been contacted?

- Was the owner arrested for another crime or suspected in a crime?

- Does the owner have any motive to falsely report the vehicle stolen?

- Was the owner involved in a hit-and-run incident or driving while intoxicated?

- Did the spouse report the vehicle missing?

- What method was used to take the vehicle?

- Has the vehicle been recovered? Where?

- Were crimes committed in the area where the vehicle was stolen or recovered?

- Was anybody seen near where the vehicle was stolen or found? When? How were they dressed? Approximate age?

- Was the vehicle seen on the street with suspects in it? Description of the suspects? Does the owner have any suspects?

- Were police field interrogation cards checked for the day of the theft and the days after to determine whether the vehicle had been stopped by police for other reasons?

- What items were inside the vehicle when it was stolen?

- Were pawnshops checked for items that were in the vehicle?

- If the vehicle was a motorcycle, were motorcycle shops checked?

- If the vehicle was a truck, have there been other truck thefts in the area or labor problems?

- Is the vehicle suspected of going interstate? Was the FBI notified?

- Has a check been made with the National Insurance Crime Bureau?

- Have junkyards been checked?

- Have known auto thieves been checked to determine whether they were in the area at the time of the theft?

- Was a check made with the DMV to determine the registered owner?

Applications

Read the following and then answer the questions:

A. On July 2, an internist finished his shift at a Veterans Administration hospital and went to the hospital parking lot to find that his Triumph TR4A was missing. He called the local police, but they refused to come, saying that because the theft occurred on federal property, it was the FBI's problem. The doctor called the FBI, which first said it would not investigate a car theft unless the car was transported out of the state. The doctor's insurance company finally convinced the FBI to investigate the theft, which it did. Two days later, local police in a town 529 miles away discovered the TR4A abandoned in the parking lot at a racetrack. Because the car had been hot-wired, they assumed it was stolen and made inquiries to the state DMV about its ownership. The car was towed to a local storage garage. When it was learned who owned the TR4A, local police contacted the police in the doctor's city.

Because that police department had no record of a stolen TR4A, officers there assumed that the message was in error. It was a holiday weekend, they were busy and the matter was dropped. Eight months later, the storage garage called the doctor to ask him when he was coming to get his car.

Questions

1. What mistakes were made in this incident?

2. Who is primarily to blame for the eight-month delay in returning the car to the owner?

B. Samuel Paris parked his 2014 Corvette Stingray in front of his home shortly after midnight when he and his wife returned from a party. He locked the car and took the keys with him. He discovered the vehicle missing the following morning at about 7:45 when he was leaving for work. He immediately called the police to report an auto theft.

Questions

1. Were his actions correct?
2. What should the police department do upon receiving the call?
3. What should the officer who is assigned to the case do?

References

Associated Press (2014, February 28). Cops take down global Luxe car theft ring. *New York Post*. Retrieved November 19, 2020, from nypost.com/2014/02/28/cops-take-down-international-auto-theft-ring/

Boat Owners Association of the United States. (2019, February). *Avoiding theft*. Alexandria, VA: Author. Retrieved December 14, 2020, from www.boatus.com/expert-advice/expert-advice-archive/2019/february/avoiding-theft

Buysse, A. (2020, February 6). Snowmobile thefts in the U.S. 2018–2019. Des Plaines, IL: National Insurance Crime Bureau. Retrieved December 14, 2020, from www.nicb.org/news/news-releases/snowmobile-thefts-us-2018-2019

Dees, T. (2019, November 15). Research review: Identifying the benefits of ALPR systems. *Police1*. Retrieved December 14, 2020, from www.police1.com/police-products/traffic-enforcement/license-plate-readers/articles/research-review-identifying-the-benefits-of-alpr-systems-wYft41yw4ONt5Wqv/

Federal Bureau of Investigation. (2018a). Crime clock statistics. *Crime in the United States, 2018*. Washington, DC: Author. Retrieved November 19, 2020, from ucr.fbi.gov/crime-in-the-u.s/2018/crime-in-the-u.s.-2018/topic-pages/crime-clock

Federal Bureau of Investigation. (2018b). *Crime in the United States, 2018*. Washington, DC: Author. Retrieved November 19, 2020, from ucr.fbi.gov/crime-in-the-u.s/2018/crime-in-the-u.s.-2018/topic-pages/motor-vehicle-theft

Federal Bureau of Investigation, New Orleans Division. (2012, December 13). *Third defendant sentenced in federal court for interstate transportation of stolen vehicles*. Washington, DC: Author. Retrieved November 19, 2020, from archives.fbi.gov/archives/neworleans/press-releases/2012/third-defendant-sentenced-in-federal-court-for-interstate-transportation-of-stolen-vehicles

Jalowiecki, P. (2019, August 8). *2018 Motorcycle thefts report*. Des Plaines, IL: National Insurance Crime Bureau. Retrieved December 14, 2020, from www.nicb.org/news/news-releases/motorcycle-thefts-declined-2018

Montoya, R. (2019, July 19). VIN lookup: How to decode your VIN. Santa Monica, CA: Edmunds. Retrieved November 19, 2020, from www.edmunds.com/how-to/how-to-quickly-decode-your-vin.html

Moss, C. (2020, May 4). *2019 watercraft theft report*. Des Plaines, IL: National Insurance Crime Bureau, Retrieved December 14, 2020, from www.nicb.org/news/news-releases/nicb-2019-watercraft-theft-report

National Equipment Register. (2016). *2015 theft report*. Jersey City, NJ: Verisk Crime Analytics. Retrieved December 14, 2020, from www.ner.net/wp-content/uploads/2017/10/Annual-Theft-Report-2015.pdf

National Insurance Crime Bureau. (n.d.). *Airbag theft and fraud: Deflating a growing crime trend*. Des Plaines, IL: Author, fact sheet. Retrieved November 19, 2020, from www.nhtsa.gov/sites/nhtsa.dot.gov/files/airbag.pdf

National Insurance Crime Bureau. (n.d.). *Vehicle theft*. Des Plaines, IL: Author, brochure. Retrieved December 14, 2020, from www.nicb.org/sites/files/2017-10/VehicleTheft.pdf

National Insurance Crime Bureau. (2015). *Vehicle cloning*. Des Plaines, IL: Author. Retrieved November 19, 2020, from www.nicb.org/sites/files/2017-10/VehicleCloning.pdf

New York City Police Department. (n.d.). Property protection services. New York, NY: Author. Retrieved June 15, 2021, from www1.nyc.gov/site/nypd/services/law-enforcement/property-protection.page

Sullivan, N. (2019, March 14). *Vehicle VIN cloning scams and ways to prevent it*. Middletown, RI: Advanced Remarketing Services. Retrieved November 19, 2020, from www.arscars.com/vehicle-vin-cloning-scams-ways-to-prevent-it/

U.S. Customs and Border Protection. (2017, February 9). *Border patrol captures cloned court truck*. Washington, DC: Author. Retrieved December 14, 2020, from www.cbp.gov/newsroom/local-media-release /border-patrol-captures-cloned-county-truck

Virginia State Police. (2017). *Virginia motor vehicle theft annual statistics*. Richmond, VA: Author. Retrieved December 14, 2020, from www.heatreward.com/Resources/Docs/2017 -Vehicle-Stats.pdf

Wagschal, G., Benitez, G., & Khoury, L. (2015, January 24). VIN cloning: How thieves can steal your car's identity. *ABC News*. Retrieved November 19, 2020, from abcnews. go.com/US/vin-cloning-thieves-masking-car-thefts /story?id=28401709

Case Cited

The People v. Gregory Shelton, No. B332259, Court of Appeals of California, Second District, Division Eight, Filed April 6, 2011.

Chapter 16
Arson, Bombs, and Explosives

Chapter Outline

Classification of Fires

Classification of Arson

Elements of the Crime: Arson

The Arsonist

Police and Fire Department Cooperation

Other Sources of Assistance in Investigating Arson

Special Challenges in Investigation

Responding to the Scene

The Preliminary Investigation

Search Warrants and Fire Investigations

Final Safety and Legal Considerations

Investigating Vehicle Arson

Prosecuting Arsonists

Preventing Arson

Bombings and Explosions

Responding to a Bomb Threat

The Bomb Scene Investigation

Learning Objectives

LO1 Define the various classifications of fires.

LO2 Explain the presumption that is made when investigating fires.

LO3 Explain how the Model Arson Law classifies arson.

LO4 Identify the criminal elements commonly included in arson statutes.

LO5 Explain how the fire department and police department cooperate in handling arson cases.

LO6 Explain what the fire triangle is and why it is important in arson investigations.

LO7 Describe the various indicators of arson.

LO8 Identify the factors to consider when determining a fire's point of origin.

LO9 Explain the different types of warrants that may be involved in a fire investigation and when they are issued.

LO10 Identify the key factors to consider when investigating suspected arson of a vehicle.

LO11 Identify what investigators should pay special attention to when working explosion and bombing cases.

© Henry Cho

Introduction

On March 25, 1990, Julio Gonzalez got into an argument with his ex-girlfriend, Lydia Feliciano, at the Happy Land nightclub where she worked as a coat check girl. He was thrown out of the Bronx club after a heated exchange with a bouncer. Gonzalez, his ego bruised by the embarrassing events, walked to a nearby service station, bought $1 worth of gas, and returned to the club for revenge. He poured the fuel around the door (the only exit from the club) and threw two matches to the ground, sparking a fire that killed 87 people inside. Only six people, one of whom was Lydia, escaped the blaze. When investigators questioned the survivors, Lydia's mention of her quarrel with Gonzalez and his subsequent ejection from the club gave the officers a suspect with a possible motive for arson. When they arrived at his apartment to question him, Gonzalez greeted them at the door reeking of gasoline. He was arrested, tried, and convicted of 174 counts of murder (two for each victim). Gonzalez was sentenced to 25 years for each count, for a total of 4,350 years (Moore & Tracy, 2015). His first bid for parole was denied in March 2015, and in 2016 he died in prison of a heart attack.

Arson, the malicious, willful burning of a building or property, is one of the oldest crimes known. It has probably been practiced since soon after fire was discovered. Arson is a combination crime against persons and property, threatening life and causing immense property losses. In October 1978 Congress mandated that the Federal Bureau of Investigation (FBI) reclassify arson as a Part One Index crime in its Uniform Crime Reporting Program, effective March 1979.

Arson is difficult to prove because in many fires the evidence is consumed and there are few witnesses. Few police officers or investigators have extensive training in investigating arson, and they are often confused by the complications involved in securing evidence and cooperating with other agencies. Because proper arson investigation typically requires knowledge of both fire and law enforcement fields, some agencies have police investigators partner with fire investigators to handle these crimes. Other agencies staff fire marshals, who also have law enforcement powers for fire-related incidents, to investigate these crimes.

Many sources gather statistics on fires, including the FBI, the National Fire Protection Association (NFPA), the U.S. Fire Administration (USFA), insurance companies, state fire marshal's offices, state crime bureaus, sheriff's offices, and local police and fire departments. The FBI's Uniform Crime Reports (UCR) show 36,127 arson offenses were reported in 2018, with an average damage of $17,406 (Federal Bureau of Investigation [FBI], 2018). Of these arson offenses, 43.1% were structure fires, 23.8% were mobile properties, and 33.1% accounted for other properties. Arson of industrial and manufacturing structures had the highest average of damage, valued at approximately $100,578.

The NFPA presents somewhat different statistics, reporting that public fire departments responded to 1,318,500 fires in 2018, of which an estimated 25,500 were intentionally set structure fires and roughly 9,500 were intentionally set vehicle fires (Evarts, 2019). These intentionally set fires resulted in 350 civilian deaths and more than $650 million in property loss. As tragic as these numbers are, it is important to recognize that the vast majority of fires are not intentionally set.

Classification of Fires

Fires can be caused by many things, and most are not the result of a criminal act that warrants a police investigation.

> **L01** Define the various classifications of fires.
>
> Fires are classified as natural, accidental, incendiary (arson), or of undetermined origin.

A *natural fire* is one caused without direct human action or intervention, such as fires caused by lightning, earthquakes, and other natural events. This category may also include fires set intentionally to destroy refuse, weeds, or waste products in industrial processes or to provide warmth. It is easy to determine that such fires are natural.

An *accidental fire*, as the name implies, is not intentional. Fires can be accidentally ignited by faulty wiring, leaking gas, a carelessly tossed cigarette, overheated Christmas tree lights, children playing with matches, and many other causes. The most common cause of accidental residential fires is cooking (U.S. Fire Administration, 2019). Arsonists usually try to make their fires appear accidental.

An **incendiary** *fire* (arson) is ignited intentionally and maliciously under circumstances in which the person knows that the fire should not be set. Such fires are often started to destroy property or buildings. Proof must be obtained that the fire was not natural or accidental.

A fire of *undetermined origin* is one in which there is no evidence to indicate whether the fire was natural, accidental, or incendiary. The cause simply cannot be proven to an acceptable level of certainty.

> **L02** Explain the presumption that is made when investigating fires.
>
> Fires are presumed natural or accidental unless proven otherwise.

The prosecution has the burden of proving that a fire is not accidental or natural. Because arson cases are hard to prove and require a great deal of work, they are unattractive to prosecutors. Moreover, a prosecutor may feel uneasy with the large amount of expert scientific testimony required.

Exercise caution in investigating fires. Most are *not* the result of arson. Do not unduly suspect property owners who have already been subjected to fire losses.

Classification of Arson

States vary in how they classify arson and related crimes. Some statutes distinguish between simple and aggravated arson. **Simple arson** is an intentional destruction by fire or explosives that does not create imminent danger to life or risk of great bodily harm. **Aggravated arson**, in contrast, is intentionally destroying or damaging a dwelling or other property by means of fire or explosives or other incendiary device—creating an imminent danger to life or great bodily harm, which risk was known or reasonably foreseeable to the suspect.

Another way states classify arson is according to the four degrees set forth in the Model Arson Law, written and promoted in the 1920s by the National Board of Fire Underwriters.

> **L03** Explain how the Model Arson Law classifies arson.
>
> The Model Arson Law divides arson into the following degrees:
>
> - *First-degree*: burning of dwellings
> - *Second-degree*: burning of buildings other than dwellings
> - *Third-degree*: burning of other property
> - *Fourth-degree*: attempting to burn buildings or property

The Model Arson Law includes within each degree the actual act and anyone who aids, counsels, or procures the act.

Still another way to classify arson is found in Section 220.1 of the Model Penal Code, drafted by the American Law Institute, which states that intentionally setting a fire or causing an explosion to destroy or damage a structure, whether their own or that of another, is a second-degree felony. Recklessly setting a fire or causing an explosion that damages property or places people in danger is a third-degree felony, and failing to control or report a dangerous fire is a misdemeanor.

Elements of the Crime: Arson

The way a state classifies and defines arson directly affects the elements of the crime that investigators need to prove. Under common law, the *crime of arson* was defined as the malicious, willful burning of another's house or outbuilding. It was once considered such a serious offense that the penalty was death. Laws have now extended arson to cover other buildings, personal property, crops, and the burning of one's own property. As in other crimes, arson laws vary from state to state but share some common elements.

> **LO4**   Identify the criminal elements commonly included in arson statutes.
>
> The elements of the crime of arson commonly include:
>
> - Willful, malicious burning of a building or property,
> - of another, or of one's own to defraud,
> - or aiding, counseling, or procuring such burning.

Willful, Malicious Burning of a Building or Property

Willful means "intentional." If a motive is determined, intent can be proven; therefore, when possible, show motive even if it is not required by law. Merchandise or household goods moved in or out immediately before the fire help to establish motive and intent.

Malicious denotes a "spiteful, vindictive desire to harm others." Malice is shown by circumstantial evidence such as statements of ill will, threats against persons or property, a recent increase in insurance coverage, or past property burned.

Burning is the prime element in the corpus delicti. There must be more than an exposure to heat, although flames need not have been visible nor the property destroyed. Heating to the ignition point is sufficient even if the fire extinguishes itself.

Of Another, or of One's Own to Defraud

The motive for burning another's property can range from revenge to economic gain. The burning of one's own property, however, is almost always to defraud, an act commonly referred to as *arson for profit*. Prove that the property was insured and show a motive for desiring the insurance money, for example recent economic hardships, impending bankruptcy, failing business, or another reason why cashing in on an insurance policy would benefit the arson "victim." Copies of the insurance policies obtained from the victim after serving proper notice show whether an excessive amount of insurance was taken out, whether recent additions or changes were made in the policy, or whether the insurance was soon to expire. Businesses are sometimes burned because they are failing financially, which can be established by business records or employee statements.

Or Aiding, Counseling, or Procuring the Burning

A person who hires a professional (a **torch**) to commit arson is also guilty of the crime. Seek evidence connecting this person with the actual arsonist.

Additional Elements That May Need to Be Proven

Recall the definition of aggravated arson—intentionally destroying or damaging a dwelling or other property by means of fire or explosives or other incendiary device, creating an imminent danger to life or great bodily harm, which risk was known or reasonably foreseeable to the suspect.

Fire does not require visible burning or an actual flame, but it must involve some extent of burning. *Explosives* include any device, apparatus, or equipment that causes damage by combustion or explosion, such as time bombs, Molotov cocktails, missiles, plastic explosives, grenades, and dynamite. *Destruction or damage* does not require total destruction or consumption. Damage that affects the value or usefulness of the property is sufficient.

Creating an imminent danger to life or risk of great bodily harm is assumed whenever the burned structure is a dwelling or is likely to have people within it. People need not be there at the time. *If the danger or risk was known or reasonably foreseeable* means that even if the suspect did not intend to harm anyone, the risk should have been known or reasonably anticipated. If a person dies in a fire set by an arsonist, the death is first-degree murder, an additional offense to be prosecuted.

Element of the Crime of Arson under the Model Penal Code, Section 220.1

Section 220.1 of the Model Penal Code defines arson, thereby delineating the elements to prove, as:

- starting a fire or causing an explosion with the purpose of

- destroying a building or occupied structure of another; or

- destroying or damaging any property, whether one's own or another's, to collect insurance for such loss.

Under the Model Penal Code, an *occupied structure* is any structure, vehicle, or location adapted for overnight accommodation of persons, or for conducting business therein, whether or not a person is actually present. *Property* is that of another, for the purposes of this section, if anyone other than the actor has a possessory or proprietary interest therein. If a building or structure is divided into separately occupied units, any unit not occupied by the actor is an occupied structure of another.

Elements of Attempted Arson

Attempted arson is also a crime in most states. The elements of attempted arson are the intent to set a fire and some preparation to commit the crime. The intent is normally specific, and the act must be overt. It must be shown that the fire would have occurred except for some intervention. Attempted arson also includes placing any combustible or explosive material or device in or near any property with the intent to set fire, to destroy, or to otherwise damage property. Putting materials together at a location where they could not cause a fire does not constitute attempted arson.

Setting Negligent Fires

Many states have statutes that include language about negligent or reckless acts that lead to fires (e.g., tossing a cigarette butt out of a car window). Setting a negligent fire is defined as causing a fire to burn or to get out of control through culpable negligence, creating an unreasonable risk and the likelihood of damage or injury to persons or property. This charge is often brought against people who leave smoldering campfires that cause forest fires.

Under Section 220.1 of the Model Penal Code (*Reckless Burning or Exploding*), a person commits a third-degree felony if they purposely start a fire or cause an explosion, whether on their own property or another's, and thereby recklessly:

(a) place another person in danger of death or bodily injury; or

(b) place a building or occupied structure of another in danger of damage or destruction.

Again, investigators must know their state's laws and whether this act constitutes a misdemeanor or felony.

Failure to Control or Report Dangerous Fire

Section 220.1 of the Model Penal Code states that it is a misdemeanor offense when a person who knows that a fire is endangering life or a substantial amount of property of another fails to take reasonable measures to put out or control the fire, when they can do so without substantial risk to themselves, or to give a prompt fire alarm, if:

(a) they know that they are under an official, contractual, or other legal duty to prevent or combat the fire; or

(b) the fire was started, albeit lawfully, by them, or with their assent, or on property in their custody or control.

The Arsonist

According to the FBI's UCR, most of those arrested for arson are white males and more than half are under age 18, a higher rate of juvenile involvement than any other Index crime. The typical adult male arsonist has been reared in a broken or unstable home, has an extensive criminal history, is below average intelligence, lacks marital ties, is socially maladjusted or a loner, is unemployed or working in an unskilled position, and is intoxicated at the time he sets the fire.

Female arsonists usually burn their own property, rarely that of an employer, neighbor, or associate. They are often self-destructive, mentally disabled, older, lonely and unhappy, and have some psychotic problems, primarily schizophrenia.

The professional torch—the arsonist for hire—is extremely difficult to identify because such individuals have no apparent link to the fire. However, the victim is also under suspicion in many instances. A guilty victim typically has an ironclad alibi.

As with other types of criminal activity, arson may be a one-time event or perpetrated by a recidivist. The classification of repetitive firesetting behavior uses terminology similar to that used when referring to those who commit multiple murders:

- **Serial arson**—three or more fires set by the same offender, with an emotional cooling-off period between fires

- **Spree arson**—three or more fires set at separate locations by the same offender, with no emotional cooling-off period between fires

- **Mass arson**—three or more fires set at the same site or location by the same offender during a limited period of time

  (National Fire Protection Association [NFPA], 2021)

Computer software can play a pivotal role in identifying serial arsonists by allowing investigators to efficiently organize and manage tips, evidence, and other information about related fires. Such case management can shorten investigations by months.

Juvenile Firesetting

Juvenile firesetting can have tragic, costly consequences. Data from the NFPA shows that from 2007 to 2011, an average of 49,300 fires involving playing with fire were reported to fire departments each year (Campbell, 2014). These fires were responsible for an average of 80 civilian deaths, 850 civilian injuries, and $235 million in direct property damage each year. A review of the literature reveals myriad terms used to describe the misuse of fire by youth, including fire lighting, match play, fireplay, youth firesetting, juvenile firesetting, child arson, and juvenile arson (U.S. Fire Administration, 2012). It is important to recognize that, regardless of the term used, misuse of fire by youths is not necessarily arson. A general distinction between fireplay and firesetting behavior lies in the individual's intent. **Fireplay** conveys a low level of intent to inflict harm and an absence of malice; rather, it involves curiosity and fascination. **Firesetting**, on the other hand, involves malice and intent to inflict harm.

Juvenile firesetters are often divided into four categories: curiosity/experimental, troubled/crisis, delinquent/criminal, and pathological/emotionally disturbed (U.S. Fire Administration, 2006). The curiosity firesetters are mainly children between ages 2 and 10 who experiment with or cause accidental fires. The troubled/crisis firesetters are mostly boys of any age whose firesetting represents "underlying psychosocial conflicts." Delinquent/criminal firesetters are adolescents between ages 13 and 18 with a long history of undetected firesetting who start fires as acts of vandalism or malicious mischief, but always with an intent to destroy. Pathological/emotionally disturbed firesetters' actions result from psychosocial conflict and may be random, ritualized, or with specific intent to destroy property. These firesetters can be boys or girls of any age and typically display a chronic history of behavioral and social problems (Howell Bowling, Merrick, & Omar, 2013).

Motivation

In arson, unlike other crimes, the victim is often the prime suspect. Motivation, although it need not be proved, has great significance in arson investigations. According to the NFPA (2021, p. 276), "The behaviors that may identify a possible motive, and thus a possible suspect, apply whether the fire is the result of a one-time occurrence or multiple occurrences, such as with a repetitive or serial firesetter." The National Center for the Analysis of Violent Crime (NCAVC) identifies six motive classifications for firesetting behavior: vandalism, excitement, revenge, crime concealment, profit, and extremism.

Vandalism, or *malicious mischief*, is a frequent motive for juveniles who burn property merely to relieve boredom or as a general protest against authority. This type of arson lacks the significant emotional component observed by the excitement- or revenge-motivated firesetters. The arsonist who vandalizes is not looking to necessarily hurt someone or destroy something valuable or deeply personal; instead, they are often looking for peer recognition or are acting on peer pressure. Many fires in schools, abandoned autos, vacant buildings, and trash containers are caused by this type of arsonist.

Excitement is another common motivation for firesetting, and the excitement-motivated offender is often a serial firesetter. These firesetters may be excited by the actual setting of the fire, watching the activities surrounding fire suppression efforts, or both, or they may have a psychological need for attention. Subcategories of excitement-motivated firesetting are:

- thrill seeking

- attention seeking

- perversion or sexual gratification (considered relatively rare)

- recognition

(NFPA, 2021)

Firesetters in this final subcategory are often referred to as *hero* or *vanity* firesetters or **strikers**, and these firesetters often remain at the fire scene in an effort to help and, thus, play "the hero." In fact, the U.S. Fire Administration (2016) recognizes the hero complex or hero syndrome as one of the causes of arson, and typical among these arsonists are security guards and firefighters themselves.

Firefighters aren't the only ones who seek to become heroes. In December 1999, a male nurse set a fire that killed billionaire banker Edmond Safra, stating he hoped to emerge as the hero who saved his employer's life. Safra was terrified that assailants were after him and locked himself in his Monaco penthouse bathroom, refusing to leave even when police and firefighters arrived. He died of asphyxiation.

Regarding excitement-motivated firesetters, the NFPA states (2021, p. 276): "Attention-seeking, recognition, and sexual gratification firesetters rarely attempt or intend to harm people, but these firesetters may disregard the safety of innocent bystanders or occupants. However, the thrill-seeking offender, whose compulsion requires the inherent sense of satisfaction, will often set a big fire or series of fires. Fires will typically involve structures, but when vegetation is involved, these fires are also large."

Revenge is a motive for someone who is retaliating against a real or perceived injustice. Revenge-motivated firesetters may direct their retaliation against an individual, an institution, or society at large. Revenge, spite, and jealousy are deeply emotional motivations for jilted lovers, feuding neighbors, disgruntled employees, quarreling spouses, people who feel cheated or abused, and those who feel racial or religious hostility. In rural areas, disagreements often result in the burning of homes or barns.

Crime concealment motivates criminals to set fires as a secondary crime to destroy evidence of a primary crime or evidence connecting them to the crime. In murder cases, arson can be used to attempt to make it impossible to identify a victim. However, it is very difficult to burn a body completely. Teeth, for example, can survive intense fires and still be used for identification purposes. In other cases, people set fires to destroy records containing evidence of embezzlement, forgery, or fraud. Arson is also used to divert attention while criminals commit another crime or cover their escape.

Profit is a common motive for arson, in which the fire is set to obtain material or monetary gain, either directly or indirectly. The gain may come from eliminating or intimidating business competition, extortion, removing unwanted structures to increase property values, insurance fraud, or from otherwise escaping financial obligations (NFPA, 2021). Intimidation, extortion, and sabotage are motives of striking workers and employers to apply pressure during a strike. Criminals, especially mobsters, use arson to intimidate witnesses and to extort money. With insurance fraud, a businessperson may wind up in dire financial straits and decide that the easiest way out is to burn the business and collect the insurance. Some people overinsure property and then burn it, collecting far more than the property was worth. For example, between 2005 and 2008, Ali Darwich and eight associates ran an arson-for-profit ring in the greater Detroit metropolitan area in which they would purchase insurance for various dwellings, businesses, and vehicles; intentionally burn, vandalize, or flood the various properties or vehicles; and then file false insurance claims seeking reimbursement for structural repairs, replacement of contents, loss of profits, and alternative living costs. Investigators discovered that the ring had defrauded seven insurance companies for more than $5 million during the course of their scheme. Darwich was sentenced to 137 years in prison for his crimes (FBI, Detroit Division, 2013).

In another arson-for-profit scheme, a father and son had received nearly $1 million after filing fraudulent insurance claims on 34 fires over 15 years (Bergazzi & Burkett, 2018). Dozens of properties directly owned by or somehow connected to the father-son duo—houses, trailers, RVs, and cars—had all caught fire, seemingly at random, the arson spree apparently perpetuated by the arsonists' ability to set fires that most investigators did not deem suspicious. Luck ran out for the father and son in 2015 when one of their houses went up in such a massive blaze just eight days after being purchased that it raised a battalion fire chief's suspicion. The fire marshal was summoned and spent days digging through the charred remains. The discovery of what looked as if something had been poured on the basement floor led investigators to reach out to the ATF, who removed a section of the tile floor for testing. The substance was confirmed to be gasoline, leading investigators to revisit other fires associated with the suspects. Comparing evidence found at the various scenes allowed investigators to discover incriminating patterns. For example, a couch that survived one fire was later found at the scene of another fire. In addition, the same clothes were discovered at two different fire scenes, which investigators were able to link because the items still retained dry cleaning tags that identified the suspects (Bergazzi & Burkett, 2018).

Extremism is the final category of firesetting motivation, where arson is committed to further a social, political, or religious cause. Extremist firesetters may work individually or as part of a group. Subcategories of this type of firesetting are terrorism and riot/civil disturbance protests. For example, an environmental group claimed responsibility for a series of fires that caused $12 million in damage in protest of Vail Associates moving forward with its controversial 885-acre ski resort expansion.

Several studies reveal revenge as the most common motive for arson. Nonetheless, many arson investigators believe that insurance fraud is the most prevalent motive for arson. It may be that arson intended to defraud is often hired out to a professional who is less likely to get caught and, if apprehended, is more likely to have better legal counsel. Also to be considered is the unintentional firesetter, that is, the individual who accidentally sets a fire and then is too embarrassed to admit it or who fears that insurance may not cover the loss if the accident is made known.

Police and Fire Department Cooperation

Arson is investigated by many agencies with joint jurisdiction: state fire marshals, state police, county sheriffs, and local police and fire departments. In addition, insurance investigators often become involved. Utility companies may also send investigators to the scene if there is concern that malfunctioning electrical or gas equipment caused the fire.

Lack of trained personnel to investigate arson is a major problem in both police and fire departments, except in large cities that have their own arson investigation squads. Although arson is a crime, police tend to give it low priority, believing that the fire department should investigate. However, many firefighters are volunteers who are not trained in arson investigation, and even many full-time fire departments do not train their personnel to investigate arson. Rural areas and cities of as many as 75,000 in population rely heavily on the state fire marshal's office, which usually does not have enough staff to conduct full investigations throughout the state. State fire marshal's offices can help local police and fire agencies by providing advice, coordinating activities, and supplying information on suspect profiles. They cannot, however, assume full responsibility for the investigation. Even fire departments that provide training in arson detection seldom include training on the criminal procedures followed in prosecuting arson.

Attitudes about the responsibility for investigating arson vary. Some fire departments feel that arson investigation and prosecution are their responsibility; others feel just as strongly that arson is a police matter.

> **LO5** Explain how the fire department and police department cooperate in handling arson cases.
>
> An arson investigation is a joint effort. Law enforcement investigators need to work with fire specialists to determine the fire's point(s) of origin and probable cause to prepare the case for prosecution.

Fire Department Expertise

Recognizing factors concerning smoke and fire conditions, detecting arson evidence, and determining the origin and cause (O&C) of a fire are specific areas of expertise for the fire department, which investigates many accidental and natural fires. To delegate this responsibility to the police department would be an unnecessary duplication of skill, especially because only a small number of fires are the result of arson.

Trained fire personnel know about buildings, how fires are started, and the various components necessary for ignition. Fire marshals also have extralegal powers to summon witnesses, subpoena records, and take statements under oath that police officers do not have. Moreover, fire personnel may enter buildings after a fire without a warrant, a benefit to criminal investigations. They also work closely with insurance companies and are apt to recognize people frequently present at fires.

The fire department's basic role is fire investigation and arson detection, rather than arson investigation. Once the cause of the fire is determined to be arson, the police are notified and the process becomes a joint investigation, with the police taking the lead on the associated criminal investigation.

Police Department Expertise

Police on patrol duty and investigators, through intelligence files, are likely to know possible arson suspects. Field-interview cards can include names of people present in an area where arson fires are being set. Specialized techniques such as interviewing witnesses and interrogating suspects are normal police operations. Moreover, police have contacts with informants and arrest power. Police also communicate with neighboring agencies, who may have had similar arson investigations and can share intelligence with the requesting agency.

Coordinating Efforts

Regardless of the actual agency assigned to an arson investigation, someone must coordinate the efforts of everyone involved. A full-time arson squad has the potential for conducting the best arson investigation. The next best arrangement is to have a well-trained arson investigator from local jurisdictions or the state fire marshal's office. However, police personnel trained in criminal investigation working with fire personnel trained in arson detection can do an effective job if they mutually agree about who is in charge. Cross-training is one way to help police and firefighters understand each other's roles.

Other Sources of Assistance in Investigating Arson

Other sources of assistance in investigating arson are the Bureau of Alcohol, Tobacco, Firearms, and Explosives (ATF); the news media; insurance companies; and arson task forces.

The Bureau of Alcohol, Tobacco, Firearms, and Explosives

On January 24, 2003, the Bureau of Alcohol, Tobacco, and Firearms became part of the Department of Justice under the Homeland Security bill and had its name expanded to the Bureau of Alcohol, Tobacco, Firearms, and Explosives to reflect the new focus on explosives-related crime and terrorism. The ATF has extensive resources for investigating arson, including the ATF National Response Team (NRT), ready to investigate within 24 hours of receiving a call, and the International Response Team (IRT), part of the NRT program, which can be deployed worldwide to investigate fires and explosions at the request of the U.S. Department of State (Bureau of Alcohol, Tobacco, Firearms, and Explosives, 2016). In December 2013, the NRT was activated to help the Denver Fire Department, Glendale Police Department, and the Colorado Bureau of Investigation investigate a massive three-alarm fire in Glendale, Colorado, that destroyed a four-story building that was under construction; melted cars, siding, and windows of adjacent structures; and caused in excess of $12 million in damage. It was the second NRT deployment in 2013 and the 749th time an NRT had been activated since its inception in 1978 (Bureau of Alcohol, Tobacco, Firearms, and Explosives, Denver Field Division, 2013).

Other ATF resources include arson profilers; national laboratories in Georgia, Maryland, and California; the Explosives Incidents Systems (EXISs) database, an intelligence division; financial auditors; accelerant-detecting canines; photograph examiners; and Certified Fire Investigators. The ATF's Fire Research Laboratory (FRL), located within the National Laboratory Center in Ammendale, Maryland, is accredited by the ANSI National Accreditation Board and is the nation's only large-scale fire science research laboratory dedicated to fire and arson criminal investigations.

News Media

One source of assistance frequently overlooked is the news media, which can publish profiles of arsonists and seek the public's help in identifying them. Media may also have photographs or videotapes of in-progress fires that can be extremely useful in investigations.

Insurance Companies

Many insurance companies have full-time fire loss investigators, which can be of tremendous benefit to those fire and police agencies that do not because they bring a wealth of knowledge, training, and experience to a fire investigation. The objective is the same for both the insurer and the authorities—obtaining the truth. For fire and police authorities, the goal is to locate the suspect. If the suspect in a fire-for-profit act is arrested, fire loss problems for the insurance company are resolved. But police must keep some things in mind. While insurance companies are often willing to bring in outside laboratories to help with forensic analyses, investigators need to be cognizant that that insurance companies risk losing significant amounts of money. Investigators must ensure that the labs are accredited.

Officers must also refrain from making requests of insurance companies that are, in actuality, attempts to get information to use against a victim/suspect. An example would be if police asked an insurance adjustor or loss investigator to get a statement from the victim/suspect or to ask for their bank statements. The courts have ruled that when police ask others to do their work, the others become agents of the state and all subsequent legal protections apply. Police must perform this part of the investigation by taking a proper statement, preceded by a *Miranda* warning if needed, and getting a subpoena or warrant for bank statements.

The property owner must work with the fire and police departments and insurance company to collect the insurance money. Consequently, interviewing and interrogating efforts are much enhanced. In addition, insurance companies usually request the insured to sign a release authorizing the company to obtain private records such as income tax returns, financial audits, bank accounts, credit reports, telephone records, and utility company records. Without this release, obtaining such records is a long, complex process. This is another place where officers need to be careful and not be the ones making such requests. Information can be provided to them for investigative reasons, but officers cannot ask insurance agents to do or collect something on their behalf.

Insurance loss investigators have the additional advantage of being able to enter the fire scene without a warrant in their efforts to examine the damage and to determine the cause of the fire. However, fire scene security is especially important in this type of investigation.

There are often many interested persons, and control must be kept. If needed, insurance loss investigators can be advised to wait until the potential crime scene is fully processed before allowing access.

Several index bureaus gather insurance-claim information in an attempt to determine whether the same claim is being made to more than one company or whether a pattern of claims exists. Law enforcement investigators can benefit from information gathered by these bureaus as well. Most states provide limited civil immunity to insurance companies that provide information to law enforcement agencies in their investigations.

Arson Task Forces

To coordinate existing forces and create new sources for combating arson and related problems in any community, county, or state, arson task forces should be developed comprising fire and police department personnel; community leaders; insurance representatives; city, county, and district attorneys; federal agency personnel; and others. Arson has the lowest clearance by arrest of the major crimes, primarily because of inadequate training of fire and police department personnel, the difficulty of locating and preserving evidence, and a lack of coordination of personnel of the various organizations involved.

The website of the City of Paducah, Kentucky, describes its Youth Firesetter Intervention Program (paducahky.gov/youth-firesetter-intervention-program) as part of a task force whose mission is to "(1) Identify the firesetting behavior of children who have been referred to the program for the unsanctioned and/or unsupervised use of fire; (2) Determine the motivation for the firesetting behavior; and (3) Provide appropriate education and/or referral for such children/families." The partner agencies comprising the task force include Paducah Fire and Police Departments, ChildWatch, the McCracken County Court System, McCracken Regional Juvenile Detention Center, Paducah Public Schools, Four Rivers Behavioral Health, Kentucky Department for Community Based Services, Necco (a multistate service provider to at-risk children and families), the local chapter of the American Red Cross, and Western Baptist Hospital.

Other task force approaches can accomplish at least three goals:

1. Detecting arson, including seeking ways to improve detection of, as well as to properly investigate and successfully prosecute the crime

2. Reducing the number of arsons and deliberately set fires, in turn reducing property damage, physical injuries, and deaths

3. Developing a preventive program aimed at educating and developing a working relationship with the people the task force serves

The Importance of the Dispatcher

Local emergency dispatchers can play an important role in arson cases because they serve as the first point of contact between the fire witness, who may actually be responsible for setting the fire, and the fire investigator. At minimum, the person who calls 9-1-1 is a witness who may hold valuable information about the fire that no one else has (InterFire, n.d.; Harpster & Adams, 2019). Such 9-1-1 calls can provide invaluable clues to investigators because, in some cases, the caller may have committed the crime.

Special Challenges in Investigation

Special challenges in investigating arson include coordinating efforts with the fire department and others; determining whether a crime has been committed; finding physical evidence, most of which is destroyed by the fire; finding witnesses; and determining whether the victim is a suspect. Investigating arson often requires even more persistence, thoroughness, and attention to minute details than do other crimes. Arson is a difficult crime to investigate because there are seldom witnesses and the evidence needed to prove that a crime has been committed is usually consumed in the fire. Moreover, arson is an easy crime to write off without being publicly criticized because the victim and the suspect are often the same person. However, the innocent victim of arson is frequently frustrated by the lack of evidence and witnesses and by the inability of the police to prove that a crime was committed.

Responding to the Scene

The fire department usually receives the initial fire call unless the departments have a joint dispatcher or are merged into a public safety department. Because of the unpredictable nature of fires, responding officers should never go into a fire scene alone as they may need assistance, especially if they get trapped or injured. While approaching a fire scene, first responders should observe, mentally note, and, when time permits, record in their notes:

- The presence, location, and conditions of victims and witnesses

- Vehicles leaving the scene, bystanders, or unusual activities near the scene

- Flame and smoke conditions (e.g., the volume of flames and smoke; the color, height, and location of flames; the direction in which the flames and smoke are moving)

- The type of occupancy, use, and condition of the structure

- Conditions surrounding the scene, including weather conditions

- Fire-suppression techniques used, including ventilation, forcible entry, portable extinguishers, outdoor hoses, and utility shutoff measures

- Status of fire alarms, security alarms, and sprinklers

(National Institute of Justice, 2000, pp. 13–14)

It is also imperative that officers responding to a structural fire have an understanding of fire dynamics, including the concept of **flashover**, an event in which surfaces and room contents exposed to the thermal radiation of a fire reach their ignition temperatures effectively simultaneously, causing the fire to spread suddenly and rapidly; how smoke itself acts as fuel; and how newer structures often burn hotter and faster because of an abundance of synthetic materials on the premises, materials which can produce toxic fumes (NFPA, 2021; Bossert, 2015). In fact, decades ago when residential structures were constructed primarily of natural furnishings and building materials, occupants had an average of 17 minutes to evacuate a burning building. But as synthetics have become more common in furnishings and construction material, that escape time has shrunk to three minutes or less (Kerber & Mandeville, 2018).

The Preliminary Investigation

The scene of a fire is dirty, messy, and complicated, making it difficult to obtain evidence of possible arson. An arson scene may be the most contaminated crime scene you will ever encounter. Piles of smoldering, blackened debris, often coated in foam or soaked with water, are difficult environments in which to locate evidence. In addition, structural damage caused by the fire may make searching for such evidence even more hazardous.

Although the fire department is responsible for establishing that arson has occurred, investigators must verify those findings by understanding what distinguishes an accidental fire from arson and by knowing what evidence and information are available for proving the elements of the crime. The NFPA has developed *NFPA 921* as the definitive national guide for fire and explosion investigations. According to the most recent *NFPA 921* (NFPA, 2021, p. 169), an investigator should seek answers to the following questions as they conduct the preliminary investigation:

- Was the creation, starting, or maintaining of a fire or the causing of an explosion intentional?

- Was another person present in or on the property?

- Who owned the property?

- If the property involved was a building, what type of building and what type of occupancy was involved in the fire?

- Did the perpetrator act recklessly, though aware of the risk involved?

- Was there actual presence of flame?

- Was actual damage to the property or bodily injury to a person caused by the fire or explosion?

The Fire Triangle

The fire triangle is a basic concept critical to an arson investigation.

> **L06** Explain what the fire triangle is and why it is important in arson investigations.
>
> The **fire triangle** consists of three elements necessary for a substance to burn: air, fuel, and heat. In arson, one or more of these elements is usually present in abnormal amounts for the structure.

Extra amounts of *air* or oxygen can result from opened windows or doors, pried-open vents, or holes knocked in walls. Because firefighters often chop holes in structures, determine whether any such openings were made by the firefighters or by someone else. *Fuel* can be added by piling up newspapers, wood, or other combustible materials found at or brought to the scene. Gasoline, kerosene, and other accelerants add sufficient *heat* to the fire to cause the desired destruction after it has been ignited.

Potential Arson Indicators

Several factors can alert investigators that the fire might be incendiary and the result of arson. However, as fire science has evolved considerably over the past two decades, many of the "facts" and factors previously deemed indicative of arson have since been debunked, discarded, or severely modified. Training and controlled experiments have contributed to an empirically derived knowledge base that can help fire investigators be better equipped to determine cause and origin. Thus, as you read through the following section, keep in mind that those who investigate potential arson must take *all* elements into account and not base a determination of arson solely on one indicator, such as the presence of a flammable liquid or an unusual burn pattern. (Note: Chapter 23 in the 2021 Edition of *NFPA 921* deals with incendiary fires.)

LO7   Describe the various indicators of arson.

A fire may be considered incendiary and, thus, the result of arson if investigation of the fire shows

- The presence of an abnormal amount of air, fuel, or heat
- Evidence of having been accelerated
- Evidence of incendiary igniters
- More than one point of origin
- Deviation from normal burning patterns
- Evidence of trailers

Accelerants. An **accelerant** is a fuel or oxidizer that promotes combustion and is intentionally used to start a fire or increase the rate of growth or spread of fire. Accelerants are often ignitable liquids, and evidence of accelerants is a primary form of physical evidence at an arson scene. Commonly used accelerants in arson are gasoline, kerosene, charcoal lighter, paint thinner, lacquer solvent, acetone, and isopropyl alcohol.

Look for residues of liquid fire accelerants on floors, carpets, and soil because the liquid accelerants run to the lowest level. In addition, these areas often have the lowest temperatures during the fire and may not have enough oxygen to support complete combustion of the accelerant. Accelerants may seep through porous or cracked floors to underlying soil that has excellent retention properties for flammable liquids. Accelerants can also be found on the clothes and shoes of the suspect if apprehended.

You can also identify fire accelerants at the scene either by your own sense of smell (olfactory detection) or by using portable equipment that detects residues of flammable liquids. The ability of the human nose to detect gasoline vapor may be hampered, however, if the odor is masked by another strong odor, such as that of burned debris. Consequently, arson investigators commonly use devices such as catalytic combustion detectors or explosimeters to reveal the presence of flammable vapors at a fire scene. Investigators must be cognizant of the fact that gasoline is often stored in garages and sheds, and the mere presence of the odor or vapor alone does not prove arson occurred.

Many substances, including oil and gasoline, do not mix with water. Instead they float on the surface of the water, giving the sheen a colorful appearance referred to as the **rainbow effect**. While rainbow effects are common at fire scenes, investigators who observe puddles with a sheen appearance should not assume they indicate the presence of an ignitable liquid or accelerant. When some building materials, such as wood and plastic, burn, they produce oily substances that can cause rainbow effects (*NFPA 921*, 6.3.12.3). If an ignitable liquid is suspected, confirm it by a laboratory analysis.

Crazing is a complicated, irregular pattern of short cracks in glass. In the past, crazing was thought to be the result of rapid, intense heat on one side of the glass, possibly indicative of the presence of a fire accelerant. However, there is no scientific basis to this claim and the NFPA strongly cautions investigators to not make conclusions about a fire based on glass morphology alone (*NFPA 921*, 6.3.17.4.5).

Spalling is the cracking, chipping, or breaking off of surface pieces of concrete, rock, or brick because of intense heat. However, spalling can result from other processes and may have occurred prior to the fire. The NFPA cautions: "The presence or absence of spalling at a fire scene should not, in and of itself, be construed as an indicator of the presence or absence of liquid fuel accelerant. The presence of ignitable liquids will not normally cause spalling beneath the surface of the liquid. Rapid and intense heat development from an ignitable liquid fire may cause spalling on adjacent surfaces, or a resultant fire may cause spalling on the surface after the ignitable liquid burns away" (*NFPA 921*, 6.3.14). Investigators should determine if there was spalling present before the fire.

Igniters. An **igniter** is a substance or device used to start fires. The most common igniters are matches. Other common igniters include candles; cigars; cigarettes; cigarette lighters; electrical, mechanical, and chemical devices; and explosives. To be carrying matches is not damaging

Myth Crazing is caused by rapid, intense heat and is a good indicator that a fire accelerant was used.

Fact Crazing can only be caused by the rapid cooling of glass, such as when water is sprayed on hot glass. The presence of crazing has no investigative value in suspected arson cases.

evidence unless some have been removed from the book or box and those found at an arson scene match those found in the suspect's possession.

Electrical devices left on, kerosene-soaked papers in waste baskets, time fuses, shorted light switches, magnifying glasses, matches tied around a lighted cigarette, and numerous other igniters have been used to commit arson. Unattended space heaters or curling irons or clothes irons that have been left on and forgotten, however, are more likely to be igniters for accidental fires.

Candles are often used in arsons because they give the suspect time to leave the scene. The average candle burns about 30–45 minutes per inch, depending on its size, shape, composition, and the amount of air in the room. Tapered candles burn faster at the top and slower toward the base. The arsonist may control the length of time by cutting off part of the candle before lighting it. The candle can be set in a material that will ignite once the candle burns down or the hot wax may be allowed to drip onto a surface to start a fire. The candle's flame can also be used to ignite other materials in the room.

Professional arsonists use a variety of methods to ignite fires, including:

- Connecting magnesium rods to timed detonators and placing them in a building's electrical system. The rods burn with extreme intensity and cause a fire that looks as though it was caused by faulty wiring.

- Connecting a timed explosive charge on one or more barrels of gasoline or other highly flammable liquid. This method is often used when large areas such as warehouses are to be burned.

- Pouring acid on key support points in steel-structured buildings to make certain the building will collapse during the fire.

Regardless of whether arsonists use direct or delayed ignition, they usually plan for the fire to consume the igniter. However, this often does not happen, and

incendiary (igniter) evidence might be discovered at the point of origin. Or, in their haste to leave the scene, arsonists may drop parts of the igniter in an area unaffected by the fire. Any igniter not normally present at the location is evidence.

Points of Origin. In stressing the importance of origin determination, the NFPA states (2021, p. 220): "The origin of a fire is one of the most important hypotheses that an investigator develops and tests during the investigation. Generally, if the origin cannot be determined, the cause cannot be determined, and generally, if the correct origin is not identified, the subsequent cause determination will also be incorrect." Knowing the fire's point, or points, of origin helps to establish how the fire spread and whether it followed a normal burning pattern. The more extensive the destruction, the more difficult it is to determine the fire's point of origin.

LO8 Identify the factors to consider when determining a fire's point of origin.

Determination of the origin of a fire involves the combined interpretation of information derived from one or more of the following: (1) witness information and/or electronic data, (2) fire patterns, and (3) fire dynamics (the physics and chemistry of the fire) (*NFPA* 921, 18.1.2). Multiple points of origin might indicate arson.

Areas of uneven burning can indicate the presence of an incendiary or that a great amount of flammable material was present at the scene.

While burn patterns may be the most readily available data for determining a fire's point of origin, investigators are cautioned to not assume that the fire at the origin burned the longest and that, therefore, a fire pattern showing the greatest damage must be at the area of origin.

Nearly all structural fires will produce charring, the cracked, and blistered remnants of when various materials, such as vinyl, gypsum wallboard, and wood, are exposed to elevated temperatures. The **depth of char**, or how deeply wood is burned, may, in limited circumstances, be useful in determining the fire's point of origin. The extent of the depth of char is more reliable for establishing the burn spread rather than length or duration of burn. Factors to consider when using depth of char to determine the direction of burn spread include whether the fire had a single fuel source or multiple sources and how ventilation factors may have influenced the burn rate (*NFPA 921*, 6.3.2.4). In addition, investigators must

Arson investigators assemble a couch on the lawn outside the scene of a suspicious fire. Such objects often provide evidence regarding a fire's point of origin, and multiple points of origin within a structure may indicate an incendiary fire.
The Star-Ledger/Murray, E./The Image Works

ensure consistency in measuring by always using the same device to take measurements. A char depth gauge is a useful tool for obtaining quick, accurate measurements.

The direction of heat impingement can sometimes be determined by the presence of distorted incandescent lightbulbs, with the side closest to the heat source appearing more damaged or softened (*NFPA 921*, 6.3.6.1). Noting the location of such evidence can help investigators assess the fire's origin.

Fire can also "jump" or arc via the electrical circuits within and throughout a structure. Studies have revealed that energized electrical circuits exposed to a spreading fire behave in a predictable manner. **Arc mapping**

Myth The presence of large shiny blisters (alligator char) occurs when a fire spreads rapidly or burns with great intensity and is evidence that a liquid accelerant was present during the fire.

Fact Contrary to old fire science beliefs, the appearance of alligatoring at a fire scene has no investigative significance. These types of blisters can be found in many different types of fires. There is no scientific basis to infer that the appearance of large, curved blisters is an indicator of an accelerated fire.

involves the survey and analysis of the locations where electrical arcing has caused damage to determine the origin of a fire (*NFPA 921*, 6.3.21.10).

Trailers. If the arsonist places a path of flammable liquid, the fire will follow that path, known as a **trailer**. Trailers can be made of paper, hay, flammable compounds, or any substance that burns readily, and they result in an abnormal pattern. Char marks will follow the trailer's path.

Documenting the Fire Scene

As with other preliminary investigations, the investigator must properly document the scene by taking photographs and videos and making sketches. Pictures taken of people at the fire scene might reveal the presence of a known arsonist or show a person who repeatedly appears in photos taken at fires and is therefore an arson suspect. Photos or videos of the fire scene are also useful for showing to the judge and jury if the case goes to trial.

Seek pictures or video of the fire in progress to show the size of the fire at different points and times. Such documentation can be especially useful if there appears to be acceleration of the fire at a specific time that would indicate arson or the presence of highly combustible substances. Many fire departments take such in-progress videos. Media crews may have also captured video of the blaze.

Photos or videos of an in-progress fire can be valuable to investigators in that they can document the size and development of a fire at different points and times.

Helen H. Richardson/The Denver Post/Getty Images

After the fire, take enough pictures to show the entire scene in detail. Start with the outside of the structure, showing all entries and exits. Look for footprints and any unusual items outside the property, keeping in mind that items may have been discarded while the suspect was running away. Also photograph any obstructions that were placed in front of windows to prevent seeing inside the building. People familiar with the structure can review the pictures for anything out of the ordinary.

Take inside pictures to show the extent of burning. These will prove the corpus delicti. Take close-up pictures of extra papers, rags, gas cans, or other suspicious substances, as well as examples of charring and burn patterns. Take pictures at each stage of the search to show the point of origin, the nature of the burning, and the direction and speed of the fire's spread.

Physical Evidence

Preserving evidence is a major problem because much of the evidence is very fragile. Follow carefully the procedures described in Chapter 5. Use disposable cellulose sponges to sop up accelerants for transfer to a container. Use hypodermic or cooking syringes to suck up accelerants between boards or crevices. Sift ashes to detect small objects such as the timing device from an igniter.

Incendiary evidence at the point of origin can be part of a candle, an empty flammable liquid container,

excessive amounts of unburned newspaper folded together, or a number of unburned matches.

Paper exposed to high temperatures and sufficient air burns with little ash to examine. However, with a limited supply of air, only partial combustion occurs, leaving charred paper evidence that can be collected for laboratory examination. Paper in a fireplace or stove may be only partially burned, even if the building was totally consumed. These papers may provide a motive for the arson. If the paper is not destroyed, a laboratory may be able to recover any messages on it.

Do not overlook electronic evidence and computer data, even if the devices have been involved in an intense fire. Hard drives may survive extreme heat and sometimes even direct flames. They may also survive the water and steam encountered during suppression efforts.

An important step in an arson investigation is identifying potential accelerants at a fire scene. The accepted method is to use gas chromatography-mass spectrometry (GC-MS), which can make identification in 95% of the cases.

Using K-9s in Arson Investigations

Dogs can be of great assistance in arson investigation. A lab-certified accelerant-detection canine can detect accelerants at fire scenes and can also search a crowd for possible suspects, search a suspect's clothing and vehicle for the presence of accelerants, and search areas for accelerant containers. Connecticut's K-9 accelerant-detection program, for example, is the result of collaboration among the ATF, the New Haven County state's attorney's office, the State Police Science Laboratory, the Emergency Services Division Canine Unit, and the Bureau of the State Fire Marshal. Their first dog, Mattie, was trained to detect extremely small quantities of highly diluted flammable and combustible liquids, including paint remover and thinner, lacquer thinner, charcoal lighter fluid, kerosene, naphtha, acetone, dry gas, heptone, gasoline, number 2 fuel, diesel fuel, gum turpentine, Heritage lamp oil, transmission fluid, octane, and Jet A fuel.

Evidence on a Suspect, at a Residence, or in a Vehicle

If you have a suspect, look for any burns they may have received while setting the fire. The suspects may have scorched hair; torn clothing; soot on their skin; stains, cuts, and other injuries; or their clothing or shoes may have traces of accelerants or charred soot. Be alert to the presence of unique odors such as gasoline or other chemicals, either on the suspect or in their vehicle. The suspect's residence or vehicle may contain clothes noticed at the fire by a witness, objects removed from the scene of the fire, or incendiary devices. You may also find insurance documents or business or financial records that provide a motive.

Observing Unusual Circumstances

Suspicious circumstances implying arson include suddenly emptied premises, evidence of selectively missing inventory from a business or missing personal items from a home, the presence of materials not normally part of the business, holes in wall plaster or drywall that expose the wood, disconnected sprinkler systems, blocked-open interior doors, nailed-open fire doors, and other alterations that would provide more air, heat, or fuel to the area.

Interviewing the Owner/Victim, Witnesses, and Firefighters

One of the most basic and valuable investigative techniques is the interview, and fire investigations are no exception. Ask questions such as: How was the fire discovered? Who discovered it? Who were witnesses? What did they see? Who owns the property, and where are they? Is there anyone else who occupies or has access to the property? What color was the smoke, and where was it coming from? What direction was the wind? Did the fire appear to suddenly accelerate? Did anything out of the ordinary occur before the fire? Were there unusual odors? Were the shades up or down? Did obstructions prevent seeing into the building? Were suspicious persons or vehicles observed at the scene before, during, or after the fire?

Also try to learn who had an opportunity to set the fire and who might benefit from it. Determine who had keys and how the property was normally guarded or protected. Check the victim's financial status and find out how much insurance was carried on the property. Make note of whether the owner is cooperative with the investigators.

Document the names of the firefighters and record their observations while suppressing the fire, including the methods used and steps taken to fight the fire. Also interview those officers who responded first to the fire. Finally, do not overlook the person who called in the fire to 9-1-1.

Search Warrants and Fire Investigations

Entry to fight a fire requires no warrant. Once in the building, fire officials may remain a reasonable time to investigate the cause of the blaze. After this time, however, a warrant is needed. The U.S. Supreme Court set forth a two-step warrant process for investigating fires involving crimes. The initial search may require an **administrative warrant** for searching the premises for cause of fire and origin determination *and* a criminal warrant when evidence of a crime is discovered. Both require probable cause for issuance.

> **LO9** Explain the different types of warrants that may be involved in a fire investigation and when they are issued.

> An administrative warrant is issued when it is necessary for a government agent to search the premises to determine the fire's cause and origin. A criminal warrant is issued on probable cause when the premises yield evidence of a crime. Entry to fight a fire requires no warrant.

Both require an affidavit in support of the warrant that states the location and legal description of the property, the purpose (to determine the fire's cause and origin), under what authority the search request is being made, the area of the search, the use of the building, and the measures taken to secure the structure or area of the fire. In criminal search warrants, investigators must state what items they are looking for and why they believe those items will be found at that location. The search must then be limited to the items specified in the warrant. Found evidence may be seized, but once the officers leave after finding the evidence, they must have a criminal warrant to return to the premises for a further search.

Administrative warrants allow civil inspections of private property to determine compliance with city ordinances such as fire codes. The Supreme Court has established guidelines for arson investigators. In *Michigan v. Clifford* (1984), the Court held, "If a warrant is necessary, the object of the search determines the type of warrant required. If the primary object is to determine the cause and origin of a fire, an administrative warrant will suffice . . . and if the primary object is to gather evidence of criminal activity, a criminal search warrant may be obtained only on a showing of probable cause to believe that relevant evidence will be found in the place to be searched."

In *Coolidge v. New Hampshire* (1971), the Court held that evidence of criminal activity discovered during a search with a valid administrative warrant may be seized under the plain view doctrine. Any evidence so seized may be used to establish the probable cause needed to obtain a criminal search warrant.

Guidelines on the current legal status of searches conducted during fire investigations include the following:

- Warrants are not required when an authorized individual consents to the search. The consent must be written and must specify the areas to be searched and the purpose of the search. This consent can be revoked at any time.

- Warrants are not required when investigators enter under "exigent circumstances," that is, if investigators enter the premises while firefighters are extinguishing the blaze or conducting overhaul. The scope of the search must be limited to determining the cause and origin. If evidence of a crime is discovered, a criminal warrant is required to continue the search.

- Without consent or an exigency, warrants are required if the premises are subject to a "reasonable expectation of privacy." This includes commercial businesses as well as private residences. Exceptions would be premises that are so utterly devastated by the fire that no expectation of privacy is reasonable and property that has been abandoned.

- Evidence of a crime discovered during an administrative search may be seized if in plain view.

- Once evidence of arson is discovered, the fire's cause and origin are assumed to be known. The scope of the administrative warrant has been exhausted. A criminal warrant is required to continue the search.

When in doubt, obtain a warrant: "At the scene of the fire, a firefighter or ranking fire official may request to take you on a 'walk-through' of the scene to explain his or her observations that led to the conclusion that the fire was arson. Before you go on that walk-through, remember that law enforcement officers must have the legal authority to enter and investigate the scene after the fire is out" (Smith & Gipson, 2008, pp. 55–56).

Final Safety and Legal Considerations

Entering a burned-out building can be a dangerous endeavor, from both a safety perspective and a legal standpoint, and requires some advanced preparation (Smith & Gipson, 2010). These are some final tips to remember before entering fire-damaged property:

- Obtain either consent from the legal owner or a search warrant.

- Turn off utilities.

- Have the structure inspected and ventilated.

- Bring a partner.

- Put on safety boots, protective eyewear, and a hard hat.

- Wash your boots with detergent to eliminate cross-contamination.

Investigating Vehicle Arson

Although vehicle fires can be caused by accident, vehicles usually do not burn readily. Accelerants are used on many vehicles to accomplish arson. A quart to a half-gallon of flammable liquid is required to cause a major vehicle fire.

Motives for vehicle arson include the desire to collect insurance, inability to make needed repairs after an unreported accident, desire to eliminate a loan on the vehicle, desire to cover up another crime committed in or with the vehicle, general dissatisfaction with the vehicle's performance, and desire to resolve arguments over the vehicle's use.

LO10 Identify the key factors to consider when investigating suspected arson of a vehicle.

When investigating vehicle fires, look for evidence of accelerants and determine whether the vehicle was insured. It is seldom arson if there was no insurance.

A close correlation exists between insurance coverage and vehicle arson. Obtain proof that the vehicle was insured against fire, that the fire was willfully set, that damage resulted, and that there was intent to defraud.

Prosecuting Arsonists

Some studies indicate that considerably more than 90% of arsonists go unpunished, probably because arson is most often committed without the benefit of witnesses. According to the International Association of Arson Investigators, approximately 25% of all fires in the United States—about 500,000 per year—result from arson, but only about 2% of all arsonists are ever arrested and convicted for their crimes.

The difficulty of investigating arson has been discussed, as has the need for cooperation between law enforcement investigators and firefighters. Equally difficult is prosecution. There is a big difference between proving a fire as arson and proving arson in court. Cooperative investigation and prosecution are required if the losses from arson are to be stemmed.

Many prosecutors fail to bring charges because all they have is circumstantial evidence. However, circumstantial evidence can be used to successfully prosecute a case. Look for evidence of planning, such as increasing insurance coverage, removing items, or making offhand remarks or unusual changes. Also look for evidence of disabled or turned-off alarms or sprinkler systems and doors left open. Finally, look for evidence of motive.

Preventing Arson

To prevent arson, various properties at risk of being set on fire might be identified by computer mapping. In some instances, crime analysis has determined that most properties that had experienced arson were either abandoned or vacant properties located near or adjacent to notably high crime locations. In one instance, six key factors were merged into one master map: (1) abandoned properties, (2) negative-equity properties, (3) properties whose gas or electric utilities were shut off, (4) sites of prior-year fires, (5) gang locales, and (6) known drug hot

spot locations. With accurate predictions, officers can be stationed close to and be more observant of targeted zones.

Some jurisdictions have implemented fire prevention and intervention programs targeting youth at risk of firesetting. An example is the Broward County (Florida) Juvenile Firesetter Prevention and Intervention Program, which provides specialized fire safety education for children between the ages of 2 and 17 as well as community outreach presentations to raise general public awareness. The program also targets at-risk children and teens who have shown an interest in or a history of starting fires, initiating bomb threats, creating destructive incendiary devices, or pulling fire alarms (Broward County Sheriff's Office, 2020).

Interfire.org is a resource for law enforcement, fire services, insurance providers, and others who conduct arson investigations. The organization offers online tutorials to help jurisdictions form interagency arson strike forces and develop operational protocol for arson response.

Bombings and Explosions

It seems hardly a week passes when the media doesn't report a bombing incident having occurred somewhere around the globe, often with significant casualties. Bombs have become a high-profile, almost routine, weapon of mass destruction. Bombs generate substantial media attention and provide an impersonal means of causing considerable damage, while either allowing bombers to be a safe distance away when detonation occurs or enabling suicide bombers to achieve martyrdom and incite other holy warriors to follow in their path. As noted, this emphasis on explosives was reflected in the addition of "and explosives" to the ATF name in 2003.

Most explosive incidents in this country fall into one of five classes:

1. Juvenile/experimentation
2. Recovered military ordnance or commercial explosives
3. Emotionally disturbed persons
4. Criminal actions
5. Terrorist or extremist activity

(Laska, 2008)

Motives for bombings include vandalism, revenge, and protest. Bombs are relatively easy to build from directions that can be found on the Internet. The following are common types of improvised explosive devices (IEDs) or homemade bombs:

- *Dry ice.* Combines dry ice and some water in a two-liter plastic soda bottle. Depending on the condition of the bottle, the amount of ice, and the weather, the device will explode in three to seven minutes, causing a dangerous, loud explosion.

- *Mailbox bomb.* Combines a bit of sugar and some water in a two-liter bottle of chlorine. The explosion can launch an average mailbox 20 feet into the air.

- *Car bomb.* A fuse is wrapped around a car's exhaust manifold. The fuse is ignited by the heat of the manifold, detonating the explosion.

- *Nail bomb.* An explosive device packed with nails to increase destructive power when detonated in crowded places. The July 7, 2005, explosion in London atop a double-decker bus near Shoreditch was thought to be this type of bomb.

- *Pipe bomb.* Consists of pipe, end caps, and smokeless powder, detonated by a spark or some heat source. Common containers are pipes, bottles, cans, boxes, pressurized cartridges, and grenade hulls. A pipe bomb laced with nails and other hardware to increase fragmentation caused two deaths in Atlanta's Centennial Park bombing.

Terrorists have long used cellular phones to trigger IEDs because they have adequate power, time synchronization capabilities, and alarm clock functions; allow for worldwide usage; and are extremely difficult if not impossible to track, especially if they're disposable.

A homemade explosive known as "TATP"—triacetone triperoxide—is the explosive that Richard Reid, the "shoe bomber," carried aboard American Airlines Flight 63 from Paris to Miami in 2001. TATP was also an ingredient in the "underwear bomb" worn by Umar Farouk Abdulmutallab during his attempt on Christmas Day 2009 to bring down Northwest Airlines flight 253 as it descended into Detroit. TATP is composed of acetone, hydrogen peroxide, and an acid, even a weak acid such as a can of Coke. The ingredients can easily be bought for about $17 at any hardware or home improvement store or online. The explosive concoction is virtually undetectable and quite easy to get past security, although restrictions on the quantity of liquids and gels passengers may carry on board make it more difficult to get the requisite materials through security checkpoints (Moore, 2007).

The threat of liquid explosives is of great concern, especially to airlines, as the aircraft environment requires very little explosive force because of the already pressurized cabin. Thus, law enforcement should be familiar with several types of liquid and gel explosives, some of which are very volatile (Morgenstern, 2007). Even picking up a bottle of nitroglycerine and shaking it could cause an explosion.

Bombers sometimes take their explosives one step further, creating a weapon known as the vehicle-borne improvised explosive device (VBIED), or the car bomb. Numerous websites give detailed instructions about how to make bombs, especially pipe bombs.

Bombs, more than any other weapon, make people feel vulnerable. Unlike a gun, a bomb does not have to be aimed. Unlike poison, it does not have to be administered. Bombs are weapons of chance. Victims are simply in the wrong place at the wrong time. For example, the 1995 bombing at the Murrah Federal Building in Oklahoma City claimed 169 lives, caused nearly 500 injuries and resulted in losses of $651 million. Bomber Timothy McVeigh was found guilty of the crime and executed. And the Boston Marathon bombing on April 15, 2013, which left three people dead and more than 260 injured, involved two pressure cookers concealed in backpacks and left on a crowded sidewalk. Terrorist acts are discussed in Chapter 20.

National attention also focused on the Unabomber case. Theodore Kaczynski, a Montana hermit who hated our technological society, expressed his social criticism through a campaign of bombing between 1978 and 1995. During this interval, his 16 separate bombs killed 3 people and injured 23 others. After 18 years of investigation, Kaczynski was arrested, found guilty and sentenced to life in prison without possibility of release. Evidence found in Kaczynski's cabin included scrap metal and wood, batteries and electric wire, 10 three-ring binders filled with writings and diagrams about constructing and concealing explosive devices, and two manual typewriters that investigators believe Kaczynski used to type his "Unabomber Manifesto."

In the late 1990s, Eric Rudolph used nail-laden bombs during the Atlanta Summer Olympics as well as at abortion clinics and at nightclubs catering to a mostly gay and lesbian clientele. His 11-page statement was devoid of remorse but rife with antiabortion and antigay rhetoric. The attack at the Olympics was meant to embarrass the government for legalizing abortion.

In 2002, Luke Helder, age 21 at the time, left a trail of 18 pipe bombs in rural mailboxes in Illinois, Iowa, Nebraska, Texas, and Colorado. The bombs were accompanied by typewritten notes in clear plastic bags indicating the bomber wanted to get people's attention. Six of the bombs exploded, injuring four letter carriers and two residents, but no one was killed. Law enforcement pulled Helder over three times during the course of his 1,500-mile journey in which he attempted to create a "smiley face" pattern of mailbox bombings. He was stopped in Nebraska and given a speeding ticket. He was stopped in Oklahoma for driving without a seatbelt. And he was stopped in Colorado for speeding. Within 48 hours of these three encounters, Helder was arrested on bombing charges after his cell phone calls were traced. The FBI was the lead agency in investigating these bombings and in apprehending Helder.

Responding to a Bomb Threat

Too often officers respond to a bomb threat call with a blasé approach. As with any other aspect of policing, a nonchalant attitude could prove fatal. Special safety precautions must be taken when responding to a bomb threat. The National Counterterrorism Center (NCTC) has developed detailed bomb threat instructions to be kept near telephones where such a threat might be received (Figure 16.1).

A caution: because many bombs are detonated using a remote electrical device, and because the possibility exists prior to a complete search that additional explosives might remain on scene and undetonated, it is critically important that officers not use the police radio or cell phones during the search. Furthermore, if any other people remain on site, they should be instructed to not use their cell phones until given the all clear.

Management should assist first responders in devising a thorough search of the building using employees to

Figure 16.1
Bomb threat call procedures.
Source: Cybersecurity and Infrastructure Security Agency (CISA). www.cisa.gov/sites/default/files/publications/Bomb-Threat-Procedure-Checklist.pdf

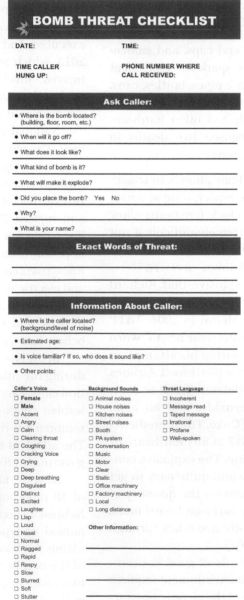

BOMB THREAT PROCEDURES

This quick reference checklist is designed to help employees and decision makers of commercial facilities, schools, etc. respond to a bomb threat in an orderly and controlled manner with the first responders and other stakeholders.

Most bomb threats are received by phone. Bomb threats are serious until proven otherwise. Act quickly, but remain calm and obtain information with the checklist on the reverse of this card.

If a bomb threat is received by phone:
1. Remain calm. Keep the caller on the line for as long as possible. DO NOT HANG UP, even if the caller does.
2. Listen carefully. Be polite and show interest.
3. Try to keep the caller talking to learn more information.
4. If possible, write a note to a colleague to call the authorities or, as soon as the caller hangs up, immediately notify them yourself.
5. If your phone has a display, copy the number and/or letters on the window display.
6. Complete the Bomb Threat Checklist immediately. Write down as much detail as you can remember. Try to get exact words.
7. Immediately upon termination of call, DO NOT HANG UP, but from a different phone, contact authorities immediately with information and await instructions.

If a bomb threat is received by handwritten note:
- Call _____
- Handle note as minimally as possible.

If a bomb threat is received by e-mail:
- Call _____
- Do not delete the message.

Signs of a suspicious package:
- No return address
- Excessive postage
- Stains
- Strange odor
- Strange sounds
- Unexpected delivery
- Poorly handwritten
- Misspelled words
- Incorrect titles
- Foreign postage
- Restrictive notes

* Refer to your local bomb threat emergency response plan for evacuation criteria

DO NOT:
- Use two-way radios or cellular phone. Radio signals have the potential to detonate a bomb.
- Touch or move a suspicious package.

WHO TO CONTACT (Select One)
- 911
- Follow your local guidelines

For more information about this form contact the Office for Bombing Prevention at: OBP@cisa.dhs.gov

BOMB THREAT CHECKLIST

DATE: _____ TIME: _____

TIME CALLER HUNG UP: _____   PHONE NUMBER WHERE CALL RECEIVED: _____

Ask Caller:
- Where is the bomb located? (building, floor, room, etc.)
- When will it go off?
- What does it look like?
- What kind of bomb is it?
- What will make it explode?
- Did you place the bomb? Yes No
- Why?
- What is your name?

Exact Words of Threat:

Information About Caller:
- Where is the caller located? (background/level of noise)
- Estimated age:
- Is voice familiar? If so, who does it sound like?
- Other points:

Caller's Voice	Background Sounds	Threat Language
☐ Female	☐ Animal noises	☐ Incoherent
☐ Male	☐ House noises	☐ Message read
☐ Accent	☐ Kitchen noises	☐ Taped message
☐ Angry	☐ Street noises	☐ Irrational
☐ Calm	☐ Booth	☐ Profane
☐ Clearing throat	☐ PA system	☐ Well-spoken
☐ Coughing	☐ Conversation	
☐ Cracking Voice	☐ Music	
☐ Crying	☐ Motor	
☐ Deep	☐ Clear	
☐ Deep breathing	☐ Static	
☐ Disguised	☐ Office machinery	
☐ Distinct	☐ Factory machinery	
☐ Excited	☐ Local	
☐ Laughter	☐ Long distance	
☐ Lisp		
☐ Loud		Other Information:
☐ Nasal		
☐ Normal		
☐ Ragged		
☐ Rapid		
☐ Raspy		
☐ Slow		
☐ Slurred		
☐ Soft		
☐ Stutter		

V2

help in the search because employees will know if anything is out of place and "doesn't fit." Management will also decide if the building is to be evacuated after the search.

Searchers pay attention to unattended bags, boxes, or briefcases as well as areas with suspended ceilings with panels that are easily pushed up to hide an IED. Other items to pay attention to are trash cans, ashtrays, and flowerpots. In addition, any incoming mail or packages should be carefully screened. Large warehouses in which an enormous quantity of inventory is stored can be extremely challenging environments to search. Again, employees familiar with the routine movement of product and equipment can help officers identify if something seems out of place.

Once responding officers establish that a suspicious package could be a threat or potential bomb, they must contact a specially trained bomb squad to handle the situation from that point. Other than the initial call, responding patrol officers do not deal with explosives. If the agency does not have a local explosives unit, the agency typically requests mutual aid assistance from the closest agency with a bomb squad.

If a bomb is found, the most important rule in handling suspect packages is to NOT TOUCH the package. The area should be cleared to a minimum 300-foot radius. Emergency personnel (fire and emergency medical personnel) should be alerted. All radios should be turned off.

Methods of Explosives Detection

Often, additional tools are needed to help responding officers determine if an explosive threat truly exists. Some of the methods are low-tech, such as using dogs to sniff out compounds used to build bombs. Other techniques employ highly advanced equipment and technology to detect explosive material.

Using K-9s in Detecting Explosives. As with arson investigations, dogs have become increasingly useful in bomb detection and in searches for evidence following explosions: "Field deployable electronic sensors or instruments can't top dogs, which have been increasingly in demand since 9/11. Canines are still our best detection technology" (Kanable, 2007, p. 68). Following the precaution of not handling the explosive, bomb dogs are trained to alert the handler by sitting near a suspect package without touching it.

Using Stationary Technology in Detecting Explosives. Airports and cargo terminals use X-ray and computed axial tomography (CAT) equipment to scan large numbers of items and people. Such methods require highly trained operators, are stationary, and

cannot readily be used on vehicles or individuals or to investigate where bomb-making activities are ongoing or have taken place. Because of this, law enforcement must rely on what is referred to as "sniffer" technology, the use of a portable device that pulls in an air sample and passes it through a chemical analyzer to calculate a profile of the elements and compounds, including explosives, that are present in the ambient environment.

Using Robots in a Bomb Threat Response. Bomb squads in larger departments are using robots to approach and detonate suspected packages. Robots can be equipped with **disrupters**, devices that use gunpowder to fire a jet of water or a projectile at a particular component of an explosive to make it safe (Cox, 2004). Other features of bomb robots include portable X-ray machines and devices to remotely cut open a car door.

The Bomb Scene Investigation

If there has been an explosion, investigators should

- Ensure that a search for secondary explosive devices has been conducted

- Ensure that the scene has been secured, that a perimeter and staging areas for the investigation have been established, and that all personnel have been advised of the need to prevent contamination of the scene

- Establish a media staging area, if needed

- Ensure that the chain of custody is initiated for evidence that may have been previously collected

- Establish procedures to document personnel entering and exiting the scene

- Determine if there were any people injured and where they are, as those close to the blast may be the best witnesses

- Establish and document procedures for evidence collection, control, and chain of custody

- Be ever mindful of safety

> **LO11** Identify what investigators should pay special attention to when working explosion and bombing cases.

When investigating explosions and bombings, pay special attention to fragments of the explosive device as well as to any powder present at the scene. Determine motive.

Bomb-scene investigations must progress logically. The first step is to determine the scene's parameters. In general, once the farthest piece of recognizable evidence is located, a radius 50% wider is established. For example, in the Oklahoma City bombing, the rear axle of the truck carrying the explosives was located three blocks from the blast site, so the scene parameters were approximately four and a half blocks in all directions.

Raising Awareness

Awareness training programs should teach employees to notice individuals wearing clothes unsuitable for the time of year, people trying to blend into a group that they clearly don't belong to, or an object protruding from a person's clothing. Other behaviors to watch for are people acting very nervous or perspiring profusely, someone obviously staying clear of security personnel, a person walking slowly while constantly glancing back, or a person running suspiciously.

Importance of the Team Approach

The teamwork of field investigators and laboratory specialists in investigating bombings is critical. Such teamwork followed a California pipe-bombing incident that killed the driver of a vehicle to which a bomb had been attached. The Rialto Police Department, the San Bernardino Sheriff's Office, and the ATF combined their efforts. They investigated and forwarded evidence from the scene to the ATF laboratory for examination. Chemists identified the type and brand of powder used in the bomb by examining intact powder particles found in the bomb's end caps. A subsequent search at the suspect's home uncovered a can of smokeless powder identical to the identified powder. Additional evidence obtained during the search provided further links between the suspect and the bombing. The suspect was arrested and charged with murder.

Investigators with technical questions about commercial explosives can receive assistance from the

---

Technology Innovations

Handheld Explosive Detectors

An increasing number of portable, handheld explosive detection devices are being developed for officers in the field. Some of the newcomers include the Fido X3 by FLIR, the TraceX Explosive Detection Kit by Morphix® Technologies, and ACE-ID from Smiths Detection (Basich, 2014). This last device uses laser technology to conduct "noncontact analysis" of a variety of powders, gels, liquids, and solids: "It can even identify two components in one sample without the device—or the officer—ever touching the substance. Materials can be identified through translucent and semi-translucent containers such as plastic and glass, and a software kit allows for remote operation. . . . [A] wide range of agencies use it for clandestine drug lab investigations and any 'white powder type calls' to determine if a substance is drugs or explosives . . . because it can detect approximately 500 substances including explosives and toxic chemicals." The device is small enough to fit in a tactical pants pocket and has an expandable library, so if an agency thinks it is facing a new threat that is not already one of the 500 detectable substances stored in the unit, new sample profiles can be added with computer software.

Source: www.policemag.com/341182/explosives-detection-in-hand

---

Institute of Makers of Explosives (IME) in Washington, D.C. This nonprofit safety organization has 31 member companies and more than 80 subsidiaries and affiliates, which together produce more than 85% of the commercial explosives used in the United States. Also of help is the ATF National Response Team (NRT), which can be deployed in the most urgent, difficult bomb cases.

Summary

Fires are classified as natural, accidental, incendiary (arson), or of undetermined origin. They are presumed to be natural or accidental unless proven otherwise. The Model Arson Law divides arson into the following degrees:

- *First-degree*: burning of dwellings

- *Second-degree*: burning of buildings other than dwellings

- *Third-degree*: burning of other property

- *Fourth-degree*: attempting to burn buildings or property

The elements of the crime of arson include (1) the willful, malicious burning of a building or property (2) of another, or of one's own to defraud (3) or aiding, counseling, or procuring such burning. Logic suggests that the fire department should work to detect arson and determine the fire's point of origin and probable cause, whereas the police department should investigate arson and prepare the case for prosecution.

The fire triangle consists of three elements necessary for a substance to burn: air, fuel, and heat. In arson, at least one of these elements is usually present in abnormal amounts for the structure. Determination of the origin of a fire involves the combined interpretation of information derived from one or more of the following: (1) witness information and/or electronic data, (2) fire patterns, and (3) fire dynamics (the physics and chemistry of the fire). Multiple points of origin might indicate arson. A fire may be considered incendiary and, thus, the result of arson if investigation of the fire shows:

- The presence of an abnormal amount of air, fuel, or heat

- Evidence of having been accelerated

Can You Define?

accelerant	fireplay	serial arson
administrative warrant	firesetting	simple arson
aggravated arson	fire triangle	spalling
arc mapping	flashover	spree arson
arson	igniter	strikers
crazing	incendiary	torch
depth of char	mass arson	trailer
disrupters	rainbow effect	

Checklist

Arson

- Who first noticed the fire?

- Who notified authorities?

- Who responded from the fire department?

- Did the fire department record the color of the smoke? The color of the flame?

- What was the fire's point of origin? Was there more than one point of origin?

- What material was used to ignite the fire?

- Was there an explosion before the fire? During the fire? After the fire?

- Was the fire's burn time normal? Did it appear to be accelerated?

- Evidence of incendiary igniters

- More than one point of origin

- Deviation from normal burning patterns

- Evidence of trailers

An administrative warrant is issued when it is necessary for a government agent to search the premises to determine the fire's cause and origin. A criminal warrant is issued on probable cause when the premises yield evidence of a crime. Entry to fight a fire requires no warrant.

When investigating vehicle fires, look for evidence of accelerants and determine whether the vehicle was insured. It is seldom arson if there is no insurance. When investigating explosions and bombings, pay special attention to fragments of the explosive device as well as to any powder present at the scene. Determine motive.

- Were any accelerants (newspapers, rags, or gasoline) found at the scene?

- Did firefighters have to move anything to fight the fire?

- What was the weather: dry, windy, snowy?

- What property was destroyed that was unusual for the premises?

- Were there any unusual circumstances?

- Was anyone injured or killed? Was an autopsy done to determine whether there were other causes for death than fire? Were carbon monoxide tests made of the victim to determine when death occurred—whether before or during the fire?

- Were regular informants checked to determine possible suspects?

- Who had access to the building?

- What appeared to be the motive for the fire? Who would benefit?

- Who owns the property destroyed? For how long?

- Was there insurance and, if so, how much?

- Who was the insurance payable to?

- How long had the insurance policy been in place?

- What is the name of the insurance company? Has a copy of the company's report been obtained?

- Does the owner have any record of other property destroyed by fire?

- Does the owner have a criminal record for this or other types of crimes?

- Were any suspicious people or vehicles observed at the scene before, during, or after the fire?

- Was the state fire marshal's office notified? Did it send an investigator? If so, obtain a copy of the investigator's report.

- Were photographs or videos taken? Are they available?

Applications

Read the following and then answer the questions:

A. It is mid-afternoon on a Sunday. The fire department has just received a call to proceed to the Methodist Church on St. Anthony Boulevard. Smoke has been reported coming out of the church's windows by a nearby resident. When the fire department arrives, the church is fully engulfed in flames. By the time the fire is brought under control, the church is gutted, with damage estimated at $320,000. Suspecting arson, the fire department asks for help from the local police department.

Questions

1. Was the request for assistance justified at this point?

2. What are the responsibilities of the investigator assigned to respond to the call?

B. Investigators Ron McNeil and Brianna Joyce worked together as part of Boston's special arson task force. Just before midnight, they received a call from the dispatcher and were told to proceed to a certain address. They arrived minutes later at a small, one-story frame house and pulled in behind the first fire rig. Orange flames were shooting from every window of the house.

While the firefighters fought the blaze, McNeil and Joyce walked among the bystanders, asking if anyone had seen anything suspicious before the fire, but no one had. When the fire was out and the smoke cleared, floodlights illuminated the house and McNeil and Joyce started their investigation. Beginning in the small front room, they noticed extensive burning and windows totally blackened from the fire. They proceeded through a small alcove, where the top portion had been destroyed, and then entered the kitchen. The glass in a window over the kitchen sink had broken and melted, with a series of intricate cracks running through each fragment. After shoveling out layers of debris and dragging in a fire hose to wash the floor, McNeil and Joyce noticed that the floor was deeply charred and spongy with water. Inspection of the wooden cabinets around the sink revealed large, rolling blisters. The investigators also discovered that the electricity to the structure had been disconnected. Then they began to photograph the fire scene.

Shortly afterward, the owner and his wife arrived. The owner calmly answered questions, informing the investigators that he had been letting a carpenter live in the house in exchange for fixing up the place. But when the tenant failed to make the repairs and instead stole the construction materials, much of the furniture and many appliances, the owner kicked him out. The carpenter threatened to "make him sorry." The owner had no fire insurance because he had intended not to live in the house but to use it as an investment property.

After filing their report, McNeil and Joyce returned to the property at 4 a.m. A heavy rain the day before had soaked the ground, and the mud in the backyard was crisscrossed with footprints. Joyce noticed some boot prints leading from the back door and took a plaster cast of them. Just then, a neighbor stopped over to say he had seen a green pickup parked behind the house with the motor running just before the fire. McNeil photographed all the tire tracks in the dirt alley where the pickup was reportedly parked. The next morning the investigators learned that the carpenter, now their prime suspect, had been in jail when the fire broke out. The green pickup was registered to a friend of his, a man who had been previously arrested for arson.

They obtained a search warrant and executed it later that morning. The tires of the carpenter's friend's truck and his boot soles resembled the impressions found at the fire scene, but the impressions were so spongy that it was difficult to match them exactly. The investigators found no further evidence linking the man to the fire. (Adapted from Krajick, K. [1979, July]. Seattle: Sifting through the ashes. *Police Magazine*, pp. 10–11.)

Questions

1. Where did the fire probably originate? What factors indicate this?
2. What indicated that the fire was probably arson?
3. Did the investigators have probable cause to arrest the carpenter's friend? Would the owner also be a possible suspect? Why, or why not?
4. What aspects of this case illustrate an effective arson investigation?

References

Basich, M. (2014, August 1). Explosives detection in hand. Police. Retrieved March 8, 2021, from www.policemag.com/341182/explosives-detection-in-hand

Bergazzi, M., & Burkett, J. (2018, June 7). Father and son's mistake brings down Va. arson ring. Scripps Media, Inc. Retrieved March 3, 2021, from www.wtvr.com/2018/06/06/serial-arson-investigation/

Bossert, J. (2015, March 1). Protecting responding police officers. Fire rescue magazine. Retrieved March 5, 2021, from www.firefighternation.com/firerescue/protecting-responding-police-officers/#gref

Broward County Sheriff's Office. (2020). Juvenile firesetter prevention and intervention program. Ft. Lauderdale, FL: Author, Web site. Retrieved March 8, 2021, from www.sheriff.org/Community/Pages/Juvenile-Firesetter.aspx

Bureau of Alcohol, Tobacco, Firearms, and Explosives, Denver Field Division. (2013, December 16). ATF NRT activated to join investigation of commercial building fire with $12 million in damage. Washington, DC: Author. Retrieved March 3, 2021, from www.atf.gov/news/pr/atf-nrt-activated-join-investigation-commercial-building-fire-12-million-damage

Bureau of Alcohol, Tobacco, Firearms, and Explosives. (2016, September 22). International response team. Washington, DC: Author. Retrieved March 8, 2021, from www.atf.gov/explosives/international-response-team

Campbell, R. (2014, March). Playing with fire. Quincy, MA: National Fire Protection Association. Retrieved February 23, 2021, from www.nfpa.org/-/media/Files/News-and-Research/Fire-statistics-and-reports/US-Fire-Problem/Fire-causes/oschildplay.ashx

Cox, J. (2004, February). Recoilless disrupter enhances EOD technology. Law Enforcement Technology, pp. 106–109.

Evarts, B. (2019, October). Fire loss in the United States during 2018. Quincy, MA: National Fire Protection Association. Retrieved February 16, 2021, from www.nfpa.org/-/media/Files/News-and-Research/Fire-statistics-and-reports/US-Fire-Problem/Old-FL-LL-and-Cat/FireLoss2019.ashx

Federal Bureau of Investigation. (2018). Crime in the United States, 2018. Washington, DC: Author. Retrieved February 23, 2021, from ucr.fbi.gov/crime-in-the-u.s/2018/crime-in-the-u.s.-2018/

Federal Bureau of Investigation, Detroit Division. (2013, May 8). *Leader of arson ring sentenced to 137 years in prison.* Detroit, MI: Author. Retrieved March 8, 2021, from archives.fbi.gov/archives/detroit/press-releases/2013/leader-of-arson-ring-sentenced-to-137-years-in-prison

Harpster, T., & Adams, S. H. (2018). Is the caller the killer? Analyzing 911 homicide calls. Chapter 12 in Behavior, truth and deception, Applying profiling and analysis to the interview process (2nd Ed.) by M. R. Napier. Boca Raton, FL: CRC Press.

Howell Bowling, C., Merrick, J., & Omar, H. A. (2013, December 9). Self-reported juvenile firesetting: Results from two national survey datasets. Frontiers in Public Health, 1(60). doi:10.3389/fpubh.2013.00060

InterFire. (n.d.). Episode one: The 911 call. Follow that case. Retrieved March 5, 2021, from www.interfire.org/features/followThatCase/episode001.asp

iRobot unveils its first multi-robot tablet controller for first responders. (2014, October 9). Police. Retrieved March 8, 2021, from www.policemag.com/353614/irobot-unveils-its-first-multi-robot-tablet-controller-for-first-responders

Kanable, R. (2007, September). The best from man's best friend. Law Enforcement Technology, pp. 68–77.

Kerber, S., & Mandeville, D. (2018, October 29). How cops can help firefighters close the door on fire. Police1. Retrieved March 5, 2021, from www.police1.com/police-training/articles/how-cops-can-help-firefighters-close-the-door-on-fire-alKrYZiggIOKh8nz/

Laska, P. R. (2008, February). Bombs and the street cop. *Law Officer Magazine*, pp. 40–43.

Moore, C. (2007, October). Improvised explosives. Law Enforcement Technology, p. 210.

Moore, T., & Tracy, T. (2015, March 18). Happy land mass murderer Julio Gonzalez denied parole on eve of horrific Bronx Inferno's tragic 25th anniversary. New York Daily News. Retrieved March 8, 2021, from www.nydailynews.com/new-york/happy-land-mass-murderer-julio-gonzalez-denied-parole-article-1.2152515

Morgenstern, H. (2007, January). Simple plot. Law Enforcement Technology, pp. 8–16.

National Fire Protection Association. (2021). NFPA 921: Guide for fire and explosion investigations. Quincy, MA: Author. Retrieved March 5, 2021, from www.nfpa.org/codes-and-standards/all-codes-and-standards/list-of-codes-and-standards/detail?code=921

National Institute of Justice. (2000, June). Fire and arson scene evidence: A guide for public safety personnel. Washington, DC: Author. (NCJ 181584). Retrieved March 5, 2021, from www.ojp.gov/pdffiles1/nij/181584.pdf

Smith, M., & Gipson, J. (2008, November). Don't get burned. Police, pp. 54–59.

Smith, M., & Gipson, J. (2010, June). Inner-agency cooperation for fire investigation. Law and Order, pp. 32–34.

U.S. Fire Administration. (2006, July). Juvenile firesetting: A growing concern. Emmitsburg, MD: Author (FA-307). Retrieved February 23, 2021, from www.waco-texas.com/pdf/fire/prevention/kids/juvenile-firesetters.pdf

U.S. Fire Administration. (2012, May 6–12). Prevent youth firesetting. Emmitsburg, MD: Author. Retrieved February 23, 2021, from www.usfa.fema.gov/downloads/pdf/arson/aaw12_media_kit.pdf

U.S. Fire Administration. (2016, April 12). Arson motives. Emmitsburg, MD: Author Retrieved March 3, 2021, from www.usfa.fema.gov/prevention/outreach/wildfire_arson/arson_motives.html

U.S. Fire Administration. (2019, November). *Fire in the United States 2008–2017* (20th Ed.). Emmitsburg, MD: Author. Retrieved February 16, 2021, from www.usfa.fema.gov/downloads/pdf/publications/fius20th.pdf

Cases Cited

Coolidge v. New Hampshire, 403 U.S. 443 (1971).

Michigan v. Clifford, 464 U.S. 287 (1984).

SECTION 5

Other Challenges to the Criminal Investigator

The two preceding sections discussed investigating violent crimes and crimes against property. Many crimes do not fall neatly into one of the eight Index crimes reported in the Federal Bureau of Investigation's Uniform Crime Reports (UCR) but involve a combination of illegal acts related to both people and property. Unique investigative challenges are presented by investigating computer and cybercrime (Chapter 17), drug-related and organized crime (Chapter 18), the criminal activities of gangs and other dangerous groups (Chapter 19), and the war against terrorism and fight for homeland security (Chapter 20). Investigating the illegal activities related to these groups is more difficult because the elements of the crimes are not neatly spelled out and statistics are not available as they are for the UCR crimes. A final and critical challenge is preparing for and presenting cases in court (Chapter 21).

Cybercrime is relatively new, but organized crime, drug- and gang-related crime, bias and hate crime, and ritualistic crime have existed in one form or another for centuries. Not until recently, however, have they had such an impact on law enforcement, straining already limited resources. A further complication is that the areas commonly overlap; people involved in organized crime, drugs, and gangs are often the same people—but not necessarily. Terrorists fund their

activities through drug sales, extortion, money laundering, and various types of fraud, including cybertheft. Although each type of crime is discussed separately, always keep this overlap in mind. Furthermore, moral and ethical issues are raised by the activities of these organizations that are not raised by the activities of, say, bank robbers, rapists, and murderers. Stealing, raping, and murdering are clearly wrong in our society. This is not necessarily true for gambling, worshiping Satan, or smoking pot.

Among the greatest challenges are the "wars" America finds itself in against drugs and terrorism, both domestic and international. Homeland defense has become a priority for law enforcement agencies at all levels. Other great challenges for investigators are preparing final reports the prosecutor can use to bring criminal cases to trial and presenting effective testimony to bring these cases to successful resolution. Without these skills, the best investigations are futile.

Chapter 17
Computer Crime and Digital Evidence

Learning Objectives

LO1   Define the three basic ways computer crime can be categorized.

LO2   List the steps taken in following a common protocol for processing a crime scene involving electronic evidence.

LO3   Explain the basic on/off tenet for first responders at a computer crime scene.

LO4   Summarize the benefits of getting a search warrant in a computer crime investigation.

LO5   Identify the various forms electronic evidence and other computer crime evidence may take.

LO6   Describe how electronic evidence should be stored.

LO7   Determine how cybercriminals may be categorized, including their differing motivations.

LO8   Understand ways in which computer crimes can be prevented.

Introduction

Barely a month passes these days without some high-profile computer-related crime making front-page news. "Not long ago, a breach that compromised the data of a few million people would have been big news. Now, breaches that affect hundreds of millions or even billions of people are far too common" (Swinhoe, 2021). In fact, in two of the biggest data breaches since 2000, approximately 3.5 billion people had their personal data stolen.

The Target data security breach that occurred during the holiday shopping season in late 2013 involved hackers gaining unauthorized access to roughly 40 million customer credit and debit cards, crimping the spending habits and rattling the trust of many consumers. The Sony Pictures hack by the "Guardians of Peace" (GOP) in December 2014 resulted in the leak of unreleased films, movie scripts, employee payroll information, actors' private contact numbers, box office projections, company passwords, and other sensitive proprietary data, as well as threats to the safety of company executives, their families, and any moviegoers who attended showings of *The Interview* (Alvarez, 2014).

Evgeniy Bogachev, one of the FBI's Most Wanted cybercriminals and mastermind of what many consider to be the most sophisticated cybercrime network to date, is considered a hero in his homeland: "[T]he man named . . . as the biggest new threat to America's banking system has never needed a gun, nor is he even thought to have set foot in the United States. Instead, under the code name 'Lucky 12345,' he carried out his entire operation via strokes of a keyboard from his house in Russia's Black Sea coast" (Freeman, 2014). The 30-year-old hacker and his cybergang allegedly used malware to infect millions of computers with the program GameOverZeus (GOZ), enabling them to capture passwords to victims' bank accounts and other sensitive websites. The FBI estimates that the GOZ virus has cost victims approximately $100 million in the United States alone.

The hackers also unleashed a ransomware program called CryptoLocker, which encrypts all of the data on a victim's computer, no matter how benign—private emails, personal photos, school homework assignments, business documents—and threatens to permanently destroy it unless a ransom, payable in **bitcoins** (an Internet currency used in online payment programs), is delivered before a deadline. Although each

ransom demand was relatively small, the number of victims who paid the ransom was enormous, and authorities believe the cybergang raked in roughly $15 million each month (Freeman, 2014).

Computers and other wireless devices are pervasive in the home, workplace, and school. According to its annual survey, CTIA (The Cellular Telecommunications and Internet Association) reported that there were 442.5 million wireless subscriber connections in the United States in 2020 and that 96% of American adults owned a cell phone. CTIA projects that by 2025, adults will interact with a connected device every 18 seconds (CTIA, 2020). Electronic devices store a staggering quantity of information that is getting exponentially larger.

Before the mid-1990s, computer crime was almost nonexistent. Computer crime typically involved actions performed on a single machine or on a small self-contained network of machines, such as stealing data off a hard drive or planting a malicious code within the software of a company's internal computer network. Whatever the specifics of the crime, the criminal had to come in close physical contact with the computer(s) and the crime scene.

Over the past two decades, however, crimes involving computers have become much more sophisticated and investigating such crimes considerably more complicated. What makes cybercrime the tremendous problem it is today is that most computers on the planet are connected via the Internet, allowing a criminal thousands of miles away from a crime scene—whether at a computer in a private residence, at an extensive database within a major corporation's mainframe, or holding a cell phone almost anywhere in the world—to carry out theft, fraud, vandalism, or any other number of crimes without ever setting foot in the same city, state, country, or even continent as the victim.

This medium also provides a higher level of anonymity to the offender, making identification of the perpetrator very challenging for investigators. The Internet also provides a medium through which pedophiles access and exchange child pornography, stalkers harass and threaten their targets, and terrorists around the globe communicate with each other. Keeping up with these techno-savvy criminals has pushed law enforcement to develop a new breed of detective—the cybercrime investigator.

The Scope and Cost of the Problem

The current hot crime tools are personal computers, laptops, tablets, or smartphones linked to the Internet. This online element has led to a fundamental change in how many law enforcement agencies refer to such offenses—from *computer crime* to *cybercrime*. It should come as no surprise that criminals are capitalizing on this technology. Numerous online communication options are available, such as email, chat rooms, Web pages, and social media or networking.

The Internet's capacity for global interconnectivity has made the scope of the cybercrime problem transnational, the extent of which, confess most experts, is not yet fully understood. Adding to the uncertainty of the extent of the problem is that a large percentage of police departments do not yet know how to address this threat and do not keep accurate records involving such incidents. What is known, however, is that cybercrime has touched countless individuals and businesses throughout the United States and the entire world, posing a significant economic and national security threat. While impossible to state the exact dollar cost of such crimes, it is estimated that cybercrime cost the global economy $3 trillion in 2015 and will reach a cost of $6 trillion annually by year-end 2021 (Cybersecurity Ventures, 2019).

Individuals can be victimized by a variety of different cybercrimes, such as email and Internet fraud, theft of financial or card payment data, and identity fraud. In 2018, roughly 14.4 million consumers in the United States, or 1 in 15 people, became victims of identity fraud, many of whom had their personal information stolen from cyberspace (Marchini & Pascual, 2019). Although this represents a 5.7% decrease in the number of consumer fraud victims from 2017, a greater percentage of victims were paying out-of-pocket for fraud losses. Internet scams continue to strip unsuspecting consumers of millions of dollars every year, along with their faith in the security of doing business online. Sources of information on the scope and cost of computer crime include the Internet Crime Complaint Center and the U.S. State of Cybercrime Survey.

The IC3 Annual Internet Crime Report

The Internet Crime Complaint Center (IC3), formerly called the Internet Fraud Complaint Center, is a partnership between the Federal Bureau of Investigation (FBI) and the National White Collar Crime Center (NW3C) designed to serve as a clearinghouse for cybercrime data for law enforcement and regulatory agencies at the federal, state, and local levels and to provide cybercrime investigation training. All sworn law enforcement can remotely access and search the IC3 database through the FBI's Law Enforcement Enterprise Portal (LEEP). The IC3 receives a broad spectrum of complaints including online fraud (e.g., elder fraud, romance fraud, tech support fraud), computer intrusions (hacking), breaches of intellectual property rights (IPR), online extortion and ransomware, international money laundering, economic espionage (theft of trade secrets), and, of course, identity theft. The proliferation of child pornography on the Internet has also become a serious concern, as thousands of young individuals are victimized every year by this type of exploitation.

According to the *2019 Internet Crime Report* (2020), the IC3 received 467,361 complaints in 2019 (Internet Crime Complaint Center [IC3], 2019). As of year-end 2019, the IC3 had received 4,883,231 complaints since its inception in May 2000. The most prevalent crime types reported were phishing/pharming, nonpayment/nondelivery, extortion, and personal data breach. The top three crime types with the highest reported losses were business email compromise (BEC)/email account compromise (EAC), confidence/romance fraud, and spoofing. Tables 17.1 and 17.2 show the reported crime types in 2019 by victim count and victim loss, respectively. IC3 Chief Donna Gregory states that these annual reports illustrate how prevalent cybercrimes are, how substantial the financial toll is, and how anyone who uses a connected device can become a victim: "Awareness is one powerful tool in efforts to combat and prevent these crimes. Reporting is another. The more information that comes into the IC3, the better law enforcement is able to respond" (Federal Bureau of Investigation [FBI], 2019).

In 2013, the FBI launched Operation Wellspring (OWS), an initiative in which the FBI, through the IC3, provides case-specific tactical intelligence and expert analysis to state and local law enforcement agencies engaged in investigating Internet crime. Through OWS, the IC3 sends targeted intelligence and fraud packages to participating state, local, and tribal law enforcement cyber task forces (CTFs) who successfully leverage FBI resources in developing successful cases. Meanwhile,

TABLE 17.1 2019 Crime Types by Victim Count

Crime Type	Victims	Crime Type	Victims
Phishing/Vishing/Smishing/Pharming	114,702	Lottery/Sweepstakes/Inheritance	7,767
Non-Payment/Non-Delivery	61,832	Misrepresentation	5,975
Extortion	43,101	Investment	3,999
Personal Data Breach	38,218	IPR/Copyright and Counterfeit	3,892
Spoofing	25,789	Malware/Scareware/Virus	2,373
BEC/EAC	23,775	Ransomware	2,047
Confidence Fraud/Romance	19,473	Corporate Data Breach	1,795
Identity Theft	16,053	Denial of Service/TDoS	1,353
Harassment/Threats of Violence	15,502	Crimes Against Children	1,312
Overpayment	15,395	Re-shipping	929
Advanced Fee	14,607	Civil Matter	908
Employment	14,493	Health Care Related	657
Credit Card Fraud	14,378	Charity	407
Government Impersonation	13,873	Gambling	262
Tech Support	13,633	Terrorism	61
Real Estate/Rental	11,677	Hacktivist	39
Other	10,842		

Descriptors*			
Social Media	29,093	*These descriptors relate to the medium or tool used to facilitate the crime, and are used by	
Virtual Currency	29,313	the IC3 for tracking purposes only. They are available as descriptors only after another crime type has been selected.	

Source: *2019 Internet Crime Report.* Washington, DC: Federal Bureau of Investigation, Internet Crime Complaint Center, pp. 19, 20. www.ic3.gov/Media/PDF/AnnualReport/2019_IC3Report.pdf

TABLE 17.2 2019 Crime Types by Victim Loss

Crime Type	Loss	Crime Type	Loss
BEC/EAC	$1,776,549,688	Employment	$42,618,705
Confidence Fraud/Romance	$475,014,032	Civil Matter	$20,242,867
Spoofing	$300,478,433	Harassment/Threats of Violence	$19,866,654
Investment	$222,186,195	Misrepresentation	$12,371,573
Real Estate/Rental	$221,365,911	IPR/Copyright and Counterfeit	$10,293,307
Non-Payment/Non-Delivery	$196,563,497	Ransomware	**$8,965,847
Identity Theft	$160,305,789	Denial of Service/TDoS	$7,598,198
Government Impersonation	$124,292,606	Charity	$2,214,383
Personal Data Breach	$120,102,501	Malware/Scareware/Virus	$2,009,119
Credit Card Fraud	$111,491,163	Re-shipping	$1,772,692
Extortion	$107,498,956	Gambling	$1,458,118
Advanced Fee	$100,602,297	Health Care Related	$1,128,838
Other	$66,223,160	Crimes Against Children	$975,311
Phishing/Vishing/Smishing/Pharming	$57,836,379	Hacktivist	$129,000
Overpayment	$55,820,212	Terrorism	$49,589
Tech Support	$54,041,053		
Corporate Data Breach	$53,398,278		
Lottery/Sweepstakes/Inheritance	$48,642,332		

Descriptors*		
Social Media	$78,775,408	*These descriptors relate to the medium or tool used to facilitate the crime, and are
Virtual Currency	$159,329,101	used by the IC3 for tracking purposes only. They are available only after another crime type has been selected.

** Regarding ransomware adjusted losses, this number does not include estimates of lost business, time, wages, files, or equipment, or any third-party remediation services acquired by a victim. In some cases victims do not report any loss amount to the FBI, thereby creating an artificially low overall ransomware loss rate. Lastly, the number only represents what victims report to the FBI via the IC3 and does not account for victim direct reporting to FBI field offices/agents.

Source: *2019 Internet Crime Report*. Washington, DC: Federal Bureau of Investigation, Internet Crime Complaint Center, pp. 19, 20. www.ic3.gov/Media/PDF/AnnualReport/2019_IC3Report.pdf

the CTFs reciprocate by providing the IC3 with a continual flow of information and updates which, ultimately, will help other federal, state, and even international law enforcement agencies realize success in developing effective investigations and prosecuting perpetrators of Internet crime. As a result of OWS, 18 investigations were opened in 2018, and the IC3 provided 123 referrals to 13 CTFs based on 1192 victim complaints (IC3, 2018). The total victim loss associated with these complaints was approximately $28.1 million.

In 2019, the IC3 created the Recovery and Investigative Development (RaID) Team, comprised of the Recovery Asset Team (RAT) and the Money Mule

Team (MMT), to partner with financial and law enforcement investigators to dismantle money mule organizations. According to the FBI, a money mule is someone who, either knowingly or unknowingly, transfers or moves illegally acquired money, often between accounts in different countries, on behalf of someone else (Garza, 2020). Criminal organizations use money mules to help launder income generated through online scams and frauds or other crimes like human trafficking, weapons trafficking, or drug trafficking. Using mules puts distance between the criminal organization and their victims, making it more difficult for investigators to "follow the money." While the RAT is primarily focused on financial recovery, the MMT performs detailed analysis and research on previously unknown targets to develop new investigations. In its first year of operation, the RAT assisted in the recovery of over $300 million lost through online scams, for a 79% return rate of reported losses (IC3, 2019).

The Annual U.S. State of Cybercrime Survey

The annual U.S. State of Cybercrime Survey, formerly called the CyberSecurity Watch Survey, is conducted jointly by *CSO Magazine*, the U.S. Secret Service (USSS), and Carnegie Mellon University's Software Engineering Institute CERT® Program. The survey is sent out annually to readers of *CSO Magazine*, visitors to the magazine's website, and members and partners of the USSS's Electronic Crimes Task Forces. The most recent survey, conducted in 2018, found that 41% of respondents reported an increase in the frequency of cybersecurity events from the previous year, and 35% reported it was taking longer to detect network intrusions due to the increasing sophistication of hackers (CSO Magazine, 2018). Of organizations that experienced at least one cyber security event in the previous 12 months, 25% were attributed to insiders. Outside hackers were considered to pose the greatest cyberthreat overall, and 40% of financial losses due to security threats during the previous year were the result of targeted attacks.

Terminology and Definitions

To fully understand and effectively investigate computer crime, officers need a working knowledge of relevant terminology, how documents are stored and retrieved, and how access to the Internet (and others' files) is obtained. The FBI previously defined **computer crime** as "that which involves the addition, deletion, change or theft of information." However, as the Internet has become an increasingly common element among crimes committed via the computer, the FBI has refocused its efforts and created the Cyber Investigations unit. Cybercrime, as part of the larger category of computer crime, has been a challenge to define. Many crimes that *involve* computers could just as easily be committed using other methods.

During the past decade, refinements have occurred in how **cybercrime** is defined. Although a single definition has yet to be agreed on, an acceptable definition is that cybercrime is part of the larger category of computer crime, a criminal act that is carried out using *cybertechnology* (the spectrum of computing and information/ communication technologies, from individual computers to computer networks to the Internet) and takes place in *cyberspace* (an intangible, virtual world existing in the network connections between two or more computers). Cybercrime has also been referred to as *electronic crime*, or **e-crime**, in describing any criminal violation in which a computer or electronic form of media is used.

Regardless of whether an agency calls such offenses computer crimes, cybercrimes, or e-crimes, the effective investigator must be familiar with basic computer terminology as well as with terms specifically related to computer crime (additional terms are defined throughout this chapter):

- **Adware**. A type of spyware used by advertisers to gather consumer and marketing information.

- Browser. A computer program that accesses and displays data from the World Wide Web, such as Internet Explorer, Google Chrome, and Firefox.

- Byte. The amount of space needed to store one character of information.

- **Click-jacking**. Concealing a hyperlink beneath legitimate clickable content which, when clicked, leads to the execution of hidden, unintentional actions, such as downloading malware or sending personal information to a website. Numerous click-jacking scams have employed "Like" and "Share" buttons on social networking websites.

- Digital evidence. Information and data that are of value to an investigation that are stored on, received, or transmitted by an electronic device.

- Disk drive. A device that reads, writes, and stores data that are accessed via computer (personal computers [PCs] generally have one or more internal disk drives and external or portable disk drives are commonly used to supplement storage needs, backup PCs, and transport or share data between PCs).

- **Doxing**. Publicly releasing a person's personal, sensitive identifying information online without authorization.

- Electronic device. A device that operates on principles governing the behavior of electrons.

- Electronic evidence. Information and data that are of value to an investigation that are stored on, received, or transmitted by an electronic device.

- **Encryption**. Any procedure used in cryptography to convert plain text into ciphertext to prevent anyone but the intended recipient from reading the data.

- **Firewall.** A software or hardware protective measure that blocks ports of access to a computer or network to prevent unauthorized access and stop malicious programs from entering.

- Gigabyte (GB). One billion bytes. A gigabyte can hold the equivalent of 10 yards of books on a shelf.

- **Hacktivism.** Using cyberspace to harass or sabotage sites that conduct activities or advocate philosophies that "hacktivists" find unacceptable.

- **Imaging.** Making a byte-by-byte copy of everything on a hard drive.

- **Keystroke logging.** A diagnostic technique that captures a user's keystrokes. Used in espionage to bypass security measures and obtain passwords or encryption keys. Also called *keylogging*.

- Kilobyte (KB). One thousand bytes.

- **Logic bomb.** A program that secretly attaches to another program in a company's computer system, and then monitors the input data and waits for an error to occur. When this happens, the new program exploits the weakness to steal money or company secrets or to sabotage the system. For example, if a specific name fails to appear in the payroll system, the logic bomb would delete the entire payroll database.

- **Malware.** A contraction of "malicious software." Software developed to cause harm.

- Megabyte (MB). One million bytes.

- Network. A group of computers connected to one another to share information and resources.

- **Piracy.** Copying and using computer programs in violation of copyrights and trade secret laws.

- **Port scanning.** Looking for access (open "doors") into a computer.

- **Ransomware.** Malicious software designed to block access to a computer system until a sum of money is paid.

- Removable media. Flash drives, thumb drives, pen drives, or other portable devices for storing electronic data, including CDs and DVDs.

- Script. A text file containing a sequence of computer commands.

- **Skimming.** A method in which a device is placed in a card reader, such as that found at an automated teller machine (ATM), to record sensitive information,

such as bank account numbers, credit cards numbers, and passwords.

- **Sniffing.** Monitoring data traveling along a network.

- **Spyware.** Malicious, covert (difficult to detect) software that infects a computer in a manner similar to viruses, collecting information or executing other programs without the user's knowledge. Some programs can track which websites a user visits; some can track and capture personal user information.

- Terabyte (TB). One thousand gigabytes.

- **Trojan horse.** A malicious program hidden inside an apparently harmless, legitimate program, intended to carry out unauthorized or illegal functions. For example, a program controlling a computer log-on process could log on a user (legitimate) but also record the user's password (unauthorized, illegal).

- **URL.** Universal Resource Locator. A string of characters representing an Internet resource.

- Virtual reality. An artificial, interactive world created by computer technology (usually involving some kind of immersion system, such as a headset).

- **Zombie.** A computer that has been taken over by another computer, typically through infection with hidden software (virus) that allows the zombie machine to be accessed and controlled remotely, often with the intention of perpetrating attacks on other computers.

The Net versus the Web

Confusion exists among many computer users regarding the differences between the Internet (aka "the Net") and the World Wide Web (aka "the Web"). Tim Berners-Lee (n.d.), creator of the Web, explains,

> The Internet ('Net) is a network of networks. Basically it is made from computers and cables.... [It] sends around little "packets" of information.... A packet is a bit like a postcard with a simple address on it. If you put the right address on a packet, and gave it to any computer which is connected as part of the Net, each computer would figure out which cable to send it down next so that it would get to its destination. That's what the Internet does. It delivers packets—anywhere in the world, normally well under a second....

> The Web is an abstract (imaginary) space of information. On the Net, you find computers—on the Web, you find documents, sounds, videos ... information. On the Net, the connections are cables between computers; on the

Web, connections are hypertext links. The Web exists because of programs which communicate between computers on the Net. The Web could not be without the Net. The Web made the Net useful because people are really interested in information (not to mention knowledge and wisdom!) and don't really want to . . . know about computers and cables.

Layers of the Web

Because a considerable amount of cybercrime uses a part of the Web that is not easily searched or accessed, a brief discussion of the layers of the Web is prudent. When most people think of "the Web," they are envisioning what is more accurately called the **surface web**, a collection of websites indexed by standard search engines (e.g., Google, Bing, Yahoo) that can be easily and readily accessed by the general public. The surface web goes by other names, such as the *common web*, the *indexed web*, the *crawlable web*, the *public web*, and the *visible web*. It is often analogized as the part of an iceberg visible above the surface of the ocean. As is commonly known, the proverbial tip of the iceberg is merely a fraction of what lies beneath the surface, with various sources estimating that the surface web accounts for roughly 10% of all content on the Web (Chertoff, 2017).

This leaves the remaining 90% of information located on the **deep web**, that much larger part of the Web beneath the surface that contains both indexed and unindexed content that cannot be found with standard search engines but can be accessed using another indexed Web address or application program interface found on the surface web. The deep web, also called the *invisible web* or *hidden web*, contains content such as that found on fee-for-service sites (e.g., Netflix), private and corporate networks and databases, file-sharing services (e.g., Dropbox), order history and financial transactions (e.g., Amazon, PayPal)—anything that the general public cannot access easily via normal online searches.

The smallest, deepest potion of the deep web is the **dark web**, an encrypted network designed specifically for anonymity and accessible only through specific software and browsers, such as Tor (an abbreviation for The Onion Router), IP2 (Invisible Internet Project), Freenet, and other darknet overlays (Chertoff, 2017; Finklea, 2017; Bermudez Villalva, Onaolapo, Stringhini, & Musolesi, 2018). Content on the dark web has been intentionally concealed, and the websites are known as *hidden services* (Weimann, 2016). Although activity on the dark web is not necessarily criminal, the privacy the dark web affords grants its users the expectation of being able to communicate and share content with little risk of detection (Finklea, 2017). The dark web has been called the "Wal-Mart of cybercrime" (Casey, 2017). One study found that the majority (57%) of the dark web is occupied by illegal content and websites devoted to child pornography, drug hubs, weapons trafficking, counterfeit currency, terrorist communication, illicit finances, and other criminal activities (Moore & Rid, 2016).

According to one data security specialist, the dark web is a pipeline for stolen personal information, such as social security and credit card numbers, where a single piece of data costs only a few dollars and can be obtained in only a few minutes (McMillan, 2018). Shillito (2019) observes that the technologies used to mask the identity of individuals and the nature of their activities make the dark web "an enabler of cross-border, truly international crime where each of the major actors, evidence, and the proceeds of crime can all be in different jurisdictions."

IP Addresses

A basic understanding of the Internet helps investigators trace suspected criminal activity and its perpetrators. To access the Internet, a user must have an **Internet Protocol (IP) address**, which is a unique number, analogous to a phone number. Typically, there is only one IP address per network connection—just as every house or building has a distinct address, every computer connected to the Internet has its own address. The original IP version, known as IPv4, uses four decimal-separated numbers (e.g., 10.1.2.3). This version was developed in the early 1980s and allows for just over 4 billion unique IP addresses. However, as the Internet continued to expand and the number of connected devices proliferated, it became clear that this growth would eventually consume this finite pool of IP addresses. In fact, according to one estimate, by 2019 there were 4.1 billion active Internet users worldwide, more than half (53.9%) of the global population (Central Intelligence Agency, 2019). Furthermore, the trend in recent years has shown that the number of devices and connections worldwide are growing faster than the actual number of users (Cisco, 2020).

The realization that available IPv4 addresses would ultimately run out led to the creation of the next-generation Internet Protocol—IPv6—which was standardized in 1996 to massively increase the number of available IP addresses (Internet Corporation for Assigned Names and Numbers, 2011). Because IPv6 uses strings of numbers that are considerably longer than IPv4, it can accommodate a staggering 340 undecillion IP addresses. (Note: An undecillion is written as a 1 followed by 36 zeros.) This version of IP address uses eight colon-separated segments (e.g., 2001:0db8:1111:2222:3333:4444:5555:6666). Although this format of IP address is still not widely used, its deployment is steadily increasing around the world, and investigators should be aware of these IP addresses and how they may help identify a country of origin for a cyber event (Internet Society, 2018).

IP addresses can be static or dynamic. A **static IP address** does not change. A **dynamic IP address**, in contrast, fluctuates and is, thus, more secure because it is changed frequently. The IP address is commonly issued by a user's **Internet service provider (ISP)**, a company that offers access to the Internet for a fee, such as Xfinity, Spectrum, CenturyLink, and more. More specifically, the ISP provides a customer with a router and an associated IP address, meaning the IP address identifies only the device, not the specific user of that device. The details of IP address distribution and registration are complex and not necessary to go into for a general understanding of cybercrime investigation. The importance lies in recognizing that an IP address and ISP, if known, can lead to a specific computer and, by extension, a specific user.

Deciphering Email and Web Addresses.

It is useful for investigators to understand the parts of an email or Web address and to accurately refer to the individual elements of each. Email addresses typically have two parts: the email name or identification (ID) and the email domain, separated by @ (e.g., janedoe@abc123.com). Be aware that it is relatively easy and common for cybercriminals to spoof or create fake email accounts to misrepresent themselves while attempting to commit fraud via the Internet.

A **domain name** is the unique name of a computer system on the Internet that distinguishes it from all other online systems. It is associated with a specific IP address and is easier to remember than a string of numbers. A domain name is not the same as a Web address, although many people incorrectly refer to it as such. A Web address, or URL, has several more elements. For example, the URL http://www.amz456.com can be broken down as follows:

> Scheme name: http (https typically denotes a secure website)—this part simply means an http request is being made to the host server
> Domain name: amz456.com
> Subdomain: www
> Domain: amz456
> Top-level domain: com

Common top-level domains include the following:

.com	Commercial
.edu	Educational
.org	Organization
.gov	U.S. government
.mil	U.S. Department of Defense
.net	Networks
.int	international organizations

Social Networking, Live Chat, and Instant Messaging

The world of social networking has opened a new forum in which people can interact and communicate. Many ISPs provide chat rooms and offer instant messaging (IM) to their subscribers, features that allow two or more people to "talk" online in real time. Such conversations can involve criminal activity, including child pornography. Some of the bigger providers, such as Facebook, Yahoo, and MSN all engage in some policing of subscriber activity to reduce undesirable or illegal activity. The Internet Relay Chat (IRC) environment is similar to other chat and messaging but offers worldwide communication and is not as closely monitored; therefore, it is common to see names such as #teensex or #newidentities (all IRC channel names begin with #). Twitter is often compared to an IRC client. All chat services allow "chatters" to leave a group room and have a private conversation over a more secure connection using Direct Channel Chat (DCC).

Classification and Types of Computer Crimes

Investigators should be familiar with the types of crimes that may involve computers. The crimes committed with computers range from students changing school records and grades to thieves embezzling millions of dollars from large corporations to pedophiles luring unsuspecting children into child pornography. Computers and other electronic devices and media can be used to commit crimes, store evidence of crimes, and provide information on suspects and victims (U.S. Secret Service, 2015).

The U.S. Secret Service's Electronic Crimes Branch (ECB) of its Financial Crimes Division has investigated matters involving credit card fraud, unauthorized computer access, cellular and landline telephone service tampering, the production of false identification, counterfeit currency, threats made against the president, narcotics, illegal firearms trafficking, and even homicides. Some even contend there will come a point when separate cybercrime laws become unnecessary because most crimes will involve computers in some way.

As computer crime evolves and specific offenses emerge, different categories are being identified. The U.S. Department of Justice (DOJ), which created a Cybersecurity Unit within the Computer Crime and Intellectual Property Section in December 2014, has delineated three basic ways computers are being used criminally:

1. *Computer as target.* A computer or network's confidentiality, integrity, or availability is attacked, resulting in the theft of services or information or the damaging of victim computers. Denial-of-service (DoS) attacks and the release of malware (viruses and worms) are examples of this type of computer crime.

2. *Computer as tool.* This includes crimes that have migrated from the physical world into cyberspace, such as child pornography, fraud, intellectual property violations, gambling, harassment, and the online sale of illegal substances and goods.

3. *Computer as incidental to an offense.* Significant for law enforcement because of the role the computer played in facilitating or executing a crime. For example, computers may be used by pedophiles to store child pornography, by drug traffickers to store business contact information, and by prostitution rings to manage payroll and customer accounts.

LO1 Define the three basic ways computer crime can be categorized.

Computer-related crimes may be categorized as computer as target, computer as tool, or computer as incidental to the offense.

However one chooses to categorize the various types of computer-related crimes, investigators should be aware of the ever-expanding ways in which computers are used for criminal endeavors.

The Computer as Target

Some cybercrimes involve the infection or infiltration of a computer system's software by a malware that, when executed, removes a degree of control of the machine from the authorized user and places it in the hands of an outsider. These crimes can involve viruses, worms, and DoS attacks and almost invariably involve hacking.

Hacking. The terms *hacking* and *cracking* are alternately used by law enforcement agencies to refer to the act of gaining unauthorized access to a computer system. However, among the people who perform these actions, a clear distinction is made between those who intrude for the challenge and status (hackers) and those who intrude to commit a crime (crackers). A **hacker** is not necessarily a negative term. A **cracker**, on the other hand, is a hacker in the negative sense, someone who cracks software protection and removes it. Crackers deliberately, maliciously intrude into a computer or network to cause damage. A **script kiddie**, or *skiddie*, is a derogatory term used to describe a less talented hacker who must use script or programs (scripts) created by others to carry out a cyberattack. Many investigative agencies refer to these people simply as "intruders" or "attackers" instead of hackers or crackers.

Viruses. A **computer virus** is a program that attacks, attaches itself to, and becomes part of another executable program. The purpose may be to replace or destroy data on the computer's hard drive or to simply leave a back door open for later entry.

Viruses can be transmitted through communication lines or by an infected disk or other removable media and can infect any PC. Just as human viruses are spread from one person to another, so computer viruses are spread from program to program. Viruses can be accidentally introduced into a system by infected media carried between home and work or passed among students or colleagues. The publicity surrounding recent mass virus attacks has raised the public's and corporate America's awareness of their computer systems' vulnerabilities and led many to install protective devices, such as antivirus or virus detection programs, downloadable software patches, and firewalls. Nonetheless, vast numbers of machines remain unprotected, and many consumers neglect to keep their virus detection subscriptions current.

Worms. Although the general computing public fears exposure to computer viruses, many are unaware that worms are actually more powerful and destructive. A **worm** is a self-contained program that travels from machine to machine across network connections, often clogging networks and information systems as it spreads. Whereas viruses require some action by the computer user (clicking or downloading), worms do not. They simply come in through an "open door" or unprotected port on a machine connected to the Internet. And, unlike a virus, a worm need not become part of another program to propagate itself.

Denial-of-Service Attacks. A **denial-of-service (DoS) attack** disrupts or degrades a computer or network's Internet connection or email service, thus interrupting the regular flow of data. Using multiple agents to create a widespread interruption is a *distributed DoS*, or DDoS. When a target company's website is flooded with requests for information or by some other onslaught of incoming data, the system is eventually overloaded and the site shuts down. At this time the company's cost clock starts ticking: either the company submits to extortion by its attackers or it is forced to incur millions of dollars in lost revenue as a result of its website being down.

Extortion. Cybercriminals may attempt to extort thousands, even millions, of dollars from companies by threatening to or actually damaging the company's computers, network, or Web presence. Extortion can be achieved via DoS attacks, ransomware, or threats to expose a company's Web vulnerabilities. A ransomware attack in early 2020 on the New Orleans city government garnered millions of dollars for the cybercriminals (Robinson, 2020). One source reports that the United States was bombarded by an unprecedented number of ransomware attacks in 2019, with at least 966 government agencies, educational institutions, and health care providers impacted and costs that exceeded $7 billion: "The incidents were not simply expensive inconveniences; the disruption they caused put people's health, safety and lives at risk" (Emsisoft, 2019). These types of crimes illustrate how cyber extortion fits both categories of computer as *target* and as *tool*.

The Computer as Tool

A computer connected to the Internet has become the tool of choice for many criminals because they have taken the traditional methods of committing their illegalities and elevated them to high-tech levels.

Fraud. Internet fraud can involve several other offenses singled out in this section, such as phishing, spamming, and identity theft. The types of fraud committed online span a wide range of businesses and topics. **Phishing**, first discussed in Chapter 14, is a method in which criminals misrepresent themselves as a trustworthy source to get victims to disclose personal, sensitive information, such as passwords, bank account numbers, and the like, which is then used by the criminals to commit fraud or other crimes.

Reshipper Schemes. Prior to the COVID-19 pandemic, the appeal of working from home was already a growing trend due to rising gas prices and the ability of many employees to telecommute. In the wake of the pandemic, after many Americans lost their jobs and others were forced to work from home, reliance on the Internet to earn a living reached unprecedented levels. Preying on this need and interest are scam artists who lure unsuspecting job seekers into reshipping schemes, transforming these citizens into "mules" who unwittingly help their "employers" commit international crime. To top it off, prospective employees must usually complete an application, on which they disclose such information as their birth date and social security number—harmless enough in the hands of a legitimate employer, but money in the pocket for identity thieves and others with a criminal bent.

Victims are attracted to the scheme through ads posted on popular employment websites seeking "correspondence managers," "freight-forwarding coordinators," or other respectable-sounding titles and they are guaranteed to earn money by working from home without even quitting their current jobs. After applicants are informed they have been hired—and nearly everyone who applies is hired—they begin receiving parcels at home with instructions on how to forward this merchandise to the company's home office abroad. The reshippers are compensated well, with one correspondence manager earning $24 for every package he reshipped. Thus, employee complaints, at this stage, are few. What employees do not know, however, is that the products they are reshipping are actually goods ordered online, purchased with fraudulent credit cards, and sent overseas to be sold on the black market, or that they (the mules) have become part of a high-end fencing operation that converts stolen personal and financial data into tangible goods and cash.

Offenders also lure victims into their scheme by establishing relationships with them in online chat rooms. Over time, offenders weave a tale of how, because of various legal restrictions, they are unable to direct business shipments from the United States into their home countries. They play up the injustice of these laws and how their government uses such restrictions to keep its citizens in poverty. Eventually, the scam artist gains the victim's trust, through either befriending or seduction. Offenders may even send small gifts to their victims as tokens of their affection. Whatever ploy is used, victims ultimately agree to have packages sent to their home, which they will then reship to their "friend" in another country.

The FBI, through IC3, has investigated numerous reshipper schemes throughout the United States and abroad. IC3 has also formed a public-private alliance with the Merchants Risk Council (MRC) in an effort to shut down such Internet fraud through use of real-time data sharing between law enforcement and private industry.

Spam.

Spam is unsolicited bulk email messages, similar to junk mail and commonly commercial. Less frequently known by its formal designation as *unsolicited commercial email* (UCE), spam is most often perceived by recipients as an annoyance and nothing more. Granted, it is a widespread, persistent annoyance. Chain letter spam is an example of the type of unsolicited email that clogs the Internet and fills people's inboxes but falls well short of criminal conduct. Sometimes, however, spam is distributed on such a massive scale, with such malicious or contentious content or with intent to defraud, that the spamming becomes criminal. For example, chain letters calling for a payment to participate may be construed as pyramid schemes, which are illegal in most states. Investment or business opportunity spam, which entices people with the promise of effortless income and financial freedom for the small price of an upfront "investment," commonly results in only the spammer getting rich and the victims filing complaints alleging theft or online fraud.

Spam that leaves no question as to its illegality is that intended to phish, commit identity theft, or otherwise extract sensitive information from a computer user with the ultimate goal of using such information to engage in criminal activity. Identity theft and phishing were discussed in Chapter 14.

Spoofing.

Spoofing, often considered synonymous with phishing, is acquiring unauthorized access to a computer or network through a message using an IP address that appears to be from a trusted host, in an attempt to commit identity theft (see Figure 17.1).

Pharming.

Pharming is a cybercrime that is catching even the most cautious, experienced Internet users off guard. Pharming involves hijacking a domain name to redirect online traffic away from a legitimate website toward a fake site, such as a bogus bank website. Cybercriminals have become very skilled at making their fraudulent sites appear quite similar to the legitimate site, so that unsuspecting victims are often unaware they are being led into a trap to steal information. Even if a computer user types in the correct domain name of a legitimate site, if that site has been pharmed, the user will be unknowingly taken to the fraudulent site, where they may unwittingly reveal account numbers, passwords, and other sensitive personal information that can be used for identity theft or other criminal endeavors.

Theft of Intellectual Property.

This offense involves the pirating of proprietary information and copyrighted material. Illegal online piracy is rampant, with criminals around the globe cashing in on the lucrative black market of illegally copied and distributed software, movies, music, and video and computer games. These offenses typically take place in un-policed peer-to-peer networks or forums where it is easy to exploit media-related intellectual property.

Because successful criminal prosecution of intellectual property theft requires reliable investigative resources, the FBI's Cyber Division and Intellectual Property Rights Division were created to investigate intellectual property theft and fraud.

Online Child Pornography and Child Sexual Abuse.

An increasingly persistent, pervasive cyber problem for law enforcement is the flow of child pornography. (Investigating crimes against children was discussed in Chapter 11.)

Pedophiles and other sex offenders around the world have discovered how quickly and surreptitiously they can exchange illegal images online. The Internet also provides a forum in which pedophiles can, using a fictitious identity, "meet" potential victims and strike up a friendship, in hopes of arranging a face-to-face meeting at some point. In an increasing number of cases that involve a missing child, a recurring common denominator is that the child's hobbies have included spending a great deal of time on the computer. By examining the computer files, detectives can often learn whether the child has been contacted by a pedophile and has unwitting agreed to meet this online acquaintance, not knowing that the new "friend" is someone who preys on children.

The development of software now enables more computer-savvy pornographers to create virtual child pornography in which an image of an actual child is manipulated, or "morphed," into an image no longer identifiable as that particular child. Some programs allow entirely computer-generated children to be depicted in

Myth Cybercrimes, while a nuisance, are not violent crimes and rarely cause physical harm to anyone.

Fact Considering the large number of cybercrimes involving child pornography, defined as the sexual exploitation of a minor, it is impossible to claim that cybercrime cannot ever be considered a violent crime.

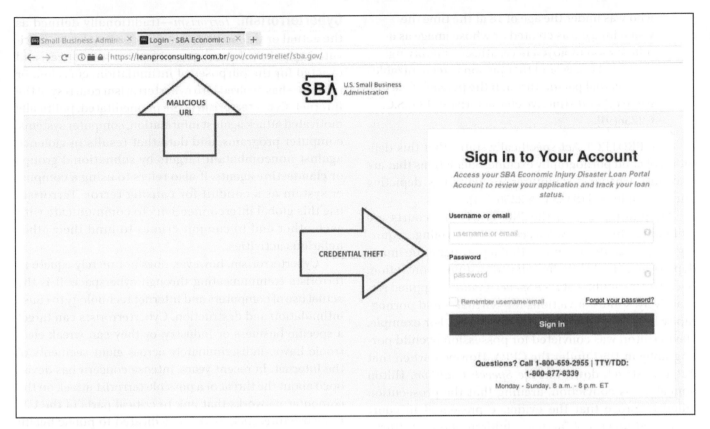

Figure 17.1
Spoofing web page via phishing email.
Source: Adapted from https://forms.us-cert.gov/report

a variety of sexual situations. As these programs become more refined, it is getting more difficult to distinguish between real children and virtual children. Such software presents considerable challenges involving how a jurisdiction defines child pornography and how investigators proceed with child pornography cases, and the legal landscape surrounding virtual child pornography continues to evolve.

When Congress passed the Child Pornography Prevention Act (CPPA) of 1996, making possession of virtual child pornography a crime, it did so on the grounds that such material, although not involving actual children or causing direct physical harm to an actual minor, presented a real and actual, albeit indirect, threat to children (Bird, 2011). Virtual child pornography, Congress reasoned, provided a tool to pedophiles for lowering the inhibitions of potential victims and "whetted" the appetites of pedophiles. Furthermore, as technology advanced, Congress asserted, it would become increasingly more difficult to prove that pornographic images portrayed actual children, thereby giving pedophiles a viable defense by which to escape prosecution. However, in *Ashcroft v. Free Speech Coalition* (2002), the Supreme Court ruled that the portion of the CPPA prohibiting the production or distribution of such virtual pornography was overly broad and an unconstitutional infringement on the First Amendment right to freedom of speech.

Shortly thereafter, Congress set to work crafting legislation with more narrow language, per the Court's mandate, and passed the Prosecutorial Remedies and Other Tools to end the Exploitation of Children Today Act of 2003 (PROTECT Act), a compilation of three statutes (18 U.S.C. § 2252, 18 U.S.C. § 2252A, and 18 U.S.C. § 2256). Specifically, the PROTECT Act describes child pornography as any visual depiction of sexually explicit conduct that includes

(a) a minor,

(b) a digital or computer image that is "indistinguishable" from that of a real minor, meaning an ordinary person viewing such an image would come to the conclusion that the image is of a real child [18 U.S.C. § 2256(11)], or

(c) an image which has been created or modified to appear to be that of an "identifiable minor" engaging in sexually explicit conduct, with an "identifiable minor" defined as either a person who was under the age of 18 at the time the visual image was created or whose image as a minor was employed in creating or modifying the visual image and that person is recognizable as an actual person through the person's face or some other distinctive characteristic [18 U.S.C. § 2256(9)].

The PROTECT Act specifically states that this definition of child pornography excludes "depictions that are drawings, cartoons, sculptures, or paintings depicting minors or adults" [18 U.S.C. § 2256(11)].

Despite passage of the PROTECT Act, courts are still guided by the *Free Speech Coalition* ruling, requiring the prosecution to prove that a pornographic image depicts an actual child in order to sustain a conviction. Because the holding of *Free Speech Coalition* applied retroactively, some convictions for "virtual" child pornography have being vacated and remanded. For example, David Hilton was convicted for possession of child pornography in 1997 under the CPPA. However, when that Act was struck down in *Free Speech Coalition*, Hilton appealed his conviction, arguing that the prosecution failed to prove that the evidence presented in court contained images of "actual" children and that, therefore, such images could have been composed merely of fictitious, computer-generated children, the possession of which is not illegal. The court agreed, concluding that in order to maintain a conviction against a defendant, the prosecution has the burden of proving that the image or images contain actual children. Hilton's conviction was vacated and remanded (*United States v. Hilton*, 2004).

The constitutionality of the PROTECT Act has yet to be weighed by the Supreme Court. Therefore, those investigating allegations of child pornography must be mindful that one element of the crime of possession of child pornography, as well as the production and distribution of such material, is proof that the images depict a *real* child or children. "The conduct portrayed in virtual child pornography is despicable and it is certainly hard to fathom any redeeming quality in such materials. Nonetheless, as the Supreme Court originally noted in *Free Speech Coalition*, the original purpose of categorizing child pornography as a separate class of unprotected speech was the compelling government interest in protecting children. And since there are no actual victims in drawings or computer-generated images, then a statute proscribing such images sweeps too broadly and oversteps the Constitution's bounds" (Bird, 2011, p. 177).

Cyberterrorism. *Terrorism*—traditionally defined as the actual or threatened use of force or violence, motivated by political or religious ideals or grievances, and exacted for the purposes of intimidation, coercion, or ransom—has evolved into cyberterrorism courtesy of the Internet. **Cyberterrorism** is the premeditated, politically motivated attack against information, computer systems, computer programs, and data that results in violence against noncombatant targets by subnational groups or clandestine agents. It also refers to using a computer system as a conduit for causing terror. Terrorists use this global interconnectivity to communicate with each other and to commit crimes to fund their other nefarious activities.

Cyberterrorism, however, does not merely equate to terrorists communicating through cyberspace. It is the actual use of computers and Internet technology to cause intimidation and destruction. Cyberterrorists can target a specific business or industry, or they can wreak electronic havoc indiscriminately across giant segments of the Internet. In recent years, intense concern has developed about the threat of a possible terrorist attack on the computer networks that link to critical parts of the U.S. infrastructure, such as those dedicated to public health and the distribution of emergency services, government and defense operations, energy and utility services, and elements that keep our economy in motion, such as shipping and cargo distribution. Figure 17.2 illustrates the number and type of entities targeted by Russian state-sponsored advanced persistent threat (APT) actors. Terrorism is the focus of Chapter 20.

Special Challenges in Investigation

Any type of criminal investigation carries potential challenges, and those involving computer crime are no exception. Special challenges in investigating computer crime include victims' reluctance or failure to report such crimes, the lack of training and understanding of computer crimes by investigators and others within the justice system, the need for specialists and teamwork, the fragility of the evidence, and jurisdictional issues. Other major challenges include determining the exact nature of the crime and gathering evidence in a way that does not disrupt an organization's regular operation.

Nonreporting of Computer Crimes

For the police to deter cybercrimes, the crimes must be reported, thoroughly investigated, and, when the

Figure 17.2
Heat Map of Cyber Attacks on Critical U.S. Infrastructure by Russian APT Actors.
Source: US-CERT Security Operations Center

evidence is sufficient, prosecuted. Law enforcement's ability to identify coordinated threats is directly tied to the amount of reporting that takes place. Too often, however, victims of computer-related crimes either are unaware that a crime has been committed or have a reason for not reporting the crime to authorities. For example, in the much publicized 2020 cybersecurity attack of Texas-based IT company SolarWinds, the breach of dozens of U.S. government agencies and private companies went unnoticed for 9 months before a private cybersecurity firm discovered that it was, itself, one of the victims (Jibilian & Canales, 2021). Security experts have assessed that the attack was carried out so stealthily that some victims may never know whether they were hacked or not.

Even when a company is aware that they have experienced a cyberattack, the IT team may be too embarrassed to report the attack to their superiors or those at the top may fear damage to the company's reputation if their cybersecurity is seen as weak or vulnerable. It is also possible that cybercrimes go unreported because a victimized organization does not understand what the reporting process entails or what is required of them by law enforcement (Rowan, 2017).

To help companies more effectively address cyberthreats and cybercrimes, the FBI, Secret Service, and *CIO Magazine* have collaborated to create a Cyberthreat Report form outlining the basic information needed by law enforcement when responding to an initial call of a suspected computer crime (Figure 17.3).

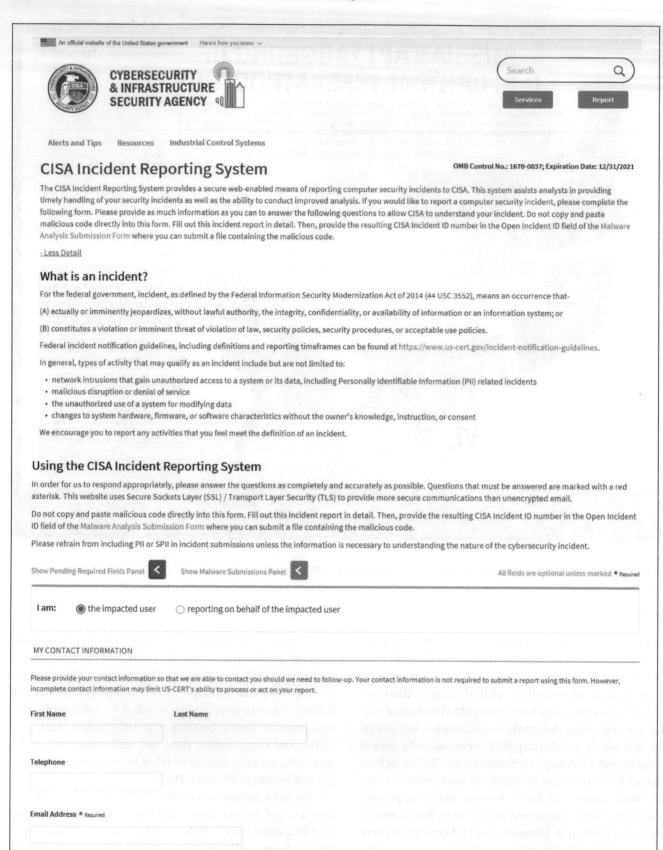

Figure 17.3
CIO cyberthreat report form.

MY ORGANIZATION

What type of organization are you? * Required

Select One ⌄

Please enter the organization's internal tracking number (if applicable):

DATE AND TIME INFORMATION

When, approximately, did the incident start?

| 7/20/2021 | 3:32:47 AM |

When was this incident detected? * Required

| 7/20/2021 | 3:32:47 AM |

From what timezone are you making this report?

Select One ⌄

INCIDENT DESCRIPTION

Please enter a brief description of the incident:

IMPACT DETAILS

Was the confidentiality, integrity, and/or availability of your organization's information systems potentially compromised? * Required

○ Yes   ○ No

Cancel   Next

Privacy Act Statement

Authority: 5 U.S.C. § 301 and 44 U.S.C. § 3101 authorize the collection of this information.

Purpose: The primary purpose for the collection of this information is to allow the Department of Homeland Security to contact you about your request.

Routine Uses: The information collected may be disclosed as generally permitted under 5 U.S.C. § 552a(b) of the Privacy Act of 1974, as amended. This includes using the information as necessary and authorized by the routine uses published in DHS/ALL-002 - Department of Homeland Security (DHS) Mailing and Other Lists System November 25, 2008, 73 FR 71659.

Disclosure: Providing this information is voluntary. However, failure to provide this information will prevent DHS from contacting you in the event there are questions about your request.

Version: 3.0 | Report ID: 2021-USCERTv34DULFB | Date: 202107200342
Email comments and feedback on the Incident Reporting Form✉

Figure 17.3 (*Continued*)
CIO cyberthreat report form.

Source: Adapted from us-cert.cisa.gov/forms/report

Lack of Investigator Training

Another challenge facing investigators assigned to computer crimes is that often they have not been adequately trained or equipped to investigate these felonies. Cybercriminals are usually more technologically sophisticated and have more resources, more access to the newest technology, and more time to devote to their crimes than do the investigators assigned to the cases. The technological disadvantage of many law enforcement agencies is painfully obvious.

Law enforcement at all levels needs additional training in the following areas: the unique requirements of computer crimes; digital evidence; identifying, marking, and storing this evidence; the capabilities of present private and state agencies to analyze this evidence; and the procedures for developing teams to conduct investigations of computer-related crimes.

Need for Specialists and Teamwork

Computer-related crimes may be relatively low tech, but for cybercrimes of a highly technical nature in which fragile digital evidence must be extracted from extensive database systems with equipment that is unfamiliar to police officers, the proactive law enforcement department has already devised a response protocol and assembled an investigative team of qualified specialists, including digital forensic investigators.

When forming a cybercrime unit, the areas to focus on are selecting the right personnel, establishing a specific protocol to guide investigators, providing the proper training for team members, and acquiring the necessary tools and equipment to do the job. Enlisting the aid of specialists is extremely critical considering the fragile nature of much computer crime evidence. Specialized cybercrime investigative teams are examined later in the chapter.

Fragility and Sensitivity of Evidence in Computer Crime

The biggest difference between traditional evidence and computer evidence is the fragility of the latter. What makes digital evidence so fragile is how easily it can be damaged, destroyed, or altered by careless handling or improper examination. Therefore, it is crucial that investigators handle digital evidence appropriately, including being mindful of the weather elements when putting such evidence into hot cars or leaving it out in extreme elements. Much the same way an officer responding to a more traditional crime may contaminate the scene by inadvertently altering the environment, an officer responding to a computer crime may destroy digital evidence simply by turning a computer or other device on or off at the wrong time. Recommended techniques and processes for collecting computer evidence are presented shortly.

Jurisdictional Issues

The global reach of the Internet poses another challenge in computer crime cases by introducing jurisdictional complications on top of an already complex area of criminal investigation. Difficulties exist in determining jurisdiction when the equipment being employed criminally is located in one community and the computer that is illegally entered electronically is in another state or even another country. For example, a 28-year-old in St. Petersburg, Russia, hacked into Citibank's cash management system in New York City and stole millions of dollars. Where did the crime take place—St. Petersburg or New York City? Who has jurisdiction?

The traditional concept of jurisdiction focuses almost exclusively on the territorial aspect of "where did the act take place?" However, traditional territorial boundaries are often complicated in cybercrime cases because the location of the acts must account for the location of the defendant and where the material originated (was uploaded from), any servers this information passed through, the location of computers where material was downloaded, and the location of any effects this material may have set in motion.

In cases of international scope, it is necessary to determine whether the act is illegal in all of the countries involved. For example, the Love Bug virus (the first "socially" engineered virus) that spread across the globe in two hours in May 2000, affecting more than 45 million users in more than 20 countries, was developed in and distributed from the Philippines, where the act of virus dissemination was not illegal at the time. The location of the defendant in such a country meant he could not be extradited to the United States, where his acts were considered illegal, because of a treaty-established requirement of double criminality in cases involving international jurisdiction, meaning the act would have needed to be criminal in both countries. This requirement of double criminality presents numerous problems for law enforcement and prosecutors trying to stem the rising tide of international cybercrime. Consider, for example, the difficulties presented by cases of child pornography:

- The age of majority (or consent) varies from country to country.

- In some countries, such as Germany, the age of consent is as low as 14.

- Virtual child pornography is legal in some countries and illegal in others.

Recognizing the need for a more unified global approach to handling cybercrime, the Council of Europe formed a Convention on Cybercrime on November 23, 2001, in Budapest. The convention set forth a framework for investigating and prosecuting cybercrimes and required that signers pass laws in their countries making specific acts, such as hacking, copyright infringement, and child pornography, illegal. As of September 2020, 64 countries, including the United States, had ratified the Budapest Convention.

When the Microsoft data warrant case made headlines in 2017, it shone a spotlight on the increasing need for new legislation and new international agreements to reform the process by which law enforcement, not just in the United States but around the world, gathered digital evidence and investigated crimes (Smith, 2018). The case began in 2013 when a U.S. judge issued a warrant under the Stored Communications Act (SCA) of 1986 ordering Microsoft to turn over the contents of an email account used by a suspected drug trafficker. Because the data being sought by investigators was actually stored on a server in Ireland, Microsoft refused the order, arguing that the court lacked authority to issue a warrant for electronic information stored outside of the United States. As the case crept through the legal system and courts went back and forth regarding the validity of the warrant under the SCA, cybercrime investigations continued to grow across the country, many of them impeded by fact that crucial electronic evidence was located in a foreign nation:

> In the Internet age, data location is often not a good basis upon which to ground requests to produce electronic data. In fact, some of the largest global companies now operate networks of storage centers in multiple countries, with the data in near-constant transit, moving between servers and across borders automatically. … Nations must ensure that law enforcement officials have reasonable legal authorities to compel production of electronic data that a CSP [Communications Service Provider] controls but that may be located in other countries. At the same time, nations also have legitimate interests in protecting data from other governments that do not adhere to appropriate legal standards or

abuse their authority for illicit purposes. The challenge is to ensure that government powers to compel production of electronic data are exercised and overseen in a way that respects the rule of law, protects privacy and human rights, and appropriately reduces conflicts between the laws of the countries concerned (U.S. Department of Justice, 2019).

As part of the effort to address these difficult issues and a situation that was becoming unsustainable, in March 2018 the U.S. Congress passed the Clarifying Lawful Overseas Use of Data Act, or "CLOUD Act":

> The CLOUD Act has two distinct parts. First, the Act authorizes the United States to enter into executive agreements with other countries that meet certain criteria, such as respect for the rule of law, to address the conflict-of-law problem. For investigations of serious crime, CLOUD agreements can be used to remove restrictions under each country's laws so that CSPs can comply with qualifying, lawful orders for electronic data issued by the other country. Second, the CLOUD Act makes explicit in U.S. law the long-established U.S. and international principle that a company subject to a country's jurisdiction can be required to produce data the company controls, regardless of where it is stored at any point in time. The CLOUD Act simply clarified existing U.S. law on this issue; it did not change the existing high standards under U.S. law that must be met before law enforcement agencies can require disclosure of electronic data (U.S. Department of Justice, 2019).

The case of *United States v. Microsoft Corp.* (2018) was being tried in the U.S. Supreme Court when the CLOUD Act was passed and signed into law, leading the Court to declare the case moot. A new warrant was subsequently issued under the CLOUD Act. The CLOUD Act amended the SCA to specifically include the cloud storage of CSPs that are subject to U.S. jurisdiction, regardless of where the cloud servers are located. It is important for investigators to understand that this amendment to the SCA does not give U.S. law enforcement any new legal authority to acquire data. It merely confirms the scope of requirements under the SCA, ensuring consistency with U.S. obligations under Article 18(1) of the Budapest Cybercrime Convention and aligning the United States with the other parties to the Convention.

A computer crime investigation may also involve domestic jurisdictional issues, between state and federal levels of jurisdiction as well as between states. Complicating the matter is that states, like nations, have varying definitions of cybercrime. Some states take a very broad approach to the issue, relying on statutes defining general criminal jurisdiction to establish jurisdiction in cybercrime cases, but other states have more specific statutes delineating the elements constituting the crime and its accompanying jurisdiction.

Another piece of the jurisdiction puzzle—one the courts have yet to reach consensus on—centers on whether cybercrime necessarily falls under federal jurisdiction because of the commerce clause and what is commonly referred to as the *nexus requirement.* Disagreement exists between the various courts regarding when a nexus, or link, exists regarding the interstate commerce clause to justify federal jurisdiction. Some courts have ruled that cybercrime automatically comes under federal jurisdiction because the Internet falls under the commerce clause as an instrumentality of interstate commerce, just as do common carriers, phone services, and so forth (*United States v. Sutcliffe,* 2007). Other courts, however, have held that digital content does not automatically come under federal jurisdiction simply because it was transmitted across the Internet and that judicial notice is required, similar to showing that a gun traveled in interstate commerce, for the case to elevate to federal jurisdiction (*United States v. Schaefer,* 2007).

In the Comprehensive Crime Control Act of 1984, Congress enacted a single new statute to address federal computer-related offenses—18 U.S.C. §1030—and in 1986, following a series of hearings on potential computer crime bills, Congress enacted the Computer Fraud and Abuse Act (CFAA) to amend 18 U.S.C. §1030: "As computer crimes continued to grow in sophistication and as prosecutors gained experience with the CFAA, the CFAA required further amending, which Congress did in 1988, 1989, 1990, 1994, 1996, 2001, 2002, and 2008" (U.S. Department of Justice, 2017, p. 2).

The original CFAA, written more than 30 years ago, was intended to address the hacking of defense department and financial institution computers, but the multiple amendments that have occurred over the last three decades have effectively expanded or, as critics contend, *overexpanded* the law such that disproportionately harsh penalties are being handed down for minor incidents. For example, under the expanded CFAA, checking personal email on a work computer could be classified as a criminal act. On June 3, 2021, the U.S. Supreme Court handed down its decision in the case of *Van Buren v. United States* (2020). In this case, officer Van Buren agreed to look up a license plate for an acquaintance, the plate belonging to a woman the acquaintance was interested in dating. The acquaintance, who was actually an FBI informant, paid Van Buren, but the officer said he would not charge the man anything to help him out. After Van Buren ran the plate, the FBI arrested him on charges of felony violation of the CFAA. The question: does a person who is authorized to access information on a computer for certain purposes violate Section 1030(a)(2) of the CFAA if that person accesses the same information for an improper purpose?

Van Buren argued that, because he was authorized to access both the computer database and the information he obtained, regardless of the purpose, he did not violate the CFAA. The court, however, rejected Van Buren's argument and sentenced him to 18 months in prison. The Eleventh Circuit upheld the conviction, and the Supreme Court granted certiorari. In a 6–3 decision, the Court held that Van Buren did, in fact, exceed his "authorized access" under the CFAA because, although he was authorized to access the computer, the specific information he then sought and acquired was contained in an area of the computer that was off-limits to him.

CFAA reform is also the impetus behind Aaron's Law, named after the late Internet activist Aaron Swartz, who was arrested after using a computer at Massachusetts Institute of Technology (MIT) to download millions of documents from the online archive site JSTOR. Prosecutors charged Swartz with violating the CFAA, his "crimes" carrying a penalty of up to 35 years in prison. Before his case went to trial, however, Swartz committed suicide. He was 26 (Eaton, 2015).

This area of law is still suffering from growing pains, as courts struggle to define jurisdiction with regard to computer crime. For this reason, we suggest investigators keep close dialogue with prosecutors on the evolving nature of jurisdiction in cybercrime cases. A valuable resource for the status of laws at the federal level; recent cases involving cybercrime; and information on computer crime, intellectual property, electronic evidence, and other high-tech legal issues is www.justice.gov/criminal-ccips, the home page for the U.S. DOJ's Computer Crime and Intellectual Property Section.

The Preliminary Investigation

As with any other crime, once a report of a cybercrime or cyberthreat has been received, the department generally conducts a preliminary investigation. Cybercrime investigations share many of the same characteristics of other felony cases, including adherence to a consistent and documented investigative methodology. However, because of the highly technical nature of computer crimes and the fragile nature of the evidence, officers must receive "first responder" training and have extensive knowledge of computers or seek the assistance of a computer expert. Several valuable resources for investigators undertaking such endeavors include the U.S. Secret Service's *Best Practices for Seizing Electronic Evidence: A Pocket Guide for First Responders* (Version 4.2, 2015), the National Institute of Justice's (NIJ) *Electronic Crime Scene Investigation: A Guide for First Responders* (2nd ed., 2008), the NIJ's *Digital Evidence Policies and Procedures Manual* (2020), and the National Forensic Science Technology Center's (NFSTC) *Crime Scene Investigation: A Guide for Law Enforcement* (2013).

When a police department receives a report of a possible computer crime, the departmental report procedure is followed for the initial information. The officer assigned to the case interviews the reporting person to obtain the information necessary to determine whether a crime has been committed. This first responder has a critical role in preserving the crime scene to protect the integrity of the evidence because this is the point where such digital evidence is most vulnerable. Recall that digital evidence was first introduced in Chapter 5.

LO2 List the steps taken in following a common protocol for processing a crime scene involving electronic evidence.

A common protocol for processing a crime scene involving electronic evidence is as follows:

- Secure and evaluate the crime scene
- Conduct preliminary interviews
- Obtain a search warrant
- Recognize and identify the evidence
- Document the crime scene
- Collect and preserve evidence
- Package, transport, and store evidence
- Submit digital evidence (such as hard drives) for analysis and data recovery
- Document the investigation in an incident report

Securing and Evaluating the Scene

As with any other crime scene, the first responder's initial priority is to ensure the safety of everyone at the scene and to protect the integrity of evidence, both conventional (physical) and electronic. Next, the responding officer should restrict access to any digital evidence, including computers, storage media, cell phones, digital cameras, and iPads and tablets; *visually* identify potential evidence (do not touch anything yet); determine whether such evidence is perishable; and formulate a search plan. When securing and evaluating the crime scene, it is recommended that the first responder

- Follow departmental policy for securing crime scenes
- Immediately secure all electronic devices, including personal or portable devices
- Ensure that no unauthorized person has access to any electronic devices at the crime scene
- Refuse offers of help or technical assistance from any unauthorized persons
- Remove all persons from the crime scene or the immediate area from which evidence is to be collected
- Ensure that the condition of any electronic device is not altered
- Leave a computer or electronic device off if it is already turned off (National Institute of Justice [NIJ], 2008, pp. 15–16)

First responders should protect perishable data on computers, tablets, cell phones, and any other storable electronic devices, physically and electronically, always keeping in mind that devices containing perishable data should be immediately secured and documented (photographed). If a device is on, take a photo of the screen immediately, before a suspect has the chance to remotely wipe the contents of the device. The time-sensitive nature of such evidence cannot be overstated: "When dealing with networked devices the amount of time it takes to secure the network and data is critical. By design many of these devices can be accessed from offsite and critical evidence can be remotely destroyed, copied, or encrypted" (National Forensic Science Technology Center [NFSTC], 2013, p. 117). Identify any communications lines (telephone, LAN/Ethernet connections) attached to devices. Document, label, and disconnect each line from the wall rather than the device, if possible. Communication via such lines must be severed to prevent remote access to data on the computers. *Do not touch* the keyboard, mouse, CDs, DVDs, removable USB or thumb/flash drives, or any other computer equipment or electronic devices (evidence) at this stage. Figure 17.4 presents a flow chart for the process of collecting digital evidence.

LO3 Explain the basic on/off tenet for first responders at a computer crime scene.

A basic tenet for first responders at computer crime scenes is to observe the ON/OFF rule: If it's on, leave it on. If it's off, leave it off.

At some point, a computer that is on will need to be turned off. At that time, investigators are advised to follow the steps outlined in the U.S. Secret Service's *Best Practices for Seizing Electronic Evidence* (2015). Before any evidence is touched, it must be properly documented (a later stage, discussed shortly). However, before identifying and documenting evidence, preliminary interviews must be conducted.

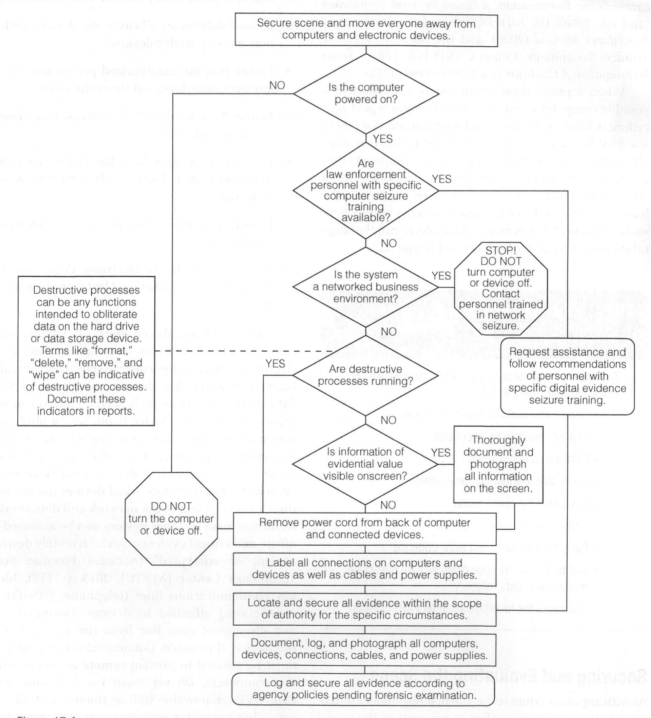

Figure 17.4
Collecting digital evidence flow chart.

Source: *Electronic crime scene investigation: A guide for first responders*, (2nd ed.). Washington, DC: U.S. Department of Justice, National Institute of Justice, April 2008, p. 29. (NIJ 187736)

Preliminary Interviews

If a crime is suspected or determined, further interviewing of the complainant and witnesses should continue. Information must be obtained as soon as possible because evidence is easily destroyed. Preliminary interviews are conducted before collecting evidence because these interviews help determine the nature of the crime and develop suspects. If the crime involves a computer user in a private residence or other type of singular victim, ask how the user became aware of the crime and who their ISP is. The victim will need to provide their username(s) and password(s) because such information is typically required to access the system. Ask about security devices or programs installed on the machine and obtain as much documentation as possible regarding the victim computer's hardware and software configurations.

If the victim is a business or other organization, interview employees and staff because they are a good source of information unless they are suspected of collusion. Internal reporting of this type of crime is the same as for any other crime within an organization, normally beginning at the lowest level and reporting upward to the supervisor and then to management. However, supervisory or management personnel are conceivably part of the collusion, so care must be used in the initial stages to eliminate those capable of being involved. Those with security clearance to access sensitive data or areas within a company's network must also be interviewed and evaluated as possible suspects. If a computer has been stolen, determine if it is protected by theft recovery software such as Absolute® Home & Office. Other apps, such as Find my iPhone or Find my iPad, can help track and locate stolen electronic devices.

The NIJ (2008, pp. 17–18) recommends the following information be obtained in the preliminary interviews:

- Names of all users of the computers and devices
- All computer and Internet user information
- All log-in names and user account names
- Purpose and uses of computers and devices
- All passwords
- Any automated applications in use
- Types of Internet access
- Any offsite storage
- Internet service provider

- Installed software documentation
- All email accounts
- Security provisions in use
- Web mail account information
- Data access restrictions in place
- All instant message screen names
- All destructive devices or software in use
- Facebook, Twitter, LinkedIn, Snapchat, or other online social networking site account information

Also during this time, the investigator should attempt to assess the skill levels of the computer users involved because proficient users may conceal or destroy evidence by employing sophisticated techniques such as encryption, which puts information in code and thus obscures a normally comprehensible message. **Steganography**, which is Greek for "hidden writing" and serves a similar purpose to encryption, involves hiding data within another digital message, medium, or file. A steganographic message often appears as some type of "cover" message—a shopping list, a picture, and so forth. Steganography should not be confused with *stenography* (shorthand).

Obtaining a Search Warrant

Before evidence can be collected, it may be necessary to obtain a warrant. Although searches may be conducted with consent, this is not always the most desirable method, particularly if the suspect is unknown at this point, because it could alert the person who committed the crime.

> **LO4** Summarize the benefits of getting a search warrant in a computer crime investigation.
>
> Having a search warrant generally decreases the amount of resistance investigators face at the scene and increases the odds of successful prosecution should the case go to court.

Be certain that the warrant includes language specific to both the seizure and the search (forensic examination) of all evidence including the computer hardware, software, electronic media, documentation, and user notes (U.S. Secret Service, 2015).

Privacy issues surrounding some or all of the information contained in the digital evidence desired may pose a legal technicality. If the organization involved is the victim of the crime, its management normally grants permission. If it is not the victim, it may be necessary to obtain permission from individuals named in the evidentiary file, which could be an enormous task. It may be better to take the evidence to a court and obtain court permission if possible.

Investigators may have both a consent search form and a search warrant, thus avoiding the possibility of destruction of evidence. Getting consent is useful if investigators do not have enough information to support a warrant or if they are in a time-sensitive situation and believe consent will be granted, but relying on consent can be problematic because it may be revoked by the owner at any time during the search. Thus, obtaining a warrant is usually the preferred route for electronic crimes investigations because it provides authority to continue with a search in the absence or revocation of consent.

The areas of search and the sought items must be specified in the warrant. Determine the computer system used and the types of physical evidence available from this system. Include this information in the search warrant application. A person connected with the computer operation in question should assist with the search warrant to provide information to the investigators, and this person should accompany the investigators with the affidavit for warrant in case the judge requires technical explanations that the investigators cannot provide regarding the equipment and the evidence desired.

Recognizing Evidence—Traditional and Digital

Computer crimes commonly involve both conventional evidence (fingerprints, documents, computer hard drive, etc.) and digital evidence (electronic computer files, emails, etc.). For physical evidence, search techniques and patterns described in Chapter 4 apply. Seal the area and search it according to the type and location of the evidence necessary for prosecution. Avoid pressures to speed up the search because of a desire for continued use of the system, but return the equipment as soon as possible and be sensitive to the company's need to get back to "business as usual" as quickly as possible.

Recall from Chapter 5 that the NIJ has defined digital evidence as "information and data that is of value to an investigation that is stored on, received, or transmitted by an electronic device" (NIJ, 2008). The NIJ also explains that digital evidence

- Is latent like fingerprints or DNA evidence
- Crosses jurisdictional borders quickly and easily
- Is easily altered, damaged, or destroyed
- Can be time sensitive

It is usually not difficult for an investigator to recognize obvious evidence such as a computer, keyboard, or mouse, but digital evidence may also exist among a host of other electronic devices too often overlooked. Some of these devices contain perishable data and thus must be immediately secured and documented. Remember: do not alter a device's condition at this point. If it is off, leave it off. Electronic devices, components, and peripherals that first responders may need to collect as digital evidence include the following:

- Audio recorders
- Bar coding machines
- Cables
- Cell phones
- Computer chips—when found in quantity may indicate chip theft
- Copy machines—usage logs, time, and date stamps
- Cordless landline telephones
- Digital cameras
- Fax machines
- GPS devices
- Hard drive duplicators
- Laptop power supplies and accessories
- Memory cards
- Modems
- Multifunction machines (printer, scanner, copier, and fax)
- Network attached storage (NAS) devices
- Printers
- Routers
- Scanners
- Smart cards
- Wireless access points

For certain crimes—such as child pornography, identity theft, and computer attacks—CDs, DVDs, flash drives, and external hard drives are likely to hold an abundance of evidence. Because criminals often keep "trophies" or collections to document their activities, investigators should search the work area around computers as well as CD and DVD storage units throughout the premises. Some offenders try to hide incriminating CDs and DVDs among legitimate ones or insert illicit data into a disk that contains otherwise aboveboard content. Refer back to Table 5.4, which lists the types of digital evidence commonly encountered during a computer crime scene search as they relate to specific crimes. Investigators should remember that digital evidence may also contain physical evidence such as DNA, fingerprints, or serology.

Documenting Digital Evidence

As with other crime scenes, thorough notes, sketches, photographs, and videos are necessary to create a detailed, permanent record of the scene. The entire scene should be documented as it was found before any collection occurs, including all activity and processes shown on display screens. Investigators should be aware that evidence may not necessarily be located right next to a computer, laptop, or other obvious digital device. The NFSTC's *Crime Scene Investigation Guide for Law Enforcement* (2013, pp. 113–134) presents very detailed procedures for documenting various types of digital evidence, including networked and non-networked computers; cell phones; loose media; and other devices such as copy and fax machines, printers, scanners, bar coding machines, digital cameras, GPS devices, and the like. Generally speaking, the following steps are suggested for documenting digital evidence:

- Video record and photograph the evidence as found using standard crime scene techniques (overall, mid-range, closeup).

- Photograph the screen, the back of the device, and the connections to all other equipment (e.g., printer, external drive), making sure to get quality images of the connections (network cables, power cables, and peripheral cables) themselves.

- Sketch a diagram of the connections between all of the electronic devices at the scene.

- Sketch a diagram of the placement of all electronic devices or media in the area relative to other devices, equipment, and objects.

- Record information that supports the photograph, including:

  - The state of the device (on, off, sleep mode) and existing connections

  - Type of device, equipment, or media

  - Location of device, equipment, or media

  - Appearance or condition of the device, equipment, or media, including visible damage or other characteristics

  - Serial or other identifying numbers

  - Media storage capacity (e.g., SanDisk® 256MB)

(NFSTC, 2013; NIJ, 2008)

The preceding guidelines are generally sufficient for most stand-alone devices and computers. However, in a business environment and an increasing number of residences, multiple computers may be connected or networked together, presenting unique challenges to investigators. Indicators of a computer network include:

- The presence of multiple computer systems

- The presence of cables and connectors running between computers or central devices such as hubs

- Information provided by those on the scene or by informants

When dealing with networked computers, investigators are advised to consult with the administrator of the system as they will be the best resource to safely access and image media, thus avoiding loss or damage of evidence. Investigators should be prepared for extended time on site to logically or physically image media and data. Recognize also that these devices can often be accessed from offsite, and critical evidence can be remotely destroyed, copied, or encrypted (NFSTC, 2013).

Collecting Physical and Digital Evidence

Investigators assigned to cybercrimes or other computer-related crimes must have ready certain tools and equipment commonly required in cases involving electronic evidence:

In most cases, items or devices containing digital evidence can be collected using standard seizure tools and materials. First responders must . . . avoid using any tools or materials that may produce or emit static electricity or a magnetic field as they may damage or destroy the evidence . . . .

In addition to tools for processing crime scenes in general, first responders should have the following items in their digital evidence collection toolkit: cameras (photo and video); cardboard boxes; notepads; gloves; evidence inventory logs; evidence tape; paper evidence bags; evidence stickers, labels or tags; crime scene tape; antistatic bags, permanent markers and nonmagnetic tools.

First responders should also have radio frequency-shielding material such as faraday isolation bags or aluminum foil to wrap cell phones, smart phones, and other mobile communication devices after they have been seized. [This] ... prevents the phones from receiving a call, text message or other communications signal that may alter the evidence.   (NIJ, 2008, pp. 13–14)

LO5	Identify the various forms electronic evidence and other computer crime evidence may take.

Digital evidence is often contained on disks, CDs, or hard drives, or on any number of peripheral electronic devices; is not readily discernible; and is highly susceptible to destruction. Other computer crime evidence may exist in the form of data reports, logs, programming, or other printed information run from information in the computer. Latent prints may be found on the keyboard, mouse, power button, or any other peripheral equipment near the computer, including the printer.

Digital evidence can be altered, damaged, or destroyed simply by turning the computer on or off at the wrong time. The NIJ (2008, p. 6) strongly cautions, "Without having the necessary skills and training, no responder should attempt to explore the contents or recover data from a computer (e.g., do not touch the keyboard or click the mouse) or other electronic device other than to record what is visible on its display." First responders and investigators must be aware that destruction of the program or of information files may be programmed in so that any attempt to access the information or to print it will cause it to self-destruct. Check for a **hardware disabler**, a device designed to ensure a self-destruct sequence of any potential evidence. It may be present on or around a computer, with a remote power switch being the most prevalent of the disabler hardware devices. If found, a disabler switch should be taped in the position in which it was found. More sophisticated criminals are using technology that allows them to remotely wipe incriminating data from electronic devices, causing considerable frustration for investigators.

Evidence in computer cases is also unique in that it is not as readily discernible as is evidence in most other criminal cases. Removable storage media, for example, although visible in the physical sense, contain "invisible" information.

Because chemicals used in processing fingerprints can damage electronic equipment and data, latent prints should be collected after electronic evidence recovery is complete.

A backup of the hard disk contents should be made as quickly as possible. A portable hard drive duplication tool is available that lets investigators quickly create a mirror image of one or more hard drives in the field without removing the original to a remote site.

Investigators must reproduce the material within the rules of evidence. Identification should include the case number, date, time, and initials of the person taking the evidence into custody. To mark a metal container, use a carbide metal scribe such as that used in marking items in the Operation Identification program. Use a permanent black-ink marker or felt-tip pen to identify disks. If the evidence is in a container, both the container and the inside disks should be identified in the same way. Marking both identically avoids interchangeability and retains the credibility of the item as evidence. Use normal evidence tape to mark containers and to seal them.

Avoid contact with the recording surfaces of computer tapes and disks. Never write on disk labels with a ballpoint pen or pencil or use paper clips or rubber bands with disks. To do so may destroy the data they contain.

Usually printouts must be made of data contained on computer disks or CDs. These printouts should be clearly identified and matched with the software they represent.

In more complex cases, the volume of evidence is significant because large amounts of information can be stored on a single disk, CD, DVD, or flash drive. In most felony investigations, the amount of evidence is not a major problem, but in the case of computer crimes, the evidence may involve hundreds of disks, CDs, DVDs, or other storage media. Copying this amount of evidence can be costly and time-consuming. In addition, taking equipment into evidence can be a major problem because some equipment is heavy and bulky.

In a very few cases, the evidence is the computer equipment. Also, it may be necessary to keep the equipment operating to continue business. Investigators must work with management to determine how to best accomplish this. If the evidence cannot be moved from the premises, management may have to provide on-premises security with their own guards or with temporarily hired security until the evidence can be copied or otherwise secured by court order or by police security.

Other nonelectronic evidence that may prove valuable to the investigation includes material found in the vicinity of the suspect computer system, such as handwritten notes, Post-It® notes with passwords written on them, blank pads of paper with the indentations from previous pages torn off, hardware and software manuals, calendars, and photographs.

Any evidence collected and removed from the premises must be entered onto an evidence log, thus creating a chain of custody that must be maintained from this point forward throughout the investigation. Investigators should be aware that the chain-of-custody issues regarding data are additional to the chain-of-custody issues regarding the physical item.

Collecting Evidence from Cyberspace.

Most, if not all, cybercrimes leave some type of cyber trail or "e-print" as evidence because ISPs maintain records of everything a subscriber does online, at least for a while. Even apps such as Snapchat, which are designed to provide short-lived content that is automatically deleted from the server after a specific length of time, do possess the capability to retain data past its normal "expiration" period. According to Snapchat's Privacy Policy, "Even after we've deleted message data from our servers, that same data may remain in backup for a limited period of time. We also sometimes receive requests from law enforcement requiring us by law to suspend our ordinary server-deletion practices for specific information."

Recall that IP addresses are assigned by the ISP when it provides a router through which a customer can access the Internet. Consequently, IP addresses can be valuable pieces of information to investigators because nearly every criminal uses the Internet at some point, leaving behind a digital trail. However, as Larson (2017) cautions, while an IP address alone can help narrow down a suspect list, it does not inherently identify an individual as the suspect. Furthermore, "As seen in cases where criminals use dark web browsers, IP addresses can easily be relayed among various different computers across the country or can be re-routed to another device." Additionally, unsecured networks in private homes may be used to commit

cybercrime unbeknownst to the homeowner, as happened in *United States v. Stanley* (2014), when Stanley hijacked ("mooched") his neighbor's unprotected IP address to download child pornography. Thus, investigators must not jump to an early conclusion that an IP address, alone, is proof of an individual's involvement in cybercrime.

Nonetheless, an IP address is a useful tool, and if an investigator knows a suspect user's screen name, it can be linked to an identifiable IP address. The IP address(es) associated with suspect pieces of data transmitted via the Internet will help track down the user's ISP. However, no law yet requires maintaining online activity data, and the storage policies of ISPs can vary tremendously. For example, large ISPs commonly maintain data for as long as 30 days, whereas others dump these records every 30 minutes. Data storage is a major expense for ISPs, and many try to save money by purging their files fairly quickly. Therefore, if a crime has involved Internet use, investigators should proceed quickly to subpoena the ISP for stored records. If the subpoena will take several days or longer to obtain, send a letter to the ISP requesting that they preserve the data until a subpoena, warrant, or court order can be obtained.

These records, once obtained, will provide such information as the suspect's billing address and log-in records, which can in turn lead to the location of the computer used, such as in a private residence, a public library, or an Internet café. Although the billing information and credit card numbers associated with a user's account can be falsified, this information may still be of value to the investigation. Investigators must know whether their state laws require that they obtain a search warrant for such evidence or if a subpoena will suffice. Once the suspect's location is known, the investigation typically expands to involve another jurisdiction because the perpetrators of cybercrimes can be thousands of miles away from their victims and the investigation's point of origin.

After the desired target information is culled from the general ISP data records, the investigator still generally needs a search warrant to delve further into a particular user's account information. These files are likely to include emails, website data, images, spreadsheets, and other digital log files that can help assess what activity the account is being used for.

Other tools available to cybersleuths are the Internet pen register and Internet Title III Intercept, the use of which requires court approval. Internet pen registers track transactions originating at the target's computer and can reveal Web surfing habits and sites commonly visited, the types of applications being used, and the email addresses of those being communicated with. Title III Intercepts are similar in function to the Internet pen register but trap more comprehensive data, allowing investigators to see where the target is surfing, with whom the target communicates, and what the target sees, as well as to read the content of the target's email and chat messages.

Understanding how to decipher email headers is a necessary skill for cyber investigators. Banday (2011) notes: "E-mail forensics dealing with the investigation of e-mail message[s] is a specialized type of network forensics which in turn is also a specialized type of cyber forensics. It refers to the study of [the] source and content of e-mail message[s] as evidence to identify the actual sender and recipient of a message, date/time

of transmission, detailed record of e-mail transaction, intent of the sender, etc."

When an Internet email message is sent, the user typically controls only the recipient line(s) (To, Cc, and Bcc) and the subject line; mail software adds the rest of the header information during processing: "The journey of the message can usually be reconstructed by reading the email header from bottom to top. As the message passes through additional mail servers, the mail server will add its information above the previous information in the header. One of the most important pieces of information for the investigator to obtain from the detailed header is the originating IP address" (NIJ, 2007, p. 19).

Figure 17.5 shows a typical email header. The pink-shaded guidelines that follow on p.621 illustrate how to trace an Internet email, reading the lines in Figure 17.5 from bottom to top.

```
12.  X-Message-Info: JGTYOYF78jEv6iDU7aTDV/xX2xdjzKcH
11.  Received: from web11603.mail.yahoo.com ([216.136.172.55]) by mc4-
     f4 with Microsoft SMTPSVC (5.0.2195.5600);
                Mon, 8 Sep 2003 18:53:07 -0700
10.  Message-ID: 20030909015303.27404.qmail@web11603.mail.yahoo.com
 9.  Received: from [165.247.94.223] by web11603.mail.yahoo.com via
     HTTP; Mon, 08 Sep 2003 18:53:03 PDT
 8.  Date: Mon, 8 Sep 2003 18:53:03 -0700 (PDT)
 7.  From: John Sender sendersname2003@yahoo.com
 6.  Subject: The Plan!
 5.  To: RecipientName_1@hotmail.com
 4.  MIME-Version: 1.0
     Content-Type: multipart/mixed; boundary="0-2041413029-
     1063072383=:26811"
 3.  Return-Path: sendersname2003@yahoo.com
 2.  X-OriginalArrivalTime: 09 Sep 2003 01:53:07.0873 (UTC)
     FILENAME=[1DBDB910:01c37675]


 1.  --0-2041413029-1063072383=:26811
     Content-Type: multipart/alternative; boundary="0-871459572-
     1063072383=:26811"


     --0-871459572-1063072383=:26811
     Content-Type: text/plain; charset=us-ascii


     Received the package. Meet me at the boat dock.
     See attached map and account numbers
```

Figure 17.5
Email header.

Source: *Special Report: Investigations Involving the Internet and Computer Networks.* Washington, DC: U.S. Department of Justice, National Institute of Justice, Jan. 2007, p. 19. (NIJ 210798)

12. **X-Message-Info: JGTYoYF78jEv6iDU-7aTDV/ xX2xdjzKcH**

   X-headers are nonstandard headers and are not essential for the delivery of mail. The usefulness of the X-header needs to be explored with the Internet Service Provider (ISP).

11. **Received: from web11603.mail.yahoo.com ([216.136.172.55]) by mc4-f4 with Microsoft SMTPSVC(5.0.2195.5600); Mon, 8 Sep 2003 18:53:07-0700**

   Received: [   ]

   *This "Received" line is the last stamp that was placed in the header. It is placed there by the last mail server to receive the message and will identify the mail server from which it was received. Note that the date and time stamp is generated by the receiving mail server and indicates its offset from **UTC** (-0700). In this example, the mail server's name is indicated. This can be accomplished by either the receiving server resolving the IP address of the last mail server or the prior mail server broadcasting its name.*

10. **Message-ID: 20030909015303.27404 .qmail@web11603.mail.yahoo.com**

   Message-ID: [   ]

   A unique identifier assigned to each message. It is usually assigned by the first e-mail server and is a key piece of information for the investigator. Unlike the originating IP address (below), which can give subscriber information, the message-id can link the message to the sender if appropriate logs are kept.

9. **Received: from [165.247.94.223] by web11603.mail.yahoo.com via HTTP; Mon, 08 Sep 2003 18:53:03 PDT**

   Received: [   ]

   The bottom "Received" line identifies the IP address of the originating mail server. It could indicate the name of the server, the protocol used, and the date and time settings of the server. Note the time zone information that is reported.

   CAUTION: If the date and time associated with the e-mail are important to the investigation, consider that this "Received" time recorded in the e-mail header comes from the e-mail server and may not be accurate.

8. **Date: Mon, 8 Sep 2003 18:53:03-0700 (PDT)**

   Date: [   ]

   This date is assigned by the sender's machine and it may not agree with the e-mail server's date and time stamp. If the creation date and time of the e-mail are important to the investigation, consider that the time recorded in the e-mail header comes from the sender's machine and may not be accurate.

7. **From: John Sender <sendersname2003 @ yahoo. com>**

   From: [   ]

   This is information usually configured in the e-mail client by the user and may not be reliable.

6. **Subject: The Plan!**

   Subject: [   ]

   This is information entered by the user.

5. **To: RecipientName_1@hotmail.com**

   To: [   ]

   This is information entered by the user.

4. **MIME-Version: 1.0 Content-Type: multipart/mixed; boundary="0-2041413029-1063072383=:26811"**

   The purpose of these two lines is to give the recipient's e-mail client information on how to interpret the content of the message.

3. **Return-Path: sendersname2003@yahoo. com**

   Return-Path: [   ]

   This is information usually configured in the e-mail client by the user and may not be reliable.

2. **X-OriginalArrivalTime: 09 Sep 2003 01:53:07.0873 (UTC) FILETIME=[1DBDB910:01C37675]**

   X-headers are nonstandard headers and are not essential for the delivery of mail.

   The usefulness of the X-header needs to be explored with the Provider ISP.

1. **–0-2041413029-1063072383=:26811**

   E-mail client information; not relevant to the investigation.

Source: Special Report: Investigations Involving the Internet and Computer Networks. Washington, DC: U.S. Department of Justice, National Institute of Justice, Jan. 2007, pp. 20-22. (NIJ 210798)

Mobile Evidence. The electronic memory devices within cell phones that store digital data have become an important source of evidence for criminal investigators. Cell phone use may factor into an investigation involving any of the crimes discussed in this text.

Evidence on a mobile or cell phone system may be found on the communication equipment (the phone itself), the subscriber identity module (SIM), a media card within the phone, a fixed base station, a switching network, the operation and maintenance system for the network, and the customer management system. It may also be possible to retrieve deleted items. Call data records (CDRs) obtained from the network service provider are also very valuable as evidence, for they can reveal the location of the mobile phone user every time a call is sent or received.

The following guidelines are offered for the proper seizure and preservation of mobile devices such as cell phones, tablets, GPS units, and associated removable media:

- If the device is "off," do not turn "on."

- With tablets or cell phones, if the device is on, leave it on. Powering down a device could enable a password, thus preventing access to evidence. However, investigators must recognize the risk of having the device remotely wiped if it is left on.

- If the device is on and unlocked, photograph the device and screen display (if available).

- If the device is on, locate and remove any SIM cards and place the device in airplane mode. Many newer phones allow the device to be placed in airplane mode even if locked.

- If the device is an Android and is unlocked, place it in "USB Debugging Mode" and "Stay Awake" mode prior to powering it down.

- Power down the device and remove the battery if possible. This helps prevent the device from receiving an alarm to "wake up" and power back on.

- If possible, place the device in a Radio Frequency (RF) shielded enclosure, such as a Faraday bag, to block connectivity to any wireless signal. Blocking access to a signal is vital in preserving evidence and preventing anyone from remotely wiping the device.

- Label and collect all cables, including the power supply, and transport them with the device.

- As always, document all steps involved in seizure of devices and components.

(adapted from U.S. Secret Service, 2015, pp. 11–12)

Packaging, Transporting, and Storing Digital and Other Computer Crime Evidence

Computer evidence—electronic devices and the data contained within them—is fragile and sensitive to temperature, humidity, physical shock, static electricity, and magnetic sources. Thus, investigators must use due diligence when packaging, transporting, and storing the evidence. Furthermore, documenting these procedures is necessary for maintaining the chain of custody.

Before electronic evidence is packaged, it must be properly documented, labeled, marked, photographed, video recorded or sketched, and inventoried. All connections and connected devices should be labeled for easy reconfiguration of the system later. All digital evidence should be packed in antistatic packaging and in a way that will prevent it from being bent, scratched, or otherwise deformed. Only paper bags and envelopes, cardboard boxes, and antistatic containers should be used. Plastic materials should not be used because plastic can produce or convey static electricity and allow humidity and condensation to develop, which may damage or destroy the evidence. All containers should be clearly labeled. At this point, cellular, mobile, or smartphone(s) should be powered down if it is safe to do so, meaning it has been confirmed there will be no loss of data if the device is turned off. If it is not possible to safely power down the device, steps should be taken to protect it from receiving or transmitting signals to cellular phone towers. Again, switching to airplane mode is the recommended way to achieve this.

If a device is powered down, investigators need to bear in mind what might happen when it is turned back on: "When a mobile device has been powered off, text messages and other data may queue for delivery when the phone is powered back on and returned to service. The queued messages and data can overwrite old and deleted messages and/or data once they are delivered to the carrier. Carrier providers may update system files and roaming services when the mobile device is connected to the system. There will also be the potential for corruption of downloaded data as well as the file system of the device during a forensic examination when the system updates are transmitted to the system" (Bennett, 2011).

During transportation, investigators must keep digital evidence away from magnetic fields such as those produced by radio transmitters, speaker magnets, and magnetic mount emergency lights. Store disks in the manufacturers' containers, and store all computer evidence in areas away from strong sources of light.

LO6 Describe how electronic evidence should be stored.

Store electronic evidence in a secure area away from temperature and humidity extremes and protected from magnetic sources, moisture, dust, and other harmful particles or contaminants. Do not use plastic bags.

Also be aware of the time-sensitive nature of perishable data evidence. Potential evidence such as dates, times, and system configurations may be lost because of prolonged storage or the depletion of a device's battery. Therefore, when submitting such evidence for examination, notify the appropriate personnel that a device powered by batteries needs immediate attention.

Crime-Specific Investigations

As mentioned, several NIJ documents provide detailed coverage of specific computer crime investigations. *Investigations Involving the Internet and Computer Networks* (2007) provides in-depth explanations of investigations involving email; websites; instant message services and chat rooms; file-sharing networks, network intrusion, or denial of service; and bulletin boards, message boards, and newsgroups. *Electronic Crime Scene Investigation: A Guide for First Responders* (2008) contains detailed discussions of electronic crime and digital evidence considerations by crime category: child abuse or exploitation; computer intrusion; counterfeiting; death investigation; domestic violence, threats, and extortion; email threats, harassment, and stalking; gaming; identity theft; narcotics; online or economic fraud; prostitution; software piracy; telecommunication fraud; and terrorism. For those interested in these in-depth discussions, search the Internet by their titles.

Forensic Examination of Digital Evidence

Digital forensics (DF) carries the potential to benefit nearly every type of criminal investigation: "DF tools are now used on a daily basis by examiners and analysts within local, state and Federal law enforcement; within the military and other U.S. government organizations; and within the private 'e-Discovery' industry. Developments in forensic research, tools, and process . . . have been very successful and many in leadership positions now rely on

these tools on a regular basis—frequently without realizing it" (Garfinkel, 2010).

Crime laboratories, either public or private, have much of the equipment necessary to examine computer evidence. Computer hardware has individual characteristics, much the same as other items of evidence, such as tools. The hardware might also contain fingerprints, but frequently the perpetrator's fingerprints are not unusual because they have legal access to the hardware. Printers also have individual characteristics, much the same as typewriters. Document examinations of printouts can be made, and these printouts can be analyzed for fingerprints. Fragments of software may be compared. And, as discussed, the entire file content of a computer's hard drive may be analyzed for incriminating text or images.

Because the skills required for some of today's complex digital and electronic forensic evidence examination are very technical and usually fall outside the realm of what is expected of the typical criminal investigator, this discussion does not delve too deeply into specific techniques required during such examinations but, rather, presents an overview of what happens to evidence once it is submitted to the lab.

Data Analysis and Recovery

In an ideal case, digital data on a seized computer's hard drive or contained on other media such as CDs or flash drives is intact, unencrypted, and has not been "deleted." In these scenarios, the digital forensic examiner can simply retrieve the data and print it. Another place to look for evidence is in the computer's recycle bin, as some less computer-savvy criminals might equate putting a file in "the trash" with deleting it. In many cases, however, the suspect has taken steps to hide evidence of criminal activity, such as through data encryption or steganography, installing booby traps or other destructive programs to keep outsiders from gaining access, or by deleting files. Sometimes computer evidence is damaged through exposure to fire, water, or physical impact.

Data recovery is a computer forensic technique that requires an extensive knowledge of computer technology and storage devices and an understanding of the laws of search and seizure and the rules of evidence, to be discussed shortly. Software programs can help investigators restore data on damaged hard drives or other computer media or recover information that a suspect may have thought had been deleted.

Modern operating systems often leave copies of "deleted" files scattered about, in temporary directories, unallocated sectors, and swap files. Although deleted files remain on the hard drive in a nonviewable format, their existence hidden from most computer users, the computer forensic expert knows where to look and how to make such files viewable again. **Data remanence** refers to the residual physical representation of data that have been erased. In addition to recovering deleted material, a qualified computer forensic analyst may be able to recover evidence of the copying of documents, whether to another computer on the network or to some removable storage device such as a flash drive; the printing of documents; the dates and times specific documents were created, accessed, or modified; the type and amount of use a particular computer has had; Internet searches run from a computer; and more.

Legal Considerations in Collecting and Analyzing Computer Evidence

Throughout the entire evidence collection and analysis processes, investigators and forensic technicians must adhere to strict standards if the evidence is to be of value in the courtroom. Individuals must testify in court to the authenticity of the disks, CDs, or printouts. The materials must be proven to be either the originals or valid substitutes in accordance with the best-evidence rule. This evidence must be tied to its source by a person qualified to testify about it (Goodison, Davis, & Jackson, 2015).

Besides adhering to authenticity standards, investigators must be alert to situations where the Privacy Protection Act (PPA) of 1980 may be implicated. Under this act, with certain exceptions, it is considered unlawful for a government agent to search for or seize materials possessed by a person reasonably believed to have a legitimate purpose for disseminating information to the public. For example, seizure of materials relating to protected First Amendment activities such as publishing or posting materials on the Internet may implicate the PPA (Computer Crime and Intellectual Property Section, 2009). The PPA prohibition on the use of a search warrant does not apply in the following circumstances:

- Materials searched for or seized are contraband, fruits, or instrumentalities of the crime.

- There is reason to believe that the immediate seizure of such materials is necessary to prevent death or serious bodily injury.

- Probable cause exists to believe that the person possessing the materials has committed or is committing a criminal offense to which the materials relate.

Technology Innovations

Improving Methods to Acquire and Analyze Digital Media

Novak, Grier, and Gonzales (2019) note: "Large-capacity media typically seized as evidence in a criminal investigation, such as computer hard drives and external drives, may be 1 terabyte (TB) or larger. This is equivalent to about 17,000 hours of compressed recorded audio. Today, media can be acquired forensically at approximately 1.5 gigabytes (GB) per minute. The forensically acquired media are stored in a RAW image format, which results in a bit-for-bit copy of the data contained in the original media without any additions or deletions, even for the portions of the media that do not contain data. This means that a 1 TB hard drive will take approximately 11 hours for forensic acquisition. Although this method captures all possible data stored in a piece of digital media, it is time-consuming and creates backlogs. In 2014, there were 7,800 backlogged cases involving digital forensics in publicly funded forensic crime labs."

Two technology innovations are expediting the way digital evidence is acquired and analyzed. Grier Forensics has developed a software application called the Rapid Forensic Acquisition of Large Media with Sifting Collectors to bypass disk regions that are blank, unused, or contain exclusively third-party, unmodified applications, instead zeroing in on the regions of a disk that contain data, artifacts, and other evidence. This technology "has the potential to significantly reduce digital forensics backlogs and quickly get valuable evidence to the people who need it. In laboratory testing, it accelerated the imaging and acquisition process by three to 13 times while still yielding 95 to 100 percent of the evidence."

After media are acquired, they must be analyzed. And as with acquisition time, the time it takes to conduct digital forensics analysis has continued to increase as the size of hard drives increases. RAND Corporation has developed an open-source digital forensics processing application called Digital Forensics Compute Cluster (DFORC2), which "takes advantage of the parallel-processing capability of stand-alone high-performance servers or cloud-computing environments. The primary advantage of DFORC2 is that it will significantly reduce the time required to ingest and process digital evidence," helping law enforcement curb the backlog of forensic digital evidence.

Source: nij.ojp.gov/topics/articles /new-approaches-digital-evidence-acquisition-and-analysis

First responders seizing electronic devices must be aware of the restrictions on searching legally privileged communication, such as that found in files of doctors, lawyers, and members of the clergy, if those persons are not implicated in the crime being investigated. Improper access of data stored within may violate provisions of certain federal laws, including the Electronic Communications Privacy Act of 1986. The recommended course of action, should this be a concern, is to consult the local prosecutor before accessing stored data on an electronic device (NIJ, 2008).

An evolving area of legal wrangling concerns copyright laws and investigative agencies that seize computers that have an operating system installed on them, as most do. Operating systems, which are copyright protected, may not be copied without the author's, or in this case the software company's, expressed permission.

Follow-Up Investigation

Once the initial report has been completed and the general information has been obtained, a plan is made for the remaining investigation. The plan should identify the problem and the crime or crimes committed. A suspect must be developed, as must other peripheral parties to the crime. Determine the areas involved in the crime, equipment used, internal and external staffing needs, approximate length of time required for the investigation, a method of handling and storing evidence, and the assignment of personnel. When developing a suspect, ascertain motive, opportunity, means of commission, the type of security system bypassed, and known bypass techniques. It may be necessary to conduct covert operations as part of the investigation. In such cases, an officer with expert-level knowledge in cybercrime is a critical factor in achieving a successful resolution. It is also necessary to determine which federal, state, or local laws apply to the specific type of computer crime committed.

Developing Suspects

A few decades ago, computer crime was the exclusive domain of a relatively small group of electronic geniuses whose incredibly specialized knowledge and programming skills afforded them unique opportunities to pry into individuals' and corporations' computers and steal money, trade secrets, or other information of value. Today, however, cybercrooks are not such an elite bunch. Today's global population of twenty-somethings and younger are often as proficient on the computer as they are with using a TV or cell phone.

Myth Cybercrimes require a high level of technical knowledge and skill to pull off.

Fact While some types of cybercrime, such as writing code for malware, may require a higher-than-average level of technical know-how, many crimes committed with a computer are very easy to execute, requiring minimal technical expertise.

A significant change from previous editions of this text is in the number of crimes committed by insiders versus outsiders. It used to be that most computer-related crimes against businesses and other organizations were committed by insiders because these people had the best access to the devices. While crimes committed by insiders continue to grow, outsiders have gained increasing levels of access, courtesy of the Internet, to the extent that today most (72%) electronic crimes are perpetrated by outsiders.

Although anyone with the requisite know-how can take up a life of cybercrime, the FBI and other organizations that have been compiling records on the perpetrators of cybercrime have developed a sort of cybercriminal profile of characteristics these individuals are likely to exhibit. A cybercriminal will likely fall into one of three categories:

- ■ *Hackers*: motivated by achieving prohibited access; inspired by boredom and the desire for intellectual challenge; no real damage done

- ■ *Vandals*: motivated to cause damage and as much harm as possible; are often disgruntled, either with their employer or with life and society in general; include hacktivists

- ■ *Criminals*: motivated by economic gain; use espionage and fraud, among other tactics, to accomplish their goals; include crackers, insiders, industrial spies, cybercriminals, and cyberterrorists

L07 Determine how cybercriminals may be categorized, including their differing motivations.

Three general categories of cybercriminals are hackers, vandals, and criminals. Motivations vary, from the hacker's need for an intellectual challenge, to the vandal's urge to cause damage, to the criminal's desire for financial or other personal gain.

Cybercriminals can generally be classified by organization level:

- Most computer criminals, although commonly active in a social underground, commit their criminal acts alone.

- A smaller percentage of cybercriminals will exist in organized groups, such as corporate spies and organized crime groups.

Normal or special audit procedures may have brought a computer crime to the attention of the proper persons, as in embezzlement cases. Because computer operations require contact with other employees in collecting computer-input information, suspicion develops when employees appear to withdraw from other normal relationships.

Overloading of the computer system or a lack of accessibility to records that the system was designed for may indicate illegal use of the computer, a crime that occurs more frequently in small computer operations, where greater opportunity exists. However, this makes an investigator's task easier because the number of suspects is reduced.

The suspect may act alone or in collusion in committing the crime. In cases of internal abuse, commission normally occurs during authorized use or during periods of overtime when the employee is working alone. Developing a suspect's work history assists in locating past opportunities for committing the offense. The suspect's training will provide information about their knowledge of computers and computer languages. Comparisons of these factors with the equipment at the crime scene will help determine whether the suspect was capable of the crime.

A complete review of everyone within the organization who has access, their type of access, and their technical capability or opportunity greatly assists the investigation if the crime is internal. Check for employees who have a history of computer crimes.

Investigators will often find that computer-related thefts originate from agencies that already have highly trained computer personnel on staff. If the theft is internal, the investigator may confidentially involve personnel of that agency who are not suspect. In internal crimes of this nature, the number of suspects will necessarily be limited, compared with a crime such as a residential burglary, in which the suspect could be a local or an outsider. In computer theft crimes, supervisory and management personnel may use computers to hide their offenses and then misdirect the investigative team toward subordinate staff who have committed relatively minor transgressions.

Internal auditing procedures are normally started with the security director involved. If an employee is suspected at this point, management must decide whether to handle the matter internally or proceed with prosecution. If the decision is to handle the matter internally, then the case is closed. If not, the investigation continues, often involving state or private investigators. Such individuals may have the expertise and anonymity not available to local police departments.

Organized Cybercrime Groups

Most cybercriminals work alone. However, on occasion these individuals may come together for a common criminal endeavor. They generally are not Mafia-style organizations and usually lack any real loyalty to one another. The transitional nature of these cybercrime rings makes prosecution an effective tool against such groups and sends a message of deterrence to other online criminals, who, because of the anonymity involved with Internet communications, often do not know who they are really dealing with.

Although cybercriminal rings have not historically been formally structured like traditional organized crime, a few hacker groups have been observed to have a Mafia-like hierarchy, with virtual godfathers mapping strategy, capos issuing orders, and soldiers carrying out the dirty work. Some cybergangs have evolved into highly organized criminal enterprises whose membership and illegal activities span the globe. Other cybergangs, like Anonymous, are an amorphous conglomerate of individuals who are members simply by virtue of claiming allegiance to the "cause." In the case of Anonymous, whose online presence has ebbed and flowed for the better part of two decades, their ability to coordinate and conduct "operations" such as targeted DDoS attacks to disable corporate websites or hacks of law enforcement servers to leak hundreds of gigabytes of internal police files has proven challenging to cybercrime investigators (Beran, 2020; Klein, 2015). Particularly difficult are cases involving cybergangs that operate in countries with weak hacking laws and lax enforcement, such as Russia, Eastern European countries, and China.

An effective tactic being used to apprehend organized cybercrime networks is undercover investigation and surveillance.

Undercover Investigation and Surveillance

Sometimes it is necessary to develop an undercover operation to further the investigation. This operation must be headed by a computer expert and coordinated with the nonsuspects. Lists must be prepared of all individuals to be used in the case and the evidence to be obtained. Undercover work can be used in nearly every aspect of cybercrime. As with undercover work in the real world, investigators must be sensitive to entrapment issues and to undercover involvement with criminal activity.

Covert investigation including ongoing surveillance operations is a method being used to gather evidence against cybercrime gangs. Undercover tactics are also commonly used in cases of online child pornography and sexual exploitation. An officer will go online, undercover, into predicted locations, and, using a fictitious screen name and profile, pose as a child or teenager and engage in real-time chat or email conversations with subjects to obtain evidence of criminal activity. Investigations of specific Internet locations can be initiated through a citizen complaint; a complaint by an ISP; a referral from another law enforcement agency; or the name of an online location, such as a chat room, which can suggest illicit activity.

Security of the Police Department's Computers

When considering computer crime, law enforcement officers should not overlook the possibility that their own computers may be accessed by criminals. Any computer attached to a phone line is accessible by unauthorized people outside the department, even thousands of miles away on a different continent. Considering the critical nature of law enforcement data and communications, such as systems that control computer-aided dispatch, records management applications, and offender databases, ensuring the security of an agency's network should be a top priority. Law enforcement departments cannot afford to have their evidence logs hacked or have reports and other valuable data hijacked in a system takeover following a virus attack.

Legislation

With the proliferation of online child pornography, phishing, and other crimes involving the computer, legislation has necessarily been developed to address the problem. For example, in 1986, President Ronald Reagan signed a bill to modernize the federal wiretap law to protect the privacy of high-tech communications. This bill makes it illegal to eavesdrop on email, video conference calls, conversations on cellular car phones, and computer-to-computer transmissions.

However, following the September 11, 2001, tragedy and the realization that the terrorists had used the Internet and other electronic means to communicate and coordinate their plans, the government took measures to allow law enforcement greater latitude in its surveilling of electronic communication if there is a reasonable suspicion that such activity involves terrorism. On October 26, 2001, President George W. Bush signed the USA PATRIOT Act (Uniting and Strengthening America by Providing Appropriate Tools Required to Intercept and Obstruct Terrorism), a major piece of legislation consisting of more than 150 sections, many of which pertain to electronic communications and other areas of cybercrime investigation.

The act made several amendments to the Foreign Intelligence Surveillance Act (FISA) of 1978, such as granting "roving" authority to FBI and other law enforcement agents to more efficiently serve orders on communications carriers and thus meet the challenges posed by individuals who rapidly switch telephone carriers, cell phones, or Internet accounts as a way of evading detection and thwarting surveillance. These amendments, while lauded by those conducting criminal investigations, raised privacy concerns among civil rights groups.

The PATRIOT Act also changed key features of existing National Security Letter (NSL) protocol. NSLs are a type of subpoena issued in foreign counterintelligence and international terrorism investigations to obtain records under the statutory authority of the Electronic Communications Privacy Act (telephone and ISP records), the Right to Financial Privacy Act of 1978 (financial institution records), and the Fair Credit Reporting Act of 1970 (records from credit bureaus). The PATRIOT Act expanded signature authority for NSLs to increase the efficiency and effectiveness of processing such subpoenas. Again, this expansion was criticized by privacy advocates.

The PATRIOT Act, and many of its most controversial sections, expired on June 1, 2015, and was replaced by Congress with the Uniting and Strengthening America by Fulfilling Rights and Ending Eavesdropping, Dragnet-collection and Online Monitoring (USA FREEDOM) Act. The Freedom Act, while restoring and modifying many of the expiring provisions of the PATRIOT Act through 2019, eliminated mass

628 Section 5 | Other Challenges to the Criminal Investigator

surveillance, placing new limits on the bulk interception of telecommunication metadata about U.S. citizens, and required more transparency in FISA (215) cases. The act did, however, reauthorize roving wiretaps and tracking of lone wolf terrorists through 2019. The USA Freedom Reauthorization Act of 2020, passed in the Senate in May 2020, included renewal of the expired lone wolf and roving wiretap provisions, but concerns at the presidential level and threats to veto the bill led the House of Representatives to withdraw the bill. As this text goes to press, no new reauthorization bill has been proposed.

Other federal statutes relevant to computer-related crimes include patent laws, espionage and sabotage laws, trade secret laws, the Copyright Act of 1976, and the Financial Privacy Act of 1978. In 1998, the Child Protection and Sexual Predator Punishment Act was passed after members of Congress cited horror stories involving sexual predators making initial contact with young children through the Internet.

In the past decade, all 50 states have enacted tough computer crime control laws. States address computer crime either by modifying existing statutes such as those pertaining to theft or by adding computer crime chapters to their criminal codes. For example, to address the growing problem of cyberstalking, some states have amended their traditional stalking laws to include threats transmitted via the Internet. Phishing schemes are likely to violate various existing state statutes on fraud and identity theft and several federal criminal laws. Those who phish may be committing identity theft (18 U.S.C. §1028[a][7]), wire fraud (18 U.S.C. §1343), credit card or "access-device" fraud (18 U.S.C. §1029), bank fraud (18 U.S.C. §1344), computer fraud (18 U.S.C. §1030[a][4]), and the criminal offenses delineated in the Controlling the Assault of Non-Solicited Pornography and Marketing (CAN-SPAM) Act (18 U.S.C. §1037). Transmission of computer viruses and worms may be prosecuted under the federal provisions of the computer fraud and abuse statute relating to damage to computer systems and files (18 U.S.C. §1028[a][5]). These federal criminal offenses can carry substantial penalties and fines, with convictions for wire fraud and bank fraud earning the offender as many as 30 years in prison and the possibility of fines as high as $250,000, plus forfeiture of the defendant's property.

Well-defined statutes are critical to investigating and prosecuting computer crimes successfully, and the area of cyber law is rapidly evolving. Lawmakers are challenged, however, by the complex nature of the technology and nontraditional jurisdictional concerns, elements that complicate the effort to define cybercrime

and cybercrooks. Through it all, cybercrime investigators must stay on top of the ever-changing body of state and federal law regarding electronic crimes.

The Investigative Team

Criminals around the world have their sticky fingers poised at the keyboard, prepared to click their way into places they don't belong and steal. The rising tide of Internet activity has washed ashore an increasing variety of old crimes in new bottles and shows no signs of ebbing. To handle this challenge, many departments have formed cybercrime investigative teams comprising various specialists, similar to the approach taken in cases involving complex art thefts, bank embezzlements, narcotics trafficking, or other types of crime in which a generalist investigator has little expertise.

Investigating computer crime often requires a team approach. The investigative team is responsible for assigning all team personnel according to their specialties, including securing outside specialists if necessary; securing the crime scene area; obtaining search warrant applications; determining the specific hardware and software involved; searching for, obtaining, marking, preserving, and storing evidence; obtaining necessary disks, storage media, printouts, and other records; and preparing information for investigative reports. In most computer-related crimes, investigators seek assistance from the victim who owns the equipment, database-processing technicians, auditors, highly trained computer experts or programmers, and others. If necessary, the team should contact the manufacturer of the equipment, the consulting services of a private computer crime investigative agency, or the technology resources found at local universities and other institutions of higher learning.

To assist in combating increasing computer crimes, government and private businesses are developing computer crime teams similar to the FBI's kidnapping crime teams and the arson investigation specialist teams of the Bureau of Alcohol, Tobacco, Firearms, and Explosives (ATF). The FBI's Computer Analysis Response Team (CART) helps state and local law enforcement as well as federal agents. CART helps write and execute search warrants, seize and catalog evidence, and perform routine examinations of digital evidence. In addition to CART, investigators working cybercrime cases may seek assistance from a growing pool of resources, both domestic and international. Figure 17.6 shows the agencies that play a critical role in U.S. cyber enforcement efforts.

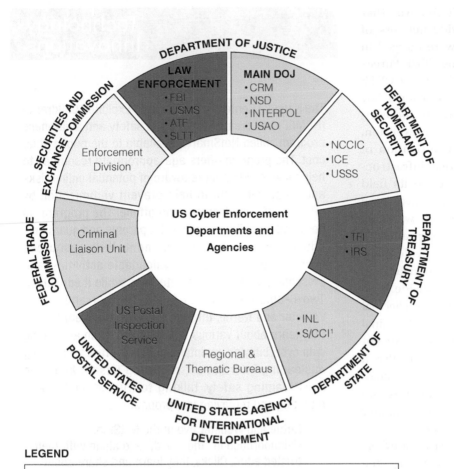

FIGURE 17.6
U.S. Cyber Enforcement Departments and Agencies.

Source: Gaskew, B. (2019, February 21). *Reader's guide to understanding the U.S. cyber enforcement architecture and budget.* Washington, DC: Third Way. www.thirdway.org/memo/readers-guide-to-understanding-the-us-cyber-enforcement-architecture-and-budget

LEGEND

- ATF: Bureau of Alcohol, Tobacco, Firearms and Explosives
- CRM: Criminal Division
- FBI: Federal Bureau of Investigation
- INTERPOL Washington
- ICE: U.S. Immigrations and Customs Enforcement
- INL: Bureau of International Narcotics and Law Enforcement
- IRS: Internal Revenue Services
- NCCIC: National Cybersecurity and Communications Integration Center
- NSD: National Security Division
- S/CCI: Office of the Coordinator for Cyber Issues
- SLTT: State, Local, Tribal and Territorial (SLTT) Law Enforcement Agencies
- TFI: Office of Terrorism and Financial Intelligence
- USAO: United States Attorney's Offices
- USMS: U.S. Marshals Service

Resources Available

Police agencies in many states are forming cooperative groups and providing training seminars on investigating computer crimes. Such groups are especially helpful for small departments, which are less likely to have the needed expertise in-house. For example, Florida's law enforcement agencies can submit computer evidence to the Computer Evidence Recovery (CER) program, which also trains the state's law enforcement agencies to prepare warrants to search computers and to follow specific procedures when seizing computer crime evidence.

Training in computer crimes investigation is also available from other sources. The U.S. DOJ has developed the Computer Crime and Intellectual Property Section (CCIPS) which, as one of its many functions, provides training to state, local, tribal, territorial, and international law enforcement agencies on how to properly collect electronic evidence and strengthen the prosecution of cybercrime cases. Another resource to help law enforcement handle comp uter crimes is the IC3, discussed earlier. The IC3 provides to cybercrime victims a convenient, user-friendly reporting mechanism that notifies authorities of suspected violations.

One mandate of the USA PATRIOT Act was that the Secret Service establish a nationwide network of Electronic Crimes Task Forces, which were merged in 2020 with the Cyber and Financial Crimes Task Forces to form the Cyber Fraud Task Forces (CFTFs). The CFTF network brings together federal, state, and local law enforcement, as well as prosecutors, private industry, and academia. The common purpose is the prevention, detection, mitigation, and aggressive investigation of attacks on the nation's financial and critical infrastructures. The USSS offers numerous services to its field agents, including technical assistance in developing cybercrime cases, help in preparing search warrants involving electronic storage devices, laboratory analysis of and courtroom testimony regarding the evidentiary contents of electronic storage devices, and educational seminars for law enforcement officers nationwide.

The website of the Computer Crime and Intellectual Property Section of the DOJ (www.justice.gov/criminal-ccips) serves as a one-stop resource for law enforcement for everything related to computer crime. The site offers a collection of documents and links to other sites and agencies that may help prevent, detect, investigate, and prosecute cybercrime. Another resource is the nonprofit Computer Crime Research Center (www.crime-research.org).

For the special challenge of handling cases of cybercrimes involving children, investigators may tap the resources of the Internet Crimes Against Children (ICAC) program, a national network of 61 coordinated task forces representing over 4,500 federal, state, and local law enforcement and prosecutorial agencies. Members of the ICAC program, which is funded by the U.S. DOJ's Office of Juvenile Justice and Delinquency Prevention, assist with proactive investigations, forensic investigations, and criminal prosecutions.

Preventing Computer Crime

Although computers and related technologies have added immeasurable benefits and value to our quality of life, this technology has opened new avenues of crime and exploitation. One reason computer crime has proliferated among businesses in the private sector is that many managers are unprepared to deal with it. They may be ignorant, indifferent, or both. They also frequently lack control over their information. Without standards to violate, there is no violation.

Management must institute organization-wide policies to safeguard its databases and must educate employees in these policies and any security measures implemented. Management should also take internal security precautions:

Technology Innovations

NetSmartz

The National Center for Missing and Exploited Children® (NCMEC) has created an Internet safety and awareness program called NetSmartz, available to the public at no cost. The program offers age-appropriate resources to help make children more aware of potential online risks and empower them to help prevent victimization by making safer choices on- and offline. The program "is designed for children ages 5–17, parents and guardians, educators, and law enforcement. With resources such as videos, games, downloadable activities, and presentations, NetSmartz entertains while it educates." Two 6-episode seasons follow brother and sister, Webster and Nettie, through a series of adventures as they learn about various safety topics, such as dealing with cyberbullying, maintaining online privacy, checking misleading information, reporting unsafe behavior, livestreaming safety, talking to trusted adults, and reporting and removing inappropriate content:

> Nettie and Webster live in the NetSmartz Neighborhood in "the cloud," and along with their trusted adult, Clicky, they learn and share about ways to keep the internet safer while fighting off the evil plots of the Webville Outlaws. After falling through an abandoned transport tube, Nettie and Webster find themselves stranded in the strange cloud realm of *Badromeda*. As they venture deeper into these unknown realms of the cloud, they'll have to rely on each other, some new friends, and everything they've learned about internet safety to make it home and stop the Webville Outlaws!

The notorious Outlaws include Wanta-Know Wally, who tries to trick people into giving up their personal information; Meet-Me Mack, who tries to get kids he talks to online to meet him face-to-face; and Potty-Mouth Pete, the biggest cyberbully around, who tries to get people to be rude and mean to each other online. Helping Webster and Nettie navigate through these issues is Officer Armstrong, a new recruit to the Badromeda Police Department. She specializes in cybercrime and uses computers and technology to catch those using the internet for illegal purposes. In her free time she likes to travel and is a recreational extreme hoverboard enthusiast.

Sources: www.netsmartzkids.org/www.missingkids.org/content/dam/netsmartz/downloadable/ITC%20Marketing%20One%20Pager.pdf firewalls and virus protection are two safeguards for computers. Data disks and removable storage media should have backup copies and be kept in locked files.

> **LO8** Understand ways in which computer crimes can be prevented.
>
> Computer crimes can be prevented by educating top management and employees and by instituting internal security precautions. Top management must make a commitment to defend against computer crime.

The *U.S. State of Cybercrime Survey* (CSO Magazine, 2018) reports that the most common strategies used by organizations to address cyber-risks and prevent attacks are adding new technologies (46%), conducting audits and assessments (34%), adding new skills and capabilities (32%), redesigning their cybersecurity system (24%), redesigning processes (18%), and participating in knowledge sharing (11%). Survey respondents also report that the majority of their employees receive cybersecurity training at least once a year.

As part of its cyber strategy, the FBI recommends that computer users take several key steps to avoid becoming a computer crime victim (n.d.):

- Keep the firewall turned on
- Install or update antivirus software
- Install or update antispyware technology
- Keep the operating system up to date
- Use caution when downloading files or other content
- Turn off the computer when not in use

One of the most important, yet most frequently overlooked, security measures is to use a paper shredder for all sensitive documents once they are no longer needed. Another technique gaining momentum in the effort to increase computer security is biometrics, using physical characteristics the user cannot lose or give away, including facial, voice, and fingerprint recognition.

Computer crimes also plague and persist among private American citizens because, like corporate managers, they remain uninformed about how to protect themselves. One of the most common ways home users become victims of cybercrime is through phishing or other scams devised to get computer users to relinquish sensitive information.

Businesses also need to become more proactive. *CIO Magazine*, the FBI, and the USSS have collaborated to produce guidelines for how businesses should plan for and respond to attacks on information systems, including viruses, hacks, and other breaches. The guidelines suggest that chief information officers (CIOs), chief information security officers (CISOs), and business leaders establish a relationship with law enforcement now, before the next attack occurs.

Besides individuals and companies, the entire U.S. population risks victimization by cybercriminals because of our increasing reliance on information technology and the role computers play in many aspects of our daily lives, including the dependence of the various components of our nation's critical infrastructure—public and private institutions in the sectors of agriculture, food, water, public health, emergency services, government, defense industrial base, information and telecommunications, energy, transportation, banking and finance, chemicals and hazardous materials, and postal and shipping—on a fully functional cyberspace. Cyberattacks on any part of this infrastructure could lead to tremendous loss of revenue and intellectual property and to loss of life. For these reasons, the scope of cybercrime, even if undetermined, has the potential to cause extreme damage.

One of the six primary missions set forth in the Department of Homeland Security's *Strategic Plan: Fiscal Years 2020–2024* (2019, p. 34) is to safeguard and secure cyberspace:

> As cyberspace increasingly pervades every facet of society, it has provided a new and complex domain for traditional criminal actors to engage in illicit activity that threatens U.S. homeland security. This borderless feature allows transnational criminal organizations and foreign criminal actors to commit cyber intrusions, bank fraud, child exploitation, data breaches, and other computer-enabled crimes without ever entering the United States. The speed of innovation further complicates this threat, since cybersecurity measures are implicitly reactionary. As a result, the United States is relying on law enforcement investigations to complement its defensive capabilities that combat this threat.

> Despite diligent efforts by the collective homeland security enterprise, the United States must do more to deter, detect, and identify cyber criminals and bring them to justice. Accordingly, DHS is applying its extensive cyber capabilities to investigate cyber criminals and take decisive actions to shield the American public from the incessant barrage of cybercrime by disrupting and dismantling criminal organizations. In particular, DHS is working to expand multilateral cooperative agreements with international partners to reach cybercriminals from regions outside the United States.

Summary

Computer-related crimes may be categorized as computer as target, computer as tool, or computer as incidental to the offense. A common protocol for processing a crime scene involving electronic evidence is

1. Secure and evaluate the crime scene
2. Conduct preliminary interviews
3. Obtain a search warrant
4. Recognize and identify the evidence
5. Document the crime scene
6. Collect and preserve evidence
7. Package, transport, and store evidence
8. Submit digital evidence (such as hard drives) for analysis and data recovery
9. Document the investigation in an incident report

A basic tenet for first responders at computer crime scenes is to observe the ON/OFF rule: If it's on, leave it on. If it's off, leave it off. Having a search warrant generally decreases the amount of resistance investigators face at the scene and increases the odds of successful prosecution should the case go to court.

Digital evidence is often contained on disks, CDs, or hard drives, or on any number of peripheral electronic devices; is not readily discernible; and is highly susceptible to destruction. Other computer crime evidence may exist in the form of data reports, logs, programming, or other printed information run from information in the computer. Latent prints may be found on the keyboard, mouse, power button, or any other peripheral equipment near the computer, including the printer.

Store electronic evidence in a secure area away from temperature and humidity extremes and protected from magnetic sources, moisture, dust, and other harmful particles or contaminants. Do not use plastic bags.

Three general categories of cybercriminals are hackers, vandals, and criminals. Motivations vary, from the hacker's need for an intellectual challenge, to the vandal's urge to cause damage, to the criminal's desire for financial or other personal gain. Computer crimes can be prevented by educating top management and employees and by instituting internal security precautions. Top management must make a commitment to defend against computer crime.

Can You Define?

adware	e-crime	port scanning
bitcoins	encryption	ransomware
click-jacking	firewall	script kiddie
computer crime	hacker	skimming
computer virus	hacktivism	sniffing
cracker	hardware disabler	spam
cybercrime	imaging	spoofing
cyberterrorism	Internet Protocol (IP) address	spyware
dark web	Internet service provider (ISP)	static IP address
data remanence	keystroke logging	steganography
deep web	logic bomb	surface web
denial-of-service (DoS) attack	malware	Trojan horse
domain name	pharming	URL
doxing	phishing	worm
dynamic IP address	piracy	zombie

Checklist

Cybercrime

- Who is the complainant?

- Has a crime been committed?

- What is the specific nature of the crime reported to the police?

- What statutes are applicable? Can the required elements of the crime be proven?

- Has the crime been terminated, or is it continuing?

- Is the origin of the crime internal or external?

- Does the reported crime appear to be a cover-up for a larger crime?

- What barriers exist to investigating the crime?

- What are the make, model, and identification numbers of the equipment involved? The hardware? The software?

- Is the equipment individually or company owned?

- Is an operations manual available for the hardware?

- Is a flowchart of computer operations available? Is a computer configuration chart available?

- Is documentation for the software available?

- What computer language is involved? What computer programs are involved?

- What is the degree of technicality involved? Simple or complex?

- What are the input and output codes?

- What accounting procedures were used?

- What is the database system? What are the system's main vulnerabilities?

- Is there a built-in security system? What is it? How was it bypassed?

- What are the present security procedures? How were they bypassed?

- Can the equipment be shut down during the search and investigation or for a sufficient time to investigate the portion essential to obtaining evidence?

- Can the computer records be "dumped" without interfering with the ongoing operations, or must the system be closed down and secured?

- Does the equipment need to be operational to conduct the investigation?

- Does the reporting person desire prosecution or only disciplinary action?

- Are there any suspects? Internal or external?

- If internal, are they presently employed by the reporting organization or person?

- Is a list of current employees and their work histories available? Are all current computer-related job descriptions available?

- What level of employees is involved? Is an organizational table available?

- How can the investigation be carried out without the knowledge of the suspect?

- What is the motive for the crime?

- What competitors might be suspect?

- What types of evidence are needed or likely to be present?

- What external experts are needed as part of the search team?

- Does the available evidence meet the best-evidence requirement?

- What are the main barriers to the continued investigation? How can they be overcome?

Applications

Read the following and then answer the questions:

A.   Ang has just enrolled in her first college course. After reading the syllabus, she purchases the required textbook, which was quite expensive, from the college online bookstore. Ang receives a digital access code to view the book online and realizes that the access code be used on multiple devices. To recoup some of the cost of the required textbook, Ang sells the access code via several online sales platforms. A law enforcement officer comes across a listing to purchase access to the textbook. He believes it is illegal and opens an investigation.

Questions

1. What crime is being committed, if any?

2. Who has jurisdiction?

3. What steps would you take to conduct this investigation?

4. How would you prepare a search warrant?

5. What types of evidence would you look for?

B. A local firm contacts your police department concerning theft of customer credit card and Social Security numbers from their computer records. This operation and theft are suspected to be internal, so present and past employees are the prime suspects.

Questions

1. How would you plan to initiate the investigation?

2. What statements would you obtain?

3. Would you use internal or external assistance?

4. What types of evidence would you need?

References

Alvarez, E. (2014, December 10). *Sony pictures hack: The whole story*. Retrieved March 9, 2021, from www.engadget.com/2014-12-10-sony-pictures-hack-the-whole-story.html

Banday, M. T. (2011). Technology corner: Analysing e-mail headers for forensic investigation. *Journal of Digital Forensics, Security and Law, 6*(2): 49–64. Retrieved March 17, 2021, from commons.erau.edu/cgi/viewcontent.cgi?article=1095&context=jdfsl

Bennett, D. W. (2011, August 20). The challenges facing computer forensics investigators in obtaining information from mobile devices for use in criminal investigations. *Forensic Focus*. Retrieved March 17, 2021, from www.forensicfocus.com/articles/the-challenges-facing-computer-forensics-investigators-in-obtaining-information-from-mobile-devices-for-use-in-criminal-investigations/

Beran, D. (2020, August 11). The return of anonymous. *The Atlantic*. Retrieved March 17, 2021, from www.theatlantic.com/technology/archive/2020/08/hacker-group-anonymous-returns/615058/

Bermudez Villalva, D. A., Onaolapo, J., Stringhini, G., & Musolesi, M. (2018). Under and over the surface: A comparison of the use of leaked account credentials in the dark and surface web. *Crime Science Journal, 7*(17). doi:10.1186/s40163-018-0092-6

Berners-Lee, T. (n.d.). *Frequently asked questions*. Retrieved March 18, 2021, from www.w3.org/People/Berners-Lee/FAQ.html#InternetWeb

Bird, P. (2011, Spring). Virtual child pornography laws and the constraint imposed by the First Amendment. *Barry Law Review, 16*(1), 160–177.

Casey, B. (2017, October 3). Dark web diary. *Cybercrime Magazine*. Retrieved March 16, 2021, from cybersecurityventures.com/dark-web-diary/

Central Intelligence Agency. (2019). *The world factbook*. McLean, VA: Author. Retrieved March 21, 2021, from www.cia.gov/the-world-factbook/field/internet-users/

Chertoff, M. (2017). A public policy perspective of the dark web. *Journal of Cyber Policy, 2*(1): 26–38. doi:10.1080/23738871.2017.1298643

Cisco. (2020, March 9). *Cisco annual internet report (2018–2023) white paper*. San Jose, CA: Author. Retrieved March 12, 2021, from www.cisco.com/c/en/us/solutions/collateral/executive-perspectives/annual-internet-report/white-paper-c11-741490.html

Computer Crime and Intellectual Property Section. (2009). *Searching and seizing computers and obtaining electronic evidence in criminal investigations*. Washington, DC: Author. Retrieved March 17, 2021, from www.justice.gov/sites/default/files/criminal-ccips/legacy/2015/01/14/ssmanual2009.pdf

CSO Magazine. (2018). *2018 U.S. state of cybercrime*. Needham, MA: International Data Group. Retrieved March 12, 2021, from images.idgesg.net/assets/2018/11/201820us20state20of20cybercrime_sample20slides_gated20for20insider.pdf

CTIA. (2020, August 25). *2020 annual survey highlights*. Washington, DC: Author. Retrieved March 10, 2021, from www.ctia.org/news/report-2020-annual-survey-highlights

Cybersecurity Ventures. (2019). *2019 official annual cybercrime report*. Toronto, Ontario, Canada: Herjavec Group. Retrieved March 11, 2021, from www.herjavecgroup.com/wp-content/uploads/2018/12/CV-HG-2019-Official-Annual-Cybercrime-Report.pdf

Eaton, J. (2015, April 27). Lawmakers revive support for Aaron's Law to reform antihacking statute. *The Christian Science Monitor*. Retrieved March 18, 2021, from www.csmonitor.com/World/Passcode/2015/0427/Lawmakers-revive-support-for-Aaron-s-Law-to-reform-anti-hacking-statute

Emsisoft. (2019, December 12). *The state of ransomware in the US: Report and statistics 2019*. British Columbia, Canada: Author. Retrieved March 15, 2021, from blog.emsisoft.com/en/34822/the-state-of-ransomware-in-the-us-report-and-statistics-2019/

Federal Bureau of Investigation. (n.d.). *Scams and safety*. Washington, DC: Author. Retrieved June 25, 2021, from www.fbi.gov/scams-and-safety/on-the-internet

Federal Bureau of Investigation. (2019, April 22). *IC3 annual report released*. Washington, DC: Author. Retrieved March 12, 2021, from www.fbi.gov/news/stories/ic3-releases-2018-internet-crime-report-042219

Finklea, K. (2017, March 10). *Dark web*. Congressional Research Service Report (R44101). Washington, DC: Federation of American Scientists. Retrieved March 16, 2021, from fas.org/sgp/crs/misc/R44101.pdf

Freeman, C. (2014, June 7). Russian hacker wanted by US hailed as hero at home. *The Telegraph*. Retrieved May 24, 2015, from www.telegraph.co.uk/news/worldnews/europe

/russia/10883333/Russian-hacker-wanted-by-US-hailed-as
-hero-at-home.html

Garfinkel, S. L. (2010, August). Digital forensics research: The
next 10 years. *Digital Investigation, 7*(Supplement): S64–S73.
doi:10.1016/j.diin.2010.05.009

Garza, C. (2020, December 11). *FBI warns of money mules.*
Houston, TX: Federal Bureau of Investigation. Retrieved
June 22, 2021, from www.fbi.gov/contact-us/field-offices
/houston/news/press-releases/fbi-warns-of-money-mules

Goodison, S. E., Davis, R. C., & Jackson, B. A. (2015). *Digital
evidence and the U.S. criminal justice system.* Santa Monica,
CA: The RAND Corporation. Retrieved March 17, 2021,
from www.ojp.gov/pdffiles1/nij/grants/248770.pdf

Internet Corporation for Assigned Names and Numbers.
(2011). *Beginner's guide to internet protocol (IP) addresses.*
Los Angeles, CA: Author. Retrieved March 12, 2021, from
www.icann.org/en/system/files/files/ip-addresses
-beginners-guide-04mar11-en.pdf

Internet Crime Complaint Center. (2018). *2018 internet crime
report.* Washington, DC: Author. Retrieved March 12, 2021,
from www.ic3.gov/Media/PDF/AnnualReport/2018
_IC3Report.pdf

Internet Crime Complaint Center. (2019). *2019 internet crime
report.* Washington, DC: Federal Bureau of Investigation.
Retrieved March 11, 2021, from www.ic3.gov/Media/PDF
/AnnualReport/2019_IC3Report.pdf

Internet Society. (2018, June 6). *State of IPv6 deployment 2018.*
Reston, VA: Author. Retrieved March 12, 2021, from www
.internetsociety.org/wp-content/uploads/2018/06/2018
-ISOC-Report-IPv6-Deployment.pdf

Jibilian, I., & Canales, K. (2021, February 25). Here's a
simple explanation of how the massive solarwinds hack
happened and why it's such a big deal. *Business Insider.*
Retrieved March 15, 2021, from www.businessinsider.com
/solarwinds-hack-explained-government-agencies-cyber
-security-2020-12

Klein, A. G. (2015). Vigilante media: Unveiling anonymous and
the hacktivism persona in the global press. *Communication
Monographs, 83*(3): 379–401. doi:10.1080/03637751.2015.10
30682

Larson, E. (2017). Tracking criminals with internet
protocol addresses: Is law enforcement correctly
identifying perpetrators? *North Carolina Journal of
Law & Technology, 18*(5): 316–358. Retrieved March 17,
2021, from scholarship.law.unc.edu/cgi/viewcontent
.cgi?article=1340&context=ncjolt

Marchini, K., & Pascual, A. (2019, March 6). *2019 identity
fraud study: Fraudsters seek new targets and victims bear
the brunt.* Pleasanton, CA: Javelin Strategy & Research.
Retrieved March 11, 2021, from www.javelinstrategy.com
/coverage-area/2019-identity-fraud-report-fraudsters-seek
-new-targets-and-victims-bear-brunt

McMillan, R. (2018, December 9). Thieves can now nab
your data in a few minutes for a few bucks. *The Wall Street
Journal.* Retrieved March 16, 2021, from www.wsj
.com/articles/what-happens-to-your-data-after-a-hack
-1544367600?mod=hp_lead_pos10

Moore, D., & Rid, T. (2016). Cryptopolitik and the darknet.
Survival, 58(1): 7–38. doi:10.1080/00396338.2016.1142085

National Forensic Science Technology Center. (2013,
September). *Crime scene investigation: A guide
for law enforcement.* Largo, FL: Author. Retrieved
March 18, 2021, from shop.nfstc.org/product
/crime-scene-investigation-guide/

National Institute of Justice. (2007, January). *Investigations
involving the Internet and computer networks.* Washington,
DC: Author. (NCJ 210798). Retrieved March 17, 2021, from
www.ojp.gov/pdffiles1/nij/210798.pdf

National Institute of Justice. (2008, April). *Electronic crime
scene investigation: A guide for first responders,* (2nd ed).
Washington, DC: Author. (NCJ 219941). Retrieved March 17,
2021, from www.ojp.gov/pdffiles1/nij/219941.pdf

National Institute of Justice. (2020, May). *Digital evidence:
Policies and procedures manual.* Washington, DC: Author.
Retrieved March 25, 2021, from www.ojp.gov/pdffiles1
/nij/254661.pdf

Novak, M., Grier, J., & Gonzales, D. (2019, January).
New approaches to digital evidence acquisition and
analysis. *NIJ Journal,* Issue 280. Retrieved March 17,
2021, from nij.ojp.gov/topics/articles
/new-approaches-digital-evidence-acquisition-and-analysis

Robinson, T. (2020, January 17). Ransomware attack cost New
Orleans $7 million and counting. *SC Magazine.* Retrieved
March 15, 2021, from www.scmagazine.com/home
/security-news/ransomware/ransomware-attack-cost
-new-orleans-7-million-and-counting/

Rowan, T. (2017, February 2). Why are organizations failing to
report cybercrime? *Infosecurity Magazine.* Retrieved March 15,
2021, from www.infosecurity-magazine.com/opinions
/organizations-failing-report/

Shillito, M. R. (2019). Untangling the "dark web": An emerging
technological challenge for the criminal law. *Information &
Communications Technology Law, 28*(2): 186–207. doi:10.1080
/13600834.2019.1623449

Smith, B. (2018, April 3). The CLOUD act is an important step
forward, but now more steps need to follow. Redmond,
WA: Microsoft Corporation. Retrieved March 18, 2021, from
blogs.microsoft.com/on-the-issues/2018/04/03/the-cloud
-act-is-an-important-step-forward-but-now-more-steps
-need-to-follow/

Swinhoe, D. (2021, January 8). The 15 biggest data breaches
of the 21st century. *CSO Digital Magazine.* Needham, MA:
International Data Group. Retrieved March 10, 2021, from
www.csoonline.com/article/2130877/the-biggest-data
-breaches-of-the-21st-century.html

U.S. Department of Homeland Security. (2019). *DHS strategic
plan: Fiscal years 2020–2024.* Washington, DC: Author.
Retrieved March 18, 2021, from www.dhs.gov/sites/default
/files/publications/19_0702_plcy_dhs-strategic-plan
-fy20-24.pdf

U.S. Department of Justice. (2017). *Prosecuting Computer
Crimes.* Scotts Valley, CA: CreateSpace Independent
Publishing Platform.

U.S. Department of Justice. (2019, April). *Promoting public safety, privacy, and the rule of law around the world: The purpose and impact of the CLOUD act*. Washington, DC: Author. Retrieved March 18, 2021, from www.justice.gov /opa/press-release/file/1153446/download

U.S. Secret Service. (2015). *Best practices for seizing electronic evidence: A pocket guide for first responders*, version 4.2. Washington, DC: U.S. Department of Homeland Security, Author. Retrieved March 13, 2021, from www.cwagweb.org/wp-content/uploads/2018/05 /BestPracticesforSeizingElectronicEvidence.pdf

Weimann, G. (2016, June). Terrorist migration to the dark web. *Perspectives on Terrorism, 10*(3): 40–44. Retrieved March 16, 2021, from www.jstor.org/stable/pdf/26297596

Cases Cited

Ashcroft v. Free Speech Coalition, 535 U.S. 234 (2002).

United States v. Hilton, 386 F.3d 13 (1st Cir. 2004).

United States v. Microsoft Corp., 584 U.S. ___ (2018).

United States v. Schaefer, 501 F.3d 1197, 1206–07 (10th Cir. 2007).

United States v. Stanley, 753 F.3d 114 (3d Cir. 2014).

United States v. Sutcliffe, 505 F.3d 944 (9th Cir. 2007).

Van Buren v. United States, 140 S.Ct. 2667 (2020).

Chapter 18
A Dual Threat: Drug-Related Crime and Organized Crime

Chapter Outline

The Threat of Drugs

Seriousness and Extent of the Drug Problem

Legal Definitions

Classification of Controlled Substances

Identification of Controlled Substances

Investigating Illegal Possession or Use of Controlled Substances

Investigating Illegal Sale and Distribution of Controlled Substances

Clandestine Drug Laboratories

Indoor Marijuana Growing Operations

Investigative Aids

Agency Cooperation

Drug Asset Forfeitures

Preventing Problems with Illegal Drugs: Community Partnerships

The National Drug Control Strategy

Organized Crime: An Overview

Applicable Laws against Organized Crime

Major Activities of Organized Crime

The Threat of Specific Organized Crime Groups

Organized Crime and Corruption

The Police Response

Agencies Cooperating in Investigating Organized Crime

Methods to Combat Organized Crime

The Decline of Organized Crime?

Learning Objectives

LO1   Name the act that made it illegal to sell or use certain narcotics and dangerous drugs and the year it was passed.

LO2   Explain when it is illegal to use or sell narcotics or dangerous drugs.

LO3   List the classes of drugs that are regulated by the CSA and provide at least two examples of each group.

LO4   Understand what drugs are most commonly observed on the street, in the possession of users, and seized in drug raids, and what the most frequent drug arrest is.

LO5   Summarize the major legal evidence to seek in prosecuting drug use and possession.

LO6   Identify the major legal evidence in prosecuting drug sale and distribution.

LO7   Discuss the circumstances under which an on-sight arrest can be made for a drug buy.

LO8   Describe the precautions to take in undercover drug buys, including how to avoid a charge of entrapment.

LO9   Identify the agency responsible for providing unified leadership in combating illegal drug activities and what its primary emphasis is.

LO10   Recognize the distinctive characteristics of organized crime.

LO11   List the three activities that can be prosecuted under Title 18 of the U.S. Code, Section 1962, as they relate to organized crime.

LO12   Understand the crimes organized crime is typically involved in.

LO13   Explain what the investigator's primary role is in dealing with the organized crime problem.

Robert Nickelsberg/Getty Images

Introduction

The headline of a Drug Enforcement Administration (DEA) News Bulletin from April 15, 2015, reads: "Joint Investigation Leads to Arrest of Doctor for Selling Assault Weapons & Drugs during Course of Murder-for-Hire Plot." This case, which started as a routine investigation of a New York doctor for the suspected diversion of prescription drugs, led investigators down a sinister trail involving arson, assault weapons, and a murder plot against a rival physician. Search warrants executed at the doctor's home on April 14, 2014, during the fourth month of an investigation that was still ongoing, led to the discovery of a hidden room containing a cache of approximately 100 weapons, including an AR-15 and an M1 Carbine, each with illegal high-capacity magazines. A 77-count indictment was filed against the doctor, and on October 25, 2017, Dr. Anthony J. Moschetto, then 56, pleaded guilty to one count each of

- Criminal Possession of a Weapon in the 1st (a class B violent felony)

- Criminal Sale of a Prescription for a Control (a C felony)

- Arson in the 3rd (a C felony)

- Conspiracy in the 4th (an E felony)

Moschetto was sentenced to five years in prison with five years of post-release supervision. The sentence led to the suspension of his medical license and his DEA-prescribing privileges as well as stripping him of his right to possess any weapons (Drug Enforcement Administration [DEA], 2017). James J. Hunt, the DEA Special Agent in Charge, described Dr. Moschetto as "a new breed of drug trafficker; one who sells blank prescription pads, assault weapons; plots attempted murders, commits arson and distributes diverted prescription pain pills out of his medical office" (DEA, 2015a).

The preceding case illustrates how drug-related crime can inspire other acts of violence including murders, arsons, drive-by shootings, car bombs, and other acts that threaten and terrorize communities across the country. Drug gangs have turned many communities into virtual war zones. Some of these acts are gang reprisals or witness intimidation; others are designed simply to frighten innocent citizens enough to ensure that they refrain from calling the police.

Similarly, organized crime groups have infiltrated some communities to the point that the people looked upon as leaders and role models, or as guardians of the law, have become corrupt themselves. Organized crime is heavily involved in the drug trade, and many drug cartels are structured and operated much like other crime syndicates. Thus, these two investigative challenges are discussed together in this chapter. Keep in mind, however, that the two topics, while overlapping, are also separate. Organized crime is involved in many more activities than just drug trafficking, and drug-related crimes, though sometimes linked to organized crime, are usually committed by other groups and individuals with no mob associations.

Another facet of these two crime problems to be aware of is the response and involvement of different jurisdictional levels. Federal law enforcement has devoted substantial investigative resources to both the illegal drug trade and organized crime. In most cases, however, local law enforcement first detects these problems and opens the cases.

The Threat of Drugs

American history is filled with drug use, including alcohol and tobacco. As the early settlers moved west, one of the first buildings in each frontier town was a saloon. Cocaine use was also common by the 1880s. At the beginning of the twentieth century, cocaine was the drug of choice, said to cure everything from indigestion to toothaches. It was added to flavor soft drinks such as Coca-Cola.

In 1909 a presidential commission reported to President Theodore Roosevelt that cocaine was a hazard, leading to loss of livelihoods and lives. As the public became increasingly aware of the hazards posed by cocaine and other drugs, it pressed for legislation against use of such drugs. This mounting pressure led congressman Francis Harrison to sponsor a bill aimed at regulating and taxing the nonmedical sale and distribution of certain narcotic substances, including opium, cocaine, and their derivatives, which Congress passed in 1914 and President Woodrow Wilson signed into law.

LO1 Name the act that made it illegal to sell or use certain narcotics and dangerous drugs and the year it was passed.

In 1914, the federal government passed the Harrison Narcotics Act, which made the sale or use of certain drugs illegal.

In 1920, every state required its students to learn about narcotics' effects. In 1937, under President Franklin Delano Roosevelt, marijuana became the last drug to be banned. For a quarter of a century, the drug problem lay dormant.

Then came the 1960s, a time of youthful rebellion, of Haight Ashbury and the flower children, a time to protest the Vietnam War. A whole culture had as its theme "tune in, turn on, and drop out"—often through marijuana and lysergic acid diethylamide (LSD). By the 1970s, marijuana had been tried by an estimated 40% of 18- to 21-year-olds and was being used by many soldiers fighting in Vietnam. Many other soldiers turned to heroin. At the same time, an estimated half million Americans began using heroin back home.

The United States became the most drug-pervaded nation in the world, with marijuana leading the way. The 1980s saw a turnaround in drug use, with celebrities advocating, "It's not cool to do drugs" and "Just say no to drugs." At the same time, however, other advertisements suggested that alcohol and smoking are where the "fun is."

Seriousness and Extent of the Drug Problem

In 2019, an estimated 57.2 million Americans age 12 years and older—or one-fifth (20.8%) of the population age 12 and older—had used illicit drugs within the past year (Substance Abuse and Mental Health Services Administration, 2020). Drug addiction and the crime it engenders weigh heavily on American society and pose a formidable challenge for law enforcement. In the United States, more accidental deaths are now caused by drug overdoses than by car accidents (DEA, 2014). According to the National Institute on Drug Abuse (NIDA), the cost of drug abuse in the United States in 2017 was nearly $272 billion, when factoring in crime, health care needs, lost work productivity, and other impacts on society (National Center for Drug Abuse Statistics, n.d.). In 2020, the federal budget for drug control was $35 billion, allocated to five functional areas of drug control: operations, prevention, treatment, interdiction, and law enforcement.

The DEA's annual *National Drug Threat Assessment* reports that Controlled Prescription Drugs (CPDs) remain a prevalent concern within the United States, even as abuse levels have dipped slightly in recent years (DEA, 2021). Misuse of CPDs renders them the second most abused illicit substance after marijuana. In 2019, 16.3 million Americans over the age of 12 reported prescription drug misuse within the past year, a decrease from 18.1 million persons in 2018 (Substance Abuse and Mental Health Services Administration, 2020). Despite this drop, the DEA predicts CPD availability and abuse will most likely persist as significant threats to the United States as CPDs continue to be involved in large numbers of overdose deaths.

Monitoring the Future (MTF), which began in 1975, is an ongoing report series by the University of Michigan's Institute for Social Research that summarizes the findings of annual surveys of American adolescents and adults:

> [T]here tends to be a continuous flow of new drugs onto the scene and of older ones being rediscovered by young people. Many drugs have made a comeback years after they first fell from popularity, often because knowledge among youth of their adverse consequences faded as generational replacement took place. We call this process "generational forgetting." Examples include LSD and methamphetamine, two drugs used widely in the 1960s that made a comeback in the 1990s after their initial popularity faded as a result of extensive media coverage of potential adverse consequences occurring primarily in periods of high use. . . .
>
> The frequent introduction of new drugs (or new forms or new modes of administration of older drugs, as illustrated by crack, crystal methamphetamine, and non-injected heroin) helps keep this nation's drug problem alive. . . .
>
> [I]t may be useful to emphasize that many newer synthetic drugs should be considered dangerous simply because such drugs are made and sold by people totally unconcerned with adverse consequences for their users. Those who manufacture synthetic drugs regularly change

the chemical formulations in order to skirt laws prohibiting their sale, and they make no effort to assess the safety of each new formulation, which may differ dramatically from the safety of previous formulations. Dealers at the distribution level, in an effort to build a reputation for selling powerful drugs, may mix highly potent drugs (e.g., fentanyl) into other drugs (e.g., heroin or other narcotics, marijuana) not attending to the danger that carries for the user. (Johnston et al., 2019, pp. 52–53)

MTF, as it is updated each year, provides a valuable resource regarding the prevalence and frequency of use of many drugs among American youth and adults, as well as historical trends in use, and also presents distinctions among important demographic subgroups in these populations based on gender, college plans, region of the country, population density, parent education, and race/ethnicity. Students are encouraged to go online and access the most recent publications available from www. monitoringthefuture.org.

The MTF authors note: "The most important finding to emerge from the 2018 survey is the dramatic increase in vaping by adolescents" (Johnston et al., 2019, p. 1). Other key findings of the 2018 survey, which involved about 44,500 students in eighth, tenth, and twelfth grades enrolled in 392 secondary schools nationwide, include:

- There was little change in marijuana use compared to previous years.

- Use of most illicit drugs held steady.

- The use of controlled prescription drugs declined, continuing the trend that began in 2010.

- Cigarette smoking continued its long decline in 2018 and is now at or very close to the lowest levels in the history of the survey.

- Alcohol remains the substance most widely used by today's teenagers. Despite recent declines, by the end of high school six out of every ten students (59%) have consumed alcohol (more than just a few sips) at some time in their lives (after a significant 3 percentage point drop in 2018); and about a quarter (24%) have done so by 8th grade. (pp. 1–4)

Legal Definitions

The legal definitions of *narcotics* and *controlled substances* as stated in local, state, and federal laws are lengthy and technical. The laws define the terms that describe the drugs, the various categories, and the agencies responsible for enforcement.

The Controlled Substances Act (CSA), signed into law in 1970 by President Nixon, placed all substances which were in some manner regulated under existing federal law into one of five schedules based on the substance's accepted medical use, potential for abuse, and safety or dependence liability (DEA, 2020a). The five schedules contain the official, common, usual, chemical, and brand names of the drugs. Schedule I drugs are considered the most dangerous, in part because of their high addictive qualities; Schedule V drugs, in contrast, present a very low chance of addiction (see Table 18.1). Under this act, if a drug does not have a potential for abuse, it cannot be controlled. The act also provides a mechanism for substances to be controlled (added to or transferred between schedules) or decontrolled (removed from control).

Laws also establish prohibited acts concerning the controlled substances and assign penalties in proportion to the drug's danger. Basically, these laws state that no person, firm, or corporation may manufacture, sell, give away, barter or deliver, exchange, distribute, or possess these substances with intent to do any of the prohibited acts. Possession of controlled substances is probably the most frequent charge in narcotics arrests. Actual or constructive possession and knowledge by a suspect that a drug was illegal must be shown. If the evidence is not on the person, it must be shown to be under the suspect's control.

> **LO2** Explain when it is illegal to use or sell narcotics or dangerous drugs.
>
> It is illegal to possess or use narcotics or dangerous drugs without a prescription and to sell or distribute them without a license.

Specific laws vary by state. For example, possessing a small amount of marijuana is a felony in some states, a misdemeanor in others, and not a crime at all in dozens of other a few states. Laws also define the type of activity drug traffickers are involved in and can be used to impose criminal sanctions even when the intended act is unsuccessful.

Classification of Controlled Substances

The CSA regulates five classes of drugs:

- Narcotics (heroin, codeine, fentanyl, methadone, meperidine [Demerol], OxyContin, Vicodin)

TABLE 18.1 **Five Federal Schedules of Controlled Substances**

	Abuse Tendency	Accepted Medical Use of Any Kind in the United States	Available by Physician Prescription?	Do Pharmacies Stock/Sell?	Other Comments	Examples
Schedule I	High	None	No	No	There is a lack of accepted safety for use of the drug under medical supervision	Marijuana Heroin Ecstasy LSD GHB
Schedule II	High	Some	Yes	Some do; even with valid prescription, some will not fill Rx	Abuse of the drug may lead to severe psychological or physical dependence	Cocaine Fentanyl Morphine Opium
Schedule III	Low	Yes	Yes	Not all	Abuse of the drug may lead to moderate or low physical dependence or high psychological dependence	Anabolic steroids Codeine Ketamine
Schedule IV	Very low, with low chance of addiction	Yes	Yes	Not all	Abuse of the drug may lead to limited physical dependence or psychological dependence relative to the drugs in Schedule III	Valium Xanax® Rohypnol
Schedule V	Very low, with very low chance of addiction	Yes	No Rx needed	Yes, very commonly, although such sales have become restricted by stores to limited quantities purchased by adults only	Abuse of the drug may lead to limited physical dependence or psychological dependence relative to the drugs in Schedule IV	Cough suppressants with codeine

For a more comprehensive list of drugs and their assigned schedules, refer to 21 U.S.C. Sec. 812 (revised 2020): U.S. Code Title 21—Food and Drugs, Chapter 13—Drug Abuse Prevention and Control, Subchapter I—Control and Enforcement, Part B—Authority to Control; Standards and Schedules.

Adapted from www.law.cornell.edu/uscode/text/21/812 (revised 11/10/2020)

Adapted from www.deadiversion.usdoj.gov/pubs/manuals/(DEA-DC-046)(EO-DEA154)_Pharmacist_Manual.pdf#search=pharmacist%27s%20manual

- Stimulants (cocaine, amphetamines, methamphetamine, khat)

- Depressants (alcohol, barbiturates, tranquilizers, benzodiazepines, GHB, Rohypnol)

- Hallucinogens (LSD, phencyclidine or PCP [angel dust], psilocybin, Ecstasy/MDMA, K2/Spice, Ketamine)

- Anabolic steroids (testosterone, nandrolone, stanozolol, methandienone, boldenone)

LO3 List the classes of drugs that are regulated by the CSA and provide at least two examples of each group.

The main drug classes regulated by the CSA are narcotics, stimulants, depressants, hallucinogens, and anabolic steroids. Controlled prescription drugs (CPDs), marijuana, and designer drugs are also regulated by the CSA and present a challenge to law enforcement. Over-the-counter (OTC) drugs and inhalants, although not regulated under the CSA, are also commonly abused, most often by youth.

Inhalants (hobby model glue, cleaning solvents, lighter fluid, aerosols) and other drugs of concern, such as bath salts, dextromethorphan (DXM), and Salvia are not regulated by the CSA, but their purchase has been restricted by various state laws in an effort to control their use. For example, consumers wishing to purchase products containing inhalants must often show a driver's license, a measure designed to keep minors from buying these products to get high.

Marijuana laws are changing rapidly across the country, and as of March 2021, marijuana was fully legal in 13 states and the District of Columbia, with enactment pending in two other states. Also, as of March 2021, 29 states had decriminalized marijuana use, but the drug remained illegal in eight states and under federal law. Even with legalization and decriminalization becoming more common, police officers in the United States continue to make more arrests for possession of marijuana than for any other drug (Federal Bureau of Investigation [FBI], 2019).

LO4 Understand what drugs are most commonly observed on the street, in the possession of users, and seized in drug raids, and what the most frequent drug arrest is.

The most commonly observed drugs on the street, in possession of users, and seized in drug raids are heroin and prescription opioids such as OxyContin and fentanyl; powder cocaine and crack; methamphetamine; and marijuana. Arrest for possession or use of marijuana is the most frequent drug arrest.

This section will discuss some of the most commonly encountered narcotics, stimulants, depressants, and hallucinogens as well as controlled prescription drugs, marijuana, designer drugs, over-the-counter drugs, and inhalants.

Narcotics

Narcotics, also called opioids, are controlled substances that vary from Schedule I (e.g., heroin) to Schedule V, depending on their medical usefulness, abuse potential, safety, and drug dependence profile. Two of the most problematic narcotics for law enforcement are heroin and fentanyl.

Heroin. Heroin, a commonly abused narcotic, is synthesized from morphine and is as much as 10 times more powerful in its effects. It is physically addictive and relatively inexpensive. Heroin can be injected, smoked, or snorted, with

intravenous injection producing the greatest intensity and most rapid onset of euphoria, usually within seven or eight seconds. Heroin that is sniffed or smoked takes longer to enter the bloodstream (10 to 15 minutes), but these methods have increased in popularity because of the availability of high-purity heroin and the growing fear of sharing needles. According to the Drug Enforcement Agency:

> Heroin availability remains high in the United States, especially in the Great Lakes, Midwest, and Northeast regions, where the largest white powder heroin markets are located. DEA Field Divisions seized 6,951 kilograms of heroin in 2019, a 30% increase from 2018, with the largest amounts of heroin seized in Texas, California, Arizona, and New York. California, Texas and Arizona are all major entry points for heroin sourced from Mexico and also serve as transshipment points for the onward movement of heroin to domestic markets throughout the United States. New York is regarded as the most significant heroin market and distribution hub in the United States. (DEA, 2021, p. 8)

Analysis conducted on retail level heroin seizures by the DEA's Special Testing and Research Lab (STRL) indicates that Mexico-sourced heroin dominates retail heroin markets throughout the United States and that heroin mixed with other controlled substances, mostly fentanyl, is increasingly widespread at the retail level. While retail-level heroin distributors have traditionally mixed or "cut" heroin with adulterants such as caffeine and lidocaine to increase profits, such additives also decreased the purity of their product. Adding fentanyl to heroin allows distributors to greatly increase their profits while maintaining product quality. Overdose data indicates that fentanyl-laced heroin is also more deadly:

> Drug-poisoning data shows that heroin-involved overdose deaths are leveling off as overdose deaths continue to increase related to synthetic opioids other than methadone (SOOTM). . . . [W]hile the rate of overdose deaths involving heroin alone decreased almost 20%, the rate of heroin-involved overdose deaths with fentanyl present increased almost 12%. (DEA, 2021, p. 11)

Fentanyl. Fentanyl, which was first introduced in the 1960s and used as an intravenous anesthetic, is a potent Schedule II synthetic opioid approved by the Food and Drug Administration (FDA) for use as an analgesic (pain relief) and anesthetic. It is approximately 100 times more potent than morphine and 50 times more potent than heroin as an analgesic (DEA, 2020a). Fentanyl can be injected, snorted/sniffed, smoked, taken orally by pill or tablet, and spiked onto blotter paper. Fentanyl patches are abused by removing their gel contents and then injecting or ingesting these contents.

Fentanyl produces effects such as relaxation, euphoria, pain relief, sedation, confusion, drowsiness, dizziness, nausea, vomiting, urinary retention, pupillary constriction, and respiratory depression. A fentanyl overdose may result in stupor, changes in pupillary size, cold and clammy skin, cyanosis, coma, and respiratory failure leading to death. The presence of a triad of symptoms such as coma, pinpoint pupils, and respiratory depression are strongly suggestive of opioid poisoning (DEA, 2020a).

Although pharmaceutical-grade fentanyl is FDA approved and acquired through a doctor's prescription, the Centers for Disease Control and Prevention (CDC) notes that most of the recent cases of fentanyl-related overdose and death have been linked to illegally made fentanyl and fentanyl analogs sold through the illegal drug market. Data from the CDC indicates that deaths from illicitly manufactured fentanyl are increasing and that overdose deaths involving synthetic opioids other than methadone, which includes fentanyl and fentanyl analogs, were nearly 12 times higher in 2019 than in 2013 (Mattson et al., 2021). More than 36,000 people died from overdoses involving synthetic opioids in 2019, and as this text goes to press, preliminary data suggests an acceleration of overdose deaths during the COVID-19 pandemic (Centers for Disease Control and Prevention, 2020).

Stimulants

Stimulants, sometimes called *uppers*, are a class of drugs that speed up, or stimulate, the body's systems. Stimulants can be pills or capsules that are swallowed. Smoking, snorting, or injecting stimulants produces a sudden sensation known as a "rush" or a "flash." Stimulants commonly encountered by law enforcement are powder cocaine, crack, methamphetamine, and khat.

Powder Cocaine and Crack.
Cocaine and its derivative, crack, are major problems for law enforcement officers, with crack consistently being ranked as the drug with the most serious consequences. **Crack**, also called *rock* or *crack rock*, is produced by mixing cocaine with baking soda and water, heating the solution in a pan, and then drying and splitting the substance into pellet-size bits or chunks. Crack is generally less expensive than powder cocaine.

Crack is most often smoked in a glass pipe and has ten times the impact of cocaine. It is described as "cocaine intensified or amplified" in its effects on the human body. The intense high produced by crack is usually followed by a severe depression, or "crash," and a deep craving for more of the drug. It is more addictive than cocaine, at a much earlier stage of use, sometimes after the first use. Some users "space-base" the drug; that is, they lace it with PCP or other drugs. PCP causes out-of-control behavior, an added hazard to the already dangerous effects of crack itself. Users may also "speedball" the drug, mixing cocaine with an opiate such as heroin.

The vast majority (90%) of cocaine powder reaching the United States comes from Colombia and is smuggled across the U.S.–Mexico border. A smaller amount comes through the Caribbean corridor (DEA, 2020a).

Concern is rising over indications that Colombian cocaine producers are increasing their use of a harmful cutting agent, levamisole, a pharmaceutical compound typically used to deworm livestock, and several sources report that the majority of the cocaine supply in the United States is now contaminated with levamisole (Lee, Ladizinski, & Federman, 2012). The danger of this additive is its apparent link to skin necrosis, or the dying of flesh due to impaired blood flow to skin, particularly in people with compromised immune systems. Levamisole has also been detected in other illicit substances, including heroin.

Methamphetamine.
Methamphetamine (meth) is now firmly entrenched as a major U.S. drug problem that is only getting bigger. Meth is a highly addictive synthetic stimulant that looks like cocaine but is made from toxic chemicals, such as drain cleaner, paint thinner, and other easily obtained OTC products, including cold medications containing pseudoephedrine.

Concocting **crank**, a street name for methamphetamine, is relatively simple and inexpensive. Typical meth users are high school and college students and working-class white men and women. A **tweaker** is a methamphetamine addict; a meth **cook** is someone who produces the drug.

The most common form is powder meth, which is usually injected or snorted but can also be ingested orally or smoked. Other forms include ice meth—which resembles shards of ice, is usually smoked, and is highly pure and very addictive—and methamphetamine tablets, commonly the size of a pencil eraser, which are typically ingested orally or smoked, but can also be crushed and snorted or mixed with water and injected.

Many sources report the particularly devastating effect meth is having on America's rural communities, where much of the production and abuse occurs and where law enforcement and public health officials lack adequate resources to effectively address the growing problems.

Because of the growing popularity of meth, the proliferation of extremely dangerous clandestine labs and the recognition that one of the main ingredients in the production of meth is pseudoephedrine, a powerful stimulant found in many OTC decongestant and allergy medications as well as in energy-boosting pills, the U.S. Congress passed the Combat Methamphetamine Epidemic Act of 2005 (aka CMEA) as an amendment to the renewal of the USA PATRIOT Act. President George W. Bush signed the amendment into law on March 9, 2006, amending 21 U.S.C. § 830 regarding the sale of products containing pseudoephedrine. The law encompasses purchasing restrictions and standards along with standards for storage, employee training, and record keeping.

Forty-five states have additional laws and restrictions regarding the sale and regulation of pseudoephedrine. Private U.S.-based companies such as Target, CVS, Walgreens, and Winn-Dixie have created their own company policies in addition to mandated laws on the sale of pseudoephedrine as well.

A chemical additive, GloTell™, can identify those who handle anhydrous ammonia fertilizer, a common ingredient in producing methamphetamine. GloTell leaves bright pink stains on the skin and clothes of anyone who comes in contact with the fertilizer and is detectable with ultraviolet light as long as 72 hours after exposure. The additive also impedes the production process of meth by making the drug very difficult to dry.

Khat. Khat (pronounced "cot"), a natural narcotic whose primary psychoactive ingredients are chemically similar to amphetamines, is a relative newcomer to the U.S. drug scene but is well known in eastern African and southern Middle Eastern countries, where its use is culturally acceptable and a part of many traditional social situations (DEA, 2020). The drug is harvested from the leaves of the khat tree. Users either chew the leaves or smoke the powder obtained from dried leaves. Cathinone, one of the main chemicals in khat, is a Schedule I narcotic in the United States and is regulated by law. The rising use of khat in the United States appears to coincide with the increased numbers of immigrants coming from eastern African and Middle Eastern countries where the substance is legal, and many immigrants may be unaware of khat's illegal status in this country.

Depressants

Depressants, also called *downers*, are used therapeutically to induce sleep, relieve anxiety and muscle spasms, and prevent seizures. Depressants come in the form of pills, syrups, and injectable liquids. Most depressants are controlled substances that range from Schedule I to Schedule IV under the CSA, depending on their risk for abuse and whether they currently have an accepted medical use (DEA, 2020a). Two depressants commonly included in a category referred to as "club drugs" are GHB and Rohypnol.

GHB. GHB, short for gamma-hydroxybutyric acid, is a Schedule I controlled substance, meaning that it has a high potential for abuse, no currently accepted medical use in treatment in the United States, and a lack of accepted safety for use under medical supervision. FDA-approved GHB products, however, are Schedule III substances under the CSA (DEA, 2020a). GHB is colorless and odorless and can come as a slightly salty liquid or white powder. It is taken orally and costs $5 to $25 per dose (capful or ounce). According to the DEA:

> GHB and its analogues are . . . misused for their ability to increase libido, suggestibility, passivity, and to cause amnesia (no memory of events while under the influence of the substance)—traits that make victims vulnerable to sexual assault and other criminal acts. GHB misuse became popular among teens and young adults at dance clubs and "raves" in the 1990s and gained notoriety as a date rape drug. GHB is taken alone or in combination with other drugs, such as alcohol (primarily), other depressants, stimulants, hallucinogens, and marijuana. (2020a, p. 73)

Investigating cases involving GHB may be very challenging, and investigators have started referring to it as a "stealth drug" because of the difficulty in detecting its use. Because GHB causes unconsciousness, victims may be unable to provide much useful information to investigators regarding any attack that may have occurred following ingestion of the drug.

Rohypnol. A second club drug that has made news in the past is the "date-rape" drug Rohypnol, also known as "roofies." Available by prescription outside the United States, Rohypnol is a central nervous system depressant 10 times more potent than Valium. The drug by itself can produce extreme lethargy and significant reduction in the brain's recall ability. Combined with alcohol, it causes memory loss, blackouts, and disinhibition. Because Rohypnol was originally colorless, odorless, and tasteless, it became used as a way to facilitate sexual assault, hence the tag "date-rape drug." Once it was learned that Rohypnol was being slipped into unwary victims' drinks as an aid for committing sexual assault, the manufacturer of the drug reformulated it to increase its detectability in clear fluid and to retard its dissolution rate.

Hallucinogens

Hallucinogens are among the oldest known group of drugs and are used for their ability to alter human perception and mood. Hallucinogens come in a variety of forms and are typically taken orally or smoked. Many hallucinogens are Schedule I under the CSA, and three of the most commonly abused hallucinogens are Ecstasy/MDMA, ketamine, and LSD.

Ecstasy. 3,4-Methylenedioxymethylamphetamine (**MDMA**), known more commonly as **Ecstasy**, XTC, or Molly, is a powerful stimulant derivative of amphetamine, or speed. MDMA, which is a Schedule I drug under the CSA, is considered a moderate threat in the United States, with reported levels of availability and abuse trending downward. Mixing drugs such as MDMA with prescription drugs has also gained popularity in the club scene. For example, consuming both Ecstasy and Viagra® is known as "Sextacy," which has been reported to produce a unique high that combines the effects of both drugs. Increased interdiction efforts and the dismantling of large MDMA trafficking organizations are credited as the major reasons for decreased use and availability.

Ketamine. A prescription general anesthetic primarily marketed for veterinary use, ketamine or "special K," is sold as both a liquid and a powder. In humans, it causes some physical effects similar to PCP and visual or hallucinogenic effects similar to LSD. At low dosage, ketamine impairs attention, learning ability, and memory. At higher doses, it can produce delirium, impaired motor function, high blood pressure, depression, and potentially fatal respiratory problems. Ketamine may also cause agitation, unconsciousness, and amnesia (DEA, 2020a). Its amnesiac effects have reportedly led to its use as a date-rape drug.

LSD. LSD (lysergic acid diethylamide), a Schedule I controlled substance with severe penalties for possession and use, is a potent hallucinogen derived from lysergic acid, a fungus that grows on rye and other grains. Often referred to as *acid* on the club scene, it is clandestinely manufactured in relatively professional laboratory settings because some chemistry background and a working knowledge of laboratory control are generally necessary to safely and successfully synthesize the drug. The initial synthesis produces a crystalline powder, which is then reduced to a liquid and placed onto blotting paper. LSD can also be sold in tablet or capsule form.

This patent-pending "Smart Straw" was invented by three young women in Florida as a way to fight date rape. The common-looking straw contains a test strip that turns blue when placed into a drink containing any of the more popular date-rape drugs, including GHB, Rohypnol, and ketamine.

C. M. Guerrero/Miami Herald

Controlled Prescription Drugs

Abuse of controlled prescription drugs (CPDs) has become a nationwide epidemic. Abuse or misuse of CPDs is defined as using a medication in a manner or dose other than as prescribed by a doctor; taking someone else's prescription, even if for a legitimate medical complaint such as pain; or taking a medication to feel euphoria (i.e., to get high). The term *nonmedical use* of prescription drugs also refers to these categories of misuse, although misuse of over-the-counter (OTC) drugs is not included (National Institute on Drug Abuse [NIDA], 2020). The three classes of CPDs most commonly misused are:

- Opioids, usually pain relievers (e.g., Vicodin, Percodan, Percocet, OxyContin, and generics such as oxycodone and hydrocone)

- Tranquilizers and depressants (e.g., Xanax® and Valium)

■ Stimulants, such as drugs used to treat ADHD (e.g., Ritalin, Adderall) or achieve weight loss (e.g., orlistat, phentermine, Desoxyn®)

The National Survey on Drug Use and Health (NSDUH) indicated that illegitimate use of CPDs rendered them the second most abused illicit substance after marijuana with 20.5 million Americans over the age of 12 reporting prescription drug misuse within the past year (Substance Abuse and Mental Health Services Administration, 2020). This number includes 9.7 million who misused prescription pain relievers, 5.9 million who misused prescription tranquilizers or sedatives, and 4.9 million who misused stimulants.

Data from the Drug Abuse Warning Network (DAWN) reveals that medical emergencies related to nonmedical use of pharmaceuticals increased 132% in the period from 2004 to 2011 (Substance Abuse and Mental Health Services Administration, 2011). CDC data show that drug overdose deaths involving prescription opioids rose from 3,442 in 1999 to a peak of 17,029 in 2017, and then began a downward trend, reaching 14,139 in 2019 (NIDA, 2021). This significant increase in opioid overdoses led to the expanded access to and use of naloxone to reverse the effects of opioid overdoses and prevent death when administered in time. The federal government now recommends that naloxone be readily available as an over-the-counter formula in most pharmacies, and as of July 2020, it was available without a prescription in 43 states (Jordan & Morrisonponce, 2020).

Diversion of lawfully made CPDs from the legitimate market is the most common way people obtain such drugs for illegitimate use. In 2019, among people aged 12 or older who misused prescription pain relievers in the past year, more than half (50.8%) obtained the pain relievers the last time from a friend or relative in some way (i.e., being given them, buying them, or taking them without asking). Specifically, 37.0% got them from a friend or relative for free, 9.2% bought them from a friend or relative, and 4.6% took their last pain reliever from a friend or relative without asking. More than one third (37.5%) of people who misused pain relievers in the past year obtained the medication the last time through prescription(s) or stole pain relievers from a health care provider, and about 1 in 15 people (6.2%) who misused pain relievers in the past year bought the last pain reliever they misused from a drug dealer or other stranger (Substance Abuse and Mental Health Services Administration, 2020).

Other means of obtaining CPDs are by faking, forging, or altering a prescription; obtaining bogus prescriptions from criminal medical practitioners; or buying drugs diverted from health care facilities by personnel. In 2019, incidents of employee theft (or suspected employee theft) increased in 48 states, Puerto Rico, and the District of Columbia (DEA, 2021).

According to DEA's Theft Loss Reporting Database, the total number of prescription drug robberies, which resulted in the loss of a variety of prescription medications, decreased over 45% in 2019 from the high of 884 armed robberies in 2017. However, events in specific jurisdictions may lead to localized surges in pharmacy thefts and robberies. For example, DEA Field Divisions indicated an uptick in pharmacy thefts, burglaries, and/or robberies during the protests that occurred in late May through June 2020. Looters took advantage of the civil unrest during the summer of 2020 to target local pharmacies and are believed to have stolen various controlled prescription drugs (DEA, 2021).

The rising cost of prescription drugs has also enticed senior citizens to join in the diversion and sell their prescriptions. Prescription drugs are also obtained through a practice called *doctor shopping*. A doctor shopper will visit multiple health care providers as a "new patient" or "visiting from out of town" and will exaggerate or feign medical problems to obtain prescriptive medications.

Myth Prescription drugs are safer to use than illegal drugs.

Fact Prescription drugs, if taken improperly, can be just as dangerous as illegal drugs.

Rogue pain management clinics, known as **pill mills**, staffed by unethical "doctors," are another source of illicit pharmaceuticals. According to the DEA, "Pill mill operations are primarily cash-based businesses and are run by operators who often don't see patients or perform any type of physical exam. It is not uncommon to see lines of people waiting to get into these pill mills" (2014, p. 6). Some have described pill mills as a form of occupational offending in which "physicians prescribe opioids for nonexistent or exaggerated pain, often with profit as a motivation, thus making such prescribing a criminal enterprise" (Moreto, Gau, & Brooke, 2020).

To address the concerning rises in opioid-related deaths, states started passing pill mill laws and law enforcement began focusing considerable efforts and resources toward cracking down on these illegal operations. In January 2020, 75-year-old Egisto Salerno, a medical doctor practicing in San Diego, pleaded guilty to opioid distribution in federal court, admitting that between November 2014 and February 2018, he signed bogus prescriptions for multiple deceased or incarcerated patients in a scheme that illegally distributed more than 78,000 hydrocodone pills (DEA, 2020b). Salerno was sentenced to 18 months in prison.

Doctors who are part of a legitimate medical practice have also been found to be running a side business dealing in prescription fraud. Frequently involved in prescription fraud are narcotics, stimulants, barbiturates, benzodiazepines, tranquilizers, and other psychoactive substances manufactured for use in legitimate medical treatment. Law enforcement officers spend a significant amount of time investigating cases involving prescription fraud, many of which also involve insurance, Medicare, or Medicaid fraud.

Marijuana

Marijuana is variously classified as a

- **Narcotic**, a drug that is physically and psychologically addicting; examples include heroin, morphine, codeine, and cocaine

- **Depressant**, a drug that reduces restlessness and emotional tension and induces sleep; most common are the barbiturates

- **Hallucinogen**, a drug that induces visions, delusions, or perceptual distortions of reality

Street names include *grass, pot, dope, joint, herb, Mary Jane, mj, reefer*, and *weed*. Marijuana is made from a plant in the genus *Cannabis* and is the most widely available and most commonly used illicit drug in the United States, with the majority of DEA Field Divisions indicating that, in 2019, marijuana availability was high in their respective areas, meaning the drug was easily obtained at any time (DEA, 2021). The NSDUH indicates that an average of 9,500 people became new marijuana users each day during 2019 (Substance Abuse and Mental Health Services Administration, 2020). The federal Marihuana [sic] Tax Act of 1937 outlawed its use.

Marijuana is the most controversial of the illicit drugs, and a wide spectrum of opinion exists regarding its harmfulness. Some feel it should be legalized; others think it is a very dangerous drug. Many opponents of legalizing marijuana contend that it is a "gateway" drug, exposing new and curious experimenters to a fairly benign drug that will eventually lead them to explore other, "harder" chemical substances. Whether marijuana users progress to hard narcotics or other

Myth Marijuana is not addictive.

Fact Contrary to common belief, marijuana can be addictive. Severe substance use disorders are also known as *addiction*. Research suggests that between 9% and 30% of those who use marijuana may develop some degree of marijuana use disorder and that people who begin using marijuana before age 18 are four to seven times more likely than adults to develop a marijuana use disorder (NIDA, 2019).

controlled substances has not been thoroughly researched. Most hard-narcotics users once used marijuana, but how many marijuana users proceed to hard drugs is unknown.

In the never-ending quest to enhance their high, some users lace marijuana with other substances, including PCP, cocaine, and even embalming fluid, or formaldehyde, stolen from funeral homes or university labs. Marijuana laced with PCP or embalming fluid, called "wet" marijuana, will likely cause hallucinations, euphoria, and, sometimes, panic or violence.

According to the DEA, three types of marijuana markets currently operate in the United States: illicit markets, state-approved medical marijuana markets, and state-approved personal use/recreational markets. While these markets operate differently, drug traffickers obtain supplies from all three markets:

Both state-licensed and illicit domestic marijuana production continue to increase and diversify. Expanding marijuana production, specifically in states that have legalized the drug, has led to saturated markets. Meanwhile, black market marijuana production continues to grow in California, Colorado, Oregon, Washington, and other states that have legalized marijuana, creating an overall decline in prices for illicit marijuana as well. This further incentivizes drug trafficking organizations operating large-scale grow sites in these states to sell to customers in markets throughout the Midwest and East Coast, where marijuana commands a higher price. Marijuana is also shipped via mail and express consignment shipping services from the United States mainland to the U.S. Virgin Islands (USVI). In the USVI, marijuana users generally desire marijuana with a higher THC and often obtain it from areas in the United States where medical and/or recreational marijuana is legal.

As domestic production and availability continue to rise, the THC potency of marijuana and marijuana concentrate products increases as well. Most states that have legalized marijuana have not placed limits on THC potency, with the exception of those states with cannabidiol (CBD)-only provisions. (DEA, 2021, p. 51)

Domestic cultivation of marijuana appears to be on an upward trend, but Mexican commercial-grade marijuana remains the most common variety in the United States. An increasing amount of "BC Bud," marijuana from British Columbia, is also being found; this variety generally has a higher concentration of the active substance tetrahydrocannabinol (THC), and thus greater potency. The DEA notes:

Large quantities of foreign-produced marijuana are smuggled into the United States via POVs [privately owned vehicles], commercial vehicles, buses, rail systems, subterranean tunnels, small boats, unmanned aerial vehicles/drones, and catapults. Backpackers also walk loads of marijuana across the SWB [Southwest Border]. Once marijuana has been smuggled into the United States, it is often stored in warehouses along the border prior to distribution throughout the United States. (2021, p. 58)

On March 19, 2020, federal agents seized more than 4,000 pounds of illicit drugs from the U.S. exit point of a 2,000-foot-long cross-border tunnel running from a warehouse in Tijuana, Mexico, to another warehouse in a San Diego suburb. The seizure included, 3,000 pounds of marijuana, 1,300 pounds of cocaine, 86 pounds of methamphetamine, 17 pounds of heroin, and more than 2 pounds of fentanyl, with a combined estimated street value of $29.6 million. The DEA Special Agent in Charge said, "These tunnels show the determination of drug trafficking organizations to subvert our border controls and smuggle deadly drugs into our community" (U.S. Immigration and Customs Enforcement, 2020).

Large quantities of marijuana are being grown hydroponically indoors, often in abandoned barns or other buildings in rural areas. Such controlled cultivation increases marijuana potency by 3 to 10 times, which increases its value and thus the growers' profits. Known as **sinsemilla**, homegrown marijuana has become extremely popular, and indoor marijuana-growing operations have proliferated, domestically and abroad.

Designer Drugs

Designer drugs, also called *New Psychoactive Substances* (NPSs), are a diverse group of illicitly synthesized drugs manufactured to mimic the pharmacological effects of certain controlled substances but with chemical structures that differ enough so as to not fall under regulation by the CSA. Designer drugs are created by adding to or omitting something from an existing drug. In many instances, the primary drug is not illegal. The illicit drugs are called **analogs** of the drug from which they are created—for example, meperidine analog or mescaline analog. These drugs may cause the muscles to stiffen and give the appearance of someone suffering from Parkinson's disease. Because designer drugs are difficult for amateurs to manufacture, they are high-profit drugs for dealers. Because of their complex natures, these drugs must be submitted to a laboratory for analysis.

According to the DEA, the NPS market is typified by new substances constantly being created and marketed to users, most often as "legal" alternatives to controlled substances. Synthetic cathinones (e.g., bath salts) and synthetic cannabinoids (e.g., K2/Spice) are the most common classes of NPSs available and abused in the United States, although many other classes of NPSs, including synthetic opioids, are responsible for overdoses across the country, thus posing a significant risk to communities (DEA, 2021).

Bath Salts. Synthetic cathinones are central nervous system stimulants designed to mimic effects similar to those produced by cocaine, methamphetamine, and MDMA. These synthetic stimulants are often referred to as *bath salts* and are usually ingested by sniffing/snorting, but they can also be taken orally, smoked, or put into a solution and injected into veins. They can be purchased online or in businesses such as smoke shops, convenience stores, adult bookstores, and gas stations. Bath salts are often marketed as "research chemicals," "plant food," "glass cleaner," and labeled "not for human consumption," in order to circumvent application of the Controlled Substance Analogue Enforcement Act and to conceal the true nature of the product as a psychoactive/stimulant substance for abuse (DEA, 2020a).

K2/Spice. A type of synthetic cannabinoid cropping up across the country is K2 or Spice, a laboratory created compound that is chemically similar to THC, the psychoactive ingredient in marijuana. K2 is often marketed as "herbal incense," "potpourri," or "fake weed" and, until recently, was legal to buy and commonly sold at many tobacco and drug paraphernalia storefronts (head shops). When the MTF study began surveying students about synthetic marijuana in 2012, it found that synthetic marijuana was the second most widely used class of illicit drug after marijuana itself among twelfth graders at that time, with 11.4% of high school seniors reporting its use. However, by 2018, the annual prevalence of synthetic marijuana use among twelfth graders was down to 1.6%, reflecting a dramatic drop in use since 2012 (Johnston et al., 2019). While it is good news that the use of Spice among teenagers has declined, the drug remains potentially deadly. Single hits of Spice have been linked to cases of irreversible brain damage and death in some users, leading to increased pressure for legislation to tighten up regulation of these substances.

In early 2011, amid rising concern over the risks posed by such uncontrolled substances, the DEA exercised its emergency scheduling authority by placing this synthetic drug, among others, into Schedule I of the CSA as a necessary measure to protect the public safety. (A provision of the Controlled Substance Analogue Enforcement Act of 1986 allows many synthetic drugs to be treated as controlled substances if they are proven to be chemically and/or pharmacologically similar to a Schedule I or Schedule II controlled substance.) This temporary "fix" concerning Spice was made permanent when President Barack Obama signed into law the Synthetic Drug Abuse Prevention Act as part of the FDA Safety and Innovation Act of 2012, placing 26 types of synthetic cannabinoids and cathinones (aka bath salts) into Schedule I of the CSA. Classification of K2/Spice as a Schedule I substance allows it to be subject to the same criminal, civil, and administrative penalties, sanctions, and regulatory controls that are imposed on the manufacture, distribution, possession, importation, and exportation of other Schedule I drugs such as heroin, Ecstasy, and GHB.

Since 2011, all 50 states have banned synthetic cannabinoids and cathinones, with the majority doing so via legislation. In 2013, three more synthetic ingredients were added via the DEA's emergency scheduling authority, and with illegal drug manufacturers constantly retooling their recipes to evade the law, it seems likely that more synthetic substances will become subject to DEA scheduling in the future. Even with such bans, NPSs continue to pose a nationwide threat, even showing up behind bars. One study reports that between March 2017 and November 2018, 54 prisoners in Florida were found to have fatally overdosed on synthetic cannabinoids (Hvozdovich, Chronister, Logan, & Goldberger, 2020). In February 2020, the DEA received a package seized from the Terre Haute federal prison. Inside the package were two legal sized envelopes containing papers, some of which appeared to have been soaked in a solution containing synthetic cannabinoids. The seizure was related to a drug trafficking organization (DTO) suspected of trafficking NPSs into at least 13 different federal prisons using a network of inmates (DEA, 2021).

Project Synergy, put into action on December 1, 2012, was a coordinated effort to address the global synthetic drug problem and brought together members of the DEA's Special Operations Division, the DEA's Office of Diversion Control, U.S. Customs and Border Protection, U.S. Immigration and Customs Enforcement (ICE), Homeland Security Investigations (HSI), the Federal Bureau of Investigation (FBI), the IRS, and state and local law enforcement, as well as law enforcement in Australia, Barbados, Canada, and Panama (DEA, 2013). During the course of the operation, more than 227 arrests were made and 416 search warrants served in 35 states, 49 cities, and 5 countries. Seizures included more than $51 million in cash and assets; 9,445 kilograms of individually packaged, ready-to-sell synthetic drugs; 299 kilograms of cathinone drugs (the falsely labeled "bath salts"); 1,252 kilograms of cannabinoid drugs (used to make the so-called fake pot or herbal incense products); and 783 kilograms of treated plant material. Emphasizing the dangerous and destructive nature of designer drugs, DEA Administrator Michele M. Leonhart stated, "DEA has been at the forefront of the battle against this trend and is targeting these new and emerging drugs with every scientific, legislative, and investigative tool at our disposal" (DEA, 2013).

A later phase of this operation—Project Synergy III—resulted in 151 arrests in 16 states following a 15-month investigation targeting the synthetic designer drug industry, including wholesalers, money launderers, and other criminal facilitators (DEA, 2015b). Seizures included more than $15 million in cash and other assets; 316 kilograms of synthetic cathinones; 3,058 kilograms of synthetic cannabinoids; 98 kilograms of treated plant material; and 39 weapons. In addition, Project Synergy III revealed the continued flow of millions of dollars in U.S. synthetic drug proceeds to countries of concern in the Middle East.

Over-the-Counter (OTC) Drugs

Some teens are turning to legal **OTC drugs** for their highs, mistakenly assuming that if something is legal and readily available, it can't be dangerous, or at least not deadly. Youths have their own language to describe the methods used to get these "legal highs." Drinking bottles of cough syrup, such as Robitussin® DM, to get high is called **robotripping. Skittling,** so named because the pills resemble small, red pieces of Skittles candy, is ingesting high doses of Coricidin® Cough and Cold ("Triple C") tablets. Perhaps the riskiest and most hazardous practice of all is **pharming**—rifling through the family medicine cabinet for pills, both OTC and prescription, combining everything in a bowl, scooping out and ingesting a handful, and waiting to see what happens. When groups of youth get together and combine their respective medicinal booty, it is called a *pharm party*.

OTC drugs taken in excessive quantities for their psychoactive effects fall into three general categories: uppers, downers, and all-arounders. The most popular upper is pseudoephedrine, a main ingredient in nasal decongestants such as Sudafed®. Benadryl® Allergy formula is the top downer choice. The biggest all-arounder is dextromethorphan, also called "DXM" or "Dex," a primary ingredient in cough and cold medicines. Depending on the dose, DXM can have effects similar to marijuana or Ecstasy. In moderate to high doses, its out-of-body effects are similar to those of ketamine or PCP (DEA, 2020a). DXM, often purchased over the Internet, has been linked to numerous overdose deaths.

Because these drugs are legal, law enforcement requires a more proactive approach to the problem, such as educating youths and their parents and networking with professional organizations such as the American Pharmacists Association, public health departments, and school administrations. In the case of pseudoephedrine, one of the ingredients used to make methamphetamine, products containing this drug are no longer considered OTC but are now sold "behind the counter." In the handful of states requiring a prescription for medication containing pseudoephedrine, limits are placed on how much one person can purchase each month (DEA, 2020a).

Inhalants

Although many drugs have shown steady or declining numbers of users during the past few years, inhalant use has increased. More than 1,000 household and commercial products can be inhaled to produce a high: adhesives, aerosols, anesthetics, cleaning agents, gases, and solvents. Methods used to inhale include sniffing or snorting the inhalant directly from the container, *huffing* the chemical from a saturated piece of cloth held firmly to the nose and mouth, and *bagging* the inhalant by spraying or pouring it into a plastic or paper bag and holding the opening over the nose and mouth. This last method is often used with metallic spray paint.

Symptoms of long-term inhalant abuse include weight loss, muscle weakness, disorientation, inattentiveness, lack of coordination, irritability, depression, and damage to the nervous system and other organs. Many of the effects from prolonged abuse are irreversible. Prolonged sniffing of the highly concentrated chemicals in solvents or aerosol sprays can induce irregular and rapid heart rhythms and lead to heart failure and death within minutes.

There is a common link between inhalant use and problems in school, such as failing grades, chronic absences, and general apathy. Other signs of inhalant use are paint or stains on the body or clothing; spots or sores around the mouth; red or runny eyes or nose; a chemical breath odor; drunk, dazed, or dizzy appearance; nausea; loss of appetite; anxiety; excitability; and irritability (DEA, 2020a).

Because inhalant intoxication lasts only a few minutes, users try to prolong the high by continuing to inhale repeatedly over the course of several hours, which is a very dangerous practice. "Sudden sniffing death" can result from a single session of inhalant use by an otherwise healthy young person. Sudden sniffing death is particularly associated with the abuse of butane, propane, and chemicals in aerosols. Inhalant abuse can also cause death by asphyxiation from repeated inhalations, which lead to high concentrations of inhaled fumes displacing the available oxygen in the lungs.

Club Drugs

Club drugs are those drugs commonly found at **raves**, dance parties that feature fast-paced, repetitive electronic music and light shows. Rave culture also uses a range of licit and illicit drugs. Although tobacco and alcohol are the most common substances found at the club scene, other substances such as Ecstasy, Rohypnol, GHB, and LSD have gained popularity with young people. Methamphetamine has also been increasingly used at raves.

Table 18.2 summarizes the various narcotics and dangerous drugs. Pay special attention to each drug's effects. This information is important in investigating the sale and use of drugs.

Identification of Controlled Substances

The sale of prescription drugs, the fastest-growing category of drugs being abused, has skyrocketed since 1990. Consequently, a major challenge for law enforcement officers is to recognize and identify drugs found in a suspect's possession. Because of the countless different types, colors, sizes, trade names, and strengths of commercial drugs, many officers rely on a pharmaceutical reference book, the *Prescribers' Digital Reference*, used widely by health care providers and available for free online. Formerly published as a hardcopy text titled the *Physicians' Desk Reference* (PDR), this electronic resource is the basis for *mobile* PDR® software apps installed on handheld devices. These portable tools provide instant access to concise monographs about thousands of commonly prescribed drugs.

A reference considered by many in law enforcement to be easier and faster to use than the PDR is the *Drug Identification Bible*. The revised, expanded 2020/2021 edition contains more than 5,600 full-color actual-size photos of prescription drugs scheduled by the DEA; tablet and capsule imprints for more than 19,800 prescription and OTC drugs; hundreds of photos of drug packaging and paraphernalia; sources, methods of use, purity levels and street prices for all major illicit drugs; and updated street slang to help officers understand the language of the drug culture. For example, "A" is a street name for LSD. "Abe" means $5 worth of a drug.

Web-based pill identifiers such as those provided on drugs.com or rxlist.com are commonly used by patrol officers in the field because of their ease of use and accessibility. These resources can be accessed on the squad car mobile data terminal (MDT) through a wireless Internet connection to quickly identify pills encountered out in the field.

In the absence of a printed field guide or reference book, street drugs can be identified with a narcotic field-test kit. These kits typically use a chemical-based color test to presumptively identify narcotics. Such colorimetric assays, or "spot tests," are fast, simple to use, portable, and affordable, providing timely answers to law enforcement officers, investigators, or crime scene analysts in the field (Symonsbergen, Kangas, Perez, & Holmes, 2018). Several brands of self-contained, single-use test kits are available that reduce the likelihood of user error and require very small samples.

TABLE 18.2 Summary of Controlled Substances

Drug	Trade or Other Names	Usual Methods of Administration	Possible Effects	Effects of Overdose	Withdrawal Syndrome
Narcotics					
Codeine	Empirin Compound with Codeine, Robitussin A-C, Tylenol with Codeine	Oral, injected	Euphoria, drowsiness, respiratory depression, constricted pupils, nausea	Slow and shallow breathing, clammy skin, convulsions, coma, possible death	Watery eyes, runny nose, yawning, loss of appetite, irritability, tremors, panic, chills and sweating, cramps, nausea
Fentanyl	Abstral, Actiq, Duragesic, Fentora, Lazanda, Subsys; Apache, China Girl, Dance Fever, Friend, Goodfellas, He-Man, Jackpot, King Ivory, Murder 8, Tango & Cash	Oral, injected, snorted/sniffed, smoked			
Heroin	Diacetylmorphine; Big H, Black Tar, Hell Dust, Horse, Smack, Thunder	Injected, sniffed, smoked			
Hydromorphone	Dilaudid	Oral, injected			
Meperidine (pethidine)	Demerol, Mepergan	Oral, injected			
Methadone	Dolophine, Methadone, Methadose	Oral, injected			
Morphine	Morphine, Pectoral Syrup	Oral, smoked, injected			
Opium	Dover's Powder, Paregoric, Parepectolin	Oral, smoked			
Other narcotics	Darvon, LAAM, Leritine, Lomotil*, Numorphan, Percodan, Talwin, Tussionex,	Oral, injected			

(*Continued*)

TABLE 18.2 *(Continued)*

Drug	Trade or Other Names	Usual Methods of Administration	Possible Effects	Effects of Overdose	Withdrawal Syndrome
Stimulants					
Amphetamines	Biphetamine, Delcobese, Desoxyn, Dexedrine, Mediatric	Oral, injected	Increased alertness, excitation, euphoria, increased pulse rate and blood pressure, insomnia, loss of appetite	Agitation, increase in body temperature, hallucinations, convulsions, possible death	Apathy, long periods of sleep, irritability, depression, disorientation
Cocaine*	Coke, Flake, Snow	Sniffed, smoked, injected			
Khat	Abyssinian Tea, African Salad, Catha, Chat, Kat, Oat	Oral, smoked			
Methamphetamine	Desoxyn; Batu, Bikers Coffee, Black Beauties, Chalk, Chicken Feed, Crank, Crystal, Glass, Go-Fast, Hiropon, Ice, Meth, Methlies Quick, Poor Man's Cocaine, Shabu, Shards, Speed, Stove Top, Tina, Trash, Tweak, Uppers, Ventana, Vidrio, Yaba, Yellow Bam	Oral, sniffed, smoked, injected			
Methylphenidate	Ritalin	Oral, injected			
Other stimulants	Adipex, Bacarate, Cylert, Didrex, Ionamin, Plegine, Pre-Sate, Sanorex, Tenuate, Tepanil, Voranil	Oral, injected			
Depressants					
Barbiturates	Amytal, Lotusate, Nembutal, Phenobarbital, Seconal, Tuinal	Oral	Slurred speech, disorientation, drunken behavior without odor of alcohol	Shallow respiration, clammy skin, dilated pupils, weak and rapid pulse, coma, possible death	Anxiety, insomnia, tremors, delirium, convulsions, possible death
Benzodiazepines	Ativan, Azene, Dalmane, Diazepam, Halcion, Klonopin, Librium, Paxipam, Restoril, Rohypnol (see Flunitrazepam below), Serax, Tranxene, Valium, Verstran, Xanax	Oral			
Chloral hydrate	Noctec, Somnos	Oral			
Flunitrazepam	Rohypnol; Circles, Forget Pill, Forget-Me-Pill, La Rocha, Lunch Money Drug, Mexican Valium, Pingus, R2, Reynolds, Roach, Roach 2, Roaches, Roachies, Roapies, Robutal, Rochas Dos, Roofies, Rophies, Ropies, Roples, Row-Shay, Ruffies, Wolfies	Oral, snorted			

TABLE 18.2 *(Continued)*

Drug	Trade or Other Names	Usual Methods of Administration	Possible Effects	Effects of Overdose	Withdrawal Syndrome
Gamma-Hydroxybutyric Acid (GHB)	Sodium Oxybate. Xyrem; Easy Lay, G, Georgia Home Boy, GHB, Goop, Grievous Bodily Harm, Liquid Ecstasy, Liquid X, Scoop	Oral			
Glutethimide	Doriden	Oral			
Methaqualone	Quaalude	Oral			
Other depressants	Equanil, Miltown, Noludar, Placidyl, Valmid	Oral			
Hallucinogens					
Amphetamine variants	2,5-DMA, PMA, STP, MDA, MDMA, TMA, DOM, DOB	Oral, injected	Illusions and hallucinations, poor perception of time and distance	Longer, more-intense "trip" episodes, psychosis, possible death	Withdrawal syndrome not reported
Ketamine	Cat Tranquilizer, Cat Valium, Jet K, Kit Kat, Purple, Special K, Special La Coke, Super Acid, Super K, Vitamin K	Oral, snorted, smoked, injected			
LSD	Acid, Microdot	Oral			
Mescaline and peyote	Mesc, Buttons, Cactus,	Oral			
Phencyclidine	PCP, Angel Dust, Hog	Smoked, oral, injected			
Phencyclidine analogs	PCE, PCP, TCP	Smoked, oral, injected			
3,4-Methylenedioxy-methamphetamine (3,4-MDMA)	Adam, Beans, Clarity, Disco Biscuit, E, Ecstasy, Eve, Go, Hug Drug, Lover's Speed, MDMA, Peace, STP, X, XTC	Oral, snorted, smoked, injected (rare)			
Other hallucinogens	Bufotenine, Ibogaine, DMT, DET, Psilocybin, Psilocyn	Oral, injected, smoked, sniffed			
Anabolic Steroids					
Boldenone	Equipoise	Oral, injected, transdermal	Muscle growth, enhanced physical performance, dramatic mood swings, hostility, aggression, stunted growth, acne, fluid retention, liver damage, facial hair growth, sterility	Not associated with overdoses	Depression
Methandrostenolone	Dianabol	Oral, injected, transdermal			
Nandrolone	Deca-Durabolin, Durabolin	Oral, injected, transdermal			
Oxandrolone	Anavar, Oxandrin	Oral, injected, transdermal			

(Continued)

TABLE 18.2 *(Continued)*

Drug	Trade or Other Names	Usual Methods of Administration	Possible Effects	Effects of Overdose	Withdrawal Syndrome
Oxymetholone	Anadrol, Anadrol-50	Oral, injected, transdermal			
Stanozolol	Winstrol	Oral, injected, transdermal			
Testosterone (synthetic)	Arnolds, juice, pumpers, roids, stackers, weight gainers	Oral, injected, transdermal			
Trenbolone	Finajet, Hexabolin	Oral, injected, transdermal			
Cannabis					
Hashish	Hash	Smoked, oral	Euphoria, relaxed inhibitions, increased appetite, disoriented behavior	Fatigue, paranoia, possible psychosis	Insomnia, hyperactivity and decreased appetite occasionally reported
Hashish oil	Hash oil	Smoked, oral			
Marijuana	Acapulco gold, grass, pot, reefer, sinsemilla, Thai sticks	Smoked, oral			
Tetrahydrocannabinol	THC	Smoked, oral			

* Designated a narcotic under the Controlled Substances Act

Identification via chemical field testing, however, can be tricky. Exposure to some substances, such as fentanyl, can be dangerous to officers, and the potential exists that valuable evidence needed for prosecution may be damaged or destroyed during the testing process (Zoch, 2018; Larkin, 2014). Because of these potential hazards, some law enforcement agencies prohibit field testing of suspected narcotics, but critics argue such policies cause unnecessary delay and create problems for arrests and convictions, which can place officers at even greater risk.

Officers must understand, however, that field testing cannot be used to *establish* probable cause, only *confirm* it. Probable cause, through observation and evaluation of other factors, must already exist before a substance can be field tested. For example, an undercover officer who buys a small bag of white powder from a suspected cocaine dealer has established probable cause and may run a substance-specific field test for cocaine. Officers must be properly trained in how to use these field-testing kits to ensure accurate results and to avoid sample contamination or waste and reduce liability concerns associated with false arrests based on faulty testing procedures. Knowing the street terms for various drugs, drug paraphernalia, and drug-related activity is also beneficial to the drug investigator.

Technology Innovations

ACE-ID

New technology, such as the ACE-ID from Smiths Detection, has been developed to counter the disadvantages of chemical field tests. This portable, handheld tool uses Raman spectroscopy, or laser energy, to rapidly identify molecules in a substance and develop a molecular fingerprint to compare against a database of materials and compounds. Because it uses light to identify substances, the device can scan through translucent and semitranslucent containers, such as plastic bags and glass bottles, allowing officers to conduct contact-free identification of solids, liquids, gels, and powders. ACE-ID can also help investigators track drug trends. Furthermore, the spectroscopic device can "read" suspected explosives and other hazardous materials with diffused laser energy, mitigating the risk of overheating or igniting the unknown substances.

Source: Zoch, R. (2018, November 16). "How to identify narcotics and other suspected threats quickly and accurately." *Police1*. Retrieved March 24, 2021, from www.police1.com/police-products/narcotics-identification /articles/how-to-identify-narcotics-and-other-suspected-threats-quickly -and-accurately-ZVQxu11QJhBhvDWK/

Investigating Illegal Possession or Use of Controlled Substances

If you observe someone using a narcotic or other dangerous drug, you may arrest the person and seize the drugs as evidence. The arrested person may be searched incidental to the arrest. If a vehicle is involved but the suspect was not in the vehicle, post a guard at the vehicle or impound it. Drugs found on a person during a legally conducted search for other crimes may also be seized, and additional charges may be made.

Take the suspect into custody quickly. Then make sure the suspect does not dispose of the drugs by swallowing them, putting them between car seat cushions, or placing them in other convenient hiding places. Suspects who are high can be extremely dangerous and difficult for officers to control. Also, while in custody, the suspect may experience withdrawal pains and other bodily ills that can create special problems for the arresting officers.

In drug crimes, the victims are implicated; thus, they usually avoid contact with the police, conspiring with the sellers to remain undetected. If apprehended and faced with charges, however, the drug addict may be willing to work with the police. In exchange for a reduced punishment or monetary compensation, such informants or confidential informants (CIs) will provide information to the police about drug sellers. Therefore, many drug investigations involve identifying those who buy drugs illegally and who can thus provide information about sources of supply.

When the United States began to recognize the serious increase in heroin- and opioid/fentanyl-related fatalities, prosecutors started going after the dealers and charging them with manslaughter and murder for supplying narcotics that resulted in a buyer's death. Several states, including Florida, New York, and North Carolina have passed "drug-induced homicide" or "death by distribution" laws (Goforth, 2019; Suffolk County District Attorney's Office, 2019; Lou, 2019; DEA, 2019). Proponents of such laws contend they are similar to felony murder laws, which allow coconspirators to be prosecuted for murder, regardless of intent, if someone dies during the commission of a dangerous felony. Critics, on the other hand, argue that such laws do little to punish high-level drug traffickers and dealers, who don't sell directly to users, and instead scoop up addicts and small-time dealers who are selling relatively small amounts of drugs (Lou, 2019).

Recognizing the Drug Addict: Drug Recognition Experts

Congress has defined a *drug addict* as "any person who habitually uses any habit-forming narcotic drug so as to endanger the public morals, health, safety, or welfare, or who is or has been so far addicted to the use of habit-forming narcotic drugs as to have lost the power of self-control with reference to the addiction" (42 U.S.C. §201). Drug addiction is a progressive disease. The victim uses increased amounts of the same drug or harder drugs. Each increase in habit has a corresponding cost increase—thus the frequent necessity for committing crime. In addition, as the addiction increases, the ability to control the habit decreases. Drug addicts become unfit for employment as their mental, emotional, and physical condition deteriorates. Because addicts often help each other obtain drugs, exercise extreme caution when addicts are in jail, to prevent visitors from getting drugs to them.

Police officers are adept at recognizing and legally charging individuals who are under the influence of alcohol, especially if they are driving. They are not always so able to recognize drug-impaired individuals. However, drug evaluation classification (DEC) programs, more commonly known as drug recognition expert (DRE) programs, have demonstrated international success in detecting and deterring drug-impaired driving. The International Association of Chiefs of Police (IACP) sets DRE program guidelines, and the National Highway Traffic Safety Administration (NHTSA) supports the program's operation.

If an officer suspects a driver is impaired, the officer begins an assessment by using the standard field sobriety tests. If impairment is noticeable, the subject is given a breath test. If the blood alcohol reading is inconsistent with the perceived impairment, a DRE evaluates the individual's appearance, performance on psychological tests, eyes, and vital signs using additional tests that go beyond the scope of a standard field sobriety test. Be aware that a patrol officer must have completed specialized DRE training to lawfully conduct drug recognition tests and assess the results.

The initial interview includes questions about the subject's behavior; response to being stopped; attitude and demeanor; speech patterns; and possible injury, sickness, or physical problems. Physical evidence such as smoking paraphernalia, injection-related material, and needle marks on the subject is sought.

The physical examination includes an eye examination, an improved walk-and-turn test, the Romberg Standing Balance test, and the one-leg stand test, as well as the finger-to-nose test. Also tested are vital signs (blood pressure, pulse rate, and temperature), reaction time, and muscle rigidity. If warranted, a toxicological examination is also conducted. However, toxicology results typically take a few days to weeks to come back; thus, in the case of a driving while intoxicated (DWI) stop, the suspect may be released pending the results of the toxicology test and then charged formally at a later time if the results come back positive.

A pupilometer allows officers to inexpensively conduct sobriety checks in the field. This lightweight, handheld binocular-type instrument measures absolute pupil dynamics to presumptively detect alcohol, drugs, inhalants, or fatigue in a suspect. If the pass/fail indicators show green, the person is not under the influence of any substances. Yellow suggests the person may be under the influence and that further testing is warranted. Red indicates the person is definitely under the influence. The name of the potential substance appears next to the pass/fail indicator along with the percentage probability level.

Physical Evidence of Possession or Use of Controlled Substances

The suspect's clothing may conceal drugs, which have been found in neckties, shirt collars, coat and pants linings and seams, shoe tongues, soles of shoes or slippers, hat or cap bands, and, naturally, pockets. Drugs can also be hidden in the hair, behind the ears, between the toes, and attached to other body parts with tape. A strip search is usually conducted because drugs can be concealed in any body opening including the rectum or vagina—a method known as **body packing**. Although states vary in their legal requirements, it is generally advised that a warrant be sought before conducting a strip search of a person, excepting such searches of inmates at correctional facilities. "Although a strip search may include some manipulation of the subject's genitals and visual inspection of body cavities, physically intruding into a subject's body cavities likely requires separate and express authorization from a court" (Welty, 2018). Some criminals smuggle drugs by body packing animal couriers. In addition to insertion into body orifices, contraband may be ingested or surgically implanted for concealment in an effort to evade detection by authorities. These methods have been used to smuggle drugs into prisons as well as to transport drugs internationally.

Objects in the suspect's possession can also contain drugs, depending on the suspect's ingenuity. Cigarette cases, lighters, holders, and packages, as well as chewing-gum wrappers, fountain pens, jewelry, eyeglass cases, lockets, pencil erasers, and many other objects can conceal illegal drugs.

Vehicles have innumerable hiding places, including under seat covers; behind cushions or seats; in heater pipes, hubcaps, or glove compartments; under floor mats; in false auto batteries and oil filters; and in secret compartments devised for great amounts of smuggled drugs. (Incidentally, it is a crime in some jurisdictions to have such a secret compartment installed or created in a vehicle.) An Internet search of where compartments have been located can provide tips to officers on where to look for out-of-place items that could lead to a hidden compartment or "trap." At minimum, put the vehicle on a hoist and examine the undercarriage.

In a residence or building, do not give the suspect a chance to flush the toilet or turn on the water in a sink to destroy evidence. Look for drugs in drawer bottoms, in fuse boxes, in bedposts, behind pictures, in tissue boxes, in overhead light fixtures, under rugs and carpets, in and under furniture, and in holes in walls. If you find evidence, attempt to locate the property owner and inform them of the arrest. Gather all correspondence addressed to the person arrested if it is not in a mailbox. Obtain rent receipts, utility bills, and other evidence that establishes that the suspect resides at that location.

One initial problem is identifying the suspected substance. As discussed earlier, pharmaceutical reference materials provide information needed to identify various drugs. Field tests can be conducted to serve as the basis for a search warrant, but such tests must always be verified by laboratory examination. A residue-detection swab can be used to test surfaces for traces of cocaine. Investigators simply wipe the swab across the area to be tested, and if cocaine residue is present, the swab instantly turns color. Individually wrapped in foil packaging, these swabs are easy to carry and to use and have a relatively long shelf life. A positive swab should be preserved as evidence. In addition, if a field test yields a positive result, take a photograph of the swab indicating the test result for prosecution purposes because the color may fade or change by the time the case goes to court. Photographs of the test help the jury to see what the officer witnessed.

If evidence of narcotics or other dangerous drugs is found on an arrested suspect, as a result of a search of the premises or even by accident, immediately place it in a container, label it, and send it to a laboratory. If it is already in a container, leave it there and process the container for fingerprints. Package uncontained drug evidence carefully to avoid a challenge to its integrity as evidence. Use special precautions to avoid contaminating or altering the drugs by exposure to humidity, light, or chemicals. As a best practice, officers should always wear gloves and change them after dealing with each area and suspected substance, again to avoid challenges to the evidence's integrity as well as to protect the officer from contact with a potentially dangerous substance.

LO5 Summarize the major legal evidence to seek in prosecuting drug use and possession.

Physical evidence of possession or use of controlled substances includes the actual drugs, apparatus associated with their use, the suspect's appearance and behavior, and urine and blood tests.

Often found along with drugs are various types of pipes, syringes, grinders, cotton, spoons, medicine droppers, safety pins, razor blades, hypodermic needles, and other drug paraphernalia.

A suspect's general appearance and signs such as dilated pupils, needle marks, or razor cuts in the veins, confusion, aggressiveness, watery eyes, runny nose, and profuse perspiration provide additional evidence of drug use. Table 18.3 lists abuse indicators of various drugs.

To establish that an arrested person is under the influence of drugs, urine and blood tests, a medical examination, and a report of personal observations are used along with an alcoholic or drug-influence test form and an admission form signed by the subject.

In-Custody Deaths

Hundreds of people die each year in the United States while in police custody, often without any obvious reason or explanation. Sometimes the cause is a medical condition; other times, it is a consequence of drug use. Most of the time, it is a combination of factors.

One serious problem that may be encountered in dealing with drug users is **excited delirium** (discussed in Chapter 7), which may occur in people under the influence of an illicit stimulant substance such as cocaine or in people with a history of mental illness who are not taking their medications. The person may exhibit extremely agitated and incoherent behavior, elevated temperature, and excessive endurance without fatigue. People in this mental state do not perceive or respond to the brain's signals to calm down before the body collapses. They continue to push past the point of exhaustion by running, fighting with officers, or resisting against restraints, until their body reaches a potentially fatal medical condition called metabolic acidosis, which can lead to shock, cardiac arrest, and sudden in-custody death in a matter of minutes.

Occasionally, a suspect in a drug case will attempt to hide or destroy evidence by ingesting it, which could lead to an in-custody overdose death. In an effort to avoid arrest, subjects have also been known to swallow entire packages

TABLE 18.3 Indicators of Drug Abuse

Drug	Physical Evidence	Observable Conditions
Cocaine	White or colorless crystalline powder, hypodermic needle, pipe	Needle marks, dilated pupils, increased heart rate, convulsions
Crack	Pellets, glass pipes, plastic bottle	Depression, euphoria, convulsions
Depressants	Pills of various shapes and sizes	Symptoms resemble those of drunkenness: slurred, indistinct speech and loss of physical coordination
Hallucinogens	Hypodermic needle, eyedropper, spoon, bottle caps, tourniquets, cotton balls, actual substances	Needle marks on inner elbow, extreme emotionalism, noticeable dilation of pupils, often causing persons to wear dark glasses even at night
Heroin	Burning spoon, candle, hypodermic needle, razor blade, eyedropper, actual substance	Needle marks or razor cuts, euphoria, starry look, constricted pupils, profuse perspiration
Marijuana	Roach holder, pipe with a fine screen placed halfway down the bowl, actual substance	Sweet smoke odor; symptoms resemble those of mild intoxication: staring off into space, glassy eyes, semiconsciousness, drowsiness
Methamphetamine	Makeshift laboratory with ingredients present	Violent behavior, paranoia, other psychotic episodes
Morphine	Burning spoon, candle, hypodermic needle, actual substance	Needle marks, euphoria
Stimulants	Pills of various shapes and sizes	Restlessness, nervousness, hand tremor, dilated pupils, dry mouth, excessive perspiration

or bags containing drugs, which results in their suffocating or choking to death. Using restrictive restraint devices and procedures, such as handcuffing subjects behind their back and placing them facedown, can lead to positional asphyxia.

Investigating Illegal Sale and Distribution of Controlled Substances

Because addiction depends on drug availability, drug control must be directed toward the supplier. This is often a joint effort among law enforcement agencies at all levels. Drug users and sellers know the local police, so it is difficult to mount undercover or surveillance operations locally. Outsiders are frequently brought in by the police to make buys and arrests, and drug task forces comprised of law enforcement personnel from multiple agencies and jurisdictions have become an increasingly popular and valuable option for such endeavors. However, local patrol officers are still responsible for investigating drug offenses because they see the users and sometimes observe drug sales. Actions these officers take against users can put pressure on sellers because their market is hurt when users are arrested and jailed.

Drug users often become sellers to support their habits. Many such individuals, called **mules**, sell or transport drugs for a regular dealer in return for being assured of a personal drug supply. Whereas some remain in small operations sufficient to support their needs, others see the profit they can make in large operations and go into business on a larger scale. Further, many drug pushers become users—an occupational hazard. This sometimes occurs accidentally as the result of testing the quality of the merchandise over an extended period.

Investigating the illegal sale and distribution of drugs requires all the basic techniques used for other crimes, plus special investigative skills related to the behavior of drug users and sellers, both of whom can be dangerous and unpredictable. An increasing challenge to narcotics investigators is the evolving use of technology by drug traffickers and street dealers. Law enforcement agencies have encountered all types of devices used by drug sellers, ranging from two-way radios and cellular phones to drones. One seller of two-way radios stated that drug dealers were his biggest customers. If a radio was confiscated in an arrest, another was immediately purchased. Drug dealers use personal computers, sophisticated encryption systems that even federal agencies have difficulty deciphering, night-vision equipment, police frequency jamming equipment, scanners, and networking systems.

The main advantages drug dealers have over government in using technology are the availability of almost unlimited funds and a lack of bureaucratic approval systems.

Other challenges concern the wide variety of drugs, the difficulty faced when trying to identify them under street conditions, and the special types of searches often required to locate minute amounts of drugs that may be hidden ingeniously. Investigators also encounter special problems in finding drugs smuggled across national borders in a variety of ways and in identifying those who transport and distribute them. It takes much time and expense to develop informants and to make a purchase or otherwise discover and confiscate drugs while ensuring that the evidence will stand up in court. In the past few years, international drug lords have benefited from lowered political and economic barriers as well as easy access to sophisticated communications technology that can be frequently changed to evade law enforcement.

> **LO6** Identify the major legal evidence in prosecuting drug sale and distribution.
>
> The actual transfer of drugs from the seller to the buyer is the major legal evidence in prosecuting drug-sale cases.

A patrol officer may see a drug transfer by chance or observe it after long surveillance or when an undercover officer makes a planned buy. Some transfers are quite intricate. In one case, a drug seller put drugs on a dog's back, and the dog brought them to the buyer and then returned to the seller with the payment. Even though the seller did not personally hand the drugs to the seller, there was a sale. In other cases, the seller leaves drugs at a predetermined location and picks up payment at another location. Such subterfuge is countered by personal testimony.

If either the buyer or seller throws the drugs away to avoid being caught with them in possession, the drugs can be recovered as abandoned property and taken into custody. If the suspect was seen discarding the drugs, they can be used as evidence.

Narcotics cases begin with a report of suspicious drug activity, a search warrant obtained on information from a reliable informant, or an on-sight observation of a drug buy. Undercover officers and informants then become central figures in obtaining evidence. Confidential informants (CIs), discussed in Chapter 6, play a crucial role in many law enforcement investigations, particularly in drug investigations, as they can often provide specific information that is simply not available from other sources. Investigators must remember that informants are often involved in criminal activity themselves and must be properly managed to protect not only the integrity of the investigation but also the department's credibility and officers' safety. To this end, investigators should follow strict department protocol when dealing with informants (Jones-Brown & Shane, 2011). Informants are often vital to making on-sight arrests.

On-Sight Arrests

Patrol officers witnessing a suspected drug buy should obtain as complete a description as possible of the persons and vehicles involved. There is usually no urgency in making a drug arrest because the seller and buyer continue to meet over time.

> **LO7** Discuss the circumstances under which an on-sight arrest can be made for a drug buy.
>
> If you observe what appears to be a drug buy, you can make a warrantless arrest if you have probable cause. Often, however, it is better to simply observe and gather information.

Probable cause is established through knowledge of the suspect's criminal record, by observing other people making contact with the suspect and finding drugs on them, by knowing of the suspect's past relationships with other drug users or sellers, and through observing actions of the suspect that indicate a drug buy. The courts usually give weight to officers' experience and to their information about the suspect and the circumstances of the arrest, including actions by the suspect before the arrest commonly associated with drug selling.

If probable cause is based on information supplied by an informant, check the information for accuracy against intelligence files. If no prior intelligence information exists, add the facts provided to the file. Check the informant's reliability by asking about other suspects in drug cases. Are these suspects already in the files? Has the informant helped before? How many arrests or convictions were based on the information?

You might ask the informant to obtain a small amount of the drug if possible. However, this request should only be made as part of a "controlled buy," discussed shortly, in which officers watch and control the environment that the drug buy occurs in. It is important that officers do not ask the informant to commit a crime.

Surveillance

Neighborhood residents often know where the drug dealers live or which houses are the crack houses. They are, however, usually reluctant to provide such information to police for fear of retributive consequences. Therefore, it may be necessary to surveil a property to develop evidence of drug dealing activity. Some common indicators of residential drug trafficking are as follows:

- A high volume of foot or vehicle traffic to and from a residence at late or unusual hours

- Periodic visitors who stay at the residence for very brief periods

- No regular schedule as to when residents come and go from the residence

- Blinds pulled closed during daylight hours

- Lights on inside at odd hours

- Property altered to maximize privacy

- Outdoor security cameras

- "Beware of Dogs" signs and dogs that often seem to be "on guard"

- Anti-social behavior with neighbors

- Putting trash out at the last minute or having no trash service at all

It is frequently best simply to watch and obtain information if you witness a drug buy. The suspected seller or the location of the buy can then be put under surveillance, an especially important technique in narcotics investigations. Surveillance can provide protection for controlled buys, protect the buy money, provide credibility for the buyer, provide information regarding the seller's contacts, and provide information to establish probable cause for an arrest or search warrant. It is not necessary to make an arrest on the first surveillance. Actually, it is generally advisable to make several surveillances to gather evidence. Surveillance officers must have patience because many controlled drug buys necessitate a long period of surveillance before the actual sale, or bust, is made.

Undercover Assignments

Undercover investigations are used more routinely in drug cases than perhaps any other type of criminal investigation. The downside to this common tactic is that drug dealers also know it is routinely used, and they have become fairly adept at sniffing out a "narc." Street dealers are also aware of the restrictions imposed on undercover agents. As a result, undercover narcotics officers have had to develop more convincing ways to fit into the drug culture.

An undercover agent might dress a certain way, use certain slang, and talk with an accent, or even gargle with beer or hard liquor just before meeting with a dealer. Applying a cologne or another marijuana-smelling product can help undercover officers gain street credibility by giving them the right smell. For example, an incense stick or diffusing oil that produces a similar odor to that of smoked marijuana can be burned inside an officer's vehicle. The scent can also permeate the undercover operative's clothing, leading the dealer to believe the buyer is a doper. A loose weed version of the stick can be rolled into an imitation marijuana cigarette and used as if it were real marijuana.

Undercover officers often have permission to consume small amounts of alcohol so they do not look out of place or suspicious. In addition, if placed in a situation where officers fear for their own safety if they do not participate in drug activity, they can do so. If this occurs, there are generally procedures in place where officers must report the incident and go through proper treatment if it is needed.

Controlled Buys. Controlled buys, also referred to as *planned buys*, usually involve working an undercover agent into a group selling or buying drugs or having an informant make the buy. Before using an informant to buy drugs, determine why the person is involved and keep a strict log of their activities. Exercise caution when using illegal drug users as buyers, as courts have challenged their reliability based on drug abuse history and related behaviors.

The enormous number of drug buys by undercover agents and informants have made drug sellers wary of new customers. Informants typically introduce the undercover officer. Informants are often involved in criminal narcotics as users or sellers and are "turned" by the police for providing information in exchange for lesser charges or monetary compensation. The prosecutor's office usually makes the decision to use an informant in this way. Most people arrested for dealing drugs to whom the options of either going to jail or becoming an informant are given choose the latter. Police departments should have written policies on using informants.

Undercover agents are usually police officers of the investigating agency (in large cities) or of cooperative agencies on the same level of government in an exchange operation or a mutual-aid agreement that provides an exchange of narcotics officers.

If working undercover, be thoroughly conversant with the language of the user and the seller, know the street prices of drugs, and have a tight cover. Talk little and listen much. Observe without being noticed. Also devise an excuse to avoid using the drugs. Work within the seller's system. Drug pushers, like other criminals, tend to develop certain methods for making their sales. Asking them to change their method can cause suspicion, whereas going along with the system establishes your credibility for subsequent buys. Avoid dangerous situations by insisting you do not want to get into a situation where you could be ripped off, injured, or killed.

Make careful plans before a drug buy. Undercover drug buys that are carefully planned, documented, witnessed, and conducted are less likely to fall victim to charges of entrapment. Document any telephone numbers called or text messages sent in setting up the buy. Select a surveillance group and fully brief group members on the signals to use and their specific assignments. Small transmitters are important communications devices for surveillance team members. Have alternate plans in case the original plan fails.

Careful preparation includes searching the buyer immediately before the transaction to avoid the defense that drugs were planted on the suspect. Any items on the buyer other than the money are retained at the police station or with other police officers until after the buy.

Prepare the buy money in advance. It must be marked, identified, counted, and recorded by serial number, date, time, and denomination. Have this procedure witnessed by one or more people. The money is not given to the buyer until immediately before the buy. Fluorescent powders can be used, but some drug sellers check money for these powders before making a transaction. All buys should be observed from a location where the movements of both the seller and buyer can be seen by the surveillance team.

At the meeting, record the seller's description, the vehicles used, and observations about the seller's personal statements and habits. If the informant and the undercover officer are both present, the officer makes the buy to protect the informant's identity if an arrest is planned. If the informant is not present, video of the meet should be taken if possible. If no arrest is planned, both the undercover officer and the informant make buys, providing additional evidence.

If several buys are made from the same seller over a period, the seller may relax security and include others higher in the organization. Even if this is not the case, the seller usually visits their drug source frequently. The route to or the actual location of the supplier can then be put under surveillance. Such an opportunity seldom arises on the first contact because sellers usually devise very clever ruses to cover their tracks.

The three things valued by dealers are the drugs, the money the drugs can bring, and their freedom to do business. In the middle of the triangle is the officer. When both the money—that is, the **flashroll**—and the drugs are present at the same time, the undercover officer faces the greatest danger.

The ability to negotiate is essential for an undercover officer. Almost everything is negotiable in a drug deal. Remaining cool and collected during the actual buy is absolutely necessary. If the situation does not look right or appears to be too dangerous, walk away from the deal; there is always another time and place. Because of the prevalence of weapons in drug trafficking, undercover officers can be in extreme danger, especially because they are usually alone.

If the buy is successful, an arrest can be made immediately, or a search warrant can be obtained based on the buyer's observation of other drugs on the premises. After the buy, the buyer is searched again and the exact amount of money and drugs on the buyer recorded.

LO8 Describe the precautions to take in undercover drug buys, including how to avoid a charge of entrapment.

Make two or more buys to avoid the charge of entrapment. The more buys documented, the weaker a suspect's defense of entrapment.

Although police are responsible for investigating narcotics offenses and arresting violators, they are equally responsible for making every reasonable effort to avoid arresting an innocent person. The illegal act involved in the sale should be voluntary, without special urging or persuasion. An agent who knows that a seller is in business and merely asks for, pays for, and receives drugs is not using entrapment. But continued requests for drugs from a person who does not ordinarily sell them *is* entrapment. If there has been more than one voluntary drug transaction, no basis for a defense of entrapment exists.

Stings. A **sting**, or **reverse buy**, is a complex operation organized and implemented by undercover agents to apprehend drug dealers and buyers and to deter other users from making drug purchases at a certain location. As with other controlled buys, reverse buys are labor intensive, complex, and require officers to be well trained. In a typical reverse buy, a team of officers conducts a street sweep to clear an area of drug dealers, and a second undercover team moves in posing as dealers. A third group of officers is stationed nearby conducting surveillance on the operation, videotaping transactions, and providing backup should a deal go awry. A fourth group of uniformed officers waits just outside the perimeter of the reverse buy, to arrest those who have just purchased drugs.

Narcotics Raids

Raids are another method used to apprehend narcotics dealers. Surveillance frequently provides enough information for obtaining a no-knock search or arrest warrant. Successful narcotics raids are rarely spontaneous; they are planned on the basis of information obtained during an extended period. They can be designed to occur in two, three, or more places simultaneously, not only in the same community but also in other communities, other states, and even multiple countries. The raid itself must be carried out forcefully and swiftly because drugs can easily be destroyed in seconds.

Narcotics raids are often dangerous; therefore, before the raid, gather information about the people involved and the premises where the drugs are located. Also determine how many officers are needed, the types of weapons needed, and the location of evidence, as discussed in Chapter 7.

Drug Paraphernalia Stores

Another avenue available to investigators concerns paraphernalia shops and their clientele. Such stores fall into two broad categories. "Head shops" sell products that help the end user ingest drugs, such as pipes, syringes, and so on. They have also begun selling "marijuana snacks" in states with legalized marijuana. "Cut or vial stores," in contrast, sell adulterants, diluents, and other "office supplies" used by drug organizations in measuring, separating, chemically altering, and packaging mass quantities of drugs. The trail of drug paraphernalia may help investigators track down drug gangs and other major drug distributors.

Online Drug Dealers

One challenge for twenty-first-century narcotics investigators involves a move from the street corner into cyberspace. Club drugs, prescription narcotics, and ultra pure forms of DXM, an ingredient found in OTC cough medication, can all be purchased online and shipped directly to the user's home—transactions that are extremely difficult for law enforcement to detect.

Online drug dealers commonly try to disguise their activities by posting their available products as some type of legitimate substance.

Clandestine Drug Laboratories

Methamphetamine is the most frequently manufactured drug seized in clandestine laboratories ("clan labs") in the United States. At the end of the 1990s and into the early 2000s, seizures of domestic methamphetamine laboratories across the country increased annually, peaking in 2004 with approximately 23,700 clandestine labs seized (DEA, 2021). Since 2004, domestic methamphetamine production has decreased annually, with a mild spike from 2007 to 2010 that has since declined significantly, with 890 seizures reported in 2019, the lowest reported in 19 years. Enactment of the Combat Methamphetamine Epidemic Act (CMEA) in 2005 reduced domestic methamphetamine production by placing restrictions on key ingredients, constraints that have kept domestic producers unable to keep up with the quantity or quality of the lower cost methamphetamine produced on an industrial scale in Mexico.

Many of the domestic methamphetamine laboratories seized in 2019 were small-capacity production laboratories, known as "one-pot" or "shake and bake" (DEA, 2021). These domestic labs often obtain the restricted precursors from China and India via maritime shipments. Most of the finished methamphetamine from foreign production is trafficked overland across the U.S.-Mexico border.

Most clandestine labs produce one or more types of amphetamine, but a few produce club drugs such as Ecstasy and LSD. The most serious challenge is posed by covert drug labs involved in the manufacture of methamphetamine, the most widely used and clandestinely produced synthetic drug in the United States. Meth labs are found across the country, in cities and rural areas, and have been found in private residences, motel rooms, storage units, garages, barns, and vehicles.

The production of meth involves a variety of hazardous ingredients, including strong acids and bases, flammable solvents, and highly explosive and toxic chemicals. Because of their volatility, these labs present a significant threat to public safety. An estimated 20% of meth labs come to the attention of law enforcement because of fire or explosion. Meth labs run out of homes can have a particularly devastating impact on the health of children living there. According to one source, the cost to treat a meth lab burn victim averages $230,000, and the age group with the highest incidence of meth lab burns is children under four years of age (Wood, 2014). Figure 18.1 lists the toxic, explosive, and hazardous chemicals commonly found in clandestine drug labs.

Identifying a Clandestine Drug Lab

Clandestine drug laboratories can be set up anywhere: private residences, motel and hotel rooms, apartments, mobile homes, campgrounds, and commercial establishments. Smaller operations are more portable and easily moved, making detection more difficult. Clan labs tend to share some common characteristics, however, and knowing what to watch for can help investigators uncover these dangerous, unlawful operations. From the outside of a structure, investigators may observe blacked out or boarded up windows, hoses sticking out through windows and doors, dead vegetation from dumped chemical wastes, and strong chemical odors, all of which may indicate a clan lab is operating inside. Inside a structure, indicators of a clan lab include coffee grinders with white residue; coffee filters with red stains; large quantities of acetone, antifreeze, camping fuel, drain cleaner, lithium batteries, matches, plastic baggies, cold tablets, or cough syrup containing the ingredient pseudoephedrine; an abundance of mixing containers such as Pyrex glassware, crock pots, and other large pots; strips of bed linen or cloth for filtering liquid drug mixtures; and general clutter, disarray and filthy living conditions (National Drug Intelligence Center, n.d.).

Because hotel rooms are commonly used for those setting up clan labs, some law enforcement agencies are training hotel managers and employees on the dangers such labs pose and ways to identify suspected "meth cooks." DEA agents profile a typical meth cook as White, trashy looking, with rotting teeth (often coined "meth mouth") and poor-quality tattoos, and with a local address on their identification. Because the chemicals, such as Drāno®, used in the production are corrosive and the cooks usually do not get all of them out before using the drug, they suffer corrosion on their teeth and skin.

Entering a Clandestine Drug Lab

Clan labs pose serious physical, chemical, and toxic hazards to law enforcement agencies conducting raids on the premises, including booby traps and assaults from attack dogs or violent drug "cooks" under the influence of their products. In addition, many of the substances, often unidentified or misidentified, are explosive and extremely flammable. Irritants and corrosives, asphyxiants, and nerve toxins also may be encountered.

When encountering a drug lab or its components, do not use matches, lighters, or items that could ignite fumes. Do not turn switches on or off, because the electric connection could produce sparks and cause an explosion. Do not taste, smell, or touch any substance, and do check for booby traps before moving or touching containers.

Typical Chemicals Found in Lab Sites	Common Legitimate Uses	Poison	Flammable	Toxic Vapors	Explosive	Corrosive	Skin Absorption	Common Health Hazards
Acetone	Fingernail polish remover, solvents	X	X	X				Reproductive disorders
Methanol	Brake cleaner fluid, fuel	X	X	X				Blindness, eye damage
Ammonia	Disinfectants	X		X		X	X	Blistering, lung damage
Benzene	Dye, varnishes, lacquers	X	X		X	X	X	Carcinogen, leukemia
Ether	Starter fluid, anesthetic	X	X		X			Respiratory disorders
Freon	Refrigerant, propellants	X		X		X	X	Frostbite, lung damage
Hydriodic acid	Driveway cleaner	X		X		X	X	Burns, thyroid damage
Hydrochloric acid (HCl gas)	Iron ore processing, mining	X		X		X	X	Respiratory, liver damage
Iodine crystals	Antiseptic, catalyst	X	X		X	X		Birth defects, kidney failure
Lithium metal	Lithium batteries	X				X	X	Burns, pulmonary edema
Muriatic acid	Swimming pool cleaners	X		X		X		Burns, toxic vapors
Phosphine gas	Pesticides	X		X			X	Respiratory failure
Pseudoephedrine	Cold medicines	X						Abuse: health damage
Red phosphorus	Matches, fireworks	X	X	X	X			Unstable, flammable
Sodium hydroxide	Drain cleaners, lye	X		X		X	X	Burns, skin ulcers
Sulfuric acid	Battery acid	X		X		X	X	Burns, thyroid damage
Toluene	Paint thinners, solvents	X	X	X	X		X	Fetal damage, pneumonia
Liquid lab waste	None	X	X	X	X	X	X	Unknown long-term effects

Figure 18.1

Toxic, explosive, and hazardous chemicals found in clandestine drug labs.

Source: *Law enforcement technology*, May 2005, p. 10. Courtesy of the Clandestine Drug Lab Program of the Division of Environmental Health in the Washington State Department of Health.

The various health and safety hazards encountered at a clandestine drug lab necessitate that only properly trained and equipped personnel proceed onto the site. A safety program developed by the DEA and the California Bureau of Narcotics Enforcement following recommendations by the Occupational Safety and Health Administration and the National Institute for Occupational Safety and Health has four basic elements: policies and procedures, equipment and protective clothing, training, and medical monitoring.

Policies and procedures are aimed at ensuring officer safety through a certification process. Only certified individuals are allowed to seize, process, and dispose of clandestine laboratories. Their procedure for conducting a raid has five stages: planning, entry, assessment, processing, and exit.

During the planning stage, certified agents and chemists identify the chemicals that may be present and arrange for the proper safety equipment and protective clothing. Entry has the most potential for danger. The entry team faces the possibility of armed resistance by owners and operators, booby traps, and exposure to hazardous chemicals. Still, the entry team wears the least protection because the gear limits mobility, dexterity, vision, and voice communications.

Once entry has been successful, the assessment team—an agent and a chemist—enter the site to deal with immediate hazards, to ventilate the site, and to segregate incompatible chemicals to halt reactions. Assessment team members wear fire-protective, chemical-resistant suits, gloves, and boots. They also use self-contained breathing devices for respiratory protection. This team determines what safety equipment and clothing the processing team will need. The processing team then enters and identifies and collects evidence. They photograph and videotape the site and collect samples of the various chemicals. The final step involves removing and disposing of hazardous materials and decontaminating and posting the site.

Training involves 40 hours of classroom instruction followed by a 24-hour in-service training course at the field level. Medical monitoring has two stages: medical screening of potential team members and annual monitoring to learn whether any team members have developed adverse health effects as a result of working with hazardous chemicals. Guidelines and training for clandestine drug laboratory investigations are available through the National Sheriffs' Association.

Processing of Clandestine Drug Labs

Proper processing of a clandestine drug lab requires taking photographs with identifying labels, completing a thorough inventory, collecting evidentiary samples, and preparing chemicals and equipment for disposal. Table 18.4 lists information to collect and steps to take when processing a clandestine drug laboratory.

Cleanup of Clandestine Drug Labs

Not only do clan labs pose a danger to officers and the public, but also they generate an enormous amount of waste and can be very expensive to clean up. Estimates suggest that for every pound of meth produced, as much as five pounds of waste are created, including empty chemical containers, contaminated cooking equipment, and other items that have become hazardous through exposure to the vapors produced during the drug manufacturing process. Such trash requires special handling and disposal, often at great expense. The U.S. Environmental Protection Agency

TABLE 18.4 Information to Be Collected during Laboratory Processing—Drawings, Photographs, Inventory, and Samples

- Drawing of clandestine drug laboratory site
- Photographs
  - Photograph everything in place
    - General overviews
    - Close-ups
    - Specific items during inventory
    - Evidentiary samples and original containers
    - Visible contamination
  - Photograph site after removal of bulk materials
- Inventory
  - Inventory all equipment and paraphernalia present in terms of quantity, size, manufacturer's serial number, condition, and location
  - Inventory all chemicals present for type, concentration, and quantity
  - Describe unknown or unlabeled materials in terms of phase (solid, liquid, or gas), color, volume/mass, and appearance
  - Describe the type, size, condition, and labeling of all containers
    - Plastic, glass, metal
    - Five-gallon, 2-ounce, etc.
    - Punctured, rusty, leaking, corroded, damaged, uncapped, bulging
    - Label, markings, etc.
  - Identify the location of leaking or broken containers
    - Describe spilled solids or liquids, specifying odor, color, appearance, location, size of spill, etc.
  - Identify leaking compressed-gas cylinders
  - Identify unstable container storage
  - Identify other concerns
- Samples
  - Take samples of appropriate items for evidence; one-ounce sample size is usually sufficient
  - Photograph samples and original containers with identifying labels
  - Maintain chain of custody

Source: Adapted from Christian, D. R. (2004). *Forensic examination of clandestine laboratories*. Boca Raton, FL: CRC Press. Retrieved March 24, 2021, from www.academia.edu/40188802/Forensic_Investigation_of_Clandestine_Laboratories

(EPA) has published guidelines for methamphetamine laboratory cleanup and suggestions for approaching meth lab remediation (2013). The Comprehensive Methamphetamine Control Act (MCA) of 1996 allows the courts to order a defendant convicted of manufacturing methamphetamine to pay the cost of cleanup of the lab site. Despite efforts to detect and shut them down, however, clan labs continue to proliferate.

Members of a clandestine lab assessment and response team, some still wearing their hazmat safety gear, display some of the evidence seized from a methamphetamine lab.
Wellphoto/Shutterstock.com

Indoor Marijuana Growing Operations

Another type of clandestinely produced drug is sinsemilla, a potent form of marijuana cultivated indoors. One good indication of indoor marijuana-growing operations is excessive use of electricity needed to run the lighting system, and a residence that pulls a great deal more electricity than the average home in a particular location may warrant a closer look. If such a residence is identified, police may observe the type and amount of traffic to and from the house and, based on the combination of information involving electricity use and traffic, obtain a search warrant. This approach has been used many times to break up large marijuana-growing operations.

Many grow operations steal electricity by diverting power from a main supply line. In addition to tampered-with electric meters and supply lines, other signs of an indoor grow operation include water lines or electrical cords running to a basement or outbuilding, an outbuilding with air conditioners, an unusual number of roof vents, excessive condensation around windows, and unusual security measures.

Inherent dangers associated with the high-energy needs of these indoor grow operations include the risk of electrocution from exposing and tampering with high-voltage wires, explosion and fire risks because of the presence and prevalence of chemicals stored inside, and upper respiratory infections caused by mold that thrives in these high-humidity environments.

Investigative Aids

One tool to help federal, state, and local law enforcement agencies investigate drug trafficking is the DEA's National Drug Pointer Index (NDPIX), a nationwide database that became operational across the United States in 1997. The NDPIX is intended to enhance agent and officer safety, eliminate duplication, increase information sharing and coordination, and minimize costs by using existing technology and 24-hour access to information through an effective, secure law enforcement telecommunications system.

Some investigative aids are not so high-tech. For example, using dogs to detect drugs has been common for decades because their keen sense of smell enables them to detect minute traces of illicit drugs. Law enforcement agencies depend on their K-9s and handlers for many tasks essential to police work. Narcotics and explosives detection dogs have become the primary growth area with respect to police dog work in the United States, partly because courts, including the U.S. Supreme Court, have set boundaries that permit dogs to perform sniffs in many situations (Ensminger, 2012). For example, an officer and his K-9 on routine patrol in a Pennsylvania township made one of the jurisdiction's biggest drug busts on record, seizing 15 kilos of heroin and 20 pounds of crystal meth worth more than $11 million (Reed, 2012). The Supreme Court ruled in *Illinois v. Caballes* (2005) that a canine sniff in a public area or during a lawful traffic stop is not a Fourth Amendment "search." However, use of a narcotics-detection dog to sniff at the door of an apartment or a home has been ruled a search within the meaning of the Fourth Amendment and therefore requires a warrant (*Florida v. Jardines*, 2013).

Another assist for investigators is a special high-accuracy laser rangefinder developed for the U.S. Customs Service that can find secret compartments that might contain drugs. Investigators use the unit to measure the interior dimensions of cargo containers in their search for hidden compartments in which drugs may be smuggled. The small laser beam allows measurements of loaded containers in which physical access to the rear wall is limited. The handheld, battery-operated laser rangefinder measures distances from 6 to 85 feet with an accuracy of 1 inch.

Agency Cooperation

Investigating illegal drug activities requires the cooperation of all law enforcement agencies, including the exchange of suspect car lists and descriptions of sellers and buyers. Local police assist state and federal narcotics investigators by sharing their knowledge of drug users and sellers in their community. In addition, many narcotics officers exchange vehicles and personnel with other agencies to have less identifiable operators and equipment.

The federal government has mobilized an all-out attack on illegal drug activities. Before 1973, several federal agencies separately investigated illegal drug activities. In 1973 these agencies were merged into the Drug Enforcement Agency (DEA).

| **LO9** | Identify the agency responsible for providing unified leadership in combating illegal drug activities and what its primary emphasis is. |

The federal DEA provides unified leadership in attacking narcotics trafficking and drug abuse. The DEA's emphasis is on the source and distribution of illicit drugs rather than on arresting abusers.

The DEA emphasis is on stopping the flow of drugs at their foreign sources, disrupting illicit domestic commerce at the highest levels of distribution, and helping state and local police prevent the entry of illegal drugs into their communities. Coordination of national drug enforcement efforts has been enhanced through the DEA's State and Local Task Force Program, which allows the DEA to draw on the expertise of state and local law enforcement; share resources with state and local officers; deputize state and local officers as federal drug agents, thus extending their jurisdiction; provide participating state and local agencies with equitable shares of forfeited drug proceeds; and pay overtime to and investigative expenses for participating state and local agencies. In 2016, the DEA State and Local Task Force Program managed 271 state and local task forces (DEA, *State and Local*, n.d.).

Another DEA initiative at the center of the Attorney General's drug supply reduction strategy is the Organized Crime and Drug Enforcement Task Force (OCDETF) Program, established in 1982 to conduct comprehensive, multilevel attacks on major drug trafficking and money laundering organizations. Today, OCDETF is the largest anticrime task force in the United States, and the agencies that participate in OCDETF, combining their resources and expertise, include the DEA; the FBI; Immigration and Customs Enforcement (ICE); the Bureau of Alcohol, Tobacco, Firearms, and Explosives (ATF); the U.S. Marshals Service (USMS); the Internal Revenue Service (IRS); the U.S. Coast Guard (USCG); and the Department of Justice's Criminal Division. The principal mission of the OCDETF program is to identify, disrupt, and dismantle the most serious drug trafficking and money laundering organizations and those primarily responsible for the nation's drug supply (DEA, *Organized Crime*, n.d.).

The National Drug Intelligence Center (NDIC) also plays a vital role in providing police administrators and officers with the latest information on drug distribution patterns.

The U.S. agencies must cooperate with law enforcement in other countries because much of the U.S. domestic drug problem originates across national borders. To overcome interjurisdictional competition and minimize duplication of effort, multijurisdictional drug task forces have been implemented across the country. Sometimes task forces and programs are created because of a need to eliminate dissention, rather than from a desire to cooperate. One benefit of working with a task force is shared forfeiture revenues.

Drug Asset Forfeitures

Asset forfeiture is a tool that allows agencies investigating various types of crimes, including drug trafficking, to seize items used in or acquired through committing that crime. The federal Comprehensive Crime Control Act of 1984 initiated procedures for asset forfeitures as a result of drug arrests. The U.S. Congress gave final approval to the Civil Asset Forfeiture Reform Act of 2000, which lowered the burden of proof from "clear and convincing" to "a preponderance of the evidence." The act also reduced the statute of limitations from 11 years to 5 years for a property owner to make a claim on the property.

Confiscating drug dealers' cash and property has been effective in reducing drug trafficking and is providing local, state, and federal law enforcement agencies with assets they need for their fight against drugs. Asset forfeiture laws provide for the confiscation of cash and other property in possession of a drug dealer at the time of the arrest. Seized vehicles, boats, or airplanes may be used directly by the agency or sold at auction to generate funds. Monetary assets may be used to purchase police equipment, to hire additional law enforcement personnel, or to provide training in drug investigation.

Currency seizures pose special challenges to law enforcement because there is no law against possessing a large quantity of cash, and many currency seizures occur in the absence of narcotics, making it difficult to link the money to criminal activity. The investigator must establish the ownership of the currency (Was it inherited? Was it won at the track? What does the person do for a living?), the origin of the currency, and the packaging and transportation methods used with the currency. An attempt to disguise or otherwise hide the currency suggests criminal involvement.

Precise recording of all proceedings is necessary to avoid allegations of abuse or misuse of these funds. Because of the required legal and judicial proceedings regarding these confiscations, six months or more often pass after an arrest before the assets are available for police agency use.

A common defense to asset seizure is the *innocent owner defense*. If an owner can prove that they had no knowledge of the prohibited activity, the property is not subject to forfeiture.

The forfeiture program has not been without problems and misunderstandings. The confiscated funds may be used only for police department efforts to increase their fight against drugs. Police budgets cannot be reduced because of the availability of the asset-forfeiture funds.

Preventing Problems with Illegal Drugs: Community Partnerships

Tremendous national, state, and local efforts are being directed to meeting the challenges of drug use and abuse in the United States. A national "drug czar" serves at the direction of the president, and many states appoint people to similar positions to direct state and local efforts. Federal funding is available through state agencies. Federal, state, and local agencies with roles in the drug war coordinate their efforts. Any successful effort to address drug-related crime and drug addiction must also necessarily involve partnerships with the community. Businesses, schools, public health departments, and individual citizens are invaluable components of an effective response.

Thousands of volunteers, groups, and agencies have joined the fight against illegal drugs. For example, Operation Weed and Seed is an initiative for marshaling the resources of a number of federal, state, and local agencies to strengthen law enforcement and revitalize communities. It is a comprehensive, coordinated approach to controlling drugs and crime in targeted high-crime neighborhoods. The Weed and Seed program links community policing and concentrated law enforcement efforts to identify, arrest, and prosecute violent offenders, drug traffickers, and other criminals (weeding) with human services such as after-school, weekend, and summer youth activities; adult literacy classes; parental counseling; and neighborhood revitalization efforts to prevent and deter further crime (seeding). Although federal funding for the national Weed and Seed program has ended, some states still have versions in place.

But crime control is only one of several drug-control strategies that individual communities and the nation as a whole have available. Figure 18.2 depicts the multifaceted drug-control strategies competing for funds and support.

Some communities are developing specific programs to address the drug problem and are recognizing the need for innovative approaches. For example, in jurisdictions facing high incidence of youths abusing OTC drugs, law enforcement can take steps to educate business owners and operators who sell these products about the risks involved. Clerks can be trained to recognize common signs of drug abuse and to understand why they should not sell a dozen packages of Coricidin® Cough and Cold medicine to a group of teenagers. Some businesses may voluntarily move the drugs behind the counter, limit the number of packages a customer may purchase at one time, or require customers to be over age 18. Although many states have passed legislation banning OTC sales of certain products deemed threats to public safety, law enforcement is limited in its ability to restrict OTC drug sales. Indeed, strategic crime-control partnerships with a range of third parties are more effective at disrupting drug problems than are law enforcement–only approaches. Addressing the drug problem has been a priority for the past half century.

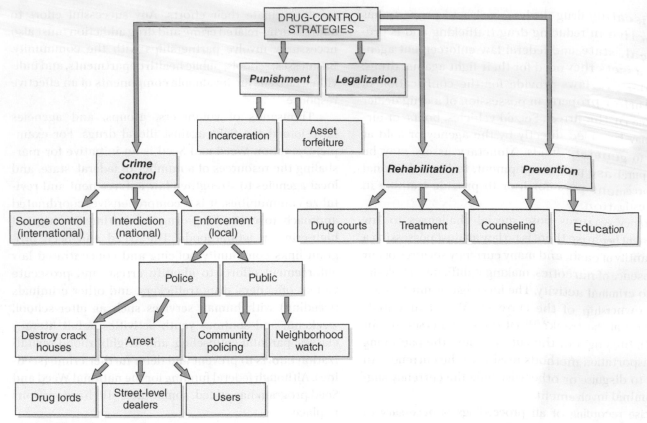

Figure 18.2
Overview of drug-control strategies.

The National Drug Control Strategy

In 1971, President Richard M. Nixon declared "war" on drugs. Since then, federal spending on this war against drug smugglers, users and sellers has increased more than 80-fold—from $420 million in 1973 to $34.6 billion in 2020 (Office of National Drug Policy, 2020). Drug arrests have nearly tripled since 1980, when the federal drug policy shifted to arresting and incarcerating users. In 2019, over 1.5 million state and local arrests were made for drug-related offenses, more than half of which involved the sale, distribution, or possession of marijuana and synthetic/manufactured drugs (FBI, 2019). In the *2020 National Drug Control Strategy*, the annual blueprint published by the Office of National Drug Control Policy (ONDCP), Director James Carroll states:

> This Strategy focuses Federal government efforts along three complementary lines of effort. First, we must continue to prevent initiates to drug use through education and evidence-based prevention programs. Second, we must continue to reduce barriers to treatment services so that access to long-term recovery is available for those suffering from substance use disorder. And finally, we must continue our work to drastically reduce the

availability of these drugs in the United States through law enforcement and cooperation with international partners to eliminate the negative effects that drug trafficking has on the safety of our communities and the well-being of our citizens. . . . The President's top priority [is] to address the current opioid crisis and reduce the number of Americans dying from these dangerous drugs.

In addition to presenting a major challenge to law enforcement in itself, the illegal drug trade is an essential source of revenue for organized crime.

Organized Crime: An Overview

Organized crime in the United States is generally thought to have begun during the 1920s and the time of Prohibition. For most of the twentieth century, law enforcement efforts in the country were focused on what were considered "traditional" organized crime networks, including the Russian Mafia, Japanese Yakuza, Chinese Tongs, and the most well-known of all, the Italian Mafia, or La Cosa Nostra. In fact, the Italian American Cosa Nostra crime families, which peaked in power during the 1970s and 1980s, are widely regarded as the longest lived and most successful organized criminal operations in our nation's history (Jacobs, 2020). These traditional organized crime networks engaged in myriad illegal activities, but the most profitable were gambling, loan sharking, narcotics trafficking, extortion, prostitution, bootlegging, and fraud (Finklea, 2010). Other crimes committed by these groups included racketeering, theft, murder, and money laundering.

For decades, the predominant organized crime family in the United States—La Cosa Nostra—operated with little risk from law enforcement, particularly because FBI Director J. Edgar Hoover denied any organized crime threat existed. However, following Hoover's death in 1972, federal law enforcement reversed course and declared as its number one priority the eradication of organized crime, embarking on years of relentless investigation and prosecution of Cosa Nostra members (Jacobs, 2020). And while the threat of the traditional Italian Mafia has waned in the United States, new organized crime groups have emerged from around the globe, ushering in a new term—**transnational organized crime (TOC)**—to describe self-perpetuating associations of individuals who operate, wholly or in part, by illegal means and irrespective of geography.

Today, organized crime is a global scourge, entangling communities around the world in a web of corruption and violence. Organized crime undermines legitimate commerce, manipulates stock markets, steals merchandise, distributes drugs, controls labor unions, and traffics and enslaves innocent women and children. These criminal enterprises have developed an online presence, with organized crime groups actively and increasingly engaged in Internet fraud and identity theft.

The FBI defines **organized crime** as any group having some manner of a formalized structure and whose primary objective is to obtain money through illegal activities. TOC groups, also called *transnational criminal networks* (TCNs), are a type of organized crime that operates across national borders for economic gain, commonly engaging in drug trafficking, migrant smuggling, human trafficking, money laundering, firearms trafficking, illegal gambling, extortion, counterfeit goods, wildlife and cultural property smuggling, and cybercrime. Organized crime groups achieve and retain their status through the use of actual or threatened violence, corruption of public officials, and other coercive tactics. A **criminal enterprise**, by FBI definition, is a group of individuals with an identified hierarchy, or comparable structure, engaged in significant criminal activity. Although *organized crime* and *criminal enterprise* are often equated and used interchangeably, several federal statutes specifically delineate the elements of an *enterprise* that must be proven to convict individuals or groups under those statutes. For example,

the Racketeering Influenced and Corrupt Organizations (RICO) Act, or Title 18 U.S.C. 1961(4), passed in 1970, defines an enterprise as "any individual, partnership, corporation, association, or other legal entity, and any union or group of individuals associated in fact although not a legal entity."

Albanese (2010, p. 4) provides a definition based on the consensus of a review of definitions of organized crime in the literature: "Organized crime is a continuing criminal enterprise that rationally works to profit from illegal activities that are often in great public demand. Its continuing existence is maintained through the use of force, threats, monopoly control, and/or the corruption of public officials." A notable distinction between organized crime and organizational or "white-collar" crime is that white-collar crime typically occurs as criminal activity that deviates from *legitimate* business activity, whereas organized crime is a continuing criminal enterprise that exists to profit from that very activity (Albanese, 2010).

Several characteristics distinguish organized crime from crimes committed by individuals or unorganized groups.

LO10 Recognize the distinctive characteristics of organized crime.

Distinctive characteristics of organized crime include the following:

- Definite organization and control
- High-profit and continued-profit crimes
- Singular control through force and threats
- Protection through corruption

Other characteristics not as frequently mentioned in definitions of organized crime include restricted membership, being nonideological, specialization, and a code of secrecy.

The organization provides direct control, leadership, and discipline. The leaders are isolated from the general operations through field or area leaders, who in turn control the everyday activities that bring in the profits. Organized crime deals primarily in high-profit crimes that are susceptible to organizational control and that can be developed into larger operations that provide the continued profit necessary for future existence.

Organized crime functions through many forms of corruption and intimidation, often through strong arm tactics, to create a singular control over specific goods and services that ultimately results in a monopoly. Monopoly provides the opportunity to set higher prices and profits for that product or service.

Organized crime flourishes most where protection from interference and prosecution exists. The first line of immunity is the indifference of the general public and their knowing or unknowing use of the services or purchase of the goods offered by organized crime. Through such activities, citizens provide the financial power that gives organized crime immunity from legal authorities. Moreover, organized crime uses enforcement tactics to ensure compliance with its decrees. Members or paid enforcers intimidate, brutalize, and even murder those who fail to obey the dictates of organized crime bosses.

In the early 1960s, Joseph Valachi became the first member of the Mafia to publicly acknowledge its existence when he testified before a Senate subcommittee about the nature of organized crime and dispelled many misconceptions about it. First, organized crime is not a single entity controlled by one superpower. Although a large share of organized crime in the United States was historically controlled by the Italian Mafia, other organizations have sprung up. As America has become more diverse, so too have the organized crime groups operating within it. Asian, Balkan, African, and Russian/Eurasian criminal groups, for example, have been spreading across the country in recent years.

Second, organized crime does not exist only in metropolitan areas. Although organized crime operates primarily in larger metropolitan areas, it has associate operations in many smaller cities, towns, and rural areas.

Third, organized crime does not involve only activities such as narcotics, prostitution, racketeering, and gambling. Rather, organized crime is involved in virtually every area where profits are to be made, including legitimate businesses.

Fourth, citizens are not isolated from organized crime. They are directly affected by it through increased prices of consumer goods controlled by behind-the-scenes activities of organized crime. In addition, citizens who buy items on the black market or knock-off products, solicit prostitutes, purchase pornography, bet through a bookie, take chances on punch boards, or participate in other innocent betting operations directly contribute to the financial success of organized crime. Millions of citizens support organized crime by knowingly or unknowingly taking advantage of the goods and services it provides.

Applicable Laws against Organized Crime

In addition to various state laws, two other distinct groups of laws seek to control organized crime: criminal laws that attack the criminal act itself and laws that make violations a criminal conspiracy. Charges have also been brought against some types of organized crime through prosecution under the Internal Revenue laws and initiation of civil lawsuits.

The major federal acts specifically directed against organized crime are the 1946 Hobbs Anti-Racketeering Act, the 1968 Omnibus Crime Control and Safe Streets Act, the RICO Act of 1970, and the Organized Crime Control Act of 1970. These acts make it permissible to use circumstantial rather than direct evidence to enforce conspiracy violations. These acts also prohibit the use of funds derived from illegal sources to enter into legitimate enterprises (commonly known as *laundering* money). Title 18 U.S. Code, Section 1962, defines three areas that can be prosecuted:

> **LO11** List the three activities that can be prosecuted under Title 18 of the U.S. Code, Section 1962, as they relate to organized crime.

It is a prosecutable conspiracy to

- Acquire any enterprise with money obtained from illegal activity.
- Acquire, maintain, or control any enterprise by illegal means.
- Use any enterprise to conduct illegal activity.

Major Activities of Organized Crime

Organized crime is involved in almost every legal and illegal activity that makes large sums of money with little risk.

> **LO12** Understand the crimes organized crime is typically involved in.

Organized crime is heavily involved in the so-called victimless crimes of gambling, drugs, pornography, and prostitution, as well as fraud, loan-sharking, money laundering, human trafficking, and infiltration of legitimate businesses.

Federal crimes prosecutable under the RICO statute include bribery, sports bribery, counterfeiting, embezzlement of union funds, mail fraud, wire fraud, money laundering, obstruction of justice, murder for hire, drug trafficking, prostitution, sexual exploitation of children, human smuggling, trafficking in counterfeit goods, theft from interstate shipment, and interstate transportation of stolen property. State crimes chargeable under RICO include murder, kidnapping, gambling, arson, robbery, bribery, extortion, and drug offenses. Thus, investigating organized crime effectively means investigating any of these other types of criminal activity in which the organization is involved.

Although the history of organized crime is filled with bloodshed, violence, and corruption, organized crime bosses no longer wield power through a Thompson submachine gun. They manipulate the business economy to their benefit. Such crimes as labor racketeering, unwelcome infiltration of unions, fencing stolen property, gambling, loan-sharking, drug trafficking, employment of illegal aliens, wire fraud, online gambling, cybercrime, and white-collar crimes of all types can signal syndicate involvement.

Victimless Crimes

A **victimless crime** is an illegal activity in which all involved are willing participants. Among the crimes categorized as "victimless" are gambling, drug use, pornography, and prostitution. Because there is no complainant, these crimes are difficult to investigate and to prosecute.

Arguments for legalizing so-called victimless crimes have been made periodically over the years, with varying degrees of success. Proponents argue that it is not the government's function to regulate morality, that the laws are ineffective as well as hypocritical and unenforceable. Further, the laws have created a whole class of "criminals" who would not otherwise be considered such. Perhaps most important, the laws create the conditions under which organized crime can thrive.

Opponents of legalizing these activities argue that it *is* the government's proper function to protect its citizens, even if from themselves. As long as the activities are illegal, law enforcement is obligated to enforce the laws. Among the most difficult laws to enforce are those making gambling illegal in some instances but not others.

Gambling is regarded by some as a vice, a sinful activity that corrupts society; others see gambling as simply a harmless form of entertainment. Within the gambling industry, the term *gambling* is being replaced with the term *gaming*, giving it the appearance of respectability. Legal "gaming" has greatly expanded throughout the country in the form of state lotteries, pari-mutuel betting on horses and greyhounds, bingo, slot machines, and casinos. The Internet has hundreds of gambling-related sites, many of which have set up operations offshore. Some contend that when casino gambling comes to a city, robberies, credit card fraud, property crimes, domestic abuse, and alcohol-related violations increase.

In addition to the problems associated with legal gambling, most reports on organized crime indicate that illegal gambling is the backbone of its activities and its largest source of income. **Bookmaking**—soliciting and accepting bets on any type of sporting event—is the most prevalent gambling operation. Furthermore, various forms of numbers/policy and other lottery games net substantial portions of the financial gain to organized crime from gambling.

Loan-Sharking

Loan-sharking—lending money at exorbitant interest rates—is supported initially by the profits from gambling operations. The upper hierarchy lends money to lower-echelon members of the organization, charging them 1% to 2% interest on large sums. These members in turn lend the money to customers at rates of 20% to 30% or more. The most likely customers are people who cannot obtain loans through legitimate sources, often to pay off illegal gambling debts.

Money Laundering and the Infiltration of Legitimate Business

In recent years, organized crime has become increasingly involved in legitimate business. The vast profits from illegal activities are given legitimacy by being invested in legal business. This is another way of turning dirty money into clean money, or "laundering" it. (Money laundering was discussed in depth in Chapter 14.) For example, a medium-sized company experiences a lack of business and is unable to get credit. Convinced that an infusion of capital will turn the business around, the president turns to a loan shark and borrows at an interest rate of 50% per week. Within months, organized crime has taken over the company. The crime boss keeps the president as a figurehead and uses his reputation to order goods worth thousands of dollars, never intending to pay for them. After a few months, the company files for bankruptcy.

Investigators must be aware that some criminal groups are more involved than others in particular activities. Familiarity with a crime group's "specialties" or crimes of preference will greatly assist in investigations and will help identify the presence of new organized crime factions.

The Threat of Specific Organized Crime Groups

Whereas Italian crime syndicates such as La Cosa Nostra (LCN) may have predominated in the early days of organized crime in the United States, groups from other parts of the world are now cashing in on America's reputation as the "land of opportunity." The rise of Asian, Latin American, African, and Eurasian/Russian gangs requires the government to redesign the fight against organized crime. Nonetheless, Italian criminal groups persist as the stereotypical organized crime threat to American society and are indeed the most organized criminal presence in America.

Italian Organized Crime

Italian organized crime groups, broadly known as the Italian Mafia, first appeared in Italy in the 1800s and consisted of four separate groups: Cosa Nostra (the Sicilian Mafia); the Neapolitan Camorra; the 'Ndrangheta (Calabrian Mafia); and Sacra Corona Unita ("United Sacred Crown"). Cosa Nostra, which means "our thing," is the original Mafia (capital M) and established the model for other mafias, including the famous *omerta* in which members pledged an oath of fealty to the family and adherence to a code of silence about the family's organization and activities (Peters, 2018; Jacobs, 2020).

In the United States, LCN originated with the immigration of Cosa Nostra members and grew into a nationwide alliance of criminals—linked by blood ties or through conspiracy—dedicated to pursuing crime and protecting its members. The LCN, which the FBI estimates has more than 3,000 members and associates, consists of different "families" or groups scattered mostly across major cities in the Northeast, Midwest, California, and the South, but their largest presence exists around New York, southern New Jersey, and Philadelphia (FBI, n.d.). LCN is one of the foremost organized criminal threats to American society, and the major threats they pose are drug trafficking—heroin, in particular—and money laundering. They also are involved in illegal gambling, political corruption, extortion, kidnapping, fraud, counterfeiting, murders, bombings, weapons trafficking, and the infiltration of legitimate businesses.

Five crime families make up New York City's LCN: the Bonanno, Colombo, Genovese, Gambino, and Lucchese families. Each family has roughly the same organizational structure and is headed by a boss (sometimes called the "godfather") who controls the family and makes executive decisions. The underboss is second in command, and the consigliere serves as a senior adviser or counselor. Surrounding the boss are captains ("capos") who supervise "crews" of soldiers. Cosa Nostra crews include "associates" who work for and with made members. To become a "made" member, an individual must be invited by the boss, typically after years of being associated with the family (Jacobs, 2020). It is the crew and their associates who carry out the actual crimes, the proceeds from which go to the capos and those of higher rank.

LCN was originally grounded on standards of conduct borrowed from southern Italian tradition, particularly loyalty to the family. In the Mafia, however, this meant that loyalty to the crime family took precedence over loyalty to one's own blood family. This loyalty began to unravel with the 1992 testimony of an underboss, Salvatore "Sammy the Bull" Gravano, of the Gambino family, against his boss, John Gotti, which sent Gotti to prison for life and set the precedent for other turncoat mobsters to inform on their crime bosses in exchange for reduced prison sentences.

The strict family loyalties that once reigned among Italian organized crime groups have relaxed over the years, as members of once rival groups increasingly put their histories aside for the sake of profit. For example, in February 2014, 24 individuals with connections to Italian organized crime were arrested in a coordinated U.S.–Italian takedown, charged with numerous counts of narcotics trafficking, money laundering, and firearms offenses based, in part, on their alleged participation in a transnational heroin and cocaine trafficking conspiracy involving the 'Ndrangheta, one of Italy's most powerful organized crime syndicates. According to a report by the FBI, the transnational investigation revealed a shipping scheme between members of the Bonanno and Gambino families and 'Ndrangheta, with ties to Mexican drug cartels and a corrupt Italian port official (FBI, 2014).

Asian Organized Crime

Asian organized crime groups, referred to as Asian criminal enterprises by the FBI, are often well run and hard to crack, using very fluid, mobile global networks of criminal associates. Asian criminal enterprises are involved in the traditional racketeering activities normally associated with organized crime—murder, kidnapping, extortion, prostitution, pornography, loan-sharking, gambling, money laundering, financial fraud alien smuggling, counterfeiting of computer and clothing products, theft of autos and computer chips, and various protection schemes (FBI, n.d.). However, Asian organized crime groups derive most of their profits from trafficking in drugs such as heroin and methamphetamine (Finklea, 2010).

Asian criminal enterprises are classified as either traditional, such as the Yakuza and Triads, or nontraditional, such as ethnic Asian street gangs. Japanese organized crime is sometimes known as Boryokudan but is more commonly known as the Yakuza. A gyangu (Japanese gangster) is a member of the Yakuza (organized crime family) and is affiliated with the Yamaguchi-gumi (Japan's largest organized crime family) as a soldier or enforcer (used primarily for muscle). Triads—which are typically based in Hong Kong, Taiwan, and Macau—are the oldest of the Chinese organized crime groups. The Triads engage in a wide range of criminal activities, including money laundering, gambling, extortion, prostitution, loan-sharking, pornography, alien smuggling, and numerous protection schemes, but have seen their greatest profits from drug trafficking. Asian criminal enterprises have been identified in more than 50 metropolitan areas throughout the United States, but they are most prevalent in Honolulu, Las Vegas, Los Angeles, New Orleans, New York, Newark, Philadelphia, San Francisco, Seattle, and Washington, DC (FBI, n.d.).

An emerging trend seen among Asian crime syndicates is a willingness to cooperate across ethnic and racial lines if it is profitable for the enterprise. For example, as with Italian organized crime, Asian organized crime has partnered with Latin American drug cartels to cash in on the lucrative drug business. One such partnership came to light following a U.S.-intelligence led raid on a Philippine cock fighting farm on December 25, 2013, in which a meth lab was discovered and three known affiliates of the Sinaloa cartel were arrested. Further investigation into their activities revealed connections between Hong Kong Triad members in China, one of the world's leading producers of meth and its chemical precursors, and the Sinaloa drug ring that supplies a large quantity of methamphetamine to users in the United States (Harris, 2014).

In another example, drug kingpin Tse Chi Lop, a Chinese-born Canadian national whom law enforcement refers to as Asia's El Chapo, is known to head a vast multinational drug trafficking syndicate comprised of five Triad families in collaboration with Japanese Yakuza, Australian biker gangs, and other various Chinese ethnic gangs across Southeast Asia (Allard, 2019). The syndicate, which the United Nations Office on Drugs and Crime (UNODC) says may bring in as much as $17 billion a year, derives most of its money from the trafficking of tons of methamphetamine to at least a dozen countries. In response to the global threat posed by Tse's syndicate, an international counter-narcotics investigation dubbed Operation Kungur was begun, bringing together authorities from Myanmar, China, Thailand, Japan, the United States, and Canada. It is, say law enforcement agents involved in the investigation, the biggest international effort ever undertaken to combat Asian drug trafficking syndicates.

Vietnamese organized crime is generally one of two kinds: roving or local. As the name suggests, roving bands travel from community to community, have a propensity for violence, and have no permanent leaders or group loyalty. They lack language and job skills and have no family in the United States. Local groups, in contrast, tend to band together in a certain area of a specific community and have a charismatic leader. They also have a propensity for violence and tend to engage in extortion, illegal gambling, and robbery.

Asian organized crime investigations present some unique challenges, primarily because of cultural and social differences. Many Asians are suspicious of the police and the U.S. criminal justice system. Asian criminals exploit this distrust by preying on other Asians, secure in the knowledge that their crimes will most likely go unreported. Another challenge is that many Asian groups are very mobile and have associates or family scattered throughout the United States.

Latin American Organized Crime

Latin American organized crime groups within the United States include Cubans, Colombians, Mexicans, Dominicans, and Salvadorans. These criminal enterprises are heavily involved in drug trafficking, typically bringing their criminal organization into this country along with the drugs they sell. For example, most of the world's cocaine market is controlled by Colombian cartels. In the United States, cartel representatives serve as brokers to coordinate cocaine deliveries to various drug networks, oftentimes by working with local street gangs.

Because of Mexico's proximity to the United States, its organized crime groups are becoming an increasing threat to the United States and are among the fastest-growing gangs in the country. Mexican drug trafficking has had an enormous impact on the United States, as organizations smuggle heroin, cocaine, marijuana, and, most recently, meth. The Mexican Mafia is a prison-based gang that has been growing within the U.S. correctional system for nearly 50 years and is found in several state prison systems. The Mexican Mafia also has links to Hispanic street gangs and controls, to varying degrees, their drug trafficking activities.

Another Latin American organized crime group is the Barrio Azteca, also called "Los Aztecas," a group born in 1986 in the El Paso facility of the Texas prison system, just over the Mexico border from Juárez. In addition to its primary activity of drug trafficking, Barrio Azteca is also involved in murder, extortion, money laundering, and human trafficking. The group is heavily allied with the Juárez Cartel, and, although it is usually described as a gang, some have observed that the group's highly organized nature and growth in membership on both sides of the U.S./Mexico border has positioned Barrio Azteca to make the leap into large-scale transnational organized crime (InSight Crime, 2018). In 2013, Barrio Azteca had an estimated 3,000 members in the United States, including members as far away from Texas as Massachusetts and Pennsylvania.

In 2017, the U.S. Justice Department led an initiative called Operation Regional Shield (ORS) to combat transnational Latin American organized crime by bringing together gang prosecutors and investigators from El Salvador, Guatemala, Honduras, Mexico, and the United States. Since its inception, ORS has coordinated numerous multicountry investigations and takedowns of various criminal entities. In 2020, authorities arrested 36 individuals in El Salvador and Honduras, including a police commissioner, a police deputy inspector, and three law enforcement agents, who were part of a human smuggling network between Central America and the United States. In November 2020, law enforcement also announced criminal charges in Central America against more than 700 members of transnational criminal organizations, primarily MS-13 and 18th Street gangs (U.S. Department of Justice, 2020). Members of these TCOs are charged with a wide range of crimes, including terrorism, murder, kidnapping, human trafficking, drug trafficking, weapons violations, extortion, money laundering, robbery, vehicle theft, and conspiracy.

African Organized Crime

African criminal enterprises, an emerging criminal threat facing law enforcement agencies worldwide and known to be operating in at least 80 other countries, have proliferated in the United States since the 1980s. Although some groups comprise members originating in Ghana, Liberia, and Somalia, by far the predominant nationality in African organized crime is Nigerian. According to the FBI, Nigerian criminal enterprises operate in more than 80 countries around the world, and in the United States, these groups are most prevalent in Atlanta, Baltimore, Chicago, Dallas, Houston, Milwaukee, Newark, New York, and Washington, DC (FBI, n.d.). They are among the most aggressive and expansionist TOCs and engage primarily in drug trafficking and financial frauds, such as health care billing scams, credit card fraud, and advance-fee schemes. Advance-fee schemes, often perpetrated over the Internet and known as "4-1-9 scams" after Section 4-1-9 of the Nigerian Penal Code relating to fraudulent schemes, prey on victims' sympathy, naïveté and, often, greed, by promising a handsome monetary reward in exchange for help in making a financial transaction. Usually received via email or fax, these frauds are often riddled with misspellings, improper grammar, and other potential "tip-offs" that the correspondence is less

than legitimate. Nonetheless, many unwary citizens fall for the scams, and estimates place the cost of Nigerian fraud-related expenses at $1 to $2 billion a year.

Eurasian/Russian Organized Crime

Russia has a 400-year history of dealing with organized crime groups, which for the most part kept their illegal activities inside the border. However, following the collapse of the Soviet Union, Russian organized crime has gone international and poses a great threat to and challenge for U.S. justice. The FBI refers to these groups as Eurasian Organized Crime (EOC). It is estimated that EOC groups have caused hundreds of billions of dollars in losses to U.S. taxpayers, businesses, and investors (FBI, n.d.).

Unlike members of organized crime groups originating from economically and educationally disadvantaged areas, EOC members tend to be well educated. EOC has had little to no involvement in some of the more traditional organized crime activities, such as loansharking and gambling, choosing instead to focus on a wide range of frauds and scams, including insurance scams, securities and investment fraud, and fuel oil scams. In the United States, EOC has become the primary purveyor of credit card scams. Contract murders, kidnappings, robbery, extortion, drug trafficking, auto theft and interstate transportation of stolen property are also common. In addition to transnational money laundering, Russian organized crime is known to traffic in women and children.

EOC members also traffic in such hazardous commodities as weapons and nuclear material smuggled out of their homeland. This removal of otherwise legal raw materials is a major concern to the Russian government because it deprives the country of export income and diminishes the global market value of these goods. The large-scale removal of funds or capital from a country is called **capital flight**. Do not confuse *money laundering* and *capital flight*, which are not interchangeable terms. Money laundering is capital flight, but not all capital flight is money laundering. Money laundering is illegal; capital flight is not.

The U.S. money laundering laws recognize only three offenses committed outside the United States as predicates for a charge of money laundering: drug violations, terrorism, and bank fraud. Any funds resulting from a theft from the Russian government, evasion of Russian taxes, or bribes received by Russian officials can legally be processed through U.S. banks. Such activities do not qualify as money laundering.

Investigating Eurasian/Russian organized crime is challenged by several factors. First, the EOC consists of hundreds of groups, all acting independently. Eurasian/Russian crime groups in the United States are loosely structured, lacking any formal hierarchy. They tend to be fluid with membership fluctuating between 5 and 20 people, depending on the operation. Most members are already hardened criminals, have military experience, and are highly educated. As with cases involving other immigrant organized crime groups, language barriers present a challenge to investigators. Another problem lies in the cooperation among and pooling of resources between Eurasian/Russian and other organized crime groups.

Organized Crime and Corruption

One of the greatest threats posed by organized crime is the corruption it engenders throughout the entire legal system. Although the police are interested in any corruption by public officials, they are especially concerned about corruption in their own department. Bribes of police officers can take many forms: offering money outright, taking care of medical bills, or providing free merchandise or free vacations. Any police officer who is offered a bribe must report it immediately to a superior and then attempt to make an arrest that will involve the person making the offer as well as those responsible higher in the organization.

Some officials repay organized crime figures by providing inside information that can be used to manipulate securities or to purchase real estate in areas of future development that can be sold for a much higher price.

The Police Response

It is frequently difficult for local law enforcement officers to understand their role in investigating or controlling organized crime. But there is a direct relationship between what officers do on assignment and investigation of organized crime activities. Local law enforcement officers are the first line of defense in controlling all crime, and organized crime is no exception. Because of the highly structured nature of many organized crime groups, law enforcement officers can seldom break into these hierarchies, but they can remain the "eyes" and "ears" of the information and intelligence system essential to combat organized crime. While local law enforcement is not usually putting together the RICO case, they do still investigate the crimes, and they will always be the one to get to the crime scene first or take the first report of the crime.

> **LO13** Explain what the investigator's primary role is in dealing with the organized crime problem.
>
> The daily observations of local law enforcement officers provide vital information for investigating organized crime. Report all suspicious activities and persons possibly associated with organized crime to the appropriate person or agency.

Because organized crime is involved in a great number of activities, information can arise from many sources. Thus, your street-level observations can be critical. Every day you observe many conditions related to crime and deal with individuals who are part of the community's activities. Seemingly unimportant details can fit into an overall picture that an intelligence unit is putting together (Figure 18.3).

Ways to become aware of people and conditions that suggest organized crime activity are provided by the International Association of Chiefs of Police:

A retail establishment seems to be doing a brisk business—many customers coming and going. But the customers do not remain in the store very long and do not leave with packages or other evidence that purchases were made. The store may have a meager selection of merchandise, which raises the question of how it can attract so many customers day after day. This could indicate the presence of a policy operation at the writer level or the place of business of a bookmaker's commission man.

At about the same time each day, a package is delivered to a newsstand, bar, or other location. Later the package is picked up by another individual. The location could be a policy drop—the place to which a policy writer sends his slips and/or day's receipts.

You are called to investigate a beating in a bar or at a location near a factory or other place of employment. The incident may occur on a payday or within a couple of days thereafter. The beating may have resulted from the impatience of a loan shark who has not been paid on schedule.

Merchants complain about another price rise by the cartage company that removes their garbage or trash. They also mention that there is either no competitor to deal with or if there is one, it will not accept their business. Frequently, this indicates that an organized crime group is trying to monopolize the cartage business or limit competition through territorial agreements.

A rash of vandalism strikes a number of establishments engaged in the same type of business—such as dry cleaning. Racketeers may be trying to coerce reluc-

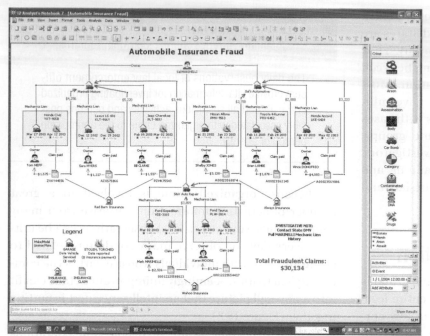

FIGURE 18.3

The progress and details of an organized crime investigation may make perfect sense to those who have spent months putting it together, but bringing others up to date can be challenging and time consuming. Analytical charts like this—made with i2 Analyst's Notebook—can quickly uncover key relationships, identify patterns/trends, and focus on important leads and clues among suspects, witnesses, vehicles, and events. This brings into focus individuals at the center of organized crime and fraud, allowing analysts and investigators to pinpoint the most significant areas of interest in an investigation and aid decision makers in targeting their resources.

i2 Inc.

tant owners into joining an association or into doing business with mob-controlled vendors. (Reprinted from *Criminal Intelligence*, Training Key #223, with permission of the International Association of Chiefs of Police)

Because conspiratorial associations are a threshold matter in classifying a group as being involved in organized crime, investigators must consider characteristics that may signal the presence and operation of organized crime in their jurisdiction. In addition to the factors of continuity and involvement in illegal activity for the primary motivation of financial profit, other "red flags" that may warrant further scrutiny by law enforcement include:

- Clannish or cultural connections

- Leadership

- Scope of membership

- Foreign nexus

- Known safe havens, both domestic and abroad

- Impact and expanse of activities

- Nature of offenses (Ott, 2012, pp. 11–12)

Make a habit of checking out new businesses in your area. If the enterprise requires a license, such as a bar, ask to see the license if for no other reason than to observe who the owners are; ascertain the identity of the company that distributes or services the jukeboxes, vending machines, video gaming machines, and so forth. If, for example, the jukebox or vending machine distributor is a company controlled by the organized underworld, so also might be the bar in which the equipment is located.

Report in writing all information pertaining to such activities, either immediately, if the activity involves an imminent meeting, or when time permits. Report as nearly as possible exact conversations with assault victims suspected of associating with organized crime members. These conversations can include names of people, including their nicknames or monikers, or organizations responsible for violence and crime in the community.

Agencies Cooperating in Investigating Organized Crime

Under the authority of the 1968 Omnibus Crime Control and Safe Streets Act and the Organized Crime Control Act of 1970, the U.S. Department of Justice established the Organized Crime and Racketeering Unit. Organized crime strike forces were formed throughout the country, mostly in major cities, to coordinate all federal organized crime investigation activities and work closely with state, county, and municipal law enforcement agencies.

Other agencies that play important roles in investigating organized crime are the FBI, which often has a member on the strike forces; the Postal Inspection Service (USPIS), which is in charge of mail fraud, embezzlements, and other crimes involving material distributed through the mails; the U.S. Secret Service (USSS), which investigates government checks and bonds as well as foreign securities; the Department of Labor, which investigates organized crime activities related to labor practices and pension funds; the Securities and Exchange Commission (SEC), which investigates organized crime activities in the purchase of securities; and the Internal Revenue Service (IRS), which investigates violations of income tax laws. Other agencies committed to sustained cooperation in investigating organized crime include U.S. Immigration and Customs Enforcement (ICE); the DEA; the Bureau of Alcohol, Tobacco, Firearms, and Explosives (ATF); the U.S. Department of State, Bureau of Diplomatic Security (DS); the U.S. Department of Labor, Office of the Inspector General (DOL-OIG); and components of the State Department, the Treasury Department, INTERPOL, and the intelligence community. In addition to these agencies, the state attorney general's office and the district attorney's office can assist police in building a case against organized crime figures who violate local and state laws.

Organized crime investigations in the United States increasingly involve agencies from other countries, as such criminal organizations rarely restrict their illegal activities to the jurisdiction of one nation. The United Nations Convention against Transnational Organized Crime (UNTOC), also called the Palermo Convention, was signed in Palermo, Italy, in December 2000 as recognition of the shared global challenges of investigating and combatting TOC (also called "international organized crime" [IOC]). UNTOC was entered into force in the United States in November 2005:

> On May 29, 2009, Attorney General Eric Holder announced the creation of the International Organized Crime Intelligence and Operations Center (IOC-2), which marshals the resources and information of nine U.S. law enforcement agencies, as well as federal prosecutors, to collectively combat the threats posed by international criminal organizations to domestic safety and security. The IOC-2 allows partner agencies to join together in a task force setting, combine data, and produce actionable leads for investigators and prosecutors working nationwide to combat international organized crime, and to coordinate the resulting multi-jurisdictional investigations and prosecutions. . . .
>
> The mission of the IOC-2 is to disrupt and dismantle transnational criminal organizations posing the greatest threat to the United States by (1) providing de-confliction and coordination of multi-jurisdictional, multi-agency, and multi-national law enforcement operations, investigations, prosecutions, and forfeiture proceedings; (2) identifying and analyzing all source information and intelligence related to transnational organized crime; and (3) disseminating such information and intelligence to support member agency investigative efforts. (FBI, n.d.)

If organized crime is suspected in a local jurisdiction, investigators should work with local prosecutors to have the case agent submit a request to IOC-2 for assistance in determining whether the case is connected to any other federal investigations occurring throughout the country (Ott, 2012).

Methods to Combat Organized Crime

Because organized crime groups often have abundant resources and international connections to help protect their interests, law enforcement must deploy a wide variety of tactics to conquer the threat. Proactive community policing and problem-solving approaches hold much promise in combating organized crime. Intra-agency cooperation is also needed because most organized crime activities cross jurisdictions. Surveillance and undercover operations are also sometimes indicated.

In addition to the IOC-2, the DOJ has, since 2008, led a multiagency effort to develop and implement the Law Enforcement Strategy to Combat International Organized Crime (IOC Strategy). The IOC Strategy established a comprehensive framework for law enforcement to address the threats posed by IOC

Another resource for combating organized crime is the local citizenry. However, victims, witnesses, and others with knowledge about organized crime activities are usually, and understandably, reluctant to come forth with information. Consequently, the government is often prepared to provide federal protection to those whose testimony is deemed crucial in building a case against organized crime.

The enterprise theory of investigation (ETI) is a combined organized crime and drug strategy the FBI uses to focus investigations and prosecutions on entire criminal enterprises rather than on individuals. ETI is a proactive approach to attack a criminal organization's structure and, when combined with appropriate federal and state laws, can enable law enforcement to effectively target and terminate a criminal enterprise with a single criminal indictment. As with other FBI initiatives, ETI focuses on major regional, national, and international crime groups that control large segments of organized crime's illegal activities.

Investigative Aids

Electronic surveillance of suspects is essential in investigating organized crime. Organized crime leaders often avoid direct involvement in criminal acts by planning and coordinating criminal activity over the phone or the Internet. Consequently, electronic surveillance can be used to build an effective case based on a criminal's own words while avoiding the risks associated with using informants or undercover agents.

Pen registers also are important in investigating sophisticated criminal networks. Pen registers record the numbers dialed from a telephone and sent via text or SMS message by monitoring the electrical impulses of the numbers dialed. In *Smith v. Maryland* (1979), the Supreme Court held that using a pen register does not constitute a search within the meaning of the Fourth Amendment, so neither probable cause nor a warrant is required to use the device. Several state courts, however, have held that using a pen register *is* a search under the respective state statutes and that a warrant supported by probable cause *is* needed. Investigators must be familiar with their state's statutes in this area. The same situation exists for trap-and-trace devices, which reveal the telephone number of the source of all *incoming* calls to a particular number. Their use may or may not require a warrant, depending on the specific state. Wiretapping is another extremely important tool, but it is also a labor intensive avenue. Caller ID and phone numbers stored in speed dialers, fax machines, and computer files can also be of assistance, as discussed in Chapter 17.

Investigators should never forget about traditional surveillance techniques. Following a suspect around can disclose much useful information with no warrant required. Finally, to minimize labor and personnel requirements, use of pole cameras can provide excellent sources of information.

The Regional Information Sharing System (RISS), a multijurisdictional intelligence sharing system comprising nearly 9,000 local, state, and federal agencies, is another tool to help investigators identify, target, and remove criminal conspiracies and activities that reach across jurisdictional boundaries.

Asset Forfeiture

An effective weapon against organized crime, as with drug crimes, is the asset-forfeiture program, which allows law enforcement agencies to seize funds and property associated with criminal activity and effectively subjects criminals to 100% tax on their earnings. Asset forfeiture was presented in detail earlier in the section on drug-related criminal investigations.

The Decline of Organized Crime?

Certainly one hopes that tougher legislation, improved investigative techniques, and increased use of tools such as asset forfeiture have brought about a decline in organized crime. Although perhaps these measures have forced a decline in the threat of *traditional* organized crime, the vacancies left by recent LCN associates and Gambino crime family members will easily be filled by any number of new criminal enterprises finding their way onto American soil.

Furthermore, in the wake of the September 11, 2001, terrorist attacks, many of the law enforcement resources previously allocated to organized crime investigations have been redirected toward counterterrorism efforts, allowing a resurgence in organized crime activity throughout the country.

It is sometimes difficult to determine whether criminal events are the work of organized crime or of gangs. Many defining characteristics of organized crime groups are strikingly similar to those of better-organized gangs, and prison gangs often have direct ties to organized crime groups. Gangs are the focus of Chapter 19.

Summary

In 1914, the federal government passed the Harrison Narcotics Act, which made the sale or use of certain drugs illegal. It is illegal to possess or use narcotics or other dangerous drugs without a prescription and to sell or distribute them without a license. The main drug classes regulated by the CSA are narcotics, stimulants, depressants, hallucinogens, and anabolic steroids. Controlled prescription drugs (CPDs), marijuana, and designer drugs are also regulated by the CSA and present a challenge to law enforcement. Over-the-counter (OTC) drugs and inhalants, although not regulated under the CSA, are also commonly abused, most often by youth. The most commonly observed drugs on the street, in possession of users, and seized in drug raids are heroin and prescription opioids such as OxyContin and fentanyl; powder cocaine and crack; methamphetamine; and marijuana. Arrest for possession or use of marijuana is the most frequent drug arrest.

Physical evidence of possession or use of controlled substances includes the actual drugs, apparatus associated with their use, the suspect's appearance and behavior, and urine and blood tests. The actual transfer of drugs from the seller to the buyer is the major legal evidence in prosecuting drug-sale cases. If you observe what appears to be a drug buy, you can make a warrantless arrest if you have probable cause. Often, however, it is better simply to observe and gather information. Undercover drug buys are carefully planned, witnessed and conducted so that no charge of entrapment can be made. Make two or more buys to avoid the charge of entrapment. The more buys documented, the weaker a suspect's defense of entrapment.

The federal DEA provides unified leadership in attacking narcotics trafficking and drug abuse. The DEA's emphasis is on the source and distribution of illicit drugs rather than on arresting abusers.

The illegal drug trade is an essential source of revenue for organized crime. Distinctive characteristics of organized crime include definite organization and control, high-profit and continued-profit crimes, singular control through force and threats, and protection through corruption. It is a prosecutable conspiracy to acquire any enterprise with money obtained from illegal activity; to acquire, maintain, or control any enterprise by illegal means; or to use any enterprise to conduct illegal activity.

Organized crime is heavily involved in the so-called victimless crimes of gambling, drugs, pornography and prostitution, as well as fraud, loan-sharking, money laundering, human trafficking, and infiltration of legitimate businesses. The daily observations of local law enforcement officers provide vital information for investigating organized crime. Report all suspicious activities and persons possibly associated with organized crime to the appropriate person or agency.

Can You Define?

analogs	Ecstasy	pill mills
body packing	excited delirium	raves
bookmaking	flashroll	reverse buy
capital flight	hallucinogen	robotripping
club drugs	loan-sharking	sinsemilla
cook	MDMA	skittling
crack	mules	sting
crank	narcotic	transnational organized crime
criminal enterprise	organized crime	(TOC)
depressant	OTC drugs	tweaker
designer drugs	pharming	victimless crime

Checklists

Drugs and Controlled Substances

- How did the complaint originate? From police? Victim? Informant? Neighbor?

- What is the specific nature of the complaint? Selling? Using? Possessing? Overdose? Are all required elements present?

- What type of narcotics are suspect?

- Is there enough evidence of sale to justify planning a buy?

- Were obtained drugs tested with a department drug-detection kit?

- Has the evidence been properly collected, identified, and preserved?

- Has the evidence been sent to a laboratory for examination?

- Has the drug been determined to be a controlled substance?

- Has everyone involved been interviewed or interrogated?

- Do those involved have prior arrests for similar offenses?

- Is surveillance necessary to obtain evidence for an arrest or a search warrant?

- Is a raid called for? (If so, review the checklist for raids in Chapter 7.)

- Have cooperating agencies been alerted?

Organized Crime

- Have people recently moved into the city and purchased businesses that obviously could not support their standard of living?

- Do any public officials appear to live beyond their means?

- Does a public official continuously vote in favor of a business that is suspected of being connected with organized crime?

- Have business owners complained of pressure to use a specific service or of threats to close the business if they do not hire certain people?

- Does a business have high-level executives with police records?

- Have there been complaints of someone on the premises operating as a bookie?

- Have families complained about loss of wages paid to a loan shark?

- Have union officials suddenly been replaced by new, nonlocal persons?

- Has there been damage or injury to property during union problems?

- Are goods being received at a store that do not fit with merchandise sold there?

- Has a discount store suddenly appeared without a clear indication of true ownership?

- Has arson suddenly increased?

- Do nonemployees hang around manufacturing plants or nonstudents hang around a school? (This could indicate a bookie operation or drug sales.)

- Is evidence of betting operations being left in public wastebaskets or trash containers on the streets?

- When assaults occur, what are the motives? Could they be a result of gambling debts owed to a loan shark?

- Are people seen going into and out of certain businesses with which they are not ordinarily associated?

- Are known gamblers or persons with other criminal records repeatedly seen in a specific location?

Application

Read the following and then answer the questions:
The Stakeout (adapted from an account of an actual narcotics investigation written by David Peterson): It is dark as the five men emerge from the plane. They haul out their luggage and walk to the parking lot of the tiny, one-strip airport. The pilot enters a white shack that is trimmed in red. When the pilot leaves, the others gather around a young man who has driven out to meet them. His name is Bruce Preece, and he looks like an outdoorsman. Bearded, he wears a suede hat and red plaid jacket.

Moments later, a camper occupied by two more men pulls into the parking lot, and most of the group pile into the back. Seated along foam-rubber benches, they are dim in the shadows as the camper moves through the empty town.

"That guy sure was an inquisitive one," the pilot remarks, referring to the man in the shack. "He knew we were here last week, and he wanted to know what we were up to."

"Tourists," someone else replies, his head silhouetted against a window. Everyone looks like a visitor—a hunter, perhaps, or a fisherman. They carry small bags and wear down jackets and jeans. The clothing is deceptive.

Four narcotics agents, or *narcs*, and four agents from the federal DEA are staked out in a camper outside the home of a man who works for a chemical firm. They suspect that at home he is manufacturing illegal drugs in a clandestine laboratory. The agents call him "No. 1."

They suspect that another man is getting illegal drugs and distributing them in nearby towns. They call him "No. 2."

No. 1 came under suspicion when a chemical supply company in Connecticut notified the feds that someone in this little town was ordering chemicals often used to make illegal substances. No. 2 came under suspicion when he told a local deputy sheriff he would be paid $2,000 if he notified him of any narcotics investigations.

The two men have been under surveillance for several weeks. One agent has even been inside the house by taking a shipment of chemicals from the Connecticut firm and making a "controlled delivery"—that is, he pretended to be the mailman and hauled the heavy boxes inside the house.

The agents have noticed a pattern. On Wednesdays, No. 1's wife goes into town and No. 2 stops by. It is Wednesday night. The plan is to watch No. 2 enter and leave the house and arrest him before he reaches his car. Assuming he is carrying illegal drugs, the agents will arrest No. 1 as well, search his home and seize the contents of the lab. Both men are known to be armed.

By 7 p.m., surveillance has begun in earnest. The eight agents are waiting for something to happen. Two agents sit in an unmarked car along the highway leading to the house. Two others are in the woods, within view of the house. The other four are in the camper, parked just off the highway. Even from inside, the camper looks normal. But its cabinets contain an array of radios, cameras,

lenses, firearms, and other gear. From the camper's bathroom, one agent takes out a telephoto lens the size of a small wastebasket and attaches it to a "night scope."

At about 7:15, the woman leaves.

Each of the three groups of agents has a radio. However, No. 1 is believed to have a police scanner, which would allow him to monitor their conversation. So they speak in a rough sort of code, as though they were squad cars checking for speeders. "401," for example, will mean that No. 2 has arrived.

Hours pass. None of the agents has eaten since noon. They pass around a bag of Halloween-sized Snickers bars and start telling narc stories.

At 10 p.m., a sober, low voice over the radio says, "You may have three visitors shortly." A few minutes later, three agents climb into the camper, shivering. One agent, who has been watching No. 1 through his kitchen window with binoculars, says, "He's busy in there. He's pouring stuff, and he's running something, like a tableting machine."

The agents know that if they could just bust into that house, they'd find a guilty man surrounded by evidence. No. 2 doesn't show. Another night wasted?

Questions

1. Do the agents have probable cause to conduct a raid at this time?

2. Could they seize the materials No. 1 is working with as plain-view evidence? Why or why not?

3. What aspects of the surveillance illustrate effective investigation?

4. Have the agents made any mistakes?

5. What should their next step be?

6. Is there likely to be a link between the suspects and organized crime? Why or why not?

References

Albanese, J. S. (2010). *Organized crime in our times* (6thEd.). Burlington, MA: Anderson Publishing.

Allard, T. (2019, October 14). The hunt for Asia's El Chapo. *Reuters*. Retrieved March 27, 2021, from www.reuters.com/investigates/special-report/meth-syndicate/

Centers for Disease Control and Prevention, (2020). Increase in fatal drug overdoses across the United States driven by synthetic opioids before and during the COVID-19 pandemic. Atlanta, GA: Author. (CDCHAN-00438). Retrieved March 22, 2021, from emergency.cdc.gov/han/2020/han00438.asp

Christian, D. R. (2004). *Forensic examination of clandestine laboratories*. Boca Raton, FL: CRC Press. Retrieved March 24, 2021, from www.academia.edu/40188802/Forensic_Investigation_of_Clandestine_Laboratories

Drug Enforcement Administration. (n.d.). *Organized crime and drug enforcement task force*. Washington, DC: Author. Retrieved May 28, 2015, from www.justice.gov/ocdetf

Drug Enforcement Administration. (n.d.). *State and local task forces*. Washington, DC: Author. Retrieved March 25, 2021, from www.dea.gov/state-and-local-task-forces

Drug Enforcement Administration. (2013, June 26). *Updated results from DEA's largest-ever global synthetic drug takedown yesterday*. Washington, DC: Author. Retrieved March 23, 2021, from www.dea.gov/divisions/hq/2013/hq062613.shtml

Drug Enforcement Administration. (2014, November). *2014 national drug threat assessment summary*. Washington, DC: Author. Retrieved March 23, 2021, from www.dea.gov/sites/default/files/2018-07/dir-ndta-unclass.pdf

Drug Enforcement Administration. (2015a, April 15). *Joint investigation leads to arrest of doctor for selling assault weapons & drugs during course of murder-for-hire plot*. Washington, DC: Author. Retrieved March 19, 2021, from www.dea.gov/press-releases/2015/04/15/joint-investigation-leads-arrest-doctor-selling-assault-weapons-drugs

Drug Enforcement Administration. (2015b, October 15). *151 arrested in DEA-led investigation of synthetic drug rings.* Washington, DC: Author. Retrieved March 23, 2021, from www.dea.gov/press-releases/2015/10/15/151-arrested-dea-led-investigation-synthetic-drug-rings

Drug Enforcement Administration. (2017, January 31). *Sands Point cardiologist sentenced for vicious assault-for-hire plot against rival doctor.* Washington, DC: Author. Retrieved March 19, 2021, from www.dea.gov/press-releases/2017/01/31/sands-point-cardiologist-sentenced-vicious-assault-hire-plot-against

Drug Enforcement Administration. (2019, November 13). *Narcotics dealer charged with fentanyl overdose death.* Washington, DC: Author. Retrieved March 24, 2021, from www.dea.gov/press-releases/2019/11/13/narcotics-dealer-charged-fentanyl-overdose-death

Drug Enforcement Administration. (2020a). *Drugs of abuse: A DEA resource guide (2020 edition).* Washington, DC: Author. Retrieved March 19, 2020, from www.getsmartaboutdrugs.gov/sites/getsmartaboutdrugs.com/files/publications/Drugs%20of%20Abuse%202020-Web%20Version-508%20compliant.pdf

Drug Enforcement Administration. (2020b). *"Pill mill" doctor pleads guilty to opioid distribution, admits signing prescriptions for dead and jailed patients.* Washington, DC: Author. Retrieved March 23, 2021, from www.dea.gov/press-releases/2020/01/21/pill-mill-doctor-pleads-guilty-opioid-distribution-admits-signing

Drug Enforcement Administration. (2021, March). *2020 National drug threat assessment.* Washington, DC: Author. Retrieved March 22, 2021, from www.dea.gov/sites/default/files/2021-02/DIR-008-21%202020%20National%20Drug%20Threat%20Assessment_WEB.pdf

Ensminger, J. J. (2012). *Police and military dogs: Criminal detection, forensic evidence, and judicial admissibility.* Boca Raton, FL: CRC Press. Retrieved March 25, 2021, from www.perrosdebusqueda.es/wp-content/uploads/2014/11/Libro-Police-dogs.pdf

Federal Bureau of Investigation. (n.d.). *Transnational organized crime.* Washington, DC: Author. Retrieved March 26, 2021, from www.fbi.gov/investigate/organized-crime

Federal Bureau of Investigation. (2019). *Crime in the United States, 2019.* Washington, DC: Author. Retrieved March 22, 2021, from ucr.fbi.gov/crime-in-the-u.s/2019/crime-in-the-u.s.-2019/

Finklea, K. M. (2010, December 22). *Organized crime in the United States: Trends and issues for congress.* (R40525). Washington, DC: Congressional Research Service. Retrieved March 26, 2021, from fas.org/sgp/crs/misc/R40525.pdf

Goforth, C. (2019, July 29). Florida in debate over murder charges for drug dealers who buyers die. *Juvenile Justice Information Exchange.* Retrieved March 24, 2021, from jjie.org/2019/07/29/florida-considers-murder-charge-for-drug-dealers/

Harris, B. (2014, January 12). Hong Kong triads supply meth ingredients to Mexican drug cartels. *South China Morning Post.* Retrieved March 29, 2021, from www.scmp.com/news/hong-kong/article/1403433/hong-kong-triads-supply-meth-ingredients-mexican-drug-cartels

Hvozdovich, J. A., Chronister, C. W., Logan, B. K., & Goldberger, B. A. (2020, April). Case report: Synthetic cannabinoid deaths in State of Florida prisoners. *Journal of Analytical Toxicology, 44* (3): 298–300. doi:10.1093/jat/bkz092

InSight Crime. (2018, July 9). *Barrio Azteca.* Medellin, Colombia: Author. Retrieved March 27, 2021, from insightcrime.org/mexico-organized-crime-news/barrio-azteca-profile/

International Association of Chiefs of Police. (n.d.). *Criminal intelligence.* Training Key #223. Alexandria, VA: Author

Jacobs, J. B. (2020). The rise and fall of organized crime in the United States. *Crime and Justice, 49*: 17–67. doi:10.1086/706895

Johnston, L. D., Miech, R. A., O'Malley, P. M., Bachman, J. G., Schulenberg, J. E., & Patrick, M. E. (2019). *Monitoring the future national survey results on drug use: 1975–2018: Overview, key findings on adolescent drug use.* Ann Arbor, MI: Institute for Social Research, University of Michigan. Retrieved March 22, 2021, from files.eric.ed.gov/fulltext/ED594190.pdf

Jones-Brown, D., & Shane, J. M. (2011, June). *An exploratory study of the use of confidential informants in New Jersey.* Newark, NJ: American Civil Liberties Union. Retrieved March 24, 2021, from www.researchgate.net/profile/Jon-Shane-2/publication/267549691_An_Exploratory_Study_of_the_Use_of_Confidential_Informants_in_New_Jersey/links/55ae23a008aee079921ebca1/An-Exploratory-Study-of-the-Use-of-Confidential-Informants-in-New-Jersey.pdf

Jordan, M. R., & Morrisonponce, D. (2020, July 10). Naloxone. In *StatPearls.* Treasure Island, FL: StatPearls Publishing. Retrieved March 23, 2021, from www.ncbi.nlm.nih.gov/books/NBK441910/

Larkin, S. (2014, January). *Presumptive field testing using portable Raman spectroscopy.* doi:10.13140/RG.2.1.1703.3689

Lee, K. C., Ladizinski, B., & Federman, D. G. (2012, June). Complications associated with use of Levamisole-contaminated cocaine: An emerging public health challenge. *Mayo Clinic Proceedings, 87*(6): 581–586.

Lou, M. (2019, July 9). Under new North Carolina law, drug dealers could be charged with second-degree murder. Retrieved March 24, 2021, from www.cnn.com/2019/07/09/us/north-carolina-hb-474-death-by-distribution-trnd/index.html

Mattson, C. L., Tanz, L. J., Quinn, K., Kariisa, M., Patel, P., & Davis, N. L. (2021). Trends and geographic patterns in drug and synthetic opioid overdose deaths—United States, 2013–2019. *Morbidity and Mortality Weekly Report, 70*: 202–207. Retrieved March 22, 2021, from www.cdc.gov/mmwr/volumes/70/wr/mm7006a4.htm#suggestedcitation

Moreto, W., Gau, J. M., & Brooke, E. (2020, June). Pill mills, occupational offending, and situational crime prevention: A framework for analyzing offender behavior and adaptation. *Security Journal, 33*(4). doi:10.1057/s41284-019-00180-y

National Center on Drug Abuse Statistics. (n.d.). *Drug abuse statistics.* Bethesda, MD: National Institute on Drug Abuse. Retrieved March 22, 2021, from drugabusestatistics.org/

National Drug Intelligence Center. (n.d.). *Methamphetamine laboratory identification and hazards: Fast facts.* Johnstown, PA: Author. Retrieved March 24, 2021, from www.justice.gov/archive/ndic/pubs7/7341/7341p.pdf

National Institute on Drug Abuse. (2017, December). *Over-the-counter medicines.* Bethesda, MD: Author. Retrieved March 24, 2021, from www.drugabuse.gov/sites/default/files/drugfacts-overthecountermedicines.pdf

National Institute on Drug Abuse. (2019, December 24). *Marijuana DrugFacts.* Bethesda, MD: Author. Retrieved March 22, 2021, from www.drugabuse.gov/publications/drugfacts/marijuana

National Institute on Drug Abuse. (2020, June). *Misuse of prescription drugs research report.* Bethesda, MD: Author. Retrieved March 23, 2021, from www.drugabuse.gov/download/37630/misuse-prescription-drugs-research-report.pdf?v=add4ee202a1d1f88f8e1fdd2bb83a5ef

National Institute on Drug Abuse. (2021, January 29). *Overdose death rates.* Bethesda, MD: Author. Retrieved March 23, 2021, from www.drugabuse.gov/drug-topics/trends-statistics/overdose-death-rates

Office of National Drug Control Policy. (2020, February). *National drug control strategy.* Washington, DC: Author. Retrieved March 25, 2021, from legislativeanalysis.org/wp-content/uploads/2020/02/2020-ONDCP-National-Drug-Control-Strategy.pdf

Ott, T. P. (2012). Responding to the threat of international organized crime: A primer on programs, profiles, and practice points. *Organized Crime, 60*(6): 1–24. Retrieved March 29, 2021, from www.justice.gov/sites/default/files/usao/legacy/2012/10/31/usab6006.pdf

Peters, L. (2018, January 28). Italian mafia: How crime families went global. *BBC News.* Retrieved March 26, 2021, from www.bbc.com/news/world-europe-42794848

Reed, B. (2012, July 17). Pa. officer, K-9 make $11.7 million drug seizure. *PoliceOne.com.* Retrieved March 29, 2021, from www.police1.com/drug-interdiction-narcotics/articles/pa-officer-k-9-make-117-million-drug-seizure-uGPGTUrpp4wTw1TJ/

Substance Abuse and Mental Health Services Administration. (2011). *Drug abuse warning network, 2011: National estimates of drug-related emergency department visits.* HHS Publication No. (SMA) 13-2760, DWN Series D-39. Rockville, MD: Author. Retrieved March 23, 2021, from www.samhsa.gov/data/sites/default/files/DAWN2k11ED/DAWN2k11ED/DAWN2k11ED.pdf

Substance Abuse and Mental Health Services Administration. (2020). *Key substance use and mental health indicators in the United States: Results from the 2019 National Survey on Drug Use and Health* (HHS Publication No. PEP20-07-01-001, NSDUH Series H-55). Rockville, MD: Center for Behavioral Health Statistics and Quality, Substance Abuse and Mental Health Services Administration. Retrieved March 22, 2021, from www.samhsa.gov/data/

Suffolk County District Attorney's Office. (2019, October 3). *Drug dealer convicted on manslaughter for causing fatal overdose death sentenced to prison.* Hauppauge, NY: Author. Retrieved March 24, 2021, from suffolkcountyny.gov/da/News-and-Public-Information/Press-Releases/drug-dealer-convicted-of-manslaughter-for-causing-fatal-overdose-sentenced-to-prison

Symonsbergen, D. J., Kangas, M. J., Perez, M., & Holmes, A. E. (2018). General advantages and disadvantages of the NIK narcotic test. *Journal of Forensic Science and Criminal Investigation, 8*(1): 555730. doi:10.19080/JFSCI.2018.08.555730

U.S. Department of Justice. (2020, November 27). *More than 700 members of transnational organized crime groups arrested in Central America in U.S. assisted operation.* Washington, DC: Author. Retrieved March 27, 2021, from www.justice.gov/opa/pr/more-700-members-transnational-organized-crime-groups-arrested-central-america-us-assisted

U.S. Environmental Protection Agency. (2013, March). *Voluntary guidelines for methamphetamine laboratory cleanup.* Washington, DC: Author. Retrieved March 24, 2021, from www.epa.gov/sites/production/files/documents/meth_lab_guidelines.pdf

U.S. Immigration and Customs Enforcement. (2020, March 31). *San Diego tunnel task force uncovers sophisticated cross-border drug tunnel under the US/Mexico border.* Washington, DC: Author. Retrieved March 22, 2021, from www.ice.gov/news/releases/san-diego-tunnel-task-force-uncovers-sophisticated-cross-border-drug-tunnel-under

Welty, J. (2018, August 13). *Does a search warrant for a person authorize a strip search?* Chapel Hill, NC: North Carolina Criminal Law. Retrieved March 24, 2021, from nccriminallaw.sog.unc.edu/does-a-search-warrant-for-a-person-authorize-a-strip-search/

Wood, C. (2014, July 1). Indiana's interactive map plots meth lab data. *Government Technology.* Retrieved May 28, 2015, from www.govtech.com/public-safety/Indianas-Interactive-Map-Plots-Meth-Lab-Data.html

Zoch, R. (2018, November 16). How to identify narcotics and other suspected threats quickly and accurately. *Police1.* Retrieved March 24, 2021, from www.police1.com/police-products/narcotics-identification/articles/how-to-identify-narcotics-and-other-suspected-threats-quickly-and-accurately-ZVQxu11QJhBhvDWK/

Cases Cited

Florida v. Jardines, 569 U.S. 1 (2013).

Illinois v. Caballes, 543 U.S. 405 (2005).

Smith v. Maryland, 442 U.S. 735 (1979).

Chapter 19
Criminal Gangs and Other Dangerous Groups

Learning Objectives

LO1 List the types of gangs identified by the National Gang Intelligence Center.

LO2 Identify the types of crimes gangs typically engage in.

LO3 Outline the first step in dealing with a gang problem.

LO4 Understand the criteria or characteristics used to identify gang members.

LO5 Describe the types of records to keep on gangs.

LO6 Explain the special challenges that may be involved in investigating illegal activities of gangs.

LO7 Summarize what strategies have been used to combat a gang problem.

LO8 Explain what two defense strategies are commonly used by gang members' lawyers in court.

LO9 Recognize the primary motivation for bias or hate crimes and who is most frequently targeted.

LO010 Define what a ritualistic crime is and identify what to investigate.

LO011 List the indicators of ritualistic crimes.

LO012 Identify what special challenges are involved in investigating ritualistic crimes.

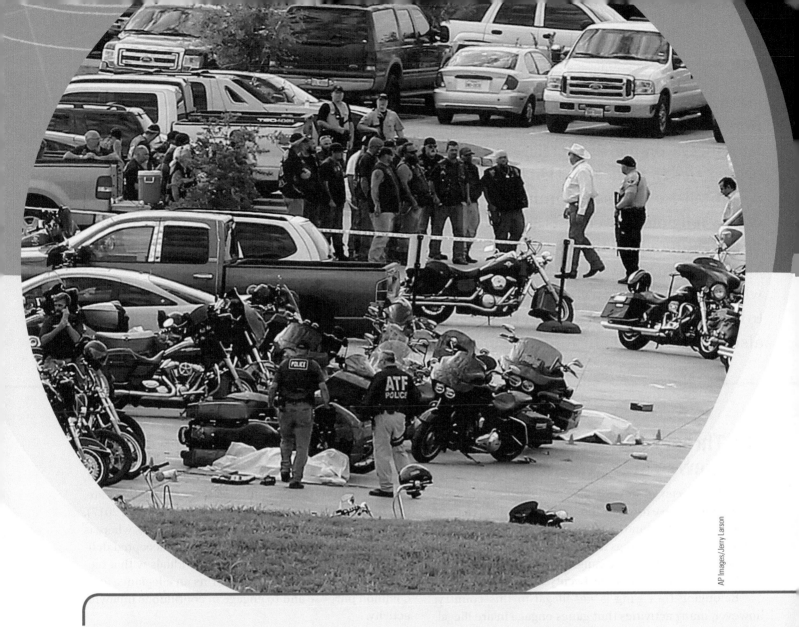

AP Images/Jerry Larson

Introduction

Gangs and the violence they sow reach across the country. In Santa Rosa, California, members of the Norteño gang Varrio South Park (VSP) wreak havoc on the community, committing armed robberies that lead to high-speed car chases, firing shots at "snitches" in restaurant parking lots, shooting at their own fellow gang members if they feel their status and authority has been challenged, and threatening to kill witnesses if they come forward or cooperate with police. In Miami, Florida, members of the fearsome Latin Kings carry out their daily business of racketeering, drug distribution, fraud, robbery, kidnapping, and murder. And in the country's heartland—Omaha, Nebraska—gunfire erupts at a party in a vacant house, leaving three people dead and witnesses refusing to cooperate with investigators because of the gang-related nature of the shootings.

But street gangs are not the only dangerous groups that bring violence and fear to the nation's neighborhoods. Bias and hate crimes touch communities throughout the country. In Jasper, Texas, a Black man is chained by his ankles to a pickup truck and dragged to his death, his head and arm ripped from his body during the incident. In Laramie, Wyoming, a gay college student is beaten, tied to a fence, and left to die alone.

Ritualistic crimes committed by cults or new religious movements also challenge investigators across the United States. On a lonely rural road in Wisconsin, a pharmacist who was a member of a voodoo cult arranges to have himself shot and killed by two friends, also cult members. In Rancho Santa Fe,

California, 39 members of a high-tech cult pack their bags and commit mass suicide, believing that in death they will rendezvous with a UFO that was trailing the Hale–Bopp comet. In Tavares, Florida, members of a teenage "vampire clan" use cigarettes to burn a "V" onto the body of a man they had just bludgeoned to death.

These actual events reflect the everyday reality of gangs, hate crime, and ritualistic crime in the United States.

The Threat of Criminal Gangs: An Overview

Gangs have been of interest and concern for centuries. Street gangs have existed in the United States for most of the country's history and have been studied since the 1920s. The 1900s saw street gangs flourishing, influenced by such mobsters as Al Capone. And gangs continue to pose a problem for law enforcement in the twenty-first century.

Belonging to a gang is *not* illegal in this country; however, many activities that gangs engage in are illegal. Criminal gangs traffic in drugs; commit shootings, assaults, robbery, extortion, and other felonies; and terrorize neighborhoods. Previously loose-knit groups of juveniles and young adults who engaged in petty crimes have, over time, become powerful, organized gangs, representing a form of domestic terrorism. Gang wars, drive-by shootings, and disregard for innocent bystanders have a chilling effect. Gangs now exist in almost every community.

To investigate gang-related crimes effectively, law enforcement personnel must understand the makeup of these organizations, what types of crimes to expect, how to identify their members, and how to deal with the special challenges of investigating such crimes.

Gangs Defined

Although most people are easily able to form an image in their mind when they think of a gang, defining a gang

is a bit more difficult, and no single, agreed-upon definition exists. Indeed, one of the largest obstacles to gathering accurate gang-related data is the lack of a national, uniform definition of a "gang" used by all federal, state, and local law enforcement agencies (Frazier et al., 2017). Some definitions emphasize criminal activity whereas others stress territoriality. One commonly accepted definition is that a *gang* is a group of individuals with a recognized name and symbol that forms an allegiance for a common purpose and to engage in continuous unlawful activity.

The National Alliance of Gang Investigators' Associations (NAGIA) defines a **gang** as "a group or association of three or more persons with a common identifying sign, symbol, or name who individually or collectively engage in criminal activity that creates an atmosphere of fear and intimidation" (n.d.). The U.S. Department of Justice (DOJ) provides an expanded definition of a gang as:

> (1) an association of three or more individuals; (2) whose members collectively identify themselves by adopting a group identity, which they use to create an atmosphere of fear or intimidation frequently by employing one or more of the following: a common name, slogan, identifying sign, symbol, tattoo or other physical marking, style or color of clothing, hairstyle, hand sign or graffiti; (3) the association's purpose, in part, is to engage in criminal activity and the association uses violence or intimidation to further its criminal objectives; (4) its members engage in criminal activity, or acts of juvenile delinquency that if committed by an adult would be

crimes; (5) with the intent to enhance or preserve the association's power, reputation, or economic resources; (6) the association may also possess some of the following characteristics: (a) the members employ rules for joining and operating within the association; (b) the members meet on a recurring basis; (c) the association provides physical protection of its members from other criminals and gangs; (d) the association seeks to exercise control over a particular location or region, or it may simply defend its perceived interests against rivals; or (e) the association has an identifiable structure; (7) this definition is not intended to include traditional organized crime groups, such as La Cosa Nostra, groups that fall within the Department's definition of "international organized crime," drug trafficking organizations or terrorist organizations. (2015a)

As of July 2020, 45 jurisdictions, including 43 states, Washington, DC, and the federal government, had laws that define gang-related terms (National Gang Center [NGC], *Highlights*, n.d.). Gang investigators must be aware that many states have legislatively enacted their own definitions of a *gang* that all local and state law enforcement agencies are mandated to follow. The National Gang Center (NGC) has compiled and posted online a state-by-state list of criteria used to define gangs and gang members (nationalgangcenter.ojp.gov /legislation).

Extent of Gangs

The last quarter of the twentieth century saw significant growth in gang problems across the country. In the 1970s, less than half the states reported youth gang problems, but by the late 1990s, every state and the District of Columbia reported gang activity. During that same period, the number of cities reporting youth gang problems mushroomed nearly tenfold.

Gangs range in size from small groups of three to five to as many as several thousand. Nationally known gangs such as the Crips number around 50,000 and the Bloods number about 20,000 to 30,000. Large gangs are normally broken down into smaller groups but are known collectively under one name. More than 90% of gangs have between 3 and 100 members, and only 4% have more than 100 members. The number of gangs in large cities ranges from 1,200 to 1,500.

Different sources vary in their estimates of the number of gangs and gang members currently active within the United States. The *2011 National Gang Threat Assessment*, published by the National Gang Intelligence Center (NGIC), estimated that 1.4 million gang members and more than 33,000 gangs were criminally active in the United States in 2011. According to the *National Youth Gang Survey* (NYGS), a 10-year project published by the Office of Juvenile Justice and Delinquency Prevention (OJJDP) which finished in 2012, an estimated 850,000 gang members belonging to 30,700 gangs were in existence across the nation during 2012 (Egley, Howell, & Harris, 2014). One explanation for the discrepancy could be the inconsistency in how various jurisdictions define a gang. Regardless of which data set one looks at, however, it is clear that gangs and gang-related crime are a serious threat to communities throughout the country. Analysis of past estimates reveals that, "Across jurisdiction types, prevalence rates of gang activity followed a marked decline in the late 1990s, increased in the early 2000s, and, with the exception of smaller cities, have generally stabilized in recent years" (Egley et al., 2014, p. 1).

The gang problem is not restricted to metropolitan areas. As society in general has become more mobile, gangs and gang members have also increased their mobility, contributing to gang migration. Whereas early gangs tended to exist primarily in large cities near the country's borders (Los Angeles, New York, Miami, Chicago), gangs are now sending members across the country and into the nation's heartland to take advantage of new territory, diminished competition from other gangs, and law enforcement agencies with less experience in dealing with gang activity.

According to the *2015 National Gang Report*, which surveyed federal, state, local, and tribal law enforcement, street gangs continue to impact communities across the United States and show no signs of decreasing membership or declining criminal activity. Survey respondents indicated that street gang membership increased in approximately 49% of jurisdictions over the past two years, stayed the same in 43%, and decreased in about 8% of jurisdictions (National Gang Intelligence Center [NGIC], 2015).

Why People Join Gangs

Gang members are not a monolithic group, and their reasons for joining gangs are numerous. The search to understand the complex dynamics of gang formation and what leads some people to join has led researchers and practitioners to study gangs from psychological, sociological, and criminological perspectives (Howell, 2010).

Discussion of the myriad theories exceeds the scope of this chapter. However, review of the literature reveals three common themes regarding why males and females join gangs:

- Neighborhood disadvantage

- Parent-child relationship problems, such as neglect, lack of supervision, and substance abuse and addiction

- Having gang-involved family and friends (Bell, 2009)

Reasons given by gang members, themselves, for joining a gang include wanting to feel a sense of belonging, to be in a "family" of supportive friends, and to feel that someone had their backs in case trouble developed (Dong & Krohn, 2016). In fact, one meta-analysis of gang research found that protection was the number one reason given by youths for joining a gang (Howell, 2010). Gang membership is also often seen as a way to obtain money, power, and drugs.

A desire to overcome and control social disparities and neighborhood disadvantage is another reason people join gangs: "The power of place and status in gang formation cannot be discounted, because these two aspects contribute directly to the generation of street gangs" (Vigil, 2019). Empirical evidence supports the argument that, in a class-based society, street gangs are often the product of multiple marginalization, with members joining in an effort to combat a sense of powerlessness over social and economic conditions.

People join gangs to feel a sense of camaraderie with others, particularly when strong connections with parents, other family members, and peers are lacking (McDaniel, Logan, & Schneiderman, 2014). It is widely understood that during adolescence, peer groups become increasingly important in a youth's journey to establish their first identity outside of the family, providing a source of one's developing social status, self-esteem, and even safety. Therefore, it comes as little surprise that association with deviant peers is one of the most potent risk factors for gang membership (Dong & Krohn, 2016).

Finally, some people join gangs because they come from a gang-involved family and it is simply what they are expected to do.

Types of Gangs

Gangs can be differentiated in many ways, such as by age (e.g., youth gangs), race or ethnicity (e.g., Latin American gangs, Native American gangs), gender composition (e.g., female gangs), setting (e.g., street or prison gangs), and type of activity (e.g., drug gangs). The NGIC notes that three basic types of gangs have been identified by gang investigators: street gangs, prison gangs, and outlaw motorcycle gangs (OMGs).

> **LO1** List the types of gangs identified by the National Gang Intelligence Center.
>
> The NGIC has identified three general types of gangs: street gangs, prison gangs, and outlaw motorcycle gangs (OMGs).

Street Gangs

As with the term *gang* in general, several definitions exist for *street gang*. A broadly applicable definition of street gangs has evolved from several years' worth of intense discussions among working groups of American and European gang researchers in an assembly that has come to be known as the *Eurogang program*. The Eurogang consensus nominal definition of a **street gang** is "any durable, street-oriented youth group whose involvement in illegal activity is part of its group identity" (Weerman et al., 2009, p. 20). The NGIC's definition differs slightly: "Street gangs are criminal organizations that formed on the street and operate in neighborhoods throughout the United States" (2015, p. 11).

Klein (2007, p. 54) states simply, "There is no *one* form of street gang." Street gangs vary widely in their size, duration of existence, level of territoriality, and criminal involvement. The NGIC, however, divides street gangs into two broad categories: neighborhood-based gangs (NBGs) that are confined to specific neighborhoods and jurisdictions and have no known leadership beyond their communities, and national-level gangs that have a presence in multiple jurisdictions, such as the Bloods, Crips, Gangster Disciples, Mara Salvatrucha (MS13), and Sureños. The vast majority of all gang members belong to these types of gangs, whether a local NBG or national street gangs. According to the *2015 National Gang Report*, NBGs and local street gangs present the greatest threat to communities throughout the country, perpetuating violence, drug distribution, and opportunistic crimes, such as robbery. NBGs are considered the most problematic type of gang, in large part due to the gun violence caused by turf wars fought for lucrative drug-trafficking territories. National-level street gangs have a high or moderate impact in approximately half of jurisdictions (NGIC, 2015).

The most violent street gang in the United States and, arguably, the world is MS13, whose 50,000 to 70,000 members are now spread throughout more than a half-dozen countries (InSight Crime & The Center for Latin American and Latino Studies, 2018). Despite being a central focus of law enforcement in two hemispheres, MS13 is thriving and shows signs of expanding its criminal portfolio. A recent study reports that MS13 has survived for nearly four decades without a master plan, one all-powerful leader, or a reliable source of income. Its core membership consists primarily of teenagers who communicate mostly via text messages, their messages conveyed with spray paint. Many of its leaders are in jail, and the majority of its members did not complete high school.

Street gangs are very often organized by ethnicity. Among the most well-known ethnic street gangs are African American gangs (Bloods, Crips, Vice Lords), Latin American gangs (Latin Kings and MS13), Asian gangs (Chinese, Filipino, Vietnamese, Hmong), and Indian Country gangs. The literature on ethnic gangs is abundant, and Howell and Moore's *History of Street Gangs in the United States* (2010) is an informative read for those seeking a more comprehensive understanding of how various gangs evolved throughout our country. Another valuable resource is *Gangs in America's Communities*, 3rd edition (2019) by Howell and Griffiths.

A type of increasingly violent street gangs are hybrid gangs, informal and fairly unstructured groupings of members from different gangs, such as NBGs and national-level gangs, that are usually considered rivals but are willing to "work" together for financial gain (Drug Enforcement Administration, 2019). Members of hybrid gangs are generally young and particularly profit-driven. They thrive in areas with relatively new gang problems and often include gangbangers who have migrated from larger cities. These gangs represent a sea change in gang culture and bear little resemblance to traditional gangs. Unlike older gangs based on race or neighborhood loyalty, this new generation is singularly profit-driven and will do whatever it takes—traffic drugs, run prostitution rings, or commit armed robbery and murder—to make money. Hybrid gangs are often temporary, but in some cases they do endure, forming their own identity with an informal set of rules and standards. This phenomenon is true for both street gangs and prison gangs (Jones, 2019).

Prison Gangs

The NGIC and U.S. DOJ define a prison gang as "a criminal organization that originates in the penal system and continues to operate within correctional facilities throughout the United States. Prison gangs are self-perpetuating criminal entities that also continue their operations outside of prison" (NGIC, 2015; U.S. Department of Justice [DOJ], 2015b). Some researchers, however, take issue with this definition, specifically the attribute of *originating* in the penal system, noting that many of the gangs operating within the correctional system were "imported" from the street. While true that gangs like the Vice Lords, Aryan Brotherhood, Black Guerilla Family, Mexican Mafia, and Ghost Face Gangsters are generally thought to have originated inside prison, it is also true that numerous others did not. Nearly every gang that exists on the street is also likely to exist and operate inside a correctional facility because many gang members choose not to disavow their gang affiliation simply upon becoming incarcerated (Knox, 2019). This is one reason why some researchers, practitioners, and jurisdictions prefer to call prison gangs by the term **security threat group** (STG), which is "is any group of three (3) or more persons with recurring threatening or disruptive behavior (i.e., violations of the disciplinary rules where said violations were openly known or conferred benefit upon the group would suffice for a prison environment), including but not limited to gang crime or gang violence (i.e., crime of any sort would automatically make the group a gang, and as a gang in custody it would logically be an STG)" (Knox, 2019, p. 5). STGs thus include any group of three or more inmates who were members of the same street gang.

While ample research indicates that gang membership is highly durable and many members retain their street affiliation while behind bars, some studies have found that the majority of juvenile offenders are more likely to leave rather than join a gang while in prison (Pyrooz & Decker, 2019; Pyrooz, Gartner, & Smith, 2017). Although there is no centralized, standardized repository of data on prison gang populations, researchers estimate that roughly 1 out of 7 inmates (14%) are gang-affiliated and that gang members in the correctional population outnumber gang members in the general population by a factor of 75 (Pyrooz & Decker, 2019).

It is important to recognize that discussions of "street gangs" and "prison gangs" can create a misleading impression that these two groups are mutually exclusive and that their activities begin and end where their members' freedoms start or stop—at the prison gate. In addressing this false dichotomy, gang researchers Pyrooz and Decker (2019, p. 19) assert: "When we refer to *street* gang or *prison* gang, we are referring to the *context of influence* of a gang. For some gangs, such influence exists on the street and in institutions; for other gangs, it exists in only one setting." For certain, iron bars and razor-wire–topped walls cannot contain the impact prison gangs can have on free society:

> Many incarcerated gang members continue to engage in gang activities following incarceration and use their connections inside prison to commit crime in the

community. Prison gang members influence and control gang activity on the street, and exploit street gangs for money and other resources. . . .

A gang member's incarceration often prompts their family to move closer to the correctional facility where the gang member is being housed. In some cases, family members assist or facilitate gang criminal activity and recruiting. Family members of gangs operate as outside facilitators, serving as messengers, drug couriers, or in any capacity benefiting the gang. Outside facilitators are provided instructions by the incarcerated gang member, often during a social or legal visit, and in turn pass this information to gang members on the streets. Family members have also been used to assist prison escapes and smuggle contraband into correctional facilities, allowing incarcerated gang members to continue their operations inside prison. (NGIC, 2011, p. 30)

Smuggling is a primary way for prison gangs to perpetuate their criminal activity, and the smuggled contraband most commonly reported, in decreasing order, are drugs, weapons, and cell phones. Drugs translate to money; weapons generate power; and cell phones enable inmates to readily direct gang members in the territories under their command (NGIC, 2015).

Outlaw Motorcycle Gangs

The NGIC defines an OMG as an ongoing organization, association, or group of three or more persons with a common interest or activity characterized by the commission of, or involvement in, a pattern of criminal conduct. Members must possess and be able to operate a motorcycle to achieve and maintain membership within the group (NGIC, 2015). OMG members comprise about 2.5% of the nation's total gang population.

Motorcycle gangs first appeared in the United States in the 1950s and have evolved from barroom brawlers to sophisticated criminals. The largest OMGs are the Hells Angels Motorcycle Club, Pagans, Vagos, Sons of Silence, Outlaws, Bandidos, and Mongols. All are classified as "one-percent" (1%) clubs, a term that originated after a riot broke out on July 4, 1947, at the Dirt Hill Climb motorcycle races in Hollister, California. In response to the riot, the American Motorcycle Association released a statement stressing that 99% of the motorcycling public was comprised of honest, law-abiding citizens, and that only one percent constituted troublemakers. OMGs took pride in the reference and adopted 1% as its symbol. Thus, many outlaw bikers prefer to refer to their groups as "one percenter" motorcycle clubs (MC) rather than gangs. Not all OMGs, however, boast the symbol (NGIC, 2015).

OMGs first formed in the United States but have since spread globally. The Hells Angels in particular are notable for their international connectivity and propensity to travel abroad. Reporting indicates street gangs, prison gangs, and extremist groups are significant recruiting pools for OMGs, with approximately equal recruitment from each category. Black OMGs recruit primarily from street gangs.

The size of an OMG influences its ability to form gang alliances and engage in criminal activities. OMGs engage primarily in violent crimes, such as assault, robbery, and homicide. And since OMGs have a well-earned reputation for violence, witnesses to their crimes are often reluctant to testify for fear of retaliation. Thus, unless an OMG commits a homicide or an assault that requires hospitalization, OMG violence frequently goes unreported to law enforcement (NGIC, 2015).

According to the *2015 National Gang Report*, weapons possession, threats and intimidation, assault, and drug trafficking were the most common criminal activities committed by OMGs over the previous two years. Rival gangs or individuals involved in other criminal activities like drug trafficking were the most common targets of OMG assaults and robberies. Methamphetamine, cocaine, and marijuana ranked respectively as the top three drugs that led to OMG arrests over the prior two years. OMG members have increasingly found employment in various white-collar professions, and many have become business owners, with tattoo shops and motorcycle and automobile repair shops comprising over half of all OMG member-owned businesses. In some instances, OMGs use their businesses to facilitate criminal activity.

Female Gang Involvement

Gangs are primarily male-dominated, with most estimates placing female gang membership at around 10% of all gang members (Coleman & McDonald, 2018; Hayward & Honegger, 2014; NGC, *National*, n.d.). It is also observed, however, that female gang membership has been rising for several decades and, as females grow more independent from their male counterparts, females are assuming greater responsibility in gang activities. Females are increasingly being forced or volunteering to commit violent acts for their gang, and some research shows that female gang crime and incarceration rates are outpacing those of their male counterparts (Gutierrez-Adams, Rios, & Case, 2020; Hayward & Honegger, 2014; Wolf, Castro, & Glesmann, 2016).

Females join gangs for many of the same reasons as males: for protection, because of family connections to a gang, as a source of income, and as a way to earn respect (Maxwell & Henning, 2017; Wolf, Castro, & Glesmann, 2016). Young women are more likely than young men, however, to join a gang because of a romantic partner's involvement. Female gang members typically support male gang members by serving as drug mules and weapons couriers and gathering intelligence for the gang, although females have increasingly begun to take more active roles as soldiers or coconspirators (Gutierrez-Adams, Rios, & Case, 2020; Wolf, Castro, & Glesmann, 2016).

Gang members flash their signs.

Myth Female gang members are only allowed into gangs to be used as girlfriends to the real gang members.

Fact Female gang members have committed serious crimes, including rape and murder, for the benefit of the gang. Female gang members are often the ones holding the drugs and guns.

The National Youth Gang Center (NYGC) reports that, during its most recent survey, a large percentage of law enforcement agencies were unable to provide quantitative data regarding female gang membership, which suggests that the issue of girls in gangs is "of secondary or lesser significance for law enforcement" (NGC, *National*, n.d.). Of those law enforcement agencies that did provide data to the survey, less than 15% reported that the gangs active in their jurisdiction had no female members. Jurisdictions in larger cities reported 22.8% of their gangs had female members, whereas the percentage of female membership in gangs that were active in smaller jurisdictions was considerably higher—45.3% of gangs in suburban counties, 43.0% of those in smaller cities, and 49.5% of gangs in rural counties reported female members (NGC, *National*, n.d.).

Gang Members in the Military

The military is not immune to the influence of gangs. It has been noted that many gang members enlist as a way out of gang life. However, some of these individuals find themselves returning to their gang following discharge from active duty, possessing specialized military skills such as those involving weapons, tactics, and attack planning. These military-trained gang members pose a serious threat not only to rival gangs but also to law enforcement and the general public (NGIC, 2015).

A military-trained gang member (MTGM) is a street gang, prison gang, OMG, or Domestic Terrorist Extremist (DTE) group member, as defined by jurisdictional statute, who has military training or experience, as perceived by a reasonable, typical, police officer (Smith, 2017). Indicators of such training or experience include the use of distinctive military skills, such as weapons and explosives training; demonstration of tactical assault techniques; and knowledge of organizational leadership strategies (Smith, 2017). According to Smith and Harms (2018), MTGMs are a threat not only within the military community because they corrupt the cohesiveness of military units, undermine the authority of military leadership, and expose military families on base to dangerous criminal activity, they also pose a danger to communities adjacent to military installations and disparage the image and perceived value of the military installation in the civilian community at large.

The Gang and Domestic Extremist Activity Threat Assessment is a regular report compiled by Army Criminal Investigation Command (CID) and submitted to Congress. In fiscal year 2018, the assessment found 83 law enforcement reports across the military with known or suspected gang or domestic extremist member involvement, which was a 66% increase from fiscal year 2017 (Seck, 2020).

Gang Culture, Membership, and Organization

Some gang experts talk about the three Rs of the gang culture: reputation, respect, and revenge. Reputation is of prime concern to gang members, both individually and collectively. They expect, indeed demand, respect.

And they are required to show disrespect for rival gang members, called a "diss" in gang slang. Disrespect inevitably leads to the third R—revenge. Every challenge must be answered, often in the form of violence, including drive-by shootings.

Most gangs are of limited numbers sufficient for the entire group to meet and discuss things in person. Incidents that happen to them or that are expressly initiated by them cause them to identify as a group. Sometimes gang members are multigenerational—that is, father and son may have been members of the same gang. Most gang members are unemployed or work at part-time jobs. Many are most active at night and sleep during the day. Some stay with their gangs into adulthood, and others may go back to school or gain full-time employment, usually in jobs with very low pay.

Myth Gang members are mostly juveniles.

Fact While the average age can fluctuate per jurisdiction, the average gang member is 20 years old. The most recent NYGSA data shows nearly two thirds (65%) of active gang members are adults over age 18 (NGC, *National*, n.d.).

Most gang members are weak academically because they lack good study habits, although they are mentally capable. This is an important factor because gangs are essentially self-operated and self-governed. Some operate by consensus, but most have leaders and a subgoverning structure. Leadership may be single or dual. Status is generally obtained by joining the gang, but equal status within the gang once joined is not automatically guaranteed.

Gang members have differing levels of commitment and involvement in gang activities. Most gang members are either hard-core, associate, or peripheral members. The hard-core members are those most dedicated to the gang. Knowing how a gang is organized and what level of involvement a member has can be of great assistance to investigators. The hard-core member is least likely to cooperate with the police; the peripheral members are most likely to be cooperative.

A gang's degree of organization influences the behavior observed among its members, with even low levels of organization having important implications regarding criminality. Research has found that even slight increases in a gang's organization correlate to increased involvement in criminal activity (Decker, Katz, & Webb, 2008).

Symbols

Gang symbols are common. Clothing, hand signals, graffiti, and tattoos are all used as symbolic representations of a person's affiliation with a specific gang. Clothing and jewelry are often the most distinguishing characteristics. Gangs also often associate themselves with certain colors. Members use jerseys, T-shirts, athletic team logos, bandanas, and belts to display their allegiance. Another form of symbolic communication typical of gang members is hand signals. Certain signs are flashed to indicate membership in a specific gang. Symbols are often displayed in graffiti to mark a gang's turf.

Turf and Graffiti

Many gangs establish a **turf**, the geographic area of domination that gang members will defend to the death. The turf includes the schools, businesses, residential areas, streets, and alleys in the area, all controlled through fear, intimidation, and violence. In the past, turf wars took the form of gang fights. Today, however, they often take the form of drive-by shootings, many of which have killed innocent citizens as well as rival gang members.

Gangs identify their turf through **graffiti**. Other gangs may challenge the turf claim by writing over or crossing out the graffiti and replacing it with their own. Such cross-outs are usually found at the edge of a gang's territory and are a sign of intentional disrespect, meant to elicit a response from a gang's rivals (Perna, 2019). Gang members caught in the act of crossing out graffiti in a rival's territory may be killed, or a turf war can result. Gangs also use graffiti to:

- Memorialize a deceased gang member

- Make a statement

- Send a message

- Conduct business

Gang graffiti is a source of frustration and expense to property owners and local governments.

In Wilson and Kelling's classic Broken Windows crime model, graffiti is a foothold crime leading to a neighborhood's decay. However, various sources estimate that at the national level, only about 10% of all graffiti is gang-related. Nonetheless, gang graffiti is meant to intimidate and challenge rivals, and when graffiti appears it can increase the sense of fear in a community. One study found that for each unit increase in the density of neighborhood gang graffiti, there existed a 40%–60% increase in the expected rate of gang homicide, gang assaults, and gang firearm offenses (Hughes, Schaible, & Kephart, 2021).

Police officers who deal with gangs can learn much by understanding wall graffiti. The center of a gang's turf will have the most graffiti. It may name members of the gang, often in order of authority, listed in neat rows under the gang's logo. Reading graffiti is discussed later in the chapter. Unchallenged graffiti affirms the gang's control. With the increasing mobility of society, graffiti no longer has to necessarily remain within a gang's turf.

Graffiti is often highly artistic and very detailed, displaying important gang symbols and weapons. Graffiti can provide investigators with important intelligence, including gang member names, monikers, and gang territory. It is important for investigators to recognize the difference between gang graffiti and tagging. Some urban artists unaffiliated with gangs have begun replicating graffiti as one type of artistic expression. These public displays are called **tagging** and are done by people who want to put their name, or "tag," on items to bring personal recognition to themselves. Mistakenly identifying such "art" as gang-affiliated graffiti can complicate or obstruct a jurisdiction's efforts to get a handle on its gang crime. Figure 19.1 shows some typical symbols used by various gangs in their graffiti.

Tattoos

Tattoos are also used by some gangs. Gang tattoos are meant to intimidate, show gang affiliation, and indicate rank, and they are a gang member's permanent record, telling who they are, what they believe, what they have done, where they have been, where they did time and for how many years, and how many people they have has killed. An officer trained to read gang tattoos can discern a suspect's history.

Gangs and Technology

According to the *2015 National Gang Report*, gang use of technology and social media has significantly increased in recent years. Widely used social media platforms, such as Facebook, YouTube, Instagram, Twitter, kik, and WhatsApp have become ubiquitous in gang activity. Gangs also use various sites, applications, and platforms to recruit new members, communicate with each other, target rivals, sell drugs, advance their criminal activities, and thwart law enforcement (Fernández-Planells, Orduña-Malea, & Pàmpols, 2021; NGIC, 2015; Pyrooz & Moule, 2019). Prison gang members, in particular, seek to acquire cell phones to stay in contact with the outside

Technology Innovations

Gang Graffiti Automatic Recognition and Interpretation (GARI) App

In early 2011, researchers at the U.S. Department of Homeland Security's Center for Visualization and Data Analytics (CVADA) partnered with the Indianapolis Metropolitan Police Department (IMPD) to create a smartphone application and image database capable of quickly translating the meaning of thousands of graffiti images. The Gang Graffiti Automatic Recognition and Interpretation (GARI) app allows law enforcement to take a picture of the graffiti and upload it, along with its GPS coordinates and date/time information, to a central database, where it undergoes sophisticated image processing and analysis methods to detect structures and symbols within the graffiti image. The user then receives an analysis of the gang affiliation, an interpretation of the message in that graffiti, and the geographic location of other similar images, allowing law enforcement to track and identify gang activity over time throughout a region. According to GARI's developer, the method for finding similar images achieves an accuracy of more than 90%, and the method for classifying gang graffiti components achieves an accuracy of more than 80%. The system is also used to analyze gang tattoo images and can match images in 84% of cases.

Source: *Law Officer*. (2016, January 8). New smartphone app interprets gang graffiti. Retrieved April 3, 2021, from www.lawofficer.com/new-smartphone-app-interprets-gang-graffiti/

world, and approximately 90% of prison gang survey respondents report that fellow inmates use at least one social media platform.

Anecdotal evidence suggests social media has fueled a new level of gang violence (Tarm, 2018). And while there is no doubt that gang members, like everyone else, are increasingly accessing and using social media, there is a significant lack of empirical research that examines how gang-associated youth actually deploy such technology within the context of gang conflict and the associated consequences of those actions (Stuart, 2020). Stuart cautions without such scientific research, criminal justice professionals risk continuing to misunderstand and overstate the violent effects of social media. He also points out that, "contrary to common belief, the

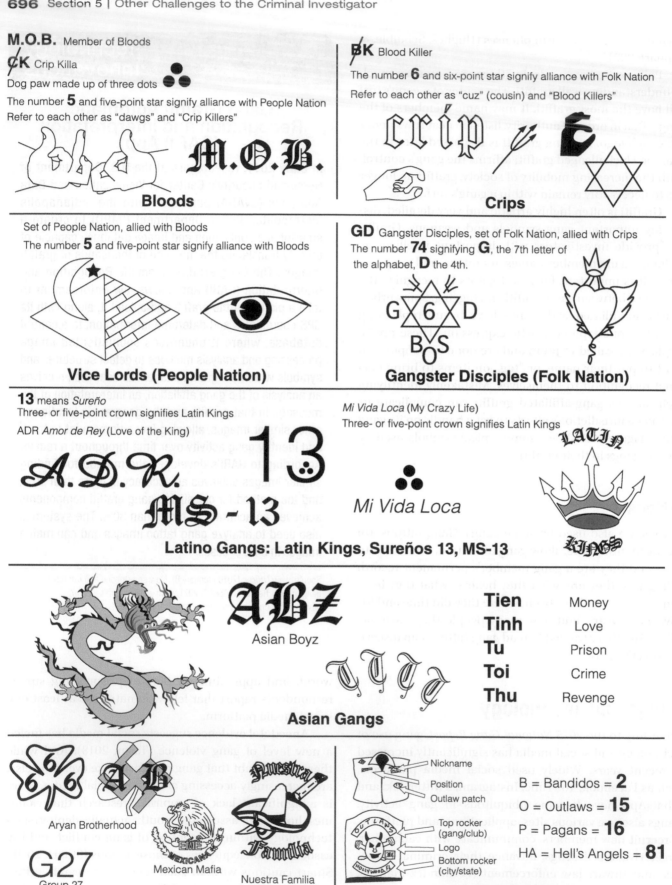

M.O.B. Member of Bloods

CK Crip Killa

Dog paw made up of three dots ●●●

The number **5** and five-point star signify alliance with People Nation

Refer to each other as "dawgs" and "Crip Killers"

Bloods

BK Blood Killer

The number **6** and six-point star signify alliance with Folk Nation

Refer to each other as "cuz" (cousin) and "Blood Killers"

Crips

Set of People Nation, allied with Bloods

The number **5** and five-point star signify alliance with Bloods

Vice Lords (People Nation)

GD Gangster Disciples, set of Folk Nation, allied with Crips

The number **74** signifying **G**, the 7th letter of the alphabet, **D** the 4th.

Gangster Disciples (Folk Nation)

13 means *Sureño*

Three- or five-point crown signifies Latin Kings

ADR *Amor de Rey* (Love of the King)

Latino Gangs: Latin Kings, Sureños 13, MS-13

Mi Vida Loca (My Crazy Life)

Three- or five-point crown signifies Latin Kings

Mi Vida Loca

Asian Boyz

Asian Gangs

Tien	Money
Tinh	Love
Tu	Prison
Toi	Crime
Thu	Revenge

Aryan Brotherhood

G27
Group 27

Mexican Mafia

Nuestra Familia

Prison

Nickname
Position
Outlaw patch
Top rocker (gang/club)
Logo
Bottom rocker (city/state)

B = Bandidos = **2**

O = Outlaws = **15**

P = Pagans = **16**

HA = Hell's Angels = **81**

Outlaw Motorcycle

Figure 19.1
A sampling of gang symbols, including graffiti and hand signs.

majority of social media challenges by gang members remain confined to online space and do not generate offline violence."

Illegal Gang Activities

Many gang activities are similar to those of other segments of society and are *not* illegal. Gangs gather informally on streets and street corners, in parks, homes, abandoned buildings, vehicles, vacant lots, or recreational areas and buildings. Indeed, many of the defining characteristics of a gang could apply to any other organization in society, with the exception of the purpose, which is to engage in antisocial or criminal behavior. Extensive documentation of gang activity shows they are involved in a full range of violent and property offenses, as well as street-level and large-scale drug trafficking, weapons trafficking, sex trafficking and prostitution, extortion, and other economic crimes to finance the gang (Langton, 2010; NGIC, 2015). The flip side to being more involved in perpetrating crime means that gang members are also more likely themselves to experience victimization. And although most gang crime consists of relatively minor offenses, such as property damage and theft, the more serious crimes, such as robbery, assault, home invasions, and murder, garner more publicity, which heightens public fear and leads to increased attention by the criminal justice system (Klein, 2007).

> **LO2** Identify the types of crimes gangs typically engage in.
>
> Gang members often engage in vandalism, arson, auto theft, shoplifting, drug trafficking, weapons trafficking, threats and intimidation, extortion, shootings, stabbings, and other forms of violence.

The nexus between gangs and crime has been well studied, with nearly a century's worth of criminological research supporting the association between the two and providing empirical evidence that gang members are more criminally active than nongang members (Gibson, Miller, Jennings, Swatt, & Gover, 2009). However, identification of causal factors has been more elusive, and questions still exist about which way, if any, the influence flows: does gang involvement lead to higher criminal activity or, in contrast, are those individuals who are already predisposed to antisocial or criminal behavior more likely to join a gang? The competing hypotheses currently circulating to explain the relationship between gangs and crime, including involvement in drug use/sales, and violence, are these:

- *The facilitation model.* Gang membership facilitates or promotes drug involvement, which, in turn, facilitates or increases violence.

- *The selection model.* Gangs attract members who are already delinquent or criminally involved, and antisocial behaviors precede joining the gang.

- *The enhancement model.* Gangs attract those who are already delinquent or criminally involved, and membership in the gang further facilitates or enhances their preexisting antisocial behavior. (Bjerregaard, 2010)

Research efforts to disentangle the forces at work have led to some interesting conclusions. For example, increases in a gang's organization have been correlated with elevated levels of criminal involvement and victimization (Brantingham, Yuan, & Herz, 2020; Decker et al., 2008). Other studies have found that increases in neighborhood disadvantage, as measured by socioeconomic conditions and indices, intensify the influence that gang membership and drug sales have on violence (Bellair & McNulty, 2009; Fabio, Tu, Loeber, & Cohen, 2011).

Although gang crime often involves only a few members at a time, occasionally the entire gang, or a large portion of it, participates in the illegal activity. For example, a surveillance video from a Las Vegas mini-market showed more than 40 teenagers flooding into the tiny store. Three youths jumped the counter and robbed the cashier at gunpoint while the others flocked to coolers. Teens clogged the doorways as they rushed out, carrying cases of beer and handfuls of food. The whole incident took less than 90 seconds. Such an incident is referred to as a **flash mob** or *mob rob*. Some police call this technique *swarming*.

Gangs and Drugs

Until the early 1980s, when crack, or rock cocaine, hit the market, gangs engaged primarily in burglary, robbery, extortion, and car theft. Although drug trafficking existed, it was nowhere near current levels. The reason: enormous profit. Economic gain is often the reason youths join gangs. It is hard to convince a youth that earning $9 an hour for busing tables or flipping burgers is preferable to making $600 for 2 hours' work as a drug courier. Thus, today, gangs are the primary retail-level distributors of most drugs throughout the United States, and drug trafficking has been identified as the most common criminal activity engaged in by today's street gangs (NGIC, 2015).

Furthermore, state and federal correctional facilities reported that drug trafficking is among the top crimes committed by prison gangs.

Some caution that drug trafficking by gangs is not as rampant as others might claim. Results of one study (Bjerregaard, 2010) found that gang membership is only weakly associated with drug use and distribution. However, the results of this study also provided empirical support for the concept that gang membership facilitates drug use, not vice versa, and promotes drug sales among the juveniles examined in the study. Furthermore, this research revealed that among youth who use and sell drugs, distinct differences exist between gang and nongang members, with gang members who use drugs doing so at higher rates than nongang members.

Aside from some expert opinions that most gangs lack the discipline, leadership, and crime skills necessary to sustain a successful drug operation, those gangs that are successful—particularly those who align with drug trafficking organizations (DTOs) and other criminal organizations—are serious forces to be reckoned with.

Gangs and Violence

The nexus between gang membership, drug trafficking, and violence has been a subject of research interest for many years, with results providing empirical support for several conclusions. Research by Bellair and McNulty (2009) found drug distribution to be a major facilitator of violence and that gang members involved in selling drugs engaged in significantly higher rates of violence than did nonselling gang members and nongang drug sellers. Another study found that although drug involvement, even among gang members, was not related to assaults, it was associated with gun-carrying behaviors, which does not necessarily correlate to actual violence but certainly increases the potential for violence (Bjerregaard, 2010).

According to the NYGS, the three factors, as reported by law enforcement, that most influence local gang violence are drug-related factors (81% of respondents identified this factor as one influencing gang violence), intergang conflict (61.8%), and a return of gang members to society from secure confinement, such as prison (55.2%) (NGC, *National*, n.d.). Factors that were reported less frequently as contributing to gang violence were intragang conflict (36.7%), emergence of new gangs (34.2%), gang-member migration within the United States (30.7%), and gang-member migration from outside the United States (14.3%).

With increased involvement in violence comes an increased risk of serious bodily harm and death.

Research shows that gang-related violence triggers twice as many additional violent retaliations (referred to as *contagious offspring*) as nongang violence, and that these gang-related subsequent acts of violence are significantly more lethal than those committed by nongang individuals (Brantingham, Yuan, & Herz, 2020). Data indicate that the homicide victimization rate for gang members is more than 100 times greater than for those in the general U.S. population. Further, researchers believe that the variable used by the National Violent Death Reporting System (NVDRS) to identify and code certain homicides as gang-related may underestimate the true level of these deaths by as much as 70% because the criteria used by law enforcement or coroner/medical examiners to attribute a homicide to gang activity differ across jurisdictions (Frazier et al., 2017).

Gang Associations with Other Criminal Organizations

Gangs, particularly those at the national and regional levels, are increasingly associating with organized crime entities, such as Mexican DTOs, Asian criminal groups, and Russian organized crime groups. These organized crime groups often turn to gangs to conduct low-level criminal activity, protect territories, and facilitate drug-trafficking activities. The primary goal of any association between these groups is financial gain. Table 19.1 summarizes the main types of criminal organizations existing within the United States, most of which are gangs, listing specific group names and the types of criminal activities they engage in. Many of these groups were discussed in Chapter 18.

Recognizing a Gang Problem

Failure to recognize or acknowledge the existence of gang activity, whether willingly or through the lack of gang identification training, dramatically increases a gang's ability to thrive and develop a power base. Many communities begin to address gang issues only after a high-profile gang-related incident occurs.

Recognizing a gang can be challenging, but law enforcement, schools, and communities can be aware of warning signs such as graffiti, obvious colors of clothing, tattoos, initiations, hand signals or handshakes, uncommon terms or phrases, and a sudden change in behavior. Communities and law enforcement may not know when a group of misbehaving youths crosses the line into becoming a bona fide gang. To answer the question, "Does

TABLE 19.1 Criminal Organizations

Type of Group	Subtype of Group	Specific Groups and Distinct Gangs	Criminal Activity
Asian gangs*	Chinese street gangs, Triads, Tongs	Flying Dragons, Fuk Ching, Ghost Shadows, Ping On, Taiwan Brotherhood, United Bamboo, Wah Ching, White Tigers	Extortion of Chinese businesses, gambling, heroin distribution, exploitation of recent immigrants, smuggling of humans
	Japanese gangs (Boryokudan or Yakuza)	Kumlai, Sumiyoshi Rengo, Yamaguchi Gumi	Gambling, prostitution and sex trade, money laundering, trafficking in weapons and drugs
	Korean gangs	AB (American Burger), Flying Dragons, Junior Korean Power, KK (Korean Killers), Korean Power	Prostitution, massage parlors; gambling; loan-sharking; extortion of Korean businesses (particularly produce markets and restaurants)
	Laotian/ Cambodian/ Vietnamese gangs	Born to Kill (BTK), Laotian Bloods (LBs), Richtown Crips, Tiny Oriental Crips, Tiny Rascal Gang (TRG)[1]	Strong-arm and violent crimes related to business extortion; home invasion for theft of gold, jewelry and money coupled with rape to deter reporting; street crimes; prostitution; drug trafficking; assault; murder
	Hmong gangs	Cobra gang, Menace of Destruction (MOD), Oriental Ruthless Boys, Totally Gangster Crips, Totally Mafia Crips, True Asian Crips, True Crip Gangster, True Lady Crips (female Hmongs), True Local Crips, Westside Crips, White Tigers	Gang rape, prostitution, burglary, auto theft, vandalism, home invasion, street crimes, strong-arm robbery of businesses, drug trafficking, assault, murder
Latin American gangs*	Mexican	18th Street gang, Sureños-Mexican Mafia, Norteños-Nuestra Family, Tijuana Cartel-Arellano Felix organization, Colima Cartel-Amezcua Contreras brothers, Juárez Cartel-Amado Carillo Fuentes group, Sonora Cartel-Miguel Caro Quintero organization, Sinaloa Cartel-Guzman/ Leora Organization, Guadalajara Cartel-Rafael Caro Quintero/Miguel Angel Felix Gallardo, Gulf Cartel	Drug trafficking (cocaine, crack, heroin, marijuana), counterfeiting, pickpocketing, money laundering, murder
	Cuban	Cuban Mafia	Drug trafficking (cocaine, crack, heroin, marijuana), counterfeiting, pickpocketing, money laundering, murder
	Puerto Rican	Latin Kings, Puerto Rican Stones	Street crimes, drug trafficking, burglary, assault, rape, murder
	Colombian gangs and cartels	Cali cartel, Medellin cartel, Norte Del Valle Cartel, North Coast Cartel, Bogota Cartel, Santander DeQuilichao Cartel, Black Eagles, AUC, ELN, FARC	Drug trafficking (cocaine, crack, heroin, marijuana), counterfeiting, pickpocketing, money laundering, murder
	Salvadoran gangs	Mara Salvatrucha 13 (MS13)	Street crimes, strong-arming businesses, assault, drug trafficking, rape, murder
	Peruvian gangs	Shining Path—guerilla organization with a mission for Maoist government	Vandalism and other property damage, assault, rape, murder
Jamaican posses		Shower posse, Spangler posse	Drug trafficking (cocaine, crack, marijuana), weapons trafficking, trafficking green cards
Native American gangs		Native Mob	Retail-level distribution of illicit drugs (primarily marijuana and meth), auto theft, assault, carjacking, drive-by shootings, extortion, robbery, murder
Nigerian gangs*		NCE (Nigerian Criminal Enterprise)	Heroin smuggling (via mules) and heroin dealing; credit card fraud, infiltration of private security, planned bankruptcy of companies, exploitation of other Africans
Somali gangs		Somali Outlaws, Somalian Hot Boys, Murda Gang, Somali Mafia, Ma Thug Boys, Ruff Tuff Somali Crips[2]	Street crimes, strong-arming businesses, drug trafficking, assault, rape, murder

(Continued)

TABLE 19.1 *(Continued)*

Type of Group	Subtype of Group	Specific Groups and Distinct Gangs	Criminal Activity
Eurasian/Russian gangs*		Evangelical Russian Mafia, Malina/Organizatsiya, Odessa Mafia, Gypsy gangs	Theft (diamonds, furs, gold) and fencing stolen goods, export and sale of stolen Russian religious art and gold; extortion, insurance fraud, money laundering, counterfeiting, daisy chain tax evasion schemes, credit card scams and fraud; smuggling illegal immigrants; drug trafficking
Street gangs	African American, Caucasian, Hispanic and others	Disciples, Latin Kings, Vice Lords, Dog Pound and many others, including variants of Bloods/Crips (e.g., Westside Crips or Rolling Crips)	Motor vehicle theft, drug sales (especially crack and marijuana), weapons trafficking, assaults, drive-by shootings, robbery; burglary, theft and fencing stolen goods, vandalism, graffiti
Drug-trafficking gangs	Traditional street gangs	Bloods, Crips, Gangster Disciples, Latin Kings and many others	Trafficking of heroin, cocaine, crack and other drugs; violence; arson; indirect prostitution; vandalism, property crime; strong-arm robbery; African American gangs known for crack; Chicano gangs known for heroin and crack
	International drug cartels	Medellin cartel, Cali cartel	Drug trafficking (cocaine, crack, heroin, marijuana)
Graffiti or tagger crews (also tagger posses, mobs, tribes and piecers)		Known by three-letter monikers such as NBT (Nothing But Trouble) or ETC (Elite Tagger Crew)	Graffiti vandalism, tag-banging accompanied by violence
Prison gangs (aka Security Threat Groups, or STGs)		Aryan Brotherhood, Barrio Azteca, Black Guerilla Family, Consolidated Crip Organization, Ghost Face Gangsters, Mexican Mafia, Mexikanemi, Ñeta, Nuestra Familia, Texas Syndicate	Drug trafficking; prostitution; extortion; protection, murder for hire
Outlaw motorcycle gangs (OMGs)		Hell's Angels, Outlaws, Mongols, Pagans, Bandidos, Sons of Silence, Vagos	Drug trafficking (methamphetamine/crank, speed, ice, PCP, LSD, angel dust), weapons trafficking, chop shops, massage parlors, strip bars, prostitution, arson
Hate groups (including militia and terrorist groups, which also share a focus on ideology)		Aryan Nation, Ku Klux Klan, skinheads (White Aryan Resistance), American Nazi Party, Christian Defense League	Bombings; counterfeiting; loan fraud; armored car and bank robberies; theft rings
La Cosa Nostra (aka the Mafia)*		Families such as Bonnano, Columbo, Gambino, Genovese, and Lucchese	Gambling; loan-sharking; corruption of public officials/institutions; extortion; money laundering; theft of precious metals, food and clothing; fencing stolen property; labor racketeering; stock manipulation; securities fraud; weapons trafficking; drug trafficking (particularly heroin distribution); systemic use of violence as a tool in business transactions; murder

Note: Although nationality and ethnicity are often unifying characteristics of criminal organizations and used to identify them, this view is overly narrow and promotes ethnic stereotypes. The organization of criminal groups by nationality and ethnicity in this table is not intended to suggest that criminal behavior is characteristic of any group; ethnicity, however, is often a marker to police.

* Groups discussed primarily in Chapter 18

[1]TRG originated as a Cambodian gang but now admits Laotian members.

[2]Somali gangs often change their name, colors, and signs every few months. For example, the Somali Outlaws, Hot Boys, and Murda Gang are all one gang that has changed its identity. Somali Mafia and Ma Thugs are break-offs of these gangs.

Source: Adapted in part from Weisel, D. L. (2003). Criminal investigation. In W. A. Geller & D. W. Stephens (Eds.), *Local government police management* (p. 270). Washington, DC: International City/County Management Association. Adapted with permission of the International city/county Management Association, 777 North Capital Street, NE, Suite 500, Washington, DC 20002. All rights reserved.

our community have a gang problem?" or "Is there gang activity occurring in our jurisdiction?" agencies may use a list of criteria. Table 19.2 lists the definitional criteria used by law enforcement agencies to identify gangs, by average rank of importance. In general, law enforcement agencies regard group criminality as the most important criterion and the presence of leadership as the least important criterion in defining a gang.

> **LO3** Outline the first step in dealing with a gang problem.
>
> The first step in dealing with a gang problem is to recognize it using such definitional characteristics as group criminality; if they self-recognize with a name, display of colors or symbols, claims of turf or territory; and identified leadership.

After a gang problem has been recognized, the next step is to identify the gang members.

Identifying Gang Members

Just as variation exists in how gangs as groups are defined, there are no consistent national criteria used to identify individual gang members. A list of criteria used by individual states to identify gang members is available online at the NGC's website (nationalgangcenter.ojp.gov/legislation). According to the *National Youth Gang Survey Analysis*, an individual's claim to belong to a gang is met with different levels of credibility and importance, depending on the size of the jurisdiction involved: "For larger and smaller cities and suburban counties, a majority of agencies emphasize the display of gang symbols compared with other criteria

(e.g., arrested or associates with known gang members; self-nomination; identified by a reliable source) in identifying and documenting individuals as gang members in their jurisdictions" (NGC, *National*, n.d.).

> **LO4** Understand the criteria or characteristics used to identify gang members.
>
> Gang members may be identified by their names, symbols (clothing and tattoos), and communication styles, including graffiti and sign language.

The Crips, for example, are associated with blue or purple bandannas, scarves, or rags. The Bloods are identified by red colors. Some gangs wear jackets and caps identified with professional sports teams, posing a problem for those youths who wear them because of actual loyalty to the particular team. However, in an effort to evade detection by law enforcement, many gang members no longer publicly display their colors. Gang members may also be identified by the hand signals they use. Tattoos (sometimes called *body art*) are another means of identifying gang members. The most respected tattoos are those earned by serving a prison sentence. Table 19.3 summarizes warning signs that an individual may be involved in a gang.

Records to Keep

Information is an essential tool for law enforcement, and an effective records system is critical in dealing with any gang problem. An effective way to keep track of information and intelligence is to sort data into two files: a gang file and a gang member file.

TABLE 19.2 Definitional Characteristics of Gangs

Definitional Characteristics	Average Rank (1 = Least Important, 6 = Most Important)			
	Larger Cities	Suburban Counties	Smaller Cities	Rural Counties
Commits Crimes Together	4.8	4.9	4.7	4.5
Has a Name	3.9	3.7	3.3	3.5
Displays Colors or Other Symbols	3.3	3.2	3.3	3.2
Hangs Out Together	3.1	3.0	3.6	3.3
Claims Turf or Territory	3.3	3.1	3.0	2.9
Has a Leader(s)	2.6	3.1	3.0	3.5

Source: National Gang Center. (n.d.). Defining gangs and designating gang membership. In *National youth gang survey analysis*. Retrieved April 6, 2021, from www.nationalgangcenter.gov/Survey-Analysis

TABLE 19.3 Warning Signs That a Youth May Be Involved with a Gang

Admits to "hanging out" with kids in gangs
Shows an unusual interest in one or two particular colors of clothing or a particular logo
Has an unusual interest in gangster-influenced music, videos, movies, or websites
Uses unusual hand signals to communicate with friends
Has specific drawings of gang symbols on school books, clothes, walls, or tattoos
Has unexplained physical injuries (fighting-related bruises or injuries to hands/knuckles)
Has unexplained cash or goods, such as clothing or jewelry
Carries a weapon
Has been in trouble with the police
Exhibits negative change in behavior such as: <ul><li>Withdrawing from family</li><li>Declining school attendance, performance, or behavior</li><li>Staying out late without reason</li><li>Displaying an unusual desire for secrecy</li><li>Exhibiting signs of drug use</li><li>Breaking rules consistently</li><li>Speaking in gang-style slang</li></ul>

Source: U.S. Department of Justice, Washington, DC. Retrieved April 6, 2021, from www.justice.gov/usao-sdfl/file/762021/download

A gang file should be maintained with the following information: type of gang (street, motorcycle, etc.), ethnic composition, number of active and associate members, territory, hideouts, types of crimes usually committed, method of operation, choice of targets or victims, leadership, and members known to be violent. If there is a group photo of the gang, which can sometimes be obtained during a search, this should be included in the file as well. Included within the record system should be a gang member pointer file that cross-references the names of suspected gang members with the gang file. This may be a card or computerized file.

A gang member file should include a photograph, or several if available, and a description and/or photo of the vehicle the member drives. It should also include the gang member's **moniker**, the nickname used by the gang member among their peers and while committing crimes for the gang. Although no two members of the same gang will have the same moniker, several gangs may have members with the same moniker. Consequently, it may be helpful to have a separate file that lists all of the gang members from different gangs who go by a certain moniker. Other

helpful information to put into the gang member file, if it becomes available, is the individual's cell phone number, address, any employment information, and known relationships, especially regarding girlfriends or boyfriends, and mothers or fathers of their children. When a gang member's girlfriend or "baby mama" gets mad, this presents an ideal opportunity for investigators to acquire inside gang information.

LO5 Describe the types of records to keep on gangs.

Maintain records on gangs, gang members, monikers, photographs, vehicles, and illegal activities. Cross-reference the records.

Patrol officers need information quickly when dealing with gang members. Information technology (IT) staff can assist with computer-aided dispatch (CAD) and records management systems (RMS) to make sure information comes fast and is accurate.

Investigating Illegal Gang Activity

The most common way to gather information about gangs is internal contacts with patrol officers, as they are the most likely to have field contact with gang members or to have observed gang activities, followed by internal departmental records and computerized files, and then by review of offense reports (O'Deane & Murphy, 2010). Illegal activities of gangs usually involve multiple suspects, which makes investigation much more difficult. Evidence may link only a few of the suspects with the crime, and, as with organized crime figures, gang members maintain fierce loyalty to each other and are often unwilling to "rat."

Gangs, particularly those that are highly organized, can be very mobile, which presents another challenge to investigators. An excellent resource for investigators working crimes that involve gangs or gang members is the National Alliance of Gang Investigators' Associations (NAGIA), which provides a forum for officers in jurisdictions throughout the country to share information and intelligence.

Most often the witnesses to gang-related crimes are gang members themselves or people who at least sympathize with the gang, which presents a challenge to investigators trying to extract credible information from such individuals as these witnesses may deliberately lie to mislead investigators and protect the suspects.

Other witnesses who are not gang-involved may be too afraid to provide any information. Because they live in the neighborhood with the gang and may fear for their lives, they may provide information and then later deny it. For this reason, tape-record or videotape all such interviews.

L06 Explain the special challenges that may be involved in investigating illegal activities of gangs.

Special challenges in investigating the illegal activities of gangs include the multitude of suspects, the potential mobility of the members, and the unreliability or fear of witnesses.

Gang investigations should proceed like most other criminal investigations. Uniformed officers should establish personal contacts with the gangs in the community and become familiar with their size, the names and monikers of as many members as possible, and each gang's identifying symbols, colors, and graffiti.

Witnesses to gang crime can come from many sources. Parents, siblings, prior romantic interests, classmates, teachers, and school counselors often have unique insight into gang members' lives. Former friends may be willing to share valuable social media posts. Some disenchanted gang members may become police informants. Recreation department personnel know what is going on in the youth community and are therefore good sources of information. Another "digital" witness can include home security technology.

The immediate area in which a crime occurs may yield much information. Any graffiti present indicates which gang controls the territory. Keep in mind that gang members do not like to be on foot in a strange area, especially one dominated by their enemies; therefore, commando-type raids on foot are very rare.

If a neighborhood canvass is conducted and information is received, it is important that the canvass not stop at that point. This would implicate the house or business at which the canvass was terminated as the source of information. In addition, more information might be available from a source not yet contacted during the canvass.

Field interviews (FI) are considered "the bread and butter of any gang investigator," and properly filled out FI cards can be an important part of a gang-related crime

investigation (O'Deane & Murphy, 2010). Certain field interview techniques are more likely to yield results than others. For instance:

- When dealing with gang members, address their expectation of respect (whether it is deserved or not) by maintaining a firm but fair attitude. This will get an investigator farther in extracting useful information from the individual.

- When talking to a gang member about a significant matter, such as a crime or another gang member, hold your conversation where other gang members can neither see nor hear you. This will encourage subject cooperation.

- Immediately isolate gang members suspected of a crime so that they cannot collaborate on their "story." This technique is similar to any police response in which multiple suspects are apprehended at the crime scene.

- Keep in mind that gang members will often attempt to discard any contraband they are carrying, such as weapons or drugs, when they see an officer approaching. Therefore, it is important to check the area surrounding the location of contact. (O'Deane & Murphy, 2010)

Crime scenes that involve gangs are unique. Often the crime scene is part of a chain of events. When a gang assault occurs, for example, often a chase precedes and follows the assault, considerably widening the crime scene. If vehicles are involved, the assault is probably by a rival gang. If no vehicles appear to have been involved, the suspects are probably local, perhaps even members of the same gang as the victim. This frequently occurs when narcotics, girlfriends, or family disputes are involved.

Evidence obtained in gang-related criminal investigations is processed in the same way as evidence related to any other crime. Photograph graffiti for later identification. If feasible, take photos of gang members and their tattoos. File FI cards on members, vehicles, territory, locations, crimes committed, drug activities, and any other information. Gang members may usually be located within their territory even after they commit a crime—because this is their "home."

A helpful source of information on gangs is the Internet. Thousands of gang-related sites have been posted. In addition, investigators can learn much about gangs in their jurisdiction by paying attention to graffiti. To document graffiti evidence, take the following steps:

- Photograph it whole and in sections.

- Analyze it while it is intact.

- Remove it (paint over it, sandblast it, etc.).

- Archive the photo.

- Record the colors used.

- Record the gang monikers.

- Record indicators of "beef" or violence.

- Create an antigraffiti program to cover over all graffiti.

Approaches to the Gang Problem

Each year, approximately 401,000 youth join gangs while another 378,000 youths leave gangs (Pyrooz & Sweeten, 2015). These youth are the target populations for gang prevention and intervention programs, two of the three fundamental approaches to addressing the gang problem. The third approach—suppression—rounds out a method identified as either the Comprehensive Community-Wide Gang Program Model or, more simply, the Spergel Model (Howell, 2010; Villanueva, 2009).

> **LO7** Summarize what strategies have been used to combat a gang problem.
>
> A three-pronged approach to address the gang problem uses a balance of prevention, intervention, and suppression strategies.

The first strategy—prevention—aims at keeping youths from becoming gang members in the first place and is divided into two tiers: primary prevention, directed at all youths living in communities where gangs are present; and secondary prevention, targeting at-risk youths. Primary prevention efforts include after-school activities, truancy and dropout prevention programs, and job programs—strategies that disrupt gang recruiting efforts by keeping kids in prosocial activities and away from unstructured social environments (NGC, 2010).

The Gang Resistance Education and Training (G.R.E.A.T.) program is an evidence-based gang prevention program that targets children in elementary and middle school and, similar to Drug Abuse Resistance Education (D.A.R.E.), uses a classroom curriculum with instruction conducted by law enforcement officers

to teach children problem-solving and life skills in an effort to immunize them from the lure of gangs, delinquent behavior, and youth violence. Information on how numerous police departments around the country have implemented G.R.E.A.T. in their jurisdictions can be found on the program's website (www.great-online.org).

Because the risk for joining a gang is greatest at age 13, efforts directed at children in elementary and middle school can be the most effective in preventing gang involvement (Pyrooz & Sweeten, 2015). Secondary prevention identifies children ages 7 to 14 at high risk, who have already displayed early signs of delinquency, and intervenes with appropriate school, community, and faith-based services before their problem behaviors can evolve into serious delinquency and gang involvement (NGC, 2010).

According to some gang experts, prevention is the weakest link in the effort to stop gang crime, and the police have a vital role to play in this endeavor. To fulfill their sworn duty to protect and serve within the context of gang prevention, law enforcement must move beyond a "hook 'em and book 'em" mentality and, instead, actively collaborate with public health, the community, schools, and other public- and private-sector partners on front-end prevention strategies (Decker, 2013).

If jurisdictions focus the majority of resources on gang members, what efforts are being made to address the at-risk youth who are being threatened and beaten up by gang members? For these kids, often the best way to stop being victimized is to join the gang. For youth living in marginalized communities where financial instability is common, the lure of gangs may seem like the only way for make money. In certain parts of the country where gangs are more prevalent and entrenched, prevention efforts are particularly crucial and can pay big dividends.

The second strategy—intervention— is directed at youths already involved in gangs, either as active members or close associates. The goal of intervention is to help youths make the decision to leave a gang, a process known as *desistance*, and provides sanctions and services designed to push these juveniles out of and away from gangs. This strategy "involves aggressive outreach and recruitment activity. Support services for gang-involved youths and their families help youth make positive choices" (NGC, 2010, p.4). This group of gang-involved youths make up a relatively large share of the population, typically range in age from 12 to 24, and are involved in significant levels of illegal activity but are not necessarily considered the more serious or chronic offenders.

Many gang members desist on their own without the need for intervention. Some grow disillusioned with gang life, others enter romantic relationships with people outside of the gang, and many others simply mature to the point where they "age out." Therefore, intervention efforts should focus on those at greatest risk of long-term persistence. Research on gang desistence has identified several crucial experiences, some of which occur abruptly while others occur over a period of time, that can lead a gang member to re-evaluate their involvement in a gang (Young & Gonzalez, 2013). These so-called leverage points include:

- Victimization by other gang members

- Negative contacts with law enforcement

- Involvement with the criminal justice system

- Periods of disruption within the framework and operations of the gang

- Life-changing events (e.g., romantic relationship, pregnancy, birth of a child, family health issues)

These leverage points are opportunities where intervention strategies may be more effective because the gang member is more receptive to options other than life in the gang.

The third strategy—suppression—targets serious and chronic offenders, those hard-core members most embedded in the gang culture, who comprise a relatively small proportion of the population but commit a disproportionately large share of crime and violence (Howell, 2010). Suppression involves both formal and informal social control procedures, such as "close supervision and monitoring of gang-involved youth by agencies of the juvenile/criminal justice system and also by community-based agencies, schools, and grassroots groups" (NGC, 2010, p. 4). Furthermore, members of this group "are candidates for targeted enforcement and prosecution because of their high level of involvement in crime and violent gangs and the small probability that other strategies will reduce their criminal behavior" (Howell, 2010, p. 12).

Civil gang injunctions (CGIs) and ordinances are legal tools used with urban gangs that focus on individuals and the locations of their routine activities. These neighborhood-level intervention strategies target specific individuals who intimidate residents and cause other public nuisance issues and restrict these gang members' activities within a specific geographic area.

However, injunctions and ordinances may be challenged as unconstitutional violations of the freedom of speech, the right of association, and due process rights if they do not clearly delineate how officers may apply such orders. For example, Chicago passed a gang congregation ordinance to combat the problems created by the city's street gangs. During the three years following passage of the ordinance, Chicago police officers issued more than

89,000 dispersal orders and arrested more than 42,000 people. But in *Chicago v. Morales* (1999), the Supreme Court struck down the ordinance as unconstitutional because its vague wording failed to provide adequate standards to guide police discretion. The lesson here is that any civil injunctions a city passes must be clear in what officers can and cannot do when they observe what they believe to be gang members congregating in public places.

Tougher legislation is also being used as a gang control approach. Because some gangs use their younger members to commit serious crimes, relying on the more lenient juvenile sentencing laws, some jurisdictions have allowed courts to raise the penalties for teenagers convicted of gang-related offenses.

Collaborative Efforts: Gang Task Forces

Collaboration among law enforcement agencies can greatly enhance efforts to cope with the gang problem. Multiagency task forces bring together differing perspectives and focus human labor efforts and resources on a common goal, providing a more effective response to the issue of gangs. Even though law enforcement unquestionably plays a major role in effectively combating the gang problem, partnerships with the community, parents, and schools significantly increase the likelihood of a successful response.

The OJJDP's Comprehensive Gang Model for a gang reduction program is based on years of experimentation and research on gang prevention. The model's key distinguishing feature is a strategic planning process that empowers communities to assess their own gang problems and fashion a complement of antigang strategies and program activities. The report, *Best Practices to Address Community Gang Problems* (NGC, 2010), presents the best practices for the Comprehensive Gang Model and highlights results of the NYGC Survey and a meeting of practitioners regarding their experiences in implementing the model. Another valuable resource available to all communities is the National Gang Crime Research Center website (www.ngcrc.com).

Prosecuting Gang-Related Crimes

One valuable and effective tactic in prosecuting gang-related crimes is to make use of conspiracy laws such as the federal Racketeering Influenced and Corrupt Organizations (RICO) Act statutes commonly used with organized crime cases. As many of the gang members ("aiders and abettors") as possible should be charged and prosecuted.

Some jurisdictions are seeing positive results by escalating the level of prosecution, particularly for higher level gang members. Mandatory minimum sentences have also become a useful tool in garnering gang member and associate cooperation during investigations. The fear of federal time due to mandatory minimum penalties provides investigators with leverage over defendants, encouraging cooperation in exchange for lesser charges or substantial-assistance benefits.

Former San Diego Police Chief William Lansdowne explains why the threat of federal prison is an important deterrent and valuable strategy for law enforcement, particularly when going after a gang leader: "It's nothing for a gang member to go to prison in California. They know they are going to be able to keep those gang connections. But if you send a gang member from California to a federal prison in Connecticut, they lose their local gang connections.... and they don't have that safety net" (PERF Report Describes Changes, 2010, p. 7).

Throughout the investigation of illegal gang activities, be aware of the most common defenses gang members use in court.

> **LO8** Explain what two defense strategies are commonly used by gang members' lawyers in court.
>
> The two most often used defense strategies are pleas of diminished capacity and self-defense.

Although some states have eliminated "diminished capacity" as a defense, many have not. Therefore, be sure to document whether the suspect was under the influence of alcohol or other drugs at the time of the crime. Likewise, document whether the suspect was threatened by the victim and could possibly have been acting in self-defense.

Federal Efforts to Combat the Gang Problem

Several entities exist to combat the nation's gang problem. The NGIC is one such collaborative effort:

> The NGIC was established by Congress in 2005 in order to support law enforcement agencies through timely and accurate information sharing and to provide strategic and tactical analysis to federal, state, and local law

enforcement. A multi-agency fusion center, the NGIC integrates its resources to investigate and study the growth, migration, and criminal networks of gangs that pose a significant threat to communities throughout the United States. The NGIC is comprised of representatives from the Federal Bureau of Investigation (FBI); U.S. Drug Enforcement Administration (DEA); U.S. Bureau of Alcohol, Tobacco, Firearms, and Explosives (ATF); Federal Bureau of Prisons (BOP); United States Marshals Service (USMS); U.S. Department of Defense (DOD); and U.S. Customs and Border Protection (CBP)....

> One of the NGIC's primary resources is NGIC Online. A web-based information system, NGIC Online supplies state, local, federal, and international law enforcement partners with an array of tools designed to facilitate research on gang-related intelligence. NGIC Online is available through the Law Enforcement Enterprise Portal (LEEP).... A digital warehouse of data, NGIC Online contains a Gang Encyclopedia; Signs, Symbols, and Tattoos Database; Gang Terms Dictionary; Intelligence Library; and a Gang Training and Events Calendar, all of which are fully searchable and provide users with a vast collection of intelligence products; images; announcements; officer safety alerts; and other materials aimed to promote gang awareness and to assist gang investigations at state, local, and federal levels. NGIC Online also features two communication platforms—a Discussion Board and a Request for Information portal—that allow users to solicit analytical assistance from the NGIC and to communicate with the NGIC's network of gang subject matter experts. (NGIC, 2015)

Another multiagency effort is the Organized Crime and Gang Section (OCGS) of the Criminal Division within the U.S. Department of Justice. OCGS was established in 2010 when the (former) Organized Crime and Racketeering Section (OCRS) merged with the Criminal Division's Gang Unit and another agency called GangTECC, itself a multiagency task force. GangTECC (which stands for Gang Targeting, Enforcement, and Coordination Center) was designed to serve as a critical catalyst in a unified federal effort to help disrupt and dismantle the most significant and violent gangs in the United States. The senior investigators at GangTECC come from the ATF, BOP, DEA, FBI, USMS, and U.S. Immigration and Customs Enforcement (ICE) at the Department of Homeland Security.

Previous editions of this text also discussed the NYGC, which was established in 1995 and funded by the OJJDP, as another "one-stop shop for information about gangs and effective responses to them." In October 2009 the NYGC merged with the NGC, which was established in 2003 and funded by the Bureau of Justice Assistance, to create a new consolidated NGC. The current NGC provides a plethora of published research about gangs; descriptions of evidence-based antigang programs; and links to tools, databases, and other resources to assist in developing and implementing effective community-based gang prevention, intervention, and suppression strategies. The center also offers a variety of antigang training courses and provides an online database of gang-related state legislation and municipal codes; a list of newspaper articles on nationwide gang activity that is updated daily; and GANGINFO, an electronic mailing list for professionals working with gangs.

Bias and Hate Crime: An Overview

In addition to youth and street gangs, law enforcement is often confronted with the criminal activities of hate groups. Hate is a complex subject that can be divided into two general categories: rational and irrational. Unjust acts inspire rational hate. Hatred of a person based on race, religion, gender, sexual orientation, ethnicity, or national origin constitutes irrational hate. Generically, a **bias crime** or a **hate crime** is a traditional criminal act, such as murder, arson, or vandalism, with the added element of bias —it is committed because of someone's actual or perceived membership in a particular group. The Matthew Shepard and James Byrd, Jr., Hate Crimes Prevention Act of 2009 (18 U.S.C. § 249) defines a hate crime as any criminal offense in which an offender intentionally selects a victim, or in the case of a property crime, the property that is the object of the crime, in whole or in part because of the actual or perceived race, color, religion, national origin, ethnicity, gender, gender identity, disability, or sexual orientation of any person. A listing of state hate crime laws is available online at the website of the Anti-Defamation League (ADL) (www.adl.org/media/13726/download).

Hate itself is not a crime; the freedom to feel hatred is a protected civil liberty. However, when that feeling is translated into action, it becomes a criminal offense. Crimes range from verbal intimidation and harassment to destruction of property, physical violence, and murder.

Hate crime is not a new development in our country. It has probably existed in America for more than 300 years; however, only recently has it become recognized as a violation of the law. The Southern Poverty Law Center (SPLC), which monitors hate groups and other extremists throughout the United States, reports that since 2000 the number of hate groups organized in the United States has increased by 30%, a surge fueled by fears of Latino immigration, by the election of the country's first African American president, and more recently, by the COVID-19 pandemic. The SPLC tracked 838 known hate groups actively operating across the country in 2020. The SPLC organizes hate groups into the following categories: Ku Klux Klan, Neo-Nazis, Racist Skinheads, White Nationalists, Christian Identity, Neo-Confederates, Anti-Immigrant, Anti-LGBTQ, and Anti-Muslim (Southern Poverty Law Center, 2020).

The FBI's Uniform Crime Report for 2019 indicates that there were 7,314 hate crime incidents reported that year involving 8,559 offenses. Further breakdown of incidents revealed that there were 7,103 single-bias incidents involving 8,302 offenses, 8,552 victims, and 6,268 known offenders. Two hundred eleven multiple-bias incidents were reported in 2019 involving 257 offenses, 260 victims, and 138 known offenders (Federal Bureau of Investigation [FBI], 2019).

Motivation for Hate Crime

According to the FBI, of the 7,103 single-bias hate incidents reported in 2019

- 55.8% of hate incidents were motivated by a race, ethnicity, or ancestry bias.

- 21.4% were motivated by religious bias.

- 16.8% were motivated by sexual-orientation bias.

- 2.8% were motivated by gender-identity bias.

- 2.2% were motivated by disability bias.

- 1.0% were motivated by gender bias. (FBI, 2019)

Figure 19.2 illustrates the distribution of hate incidents by bias type.

> **LO9** Recognize the primary motivation for bias or hate crimes and who is most frequently targeted.
>
> Bias or hate crimes are motivated by bigotry and hatred against a specific group of people. Race is usually the primary motivation for hate crimes, and African Americans are most often the victims.

The groups most likely to be victims of hate crime are (in alphabetical order) African Americans, Arabs, Asians, gay males, Jews, Latinos, lesbians, Native Americans, and White women in interracial relationships. Following the events of September 11, 2001, concern has arisen over an increase of hate crimes against young men of Middle Eastern descent, leading the SPLC to create a new category of hate crimes by anti-Muslims.

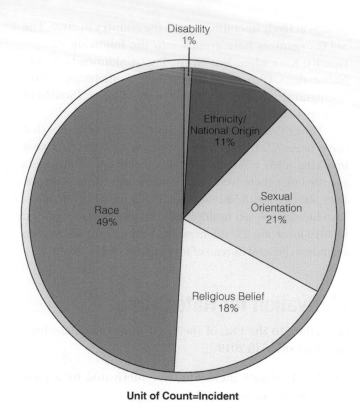

Unit of Count=Incident

Figure 19.2
Distribution of hate incidents by bias type, 2019.

Source: Adapted from Federal Bureau of Investigation. (2019). *Hate crime statistics, 2019.* Washington, DC: Author. Retrieved April 6, 2021, from ucr.fbi.gov/hate-crime/2019/hate-crime

A group often overlooked in discussions of hate crime is the homeless. Homeless people have been run over; hit with stun guns, pellet guns, paint guns, and pepper balls; set on fire; beaten; robbed; raped; and firebombed. Some characteristics typical of hate-motivated violence are relatively rare in other crimes of violence, as shown in Table 19.4.

The SPLC (2018) notes that differentiating between hate crimes and terrorist attacks is important to understanding an offender's motive, addressing the root causes of an offense, and successfully prosecuting offenders: "Hate crimes are motivated at least in part by an offender's personal bias and are sometimes committed by nonpolitical youths simply for the thrill of it. Terrorist attacks, on the other hand, are violent acts inspired primarily by extremist beliefs and intended as political or ideological statements. Rather than target a specific identity—such as Jews or Muslims, as in a hate crime—offenders typically target government installations or groups of civilians related more by proximity than by their individual identity." Some violent crimes, such as the 2015 massacre of nine African Americans in a Charleston church by White supremacist Dylann Roof, can be classified as both a hate crime and a terrorist attack. Terrorism, including that committed by domestic violent extremists (DVEs) and other hate groups, is the focus of Chapter 20.

Offenses

Of the 8,559 hate crimes reported to law enforcement in 2019, 5,512 (64.4%) were crimes against persons: 40.0% of these were intimidation; 36.7%, simple assault;

TABLE 19.4 Nonhate-Based Crime versus Hate-Based Crime

Characteristics	Nonhate-Based Incidents	Hate-Based Incidents
Relationship of victim to perpetrator	Most assaults involve two people who know each other	Assaults tend to be "stranger" crimes
Number of perpetrators	Most assaults have one perpetrator and one victim	Involve an average of four assailants for each victim
Nature of the conflict	Tend to be even	Tend to be uneven—hate crime perpetrators often attack younger or weaker victims or arm themselves and attack unarmed victims
Amount of physical damage inflicted	Not typically "excessive"	Extremely violent, with victims being three times more likely to require hospitalization than "normal" assault victims
Treatment of property	In most property crimes, something of value is taken	More likely that valuable property will be damaged or destroyed
Perpetrator's personal gain	Attacker settles a score or profits from the crime	In most, no personal score is settled and no profit is made
Location of crime	No place with any symbolic significance	Frequently occur in churches, synagogues, mosques, cemeteries, monuments, schools, camps, and in or around the victim's home

Source: Adapted from Bodinger-deUriarte, C. (1991, December). Hate crime: The rise of hate crime on school campuses. *Research Bulletin* No.10 of Phi Delta Kappa, Center for Evaluation, Development, and Research, p. 2. Reprinted by permission of Phi Delta Kappa International. All rights reserved. Retrieved April 6, 2021, from files.eric.ed.gov/fulltext/ED368994.pdf

21.0%, aggravated assault; 1.5% were the violent crimes of murder (51 offenses) and forcible rape (30 offenses); and 0.7% involved the offense category "other," which is collected only in the National Incident-Based Reporting System (NIBRS) (FBI, 2019). Of the 2,811 hate crimes (32.8%) committed against property, 76.6% were acts of destruction, damage, or vandalism. The remaining 23.4% of crimes against property consisted of robbery, burglary, larceny-theft, motor vehicle theft, arson, and other crimes. A total of 236 offenses defined as crimes against society (e.g., drug or narcotic offenses or prostitution) were reported in 2019 (FBI, 2019).

Offenders

Of the 6,406 known hate crime offenders for whom race was reported in 2019, 52.5% were White, 23.9% were Black, 6.6% were groups made up of individuals of various races, 1.1% were American Indian or Alaska Native, 0.9% were Asian, and 0.3% were Native Hawaiian or other Pacific Islander. Approximately 1 out of 7 (14.6%) of hate crime offenders were of unknown race.

Hate Groups versus Other Dangerous Groups

As with making the distinction between terrorists and hate groups, the SPLC also differentiates between extremists and hate groups, noting that not all extremist groups fit within the SPLC-designated "hate groups." For example, by SLPC standards, the Oath Keepers and Aryan Brotherhood are extremist groups, whereas the Proud Boys and Knights of the Ku Klux Klan are both extremist *and* hate groups. The SPLC also monitors a sector of radical right extremists known as antigovernment "patriot" groups, which include militias. These patriot groups reject the authority of government, consider the federal government to be an enemy of the people, and promote baseless conspiracy theories typically involving a secret cabal of elites who wish to create a "New World Order" of totalitarian government. Militia movements, such as the Oath Keepers, are patriot groups that actively engage in paramilitary activities. Domestic violent extremism is discussed in Chapter 20.

The main hate groups in the United States are "skinheads," Christian Identity groups, the Ku Klux Klan (KKK), White supremacists, and neo-Nazis. Such hate crime groups terrorize innocent civilians and spread fear throughout communities nationwide. Several watchdog organizations such as the SPLC and the ADL track the size and activities of racist groups and are good resources for law enforcement.

The Police Response

Respond promptly to reports of hate crime, attempt to reduce the victims' fears, and determine the exact type of prejudice involved. Investigators should ask the following questions to determine whether an incident was hate or bias motivated:

- Was the victim a member of a targeted class and outnumbered?

- Were the offenders from a different racial or ethnic group than the victim(s)?

- Did the offender use biased language, including slang?

Always provide follow-up information to the victims. Include in the report the exact words or language used reflecting racial, religious, ethnic, or sexual orientation bias; the perpetrators' actions, symbols, colors, and dress; or any other identifying characteristics or actions.

The International Association of Chiefs of Police (IACP) has outlined key indicators that a hate crime may have been committed:

- The victim(s) and witnesses perceptions about the crime

- Comments, gestures, or written statements made by the perpetrator that reflect bias, including graffiti or other symbols

- Any differences between perpetrator and victim, whether actual or perceived by the perpetrator

- Similar incidents in the same area, indicating a pattern may exist

- If the victim was engaged in activities promoting their group or community

- If the incident occurred on a holiday or coincided with a date of particular significance to the victim's group

- Known involvement by the perpetrator in an organized hate group

- Absence of any other motive, such as economic gain (IACP, 2021)

Symbols commonly associated with extremist or hate groups are shown in Figure 19.3.

American Front

American Nazi Party

Aryan Nation

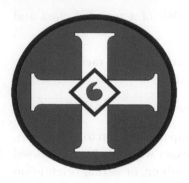

Ku Klux Klan

New Black Panther Party

National Socialist Movement

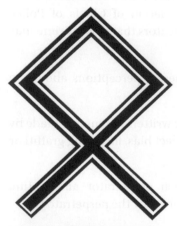

Odin Rune

Posse Comitatus

Storm Front

Nationalist Movement

Triskele

Volksfront

Figure 19.3

A sampling of extremist group symbols. Their origins and meanings may be found online at the Anti-Defamation League's website.

Source: www.adl.org/hate_symbols/default_graphics.asp

Officers and investigators must be able to differentiate between hate crimes and hate incidents. **Hate incidents** involve actions by an individual or group that, while motivated by bias against a victim's race, religion, ethnicity, national origin, gender, gender identity, sexual orientation, age, or disability, do *not* rise to the level of a statutorily defined criminal offense (International Association of Chiefs of Police, 2021). For example, hostile or hateful speech or other disrespectful or discriminatory behavior may be motivated by bias but is not illegal.

The passage of the Hate Crime Statistics Act of 1990 requires the attorney general to collect data about crimes that manifest evidence of prejudice based on race, religion, sexual orientation, or ethnicity. The responsibility for developing the procedures for implementing, collecting, and managing hate crime data was delegated to the director of the FBI, who in turn assigned the tasks to the Uniform Crime Reporting (UCR) program. In 2009, Congress further amended the Hate Crime Statistics Act with the passage of the Matthew Shepard and James Byrd, Jr. Hate Crime Prevention Act. This amendment includes the collection of data for crimes motivated by bias against a particular gender and gender identity, as well as for crimes committed by, and crimes directed against, juveniles.

In 2019, 15,588 law enforcement agencies throughout the country participated in the UCR's Hate Crime Statistics Program, representing more than 305 million inhabitants (FBI, 2019). Appendix G contains a form for collecting data for a bias offense report. Such forms can help ensure quality field reports that properly identify the crime, the elements of the offense, and the evidence clearly demonstrating that a hate crime was committed.

The FBI has also published manuals concerning the types of statistics needed and has established training programs in major cities. Nonetheless, it is difficult to establish hate crime records because some hate crimes involve groups rather than individuals. Table 19.5 summarizes the variables that may encourage or discourage an agency from reporting hate crimes.

TABLE 19.5 Variables That Affect whether Agencies Report Hate Crimes

Agency Encouragers	Agency Discouragers
Ability to assess intergroup tensions in community	Perception that some minority groups complain unnecessarily
Desire to give support to communities	Perceived as not being real police work in the community
Belief that hate crime reporting will improve police/community relations	Belief that hate crime reporting will result in negative publicity for the community
Belief that police help set level of acceptable behavior	Agency does not have the adequate technological resources
Understanding that community wants police to report	Belief that reporting hate crimes will make things worse for communities
Need to know extent of problem as first step to developing solutions	Perception on part of police that no problem exists
Let community know that department takes hate crimes seriously	Belief that hate crimes are not as serious as other crimes (i.e., lower priority)
Belief that victims will get help	Belief that reporting hate crimes will make things worse for hate violence victim
Will help diffuse racial tensions within the police department	Creates too much additional work
The right thing to do politically	Belief that hate crime reporting supports the political agendas of gay and minority groups (which is seen as a negative outcome)
The right thing to do morally	Belief that it is wrong to make these types of crimes special
Will help maintain department's good relationship with diverse groups	Not a priority of local government
Consistent with values of department	Not deemed important by department
Belief that identifying problem will keep others safe	Belief that identifying a crime as a hate crime will have no effect on the outcome
Citizens appreciate the hate crime reporting efforts of police	Insufficient support staff to process, record and submit hate crime data

Source: Adapted from Nolan, J. J., & Yoshio, A. (1999). An analysis of factors that affect law enforcement participation in hate crime reporting. *Journal of Contemporary Criminal Justice*, 15(1), 118. Sage Publications.

Efforts to Combat Bias and Hate Crimes

An ideal place to start in the efforts to combat bias and hate crimes is within the police department itself. One of the recommendations of the President's Task Force on 21st Century Policing (2015) is for law enforcement agencies to strive to create a workforce that encompasses a broad range of diversity including race, gender, language, life experience, and cultural background to improve understanding and effectiveness in dealing with all communities. A diverse police force that more closely resembles and identifies with the communities it serves can help build trust and legitimacy and foster partnerships to better fight crime (Matthies, Keller, & Lim, 2012).

Regardless of how an agency or individual officer views hate crime, it remains a criminal offense that requires a law enforcement response. Two responses have been taken: legislation to expand the scope of the law and increase the severity of punishment for hate crimes and more police focus on and full investigation of such crimes. Other efforts include community-based programs to increase awareness of and offer solutions to the problem of hate crime.

No national consensus exists about whether hate crimes should be a separate crime, and those supporting hate crime statutes disagree about what should be included. States vary greatly in legislation related to hate crimes. The most common elements of hate crime legislation include:

- Enhanced penalties
- Criminal penalties for vandalism of religious institutions
- Collection of data

Legislation must also keep up with the technology used to spread messages of hate. Despite such legislation, those who propagate messages of bigotry, intolerance, and hatred claim they have a constitutionally protected right to do so, citing free speech, due process, and equal protection challenges. And although state courts have repeatedly upheld the constitutionality of legislation that enhances penalties for hate-motivated violence, the U.S. Supreme Court struck down a Virginia law banning cross burning in 2003, saying the statute violated the First Amendment (*Virginia v. Black*, 2003).

Furthermore, research has found minimal public support for harsher penalties for offenders who commit hate crimes than for offenders who commit identical crimes with no biased motivation.

Sometimes, the hideous nature of hate crimes leaves investigators wondering whether the offense is truly based on bias or whether some type of ritualistic torture was involved.

Ritualistic Crime: An Overview

Ritualistic crimes are most often associated with cults or occult groups. A **cult** is a system of religious beliefs and rituals. It also refers to those who practice such beliefs. One informal definition of a *cult* is "any religion other than your own." The term is often applied to religious or mystical groups that society does not understand. Most cults involve some form of worship and followers dedicated to the concepts promoted by the leader.

Cults range in size from a few followers to worldwide organizations directed by a complex chain of command. According to some estimates, 3,000 cults exist throughout the world, claiming a total estimated membership of more than 3 million people, mostly young adults.

One cult in the late 1970s was the People's Temple, led by Jim Jones, a Protestant clergyman. Hundreds of his followers moved into Jonestown, a rural commune in Guyana, South America, and lived under his absolute rule. In 1978, cult leaders killed a U.S. congressman and three journalists investigating activities in Jonestown. Jones then ordered his followers to commit suicide, resulting in the deaths of more than 900 people.

Another well-known group regarded as a cult is the International Society for Krishna Consciousness, better known as the Hare Krishna movement. This cult came from India in 1954. Most members wear orange robes, and the men shave their heads.

Some scholars refer to cults as "new religious movements," or NRMs, because most cults are young religious movements still in their first generation (Arweck, 2006; Cowan & Bromley, 2015; Lewis & Tøllefsen, 2016). As such, these authors stress, most NRMs are law abiding. For example, the neo-pagan Wicca movement, although it may have aspects of a cult, continually disclaims association with witchcraft and insists on its status as a religion.

Moreover, the pervasive effect of mass media has elevated some superficial characteristics of cults—such as goth/vampire makeup and clothing—to an almost pop-culture status; consequently, the display of such trappings may not be indicative of serious involvement.

Normally, NRMs have a charismatic leader who develops an idea that attracts people looking for fulfillment. The leader is usually self-appointed and claims the

Graves scribbled with swastikas and other anti-Semitic graffiti in a Jewish cemetery. One of the results of increased awareness of hate crimes is the creation of laws that exact higher penalties from convicted hate-crime offenders.

Vincent Kessler/Reuters/Alamy Stock Photo

right of rule because of a supernatural power of appointment. NRM membership may include males and females, and there is normally no room for democratic participation. Leadership is most often exerted through fear and mysticism. Charles Manson and Jim Jones are examples of such leaders.

An NRM in Waco, Texas, the "Branch Davidians" headed by David Koresh, clashed with federal agents attempting a raid in February 1993. The raid turned into a gun battle in which four federal agents and at least two Branch Davidian members were killed. Sixteen agents were wounded. Weapons inside the compound included at least one tripod-mounted .50-caliber machine gun and many semiautomatic weapons. A child released from the compound who had lived there for four years said she had been taught to put a gun into her mouth and told how to commit suicide by taking cyanide.

A 51-day standoff between the federal government and Koresh's armed followers ended in April 1993, when fire engulfed the compound. The FBI had sent an armored combat vehicle to ram holes into the buildings and pump tear gas into them. The FBI asserted that Davidians started the blaze, an apparent mass suicide that killed at least 70, including women and children.

Survivors of the fire, however, insisted that it was caused by the tank's hitting a barrel of propane and tipping over lit camping lanterns. The FBI has been cleared of wrongdoing in this incident.

Terminology and Symbols of Cults

Over the years, a number of terms have been associated with cults. Among the terms law enforcement officers should be familiar with are the following:

- **Antichrist**—the son of Satan

- **Beelzebub**—a powerful demon, directly under Satan

- **Coven**—a group of witches or Satanists

- **Hand of Glory**—the left hand of a person who has died

- **Incantation**—verbal spell

- **Magick**—the "glue" that binds occult groups, a supernatural act or force that causes a change in the environment

- **Occult**—secret knowledge of supernormal powers

- **Ritual**—prescribed form of religious or mystical ceremony

- **Sabbat**—a gathering of witches

Among the satanic and occult symbols are the circle, which symbolizes totality and wholeness and within which ceremonies are often performed; the inverted cross, which mocks the Christian cross; the goat's head, symbolizing the devil; the heart, symbolizing the center of life; the hexagram (six-pointed star), purported to protect and control demons; the pentagram (five-pointed star), representing the four elements of the earth surmounted by "the Spirit"; and the horned hand, a hand signal of recognition used between those members. This is similar to the hand signals used by street gangs. Figure 19.4 illustrates symbols commonly associated with satanic and occult groups.

Colors also have significance to many cults:

- Black—darkness, night, sorrow, evil, the devil

- Blue—water, tears, sadness

- Green—vegetation, nature, restfulness

- Red—blood, physical life, energy, sexuality

- White—cleanliness, purity, innocence, virginity

- Yellow—perfection, wealth, glory, power

The Nature of Ritualistic Crimes

Cults and the occult have created great interest because of recurring stories from children and adults in different areas of the United States concerning bizarre satanic rituals and behaviors. Although some may be fantasies, there appears to be some truth, especially

Figure 19.4
Common satanic and occult symbols.

Symbol	Meaning
AC/DC	ANTICHRIST/DEVIL CHILD
ZOSO	THREE-HEADED DOG THAT GUARDS GATE TO HELL
S	SATAN/STONER
MARKOS	ABRACADABRA
FFF	ANTICHRIST
666	ANTICHRIST
ANTICHRIST
NATAS	SATAN REVERSED
6, 9, 13, XIII	OCCULT NUMBERS
HORN AND TAIL ADDED TO ANY LETTER
LIGHTNING BOLT HEAVEN TO HELL STRENGTH
SWASTIKA
ANTICHRIST CROSS OF CONFUSION
PENTAGRAM WHITE MAGIC
PENTAGRAM UPSIDE-DOWN STAR SIGN OF OCCULT
HEXAGRAM CIRCLE
INFINITY-CONTAINMENT CONTROL OF EVIL POWER
ANK
LUCIFER MORNING STAR

regarding the danger to children of the members of satanic groups.

A **ritualistic crime** is an unlawful act committed within the context of a ceremony. Investigate the crime, not the belief system.

Like gangs, occult groups have three levels of activity: dabbling, serious involvement, and criminal involvement. Ritualistic crimes include vandalism, destruction, or theft of religious artifacts; desecration of cemeteries; the maiming, torturing, or killing of animals and people; and the sexual abuse of women and children.

The "Black Masses" of satanism often incorporate religious articles stolen from churches. A **Black Mass** mocks the Christian ritual of communion by substituting blood and urine for the wine and feces for the bread. The cross is usually inverted, and candles and cups may be used in sexual acts. "Hymns" either obscene or praising Satan may be sung, and heavy-metal music may be played.

The Black Mass frequently involves animal mutilation and sacrifice and sometimes torture and sacrifice of humans, often babies or virgins. The sacrifice often incorporates ritualistic incantations. Victims, animal or human, are tortured and mutilated because it is believed that while the victim struggles, the life forces given off can be captured and stored for later use. Such sacrifices may be followed by a dance and an orgy.

"Stoner" gangs consist of middle-class youths involved in drugs, alcohol, and often satanism. Although stoners are not as apt to engage in the violent crimes associated with other street gangs, they may mutilate animals, rob graves, and desecrate churches and human remains. Their graffiti frequently depicts satanic symbolism such as inverted crosses and the number 666.

Who Commits Ritualistic Crime?

A psychological profile of males and females involved in the occult reveals that they tend to be creative, imaginative, curious, daring, and thus intelligent and well educated, yet are frequently underachievers. Although they are egocentric, they also have low self-esteem and have suffered peer rejection or persecution. They come from various social and economic backgrounds, can be any age (although the age range of 13 to 24 is the most common), and are of a variety of races, nationalities, and religions. Interestingly, few Jews are involved in satanism, because Judaism does not emphasize the devil.

A number of factors may lead an individual to occult involvement, including family alienation, insecurity and a quest for personal power, unfulfilled ambitions, a spiritual search for answers, idealism, nonconformity, adolescent rebellion, a desire for adventure and excitement, a need for attention and recognition, and a need to escape reality or the circumstances of their own birth.

Although the personal appearance of those involved in occult activity is often quite normal, some adopt a less mainstream look. For example, they may dress entirely in black or other dark clothing; pierce various parts of their bodies; grow their hair long and dye it; wear chains as implements of confinement; wear heavy eye shadow and white makeup to appear more ashen or deathlike; wear heavy boots; display tattoos depicting serpents, skulls, or other occult symbols; and have scars indicating cuttings, burnings, or whippings.

Dawn Perlmutter, director of the Institute for Research of Organized and Ritualistic Crime, categorizes perpetrators of ritualistic crime as dabblers, true believers, and "true criminals," and asserts that knowledge of how these various groups approach their crimes can help investigators focus their efforts in locating suspects and solving cases. Dabblers are intermittently involved in the occult and have a strong, curious interest in supernatural belief systems. They usually act alone or in small, loosely organized groups. Dabblers often create their own belief system based on some occult ideology and then commit crimes that conform to that ideology (Perlmutter, 2016). The crime scene of a dabbler is generally disorderly and considered by experts to be "sloppy."

True believers are committed to their religion and commit ritualistic crimes because the acts are required by their belief system. According to Perlmutter, true believers understand that their actions are illegal but do not consider such acts to be criminal because they are a necessary part of a religious ritual. True *criminals*, on the other hand, are not committed to a belief system, but rather "use the occult as an excuse to justify or rationalize their criminal behavior (Perlmutter, 2016). A well-known example of a true criminal was Richard Ramirez, also known as the Night Stalker:

> Self-styled Satanists such as Ramirez are not viewed as true believers since their primary interest is usually the acquisition of personal power, material gain, or gratification through criminal activity rather than spiritual Satanic worship. This does not mean that Richard Ramirez was not conducting ritualistic crimes; his crimes involved obvious ritual activities and contained Satanic symbolism, and he clearly

identifies himself as a Satanist. Although dabblers, true criminals, and true believers can all be identified as Satanists, the differences in motivation significantly affect the types of rituals they conduct—hence the investigation and the evidence sought at the crime scene. For example, true criminals are not as concerned about the accurate symbolism, place, date, or victim of the rituals and are not connected to any organized group or specific Satanic tradition; consequently the symbolic evidence will be unique to that person. Dabblers most often are true believers who are emulating a particular tradition or theology but are not yet experienced enough to accurately conduct the ritual. Occasionally dabblers are true criminals who use the occult as a method to gain followers; in either case, the crime scene reflects a lack of knowledge or skill in sacred rites. (Perlmutter, 2016)

Investigating Ritualistic Crimes

Occult reports and activities are investigated in much the same way as any other crime. Interview the people who report these incidents, and prepare reports concerning witnesses or alleged victims of criminal activity. Take photos, sketch symbols, describe colors found, and measure objects. Preserve all objects at the scene as evidence. Work from the outside perimeter to the center or the focus point of the site.

Numerous books and websites are dedicated to discussing the beliefs and rituals of various cults. The background contained in such reference material is beyond the scope of this book, but investigators should be alert to signs that criminal activity may be cult related and know what resources to seek if more information is needed.

One challenge in investigating ritualistic crime is determining that an act is, in fact, motivated by a religious belief system, rather than by hate or bias. Some crimes, such as arson or vandalism, may not initially present clearly as one type of crime or the other, particularly when the victim or target has some religious component, such as a church or cemetery. Understanding the motivations behind these crimes will help investigators distinguish whether an act is rooted in hate or ritualism. Most of the signs, symbols, and other indicators of ritualistic crime discussed next are rarely found at the scene of a hate crime, whereas derogatory or hate-filled verbalizations, graffiti, or other written evidence are often present in bias

crimes. Victim statements, if available, can provide valuable information regarding possible offender motivations. For example, did the offender(s) use racially charged language or other words indicating a hatred for the victim or others in the victim's perceived group (homosexuals, immigrants, religious groups, etc.), or did the offender's words and actions convey more of a ceremonial tone, mentioning sacrifices, or other ritualistic purposes, including prayers or incantations? Did the offenders wear ceremonial-looking clothing or use any type of ceremonial or symbolic item, or were they brandishing baseball bats and other nonsymbolic weapons? These elements help investigators distinguish between hate crimes and ritualistic crimes.

Signs of Cult-Related Activity

The following items may be important indicators of satanic or cult activity. If you suspect ritualistic crime, list these items in any search warrant sought:

- Altars (stone or metal) or a wooden stand for an altar
- Animal parts (anus, heart, tongue, ears, front teeth, front legs, genitals), cages
- Ashes or bowls with powder, colored salt, drugs, or herbs
- Bells, gongs, drums
- Blood, bottles containing blood (may be in a refrigerator), hypodermic needles (for removing blood)
- Body paint, painted rocks
- Body parts (may be in a freezer), skulls and bones, perhaps taken from graves (femur, fibula, index finger, skull and other large bones; the upper right leg and joints of the right-hand fingers are valued)
- Booby traps
- Books on satanism (especially *Book of Shadows*)
- Bullwhips, cat-o'-nine-tails
- Candles, candle holders, candle drippings, incense
- Cauldron for a fire
- CDs or DVDs involving music associated with or depicting acts of satanic violence
- Chalices

- Circle with a 9-foot diameter (may contain a pentagram)

- Coffins

- Cords (colored and knotted) and ligatures

- Crystals

- Daggers, knives, swords (particularly double-edged short swords), martial arts weaponry, and clothing

- Effigy-like clay figures or voodoo dolls stuck with pins or otherwise mutilated

- Flash powder, smoke bombs

- Hoods, robes (especially red, white, or black), hats, helmets, gloves (black satin or velvet) for the right hand, masks

- Inverted crosses, vandalized Christian artifacts

- Jewelry such as amulets or medallions with satanic symbols

- Nondiscernible alphabet, satanic symbols painted on rocks or trees, unusual drawings, or symbols on walls or floors (hexagrams, pentagrams, horns of death, etc.)

- Occult games, Ouija boards, tarot cards

- Parchment (for making contracts)

- Pillows

- Rooms draped in black or red (or nail holes in walls and ceiling indicating that such drapes may have been used)

Indicators of Ritualistic Crimes

> **LO11** List the indicators of ritualistic crimes.

> Indicators that criminal activity may be cult related include symbols, candles, makeshift altars, bones, cult-related books, swords, daggers, and chalices.

If evidence is found to support the commission of a crime, submit the case to the prosecuting attorney's office, as with other crimes. Also as with other crimes, if illegal acts are being committed in the presence of an officer who arrives at the scene, an immediate arrest may be executed. However, many authorities on cult activity warn that no one, including a police officer, should ever approach or try to stop an occult ritual alone because the officer would likely be dealing with mentally deranged people high on drugs.

Investigating Animal Deaths

Unusual circumstances surrounding animal deaths may be important indicators of satanic or cult activity. The following circumstances connected with dead animals should be noted:

- No blood (the blood has been drained from the animal)

- An inverted cross carved on the animal's chest

- Surgically removed head

- Intestines or other body organs removed

If a rash of missing-animal reports occurs, gather information on the kind of animals they are, when they disappeared, and from what area. Look for patterns, and coordinate efforts with the local humane society, American Society for the Prevention of Cruelty to Animals (ASPCA), and veterinarians.

Investigating Homicides

According to Perlmutter (2016), when a true believer commits a ritual homicide, the crime scene will reflect a high level of skill and meticulous attention to detail, reflecting the perpetrator's serious knowledge of a particular theology and the belief that the murder was a sacred act. At the scene of a homicide investigation, the following may suggest a ritualistic death:

- Missing body parts—heart, genitals, left hand, tongue, index finger

- Scarring between index finger and thumb or inside the wrist from past rituals involving members' blood

- Blood drained from body

- Ritualistic symbols such as a pentagram associated with satanic worshipers carved on the body or surrounding area

- Tattoos on armpits or the bottom of feet

- Wax drippings, oils, incense, or powders of ritual on the body

- Urine or human or animal feces smeared on body or found in body cavities

- Semen inside, on, or near body cavities or smeared on the body

- Victim undressed

- Body painted or tied up

- Neck wounds, branding-iron marks, or burn marks on body

- Colored strings near the body

Ritualistic murders are usually stabbings or cuttings—seldom are they gunshot wounds—and many victims are cult members or former members. The murderer is typically a White male from a middle- to upper-class family with above-average intelligence and using some form of drug. A high level of experience is required to drain blood from a person or animal without soiling the scene. A blood-soaked scene is more likely the work of a dabbler. In contrast, an experienced high priest who serves in the honored and privileged role of sacrificer will remove blood from a body with "the skills of a surgeon" (Perlmutter, 2016).

Guard against reacting emotionally when confronted with ritualistic crimes, for they tend to be emotionally and spiritually repulsive. Also bear in mind that unusual crimes are also committed by individuals with mental problems who are not connected with cults.

During postmortem examination, the stomach contents can be of great importance in determining what occurred just before death. In many ritualistic homicides, the body is not available because it has been burned, leaving little evidence. Further, most juries disbelieve seemingly outlandish charges of satanism and human sacrifice, and some judges do not regard satanism as a real problem. Hence, cases often get dismissed.

Investigating Satanic Serial Killings

Serial killings may be linked to satanic-like rituals in the murder act itself as well as in the killer's behavior following the murder. Some brutal, vicious serial killers find satanism a justification for their bizarre antisocial

behavior. Some infamous serial killings have been linked to satanism:

- Charles Manson had links with the Process, a satanic group. Many of the murders committed by Manson and his followers had ritualistic overtones.

- The "Son of Sam" murders involving David Berkowitz are claimed by author Maury Terry in *The Ultimate Evil* to have been a conspiracy among satanic cult members of the Process group.

- "Night Stalker" Richard Ramirez had a pentagram on the palm of his hand, wrote satanic graffiti on the walls of some of his victims' homes, and was obsessed with AC/DC's *Highway to Hell* album featuring the song "Night Stalker." Ramirez shouted "Hail, Satan" as he left the courtroom.

Special Challenges in Ritualistic Crime Investigations

Just as law enforcement officers may have difficulty relating to gang members and not reacting with scorn toward them because of their gang associations, they will almost certainly have difficulty relating to those who engage in ritualistic activity. This is also true of the general public and the media, which frequently sensationalize cases involving ritualistic or cult-related crimes, particularly sexual abuse of children and homicides.

> **LO12** Identify what special challenges are involved in investigating ritualistic crimes.
>
> Special challenges involved in investigating ritualistic or cult-related crimes include separating the belief system from the illegal acts, the sensationalism that frequently accompanies such crimes, and the "abnormal" personalities of some victims and suspects.

Frequently, the victims of cult-related crimes are former cult participants. Many have been or are currently undergoing psychological counseling, which makes their testimony less than credible to some people. Likewise, many suspects, the leaders in particular, are beyond the pale of what most people would consider to be normal and consequently may be treated differently because of how they look and what they believe rather than because of their actions.

Summary

Belonging to a gang is not illegal in this country; however, the activities of gang members frequently *are* illegal. The National Gang Intelligence Center has identified three general types of gangs: street gangs, prison gangs, and outlaw motorcycle gangs (OMGs). Gang members often engage in vandalism, arson, auto theft, shoplifting, drug trafficking, weapons trafficking, threats and intimidation, extortion, shootings, stabbings, and other forms of violence.

The first step in dealing with a gang problem is to recognize it using such definitional characteristics as group criminality, if they self-recognize with a name, display of colors or symbols, claims of turf or territory, and identified leadership. Gang members may be identified by their names, symbols (clothing and tattoos), and communication styles, including graffiti and sign language. Maintain records on gangs and gang members, including monikers, photographs, vehicles, and illegal activities. Cross-reference the records.

Special challenges in investigating the illegal activities of gangs include the multitude of suspects, the potential mobility of members, and the unreliability or fear of witnesses. A three-pronged approach to address the gang problem uses a balance of prevention, intervention, and suppression strategies. The two most often used defense strategies in gang-related crime prosecutions are pleas of diminished capacity and of self-defense.

Other challenges are investigating bias or hate crimes and ritualistic crimes. Bias or hate crimes are acts motivated by bigotry and hatred against a specific group of people. Race is usually the primary motivation for bias and hate crime, and African Americans are most often the victims.

A ritualistic crime is an unlawful act committed within the context of a ceremony. Investigate the crime, not the belief system. Indicators that criminal activity may be cult related include symbols, candles, makeshift altars, bones, cult-related books, swords, daggers, and chalices. Special challenges involved in investigating ritualistic or cult-related crimes include separating the belief system from the illegal acts, the sensationalism that frequently accompanies such crimes, and the "abnormal" personalities sometimes found in both victims and suspects.

Can You Define?

Antichrist	graffiti	ritual
Beelzebub	Hand of Glory	ritualistic crime
bias crime	hate crime	sabbat
Black Mass	hate incidents	security threat group
coven	incantation	street gang
cult	magick	tagging
flash mob	moniker	turf
gang	occult	

Checklists

Gangs

- What illegal activities have been committed?

- Who reported the activities?

- What evidence is there?

- Who are the suspects?

- What signs tend to implicate a specific gang?

- Who are the leaders of this gang?

- What records exist on this gang?

- Who might provide additional information?

Bias and Hate Crimes

- What specific crime was involved?

- What were the victims' and witnesses' perceptions of motivation for the crime?

- Was there more than one perpetrator?

- What was the relationship between the victim and the perpetrator(s)?

- Was the perpetrator associated with an organized hate group?

- How much physical damage was inflicted?

- Did the perpetrator make any comment, gesture, or written statement reflecting bias, including graffiti?

- Were there any differences between the perpetrator and the victim, whether actual or perceived?

- Have similar incidents occurred in the same location or neighborhood, indicating a pattern?

- Was the victim engaged in activities promoting a group, either by appearance or conduct?

- Did the incident coincide with a holiday or date of particular significance?

- In destruction of property crimes, was there an absence of any other motive such as economic gain?

Cults

- What type of activity brought the cult to the attention of the police?

- Is the activity illegal?

- What statutes or ordinances are applicable?

- Who reported the activity? What is their connection to the cult?

- What evidence is there that the illegal activity is part of a ritual?

- Who are suspected cult members?

- What records exist on the cult?

- Who might provide additional information?

Applications

Read the following and then answer the questions:

A. Graffiti has suddenly appeared in increasing amounts in specific areas on walls, public buildings, telephone poles, and streetlights in your community. Some are in blue paint and some are in red. Groups in the local park have been seen wearing blue bandannas, whereas in another park they are wearing red bandanas. Some of them have been seen flashing particular hand signals to each other. Some of the graffiti symbols represent animals and insects. A blue word *Crips* has the letter C crossed out with a red X.

Question

If graffiti is truly the "newspaper of the street gangs," what information should the preceding description give to a police officer?

B. While looking for a stolen safe in a wooded area, the police discover a circular clearing about 200 feet in diameter with candles placed around the circumference. A rough altar has been constructed with a cross. A fire has been burned beneath the cross. A five-pointed star is scratched in the dirt, and the word *NATAS* is scrawled on several trees and on the cross. The number 6 also appears on several trees. What appear to be bones are found in the ashes of the fire below the altar.

Question

What do these findings suggest? Is this something the police should investigate further? Why or why not?

References

Arweck, E. (2006). *Researching new religious movements*. London, United Kingdom: Taylor & Francis. Retrieved June 29, 2021, from library.oapen.org /handle/20.500.12657/24148

Bell, K. E. (2009, July). Gender and gangs: A quantitative comparison. *Crime & Delinquency, 55*(3), 363–387.

Bellair, P. E., & McNulty, T. L. (2009, December). Gang membership, drug selling, and violence in neighborhood context. *Justice Quarterly, 26*(4), 644–669.

Bjerregaard, B. (2010, January). Gang membership and drug involvement: Untangling the complex relationship. *Crime & Delinquency, 56*(1), 3–34.

Brantingham, P. J., Yuan, B., & Herz, D. (2020, September). Is gang violent crime more contagious than non-gang violent crime? *Journal of Quantitative Criminology.* doi:10.1007/s10940-020-09479-1

Coleman, B. R., & McDonald, M. M. (2018). Urban gangs. In Shackelford, T., & Weekes-Shackelford, V. (eds.) *Encyclopedia of evolutionary psychological science.* Springer, Cham. doi:10,1007/978-3-391-16999-6_886-1

Cowan, D. E., & Bromley, D. G. (2015). *Cults and new religions: A brief history* (2nd ed.). West Sussex, United Kingdom: John Wiley & Sons, Ltd.

Decker, S. H. (2013). What is the role of police in preventing gang membership? Chapter 4 in *Changing course: Preventing gang membership.* T. R. Simon, N. M. Ritter, & R. R. Mahendra (Eds.), pp. 51–62. U.S. Department of Justice and U.S. Department of Health and Human Services. Retrieved April 5, 2021, from www.ojp.gov/pdffiles1/nij/239234.pdf

Decker, S. H., Katz, C. M., & Webb, V. J. (2008, January). Understanding the black box of gang organization. *Crime & Delinquency, 54*(1), 153–172.

Dong, B., & Krohn, M. D. (2016, April). Dual trajectories of gang affiliation and delinquent peer association during adolescence: An examination of long-term offending outcomes. *Journal of Youth and Adolescence, 45*(4): 746–762. doi:10.1007/s10964-016-0417-2

Drug Enforcement Administration. (2019). *2019 National Drug Threat Assessment.* Washington, DC: Author. Retrieved April 1, 2021, from www.dea.gov/sites/default/files/2020-02/DIR-007-20%202019%20National%20Drug%20Threat%20Assessment%20-%20low%20res210.pdf

Egley, A. Jr., Howell, J. C., & Harris, M. (2014, December). *Highlights of the 2012 national youth gang survey.* Washington, DC: Office of Juvenile Justice Delinquency Prevention. (NCJ 248025)

Fabio, A., Tu, L., Loeber, R., & Cohen, J. (2011, December). Neighborhood socioeconomic disadvantage and the shape of the age-crime curve. *American Journal of Public Health, 101*(Suppl 1): S325–S332. doi:10.2105/AJPH.2010.300034

Federal Bureau of Investigation. (2019). *Hate crime statistics, 2019.* Washington, DC: Author. Retrieved April 6, 2021, from ucr.fbi.gov/hate-crime/2019/hate-crime

Fernández-Planells, A., Orduña-Malea, E., & Pàmpols, C. F. (2021, February). Gangs and social media: A systematic literature review and an identification of future challenges, risks and recommendations. *New Media & Society.* doi:10.1177/1461444821994490

Frazier, L., Jr., Ortega, L., Patel, N., Barnes, J., Crosby, A. E., & Hempstead, K. (2017, Winter). Methods and findings from the national violent death reporting system for identifying gang-like homicides, 2005–2008. *Journal of the National Medical Association, 109*(4): 272–278. Retrieved March 29, 2021, from www.ncbi.nlm.nih.gov/pmc/articles/PMC5878039/

Gibson, C. L., Miller, J. M., Jennings, W. G., Swatt, M., & Gover, A. (2009, December). Using propensity score matching to understand the relationship between gang membership and violent victimization: A research note. *Justice Quarterly, 26*(4), 625–643.

Gutierrez-Adams, E., Rios, D., & Case, K. A. (2020). Female gang members negotiating privilege, power, and oppression within family and gang life. *Women & Therapy, 43*(3–4): 287–308. doi:10.1080/02703149.2020.1729474

Hayward, R. A., & Honegger, L. (2014). Gender differences in juvenile gang members: An exploratory study. *Journal of Evidence-Based Social Work, 11*(4): 373–382. doi:10.1080/10911359.2014.897110

Howell, J. C. (2010, December). *Gang prevention: An overview of research and programs.* Washington, DC: Office of Juvenile Justice and Delinquency Prevention, Juvenile Justice Bulletin. (NCJ 231116)

Howell, J. C., & Moore, J. P. (2010, May). *History of street gangs in the United States.* Washington, DC: National Gang Center, Bulletin No.4.

Howell, J. C., & Griffiths, E. (2019). *Gangs in America's communities* (3rd ed.) Thousand Oaks, CA: Sage Publications, Inc.

Hughes, L. A., Schaible, L. M., & Kephart, T. (2021). Gang graffiti, group process, and gang violence. *Journal of Quantitative Criminology.* doi:10.1007/s10940-021-09507-8

InSight Crime & the Center for Latin American and Latino Studies. (2018). *MS13 in the Americas: How the world's most notorious gang defies logic, resists destruction.* Retrieved March 31, 2021, from www.justice.gov/eoir/page/file/1043576/download

International Association of Chiefs of Police. (2021, March). *Investigation of hate crimes.* Alexandria, VA: Author. Retrieved April 6, 2021, from www.theiacp.org/resources/policy-center-resource/hate-crimes

Jones, R. (2019, January 15). The rise of hybrid gangs. *Police.* Retrieved April 1, 2021, from www.policemag.com/502065/the-rise-of-hybrid-gangs

Klein, M. W. (2007). *Chasing after street gangs: A forty-year journey.* Upper Saddle River, NJ: Pearson/Prentice Hall.

Knox, G. W. (2019, Fall). Gangs and other problems in American jails today: A special report of the NGCRC. *Journal of Gang Research, 27*(1): 1–76. Retrieved April 1, 2021, from ngcrc.com/2019jail.report.pdf

Langton, L. (2010, October). *Gang units in large local law enforcement agencies, 2007.* Washington, DC: Bureau of Justice Statistics. (NCJ 230071). Retrieved April 4, 2021, from www.bjs.gov/content/pub/pdf/gulllea07.pdf

Lewis, J. R., & Tøllefsen, I. B. (2016). *The Oxford handbook of new religious movements, Vol II* (2nd ed.). New York, NY: Oxford University Press.

Matthies, C. F., Keller, K. M., & Lim, N. (2012). Identifying barriers to diversity in law enforcement agencies. Santa Monica, CA: Rand Corporation. Retrieved April 6, 2021, from www.rand.org/content/dam/rand/pubs/occasional_papers/2012/RAND_OP370.pdf

Maxwell, E., & Henning, A. (2017, December 20). Female gang membership: Trends and future directions. *Police Chief Online*. Retrieved April 3, 2021, from www.policechiefmagazine.org/female-gang-membership/

McDaniel, D. D., Logan, J. E., & Schneiderman, J. U. (2014, January). Supporting gang violence prevention efforts: A public health approach for nurses. *Online Journal of Issues in Nursing, 19*(1): 3. Retrieved March 31, 2021, from www.ncbi.nlm.nih.gov/pmc/articles/PMC4703334/

National Alliance of Gang Investigators' Associations. (n.d.). Retrieved March 29, 2021, from www.nagia.org/about-nagia.html

National Gang Center. (n.d.). *Highlights of gang-related legislation* (as of July 2020). Washington, DC: Author. Retrieved March 30, 2021, from www.nationalgangcenter.gov/Legislation/Highlights

National Gang Center. (n.d.). *National youth gang survey analysis*. Washington, DC: Author. Retrieved April 3, 2021, from www.nationalgangcenter.gov/Survey-Analysis

National Gang Center. (2010, October). *Best practices to address community gang problems*, 2nd ed. Washington, DC: Author.

National Gang Intelligence Center. (2011). *2011 National gang threat assessment—emerging trends*. Washington, DC: Author. Retrieved April 1, 2021, from www.fbi.gov/file-repository/stats-services-publications-2011-national-gang-threat-assessment-2011%20national%20gang%20threat%20assessment%20%20emerging%20trends.pdf/view

National Gang Intelligence Center. (2015). *2015 National gang report*. Washington, DC: Author. Retrieved March 31, 2021, from www.fbi.gov/file-repository/stats-services-publications-national-gang-report-2015.pdf/view

O'Deane, M., & Murphy, W. P. (2010, September). Identifying and Documenting gang members. *Police*, pp. 52–61.

PERF Report Describes Changes in Gang Dynamics. (2010, February). *Subject to Debate, 24*(2), 1, 7

Perlmutter, D. (2016). The forensics of sacrifice: A symbolic analysis of ritualistic crime. *Anthropoetics*. Retrieved April 6, 2021, from www.tritechtraining.com/ritualistic-and-occult-crimes.html

Perna, N. (2019, April 25). How police can gain intelligence from gang graffiti. *Police1.com*. Retrieved April 3, 2021, from www.police1.com/gangs/articles/how-police-can-gain-intelligence-from-gang-graffiti-MvdTDCKoViQkvbMf/

President's Task Force on 21st Century Policing. (2015, May). *Final Report of the President's Task Force on 21st Century Policing*. Washington, DC: Office of Community Oriented Policing Services. Retrieved April 6, 2021, from cops.usdoj.gov/pdf/taskforce/taskforce_finalreport.pdf

Pyrooz, D. C., & Decker, S. H. (2019). *Competing for control: Gangs and the social order of prisons*. Cambridge, United Kingdom: Cambridge University Press.

Pyrooz, D. C., Gartner, N., & Smith, M. (2017, March 14). Consequences of incarceration for gang membership: A longitudinal study of serious offenders in Philadelphia and Phoenix. *Criminology, 55*(2): 273–306. doi:10.1111/1745-9125.12135

Pyrooz, D. C,, & Moule, R. K. (2019). Gangs and social media. In Rafter, N., & Brown, M. (eds). *Oxford research encyclopedia of criminology and criminal justice*. Oxford: Oxford University Press, pp. 1–21.

Pyrooz, D. C., & Sweeten, G. (2015). Gang membership between ages 5 and 17 years in the United States. *Journal of Adolescent Health*. Retrieved April 5, 2021, from jjie.org/wp-content/uploads/2015/02/Pyrooz_Sweeten_Gang-Membership-Between-Ages-5-and-17-Years-in-the-United-States.pdf

Seck, H. H. (2020, August 17). Army street gang activity is increasing, internal report shows. *Military.com*. Retrieved April 3, 2021, from www.military.com/daily-news/2020/08/17/army-street-gang-activity-increasing-internal-report-shows.html

Smith, C.F. (2017). *Gangs and the military: Gangsters, bikers, and terrorists with military training*. Lanham, MD: Rowman & Littlefield.

Smith, C. F., & Harms, J. (2018, March). The threat of street gangs, outlaw motorcycle groups, and domestic terrorist/extremist groups with military-trained members. *Small Wars Journal*. Retrieved April 3, 2021, from www.researchgate.net/publication/324014881_The_Threat_of_Street_Gangs_Outlaw_Motorcycle_Gangs_and_Domestic_TerroristExtremist_Groups_with_Military-Trained_Members

Southern Poverty Law Center. (2020). *The year in hate and extremism 2020*. Montgomery, AL: Author. Retrieved April 6, 2021, from www.splcenter.org/year-hate-and-extremism-2020

Stuart, F. (2020, May). Code of the tweet: Urban gang violence in the social media age. *Social Problems, 67*(2): 191–207. doi:10.1093/socpro/spz010

Tarm, M. (2018, June 11). Gangs embrace social media with often deadly results. *Associated Press*. Retrieved April 3, 2021, from apnews.com/article/f8aad489997c4eb5b652f4fa9573685e

U.S. Department of Justice. (2015a, May 28). *About violent gangs*. Washington, DC: Author. Retrieved March 30, 2021, from www.justice.gov/criminal-ocgs/about-violent-gangs

U.S. Department of Justice. (2015b, May 11). *Prison gangs*. Washington, DC: Author. Retrieved April 1, 2021, from www.justice.gov/criminal-ocgs/gallery/prison-gangs

Vigil, J. D. (2019, May 23). Street gangs: A multiple marginality perspective. *Oxford Research Encyclopedia of Criminology*. doi:10.1093/acrefore/9780190264079.013.425

Villanueva, A. (2009, July). Ends-based model of multi-dimensional policing. *Law and Order*, pp. 70–74.

Weerman, F. M., Maxson, C. L., Esbensen, F-A., Aldridge, J., Medina, J., & van Gemert, F. (2009, February). *Eurogang program manual*. St. Louis, MO: The Eurogang Project. Retrieved March 31, 2021, from eurogangproject.files. wordpress.com/2018/06/eurogang-manual.pdf

Wolf, A. M., Castro, E., & Glesmann, C. (2016, Fall). Improving understanding of and responsiveness to gang-involved girls. *National Gang Center Newsletter*. Retrieved April 2, 201 from www.nationalgangcenter.gov/Content/Newsletters /NGC-Newsletter-2016-Fall.pdf

Young, M. A., & Gonzalez, V. (2013, January). *Getting out of gangs, staying out of gangs: Gang intervention and desistance strategies*. Tallahassee, FL: National Gang Center. Retrieved April 5, 2021, from www.nationalgangcenter.gov/Content /Documents/Getting-Out-Staying-Out.pdf

Cases Cited

Chicago v. Morales, 527 U.S. 41 (1999).

Virginia v. Black, 538 U.S. 343 (2003).

Chapter 20
Terrorism, Extremism, and Homeland Security

Chapter Outline

Learning Objectives

LO1 Identify what most definitions of terrorism have in common.

LO2 Understand the motivations for terrorist attacks.

LO3 List the groups commonly identified as Islamic terrorist organizations.

LO4 Recognize the domestic terrorist groups that exist in the United States.

LO5 Name the federal office that was established as a result of the 9/11 terrorist attacks on the United States.

LO6 Identify the two lead agencies in combating terrorism and how they are involved.

LO7 Explain how the USA PATRIOT Act and USA FREEDOM Act enhance counterterrorism efforts by the United States.

Introduction

The terrorist attacks of September 11, 2001, sounded a wake-up call to Americans. And although the 9/11 attacks were a shock, they should not have been a surprise. Islamist extremists had given ample warning that they meant to kill Americans. The critical failures were not believing the gravity of the threat or piecing together quickly enough the intelligence that had been gathered about the impending attack. However, in his speech before Congress, the country, and the world on September 20, 2001, President George W. Bush stated, "Tonight we are a country awakened to danger and called to defend freedom. Our grief has turned to anger, and anger to resolution."

In addition to galvanizing the nation, the events of that tragic day had other ramifications, such as changing how our nation views its security, with law enforcement working to redefine its role as traditional crime fighters while taking on tremendous new counterterrorism activities. But the threat remains.

The terrorist attacks of September 11, 2001, rocked the entire nation. First responders to the World Trade Center crime scene, including law enforcement officers and firefighters, were invaluable in saving countless lives but were also among the many casualties of the horrific event. A positive consequence of this tragedy was the galvanization of American patriotism and a resolve of citizens to join law enforcement in the daily efforts to protect our freedoms and valued way of life.

Left: Ash and debris lie thick in the streets of New York City following the collapse of the Twin Towers, as first responders gather to discuss how to approach the scene safely.

Philippe Filion/Getty Images

Right: New York City firefighters share in a moment of silence during a prayer service on October 7, 2001, at ground zero, where the World Trade Center twin towers once stood in New York, NY.

Tony Gutierrez/AFP/Getty Images

On May 3, 2015, two heavily armed men from Phoenix, Arizona, arrived outside a controversial art show in Garland, Texas, and began firing semiautomatic weapons at whatever they could hit, intending to kill the hundreds of people attending the show. Their motive: they were incensed about the show's featured contest in which cartoon depictions of the Prophet Muhammad were on display.

On April 21, 2015, six friends from Minnesota, all between the ages of 19 and 21, were arrested after conspiring to travel to Syria to join ISIS. The U.S. Attorney of the District of Minnesota, Andrew M. Luger, characterized the young men as focused and intent, not confused or easily influenced, and said the group came together through peer-to-peer recruiting (Levs & Vercammen, 2015).

In October 2020, all 13 members of the Wolverine Watchmen, a far-right militia group, were arrested and charged, six of them federally, with conspiring to kidnap and possibly kill the governor of Michigan. The group, which did not even exist at the beginning of 2020, grew out of the men's shared anger and frustration with the governor's strict lockdown policy in the wake of the COVID-19 pandemic. The Watchmen, many of whom first met online, used social media extensively to communicate with each other and recruit new members into their plot to abduct the governor from her vacation home while other members stormed the state capitol building.

These incidents highlight the reality that terrorism—both domestic and foreign—is a concern for all law enforcement, for whom the challenge is to remain aware and alert, especially when things appear to not be a concern in their communities. The Justice Department's top priority is to support law enforcement and intelligence agencies in the fight against terrorism.

Major changes that have occurred in the post-9/11 era of policing include the creation of new security-focused federal agencies, including the Transportation Security Administration (TSA) and the U.S. Department of Homeland Security (DHS); the reorganization of existing federal law enforcement agencies; the reallocation of resources to equip and train first responders for a wider range of disasters, including terrorist incidents; and a heavy emphasis on improving interoperability and data sharing.

Risk assessments regarding local targets and written response plans to terrorist events have been added to law enforcement agencies' emergency preparedness protocols, with many jurisdictions entering into mutual aid agreements and joint-training activities (Burruss, Giblin, & Schafer, 2010). Despite the necessity to ramp up our strategy to address the threat of terrorism, we cannot afford to neglect the attention and resources devoted to traditional crimes. Many have voiced concern over the increased attention and funding given to terrorism and whether the allocation of such funds divert resources away from other equally urgent law enforcement priorities, including drug trafficking, gangs, and violent crime. Such concerns fail to consider that terrorist organizations routinely participate in other criminal activities, including drug and weapons trafficking, fraud, and extortion, to fund their operations, and resources directed toward preventing, detecting, and responding to terrorism will often also help efforts to combat these more "traditional" crimes. Furthermore, some criminal justice scholars posit that the strong police-community connections that produce the best results for preventing and responding to crime in general may also be the most useful in preventing and responding to terrorist attacks (LaFree, 2012). The need for balancing crime fighting efforts with counterterrorism efforts should be kept in mind while reading this chapter.

Terrorism: An Overview

The United States has not been immune from terrorist attacks from within and without. Consider, for example, the raids of the Ku Klux Klan (KKK), the mail bombings of the Unabomber, the 1993 attack on the World Trade Center, and the 1995 bombing of the Alfred P. Murrah Federal Building in Oklahoma City. Most terrorist acts result from dissatisfaction with a religious, political, or social system or policy and an inability to change it through acceptable, nonviolent means.

The United States paid lip service to fighting terrorism in 1995 when the Federal Bureau of Investigation (FBI) established a Counterterrorism Center. In 1996, the Antiterrorism and Effective Death Penalty Act was passed, enhancing the federal government's powers to deny visas to individuals belonging to terrorist groups and simplifying the process for deporting aliens convicted of crimes. On February 23, 1998, Osama bin Laden (alternately spelled Usama bin Ladin by some government agencies) called for **jihad**, a holy war, on the United

States, calling on every Muslim to comply with God's order to kill Americans and plunder their money wherever and whenever they find it.

In 1999, FBI Director Louis Freeh announced that his agency's number-one priority was preventing terrorism. But it took the horrendous attacks of September 11, 2001, to truly get the nation's attention. Those attacks were criminal. It is up to law enforcement throughout the country to investigate possible terrorist activities. To do so, it is important to "know the enemy" and to understand terrorism and those who engage in it.

Terrorism Defined

Terrorism is difficult to define because, as the saying goes, "One man's terrorist is another man's freedom fighter." While there is no single, universally accepted, definition, **terrorism** is generally thought of as "the unlawful use of force and violence against persons or property to intimidate or coerce a government, the civilian population, or any segment thereof, in furtherance of political or social objectives" (28 C.F.R. Section 0.85). The FBI classifies terrorism as either domestic or international, in accordance with federal law (18 U.S.C. § 2331). For the purposes of Chapter 113B of the Code, entitled "Terrorism," these subsets are defined as follows:

- **Domestic terrorism** means activities with the following three characteristics:
  - Involve acts dangerous to human life that violate federal or state law;
  - Appear intended (i) to intimidate or coerce a civilian population; (ii) to influence the policy of a government by intimidation or coercion; or (iii) to affect the conduct of a government by mass destruction, assassination. or kidnapping; and
  - Occur primarily within the territorial jurisdiction of the United States.

- **International terrorism** means activities with the following three characteristics:
  - Involve violent acts or acts dangerous to human life that violate federal or state law;
  - Appear to be intended (i) to intimidate or coerce a civilian population; (ii) to influence the policy of a government by intimidation or coercion; or (iii) to affect the conduct of a government by mass destruction, assassination, or kidnapping; and

  - Occur primarily outside the territorial jurisdiction of the United States, or transcend national boundaries in terms of the means by which they are accomplished, the persons they appear intended to intimidate or coerce, or the locale in which their perpetrators operate or seek asylum.

The code further defines the term *federal crime of terrorism* as an offense that:

- Is calculated to influence or affect the conduct of government by intimidation or coercion, or to retaliate against government conduct; and

- Is a violation of one of several listed statutes, including § 930(c) (relating to killing or attempted killing during an attack on a federal facility with a dangerous weapon); and § 1114 (relating to killing or attempted killing of officers and employees of the United States). (18 U.S.C. § 2332b)

The U.S. Code, Title 22, defines terrorism as the "premeditated, politically motivated violence perpetrated against noncombatant targets by subnational groups or clandestine agents" (22 U.S.C. § 2656f(d)(2)).

> **LO1** Identify what most definitions of terrorism have in common.
>
> Most definitions of terrorism have common elements, including involving acts dangerous to human life that violate federal or state law and are intended to intimidate or coerce a civilian population, or to influence the policy or affect the conduct of a government.

Two decades after the 9/11 attacks, terrorism and targeted violence continue to pose serious threats to this country. The DHS notes that while most Americans are familiar with the term *terrorism*, a less familiar term is **targeted violence**, which refers to "any incident of violence that implicates homeland security and/or U.S. Department of Homeland Security (DHS) activities, and in which a known or knowable attacker selects a particular target prior to the violent attack" (U.S. Department of Homeland Security [DHS], 2019c). Targeted violence, unlike terrorism, includes attacks that, while lacking a clearly discernible political, ideological, or religious motivation, are so severe and of such great magnitude as to suggest "an intent to inflict a degree of mass injury, destruction, or death commensurate with known terrorist tactics" (DHS, 2019c).

Violent Extremism

Consider briefly the relationship between extremism and terrorism, two different and independent concepts that are interconnected and inseparable by virtue of the fact that terrorism can be viewed as a continuation of extremism, or its "next step" (Baisagatova, Kemelbekov, Smagulova, & Kozhamberdiyeva, 2016). **Extremism** is a radical mental attitude or ideology, a main driving idea or purpose, that one holds internally. It is a concept used to describe a religious, social, or political belief system that falls outside the margins of mainstream societal beliefs, often because it espouses views or tactics that society at large finds objectionable (Anti-Defamation League [ADL], *Defining extremism,* n.d.).

Extremism, in and of itself, is not a crime, and not every extremist is automatically violent or terroristic. But extremism often precedes terrorism and can serve as the driving force behind violent acts. Terrorism then becomes the external manifestation of the violent extremist ideology. Consequently, much of the focus on counterterrorism looks "upstream" to extremist groups, especially those with a penchant for violence.

Motivations for Terrorism

Many people see terrorism as irrational attacks by individuals from one country against innocent civilians from another country. Terrorism experts, however, note that many terrorist attacks involve relatively rational motivations or disputes over religious, political, or social policies, often involving racial, ethnic, economic, health, and other grievances.

> **LO2** Understand the motivations for terrorist attacks.
>
> Most terrorist acts result from dissatisfaction with a religious, political, or social system or policy and frustration resulting from an inability to change it through acceptable, nonviolent means.

Religious motives are seen in Islamic extremism. Political motives are seen in such elements as the Red Army Faction. Social motives are seen in single-issue groups such as those against abortion or active in animal-rights or environmentalist movements. The DHS reports that throughout 2020, a range of issues motivated domestic violent extremists throughout the country, including anger over COVID-19 restrictions, the 2020 election results, police use of excessive force, and long-standing racial and ethnic tension, some rooted in anti-immigration sentiments (DHS, 2021).

Before looking at specific terrorist groups, consider how they might be classified.

Classification of Terrorist Acts

As mentioned, the FBI categorizes terrorism in the United States as either domestic or international.

Domestic Terrorism

Domestic terrorism is the unlawful use, or threatened use, of force or violence by a group or individual based and operating entirely within the United States or its territories, without foreign direction, committed against persons or property, to intimidate or coerce a government, the civilian population, or any segment thereof, to further a political or social objective. Most domestic terrorism in the United States falls into one of four categories: racially motivated violent extremism (RMVE), anti-government/anti-authority extremism, animal rights/environmental extremism, and abortion extremism (Alcoke, 2019).

The bombing of the Murrah Federal Building in Oklahoma City and the 2015 shooting at the Garland, Texas art show highlight the threat of domestic terrorists. These terrorists represent extreme right- or left-wing and special-interest beliefs. And while the threat from domestic terrorism is not new, the radicalization and communication of domestic terrorism actors, primarily by way of social media and online forums, has evolved rapidly in recent years and presents an ever-growing challenge to law enforcement and all levels (Jones, Doxsee, Harrington, Hwang, & Suber, 2020; National Counterterrorism Center, 2020). Domestic terrorist groups are discussed later in the chapter.

International Terrorism

International terrorism is foreign based or directed by countries or groups outside the United States against the United States. Three general categories of international terrorists are: (1) foreign state sponsors using terrorism as a tool of foreign policy; (2) formalized terrorist groups, also referred to as foreign terrorist organizations (FTOs), such as the Lebanese Hizballah, the Egyptian al-Gama'a al-Islamiyya, the Palestinian Harakat al-Muqawamah al-Islamiyyah (HAMAS), al-Qa'ida, and ISIS/ISIL; and (3) loosely affiliated international radical extremists who have a variety of identities and travel freely in the United States, unknown to law enforcement or the government. Included in this last group are **homegrown violent extremists (HVEs)**, U.S.-based individuals who have been radicalized primarily in the United States and are inspired by global jihadists but are not generally receiving individualized direction from FTOs (McGarrity, 2019).

According to the most recent *Worldwide Threat Assessment of the U.S. Intelligence Community* (Coats, 2019, p. 12): "Homegrown violent extremists (HVEs) are likely to present the most acute Sunni terrorist threat to the United States, and HVE activity almost certainly will have societal effects disproportionate to the casualties and damage it causes." The U.S. Department of Justice (DOJ) asserts that most successful HVEs, who are typically inspired by a mix of ideological, sociopolitical, and personal factors, undergo a radicalization period that can take one to four years but, once that process is complete, can be mobilized to violence in less than six months. This timeline suggests there may be more time for law enforcement to detect plotters during the radicalization phase than the mobilization phase (U.S. Department of Justice [DOJ], 2020a). The DOJ has observed that HVE plotters and attackers have trended younger in recent years, underscoring the susceptibility of some youth to violent extremist ideologies that appeal to their desire for belonging, identity, or attention.

International terrorist groups are likely to engage in what is often referred to as **asymmetric warfare**, combat in which a weaker group attacks a superior group not head-on but by targeting areas where the adversary least expects to be hit, causing great psychological shock, along with loss of life among random victims. Asymmetric warfare aims to empower the powerless and nullify the stronger adversary's ability to use its conventional weapons. A prime example was the use by the 9/11 al-Qa'ida terrorists of ordinary box cutters to overpower flight personnel and convert airplanes into weapons of mass destruction, costing billions of dollars of losses to the U.S. economy and tremendous loss of life (at a total estimated cost to the terrorists of $500,000).

The U.S. government's National Counterterrorism Center (NCTC) is a knowledge bank on international terrorism staffed by more than 1,000 personnel from more than 20 departments and agencies, including the Central Intelligence Agency (CIA), FBI, Department of Defense (DoD), DHS, the Nuclear Regulatory Commission (NRC), the U.S. Capitol Police, and the departments of Energy, Treasury, Agriculture, Transportation, and Health and Human Services. The NCTC maintains a national repository of known and suspected terrorists and operates a secure website, NCTC Online CURRENT, which serves as the primary dissemination mechanism for terrorism information produced by the NCTC and other counterterrorism mission partners, including international partners. Among their various products, the NCTC's Interagency Threat Assessment and Coordination Group (ITACG) has developed an *Intelligence Guide for First Responders* (2015) to assist state, local, and tribal law enforcement; firefighters; and private sector personnel in accessing and understanding federal counterterrorism, homeland security, and weapons of mass destruction intelligence reporting.

Although secular, political, and anarchist groups do commit a considerable amount of global terrorism, the majority of worldwide terrorist attacks have historically been perpetrated by religious extremists, with Islamic extremists accounting for the largest percentage of all attacks around in the globe (Institute for Economics & Peace, 2020; Miller, 2019; National Counterterrorism Center [NCTC], 2019). Often these attacks disproportionately affect Muslims; in 2020, 5 of the top 10 countries most impacted by terrorism were countries where Islam was the state religion (see Figure 20.1).

In 2015, however, nations began witnessing a rise in terrorism involving racially or ethnically motivated terrorism (REMT), particularly White supremacist terrorism, and numerous deadly REMT attacks were reported around the world in 2019, including in Christchurch, New Zealand; Halle, Germany; and El Paso, Texas (Institute for Economics & Peace, 2020; U.S. Department of State, 2020). One study of 560 terrorist groups active over a 10-year period found that Islamist groups, while second in global prevalence to groups based on a nationalist ideology, were responsible for more fatalities than all secular nationalist groups combined (Romano, Rowe, & Phelps, 2019). Such data help explain why much of the international antiterrorism effort is focused on radical Islamic groups and their jihadist ideology.

Confusion often exists when the term *Islamic jihad* is used because several Middle Eastern groups go by that name. These terrorist groups are all parts of the Palestine Liberation Organization's (PLO) military branch but have different ideas about how to go about their militant actions. They share a similar beginning, however, born of the first **intifada**, or uprising, which was a spontaneous Palestinian revolt in Gaza and the West Bank against Israeli crackdowns on rioting (White, 2012).

Keep in mind as you read this section that radical Islamist groups are ever changing—joining together, fracturing and separating, renaming themselves, etc.

Figure 20.1
Global Incidents of Terrorist Attacks in 2018, by Concentration and Intensity.
Courtesy of University of Maryland

LO3	List the groups commonly identified as Islamic terrorist organizations.

Islamic terrorist groups include Hizballah, Palestinian Islamic Jihad (PIJ), core al-Qa'ida (AQ) groups and their affiliates, ISIS/ISIL, and the Taliban.

This discussion will focus on some of the more enduring groups of concern to the United States.

Hizballah. Hizballah, literally the Party of God, is a militia group and political party that first emerged in Lebanon following the Israeli invasion of that country in 1982 and was named an FTO on October 8, 1997. Hizballah began with a group of Lebanese Shi'ite clerics determined to drive Israel from their homeland. They found assistance from Iran, which provided logistical support and an ample supply of recruits, primarily disaffected, younger, more radical Muslims. Hizballah's tactics include kidnappings and car bombings directed predominantly against Westerners. In June 2017, two Hizballah operatives were arrested in the United States. One operative, who was arrested in Michigan, had identified the availability of explosives precursors in Panama in 2011 and surveilled U.S. and Israeli targets in Panama as well as the Panama Canal from 2011 to 2012. Another operative arrested in New York had surveilled U.S. military and law enforcement facilities from 2003 to 2017 (U.S. Department of State, 2020).

Palestinian Islamic Jihad. Palestine Islamic Jihad (PIJ) was formed by militant Palestinians in Gaza during the 1970s and was designated as an FTO on October 8, 1997. PIJ is committed to the destruction of Israel and to the creation of an Islamic state in historic Palestine, including present-day Israel. PIJ terrorists have conducted numerous attacks, including large-scale suicide bombings, against Israeli civilian and military targets. PIJ claimed responsibility for launching rockets into Israel throughout 2018 and 2019 (U.S. Department of State, 2019). The group has strong links in the United States, allegedly in Florida, and is one of the groups that have mastered suicide bombing (White, 2012).

Al-Qa'ida: Core and Affiliates. A very different terrorist group is al-Qa'ida, meaning "the base." Al-Qa'ida (AQ) was founded in 1988 by now-deceased Osama bin Laden and designated as an FTO on October 8, 1999, nearly two years before the 9/11 terrorist attacks on the United States. Al-Qa'ida is a broad-based Islamic militant organization that, in its early days, helped finance, recruit, transport, and train Muslim fighters during the Afghan War against the Soviet Union. When the Soviets withdrew from Afghanistan in 1989, the organization dispersed but continued to oppose what its leaders considered corrupt Islamic regimes and foreign presence in Islamic lands. The group eventually reestablished its headquarters in Afghanistan under the patronage of the Taliban militia.

Al-Qa'ida merged with other Islamic extremist organizations, and in 1996, its leaders openly declared jihad on the United States, issuing a statement later in 1998 saying it was the duty of all Muslims to kill U.S. citizens—civilian and military—and their allies everywhere. Tens of thousands of Muslim militants throughout the world were trained in military skills, and its agents have engaged in numerous terrorist attacks, including the 1998 bombings of the U.S. embassies in Dar es Salaam, Tanzania, and Nairobi, Kenya—attacks that killed more than 200 people. Bin Laden was indicted for his role in planning the attacks and added to the FBI's Ten Most Wanted Fugitives list in 1999. After 9/11, when intelligence agencies learned that the attacks were carried out by bin Laden's terrorist organization, his name was added to the U.S. Department of State's Most Wanted Terrorists list and a nearly decade-long global search for bin Laden began.

By August 2010, intelligence had developed to a point where there existed a "high probability" that bin Laden was hiding at a compound deep inside Pakistan. For the next eight months, intelligence and counterterrorism agencies worked tirelessly to confirm the data, while special forces trained for their anticipated mission involving a "high value target." On May 1, 2011, President Barack Obama authorized U.S. special forces to raid the compound in Abbottabad, Pakistan, where bin Laden was located and executed. His body was removed from the compound by the highly classified and now infamous Seal Team 6, his identity was verified, and he was then immediately buried at sea.

Al-Qa'ida leaders moved quickly to name Ayman al-Zawahiri as bin Laden's successor, who remains at large as this text goes to press. In August 2011, al-Qa'ida suffered another major blow when its second-in-command, Atiyah Abd al-Rahman, was killed in Pakistan. In 2019, emerging al-Qa'ida leader Hamza bin Laden, Osama bin Laden's son, was killed in a United States counterterrorism attack in the Afghanistan/Pakistan region.

Despite leadership losses and sustained pressure from counterterrorism efforts, al-Qa'ida remains a cohesive organization and what is widely called al-Qa'ida's Core leadership continues to be important to the global movement. Al-Qa'ida senior leaders are strengthening the network's global command structure and continuing to encourage attacks against the West, including the United States, although most al-Qa'ida affiliates' attacks to date have been small scale and limited to their regional areas (Coats, 2019). In July 2019, a 30-year-old Kenyan national was arrested in the Philippines as part of a plot to carry out a 9/11-style attack in the United States. The man was acting at the direction of Al Shabaab, an FTO considered one of the deadliest in the world that has sworn allegiance to al-Qa'ida and serves as AQ's principal wing in East Africa (Institute for Economics & Peace, 2020; DOJ, 2020b).

The al-Qa'ida affiliate al-Qa'ida in the Arabian Peninsula (AQAP), which emerged in January 2009 and was designated as an FTOP on January 19, 2010, is a Sunni extremist group based in Yemen that has orchestrated numerous high-profile terrorist attacks, including the attempt by "underwear bomber" Umar Farouk Abdulmutallab to detonate an explosive device aboard a Northwest Airlines flight on Christmas Day 2009.

ISIS/ISIL. Although al-Qa'ida has been considered by many in the United States to be the greatest threat since 9/11, other jihadist groups are gaining prominence and are challenging the global leadership of al-Qa'ida's Core. One in particular, the Islamic State of Iraq and the Levant, often referred to as ISIL, was the third deadliest terrorist organization in 2019 (Institute for Economics & Peace, 2020). But before ISIL, there was ISIS.

The Islamic State of Iraq and Syria (ISIS) was originally named Al-Qa'ida in Iraq (AQI), which was designated as an FTO on December 17, 2004. After its leader, Abu Mus'ab al-Zarqawi, was killed in June 2006, AQI publicly renamed itself in October 2006 as the Islamic State in Iraq, then again in 2013 as ISIS to express its expanded operations into Syria. ISIS was led by Abu Bakr al-Baghdadi, who declared an Islamic caliphate in June 2014, until he killed himself and three of his children by detonating a suicide vest to avoid capture during a U.S.-led raid. October 27, 2019. Shortly thereafter, ISIS announced Abu Ibrahim al-Hashimi al-Qurashi as its new leader.

ISIS has conducted numerous high-profile attacks, including IED attacks against U.S. military personnel and Iraqi infrastructure, videotaped beheadings of U.S. citizens, suicide bombings against both military and civilian targets, and rocket attacks. Since at least 2015, the group has integrated local children and children of adult fighters, also known as foreign terrorist fighters (FTFs), into its forces and used them as executioners and suicide attackers.

ISIS also directs, enables, and inspires individuals to conduct attacks on behalf of the group around the world, including in the United States and Europe. The coordinated attacks on November 13, 2015, in Paris, France, killed about 130 people, including a 23-year-old U.S. citizen. In March 2016, ISIS directed two simultaneous attacks in Brussels, Belgium, that killed 32 people, including four U.S. citizens. In June 2016, a gunman who pledged allegiance to ISIS killed 49 individuals and injured 53 others at the Pulse nightclub in Orlando, Florida, and one months later, ISIS claimed responsibility for an attack in which a terrorist driving a cargo truck barreled into a crowd in Nice, France, during Bastille Day celebrations, killing 86 people, including three U.S. citizens. In January 2019, ISIS claimed responsibility for the suicide bombing of a restaurant in Manbij,

Syria, that killed 19 people, including four Americans. And in August 2019, ISIS claimed responsibility for killing a U.S. service member while he was participating in a combat operation in Iraq.

Despite significant leadership and territorial losses, ISIS currently commands thousands of fighters in Iraq and Syria across eight branches and more than a dozen networks, as well as thousands of dispersed supporters around the world. ISIS very likely will continue to pursue external attacks from Iraq and Syria against regional and Western adversaries, including the United States (Coats, 2019).

In 2014, then-ISIS leader Abu Bakr al-Baghdadi dispatched a group of ISIS operatives from Syria to Libya to establish a branch of the terrorist group. In October 2014, several hundred operatives set up a base in Darnah, and the following month, after accepting the oath of allegiance from fighters in Libya, Baghdadi formally established the Islamic State of Iraq and the Levant (ISIL). Since 2014, ISIL has been responsible for over 30,000 terrorist deaths. Of these, 79% were in Iraq and 17% in Syria. ISIL was designated as an FTO on May 20, 2016.

Taliban. Although not designated as an FTO by the U.S. State Department, the Taliban became relevant to the United States in 2001 when it was found to have offered Osama bin Laden and al-Qa'ida a safe refuge in which to plan their attack on the United States. A U.S.-led invasion in October 2001 toppled the Taliban regime for its role in providing safe harbor to al-Qa'ida, although it was later learned that the Taliban had had no prior knowledge of the attacks and had publicly condemned the attacks (Schott, 2012). In fact, subsequent examination of the two groups revealed significant distinctions in their goals, ideologies, and sources of recruits.

Although it signed a peace agreement with the United States in 2020 and entered into power-sharing negotiations with the Afghan government, the Taliban continues to launch attacks against government and civilian targets and maintains control over dozens of Afghan districts. In fact, the Taliban was identified as the deadliest terrorist group in the world for both 2018 and 2019 (Institute for Economics & Peace, 2020; Miller, 2019). It is also worth noting that the Tehrik-e Taliban Pakistan (TTP), a Pakistan- and Afghanistan-based terrorist organization formed in 2007 to oppose Pakistani military efforts in Khyber Pakhtunkhwa province, has been designated as an FTO as of September 1, 2010 (U.S. Department of State, 2019). The TTP has carried out and claimed responsibility for numerous terrorist acts against Pakistani and U.S. interests, including a December 2009 suicide attack on a U.S. military base in Khost, Afghanistan, which killed seven U.S. citizens, and an April 2010 suicide bombing against the U.S. Consulate in Peshawar, Pakistan, which

killed six Pakistani citizens. TTP is suspected of involvement in the 2007 assassination of former Pakistani Prime Minister Benazir Bhutto. TTP directed and facilitated Faisal Shahzad's failed attempt to detonate an explosive device in New York City's Times Square on May 1, 2010. Between 2011 and 2018, TTP continued to carry out attacks against the government of Pakistan and Pakistani civilian targets, as well as against U.S. targets in Pakistan.

Domestic Terrorist Groups in the United States

While the United States must continue to protect itself from international terrorist groups such as al-Qa'ida and ISIL, it must also protect its citizens from those among us who would like nothing better than to tear the country apart from within and recast it in their own image. In fact, the primary terrorist threat currently facing the country is not from FTOs but, rather, from lone offenders and small cells of individuals categorized as domestic violent extremists (DVEs) (DHS, 2020). Data from the Center for Strategic and International Studies (CSIS) indicate that far-right DVEs, including White supremacists and militia members, were responsible for the majority (66%) of domestic terror attacks and plots in 2020, and that far-left DVEs, including anarchists and antifascists, conducted 23% of terrorist attacks and plots in 2020 (Jones, Doxsee, Hwang, & Thompson, 2021).

Domestic terrorists commit violent criminal acts to further ideological goals stemming from domestic issues, whether political, religious, social, economic, or other. It must also be pointed out that domestic terrorism and hate crimes are not mutually exclusive. Some of the groups discussed in this section were introduced in Chapter 19 as hate groups or cults.

LO4 Recognize the domestic terrorist groups that exist in the United States.

Domestic terrorist groups in the United States are categorized as far-right, far-left, religious, ethnonationalist, and "other."

According to the CSIS, terrorist incidents perpetrated by ethnonationalist groups—those who commit violence in support of ethnic or nationalist goals—are relatively insignificant in the U.S. (no incidents occurred in 2020) compared to those committed by far-right and far-left groups (Jones et al., 2020). Therefore, ethnonationalist terrorism is not discussed in this text.

Far-Right Terrorism

Far-right terrorist groups have been the predominant domestic threat for more than two decades, and during that time, violent far-right extremists have consistently accounted for more terrorist attacks and plots than any other domestic terrorist group (see Figure 20.2). A national survey of state law enforcement agencies found that the majority reported a greater presence of White supremacists and other far-right extremist groups in their jurisdictions than far-left or religious extremist groups (Freilich, Chermak, & Simone, 2009).

Three events in the early 1990s rejuvenated the extreme right and inspired the growth of the militia movement in the United States: the Ruby Ridge standoff, the Waco siege, and the passage of the Brady Bill (White, 2012). The Ruby Ridge incident began on August 21, 1992, when U.S. Marshals attempted to arrest self-proclaimed White separatist Randy Weaver at his Idaho cabin for failing to appear in court to face federal firearms charges. A shootout ensued that resulted in the death of a U.S. marshal and Weaver's young son and wife. Following an 11-day standoff, Weaver surrendered.

The second event began on February 28, 1993, when agents from the Bureau of Alcohol, Tobacco, Firearms, and Explosives (ATF) attempted to serve a search warrant at the Branch Davidian compound near Waco, Texas, and were met with a hail of gunfire.

Four federal agents were killed in the exchange, and several others were wounded. After a 51-day standoff, FBI agents moved in with tear gas, unaware that the compound had been laced with gasoline. Rather than surrender to the FBI, the Branch Davidians set fire to their compound, killing more than 70 people inside, including several young children. Claims by compound survivors that government tanks started the fire have been unfounded.

The third galvanizing incident occurred when the Brady Bill was passed into law on February 28, 1994, causing militia groups to fear federal gun control legislation. This panic was reignited in 2013 when President Obama added 23 items to gun control legislation.

Those who study terrorism have defined far-right extremists as being individuals who subscribe to aspects of the following ideals:

- They are fiercely nationalistic (as opposed to universal and international in orientation) and antiglobal.

- They are highly suspicious of centralized federal authority.

- They revere individual liberty, especially their right to own guns and be free of taxes.

- They believe in conspiracy theories that involve a grave threat to national sovereignty and/or personal liberty.

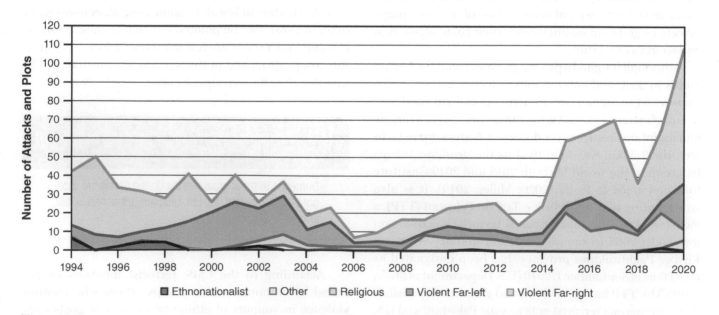

Figure 20.2

Number of U.S. Terrorist Attacks and Plots by Perpetrator Orientation, 1994–2020.

Source: Jones, S. G., Doxsee, C., Hwang, G., & Thompson, J. (2021, April). *The military, police, and the rise of terrorism in the United States.* Washington, DC: Center for Strategic and International Studies. Retrieved April 12, 2021, from csis-website-prod.s3.amazonaws.com/s3fs-public/publication/210412_Jones_Military_Police_Rise_of_Terrorism_United_States_1.pdf?

- They believe that their personal and/or national "way of life" is under attack and is either already lost or that the threat is imminent (the threat often coming from a specific ethnic, racial, or religious group).

- They believe in survivalism and the need to be prepared for an attack and may participate in paramilitary preparations and training.

(Chermak, Freilich, & Suttmoeller, 2013)

A far-right extremist group is defined as an identifiable organization (i.e., has a name) consisting of two or more individuals who adhere to a far-right extremist ideology and seek political objectives to further the ideology (Chermak, Freilich, & Suttmoeller, 2013). It is important to note that the mainstream conservative movement and the mainstream Christian right are not included in such groups.

Far-right extremist ideologies may be further subcategorized as motivated by:

- Racial or ethnic supremacy (e.g., White nationalists; neo-Nazis, racist skinheads, Christian Identity, White supremacist prison gangs)

- Opposition to government authority (e.g., Patriot groups, militia groups)

- Other right-wing extremists (e.g., anti-abortion, anti-Muslim, anti-LGBTQ, anti-Semitic, anti-immigration, anti-public lands, "InCel" (involuntary celibate), believers in conspiracy theories (e.g., QAnon)

Some extremists on the violent far-right support "accelerationism," which includes taking deliberate actions to promote social upheaval and incite a civil war (Jones et al., 2020).

Racially and Ethnically Motivated Violent Extremists (RMVE).

According to the *Homeland Threat Assessment*, racially and ethnically motivated violent extremists, and White supremacist extremists (WSEs) in particular, are predicted to remain the most persistent and deadly threat to the United States in the foreseeable future (DHS, 2020). RMVEs include a wide range of extremists, most notably those who advocate for the superiority of the White race. Some have observed that members of RMVE groups are adopting strategies similar to those used by FTOs, including strict membership guidelines, online propaganda, and inspiring lone offenders (DOJ, 2019).

The KKK is one of America's original terrorist organizations and perhaps the most well-known WSE group. Founded by Confederate cavalry commander Nathan Bedford Forrest, the Klan's original purpose was to create an anti-unionist organization to preserve Southern culture and tradition and exert political influence over the Reconstruction south. When the newly formed Klan became violent toward freed slaves, Forrest tried unsuccessfully to disband the group. But the momentum was too strong, and the KKK became a campaign of hate (White, 2012). The strength and organization of the Klan have waxed and waned over the years, and the modern Klan is fragmented and decentralized, yet still dominated by hate-filled rhetoric aimed at racial minorities. Neo-Nazi groups also espouse White supremacy, as do "skinheads." Over many decades, WSEs have shown their steadfast intent to target racial and religious minorities, members of the LGBTQ+ community, politicians, and anyone they believe promotes multiculturalism and globalization at the expense of the White identity. Since 2018, WSEs have conducted more lethal attacks in the United States than any other DVE movement (DHS, 2020).

In 2008, Richard Spencer coined the term "alternative right," which has since evolved into simply "the alt right," in an effort to promote White identity and an ultraconservative political faction the embraces racism and anti-Semitism (ADL, 2018). Spencer helped promote the August 12, 2017, Unite the Right rally in Charlottesville, Virginia, which attracted more than 500 White supremacists as well as hundreds of counterprotesters. It was during the violent clashes between the two groups that a White supremacist drove his car into a crowd of counterprotesters and killed Heather Heyer, injuring several others.

Anti-Government Extremists.

The Anti-Defamation League (*Anti-government extremism*, n.d.) notes that, while the term *anti-government extremism* can be used in a general sense to refer to any fringe movement opposed to the government, or even just the *idea* of government, in the United States it typically describes a specific cohort of right-wing extremist groups who hold a shared belief that part or all of the U.S. government has been taken over by a conspiracy and is, as a consequence, illegitimate. These groups are often collectively referred to as the "Patriot" movement.

The *Homeland Threat Assessment* reports that anti-government/anti-authority violent extremists, who are sometimes influenced by anarchist ideology, have been associated with multiple plots and attacks and a significant uptick in violence against law enforcement and government symbols in 2020 (DHS, 2020). As the COVID-19 pandemic swept across the United States in 2020, prompting state and local officials to impose widespread lockdowns in their jurisdictions, extremists, some heavily armed, took to the streets to hold rallies and protests outside capitol buildings around the country to decry what they saw as government overreach and infringement on their liberties.

A subset of anti-government extremism is the militia movement. Though deeply rooted in far-right ideologies dating back many decades earlier, the militia movement really took hold around 1993, focusing heavily on paramilitary activities, especially shooting skills. Militia movement supporters have traditionally believed that the federal government is conspiring to strip Americans of their rights, beginning with the right to keep and bear arms, as a way to render U.S. citizens defenseless and force the unarmed population into a tyrannical socialist one-world government known as the "New World Order" (ADL, 2020b).

Militia groups, who often serve as security for other anti-government groups, have a long history of serious criminal activity, including murders, terroristic threats against public officials, trafficking in illegal weapons or explosives, armed standoffs, and terrorist plots or acts. They also serve as inspiration for others who may not actually belong to a militia group but share the same anti-government ideology. Such was the case in April 1995, when Timothy McVeigh and Terry Nichols bombed the Murrah Federal Building in Oklahoma City, motivated by an antagonism toward the government for its roles in the Ruby Ridge and Waco incidents. The blast killed 168 people, including 19 children who were in the building's day care center at the time of the explosion.

The militia movement also has ties to an emerging anti-government extremist faction known as the *boogaloo movement*, whose followers aim to start a civil war (a "**boogaloo**" is a slang term for a future civil war) in the United States. Although the ideology of the boogaloo movement is still developing, its basic nature is anti-government, anti-authority, and anti-police (ADL, *Boogaloo*, n.d.).

Other far-right anti-government extremist groups of concern to law enforcement include:

- The Oath Keepers—one of the largest anti-government groups in the country, whose membership consists of thousands of current and former law enforcement officers and military personnel. Under the motto "Guardians of the Republic," the group takes its name from the core idea that its members vow to forever keep the oaths taken when they joined the service or law enforcement: "to support and defend the Constitution of the United States against all enemies, foreign and domestic." Oath Keepers rally around a conspiracy theory that the federal government has become a domestic enemy of the Constitution and seeks to seize citizens' guns, force

resisters into concentration camps, impose martial law, and surrender America to the New World Order. (Southern Poverty Law Center, *Oath Keepers*, n.d.)

- The Three Percenters—part of the militia movement, they equate their mission to that of the American patriots who fought to liberate themselves from a tyrannical British government during the Revolutionary War. They derive their name from the belief, however inaccurate, that the number of American colonists who fought against the British during that war amounted to only 3% of the population at the time, but their heroism won freedom for everyone. Historians generally agree that percentage was actually far higher. The Three Percenter logo—a Roman numeral III often surrounded by a field of 13 stars—is readily identifiable, easy to replicate, and often added after a member's name (e.g., Joe Smith III). (ADL, 2020b)

- The Proud Boys—a group that became a household name after a mention at the September 29, 2020, presidential debate, are self-described "Western chauvinists" who strongly reject any connection to the racist "alt-right," insisting they are merely a fraternal group who support an "anti–political correctness" and "anti–White guilt" agenda. Nonetheless, they often appear with other hate groups such as Neo-Nazis and anti-Semites at extremist events such as the "Unite the Right" rally in Charlottesville, Virginia. Proud Boys are known for misogynistic rhetoric, believing women are ill-suited for the workplace, should not be involved in politics, and are happier when they stay home and have children. In February 2021, the Canadian government designated the Proud Boys as a terrorist organization, citing the role the group played in the events that took place January 6, 2021, at the U.S. Capitol in Washington, DC (Southern Poverty Law Center, *Proud Boys*, n.d.).

The United States has stopped short of designating the Proud Boys a domestic terror group, instead calling them a nationalist organization. On February 26, 2021, six individuals associated with the Proud Boys were indicted by a grand jury for conspiring to obstruct or impede an official proceeding at the U.S. Capitol on January 6, 2021, and to impede or interfere with law enforcement during the commission of a civil disorder, among other charges (U.S. Attorney's Office, 2021). The FBI has confirmed that multiple investigations into the roles alleged right-wing violent extremists played prior to and during the January 6 Capitol riot are ongoing as this text goes to press, but the federal government has, to date, declined to designate these groups as domestic terrorist groups, focusing instead on the violent criminal acts of individuals, whether members of any groups or not (Sacco, 2021).

Other Right-Wing Extremists. Other extremist groups holding far-right ideologies include pro-life/anti-abortion group and QAnon. Although many pro-life, anti-abortion advocates stay within the law in promoting their beliefs, some groups do not, choosing instead to commit violent, criminal acts against abortion providers. Using their belief that human life begins at conception, anti-abortion extremists rationalize that those performing abortions are murdering other human beings and, therefore, are worthy of death. This principle is found in the Army of God (AOG) manual, which holds that the killing of abortion providers is morally acceptable and justified as "doing God's work" (Johnson, 2018). The Army of God, which for decades has targeted abortion clinics and their staffs and terrorized them through arson, assault, and murder, made headlines in 2015, when Robert Lewis Dear Jr. opened fire in a Planned Parenthood clinic in Colorado Springs, Colorado, killing two civilians and a police officer. Four civilians and five officers were also injured. Dear told the arresting officers "no more baby parts" (Police1 Staff, 2017).

QAnon, which the FBI labeled in 2019 as a domestic terror threat because of its potential to incite violence, was born on October 28, 2017, when an individual calling themselves Q began leaving a series of cryptic posts in the "politically incorrect" section of the website 4chan. 4chan is an Internet forum with a "no rules" policy, where anyone can post comments and share images anonymously. Q claimed to hold a high-level security clearance and wanted to use this forum to expose the "deep state," the alleged secret network of influential, nonelected government and military officials, and sometimes private entities (e.g., the financial services and defense industries), conspiring against the president to manipulate and enact their own government policies. Q also claimed that within the "deep state" there existed a global cabal of child-trafficking, Satan-worshipping pedophiles, including national Democrats, Hollywood celebrities, and global elites, who had been running the world clandestinely for decades and that then-President Trump was the only one who could bring this sinister group to justice (GNET, 2020).

Since its inception, users claiming to be Q have made more than 4,000 posts, known as "Qdrops." And as the QAnon movement has grown more vast, it has absorbed a tangled variety of other conspiracies into its ideology, including anti-5G conspiracies, COVID-19 and anti-vaccine conspiracies, and the assertion that the George Floyd killing was staged (Gallagher, Davey, & Hart, 2020).

It remains to be seen how QAnon will adapt following the 2021 change in executive administration.

Far-Left Terrorism

During the 1970s, the most active perpetrators of terrorist attacks in the United States were members of left-wing extremist groups, many of whom emerged as radical elements of the civil rights, feminist, and antiwar movements of the 1960s (Miller, 2014). Attacks by far-left extremists dropped sharply in the 1980s, while attacks by right-wing anti-abortionists became the most prevalent type of DVE. During the 1990s and into the 2000s, however, left-wing single-issue extremist groups such as the Animal Liberation Front (ALF) and Earth Liberation Front (ELF) became more active, posing greater threats to the country. In fact, in a 2014 survey of all state, county, and municipal law enforcement agencies with more than 200 sworn officers, one-third of respondents reported environmental extremism as a top threat (Kurzman & Schanzer, 2015).

The nature of leftist ideology is quite malleable, making it difficult for researchers and practitioners to agree on a uniform conceptualization of "left-wing" (Windisch, Ligon, & Simi, 2017). However, in general, left-wing extremists subscribe to a Marxist-Leninist point of view; espouse pro-communist or pro-socialist beliefs; and oppose capitalism, imperialism, colonialism, and globalization. They believe that the political and social structure of the United States is corrupt and that the status quo should be destroyed to redistribute economic wealth and services to lower classes. Therefore, they often consider actions such as bombings, arson, and sabotage to be legitimate political tactics in their war against an oppressive government (Chermak et al., 2013).

Today, the threat posed by far-left extremism is a shadow of what it was during the 1970s. However, it is not nonexistent. Contemporary far-left extremist ideology covers a broad spectrum of issues, with some left-wing extremists advocating for Black nationalism, others pursuing environmental or animal rights issues, and others supporting a decentralized social and political system such as anarchism (Jones et al., 2020). Two movements that have been garnering a lot of attention in recent years are anarchists and Antifa.

Anarchists. Anarchism is a philosophy and social movement based on a core belief that government is both harmful and unnecessary and grounded in moral assertions about the importance of individual liberty (Fiala, 2018). Anarchists advocate for stateless societies based on free and voluntary associations and believe that government institutions such as the police, the military, and prisons are inherently oppressive and should be abolished.

Anarchist violence was observed at many of the social justice reform protests and rallies that took place throughout the nation following George Floyd's murder, with violent extremists taking advantage of the large protest crowds to conduct violence against government officials, facilities, and counterprotestors. For example, during the months of nightly unrest in Portland, Oregon, law enforcement officers suffered more than 300 separate injuries at the hands of anti-government extremists (DHS, 2020).

Antifa. Short for *anti-fascist*, Antifa is a decentralized, leaderless network of far-left militants who vehemently oppose fascists, racists, and anyone else supporting the far-right agenda. Many in Antifa come from the anarchist movement, but as far-right protests increased in recent years, Antifa saw more people with mainstream political views join their ranks (ADL, *Who are Antifa?*, n.d.). Antifa has been increasingly present at far-right gatherings and rallies, attempting to disrupt such events with their own counterprotests. Although Antifa has been blamed for much of the violence, looting, and destruction that has occurred during and after various protests across the country, law enforcement and intelligence officials believe the amount of violence actually attributable to the group is minor and that the overall threat from Antifa and other far-left extremist groups remains low (Jones, 2020).

Animal-Rights Extremists. The animal-rights movement was born in England during the nineteenth century but did not come to the United States until the 1970s. The largest and most notorious animal-rights extremist group in the country is the Animal Liberation Front (ALF), founded in 1976 by Ronnie Lee with the main purpose of fighting all forms of human exploitation of animals (Posłuszna, 2020). This clandestine, decentralized group is one of the most active domestic terrorist assemblages in the United States. Responsible for millions of dollars in damage, their actions account for 20% of all terror attacks committed in the United States from 2000 to 2013 (Miller, 2014).

ALF commonly uses arson, vandalism, and harassment, and their most frequent targets are meat and food processing plants, research labs at universities, and fur and leather companies (Chermak, Freilich, Duran, & Parkin, 2013). ALF's objective to eliminate animal euthanasia and prevent the use of animals in scientific lab testing has led to numerous attacks on labs and farms where the extremist activists "liberated" the caged animals. In 2016, a 28-year-old animal rights activist was sentenced to three years in federal prison for vandalizing a fur farm and releasing more than 2,000 mink from their cages (U.S. Attorney's Office, Northern District of Illinois, 2016).

While ALF claims to avoid direct attacks on civilians, terrorism researchers have found that most (91.6%) of their attacks that involved the use of weaponry were directed at businesses, educational institutions, and private citizens or property, with some attacks occurring at the homes of researchers (Miller, 2014). Although no deaths have been attributed to the ALF thus far, its members have committed crimes of increasing severity, including the mailing of letter bombs and the use of incendiary devices (Police1 Staff, 2017).

Data indicate that a relatively small group of individuals is responsible for a large number of offenses. Law enforcement has reported difficulty in identifying animal-rights extremists because most stay well "under the radar," not actively engaging in legal protests or movement-related activities prior to committing their crimes (Chermak et al., 2013). ALF members usually come together through personal contact and carry out their attacks as small, autonomous cells. These tactics make the collection of intelligence and investigation of such activities particularly challenging.

Those who study domestic terrorism have observed that many who participate in animal-rights extremism are also affiliated with environmental extremist groups (Chermak et al., 2013).

Environmental Extremists. Environmental extremists fight for the protection and conservation of the natural environment. The beginning of environmental extremism in the United States can be traced to the early 1960s, when people started to question for the first time whether the increasing exploitation of natural resources was actually beneficial for humans' long-term prosperity. With this emerging environmental awareness came the realization that an ecological crisis was a real possibility, one that would threaten every species on earth. Thus was born the environmental extremism movement, whose sole objective was to decisively, albeit not necessarily lawfully, combat the growing indifference towards the natural environment (Posłuszna, 2015).

The best-known radical environmental group in the United States is the Earth Liberation Front (ELF), which often works with the ALF. Arson is a favorite weapon, responsible for tens of millions of dollars of property damage, including a U.S. Department of Agriculture building, a U.S. Forest Service ranger station, and a Colorado ski resort. The group has claimed responsibility for releasing 5,000 mink from a Michigan fur farm, releasing 600 wild horses from an Oregon corral, and burning the Michigan State University's genetic engineering research offices.

Animal-rights and environmental extremists are considered two subgroups within the larger radical ecological movement, and their members are collectively referred to as "ecoterrorists," with *eco* being derived from *ecology*—the study of the interrelationships of organisms and their environment. **Ecoterrorism** seeks to inflict economic damage on those who exploit and profit from the destruction of the natural environment, often through criminal violence. Ecologically motivated violence is not a declining phenomenon (Kurzman & Schanzer, 2015; Posłuszna, 2020;). An uptick in ecoterrorism has presumably been fueled by the rising success of genetically modified crops. Criminal vandalism, or what the FBI terms *economic sabotage*, has been leveled at several research fields where trials of genetically engineered plants are being performed (Byrne & Miller, 2013).

Religious Extremism

In the United States, discussions of religious extremism typically focus on Islamist extremism, although White Christian extremists, which were discussed with other far-right extremists, are also of concern. Islamist extremism reflects an adherence to the Salafi-jihadist ideology espoused by FTOs like al-Qa'ida and ISIS, rather than nationalist or other ideological motivations. Salafi-jihadism encourages violent means to achieve their goals, such as establishing an Islamic state, and it is this type of religious extremism that poses the greatest threat to the United States (Baffa, Vest, Chan, & Fanlo, 2019; Jones, Doxsee, & Harrington, 2020).

Homegrown violent extremists (HVEs), which were mentioned earlier, are so influenced and motivated by the rhetoric and ideology of foreign extremist groups that most terrorism experts categorize these types of terrorists as international terrorists, even though they are operating domestically. Considerable concern exists about the number of U.S. citizens who travel to Syria, Iraq, and other radicalized hotbeds to receive training and weapons to use against this country upon their return. It is estimated that roughly 3,400 fighters from Western countries, including more than 150 people from the United States, have either traveled to Syria and surrounding conflict zones or have attempted to do so (Rasmussen, 2015).

HVEs may also attempt to harm U.S. citizens and interests abroad, including deployed military personnel. On January 21, 2021, a 20-year-old private in the U.S. Army, based at Fort Stewart, Georgia, was arrested on federal terrorism charges for allegedly attempting to provide material support to ISIS in their efforts to attack and kill U.S. soldiers in the Middle East. According to the criminal complaint, Private First Class Cole Bridges had grown frustrated with the U.S. military and had become radicalized after researching and consuming online propaganda promoting jihadists and their violent ideology. Fortunately, the "ISIS sympathizer" Bridges was communicating with online was, in reality, an FBI online covert employee (OCE) (U.S. Attorney's Office, Southern District of New York, 2021).

Other Extremist Groups

Another extremist group that does not fit neatly into any of the above categories is Black Separatists, such as the New Black Panther Party (NBPP), a militant, highly racist group that believes Black Americans should form their own nation and that advocates for violence against Whites, Jews, and law enforcement officers. Founded in Dallas in 1990, the NBPP is particularly active along the East Coast of the United States, its members identifiable by their coordinated, military-style uniforms comprised of black boots, black pants, a black shirt with NBPP patches on it, and black berets (Southern Poverty Law Center, *New Black Panther Party*, n.d.). It should be noted that the original Black Panther Party, which was especially strong during the 1960s and 1970s and, while militant, was not racist, is not affiliated with the NBPP and is, in fact, heavily critical of the NBPP, calling them "a black racist hate group" (Southern Poverty Law Center, *New Black Panther Party*, n.d.). The NBPP has garnered considerable media attention over the years, making headlines in 2012 when one of the organization's leaders placed a $10,000 "bounty" on George Zimmerman, the neighborhood watch volunteer who shot and killed 17-year-old Trayvon Martin.

Myth Terrorism is a federal law enforcement problem.

Fact Local level law enforcement is our first line of defense and the eyes and ears to federal law enforcement. Local level law enforcement has thwarted terrorist attacks by responding to suspicious behavior.

Terrorists as Criminals

A critical difference in approach exists between dealing with a terrorist and a street criminal: when fighting terrorists, it's kill or be killed, not capture and convict. Law enforcement agencies and officers who have been trained and equipped to deal with traditional crimes are now focusing on apprehending individuals operating with different motivations, different objectives, and much deadlier weapons than those used by traditional criminals. While terrorism is certainly a form of crime, and terrorists and common criminals share certain similarities (e.g., the offender pool is generally comprised of young males, and their actions have serious, harmful effects on social trust and community cohesion), important differences also exist. Whereas conventional criminals generally seek personal financial or material gain driven by selfishness, take measures to avoid detection, and plan an escape route, terrorists are most often motivated by the furtherance of political causes or what they believe to be "the greater good." Terrorists commit their acts brazenly, seek to cause wide-scale damage and inflict fear, welcome media attention and the largest audiences possible, and may be less concerned with escape—suicide bombers being the extreme type of terrorists, willing to sacrifice their lives and become martyrs for their cause (LaFree & Greuenwald, 2018). In fact, among the documents recovered during the raid on bin Laden's compound, a sizeable collection of which was released by the Office of the Director of National Intelligence on May 20, 2015, was an "application" in which potential fighters were asked if they would be willing to perform as suicide bombers. Other findings from the raid can be accessed on the DNI website (www.dni.gov), under the "Resources" tab, and cataloged as "Bin Laden's Bookshelf."

Methods Used by Terrorists

Terrorists have employed a variety of techniques in furtherance of their cause. In addition to armed attacks, terrorists use arson, explosives, and bombs; weapons of mass destruction (biological, chemical, or nuclear agents); or technology. However, many experts believe the next terrorist assault on the United States is most likely to consist of relatively unsophisticated, near-simultaneous attacks similar to the November 2015 Paris attacks or those attempted in Britain in June, 2007, which were intended to cause widespread fear and panic rather than to cause major losses (Deloughery, 2013).

Law enforcement agencies use the term *CBRN* to include all potential terrorist threats that can have consequences for the health of large numbers of people. These threats include chemical agents (C), biological agents (B), radiation/nuclear exposure (RN). Figure 20.3 presents the most likely to least likely terrorist threats; Figure 20.4 illustrates the relative level of impact by weapon used. Although explosives are considered the most likely to be used by terrorists, they also carry the least amount of impact relative to the other threats.

Explosives and Bombs

Directions for making pipe bombs and other incendiary devices can be found easily on the Internet, and the use of improvised explosive devices (IEDs) by terrorists and conventional criminals is recognized as the most dangerous emerging threat to our homeland defense. IEDs are cheap, lethal, and relatively low-tech, generally composed of five basic components: a switch, a power source, an initiator, a container and an explosive charge (Vanderheyden, Verhoeven, Vermeulen, & Bekaert, 2020). Data gathered by the Action on Armed Violence (AOAV) recorded 19,246 deaths and injuries in 2016 alone as a result of IEDs being used around the world. From 2011 to 2016, 38 people in the United States were killed or injured by IEDs (Overton & Dathan, 2017). Explosives, bombs, and dynamite were the weapons used in 53% of terrorist attacks in the United States from 1970 to 2013 (Miller, 2014).

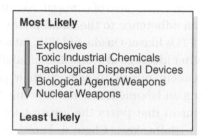

Figure 20.3
Terrorist threats from most likely to least likely.
Source: Reuland, M., & Davis, H. J. (2004, September). *Protecting your community from terrorism: Strategies for local law enforcement, Vol. 3. Preparing for and responding to bioterrorism.* Washington, DC: Community Oriented Policing Services Office and the Police Executive Research Forum, p. 7.

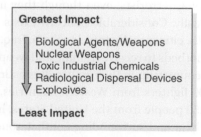

Figure 20.4
Level of impact by weapon used.
Source: Reuland, M., & Davis, H. J. (2004, September). *Protecting your community from terrorism: Strategies for local law enforcement, Vol. 3. Preparing for and responding to bioterrorism.* Washington, DC: Community Oriented Policing Services Office and the Police Executive Research Forum, p. 8. Reprinted by permission of the Police Executive Research Forum.

Incendiary devices and explosives are commonly used because they are easy to make. Bombing does require a certain level of organization, equipment, and materials, as well as a place to put the bomb together, all aspects that an investigator's knowledge can help detect, helping prevent these crimes. Furthermore, to be a good bomber, practice is more important than intelligence: "Well-educated people do not necessarily make good terrorists. The medical doctors behind the failed 2007 car bombings in London and Glasgow, Scotland, lacked the bomb making skills of the petty criminals who killed 56 people in the London Tube and bus bombings two years before" (Kenney, 2010, p. 18). Successful bombers must hone their skills through practical application and detonation of their work, which necessarily exposes them to detection and apprehension by authorities.

Investigating bombings was discussed in Chapter 16. The following discussion is intended to provide supplemental information within the context of investigating terrorist activities.

Suspicious Packages.

Security officers responding to a suspicious package, unattended bag, or other such items must understand the threat because knowledge can save lives. Knowing what to do prior to or following an explosion can be what ensures the survival of officers as well as those around them. If the presence of an IED is suspected, it is important that no one uses a cell phone near the suspicious package because if there an explosive device inside, a phone's radio frequency (RF) signal could possibly detonate it. Further, no switches or fire alarms should be activated in the vicinity of the package. The area should be immediately evacuated (Cybersecurity and Infrastructure Security Agency, 2020).

Vehicle Bombs.

Cars and large vehicles are also commonly used by both domestic and foreign terrorists as bombs (Griffith, 2010). The Oklahoma City bombing that killed 168 people resulted from an enormous bomb ignited inside a rental truck that had been parked in a drop-off zone underneath the building's day care center. The 2010 attempted bombing in Times Square involved a parked vehicle, from which smoke was coming. Two street vendors reported the suspicious vehicle to police before any damage occurred. Two critical pieces of advice to always bear in mind: (1) a vehicle you observe for a simple parking violation could, in actuality, be a car bomb, and (2) the initial explosion may not be the only one (Griffith, 2010). A bomb attack will draw a lot of attention, including first responders. Having a multitude of police, firefighters, and other emergency response personnel in one place presents an attractive target for a follow-up attack. It is

also important to keep this multiple-explosion scenario in mind when evacuating a building on the report of a bomb threat. Do not send evacuees out into a parking lot where a vehicle bomb might be located.

Suicide Bombers.

A suicide bombing is commonly defined as "an attack where the death of the bomber is the means by which the attack is accomplished" (Horowitz, 2015). For decades, suicide bombing has been a prominent weapon in the terrorist's toolkit because it generates a significantly higher body count per attack than other uses of force. Whereas a typical criminal will very rarely look to lay down their life for the sake of crime, suicide bombers go to their targets knowing that they will die there. Most believe the act makes them martyrs and ensures them a place in their version of heaven. Their families are usually held in reverence and taken care of.

The notion of a suicide bomber as a young male fundamentalist fanatic is dangerously narrow-minded. Potential suicide terrorists may come from different backgrounds and different age groups, can be male or female, educated or uneducated, upstanding citizen or deviant. Among the warning signs revealing a suicide bomber are unseasonable garb; profuse sweating; obvious disguises (such as a police uniform with a security badge); and a well-dressed, perfumed appearance and demeanor fitting for one who is going to meet their maker.

Individuals chose to become suicide bombers for a variety of social, organizational, economic, religious, and other reasons. Most scholars agree that the decision to be a suicide bomber is not made spontaneously or irrationally but, rather, strategically during the course of radicalization (Horowitz, 2015). Researchers who study the process of terrorist radicalization explain that the journey someone takes to become a suicide bomber typically involves a series of phases that build upon each other, deepening a person's commitment to a violent ideology over time (Sugara, 2018). The transformation generally starts from a base where an individual feels a sense of oppression and injustice; for example, Islamist extremists begin with feeling the injustice of a system that oppresses Muslims. Those who wish to find the perpetrators of the injustice move to the next phase. Again, for Islamist extremists, they blame democracy, and the United States in particular, for such oppression and vow to fight against the democratic system. During the next phase, extremists start to agree to resist using all means available, including suicide bombings. People who sympathize with what terrorist groups do may be in this stage. At the next phase, extremists start to prepare their attack, and the final phase is actual attack itself.

A significant new tactic being used by terrorists are body cavity bombs (BCBs) and surgically implanted IEDs (SIIEDs) carried inside human or animal hosts and capable of evading detection technologies devices (Bunker & Flaherty, 2013). The Police Executive Research Forum (PERF) has developed guidelines for a patrol-level response to a suicide bomb threat, stressing that any protocol should be consistent with the agency's policies and procedures for use of force, active shooter situations, and bomb threats.

Weapons of Mass Destruction (WMDs)

Much concern centers around potential use by terrorists of chemical, biological, radiological/nuclear (CBRN) agents. Because such agents carry the potential to cause widespread devastation, they are also referred to as weapons of mass destruction (WMDs). Biological WMDs have actually been in use since the 1300s. The twentieth century brought the first use of artificially produced WMDs—or chemical agents—during World War I. Today, the means for developing chemical, biological, radiological, and nuclear weapons are well known. Some experts suggest that, of these CBRN means, bioterrorism is the least likely to occur whereas chemical attacks are the most likely because the raw materials are easy to get and the devices are simple to assemble and use.

Biological Agents. Bioterrorism involves dissemination of anthrax, botulism, smallpox, or other pathogens as WMDs, and is a potential reality following the anthrax scare of 2001 on the heels of the 9/11 attacks. Especially susceptible to bioterrorism are the nation's food and water supplies, which might also be attacked using chemical agents.

Chemical Agents. A chemical attack has the potential for mass casualties and significant economic loss. The four common types of chemical weapons are nerve agents, blood agents, choking agents, and blistering agents. One agent, ricin toxin, is both a biological and a chemical weapon. Ricin is 1,000 times more poisonous than cyanide and in its purest form, a grain of ricin no bigger than a grain of table salt can kill an adult.

The attention of security experts was riveted on the potential for chemical terrorism in 1995 when members of Aum Shinrikyo, a new-age cult, released deadly sarin gas into the Tokyo subway system, killing 12 and sending 5,000 to the hospital. It was what many considered their worst nightmare. Unfortunately, anyone with Internet access and a Web browser can, in less than 40 minutes, obtain the chemical formula for the invisible, odorless, and highly toxic sarin gas.

One chemical agent receiving increased attention in security periodicals is chlorine, a toxic gas with corrosive properties. It is widely used in the manufacture of paper, cloth, industrial solvents, pesticides, synthetic rubber, and refrigerants, but chlorine has also been used in chemical warfare as a choking agent (National Institute for Occupational Safety and Health, 2011).

The DHS has implemented the Chemical Facility Anti-Terrorism Standards (CFATS) program to identify and regulate high-risk chemical facilities in an effort to ensure they have security measures in place to reduce the risks associated with these chemicals. Initially authorized by Congress in 2007, the program uses a dynamic multitiered risk assessment process, requiring identified high-risk facilities to meet and maintain performance-based security standards. DHS chemical security inspectors operate in all 50 states to help ensure facilities meet CFATS requirements. On December 18, 2014, President Obama signed into law the Protecting and Securing Chemical Facilities from Terrorist Attacks Act of 2014 ("the CFATS Act of 2014"), which recodifies and reauthorizes the CFATS program for four years. A CFATS Extension Act was signed in 2019, and the CFATS Act itself was amended and reauthorized on July 22, 2020, extending the CFATS program to July 27, 2023.

Radiological/Nuclear Terrorism. Considering the devastating capability of nuclear weapons, and the economic destruction that follow in the wake of a detonation, it comes as no surprise that terrorists seek to acquire these devices. With more than 16,000 nuclear weapons worldwide, and given the fact that Islamic State groups are already in possession of low-grade nuclear material seized from a Mosul facility, many consider it well within the realm of possibility that weapons-grade nuclear materials could fall into the hands of international terrorists who would not hesitate to deploy them (Plame, 2014).

The U.S. NRC estimates that an average of 375 devices of all kinds containing radioactive material are reported lost or stolen each year. Such devices are also called "dirty bombs." Although this may seem another horrific addition to a terrorist arsenal as a weapon of choice, the most destruction and disruption from a dirty bomb detonation will be caused by public panic, not radiation.

Detecting Radiation and Other Bioterrorism Agents.
Dosimeters are small, lightweight devices that use silicon diode technology to instantaneously detect and display the accumulated exposure dose and dose rate. They can identify the specific radionuclide(s) involved and let investigators calculate how long they can safely remain on the scene.

Another advance in detecting hazardous agents is the *electronic nose*. Already used to select fragrant wines and diagnose diseases, electronic noses are now "sniffing" their way into the market for detecting hazardous agents. Electronic nose technology is designed to detect all chemicals within an aroma or fragrance and miss nothing. Some electronic noses already use wireless technology, allowing an investigator more than a mile away from the device to use a computer to monitor the vapors, smells, odors, and chemistry of the air remotely.

Robotic detection and identification technology can warn responders of CBRN agents' presence and strength. Global positioning systems (GPS) can be applied to determine the coordinates of an CBRN release relative to the position of responders, residential or other civilian centers, or other critical location information. GPS can also track vehicles charged with transporting CBRN materials to and from the site. Finally, weather data, such as wind direction and speed, barometric pressure, and relative humidity, is critical to responders at CBRN scenes.

A WMD Team. Law enforcement agencies should select and train officers to form a WMD team to be ready if needed. Members of the team must have adequate personal protective equipment (PPE). Implementing a PPE program protects first responders and eliminates "blue canaries." (Police officers who walk into hazardous situations and die are sometimes described as blue canaries from the practice of coal miners releasing a canary into a mine shaft to see whether the shaft was safe for breathing—if the canary died, more ventilation was needed.) Table 20.1 outlines the level of protection, description, type of protection afforded, and circumstance for use of each level of equipment.

Cyberterrorism

Cyberterrorism is where cybercrime intersects with terrorism. **Cyberterrorism** is defined by the FBI as "a premeditated, politically motivated attack against information, computer systems, computer programs and data which results in violence against non-combatant targets by subnational groups or clandestine agents." Cyberterrorism is a form of technological terrorism, which involves attacks *on* technology *by* technology. The most basic technological capability—access to the Internet—has transformed the way terrorists radicalize others and operationalize their attacks: while a conventional terrorist will use an IED, a cyberterrorist will use the Internet (Harrison, 2018).

A report by the United Nations Office on Drugs and Crime (2012) states:

> Technology is one of the strategic factors driving the increasing use of the Internet by terrorist organizations and their supporters for a wide range of purposes, including recruitment, financing, propaganda, training, incitement to commit acts of terrorism, and the gathering and dissemination of information for terrorist purposes. Terrorist organizations and their affiliates have been particularly clever in designing propaganda to disseminate over the Internet for recruiting minors, such as popular music videos, cartoons, children's stories, and video games. Such targeted propaganda has been found to effectively assimilate radical ideologies into a medium that youth consider as entertainment, subtly delivering messages that promote and glorify acts of terrorism, including suicide attacks. (U.N. Office on Drugs and Crime, 2012)

The Worldwide Threat Assessment (Coats, 2019) warns that an attack by cybercriminals could seriously

TABLE 20.1	**Personal Protective Equipment**		
Level	**Description**	**Protection**	**Circumstance**
D	Work uniform	Provides no respiratory protection and minimal skin protection	Should not be worn on any site where respiratory or skin hazards exist
C	Full facepiece, air-purifying, canister-equipped respirator, and chemical-resistant clothing	Same skin protection as level B, but a lower level respiratory protection	Worn when airborne substance is known, concentration is measured, criteria for using air-purifying respirators are met, and skin and eye exposures are unlikely
B	Chemical-resistant clothing (overalls and long sleeves) and self-contained breathing apparatus (SCBA)	Provides splash protection	Worn when the highest level of respiratory protection is needed but a lesser level of skin and eye protection is sufficient
A	Fully encapsulating chemical-resistant suit and SCBA can be worn for only 15 to 30 minutes due to overheating; special training is required	Provides full protection	Worn when the highest level of respiratory, skin, eye, and mucous membrane protection is needed

Source: Adapted from OSHA: www.osha.gov/laws-regs/regulations/standardnumber/1910/1910.120AppB

disrupt a wide range of critical U.S. infrastructure sectors, including health care, financial services, energy, transportation systems, food and agriculture, and emergency service sectors. For example, we rely on energy to drive our technology, and our energy sector fuels the 21st century economy. The cyberattack on the Colonial Pipeline during the spring of 2020 showed how disruptive such a security breach could be, by shutting down fuel supplies stretching from Texas all along the southeastern United States and up to New Jersey, causing gas shortages and panic buying, and prompting the company to pay a ransom to get their operation back online. Likewise, an attack on the information technology systems and networks critical to the functioning of businesses, health care facilities, educational institutions, the military, and all governmental agencies would be catastrophic, putting our safety and national security in jeopardy.

The Federal Response to Terrorism

On October 19, 1984, President Ronald Reagan signed into law the Act to Combat International Terrorism (ACIT), which established a monetary reward program for information involving terrorism. In 1996, the FBI established the NCTC. Also in 1996 the Antiterrorism and Effective Death Penalty Act was passed, including several specific measures aimed at terrorism. It enhanced the federal government's power to deny visas to individuals belonging to terrorist groups and simplified the process for deporting aliens convicted of crimes.

Having announced in 1999 that preventing terrorism was its top priority, the FBI added a new Counterterrorism Division with four subunits: the International Terrorism Section, the Domestic Terrorism Section, the National Infrastructure Protection Center, and the National Domestic Preparedness Office. But this was not enough to avert the tragic events of 9/11. It took a disaster of that magnitude to make the war on terrorism truly the number-one priority of the United States. In the immediate aftermath of September 11, 2001, Attorney General John Ashcroft announced that all U.S. attorneys were establishing antiterrorism task forces to serve as conduits for information about suspected terrorists between federal and local agencies. Another initiative was establishing a new federal agency at the cabinet level.

The U.S. Department of Homeland Security (DHS)

On October 8, 2001, President George W. Bush signed Executive Order 13228 establishing the Department of Homeland Security to be headed by Tom Ridge, who resigned as governor of Pennsylvania to take the post.

LO5 Name the federal office that was established as a result of the 9/11 terrorist attacks on the United States.

The Department of Homeland Security was established as a result of the 9/11 terrorist attacks on the United States, reorganizing the departments of the federal government.

Homeland security is an amalgamation of law enforcement, immigration, disaster, and terrorism issues. Homeland security is the responsibility of civilian agencies at all levels and a coordination of efforts of government at all levels (Reese, 2013). The mission of the DHS is six-fold: prevent terrorism and other threats to homeland security, secure and manage our borders, preserve and uphold our economic security, safeguard and secure cyberspace and critical infrastructures, ensure preparedness for and resilience to disaster, and support and strengthen the workforce of the DHS (DHS, 2019b). Figure 20.5 shows the organization of the DHS.

LO6 Identify the two lead agencies in combating terrorism and how they are involved.

At the federal level, the FBI is the lead agency for responding to acts of domestic terrorism. The Federal Emergency Management Agency (FEMA) is the lead agency for consequence management (after an attack).

The DHS serves in a broad capacity, facilitating collaboration between local and federal law enforcement to develop a national strategy to detect, prepare for, prevent, protect against, respond to, and recover from terrorist attacks within the United States. In April 2011, DHS Secretary Janet Napolitano announced that the five-tiered color-coded security advisory system that had been used since 2002 would be replaced by a two-level threat advisory:

- *Elevated threat*—warns of a credible terrorist threat against the United States

- *Imminent threat*—warns of a credible, specific, and impending terrorist threat against the United States

The basic difference between the two levels is that "elevated" applies when no specific information exists about the timing or location of a credible threat, and

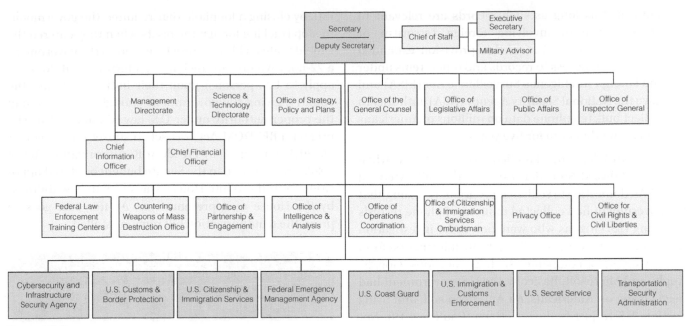

Figure 20.5
Organization of the Department of Homeland Security.
Source: https://www.dhs.gov/sites/default/files/publications/19_1205_dhs-organizational-chart.pdf

"imminent" applies when the timing of the threat is believed to be in the very near future (DHS, 2021).

The USA PATRIOT Act

On October 26, 2001, President Bush signed into law the Uniting and Strengthening America by Providing Appropriate Tools Required to Intercept and Obstruct Terrorism (USA PATRIOT) Act, giving police unprecedented ability to search, seize, detain, and eavesdrop in their pursuit of possible terrorists. The law expanded the FBI's wiretapping and electronic surveillance authority and allowed nationwide jurisdiction for search warrants and electronic surveillance devices, including legal expansion of those devices to email and the Internet. The act included money laundering provisions, set strong penalties for anyone who harbors or finances terrorists, and established new punishments for possessing biological weapons. Further, it made it a federal crime to commit an act of terrorism against a mass transit system.

Prior to 9/11, the Foreign Intelligence Surveillance Act (FISA) of 1978, which was enacted well before the proliferation of the Internet, was the principal federal law governing both the physical and electronic surveillance of primarily foreign powers and agents. The PATRIOT Act essentially amended FISA to expand surveillance to individuals not directly linked to terrorist groups. In addition to the increased scope of surveillance, the USA PATRIOT Act significantly improved the nation's counterterrorism efforts by:

- Allowing investigators to use the tools already available to investigate organized crime and drug trafficking

- Facilitating information sharing and cooperation among government agencies so they can better "connect the dots"

- Updating the law to reflect new technologies and new threats

- Increasing the penalties for those who commit or support terrorist crimes

President Obama signed a four-year sunset extension of the USA PATRIOT Act on May 26, 2011, which included three key provisions:

- Use of roving wiretaps—allows monitoring of a person rather than a specific device, to defeat suspected terrorists who constantly switch out electronic communication devices such as cellphones

- Surveillance of "lone wolf" terror suspects—allows U.S. intelligence and law enforcement agencies to target surveillance at suspected terrorists even in the absence of any direct connection to a terrorist group. This provision specifically states that it does not apply to U.S. citizens and, during its four-year tenure, was never used.

- Searches of business records—permits the government to obtain a wide array of records on an individual as long as such records are relevant to an investigation involving foreign terrorism or espionage. Section 215 of this provision expanded government access to records and other items under the Foreign Intelligence Surveillance Act (FISA) and gave the National Security Agency (NSA) authority to collect bulk telephone data on millions of Americans and retain that data for five years.

The 2013 leak of classified documents by whistleblower Edward Snowden exposed the full extent of the NSA's domestic surveillance program, revealing that the government had collected millions of phone records involving U.S. citizens who were not under investigation for terrorist activities, as well as private information from the customers of companies such as Facebook, Google, Apple, and Microsoft. Basically, the U.S. government had been spying on Americans, on American soil, and using Section 215 to justify those actions (Cauley, 2018). Not surprisingly, this revelation caused considerable controversy and attacks from groups across the political spectrum, helping to fuel the effort to reform the PATRIOT Act and leading to the creation of the USA FREEDOM Act.

The USA FREEDOM Act

The Uniting and Strengthening America by Fulfilling Rights and Ending Eavesdropping, Dragnet-collection and Online Monitoring (USA FREEDOM) Act was enacted June 2, 2015, to replace the PATRIOT Act, which had expired the day before. Critics of the PATRIOT Act had long contended that the measures had been passed too hastily in the wake of 9/11 and had cast a wider net than should have been Constitutionally allowed with respect to U.S. citizens' First and Fourth Amendment rights. The FREEDOM Act, which was first introduced in Chapter 17, revised several key provisions of the PATRIOT Act, including curtailing the controversial bulk metadata collection allowed by Section 215, in an effort to better protect civil liberties, improve transparency, prevent government overreach, enhance information sharing with American people, and strengthen national security (Cauley, 2018). The act did, however, reauthorize roving wiretaps and tracking of lone wolf terrorists.

As part of the revised provisions, the USA FREEDOM Act imposes new limitations on the bulk collection of metadata on U.S. citizens and requires the government to obtain a targeted warrant to collect phone metadata. Further, the Foreign Intelligence Surveillance Court (FISC), the body charged with reviewing those warrant requests, must provide greater transparency. The FREEDOM Act also contains an additional tool to combat

ISIL by closing a loophole that required the government to stop tracking foreign terrorists when they entered the United States. This new provision allows the government a 72-hour window to track foreign terrorists (it does not apply to U.S. persons) upon their initial entry into the country, giving the government enough time to obtain the proper authority under U.S. law (Cauley, 2018). The original FREEDOM Act was set to sunset on December 15, 2019, and the USA Freedom Reauthorization Act of 2020, which passed in the Senate but encountered opposition from the White House, was ultimately withdrawn by the House of Representatives. As this text goes to press, the reauthorization bill remains stalled.

LO7 Explain how the USA PATRIOT Act and USA FREEDOM Act enhance counterterrorism efforts by the United States.

The PATRIOT Act of 2001 aimed to significantly improving the nation's counterterrorism efforts by greatly expanding the scope of surveillance allowed under U.S. law, enabling the government to collect intelligence information on both Americans and foreigners without the need to prove that the target was an agent of a foreign power. It also lengthened the maximum duration of surveillance and investigations, implemented roving wiretaps, and allowed intelligence agencies to conduct investigations of "lone wolves."

After several amendments and reauthorizations, the PATRIOT Act was replaced by the FREEDOM Act in 2015. The FREEDOM Act revised several key provisions of the PATRIOT Act, including the controversial Section 215, in an effort to better protect civil liberties, improve transparency, prevent government overreach, enhance information sharing with American people, and strengthen national security.

Congress and other legislators continue to grapple with how to provide federal agents the right amount of power to pursue suspected terrorists without threatening the civil rights and privacy of Americans. Several other federal initiatives are aimed at preventing terrorist attacks or at least mitigating their effects.

The National Infrastructure Protection Plan (NIPP)

The *National Infrastructure Protection Plan (NIPP)* is a comprehensive risk management framework defining critical infrastructure protection roles and responsibilities of federal, state, local, tribal, and private security partners:

Our national well-being relies upon secure and resilient critical infrastructure—those assets, systems and networks that underpin American society. The purpose of the *NIPP 2013*... is to guide the national effort to manage risks to the Nation's critical infrastructure. To achieve this end, critical infrastructure partners must collectively identify national priorities; articulate clear goals; mitigate risk; measure progress; and adapt based on feedback and the changing environment. Success in this complex endeavor leverages the full spectrum of capabilities, expertise, and experience from across a robust partnership. (DHS, 2013, p. 3)

The 16 specific sectors included in the plan include: chemical; commercial facilities; communications; critical manufacturing; dams; defense industrial base; emergency services; energy; financial services; food and agriculture; government facilities; health care and public health; information technology; nuclear reactors, materials, and waste; transportation systems; and water and wastewater systems.

Investigating Possible Terrorist Activities

Investigating possible terrorist activities is facilitated by the fact that terrorists also often engage in other criminal activities: "A growing body of literature supports the hypothesis of a crime–terror nexus, especially as a result of the post–9/11 alarm on terrorism financing" (Belli, 2011, p. 12). One way to address terrorism is to modify laws that deal with white-collar crimes, traditionally nonviolent and involving some form of fraud to achieve financial gain. These crimes include credit card fraud, insurance fraud, identity theft, money laundering, immigration fraud, and tax evasion. This approach rests on the assumption that terrorist activities require funding for weaponry, training, travel, and living expenses. (Funding terrorism is discussed shortly.) Cases involving money laundering should be looked at as a white-collar crime but also as potentially linked to terrorism. The investigative techniques described in Chapter 18 would be applicable in this counterterrorism strategy.

Terrorists also commonly create and use false identifications to enter the country, gain employment, acquire equipment, and accumulate money. Ernst (2014) states: "One thing we have learned is that terrorism and fake identification documents go hand in hand." He suggests all officers learn how to identify a fake passport. The *Counterterrorism 2015 Calendar* provides a list of indicators of fraudulent travel documents (NCTC, 2015).

A major challenge in the war on terrorism is ensuring that individual officers remain vigilant and cognizant of their critical role in homeland security. For example, law enforcement officers should be on the watch during traffic stops and other contacts for certain logos suggesting membership in a terrorist group or financial or general support for them (Figure 20.6). These emblems may be noticed on jewelry, documents, posters, or other materials.

Law enforcement officers should also be aware of terrorist *indicators* such as negative rhetoric, excessive physical training, anti-American literature, or a disregard for U.S. laws. Terrorists and their supporters tend to act alike because many have trained in the same camps and share the same negative beliefs. The New York Police Department (NYPD) has published *Radicalization in the West: The Homegrown Threat* (New York Police Department, 2007), a useful reference for investigators to familiarize themselves with the characteristics of someone undergoing the radicalization process.

Investigators should also be knowledgeable of vulnerable, valuable targets for a terrorist attack, such as any high-occupancy structure or any site where a significant number of lives are affected; a structure containing dangerous substances or articles; any vital, high-use structure composing an infrastructure; a site of significant historical, symbolic, strategic, defensive, or functional value to the nation, including government buildings and structures holding highly sensitive, rare, historical, or irreplaceable artifacts, documents, or other such content.

Although focusing on logical targets for terrorist attacks, "soft" targets—that is, those that are relatively unguarded or difficult to guard—should not be overlooked, including shopping malls, subways, trains, sports stadiums, theaters, schools, hospitals, restaurants, entertainment parks, compressed gas and oil storage areas, chemical plants, pharmaceutical companies, and many others.

Finally, when investigating possible terrorist activities, it is important to understand that domestic terrorism is often not a chargeable offense on its own. While many states do have legislation pertaining to domestic terrorism, there is currently no federal criminal statute that establishes criminal penalties solely for "domestic terrorism," although it may be an element of other federal crimes or provide an enhanced sentence. In other words, an individual may commit criminal acts that are widely considered domestic terrorism and be prosecuted for the criminal acts themselves, but an individual cannot be charged with committing an act of domestic terrorism under current federal law. For example, Timothy McVeigh, widely considered a

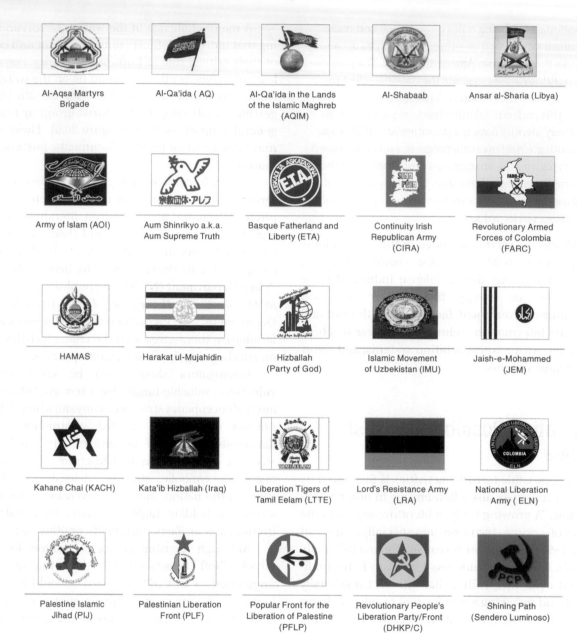

Figure 20.6
Logos Associated with Foreign Terrorist Organizations.
Office of the Director of National Intelligence

domestic terrorist, was convicted of murder, conspiracy, and using a weapon of mass destruction in the 1995 bombing of the Murrah Federal Building, but he was not convicted of domestic terrorism (Congressional Research Service, 2021). Remember: terrorism is extremist ideology translated into criminal action. The bottom line for officers and investigators is to focus on the crime, not the ideology.

Funding Terrorism

It takes money for both weapons and general operating expenses to carry out terrorism. Illegal activities undertaken to generate funds present an opportunity for terrorists to appear on law enforcement's radar. Terrorist groups commonly collaborate with organized criminal groups to deal drugs, arms, and, in some instances, people. The concept of **narcoterrorism** refers to the use of terrorist tactics to support drug operations or the use of drug trade profits to finance terrorism (White, 2012). To finance their operations, terrorist groups smuggle stolen goods and contraband, forge documents, profit from the diamond trade, and engage in extortion and protection rackets.

Many terrorist operations are financed by charitable groups and wealthy patrons sympathetic to the group's cause. To investigate local charities, any interested individual can access the information by contacting the Better Business Bureau or the Wise Giving Alliance.

Fraud has become increasingly common among terrorists—as a way to generate revenue and as a way to gain access to their targets. Fraudulently obtained driver's licenses, passports, and other identification documents are often found among terrorists' belongings. No matter how terrorist groups are financed, they usually need to hide where the money came from.

Money laundering was discussed in Chapter 14. However, one tactic is especially important in hiding the money trail of terrorist financing—*hawala*. **Hawala** is an informal banking system based on trust and often bartering, common throughout the Middle East and used to transfer billions of dollars every year. No tax records or paper trails exist. This practice has been used for many years to move terrorist money without a trace of banking records or currency transaction reports. Hawala allows money launderers to secretly hide and send money out of the country without detection.

Some differences have been observed to exist in the types of crimes terrorists use to fund their operations. For example, one study of financial crimes linked to al-Qa'ida and affiliated movements (AQAM) found that these material support schemes were more likely than other financial crime schemes to be motivated by ideology than by profit or greed (Sullivan, Freilich, & Chermak, 2014). AQAM-linked financial crimes and material support schemes carried out in the United States between 1990 and mid-2014 involved a wide range of activities, including check, loan, and credit card fraud; money laundering; currency counterfeiting; cybercrime; identity theft; and tax avoidance. The techniques used to carry out these schemes included identity theft (stealing, selling, or using other people's names and social security numbers); credit card theft; falsification of documents for government assistance, bank loans, or insurance claims; passing insufficient funds checks or checks drawn from false accounts; and money laundering. Other crimes engaged in by terrorists have included weapons trafficking, extortion, and insurance fraud.

The Typical Stages in a Terrorist Attack

Terrorist attacks typically have three stages: research, planning and preparation, and execution. Each stage provides unique opportunities for officers conducting an investigation into terrorist activities. Often these attacks are carried out by a **sleeper cell**, a group of terrorists who blend into a community and who may share or divide responsibilities for various stages of the attack. Other attacks are carried out by lone actor terrorists.

The first stage—research—includes surveillance, stakeouts, and local inquiries. Local law enforcement officers can best serve the counterterrorism effort at this stage because the terrorists are out in public, watching us, studying our habits, discovering our vulnerabilities, and reporting back to their handlers with prospective targeting data to begin the planning stage. Interestingly, a study of terrorist attack sites found that nearly half of the attackers lived within 30 miles of their selected target (Smith, 2008).

The second stage is planning and preparation, often conducted behind closed doors. The average planning cycle for international terrorists is 92 days, compared with 14 days for environmental terrorists (Smith, 2008). Part of this stage involves the training necessary to carry out an attack. One study found that approximately one-fifth (21%) of lone-actor terrorists received some form of hands-on training, while just under half (46.2%) learned through virtual sources (Gill, Horgan, & Deckert, 2014). Nearly one-third (29.4%) of offenders engaged in dry runs or preparatory trips to the site of their intended attack, with more than half (57.1%) of them doing so within a year of the eventual attack.

Terrorism researchers have observed changing patterns in attackers' social interactions in the days, weeks, and months leading up to an attack, noting that these individuals tend to become progressively more isolated from those not involved in the impending attack, including family and friends (Davis et al., 2013). This isolation serves not only to shield the attacker from potential ideas that might undermine or disrupt the radical master narrative calling for violence but also to bolster secrecy and operational security by limiting contact with those outside the plot who might leak information or otherwise interfere with the execution of the attack. It stands to reason that the more people involved in a potential plot, the greater the risk of exposure to outsiders and the interception of attackers by law enforcement. In fact, research has found that those who remained most isolated in the run-up to an attack were significantly more successful in executing their attack (Gill et al., 2014).

One study examined operational security (actions taken to minimize the chances of detection while planning or preparing an attack) and leakage behavior (actions that intentionally or unintentionally divulge one's motivation or capability to commit acts of violence) of lone wolf terrorists, two factors related to the opportunity for early detection and intervention of impending attacks. The study found that a vast majority (86%) of these lone actors communicated their radical or extremist convictions to others, such as family members, friends, and colleagues (Schuurman, Bakker, Gill, & Bouhana, 2018). These researchers also report that, from a threat assessment perspective, it is noteworthy that more than half (58%) of the lone wolf attackers gave others the idea that they were involved in suspicious and potentially violent activities, and one-fourth (26%) divulged specific details of the planned attack.

One of the more significant findings of the study was the general lack of operational security precautions taken by lone actor terrorists. For example, only one in four (26%) took measures to maintain plot secrecy; most (76%) were found to have stored weapons, explosives, or the precursor components for making bombs at their own place of residence; and nearly all (94%) had left incriminating evidence such as bomb-making manuals in plain sight for the authorities (Schuurman et al., 2018). The researchers suggest that this disregard for operational security might stem from the attackers' expectation of dying during the attack itself, removing any concern about the discovery of evidence during the post-attack investigation.

Finally, this study found that nearly half (49%) of all lone actor terrorists had come into contact with police or members of intelligence agencies during the planning and preparation phase, but researchers caution that this does not mean that the authorities were necessarily aware of such individuals' extremist convictions or terrorist intent. However, just over one-fourth (27%) of lone actors were, *while* they were engaged in planning and preparatory activities, already on authorities' radar as potential terrorist threats (Schuurman et al., 2018).

The third stage of a terrorist attack is execution, possibly followed by escape. Occasionally the terrorist(s) will deploy a feint attack, a diversionary tactic to draw protective measures away from the main attack area. Hostages may also be taken during the attack, signaling plans for a lengthy standoff (Davis et al., 2013)

One approach to identifying potential terrorists is to use behavior pattern recognition (BPR), observing irregular behaviors for the environment as well as targeted conversations with suspects. For instance, the TSA has trained more than 3,000 screeners at 161 airports who look for signs of stress, fear, and deception among airline passengers. In 2012, TSA made 2,116 referrals to law enforcement based on BPR which resulted in 30 boarding denials, 79 law enforcement investigations, and 183 arrests (Pistole, 2013). However, a recent assessment by the U.S. Government Accountability Office (GAO) was critical of the TSA's behavior detection process, reporting that 28 of the 36 behavioral indicators lacked valid empirical evidence to support their use in identifying individuals who may pose a threat to aviation security (Kingsbury & Grover, 2017).

The New York City Police Department is using a different tactic, having detectives visit scuba shops and hardware stores, talk to parking garage attendants and plastic surgeons, hotel managers and tool rental companies, bulk fuel dealers, and trade schools. Although admittedly somewhat of a "needle-in-a-haystack approach," the program, called Operation Nexus, has the potential to identify terrorists. Information from an al-Qa'ida manual for terrorist operatives and debriefings of some of the group's leaders and foot soldiers suggest that al-Qa'ida has considered using scuba divers to blow up bridges, riding in tourist helicopters for surveillance, turning trucks and limousines into rolling bombs, and using special torches to cut the cables of the Brooklyn Bridge.

Terrorists might be hunted down using confidential informant reward programs established by the 1984 ACIT. The PATRIOT Act amended the reward program by increasing the amount offered to an informant to $250,000.

Surveillance Cameras as Investigative Tools

When terrorists attacked London's transit system in 2005, four homemade bombs stuffed into backpacks failed to fully explode. Only one person was injured. A day later, photographs of four suspects captured on surveillance cameras near the sites of the attempted attacks were broadcast on television. The remarkable speed of that investigation was repeated on July 7, 2007, following another attack. British investigators, aided by surveillance cameras, tracked the suspects to Glasgow, Scotland, and arrested several individuals. Surveillance camera footage also played a crucial role in the rapid identification of the two Boston Marathon bombing suspects.

Information Gathering and Intelligence Sharing

An important distinction differentiates information and intelligence. Information is simply raw, unanalyzed data. Information is a packet of knowledge or facts about persons, evidence, events, etc. Intelligence, on the other hand, is "the end product of an analytic process that evaluates information collected from diverse sources; integrates the relevant information into a logical package; and produces a conclusion, estimate, or forecast about a criminal phenomenon [that can then be disseminated to other parties] . . . Intelligence, therefore, is a synergistic product intended to provide meaningful and trustworthy actionable knowledge to law enforcement decision makers about complex criminality, criminal enterprises, criminal extremists, and terrorists" (Carter, 2009, p. 9). One way to conceptualize the difference is to think of raw information as a fluid poured into a funnel that gets passed through various filters, sieves, and other analytical processes; the more meaningful, relevant, or useful bits of data that are extracted at the end are referred to as *intelligence*. The process of extracting intelligence from raw data is referred to as the *intelligence cycle* (Figure 20.7).

The Intelligence Cycle

The cycle begins with knowing the *intelligence requirements* needed for an investigation. What do investigators need to know to effectively safeguard the nation? These requirements are established by the director of National Intelligence under the guidance of the president and the national and homeland security advisors and are based on critical information necessary for homeland security. The second step—*planning and direction*—is a function of the FBI and is led by the executive assistant director of the National Security Branch.

The third step is *collecting raw information* from local, state, and federal investigations. Such information may come from interviews, technical and physical surveillance, searches, human source operations, and liaison relationships. Fourth is *processing and exploiting* the raw information into a form usable by analysts. Fifth is *analysis and production*, which converts the raw information into intelligence. The final step is *dissemination* of intelligence to consumers, who make decisions based on the intelligence. These decisions may levy further requirements, thus continuing the intelligence cycle.

Local and state law enforcement agencies are critical to the third step in the intelligence cycle and benefit

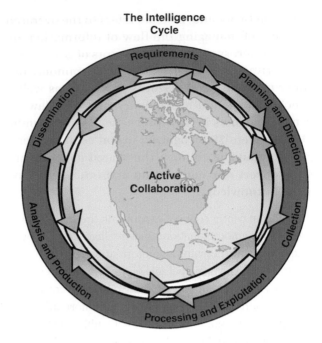

Figure 20.7
The intelligence cycle.
Source: www.fbi.gov/about-us/intelligence/intelligence-cycle/

from the sixth step as well. Many day-to-day duties of local law enforcement officers bring them into proximity with sources of information about terrorism. Patrol operations, especially traffic officers, properly trained in what to look for and what questions to ask when interacting with citizens, can be a tremendous source of intelligence for their state and federal homeland security counterparts as well as for local investigators.

The difficult tasks of counterterrorism and antiterrorism are made even harder by the operational style that pervades law enforcement—that of withholding, rather than sharing, intelligence. Fusion centers are one way to address and overcome this obstacle.

Fusion Centers

An initiative aimed at promoting and facilitating information and intelligence sharing among federal and local law enforcement agencies is the development of fusion centers throughout the country. **Fusion centers** are "state-owned and operated centers that serve as a focal point in states and major urban areas for the receipt, analysis, gathering, and sharing of threat-related information between State, Local, Tribal and Territorial (SLTT), federal, and private sector partners" (DHS, n.d.). The term *fusion* conveys the concept that the collaborative effort goes beyond simply establishing an information/intelligence center or creating a computer network and, instead, refers to the overarching process of managing the flow of information and intelligence across *all* levels and sectors of government and the private sector. Fusion centers commonly take an all-crimes and/or all-hazards approach, as well as the inclusion of multidisciplinary and non–law enforcement partners in their processes. As of December 2020, there were 78 recognized fusion centers operating throughout the country, the shared goal of which was to convert raw information and intelligence into actionable knowledge:

> The fusion center concept expands on the traditional role of law enforcement criminal intelligence units by expanding partnerships and information sharing opportunities. The principal role of the fusion center is to compile, analyze, and disseminate criminal/terrorist information and intelligence and other information (including, but not limited to, threat, public safety, law enforcement, public health, social services, and public works) to support efforts to anticipate, identify, prevent, and/or monitor criminal/terrorist activity. This information and intelligence should be both strategic (i.e., designed to provide general guidance of patterns and trends) and tactical (i.e., focused on a specific criminal event). (National Fusion Center Association, 2014, p. 8)

Crucial Collaborations and Partnerships

The importance of partnerships between law enforcement agencies at all levels cannot be overstated as it applies to the war on terrorism. The issue of effective partnerships has deserved attention for at least half a century; it now demands attention. Local networking modules developed among local, state, tribal, and federal law enforcement agencies are the most effective way to discuss and share investigative and enforcement endeavors to combat terrorism. This networking module approach avoids compromising existing investigations or conducting conflicting cases and should have a built-in **deconfliction** protocol, which essentially means guidelines to avoid conflict. Deconfliction can be applied to declassified and confidential investigations.

A subtitle of the Homeland Security Act of 2002, called the Homeland Security Information Sharing Act, required the president to develop new procedures for sharing classified information, as well as unclassified but otherwise sensitive information, with state and local police. This charge was fulfilled in May 2002

when the IACP, the Department of Justice (DOJ), the FBI, the DHS, and other representatives of the federal, state, tribal, and local law enforcement communities endorsed the National Criminal Intelligence Sharing Plan (NCISP). The NCISP unites law enforcement agencies of all sizes and geographic locations in a national effort to prevent terrorism and criminal activity. In 2004, the Criminal Intelligence Coordinating Council (CICC), a group under the U.S. DOJ's Global Justice Information Sharing Initiative, was established as a top priority of NCISP to serve as the central point of collaboration among local, state, and tribal agencies and organizations. More than a decade later, the CICC continues to serve local, state, and tribal law enforcement and homeland security agencies in national criminal intelligence sharing efforts (Brooks, 2011). Another extremely valuable resource for investigators is the Regional Information Sharing Systems (RISS) program, which assists state and local agencies by sharing information and intelligence regarding terrorism.

Limitations on information sharing have caused tensions in the past, as often information received by the FBI is classified. Rules of federal procedure and grand jury classified material are two other limitations to how much information can be shared. Since 9/11, more than 6,000 state and local police officers have been granted access to classified material involving terrorist threats.

Initiatives to Assist in the Fight against Terrorism

Several initiatives have been undertaken to help in the fight against terrorism. One such initiative is production of the *FBI Intelligence Bulletin*, a weekly online publication containing information related to terrorism in the United States. Recipients include duly authorized members of all law enforcement agencies who have registered with a law enforcement network. Another initiative that indirectly supports the fight against terrorism is passage of the Law Enforcement Officers Safety Act (LEOSA) of 2004, which gives qualified active duty as well as qualified retired police officers the right to carry their firearms concealed in all 50 states.

Other initiatives include increased security at our borders; the Community Vulnerability Assessment Methodology (C-VAM), the National Memorial Institute for the Prevention of Terrorism, the Center for Food Protection and Defense, the National Incident Management System, and joint terrorism task forces.

Increased Border Security

The U.S. Visitor and Immigrant Status Indicator Technology (US-VISIT) was implemented in January 2005 to capture biometric data, such as inkless finger scans and digital photographs, as a tool to help Customs and Border Protection (CBP) officers to determine whether the person applying for entry at our nation's border was the same one who was issued a visa by the State Department. In March 2013, the Office of Biometric Identity Management (OBIM) replaced the US-VISIT program as the technology source for collecting and storing biometric data, providing analysis, updating the terrorist watchlist, and ensuring the integrity of the data. OBIM supports the DHS's responsibility to protect the nation by providing biometric identification services that help federal, state, and local government decision makers accurately identify the people they encounter and determine whether those people pose a risk to the United States.

The National Memorial Institute for the Prevention of Terrorism

The National Memorial Institute for the Prevention of Terrorism (MIPT) grew out of the desire of the survivors and families of the Murrah Federal Building bombing to have a living memorial in the form of an online, national network of best practices and lessons learned. Since 2000 this nonpartisan, nonprofit organization, located in Oklahoma City, Oklahoma, has amassed the largest national open source collection of documents on counterterrorism and functions as a terrorism prevention training center for police officers and other first responders, investigators, and intelligence analysts from throughout the country.

The National Center for Food Protection and Defense

The mission of the National Center for Food Protection and Defense is to safeguard the security of the food system through research and education. Its goals are to reduce the vulnerability of the nation's food system to terrorist attack by contamination with biological, chemical, or radiological agents at any point along the food supply chain; to strengthen the food system's preparedness and resiliency to threats, disruption, and attacks; and to mitigate the potentially catastrophic public health and economic effects of food system attacks (National Center for Food Protection and Defense, n.d.). This effort is led by the University of Minnesota.

The National Incident Management System

In October 2003, the DHS created the Initial Response Plan (INRP), an interim plan designed to help develop a unified approach to domestic incident management across the nation. On March 1, 2004, then-Secretary Ridge announced the approval of the National Incident Management System (NIMS), the country's first standardized management approach unifying federal, state, and local governments for incident response. NIMS establishes standardized incident management processes, protocols, and procedures that all responders—federal, state, tribal, and local—use to coordinate and conduct response action. Online training courses are available on the FEMA website.

Joint Terrorism Task Forces

The FBI has approximately 200 joint terrorism task forces (JTTFs) throughout the country, including at least one in each of its 56 field offices. JTTFs are the nation's front line on terrorism and consist of small cells of highly trained, locally based investigators, analysts, linguists, special weapons and tactics (SWAT) experts, and other specialists from dozens of U.S. law enforcement and intelligence agencies. In a JTTF, all investigators, whether FBI agents, other federal officers, or state or local officers, are equal partners. Every investigator is assigned substantive cases and works from established FBI protocols for investigating terrorism, completing paperwork requirements, and using data systems.

The Role of the Media in the War on Terrorism

The Terrorism Research Center suggests that terrorists and the media have a symbiotic relationship, both benefitting from the actions of the other. For the media, stories about terrorism generate high viewer ratings. For terrorists, the media provide publicity—a way to spread the word about their cause and generate public fear. Indeed, terrorism is futile if no one knows about it. White (2012) raises the question of the **contagion effect**: that is, coverage of terrorism inspires more terrorism, thus making terrorism, in effect, contagious. This controversial issue leads to discussions about censorship in the war on terrorism.

Concerns Related to the War on Terrorism

Two pressing concerns related to the "war on terrorism" are that civil liberties may be jeopardized and that people of Middle Eastern descent may be discriminated against or become victims of hate crimes. These two concerns were explored by Getlin (2005), who found that some of those he interviewed saw the searches at New York City's Penn Station as an intrusion on personal freedom, whereas other people wanted police to be able to openly focus on Muslim commuters.

In its *Strategic Plan for Fiscal Years 2020–2024*, the DHS (2019a) has addressed this first concern in one of its five guiding principles: "DHS will continue to implement safeguards for privacy, transparency, civil rights, and civil liberties when developing and adopting policies and throughout the performance of its mission to ensure that homeland security programs uphold privacy, civil rights, and civil liberties."

Concern for Civil Rights

Civil libertarians are concerned that valued American freedoms will be sacrificed in the interest of national safety. For example, the Justice Department has issued a regulation giving itself the authority to monitor inmate-attorney communications if "reasonable suspicion" exists that inmates are using such communications to further or facilitate acts of terrorism. However, criminal defense lawyers and members of the American Civil Liberties Union (ACLU) have protested the regulation, saying that it effectively eliminates the Sixth Amendment right to counsel because, under codes of professional responsibility, attorneys cannot communicate with clients if confidentiality is not ensured. The ACLU has vowed to monitor police actions closely to see that freedoms protected under the Constitution are not jeopardized.

The government must preserve the rights and freedoms guaranteed by America's democracy, but, at the same time, ensure that the fight against terrorism is vigorous and effective.

Retaliation or Discrimination against People of Middle Eastern Descent

Another concern is that some Americans may retaliate against innocent people of Middle Eastern descent, many of whom were either born in the United States or are naturalized citizens, or that police may unlawfully profile Arab Americans. Henderson, Ortiz, Sugie, & Miller (2008) identified four significant obstacles to improved relations between police and Arab American communities:

- Distrust between Arab American communities and law enforcement

- Lack of cultural awareness among law enforcement officers

- Language barriers

- Concerns about immigration status and fear of deportation

Community policing efforts can do much to overcome these obstacles.

Several studies provide evidence that, thus far, the relationship between Arab Americans and local law enforcement is generally positive. One study found that, in the Detroit area, the majority of Arab Americans expressed confidence in their local police (Sun & Wu, 2015). Another study found that Arab Americans' confidence in the federal government was positively associated with support for antiterrorism practices in general, but that aggressive law enforcement practices targeting Arab Americans received less favorable attitudes toward counterterrorism measures (Sun, Wu, & Poteyeva, 2011).

Closely related concerns are the rights of citizens detained as enemy combatants and the rights of detained foreign nationals. In *Hamdi v. Rumsfeld* (2004), the Supreme Court ruled that a citizen detained in the United States as an enemy combatant must be afforded the opportunity to rebut such a designation. Petitioner Hamdi was captured in an active combat zone in Afghanistan following the September 11, 2001, attacks on the United States and surrendered an assault rifle. The U.S. District Court found that the declaration from the Defense Department did not support Hamdi's detention and ordered the government to turn over numerous materials for review. The U.S. Court of Appeals for the Fourth Circuit reversed the decision, stressing that because it was undisputed that Hamdi was captured in an active combat zone, no factual inquiry or evidentiary hearing allowing Hamdi to rebut the government's assertions was necessary. The U.S. Supreme Court voted 6–3 to vacate and remand, concluding that Hamdi should have a meaningful opportunity to offer evidence that he was not an enemy combatant.

In *Rasul v. Bush* (2004), the Supreme Court ruled that U.S. courts have jurisdiction to consider challenges to the legality of the detention of foreign nationals captured in Afghanistan in a military campaign against al-Qa'ida and the Taliban regime that supported it. The petitioners, 2 Australians and 12 Kuwaitis, were being held at Guantánamo Bay, Cuba, without charges. These and other legal issues regarding civil rights will continue to be debated as the country seeks to balance the need for security with civil rights.

Community Policing, Hometown Security, and Homeland Security

The criticality of local law enforcement has been recognized ever since homeland security became a focus. Local, state, and tribal law enforcement personnel have realized that, in our post-9/11 society, their duties have expanded considerably, and they are no longer looking to federal agencies and the military as the sole source of our county's protection. The nearly 18,000 state and local law enforcement agencies in the United States employ roughly 655,000 sworn officers who patrol the city streets daily and know their communities intimately (Banks, Hendrix, Hickman, & Kyckelhahn, 2016; U.S. Bureau of Labor Statistics, 2020). A crucial component of homeland security is hometown security. Thus, it makes sense that the first line of defense against terrorism is the uniformed patrol officer in the field.

The International Association of Chiefs of Police (IACP), in recognizing that terrorism, violent extremism, and precursor crimes are problems that begin at the local level, advocates for law enforcement to apply the principles of community policing in their efforts to detect and prevent future attacks (2014). The IACP calls community members "an important force multiplier," because their proximity to those who are becoming radicalized into violent terrorist extremists can help law enforcement identify, prevent, and eliminate terrorist ideologies and behaviors before they turn into violence. Homeland security depends on alert, aware, vigilant citizens. Information they provide officers on their beat can be invaluable to investigators. The Nationwide Suspicious Activity Reporting (SAR) Initiative (NSI) encourages individual citizens to take an active role in reporting any type of suspicious or criminal activity, including extremist behavior, to authorities.

Officers in departments that fully embrace community policing will have an advantage in recognizing potential terrorist threats and targets in their jurisdictions because their daily work requires and imparts an intimate familiarity with their regularly assigned patrol area. Officers must keep their ears to the ground and establish a rapport with the various sources of information in their community, including storage facilities, religious groups, real estate agents, hotels and motels, colleges and universities, transportation centers, and tourist attractions.

Any law enforcement officer can potentially come in contact with a terrorist at any time, whether investigating an unrelated crime, conducting routine duties, or backing up another officer. Many of the 9/11 hijackers had prior contact with law enforcement officers in various parts of the country. For example, on September 9, 2001, Ziad Jarrah, hijacker of the plane that crashed in Shanksville, Pennsylvania, was stopped by police in Maryland for driving 90 mph in a 65 mph zone. Jarrah was issued a ticket and released. Similarly, in August 2001, Hani Hanjour, hijack pilot of the plane that crashed into the Pentagon and killed 289 people, was stopped for speeding by police in Arlington, Virginia, and was issued a ticket and released. Hanjour paid the ticket to avoid having to show up in court.

In 2010, the FBI confirmed that 4,876 alleged terrorists had contacts with U.S. law enforcement, usually for reasons not related to terrorism (Kephart, 2013). Research by Ernst (2014) indicates that 36 U.S. states have either been the intended target of a terrorist plot or have been the location where terrorists have been arrested, lived, worked, or gone to school. He offers two key points for street cops to bear in mind:

- Those embracing a radical or extremist ideology can be found throughout the United States, not just in major metropolitan areas such as New York City or Los Angeles.

- The radicalization process, indoctrination and training activities, and financing activities need not necessarily occur in the same jurisdiction as the intended target of an attack.

Frank Straub, Director of the National Police Foundation's Center for Mass Violence Response Studies, as well as a former member of the FBI-NYPD Joint Terrorist Task Force in New York City and a first responder to the 9/11 attack on the World Trade Center, offers this final comment (2020): "As a collective group, law enforcement needs to recognize the importance of community relationships if we are going to identify individuals who pose a threat to our national security. Developing and maintaining trusting relationships are the foundation of community policing and are essential to preventing crime, terrorism, and targeted violence."

Summary

The threat of terrorism has become a reality in America. Most definitions of terrorism have common elements, including involving acts dangerous to human life that violate federal or state law and are intended to intimidate or coerce a civilian population, or to influence the policy or affect the conduct of a government. Most terrorist acts result from dissatisfaction with a religious, political, or social system or policy and frustration resulting from an inability to change it through acceptable, nonviolent means.

The FBI classifies terrorist acts as either domestic or international. Islamic terrorist groups include Hizballah, Palestinian Islamic Jihad (PIJ), core al-Qa'ida (AQ) groups and their affiliates, ISIS/ISIL, and the Taliban. Domestic terrorist groups in the United States are categorized as far-right, far-left, religious, ethnonationalist, and "other."

The U.S. Department of Homeland Security was established as a result of the 9/11 terrorist attacks against the United States, reorganizing the departments of the federal government. At the federal level, the FBI is the lead agency for responding to domestic terrorism. The Federal Emergency Management Agency (FEMA) is the lead agency for consequence management (after an attack).

After several amendments and reauthorizations, the PATRIOT Act was replaced by the FREEDOM Act in 2015. The FREEDOM Act revised several key provisions of the PATRIOT Act, including the controversial Section 215, in an effort to better protect civil liberties, improve transparency, prevent government overreach, enhance information sharing with the American people, and strengthen national security.

Can You Define?

asymmetric warfare

bioterrorism

boogaloo

contagion effect

cyberterrorism

deconfliction

domestic terrorism

ecoterrorism

extremism

fusion center

hawala

homegrown violent extremists (HVEs)

international terrorism

intifada

jihad

narcoterrorism

sleeper cell

targeted violence

terrorism

Checklist

Terrorism

- What method of attack was used?

- What was the target of the attack?

- Have additional target areas been identified? If so, has a response been initiated?

- Who had access to the location(s)?

- What was the likely motivation?

- Has any group claimed responsibility?

- What was the damage?

- Were there injuries? Fatalities?

- Who notified authorities?

- Who responded first?

- Were there any witnesses?

- Were any suspicious individuals or vehicles observed at the location before the attack? During the attack? After the attack?

- Was the scene photographed or videotaped?

- What evidence was found at the scene?

- Were there any unusual circumstances?

- Was a canvass of the area conducted?

Application

Read the following and then answer the questions:

Detective Smith has had a young Middle Eastern–appearingmale under surveillance as a suspected terrorist. She has followed him for several days and has observed him buy a newspaper from a machine every morning, walk to the state capitol building several times each day and take pictures from various angles, enter the building, and come out shortly. He then returns to an inexpensive motel on the edge of town. He has visits from other Middle Eastern–appearing young males who bring him packages. He does not appear to be employed but wears expensive clothing and eats at expensive restaurants.

On this particular day, she sees that the suspect is carrying a briefcase, something he has not done before. He goes directly to the state capitol building and enters. Approximately one hour later, he comes out, but without the briefcase.

Questions

1. Does Detective Smith have reasonable suspicion to stop the suspect and question him?

2. If so, based on what?

3. What should be the next step?

References

Alcoke, M. (2019, November 19). *The evolving and persistent terrorism threat to the homeland.* Washington, DC: Federal Bureau of Investigation. Retrieved April 10, 2021, from www.fbi.gov/news/speeches/the-evolving-and-persistent-terrorism-threat-to-the-homeland-111919

Anti-Defamation League. (n.d.). *Anti-Government Extremism.* New York, NY: Author. Retrieved April 13, 2021, from www.adl.org/resources/glossary-terms/anti-government-extremism

Anti-Defamation League. (n.d.). *The boogaloo movement.* New York, NY: Author. Retrieved April 14, 2021, from www.adl.org/boogaloo

Anti-Defamation League. (n.d.). *Defining extremism: A glossary of white supremacist terms, movements and philosophies.* New York, NY: Author. Retrieved April 12, 2021, from www.adl.org/education/resources/glossary-terms/defining-extremism-white-supremacy

Anti-Defamation League. (n.d.). *Who are antifa?* New York, NY: Author. Retrieved April 15, 2021, from www.adl.org/antifa

Anti-Defamation League. (2018, March 29). *Richard Spencer: Five things to know.* New York, NY: Author. Retrieved April 13, 2021, from www.adl.org/news/article/richard-spencer-five-things-to-know

Anti-Defamation League. (2020a, April 20). *Extremists involved in nationwide protests against Coronavirus restrictions.* New York, NY: Author. Retrieved April 13, 2021, from www.adl.org/blog/extremists-involved-in-nationwide-protests-against-coronavirus-restrictions

Anti-Defamation League. (2020b). *The militia movement.* New York, NY: Author. Retrieved April 13, 2021, from www.adl.org/resources/backgrounders/the-militia-movement-2020

Baffa, R. C., Vest, N., Chan, W. Y., & Fanlo, A. (2019, August). *Defining and understanding the next generation of Salafi-Jihadis.* Santa Monica, CA: Rand Corporation. Retrieved April 16, 2021, from www.rand.org/content/dam/rand/pubs/perspectives/PE300/PE341/RAND_PE341.pdf

Baisagatova, D. B., Kemelbekov, S. T., Smagulova, D. A., & Kozhamberdiyeva, A. S. (2016). Corrections of concepts "extremism" and "terrorism" in countering the financing of terrorism and extremism. *International Journal of Environmental & Science Education, 11*(13): 5903–5915. Retrieved April 12, 2021, from files.eric.ed.gov/fulltext/EJ1115522.pdf

Banks, D., Hendrix, J., Hickman, M., & Kyckelhahn, T. (2016, October). *National sources of law enforcement employment data.* Washington, DC: Bureau of Justice Statistics. (NCJ 249681). Retrieved April 20, 2021, from www.bjs.gov/content/pub/pdf/nsleed.pdf

Belli, R. (2011). *Where political extremists and greedy criminals meet: A comparative study of financial crimes and criminal networks in the United States.* Unpublished doctoral dissertation. Retrieved April 20, 2021, from www.ojp.gov/pdffiles1/nij/grants/234524.pdf

Brooks, R. E. (2011, February). Improving criminal intelligence sharing: How the criminal intelligence coordinating council supports law enforcement and homeland security. *The Police Chief,* pp. 34–38.

Bunker, R. J., & Flaherty, C. J. (2013). *Body cavity bombers: The new martyrs.* Bloomington, IN: iUniverse LLC.

Burruss, G. W., Giblin, M. J., & Schafer, J. A. (2010, February). Threatened globally, acting locally: Modeling law enforcement homeland security practices. *Justice Quarterly, 27*(1), 77–101.

Byme, J., & Miller, H. I. (2013, July 10). Domestic eco-terrorism has deep pockets. And many enablers. *Forbes* online. Retrieved April 20, 2021, from geneticliteracyproject.org/2013/05/15/viewpoint-domestic-eco-terrorism-has-deep-pockets-and-many-enablers/

Carter, D. L. (2009, May). *Law enforcement intelligence: A guide for state, local, and tribal law enforcement agencies* (2nd ed.). Washington, DC: Office of Community Oriented Policing Services. Retrieved April 20, 2021, from cops.usdoj.gov/RIC/ric.php?page=detail&id=COPS-P064

Cauley, A. (2018, May 1). *USA Freedom Act replaces USA Patriot Act*. Retrieved April 19, 2021, from civil-liberties-ite.blogs .rutgers.edu/author/cauley-alicia/

Chermak, S. M., Freilich, J., Duran, C., & Parkin, W. S. (2013). *An overview of bombing and arson attacks by environmental and animal rights extremists in the United States, 1995–2010*. College Park, MD: START. Retrieved April 16, 2021, from start.umd.edu/sites/default/files/files/publications /START_Bombing And Arson Attacks By Environmental And Animal Rights Extremists_May2013.pdf

Chermak, S. M., Freilich, J. D., & Suttmoeller, M. (2013, December). The organizational dynamics of far-right hate groups in the United States: Comparing violent to non -violent organizations. *Studies in Conflict & Terrorism, 36*: 193–218. doi:10.1080/1057610X.2013.755912

Coats, D. R. (2019, January 29). *Statement for the record: Worldwide threat assessment of the U.S. intelligence community*. Washington, DC: Office of the Director of National Intelligence, Senate Select Committee on Intelligence. Retrieved April 10, 2021, from www.dni.gov /files/ODNI/documents/2019-ATA-SFR---SSCI.pdf

Cybersecurity and Infrastructure Security Agency. (2020). What to do—Bomb threat. Washington, DC: Author. Retrieved April 18, 2021, from www.cisa.gov /what-to-do-bomb-threat

Davis, P. K., Perry, W. L., Brown, R. A., Yeung, D., Roshan, P., & Voorhies, P. (2013) *Using behavioral indicators to help detect potential violence acts: A review of the science base*. Santa Monica, CA: RAND Corporation. Retrieved April 20, 2021, from www.rand.org/content/dam/rand/pubs/research _reports/RR200/RR215/RAND_RR215.pdf

Deloughery, K. (2013, December). Simultaneous attacks by terrorist organisations. *Perspectives on Terrorism, 7*(6): 79–83. Retrieved April 17, 2021, from terrorismanalysts.com /pt/index.php/pot/article/view/312

Ernst, M. (2014, March 20). How local and state cops fit into local counterterrorism. *PoliceOne.com*. Retrieved June 2, 2015, from www.policeone.com/counterterrorism /articles/6994276-How-local-and-state-cops-fit-into -counterterrorism/

Fiala, A. (2018, Spring). Anarchism. In *The Stanford Encyclopedia of Philosophy*, Edward N. Zalta (ed.). Retrieved April 15, 2021, from plato.stanford.edu/cgi-bin /encyclopedia/archinfo.cgi?entry=anarchism

Freilich, J. D., Chermak, S. M., & Simone, J., Jr. (2009). Surveying American state police agencies about terrorism threats, terrorism sources, and terrorism definitions. *Terrorism and Political Violence, 21*(3): 450–475. doi:10.1080/09546550902950324

Gallagher, A., Davey, J., & Hart. M. (2020). *The genesis of a conspiracy theory: Key trends in QAnon activity since 2017*. London, UK: Institute for Strategic Dialogue. Retrieved April 15, 2021, from www.isdglobal.org/wp-content /uploads/2020/07/The-Genesis-of-a-Conspiracy-Theory. pdf

Getlin, J. (2005, August 8). Profiling fears surface in subway. *Los Angeles Times*. Retrieved April 20, 2021, from articles. latimes.com/2005/aug/08/nation/na-subway8

Gill, P., Horgan, J., & Deckert, P. (2014, March). Bombing alone: Tracing the motivations and antecedent behaviors of lone-actor terrorists." *Journal of Forensic Science, 59*(2): 425–435. doi:10.1111/1556-4029.12312

GNET Team. (2020, October 15). *What is QAnon?* London, UK: Global Network on Extremism and Technology. Retrieved April 15, 2021, from gnet-research.org/2020/10/15 /what-is-qanon/

Griffith, D. (2010, September). Global terror, local targets. *Police*, pp. 48–51.

Harrison, S. (2018, Spring). Evolving tech, evolving terror. *New Perspectives in Foreign Policy, 15*: 28–33. Retrieved April 19, 2021, from csis-website-prod.s3.amazonaws .com/s3fs-public/180322_evolving_tech_terror_harrison .pdf?GpUN2x6.58_hIq86bS0INpCOAq4efJ7Y

Henderson, N. J., Ortiz, C. W., Sugie, N. F., & Miller, J. (2008, July). *Policing in Arab-American communities*. Washington, DC: National Institute of Justice. (NCJ 221706)

Horowitz, M. C. (2015). The rise and spread of suicide bombing. *Annual Review of Political Science, 18*: 69–84. Retrieved April 18, 2021, from www.annualreviews.org/doi /pdf/10.1146/annurev-polisci-062813-051049

Institute for Economics & Peace. (2020, November). *Global terrorism index 2020: Measuring the impact of terrorism*. Sydney, Australia. Retrieved April 11, 2021, from www. visionofhumanity.org/wp-content/uploads/2020/11/GTI -2020-web-1.pdf

International Association of Chiefs of Police. (2014). *Using community policing to counter violent extremism: Five key principles for law enforcement*. Washington, DC: Office of Community Oriented Policing Services. Retrieved April 20, 2021, from www.theiacp.org/sites/default/files/all/f-h /Final%20Key%20Principles%20Guide.pdf

Johnson, D. (2018, Spring). Holy hate: The far right's radicalization of religion. *Intelligence Report*. Montgomery, AL: Southern Poverty Law Center. Retrieved April 15, 2021, from www.splcenter.org /fighting-hate/intelligence-report/2018 /holy-hate-far-right%E2%80%99s-radicalization-religion

Jones, S. G. (2020, June 4). *Who are Antifa, and are they a threat?* Washington, DC: Center for Strategic and International Studies. Retrieved April 15, 2021, from www .csis.org/analysis/who-are-antifa-and-are-they-threat

Jones, S. G., Doxsee, C., & Harrington, N. (2020, June). *The escalating terrorism problem in the United States*. Washington, DC: Center for Strategic and International Studies. Retrieved April 16, 2021, from csis-website-prod.s3.amazonaws.com/s3fs-public /publication/200612_Jones_DomesticTerrorism_v6.pdf

Jones, S. G., Doxsee, C., Harrington, N., Hwang, G., & Suber, J. (2020, October). *The war comes home: The evolution of domestic terrorism in the United States*. Washington, DC: Center for Strategic and International Studies. Retrieved April 12, 2021, from csis-website-prod.s3.amazonaws.com/s3fs-public /publication/201021_Jones_War_Comes_Home_v2.pdf

Jones, S. G., Doxsee, C., Hwang, G., & Thompson, J. (2021, April). *The military, police, and the rise of terrorism in* the United States. Washington, DC: Center for Strategic and International Studies. Retrieved April 12, 2021, from csis-website-prod.s3.amazonaws.com/s3fs-public/publication/210412_Jones_Military_Police_Rise_of_Terrorism_United_States_1.pdf?

Kenney, M. (2010, April). Organizational learning and Islamic militancy. *NIJ Journal*, 265, pp. 18–21.

Kephart, J. (2013, April 19). *Update: Most terrorist incidents in the past five years committed by foreign-born individuals.* Washington, DC: Center for Immigration Studies. Retrieved April 20, 2021, from cis.org/kephart/update-most-terrorist-incidents-past-five-years-committed-foreign-born

Kingsbury, N. R., & Grover, J. A. (2017, July 20). *Aviation security: TSA does not have valid evidence supporting most of the revised behavioral indicators used in its behavior detection activities.* Washington, DC: U.S. Government Accountability Office. Retrieved April 20, 2021, from www.gao.gov/assets/gao-17-608r.pdf

Kurzman, C., & Schanzer, D. (2015, June 25). *Law enforcement assessment of the violent extremism threat.* Durham, NC: Triangle Center on Terrorism and Homeland Security. Retrieved April 15, 2021, from sites.duke.edu/tcths/files/2013/06/Kurzman_Schanzer_Law_Enforcement_Assessment_of_the_Violent_Extremist_Threat_final.pdf

LaFree, G. (2012, July). Policing terrorism. *Ideas in American Policing, 15.* Retrieved April 10, 2021, from www.policefoundation.org/wp-content/uploads/2015/06/Ideas_15_LaFree_1.pdf

LaFree G., & Gruenewald, J. (2018). The intersection of homicide, terrorism, and violent extremism. *Homicide Studies, 22*(1): 3–7. Retrieved April 17, 2021, from journals.sagepub.com/doi/pdf/10.1177/1088767917737809

Levs, J., & Vercammen, P. (2015, April 20). Arrests of ISIS supporters in Minnesota shed light on recruiting, U.S. says. *CNN* online. Retrieved April 20, 2021, from www.cnn.com/2015/04/20/us/fbi-terrorism-probe

McGarrity, M. C. (2019, May 8). *Confronting the rise of domestic terrorism in the homeland.* Washington, DC: Federal Bureau of Investigation. Retrieved April 10, 2021, from www.fbi.gov/news/testimony/confronting-the-rise-of-domestic-terrorism-in-the-homeland

Miller, E. (2014). *Patterns of terrorism in the United States, 1970–2013: Final report to the resilient systems division, DHS science and technology directorate.* College Park, MD: START. Retrieved July 1, 2021, from www.dhs.gov/sites/default/files/publications/OPSR_TP_TEVUS_Patterns-of-Terrorism-Attacks-in-US_1970-2013-Report_Oct2014-508_0.pdf

Miller, E. (2019). *Global terrorism in 2018.* College Park, MD: START. Retrieved April 11, 2021, from www.start.umd.edu/sites/default/files/publications/local_attachments/START_GTD_TerrorismIn2018_Oct2018.pdf

National Center for Food Protection and Defense Web site. (n.d.). Retrieved April 20, 2021, from foodprotection.umn.edu/

National Counterterrorism Center. (2015). *Counterterrorism 2015 calendar.* Washington, DC: Author. Retrieved April 19, 2021, from www.hsdl.org/?abstract&did=767348

National Counterterrorism Center. (2020, January). *Domestic terrorism conference report.* Washington, DC: Author. Retrieved April 10, 2021, from www.dni.gov/files/2020-01-02-DT_Conference_Report.pdf

National Fusion Center Association. (2014, July). *2014–2017 National strategy for the national network of fusion centers.* Retrieved April 20, 2021, from info.publicintelligence.net/NationalFusionCenterStrategy-2014-2017.pdf

National Institute for Occupational Safety and Health. (2011, May 12). *Chlorine: Lung damaging agent.* Washington, DC: Author. Retrieved April 18, 2021, from www.cdc.gov/niosh/ershdb/emergencyresponsecard_29750024.html

New York Police Department. (2007). *Radicalization in the West: The homegrown threat.* New York: Author. Retrieved April 20, 2021, from www.nypdshield.org/public/SiteFiles/documents/NYPD_Report-Radicalization_in_the_West.pdf

Office of the Director of National Intelligence. (n.d.). *Bin Laden's bookshelf.* Washington, DC: Author. Retrieved April 17, 2021, from www.dni.gov/index.php/features/bin-laden-s-bookshelf

Overton, I., & Dathan, J. (2017). The global burden of improvised explosive devices. *Improvised Explosive Device (IED) Monitor*: 1–14. Retrieved April 17, 2021, from reliefweb.int/sites/reliefweb.int/files/resources/IED-Monitor-Report-for-web-final.pdf

Pistole, J. S. (2013, November 14). Statement of Administrator John S. Pistole, Transportation Security Administration, U.S. Department of Homeland Security, Before the United States House of Representatives Committee on Homeland Security Subcommittee on Transportation Security. Retrieved April 20, 2021, from www.apfa.org/wp-content/uploads/2013/05/17_3_14_pistole_testimony.pdf

Plame, V. (2014, September 26). Nuclear terrorism: Most immediate and extreme threat to global security. *The Hill* online. Retrieved April 20, 2021, from thehill.com/opinion/op-ed/218959-nuclear-terrorism-most-immediate-and-extreme-threat-to-global-security

Police1 Staff. (2017, February 2). 5 domestic terrorism threats you haven't thought of in a while, but are still here. *Police1.com.* Retrieved April 15, 2021, from www.police1.com/ambush/articles/5-domestic-terrorism-threats-you-havent-thought-of-in-a-while-but-are-still-here-rDq4uhfWVo72qc6l/

Posłuszna, E. (2015). *Environmental and animal rights: Extremism, terrorism, and national security.* Amsterdam, The Netherlands: Elsevier.

Posłuszna, E. (2020, August). A prognostic view on the ideological determinants of violence in the radical ecological movement. *Sustainability, 12*(16): 6536. doi:10.3390/su12166536

Rasmussen, N. J. (2015, February 11). *Countering violent Islamist extremism: The urgent threat of foreign fighters and homegrown terror.* Washington, DC: National Counterterrorism Center. Retrieved April 20, 2021, from www.dni.gov/files/NCTC/documents/news_documents/Countering_Violent_Islamist_Extremism.pdf

Reese, S. (2013, January 8). *Defining homeland security: Analysis and congressional considerations.* Washington, DC: Congressional Research Service. (R42462) Retrieved June 2, 2015, from fas.org/sgp/crs/homesec/R42462.pdf

Romano, D., Rowe, S., & Phelps, R. (2019). Correlates of terror: Trends in types of terrorist groups and fatalities inflicted. *Cogent Social Sciences, 5*(1). doi:10.1080/23311886.2019.1584957

Sacco, L. N. (2021, January 13). *Domestic terrorism and the attack on the U.S. Capitol.* Washington, DC: Congressional Research Service. Retrieved April 19, 2021, from fas.org/sgp/crs/terror/IN11573.pdf

Schott, J. (2012, November 17). *The differences between the Taliban and al-Qaeda.* Retrieved April 11, 2021, from www.e-ir.info/pdf/29963

Schuurman, B., Bakker, E., Gill, P., & Bouhana N. (2018, July). Lone actor terrorist attack planning and preparation: A data-driven analysis. *Journal of Forensic Science, 63*(4): 1191–1200. doi:10.1111/1556-4029.13676

Smith, B. (2008, July). A look at terrorist behavior: How they prepare, where they strike. *NIJ Journal,* 260, pp. 2–7.

Southern Poverty Law Center. (n.d.). *New Black Panther Party.* Montgomery, AL: Author. Retrieved April 20, 2021, from www.splcenter.org/get-informed/intelligence-files/groups/new-black-panther-party

Southern Poverty Law Center. (n.d.). *Oath Keepers.* Montgomery, AL: Author. Retrieved April 14, 2021, from www.splcenter.org/fighting-hate/extremist-files/group/oath-keepers

Southern Poverty Law Center. (n.d.). *Proud Boys.* Montgomery, AL: Author. Retrieved April 14, 2021, from www.splcenter.org/fighting-hate/extremist-files/group/proud-boys

Straub, F. (2020, March 3). *The importance of community policing in preventing terrorism.* Washington, DC: National Institute of Justice. Retrieved April 20, 2021, from nij.ojp.gov/topics/articles/importance-community-policing-preventing-terrorism

Sugara, R. (2018, May 22). How people become suicide bombers: the six steps to terrorism. *The Conversation.* Retrieved April 18, 2021, from theconversation.com/how-people-become-suicide-bombers-the-six-steps-to-terrorism-96944

Sullivan, B.A., Freilich, J. D., & Chermak, S. M. (2014). *Financial crime and material support schemes linked to al-Qa'ida and affiliated movements (AQAM) in the United States, 1990 to June 2014.* College Park, MD: START. Retrieved April 19, 2021, from www.dhs.gov/sites/default/files/publications/OPSR_TP_Financial-Crime-Material-Support-Schemes-Linked-AQAM-US-1990-June2014_Nov2014-508.pdf

Sun, I. Y., & Wu, Y. (2015). Arab Americans' confidence in police. *Crime & Delinquency, 61*(4): 483–508. doi:10.1177/0011128711420103

Sun, I. Y., Wu, Y., & Poteyeva, M. (2011). Arab Americans' opinion on counterterrorism measures: The impact of race, ethnicity, and religion. *Studies in Conflict & Terrorism, 34*(7): 540–555. doi:10.1080/1057610X.2011.578550

United Nations Office on Drugs and Crime. (2012). *The use of the Internet for terrorist purposes.* New York, NY: Author. Retrieved April 18, 2021, from www.unodc.org/documents/frontpage/Use_of_Internet_for_Terrorist_Purposes.pdf

U.S. Attorney's Office. (2021, February 26). *Individuals associated with Proud Boys charged with conspiring to obstruct an official proceeding and interfering with law enforcement, and other charges related to the Jan. 6 riots.* Washington, DC: Author. Retrieved April 15, 2021, from www.justice.gov/usao-dc/pr/individuals-associated-proud-boys-charged-conspiring-obstruct-official-proceeding-and

U.S. Attorney's Office, Northern District of Illinois. (2016, February 29). *Animal rights activist sentenced to three years in prison for vandalizing a farm and releasing 2,000 mink from their cages.* Chicago, IL: Author. Retrieved April 16, 2021, from www.justice.gov/usao-ndil/pr/animal-rights-activist-sentenced-three-years-prison-vandalizing-farm-and-releasing-2000

U.S. Attorney's Office, Southern District of New York. (2021, January 19). *U.S. Army soldier arrested for attempting to assist ISIS to conduct deadly ambush on U.S. troops.* New York, NY: Author. Retrieved April 16, 2021, from www.justice.gov/usao-sdny/pr/us-army-soldier-arrested-attempting-assist-isis-conduct-deadly-ambush-us-troops

U.S. Bureau of Labor Statistics. (2020, May). *Occupational employment and wage statistics.* Washington, DC: Author. Retrieved April 20, 2021, from www.bls.gov/oes/current/oes333051.htm#nat

U.S. Department of Homeland Security. (n.d.). *Fusion centers.* Washington, DC: Author. Retrieved April 20, 2021, from www.dhs.gov/fusion-centers

U.S. Department of Homeland Security. (2013). *National infrastructure protection plan 2013: Partnering for critical infrastructure security and resilience.* Washington, DC: Author. Retrieved April 20, 2021, from www.cisa.gov/national-infrastructure-protection-plan

U.S. Department of Homeland Security. (2019a). *The DHS strategic plan: Fiscal years 2020–2024.* Washington, DC: Author. Retrieved April 20, 2021, from www.dhs.gov/strategic-planning

U.S. Department of Homeland Security. (2019b). *Mission.* Washington, DC: Author. Retrieved July 2, 2021, from www.dhs.gov/mission

U.S. Department of Homeland Security. (2019c, September). *Strategic framework for countering terrorism and targeted violence.* Washington, DC: Author. Retrieved April 10, 2021, from www.dhs.gov/sites/default/files/publications/19_0920_plcy_strategic-framework-countering-terrorism-targeted-violence.pdf

U.S. Department of Homeland Security. (2020, October). *Homeland threat assessment 2020.* Washington, DC: Author. Retrieved April 11, 2021, from www.dhs.gov/sites/default/files/publications/2020_10_06_homeland-threat-assessment.pdf

U.S. Department of Homeland Security. (2021, January 27). *National terrorism advisory system bulletin.* Washington, DC: Author. Retrieved April 12, 2021, from www.dhs.gov/sites/default/files/ntas/alerts/21_0127_ntas-bulletin.pdf

U.S. Department of Justice. (2020a, June 15). *Homeland Security.* Washington, DC: Author. Retrieved April 10, 2021, from www.justice.gov/file/1354566

U.S. Department of Justice. (2020b, December 16). *Kenyan national indicted for conspiring to hijack aircraft on behalf of al Qaeda-affiliated terrorist organization Al Shabaab.* Washington, DC: Author. Retrieved April 12, 2021, from www.justice.gov/opa/pr/kenyan-national-indicted -conspiring-hijack-aircraft-behalf-al-qaeda-affiliated -terrorist

U.S. Department of State. (2019). *Country reports on terrorism 2019.* Washington, DC: Author. Retrieved April 11, 2021, from www.state.gov/wp-content/uploads/2020/06 /Country-Reports-on-Terrorism-2019-2.pdf

Vanderheyden, N., Verhoeven, E., Vermeulen, S., & Bekaert, B. (2020, July). Survival of forensic trace evidence on improvised explosive devices: Perspectives on individualization. *Scientific Reports, 10*(12813). doi:10.1038 /s41598-020-69385-1

White, J. R. (2012). *Terrorism and homeland security*, 7th ed. Belmont, CA: Wadsworth Publishing Company.

Windisch, S., Ligon, G. S., & Simi, P. (2017). Organizational [dis] trust: Comparing disengagement among former left -wing and right-wing violent extremists. *Studies in Conflict & Terrorism.* doi:10.1080/1057610X.2017.1404000

Cases Cited

Hamdi v. Rumsfeld, 542 U.S. 507 (2004).

Rasul v. Bush, 542 U.S. 466 (2004).

Useful Resources

- Centers for Disease Control and Prevention: www .cdc.gov

- Director of National Intelligence: www.dni.gov

- Federal Bureau of Investigation: www.fbi.gov

- Federal Emergency Management Agency: www.fema .gov

- Global Terrorism Database: www.start.umd.edu/gtd

- National Counterterrorism Center: www.nctc.gov

- U.S. Department of Homeland Security: www.ready.gov

Chapter 21
Preparing for and Presenting Cases in Court

Chapter Outline

The Final Report

The Role of the Prosecutor

Preparing a Case for Prosecution

The Trial

Final Lessons from a Seasoned Investigator's Experience

Learning Objectives

LO1   Identify the most important rule to eradicate fear of testifying in court.

LO2   List the items to include in the final report.

LO3   Explain the relative importance of the prosecutor in the court system.

LO4   Understand the reasons why some cases are not prosecuted.

LO5   Outline the necessary steps to take to prepare a case for court.

LO6   Summarize what to concentrate on when reviewing a case.

LO7   Discuss what occurs during the pretrial conference.

LO8   Diagram the usual sequence of a criminal trial.

LO9   Explain what the "win" is for an investigator who testifies in court.

LO010   Describe the kinds of statements that are inadmissible in court.

LO011   List the guidelines for effective testimony.

LO012   Determine when to use notes while testifying.

LO013   Recognize what nonverbal elements can influence courtroom testimony positively and negatively.

LO014   Know the defense attorney tactics to anticipate during cross-examination.

LO015   Identify the ways to avoid objections to your testimony.

Introduction

On Monday, March 31, 2014, five veteran police officers took the witness stand, one by one, at a hearing in the Skokie, Illinois, courthouse to give testimony regarding the seizure of evidence in a drug case. Everything seemed routine, the officers providing their sworn accounts of how they had legally stopped, searched, and arrested the defendant. But the inquiry made an abrupt and unanticipated turn when the defense attorney played video captured unintentionally by one of the officer's squad cameras, evidence that clearly contradicted the testimony each of the five officers had just given.

Cook County Circuit Judge Catherine Haberkorn, furious at this turn of events, suppressed the officers' search and arrest, prosecutors immediately dismissed the felony charges, and all five officers were placed on administrative duty, stripped of their police powers, pending an internal investigation (Schmadeke, 2014). In a hearing transcript, Judge Haberkorn was quoted as saying, "Obviously, this is very outrageous conduct. All officers lied on the stand today.... All their testimony was a lie. So there's strong evidence it was conspiracy to lie in this case, for everyone to come up with the same lie.... Many, many, many, many times they all lied."

As media accounts bear out, law enforcement officers across the country have faced their own trials after being found to have lied under oath. For example, on June 27, 2018, a former NYPD detective pleaded guilty to perjury and falsifying facts to cover up a warrantless search (Goldstein, 2018). On October 31, 2019, a Baltimore police officer was convicted of perjury for lying about a criminal case (Prudente, 2019). And these incidents are not isolated cases.

In the early 1990s, the Mollen Commission was convened to investigate allegations of police corruption in the New York Police Department. In the initial report, the Commission noted that police perjury "is so common in certain precincts that it has spawned its own word: 'testilying.' A large part of the problem is that once officers falsify the basis for an arrest, search, or other action in a Department record . . . . [T]o avoid Departmental or criminal charges, they must stick to their story even under oath when swearing to a criminal complaint or giving testimony before a trial jury" (1994, pp. 36–37). This spotlight on testilying led many departments across the country to re-examine their policies pertaining to ethical conduct, including false statements, and prompted some administrators, such as the Boston Police Commissioner, to make lying by an officer a fireable offense. False statements may also be put into written reports; some officers refer to these as acts of "creative writing" (Lyons, 2013).

Sometimes officers believe that the ends justify the means, and that getting a drug offender—the defendant in the Skokie case happened to have several prior drug-related arrests and a drug conviction—or any other criminal off the streets is worth stretching the truth. However, when police perjure themselves, they commit more than a miscarriage of justice; their actions erode public trust and confidence in the entire criminal justice system. As one public defender puts it, "The dangerous part of it is an innocent person could go to jail. What we're trying to find is the truth. It's what the whole system is supposed to be about" (Schmadeke, 2014).

After all the leads in a case have been exhausted, all the witnesses interviewed, all the suspects interrogated, and all the evidence properly collected and stored, if the investigation has been successful, the case will be ready for prosecution. Before this can occur, however, a final report on the case must be written, establishing the elements of the crime and proving the corpus delicti. Officers and prosecutors must ensure that the evidence has not been contaminated, that the witnesses have not been corrupted, and that the suspect's constitutional rights have not been violated. With these assurances in place, the case can proceed to court, where the investigator's testimony is almost always critical to a successful outcome. Even the most experienced investigator may worry about having to testify, perhaps fearing the responsibility.

The most important rule to eradicate fear of testifying in court is to always tell the truth, beginning with the final report.

The Final Report

Recall from Chapter 3 the importance of well-written reports and the skills required to craft them: "Report writing skills are just as important for career survival as any other police skill, such as defensive tactics, firearms handling, and knowledge of statutes and codes" (Bertomen, 2019). The most skillful investigation may fail to bring "the bad guy" to justice if the final report is weak, because the effectiveness of that report is often the determining factor in whether a case is prosecuted. A final report forms the basis for a criminal trial and must be able to withstand heavy scrutiny by prosecutors, defense attorneys, civil attorneys, judges, citizens, and the media if it is to serve the interest of justice (Savelli, 2018). The recommendations and guidelines presented in Chapter 3 apply to the final report as well. Therefore, you might review that chapter.

The final report presents the facts of the case, a criminal history of the person charged, the types of evidence available, the names of those who can support such evidence by testimony in court, the names of people the prosecutor can talk to for further information, and a chronological account of the crime and subsequent investigation.

The final report contains (1) the complaint; (2) the preliminary investigation report; (3) all follow-up, supplemental, and progress reports; (4) statements, admissions, and confessions; (5) laboratory and other professional reports (e.g., autopsy); (6) photographs, sketches, and drawings; and (7) a summary of all exculpatory evidence. The quality of the content and writing of the report influences its credibility.

Prepare the report after a careful review of all information. Organize the facts logically.

The Complaint

Include a copy of the original complaint. This should include the date and time of the complaint, location of the incident, brief details, times when officers were dispatched and when they arrived on scene, and the names of the officers assigned to the initial call.

The Preliminary Investigation Report

The report of the officer's initial investigation at the crime scene provides essential information about the time of arrival, lighting and weather conditions, observations at the scene, and immediate and subsequent actions taken by officers responding to the call.

Follow-Up Reports

Assemble each contact and follow-up report in chronological order, presenting the sequence of the investigation and the pattern used to follow leads. These reports contain the essential information gathered in proving the elements of the crime and in linking the crime to the suspect. The reports can be in the form of progress notes.

Statements, Admissions, and Confessions

Include the statements of all witnesses interviewed during the investigation, as discussed in Chapter 6. If written statements were not obtained, report the results of oral interviews with witnesses. Assemble all statements, admissions, or confessions by suspects in a separate part of the report. Include the reports of all polygraphs or other examinations used to determine the truth of statements, admissions, or confessions.

Laboratory and Other Professional Reports

Assemble laboratory results, including those from a medical examination or autopsy, in one segment of the final report. Make recommendations regarding how these results relate to other areas of the report.

Photographs, Sketches, and Drawings

Include photographs, sketches, and drawings of the crime scene to show conditions when officers arrived and the available evidence, as discussed in Chapter 2.

Summary of Exculpatory Evidence

Include a summary of all exculpatory evidence developed during the investigation. Statements of witnesses who claim the suspect was elsewhere at the time of the crime are sometimes proved false, but the prosecution must consider such statements and develop a defense. If information exists that the suspect committed the crime but did so in self-defense or accidentally, state this in the report. Include all recognizable weaknesses in proving the corpus delicti or the offender's identity.

Write the report clearly and accurately, following the guidelines presented in Chapter 3. The quality of the final report influences its credibility. Arrange the material in a logical sequence and a convenient format. If the report is not submitted electronically, use a binder or loose-leaf notebook because it allows the various units of information to be separated, with a labeled, tabbed divider for each unit. For a digital submission, be sure all sections are labeled and easy to find and that the report is presented in a clear and concise manner. Many agencies prefer electronic report submission.

Although the prosecutor may have been consulted at various stages of the investigation, at this point the prosecutor might offer a plea bargain to the defendant based on the strength of the case and of the final report. It has been said that some cases are, in effect, trial by report.

The Role of the Prosecutor

The prosecutor is the gatekeeper of the court system, determining which cases are prosecuted and which are not: "The prosecutor is of critical importance because of the office's central position in the criminal justice system. Whereas police, defense attorneys, judges, and probation officers specialize in specific phases of the criminal justice process, the duties of the prosecutor bridge all of these areas. This means that on a daily basis, the prosecutor is the only official who works with all actors of the criminal justice system" (Neubauer & Fradella, 2014, p. 150). Indeed, as Justice Robert Jackson has asserted, "The prosecutor has more control over life, liberty, and reputation than any other person in America" (1940, p. 18).

> **LO3** Explain the relative importance of the prosecutor in the court system.
>
> The prosecutor is the most powerful official in the court system.

At the county level, the prosecutor, or district attorney (DA), is the chief law enforcement official. DAs may be appointed or elected and are responsible for prosecuting felonies and serious misdemeanors in the trial courts of general jurisdiction. At the federal level, the prosecutor is called the U.S. attorney, a position appointed by the president, approved by Congress, and confirmed by the Senate. Although prosecutors' offices at the local level generally do not have in-house investigators, federal prosecutors' offices commonly have staff investigators and are in frequent contact with other federal investigative agencies, such as the Federal Bureau of Investigation (FBI); Drug Enforcement Administration (DEA); Bureau of Alcohol, Tobacco, Firearms, and Explosives (ATF); and U.S. Secret Service. Also, unlike local prosecutors, federal prosecutors are typically those who initiate a federal criminal investigation, whereas by the time a case comes to a local prosecutor or DA, the investigation has already been completed by local law enforcement.

The ability to wield broad discretion is a key characteristic of prosecutors in our justice system, and the various actors in a trial often have conflicting views about how this discretion should be used. The police advocate for the maximum penalty possible for criminals; defense attorneys aim for leniency, trying to get the lowest sentence for their client or, better yet, an acquittal; and the judge is motivated to keep case moving in an effort to clear the docket (Neubauer & Fradella, 2014). In addition, although the prosecutor tries cases in the court, the office is part of the executive branch of government, independent from the judiciary. This independence is crucial for the adversary system to function because prosecutors often challenge judicial decisions. The adversary system is discussed later in the chapter.

Tensions and conflicts sometimes exist between investigators and prosecutors. An investigator may feel a case is strong and the suspect should be brought to trial, but the prosecutor may disagree. In these cases, officers must remain cognizant of the varying standards of proof at work when considering legal arrests and prosecutable offenses. Crime-charging gaps may occur when the prosecutor thinks a reduced charge is more likely to obtain a conviction than is the charge the defendant was originally arrested on. Although officers can arrest based on probable cause, prosecutors are held to a much higher standard—proof *beyond a reasonable doubt*—in the courtroom. If the prosecutor feels that this higher burden of proof cannot be met, criminal proceedings cannot ethically be commenced. Consequently, charges may be reduced or dismissed because the evidence is insufficient to establish the necessary guilt at a trial. However, this burden of proof is often misunderstood. Many cases are won on circumstantial evidence alone. There is a significant difference between *reasonable doubt* and *reason to doubt*. Many defense lawyers exploit that reason to doubt, which is very easy to do in most cases.

One of the facets of prosecution that frustrates law enforcement is the fact that the chief prosecutor holds a political position, whether appointed or elected, and is expected to have a successful track record of charged cases that win. Because of this, prosecutors can be very selective and conservative on cases they decide to pursue, not wanting to take chances on cases that they are not certain can be won. Regardless of the politics, the prosecutor is an investigator's legal adviser throughout the process—during the investigation, the pretrial conference, and the court presentation. It is ultimately the prosecutor's decision. Investigators should follow prosecutors' advice even if they disagree, for it is best to work out the issues of cases together. Investigators should listen to and learn from prosecutors. There may be valid reasons for not prosecuting a case.

Myth A plea bargain means the law enforcement investigation failed to provide a strong enough case for trial.

Fact Not necessarily. For many reasons, most criminal cases are resolved without a trial. An excellent investigation and report may cause the defendant to plead guilty, the defendant may desire to plead guilty without going through a trial, or the plea-bargaining process may bring about a satisfactory resolution.

LO4 Understand the reasons why some cases are not prosecuted.

Cases are not prosecuted if

- The complaint is invalid
- The prosecutor declines after reviewing the case
- The complainant refuses to prosecute
- The offender dies
- No evidence or leads exist

Administrative policy sometimes closes cases to further investigation. Specific criteria are established for these decisions. The caseload of investigative personnel

has grown so large that cases with little probability of successful prosecution must be closed as a matter of maintaining priorities.

Many police departments have incorporated such criteria into their crime report forms. If enough criteria are met, the department closes the case to further investigation and notifies the complainant. This often happens when complainants file reports only because their insurance companies require them to report the loss to police. The loss may have occurred many days before the report, or there may be no leads. In some cases, there are insufficient facts to support the complaint, but the victim insists on filing a complaint and has the right to do so.

In other cases, the report is valid but investigation reveals that witnesses have left the area or that no physical evidence remains at the crime scene. Without physical evidence, witnesses, identifiable leads, or information to follow up, it is unwise to pursue the case when more pressing cases abound. Such a case is placed in an inactive file and is reopened only if time is available or new information is received. Occasionally, such cases are cleared by the admission or confession of a suspect arrested for another crime. Cases are **exceptionally cleared** when circumstances outside the investigation result in no charges being filed—for example, the suspect dies.

A motion is a request to the court for a decision on a specific legal issue. A motion can lead to a hearing, an appearance before the court to resolve the issue raised in the motion. Hearings are typically less formal and shorter than a full trial. Motions can be filed before, during, or after trial, but one type of pretrial motion investigators should be aware of is the *motion to suppress*. If the defense files such a motion, claiming that evidence was illegally obtained or a confession unconstitutionally extracted, and an evidentiary hearing is granted by the court, the possibility exists for the case to fold before ever going to trial, effectively resulting in nonprosecution. If the court ruling is favorable to the defense and the evidence is excluded from trial, the prosecution has the option to appeal the court's decision, generally the only point in the judicial process when such an appeal by the state is allowed.

If no motions have been submitted to the court and the prosecutor decides to bring the case to trial, the investigator must thoroughly prepare for testifying in court.

Preparing a Case for Prosecution

Once the decision is made to prosecute a case, more than "probable cause" is required. The prosecution must prove the case *beyond a reasonable doubt*—the degree of proof necessary to obtain a conviction. To do so, the prosecution must know what evidence it can introduce, what witnesses will testify, the strengths and weaknesses of the case, and the type of testimony police investigators can supply.

LO5 Outline the necessary steps to take to prepare a case for court.

To prepare a case for court

- Review and evaluate all evidence, including exculpatory, and the chain of custody.
- Review all reports on the case, including transcripts of any depositions you have given.
- Prepare witnesses.
- Hold a pretrial conference with the prosecutor.

Review and Evaluate Evidence

Each crime consists of one or more elements that must be proven. The statutes and ordinances of the particular jurisdiction define these elements.

Review physical evidence to ensure that it has been properly gathered, identified, transported, and safeguarded between the time it was obtained and the time of the trial. Make sure the evidence is available for the

trial and is taken to the courtroom and turned over to the prosecuting attorney. Arrange for trained laboratory technicians' testimony if necessary. As discussed in detail in Chapter 5, select evidence that is material, relevant, and competent and that helps establish the corpus delicti: what happened and who is responsible. How evidence is moved along in the system is shown in Figure 21.1.

LO6 Summarize what to concentrate on when reviewing a case.

Concentrate on proving the elements of the crime and establishing the offender's identity.

The pretrial **discovery process** requires the prosecution and defense to disclose to each other certain evidence they intend to use at trial, thus avoiding surprises. There is no general constitutional right to discovery in criminal trials (*Weatherford v. Bursey,* 1977). Courts have expressed concern that requiring too much prosecutorial disclosure might put the prosecution at a disadvantage or that witnesses for the defense might be intimidated. The type of information that is discoverable varies greatly from state to state, with some states allowing only limited discovery, others taking a middle ground, and yet others adopting liberal discovery rules.

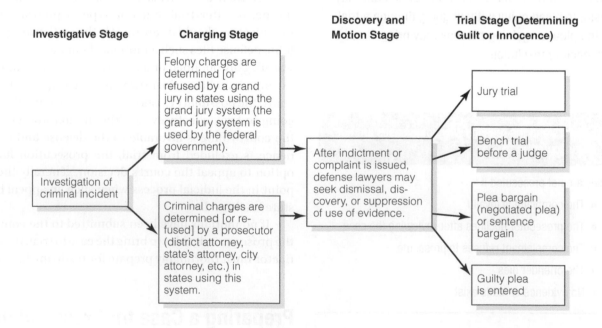

Figure 21.1

The use of evidence in the stages of the criminal justice process.

Source: From Gardner, T. J., & Anderson, T. M. (2010). *Criminal evidence: Principles and cases,* 7th ed. Belmont, CA: Wadsworth Publishing Company, a part of Cengage Learning, Inc.

The landmark Supreme Court case in the discovery process is *Brady v. Maryland* (1963), in which the Court held, "The suppression by the prosecution of evidence favorable to the accused upon request violates due process where the evidence is material either to guilt or to punishment, irrespective of the good faith or bad faith of the prosecution." This is known as the **Brady rule**—exculpatory evidence, that is, evidence that tends to show innocence of the accused, must be disclosed by the prosecution to the defense.

Investigators who are aware of such evidence are obligated to bring it to the prosecutor's attention. When officers intentionally withhold exculpatory material from the prosecution, they leave themselves open to personal liability for violating a defendant's due process rights. In most states, "missing" evidence or failure to turn over evidence violates the Brady rule only if it can be shown it was done in bad faith; that is, it was known the evidence was exculpatory and was intentionally withheld. The defense must prove a "conscious effort" to suppress exculpatory evidence.

The Supreme Court has held that due process requires the government to disclose information regarding witness credibility before trial, extending *Brady* to impeachment material in *Giglio v. United States* (1972). Defense attorneys will try to **impeach** the testimony of prosecution witnesses; that is, they will try to discredit the testimony, to challenge the truth or accuracy of what a prosecution witness testified to under direct examination. This applies to police officers and investigators who testify. Recall from the discussion in Chapter 3 that officers who knowingly report false information or selectively exclude from their reports any information favorable to the defendant may find themselves caught in a "Brady/Giglio" situation where their testimony is considered unreliable or impeachable by the court.

In 1996 the U.S. Department of Justice (DOJ) issued a policy for all DOJ investigative agencies obligating each of their employees to inform prosecutors of potential impeachment material as early as possible before providing a sworn statement or testimony in any criminal investigation. The DOJ guidelines suggest that the following must be disclosed: substantiated allegations; pending investigations or allegations; and criminal charges, past or pending.

There are limits on what the defense is entitled to learn about law enforcement witnesses. In *Pennsylvania v. Ritchie* (1987), the Supreme Court held, "Evidence is material only if there is a reasonable probability that had the evidence been disclosed to the defense, the result of the proceeding would have been different. . . . The government has the obligation to turn over evidence in its possession that is both favorable to the accused and *material* to guilt or punishment." The issue of credibility also applies to witnesses other than those of law enforcement who may testify for the prosecution.

Review and evaluate witnesses' statements for credibility. If a witness claims to have seen a specific act, determine whether the light was sufficient and whether the witness has good eyesight and was in a position to see the act clearly. Also assess the witness's relationship to the suspect and the victim.

Establish the suspect's identity by eyewitness testimony, transfer evidence, and supporting evidence such as motive, prior knowledge, opportunity, and known modus operandi.

Video recordings are being used increasingly in court, especially in child abuse and sex crime cases. Body worn police cameras, wireless doorbell videos, and cell phone data are all sources of information being seen in the courtroom for all types of crimes. However, a fair trial requires the ability of opposing counsel to cross-examine a witness, and videotaped testimony impedes that ability. Expert witnesses with heavy time commitments may be allowed to testify via prerecorded video or by remote video chat, saving the time and expense of a trip to the city where the trial is taking place, but this allowance varies by state and may require a judge to waive a rule that testimony must be done in person. Video-recorded testimony is also sometimes allowed by witnesses who are severely injured and cannot appear in court. In addition, video recordings of suspects' confessions and of crime scenes are invaluable.

Reviewing every aspect of the case before entering the courtroom is excellent preparation for testifying. Do not memorize answers to imagined questions, but be prepared.

Depositions. In many states, officers must provide a deposition before trial as part of the discovery. A **deposition** is an oral statement given under oath that is recorded and transcribed word-for-word. The primary purpose of a deposition is to allow discovery of the facts and evidence of a case, but it also serves to memorialize the testimony of the witness and may be used in place of live courtroom testimony (Penrod, 2015).

Testifying at a "depo" can be particularly stressful for the unprepared officer and, consequently, quite damaging to the prosecution. Therefore, preparing for a deposition must be taken seriously; what you say at a depo is as crucial as what you say in a court trial. As one lawyer and former military police officer who has been through the procedure more than 150 times stresses: "Being deposed is not for the faint-of-heart . . . . [A] deposition can cost you your case as a plaintiff or defendant and cost you your job and career as an expert witness. Even as 'just' a witness, a deposition can set you up for a perjury charge" (Lewis, 2019).

The deposition is a fact-finding mission, but some have characterized it as more of a "fishing expedition," as the other side tries to get any information they can to discredit or use against you later. The defense counsel will likely dig deep into your professional background and work history, including formal education and law enforcement training, and may venture into your personal life. They will ask detailed questions about your observations, thoughts, and actions before, during, and after the incident in question. They will likely ask you to describe with great specificity the threat a suspect posed to you and others during the incident and why you believe your response to that threat was reasonable. It is also prudent to refamiliarize yourself with all departmental policies that pertain to the incident as well as the relevant key case law so that you are able to articulate how your actions comported with both (Williams, 2013.

Keep in mind that depositions may occur months or years after an event, so preparation to recall the details is crucial: "Those who fail to ready themselves rarely do well, and sometimes literally lose what was a winnable case for themselves and their agencies by giving terrible deposition testimony" (Williams, 2013, p. 2). Officers should also know that a deposition can take an hour or two, or may last several days.

Review Reports

Review written reports of everything done during the investigation. This includes the preliminary report, memorandums, summary reports, progress reports, evidence records and receipts, photographs and sketches, medical examiner's reports, emergency squad records, laboratory test reports on evidence, statements of witnesses (positive and negative), and any other reports on actions taken during the investigation. This also includes the transcript of your own deposition. It is not uncommon for a year or more to pass between the time you give a deposition and the time you are called as a witness during a criminal trial, and the defense attorney will be waiting for your testimony to contradict, even slightly, any statements you made in your depo.

Finally, although it should not happen at this stage, if you find any errors in your report during your review, address them immediately and write a supplemental report explaining how you discovered the error and what the correction should be. While it can be stressful and embarrassing to admit that an error slipped through unnoticed for so long, it is far preferable and less damaging to deal with it before trial.

Prepare Witnesses

Reinterview witnesses to refresh their memories. Read their previous statements to them and ask if this is the evidence they will present in court. Such a review also helps allay any fears witnesses have about testifying. Describe trial procedures to witnesses so they understand what will occur. Explain that they can testify only to facts from their own personal knowledge or from common knowledge. Emphasize that they must tell the truth and present the facts as they know them. Explain the importance of remaining calm; having a neat, clean appearance; and remaining impartial.

By experience, police officers know of the many delays in court proceedings and of the waits in the courtroom or in the hall outside before they can testify. This should also be explained to witnesses who may be testifying for the first time so they can make flexible arrangements for the day. In addition, complainants should be prepared for the possible delays and continuances that may be part of the defense's strategy to wear them down so they will drop the charges.

Pretrial Conference

Before testifying in court and after you have made the final case preparation, arrange for a pretrial conference with the prosecuting attorney. Organize the facts and evidence and prepare a summary of the investigation. Include in this summary the focal points and main issues of the case, an envelope containing copies of all reports, and all other relevant documents.

LO7 Discuss what occurs during the pretrial conference.

At the pretrial conference with the prosecutor

- Review all the evidence.
- Discuss the strengths and weaknesses of the case.
- Discuss the probable line of questioning by the prosecutor and the defense.

Discuss complicated or detailed information fully to avoid misunderstanding. Discuss any legal questions concerning admissibility of evidence or testimony. The prosecutor may be able to offer insights into the style of the defense attorney as well as the judge hearing the case.

Sometimes witnesses are included in the pretrial conference. If so, listen carefully to what each witness says to the prosecuting attorney and to what the prosecuting attorney says in response. During the trial, the judge may exclude all witnesses from the courtroom except the person testifying, a practice called **sequestering**. Therefore, you may have no opportunity to hear the testimony of other witnesses or the approach used by the prosecuting attorney.

It is also a good idea to review the case with other officers who are going to testify. You may not hear their actual testimony, and it will help you if you know in advance what they are going to say.

Final Preparations

Shortly before the trial, again review your notes and your final report. Take with you only those notes you want to use in testifying. Be certain the physical evidence is being taken to the courtroom and will be available for the prosecuting attorney when needed. Also make sure that laboratory technicians are available to appear when necessary. Find out which courtroom you will be testifying in and look it over before the trial. If you are asked to bring physical evidence with you to the trial, use an appropriate container to prevent passersby from seeing it.

Know What Is Expected and the Rules of the Court.
When an officer receives a **subpoena**, an order to appear before the court, it may not indicate what kind of hearing it is. It might be a grand jury or a preliminary hearing or a criminal trial. The rules of evidence are different, as is the burden of proof required. If the subpoena does not specify the type of hearing, call the prosecutor or the attorney who sent the subpoena to determine the nature of the hearing.

The subpoena will also usually indicate whether the officer is to make a personal appearance or be on call, meaning the officer need not appear personally unless called by the prosecution. On-call officers should provide the prosecutor or county clerk with a phone number where they can be reached and should be available to receive the call and respond within a relatively short time.

Witnesses usually are excluded from the courtroom during a trial to prevent one witness from hearing

Victims and witnesses may have the opportunity to speak to the court during the sentencing phase of a trial, should a conviction occur. Statements made during this stage are often emotionally charged and intended to provide the court with insight about the impact of the crime on the victim(s) or witness(es). Preparation is also important in making the most of these "statement of opinion" opportunities.

Brendan Costin, shown here speaking at the sentencing trial of Thomas Junta, the man found guilty of beating Brendan's father to death at the boy's hockey practice, is noticeably choked up as he states, "I can still remember being hysterical, trying to wake him up as the blood streamed down his face. Rushed to the hospital in the ambulance, my father had stopped breathing and had no pulse and his heart stopped beating. After two days in the hospital I realized I had just witnessed my dad literally getting beaten to death."

The 6-foot-1, 270-pound Junta was convicted of involuntary manslaughter for beating 160-pound Michael Costin to death at a Reading, Massachusetts, ice rink in 2000, after Junta got angry over rough play on the ice. Junta testified that he struck Costin only in self-defense. Others said Junta was red-faced with rage. After hearing both sides, the judge determined there were aggravating circumstances surrounding Costin's death, including the fact that the beating took place in front of children.
Jim Bourg/Reuters/Corbis

another witness's testimony. This is known as the **rule on witnesses** or **witness sequestration rule**. Find out before going into the courtroom whether witnesses have been excluded. If they have and an investigator goes into the courtroom and sits, the investigator may be severely reprimanded or, worse, be the cause for a mistrial.

Be familiar with any pretrial rulings a judge has issued. In some instances, a judge may have issued a **motion in limine**, a motion requesting the judge to issue a protective order against prejudicial questions or statements. For example, a defense attorney may ask a judge to restrict any reference to his client's criminal record during the trial. An investigator who is unaware of this motion and violates it may cause the judge to order a mistrial.

Dress Appropriately. Most police departments have regulations regarding attire when officers appear in court. Some departments specify that officers should appear in uniform. If you wear street clothes, dress conservatively. Avoid bright colors and large plaids. Do not overdo on accessories, and avoid bizarre haircuts. Do not wear dark or deeply tinted glasses. Your personal appearance reflects your attitude and your professionalism and will have a definite effect on the jury.

Be on Time. If you are delayed for any reason, phone the prosecutor or the court clerk, explain the reason, and give an approximate time when you can be expected to appear.

The Trial

Trials occur within a construct called the **adversary system**, which establishes clearly defined roles for both the prosecution and the defense and sets the judge as the neutral party. This has important implications for the investigator, who is on the "side" of the prosecutor in the proceeding, as will be discussed shortly. The main participants in a trial are the judge, jury, attorneys, defendant, and witnesses (Figure 21.2).

The *judge,* or *magistrate,* presides over the trial; determines whether a witness is qualified and competent; addresses questions of law, including motions, objections, and procedures; rules on the admissibility of evidence; keeps order; interprets the law for the jurors; and passes sentence if the defendant is found guilty.

The *jurors* hear and evaluate the testimony of all witnesses. Called *fact finders,* jurors consider many factors other than the words spoken. The attitude and behavior of witnesses, suspects, and attorneys are constantly under the jury's scrutiny. Jurors notice how witnesses respond to questions and their attitudes toward the prosecution and the defense. Jurors reach their verdict based on what they see, hear, and feel during the trial. Typical jurors will have had limited or no experience with the criminal justice system outside of what they have read in the newspaper and seen on television.

Legal counsel presents the prosecution and defense evidence before the court and jury. Lawyers act as checks against each other and present the case as required by court procedure and the rulings of the presiding judge.

Defendants may or may not take the witness stand. The Fifth Amendment protects defendants against self-incrimination. If a defendant chooses not to testify,

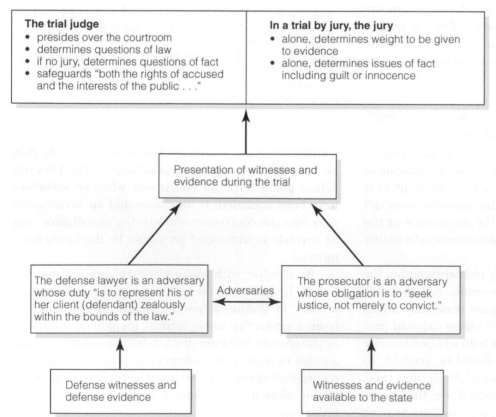

Figure 21.2
The American adversary system.

Source: From Gardner, T. J., & Anderson, T. M. (2010). *Criminal evidence: Principles and cases,* 7th ed. Belmont, CA: Wadsworth Publishing Company, a part of Cengage Learning, Inc.

The trial judge
- presides over the courtroom
- determines questions of law
- if no jury, determines questions of fact
- safeguards "both the rights of accused and the interests of the public . . ."

In a trial by jury, the jury
- alone, determines weight to be given to evidence
- alone, determines issues of fact including guilt or innocence

Presentation of witnesses and evidence during the trial

The defense lawyer is an adversary whose duty "is to represent his or her client (defendant) zealously within the bounds of the law."

Adversaries

The prosecutor is an adversary whose obligation is to "seek justice, not merely to convict."

Defense witnesses and defense evidence

Witnesses and evidence available to the state

this fact cannot be used against them. However, if a defendant does choose to testify, waiving the privilege against self-incrimination, that defendant cannot tell only a part of the story. If a defendant testifies, the state can ask questions about all the facts surrounding the event testified to. In addition, once the defendant takes the stand, the state may try to impeach the defendant's credibility by introducing any prior felony convictions. A jury might become suspicious if a defendant chooses not to testify on their own behalf, but the defense attorney might decide it is safer to keep the accused off the stand than to open them up to potentially damaging cross-examination.

Witnesses present the facts as they know them: "To qualify as a witness, a person must have relevant information, must be competent and must declare that he or she will testify truthfully. To be competent, a witness must be able to remember and tell what happened, must be able to distinguish fact from fantasy and must know that he or she must tell the truth. . . . Anglo-Saxon law seeks to keep witnesses honest by having them testify under oath or affirmation in the presence of the fact finder and the accused, subject to cross-examination and subject to possible perjury charges for failure to tell the truth" (Gardner & Anderson, 2010, p. 107).

Police officers are witnesses for the prosecution. Law enforcement witnesses present a challenge to the prosecution's case because the prosecuting attorney must establish the burden of proof beyond a reasonable doubt.

Sequence of a Criminal Trial

A trial begins with a case being called from the court docket. If both the prosecution and the defense are ready, the case is presented before the court.

If the trial is before a judge *without a jury*, called a **bench trial**, the prosecution and the defense make their opening statements directly to the judge. The opening statements are brief summaries of both the prosecution and defense attorneys' plans. In a *jury trial*, the jury is selected and then both counsels make their opening statements before the judge and jury.

The prosecution presents its case first. Witnesses for the prosecution are sworn in, and the prosecuting attorney asks them questions. Then the defense attorney may cross-examine the witnesses. After this cross-examination, the prosecuting attorney may redirect-examine, and then the defense attorney may re-cross-examine.

Direct examination is the initial questioning of a witness or defendant by the lawyer who is using the person's testimony to further their case. **Cross-examination**

is questioning by the opposing side to assess the validity of the testimony.

After the prosecutor has completed direct examination of all prosecution witnesses, the defense presents its case. After the direct examination of each defense witness, the prosecutor may cross-examine, the defense counsel may redirect-examine, and the prosecutor may re-cross-examine.

After each side has presented its regular witnesses, both sides may present *rebuttal* and *surrebuttal* witnesses. The prosecution can call **rebuttal** witnesses to contradict the testimony (or evidence) presented by the defense. The defense, in turn, can call **surrebuttal** witnesses to contradict the testimony (or evidence) presented by the prosecution. When the entire case has been presented, prosecution and defense counsel present their closing arguments. In these arguments, the lawyers review the trial evidence of both sides and tell the jury why the defendant should be convicted or acquitted. Sometimes the lawyers also make recommendations for penalty.

The judge instructs the jury on the laws applicable to the case and on how they are to arrive at a decision. The jury then retires to the jury room to deliberate and arrive at a verdict. When the jury reaches a verdict, court is reconvened and the verdict is read. If the verdict is for acquittal, the defendant is released from charges. If the verdict is guilty, the judge passes sentence or sets a time and date for sentencing. During a bench trial, it is common for the judge to take the matter under review and arrive at a decision later (time determined by local law).

LO8 Diagram the usual sequence of a criminal trial.

The sequence in a criminal trial is as follows:

- Jury selection
- Opening statements by the prosecution and the defense
- Presentation of the prosecution's case; cross-examination by the defense
- Presentation of the defense's case; cross-examination by the prosecution
- Rebuttal and surrebuttal testimony
- Closing statements by the prosecution and the defense
- Instructions to the jury
- Jury deliberation to reach a verdict
- Reading of the verdict
- Acquittal or passing of sentence

While Waiting to Testify

Do not discuss the case while waiting in the hallway to testify. If a juror or another witness hears your statements, you may have created grounds for a mistrial. Although it may be impractical or impossible to avoid all contact with jurors, such as chance encounters in a crowded elevator or passing each other in the hallway, **de minimus communication**, that is, a simple hello or giving of directions, is allowable. It is important not to appear aloof or unfriendly.

Testifying Under Direct Examination

As you enter the courtroom, keep in mind your goal, which is similar to that sought on the street—to win. However, this does not mean winning the case with a conviction but, instead, winning the trust of the court and the jury. You are on trial. The way you treated the suspect, how you followed policies and procedures, and your professional demeanor and knowledge are all on trial. They all factor into whether the jury trusts and believes you. To win, the jury must find you credible. Your success as an investigator depends not only on conducting a thorough investigation, making a good arrest, and producing a well-written, well-documented report, but also on presenting yourself on the stand as a competent and credible witness. As Van Brocklin (2020) states succinctly, "The win for an officer in court—whether in a criminal prosecution or civil litigation—is that at the end of testimony, the jury or judge must believe you. That's it."

> **LO9** Explain what the "win" is for an investigator who testifies in court.
>
> The "win" for an investigator who testifies is to have established credibility with the court and the jury.

First impressions are critical. Know what you are doing when you enter the courtroom. When your name is called, answer "Here" or "Present" and move directly to the front of the courtroom. Do not walk between the prosecutor and the judge; go behind the attorneys. Never walk in front of the judge or between the judge and the attorneys' tables. This area, called **the well**, is off-limits and is to be entered only if the judge so directs or permission is granted. Traditionally, the area is a sword's length and was intended for the judge's protection.

Walk confidently; the jurors are there to hear the facts from you. If your investigation has been thorough and properly conducted, the jury will give a great deal of weight to your testimony.

If you have notes or a report, carry them in a clean manila file folder in your left hand so your right hand is free for taking the oath. Taking the oath in court is basically the same as taking your oath of office. Stand straight and face the clerk of the court, holding the palm of your hand toward the clerk. Use a clear, firm voice to answer "I do" to the question "Do you promise to tell the truth, the whole truth, and nothing but the truth, so help you God?" Do not look at the judge, either legal counsel, or the jury.

Sit with your back straight but in a comfortable position, usually with your hands folded in your lap or held on the arms of the chair. Do not move the chair around or fidget because this is distracting. Hold notes and other reports in your lap. If the reports are bulky, many experts on testifying recommend placing them under the chair until needed.

The witness chair in all courtrooms is positioned so you can face the judge, legal counsel, jury, or the audience, depending on to whom your answers are directed. In most instances, if the judge asks you a question, look directly at the judge to answer. If either the prosecutor or defense counsel asks you a question, look either at them or the jury to give your answer. The prosecutor will ask you to state your name, department, and position. As you respond, keep in mind the types of statements that are not admissible.

> **LO10** Describe the kinds of statements that are inadmissible in court.
>
> Inadmissible statements include
> - Opinions and conclusions (unless the witness is qualified as an expert)
> - Hearsay
> - Privileged communication
> - Statements about character and reputation, including the defendant's criminal record

Testify only to what you actually saw, heard, or did, not what you believe, heard from others (**hearsay**), or were told about (also hearsay). You can testify to what a defendant told you directly, but any other statements must be testified to by the person making them.

Preparation is the key to being a good witness. After a review of your personal notes and all relevant reports, you will be familiar with the case and can "tell it like it is." This will come across well to the jury and establish your credibility.

LO11 List the guidelines for effective testimony.

Guidelines for effective testimony are:

- Speak clearly, firmly, and with expression.
- Answer questions directly. Do *not* volunteer information.
- Pause briefly before answering.
- Refer to your notes if you do not recall exact details.
- Admit calmly when you do not know an answer.
- Admit any mistakes you make in testifying.
- Avoid police jargon, sarcasm, and humor.
- Tell the complete truth as you know it.

How you speak is often as important as what you say. Talk slowly, deliberately, and loudly enough to be heard by everyone. Never use obscenity or vulgarity unless the court requests a suspect's or victim's exact words. In such cases, inform the court before you answer that the answer requested includes obscenity or vulgarity.

Myth The investigator's primary objective during testimony is to provide convincing evidence of the defendant's guilt.

Fact The investigator's only objective during testimony should be to tell the truth as they know it.

Ignore the courtroom's atmosphere. Devote your entire attention to giving truthful answers to questions. Answer all questions directly and politely with "yes" or "no" unless asked to relate an action taken, an observation made, or information told to you directly by the defendant. Refer to the judge as "Your Honor" and to the defendant as "the defendant." Do not volunteer information. Instead, let the prosecution decide whether to pursue a particular line of questioning.

Take a few seconds after hearing the question to form your answer. If the counsel or the court objects to a question, wait until instructed to proceed. If it takes some time for the judge to rule on an objection, ask to have the question repeated.

Reviewing the case thoroughly before your courtroom appearance does not mean that you should memorize specific dates, addresses, or spellings of names and places. Memorization can lead to confusion. Instead, use notes to help avoid contradictions and inconsistencies. An extemporaneous answer is better received by the judge and jury than one that sounds rehearsed.

LO12 Determine when to use notes while testifying.

Refer to your notes if you are uncertain of specific facts, but do not rely on them excessively.

Using notes too much detracts from your testimony, weakens your presentation, and gives the impression you have not adequately prepared for the case. It can also lead to having your notes introduced into the record. If, as you refer to your notes, you discover you have given erroneous testimony such as an incorrect date or time, notify the court immediately. Do not try to cover up the discrepancy. Everyone makes mistakes. If you admit them in a professional manner, little harm results. Do not hesitate to admit that you do not know the answer to a question or that you do not understand a question. Never bluff or attempt to fake your way through an answer.

In addition, be aware of certain phrases that may leave a negative impression on the jury. Phrases such as "I believe" or "to the best of my recollection" will not impress a jury. Do not argue or use sarcasm, witticisms, or "smart" answers. Be direct, firm, and positive. Be courteous, whether in response to a question from the prosecutor or an objection from the defense or the judge. Do not hesitate to give information favorable to the defendant. Your primary responsibility is to state what you know about the case.

If asked to identify evidence with your personal mark, take time to examine the item thoroughly. Make sure that all marks are accounted for and that your mark has not been altered. A rapid identification may make a bad impression on the jury and may lead you into an erroneous identification.

Nonverbal Factors. Do not underestimate the power of nonverbal factors as you testify. More than 50 years ago, Dr. Albert Mehrabian (1972) conducted his famous, often-cited study at the University of California, Los Angeles (UCLA), and concluded that communication is made up of several components:

- *What* is said—the actual words spoken (7% of the total message communicated)
- *How* it is said—tone of voice, pitch, modulation, and the like (38% of the message)
- *Nonverbal factors*—body language, gestures, demeanor (55%)

Mehrabian was clear, however, that the 7-38-55% communication formula was developed for a specific context—when the nonverbal channel and the verbal channel are incongruent (not matching): "When there are inconsistencies between attitudes communicated verbally and posturally, the postural component should dominate in determining the total attitude that is inferred" (1972, p. 108). If your words seem to align with your nonverbal cues, people will likely pay attention to those words. If however, they detect, even subconsciously, that your body language and words aren't matched, people tend to discount the veracity of those words and, instead, believe the message conveyed by the nonverbal factors. Never overlook the importance of how you present information and nonverbal factors when testifying.

> **LO13** Recognize what nonverbal elements can influence courtroom testimony positively and negatively.
>
> Important nonverbal elements include dress, eye contact, posture, gestures, mannerisms, rate of speech, tone of voice, and facial expressions.

Make brief, periodic eye contact with jurors as you testify, but do not stare (Heldmyer, 2018). Be aware of facial expressions that might indicate indifference, disgust, displeasure, or arrogance. Avoid actions associated with deception such as putting a hand over your mouth, nodding your head (in agreement), rubbing your nose, straightening your hair, buttoning your coat, picking lint off your clothing, or tugging at your shirt or a pant leg.

In some instances, officers may qualify to testify as *expert witnesses*. In such cases, the restrictions on testimony are somewhat more relaxed.

Expert Testimony. Rule 702 of the Federal Rules of Evidence states, "If scientific, technical or other specialized knowledge will assist the trier of fact to understand the evidence or to determine a fact in issue, a witness qualified as an expert by knowledge, skill, experience, training or education, may testify thereto in the form of an opinion or otherwise, if (1) the testimony is based upon sufficient facts of data, (2) the testimony is the product of reliable principles and methods, and (3) the witness has applied the principles and methods reliably to the facts of the case."

Expert testimony is that presented by a person deemed to have specialized training, skills, or experience in a particular area that will help the jury understand the topic and evidence presentation. *Daubert v. Merrell Dow Pharmaceuticals, Inc.* (1993) established standards for the admission of expert testimony in federal courts. Under *Daubert*, an expert's testimony must be specialized and relate directly to some fact at issue in the case: "Expert testimony which does not relate to any issue in the case is not relevant and, ergo, non-helpful." The Supreme Court noted that expert testimony must fit the case. Fitness is determined by examining how helpful the testimony is. This "helpfulness" standard requires a valid connection between the expert testimony and the inquiry.

Officers who qualify as experts in an area are allowed to give opinions and conclusions, but the prosecution must qualify the officer as an expert on the stand. The prosecution must establish that the person has special knowledge that others of moderate education or experience in the same field do not possess. To qualify as an expert witness, one must have as many of the following as possible:

- Present or prior employment in the specific field
- Active membership in a professional group in the field
- Research work in the field
- An educational degree directly related to the field
- Direct experience with the subject if not employed in the field
- Papers, treatises, or books published on the subject or teaching experience in it

Police officers can become experts on sounds, firearms, distances, lengths of time, speed, visibility problems, and so on simply by years of experience in police work. Other areas, such as firearms identification, fingerprint classification, and handwriting analysis require specialized training. Just who qualifies as an expert is not always clear, and different qualifications may exist for scientific and nonscientific evidence.

It is strongly recommended that officers document their training, studies, and experience in a format such as that shown in Figure 21.3. Take this record to court to establish yourself as an expert witness.

Testifying Under Cross-Examination

Because investigators are typically called as witnesses for the prosecution, cross-examination by the defense attorney is usually the most difficult part of testifying. It is the

IN-SERVICE TRAINING				
	Date	Place	Subject	# of Hours
Basic Academy				
Advanced Academy				
Special Schools				
Roll-Call Training				

SPECIAL STUDIES/EXPERIMENTS			
Dates	Place	Subject	Description

COLLEGE, UNIVERSITY, TECH SCHOOL			
Dates	Place	Subject	Description

READINGS			
Dates	Title	Subject	Description

PROFESSIONAL ASSOCIATIONS

OJT Supervised Training			
Dates	Supervisor	Subject	# of Hrs or Cases

INVESTIGATIONS, ARRESTS, EVALUATIONS, ETC. Approximate Number							
Narc.	Prints	T/A	Bkmkg	Ballis.	DWI	Handwriting	Poly.

Figure 21.3

Record of training, studies, and experience.

Source: From Rutledge, D. (2000). *Courtroom survival: The officer's guide to better testimony.* Belmont, CA: Wadsworth Publishing Company, a part of Cengage Learning, Inc.

PRIOR EXPERT TESTIMONY (Number)								
Court	Narc.	Prints	T/A	Bkmkg	Ballis.	DWI	Handwriting	Poly.
Justice								
Municipal								
Superior								
Supreme								
Federal								
Other States								
OTHER QUALIFICATION(S)								

Figure 21.3 (*Continued*)
Record of training, studies, and experience.
Source: From Rutledge, D. (2000). *Courtroom survival: The officer's guide to better testimony.* Belmont, CA: Wadsworth Publishing Company, a part of Cengage Learning, Inc.

defense attorney's job to inject reasonable doubt into the case, to undermine the state's argument that the defendant is guilty, and to win a "not guilty" verdict from the court. One of the most effective ways to create doubt in a jury's mind is to harm your credibility and make you look incompetent. The defense will try to attack and manipulate you, spin you up to make you lose your composure, turn questions around so that they confuse you and get you to elicit an answer that contradicts something you stated earlier.

One testimony expert noted that when officers were given a word-association test and the words *defense attorney* were given, a plethora of derogatory terms flew from the officers' mouths—*snake, shark, weasel, slime, liar* (Van Brocklin, 2007). This negative attitude explains why an officer can do a competent job in the investigation, be truthful, and still not be believed by the jury. If jurors perceive that an investigator is acting defensively, they may think the investigator is not testifying truthfully, as it is often presumed that only someone with something to hide acts defensively. The key is to recognize this tendency and remain professional and objective.

The defense attorney will attempt to cast doubt on your direct testimony in an effort to win an acquittal for the defendant. Know the methods of attack for cross-examination to avoid being trapped.

The defense attorney can be extremely friendly, hoping to put you off guard by making the questioning appear to be just a friendly chat. The attorney may praise your skill in investigation and lead you into boasting or a show of self-glorification that will leave a very bad impression on the jury. The "friendly" defense attorney may also try to lead you into testifying about evidence of which you have no personal knowledge. This error will be immediately exposed and your testimony tainted, if not completely discredited.

At the opposite extreme is the defense attorney who appears outraged by statements you make and goes on the attack immediately. This kind of attorney appears very excited and outraged, as though the trial is a travesty of justice. A natural reaction to such an approach is to exaggerate your testimony or lose your temper, which is exactly what the defense attorney wants. If you show anger, the jury may believe you are more interested in obtaining a conviction than determining the truth. It is often hard for a jury to believe that the well-dressed, meek-appearing defendant in court is the person who, armed with a gun, robbed a store and assaulted several bystanders. Maintain your dignity and impartiality, and show concern for only the facts.

The credibility of your testimony can be undermined in many ways. The defense may attempt to show that you are prejudiced, have poor character, or are interested only in seeing your arrest "stick." If asked, "Do you want to see the defendant convicted?" reply that you are there to present the facts you know and that you will abide by the court's decision. No case demonstrated these cross-examination attacks on police credibility more effectively than the O. J. Simpson murder trial. The defense was successful in shifting the focus away from the issue of the defendant's guilt and putting it directly on the incompetence of the police investigators.

The defense may also try to show that your testimony itself is erroneous because you are incompetent, lack information, are confused, have forgotten facts, or could not have had personal knowledge of the facts you have testified to. Do not respond to such criticism. Let your testimony speak for itself. If the defense criticizes your reference to notes, state that you simply want to be completely accurate. Be patient. If the defense counsel becomes excessively offensive, the prosecutor will intervene. Alternatively, the prosecutor may see that the defense is hurting its own case by such behavior and will allow the defense attorney to continue.

The defense attorney may further try to force contradictions or inconsistencies by incessantly repeating questions using slightly different wording. Repeat your previous answer. If the defense claims that your testimony does not agree with that of other officers, do not change your testimony. Whether your testimony is like theirs or different is irrelevant. The defense will attack it either way. If it is exactly alike, the defense will allege collusion. If it is slightly different, the defense will exaggerate this to convince the jury that the differences are so great that the officers are not even testifying about the same circumstances.

A common tactic of defense lawyers to destroy credibility is to try to get you to commit yourself to something and then later have to admit you could be wrong about it. When something like age, weight, or distance is unknown and approximate, it should be stated that it is an approximation or put into brackets. **Brackets** provide a range—for example, "he was 40 to 50 feet away." If the defense tries to trap you with a question like, "How many times did you ask my client where he was the night of June 14?" do not take the bait. It may be tempting to give a number, any number, to avoid sounding clueless, but the reality is there are some things you cannot be expected to know, and it is okay to politely admit it. In a situation like this, a good response would be "I don't know. When I am interviewing someone, I pay more attention to what they are saying than to how many times I ask something."

Another defense tactic is to use an accusatory tone in asking whether you talked with others about the case and what they told you about how to testify. Such accusations may make inexperienced officers feel guilty because they know they have talked about the case with many people. Because the accusing tone implies that this was legally incorrect, the officers may reply that they talked to no one. Such a response is a mistake because you may certainly discuss the case before testifying. Simply state that you have discussed the case with several people in an official capacity, but that none of them told you how to testify.

If defense counsel asks whether you have refreshed your memory before testifying, do not hesitate to say "yes." You would be a poor witness if you had not done so. Discussions with the prosecution, officers, and witnesses and a review of notes and reports are entirely proper. They help you tell the truth, the main purpose of testimony.

Leading questions are another defense tactic. For example, defense counsel may ask, "When did you first strike the defendant?" This implies that you did in fact strike the defendant. Defense attorneys also like to ask questions that presume you have already testified to something when in fact you may not have done so. If you are misquoted, call it to the counsel's attention and then repeat the facts you testified to. If you do not remember your exact testimony, have it read from the court record.

In addition, defense counsel may ask complicated questions and then say, "Please answer 'yes' or 'no.'" Obviously, some questions cannot be answered that simply. Ask to have the question broken down. No rule requires a specific answer. If the court does not grant your request, answer the question as directed and let the prosecutor bring out the information through redirect examination.

Rapid-fire questioning is yet another tactic that defense attorneys use to provoke unconsidered answers. Do not let the attorney's pace rush you. Take time to consider your responses.

Do not be taken in by the "silent treatment." The defense attorney may remain silent for what seems like many seconds after you answer a question. If you have given a complete answer, wait patiently. Do *not* attempt to fill the silence by saying things such as, "At least that's how I remember it" or "It was something very close to that."

LO14 Know the defense attorney tactics to anticipate during cross-examination.

During cross-examination the defense attorney may

- Be disarmingly friendly or intimidatingly rude.
- Attack your credibility and impartiality.
- Attack your investigative skill.
- Attempt to force contradictions or inconsistencies.
- Ask leading questions or deliberately misquote you.
- Ask for a simple answer to a complex question.
- Use rapid-fire questioning.
- Use the silent treatment.

Another tactic frequently used by defense attorneys is to mispronounce officers' names intentionally or address them by the wrong rank. This is an attempt to rile or distract the officer.

Regardless of how your testimony is attacked, treat the defense counsel as respectfully as you do the prosecutor. Do not regard the defense counsel as your enemy. You are in court to state the facts and tell the truth. Your testimony should exhibit no personal prejudice or animosity, and you should not become excited or provoked at defense counsel. Be professional.

Few officers are prepared for the rigor of testifying in court, even if they have received training in this area. Until officers have actually testified in court, they cannot understand how difficult it is. Because police officers are usually the primary and most damaging witnesses in a criminal case, defense attorneys know they must attempt to confuse, discredit, or destroy the officers' testimony. The best testimony is accurate, truthful, and in accordance with the facts. Every word an officer says is recorded and may be played back or used by the defense.

One key to testifying during cross-examination is to *never* volunteer any information. During cross-examination, the defense attorney can ask questions about only subjects raised by the prosecution during direct examination. If an investigator volunteers additional information, they may open up areas the prosecution did not intend to present and may not be prepared for.

Handling Objections

Three general types of objections common during trials are:

- Objections to the *form of the question* argue that the question, as asked, is leading, speculative, argumentative, misstates facts in evidence, assumes facts not in evidence, is vague and ambiguous, repetitive or cumulative, or is misleading.

- Objections to the *substance of the question* argue that the question is irrelevant, immaterial, incompetent, calls for hearsay, has insufficient foundation, calls for inadmissible opinion, or is beyond the scope of the direct examination.

- Objections to the *answer* argue that it is either unresponsive, an inadmissible opinion, or an inadmissible hearsay statement.

While some sources cite in excess of 150 possible objections that might come up during a trial, Bucklin (2013) contends only two dozen are routinely used:

1. Admitted
2. Argumentative

3. Assumes facts not in evidence
4. Best evidence rule
5. Beyond the scope of direct/cross/redirect examination
6. Completeness
7. Compound/double question
8. Confusing/vague/ambiguous
9. Counsel is testifying
10. Form
11. Foundation
12. Hearsay (rules 801, 802, 803, and 804)
13. Improper impeachment
14. Incompetent
15. Lack of personal knowledge
16. Leading
17. Misstates evidence/misquotes witness /improper characterization of evidence
18. Narrative
19. Opinion (rules 701 and 702)
20. Pretrial ruling
21. Privileged communication
22. Public policy
23. Rule 403 (undue waste of time/immaterial /irrelevant/repetitive/asked and answered /cumulative/surprise)
24. Speculative

In his text, Bucklin (2013) provides examples of when each type of objection might be used, a discussion of the context, and a possible response to the objection.

> **LO15** Identify the ways to avoid objections to your testimony.
>
> To avoid objections to your testimony, avoid conclusions and nonresponsive answers. Answer yes-or-no questions with "yes" or "no."

Concluding Your Testimony

Do not leave the stand until instructed to do so by counsel or the court. As you leave the stand, do not pay special attention to the prosecution, defense counsel, defendant, or jury. Return immediately to your seat in the courtroom or leave the room if you have been sequestered. If you are told you may be needed for further testimony, remain available. If told you are no longer needed, leave the courtroom and resume your normal activities. To remain gives the impression that you have a special interest in the case.

If you are in the courtroom at the time of the verdict, show neither approval nor disapproval at the outcome. If you have been a credible witness and told the truth, win or lose in court, you have done your job and should not take the outcome personally.

The complainant should be notified of the disposition of the case. A form such as the one shown in Figure 21.4 is frequently used.

Final Lessons from a Seasoned Investigator's Experience

You were introduced to Captain Asha Mohammed at the beginning of the text. She returns to discuss lessons learned as a young detective, emphasizing the areas to focus on when giving courtroom testimony and providing examples of some of her experiences testifying. Although everything in this chapter is important, Mohammed emphasizes three major areas:

1. **Preparation.** While testifying, an investigator should not use their report as a crutch or a script.

Figure 21.4
Case disposition notice.

CASE DISPOSITION REPORT

Date Disposition Made: 4-25-20__   D.R. #: 97-1002
Date of Incident: 2-10-20__   Type of Incident: Burglary

DISPOSITION:
(x) Case Clearance
(x) Property Recovered
( ) Disposition of Property: (x) Owner ( ) Police Evidence
( ) Other
If <u>Other</u>, specify type:_____

VICTIM: (If Runaway Juvenile or Missing Adult, disregard this section)
Name__Jerome Slater__   Address_3041 Harding St., Edina, Minn._

SUSPECT(S):
NO. 1: __John Toben__   Arrested?__Yes__   BCPD I.D. # 20146
NO. 2: __William Moss__   Arrested?__Yes__   BCPD I.D. # 20147
NO. 3:_____   Arrested?_____   BCPD I.D. #_____

PROPERTY RECOVERED:
Item No. 1: _One car radio, Sears_____   Value $87.00
Item No. 2: _One car battery, Sears_____   Value $60.00
Item No. 3: _Microwave oven, GE_____   Value $250.00
Item No. 4: _One 17" TV, Sears Solid State_   Value $350.00
Recovering Agency: _Edina Police Department_   Total Value Recovered Property: $747.00

CANCELLATIONS: (Specify date, time, agency and officer receiving cancellation and officer making cancellation)

NCIC:_____
Other Agencies:_Hennepin County Sheriff's Office_____
Other Agencies:_____

OFFICER MAKING DISPOSITION: _____
SUPERVISOR APPROVING: _____
DETAILS: _Full recovery of property_____

It should be a safety net—seldom used. Constantly referring to a report gives the jury the impression that you do not know the case. Officers should *study* their reports and the reports of fellow officers before testifying.

2. **Communication**. Understand that words are a small part of communicating. Expressions, demeanor, personality, appearance, and more are what jurors use to form an opinion. If you remind them of the obstinate cop who wrote them a ticket for going two miles over the speed limit, they're going to sympathize with the defendant.

3. **Credibility**. If jurors question your credibility, the case is in big trouble. If you are caught in a lie, an embellishment, or an obvious omission, why should a juror believe anything you say? For those who remember the O. J. Simpson murder trial, a detective called for the prosecution denied repeatedly under oath that he had ever used racial slurs. The defense team, however, was able to introduce recorded interviews and witnesses that showed the detective had, many times, openly used racist language. Even though it had nothing to do with the evidence he was presenting, once he lost his credibility, his testimony lost its value and, indeed, severely damaged the prosecution's case.

Detective Mohammed was nervous the night before her first major trial, her mind filled with stories of defense attorneys ripping cops to shreds during cross-examination—stories artfully embellished by fellow cops—and the knowledge that a bad day testifying can lose a case. She had good reason to be nervous; the defense attorney assigned to the case was infamous for picking apart police reports. She studied her reports as if she were taking a final exam and rehearsed responses to every dirty trick a defense attorney could throw at her. She wasn't going to be some ill-prepared cop referring to her report for the suspect's name or the location of an arrest.

She took the stand, scanned the packed courtroom, and hoped her voice would not crack. The direct testimony went smoothly, but she knew what was coming. The defense attorney smiled and greeted her. His voice was calm and reassuring. He knew all about the detective's background and that she had reached the rank of detective at a very young age. The attorney's tone was complimentary, and Mohammed's fear of being ripped to shreds was replaced with a sense of importance. She began to enjoy the cross-examination.

Most of the initial questions were general and easy to answer. The defense attorney asked several questions about the defendant's level of cooperation. He cited things that his client had done at their request, including having his hands swabbed for gunpowder residue. Mohammed acknowledged that the defendant had been cooperative. The defense attorney asked if his client had refused any of their requests. Mohammed paused to think, and the defense attorney quickly added, "Did you ask him to do anything else?"

It seemed to Mohammed that the defense attorney was helping her remember something in her report without making her look stupid. Then Mohammed remembered, "Oh, yes. He agreed to take a polygraph test." The defense attorney thanked Mohammed and sat down. The prosecutor slowly slumped in his chair. Mohammed had been tricked into telling the jury that the defendant was willing to take a lie-detector test— something that wasn't admissible and that the defense could not have presented without the detective's help. In fact, the defendant offered to take the test, but later refused—something the jury would never hear. Her mistake left the jury with the impression that the defendant had passed a polygraph test. The jury returned a guilty verdict for a lesser charge and left Mohammed wondering what role her mistake on the stand had played in its decision.

Another defense attorney had taught Detective Mohammed a more positive lesson. She was testifying at her first rape trial, a case in which four men had followed a college student home from a bar one night, grabbed her before she reached her front door, and took her to a wooded area, where they beat and raped her, leaving her for dead. She was found the next day, naked and unconscious, by two hikers. The victim was taken to the hospital, where she lay in a coma for more than a week. Mohammed spent that time getting to know the victim's roommates and learned a lot about the woman's life. Mohammed was elated when she was able to tell the roommates that victim had woken up and was going to survive. This was a case that Mohammed would remember forever.

Experienced detectives do not allow their emotions to influence their professionalism. But at age 26, Mohammed was inexperienced and emotional. During the investigation, which involved a review of surveillance video of the victim's housing complex, Mohammed and a team of detectives were able to capture some rough images of the men involved, one of whom had a distinctive tattoo on his exposed forearm. The video also captured images of the car used by the suspects, including the plate number, which led to an address. When officers arrived at the residence to conduct a search warrant, they found four men inside. Mohammed approached one man bearing a tattoo that matched the one seen in the surveillance video. The suspect stood tall and defiant, demanding to know why the officers were there. When Mohammed informed him of investigation, the suspect looked at one of the other men and smirked before saying, "That cheating little bitch deserved what she got." Mohammed was enraged and made a stupid and unprofessional mistake. She slapped the suspect and told him to shut up, a lapse in judgment that could put the entire case in jeopardy.

Seasoned detectives interviewed the suspects for several hours, each denying any involvement in the rape. During a break in the questioning, the tattooed suspect and Detective Mohammed were left alone in an interview room. They began small talk about things unrelated to the case, learned they were the same age and actually worked out at the same gym. After developing a little rapport, the suspect began to feel more comfortable talking with Mohammed and eventually confessed to the rape.

Mohammed did not include the slapping incident in her report, but it was ever-present in her mind. She was one of the key witnesses at the trial, and the confession was the most important evidence. The defense attorney was one of the very best. He methodically questioned the detective about various aspects of the investigation, then paused and switched legal pads. "Detective, did you slap or hit my client before he confessed to you?"

Mohammed's heart pounded so loudly she was sure everyone could hear it. The confession, the case,

and her job were all about to be lost. Would the disgusting rapist get off because of Mohammed's stupidity? The courtroom was silent. The jury, the prosecutor, the judge, the press, and the victim's family all stared at her, waiting for her answer. For the sake of justice, Mohammed wondered if one lie would really hurt. She looked squarely into the defense attorney's eyes and responded, "Yes sir, I did."

For a moment the defense attorney looked perplexed. He asked a few more questions and sat down. The prosecutor was furious that Mohammed had neglected to share that damaging information with him. Fortunately, the defendants were found guilty and sentenced to lengthy prison terms. After the trial, the defense attorney asked to meet with Mohammed in the prosecutor's office. Mohammed arrived expecting some type of sanctions. Instead, the defense attorney extended his hand and commended her for telling the truth on the stand. The attorney said he had hoped Mohammed would deny slapping his client, for if she had, the attorney was prepared to show that the detective was lying and ruin her credibility with the jury. When Mohammed told the truth, the attorney's strategy failed, and the detective's credibility with the jury was actually enhanced.

The lesson to be learned is never lie, exaggerate, or embellish your testimony. It is more obvious to a jury than you may realize. Once you lose your credibility, it is nearly impossible to recover it. The truth can only strengthen a good case.

Summary

The most important rule to eradicate fear of testifying in court is to always tell the truth, beginning with the final report.

Before any trial, the final report must be written and presented to the prosecutor. The final report contains (1) the complaint; (2) the preliminary investigation report; (3) all follow-up, supplemental, and progress reports; (4) statements, admissions, and confessions; (5) laboratory and other professional reports (e.g., autopsy); (6) photographs, sketches, and drawings; and (7) a summary of all exculpatory evidence. The quality of the content and writing of the report influences its credibility.

The prosecutor is the most powerful official in the court system. Some cases are never prosecuted because the complaint is invalid, the prosecutor declines after reviewing the case, the complainant refuses to prosecute, the offender dies, or no evidence or leads exist. If the

decision is made to prosecute, thorough preparation is required. To prepare a case for court, (1) review and evaluate all evidence, including exculpatory, and the chain of custody; (2) review all reports on the case, including transcripts of any depositions you have given; (3) prepare witnesses; and (4) hold a pretrial conference with the prosecutor. Concentrate on proving the elements of the crime and establishing the offender's identity.

At the pretrial conference with the prosecutor, review all the evidence, discuss the strengths and weaknesses of the case, and discuss the probable line of questioning by the prosecutor and the defense.

The sequence in a criminal trial is jury selection, opening statements by the prosecution and the defense, presentation of the prosecution's case and cross-examination by the defense, presentation of the defense's case and cross-examination by the prosecution, rebuttal and surrebuttal testimony, closing statements by the prosecution and the defense, the judge's instructions to the jury, jury deliberation to reach a verdict, reading of the verdict, and acquittal or passing of sentence.

The "win" for an investigator who testifies is to have established credibility with the court and the jury. Inadmissible statements include opinions and conclusions (unless the witness is qualified as an expert), hearsay, privileged communications, and statements about the defendant's character and reputation, including the defendant's criminal record. To present testimony effectively, speak clearly, firmly, and with expression; answer questions directly, and do *not* volunteer information; pause briefly before answering; refer to your notes if you do not recall exact details; admit calmly when you do not know an answer; admit any mistakes you make

in testifying; avoid police jargon, sarcasm, and humor; and tell the complete truth as you know it. Refer to your notes if you are uncertain of specific facts, but do not rely on them excessively. Important nonverbal elements include dress, eye contact, posture, gestures, mannerisms, rate of speech, tone of voice, and facial expressions.

During cross-examination the defense attorney may be disarmingly friendly or intimidatingly rude, attack your credibility and impartiality, attack your investigative skill, attempt to force contradictions or inconsistencies, ask leading questions or deliberately misquote you, ask for a simple answer to a complex question, use rapid-fire questioning, or use the "silent treatment." To avoid objections to your testimony, avoid conclusions and nonresponsive answers. Answer yes-or-no questions with "yes" or "no."

Can You Define?

adversary system	direct examination	rebuttal
bench trial	discovery process	rule on witnesses
brackets	exceptionally cleared	sequestering
Brady rule	expert testimony	subpoena
cross-examination	hearsay	surrebuttal
de minimus communication	impeach	the well
deposition	motion in limine	witness sequestration rule

Checklists

Final Report

- Have all the criteria for an effective report been met? (See Chapter 3)

- Has all relevant information been included?

- Does the report include headings?

- Has the report been proofread to eliminate content and composition errors?

Preparing to Testify

- Have all reports been reviewed?

- Have all reports been organized for presentation to the prosecutor?

- Has all evidence, including exculpatory evidence, been located and made available for court presentation?

- Has all evidence been examined by competent laboratories and the results obtained? Are copies of the reports available?

- Have all known leads been developed?

- Have both negative and positive information been submitted to the prosecuting attorney?

- Has all arrest information been submitted?

- Has a list of witnesses been prepared? Addresses? Telephone numbers?

- Has the final report been assembled? Does it contain copies of investigators' reports? Photographs? Sketches? Evidence? Lab reports? Medical examiner's reports? Statements? Confessions? Maps? All other pertinent information?

- Has the deposition transcript been reviewed?

- Has a pretrial conference been held with the prosecutor's office?

- Have all witnesses been reinterviewed? Notified of the date and time of the trial?

- Have all expert witnesses been notified of the date and time of the trial?

- Has someone been designated to take the evidence to court?

- Have notes needed for testimony been removed from your notebook?

- Is your personal appearance professional?

References

Bertomen, L. J. (2019, June 13). The importance of report writing skills for career development. *Police1.com.* Retrieved April 21, 2021, from www.police1.com/police -training/articles/the-importance-of-report-writing-skills -for-career-development-TbzxehM8Z0r0lzfG/

Bucklin, L. (2013). *Building trial notebooks.* Costa Mesa, CA: James Publishing, Inc.

Gardner, T. J., & Anderson, T. M. (2010). *Criminal evidence: Principles and cases,* 7th ed. Belmont, CA: Wadsworth Publishing Company.

Goldstein, J. (2018, June 27). A detective lied to the grand jury. Now she's going to jail. *The New York Times.* Retrieved April 21, 2021, from www.nytimes.com/2018/06/27/nyregion /perjury-detective-nypd.html

Heldmyer, M. M. (2018, April 20). *The art of law enforcement testimony: Fine tuning your skills as a witness.* Glynco, GA: Federal Law Enforcement Training Center. Retrieved April 21, 2021, from www.fletc.gov/sites/default/files/the_art _of_testimony_4.20.18.pdf

Jackson, R. H. (1940). The federal prosecutor—His temptations. *Journal of the American Judicature Society, 24*: 18–25.

Lewis, J. E. (2019, April 12). The dangers of depositions. *Law Enforcement Today.* Retrieved April 21, 2021, from www .lawenforcementtoday.com/the-dangers-of-depositions/

Lyons, N. (2013, August). Presumed guilty until proven innocent: California penal code section 851.8 and the injustice of imposing a factual innocence standard on arrested persons. *Golden Gate University Law Review, 43*(3): Article 6. Retrieved April 21, 2021, from digitalcommons .law.ggu.edu/ggulrev/vol43/iss3/6/

Mehrabian, A. (1972). *Nonverbal communication.* Piscataway, NJ: Aldine Transaction.

Mollen Commission. (1994, July 7). *The City of New York Commission to investigate allegations of police corruption and the anti-corruption procedures of the police department.*

New York, NY: Author. Retrieved April 21, 2021, from web.archive.org/web/20110721230958/www.parc.info /client_files/Special%20Reports/4%20-%20Mollen%20 Commission%20-%20NYPD.pdf

Neubauer, D. W., & Fradella, H. F. (2014). *America's courts and the criminal justice system,* 11th ed. Belmont, CA: Cengage Learning.

Penrod, E. G. (2015, April). Preparing for depositions. *The LEL,* the newsletter for the National Law Enforcement Liaison Program, p. 11. Retrieved April 21, 2021, from www.nlelp.org /wp-content/uploads/2015/04/TheLEL_Apr2015_Final.pdf

Prudente, T. (2019, October 31). Judge convicts Baltimore police officer of lying in court, misconduct in office. *Baltimore Sun.* Retrieved April 21, 2021, from www .baltimoresun.com/news/crime/bs-md-ci-cr-20191031 -lqbxdeclj5eahkqfh5t4thganq-story.html

Savelli, L. (2018, April 5). Writing effective police reports. *CopBlue.com.* Retrieved April 21, 2021, from copblue.com /writing-effective-police-reports/

Schmadeke, S. (2014, April 15). 5 cops caught in lies on witness stand, judge says. *Chicago Tribune* online. Retrieved June 3, 2015, from articles.chicagotribune.com/2014-04-15 /news /ct-police-testimony-lies-met-20140415_1_police-officers -five-officers-chicago-police/2

Van Brocklin, V. (2007, December 26). Winning courtroom confrontations. *Officer.com.* Retrieved April 21, 2021, from www.officer.com/home/article/10249217 /winning-courtroom-confrontations

Van Brocklin, V. (2020, May 25). How cops can best prepare for a court appearance. *Police1.com.* Retrieved April 21, 2021, from www.police1.com/police-training/articles /how-cops-can-best-prepare-for-a-court-appearance -aZZlcOKb9pP1h6Ra/

Williams, G. T. (2013). *Preparing for your civil disposition: A guide for the law enforcement professional.* Bellingham, WA: Cutting Edge Training.

Cases Cited

Brady v. Maryland, 373 U.S. 83 (1963).

Daubert v. Merrell Dow Pharmaceuticals, Inc., 509 U.S. 579 (1993).

Giglio v. United States, 405 U.S. 150 (1972).

Pennsylvania v. Ritchie, 480 U.S. 39 (1987).

Weatherford v. Bursey, 429 U.S. 545 (1977).

Sudden In-Custody Death:
An Investigator's Checklist

The following checklists are designed to help investigators organize the collection of evidence suggested by this protocol—especially transient evidence, which can become altered within a few minutes—during the first few minutes after a subject dies in custody.

Subject's History

- ❑ Residential
- ❑ Educational
- ❑ Family
- ❑ Medical
- ❑ Behavioral
- ❑ Employment
- ❑ Financial
- ❑ Police Contact
- ❑ Nutritional
- ❑ Substance Abuse
- ❑ The Common Link

The Incident

❑ Duration of unusual behavior prior to police contact? _____

_____

_____

_____

❑ Detailed history of behavior immediately before police intervention? _____

_____

_____

_____

_____

❑ Subject utterances _____

_____

_____

❑ Subject actions, activities _____

_____

_____

_____

- ❑ Hyperventilation
- ❑ Shouting
- ❑ Other _____
- ❑ Running
- ❑ Pacing furiously

❑ Type of resistance _____

❑ Duration of resistance _____

❑ Length of time taken to subdue subject _____

❑ Time transport begins _____ Time transport ends _____

❑ Struggle against restraints during transport? _____

❑ Describe struggle _____
_____
_____
_____
_____

❑ Describe breathing pattern _____
_____
_____
_____
_____

❑ Shouting? _____
_____
_____
_____

❑ Presence or absence of sweating by the subject? _____
❑ Pulse rate during incident _____
❑ Strength during incident _____
❑ Determined by _____
❑ Time _____
❑ Name _____
❑ Presence or absence of sweating by persons involved with subject? _____
_____
_____
_____

The Scene
❑ Air temperature _____
❑ Relative humidity _____
❑ Determined by _____
❑ Time _____
❑ Name _____
❑ Transport vehicle interior temperature _____
❑ Climate control settings _____
❑ Functional? _____
❑ Used _____
❑ Determined by _____
❑ Time _____
❑ Name _____
❑ Treatment facility temperature _____
❑ Relative humidity _____
❑ Climate control settings _____
❑ Functional? _____
❑ Used _____
❑ Determined by _____
❑ Time _____
❑ Name _____
❑ Describe surface where subject was restrained _____
_____
❑ Surface temperature _____
❑ Determined by _____
❑ Time _____
❑ Name _____

Resuscitation Efforts

❏ Describe _____

_____

_____

_____

_____

❏ **Subject's core temperatures**	**Before**	**Upon death**	**PM**
Time	_____	_____	_____
Determined by	_____	_____	_____
Name	Name _____	Name _____	Name _____

Thyroid/cricoid pressure (pressure over the front of the windpipe used) _____

Number of times the attempt was made _____

ID of person making efforts _____

_____

_____

_____

_____

Environmental Factors

❏ External air temperature _____ ❏ Humidity _____

❏ Humidex _____ ❏ Wind chill _____

❏ Wind speed _____ ❏ Direction _____

❏ Determined by _____

❏ Time _____

❏ Name _____

❏ Weather trend _____

❏ Surface temperature of the ground _____

❏ Determined by _____

❏ Time _____

❏ Name _____

❏ Duration of contact with ground _____

❏ Position _____

❏ Other _____

_____

_____

_____

_____

Appendix B

Death Scene Record

This form is to be used as a supplementary source sheet for readily available information and is not intended to replace conventional reports. Copies should be distributed to investigating officers and medical examiners.

Name of deceased:

First   Middle   Last

Address:

Age: **Race:**   White   Black   Hispanic   Asian   Native   American   Unknown

Sex: Male   Female

Telephone number:

Marital status: S   M   W   D   Separated   Unknown

Next-of-kin:

Name:

Address:

Telephone number:

Policy notified by:

Date: Time:

Name:

Address:

Telephone number:

Relationship to deceased:

Deceased found:

Date: Time:

Address: (if different from above)

Location: Apartment   House   Townhouse   Other (describe)

Entrance by: Key   Cutting chain   Forcing door   Other (describe)

Type of lock on door:

Condition of other doors and windows: Open   Closed   Locked   Unlocked

Body found:

Living Room   Dining Room   Bedroom   Kitchen   Attic   Basement   Other (describe)

Location in room:

Position of body: On back   Face down   Other:

Condition of body:

Fully clothed   Partially clothed   Unclothed

Preservation: Well preserved   Decomposed

Estimated Rigor: Complete   Head   Arms   Legs

Livor: Front   Back   Localized

Color:

Blood: Absent   Present   Location

Ligatures: Yes   No

Apparent wounds: None   Gunshot   Stab   Blunt force

Number:

Location: Head   Neck   Chest   Abdomen   Extremities

Hanging: Yes   No   Means:

Weapon(s) present: Gun (estimate caliber)

Type:

Knife:

Other (describe)

Condition of surroundings: Orderly   Untidy   Disarray

Odors: Decomposition   Other

Evidence of last food preparation:

Where:

Type:

Dated material:

Mail:

Newspapers:

TV guide:

Liquor bottles:

Last contact with deceased:

Date:

Type of contact:

Name of contact:

Evidence of robbery: Yes   No   Not determined

Identification of deceased: Yes   No

If yes, how accomplished:

If no, how is it to be accomplished:

Evidence of drug use: (prescription and nonprescription)   Yes   No

If drugs present, collect them and send with body.

Evidence of drug paraphernalia: Yes   No

Type:

Evidence of sexually deviant practices: Yes   No

Type: (collect and send with body)

Name and telephone number of investigating officer:

Washington, DC, Metropolitan Police Department Homicide Case Review Solvability Chart

Suspect Comments

❑ Arrested but released _____

❑ Named, no arrest _____

❑ Incarcerated/other charge _____

❑ Under investigation/other charge _____

❑ Deceased _____

❑ Seen but unidentified _____

❑ No suspects _____

Witness

❑ Witness under investigation/trial _____

❑ Witness incarcerated _____

❑ Multiple eyewitnesses _____

❑ Other _____

Firearm Evidence

❑ Shell casings recovered _____

❑ Slugs recovered _____

❑ Linked to another crime _____

❑ No firearm evidence recovered _____

Fingerprint Evidence

❑ Unidentified prints recovered _____

❑ No fingerprint evidence recovered _____

DNA Evidence

❑ Potential suspect DNA recovered _____

❑ Potential probative victim DNA _____

❑ No DNA evidence recovered _____

Other Crimes

❏   Potential link to another crime   _____

Miscellaneous Solvability Factors

❏   _____

❏   _____

Source: Cronin, J. M., Murphy, G. R., Spahr, L. L., Toliver, J. I, & Weger, R. E. (2007, August). *Promoting Effective Homicide Investigations*. Police Executive Research Forum. Washington, DC: U.S. Department of Justice. pp. 173–174. www.policeforum.org/upload/homicide_759980432_1282008145753.pdf

Las Vegas Metropolitan Police Department Cold Case Solvability Criteria

Level 1

- Named suspect
- Forensic evidence (DNA, latent prints [AFIS], firearms)
- Witness identification of suspect
- Physical evidence that connects suspect to the victim (photographs, writing, fibers, etc.)

Level 2

- Unknown suspect
- Forensic evidence (DNA, latent prints [AFIS], firearms)
- Witness identification of suspect
- Physical evidence that connects suspect to the victim

Level 3

- Unknown suspect
- Forensic evidence (DNA, latent prints [AFIS], firearms)
- Physical evidence
- Witnesses unable to identify

Level 4

- Unknown suspect
- Physical evidence
- Witnesses unable to identify
- Unidentified victim

Level 5

- Unknown suspect
- Little or no physical evidence
- No witnesses
- Unidentified victim

Source: Cronin, J. M., Murphy, G. R., Spahr, L. L., Toliver, J. I, & Weger, R. E. (2007, August). *Promoting Effective Homicide Investigations*. Police Executive Research Forum. Washington, DC: U.S. Department of Justice. pp. 171–172. www.policeforum.org/upload/ homicide_759980432_1282008145753.pdf

Appendix E

Domestic Violence Report Review Checklist

- **Does the report include all needed information?**
  - ❑ How was the case received?
  - ❑ Is the time of the call recorded (including time of incident, time of dispatch, time of arrival)?
  - ❑ Are the elements of the crime(s) articulated to meet state and/or federal laws that address domestic violence? Firearms?
  - ❑ What were the observations upon approach?
  - ❑ Is there a valid protection order in place?
  - ❑ Is the scene concisely described/diagramed?
  - ❑ Were photos taken and details recorded?
  - ❑ Is the relationship of the parties identified?
  - ❑ What is the history of the relationship? (include frequency of any violence, intimidation, and threats)
  - ❑ Were all witnesses interviewed and documented?
  - ❑ Were there children on the scene?
  - ❑ Was information about previous incidents documented?
  - ❑ Were weapons/objects used?
  - ❑ What was the emotional state of the victim (what did they report they were thinking and feeling)?
  - ❑ What evidence was collected?
  - ❑ Is evidence of fear articulated in the report?
  - ❑ Have all threats been clearly documented?
  - ❑ Is the use of coercion and/or force articulated?
  - ❑ Have all injuries (visible and non-visible) been documented? Were injuries existing or new?
  - ❑ Was there any property damage? Theft? Burglary?
  - ❑ Are stalking behaviors identified? (e.g., following, repeated calling, sending unwanted gifts)
  - ❑ Did the officer inquire about possible strangulation (hands, ligature, etc.)?
  - ❑ Did the victim report being strangled ("choked")? If so, was it described in detail?
  - ❑ Did the victim request/need medical attention?
  - ❑ Did the victim report sexual violence?
  - ❑ Were all spontaneous statements captured?

- **Did the officer ask about firearms? Is the officer aware of the laws that address domestic violence and firearms?**
  - ❑ Did the suspect use firearms during the incident that occurred? In previous incidents?
  - ❑ Did the suspect make threats— real or implied— to use firearms during the incident that occurred? In previous incidents?
  - ❑ Does the suspect have access to firearms? If so, what are the details of the firearms? Where are they located?
  - ❑ Did the victim express fear about the suspect's access to firearms? If so, how was this captured in the report?

❏ Were firearms/weapons confiscated? If so, on what grounds?
❏ Is this individual prohibited from possessing firearms due to:
- a conviction for a misdemeanor crime of domestic violence
- a qualifying order of protection
- dishonorable discharge from the military

- **Did the officer assist the victim with safety planning?**
  ❏ Was information provided about obtaining an order of protection (if laws permit)?
  ❏ Was information provides to the victim about local service providers?
  ❏ Was a threat/risk assessment tool used with the victim? to determine if one acted in self-defense? the suspect?

- **If both parties used force, were the proper steps taken to determine if one acted in self-defense?**

- **Did the officer gather comprehensive information about the suspect?**
  ❏ Was an arrest made?
  - If an arrest was **not** made, is a detailed explanation of the reasoning in the report?
  ❏ Was more than one arrest made? If so, was probable cause articulated for the arrests in separate reports?
  ❏ What was the emotional state of the suspect (what did they report they were thinking and feeling)?
  ❏ Was a threat/risk assessment tool used with the suspect?
  ❏ Was the proper protocol followed if the suspect was not on the scene?
  ❏ Are there any active warrants out for the suspect?
  ❏ Has the suspect been the respondent to a protection order in the past?

- **Additional Notes**

Appendix F

Law Enforcement Request Letter for Identity Theft Investigations

To:

Regarding: Account Number:
                   Name on Account:

Description of fraudulent [transaction/account]:

From: [Law Enforcement Officer's Name]
          [Law Enforcement Agency's Name]
          [Agency/Department Address]
          [Telephone Number]

I am contacting you on behalf of an identity theft victim, [Victim's Name], whose case I am investigating. [Victim's Name]'s personal information was used by someone else to make a fraudulent transaction or open a fraudulent account with your company. In accordance with section 609(e) of the Fair Credit Reporting Act, I am requesting that you provide me copies of application and business records relating to the fraudulent [transaction/account] identified above. The victim's letter authorizing me to receive copies of such documents is enclosed. Federal law provides that, upon request of the victim, you make these documents available to me, as a law enforcement officer, free and without the need to issue a subpoena.

Please provide all information relating to the fraudulent account or transaction, including:

- Application records or screen prints of Internet/phone applications
- Statements/invoices
- Payment/charge slips
- Investigator's summary
- Delivery addresses
- All records of phone numbers used to activate the account or used to access the account
- Any other documents associated with the account.

Please send the information to me at the above address. You can contact me at [telephone number] if you need further information.

Enclosure:

- Request Letter of [Victim's name] Authorizing Law Enforcement Officer to Receive Fraudulent Transaction/Account Information, dated [insert date], with Victim's Enclosures

Appendix G

Sample Form for Reporting Bias Crime

BIAS OFFENSE REPORT

MONTH AND YEAR_____

AGENCY IDENTIFIER (ORI)_____
AGENCY NAME_____

This form is to be used to report any bias motivated crimes in violation of Minnesota State Statute 626.5531. The chief law enforcement officer for an agency must complete form and return to the Department of Public Safety, Office of Information Systems Management, 314 Transportation Building, 395 John Ireland Blvd., St. Paul, Minnesota 55155 within 30 days (Laws of Minnesota, 1996, Chapter 643).

A. GENERAL OFFENSE INFORMATION

1) Agency Case Number: _____   2) Date of Offense: _____
3) Bias offense base on: ☐ Officer's belief   ☐ Victim's belief
4) *Description of Offense: _____   5) *Disposition: _____
6) *Type of Bias and Description: _____ / _____
　　　　　　　　　　　　　　Type Code　　　　　　　　　Description Code or Literal
7) *Target: _____   8) Place of Occurrence: _____

B. VICTIM/OFFENDER INFORMATION

9) VICTIMS				10) OFFENDERS			11) *RELATIONSHIP TO VICTIM	12) AFFILIATION (if any)
#	Age	Sex	Race	Age	Sex	Race		
1								
2								
3								
4								
5								
6								
7								
8								
9								
10								
11								
12								
13								
14								
15								

COMMENTS: _____
_____
_____
_____

*Use code tables on reverse.

Return to:　DPS/OISM
　　　　　　314 DOT Building
　　　　　　395 John Ireland Blvd.
　　　　　　St. Paul, MN 55155

Source: Minnesota Bureau of Criminal Apprehension.

CODE TABLES

4) *DESCRIPTION of OFFENSE*:

To be used in further identifying offense
01-Cross Burning
02-Swastika
03-Bombing
04-Hanging in Effigy
05-Disturbing Public Meeting
06-Graffiti
07-Spitting
08-Letter
09-Verbal Abuse (Person to Person)
10-Telephone
11-Homicide
12-Criminal Sexual Conduct
13-Robbery
14-Burglary
15-Aggravated Assault
16-Arson
17-Larceny Theft
18-Disturbing the Peace
19-Property Damage
20-Simple Assault
00-Other (Describe)

5) *DISPOSITION:* Based on CJRS Reporting System—Major Offenses

A-Arrest of Adult and/or Adult & Juvenile
J-Arrest of Juvenile
E-Exceptionally Cleared
U-Unfounded
P-Pending

6) *TYPE of BIAS and DESCRIPTION:*

Type	*Description*
01-Racial	W-White
	H-White/Hispanic Origin
	N-Negro/Black
	B-Black/Hispanic Origin
	I-Indian or Alaskan Native
	M-Indian w/Hispanic Origin
	O-Asian or Pacific Islander
	A-Asian or Pacific Islander w/Hispanic Origin
02-Religious	01-Catholic
	02-Hindu/Buddhist
	03-Islamic/Moslem
	04-Jewish
	05-Protestant
	06-Fundamentalist
	07-Other (Describe)
03-National Origin	Specify
04-Sex	M-Male
	F-Female
05-Age	Specify age(s)
06-Disability	Specify disability
07-Sexual Orientation	01-Homosexual Male
	02-Homosexual Female
	03-Heterosexual Male
	04-Heterosexual Female

7) *TARGET CODES:*

01-Person
02-Private Property
03-Public Property

8) *PLACE of OCCURRENCE:*

01-Residence
02- Hotel, Motel or Other Commercial Short-Term Residence
03-Parking Lot Areas
04-Business
05-Vehicle
06-Street/Sidewalk
07-Highway/Freeway
08-Park/School Ground
09-Vacant Lot
10-Jail
11-Rural Area/Country Road
12-Cemetery
13-Religious Building
14-Government Building
15-School Building
16-Private Club
17-Other (Describe)

11) *RELATIONSHIP of OFFENDER to VICTIM:*

01-Family Member
02-Neighbor
03-Acquaintance
04-Boyfriend/Ex-Boyfriend
05-Girlfriend/Ex-Girlfriend
06-Ex-Husband
07-Ex-Wife
08-Employee
09-Employer
10-Friend
11-Homosexual Relation
12-Other-Known to Victim
13-Stranger
14-Gang Member
15-Peace Officer Related
16-Unknown
17-Other (Describe)

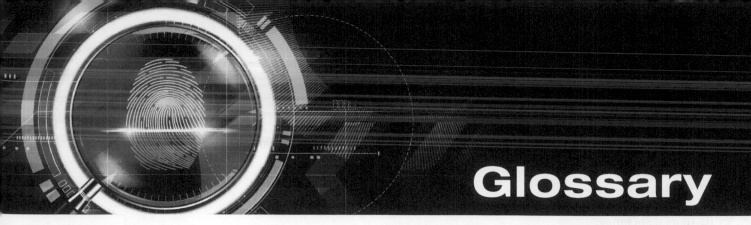

Number in parentheses is the chapter in which the term is discussed.

A

accelerant a fuel or oxidizer that promotes combustion and is intentionally used to start a fire or increase the rate of growth or spread of fire. (16)

active voice that in which the subject performs the action of the sentence; contrasts with passive voice. (3)

adipocere the soapy appearance that develops on a dead body that has been left for weeks in a hot, moist location. (8)

administrative warrant one that grants official permission to inspect a given property to determine compliance with city regulations and is issued when it is necessary for a government agent to search a premises to determine a fire's cause and origin. (16)

admission a statement containing some information concerning the elements of a crime but falling short of a full confession. (6)

adoptive admission occurs when someone else makes a statement in a person's presence and under circumstances where it would be logical to expect the person to make a denial if the statement falsely implicated them, but the person does not deny the allegations. (6)

Advanced Fingerprint Information Technology (AFIT) an integrated system, the precursor to which was the FBI's AFIS, that can also incorporate additional biometric data such as latent palmprints and facial recognition technology. (5)

adversary system the justice system used in the United States which establishes clearly defined roles for both the prosecution and the defense and sets the judge as the neutral party. (21)

adware a type of spyware used by advertisers to gather consumer and marketing information. (17)

aggravated arson intentionally destroying or damaging a dwelling or other property, real or personal, by means of fire, explosives, or other incendiary device, creating an imminent danger to life or great bodily harm, which risk was known or reasonably foreseeable to the suspect. (16)

aggravated assault an unlawful attack by one person on another to inflict severe bodily injury; also called *felonious assault*. (9)

algor mortis the postmortem cooling process of the body. (8)

analogs drugs created by adding to or omitting something from an existing drug. (18)

Antichrist the son of Satan. (19)

anticipatory warrant one based upon prior knowledge or an affidavit showing probable cause that at some future time (but not presently) certain evidence of crime will be located at a specified place; such warrants are constitutional if a proper showing is made that contraband or evidence will likely be found at the target location at a given time or when a specific triggering event occurs. (4)

apple picking a particularly brazen type of robbery in which a suspect snatches an iPhone, iPad, or other mobile device directly from the hands of its user. (12)

arc mapping involves the survey and analysis of the locations where electrical arcing has caused damage to determine the origin of a fire. (16)

arrest the taking of a person into custody in the manner authorized by law to present that person before a magistrate to answer for the commission of a crime. (7)

arson the malicious, willful burning of a building or property; *see also* **aggravated arson**. (16)

asphyxiation death or unconsciousness resulting from insufficient oxygen to support the red blood cells reaching the body tissues and the brain. (8)

assault unlawfully threatening to harm another person, actually harming another person, or attempting unsuccessfully to do so; formerly referred to threats of or attempts to cause bodily harm, but now usually includes *battery*. (9)

associative evidence links a suspect with a crime. (5)

asymmetric warfare combat in which a weaker group attacks a superior group not head-on but by targeting areas where the adversary least expects to be hit, causing great psychological shock, along with loss of life among random victims. (20)

attenuation doctrine allows for the admission of evidence when the connection between unconstitutional police conduct and the evidence is remote or has been interrupted (attenuated) by some intervening circumstance, so that the interest protected by the constitutional guarantee that has been violated would not be served by suppression of the evidence obtained. (4)

autoerotic asphyxiation accidental death from suffocation, strangulation, or chemical asphyxia resulting from a combination of ritualistic behavior, oxygen deprivation, danger, and fantasy for sexual gratification. (8)

B

bait car a model of a vehicle with a high theft rate that is selected and placed in a high crime area as "bait" for motor vehicle theft. (15)

bait money currency with recorded serial numbers that is placed at each bank teller position so it can be added to any robbery loot. (12)

ballistics the study of the dynamics of projectiles, from propulsion through flight to impact; a narrower definition is the study of the functioning of firearms. (5)

baseline (plotting) method establishes a straight line from one fixed point to another, from which measurements are taken at right angles. (2)

battery actually hitting or striking someone; is synonymous with assault in many states. (9)

beachheading an unconstitutional interrogation technique where an officer questions a custodial suspect without giving the *Miranda* warnings and obtains incriminating statements; the officer then gives the warning, gets a waiver, and repeats the interrogation to obtain the same statement. (6)

Beelzebub a powerful demon, subordinate only to Satan, according to Satanists. (19)

bench trial a trial before a judge without a jury. (21)

best evidence original object, or the highest available degree of proof that can be produced. (5)

bias crime one motivated by bigotry and hatred against a specific group of people and committed because of someone's actual or perceived membership in a particular group; also called *hate crime*. (19)

bigamy marrying another person when one or both of the parties are already married. (10)

biometrics the statistical study of biological data and a means to positively identify an individual by measuring that person's unique physical or behavioral characteristics, such as fingerprints or iris recognition. (5)

bioterrorism involves dissemination of such biological weapons of mass destruction (WMDs) as anthrax, botulism, and smallpox. (20)

bitcoins an Internet currency used in online payment programs. (17)

Black Mass a ceremony performed by Satanists that mocks the Christian ritual of communion by substituting blood and urine for wine and feces for bread. (19)

blind reporting allows sexual assault victims to retain their anonymity and confidentiality while sharing critical information with law enforcement; also permits victims to gather legal information from law enforcement without having to commit immediately to an investigation. (10)

bloodstain pattern analysis the study of bloodstains to assist in establishing spatial and sequential events that occurred during, and sometimes after, the act of bloodshed. (5)

blowing (a safe) a dangerous and noisy method of opening a safe using cotton, primer cap, copper wire, and nitroglycerin. (13)

body packing a method of smuggling or otherwise concealing drugs inside a body opening, including the rectum or vagina. (18)

boogaloo a slang term for a future civil war in the United States; the basic nature of the boogaloo movement is anti-government, anti-authority, and anti-police. (20)

bookmaking soliciting and accepting bets on any type of sporting event. (18)

boosters professional shoplifters. (14)

bore the inside portion of a weapon's barrel, which is surrounded by raised ridges called *lands* and recessed areas called *grooves*. (5)

brackets testimony tactic that allows the witness some leeway and helps them retain credibility; provides a range or approximation, for example, "He was 40 to 50 feet away." (21)

Brady rule entitles the accused to information as provided by the statutes of the state and disclosure of exculpatory evidence by the prosecution. (21)

bugging an audio surveillance technique that uses a machine to record conversations within a room without the consent of those involved. (7)

Buie **sweep** the authorized search by police of areas immediately adjoining the place of arrest, justified when reasonable suspicion exists that another person might be present who poses a danger to the arresting officers; held constitutional in *Maryland v. Buie* (1990); synonymous with *protective sweep*. (4)

bullying repeated, intentional aggression perpetrated by a more powerful individual or group against a less powerful victim. (11)

bump key a burglary tool; a generic key used along with another mechanism to apply force to open a lock. (13)

burglary the unlawful entry of a structure to commit a felony or theft, even if no force was used to gain entry. (13)

burning (a safe) opening a safe using a burn bar or other safe-cracking device to burn a hole into the safe to gain entry. (13)

bustout a type of check fraud in which a perpetrator first deposits a fictitious check that appears to be genuinely drawn on a real account into a checking or credit card account at a financial institution. Immediately thereafter, the subject withdraws funds from the account into which the fictitious check was deposited. Once the fraudulent nature of the check is discovered and the check is dishonored by the institution, the account has been "busted." (14)

C

caliber the diameter of a weapon's bore as measured between lands, as well as the size of bullet intended for use with a specific weapon. (5)

capital flight the legal large-scale removal of funds or capital from a country; not to be confused with money laundering, which is illegal. All money laundering is capital flight, but not all capital flight is money laundering. (18)

carjacking a category of robbery involving the taking of a motor vehicle from a person by force or the threat of force. (12)

car shopping the theft of items from unlocked cars. (14)

cast to make an impression using plaster of Paris or a similar substance; also, the physical reproduction of such an impression. (5)

chain of custody *see* **chain of evidence**. (5)

chain of evidence documentation of what has happened to evidence from the time it was discovered until it is needed in court, including every person who has had custody of the evidence and why. (5)

chicken hawk an adult who has either heterosexual or homosexual preferences for young boys or girls of a specific, limited age range; used synonymously with *pedophile*. (11)

child molestation the violation of a child, male or female, under age 14, by lewd or lascivious acts, indecent exposure, incest, or statutory rape; usually a felony. (10)

chopping (a safe) opening a safe by using a sledge and chisel or other tools to chop a hole in the bottom of the safe large enough to remove the contents; also called *ripping* or *peeling*. (13)

chop shop a business, usually an auto body shop, that disassembles stolen vehicles and sells the parts. (15)

chronological order in time sequence. (3)

circumstantial evidence evidence from which inferences are drawn; a fact or event that tends to incriminate a person in a crime; for example, being seen running from a crime scene; also called *indirect evidence*. (5)

civil liability a person's degree of risk of being sued; any person acting under the authority of law who violates another person's constitutional rights can be sued. (1)

class characteristics features that place an item into a specific category; for example, the size and shape of a tool the distinguishes a screwdriver from a pry bar. (5)

clearance rate the ratio of crimes resolved to the number of crimes reported. (8)

click-jacking concealing a hyperlink beneath legitimate clickable content which, when clicked, leads to the execution of hidden, unintentional actions, such as downloading malware or sending personal information to a website. (17)

cloning a crime in which a stolen vehicle is given a copied VIN to assume the identity of a legally owned, or "non-stolen," vehicle of a similar make and model. (15)

closed-ended question one that requires only a "yes" or "no," or other short, simple answer and should be avoided during interviews; not to be confused with a direct question. (6)

close surveillance staying within a few steps of the subject or keeping the subject in sight; moving surveillance that is used when it is extremely important not to lose the subject; also called *tight surveillance*. (7)

closing robbery a robbery carried out at the end of the business day. (12)

club drugs those commonly found at raves (dance parties), including Ecstacy, GHB, Rohypnol, and LSD. (18)

cocooning the idea that victims of domestic violence need to surround themselves with others who are aware of the situation and can be an extra set of eyes and ears, a layer of protection to alert authorities if the victim is unable to call for help. (9)

cognitive interview an approach that uses simple mnemonic techniques aimed at encouraging focused retrieval of memories with minimal loss in accuracy; a technique that helps victims or witnesses put themselves mentally at the scene of the crime. (6)

cold case a case, such as a violent crime, missing person, or unidentified person, that has remained unsolved for at least three years and has the potential to be solved through newly acquired information or advanced technologies to analyze evidence. (8)

commercial burglary one that occurs at a business or other nonresidential property, including churches, schools, barns, public buildings, shops, offices, stores, factories, warehouses, pharmacies, veterinary clinics, stables, ships, or railroad cars; also referred to as a *nonresidential burglary*. (13)

community policing the philosophy that the police must work with the community through partnerships and problem solving to address problems of crime and disorder; a belief that by working together, the police and the community can accomplish what neither can accomplish alone. (1)

compass-point (plotting) method uses a protractor to measure the angle formed by two lines. (2)

competent evidence that which has been properly collected, identified, filed, and continuously secured. (5)

competent photograph an image that accurately represents what it purports to represent, is properly identified, and is properly placed in the chain of evidence and secured until court presentation. (2)

complainant a person who requests an investigation or that action be taken; is often the victim of a crime. (6)

computer crime an offense which involves the addition, deletion, change, or theft of information via a computer. (17)

computer virus a program created specifically to "infect" other programs with copies of itself; it attacks, attaches itself to, and becomes part of another executable program. (17)

concise avoiding wordiness; making every word count without leaving out important facts. (3)

conclusionary language nonfactual; drawing inferences; for example, "The man was nervous"; to be avoided in police reports. (3)

confession information supporting the elements of a crime that is provided and attested to by any person involved in committing the crime; can be oral or written and must be voluntary and not given in response to threats, promises, or rewards. (6)

confidence game obtains money or property by a trick, device, or swindle that takes advantage of a victim's trust in the swindler; the confidence game offers a get-rich-quick scheme. (14)

confidential (reliable) informant (CRI) an individual who has previously provided to police information that was corroborated and used. (6)

connotative adjective describing words that have an emotional effect, with meanings that impart either positive or negative overtones. (3)

contagion effect a phenomenon in which media publicity of an act or event inspires more such acts or events; for example, the belief that coverage of terrorism inspires more terrorism. (20)

contamination postcrime transfer of material to or from evidence. (5)

content *what* is said in a narrative; as opposed to form, which is *how* a narrative is written; the content of an effective report is factual, accurate, objective, and complete. (3)

cook someone who produces methamphetamine. (18)

corporal punishment the intentional infliction of pain or injury in an effort to correct or discipline children. (11)

corporate crime *see* **white-collar crime**. (14)

corpus delicti "body of the crime"; elements of a specific crime; evidence establishing that a specific crime has been committed. (5)

corpus delicti evidence establishes that a crime was committed. (5)

coven a group of witches or Satanists. (19)

cover an assumed identity used while on an undercover assignment. (7)

crack cocaine mixed with baking soda and water, heated in a pan, and then dried and split into pellet-size bits or chunks, which are smoked to produce effects reportedly ten times greater than powder cocaine at a fraction of the cost; also called *rock* or *crack rock*. (18)

cracker a computer hacker in the negative sense; someone who cracks software protection and removes it, deliberately and maliciously intruding into a computer or network to cause damage. (17)

cramming the placement by a third party of unauthorized charges on a consumer's wired, wireless, or bundled services telephone bill. (14)

crank the street name for methamphetamine, not to be confused with crack. (18)

crazing the complicated, irregular pattern of short cracks in glass. (16)

crime an act or omission forbidden by law and punishable by a fine, imprisonment, or even death; crimes are an offense against the state and their penalties are established and defined by state and federal statutes and local ordinances. (1)

crime mapping focuses on the location of crimes—the hot spots where most crimes occur—rather than on the criminal. (1)

crime prevention through environmental design (CPTED) altering the physical characteristics of a property to make it less attractive to criminals—for example, removing dense shrubbery next to windows and doors, improving lighting, and closing garage doors; also called *target hardening*. (13)

criminal enterprise by FBI definition, a group of individuals with an identified hierarchy, or comparable structure, engaged in significant criminal activity; although *organized crime* and *criminal enterprise* are often equated and used interchangeably, several federal statutes specifically delineate the elements of an *enterprise* that must be proven to convict individuals or groups under those statutes. (18)

criminal homicide the felonious killing of one person by another; includes murder and manslaughter. (8)

criminal intent performing an unlawful act on purpose, knowing the act to be illegal. (8)

criminal investigation the process of discovering, collecting, preparing, identifying, and presenting evidence to determine what happened and who is responsible. (1)

criminalist a person who searches for, collects, and preserves physical evidence in the investigations of crime and suspected criminals; also called a *crime scene technician, examiner,* or *investigator.* (1)

criminalistics a branch of forensic science that employs specialists trained in recording, identifying, and interpreting the *minutiae* (minute details) of physical evidence. (1)

criminal negligence acts of commission or omission creating situations resulting in unreasonable risk of death or great bodily harm. (8)

criminal profiling a method of suspect identification that attempts to describe an individual's mental, emotional, and psychological characteristics in an effort to provide investigators with corroborative information about a known suspect or possible leads to an unknown suspect; also called *psychological profiling.* (7)

criminal statute a legislative act that defines a crime and attaches a penalty or punishment to that offense. (1)

cross-contamination occurs when items of evidence touch one another and thus exchange matter. (5)

cross-examination the questioning by the opposite side in a trial that attempts to assess the validity of testimony given under direct examination. (21)

cross-projection sketch a plotting method that presents the floor and walls of a room as though they were on the same surface. (2)

CSI effect the perception in the criminal justice system, popular media, and general population that widespread viewing of crime-based television programs has created a juror bias toward the requirement of forensic evidence at trial to justify a conviction, and that these unreasonable juror expectations increase the burden of proof faced by prosecutors as well as the chance of acquittal. (5)

cult a system of religious beliefs and rituals and its body of adherents; also called *New Religious Movement (NRM).* (19)

culturally adroit skilled in interacting across gender, ethnic, generational, social, and political group lines. (1)

cunnilingus sexual activity involving oral contact with the female genitals. (10)

curtilage the portion of a residence that is not open to the public, retains an expectation of privacy, and is reserved for private owner or family use, in contrast to sidewalks and alleys, which are used by the public and which hold no reasonable expectation of privacy. (4)

custodial arrest occurs when an officer has decided a suspect is not free to leave, there has been considerable deprivation of the suspect's liberty, or the officer has arrested the suspect; also referred to as having the suspect *in custody.* (6)

custodial interrogation questioning by law enforcement officers after a person has been taken into custody or otherwise deprived of freedom in a significant way; requires that the *Miranda* warning be given. (6)

cyberbullying the willful and repeated use of cell phones, computers, and other electronic communication devices to harass and threaten others; essentially cyberstalking or cyberharassment involving minors. (9)

cybercrime part of the larger category of *computer crime*, a criminal act that is carried out using cybertechnology (the spectrum of computing and information/communication technologies, from individual computers to computer networks to the Internet) and takes place in cyberspace (an intangible, virtual world existing in the network connections between two or more computers); also called *electronic crime* or *e-crime.* (17)

cyberstalking the repeated use of the Internet, email, or other digital electronic communications devices to stalk another person. (9)

cybersuicide a completed or attempted suicide influenced or mediated by the Internet. (9)

cyberterrorism the premeditated, politically motivated attack against information, computer systems, computer programs, and data that results in harm to noncombatant targets by subnational groups or clandestine agents; also refers to the use of a computer system as a conduit for causing terror. (17, 20)

cycle of violence a three-phase cycle of domestic violence—the tension-building stage, the acute battering episode, the honeymoon, and back to the tension-building stage—which typically increases in both frequency and severity. (9)

D

dark web an encrypted network designed specifically for anonymity and accessible only through specific software and browsers, such as Tor (The Onion Router), IP2 (Invisible Internet Project), Freenet, and other darknet overlays. (17)

data mining a process that uses powerful analytical tools to quickly and thoroughly explore mountains of data related to a criminal case to discover new patterns or confirm suspected patterns or trends. (1)

data remanence refers to the residual physical representation of data that have been erased from a computer's hard drive. (17)

date rape a type of sexual assault where the victim knows the suspect; sometimes called *acquaintance rape.* (10)

Daubert standard the two-pronged requirement that an expert's testimony be both reliable and relevant. (5)

deconfliction protocol or guidelines used to avoid conflict and can be applied to declassified and confidential investigations. (20)

deductive reasoning a logical process in which a conclusion follows from specific facts; a reconstructive process based on specific pieces of evidence to establish proof that a suspect is guilty of an offense; flows from general to specific. (1)

deep web that much larger part of the Web beneath the surface that contains both indexed and unindexed content that cannot be found with standard search engines but can be accessed using another indexed Web address or application program interface found on the surface web. (17)

de facto **arrest** the functional equivalent of an arrest that occurs by illegally bringing someone in for questioning without probable cause; any evidence obtained through this method is inadmissible in court. (7)

defense wounds nonfatal injuries—cuts on the hands, arms, and legs—incurred by victims as they attempt to ward off attackers; indicative of murder. (8)

de minimus communication allowed or acceptable contact between a witness and a juror, such as exchanging a simple hello or giving directions. (21)

denial-of-service (DoS) attack the disruption or degradation of a computer or network's Internet connection or email service that interrupts the regular flow of data; using multiple agents to create a widespread interruption is a distributed DoS, or DDoS. (17)

denotative an adjective describing words that have little emotional effect and are objective in their meaning. (3)

deposition an oral statement given under oath that is recorded and transcribed word-for-word. (21)

depressant a drug that reduces restlessness and emotional tension and induces sleep; most common are the barbiturates. (18)

depth of char a measure of how deeply wood is burned; indicates the burn spread and in limited circumstances may be useful in determining a fire's point of origin. (16)

designer drugs substances created by adding to or taking something away from an existing drug; also called *New Psychoactive Substances (NPSs)*. (18)

digital evidence information and data of value to an investigation that are stored on, received, or transmitted by an electronic device. (5)

digital penetration the act of using fingers (digits) to penetrate or manipulate sexual organs that include the penis, vagina, and anus. (10)

direct evidence establishes proof of a fact without any other evidence. (5)

direct examination the initial questioning of a witness or defendant during a trial by the lawyer who is using the person's testimony to further their case. (21)

direct question one that is to the point with little chance of misinterpretation; for example, "What time did you leave?" (6)

discovery process pretrial disclosure between prosecution and defense about the evidence they intend to use at trial, thus avoiding "trial by surprise." (21)

disposition how a case is disposed of—for example, referred, closed (inactive), open (active), dismissed, pending further information, and so on. (3)

disrupters devices that use gunpowder to fire a jet of water or a projectile at a particular component of an explosive to make it safe. (16)

DNA (deoxyribonucleic acid) an organic substance found in the nucleus of living cells that provides the genetic code determining a person's individual characteristics. (5)

DNA profiling the forensic analysis of blood, hair, saliva, semen, or cells from almost any part of the body to ascertain a positive identity or match. (5)

domain name the unique name of a computer system on the Internet that distinguishes it from all other online systems; associated with a specific IP address and easier to remember than a string of numbers; not the same as a Web address or URL. (17)

domestic terrorism activities that involve acts dangerous to human life that violate federal or state law; appear intended (i) to intimidate or coerce a civilian population, (ii) to influence the policy of a government by intimidation or coercion, or (iii) to affect the conduct of a government by mass destruction, assassination, or kidnapping; and that occur primarily within the territorial jurisdiction of the United States. (20)

domestic violence a pattern of behaviors involving physical, sexual, economic, and emotional abuse, used alone or in combination, to establish and maintain power and control over another person within a household or family environment. (9)

doxing publicly releasing a person's personal, sensitive identifying information online without authorization. (17)

dragging (a safe) opening a safe by inserting a V plate behind the dial and tightening screw bolts on the edges of the V plate until the dial and the spindle are pulled out; this method, the opposite of punching, works on many older safes but not on newer ones; also called *pulling*. (13)

dye pack a bundle of currency containing a colored dye and tear gas that, if taken during a robbery, is activated when the robber crosses an electromagnetic field at the facility's exit, staining the money with brightly colored dye and emitting a cloud of colored smoke. (12)

Dyer Act legislation that made interstate transportation of a stolen motor vehicle a federal crime and allowed for federal assistance in prosecuting such cases. (15)

dying declaration a statement that can provide valuable information to investigators and usually qualifies as a hearsay exception, making it admissible as evidence. (6)

dynamic IP address an IP address that fluctuates and is, thus, more secure because it is changed frequently. (17)

E

economic crime *see* **white-collar crime.** (14)

ecoterrorism seeks to inflict economic damage, often through criminal violence, to those who exploit or profit from the destruction of the natural environment. (20)

e-crime short for *electronic crime*; part of the larger category of *computer crime*, it is a criminal act that is carried out using cybertechnology (the spectrum of computing and information/communication technologies, from individual computers to computer networks to the Internet) and takes place in cyberspace (an intangible, virtual world existing in the network connections between two or more computers); also called *cybercrime*. (17)

Ecstasy (MDMA) a derivative of amphetamine or speed, a powerful stimulant; an increasingly popular club drug. (18)

elder abuse multiple intentional or neglectful acts by a caregiver or other trusted individual that lead to, or may lead to, harm of a vulnerable elderly person; includes physical or mental mistreatment, financial exploitation, and general neglect of the elderly; may include fraud as well as assault, battery, and even murder. (9)

elements of the crime the specific conditions that must occur for an act to be called a specific kind of crime. (1)

"elephant-in-a-matchbox" doctrine the requirement that searchers consider the probable size and shape of evidence they seek because, for example, large objects cannot be concealed in tiny areas. (4)

elimination prints prints of persons with reason to be at the crime scene but who are not suspects. (5)

embezzlement the fraudulent appropriation of property by a person to whom it has been entrusted. (14)

emotional abuse psychological or social abuse that causes fear or feelings of unworthiness in others; with children, this occurs by such means as name calling, locking them in closets, ignoring them, constantly belittling or insulting them, threatening violence, or exposing them to harmful psychological situations. (11)

encryption any procedure used in cryptography to convert plain text into ciphertext to prevent anyone but the intended recipient from reading the data; a technique that puts information in code and thus obscures a normally comprehensible message. (17)

entrapment the conception and planning of an offense by an officer to trick someone into committing a crime that they would not normally commit. (7)

equivocal death situations that are open to interpretation in investigations; the case may present as homicide, suicide, or accidental death depending on the circumstances. (8)

evidence data on which a judgment or conclusion may be based; used for determining the facts in a case, for later laboratory examination, and for direct presentation in court. (5)

exceptionally cleared disposition of a case when circumstances outside the investigation result in no charges being filed (e.g., if the suspect dies). (21)

excessive force more than ordinary force, going above and beyond what is required to control the situation or behavior of an individual, and justified only when exceptional resistance occurs and there is no other way to gain compliance by the subject. (7)

excited delirium describes the manifestations of extreme drug abuse; may occur in people under the influence of an illicit stimulant substance such as cocaine or in people with a history of mental illness who are not taking their medications. (18)

exclusionary rule legal principle that established that the courts cannot accept evidence obtained by unreasonable searches and seizures, regardless of its relevance to the case (*Weeks v. United States; Mapp v. Ohio*). (4)

exculpatory evidence evidence favorable to the accused that would clear the accused of blame; for example, having a blood type different from that found at a homicide. (1)

excusable homicide the unintentional, truly accidental killing of another person. (8)

exhibitionists people who gain sexual satisfaction by exposing themselves. (10)

exigent circumstances emergency situations; they do not require a warrant. (4)

expert testimony that presented by a person deemed to have specialized training, skills, or experience in a particular area that will help the jury understand the topic and evidence presentation. (21)

exploitation taking unfair advantage of children or using them illegally. (11)

expressive violence that which stems from hurt feelings, anger, or rage, in contrast to instrumental violence, which is goal-directed predatory behavior used to exert control. (8)

extremism a radical mental attitude or ideology, a main driving idea or purpose, that one holds internally. (20)

F

fellatio sexual activity involving oral contact with the male genitals. (10)

felonious assault an unlawful attack by one person on another to inflict severe bodily injury; also called *aggravated assault*. (9)

felony a serious crime such as homicide, aggravated assault, or robbery; generally punishable by death or imprisonment of more than one year in a penitentiary. (1)

female genital mutilation (FGM) a procedure that involves partial or total removal of the external female genitalia, or other injury to the female genital organs for nonmedical reasons. (11)

femicide the murder of a woman. (9)

fence a go-between who receives stolen goods for resale. (12)

field identification on-the-scene identification of a suspect by the victim of or witnesses to a crime, conducted within a short time after the crime was committed; also called *show-up identification*. (7)

field interview questioning that occurs spontaneously at or near the scene. (6)

finished scale drawing crime scene documentation done in ink on a good grade of paper and drawn to scale, using exact measurements. (2)

fireplay behavior that conveys a low level of intent to inflict harm and an absence of malice; rather, it involves curiosity and fascination. (16)

firesetting behavior that involves malice and intent to inflict harm. (16)

fire triangle the three elements necessary for a substance to burn: air, fuel, and heat. (16)

firewall software or hardware protective measure that blocks ports of access to a computer or network to prevent unauthorized access and stop malicious programs from entering. (17)

first-degree murder the premeditated, intentional killing of another person or killing someone while committing or attempting to commit a felony. (8)

first person the use of *I, me, we*, and *us* in speaking and writing; in contrast to the second person (*you*) and the third person (*he* or *this officer*). (3)

fixed surveillance observing a location from a fixed location; also called *plant* and *stakeout*. (7)

flaggers thieves who go around neighborhoods targeting mailboxes with their flags up, searching for envelopes containing checks and other forms of payment. (14)

flash mob a theft technique where a mass of individuals rapidly enter, steal from, and exit an establishment, overwhelming employees' capabilities to do anything about the situation; also called a *mob rob* or *swarming*. (19)

flashover an event in which surfaces and room contents exposed to the thermal radiation of a fire reach their ignition temperatures effectively simultaneously, causing the fire to spread suddenly and rapidly. (16)

flashroll money used in an undercover drug buy. (18)

flipping *see* **property flipping**. (14)

floor-release limit the maximum dollar amount that may be paid with a check or credit card without authorization from the central office unless the business assumes liability for any loss. (14)

fluffing increasing telephone rates without notification. (14)

force the amount of effort required by police to compel compliance by an unwilling subject; need not necessarily be "hands on." (7)

forcible rape sexual intercourse against a person's will by the use or threat of force. (10)

forensic photogrammetry the technique of extrapolating three-dimensional measurements directly from two-dimensional photographs. (2)

forensic science the application of science, technology, and the scientific process to matters of law; includes the branch of criminalistics. (1, 5)

forgery signing someone else's name to a document or altering the name or amount on a check or document with the intent to defraud. (14)

form *how* a narrative is written; in contrast to content, which is *what* is said in a narrative; the form of a well-written report is concise, clear, grammatically and mechanically correct, and written in Standard English. (3)

fraud the intentional deception to cause a person to give up property or some lawful right. (14)

frisk an external search of an individual's clothing; also called a *patdown.* (4)

"fruit-of-the-poisonous-tree" doctrine the basis for the exclusionary rule which established that evidence obtained as a result of an earlier illegality must be excluded from trial. (4)

full faith and credit the legal status wherein a document, contract, license, or court order issued anywhere in the country is legally binding and enforceable nationwide. (9)

fusion center a state-owned and operated center that serves as a focal point in states and major urban areas for the receipt, analysis, gathering, and sharing of threat-related information and intelligence between State, Local, Tribal and Territorial (SLTT); federal; and private sector partners. (20)

G

gang a group or association of three or more persons with a common identifying sign, symbol, or name who individually or collectively engage in criminal activity that creates an atmosphere of fear and intimidation. (19)

geographic profiling a technique based on the fact that everyone has a pattern to their lives, particularly in relation to the geographical areas they frequent, and used to help identify suspects who commit multiple crimes (serial criminals). (7)

Giglio-impaired a condition in which an officer's credibility is compromised because there exists potential impeachment evidence that would render that officer's testimony in a case, or any future case, of marginal value. (3)

good faith doctrine a principle that established that illegally obtained evidence may be admissible if the police were truly not aware that they were violating the suspect's Fourth Amendment rights. (4)

gouging charging undisclosed fees for use or equipment. (14)

graffiti wall writing; used to identify gang turf and send messages; sometimes called the "newspaper of the street." (19)

grand larceny a felony based on the substantial value of the property stolen. (14)

H

hacker a computer buff; one who intrudes into another's computer or network for the challenge and status; not necessarily a negative term; in contrast to a *cracker*, who is someone who intrudes to commit a crime. (17)

hacktivism using cyberspace to harass or sabotage sites that conduct activities or advocate philosophies that hacktivists find unacceptable. (17)

hallucinogen a drug that induces visions, delusions, or perceptual distortions of reality; for example, LSD, DMT, and PCP or angel dust. (18)

Hand of Glory the left hand of a person who has died. (19)

hardware disabler a device designed to ensure a self-destruct sequence of any potential evidence; it may be present on or around a computer, with a remote power switch being the most prevalent of the disabler hardware devices. (17)

hate crime one motivated by bigotry and hatred against a specific group of people and committed because of someone's actual or perceived membership in a particular group; also called *bias crime.* (19)

hate incidents behaviors that, while motivated by bias against a victim's race, religion, ethnic/national origin, gender, age, disability, or sexual orientation, do *not* rise to the level of a statutorily defined criminal offense; for example, hostile or hateful speech, or other disrespectful or discriminatory behavior motivated by bias. (19)

hawala an informal banking system based on trust and often bartering, common throughout the Middle East and used to transfer billions of dollars every year. (20)

hearsay what one has heard from others or was told about by others. (21)

heat of passion an element of criminal homicide that results from an extremely volatile emotional condition; the alternative to premeditation. (8)

hebephile a person who selects high school–age youths as sex victims. (11)

hesitation wounds less severe, superficial cutting marks caused by an individual's attempts to build up nerve before making a fatal cutting wound; indicates suicide. (8)

hit-and-run burglary a theft in which a window is smashed to steal merchandise; also called *smash and grab.* (13)

holder the person to whom a credit or debit card is issued and who agrees to pay obligations arising from its use. (14)

homegrown violent extremists (HVEs) U.S.-based individuals who have been radicalized primarily in the United States and are inspired by global jihadists but are not generally receiving individualized direction from foreign terrorist organizations. (20)

home invasion a forced entry into an occupied dwelling to commit a violent crime, whether robbery, sexual assault, murder, or some combination of violent offenses. (12)

homicide the killing of one person by another. (8)

hot sheet a list of stolen vehicles. (15)

hot spots geographic areas with a higher incidence rate of criminal activity. (1)

human trafficking the act of recruiting, harboring, transporting, providing, or obtaining a person for compelled labor or commercial sex acts through the use of force, fraud, or coercion; modern-day slavery; also called *trafficking in persons.* (10)

I

identity fraud the unauthorized use or attempted use of personally identifiable information (PII) to commit theft or fraud. (14)

identity theft the criminal act of illegally obtaining someone else's personally identifiable information (PII) for some type of gain, normally financial. (14)

igniter a substance or device used to start a fire. (16)

imaging making a byte-by-byte copy of everything on the hard drive. (17)

immediate control the area within a person's reach. (4)

immersive imaging 360-degree photographic view of a crime scene that allows viewers to virtually "walk through it" as though they were there. (2)

immobilizer a device that allows a vehicle's engine to recognize only the preprogrammed key(s) assigned to the vehicle, in an effort to prevent auto theft. (15)

impeach to discredit testimony; to challenge the truth or accuracy of what a prosecution witness testified to under direct examination. (21)

implicit bias subtle, largely unconscious or semiconscious attitudes that influence a person's behavior, judgments, and decisions. (6)

incantation a verbal spell or ritualistic prayer. (19)

incendiary describes a fire ignited intentionally and maliciously under circumstances in which a person knows that the fire should not be set; arson. (16)

incest sexual intercourse between family members or close relatives, including children related by adoption. (10)

in custody that point at which an officer has decided a suspect is not free to leave, there has been considerable deprivation of the suspect's liberty, or the officer has arrested the suspect; also referred to as *custodial arrest*. (6)

indecent exposure revealing one's genitals to another person to such an extent as to shock the other's sense of decency. (10)

independent source doctrine allows the admission of evidence initially discovered during an unlawful search if officers were later able to acquire the same evidence from a separate, wholly independent source, such as the execution of a valid search warrant (*Murray v. United States*, 1988). (4)

indicator crimes offenses that, in situations involving the same victim and suspect, can establish a pattern of events indicative of an abusive relationship; can range from harassing phone calls to hit-and-run. (9)

indirect evidence that from which inferences are drawn; a fact or event that tends to incriminate a person in a crime; for example, being seen running from a crime scene; also called *circumstantial evidence*. (5)

indirect question one that skirts the issue; for example, "How do you and the victim get along?" (6)

individual characteristics features that distinguish one item from others of the same type; for example, a gouge or scratch at the flat end of a screwdriver can distinguish it from all other screwdrivers; also called *identifying characteristics*. (5)

inductive reasoning using specific facts and observations to establish broad generalizations. (1)

inevitable discovery doctrine principle that established that if illegally obtained evidence would in all likelihood eventually have been discovered legally, it may be used and admitted in court. (4)

informant any individual who can provide information related to a case but who is not a complainant, witness, victim, or suspect. (6)

information age the time period driven by knowledge and information rather than by agriculture or industry as in the past. (6)

inkless fingerprint a digital, live-scan capture of a fingerprint that can be stored in a database for rapid retrieval. (5)

in loco parentis having the authority to take the place of the parent; teachers have historically had this right. (9)

instrumental violence goal-directed predatory behavior used to exert control, in contrast to expressive violence, which stems from hurt feelings, anger, or rage. (8)

integration the third and final step in the money laundering cycle, where criminals reclaim their money through seemingly legitimate business transactions. (14)

integrity of evidence refers to the requirement that any item introduced in court must be in the same condition as when it was found at the crime scene. (5)

international terrorism activities that involve violent acts or acts dangerous to human life that violate federal or state law; appear to be intended (i) to intimidate or coerce a civilian population, (ii) to influence the policy of a government by intimidation or coercion, or (iii) to affect the conduct of a government by mass destruction, assassination, or kidnapping; and occur primarily outside the territorial jurisdiction of the United States, or transcend national boundaries in terms of the means by which they are accomplished, the persons they appear intended to intimidate or coerce, or the locale in which their perpetrators operate or seek asylum. (20)

Internet Protocol (IP) address a unique number, analogous to a phone number, needed to access the Internet; commonly issued by a user's Internet service provider (ISP). (17)

Internet service provider (ISP) a company that offers access to the Internet for a fee. (17)

interrogation the questioning of people suspected of direct or indirect involvement in the crime being investigated. (6)

interview the questioning of people not suspected of being involved in a crime but who know something about the crime or the individuals involved in it. (6)

intifada an armed uprising of Palestinians against Israel's occupation of the West Bank and the Gaza strip. (20)

intimate partner violence (IPV) domestic abuse directed by one partner against another. (9)

intimate parts usually refers to the primary genital areas, groin, inner thighs, buttocks, and breasts. (10)

intuition a "sudden knowing" without any conscious reasoning or apparent logic; based on knowledge and experience or what is commonly called *street sense*; a "gut feeling" developed by experience. (1)

investigate to observe or study closely; to inquire into something systematically in a search for truthful information. (1)

involuntary manslaughter an accidental homicide that results from extreme (culpable) negligence. (8)

J

jargon the shorthand vocabulary and technical terminology specific to a particular profession or trade that allows colleagues within that area of work to communicate quickly and concisely. (3)

jihad holy war. (20)

joyriding simply taking a vehicle for fun, often driving recklessly and without regard for any damage caused to the vehicle itself or other property, and then abandoning it. (15)

justifiable homicide the killing of another person under authorization of the law. (8)

K

keystroke logging a diagnostic technique that captures a user's keystrokes; used in espionage to bypass security measures and obtain passwords or encryption keys; also called *keylogging*. (17)

kidnapping taking someone away by force, often for ransom. (11)

L

larceny/theft the unlawful taking, carrying, leading, or driving away of property from the possession of another. (14)

laser-beam photography an imaging process that reveals evidence indiscernible to the naked eye, such as the outline of a footprint in a carpet, even though the fibers have returned to normal position. (2)

latent fingerprints impressions transferred to a surface, either by sweat on the ridges of the fingers or because the fingers carry residue of oil, dirt, blood, or other substances. (5)

layering the second step in the money laundering process, where the money is "cleaned" by moving it around through a series of elaborate transactions, often involving offshore bank accounts and international business companies (IBCs). (14)

leading question one that prompts or leads a person to a specific response and often implies an answer; a useful interrogation technique. (6)

leads avenues bearing clues or potential sources of information relevant to solving a crime. (1)

leakage the illegal or unauthorized removal of cargo from the supply chain; a concept similar to that of *shrinkage*. (14)

legend that part of a crime scene sketch containing the case number, type of crime, name of victim or complainant, location, date, time, investigator, anyone assisting, scale of the sketch, direction of north, and name of the person making the sketch. (2)

legibility refers to the ease with which a handwritten or typeprinted character is recognizable based on its appearance. (3)

lewdness (with a minor) touching a minor to arouse, appeal to, or gratify the perpetrator's sexual desires; the touching may be done by the perpetrator or by the minor under the perpetrator's direction. (11)

livor mortis the dark blue or purple discoloration caused when blood no longer circulates after death and gravity drains the blood to the lowest level of the body; also called *postmortem lividity* or simply *lividity*. (8)

loan-sharking lending money at exorbitant interest rates. (18)

Locard's principle of exchange a basic forensic theory that postulates that when objects come in contact with each other, there is always a transfer of material, however minute, between them. (1)

lock bumping an easy, quiet burglary technique used on standard pin tumbler locks in which a generic (bump) key is used along with another mechanism to apply force to open the lock. (13)

logic bomb a program that secretly attaches another program to a company's computer system; the attached program monitors the input data and waits for some type of error to occur; when this happens, the new program exploits the weakness to steal money or company secrets or to sabotage the system. (17)

long-con games schemes in which the victims are strung along and allowed to win several small stakes before being convinced to place the "big bet," in which they inevitably lose far more than they had won previously. (14)

loose surveillance moving surveillance used when it is more important to remain undetected than to keep the subject under constant observation. (7)

lust murder a sex-related homicide involving a sadistic, deviant assault, where the killer depersonalizes the victim, sexually mutilates the body, and may displace body parts. (8)

M

macrophotography the photographic enlargement of a subject to show details of evidence such as fingerprints or tool marks. (2)

magick the glue that binds occult groups; a supernatural act or force that causes a change in the environment. (19)

malicious intent (malice) an element of first- and second-degree murder; implies ill will, wickedness, cruelty, or recklessness. (8)

maltreatment literally to treat roughly or abuse; includes neglect, medical neglect, physical abuse, sexual abuse, and psychological maltreatment. (11)

malware software developed to cause harm; a contraction of "malicious software." (17)

mandated reporters certain individuals—including teachers, school authorities, child care personnel, camp personnel, clergy, physicians, dentists, chiropractors, nurses, psychologists, medical assistants, attorneys, and social workers—who work with or treat children and are required by law to report cases of suspected neglect or abuse. (11)

manslaughter the unlawful killing of another person with no prior malice; can be voluntary or involuntary. (8)

marker (photographic) item included in a photograph to show accurate or relative size. (2)

mass arson the setting of three or more fires at the same site or location by the same offender during a limited period of time. (16)

mass murder a number of murders (four or more) occurring during the same incident by one or a few suspects, with no distinctive time period between the murders. (8)

material evidence that which is relevant to the specific case and forms a substantive part of the case presented or that has a legitimate and effective influence on the decision of the case. (5)

material photograph an image that relates to the specific case and the subject being discussed. (2)

MDMA 3,4-Methylenedioxymethylamphetamine, known more commonly as *Ecstasy*; a powerful stimulant derivative of amphetamine or speed. (18)

mechanics the use of spelling, capitalization, and punctuation in written communication. (3)

megapixel pixels are the dots making up a digital image; one megapixel is about one million dots. (2)

microaggression a subtle condescending, hostile, or derogatory comment or action that, while not blatantly racist, conveys a negative message to a person that they are viewed as "less than" others. (6)

microphotography the technique of taking pictures through a microscope to help identify minute particles of evidence (e.g., hair or fiber). (2)

minor a person under the legal age for becoming an adult, the most common being under the age of 16 or 18, depending on the state. (11)

Miranda **warning** a statement read by an arresting officer that informs a suspect of their Fifth Amendment right to remain silent, to have counsel present, and to have the state appoint and pay counsel if they cannot afford one; it also warns the suspect that anything they say can and will be used against them in court. (6)

misdemeanor a crime or offense that is less serious than a felony and is punishable by a fine or imprisonment of as long as one year in an institution other than a penitentiary. (1)

misoped a person who hates children, has sex with them, and then brutally murders them. (11)

modus operandi (MO) the characteristic way or preferred method used by a criminal when committing a specific type of crime. (1)

molestation any act motivated by an unnatural or abnormal sexual interest in minors that would reasonably be expected to disturb, irritate, or offend the victim; no touching of the victim is necessary. (11)

money laundering the process of converting illegally earned (dirty) cash to one or more alternative (clean) forms to conceal its illegal origin and true ownership. (14)

moniker a gang member's street name or nickname. (19)

morning glory robbery a robbery that occurs first thing in the morning and catches arriving employees off guard. (12)

motion in limine a request for the judge to issue a protective order against prejudicial questions or statements. (21)

motor vehicle any self-propelled device for moving people or property or pulling implements, whether operated on land, on water, or in the air; includes automobiles, trucks, buses, motorcycles, motor scooters, mopeds, snowmobiles, vans, self-propelled watercraft, and aircraft. (15)

mug shots photographs of those who have been taken into custody and booked. (2)

mules individuals who sell or transport drugs for a regular dealer in return for being assured of a personal drug supply. (18)

mummification the complete dehydration of all body tissues that occurs when a cadaver is left in an extremely dry, hot area. (8)

Munchausen by proxy syndrome (MBPS) a form of child abuse in which the parent or adult caregiver deliberately provides false medical histories, manufactures symptoms and evidence of an illness, or causes real symptoms to create medical distress in a child. (11)

Munchausen syndrome involves self-induced or self-inflicted injuries. (11)

murder *see* **first-**, **second-**, and **third-degree murder**. (8)

N

narcoterrorism the use of terrorist tactics to support drug operations or the use of drug trade profits to finance terrorism. (20)

narcotic a drug that is physically and psychologically addicting; examples include heroin, morphine, codeine, and cocaine. (18)

narrative the body of a technical report that is structured in chronological order and describes a sequence of investigative events. (3)

neglect the failure to meet a child's basic needs, including housing, food, clothing, education, and access to medical care. (11)

network a body of personal contacts and relationships; links between people or between people and their beliefs; two or more computers connected for the purpose of sharing data and resources. (6)

nightcapped warrant a court-approved stipulation authorizing officers to carry out an arrest or search warrant at any time, day or night. (4)

no-knock warrant a warrant issued with a special provision permitting officers to execute the warrant without first announcing themselves. (4)

noncriminal homicide the nonfelonious killing of one person by another; includes excusable and justifiable homicide. (8)

nonverbal communication messages conveyed by dress, eye contact, posture, gestures, distance, mannerisms, rate of speech, and tone of voice; body language. (6)

O

objective nonopinionated, fair, and impartial. (3)

occult the secret knowledge of supernormal powers; many cults claim to have such knowledge. (19)

open-ended question one that gives the victim, witness, or suspect the opportunity to provide a much fuller response, allowing the investigator greater insight into the person's knowledge and feelings; often begins with "Why," "How," or "Tell me about"; should be asked liberally during interrogation. (6)

open surveillance moving surveillance in which it does not matter if the surveillant is detected and no extraordinary means are used to remain undetected; also called a *rough surveillance*. (7)

oral copulation the act of joining the mouth of one person with the sexual organ of another person; *see* **cunnilingus** and **fellatio**. (10)

ordinance an act of the legislative body of a municipality or county relating to all the rules governing the municipality or county, including misdemeanor crimes. (1)

organized crime any group having some manner of a formalized structure and whose primary objective is to obtain money through illegal activities. (18)

organized retail crime (ORC) an umbrella term used to describe large-scale retail theft and fraud activity by organized groups of professional shoplifters; alternately called *organized retail theft*. (14)

osteogenesis imperfecta (OI) a genetic disorder characterized by bones that break easily, often from little or no apparent cause; also called *brittle bone disease*. (11)

OTC drugs over-the-counter drugs, no prescription required. (18)

overlapping a photographic technique whereby the entire scene is photographed in a clockwise direction so that a specific object is on the right side of the first photograph, on the next photo the same object is on the left side of the photo, and so on until the entire scene is photographed. (2)

P

parallel proceedings pursing civil and criminal sanctions at the same time. (14)

particularity requirement dictates that a search conducted with a warrant must be limited to the specific area and specific items named in the warrant, as held in *Stanford v. Texas* (1965). (4)

past tense the use of verbs to indicate that events have already occurred; for example, *lived* rather than *lives*. (3)

patdown an external search of an individual's clothing; also called a *frisk*. (4)

pedophile an adult who is sexually attracted to young children and has either heterosexual or homosexual preferences for boys or girls of a specific, limited age range. (10, 11)

peeling (a safe) opening a safe by drilling a hole in a corner of the safe and then making the hole successively larger by using other drills until the narrow end of a jimmy can be inserted in the hole to pry the door partially open. (13)

penetration any intrusion, however slight, of any part of a person's body or any object manipulated or inserted by a person into the genital or anal openings of another's body, including sexual intercourse in its ordinary meaning; *see also* **sexual penetration**. (10)

petty (petit) larceny a misdemeanor based on the value of the property stolen. (14)

pharming a cybercrime that involves the hijacking of a domain name for the purpose of redirecting online traffic away from a legitimate website toward a fake site, such as a bogus bank website; also refers to the dangerous act of rifling through the family medicine cabinet for pills, both OTC and prescription, combining everything in a bowl, scooping out and ingesting a handful, and waiting to see what happens. (17, 18)

phishing a method of cybercrime in which criminals misrepresent themselves as a trustworthy source to get victims to disclose personal, sensitive information, such as passwords, bank account numbers, and the like, which is then used by the criminals to commit fraud or other crimes. (17)

physical abuse beating, whipping, burning, or otherwise inflicting physical harm upon a child. (11)

physical evidence anything real—that has substance—and helps establish the facts of a case. (5)

pill mills rogue pain management clinics staffed by unethical "doctors" who supply users with illicit pharmaceuticals. (18)

piracy copying and using computer programs in violation of copyrights and trade secret laws. (17)

pixel the smallest unit of a digital image, also referred to as a *dot*. (2)

placement the first step in the process of laundering money that inserts the ill-gotten funds into the legitimate U.S. market; common methods include *smurfing* (technically known as *structuring*) whereby large amounts of cash are broken into increments less than $10,000 to avoid federal reporting requirements and then deposited into various bank accounts. (14)

plain feel/touch evidence any object discovered by a police officer who is lawfully patting down a suspect's outer clothing and that is *immediately* identified, by touch, as contraband; a warrantless seizure is justified because there is no invasion of the suspect's privacy beyond that already authorized by the officer's search for weapons (*Minnesota v. Dickerson*, 1993). (4)

plain-view evidence unconcealed evidence that is seen by an officer engaged in a lawful activity. (4)

plant observing a location from a fixed location; also called *fixed surveillance* and *stakeout*. (7)

plastic fingerprints impressions left in soft substances such as putty, grease, tar, butter, or soft soap; *see also* **visible fingerprints**. (5)

poaching illegally taking or possessing fish, game, or other wildlife, including deer, elk, bear, pheasant, ducks, wild turkeys, and grouse. (14)

polygraph a devise that scientifically measures respiration and depth of breathing, changes in the skin's electrical resistance, blood pressure, and pulse rate; also called *lie detector*. (6)

Ponzi scheme a pyramid-type fraud scheme, named after Charles Ponzi, that involves using capital from new investors to pay off earlier investors, requiring an ever-expanding base of new investors to support the financial obligations to the existing "higher ups," which, eventually and inevitably, will collapse. (14)

port scanning looking for access (open "doors") into a computer. (17)

postmortem artifact an injury sustained after death from an outside source that can look like it was related to the homicide; for example, animal bites on a victim left in the woods. (8)

postmortem lividity the dark blue or purple discoloration caused when blood no longer circulates after death and gravity drains the blood to the lowest level of the body; also called *livor mortis* or simply *lividity*. (8)

PPI pixels per inch; relates to image resolution or sharpness. (2)

premeditation considering, planning, or preparing for an act, no matter how briefly, before committing it. (8)

presumptive evidence that which provides a reasonable basis for believing a crime was intended. (13)

pretext stop occurs when an officer stops a vehicle for a relatively minor offense when the real motivation is to search for evidence of a more serious crime; also called *pretextual traffic stop*. (4)

pretextual traffic stop the stop of a vehicle when an officer's intent (pretext) was not the real reason for the stop; the presence of an ulterior motive by an officer for the stop. (7)

prima facie **evidence** that which is established by law; for example, the blood alcohol level for intoxication; also called *direct evidence*. (5)

primary transfer occurs when DNA is initially deposited on an item by a victim, suspect, or other individual. (5)

probable cause a level of certainty that exists when facts and circumstances are sufficient to lead a person of "reasonable caution" to believe that something connected with a crime is on the premises or person to be searched. (4)

probative evidence that which tends to prove or actually proves guilt or innocence; vital for the investigation or prosecution of a case. (5)

profiling *see* **psychological profiling**. (7)

property flipping a practice whereby an offender buys a property near its estimated market value, artificially inflates the property value through a false appraisal, and then resells (flips) the property, often within days of the original purchase, for a greatly increased price; although flipping *per se* is not illegal, it often involves mortgage fraud, which is illegal. (14)

prostitution a sexual act or contact with another person in return for giving or receiving a fee or anything of value. (10)

protective sweep the authorized search by police of areas immediately adjoining the place of arrest, justified when reasonable suspicion exists that another person might be present who poses a danger to the arresting officers; held constitutional in *Maryland v. Buie* (1990); also called a *Buie sweep*. (4)

proximity informant someone who can keep tabs on a domestic violence victim's normal schedule and who can establish a routine of contact with the victim, with the principle being to serve as a lifeline to police if something seems wrong or "off." (9)

proxy data remnants of an interaction, transfer, or exchange of material between two items (*see Locard's exchange principle*); the evidence analyzed by forensic scientists to uncover the relationships between people, places, and objects. (5)

psychological profiling a method of suspect identification that attempts to describe an individual's mental, emotional, and psychological characteristics in an effort to provide investigators with corroborative information about a known suspect or possible leads to an unknown suspect; also called *criminal profiling* or simply *profiling*. (7)

public safety exception a Court ruling that police may interrogate a suspect without first giving the *Miranda* warning, if a substantial public threat exists that might be removed by having the suspect talk. (6)

pulling (a safe) opening a safe by inserting a V plate behind the dial and tightening screw bolts on the edges of the V plate until the dial and the spindle are pulled out; this method, the opposite of punching, works on many older safes but not on newer ones; also called *dragging*. (13)

punching (a safe) opening a safe by shearing the dial from the safe door using a downward blow with a sledge or by holding a chisel to the dial and using a sledge to knock it off, exposing the safe mechanism spindle. (13)

R

racial profiling occurs when an officer focuses on an individual as a suspect based solely on that person's race or ethnicity, excluding legitimate factors such as behavior; this is unconstitutional. (7)

raid a planned, organized operation based on the element of surprise to recover stolen property, seize evidence, or arrest a suspect. (7)

rainbow effect refers to the sheen or colorful appearance caused when substances, such as oil and gasoline, float on the surface of water. (16)

ransomware malicious software designed to block access to a computer system until a sum of money is paid. (17)

rape nonconsensual sexual intercourse or sexual penetration of one person by another; also called *sexual assault*. (10)

rapport an understanding between individuals created by genuine interest and concern. (6)

raves dance parties that feature fast-paced, repetitive electronic music and accompanying light shows and usually entail the use of alcohol, tobacco, and drugs. (18)

reasonable sensible, rational, and justifiable. (4)

reasonable force that amount of force a prudent person would use in similar circumstances. (7)

rebuttal testimony by a witness for the prosecution given to contradict the testimony (or evidence) presented by the defense. (21)

rectangular-coordinate (plotting) method uses two adjacent walls of a room as fixed points from which distances are measured at right angles from each wall. (2)

relevant evidence that which applies to the matter in question. (5)

relevant photograph an image that assists or explains. (2)

res gestae **statements** spontaneous, unrehearsed statements made at the time a crime is committed and closely related to actions involved in the crime; considered more truthful than later, planned responses. (1)

residential burglary one that occurs in buildings, structures, or attachments that are used as or are suitable for dwellings, even though they may be unoccupied at the time of the burglary. (13)

resolution the fineness of image detail either captured with a camera, displayed on a monitor, or printed on paper, commonly quantified by pixels. (2)

restraining order (RO) a court-issued document that aims to restrict an alleged abuser's behavior and protect the intended victim; alternately called an *order for protection* or *civil protective order*. (9)

reverse buy a complex operation organized and implemented by undercover agents to apprehend drug dealers and buyers and to deter other users from making drug purchases at a certain location; also called a *sting*. (18)

rifling the spiral pattern created by lands and grooves inside a weapon's barrel, which grip and spin the bullet as it passes through the bore, providing greater projectile control and accuracy. (5)

rigor mortis the stiffening of the joints of the body after death because of partial skeletal muscle contraction. (8)

ritual a prescribed form of religious or mystical ceremony. (19)

ritualistic crime an unlawful act committed within the context of a ceremony. (19)

robbery the felonious taking of another's property, either directly from the person or in that person's presence, through force or intimidation. (12)

robbery-by-appointment a robbery that occurs when a victim willingly meets with the offender, believing a legitimate transaction will occur; also called *buy-and-sell* robberies. (12)

robotripping slang for the act of drinking bottles of cough syrup, such as Robitussin DM, to get high. (18)

rogues' gallery a collection of mug shots gathered in files and displayed in groups. (2)

Rohypnol the "date rape drug," a Schedule IV drug which is illegal to manufacture, sell, possess, or use in the United States; that dissolves rapidly when placed in a carbonated drink; and acts quickly (20 to 30 minutes) to produce physical as well as mental incapacitation after ingestion. (10)

rough sketch the first, pencil-drawn outline of the crime scene, not usually drawn to scale, which shows the location of objects and evidence within this outline. (2)

rough surveillance moving surveillance in which it does not matter if the surveillant is detected; also called an *open surveillance*. (7)

routine activity theory the hypothesis that crime results from the convergence of three elements in time and space: the presence of likely or motivated offenders; the presence of suitable targets; and an absence of guardians to prevent the criminal act. (13)

rule on witnesses the common practice of excluding witnesses from the courtroom during a trial, in an effort to keep witnesses from hearing each other's testimony; also called the *witness sequestration rule*. (21)

S

sabbat a gathering of witches. (19)

sadist a person who derives sexual gratification from causing pain to others, often through mutilation. (10)

sadomasochistic abuse fettering, binding, or otherwise physically restraining; whipping; or torturing for sexual gratification. (10)

safe a semiportable strongbox with a combination lock. (13)

scale a reference used in sketching to show relative distance, location, or size, and is determined by taking the longest measurement at the scene and dividing it by the longest measurement of the paper used for sketching. (2)

script kiddie a derogatory term used to describe a less talented hacker who must use script or programs (scripts) created by others to carry out a cyberattack; also called a *skiddie*. (17)

search an examination of a person, place, or vehicle for contraband, illicit or stolen property, or some evidence of a crime to be used in prosecuting a criminal action or offense; by its very nature an intrusion into one's privacy. (4)

secondary transfer a form of evidence contamination in which DNA from the original object is moved to another object by an intermediate agent or vector, such as a hand or instrument. (5)

second-degree murder the intentional killing of another, but without premeditation. (8)

security threat group (STG) any group of three or more persons with recurring threatening or disruptive behavior (i.e., violations of the disciplinary rules where said violations were openly known or conferred benefit upon the group would suffice for a prison environment), including but not limited to gang crime or gang violence (i.e., crime of any sort would automatically make the group a gang, and as a gang in custody it would logically be an STG); includes any group of three or more inmates who were members of same street gang. (19)

seizure a taking by law enforcement or other government agent of contraband, evidence of a crime, or even a person (via arrest) into custody. (4)

sequestering a practice used during the trial whereby the judge excludes all witnesses from the courtroom except the person testifying. (21)

serial arson the setting of three or more fires by the same offender, with an emotional cooling-off period between the fires. (16)

serial murder the killing of three or more separate victims with a "cooling off" period between the killings. (8)

sexting the act of sending, receiving, or forwarding nude or sexually explicit pictures or messages vie email or text message or posting of a nude picture of oneself to another person or on the Internet, using a cell phone to transmit the image. (10, 11)

sextortion the crime that occurs when an offender threatens to distribute a victim's private and sensitive material unless the victim provides images of a sexual nature, sexual favors, or money. (10)

sexual abuse a violent crime that includes sexually molesting a child, performing sexual acts with a child, and statutory rape and seduction. (11)

sexual contact any act committed without the complainant's consent for the suspect's sexual or aggressive satisfaction, such as touching the complainant's intimate parts, forcing another person to touch one's intimate parts, or forcing another person to touch the complainant's intimate parts; the body area may be clothed or unclothed. (10)

sexual exploitation (of a minor) to employ, use, persuade, induce, entice, or coerce any minor to engage or assist in engaging in any sexually explicit conduct for the purpose of producing any visual or print medium, knowing that such visual or print medium will be transported interstate or in foreign commerce or mailed; for example, prostitution and pornography. (11)

sexually explicit conduct any type of sexual intercourse between persons of the same or opposite sex, bestiality, sadomasochistic abuse, lewd exhibition, or mutual masturbation. (10)

sexual penetration includes sexual intercourse, cunnilingus, fellatio, anal intercourse, or any other intrusion, no matter how slight, into the victim's genital, oral, or anal openings by the suspect's body or by an object; an emission of semen is not required. (10)

sexual seduction (of a minor) ordinary sexual intercourse, anal intercourse, cunnilingus, or fellatio committed by a nonminor with a consenting minor. (11)

short-con games schemes in which victims are taken for whatever money they have on their person at the time of the swindle. (14)

show-up identification on-the-scene identification of a suspect by the victim of or witnesses to a crime, conducted within a short time after the crime was committed; also called *field identification*. (7)

shrinkage the unexplained or unauthorized loss of inventory, merchandise, cash, or any other asset from a retail establishment, due to employee theft, shoplifting, organized retail crime, administrative errors, and vendor fraud. (14)

silver alert public notification systems similar to amber alerts for missing children but that aim to recover missing seniors. (9)

simple arson the intentional destruction by fire or explosives that does not create imminent danger to life or risk of great bodily harm. (16)

simple assault the act of intentionally causing another person to fear immediate bodily harm or death or intentionally inflicting or attempting to inflict bodily harm on another; usually a misdemeanor. (9)

sinsemilla homegrown marijuana. (18)

sketch a drawing (noun), or to create a drawing (verb); may be rough or finished and accurately portrays the physical facts, relates to the sequence of events at the scene, establishes the precise location and relationship of objects and evidence at the scene, helps to create a mental picture of the scene for those not present, is a permanent record of the scene, and is usually admissible in court. (2)

skimming an electronic crime method in which a device is placed in a card reader, such as that found at an ATM, to record sensitive information, such as bank account numbers, credit cards numbers, and passwords. (14, 17)

skittling ingesting high doses of Coricidin Cough and Cold ("Triple C") tablets to get high. (18)

slamming the illegal practice of switching a consumer's traditional wireline telephone company for local, local toll, or long-distance service without permission. (14)

slanting including only one side of a story or only facts that tend to prove or support one side's theory; result of a lack of objectivity. (3)

sleeper cell a group of terrorists who blend into a community and who may share or divide responsibilities for various stages of the attack. (20)

smash and grab in burglary, breaking a window and taking items from the window display. (13)

smurfing a method of money laundering whereby large amounts of cash are broken into increments less than $10,000 to avoid federal reporting requirements and deposited into various bank accounts; more technically known as *structuring*. (14)

sniffing monitoring data traveling along a network. (17)

sodomy any form of anal or oral copulation. (10)

solvability factors elements of information relating to a crime that are known to increase the likelihood of that crime being solved. (1, 7)

sources-of-information file a reference that contains the name and location of persons, organizations, and records that can assist in a criminal investigation. (6)

spalling the cracking, chipping, or breaking off of surface pieces of concrete, rock, or brick because of intense heat. (16)

spam unsolicited bulk email messages, similar in concept to junk mail and commonly commercial in nature; less commonly known by its formal designation as *unsolicited commercial email* (UCE). (17)

spoofing acquiring unauthorized access to a computer or network through a message using an IP address that appears to be from a trusted host; often considered synonymous with *phishing*. (17)

spree arson the setting of three or more fires at separate locations by the same offender, with no emotional cooling-off period between fires. (16)

spyware malicious, covert (difficult to detect) software that infects a computer in a manner similar to viruses, collecting information or executing other programs without the user's knowledge; some programs can track which websites a user visits and some can track and capture personal user information. (17)

stake in conformity a constellation of variables that, in effect, influence someone to take a particular course of action; for offenders, it constitutes what they stand to lose if convicted, such as marital status, residential stability, or employment. (9)

stakeout observing a location from a fixed location; also called *fixed surveillance* and *plant*. (7)

stalking a pattern of repeated and unwanted attention and contact that causes fear or concern for one's own safety or the safety of someone else. (9)

standard of comparison an object, measure, or model with which evidence is compared to determine whether both originated from the same source. (5)

statement a legal narrative description of events related to a crime. (6)

statement analysis a technique used to determine whether a person's verbal or written statement is truthful or deceptive. (6)

static IP address an IP address that does not change. (17)

statutory rape sexual intercourse with a minor, with or without consent. (10)

steganography Greek for "hidden writing"; serves to keep everyone except the intended recipient of a message oblivious to its very existence by making the message appear as some type of "cover" message—a shopping list, a picture, etc. (17)

sting a complex operation organized and implemented by undercover agents to apprehend drug dealers and buyers and to deter other users from making drug purchases at a certain location; also called a *reverse buy*. (18)

Stockholm syndrome a psychological phenomenon where hostages bear no ill feelings toward the hostage takers and fear the police more than their captors. (12)

street gang any durable, street-oriented youth group whose involvement in illegal activity is part of its group identity; a criminal organization that forms on the street and operates in neighborhoods throughout the United States. (19)

striations highly individualized and characteristic scratches made on a projectile (bullet) as it passes through a weapon's rifling; provide valuable comparison evidence on recovered bullets. (5)

strikers vanity firesetters who often remain at the scene in an effort to help put out the fire and become a hero; can include firefighters. (16)

structuring a common method of money laundering whereby large amounts of cash are broken into increments less than $10,000 to avoid federal reporting requirements and deposited into various bank accounts; also called *smurfing*. (14)

subject who or what is observed during surveillance; for example, a person, place, property, vehicle, group of people, organization, or object. (7)

subpoena a written order to appear before the court. (21)

sudden infant death syndrome (SIDS) a diagnosis of exclusion and is the most frequently determined cause of sudden unexplained infant death; a tragic condition for which parents may become suspected of child abuse. (11)

suicide the intentional taking of one's own life. (8)

suicide by police a situation where a person decides they want to die but doesn't want to pull the trigger and so, therefore, creates a situation where police are forced to shoot. (8)

surface web a collection of websites indexed by standard search engines (e.g., Google, Bing, Yahoo) that can be easily and readily accessed by the general public. (17)

surrebuttal testimony by a witness for the defense given to contradict the testimony (or evidence) presented by the prosecution. (21)

surveillance the covert, discreet observation of people or places. (7)

surveillant a plainclothes investigator assigned to surveillance, to make observations of people or places. (7)

T

tagging public displays by urban artists who are unaffiliated with gangs; artistic expressions that replicate graffiti. (19)

tail a counter-surveillance technique in which the watcher becomes the watched; the practice of following people or vehicles on foot or in a vehicle to observe their actions or destinations. (7)

takeover robbery the type commonly portrayed in movies in which multiple perpetrators, heavily armed and wearing masks or disguises, conduct a hostile and violent takeover of a bank lobby, ordering patrons to the floor and often jumping over teller counters to demand money at gunpoint. (12)

targeted violence refers to any incident of violence that implicates homeland security and/or U.S. Department of Homeland Security activities, and in which a known or knowable attacker selects a particular target prior to the violent attack. (20)

target hardening an act of altering physical characteristics of a property to make it less attractive to criminals; also called *crime prevention through environmental design (CPTED)*. (13)

tech effect a broad public awareness of and familiarity with the capabilities of modern technology that indirectly influences jurors' expectations regarding forensic evidence. (5)

telematic technology transfers data between a remote vehicle and a host computer, allowing officers to track a bait car and then remotely kill the engine, lock the doors, and trap the thief inside. (15)

temporary custody without hearing removing a child from the custody of parents or guardians for a brief period, usually 48 hours, for the child's protection. (11)

terrorism the unlawful use of force and violence against persons or property to intimidate or coerce a government, the civilian population, or any segment thereof, in furtherance of political or social objectives. (20)

Terry **stop** the detaining, questioning, and possible frisking of an individual based on an officer's *reasonable suspicion* of that individual's involvement in criminal activity. (4)

testimonial hearsay prior testimony or statements made as a result of police interrogation; a witness's statement obtained through "structured questioning" by police officers that is inadmissible in a criminal trial unless the witness is unavailable to testify and was previously cross-examined by the defendant. (6)

theft *see* **larceny/theft**. (14)

the well the area within the courtroom that exists in front of the judge and between the judge and the attorneys' tables; normally off-limits and to be entered only if the judge so directs or permission is granted; traditionally, the area is a sword's length and was intended for the judge's protection. (21)

third degree the use of physical force, threats of force, or other physical, mental, or psychological abuse to induce a suspect to confess. (6)

third-degree murder a death that results from an imminently dangerous act but does not involve premeditation or intent. (8)

tight surveillance staying within a few steps of the subject or keeping the subject in sight; used when it is extremely important not to lose the subject; also called *close surveillance*. (7)

tool mark an impression left on a surface by a tool. (5)

torch a professional arsonist. (16)

totality of circumstances a test principle upon which a number of legal assessments are made, including probable cause; refers to the sum total of factors leading a reasonable person to a course of action. (4)

toxicology the study of poisons; toxicologists are consulted if food or drink poisoning is suspected. (8)

trace evidence extremely small physical matter, such as hairs and fibers. (5)

trailer a path made of paper, hay, flammable compounds, or any other substance that burns, that is set down for a fire to follow; indicates arson. (16)

transnational organized crime (TOC) a self-perpetuating association of individuals who operate, wholly or in part, by illegal means and irrespective of geography. (18)

trap photography photos that prove an incident occurred, can assist in identifying suspects and the weapons used, and can also corroborate witness testimony and identification; also called *surveillance photography*. (2)

trauma bond a dysfunctional attachment formed in the presence of danger, shame, or exploitation; commonly referred to as the *Stockholm syndrome*. (10)

triangulation (plotting method) uses straight-line measurements from two fixed objects to the evidence to create a triangle, with the evidence in the angle formed by the two straight lines; the degree of the angle formed at the location of the object or evidence can then be measured with a protractor. (2)

Trojan horse a malicious program hidden inside an apparently harmless, legitimate program and intended to carry out unauthorized or illegal functions. (17)

true scene a crime scene where no evidence has been introduced or removed except by the person(s) committing the crime; also called an *uncontaminated scene*. (4)

turf the geographic area claimed by a gang; often marked by graffiti. (19)

tweaker a methamphetamine addict. (18)

U

ultraviolet-light photography uses the low end of the color spectrum, which is invisible to human sight, to make visible the impressions of bruises and injuries long after their occurrence; the type of weapon used can often be determined by examining its impression, developed using ultraviolet light. (2)

uncontaminated scene a crime scene where no evidence has been introduced or removed except by the person(s) committing the crime; also called a *true scene*. (4)

undercover a type of surveillance in which the officer uses an assumed identity to make personal contact with the subject to obtain information or evidence. (7)

URL Uniform Resource Locator; a string of characters representing an Internet resource. (17)

V

vault a stationary security chamber of reinforced concrete, often steel lined, with a combination lock. (13)

vehicle identification number the primary nonduplicated, serialized number assigned by the manufacturer to each vehicle made; this number—critical in motor vehicle theft investigations—identifies the specific vehicle in question; also called the *VIN*. (15)

verified response policy a procedure implemented by some law enforcement agencies, whereby they will not respond to a burglary alarm unless criminal activity is first confirmed through either an onsite security officer, verbal communication with a resident or employee on-site, or some method of electronic surveillance, such as CCTV. (13)

victimless crime an illegal activity in which the victim is a willing participant; for example, a person who bets. (18)

victimology the collection of significant and relevant information related to a victim and that victim's lifestyle which helps investigators develop and ascertain suspects, motives, and risk factors. (8)

VIN the primary nonduplicated, serialized number assigned by the manufacturer to each vehicle made; this number—critical in motor vehicle theft investigations—identifies the specific vehicle in question; the acronym for *vehicle identification number*. (15)

visible fingerprints prints made when fingers are dirty or stained and leave their impression on a glossy or light-colored surface, which can then be dusted and lifted. (5)

voiceprint the graphic record of an individual's unique voice characteristics made by a sound spectrograph of the energy patterns emitted by speech. (5)

voluntary manslaughter the intentional causing of the death of another person in the heat of passion or with adequate provocation. (8)

voyeurism the act of gaining sexual pleasure from watching others when they are naked or engaged in sexual activity; a voyeur is often called a peeping Tom. (10)

W

waiver a giving up of a certain right. (6)

white-collar crime involves illegal, prohibited, and demonstrably harmful acts characterized by fraud, concealment, or a violation of private or public trust, committed by individuals or organizations in the conduct of their legitimate occupational roles or organizational functions, and directed toward financial advantage or to maintain and extend power and privilege; also called *corporate crime* or *economic crime*. (14)

wiretapping the intercepting and recording of telephone conversations by a mechanical device without the consent of either party in the conversation. (7)

witness sequestration rule the common practice of excluding witnesses from the courtroom during a trial, in an effort to keep witnesses from hearing each other's testimony; also called the *rule on witnesses*. (21)

worm (computer) a self-contained program that travels from machine to machine across network connections, often clogging networks and information systems as it spreads; need not become part of another program to propagate itself. (17)

Z

zero floor release the requirement that all transactions by credit card be authorized. (14)

zombie a computer that has been taken over by another computer, typically through infection with hidden software (virus) that allows the zombie machine to be accessed and controlled remotely, often with the intention of perpetrating attacks on other computers. (17)

Author Index

A

Adair, T., 176
Adams, S. H., 572
Adams, S. M., 428, 429
Adams, W., 165, 169, 428, 434
Adcock, J. M., 328
Adlam, D., 306, 314
Ahern, T. L., 277, 298
Ahmad, Z., 310
Albanese, J. S., 671
Albrecht, L., 367, 368
Albright, T. D., 177, 246
Alcoke, M., 729
Aldred, J., 514
Aldridge, J., 690
Alexa, I. D., 368
Allain, C., 160
Allard, T., 674
Allardyce, S., 433
Allen, J., 262
Allen, M., 187
Alper, M., 28, 403
Alvarez, E., 594
Amir, A., 172
Amrom, A. D., 212
Anderson, G., 311
Anderson, L., 387
Anderson, L. J., 394
Anderson, T. M., 289, 768, 772, 773
Araujo, W. J., 22
Aravanis, S. C., 367
Archambault, J., 390, 396
Ariel, B., 22
Arkow, P., 348
Armstrong, E. J., 311, 316
Arp, D., Jr., 90, 92, 95
Arweck, E., 712
Ascione, F. R., 352
Ashley, S., 274
Aspland, M., 92

B

Babu, N. A., 177
Bachman, J. G., 642, 651
Backes, B. L., 360
Baffa, R. C., 739
Bagdure, S., 298
Bailey, P. J., 255
Baisagatova, D. B., 729
Bakker, E., 750
Balanchander, N., 177
Baldwin, K., 427
Ball, J., 416
Ballou, S., 171
Bang, B. L., 212
Banks, D., 275, 383, 384, 755
Barak, G., 143
Barcus, J., 329

Barnes, J., 688, 698
Barnes, J. G., 157
Barnes, S., 482
Barrie, J., 348, 355, 357
Basich, M., 583
Basile, K. C., 345, 347, 350, 359, 390
Baskin, D., 393
Baum, K., 359
Beach, S. R., 369
Beauregard, E., 381, 402
Bekaert, B., 740
Bell, A., 89
Bell, K. E., 690
Bellair, P. E., 697, 698
Belli, R., 747
Benavides, M. O., 350
Benitez, G., 549
Bennett, D. W., 622
Beran, D., 626
Berg, G. R., 40
Bergazzi, M., 569
Berk, R. A., 354
Bermudez Villalva, D. A., 600
Berry, A. M., 428
Berry, O. O., 350
Bertomen, L. J., 765
Bertrand, M., 245
Bettelheim, K. A., 428
Betz, C. J., 305
Bhattacharya, S., 178
Bibb, T., 515
Bieler, D., 418
Bierer, B. E., 177
Bird, P., 605, 606
Bishop, K., 403
Bitton, Y., 297
Bjerregaard, B., 697, 698
Black, D. J., 326
Black, M. C., 345, 347, 350, 357
Blackstone, E., 483
Blakelock, H., 352
Blevins, K. R., 495
Bliss, K., 264, 265
Boehmer, M., 508
Boehnlein, T., 360
Boetig, B. P., 31, 204
Bohan, T. L., 177
Bolger, P., 271
Booth, L. J., 352
Borrello, N., 388
Bossert, J., 573
Bouhana, N., 750
Bouslimani, A., 172
Bowen, R., 183, 185, 186
Bowers, C. M., 177
Boyle, D. J., 301
Bradway, W. C., 401
Braga, A. A., 327
Brandl, B., 363

Brannan, D., 435
Brantingham, P. J., 697, 698
Brantner Smith, B., 27
Brasfield, H., 352
Brave, M. A., 274, 275, 298
Breckman, R., 363
Breiding, M. J., 345, 347, 350, 357
Brewer, B., 93
Brick, J. M., 441
Bromley, D. G., 712
Brooke, E., 648
Brooks, R. E., 752
Brown, K. M., 446
Brown, R. A., 749, 750
Bucklin, L., 780
Bulman, P., 274
Bumpas, S., 27
Bunker, R. J., 742
Burch, A. M., 29
Burkett, J., 569
Burnes, D., 525
Burruss, G. W., 727
Bush, M. A., 177
Buysse, A., 557
Byme, J., 739

C

Cameron, R., 188
Camp, N. P., 208
Campbell, R., 568
Canales, K., 607
Carey, K. B., 390
Carey, M. P., 390
Carter, D. L., 304, 326, 327, 328, 751
Carter, J. G., 326, 327, 328
Cartwright, A., 93, 94
Case, K. A., 692, 693
Casey, B., 600
Castro, E., 692, 693
Catalano, S., 340, 358, 359, 360
Catanzaro, M., 164
Cauley, A., 746
Cawley, D. F., 22
Cevik, C., 298
Chae, M. H., 301
Chaffin, M., 433
Chainey, S. P., 495
Chalfin, A., 165, 169
Chan, H. C. O., 381
Chan, W. Y., 739
Chanana, A., 310
Chapman, J. E., 143
Charman, S. D., 254, 255
Chase, R., 29
Chaumont Menendez, C. K., 460
Chen, J., 350, 357, 390
Chermak, S. M., 734, 735, 737, 738, 749
Chertoff, M., 600

Chettiar, I. M., 391
Chew, S. L., 205
Chin, J. M., 143
Cho, H. L., 15, 34, 324, 432
Chouhy, C., 529
Christian, C. W., 427
Christian, D. R., 666
Christman, D., 173
Chronister, C. W., 651
Ciminelli, M. L., 273
Cissner, A. B., 355
Clark, A., 208
Clark, D. W., 301
Clark, R., 301
Clark, S. C., 428
Clayton, H. B., 359
Cleary, H., 212
Clement, J., 359
Coats, D. R., 730, 732, 733, 743
Cohen, J., 697
Cohen, M. A., 533
Cohn, A. M., 391
Colard, T., 160
Coleman, B. R., 692
Connolly, M. T., 363
Conrad, K. J., 369
Cornell, S., 515
Coull, B. A., 271
Coupe, R. T., 22
Cowan, D. E., 712
Cox, J., 583
Crandall, S., 261
Crenshaw, Z., 262
Cronin, J. M., 275
Crosby, A. E., 363, 688, 698
Cross, T. P., 424, 425
Cuevas, C. A., 416
Cullen, F. T., 396, 529
Cunha, E., 306

D

Daigle, L. E., 396
Dake, D., 318
Damphouse, K. R., 230
Dandu, M., 273, 274
Dasgupta, N., 208
da Silva, B. F. A., 495
da Silva, R. R., 172
Dathan, J., 740
Daus, M. W., 460
Davey, J., 737
David, M. P., 178
Davidson, M. L., 278
Davies, H. J., 31, 32
Davis, D., 226
Davis, E., 271
Davis, J. A., 318, 358
Davis, K., 301

Subject Index